Statistical
Record
OF Older
Americans

Statistical Record OF Older Americans

Arsen J. Darnay, Editor

Gale Research Inc. • *DETROIT* • *WASHINGTON, D.C.* • *LONDON*

Arsen J. Darnay, *Editor*

Editorial Code & Data Inc. Staff

Gary Alampi, Helen S. Fisher, Marlita A. Reddy, *Associate Editors*
Beatrice Darnay and Susan M. Turner, *Contributing Editors*
Sherae R. Fowler and Nancy Ratliff, *Data Entry*
Gary Alampi, *Data Processing*

Gale Research Inc. Staff

Allison McNeill, *Developmental Editor*
Lawrence W. Baker, *Senior Developmental Editor*

Mary Beth Trimper, *Production Director*
Shanna Heilveil, *Production Assistant*

Cynthia Baldwin, *Art Director*
Arthur Chartow, *Technical Design Services Manager*
Bernadette M. Gornie, *Cover Designer*

ISBN 0-8103-9198-8
10 9 8 7 6 5 4 3 2 1
Printed in the United States of America
Published simultaneously in the United Kingdom
by Gale Research International Limited
(An affiliated company of Gale Research Inc.)

I(T)P™

The trademark **ITP** is used under license.

TABLE OF CONTENTS

CHAPTER 2 - DEMOGRAPHICS continued:

CHAPTER 5 - INCOME, ASSETS, AND SPENDING continued:

CHAPTER 5 - INCOME, ASSETS, AND SPENDING continued:

CHAPTER 6 - PENSIONS AND RETIREMENT continued:

CHAPTER 6 - PENSIONS AND RETIREMENT continued:

CHAPTER 7 - SOCIAL SECURITY 323

CHAPTER 8 - LABOR AND EMPLOYMENT continued:

CHAPTER 9 - HOUSING continued:

CHAPTER 10 - HEALTH AND HEALTH CARE continued:

CHAPTER 10 - HEALTH AND HEALTH CARE continued:

CHAPTER 10 - HEALTH AND HEALTH CARE continued:

CHAPTER 11 - HEALTH INSURANCE continued:

CHAPTER 12 - NURSING HOMES AND RESIDENT CARE continued:

CHAPTER 15 - OPINIONS continued:

PREFACE

The editor of *Statistical Record of Older Americans* (*SROA*) reached the honorable age of three-score years less two during the compilation of this book. One of his contributors was his mother, a still active lady who knows the meaning of the word "octogenarian." This book is dedicated to her with appreciation for a long life of unselfish service.

With age comes wisdom — and the cunning to know when to delegate. Thus most of the heavy lifting on *SROA* — including research, editorial labors, and data processing — was carried out by the next generation: those in their forty-, thirty- and twenty-somethings. The merits of the book belong to them. It's shortcomings are solidly the responsiblity of "older Americans."

INTRODUCTION

Statistical Record of Older Americans (SROA) is a compilation of information on the elderly component of the U.S. population drawn from governmental, academic, association, technical, trade, and journalistic sources. The book features:

- More than 900 statistical tables

- More than 140 sources

- Broad subject coverage ranging from demographics to opinion

- National, state, and metropolitan statistical presentations

- Comparative statistics from selected foreign countries

- Selected textual materials

- Graphic highlighting of selected tables

- Comprehensive keyword index

- Source listing with table references

- Explanation of acronyms and abbreviations

This introduction is intended to provide an overview—of the scope and coverage of the book, sources used, organization of the contents, organization of tables, and an explanation of the appended materials.

SCOPE AND COVERAGE

What is an Older American? The phrases "older Americans," "seniors," "the elderly," and others are nowhere officially defined—or, more to the point, are defined with different starting ages all depending on the subject, the agency, the program, or the particular survey that places its focus on the aging.

The strategy adopted in *SROA* has been one of flexibility: for purposes of selection, the minimum age for inclusion has been 55. However, the bulk of the materials either presents data on all age groups, including the elderly, or has its focus on those aged 65 years or older (frequently shown, in the tables, as 65 +). A minority of tables provide additional focus on those aged 85 +; and *SROA* also provides some information on centenarians.

No attempt was made to force materials into an arbitrary arrangement by age. In the case of some well-documented subjects, however, data were available for large sub-groups of the elderly. In these instances, the presentation is from younger age groups down to the oldest. Where at all possible, data for the population as a whole or for the younger ranges are presented to provide comparison and context.

The Greying of America. Interest in the elderly has surfaced in recent years because—

- Older Americans are a growing segment of the population—and expected to grow even faster as the Baby Boomers move into the aging "zone."

- Because of their numbers, the elderly represent a new and potent force in politics and—because they own most of the nation's assets—in the marketplace as well.

- A large elderly population is a new phenomenon created by advances in medicine.

- The elderly pose problems and opportunities not before encountered; these include the problems of supporting a large retired community with the income of a smaller younger workforce (at the heart of the debates about Social Security), the relatively high demand for health care services that the elderly represent, and the opportunity to employ usefully an experienced body of people at a time when, according to recent federal releases, half of the population cannot effectively calculate or read.

Subject Coverage. The demographic phenomenon of the changing age-stratification in the United States cuts across a wide range of subjects. This is fully reflected in *SROA*. Substantial and detailed coverage is provided on the major issues: the demographic phenomenon itself, health care, income and assets, pensions and retirement, and the Social Security system. A wide range of other subjects of interest is also covered to varying levels of depth (see inset).

Materials have been selected to satisfy both the needs of the interested layperson and the researcher/analyst. Thus tables of a summary nature—or tables drawn from journalistic sources and thus reflecting journalistic summations—will be found alongside detailed and in some cases relatively technical presentations. An attempt has been made to place materials that provide access to a topic at the beginning of sections; these are sometimes followed by the "heavier" material. A brief introductory chapter, titled *Summary Indicators*, provides quick access to some of the more "topical" materials in the form of extracts.

Geographic Coverage. *SROA* covers older Americans in the United States. In some of the chapters, a few tables are included to profile the subject on a worldwide basis for purposes of comparison. Foreign countries selected are usually similar to the United States in economic development.

For U.S. data, additional detailed presentations are provided for states, metropolitan areas, and selected counties.

Period of Coverage. Most of the materials in *SROA* are from the late 1980s to the early 1990s. In some tables, historical data are presented going back to 1900 or to the immediate post-War era (1946) in order to illustrate changes in demographic or other characteristics of older Americans. With but few exceptions, the 1990 Census of Population was not available in sufficient detail during the compilation of

---

Chapters

Summary Indicators

Demographics

Education

Families

Income, Assets, and Spending

Pensions and Retirement

Social Security

Labor and Employment

Housing

Health and Health Care

Health Insurance

Nursing Homes and Resident Care

Culture and Lifestyle

Public Life

Opinions

Criminals and Victims

---

this book to reflect that new and comprehensive database. Available portions of the 1990 Census data, however, are included.

SOURCES USED

The overwhelming majority of all statistical materials available on the population in the United States is collected by the federal government or—in many cases—by state or other government levels under federal mandate. *SROA* reflects this state of the statistics in its sources. Most of the tables were drawn from the statistical services (or from special reports) of major federal departments (U.S. Department of Commerce, which administers the Census; the departments of Labor, Education, Housing and Urban Development, Health and Human Services, and Justice; and other functionalities of government, including the legislative branch).

In addition to federal materials, *SROA* includes materials collected by associations, special surveys conducted by academic researchers, the results of market research studies, opinion polls, and election statistics.

Last but not least, *SROA* presents "clippings" from journalistic sources, including dailies, business periodicals, trade magazines, journals, and association publications. These sources, in their turn, draw information from federal and sometimes other sources.

The manner in which periodicals present data is, however, indicative of current tendencies, anxieties, and hopes — which adds an extra element of information to the statistics.

All told, *SROA* draws its materials from 143 sources. Approximately 230 sources were consulted before the selections were made. Materials were obtained in the form of printed reports, as personal communications, as telephone conversations, and in the form of electronic media.

ORGANIZATION OF CONTENTS

SROA is organized into 16 chapters, of which the first is a summary. A listing of chapters is provided in the inset on the previous page. Chapters are further subdivided by topic. The arrangement of the topics and the logic of their placement is explained in brief chapter notes. The topic of each table is shown above the table in italic type.

Some subjects, e.g., health care and retirement, were too big for single chapters and are subdivided. Thus, for instance, the chapter on *Health and Health Care* is followed by a related chapter on *Health Insurance* and by *Nursing Homes and Residential Care.* Similarly, the chapter on *Retirement and Pensions* is followed by a separate chapter on *Social Security.*

ORGANIZATION OF TABLES

Each table is assigned to a broad topic. Topic headers are placed above groups of tables between distinctive rules. On succeeding pages, the name of the topic appears in italic type beneath the table number and above the table title so that the user can always determine the topic under which the table is ordered.

Tables are numbered and may be located from the *Table of Contents,* the *Keyword Index,* or the *Sources* appendix by table number. Page numbers are also provided in the *Table of Contents* and in the *Keyword Index.*

The table title follows the topic designation. Thereafter, the table may display a graphical presentation as a bar chart or a pie chart. If the table has more than one column of data, the number of the column from which the data were drawn for charting is identified on the graphic. Tabular data follow whatever graphic is used.

If the table requires some explanation, a brief headnote is presented. Please note that *these notes, unless within quotes, were prepared by the editors and are not taken from the source unless that is expressly stated.* To the extent possible, the headnotes provide information needed to understand unusual terminology.

At the bottom of the table, the source of the table is identified. If the authors used another source, that source (the primary source) is identified following the word *from* or the phrase *primary source.* Footnotes or other explanatory notes are placed after the source information. Wherever possible, we have attempted to define abbreviations used in the source note of the table itself. These may be explicitly footnoted or shown without footnotes.

A selection of tables is in the form of pure text. These tables were included because they contain statistical information or provide explanatory materials.

APPENDED MATERIALS

SOURCES

Sources are shown in this appendix arranged alphabetically by author, title, or agency. In the case of periodicals, dates of issues consulted are shown. Table references are provided showing all tables which cite the source.

KEYWORD INDEX

SROA features a *Keyword Index* by means of which the user can locate all subjects, companies, institutions, agencies, and geographical entities. Items are followed by table and page numbers. Cross-references are provided. Page references do not necessarily identify the page on which the table begins. In the case of tables that span two or more pages, items shown on the second or subsequent page of the table will point the user to the page on which the reference is used.

ABBREVIATIONS AND ACRONYMS

This appendix lists abbreviations, acronyms, and initialisms. While efforts have been made to provide the user explanations of abbreviations within the source block of each table, a general listing of all abbreviations is also provided in *Abbreviations and Acronyms.* Abbreviations appear in alphabetical order followed by an explanation.

ACKNOWLEDGEMENTS

Many people helped in the compilation of *SROA* by providing unusual data, suggestions, and advice. Special thanks to Dr. Ronald Manheimer, Center for Creative Retirement, University of North Carolina at Asheville, who served as an advisor on the project and Alison Gallup, Princeton Religion Research Organization, for timely and unusual help. The editor would also like to acknowledge help and guidance provided by The American Association of Retired Persons (AARP) and the U.S. Administration on Aging in the early stages of the project.

COMMENTS AND SUGGESTIONS

Comments on *SROA* or suggestions for improvement of its usefulness, format, and coverage are always welcome. Although every effort is made to maintain accuracy, errors may occasionally occur; the editors will be grateful if these are called to their attention. Please contact:

Editors, *Statistical Record of Older Americans*, Gale Research Inc., 835 Penobscot Building, Detroit, MI 48226-4094; Phone: (313) 961-2242 or (800) 347-GALE; Fax: (313) 961-6815

Chapter 1
SUMMARY INDICATORS

This chapter presents 11 tables which were compiled from tables presented throughout *Statistical Record of Older Americans*. The objective in this chapter is to present some highlights by major topical category. These tables also serve as an illustration of the kinds of information available in the rest of the book. Each item in each table is coded so that the source of the data is shown by entry number.

★ 1 ★

Census of the Elderly

Item	Value	Denomination	Date	Table
Population				
65 years + in 1900	3.084	million	1900	12
	4.0	% of population	1900	12
65 years + in 1990	31.559	million	1990	12
	12.6	% of population	1990	12
65 years + in 2000	34.882	million	2000	12
	13.0	% of population	2000	12
65 years + by race in 1990				
White	28.000	million	1990	18
Black	2.500	million	1990	18
Other	.600	million	1990	18
Geographic Distribution				
Counties with lowest and highest population 55+				
Lowest - Chattahoochee County, GA	3.85	% over 55	1990	33
Highest - Kalawao County, HI	74.62	% over 55	1990	33
States with highest and lowest populations 65+				
Lowest - Alaska	4.1	% over 65	1990	35
Highest - Florida	18.3	% over 65	1990	35
Elderly living on farms	702,000	number	1990	34

[Continued]

1

★ 1 ★

Census of the Elderly
[Continued]

Item	Value	Denomination	Date	Table
Support Ratios				
Number of people 65+ per 100				
people aged 18-64				
1900	7	number	1900	214
1920	8	number	1920	214
1940	11	number	1940	214
1960	17	number	1960	214
1980	19	number	1980	214
1990	20	number	1990	214
2000	21	number	2000	214

Source: Data are drawn from tables in the rest of *Statistical Record of Older Americans*.

★ 2 ★

Life Expectancy and Mortality

Item	Value	Denomination	Date	Table
Life Expectancy at Birth				
1900	47.3	year	1900	71
1950	68.2	year	1950	71
1960	69.7	year	1960	71
1970	70.9	year	1970	71
1980	73.7	year	1980	71
1989	75.3	year	1989	71
Leading Causes of Death in 1985				
55-59 - Cancer	36.0	% of deaths	1985	81
60-64 - Cancer	35.0	% of deaths	1985	81
65-69 - Heart disease	36.2	% of deaths	1985	81
70-74 - Heart disease	34.8	% of deaths	1985	81
75-79 - Heart disease	40.3	% of deaths	1985	81
80-84 - Heart disease	43.8	% of deaths	1985	81
85+ - Heart disease	46.6	% of deaths	1985	81

Source: Data are drawn from tables in the rest of *Statistical Record of Older Americans*.

★ 3 ★

Educational Attainment

Item	Value	%	Date	Table
High School Graduates				
65+ group	55	%	1989	129
65-69	63	%	1989	129
70-74	57	%	1989	129
75+	46	%	1989	129
25+ population	77	%	1989	129
College Graduates				
65+ group	11	%	1989	129
65-69	13	%	1989	129
70-74	11	%	1989	129
75+	10	%	1989	129
25+ population	21	%	1989	129

Source: Data are drawn from tables in the rest of *Statistical Record of Older Americans.*

★ 4 ★

Marital Status and Living Arrangements

Item	Value	%	Date	Table
Marital Status of Households in 1990				
Married	45.9	%	1990	139
Widowed	40.3	%	1990	139
Divorced/separated	9.7	%	1990	139
Never married	4.1	%	1990	139
Living Arrangements				
Persons aged 65 years +				
Alone	30.5	%	1989	157
With spouse	54.3	%	1989	157
With other relatives	13.1	%	1989	157
With nonrelatives	2.1	%	1989	157
Persons aged 85 years +				
Alone	32.6	%	1989	157
With spouse	48.2	%	1989	157
With other relatives	17.5	%	1989	157
With nonrelatives	1.7	%	1989	157

[Continued]

★ 4 ★

Marital Status and Living Arrangements
[Continued]

Item	Value	%	Date	Table
Persons 65 years + living alone by race/ethnicity				
White	31.0	%	1989	162
Black	33.0	%	1989	162
Hispanic	22.0	%	1989	162

Source: Data are drawn from tables in the rest of *Statistical Record of Older Americans.*

★ 5 ★

Income and Net Worth

Item	Value	Denomination	Date	Table
Household Earnings of Persons 65 Years +				
Under $10,000	36.7	% of 65 years +	1990	135
$10,000-$14,999	19.6	% of 65 years +	1990	135
$15,000-$19,999	12.4	% of 65 years +	1990	135
$20,000-$29,999	16.2	% of 65 years +	1990	135
$30,000 +	15.1	% of 65 years +	1990	135
Total Income Size of Persons 65 Years +				
Less than $5,000	10.0	% of 65 years +	1990	209
$5,000-$14,999	44.0	% of 65 years +	1990	209
$15,000-$39,999	35.0	% of 65 years +	1990	209
$40,000 +	11.0	% of 65 years +	1990	209
Sources of Income				
Sources of income for persons 65 years +				
Social Security	38.0	% of total income	1988	206
Assets	25.0	% of total income	1988	206
Pensions	28.0	% of total income	1988	206
Earnings	17.0	% of total income	1988	206
Supplemental Social Security	1.0	% of total income	1988	206
Other	2.0	% of total income	1988	206
Sources of Income in 1962 and 1990				
Percent of persons receiving income from source:				
Social Security	69.0 - 92.0	% receiving from source	1962 - 1990	261
Assets	54.0 - 69.0	% receiving from source	1962 - 1990	261
Pensions	18.0 - 44.0	% receiving from source	1962 - 1990	261
Earnings	36.0 - 22.0	% receiving from source	1962 - 1990	261
Public assistance	14.0 - 7.0	% receiving from source	1962 - 1990	261
Net Worth of the Elderly				
All ages	35,752	dollars	1988	220

[Continued]

★ 5 ★

Income and Net Worth
[Continued]

Item	Value	Denomination	Date	Table
65 years +	73,471	dollars	1988	220
65-69	83,478	dollars	1988	220
70-74	82,111	dollars	1988	220
75+	61,491	dollars	1988	220

Source: Data are drawn from tables in the rest of *Statistical Record of Older Americans*.

★ 6 ★

Retirement and Social Security

Item	Value	Denomination	Date	Table
Retirement Plans				
Number of participants in private plans	12.584	million	1989	322
Number of participants in state and local government plans	11.959	million	1989	322
Percent of employees covered in industry				
All firms	41.8	%	1990	346
Mining, construction, transportation, communications,				
public utilities	52.8	%	1990	346
Trade	28.8	%	1990	346
Finance, insurance, and real estate	82.1	%	1990	346
Services	33.5	%	1990	346
Social Security Beneficiaties				
Total beneficiaries	41.2	million	1992	353
Age 65 or older	30.2	million	1992	353
Age 65 or older as percent of total	73.3	%	1992	353
Social Security Monthly Benefits, 60 Years +				
Average both sexes	594.30	dollars per month	1991	356
Average for men	707.30	dollars per month	1991	356
Average for women	517.90	dollars per month	1991	356
Average Monthly Social Security Benefit by State				
Top 5				
Connecticut	690.90	dollars per month	1991	397
New Jersey	689.40	dollars per month	1991	397
New York	673.10	dollars per month	1991	397
Michigan	672.10	dollars per month	1991	397
Illinois	667.80	dollars per month	1991	397
Bottom 5				
Kentucky	579.10	dollars per month	1991	397
Maine	578.10	dollars per month	1991	397

[Continued]

★ 6 ★

Retirement and Social Security
[Continued]

Item	Value	Denomination	Date	Table
Arkansas	565.20	dollars per month	1991	397
Mississippi	546.30	dollars per month	1991	397
District of Columbia	536.60	dollars per month	1991	397

Source: Data are drawn from tables in the rest of *Statistical Record of Older Americans.*

★ 7 ★

Labor and Employment

Item	Value	%	Date	Table
Labor Force Participation				
Participation of those 65 years and over				
Male				
1950	45.8	%	1950	412
1990	16.0	%	1990	412
Female				
1950	9.7	%	1950	412
1990	8.7	%	1950	412
Occupations of Employees 65 Years and Over				
Managerial and professional workers	26.0	%	1989	423
Technical, sales, and administrative workers	30.0	%	1989	423
Service workers	18.0	%	1989	423
Precision production workers	7.0	%	1989	423
Operators, fabricators, laborers	10.0	%	1989	423
Farm, forestry, and fishing workers	9.0	%	1989	423
Industry of Employees 65 Years and Over				
Agriculture	9.0	%	1989	424
Mining	-	%	1989	424
Construction	4.0	%	1989	424
Manufacturing	11.0	%	1989	424
Transportation/public utilities	3.0	%	1989	424
Trade	21.0	%	1989	424
Finance, insurance, and real estate	8.0	%	1989	424
Services	8.0	%	1989	424
Public administration	4.0	%	1989	424

Source: Data are drawn from tables in the rest of *Statistical Record of Older Americans.*

★ 8 ★

Health Care

Item	Value	Denomination	Date	Table
Self-Assessment of Health Status				
Persons 65 years + rating their health as:				
Excellent	16.4	%	1989	566
Very good	23.1	%	1989	566
Good	31.9	%	1989	566
Fair	19.3	%	1989	566
Poor	9.2	%	1989	566
Percent of Persons 65 Years + Suffering From:				
Arthritics	48.3	%	1989	510
Hypertension	38.1	%	1989	510
Hearing impairment	28.7	%	1989	510
Heart disease	27.9	%	1989	510
Cataracts	15.7	%	1989	510
Hospitalization				
Length of stay in the 1985-1987 period				
Whites				
All ages	8.2	days per year per person	1985-87	616
65 years +	11.7	days per year per person	1985-87	616
Blacks				
All ages	9.5	days per year per person	1985-87	616
65 years +	14.0	days per year per person	1985-87	616
Hospital useage in 1965 and 1988				
Average length of stay in 1965	13.1	days	1965	622
Average length of stay in 1988	8.9	days	1988	622
Health Care Expenditures in 1970 and 1990				
Dollar expenditures				
Hospital care	27.9 - 256.0	billion dollars	1970-1990	672
Nursing home care	4.9 - 53.1	billion dollars	1970-1990	672
Physician services	13.6 - 125.7	billion dollars	1970-1990	672
All other	18.5 - 150.5	billion dollars	1970-1990	672
Percent increase 1970 to 1990				
Hospital care	817.6	% increase in period	1970-1990	672
Nursing home care	983.7	% increase in period	1970-1990	672
Physician services	824.3	% increase in period	1970-1990	672
All other	713.5	% increase in period	1970-1990	672

Source: Data are drawn from tables in the rest of *Statistical Record of Older Americans.*

★ 9 ★

Nursing Homes

Item	Value	Denomination	Date	Table
People in Nursing Homes, 1980 and 1990				
1980	1.426	million	1980	753
1990	1.772	million	1990	753
Percent change 1980 to 1990	24.2	%	1980-1990	753
Number of Nursing Homes with 25 or More Beds				
1982	14,565	number	1982	754
1986	16,033	number	1986	754
Number of Beds in Nursing Homes with 25+ Beds				
1982	1.469	million	1982	754
1986	1.616	million	1986	754
Nursing Home Expenditures, 1990 and 2005				
Medicare	1.1 - 1.8	billion dollars	1990-2050	764
Medicaid	15.7 - 27.0	billion dollars	1990-2050	764
Out-of-pocket	20.8 - 35.2	billion dollars	1990-2050	764
Total	37.6 - 64.0	billion dollars	1990-2050	764

Source: Data are drawn from tables in the rest of *Statistical Record of Older Americans.*

★ 10 ★

Culture and Politics

Item	Value	Denomination	Date	Table
Religious Affiliation				
Protestant	64.0	%	1993	825
Roman Catholic	23.0	%	1993	825
Jewish	2.0	%	1993	825
Other	1.0	%	1993	825
Voter Registration				
Number registered to vote	22.580	million	1988	842
Percent of age group	78.4	%	1988	842
Party Affiliation				
64 to 79				
Democratic	59.0	%	1990	847
Republican	36.0	%	1990	847
Independent	6.0	%	1990	847

[Continued]

★ 10 ★

Culture and Politics
[Continued]

Item	Value	Denomination	Date	Table
80 to 95				
Democratic	66.0	%	1990	847
Republican	30.0	%	1990	847
Independent	5.0	%	1990	847

Source: Data are drawn from tables in the rest of *Statistical Record of Older Americans.*

★ 11 ★

Crime and Crime Victims

Item	Value	Denomination	Date	Table
Arrests of Persons 65 Years +				
Violent crimes	3,266	number	1990	893
Percent of total violent crimes	0.6	%	1990	893
Property crimes	15,695	number	1990	893
Percent of total	0.9	%	1990	893
All crimes	84,251	number	1990	893
Percent of total	0.7	%	1990	893
State Prison Population				
All ages	450,416	number	1986	901
65 years +	2,808	number	1986	901
65 + as percent of total	0.6	%	1986	901
Victimization Rates in 1990				
Personal crimes				
Age 12-15	160.3	rate per 1,000 people	1990	906
Age 16-19	187.8	rate per 1,000 people	1990	906
Age 20-24	174.8	rate per 1,000 people	1990	906
Age 25-34	114.0	rate per 1,000 people	1990	906
Age 35-49	76.6	rate per 1,000 people	1990	906
Age 50-64	44.0	rate per 1,000 people	1990	906
65 years +	24.6	rate per 1,000 people	1990	906
Crimes of theft				
Age 12-15	91.5	rate per 1,000 people	1990	906
Age 16-19	113.4	rate per 1,000 people	1990	906
Age 20-24	111.6	rate per 1,000 people	1990	906
Age 25-34	77.5	rate per 1,000 people	1990	906
Age 35-49	57.5	rate per 1,000 people	1990	906
Age 50-64	36.5	rate per 1,000 people	1990	906
65 years +	21.2	rate per 1,000 people	1990	906

Source: Data are drawn from tables in the rest of *Statistical Record of Older Americans.*

Chapter 2
DEMOGRAPHICS

This chapter presents information generally on population, life expectancy, and mortality of older people. The chapter begins with data for the historical, current, and projected population of older Americans, on trends in the growth of the elderly population, and—provided for purposes of comparison—world statistics on older populations. Data on life expectancy and mortality follow. The section on mortality shows death rates associated with various diseases and thus overlaps somewhat in coverage with the chapter on *Health and Health Care* where other aspects of these diseases are documented. The chapter ends with a brief section on the mobility of elderly people.

Related data may be found in the chapters on *Families*, *Labor and Employment*, and *Housing*. Detailed profiling on nursing home populations will be found in the chapter on *Nursing Homes and Resident Care*.

Population

★ 12 ★

Actual and Projected Growth of the Older Population: 1900-2050[1]

The table shows the elderly population (65 and older) rising steadily from a 1900 level of 4.0 percent of total population through 12.6 percent in 1990 to 22.9 percent by 2050. These trends assume continuing improvement in life expectations.

[Data are in 1,000]

Year	Total population all ages	55 to 64		65 to 74		75 to 84 years		85 +		65 +	
		No.	%	No.	%	No.	%	No.	%	No.	%
1900	76,303	4,009	5.3	2,189	2.9	772	1.0	123	0.2	3,084	4.0
1910	91,972	5,054	5.5	2,793	3.0	989	1.1	167	0.2	3,950	4.3
1920	105,711	6,532	6.2	3,464	3.3	1,259	1.0	210	0.2	4,933	4.7
1930	122,775	8,397	6.8	4,721	3.8	1,641	1.3	272	0.2	6,634	5.4
1940	131,669	10,572	8.0	6,375	4.8	2,278	1.7	365	0.3	9,019	6.8
1950	150,967	13,295	8.8	8,415	5.6	3,278	2.2	577	0.4	12,270	8.1
1960	179,323	15,572	8.7	10,997	6.1	4,633	2.6	929	0.5	16,560	9.2

[Continued]

★ 12 ★

Actual and Projected Growth of the Older Population: 1900-2050
[Continued]

Year	Total population all ages	55 to 64		65 to 74		75 to 84 years		85 +		65 +	
		No.	%	No.	%	No.	%	No.	%	No.	%
1970	203,302	18,608	9.2	12,447	6.1	6,124	3.0	1,409	0.7	19,980	9.8
1980	226,546	21,703	9.6	15,580	6.9	7,729	3.4	2,240	1.0	25,549	11.3
1990	250,410	21,364	8.5	18,373	7.3	9,933	4.0	3,254	1.3	31,559	12.6
2000	268,266	24,158	9.0	18,243	6.8	12,017	4.5	4,622	1.7	34,882	13.0
2010	282,575	35,430	12.5	21,039	7.4	12,208	4.3	6,115	2.2	39,362	13.9
2020	294,364	41,087	14.0	30,973	10.5	14,443	4.9	6,651	2.3	52,067	17.7
2030	300,629	34,947	11.6	35,988	12.0	21,487	7.1	8,129	2.7	65,604	21.8
2040	301,807	35,537	11.8	30,808	10.2	25,050	8.3	12,251	4.1	68,109	22.6
2050	299,849	37,004	12.3	31,590	10.5	21,655	7.2	15,287	5.1	68,532	22.9

Source: Aging America, Trends and Projections, prepared by the U.S. Senate Special Committee on Aging, the American Association of Retired Persons, the Federal Council on the Aging, and the U.S. Administration on Aging, 1991, Washington, D.C., p. 7. Primary source: 1900 to 1980 data are tabulated from the Decennial Censuses of the population and exclude Armed Forces overseas. Projections, which are middle series projections and include Armed Forces overseas, are from U.S. Bureau of the Census, "Projections of the Population of the United States, by Age, Sex, and Race: 1988 to 2080," by Gregory Spencer. *Current Population Reports* Series P-25, No. 1018, January 1989. *Note:* 1. Numbers in thousands.

★ 13 ★

Population

Population Distribution by Age, 1900-2050, Number
[Numbers in thousands]

Age	1900	1950	1990[1]	2050[1]
All ages	76,212	151,326	250,409	299,847
Under 15	26,171	40,673	54,070	49,420
15-24	14,930	22,221	36,107	34,754
25-44	21,386	45,413	81,822	74,043
45-64	10,422	30,724	46,851	73,098
65 and over	3,085	12,295	31,559	68,532

Source: "Historical Perspectives," *Statistical Bulletin* 71, No. 3, July-September, 1990, p. 33. Primary source: U.S. Bureau of the Census. As of July 1. *Note:* 1. Includes Armed Forces overseas.

★ 14 ★

Population

Population Distribution by Age, 1900-2050, Percent

[Values are in percent]

Age	1900	1950	1990[1]	2050[1]
All ages	100.0	100.0	100.0	100.0
Under 15	34.4	26.9	21.6	16.4
15-24	19.7	14.7	14.4	11.6
25-44	28.1	30.0	32.7	24.7
45-64	13.7	20.3	18.7	24.4
65 & over	4.1	8.1	12.6	22.9

Source: "Historical Perspectives," *Statistical Bulletin* 71, No. 3, July-September, 1990, p. 33.
Primary source: U.S. Bureau of the Census. As of July 1. *Note:* 1. Includes Armed Forces overseas.

★ 15 ★

Population

Population by Marital Status and Age, 1987-2080

Includes the populations of Puerto Rico, Guam, American Samoa, the Virgin Islands, and U.S. citizens living abroad. The disunity ratio is defined as "the ratio of the number of divorced persons to the number of married and widowed persons." Alternatives in the table below are "based on three different sets of assumptions about future net immigration, birth rates, and death rates.... Alternative I is designated as optimistic because among the three projections the assumptions selected produce the most favorable financial effect for the OASDI program. Conversely, the assumptions chosen for Alternative III, designated pessimistic, produce the most unfavorable financial effect."

[Numbers in thousands]

Alternative and Calendar year	Marital status				Age				Disunity ratio
	Single	Married	Widowed	Divorced	Total	0-19	20-64	65 or older	
Alternative I									
1987	107,222	113,472	14,832	16,217	251,743	73,418	148,183	30,142	.126
1988	107,915	114,242	14,897	16,971	254,025	73,663	149,632	30,730	.131
1989	108,669	114,982	14,963	17,684	256,297	73,887	151,109	31,302	.136
1990	109,478	115,695	15,030	18,348	258,551	74,041	152,668	31,841	.140
1991	110,339	116,357	15,096	18,985	260,777	74,215	154,237	32,325	.144
1992	111,247	116,948	15,161	19,615	262,971	74,566	155,629	32,777	.148
1993	112,200	117,476	15,224	20,229	265,129	75,097	156,830	33,202	.152
1994	113,192	117,952	15,284	20,820	267,249	75,682	157,988	33,579	.156
1995	114,224	118,385	15,343	21,383	269,335	76,252	159,177	33,906	.160
1996	115,290	118,774	15,399	21,925	271,389	76,790	160,423	34,176	.163
1997	116,389	119,124	15,452	22,451	273,417	77,264	161,781	34,372	.167
1998	117,518	119,444	15,504	22,960	275,425	77,671	163,246	34,508	.170
1999	118,673	119,744	15,553	23,450	277,420	78,005	164,784	34,631	.173
2000	119,854	120,033	15,600	23,921	279,408	78,258	166,377	34,773	.176
2010	133,787	122,270	16,098	27,798	299,953	81,581	179,700	38,671	.201
2020	149,910	124,232	17,168	29,657	320,967	88,266	182,280	50,422	.210

[Continued]

★ 15 ★

Population by Marital Status and Age, 1987-2080
[Continued]

Alternative and Calendar year	Marital status				Age				Disunity ratio
	Single	Married	Widowed	Divorced	Total	0-19	20-64	65 or older	
2030	164,110	126,124	19,025	29,864	339,124	94,119	182,062	62,942	.206
2040	177,228	128,722	20,167	29,739	355,856	99,607	191,882	64,367	.200
2050	189,909	133,331	19,838	30,046	373,124	106,490	202,606	64,027	.196
2060	202,404	140,560	19,319	31,102	393,385	112,804	214,663	65,917	.195
2070	215,168	149,518	19,757	32,796	417,239	119,664	228,820	68,755	.194
2080	228,198	159,115	20,768	34,815	442,895	126,975	241,816	74,105	.194
Alternative II									
1987	107,113	113,519	14,823	16,184	251,639	73,374	148,121	30,144	.126
1988	107,550	114,424	14,869	16,865	253,707	73,518	149,446	30,743	.130
1989	107,979	115,369	14,915	17,490	255,753	73,616	150,800	31,337	.134
1990	108,402	116,350	14,962	18,055	257,769	73,619	152,239	31,911	.137
1991	108,819	117,335	15,008	18,584	259,745	73,616	153,691	32,438	.140
1992	109,230	118,297	15,053	19,097	261,677	73,767	154,965	32,945	.143
1993	109,636	119,237	15,096	19,590	263,559	74,074	156,051	33,434	.146
1994	110,038	120,161	15,139	20,053	265,391	74,413	157,094	33,884	.148
1995	110,435	121,075	15,180	20,485	267,175	74,715	158,169	34,290	.150
1996	110,827	121,974	15,220	20,891	268,912	74,963	159,302	34,647	.152
1997	111,209	122,862	15,259	21,278	270,608	75,125	160,548	34,935	.154
1998	111,578	123,746	15,298	21,646	272,267	75,200	161,902	35,166	.156
1999	111,930	124,634	15,336	21,993	273,894	75,177	163,331	35,386	.157
2000	112,265	125,534	15,375	22,320	275,493	75,053	164,814	35,626	.158
2010	115,211	134,802	15,894	24,772	290,681	73,488	176,764	40,429	.164
2020	118,611	141,870	17,193	26,025	303,698	74,816	175,784	53,099	.164
2030	121,066	144,822	19,607	26,381	311,875	75,442	169,712	66,722	.160
2040	122,313	145,635	21,681	26,377	316,005	75,404	171,551	69,051	.158
2050	123,286	146,023	22,139	26,328	317,776	76,327	172,285	69,163	.157
2060	124,161	147,385	21,752	26,487	319,785	76,678	172,726	70,381	.157
2070	125,155	149,480	21,771	26,857	323,264	77,143	174,975	71,146	.157
2080	126,217	151,535	22,014	27,275	327,041	77,781	175,776	73,484	.157
Alternative III									
1987	106,999	113,564	14,814	16,152	251,529	73,324	148,059	30,146	0.126
1988	107,168	114,594	14,841	16,762	253,365	73,349	149,260	30,755	.130
1989	107,253	115,733	14,868	17,302	255,156	73,293	150,491	31,372	.132
1990	107,260	116,967	14,895	17,772	256,894	73,106	151,810	31,978	.135
1991	107,195	118,257	14,920	18,197	258,570	72,880	153,141	32,548	.137
1992	107,066	119,568	14,945	18,599	260,178	72,775	154,297	33,106	.138
1993	106,877	120,895	14,969	18,973	261,714	72,795	155,264	33,655	.140
1994	106,634	122,241	14,993	19,311	263,178	72,818	156,189	34,171	.141
1995	106,340	123,604	15,016	19,611	264,572	72,775	157,145	34,651	.141
1996	105,996	124,979	15,040	19,882	265,897	72,650	158,161	35,086	.142
1997	105,599	126,365	15,063	20,129	267,157	72,412	159,288	35,457	.142
1998	105,146	127,770	15,088	20,353	268,358	72,059	160,525	35,774	.142
1999	104,634	129,201	15,114	20,553	269,501	71,582	161,836	36,083	.142

[Continued]

★ 15 ★

Population by Marital Status and Age, 1987-2080
[Continued]

Alternative and Calendar year	Marital status				Age				Disunity ratio
	Single	Married	Widowed	Divorced	Total	0-19	20-64	65 or older	
2000	104,060	130,663	15,141	20,730	270,593	70,977	163,202	36,415	.142
2010	95,627	146,366	15,585	21,621	279,198	63,283	173,665	42,250	.134
2020	87,791	156,588	16,868	22,101	283,348	58,497	168,433	56,419	.127
2030	81,448	158,215	19,441	22,352	281,455	54,026	155,251	72,179	.126
2040	74,810	154,660	22,107	22,106	273,683	49,324	147,630	76,729	.125
2050	68,686	148,067	23,219	21,404	261,376	45,671	137,170	78,534	.125
2060	63,232	140,698	22,813	20,554	247,298	42,127	125,578	79,592	.126
2070	58,466	133,317	22,118	19,692	233,593	38,870	116,953	77,769	.127
2080	54,315	125,669	21,315	18,773	220,072	36,051	108,177	75,844	.128

Source: "Social Security Area Population Projections," Alice H. Wade (Office of the Actuary, Social Security Administration), *Social Security Bulletin* 51, No. 2, February, 1988, p. 26-7. *Note:* OASDI stands for Old Age, Survivors, and Disability Insurance.

★ 16 ★

Population

Resident U.S. Elderly Population as a Percentage of Total Population, by Race/ Ethnicity, Selected Years 1950-89

Data are based on decennial census updated by data from multiple sources.

[Numbers in thousands]

Sex, race, Hispanic origin, and year	Total resident population	55-64 years		65-74 years		75-84 years		85 years and over	
		Number	%	Number	%	Number	%	Number	%
All persons									
1950	150,697	13,370	8.9	8,340	5.5	3,278	2.2	577	0.4
1960	179,323	15,572	8.7	10,997	6.1	4,633	2.6	929	0.5
1970	203,212	18,590	9.1	12,435	6.1	6,119	3.0	1,511	0.7
1980	226,546	21,703	9.6	15,581	6.9	7,729	3.4	2,240	1.0
1987	243,400	22,019	9.0	17,668	7.3	9,301	3.8	2,867	1.2
1988	245,807	21,831	8.9	17,897	7.3	9,522	3.9	2,948	1.2
1989	248,239	21,593	8.7	18,182	7.3	9,761	3.9	3,042	1.2
White male									
1950	67,129	6,180	9.2	3,736	5.6	1,406	2.1	218	0.3
1960	78,367	6,850	8.7	4,702	6.0	1,875	2.4	331	0.4
1970	86,721	7,958	9.2	4,916	5.7	2,243	2.6	487	0.6
1980	94,976	9,151	9.6	6,096	6.4	2,600	2.7	621	0.7
1987	100,589	9,180	9.1	7,028	7.0	3,154	3.1	723	0.7
1988	101,389	9,087	9.0	7,124	7.0	3,240	3.2	739	0.7
1989	102,223	8,978	8.8	7,250	7.1	3,336	3.3	761	0.7

[Continued]

★ 16 ★

Resident U.S. Elderly Population as a Percentage of Total Population, by Race/ Ethnicity, Selected Years 1950-89
[Continued]

Sex, race, Hispanic origin, and year	Total resident population	55-64 years		65-74 years		75-84 years		85 years and over	
		Number	%	Number	%	Number	%	Number	%
White female									
1950	67,813	6,168	9.1	4,031	5.9	1,669	2.5	314	0.5
1960	80,465	7,327	9.1	5,428	6.7	2,441	3.0	527	0.7
1970	91,028	8,853	9.7	6,366	7.0	3,429	3.8	890	1.0
1980	99,835	10,325	10.3	7,951	8.0	4,457	4.5	1,440	1.4
1987	105,231	10,202	9.7	8,788	8.4	5,284	5.0	1,887	1.8
1988	105,988	10,064	9.5	8,867	8.4	5,389	5.1	1,940	1.8
1989	106,738	9,901	9.3	8,973	8.4	5,502	5.2	2,000	1.9
Black male									
1950	7,300	460	6.3	299	4.1	...	...	...	...
1960	9,114	617	6.8	382	4.2	137	1.5	29	0.3
1970	10,748	739	6.9	461	4.3	169	1.6	46	0.4
1980	12,585	854	6.8	567	4.5	228	1.8	53	0.4
1987	14,103	961	6.8	647	4.6	268	1.9	69	0.5
1988	14,325	969	6.8	660	4.6	272	1.9	70	0.5
1989	14,545	975	6.7	676	4.6	278	1.9	72	0.5
Black female									
1950	7,745	443	5.7	322	4.2	...	...	...	...
1960	9,758	663	6.8	430	4.4	160	1.6	38	0.4
1970	11,832	868	7.3	582	4.9	230	1.9	71	0.6
1980	14,046	1,059	7.5	776	5.5	360	2.6	106	0.8
1987	15,633	1,164	7.4	871	5.6	442	2.8	152	1.0
1988	15,877	1,170	7.4	886	5.6	454	2.9	158	1.0
1989	16,115	1,175	7.3	901	5.6	464	2.9	165	1.0
Hispanic male									
1980	7,280	364	5.0	201	2.8	86	1.2	19	0.3
1987	9,637	514	5.3	260	2.7	117	1.2	28	0.3
1988	9,973	528	5.3	275	2.8	120	1.2	30	0.3
1989	10,317	542	5.3	291	2.8	123	1.2	32	0.3
Hispanic female									
1980	7,329	411	5.6	257	3.5	116	1.6	30	0.4
1987	9,535	583	6.1	339	3.6	178	1.9	50	0.5

[Continued]

★ 16 ★

Resident U.S. Elderly Population as a Percentage of Total Population, by Race/Ethnicity, Selected Years 1950-89

[Continued]

Sex, race, Hispanic origin, and year	Total resident population	55-64 years		65-74 years		75-84 years		85 years and over	
		Number	%	Number	%	Number	%	Number	%
1988	9,857	603	6.1	356	3.6	186	1.9	54	0.5
1989	10,188	620	6.1	373	3.7	194	1.9	59	0.6

Source: U.S. Bureau of the Census: *1950 Nonwhite Population by Race. Special Report P-E, No. 3B.* Washington. U.S. Government Printing Office, 1951; *Population estimates and projections. Current Population Reports. Series P-25, Nos. 499, 1022, 1045, 1046, and 1057.* Washington. U.S. Government Printing Office, May 1973, Mar. 1988, Sept. 1989, Jan. 1990, and Mar. 1990; U.S. Bureau of the Census, *U.S. Census of Population: 1960, Number of Inhabitants, PC(1)- A1, United States Summary, 1964.* U.S. Bureau of the Census, *U.S. Census of Population: 1970, Number of Inhabitants, Final Report PC(1)- A1, United States Summary, 1971;* Unpublished data from the U.S. Bureau of the Census. *Notes:* Three periods (...) indicates that data were not available. The race groups, White and Black, include persons of both Hispanic and non-Hispanic origin. Conversely, persons of Hispanic origin may be of any race. Population figures are census counts as of April 1 for 1950, 1960, 1970, and 1980 and estimates as of July 1 for other years.

★ 17 ★

Population

Ratios of White and Black Youth and Elderly to Other Adults, by Race, and Hispanic Origin: 1990 and 2050

From the source: "Youth ratio is the number of persons under age 20 divided by the number of persons aged 20-64 times 100. Elderly ratio is the number of persons age 65 years and over divided by the number of persons aged 20-64 times 100."

[Data are shown in number of persons of given age per 100 persons aged 20 to 64]

Race/ethnicity	1990		2050	
	Youth ratio	Elderly ratio	Youth ratio	Elderly ratio
Total	49.2	21.3	40.5	41.6
White	46.7	22.7	39.8	43.7
Black	64.8	14.7	44.5	36.8
Other races	57.1	9.9	39.5	33.4
Hispanic origin[1]	69.8	9.2	47.3	27.2

Source: *Sixty-Five Plus in America*, Cynthia M. Taeuber, U.S. Department of Commerce, Economics and Statistics Administration, Bureau of the Census, U.S. Government Printing Office, Washington, D.C., 1992, p. 2-19. Primary source: U.S. Bureau of the Census, 1990 from 1990 Census of Population and Housing, Series CPH-L-74, *Modified and Actual Age, Sex, Race, and Hispanic Origin Data*; 2050 from *Projections of the Population of the United States, by Age, Sex, and Race: 1988 to 2080*, Current Population Reports, Series P-25, No. 1018. U.S. Government Printing Office, Washington, D.C., 1989 (middle series projections). Hispanic projections from *Projections of the Hispanic Population: 1983 to 2080*, Current Population Reports, Series P-25, No. 995, U.S. Government Printing Office, Washington, D.C., 1988 (middle series projections). *Note:* 1. Hispanic origin may be of any race.

★ 18 ★

Population

Persons 65 Years and Over, by Age, Race, and Hispanic Origin: 1990

[Data are shown in millions]

Race/ethnicity	65 years and older	65 to 79 years	80 years and older
All races	31.1	24.1	6.9
White	28.0	21.7	6.3
Black	2.5	2.0	0.5
Other races[1]	0.6	0.5	0.1
Hispanic origin[2]	1.1	0.9	0.2

Source: Sixty-Five Plus in America, Cynthia M. Taeuber, U.S. Department of Commerce, Economics and Statistics Administration, Bureau of the Census, U.S. Government Printing Office, Washington, D.C., 1992, p. 2-12. Primary source: U.S. Bureau of the Census, 1990 from 1990 Census of Population and Housing, Series CPH-L-74, *Modified and Actual Age, Sex, Race, and Hispanic Origin Data*; Hispanic from *Projections of the Hispanic Population: 1983 to 2080*, Current Population Reports, Series P-25, No. 995. U.S. Government Printing Office, Washington, DC, 1988 (middle series projections). *Notes:* 1. Includes Asians and Pacific Islanders, American Indians, Eskimos, and Aleuts. 2. Hispanic origin may be of any race.

★ 19 ★

Population

Persons 65 Years and Over, by Specific Race and Hispanic Origin: 1980 and 1990

[Data are shown in millions]

Race/ethnicity	1980	1990
All races	25.6	31.1
White	22.9	28.0
Black	2.1	2.5
American Indian, Eskimo, or Aleut	0.1	0.1
Asian or Pacific Islander	0.2	0.5
Hispanic origin[1]	0.7	1.1

Source: Sixty-Five Plus in America, Cynthia M. Taeuber, U.S. Department of Commerce, Economics and Statistics Administration, Bureau of the Census, U.S. Government Printing Office, Washington, D.C., 1992, p. 2-11. Primary source: U.S. Bureau of the Census, 1980 Census of Population, General Social and Economic Characteristics, PC-80-1-C1, U.S. Summary, U.S. Government Printing Office, Washington, D.C., 1983, Tables 120 and 130; 1990 Census of Population and Housing, Series CPH-L-74, *Modified and Actual Age, Sex, Race, and Hispanic Origin Data. Notes:* 1. Hispanic origin may be of any race. The 1980 data does not distribute persons of unspecified races among the specified races as has been done in the 1990 data. Therefore, those elderly who marked "other race" on the 1980 Census questionnaire are not included here. In data for 1990 from the CPH- L-74 Series used here, persons who marked "other race" were assigned the race reported by a nearby person with an identical response to the Hispanic origin question.

★ 20 ★

Population

Population 65 Years and Older by Race, 1950-2020

[Numbers in percent]

Race and age	1950	1960	1970	1980	1990	2000	2010	2020
White								
65 +	8.4	9.6	10.2	11.9	13.6	14.0	14.9	18.6
70 +	5.0	6.0	6.7	7.9	9.3	10.4	10.5	12.7
75 +	2.7	3.3	3.9	4.7	5.9	7.0	7.3	7.9
80 +	1.2	1.5	1.9	2.5	3.2	4.1	4.7	4.7
85 +	0.4	0.5	0.7	1.1	1.5	2.7	3.4	3.5
Black								
65 +	5.7	6.3	6.8	7.8	8.2	8.4	8.9	11.6
70 +	3.0	3.7	4.1	4.9	5.6	6.0	6.1	7.4
75 +	1.6	1.9	2.2	2.8	3.5	3.9	4.1	4.5
80 +	0.8	0.9	1.1	1.4	1.8	2.3	2.6	2.7
85 +	0.3	0.4	0.5	0.6	0.9	1.2	1.4	1.5

Source: "Black Americans' Health," *A Common Destiny: Blacks and American Society*, Gerald David Jaynes and Robin M. Williams, eds., National Academy Press, Washington, D.C., 1989, p. 426. Primary source: Decennial censuses and Census Bureau projections.

★ 21 ★

Population

Population of Persons 65+ in the Top 200 Metropolitan Areas, for Selected Minorities: 1990 - Part I

For figures relating to American Indians, Asians, and Hispanics see *Part II*.

[Rank based on total of all races and ages in places of 100,000 or more]

Place	Rank	State	Total, all races			Black	
			All ages	65 and over	85 and over	65 and over	85 and over
New York	1	NY	7,322,564	953,317	102,554	174,798	13,828
Los Angeles	2	CA	3,485,398	347,713	35,419	51,893	4,535
Chicago	3	IL	2,783,726	330,182	30,522	98,181	8,174
Houston	4	TX	1,630,553	135,077	12,129	32,586	2,840
Philadelphia	5	PA	1,585,577	240,714	22,801	70,253	5,822
San Diego	6	CA	1,110,549	113,495	10,203	5,368	384
Detroit	7	MI	1,027,974	124,933	12,506	77,444	7,005
Dallas	8	TX	1,006,877	97,891	10,131	18,565	1,643
Phoenix	9	AZ	983,403	95,226	7,832	3,379	343
San Antonio	10	TX	935,933	98,365	9,421	6,895	667
San Jose	11	CA	782,248	56,358	5,022	1,105	83

[Continued]

★ 21 ★

Population of Persons 65+ in the Top 200 Metropolitan Areas, for Selected Minorities: 1990 - Part I

[Continued]

Place	Rank	State	Total, all races			Black	
			All ages	65 and over	85 and over	65 and over	85 and over
Baltimore	12	MD	736,014	100,916	9,695	41,981	3,267
Indianapolis	13	IN	731,327	83,628	8,505	15,330	1,551
San Francisco	14	CA	723,959	105,380	12,148	9,932	763
Jacksonville (remainder)	15	FL	635,230	67,343	5,792	14,182	1,199
Columbus	16	OH	632,910	57,939	5,961	10,761	911
Milwaukee	17	WI	628,088	78,145	8,781	8,578	611
Memphis	18	TN	610,337	74,597	7,341	27,969	2,843
Washington	19	DC	606,900	77,847	7,847	52,263	4,253
Boston	20	MA	574,283	65,950	8,219	9,864	806
Seattle	21	WA	516,259	78,400	9,271	4,577	311
El Paso	22	TX	515,342	45,016	3,770	768	52
Cleveland	23	OH	505,616	70,753	6,612	27,266	2,272
New Orleans	24	LA	496,938	64,658	6,656	27,279	2,346
Nashville-Davidson (remainder)	25	TN	488,374	55,826	5,747	10,087	1,008
Denver	26	CO	467,610	64,805	7,648	5,207	486
Austin	27	TX	465,622	34,577	3,709	3,858	420
Fort Worth	28	TX	447,619	50,225	5,133	8,195	791
Oklahoma City	29	OK	444,719	52,779	5,310	5,653	570
Portland	30	OR	437,319	63,657	7,551	2,730	164
Kansas City	31	KS	435,146	56,166	6,393	11,910	1,119
Long Beach	32	CA	429,433	46,463	5,426	2,087	162
Tucson	33	AZ	405,390	51,198	5,228	1,360	120
St. Louis	34	MO	396,685	66,001	8,389	23,236	2,515
Charlotte	35	NC	395,934	38,802	3,603	8,188	642
Atlanta	36	GA	394,017	44,432	5,071	24,039	2,157
Virginia Beach	37	VA	393,069	23,214	1,846	2,062	164
Albuquerque	38	NM	384,736	42,767	3,761	668	58
Oakland	39	CA	372,242	44,855	5,303	16,038	1,243
Pittsburgh	40	PA	369,879	66,336	6,624	12,115	1,249
Sacramento	41	CA	369,365	44,619	4,464	3,748	272
Minneapolis	42	MN	368,383	47,718	7,475	2,006	171
Tulsa	43	OK	367,302	46,684	4,828	4,196	479
Honolulu CDP[1]	44	HI	365,272	58,279	5,312	169	17
Cincinnati	45	OH	364,040	50,726	6,230	14,220	1,269
Miami	46	FL	358,548	59,347	6,284	7,084	527
Fresno	47	CA	354,202	35,804	3,989	2,453	212
Omaha	48	NE	335,795	43,297	4,980	3,284	328
Toledo	49	OH	332,943	45,201	4,421	5,507	472
Buffalo	50	NY	328,123	48,703	5,083	9,191	709

[Continued]

★ 21 ★

Population of Persons 65+ in the Top 200 Metropolitan Areas, for Selected Minorities: 1990 - Part I

[Continued]

Place	Rank	State	Total, all races			Black	
			All ages	65 and over	85 and over	65 and over	85 and over
Wichita	51	KS	304,011	37,655	3,894	2,393	193
Santa Ana	52	CA	293,742	16,522	1,776	379	24
Mesa	53	AZ	288,091	35,713	2,933	241	31
Colorado Springs	54	CO	281,140	25,781	2,545	605	39
Tampa	55	FL	280,015	40,934	4,104	6,130	600
Newark	56	NJ	275,221	25,547	2,139	12,882	943
St. Paul	57	MN	272,235	37,412	5,309	1,112	111
Louisville	58	KY	269,063	44,641	5,064	9,750	970
Anaheim	59	CA	266,406	22,292	2,266	104	5
Birmingham	60	AL	265,968	39,480	4,452	19,254	1,988
Arlington	61	TX	261,721	13,012	1,038	171	7
Norfolk	62	VA	261,229	27,458	2,313	8,970	660
Las Vegas	63	NV	258,295	26,532	1,566	1,761	119
Corpus Christi	64	TX	257,453	25,933	2,186	1,439	116
St. Petersburg	65	FL	238,629	52,945	7,975	4,034	340
Rochester	66	NY	231,636	28,135	4,036	3,542	265
Jersey City	67	NJ	228,537	25,287	2,384	4,145	292
Riverside	68	CA	226,505	20,266	2,116	975	85
Anchorage	69	AK	226,338	8,258	374	328	14
Lexington-Fayette	70	KY	225,366	22,312	2,308	2,778	285
Akron	71	OH	223,019	33,171	3,470	5,179	401
Aurora	72	CO	222,103	15,044	1,135	445	26
Baton Rouge	73	LA	219,531	25,161	2,356	7,685	662
Stockton	74	CA	210,943	22,107	2,213	1,741	124
Raleigh	75	NC	207,951	18,332	1,814	3,814	358
Richmond	76	VA	203,056	31,181	3,435	12,345	934
Shreveport	77	LA	198,525	27,206	3,105	8,203	947
Jackson	78	MS	196,637	22,851	2,247	8,080	815
Mobile	79	AL	196,278	26,900	2,618	7,718	672
Des Moines	80	IA	193,187	25,884	3,053	1,325	123
Lincoln	81	NE	191,972	21,005	2,674	198	13
Madison	82	WI	191,262	17,831	2,211	210	15
Grand Rapids	83	MI	189,126	24,711	3,508	2,077	159
Yonkers	84	NY	188,082	30,935	2,979	1,684	158
Hialeah	85	FL	188,004	26,338	2,362	292	20
Montgomery	86	AL	187,106	21,884	2,185	6,574	680
Lubbock	87	TX	186,206	18,299	1,842	1,143	98
Greensboro	88	NC	183,521	21,591	2,239	4,736	442
Dayton	89	OH	182,044	23,929	2,060	7,931	568

[Continued]

★ 21 ★

Population of Persons 65+ in the Top 200 Metropolitan Areas, for Selected Minorities: 1990 - Part I

[Continued]

Place	Rank	State	Total, all races			Black	
			All ages	65 and over	85 and over	65 and over	85 and over
Huntington Beach	90	CA	181,519	15,088	1,211	24	2
Garland	91	TX	180,650	9,970	715	381	33
Glendale	92	CA	180,038	23,977	3,208	78	10
Columbus (remainder)	93	GA	178,681	19,254	1,570	5,138	442
Spokane	94	WA	177,196	28,788	3,539	296	17
Tacoma	95	WA	176,664	24,258	3,235	1,118	72
Little Rock	96	AR	175,795	22,071	2,497	4,461	545
Bakersfield	97	CA	174,820	15,998	1,696	1,323	144
Fremont	98	CA	173,339	11,541	951	123	4
Fort Wayne	99	IN	173,072	23,091	2,807	1,637	117
Arlington CDP[1]	100	VA	170,936	19,409	1,738	1,357	106
Newport News	101	VA	170,045	15,804	1,192	4,400	254
Worcester	102	MA	169,759	27,287	3,466	301	27
Knoxville	103	TN	165,121	25,441	2,708	2,979	271
Modesto	104	CA	164,730	17,268	1,769	260	22
Orlando	105	FL	164,693	18,755	2,180	3,101	262
San Bernardino	106	CA	164,164	16,396	1,616	1,658	153
Syracuse	107	NY	163,860	24,394	3,327	1,784	189
Providence	108	RI	160,728	21,802	2,659	1,379	111
Salt Lake City	109	UT	159,936	23,192	2,832	228	13
Huntsville	110	AL	159,789	15,982	1,351	2,137	240
Amarillo	111	TX	157,615	18,974	1,876	771	73
Springfield	112	MA	156,983	21,568	2,384	2,024	166
Irving	113	TX	155,037	8,413	645	122	10
Chattanooga	114	TN	152,466	23,269	2,584	5,713	577
Chesapeake	115	VA	151,976	12,844	991	3,223	230
Kansas City	116	KS	149,767	19,489	2,022	4,163	503
Metairie CDP[1]	117	LA	149,428	21,013	1,474	537	35
Fort Lauderdale	118	FL	149,377	26,562	3,351	2,156	145
Glendale	119	AZ	148,134	11,675	1,154	143	7
Warren	120	MI	144,864	21,555	1,677	35	2
Winston-Salem	121	NC	143,485	20,331	2,355	5,497	531
Garden Grove	122	CA	143,050	12,512	1,083	60	5
Oxnard	123	CA	142,216	11,003	876	445	21
Tempe	124	AZ	141,865	9,305	850	90	4
Bridgeport	125	CT	141,686	19,245	2,064	2,190	133
Paterson	126	NJ	140,891	13,551	1,197	2,706	170
Flint	127	MI	140,761	15,100	1,619	4,294	300

[Continued]

★ 21 ★

Population of Persons 65+ in the Top 200 Metropolitan Areas, for Selected Minorities: 1990 - Part I
[Continued]

| Place | Rank | State | Total, all races | | | Black | |
			All ages	65 and over	85 and over	65 and over	85 and over
Springfield	128	MO	140,494	21,329	2,696	301	30
Hartford	129	CT	139,739	13,809	1,536	3,453	240
Rockford	130	IL	139,426	20,535	2,644	1,167	80
Savannah	131	GA	137,560	18,957	1,576	7,758	635
Durham	132	NC	136,611	15,443	1,677	5,405	522
Chula Vista	133	CA	135,163	15,767	1,417	199	13
Reno	134	NV	133,850	15,802	1,264	251	16
Hampton	135	VA	133,793	12,801	898	3,985	290
Ontario	136	CA	133,179	8,489	706	267	13
Torrance	137	CA	133,107	15,900	1,546	56	7
Pomona	138	CA	131,723	9,191	1,036	883	68
Pasadena	139	CA	131,591	17,338	2,500	2,372	289
New Haven	140	CT	130,474	16,067	1,965	2,925	225
Scottsdale	141	AZ	130,069	21,199	1,901	42	1
Plano	142	TX	128,713	4,577	437	152	15
Oceanside	143	CA	128,398	18,010	1,193	186	8
Lansing	144	MI	127,321	12,171	1,205	1,131	90
Lakewood	145	CO	126,481	13,343	1,448	66	5
East Los Angeles CDP[1]	146	CA	126,379	9,617	1,017	25	3
Evansville	147	IN	126,272	21,661	2,464	1,369	142
Boise City	148	ID	125,738	14,970	1,627	25	5
Tallahassee	149	FL	124,773	10,946	1,035	2,546	245
Paradise CDP[1]	150	NV	124,682	15,864	692	373	13
Laredo	151	TX	122,899	10,020	1,019	4	0
Hollywood	152	FL	121,697	28,101	3,817	557	55
Topeka	153	KS	119,883	17,681	2,100	1,236	153
Pasadena	154	TX	119,363	9,142	677	25	3
Moreno Valley	155	CA	118,779	4,734	211	369	18
Sterling Heights	156	MI	117,810	10,872	856	16	0
Sunnyvale	157	CA	117,229	12,191	1,015	81	4
Gary	158	IN	116,646	13,261	992	9,059	663
Beaumont	159	TX	114,323	15,737	1,668	4,405	430
Fullerton	160	CA	114,144	11,668	1,251	68	5
Peoria	161	IL	113,504	16,381	1,756	1,359	93
Santa Rosa	162	CA	113,313	18,472	1,960	64	5
Eugene	163	OR	112,669	14,276	1,710	43	2
Independence	164	MO	112,301	16,148	1,547	92	17
Overland Park	165	KS	111,790	11,068	950	43	3

[Continued]

★ 21 ★

Population of Persons 65+ in the Top 200 Metropolitan Areas, for Selected Minorities: 1990 - Part I

[Continued]

Place	Rank	State	Total, all races			Black	
			All ages	65 and over	85 and over	65 and over	85 and over
Hayward	166	CA	111,498	11,910	1,076	296	29
Concord	167	CA	111,348	10,543	1,009	63	3
Alexandria	168	VA	111,183	11,406	1,380	1,615	133
Orange	169	CA	110,658	9,631	1,070	33	2
Santa Clarita	170	CA	110,642	6,916	563	42	6
Irvine	171	CA	110,330	6,357	527	30	1
Elizabeth	172	NJ	110,002	13,270	1,289	1,278	111
Inglewood	173	CA	109,602	7,494	778	3,291	265
Ann Arbor	174	MI	109,592	7,881	990	620	58
Vallejo	175	CA	109,199	11,851	978	1,725	97
Waterbury	176	CT	108,961	17,925	1,864	1,037	87
Salinas	177	CA	108,777	9,048	853	129	10
Cedar Rapids	178	IA	108,751	14,324	1,732	157	14
Erie	179	PA	108,718	17,488	1,638	789	56
Escondido	180	CA	108,635	14,074	1,778	23	3
Stamford	181	CT	108,056	14,333	1,521	1,244	96
Salem	182	OR	107,786	15,679	1,862	26	3
Citrus Heights CDP[1]	183	CA	107,439	10,326	708	75	4
Abilene	184	TX	106,654	12,568	1,533	527	59
Macon	185	GA	106,612	15,521	1,401	5,416	491
El Monte	186	CA	106,209	6,824	620	26	4
South Bend	187	IN	105,511	17,740	1,932	2,067	161
Springfield	188	IL	105,227	15,632	1,878	986	94
Allentown	189	PA	105,090	17,767	1,950	186	6
Thousand Oaks	190	CA	104,352	9,427	958	34	2
Portsmouth	191	VA	103,907	14,399	1,083	5,687	415
Waco	192	TX	103,590	15,450	1,854	2,424	273
Lowell	193	MA	103,439	12,510	1,449	80	8
Berkeley	194	CA	102,724	11,252	1,459	3,313	325
Mesquite	195	TX	101,484	5,365	568	39	3
Rancho Cucamonga	196	CA	101,409	5,125	332	138	9
Albany	197	NY	101,082	15,495	2,338	1,267	104
Livonia	198	MI	100,850	13,180	1,395	17	4
Sioux Falls	199	SD	100,814	11,775	1,520	32	3
Simi Valley	200	CA	100,217	5,273	389	38	0

Source: *Sixty-Five Plus in America*, Cynthia M. Taeuber, U.S. Department of Commerce, Economics and Statistics Administration, Bureau of the Census, U.S. Government Printing Office, Washington, D.C., 1992, pp. 8-18 - 8-21. Primary source: U.S. Bureau of the Census, 1990 Census of Population and Housing, Summary Tape File 1-A. *Note:* 1. CDP stands for Census Designated Place.

★ 22 ★

Population

Population of Persons 65+ in the Top 200 Metropolitan Areas, for Selected Minorities: 1990 - Part II

For figures relating to Blacks and a total of all groups shown here see *Part I*.

[Rank based on total of all races and ages in places of 100,000 or more]

Place	Rank	State	American Indian, Eskimo and Aleut		Asian and Pacific Islander		Hispanic origin[1]	
			65 and over	85 and over	65 and over	85 and over	65 and over	85 and over
New York	1	NY	1,771	148	33,214	2,112	108,702	8,480
Los Angeles	2	CA	958	84	31,891	2,374	50,058	4,365
Chicago	3	IL	414	36	8,361	499	19,283	1,262
Houston	4	TX	236	15	2,848	118	15,303	1,091
Philadelphia	5	PA	361	29	2,225	128	4,076	273
San Diego	6	CA	351	27	7,246	281	10,388	826
Detroit	7	MI	295	24	498	31	1,897	168
Dallas	8	TX	263	21	636	31	6,470	513
Phoenix	9	AZ	469	31	864	64	7,856	576
San Antonio	10	TX	235	17	513	31	38,524	3,272
San Jose	11	CA	180	11	8,810	451	7,894	639
Baltimore	12	MD	160	20	439	38	698	51
Indianapolis	13	IN	125	12	248	16	366	28
San Francisco	14	CA	196	16	27,168	2,163	9,094	1,013
Jacksonville (remainder)	15	FL	94	5	517	21	996	78
Columbus	16	OH	92	11	369	14	294	17
Milwaukee	17	WI	197	12	410	15	1,375	103
Memphis	18	TN	72	4	193	8	243	21
Washington	19	DC	184	14	785	69	1,585	149
Boston	20	MA	136	13	2,191	201	2,380	184
Seattle	21	WA	391	20	6,062	505	988	83
El Paso	22	TX	130	8	283	11	23,938	2,055
Cleveland	23	OH	119	9	297	23	1,029	65
New Orleans	24	LA	64	7	478	41	2,244	230
Nashville-Davidson (remainder)	25	TN	64	6	175	8	205	15
Denver	26	CO	267	25	912	63	6,547	537
Austin	27	TX	66	6	251	14	3,966	309
Fort Worth	28	TX	120	7	201	13	2,979	234
Oklahoma City	29	OK	1,277	86	317	20	768	65
Portland	30	OR	270	16	1,640	121	674	69
Kansas City	31	KS	139	10	247	17	1,143	109
Long Beach	32	CA	165	12	3,130	142	2,741	201
Tucson	33	AZ	315	38	325	16	7,350	635
St. Louis	34	MO	98	11	125	18	525	75

[Continued]

★ 22 ★

Population of Persons 65+ in the Top 200 Metropolitan Areas, for Selected Minorities: 1990 - Part II
[Continued]

Place	Rank	State	American Indian, Eskimo and Aleut		Asian and Pacific Islander		Hispanic origin[1]	
			65 and over	85 and over	65 and over	85 and over	65 and over	85 and over
Charlotte	35	NC	56	3	175	6	272	17
Atlanta	36	GA	43	4	143	9	442	40
Virginia Beach	37	VA	31	1	724	13	261	20
Albuquerque	38	NM	445	28	250	10	9,066	746
Oakland	39	CA	154	13	5,555	395	2,692	276
Pittsburgh	40	PA	67	7	143	12	330	36
Sacramento	41	CA	260	14	5,144	400	3,453	284
Minneapolis	42	MN	285	11	508	32	319	38
Tulsa	43	OK	1,344	111	156	4	431	30
Honolulu CDP[2]	44	HI	49	2	43,075	3,922	1,318	107
Cincinnati	45	OH	51	7	186	13	132	19
Miami	46	FL	42	5	171	27	43,710	4,254
Fresno	47	CA	193	12	2,003	130	4,664	389
Omaha	48	NE	114	4	107	10	580	45
Toledo	49	OH	51	2	140	12	613	52
Buffalo	50	NY	144	9	80	4	723	65
Wichita	51	KS	205	12	199	16	666	45
Santa Ana	52	CA	85	7	1,424	65	4,216	320
Mesa	53	AZ	88	5	112	4	992	78
Colorado Springs	54	CO	109	12	292	8	1,115	85
Tampa	55	FL	80	7	130	4	7,916	818
Newark	56	NJ	54	6	138	10	3,421	259
St. Paul	57	MN	120	12	556	22	540	55
Louisville	58	KY	45	5	75	5	172	18
Anaheim	59	CA	69	7	1,257	77	2,123	165
Birmingham	60	AL	29	3	31	3	95	8
Arlington	61	TX	57	7	188	11	330	18
Norfolk	62	VA	43	1	321	11	245	18
Las Vegas	63	NV	114	5	525	20	1,406	71
Corpus Christi	64	TX	71	5	119	2	9,035	680
St. Petersburg	65	FL	49	8	143	12	828	89
Rochester	66	NY	73	6	112	4	770	49
Jersey City	67	NJ	46	1	1,307	53	2,384	154
Riverside	68	CA	101	3	411	14	2,143	173
Anchorage	69	AK	420	24	538	17	141	10
Lexington-Fayette	70	KY	17	2	66	3	81	6

[Continued]

★ 22 ★

Population of Persons 65+ in the Top 200 Metropolitan Areas, for Selected Minorities: 1990 - Part II

[Continued]

Place	Rank	State	American Indian, Eskimo and Aleut		Asian and Pacific Islander		Hispanic origin[1]	
			65 and over	85 and over	65 and over	85 and over	65 and over	85 and over
Akron	71	OH	42	6	62	2	124	17
Aurora	72	CO	45	2	424	19	414	31
Baton Rouge	73	LA	26	4	92	5	281	19
Stockton	74	CA	131	5	3,346	295	2,873	204
Raleigh	75	NC	20	2	102	8	110	7
Richmond	76	VA	44	2	91	4	141	16
Shreveport	77	LA	34	9	31	3	151	15
Jackson	78	MS	12	2	31	3	86	7
Mobile	79	AL	31	3	59	3	199	18
Des Moines	80	IA	40	5	167	11	251	22
Lincoln	81	NE	29	2	92	2	148	8
Madison	82	WI	14	0	155	5	104	5
Grand Rapids	83	MI	48	2	65	7	281	27
Yonkers	84	NY	13	2	256	9	1,410	118
Hialeah	85	FL	14	0	52	8	22,747	1,912
Montgomery	86	AL	21	0	33	1	87	10
Lubbock	87	TX	32	3	40	1	1,580	91
Greensboro	88	NC	43	4	71	2	96	7
Dayton	89	OH	28	0	56	6	71	5
Huntington Beach	90	CA	33	4	825	46	660	74
Garland	91	TX	30	2	263	4	416	24
Glendale	92	CA	32	7	1,306	59	2,075	221
Columbus (remainder)	93	GA	15	0	67	2	191	8
Spokane	94	WA	160	8	344	24	195	16
Tacoma	95	WA	178	13	553	24	278	18
Little Rock	96	AR	32	2	62	3	58	6
Bakersfield	97	CA	115	14	368	25	1,160	94
Fremont	98	CA	42	3	1,705	67	1,023	71
Fort Wayne	99	IN	19	0	47	5	200	11
Arlington CDP[2]	100	VA	27	3	542	29	700	61
Newport News	101	VA	17	1	123	5	140	7
Worcester	102	MA	37	3	96	4	508	35
Knoxville	103	TN	40	5	29	3	58	4
Modesto	104	CA	99	4	441	24	1,001	70
Orlando	105	FL	15	0	98	10	1,111	88
San Bernardino	106	CA	99	9	266	11	2,754	228

[Continued]

★ 22 ★

Population of Persons 65+ in the Top 200 Metropolitan Areas, for Selected Minorities: 1990 - Part II
[Continued]

Place	Rank	State	American Indian, Eskimo and Aleut		Asian and Pacific Islander		Hispanic origin[1]	
			65 and over	85 and over	65 and over	85 and over	65 and over	85 and over
Syracuse	107	NY	86	7	81	2	175	16
Providence	108	RI	90	17	263	19	839	55
Salt Lake City	109	UT	43	3	468	45	878	63
Huntsville	110	AL	30	1	85	0	79	4
Amarillo	111	TX	77	5	77	4	745	57
Springfield	112	MA	22	3	64	1	744	52
Irving	113	TX	22	1	172	11	412	24
Chattanooga	114	TN	29	6	44	2	67	4
Chesapeake	115	VA	24	0	73	5	95	7
Kansas City	116	KS	67	8	73	1	614	52
Metairie CDP[2]	117	LA	11	0	129	6	903	79
Fort Lauderdale	118	FL	21	2	60	2	991	89
Glendale	119	AZ	42	1	194	16	882	77
Warren	120	MI	30	1	98	6	172	8
Winston-Salem	121	NC	21	0	37	0	55	4
Garden Grove	122	CA	53	1	1,400	71	917	72
Oxnard	123	CA	61	2	925	45	2,924	200
Tempe	124	AZ	25	2	136	13	506	41
Bridgeport	125	CT	16	0	90	3	1,592	117
Paterson	126	NJ	24	0	57	2	2,245	129
Flint	127	MI	55	7	28	3	199	27
Springfield	128	MO	77	4	45	4	60	9
Hartford	129	CT	32	4	72	8	1,475	108
Rockford	130	IL	14	1	68	5	213	18
Savannah	131	GA	16	2	79	6	98	12
Durham	132	NC	17	2	60	0	52	3
Chula Vista	133	CA	50	3	833	55	2,903	197
Reno	134	NV	80	3	334	13	556	39
Hampton	135	VA	32	2	75	6	106	5
Ontario	136	CA	47	0	188	7	1,459	111
Torrance	137	CA	28	2	1,620	97	831	69
Pomona	138	CA	43	1	409	12	1,777	125
Pasadena	139	CA	43	7	974	58	1,522	128
New Haven	140	CT	40	7	53	6	546	50
Scottsdale	141	AZ	54	6	82	1	302	23

[Continued]

★ 22 ★

Population of Persons 65+ in the Top 200 Metropolitan Areas, for Selected Minorities: 1990 - Part II

[Continued]

Place	Rank	State	American Indian, Eskimo and Aleut		Asian and Pacific Islander		Hispanic origin[1]	
			65 and over	85 and over	65 and over	85 and over	65 and over	85 and over
Plano	142	TX	11	1	142	1	123	8
Oceanside	143	CA	43	3	377	15	1,072	78
Lansing	144	MI	45	1	68	2	351	18
Lakewood	145	CO	24	3	155	9	493	68
East Los Angeles CDP[2]	146	CA	38	2	417	32	8,255	879
Evansville	147	IN	33	2	18	2	67	7
Boise City	148	ID	30	4	63	5	188	23
Tallahassee	149	FL	9	1	59	3	119	16
Paradise CDP[2]	150	NV	47	1	279	9	716	35
Laredo	151	TX	9	2	14	1	9,253	943
Hollywood	152	FL	15	0	88	5	1,287	122
Topeka	153	KS	90	3	59	3	515	37
Pasadena	154	TX	27	2	46	1	952	56
Moreno Valley	155	CA	27	4	338	10	616	27
Sterling Heights	156	MI	10	2	163	8	76	3
Sunnyvale	157	CA	17	0	1,374	59	1,047	85
Gary	158	IN	17	2	13	0	571	38
Beaumont	159	TX	21	1	80	5	349	26
Fullerton	160	CA	36	2	604	28	878	85
Peoria	161	IL	12	2	53	4	116	11
Santa Rosa	162	CA	72	1	184	12	453	43
Eugene	163	OR	31	3	61	5	116	8
Independence	164	MO	45	2	42	2	75	7
Overland Park	165	KS	23	1	82	3	77	8
Hayward	166	CA	57	4	1,091	74	1,572	128
Concord	167	CA	41	5	524	27	563	53
Alexandria	168	VA	7	2	262	6	236	12
Orange	169	CA	33	2	436	27	759	76
Santa Clarita	170	CA	48	3	202	4	390	18
Irvine	171	CA	8	1	671	27	210	10
Elizabeth	172	NJ	17	2	136	9	2,524	164
Inglewood	173	CA	27	1	194	14	1,050	72
Ann Arbor	174	MI	8	1	139	11	74	13
Vallejo	175	CA	48	6	1,802	95	684	57
Waterbury	176	CT	23	0	22	0	565	49
Salinas	177	CA	68	4	894	69	1,667	111
Cedar Rapids	178	IA	11	0	25	0	72	6

[Continued]

★ 22 ★

Population of Persons 65+ in the Top 200 Metropolitan Areas, for Selected Minorities: 1990 - Part II

[Continued]

Place	Rank	State	American Indian, Eskimo and Aleut		Asian and Pacific Islander		Hispanic origin[1]	
			65 and over	85 and over	65 and over	85 and over	65 and over	85 and over
Erie	179	PA	14	1	24	1	86	4
Escondido	180	CA	58	7	189	15	774	70
Stamford	181	CT	12	1	141	9	476	39
Salem	182	OR	80	10	100	5	167	16
Citrus Heights CDP[2]	183	CA	54	3	140	3	287	11
Abilene	184	TX	19	1	34	3	647	43
Macon	185	GA	17	4	12	2	51	1
El Monte	186	CA	30	3	828	34	2,404	186
South Bend	187	IN	20	1	40	1	127	9
Springfield	188	IL	23	5	38	4	81	6
Allentown	189	PA	9	0	53	3	323	14
Thousand Oaks	190	CA	24	0	247	14	327	36
Portsmouth	191	VA	21	1	45	4	74	8
Waco	192	TX	20	0	19	1	965	79
Lowell	193	MA	7	0	218	13	290	21
Berkeley	194	CA	30	1	1,239	119	344	38
Mesquite	195	TX	15	2	102	2	202	10
Rancho Cucamonga	196	CA	20	3	224	9	644	41
Albany	197	NY	19	2	64	3	139	17
Livonia	198	MI	17	1	81	7	96	9
Sioux Falls	199	SD	36	0	12	0	32	3
Simi Valley	200	CA	18	0	226	11	380	28

Source: *Sixty-Five Plus in America*, Cynthia M. Taeuber, U.S. Department of Commerce, Economics and Statistics Administration, Bureau of the Census, U.S. Government Printing Office, Washington, D.C., 1992, pp. 8-18 - 8-21. Primary source: U.S. Bureau of the Census, 1990 Census of Population and Housing, Summary Tape File 1-A. *Notes:* 1. Hispanic origin may be of any race. 2. CDP stands for Census Designated Place.

★ 23 ★

Population

Minority Age 65+ as a Percent of Total 65+ Population

Year	Percent
1990	14.0
2000	16.0
2010	20.0
2020	22.0
2030	25.0
2040	28.0
2050	32.0

Source: Aging America, Trends and Projections, prepared by the U.S. Senate Special Committee on Aging, the American Association of Retired Persons, the Federal Council on the Aging, and the U.S. Administration on Aging, 1991, Washington, D.C., p. 16. Primary source: Figures computed by Donald G. Fowles, U.S. Administration on Aging, from data in U.S. Bureau of the Census, "Projections of the Hispanic Population: 1983-2080," by Gregory Spencer. *Current Population Reports* Series P-25, No. 995, November 1986 and in U.S. Bureau of the Census, "Projections of the Population of the United States by Age, Sex, and Race: 1988 to 2080," by Gregory Spencer. *Current Population Reports* Series P-25, No. 1018, January 1989.

★ 24 ★

Population

Population 80 Years and Over: 1900-90

[Data are for resident population]

Year[1]	80-84	85+
1900	0.3	0.1
1910	0.3	0.2
1920	0.4	0.2
1930	0.5	0.3
1940	0.8	0.4
1950	1.1	0.6
1960	1.6	0.9
1970	2.3	1.4
1980	2.9	2.2
1990	3.9	3.0

Source: U.S. Department of Health and Human Services, National Institute on Aging, *Profiles of America's Elderly: Growth of America's Elderly in the 1980's*, December 1991. Primary source: U.S. Bureau of the Census. Data for 1900 to 1940, 1960, and 1980 shown in *1980 Census of Population*, PC80-B1, General Population Characteristics, tables 42 and 45; Data for 1990 from *1990 Census of Population and Housing*, Series CPH-L-74, "Modified and Actual Age, Sex, Race, and Hispanic Origin Data." Data for 1950 shown in "Estimates of the Population of the United States and Components of Change, by Age, Color, and Sex: 1950 to 1960," *Current Population Reports*, Series P-25, No. 310, U.S. Government Printing Office, Washington, DC, 1965. Data for 1970 from unpublished table consistent with "United States Population Estimates by Age, Race, Sex, and Hispanic Origin: 1988," Series P-25, No. 1045, U.S. Government Printing Office, Washington DC, 1990. *Note:* 1. Figures for 1900 to 1950 exclude Alaska and Hawaii.

★ 25 ★
Population

Population 80 Years and Over, by Sex: 1990
[Numbers are in thousands]

Age	Total	Women	Men
80 to 84 years	3,909	2,553	1,356
85 to 89 years	2,035	1,429	606
90 to 94 years	748	564	184
95 to 99 years	203	159	44
100 years +	36	28	8

Source: U.S. Department of Health and Human Services, National Institute on Aging, *Profiles of America's Elderly: Growth of America's Elderly in the 1980's*, December 1991. Primary source: U.S. Bureau of the Census, 1990 Census of Population and Housing, Series CPH-L-74, "Modified and Actual Age, Sex, Race, and Hispanic Origin Data."

★ 26 ★
Population

Ratio of Persons Aged 80+ to the Total Aged Population (65+) in Selected Countries, 1990 and 2025
[Number of people age 80+ per 100 people 65+]

Country	Ratio 80+:65+	
	1990	2025
Canada	20.8	25.8
France	26.7	24.5
Germany	24.9	26.8
Italy	20.9	32.2
Japan	19.3	33.1
Sweden	24.5	31.5
United Kingdom	23.1	29.8
United States	22.4	22.9

Source: Aging America, Trends and Projections, prepared by the U.S. Senate Special Committee on Aging, the American Association of Retired Persons, the Federal Council on the Aging, and the U.S. Administration on Aging, 1991, Washington, D.C., p. 256. Primary source: U.S. Bureau of the Census. International Data Base.

★ 27 ★
Population

Balance of Males and Females 85 Years and Over: 1930 to 2050

[Sex ratio is males per 100 females 85 years old and over]

Year	Sex ratio	Excess of females (thousands)
1930	75.4	38
1940	75.0	52
1950	69.7	103
1960	63.9	205
1970	53.3	430
1980	43.7	877
1990	38.6	1,339
2030	46.0	3,008
2050	49.9	5,115

Source: Sixty-Five Plus in America, Cynthia M. Taeuber, U.S. Department of Commerce, Economics and Statistics Administration, Bureau of the Census, U.S. Government Printing Office, Washington, D.C., 1992, p. 2-10. Primary source: U.S. Bureau of the Census, 1930 and 1940 from 1940 Census of Population, Volume IV, Part 1, *Characteristics by Age*, table 2; 1950 from *Estimates of the Population of the United States and Components of Change, by Age, Color, and Sex: 1950 to 1960*, Current Population Reports Series P-25, No. 310, U.S. Government Printing Office, Washington, DC 1965; 1960 and 1980 from 1980 Census of Population, PC80-B1, *General Population Characteristics*, table 45; 1970 from unpublished tables consistent with *United States Population Estimates by Age, Race, Sex and Hispanic Origin: 1988*, Series P-25, No. 1045. U.S. Government Printing Office, Washington, DC, 1990; 1990 from 1990 Census of Population and Housing Series CPH-L-74, *Modified and Actual Age, Sex, Race and Hispanic - Origin Data*; 2030 and 2050 from *Projections of the Population of the United States by Age, Sex, and Race: 1988 to 2080*, Current Population Reports, P-25, No. 1018. U.S. Government Printing Office, Washington, DC, 1989 (middle series projections).

★ 28 ★

Population

Population 85 Years and Older, 1990 and 2080

From the source: "If the Census Bureau is right, the number of people aged 85 or older will grow from 3.3 million today to 18.7 million in 2080. But if a Duke University demographer working with the National Institute on Aging is correct, the number of these oldest old in 2080 could actually be 72 million, a figure nearly four times as great as the Census Bureau projection."

	Millions
1990	3.3
2080	
Estimate by Dr. Gregory Spencer, Census Bureau	18.7
Estimate by Dr. James Vaupel, Duke University	72.0

Source: "New Views on Life Spans Alter Forecasts on Elderly," Gina Kolata, *The New York Times* CXLII, No. 49, 152, November 16, 1992, p. A1. Primary source: First projection by Dr. Gregory Spencer, U.S. Bureau of the Census; second by Dr. James Vaupel, Duke university.

★ 29 ★

Population

Population 85 Years and Older, by Race: 1990

[Numbers are in thousands]

Race/ethnicity	Pop.
Total	3,021
White	2,761
Black	223
Hispanic origin (of any race)	91
Asian and Pacific Islander	29
American Indian, Eskimo, and Aleut	9

Source: U.S. Department of Health and Human Services, National Institute on Aging, *Profiles of America's Elderly: Growth of America's Elderly in the 1980's*, December 1991. Primary source: U.S. Bureau of the Census, 1990 Census of Population and Housing, Series CPH-L-74, "Modified and Actual Age, Sex, Race, and Hispanic Origin Data."

★ 30 ★

Population

African-American Age Distribution, 1985-2000

[Numbers in millions except where noted]

Age range	1985		1990		2000	
	Number	Percent	Number	Percent	Number	Percent
All ages	29.1	100.0	31.4	100.0	35.8	100.0
Male	13.8		14.9		17.0	
Female	15.3		16.5		18.7	
Infants/toddlers						
Under 5	3.1	11.0	3.2	10.0	3.1	9.0
Male	1.5		1.6		1.6	
Female	1.5		1.6		1.5	
Childhood						
5-9 years	2.5	8.0	3.1	10.0	3.2	9.0
Male	1.3		1.6		1.6	
Female	1.2		1.5		1.6	
Early adolescence						
10-14 years	2.5	8.0	2.5	8.0	3.2	9.0
Male	1.3		1.3		1.6	
Female	1.2		1.2		1.6	
Late adolescence						
15-19 years	2.7	9.0	2.5	8.0	3.1	9.0
Male	1.4		1.3		1.6	
Female	1.3		1.3		1.5	
Young adulthood						
20-24 years	3.0	10.0	2.7	9.0	2.6	7.0
Male	1.5		1.4		1.3	
Female	1.5		1.4		1.3	
Adulthood						
25-39 years	7.1	24.0	8.2	26.0	8.3	23.0
Male	3.4		3.9		4.1	
Female	3.8		4.3		4.2	
Middle Years						
40-64	5.8	20.0	6.5	21.0	9.2	26.0
Male	2.7		2.8		4.2	
Female	3.1		3.7		5.0	
Seniors						
65-84 years	2.2	8.0	2.2	7.0	2.6	7.0
Male	1.0		.8		.9	
Female	1.3		1.4		1.7	
Elders						
85-over	189[1]	1.0	257[1]	1.0	412[1]	1.0
Male	60[1]		77[1]		110[1]	
Female	129[1]		180[1]		302[1]	
Median	26.2		27.7		30.2	

Source: "Understanding African-American Family Diversity," Andrew Billingsley, *State of Black America*, Janet Dewart, ed., National Urban League, Inc., 1990, p. 107. Primary source: U.S. Bureau of the Census, *Current Population Reports*, series P-25, No. 952. *Note:* 1. Numbers in thousands.

★ 31 ★
Population

Blacks as a Percentage of the Total Population by Age Group, 1940-2020

According to the Bureau of the Census the black population will rise from about one in eight in the 1980s to one in six by the middle of the next century.

Year	All	Under 15	25-54	65 and over
1940	9.7	11.5	9.4	6.8
1960	10.5	12.7	8.7	7.0
1980	11.7	14.8	10.7	8.2
2000	13.3	17.0	13.0	8.5
2020	14.9	18.4	15.3	9.9

Source: "Children and Families," *A Common Destiny: Blacks and American Society,* edited by Gerald David Jaynes and Robin M. Williams, Jr., National Academy Press, Washington, D.C., 1989, p. 548. Primary source: Decennial censuses (for 1940-1980) and U.S. Bureau of the Census projections (for 2000 and 2020).

★ 32 ★
Population

Counties with the Lowest Percentage of Americans Over 55 Years Old, 1990

Under 4% of the residents in Chattahoochee County, Georgia reported being over 55 years old to the United States Census Bureau.

County and State	Rank	% over 55	Total population
Chattahoochee County, GA	1	3.85	150,490
Aleutians West Census Area, AK	2	5.91	13,955
Liberty County, GA	3	9.28	10,441
Eagle County, CO	4	10.33	6,443
Summit County, CO	5	10.37	10,058
Kodiak Island Borough, AK	6	11.17	3,296
Fairbanks North Star Borough, AK	7	11.17	89,291
Bristol Bay Borough, AK	8	11.71	99,962
Onslow County, NC	9	12.14	6,526
Aleutians East Borough, AK	10	12.27	4,382
Prince William County, VA	11	12.37	3,406
Campbell County, FL	12	12.74	13,720
Wade Hampton Census Area, AK	13	12.79	3,687
San Miguel County, CO	14	13.01	13,073
Bethel Census Area, AK	15	13.02	4,256
Northwest Arctic Borough, AK	16	13.06	209,460
North Slope Borough, AK	17	13.08	3,823
Camden County, GA	18	13.22	3,862

[Continued]

★ 32 ★

Counties with the Lowest Percentage of Americans
Over 55 Years Old, 1990
[Continued]

County and State	Rank	% over 55	Total population
Riley County, KS	19	13.25	19,167
Anchorage Borough, AK	20	13.34	3,574

Source: U.S. Department of Commerce, Bureau of the Census, *1990 Census of Population and Housing, Summary Tape File 1C, United States Summary,* CD900- 1C, February 1992.

★ 33 ★

Population

Counties with the Highest Percentage of Americans
Over 55 Years Old, 1990

According to the United States Census Bureau, over 74% of the residents in Kalawao County, Hawaii reported being over 55 years old.

County and State	Rank	% over 55	Total population
Kalawao County, HI	1	74.62	130
Llano County, TX	2	55.93	11,567
Charlotte County, FL	3	53.60	109,983
Highlands County, FL	4	51.65	67,854
Sierra County, NM	5	51.42	9,835
Citrus County, FL	6	51.14	92,823
Hickory County, MO	7	50.79	7,271
Hernando County, FL	8	49.98	100,169
Sarasota County, FL	9	49.43	275,186
McIntosh County, ND	10	49.09	4,001
Pasco County, FL	11	48.66	278,322
McPherson County, SD	12	47.43	3,209
Baxter County, AR	13	47.31	30,899
Elk County, KS	14	47.18	3,302
Keweenaw County, MI	15	47.16	1,688
Flagler County, FL	16	46.98	28,419
Sabine County, TX	17	46.91	9,488
Roscommon County, MI	18	45.69	19,570
Lancaster County, VA	19	45.53	10,795
Smith County, KS	20	45.40	5,044
Lake County, FL	21	45.19	150,490
Sharp County, AR	22	45.11	13,955
Northumberland County, VA	23	45.08	10,441
Republic County, KS	24	44.92	6,443
Alcona County, MI	25	44.72	10,058
Pawnee County, NE	26	44.69	3,296
Indian River County, FL	27	44.59	89,291

[Continued]

★ 33 ★

Counties with the Highest Percentage of Americans Over 55 Years Old, 1990

[Continued]

County and State	Rank	% over 55	Total population
Martin County, FL	28	44.57	99,962
Towns County, GA	29	44.50	6,526
Nelson County, ND	30	44.41	4,382

Source: U.S. Department of Commerce, Bureau of the Census, *1990 Census of Population and Housing, Summary Tape File 1C, United States Summary,* CD900- 1C, February 1992.

★ 34 ★

Population

Farm Population, by Age: 1980 to 1990

[1980, April-centered five-quarter average; 1985 and 1990 ann. averages]

Age	Farm population (1,000)					Percent distribution		
	1980	1985	1990			1980	1985	1990
			Total	Male	Female			
Under 15 years old	1,146[1]	1,100	940	480	459	18.9[1]	20.5	20.5
15-19 years old	790[2]	456	356	190	166	13.1[2]	8.5	7.8
20-24 years old	444	381	232	134	99	7.3	7.1	5.1
25-34 years old	606	640	532	285	247	10.0	12.0	11.6
35-44 years old	712	687	633	314	319	11.8	12.8	13.8
45-64 years old	1,607	1,342	1,197	616	582	26.6	25.1	26.1
65 years old and over	746	747	702	365	338	12.3	13.9	15.3

Source: U.S. Bureau of the Census, *Statistical Abstract of the United States: 1992* (112th edition.) Washington, DC, 1992, p. 643. Primary source: U.S. Bureau of the Census, *Current Population Reports*, series P-20, No. 457; series P-27, No. 59 and earlier reports; and unpublished data. *Notes:* 1. Persons under 14 years old. 2. Persons 14 to 19 years old.

★ 35 ★

Population

Elderly Population in 1990 and 2010 by State

The table shows that elderly Americans (65 or older) are 12.6 percent of the population today. That number will more than double by 2010.

State	Percentage of total population	1990	2010	Change 1990 to 2010
U.S. total	12.6	21,242,000	39,362,000	26
Alabama	12.9	523,000	645,000	23.4
Alaska	4.1	22,000	40,000	80.5
Arizona	13.1	479,000	840,000	75.4
Arkansas	14.9	350,000	422,000	20.4
California	10.5	3,136,000	4,680,000	49.3
Colorado	10.0	329,000	433,000	31.4
Connecticut	13.6	446,000	512,000	14.7
Delaware	12.1	81,000	119,000	47.6
District of Columbia	12.8	78,000	87,000	11.1
Florida	18.3	2,369,000	3,917,000	65.3
Georgia	10.1	654,000	1,054,000	61.1
Hawaii	11.3	125,000	225,000	79.7
Idaho	12.0	121,000	132,000	8.6
Illinois	12.6	1,437,000	1,532,000	6.6
Indiana	12.6	696,000	765,000	9.8
Iowa	15.3	426,000	391,000	-8.2
Kansas	13.8	343,000	381,000	11.1
Kentucky	12.7	467,000	526,000	12.6
Louisiana	11.1	469,000	537,000	14.5
Maine	13.3	163,000	191,000	17.0
Maryland	10.8	517,000	757,000	46.3
Massachusetts	13.6	819,000	894,000	9.1
Michigan	11.9	1,108,000	1,184,000	6.8
Minnesota	12.5	547,000	643,000	17.6
Mississippi	12.5	321,000	396,000	23.2
Missouri	14.0	718,000	839,000	16.9
Montana	13.3	106,000	103,000	-3.2
Nebraska	14.1	223,000	232,000	4.2
Nevada	10.6	128,000	191,000	49.3
New Hampshire	11.3	125,000	189,000	51.2
New Jersey	13.4	1,032,000	1,259,000	22.0
New Mexico	10.8	163,000	228,000	40.0
New York	13.1	2,364,000	2,583,000	9.3
North Carolina	12.1	804,000	1,210,000	50.4
North Dakota	14.3	91,000	82,000	-10.0
Ohio	13.0	1,407,000	1,513,000	7.5
Oklahoma	13.5	424,000	446,000	5.2
Oregon	13.8	391,000	412,000	5.4
Pennsylvania	15.4	1,829,000	1,845,000	0.9
Rhode Island	15.0	151,000	156,000	3.9

[Continued]

★ 35 ★

Elderly Population in 1990 and 2010 by State

[Continued]

State	Percentage of total population	1990	2010	Change 1990 to 2010
South Carolina	11.4	397,000	562,000	41.7
South Dakota	14.7	102,000	104,000	1.7
Tennessee	12.7	619,000	829,000	33.9
Texas	10.1	1,717,000	2,351,000	37.0
Utah	8.7	150,000	182,000	21.1
Vermont	11.8	66,000	81,000	21.9
Virginia	10.7	664,000	985,000	48.2
Washington	11.8	575,000	710,000	23.4
West Virginia	15.0	269,000	241,000	-10.5
Wisconsin	13.3	651,000	690,000	6.0
Wyoming	10.4	47,000	39,000	-17.4

Source: Population Census, 1990, U.S. Bureau of the Census.

★ 36 ★

Population

Number of Older Americans, by State and Detailed Age Group, 1990

California leads the nation in the number of residents who are over 55 years old, followed by Florida and Texas.

State	1 to 54	Older Americans								Total	Total all ages
		55 to 59	60 and 61	62 to 64	65 to 69	70 to 74	75 to 79	80 to 84	85+	Total	
Total	196,160,189	10,531,756	4,228,303	6,387,864	10,111,735	7,994,823	6,121,369	3,933,739	3,080,165	52,389,754	248,549,943
Alabama	2,993,681	183,677	71,033	109,277	168,309	132,909	105,571	67,693	48,507	886,976	3,880,657
Alaska	498,182	16,595	5,689	7,208	9,626	5,922	3,639	1,931	1,251	51,861	550,043
Arizona	2,886,922	146,658	59,996	92,878	160,163	129,881	94,769	56,244	37,717	778,306	3,665,228
Arkansas	1,787,272	105,811	41,795	65,789	106,650	89,311	71,560	47,321	35,216	563,453	2,350,725
California	24,391,243	1,133,907	443,446	655,873	1,055,174	802,047	601,809	377,415	299,107	5,368,778	29,760,021
Colorado	2,713,398	130,193	49,657	71,703	111,246	83,281	61,855	40,108	32,953	580,996	3,294,394
Connecticut	2,545,934	147,022	59,475	88,778	140,359	115,878	87,354	55,323	46,993	741,182	3,287,116
Delaware	525,669	29,861	11,980	17,923	28,474	21,122	14,814	9,183	7,142	140,499	666,168
D.C.	478,153	25,441	10,409	15,050	24,841	19,712	15,662	9,785	7,847	128,747	606,900
Florida	9,300,905	588,552	257,504	421,534	741,225	628,427	485,393	304,276	210,110	3,637,021	12,937,926
Georgia	5,325,432	259,735	96,499	142,280	218,078	169,973	128,526	80,449	57,244	1,152,784	6,478,216
Hawaii	889,121	45,375	19,275	29,453	45,584	33,069	22,694	13,261	10,397	219,108	1,108,229
Idaho	807,527	39,407	15,287	23,263	37,986	31,769	24,529	15,583	11,398	199,222	1,006,749
Illinois	9,019,372	485,581	195,755	293,349	455,752	366,188	284,280	182,776	147,549	2,411,230	11,430,602
Indiana	4,365,907	239,692	96,812	145,552	225,935	176,106	134,740	87,664	71,751	1,178,252	5,544,159
Iowa	2,100,961	122,335	50,049	77,304	122,454	104,507	84,486	59,404	55,255	675,794	2,776,755
Kansas	1,925,994	103,821	41,529	63,659	101,421	83,243	67,620	48,046	42,241	551,580	2,477,574
Kentucky	2,895,631	162,821	63,785	96,214	150,972	117,254	92,163	60,089	46,367	789,665	3,685,296
Louisiana	3,408,078	171,927	67,728	103,249	155,859	119,149	91,394	58,956	43,633	811,895	4,219,973
Maine	956,105	54,216	21,622	32,612	50,835	40,765	31,701	21,846	18,226	271,823	1,227,928
Maryland	3,866,519	202,170	79,094	116,203	180,204	134,287	96,328	60,167	46,496	914,949	4,781,468
Massachusetts	4,682,086	253,458	103,605	157,992	252,266	207,615	160,309	106,885	92,209	1,334,339	6,016,425
Michigan	7,392,113	392,787	160,021	241,915	369,111	286,727	212,494	133,222	106,907	1,903,184	9,295,297
Minnesota	3,483,879	173,066	68,308	102,912	160,036	134,486	108,433	75,144	68,835	891,220	4,375,099
Mississippi	2,037,436	107,784	42,033	64,679	99,777	80,372	65,389	43,411	32,335	535,780	2,573,216
Missouri	3,942,007	228,556	90,491	138,338	218,973	175,229	143,185	99,077	81,217	1,175,066	5,117,073
Montana	624,247	34,005	13,894	20,422	32,496	28,388	21,408	13,529	10,676	174,818	799,065

[Continued]

★ 36 ★

Number of Older Americans, by State and Detailed Age Group, 1990

[Continued]

State	1 to 54	Age in years Older Americans									Total all ages
		55 to 59	60 and 61	62 to 64	65 to 69	70 to 74	75 to 79	80 to 84	85+	Total	
Nebraska	1,220,308	67,281	26,976	40,752	64,063	53,580	44,225	31,998	29,202	358,077	1,578,385
Nevada	966,185	54,681	21,466	31,870	50,112	35,673	22,564	11,819	7,463	235,648	1,201,833
New Hampshire	896,027	44,703	17,518	25,975	39,753	31,718	24,016	16,256	13,286	213,225	1,109,252
New Jersey	5,978,965	355,677	145,713	217,808	340,232	269,960	201,441	124,845	95,547	1,751,223	7,730,188
New Mexico	1,230,479	62,038	24,205	35,285	55,478	42,129	31,723	19,500	14,232	284,590	1,515,069
New York	13,989,766	811,857	335,402	489,708	755,342	592,937	461,880	305,390	248,173	4,000,689	17,990,455
North Carolina	5,237,393	295,739	116,081	175,083	274,530	208,575	155,430	95,837	69,969	1,391,244	6,628,637
North Dakota	494,357	26,268	10,975	16,145	24,950	22,591	18,990	13,284	11,240	144,443	638,800
Ohio	8,460,648	482,526	196,535	300,445	466,113	361,915	268,897	172,006	138,030	2,386,467	10,847,115
Oklahoma	2,442,931	141,214	54,286	82,941	131,555	103,580	84,855	58,375	45,848	702,654	3,145,585
Oregon	2,214,648	116,011	46,467	73,871	122,912	101,526	78,546	49,525	38,815	627,673	2,842,321
Pennsylvania	8,892,753	552,378	236,135	371,271	590,557	479,464	361,306	225,943	171,836	2,988,890	11,881,643
Rhode Island	763,714	42,077	18,287	28,839	47,210	38,406	29,669	19,246	16,016	239,750	1,003,464
South Carolina	2,796,986	148,762	56,803	87,217	140,455	105,850	74,914	44,967	30,749	689,717	3,486,703
South Dakota	533,873	29,218	12,176	18,406	29,466	25,005	20,307	14,210	13,343	162,131	696,004
Tennessee	3,823,778	220,952	85,467	128,170	200,986	156,437	122,539	80,062	58,794	1,053,407	4,877,185
Texas	13,980,513	661,590	255,420	372,411	571,269	426,970	334,014	217,718	166,605	3,005,997	16,986,510
Utah	1,465,481	54,930	21,224	31,257	48,676	39,511	29,266	18,894	13,611	257,369	1,722,850
Vermont	451,327	22,787	9,036	13,445	20,618	16,454	12,825	8,743	7,523	111,431	562,758
Virginia	5,020,245	257,207	99,166	146,270	228,730	171,892	125,298	78,841	59,709	1,167,113	6,187,358
Washington	3,910,420	191,602	75,747	113,635	186,679	149,355	112,448	70,505	56,301	956,272	4,866,692
West Virginia	1,347,693	85,265	35,697	55,925	87,215	68,528	53,708	33,995	25,451	445,784	1,793,477
Wisconsin	3,827,022	204,647	83,496	125,383	195,309	163,110	131,296	87,213	74,293	1,064,747	4,891,769
Wyoming	370,903	17,893	7,254	10,343	15,719	12,040	9,107	5,779	4,550	82,685	453,588

Source: U.S. Department of Commerce, Bureau of the Census, *1990 Census of Population and Housing, Summary Tape File 1C, United States Summary,* CD900-1C, February 1992.

★ 37 ★

Population

Population by State of People 65 and Over, 1990

Older Americans, 65 years old and older, were 12.5 percent of the U.S. population in 1990, 31.1 million people. Percent distribution by state varies widely as shown in this table.

State	Percent
Alabama	12.6 to 15.0
Alaska	9.9 or less
Arizona	12.6 to 15.0
Arkansas	12.6 to 15.0
California	10.0 to 12.5
Colorado	10.0 to 12.5
Connecticut	12.6 to 15.0
Delaware	12.6 to 15.0
Florida	15.0 or more
Georgia	9.9 or less
Hawaii	10.0 to 12.5
Idaho	10.0 to 12.5
Illinois	12.6 to 15.0
Indiana	12.6 to 15.0
Iowa	15.0 or more

[Continued]

★ 37 ★

Population by State of People 65 and Over, 1990
[Continued]

State	Percent
Kansas	12.6 to 15.0
Kentucky	12.6 to 15.0
Louisiana	10.0 to 12.5
Maine	12.6 to 15.0
Maryland	9.9 or less
Massachusetts	12.6 to 15.0
Michigan	9.9 or less
Minnesota	9.9 or less
Mississippi	10.0 to 12.5
Missouri	15.0 or more
Montana	12.6 to 15.0
Nebraska	15.0 or more
Nevada	10.0 to 12.5
New Hampshire	9.9 or less
New Jersey	12.6 to 15.0
New Mexico	10.0 to 12.5
New York	12.6 to 15.0
North Carolina	9.9 or less
North Dakota	15.0 or more
Ohio	12.6 to 15.0
Oklahoma	12.6 to 15.0
Oregon	12.6 to 15.0
Pennsylvania	15.0 or more
Rhode Island	15.0 or more
South Carolina	9.9 or less
South Dakota	15.0 or more
Tennessee	12.6 to 15.0
Texas	10.0 to 12.5
Utah	9.9 or less
Vermont	9.9 or less
Virginia	9.9 or less
Washington	10.0 to 12.5
West Virginia	15.0 or more
Wisconsin	12.6 to 15.0
Wyoming	10.0 to 12.5

Source: New York Times, November 10, 1992, p. A9. Primary source: 1990 census.

★ 38 ★

Population

Elderly Population Density, by State, 1990

Data show elderly as percentage of total state population.

State	Percent
Alabama	12.0-3.9
Alaska	4.0-11.9
Arizona	12.0-13.9
Arkansas	14.0 or more
California	4.0-11.9
Colorado	4.0-11.9
Connecticut	12.0-13.9
Delaware	4.0-11.9
District of Columbia	14.0 or more
Florida	14.0 or more
Georgia	14.0 or more
Hawaii	4.0-11.9
Idaho	12.0-13.9
Illinois	12.0-13.9
Indiana	12.0-13.9
Iowa	14.0 or more
Kansas	12.0-13.9
Kentucky	12.0-13.9
Louisiana	4.0-11.9
Maine	12.0-13.9
Maryland	4.0-11.9
Massachusetts	12.0-13.9
Michigan	4.0-11.9
Minnesota	12.0-13.9
Mississippi	12.0-13.9
Missouri	14.0 or more
Montana	12.0-13.9
Nebraska	14.0 or more
Nevada	4.0-11.9
New Hampshire	4.0-11.9
New Jersey	4.0-11.9
New Mexico	4.0-11.9
New York	12.0-13.9
North Carolina	12.0-13.9
North Dakota	14.0 or more
Ohio	12.0-13.9
Oklahoma	12.0-13.9
Oregon	12.0-13.9
Pennsylvania	14.0 or more
Rhode Island	14.0 or more
South Carolina	14.0 or more
South Dakota	14.0 or more
Tennessee	12.0-13.9
Texas	4.0-11.9
Utah	4.0-11.9

[Continued]

★ 38 ★

Elderly Population Density, by State, 1990
[Continued]

State	Percent
Vermont	4.0-11.9
Virginia	4.0-11.9
Washington	4.0-11.9
West Virginia	14.0 or more
Wisconsin	12.0-13.9
Wyoming	4.0-11.9

Source: Advertising Age, November 16, 1992, p. S-1. Primary source: U.S. Bureau of the Census.

★ 39 ★

Population

Selected Population Characteristics of Newark and Delaware

Data for population is shown in numbers except where indicated. Age groups are shown as a percentage of the total population of Wilmington, DE-NJ-MD SMSA, except the median age.

Characteristic	
Population	
Total 1970[1]	21,298
Total 1980[1]	25,247
Growth 1970-80 (%)	+18.5
Estimated	
1985[2]	25,515
1990[2]	26,435
2000[2]	27,378
Age groups[1]	
0 to 4	3.4
5 to 9	3.9
10 to 14	4.9
15 to 19	22.2
20 to 24	26.8
25 to 34	11.7
35 to 44	8.4
45 to 54	7.2
55 to 64	5.9

[Continued]

★ 39 ★

Selected Population Characteristics of Newark and Delaware
[Continued]

Characteristic	
65 plus	5.6
Median age	21.7

Source: U.S. Congress, "Crimes Committed Against the Elderly," Hearing before the Special Committee on Aging, United States Senate, August 6, 1991, 102-11, U.S. Government Printing Office, Washington, D.C., p. 114. Notes: 1. Data is from the U.S. Department of Commerce, 1980 Census of the Population, Summary Tape File 3-C. 2. From Delaware population Consortium, Population Projection Series, Version October, 1984.

★ 40 ★

Population

States with the Highest and Lowest Percentage of Persons Over 85 Years Old, 1990

There is no state that has more than 2% percent of its total population over 85 years old. Alaska has the lowest proportion, with only .23% of the population over 85 years old.

| State | Most | | | State | Least | | |
| | Population 85+ | | Total population | | Population 85+ | | Total population |
	Number	Percent			Number	Percent	
Total	3,080,165	1.24	248,549,943				
Iowa	55,255	1.99	2,776,755	Alaska	1,251	0.23	550,043
South Dakota	13,343	1.92	696,004	Nevada	7,463	0.62	1,201,833
Nebraska	29,202	1.85	1,578,385	Utah	13,611	0.79	1,722,850
North Dakota	11,240	1.76	638,800	South Carolina	30,749	0.88	3,486,703
Kansas	42,241	1.70	2,477,574	Georgia	57,244	0.88	6,478,216
Florida	210,110	1.62	12,937,926	Hawaii	10,397	0.94	1,108,229
Rhode Island	16,016	1.60	1,003,464	New Mexico	14,232	0.94	1,515,069
Missouri	81,217	1.59	5,117,073	Virginia	59,709	0.97	6,187,358
Minnesota	68,835	1.57	4,375,099	Maryland	46,496	0.97	4,781,468
Massachusetts	92,209	1.53	6,016,425	Texas	166,605	0.98	16,986,510

Source: U.S. Department of Commerce, Bureau of the Census, *1990 Census of Population and Housing, Summary Tape File 1C, United States Summary,* CD900-1C, February 1992.

★ 41 ★

Population

States with the Highest Proportion of Persons Over 65 Years Old, 1990

Nearly 1 in 3 residents in Florida are over 65 years old, followed by Pennsylvania and West Virginia, where about 1 in 4 are over that age.

State	Rank	Population		Total
		Persons 65 +		
		Number	%	
Total	-	52,389,754	21.08	248,549,943
Florida	1	3,637,021	28.11	12,937,926
Pennsylvania	2	2,988,890	25.16	11,881,643
West Virginia	3	445,784	24.86	1,793,477
Iowa	4	675,794	24.34	2,776,755
Arkansas	5	563,453	23.97	2,350,725
Rhode Island	6	239,750	23.89	1,003,464
South Dakota	7	162,131	23.29	696,004
Missouri	8	1,175,066	22.96	5,117,073
Alabama	9	886,976	22.86	3,880,657
Nebraska	10	358,077	22.69	1,578,385

Source: U.S. Department of Commerce, Bureau of the Census, *1990 Census of Population and Housing, Summary Tape File 1C, United States Summary,* CD900- 1C, February 1992.

★ 42 ★

Population

Veteran Population Age 16 and Older, by State

From the source: "[The] number of veterans ages 16-64 exclude those who entered active duty military since September, 1980 but served less than two years. The number in this excluded group was not given by sex. Males and females might not add to total because of rounding error. Numbers released by the Census Bureau might include those serving less than two years."

[Number]

State	All veterans				Male				Female			
	Total	Less than 65 years	65 years and over	Percent 65 years and over	Total	Less than 65 years	65 years and over	Percent 65 years and over	Total	Less than 65 years	65 years and over	Percent 65 years and over
U.S. Total (Millions)	27.2	20.0	7.2	26.3	26.1	19.2	6.8	26.2	1.1	.8	.3	29.7
Alabama	430,029	318,432	111,597	26.0	413,053	305,665	107,388	26.0	16,976	12,767	4,209	24.8
Alaska	67,404	60,611	6,793	10.1	62,354	55,965	6,389	10.2	5,050	4,646	404	8.0
Arizona	458,635	328,490	130,145	28.4	433,619	312,090	121,529	28.0	25,016	16,400	8,616	34.4
Arkansas	261,871	184,465	77,406	29.6	252,040	177,686	74,354	29.5	9,831	6,779	3,052	31.0
California	2,970,114	2,222,245	747,869	25.2	2,823,904	2,121,137	702,767	24.9	140,210	101,108	45,102	30.8
Colorado	405,138	319,753	85,385	21.1	384,135	303,507	80,628	21.0	21,003	16,246	4,757	22.6
Connecticut	371,253	267,647	103,606	27.9	357,164	258,536	98,628	27.6	14,089	9,111	4,978	35.3
Delaware	80,029	59,752	20,277	25.3	76,429	57,168	19,261	25.2	3,600	2,584	1,016	28.2
D.C.	57,066	40,143	16,923	29.7	53,403	37,693	15,710	29.4	3,663	2,450	1,213	33.1
Florida	1,701,684	1,119,171	582,513	34.2	1,616,248	1,065,760	550,488	34.1	85,436	53,411	32,025	37.5
Georgia	684,488	543,510	140,978	20.6	653,520	518,256	135,264	20.7	30,968	25,254	5,714	18.5

[Continued]

★ 42 ★

Veteran Population Age 16 and Older, by State

[Continued]

State	All veterans				Male				Female			
	Total	Less than 65 years	65 years and over	Percent 65 years and over	Total	Less than 65 years	65 years and over	Percent 65 years and over	Total	Less than 65 years	65 years and over	Percent 65 years and over
Hawaii	118,191	93,553	24,638	20.8	111,106	87,446	23,660	21.3	7,085	6,107	978	13.8
Idaho	115,427	85,651	29,776	25.8	110,862	82,532	28,330	25.6	4,565	3,119	1,446	31.7
Illinois	1,148,732	838,719	310,013	27.0	1,113,976	815,964	298,012	26.8	34,756	22,755	12,001	34.5
Indiana	614,366	463,197	151,169	24.6	594,925	449,344	145,581	24.5	19,441	13,853	5,588	28.7
Iowa	307,007	222,219	84,788	27.6	298,360	216,623	81,737	27.4	8,647	5,596	3,051	35.3
Kansas	277,575	202,749	74,826	27.0	268,281	196,084	72,197	26.9	9,294	6,665	2,629	28.3
Kentucky	375,782	277,966	97,816	26.0	363,927	269,341	94,586	26.0	11,855	8,625	3,230	27.2
Louisiana	399,318	296,340	102,978	25.8	384,989	285,908	99,081	25.7	14,329	10,432	3,897	27.2
Maine	157,663	118,513	39,150	24.8	150,246	113,188	37,058	24.7	7,417	5,325	2,092	28.2
Maryland	553,444	427,948	125,496	22.7	524,508	404,940	119,568	22.8	28,936	23,008	5,928	20.5
Massachusetts	650,499	459,853	190,646	29.3	623,966	444,596	179,370	28.7	26,533	15,257	11,276	42.5
Michigan	993,153	748,618	244,535	24.6	960,094	725,769	234,325	24.4	33,059	22,849	10,210	30.9
Minnesota	484,635	367,089	117,546	24.3	469,552	357,494	112,058	23.9	15,083	9,595	5,488	36.4
Mississippi	234,391	167,224	67,167	28.7	225,281	160,401	64,880	28.8	9,110	6,823	2,287	25.1
Missouri	606,236	445,781	160,455	26.5	586,416	431,530	154,886	26.4	19,820	14,251	5,569	28.1
Montana	101,544	75,253	26,291	25.9	96,804	71,920	24,884	25.7	4,740	3,333	1,407	29.7
Nebraska	175,869	130,263	45,606	25.9	169,018	125,231	43,787	25.9	6,851	5,032	1,819	26.6
Nevada	180,128	139,150	40,978	22.7	170,965	132,157	38,808	22.7	9,163	6,993	2,170	23.7
New Hampshire	140,254	108,029	32,225	23.0	133,096	102,839	30,257	22.7	7,158	5,190	1,968	27.5
New Jersey	810,901	570,281	240,620	29.7	784,863	554,401	230,462	29.4	26,038	15,880	10,158	39.0
New Mexico	175,961	132,368	43,593	24.8	166,357	125,249	41,108	24.7	9,604	7,119	2,485	25.9
New York	1,690,365	1,195,201	495,164	29.3	1,634,088	1,159,270	474,818	29.1	56,277	35,931	20,346	36.2
North Carolina	711,947	539,918	172,029	24.2	681,394	516,469	164,925	24.2	30,553	23,449	7,104	23.3
North Dakota	64,056	48,405	15,651	24.4	61,434	46,365	15,069	24.5	2,622	2,040	582	22.2
Ohio	1,243,714	917,241	326,473	26.2	1,203,220	889,686	313,534	26.1	40,494	27,555	12,939	32.0
Oklahoma	372,829	275,924	96,905	26.0	359,043	265,366	93,677	26.1	13,786	10,558	3,228	23.4
Oregon	380,468	277,872	102,596	27.0	363,478	266,909	96,569	26.6	16,990	10,963	6,027	35.5
Pennsylvania	1,438,997	1,011,318	427,679	29.7	1,392,744	982,379	410,365	29.5	46,253	28,939	17,314	37.4
Rhode Island	117,160	81,176	35,984	30.7	112,561	78,256	34,305	30.5	4,599	2,920	1,679	36.5
South Carolina	377,225	288,035	89,190	23.6	360,410	275,018	85,392	23.7	16,815	13,017	3,798	22.6
South Dakota	76,067	56,187	19,880	26.1	73,086	53,956	19,130	26.2	2,981	2,231	750	25.2
Tennessee	525,163	392,862	132,301	25.2	508,140	379,770	128,370	25.3	17,023	13,092	3,931	23.1
Texas	1,705,748	1,299,888	405,860	23.8	1,632,989	1,243,777	389,212	23.8	72,759	56,111	16,648	22.9
Utah	145,153	107,541	37,612	25.9	140,329	104,157	36,172	25.8	4,824	3,384	1,440	29.9
Vermont	64,063	49,166	14,897	23.3	60,677	46,747	13,930	23.0	3,386	2,419	967	28.6
Virginia	725,251	567,167	158,084	21.8	682,397	532,504	149,893	22.0	42,854	34,663	8,191	19.1
Washington	646,050	497,349	148,701	23.0	612,524	472,274	140,250	22.9	33,526	25,075	8,451	25.2
West Virginia	209,160	149,137	60,023	28.7	203,445	145,494	57,951	28.5	5,715	3,643	2,072	36.3
Wisconsin	527,680	393,616	134,064	25.4	510,309	382,393	127,916	25.1	17,371	11,223	6,148	35.4
Wyoming	53,779	42,022	11,757	21.9	51,490	40,277	11,213	21.8	2,289	1,745	544	23.8

Source: Department of Veterans Affairs, Demographics Division, *1990 Census Data on Veterans, United States.*

★ 43 ★
Population

Veterans Living in the United States and Puerto Rico, by Age and Service: 1991

Data are estimated and exclude 487,000 veterans whose only active duty military service occurred since September 30, 1980.

[In thousands, except as indicated. As of Sept. 30]

| Age | Total veterans | Wartime veterans | | | | | | | Peacetime veterans | |
| | | Total[1] | Vietnam era | | Korean conflict | | World war II[3,4] | World war I | Total | Post Vietnam era[5] |
			Total[2,3]	No prior wartime service	Total[2,3,4]	No prior wartime service[2]				
All ages	26,629[6]	20,370	8,303	7,730	4,726	3,889	8,469	65	6,259	3,043
Under 30 years old	1,132	180	-	-	-	-	-	-	953	953
30 to 34 years old	1,458	158	131	131	-	-	-	-	1,299	1,299
35 to 39 years old	1,787	1,198	1,190	1,190	-	-	-	-	590	590
40 to 44 years old	3,268	3,119	3,117	3,117	-	-	-	-	149	131
45 to 49 years old	2,952	2,434	2,434	2,434	-	-	-	-	518	35
50 to 54 years old	2,378	845	707	685	161	161	-	-	1,532	20
55 to 59 years old	2,815	1,951	305	132	1,812	1,810	-	-	864	11
60 to 64 years old	3,194	3,027	228	30	2,023	1,792	1,204	-	167	3
65 years old and over	7,646	7,458	192	10	730	126	7,257	65	187	(Z)

Source: U.S. Bureau of the Census, *Statistical Abstract of the United States: 1992* (112th edition.) Washington, DC, 1992, p. 348. Primary source: U.S. Dept. of Veterans Affairs, Office of Information Management and Statistics, Veteran Population, annual. *Notes:* (-) A dash represents zero. (Z) indicates less than 500. 1. Veterans who served in more than one wartime period are counted only once. Includes Vietnam era (no prior wartime service), Korean conflict (no prior wartime service), World War II, and World War I. 2. Includes 339,000 who served in both the Korean conflict and the Vietnam era. 3. Includes 269,000 who served in the Vietnam era, Korean conflict and World War II. 4. Includes 649,000 who served in both World War II and the Korean conflict. 5. Service only after May 7, 1975. 6. There is also one living Spanish-American War veteran and an estimated 65 living Mexican Border conflict veterans.

Population Growth

★ 44 ★

Growth of Older Population: 1900 to 1990

[Data are in thousands. Data for 1900 to 1990 are April 1 census figures]

| | Year | | | | | | | | | |
	1900	1910	1920	1930	1940	1950	1960	1970	1980	1990
Total number (all ages)	75,995	91,972	105,711	122,775	131,669	150,697	179,323	203,302	226,546	248,710
65 to 74 years										
Number	2,187	2,793	3,464	4,721	6,376	8,415	10,997	12,447	15,581	18,045
Percent	2.9	3.0	3.3	3.8	4.8	5.6	6.1	6.1	6.9	7.3
75 to 79 years										
Number	520	667	856	1,106	1,504	2,128	3,054	3,838	4,794	6,103
Percent	0.7	0.7	0.8	0.9	1.1	1.4	1.7	1.9	2.1	2.5

[Continued]

★ 44 ★

Growth of Older Population: 1900 to 1990
[Continued]

	Year									
	1900	1910	1920	1930	1940	1950	1960	1970	1980	1990
80 to 84 years										
Number	252	322	403	535	774	1,149	1,580	2,286	2,935	3,909
Percent	0.3	0.4	0.4	0.4	0.6	0.8	0.9	1.1	1.3	1.6
80 years and over										
Number	374	489	613	807	1,139	1,726	2,509	3,695	5,175	6,930
Percent	0.5	0.5	0.6	0.7	0.9	1.1	1.4	1.8	2.3	2.8
85 years and over										
Number	122	167	210	272	365	577	929	1,409	2,240	3,021
Percent	0.2	0.2	0.2	0.2	0.3	0.4	0.5	0.7	1.0	1.2
65 years and over										
Number	3,080	3,949	4,933	6,634	9,019	12,269	16,560	19,980	25,550	31,079
Percent	4.1	1.3	4.7	5.4	6.8	8.1	9.2	9.8	11.3	12.5

Source: *Sixty-Five Plus in America*, Cynthia M. Taeuber, U.S. Department of Commerce, Economics and Statistics Administration, Bureau of the Census, U.S. Government Printing Office, Washington, D.C., 1992, pp. 2-2 - 2-3. *Notes:* Figures for 1900 to 1950 exclude Alaska and Hawaii. Figures are for the resident population.

★ 45 ★

Population Growth

Projected Growth in Population, by Age Group: 1980-2050

Age	Percent increase		
	1980-2000	1980-2030	1980-2050
Under 55	16.0	11.0	8.0
55 to 64	11.0	61.0	70.0
65 to 74	17.0	130.0	102.0
75 to 84	54.0	176.0	178.0
85 +	104.0	258.0	574.0

Source: *Aging America, Trends and Projections*, prepared by the U.S. Senate Special Committee on Aging, the American Association of Retired Persons, the Federal Council on the Aging, and the U.S. Administration on Aging, 1991, Washington, D.C., p. 11. Primary source: U.S. Bureau of the Census. "Projections of the Population of the United States, by Age, Sex, and Race: 1988 to 2080," by Gregory Spencer. *Current Population Reports* Series P-25, No. 1018, January 1989.

★ 46 ★

Population Growth

Total Population Projections by Age, Sex, and Race, 1995-2010

Age, sex, and race	Population (1,000)				Percent distribution		Percent change	
	1995	2000	2005	2010	2000	2010	1990-2000	2000-2010
Total	260,138	268,266	275,604	282,575	100.0	100.0	7.1	5.3
Under 5 years old	17,799	16,898	16,611	16,899	6.3	6.0	-8.2	(Z)
5-17 years old	48,374	48,815	47,471	45,747	18.2	16.2	7.0	-6.3
18-24 years old	24,281	25,231	26,918	27,155	9.4	9.6	-3.5	7.6
25-34 years old	40,962	37,149	35,997	37,572	13.8	13.3	-15.4	1.1
35-44 years old	42,336	43,911	40,951	37,202	16.4	13.2	15.9	-15.3
45-54 years old	31,297	37,223	41,619	43,207	13.9	15.3	46.0	16.1
55-64 years old	21,325	24,158	29,762	35,430	9.0	12.5	13.1	46.7
65-74 years old	18,930	18,243	18,410	21,039	6.8	7.4	-0.7	15.3
75 years old and over	14,834	16,639	17,864	18,323	6.2	6.5	26.2	10.1
16 years old and over	201,018	210,134	219,301	227,390	78.3	80.5	8.9	8.2
Male, total	127,123	131,191	134,858	138,333	100.0	100.0	7.3	5.4
Under 5 years old	9,118	8,661	8,517	8,668	6.6	6.3	-8.1	0.1
5-17 years old	24,787	25,027	24,350	23,473	19.1	17.0	7.1	-6.2
18-24 years old	12,290	12,770	13,628	13,752	9.7	9.9	-3.4	7.7
25-34 years old	20,579	18,662	18,091	18,878	14.2	13.6	-15.5	1.2
35-44 years old	21,104	21,945	20,458	18,586	16.7	13.4	16.8	-15.3
45-54 years old	15,292	18,296	20,585	21,432	13.9	15.5	47.5	17.1
55-64 years old	10,149	11,557	14,321	17,173	8.8	12.4	14.4	48.6
65-74 years old	8,476	8,242	8,407	9,691	6.3	7.0	0.9	17.6
75 years old and over	5,326	6,032	6,501	6,681	4.6	4.8	28.9	10.8
16 years old and over	96,834	101,392	105,984	110,024	77.3	79.5	9.2	8.5
Female, total	133,016	137,076	140,746	144,241	100.0	100.0	7.0	5.2
Under 5 years old	8,681	8,237	8,094	8,231	6.0	5.7	-8.3	-0.1
5-17 years old	23,587	23,788	23,121	22,274	17.4	15.4	6.9	-6.4
18-24 years old	11,991	12,461	13,290	13,402	9.1	9.3	-3.6	7.6
25-34 years old	20,384	18,487	17,906	18,694	13.5	13.0	-15.4	1.1
35-44 years old	21,233	21,966	20,493	18,616	16.0	12.9	14.9	-15.3
45-54 years old	16,005	18,927	21,034	21,775	13.8	15.1	44.7	15.0
55-64 years old	11,175	12,601	15,441	18,257	9.2	12.7	11.9	44.9
65-74 years old	10,454	10,001	10,004	11,348	7.3	7.9	-2.0	13.5
75 years old and over	9,507	10,607	11,364	11,642	7.7	8.1	24.7	9.8
16 years old and over	104,184	108,742	113,317	117,366	79.3	81.4	8.6	7.9
White, total	216,820	221,514	225,424	228,978	100.0	100.0	5.2	3.4
Under 5 years old	14,251	13,324	12,936	13,084	6.0	5.7	-10.5	-1.8
5-17 years old	38,493	38,569	37,118	35,258	17.4	15.4	5.6	-8.6
18-24 years old	19,452	19,998	21,188	21,298	9.0	9.3	-6.2	6.5
25-34 years old	33,680	29,988	28,603	29,585	13.5	12.9	-18.1	-1.3

[Continued]

49

★ 46 ★

Total Population Projections by Age, Sex, and Race, 1995-2010
[Continued]

Age, sex, and race	Population (1,000)				Percent distribution		Percent change	
	1995	2000	2005	2010	2000	2010	1990-2000	2000-2010
35-44 years old	35,635	36,574	33,639	29,997	16.5	13.1	13.2	-18.0
45-54 years old	26,879	31,618	34,911	35,860	14.3	15.7	44.0	13.4
55-64 years old	18,327	20,667	25,407	29,913	9.3	13.1	10.9	44.7
65-74 years old	16,681	15,811	15,708	17,875	7.1	7.8	-3.5	13.1
75 years old and over	13,421	14,965	15,914	16,108	6.8	7.0	25.1	7.6
16 years old and over	169,665	175,579	181,478	186,417	79.3	81.4	6.8	6.2
Male	106,365	108,774	110,785	112,610	49.1	49.2	5.4	3.5
Female	110,455	112,739	114,639	116,368	50.9	50.8	4.9	3.2
Black, total	33,199	35,129	37,003	38,833	100.0	100.0	12.8	10.6
Under 5 years old	2,790	2,748	2,764	2,820	7.8	7.3	-2.3	2.6
5-17 years old	7,697	7,895	7,889	7,809	22.5	20.1	10.1	-1.1
18-24 years old	3,703	3,924	4,198	4,314	11.2	11.1	2.9	9.9
25-34 years old	5,534	5,264	5,299	5,590	15.0	14.4	-7.4	6.2
35-44 years old	5,041	5,481	5,332	5,076	15.6	13.1	30.2	-7.4
45-54 years old	3,261	4,106	4,928	5,369	11.7	13.8	52.9	30.8
55-64 years old	2,288	2,578	3,155	3,995	7.3	10.3	19.6	55.0
65-74 years old	1,762	1,848	1,994	2,277	5.3	5.9	14.9	23.2
75 years old and over	1,122	1,283	1,445	1,584	3.7	4.1	27.7	23.5
16 years old and over	23,860	25,708	27,638	29,467	73.2	75.9	15.7	14.6
Male	15,840	16,787	17,707	18,602	47.8	47.9	13.2	10.8
Female	17,359	18,342	19,296	20,231	52.2	52.1	12.4	10.3
Other races, total	10,119	11,624	13,177	14,764	100.0	100.0	34.5	27.0
Under 5 years old	758	826	911	995	7.1	6.7	17.8	20.4
5-17 years old	2,184	2,350	2,464	2,680	20.2	18.2	22.2	14.1
18-24 years old	1,126	1,309	1,532	1,542	11.3	10.4	31.1	17.9
25-34 years old	1,748	1,897	2,095	2,396	16.3	16.2	17.1	26.3
35-44 years old	1,660	1,856	1,980	2,129	16.0	14.4	34.5	14.7
45-54 years old	1,156	1,500	1,780	1,979	12.9	13.4	76.2	32.0
55-64 years old	711	912	1,200	1,523	7.8	10.3	59.9	67.1
65-74 years old	487	584	708	886	5.0	6.0	51.9	51.8
75 years old and over	290	391	506	632	3.4	4.3	79.3	61.8
16 years old and over	7,493	8,847	10,186	11,506	76.1	77.9	40.5	30.1
Male	4,918	5,629	6,366	7,122	48.4	48.2	33.3	26.5
Female	5,202	5,995	6,811	7,642	51.6	51.8	35.6	27.5

Source: "Projections of the Total Population by Age, Sex, and Race: 1995 to 2010," *Statistical Abstract of the United States,* 1991, p. 16. Primary source: U.S. Bureau of the Census, *Current Population Reports,* series P-25, No. 1018. As of July 1. Includes armed forces overseas. Data are for middle series. *Note:* - indicates decrease. (Z) indicates less than .05 percent.

★ 47 ★

Population Growth

Population at Retirement Age, 2008-2020

Between July 2008 and July 2009, 3.5 million people will celebrate their 62nd birthday as the first baby boomers pass this milestone. That's 37 percent more than in the previous year, and 63 percent more than in 1990. Economic incentives could push the average age of retirement up as much as seven years. But despite delayed retirement plans, the boom will continue for several decades and peak around 2020.

Source: "You'll Know It's the 21st Century When...," Judith Waldrop, *American Demographics* 12, No. 12, December, 1990, p. 25.

★ 48 ★

Population Growth

Projections of the Hispanic Population by Age and Sex, 1995-2010

Age and sex	Population (1,000)				% distribution		% change	
	1995	2000	2005	2010	2000	2010	1990-2000	2000-2010
Total	22,550	25,223	27,959	30,795	100.0	100.0	26.8	22.1
Under 5 years old	2,412	2,496	2,644	2,852	9.9	9.3	9.4	14.3
5-17 years old	5,555	6,207	6,551	6,848	24.6	22.2	28.6	10.3
18-24 years old	2,511	2,767	3,254	3,599	11.0	11.7	15.9	30.1
25-34 years old	3,717	3,804	4,036	4,526	15.1	14.7	4.8	19.0
35-44 years old	3,430	3,803	3,894	3,983	15.1	12.9	36.4	4.7
45-54 years old	2,165	2,811	3,440	3,806	11.1	12.4	68.5	35.4
55-64 years old	1,342	1,619	2,093	2,704	6.4	8.8	36.9	67.0
65-74 years old	894	1,041	1,183	1,432	4.1	4.7	47.2	37.6
75 years old and over	525	678	864	1,045	2.7	3.4	61.8	54.1
16 years old and over	15,322	17,419	19,753	22,131	69.0	71.9	29.5	27.1
Male	11,285	12,627	14,000	15,419	50.1	50.1	26.9	22.1
Female	11,265	12,596	13,960	15,376	49.9	49.9	26.7	22.1

Source: "Projections of the Hispanic Population, by Age and Sex: 1995 to 2010," *Statistical Abstract of the United States*, 1991, p. 14. Primary source: U.S. Bureau of the Census, *Current Population Reports*, series P-25, No. 995. As of July 1. Includes Armed Forces overseas. Data are for the middle series fertility at 1.9 birth per woman, mortality at 81.0, and net immigration of 143,000. These projections were prepared prior to the release of 1990 census results and are therefore not based on 1990 census data.

★ 49 ★

Population Growth

Percent Change of U.S. Population 65 Years and Over, by Region, Division, and State: 1980 and 1990

Region, division, and State	Number			Percent change, 1980 to 1990
	1990	1980	Change 1980 to 1990	
United States	31,241,831	25,549,427	5,692,404	22.3
Northeast	6,995,156	6,071,839	923,317	15.2
New England	1,770,303	1,520,368	249,935	16.4
Middle Atlantic	5,224,853	4,551,471	673,382	14.8
Midwest	7,749,130	6,691,869	1,057,261	15.8
East North Central	5,299,384	4,493,184	806,200	17.9
West North Central	2,449,746	2,198,685	251,061	11.4
South	10,724,182	8,487,891	2,236,291	26.3
South Atlantic	5,834,408	4,367,060	1,467,348	33.6
East South Central	1,929,936	1,656,788	273,148	16.5
West South Central	2,959,838	2,464,043	495,795	20.1
West	5,773,363	4,297,828	1,475,535	34.3
Mountain	1,523,825	1,060,983	462,842	43.6
Pacific	4,249,538	3,236,845	1,012,693	31.3
New England	1,770,303	1,520,368	249,935	16.4
Maine	163,373	140,918	22,455	15.9
Vermont	66,163	58,166	7,997	13.7
New Hampshire	125,029	102,967	22,062	21.4
Massachusetts	819,284	726,531	92,753	12.8
Rhode Island	150,547	126,922	23,625	18.6
Connecticut	445,907	364,864	81,043	22.2
Middle Atlantic	5,224,853	4,551,471	673,382	14.8
New York	2,363,722	2,160,767	202,955	9.4
New Jersey	1,032,025	859,771	172,254	20.0
Pennsylvania	1,829,106	1,530,933	298,173	19.5
East North Central	5,299,384	4,493,184	806,200	17.9
Ohio	1,406,961	1,169,460	237,501	20.3
Indiana	696,196	585,384	110,812	18.9
Illinois	1,436,545	1,261,885	174,660	13.8
Michigan	1,108,461	912,258	196,203	21.5
Wisconsin	651,221	564,197	87,024	15.4
West North Central	2,449,746	2,198,685	251,061	11.4
Minnesota	546,934	479,564	67,370	14.0
Iowa	426,106	387,584	38,522	9.9
Missouri	717,681	648,126	69,555	10.7

[Continued]

★ 49 ★

Percent Change of U.S. Population 65 Years and Over, by Region, Division, and State: 1980 and 1990
[Continued]

Region, division, and State	Number			Percent change, 1980 to 1990
	1990	1980	Change 1980 to 1990	
North Dakota	91,055	80,445	10,610	13.2
South Dakota	102,231	91,019	11,312	12.4
Nebraska	223,068	205,684	17,384	8.5
Kansas	342,571	306,263	36,308	11.9
South Atlantic	5,834,408	4,367,060	1,467,348	33.6
Delaware	80,735	59,179	21,556	36.4
Maryland	517,482	395,609	121,873	30.8
District of Columbia	77,847	74,287	3,560	4.8
Virginia	664,470	505,304	159,166	31.5
West Virginia	268,897	237,868	31,029	13.0
North Carolina	804,341	603,181	201,160	33.3
South Carolina	396,935	287,328	109,607	38.1
Georgia	654,270	516,731	137,539	26.6
Florida	2,369,431	1,687,573	681,858	40.4
East South Central	1,929,936	1,656,788	273,148	16.5
Kentucky	466,845	409,828	57,017	13.9
Tennessee	618,818	517,588	101,230	19.6
Alabama	522,989	440,015	82,974	18.9
Mississippi	321,284	289,357	31,927	11.0
West South Central	2,959,838	2,464,043	495,795	20.1
Arkansas	350,058	312,477	37,581	12.0
Louisiana	468,991	404,279	64,712	16.0
Oklahoma	424,213	376,126	48,087	12.8
Texas	1,716,576	1,371,161	345,415	25.2
Mountain	1,523,825	1,060,983	462,842	43.6
Montana	106,497	84,559	21,938	25.9
Idaho	121,265	93,680	27,585	29.4
Wyoming	47,195	37,175	10,020	27.0
Colorado	329,443	247,325	82,118	33.2
New Mexico	163,062	115,906	47,156	40.7
Arizona	478,774	307,362	171,412	55.8
Utah	149,958	109,220	40,738	37.3
Nevada	127,631	65,756	61,875	94.1
Pacific	4,249,538	3,236,845	1,012,693	31.3
Washington	575,288	431,562	143,726	33.3
Oregon	391,324	303,336	87,988	29.0
California	3,135,552	2,414,250	721,302	29.9

[Continued]

★ 49 ★

Percent Change of U.S. Population 65 Years and Over, by Region, Division, and State: 1980 and 1990

[Continued]

Region, division, and State	Number			Percent change, 1980 to 1990
	1990	1980	Change 1980 to 1990	
Alaska	22,369	11,547	10,822	93.7
Hawaii	125,005	76,150	48,855	64.2

Source: U.S. Bureau of the Census, 1980 and 1990 Censuses of Population: for 1980, *General Population Characteristics*, PC80-1-B1, Table 67; for 1990, Summary Tape File 1A.

★ 50 ★

Population Growth

Percent White and Black of the Total Population 65 Years and Over: 1980 to 2050

Year	White	Black
1980	89.8	8.2
1990	90.2	8.0
2000	88.2	9.0
2010	86.3	9.8
2020	84.7	10.7
2030	83.0	11.9
2040	81.0	12.9
2050	78.7	14.0

Source: *Sixty-Five Plus in America*, Cynthia M. Taeuber, U.S. Department of Commerce, Economics and Statistics Administration, Bureau of the Census, U.S. Government Printing Office, Washington, D.C., 1992, p. 2-13. Primary source: U.S. Bureau of the Census, 1980 from 1980 Census of Population; 1990 from 1990 Census of Population and Housing, Series CPH-L-74, *Modified and Actual Age, Sex, Race, and Hispanic Origin Data*; 2000 to 2050 from *Projections of the Population of the United States, by Age, Sex, and Race: 1988 to 2080*, Current Population Reports, Series P-25, No. 1018. U.S. Government Printing Office, Washington, DC, 1989 (middle series projections). Current Population Reports, Special Studies, P23-178, *Sixty-Five Plus in America*, U.S. Government Printing Office, Washington, D.C., 1992.

★ 51 ★

Population Growth

Persons 65 Years and Over, by Age, Race, and Hispanic Origin: 2050

[Data are shown in millions]

Race/ethnicity	65 years and older	65 to 79 years	80 years and older
All races	68.5	43.6	24.9
White	53.9	33.6	20.3
Black	9.6	6.6	3.0
Other races[1]	5.0	3.4	1.6
Hispanic origin[2]	7.9	5.3	2.6

Source: Sixty-Five Plus in America, Cynthia M. Taeuber, U.S. Department of Commerce, Economics and Statistics Administration, Bureau of the Census, U.S. Government Printing Office, Washington, D.C., 1992, p. 2-12. Primary source: U.S. Bureau of the Census, from *Projections of the Population of the United States, by Age, Sex, and Race: 1988-2080*, Current Population Reports, Series P-25, No. 1018. U.S. Government Printing Office, Washington, DC, 1989 (middle series projections). Hispanic from *Projections of the Hispanic Population: 1983 to 2080*, Current Population Reports, Series P-25, No. 995. U.S. Government Printing Office, Washington, DC 1988 (middle series projections). *Notes:* 1. Includes Asians and Pacific Islanders, American Indians, Eskimos, and Aleuts. 2. Hispanic origin may be of any race.

★ 52 ★

Population Growth

Population 65 Years and Over for States, by Age: 1990, 2000, and 2010

[Data are shown in thousands]

Region and state	Persons 65 years and over				Persons 85 years and over			
	Number			Percent change,	Number			Percent change,
	1990	2000[1]	2010[1]	1990 to 2010	1990	2000[1]	2010[1]	1990 to 2010
United States	31,242	34,882	39,362	26.0	3,080	4,622	6,115	98.5
Northeast	6,995	7,350	7,709	10.2	710	1,000	1,266	78.4
New England	1,770	1,884	2,023	14.3	194	275	351	80.7
Middle Atlantic	5,225	5,465	5,687	8.8	516	725	915	77.5
Midwest	7,749	8,013	8,356	7.8	840	1,155	1,409	67.8
East North Central	5,299	5,478	5,683	7.2	539	758	940	74.5
West North Central	2,450	2,535	2,672	9.1	301	398	469	55.7
South	10,724	12,735	15,083	40.6	992	1,614	2,229	124.7
South Atlantic	5,834	7,294	8,932	53.1	515	891	1,313	155.0
East South Central	1,930	2,135	2,395	24.1	186	287	362	94.7
West South Central	2,960	3,306	3,756	26.9	291	436	554	90.3

[Continued]

★ 52 ★

Population 65 Years and Over for States, by Age: 1990, 2000, and 2010
[Continued]

Region and state	Persons 65 years and over				Persons 85 years and over			
	Number			Percent change,	Number			Percent change,
	1990	2000[1]	2010[1]	1990 to 2010	1990	2000[1]	2010[1]	1990 to 2010
West	5,773	6,784	8,214	42.3	538	852	1,211	124.9
Mountain	1,524	1,774	2,147	40.9	133	215	305	130.2
Pacific	4,250	5,009	6,068	42.8	406	637	906	123.2
New England	1,770	1,884	2,023	14.3	194	275	351	80.7
Maine	163	176	191	17.0	18	26	33	81.4
Vermont	66	72	81	21.9	8	11	13	77.5
New Hampshire	125	153	189	51.2	13	20	28	107.8
Massachusetts	819	854	894	9.1	92	128	162	75.2
Rhode Island	151	152	156	3.9	16	22	28	76.6
Connecticut	446	478	512	14.7	47	68	87	85.4
Middle Atlantic	5,225	5,465	5,687	8.8	516	725	915	77.5
New York	2,364	2,459	2,583	9.3	248	330	407	64.2
New Jersey	1,032	1,152	1,259	22.0	96	141	186	94.9
Pennsylvania	1,829	1,855	1,845	0.9	172	254	321	87.1
East North Central	5,299	5,478	5,683	7.2	539	758	940	74.5
Ohio	1,407	1,469	1,513	7.5	138	200	256	85.3
Indiana	696	727	765	9.8	72	101	126	75.2
Illinois	1,437	1,477	1,532	6.6	148	203	246	66.5
Michigan	1,108	1,140	1,184	6.8	107	152	194	81.8
Wisconsin	651	665	690	6.0	74	101	118	59.3
West North Central	2,450	2,535	2,672	9.1	301	398	469	55.7
Minnesota	547	584	643	17.6	69	92	111	61.7
Iowa	426	404	391	-8.2	55	69	76	38.0
Missouri	718	769	839	16.9	81	112	136	67.6
North Dakota	91	85	82	-10.0	11	15	15	37.5
South Dakota	102	103	104	1.7	13	17	19	45.3
Nebraska	223	228	232	4.2	29	37	42	45.3
Kansas	343	361	381	11.1	42	56	68	61.3
South Atlantic	5,834	7,294	8,932	53.1	515	891	1,313	155.0
Delaware	81	101	119	47.6	7	12	19	163.6
Maryland	517	622	757	46.3	46	75	109	135.2
District of Columbia	78	80	87	11.1	8	11	14	72.6
Virginia	664	807	985	48.2	60	97	140	134.0
West Virginia	269	251	241	-10.5	25	37	43	67.0
North Carolina	804	997	1,210	50.4	70	121	176	151.0
South Carolina	397	469	562	41.7	31	55	80	159.1
Georgia	654	825	1,054	61.1	57	101	142	147.5
Florida	2,369	3,142	3,917	65.3	210	384	592	181.6

[Continued]

★ 52 ★

Population 65 Years and Over for States, by Age: 1990, 2000, and 2010
[Continued]

Region and state	Persons 65 years and over				Persons 85 years and over			
	Number			Percent change,	Number			Percent change,
	1990	2000[1]	2010[1]	1990 to 2010	1990	2000[1]	2010[1]	1990 to 2010
East South Central	1,930	2,135	2,395	24.1	186	287	362	84.7
Kentucky	467	491	526	12.6	46	67	82	77.1
Tennessee	619	714	829	33.9	59	94	123	109.6
Alabama	523	578	645	23.4	49	76	96	97.0
Mississippi	321	352	396	23.2	32	50	61	89.5
West South Central	2,960	3,306	3,756	26.9	291	436	554	90.3
Arkansas	350	379	422	20.4	35	55	67	91.2
Louisiana	469	501	537	14.5	44	64	80	82.9
Oklahoma	424	423	446	5.2	46	62	71	55.2
Texas	1,717	2,003	2,351	37.0	167	255	336	101.7
Mountain	1,524	1,774	2,147	40.9	133	215	305	130.2
Montana	106	100	103	-3.2	11	15	18	67.4
Idaho	121	118	132	8.6	11	17	21	84.8
Wyoming	47	38	39	-17.4	5	6	6	42.3
Colorado	329	370	433	31.4	33	47	63	92.1
New Mexico	163	193	228	40.0	14	23	32	126.4
Arizona	479	649	840	75.4	38	72	115	205.4
Utah	150	159	182	21.1	14	22	29	109.9
Nevada	128	149	191	49.3	7	13	21	174.7
Pacific	4,250	5,009	6,068	42.8	406	637	906	123.2
Washington	575	602	710	23.4	56	87	114	101.8
Oregon	391	375	412	5.4	39	59	72	85.9
California	3,136	3,829	4,680	49.3	299	471	682	128.0
Alaska	22	29	40	80.5	1	2	3	142.4
Hawaii	125	175	225	79.7	10	18	35	236.8

Source: U.S. Bureau of the Census, 1990 from 1990 Census of Population and Housing, Summary Tape File 1A; 2000 and 2010 from *Projections of the Population of the United States, by Age, Sex, and Race: 1989 to 2010*, Current Population Reports, series P-25, No. 1053, U.S. Government Printing Office, Washington, D.C., 1990. *Notes:* Totals may not add due to independent rounding and percents are computed on unrounded numbers. 1. State projections produced by Census Bureau consist of four series. Series A was chosen for use in this report but this does not imply in any way that Series A is preferable to the other three series.

★ 53 ★

Population Growth

Population 65 Years Old and Older by Age Group and Sex, 1960-2000

Age group and sex	Number (1,000)					Percent distribution				
	1960	1970	1980	1989	2000 proj.	1960	1970	1980	1989	2000 proj.
Persons 65 years and over	16,675	20,107	25,704	30,984	34,882	100.0	100.0	100.0	100.0	100.0
65-69 years old	6,280	7,026	8,812	10,170	9,491	37.7	34.9	34.3	32.8	27.2
70-74 years old	4,773	5,467	6,841	8,012	8,752	28.6	27.2	26.6	25.9	25.1
75-79 years old	3,080	3,871	4,828	6,033	7,282	18.5	19.3	18.8	19.5	20.9
80-84 years old	1,601	2,312	2,954	3,728	4,735	9.6	11.5	11.5	12.0	13.6
85 years old and over	940	1,430	2,269	3,042	4,622	5.6	7.1	8.8	9.8	13.2
Males, 65 years and over	7,542	8,413	10,366	12,636	14,273	100.0	100.0	100.0	100.0	100.0
65-69 years old	2,936	3,139	3,919	4,631	4,382	38.9	37.3	37.8	36.7	30.7
70-74 years old	2,197	2,322	2,873	3,464	3,860	29.1	27.6	27.7	27.4	27.0
75-79 years old	1,370	1,573	1,862	2,385	2,971	18.2	18.7	18.0	18.9	20.8
80-84 years old	673	883	1,026	1,306	1,739	8.9	10.5	9.9	10.3	12.2
85 years old and over	366	496	688	850	1,322	4.9	5.9	6.6	6.7	9.3
Females, 65 years and over	9,133	11,693	15,338	18,348	20,608	100.0	100.0	100.0	100.0	100.0
65-69 years old	3,344	3,887	4,894	5,538	5,109	36.6	33.2	31.9	30.2	24.8
70-74 years old	2,577	3,145	3,968	4,549	4,892	28.2	26.9	25.9	24.8	23.7
75-79 years old	1,711	2,298	2,966	3,648	4,311	18.7	19.7	19.3	19.9	20.9
80-84 years old	928	1,429	1,928	2,422	2,996	10.2	12.2	12.6	13.2	14.5
85 years old and over	574	934	1,582	2,192	3,300	6.3	8.0	10.3	11.9	16.0

Source: "Population 65 Years Old and Over, by Age Group and Sex, 1960 to 1989, and Projections, 2000," *Statistical Abstract of the United States,* 1991, p. 37. Primary source: U.S. Bureau of the Census, *Current Population Reports,* series P-25, Nos. 519, 917, 1018, and 1057. As of July 1. Includes Armed Forces overseas. Projections are for middle series. These projections were prepared prior to the release of 1990 census results and are therefore not based on 1990 census data.

★ 54 ★

Population Growth

Projections of the 65+ Population, by State: 2010

State	Number of 65+		Percent of total population	Percent change, 1989-2010
	Rank	Value (000's)		
U.S., total	(x)	39,362	14.0	27.0
Alabama	21	645	14.4	23.4
Alaska	50	40	6.0	84.0
Arizona	14	841	15.2	81.1
Arkansas	29	422	16.5	18.6
California	1	4,680	12.3	52.4
Colorado	28	433	12.8	33.5
Connecticut	26	513	14.6	16.4
Delaware	44	120	12.8	51.0
District of Columbia	47	87	13.9	15.1
Florida	2	3,917	19.9	72.1
Georgia	11	1,055	11.2	61.6
Hawaii	37	225	14.1	88.7
Idaho	43	131	13.3	8.2
Illinois	6	1,532	13.2	6.6
Indiana	17	765	13.5	10.3
Iowa	32	391	17.4	-8.7
Kansas	33	381	15.3	11.1
Kentucky	25	526	14.8	11.6
Louisiana	24	536	13.8	10.1
Maine	38	192	13.4	17.3
Maryland	18	757	11.7	48.7
Massachusetts	13	895	13.9	10.0
Michigan	10	1,184	12.7	7.7
Minnesota	22	644	13.9	17.3
Mississippi	31	395	13.8	21.1
Missouri	15	838	14.8	16.6
Montana	45	103	14.9	-2.9
Nebraska	35	232	16.1	3.4
Nevada	39	192	11.9	58.3
New Hampshire	40	190	11.5	50.7
New Jersey	8	1,258	14.2	23.2
New Mexico	36	228	11.9	42.0
New York	3	2,583	14.2	10.3
North Carolina	9	1,209	13.8	51.4
North Dakota	48	82	15.4	-10.6
Ohio	7	1,512	14.0	8.1
Oklahoma	27	448	16.8	4.6
Oregon	30	413	14.1	5.3
Pennsylvania	5	1,845	15.3	1.4
Rhode Island	42	155	14.1	4.9
South Carolina	23	563	13.1	44.2
South Dakota	46	103	14.7	0.2
Tennessee	16	828	14.5	32.5

[Continued]

★ 54 ★

Projections of the 65+ Population, by State: 2010
[Continued]

State	Number of 65+		Percent of total population	Percent change, 1989-2010
	Rank	Value (000's)		
Texas	4	2,351	13.1	37.2
Utah	41	181	9.6	23.6
Vermont	49	80	12.2	18.5
Virginia	12	983	12.0	49.7
Washington	19	711	13.2	25.3
West Virginia	34	240	16.2	-11.7
Wisconsin	20	690	14.8	5.9
Wyoming	51	39	10.7	-16.0

Source: *Aging America, Trends and Projections*, prepared by the U.S. Senate Special Committee on Aging, the American Association of Retired Persons, the Federal Council on the Aging, and the U.S. Administration on Aging, 1991, Washington, D.C., pp. 32-33. Primary source: U.S. Bureau of the Census, "Projections of the Population of States, by Age, Sex, and Race: 1989 to 2010," by Signe I. Wetrogan. *Current Population Reports* Series P-25, No. 1053, January, 1990, and unpublished data. *Note:* (x) stands for not applicable.

★ 55 ★

Population Growth

Population 85 Years and Over: 1900-2050

Data in this table show actual counts (in millions) for the United States through 1990 and projections beyond that date.

Year	Millions
1900	0.1
1910	0.2
1920	0.2
1930	0.3
1940	0.4
1950	0.6
1960	0.9
1970	1.4
1980	2.2
1990	3.0
2000	4.6
2010	6.1
2020	6.7
2030	8.1

[Continued]

★ 55 ★

Population 85 Years and Over: 1900-2050
[Continued]

Year	Millions
2040	12.3
2050	15.3

Source: U.S. Department of Health and Human Services, National Institute on Aging, *Profiles of America's Elderly: Growth of America's Elderly in the 1980's*, December 1991. Primary source: U.S. Bureau of the Census, Decennial Census for specified years; and "Projections of the Population of the United States by Age, Sex, and Race: 1988 to 2080," *Current Population Reports*, P-25 No. 1018, Washington, DC: U.S. Government Printing Office, 1989 (middle series projections). Data for 1990 from 1990 Census of Population and Housing, Series CPH-L-74, "Modified and Actual Age, Sex, Race, and Hispanic Origin Data."

★ 56 ★

Population Growth

Percent Change of U.S. Population 85 Years and Over, by Region, Division, and State: 1980 and 1990

Region, division, and State	Number			Percent change, 1980 to 1990
	1990	1980	Change 1980 to 1990	
United States	3,080,165	2,240,067	840,098	37.5
Northeast	709,809	546,545	163,264	29.9
New England	194,253	151,371	42,882	28.3
Middle Atlantic	515,556	395,174	120,382	30.5
Midwest	839,863	649,375	190,488	29.3
East North Central	538,530	414,808	123,722	29.8
West North Central	301,333	234,567	66,766	28.5
South	992,022	663,741	328,281	49.5
South Atlantic	514,717	326,842	187,875	57.5
East South Central	186,003	134,007	51,996	38.8
West South Central	291,302	202,892	88,410	43.6
West	538,471	380,406	158,065	41.6
Mountain	132,600	86,302	46,298	53.6
Pacific	405,871	294,104	111,767	38.0
New England	194,253	151,371	42,882	28.3
Maine	18,226	14,099	4,127	29.3
Vermont	7,523	6,007	1,516	25.2
New Hampshire	13,286	9,650	3,636	37.7
Massachusetts	92,209	73,908	18,301	24.8
Rhode Island	16,016	11,978	4,038	33.7

[Continued]

★ 56 ★

Percent Change of U.S. Population 85 Years and Over, by Region, Division, and State: 1980 and 1990

[Continued]

Region, division, and State	Number			Percent change, 1980 to 1990
	1990	1980	Change 1980 to 1990	
Connecticut	46,993	35,729	11,264	31.5
Middle Atlantic	515,556	395,174	120,382	30.5
New York	248,173	192,983	55,190	28.6
New Jersey	95,547	72,231	23,316	32.3
Pennsylvania	171,836	129,960	41,876	32.2
East North Central	538,530	414,808	123,722	29.8
Ohio	138,030	108,426	29,604	27.3
Indiana	71.751	54,410	17,341	31.9
Illinois	147,549	114,682	32,867	28.7
Michigan	106,907	81,653	25,254	30.9
Wisconsin	74,293	55,637	18,656	33.5
West North Central	301,333	234,567	66,766	28.5
Minnesota	68,835	52,789	16,046	30.4
Iowa	55,255	44,940	10,315	23.0
Missouri	81,217	61,072	20,145	33.0
North Dakota	11,240	8,140	3,100	38.1
South Dakota	13,343	10,427	2,916	28.0
Nebraska	29,202	23,744	5,458	23.0
Kansas	42,241	33,455	8,786	26.3
South Atlantic	514,717	326,842	187,875	57.5
Delaware	7,142	5,269	1,873	35.5
Maryland	46,496	32,665	13,831	42.3
District of Columbia	7,847	6,385	1,462	22.9
Virginia	59,709	41,131	18,578	45.2
West Virginia	25,451	19,409	6,042	31.1
North Carolina	69,969	45,203	24,766	54.8
South Carolina	30,749	20,004	10,745	53.7
Georgia	57,244	39,434	17,810	45.2
Florida	210,110	117,342	92,768	79.1
East South Central	186,003	134,007	51,996	38.8
Kentucky	46,367	35,036	11,331	32.3
Tennessee	58,794	41,443	17,351	41.9
Alabama	48,507	34,019	14,488	42.6
Mississippi	32,335	23,509	8,826	37.5
West South Central	291,302	202,892	88,410	43.6
Arkansas	35,216	26,354	8,862	33.6
Louisiana	43,633	30,535	13,098	42.9

[Continued]

★ 56 ★

Percent Change of U.S. Population 85 Years and Over, by Region, Division, and State: 1980 and 1990

[Continued]

Region, division, and State	Number			Percent change, 1980 to 1990
	1990	1980	Change 1980 to 1990	
Oklahoma	45,848	33,981	11,867	34.9
Texas	166,605	112,022	54,583	48.7
Mountain	132,600	86,302	46,298	53.6
Montana	10,676	8,837	1,839	20.8
Idaho	11,398	8,476	2,922	34.5
Wyoming	4,550	3,473	1,077	31.0
Colorado	32,953	24,363	8,590	35.3
New Mexico	14,232	8,783	5,449	62.0
Arizona	37,717	19,878	17,839	89.7
Utah	13,611	8,852	4,759	53.8
Nevada	7,463	3,640	3,823	105.0
Pacific	405,871	294,104	111,767	38.0
Washington	56,301	41,476	14,825	35.7
Oregon	38,815	28,431	10,384	36.5
California	299,107	218,017	81,090	37.2
Alaska	1,251	619	632	102.1
Hawaii	10,397	5,561	4,836	87.0

Source: U.S. Bureau of the Census, 1980 and 1990 Censuses of Population: for 1980, *General Population Characteristics*, PC80-1-B1, Table 67; for 1990, Summary Tape File 1A.

★ 57 ★

Population Growth

Parent and Sandwich Generation Support Ratios: 1950 to 2050

Support ratios are ratios between those able to earn an income and those who are dependent on the earning segments for their support for reasons of youth or old age. Specific ratios shown here are explained in the notes.

Ratio/race	1950	1990	2010	2030	2050
Parent support ratio[1]					
Total	3	9	11	15	28
White	3	10	11	17	30
Black	3	7	7	11	22
Other races	2	4	6	12	21
Hispanic origin[2]	(NA)	5	6	11	18
Sandwich generation[3]					
Total	144	228	164	289	279

[Continued]

★ 57 ★

Parent and Sandwich Generation Support Ratios:
1950 to 2050
[Continued]

Ratio/race	1950	1990	2010	2030	2050
White	148	235	167	301	286
Black	97[4]	195	142	260	267
Hispanic origin[2]	(NA)	159	122	194	192

Source: Sixty-Five Plus in America, Cynthia M. Taeuber, U.S. Department of Commerce, Economics and Statistics Administration, Bureau of the Census, U.S. Government Printing Office, Washington, D.C., 1992, p. 2-16. Primary source: U.S. Bureau of the Census, 1950 from 1950 Census of Population, Volume 2, Part 1, Chapter C, Table 112; 1990 from 1990 Census of Population and Housing, Series CPH-L-74, Modified and Actual Age, Sex, Race, and Hispanic Origin Data; 2010 to 2050 from Projections of the Population of the United States, by Age, Sex, and Race: 1988 to 2080, Current Population Reports, Series P-25, No. 1018. U.S. Government Printing Office, Washington, D.C., 1989 (middle series projections). Hispanic projections from Projections of the Hispanic Population: 1983 to 2080, Current Population Reports, Series P-25, No. 995, U.S. Government Printing Office, Washington, D.C., 1988 (middle series projections). Notes: 1. Ratio of persons 85 years old and over to persons 50 to 64 years old. 2. Hispanic origin may be of any race. 3. Ratio of persons aged 18 to 22 enrolled in college plus persons aged 65 to 79 to persons aged 45 to 49 years. College enrollment for 1990-2050 is based on 1989 rates for 18 to 22 year olds (total, 37.3 percent; White, 38.7 percent; Blacks, 27.9 percent; Hispanics, 24.7 percent). 4. 1950 data are for "Blacks and other races" combined. Over 90 percent of "Black and other races" were Black in 1950.

Population: Worldwide

★ 58 ★

Average Annual Growth Rates of the Elderly Population,
by Age in Selected Countries: 1990-2005 and 2005-2025
[Numbers in percent]

Country	1990-2005		2005-2025	
	65 to 79	80+	65 to 79	80+
Japan	3.00	4.30	0.70	3.40
Canada	1.60	3.80	2.90	2.60
France	1.30	1.30	1.70	1.10
Germany	1.90	0.80	0.60	1.90
Italy	1.50	3.10	0.60	2.20
Sweden	-0.60	2.00	1.40	1.20
United Kingdom	-.01	2.10	1.40	1.60
United States	0.30	2.70	2.90	1.30

Source: Aging America, Trends and Projections, prepared by the U.S. Senate Special Committee on Aging, the American Association of Retired Persons, the Federal Council on the Aging, and the U.S. Administration on Aging, 1991, Washington, D.C., p. 252. Primary source: U.S. Bureau of the Census. International Data Base.

★ 59 ★

Population: Worldwide

The 20 Countries with the Greatest Number of Elderly Persons: 1992

[Percent of population 65 years and over]

Country	Percent
Sweden	17.9
Norway	16.3
United Kingdom	15.7
Belgium	15.4
Denmark	15.4
Austria	15.3
Italy	15.2
France	15.0
Germany	15.0
Switzerland	14.9
Greece	14.8
Spain	14.1
Finland	13.9
Luxembourg	13.8
Bulgaria	13.8
Hungary	13.7
Portugal	13.6
Netherlands	13.2
Japan	12.8
United States	12.6

Source: U.S. Department of Commerce, Economics and Statistics Administration, Bureau of the Census, International Population Reports P95/92-3: *An Aging World II*, by Kevin Kinsella and Cynthia M. Taeuber, February 1993, p. 11. Primary source: U.S. Bureau of the Census, Center for International Research, International Data Base on Aging.

★ 60 ★

Population: Worldwide

Aging Population in European Community

Percentage of people 60 years old and older in each country of the European Community.

Country	1991	2020 projection
Britain	20.7	36.4
Italy	20.8	29.9
Germany	20.6	29.7
Belgium	20.8	28.2
Luxembourg	19.3	26.8
France	19.4	26.1

[Continued]

★ 60 ★

Aging Population in European Community
[Continued]

Country	1991	2020 projection
Greece	20.5	26.0
Denmark	20.4	25.8
Portugal	18.5	25.5
The Netherlands	17.6	25.2
Spain	19.0	24.9
Ireland (1990)	15.1	22.9

Source: New York Times, July 13, 1993, p. A5 Eurolink Age Bulletin, November 1992, from International Database, Center for International Research (1991 figures); Eurostat (Ireland and 2020 figures).

★ 61 ★

Population: Worldwide

Countries with More Than Two Million Elderly Persons in 1991
[Data are shown in thousands]

Country	Population aged 65 and over
China, Mainland	67,967
India	32,780
United States	32,045
Japan	15,253
Germany	12,010
United Kingdom	9,025
Italy	8,665
France	8,074
Brazil	6,680
Indonesia	5,962
Spain	5,378
Pakistan	4,734
Poland	3,851
Mexico	3,522
Bangladesh	3,492
Vietnam	3,196
Canada	3,140
Argentina	3,012
Turkey	2,789
Nigeria	2,676
Romania	2,489
Philippines	2,380
Thailand	2,350

[Continued]

★ 61 ★

Countries with More Than Two Million Elderly Persons in 1991

[Continued]

Country	Population aged 65 and over
Yugoslavia	2,328
South Korea	2,135
Egypt	2,077
Iran	2,052

Source: *Sixty-Five Plus in America*, Cynthia M. Taeuber, U.S. Department of Commerce, Economics and Statistics Administration, Bureau of the Census, U.S. Government Printing Office, Washington, D.C., 1992, p. 2-21. Primary source: U.S. Bureau of the Census, Kevin Kinsella, Center for International Research, International Data Base.

★ 62 ★

Population: Worldwide

Countries with More Than Five Million Persons 65+ and One Million Persons Over 80+, 1990

In 1990, the United States ranked second in the world both in population of persons over 65 and persons over 80 years old. The United States is expected to maintain this second ranking behind China well into the twenty-first century.

[Numbers in thousands]

Age and country	Population
Age 65+	
China	63,398
United States	31,560
India	29,518
Soviet Union	27,461
Japan	14,655
Germany[1]	11,779
United Kingdom	8,977
Italy	8,472
France	7,928
Brazil	6,430
Indonesia	5,655
Spain	5,246
80+	
China	7,716
United States	7,082
Soviet Union	6,398
Germany[1]	2,938
Japan	2,824

[Continued]

★ 62 ★

Countries with More Than Five Million Persons 65+ and One Million Persons Over 80+, 1990

[Continued]

Age and country	Population
India	2,389
France	2,119
United Kingdom	2,087
Italy	1,770
Spain	1,116

Source: *Aging America, Trends and Projections*, prepared by the U.S. Senate Special Committee on Aging, the American Association of Retired Persons, the Federal Council on the Aging, and the U.S. Administration on Aging, 1991, Washington, D.C., p. 249. Primary source: U.S. Bureau of the Census. International Data Base. *Note:* 1. Figures are for a unified Germany.

★ 63 ★

Population: Worldwide

Percent of Population Aged 65+, for Major World Regions

Data are generally for 1988, 1989 or most recently available year.

Region	Persons aged 65+
World	6.0
More developed countries	12.0
Developing countries	4.0
Developing countries (excl. China)	4.0
Africa	3.0
Northern Africa	4.0
Western Africa	2.0
Eastern Africa	3.0
Middle Africa	3.0
Southern Africa	4.0
Asia	5.0
Asia (excl. China)	4.0
Western Asia	4.0
Southern Asia	3.0
Southeast Asia	4.0
Eastern Asia	6.0
North America	12.0
Latin America	5.0
Central America	4.0

[Continued]

★ 63 ★

Percent of Population Aged 65+, for Major World Regions
[Continued]

Region	Persons aged 65+
Caribbean	6.0
Tropical South America	4.0
Temperate South America	8.0
Europe	13.0
Northern Europe	15.0
Western Europe	14.0
Eastern Europe	11.0
Southern Europe	12.0
USSR	9.0
Oceania	9.0

Source: Aging America, Trends and Projections, prepared by the U.S. Senate Special Committee on Aging, the American Association of Retired Persons, the Federal Council on the Aging, and the U.S. Administration on Aging, 1991, Washington, D.C., p. 273. Primary source: 1990 World Population Data Sheet, Washington, D.C.: Population Reference Bureau, 1990.

★ 64 ★

Population: Worldwide

Population Aged 65+ and Aged 80+ in Selected Countries, 1990 and 2025

Country	65+						80+					
	Number (in thousands)			Percent of total			Number (in thousands)			Percent of total		
	1990 (esti-mated)	2025 (pro-jected)	Percent change 1990 to 2025	1990 (esti-mated)	2025 (pro-jected)	Percent change 1990 to 2025	1990 (esti-mated)	2025 (pro-jected)	Percent change 1990 to 2025	1990 (esti-mated)	2025 (pro-jected)	Percent change 1990 to 2025
Canada	3,053	7,350	140.7	11.5	21.8	89.6	634	1,894	198.7	2.4	5.6	133.3
France	7,928	13,102	65.3	14.1	21.8	54.6	2,119	3,208	51.4	3.8	5.3	39.5
Germany	11,779	18,182	54.4	15.0	24.4	62.7	2,938	4,875	65.9	3.7	6.5	75.7
Italy	8,472	13,771	62.5	14.7	25.1	70.7	1,770	4,428	150.1	3.1	8.1	161.3
Japan	14,655	31,897	117.7	11.8	26.3	123.0	2,824	10,559	273.9	2.3	8.7	278.3
Sweden	1,527	2,032	33.1	17.9	23.7	32.4	375	640	70.8	4.4	7.5	70.4
U.K.	8,977	13,016	45.0	15.6	21.9	40.4	2,078	3,880	86.7	3.6	7.5	80.6
U.S.	31,560	59,713	89.2	12.6	20.0	58.7	7,082	13,658	92.8	2.8	4.6	64.3

Source: Aging America, Trends and Projections, prepared by the U.S. Senate Special Committee on Aging, the American Association of Retired Persons, the Federal Council on the Aging, and the U.S. Administration on Aging, 1991, Washington, D.C., p. 250. Primary source: U.S. Bureau of the Census, International Data Base.

★ 65 ★

Population: Worldwide

Percent Distribution of World Population, 80 Years and Older: 1990

Country	Percent
United States	12.8
China	15.8
India	6.2
Japan	5.2
Other Asia	6.5
Former USSR	11.8
Germany	5.4
France	4.1
United Kingdom	3.8
Italy	3.3
Spain	2.0
Poland	1.4
Other Europe	8.4
Latin America/Caribbean	6.1
Africa/Near East	5.1
All remaining countries	1.9

Source: U.S. Department of Commerce, Economics and Statistics Administration, Bureau of the Census, International Population Reports P95/92-3: *An Aging World II*, by Kevin Kinsella and Cynthia M. Taeuber, February 1993, p. 15. Primary source: U.S. Bureau of the Census, Center for International Research, International Data Base on Aging.

★ 66 ★

Population: Worldwide

Persons Over 80 as Percent of Total Elderly Population: Selected Countries, 1990 and 2025

Percentage of population 65 years and older who are 80 years and older.

Country	1990	2025
Japan	19.8	34.6
Sweden	24.6	31.5
France	27.7	27.7
United States	22.4	23.0
Brazil	14.4	17.6

Source: U.S. Department of Commerce, Economics and Statistics Administration, Bureau of the Census, International Population Reports P95/92-3: *An Aging World II*, by Kevin Kinsella and Cynthia M. Taeuber, February 1993, p. 16. Primary source: U.S. Bureau of the Census, Center for International Research, International Data Base on Aging.

★ 67 ★

Population: Worldwide

Sex Ratios, by Age in Selected Countries, 1990 and 2025

[Number of men per 100 women in age group]

Country	1990			2025		
	All ages	65 +	85 +	All ages	65 +	85 +
Canada	97.2	71.9	52.4	95.7	77.4	59.4
France	95.1	64.4	44.3	95.6	74.0	55.0
Germany	92.7	50.5	39.0	96.5	76.0	52.9
Italy	94.4	67.1	49.5	95.4	75.3	56.1
Japan	96.7	67.6	55.1	96.1	78.5	61.6
Sweden	97.3	74.1	53.7	97.3	79.6	61.2
United Kingdom	95.3	66.3	42.4	97.1	77.7	57.8
United States	95.4	68.7	47.1	95.5	77.1	53.3

Source: Aging America, Trends and Projections, prepared by the U.S. Senate Special Committee on Aging, the American Association of Retired Persons, the Federal Council on the Aging, and the U.S. Administration on Aging, 1991, Washington, D.C., p. 259. Primary source: U.S. Bureau of the Census. international Data Base.

Life Expectancy

★ 68 ★

Average Number of Years of Life Remaining at Beginning of Age Interval: Abridged Life Table for 1988

Period of life between two exact ages	Male		Female	
	White	Black	White	Black
0 to 1 year	72.3	64.9	78.9	73.4
65 to 70 years	14.9	13.4	18.7	16.9
70 to 75 years	11.8	10.9	15.0	13.8
75 to 80 years	9.1	8.6	11.7	10.9
80 to 85 years	6.8	6.8	8.7	8.4
85 years and over	5.1	5.5	6.3	6.6

Source: Sixty-Five Plus in America, Cynthia M. Taeuber, U.S. Department of Commerce, Economics and Statistics Administration, Bureau of the Census, U.S. Government Printing Office, Washington, D.C., 1992, p. 3-3. Primary source: National Center for Health Statistics, *Vital Statistics of the United States 1988*, Vol. II, Part A, Life Tables, Table 6-1.

★ 69 ★

Life Expectancy

Life Expectancy at Age 65, by Race and Sex: United States, Selected Years, 1900-1990

Data are based on the National Vital Statistics System.

Specified age and year	All races			White			Black		
	Both sexes	Sex		Both sexes	Sex		Both sexes	Sex	
		Male	Female		Male	Female		Male	Female
1900-1902[1,2]	11.9	11.5	12.2	-	11.5	12.2	-	10.4	11.4
1950[2]	13.9	12.8	15	-	12.8	15.1	13.9	12.9	14.9
1960[2]	14.3	12.8	15.8	14.4	12.9	15.9	13.9	12.7	15.1
1970	15.2	13.1	17	15.2	13.1	17.1	14.2	12.5	15.7
1975	16.1	13.8	18.1	16.1	13.8	18.2	15	13.1	16.7
1980	16.4	14.1	18.3	16.5	14.2	18.4	15.1	13	16.8
1981	16.7	14.3	18.6	16.7	14.4	18.7	15.5	13.4	17.3
1982	16.8	14.5	18.7	16.9	14.5	18.8	15.7	13.5	17.5
1983	16.7	14.5	18.6	16.8	14.5	18.7	15.5	13.4	17.3
1984	16.8	14.6	18.6	16.9	14.6	18.7	15.5	13.5	17.2
1985	16.7	14.6	18.6	16.8	14.6	18.7	15.3	13.3	17
1986	16.8	14.7	18.6	16.9	14.8	18.7	15.4	13.4	17
1987	16.9	14.8	18.7	17	14.9	18.8	15.4	13.5	17.1
1988	16.9	14.9	18.6	17	14.9	18.7	15.4	13.4	16.9
1989	17.2	15.2	18.8	17.3	15.2	19	15.5	13.6	17
Provisional data:									
1988[2]	16.9	14.8	18.6	17	14.9	18.7	15.5	13.6	17.1
1989[2]	17.2	15.2	18.8	17.3	15.2	18.9	15.8	13.8	17.4
1990[2]	17.3	15.3	19	17.3	15.3	19	16.1	14.2	17.6

Source: U.S. Department of Commerce, Economics and Statistics Administration, *National Economic, Social, and Environmental Data Bank, CD-ROM,* November 1992. Primary source: U.S. Bureau of the Census: *U.S. Life Tables 1890, 1901, 1910, and 1901-1910,* by J. W. Glover. Washington. U.S. Government Printing Office, 1921; National Center for Health Statistics: *Vital Statistics Rates in the United States, 1940-1960,* by R. D. Grove and A. M. Hetzel. DHEW Pub. No. (PHS) 1677. Public Health Service. Washington. U.S. Government Printing Office, 1968; *Annual summary of births, marriages, divorces, and deaths, United States, 1988.* Monthly Vital Statistics Report. Vol. 37, No. 13. DHHS Pub. No. (PHS) 89-1120. July 26, 1989; *Annual summary of births, marriages, divorces, and deaths, United States, 1989.* Monthly Vital Statistics Report. 1991; and *Annual summary of births, marriages, divorces, and deaths, United States, 1990.* Monthly Vital Statistics Report. Vol. 39, No. 13. DHHS Pub. No. (PHS) 91-1120. 1991. Public Health Service. Hyattsville, MD.; Unpublished data from the Division of Vital Statistics; Data computed by the Office of Research and Methodology from data compiled by the Division of Vital Statistics. *Notes:* A dash (-) indicates that data were not given in the original source. 1. Death registration area only. The death registration area increased from 10 States and the District of Columbia in 1900 to the coterminous United States in 1933. 2. Includes deaths of nonresidents of the United States.

★ 70 ★

Life Expectancy

Life Expectancy at Birth and Age 65, by Race and Sex: 1900-1987

[Values are in years]

Year	All races			White			Black		
	Both sexes	Men	Women	Both sexes	Men	Women	Both sexes	Men	Women
At birth									
1900[1,2]	47.3	46.3	48.3	47.6	46.6	48.7	33.0[3]	32.5[3]	33.5[3]
1950[2]	68.2	65.6	71.1	69.1	66.5	72.2	60.7	58.9	62.7
1960[2]	69.7	66.6	73.1	70.6	67.4	74.1	63.2	60.7	65.9
1970	70.9	67.1	74.8	71.7	68.0	75.6	64.1	60.0	68.3
1980	73.7	70.0	77.4	74.4	70.7	78.1	68.1	63.8	72.5
1987	75.0	71.5	78.4	75.6	72.2	78.9	69.4	65.2	73.6
At age 65									
1900-02[1,2]	11.9	11.5	12.2	-	11.5	12.2	-	10.4[3]	11.4[3]
1950[2]	13.9	12.8	15.0	-	12.8	15.1	13.9	12.9	14.9
1960[2]	14.3	12.8	15.8	14.4	12.9	15.9	13.9	12.7	15.1
1970	15.2	13.1	17.0	15.2	13.1	17.1	14.2	12.5	15.7
1980	16.4	14.1	18.3	16.5	14.2	18.4	15.1	13.0	16.8
1987	16.9	14.8	18.7	17.0	14.9	18.8	15.4	13.5	17.1

Source: *Aging America, Trends and Projections*, prepared by the U.S. Senate Special Committee on Aging, the American Association of Retired Persons, the Federal Council on the Aging, and the U.S. Administration on Aging, 1991, Washington, D.C., p. 20. Primary source: 1900 to 1980 data: National Center for Health Statistics. *Health United States, 1988*, DHHS Pub. No. (PHS)89-1232,Department of Health and Human Services, Washington, March, 1989. 1987 data: National Center for Health Statistics. "Life Tables," *Vital Statistics of the United States, 1987* Vol. II, Section 6, February 1990. *Notes:* 1. 10 states and the District of Columbia. 2. Includes deaths of nonresidents of the United States. 3. Figure is for the nonwhite population.

★ 71 ★

Life Expectancy

Life Expectancy at Birth and Age 65, by Race and Sex: Selected Years 1900 to 1989

Specified age and year	All races			White		Black	
	Both sexes	Male	Female	Male	Female	Male	Female
At birth							
1900[1,2]	47.3	46.3	48.3	46.6	48.7	32.5[3]	33.5[3]
1950[2]	68.2	65.6	71.1	66.5	72.2	58.9	62.7
1960[2]	69.7	66.6	73.1	67.4	74.1	60.7	65.9
1970	70.9	67.1	74.8	68.0	75.6	60.0	68.3
1980	73.7	70.0	77.4	70.7	78.1	63.8	72.5
1989	75.3	71.8	78.6	72.7	79.2	64.8	73.5
At 65 years							
1900-1902[1,2]	11.9	11.5	12.2	11.5	12.2	10.4	11.4

[Continued]

★ 71 ★

Life Expectancy at Birth and Age 65, by Race and Sex: Selected Years 1900 to 1989
[Continued]

Specified age and year	All races			White		Black	
	Both sexes	Male	Female	Male	Female	Male	Female
1950[2]	13.9	12.8	15.0	12.8	15.1	12.9	14.9
1960[2]	14.3	12.8	15.8	12.9	15.9	12.7	15.1
1970	15.2	13.1	17.0	13.1	17.1	12.5	15.7
1980	16.4	14.1	18.3	14.2	18.4	13.0	16.8
1989	17.2	15.2	18.8	15.2	19.0	13.6	17.0

Source: Sixty-Five Plus in America, Cynthia M. Taeuber, U.S. Department of Commerce, Economics and Statistics Administration, Bureau of the Census, U.S. Government Printing Office, Washington, D.C., 1992, p. 3-1. Primary source: National Center for Health Statistics, Health, United States, 1990, Hyattsville, MD: Public Health Service, 1991, Table 15. 1989 "At birth" data from Monthly Vital Statistics Report, Vol. 40, No. 8(S)2, January 7, 1992. 1989 "At 65 years" data unpublished final data from Mortality Statistics Branch. Notes: 1. Death registration area only. The death registration area increased from 10 states and the District of Columbia in 1900 to the coterminous United States in 1933. 2. Includes deaths of nonresidents of the United States. 3. Figure is for the all other population.

★ 72 ★

Life Expectancy

Life Expectancy at Birth and Age 65, by Sex: Selected Countries, 1983 and 1988
[Life expectancy in years]

Country	At birth		At 65 years	
	1983[1]	1988[2]	1983[1]	1988[2]
MALE				
Japan	74.5	75.8	15.5	16.2
Hong Kong	72.3	74.4	14.0	15.3
Greece	73.6	74.3	15.4	15.6
Sweden	73.6	74.2	14.7	15.0
Switzerland	72.7	74.0	14.6	15.4
Israel	73.0	73.9	14.9	15.1
Netherlands	73.0	73.7	14.0	14.4
Canada	72.0	73.4	14.5	15.0
Italy	71.3	73.3	13.7	14.7
Australia	72.2	73.2	14.3	15.0
Spain	72.6	73.1	14.8	15.0
Norway	72.8	73.1	14.5	14.6
France	70.7	72.9	14.2	15.7
England and Wales	71.6	72.7	13.3	14.0
Kuwait	69.0	72.5	12.5	14.5
Federal Republic of Germany	70.7	72.3	13.3	14.1
Austria	69.5	72.1	13.1	14.5
Costa Rica	74.5	72.1	17.3	14.0

[Continued]

★ 72 ★

Life Expectancy at Birth and Age 65, by Sex: Selected Countries, 1983 and 1988

[Continued]

Country	At birth		At 65 years	
	1983[1]	1988[2]	1983[1]	1988[2]
Cuba	72.2	72.0	15.3	15.3
Denmark	71.5	72.0	13.9	14.1
Ireland	70.3	71.6	12.6	13.0
United States	71.0	71.5	14.5	14.9
Singapore	69.4	71.5	12.5	13.5
Belgium	70.6	71.4	13.1	13.5
Puerto Rico	71.6	71.1	16.3	16.8
New Zealand	70.8	71.0	13.6	13.7
Northern Ireland	69.3	70.9	12.4	12.9
Finland	70.2	70.7	13.0	13.6
Portugal	69.3	70.5	13.6	14.2
Scotland	69.6	70.5	12.5	13.0
Chile	67.8	70.0	13.3	13.7
German Democratic Republic	69.5	69.7	12.5	12.6
Yugoslavia	67.1	68.7	12.5	13.3
Bulgaria	68.4	68.3	12.6	12.6
Czechoslovakia	66.9	67.7	11.5	11.9
Romania	66.9	67.1	12.6	12.8
Poland	67.1	67.1	12.6	12.5
Hungary	65.1	66.1	11.6	12.3
U.S.S.R.	62.9	64.7	12.0	12.4
FEMALE				
Japan	80.3	81.9	18.9	20.2
France	78.8	81.3	18.4	20.4
Switzerland	79.8	81.1	18.7	19.8
Netherlands	79.8	80.5	19.0	19.3
Canada	79.0	80.3	18.7	19.6
Sweden	79.6	80.0	18.5	18.7
Italy	77.9	79.9	17.2	18.7
Hong Kong	78.4	79.9	17.9	18.6
Australia	79.0	79.8	18.6	19.1
Norway	79.8	79.7	18.7	18.7
Spain	78.8	79.7	18.1	18.4
Greece	78.3	79.4	17.6	18.0
Puerto Rico	78.3	79.4	18.8	19.6
Federal Republic of Germany	77.5	79.1	17.1	18.1
Finland	78.5	78.8	17.5	17.7
Austria	76.6	78.7	16.6	17.8
England and Wales	77.6	78.4	17.4	17.9

[Continued]

★ 72 ★

Life Expectancy at Birth and Age 65, by Sex: Selected Countries, 1983 and 1988
[Continued]

Country	At birth		At 65 years	
	1983[1]	1988[2]	1983[1]	1988[2]
United States	78.1	78.3	18.6	18.6
Belgium	77.2	78.1	17.0	17.5
Denmark	77.5	77.7	17.8	17.9
Portugal	76.2	77.7	16.7	17.5
Israel	76.4	77.4	16.2	16.7
New Zealand	77.0	77.3	17.5	17.6
Ireland	76.0	77.1	15.9	16.6
Northern Ireland	75.7	76.9	16.1	17.0
Costa Rica	78.4	76.9	19.0	16.8
Scotland	75.8	76.8	16.2	16.8
Singapore	75.0	76.2	15.5	16.0
German Democratic Republic	75.4	76.0	15.4	15.6
Kuwait	73.8	75.8	15.2	16.2
Poland	75.2	75.7	16.1	16.3
Chile	74.7	75.7	16.8	16.7
Czechoslovakia	74.3	75.3	14.7	15.5
Cuba	75.3	75.3	16.7	16.6
Yugoslavia	73.0	74.7	14.9	15.9
Bulgaria	74.4	74.6	14.9	15.0
Hungary	73.0	74.2	14.8	15.6
U.S.S.R.	72.7	73.4	15.6	15.8
Romania	72.5	72.7	14.4	14.7

Source: U.S. Department of Commerce, Economics and Statistics Administration, *National Economic, Social, and Environmental Data Bank, CD-ROM,* November 1992. Primary source: World Health Organization: *World Health Statistics Annuals.* Vols. 1984-1990. Geneva. United Nations: *Demographic Yearbook 1984 and 1986.* New York. National Center for Health Statistics: *Vital Statistics of the United States, 1983,* Vol. II, Mortality, Part A. DHHS Pub. No. (PHS) 87-1101. Public Health Service. Washington. U.S. Government Printing Office, 1988; *Vital Statistics of the United States, 1988,* Vol. II, Mortality, Part A. DHHS Pub. No. (PHS) 91-1101. Public Health Service. Washington. U.S. Government Printing Office, 1991. *Notes:* Rankings are from highest to lowest life expectancy based on the latest available data for countries or geographic areas with at least 1 million population. This table is based on official mortality data from the country concerned, as submitted to the United Nations Demographic Yearbook or the World Health Statistics Annual. 1. Data for Spain are for 1981; data for Canada, Chile, Greece, and Kuwait are for 1982; data for Denmark are for 1982-1983; data for England and Wales are for 1982-1984; data for Portugal are for 1982-1985; and data for U.S.S.R. are for 1984-85. 2. Data for Romania are for 1984; data for Belgium are for 1986; data for New Zealand are for 1986-1988; data for Bulgaria, Chile, Kuwait, and Spain are for 1987; and data for Portugal are for 1987-1988.

★ 73 ★

Life Expectancy

Life Expectancy at Birth and Age 65, by Sex: Selected Countries, 1987[1]

[Data are based on reporting by countries]

Country	Life expectancy at birth	Life expectancy at 65 years	Country	Life expectancy at birth	Life expectancy at 65 years
MALE			FEMALE		
Japan	75.9	16.4	Japan	82.1	20.4
Sweden	74.2	15.1	France	81.1	20.2
Hong Kong	74.2	15.0	Switzerland	81.0	19.7
Greece	74.1	15.4	Sweden	80.4	19.1
Switzerland	74.0	15.4	Netherlands	80.3	19.3
Netherlands	73.6	14.4	Canada	80.2	19.6
Israel	73.4	14.9	Australia	79.8	19.0
Canada	73.3	15.1	Norway	79.8	18.8
Australia	73.2	14.9	Hong Kong	79.7	18.5
Spain	73.1	15.0	Spain	79.7	18.4
Cuba	73.0	16.2	Italy	79.2	18.2
Norway	72.8	14.4	Greece	78.9	17.7
Italy	72.7	14.3	Finland	78.9	17.7
England and Wales	72.6	13.9	Federal Republic of		
France	72.6	15.4	Germany	78.9	18.1
Kuwait	72.5	14.5	Puerto Rico[2]	78.9	19.2
Federal Republic of			UNITED STATES	78.4	18.7
Germany	72.2	14.0	England and Wales	78.3	17.9
Costa Rica	72.1	14.0	Austria	78.2	17.6
Denmark	71.9	14.2	Belgium	78.2	17.8
Ireland	71.6	13.1	Denmark	78.0	18.2
Austria	71.6	14.3	Portugal	77.5	17.6
UNITED STATES	71.5	14.8	New Zealand	77.3	17.6
Belgium	71.4	13.6	Ireland	77.3	16.6
Singapore	71.3	13.5	Northern Ireland	77.2	16.9
Northern Ireland	71.1	13.0	Israel	77.0	16.0
New Zealand	71.0	13.7	Costa Rica	76.9	16.8
Puerto Rico[2]	70.7	16.3	Scotland	76.6	16.7
Finland	70.7	13.5	Singapore	76.5	16.6
Portugal	70.6	14.3	Cuba	76.5	17.9
Scotland	70.5	12.8	German Democratic		
Chile	70.0	13.7	Republic	76.0	15.6
German Democratic			Kuwait	75.8	16.2
Republic	69.9	12.7	Chile	75.7	16.7
Yugoslavia	68.5	13.3	Czechoslovakia	75.3	15.5
Bulgaria	68.3	12.6	Poland	75.2	15.9
Czechoslovakia	67.7	11.9	Bulgaria	74.6	15.0

[Continued]

★ 73 ★

Life Expectancy at Birth and Age 65, by Sex: Selected Countries, 1987
[Continued]

Country	Life expectancy at birth	Life expectancy at 65 years	Country	Life expectancy at birth	Life expectancy at 65 years
Romania	67.1	12.8	Yugoslavia	74.3	15.6
Poland	66.8	12.3	Hungary	73.9	15.4
Hungary	65.7	12.1	U.S.S.R.	73.9	16.2
U.S.S.R.	65.1	12.5	Romania	72.7	14.7

Source: Sixty-Five Plus in America, Cynthia M. Taeuber, U.S. Department of Commerce, Economics and Statistics Administration, Bureau of the Census, U.S. Government Printing Office, Washington, D.C., 1992, pp. 3-5 - 3-6. Primary source: National Center for Health Statistics, *Health, United States, 1990*, Hyattsville, MD, Public Health Service, 1991, Table 22. *Notes:* This table was compiled before Germany became unified and U.S.S.R. became a commonwealth. Rankings are from highest to lowest life expectancy based on the latest data for countries or geographic areas with at least 1 million population. This table is based on official mortality data from the country concerned, as submitted to the United Nations Demographic Yearbook or the World Health Statistics Annual. 1. Data for Romania are for 1984; data for Spain are for 1985; data for Puerto Rico are for 1985-1987; data for Belgium, Greece, Israel and Italy are for 1986; data for New Zealand are for 1986-1988; and data for Costa Rica and Czechoslovakia are for 1988. 2. Data are from the Informe Annual de Estadisticas Vitales, 1983 and 1987, University of Puerto Rico.

★ 74 ★

Life Expectancy

Life Expectancy at Birth by Sex and Race, 1960-2010
[In years]

Year	Total			White			Black and other			Black		
	Total	M	F	Total	M	F	Total	M	F	Total	M	F
1960	69.7	66.6	73.1	70.6	67.4	74.1	63.6	61.1	66.3	na	na	na
1970	70.8	67.1	74.7	71.7	68.0	75.6	65.3	61.3	69.4	64.1	60.0	68.3
1975	72.6	68.8	76.6	73.4	69.5	77.3	68.0	63.7	72.4	66.8	62.4	71.3
1976	72.9	69.1	76.8	73.6	69.9	77.5	68.4	64.2	72.7	67.2	62.9	71.6
1977	73.3	69.5	77.2	74.0	70.2	77.9	68.9	64.7	73.2	67.7	63.4	72.0
1978	73.5	69.6	77.3	74.1	70.4	78.0	69.3	65.0	73.5	68.1	63.7	72.4
1979	73.9	70.0	77.8	74.6	70.8	78.4	69.8	65.4	74.1	68.5	64.0	72.9
1980	73.7	70.0	77.4	74.4	70.7	78.1	69.5	65.3	73.6	68.1	63.8	72.5
1981	74.2	70.4	77.8	74.8	71.1	78.4	70.3	66.1	74.4	68.9	64.5	73.2
1982	74.5	70.9	78.1	75.1	71.5	78.7	71.0	66.8	75.0	69.4	65.1	73.7
1983	74.6	71.0	78.1	75.2	71.7	78.7	71.1	67.2	74.9	69.6	65.4	73.6
1984	74.7	71.2	78.2	75.3	71.8	78.7	71.3	67.4	75.0	69.7	65.6	73.7
1985	74.7	71.2	78.2	75.3	71.9	78.7	71.2	67.2	75.0	69.5	65.3	73.5
1986	74.8	71.3	78.3	75.4	72.0	78.8	71.2	67.2	75.1	69.4	65.2	73.5
1987	75.0	71.5	78.4	75.6	72.2	78.9	71.3	67.3	75.2	69.4	65.2	73.6
1988	74.9	71.5	78.3	75.6	72.3	78.9	71.2	67.1	75.1	69.2	64.9	73.4
1989, prel.	75.2	71.8	78.5	75.9	72.6	79.1	71.7	67.5	75.7	69.7	65.2	74.0
Projections[1]												
1990	75.6	72.1	79.0	76.2	72.7	79.6	na	na	na	71.4	67.7	75.0

[Continued]

★ 74 ★

Life Expectancy at Birth by Sex and Race, 1960-2010
[Continued]

Year	Total			White			Black and other			Black		
	Total	M	F	Total	M	F	Total	M	F	Total	M	F
1995	76.3	72.8	79.7	76.8	73.4	80.2	na	na	na	72.4	68.8	76.0
2000	77.0	73.5	80.4	77.5	74.0	80.9	na	na	na	73.5	69.9	77.1
2005	77.6	74.2	81.0	78.1	74.6	81.5	na	na	na	74.6	71.0	78.1
2010	77.9	74.4	81.3	78.3	74.9	81.7	na	na	na	75.0	71.4	78.5

Source: Statistical Abstract of the United States, 1991, p. 73. Primary source: Except as noted, U.S. National Center for Health Statistics, Vital Statistics of the United States, annual; and unpublished data. Notes: Beginning with 1970, data exclude deaths of nonresidents of the United States. na stands for not available. 1. Based on median mortality assumptions, U.S. Bureau of the Census, Current Population Reports, series P-25, No. 1018.

★ 75 ★

Life Expectancy

Life Expectancy at Birth, by Sex and Differential for Selected Countries, 1990

From the source: "As of 1990, life expectancy at birth was highest in Japan—79.3 years... Americans born in 1990 could expect to live an average of 75.6 years, which was a lower life expectancy than that of many other developed nations. The nearly four-year difference in life expectancy between the United States and Japan has more to do with infant mortality than aging. At age 65, life expectancy is about the same in the two countries (Japanese men at that age could expect to live about six months longer and Japanese women about six months less than their counterparts in the United States in 1985). However, the infant mortality rate in Japan is about one-half the U.S. rate."

[Numbers in years]

Country	Both sexes	Men	Women	Difference (women minus men)
Canada	77.3	74.0	80.6	6.6
France	77.6	73.4	81.9	8.5
Germany	77.2	73.4	80.6	7.2
Italy	78.0	74.5	81.4	6.9
Japan	79.3	76.4	82.1	5.7
Sweden	77.7	74.7	80.7	6.0
United Kingdom	76.2	73.2	79.2	6.0
United States	75.6	72.1	79.0	6.9

Source: Aging America, Trends and Projections, prepared by the U.S. Senate Special Committee on Aging, the American Association of Retired Persons, the Federal Council on the Aging, and the U.S. Administration on Aging, 1991, Washington, D.C., p. 258. Primary source: U.S. Bureau of the Census. International Data Base.

★ 76 ★

Life Expectancy

Life Expectancy for Blacks and Whites in 1987

Age	Black (Years)	White (Years)	Percentage longer for Whites than Blacks
At birth			
Males	65.2	72.2	10.7
Females	73.6	78.9	7.2
Age 45			
Males	26.6	30.6	15.0
Females	32.3	35.9	11.1
Age 65			
Males	13.5	14.9	10.4
Females	17.1	18.8	9.9

Source: U.S. Congress, "Profiles in Aging America: Meeting the Health Care Needs of the Nation's Black Elderly," Joint Hearing Before the Special Committee on Aging and the Congressional Black Caucus Health Braintrust, United States Senate, September 28, 1990, 101-29, U.S. Government Printing Office, Washington, D.C., p. 117. Primary source: Unpublished final data, Dept. of Health and Human Services, Public Health Service, Division of Vital Statistics.

★ 77 ★

Life Expectancy

Life Expectancy at Age 85, by Sex and Race: 1900 to 1988

[Data are shown in average number of years of life remaining]

Year	Male		Female	
	White	Black	White	Black
1900 to 1902	3.8	4.0	4.1	5.1
1909 to 1911	3.9	4.5	4.1	5.1
1919 to 1921	4.1	4.5	4.2	5.2
1929 to 1931	4.0	4.3	4.2	5.5
1939 to 1941	4.0	5.1	4.3	6.4
1949 to 1951	4.4	5.4	4.8	6.2
1959 to 1961	4.3	5.1	4.7	5.4
1969 to 1971[1]	4.6	6.0	5.5	7.1

[Continued]

★ 77 ★

Life Expectancy at Age 85, by Sex and Race: 1900 to 1988

[Continued]

Year	Male		Female	
	White	Black	White	Black
1979 to 1981[1]	5.1	5.7	6.3	7.2
1988[1]	5.1	5.5	6.3	6.6

Source: Sixty-Five Plus in America, Cynthia M. Taeuber, U.S. Department of Commerce, Economics and Statistics Administration, Bureau of the Census, U.S. Government Printing Office, Washington, D.C., 1992, p. 3-3. Primary source: National Center for Health Statistics. Data for 1900-1971 from *Vital Statistics of the United States 1978*, Volume II-Section 5, Life Tables. Data for 1979-1981 from U.S. Decennial Life Tables for 1979-1981, Volume 1, No. 1, U.S. Life Tables. Data for 1988 from *Vital Statistics of the United States 1988*, Volume II, Life Tables, Table 6-1. *Notes:* 1. Deaths of nonresidents of the United States were excluded beginning in 1970.

★ 78 ★

Life Expectancy

Percent Surviving from Birth to Age 65 and 85, by Sex and Race: 1900-1902 and 1987

	White female	Other female	White male	Other male
Birth to 65				
1900-02	44.0	22.0	39.0	19.0
1987	86.0	78.0	75.0	63.0
65 to 85				
1900-02	16.0	16.0	13.0	11.0
1987	47.0	42.0	28.0	26.0
Birth to 85				
1900-20	7.0	4.0	5.0	2.0
1987	41.0	32.0	21.0	16.0

Source: Aging America, Trends and Projections, prepared by the U.S. Senate Special Committee on Aging, the American Association of Retired Persons, the Federal Council on the Aging, and the U.S. Administration on Aging, 1991, Washington, D.C., p. 24. Primary source: National Center for Health Statistics. "Life Tables," *Vital Statistics of the United States, 1987* Vol. II, Section 6, February 1990.

★ 79 ★

Life Expectancy

Projected Life Expectancy at Birth and Age 65, by Sex: 1990-2050[1]

[Values are in years]

Year	At birth			At age 65		
	Men	Women	Difference	Men	Women	Difference
1990	72.1	79.0	6.9	15.0	19.4	4.4
2000	73.5	80.4	6.9	15.7	20.3	4.6
2010	74.4	81.3	6.9	16.2	21.0	4.8
2020	74.9	81.8	6.9	16.6	21.4	4.8
2030	75.4	82.3	6.9	17.0	21.8	4.8
2040	75.9	82.8	6.9	17.3	22.3	5.0
2050	76.4	83.3	6.9	17.7	22.7	5.0

Source: Aging America, Trends and Projections, prepared by the U.S. Senate Special Committee on Aging, the American Association of Retired Persons, the Federal Council on the Aging, and the U.S. Administration on Aging, 1991, Washington, D.C., p. 23. Primary source: U.S. Bureau of the Census, "Projections of the Population of the United States, by Age, Sex, and Race: 1988 to 2080," by Gregory Spencer. *Current Population Reports* Series P-25, No. 1018, January 1989. *Note:* 1. In years.

★ 80 ★

Life Expectancy

Projections of Life Expectancy and Population Age 65+: 2040

The projections shown in this table are based on projection series used by the Bureau of the Census using different assumptions. The middle series is the most probable.

Subject	Bureau of the Census			NIA/USC
	Middle series (series 14)	High mortality (series 23)	Low mortality (series 5)	
Life expectancy at birth (years)				
Men	75.9	73.0	80.8	85.9
Women	82.8	80.3	87.1	91.5
Population (000)				
65+, total	68,109	60,936	80,110	86,805
65 to 74	30,808	29,111	33,205	32,075
75 to 84	25,050	22,516	29,224	31,212
85+	12,251	9,309	17,681	23,519

[Continued]

★ 80 ★

Projections of Life Expectancy and Population Age 65+: 2040
[Continued]

Subject	Bureau of the Census			NIA/USC
	Middle series (series 14)	High mortality (series 23)	Low mortality (series 5)	
Percent change, 1989-2040				
65+, total	120	97	159	180
65 to 74	69	60	83	76
75 to 84	157	131	199	220
85+	303	206	481	673

Source: *Aging America, Trends and Projections*, prepared by the U.S. Senate Special Committee on Aging, the American Association of Retired Persons, the Federal Council on the Aging, and the U.S. Administration on Aging, 1991, Washington, D.C., p. 10. Primary source: U.S. Bureau of the Census "Projections of the Population of the United States, by Age, Sex, and Race: 1988 to 2080," by Gregory Spencer, *Current Population Reports* Series P-25, No. 1018, January 1989; "U.S. Population Estimates, by Age, Sex, Race, and Hispanic Origin: 1989," by Frederick W. Hollman, *Current Population Reports* Series P-25, No. 1057, March 1990; Jack M. Guralnik, Machiko Yanagishita, and Edward L. Schneider, "Projecting the Older Population of the United States: Lessons from the Past and Prospects for the Future," *The Milbank Quarterly*, Vol. 66, No. 2, 1988. *Notes:* NIA/USC stands for National Institute on Aging and the University of Southern California.

Mortality

★ 81 ★

Ten Leading Causes of Death

Data are based on the National Vital Statistics System.

Age and cause of death	Rank	Number of deaths per 100,000 resident population
55-59 years		
All causes		978.8
Malignant neoplasms, including neoplasms of lymphatic and hematopoietic tissues	1	352.7
Diseases of heart	2	318.9
Cerebrovascular diseases	3	39.4
Accidents and adverse effects	4	32.5
Chronic obstructive pulmonary disease and allied conditions	5	31.3
Chronic liver disease and cirrhosis	6	29.5

[Continued]

★ 81 ★

Ten Leading Causes of Death
[Continued]

Age and cause of death	Rank	Number of deaths per 100,000 resident population
Diabetes mellitus	7	19.8
Suicide	8	17.0
Pneumonia and influenza	9	13.4
Septicemia	10	6.8
60-64 years		
All causes		1,539.1
Malignant neoplasms, including neoplasms of lymphatic and hematopoietic tissues	1	538.7
Diseases of heart	2	532.5
Cerebrovascular diseases	3	67.0
Chronic obstructive pulmonary disease and allied conditions	4	63.4
Accidents and adverse effects	5	37.1
Chronic liver disease and cirrhosis	6	35.0
Diabetes mellitus	7	32.4
Pneumonia and influenza	8	24.0
Suicide	9	17.0
Nephritis, nephrotic syndrome, and nephrosis	10	12.7
65-69 years		
All causes		2,263.0
Diseases of heart	1	820.4
Malignant neoplasms, including neoplasms of lymphatic and hematopoietic tissues	2	736.2
Cerebrovascular diseases	3	116.3
Chronic obstructive pulmonary disease and allied conditions	4	113.6
Diabetes mellitus	5	48.3
Accidents and adverse effects	6	41.4
Pneumonia and influenza	7	41.0
Chronic liver disease and cirrhosis	8	36.9
Nephritis, nephrotic syndrome, and nephrosis	9	20.0
Septicemia	10	17.8
70-74 years		
All causes		3,797.7
Diseases of heart	1	1,323.4
Malignant neoplasms, including neoplasms of lymphatic and hematopoietic tissues	2	986.6
Cerebrovascular diseases	3	224.4

[Continued]

★ 81 ★
Ten Leading Causes of Death
[Continued]

Age and cause of death	Rank	Number of deaths per 100,000 resident population
Chronic obstructive pulmonary disease and allied conditions	4	194.1
Pneumonia and influenza	5	80.8
Diabetes mellitus	6	73.1
Accidents and adverse effects	7	58.6
Chronic liver disease and cirrhosis	8	37.7
Nephritis, nephrotic syndrome, and nephrosis	9	35.4
Septicemia	10	28.6
75-79 years		
All causes		5,206.1
Diseases of heart	1	2,098.1
Malignant neoplasms, including neoplasms of lymphatic and hematopoietic tissues	2	1,188.4
Cerebrovascular diseases	3	422.0
Chronic obstructive pulmonary disease and allied conditions	4	271.2
Pneumonia and influenza	5	172.7
Diabetes mellitus	6	103.9
Accidents and adverse effects	7	86.5
Nephritis, nephrotic syndrome, and nephrosis	8	62.0
Septicemia	9	50.3
Atherosclerosis	10	49.3
80-84 years		
All causes		8,230.0
Diseases of heart	1	3,526.1
Malignant neoplasms, including neoplasms of lymphatic and hematopoietic tissues	2	1,450.3
Cerebrovascular diseases	3	823.7
Pneumonia and influenza	4	358.3
Chronic obstructive pulmonary diseases and allied conditions	5	333.7
Diabetes mellitus	6	151.7
Accidents and adverse effects	7	139.0
Atherosclerosis	8	116.9
Nephritis, nephrotic syndrome, and nephrosis	9	108.1
Septicemia	10	88.3
85 years and over		
All causes		15,398.9
Diseases of heart	1	7,178.7

[Continued]

★ 81 ★

Ten Leading Causes of Death
[Continued]

Age and cause of death	Rank	Number of deaths per 100,000 resident population
Cerebrovascular diseases	2	1,762.8
Malignant neoplasms, including neoplasms of lymphatic and hematopoietic tissues	3	1,612.0
Pneumonia and influenza	4	1,032.1
Atherosclerosis	5	432.6
Chronic obstructive pulmonary diseases and allied conditions	6	362.9
Accidents and adverse effects	7	252.2
Nephritis, nephrotic syndrome, and nephrosis	8	216.4
Diabetes mellitus	9	213.9
Septicemia	10	181.9

Source: Health Data on Older Americans: United States, 1992, Centers for Disease Control and Prevention/National Center for Health Statistics, Vital and Health Statistics, Series 3: Analytic and Epidemiological Studies, No. 27, pp. 91-92. Primary source: National Center for Health Statistics. *Vital Statistics of the United States, Vol. II, Mortality, Part A*, Washington: Public Health Service, 1986.

★ 82 ★

Mortality

Ten Leading Causes of Death Among Older Americans, 1988

Heart disease is the number one killer for all age groups of Older Americans.

[Rate per 100,000 population in age group]

Cause of death	65+	65 to 74	75 to 84	85+
All causes	5,105	2,730	6,321	15,594
Diseases of the heart	2,066	984	2,543	7,098
Malignant neoplasms	1,068	843	1,313	1,639
Cerebrovascular diseases	431	155	554	1,707
Chronic obstructive pulmonary disease	226	152	313	394
Pneumonia and influenza	225	60	257	1,125
Diabetes	97	62	125	222
Accidents	89	50	107	267
Atherosclerosis	69	15	70	396

[Continued]

★ 82 ★

Ten Leading Causes of Death Among Older Americans, 1988
[Continued]

Cause of death	65 +	65 to 74	75 to 84	85 +
Nephritis, nephrotic syndrome, nephrosis	61	26	78	217
Septicemia	56	24	71	199

Source: Aging America, Trends and Projections, prepared by the U.S. Senate Special Committee on Aging, the American Association of Retired Persons, the Federal Council on the Aging, and the U.S. Administration on Aging, 1991, Washington, D.C., p. 120. Primary source: National Center for Health Statistics, "Advanced Report of Final Mortality Statistics, 1988," Monthly Vital Statistics Report, Vol. 39, No. 7, Supplement, November 28, 1990.

★ 83 ★

Mortality

Top Causes of Death Among Persons Aged 65+, 1988
[Rate per 100,000 people in age group]

Cause	1988
All causes	5,105
Heart disease	2,066
Malignant neoplasms	1,068
Cerebrovascular disease	431

Source: Aging America, Trends and Projections, prepared by the U.S. Senate Special Committee on Aging, the American Association of Retired Persons, the Federal Council on the Aging, and the U.S. Administration on Aging, 1991, Washington, D.C., p. 122. Primary source: National Center for Health Statistics, "Advance Report of Final Mortality Statistics, 1988," Monthly Vital Statistics Report, Vol. 39, No. 7, Supplement, November 28, 1990. Notes: Data for causes of death are based on information taken from death certificates. A secondary illness will frequently be recorded as the cause of death and the underlying cause of death is not listed.

★ 84 ★

Mortality

Central Death Rate Projections by Age, Sex, and Alternative, 1985-2080

Includes the populations of Puerto Rico, Guam, American Samoa, the Virgin Islands, and U.S. citizens living abroad. The central death rate is defined as "the ratio of the number of deaths during the year for persons at the tabulated age to the midyear population at that age." Alternatives in the table below are "based on three different sets of assumptions about future net immigration, birth rates, and death rates.... Alternative I is designated as optimistic because among the three projections the assumptions selected produce the most favorable financial effect for the OASDI program. Conversely, the assumptions chosen for Alternative III, designated pessimistic, produce the most unfavorable financial effect."

[Per hundred thousand]

Alternative, sex, and age group	Calendar year										
	1985	1990	2000	2010	2020	2030	2040	2050	2060	2070	2080
Alternative I:											
Male:											
0	1,177.6	1,042.1	890.7	834.4	795.5	759.5	726.2	695.4	666.8	640.4	615.8
1-4	56.8	53.0	48.1	46.1	44.9	43.9	42.9	41.9	41.0	40.1	39.3
5-9	31.3	28.3	24.4	23.3	22.8	22.4	22.0	21.7	21.3	21.0	20.6
10-14	35.2	32.4	28.4	27.2	26.7	26.2	25.8	25.3	24.9	24.4	24.0
15-19	116.4	110.5	102.1	98.3	96.4	94.6	92.8	91.0	89.3	87.6	86.0
20-24	163.6	156.1	145.1	140.0	137.2	134.6	132.0	129.5	127.0	124.7	122.3
25-29	172.5	168.0	161.4	157.3	154.3	151.5	148.7	146.0	143.3	140.8	138.3
30-34	185.6	177.3	165.3	159.7	156.7	153.8	151.0	148.2	145.6	143.0	140.5
35-39	236.5	219.6	196.2	187.7	183.8	180.1	176.5	173.0	169.7	166.5	163.4
40-44	348.1	321.2	284.1	270.9	264.9	259.1	253.6	248.4	243.3	238.4	233.8
45-49	509.0	473.1	423.7	404.9	395.5	386.7	378.2	370.2	362.5	355.1	348.1
50-54	844.7	796.2	730.7	704.6	688.7	673.5	659.1	645.4	632.3	619.8	608.0
55-59	1,316.2	1,238.8	1,134.0	1,092.9	1,068.3	1,045.0	1,022.8	1,001.7	981.6	962.5	944.4
60-64	2,078.4	1,965.1	1,831.3	1,750.8	1,710.6	1,672.5	1,636.3	1,601.9	1,569.2	1,538.2	1,508.6
65-69	3,186.6	3,081.1	2,953.8	2,872.9	2,806.5	2,743.5	2,683.7	2,626.9	2,572.9	2,521.6	2,472.9
70-74	4,792.8	4,674.9	4,550.5	4,437.7	4,330.8	4,229.4	4,133.2	4,041.9	3,955.3	3,873.1	3,795.0
75-79	7,308.7	7,172.3	7,057.8	6,895.1	6,720.3	6,554.6	6,397.6	6,248.7	6,107.5	5,973.6	5,846.5
80-84	10,935.3	10,761.4	10,666.1	10,416.8	10,135.6	9,869.1	9,616.6	9,377.3	9,150.4	8,935.3	8,731.3
85-89	15,749.1	15,506.5	15,402.8	15,024.7	14,594.9	14,187.7	13,802.0	13,436.5	13,090.1	12,761.8	12,450.3
90-94	22,547.1	22,142.2	21,867.5	21,261.9	20,605.5	19,984.0	19,395.6	18,838.3	18,310.4	17,810.1	17,335.9
Alternative II:											
Male:											
0	1,177.6	955.9	714.1	644.5	593.7	549.0	509.7	474.9	444.1	416.7	392.3
1-4	56.8	50.3	41.3	38.4	36.7	35.1	33.7	32.3	31.1	29.9	28.8
5-9	31.3	26.5	19.9	18.6	17.9	17.4	16.8	16.3	15.8	15.3	14.8
10-14	35.2	30.6	24.0	22.4	21.6	20.9	20.3	19.6	19.0	18.4	17.9
15-19	116.4	106.8	91.9	86.7	84.0	81.4	78.9	76.5	74.2	72.0	69.8
20-24	163.6	151.3	131.8	124.6	120.7	117.1	113.5	110.1	106.8	103.6	100.5
25-29	172.5	165.1	153.2	146.8	142.3	138.0	133.8	129.8	125.9	122.1	118.5
30-34	185.6	172.0	150.9	142.9	138.4	134.1	130.0	126.1	122.2	118.6	115.0
35-39	236.5	209.0	169.3	158.3	152.8	147.7	142.7	138.0	133.5	129.2	125.1
40-44	348.1	304.4	242.1	225.3	216.9	209.0	201.5	194.4	187.5	181.1	174.9
45-49	509.0	450.8	368.0	343.8	330.5	317.9	306.1	294.8	284.1	274.0	264.3
50-54	844.7	763.7	648.9	613.3	589.6	567.3	546.1	526.0	506.9	488.9	471.7
55-59	1,316.2	1,188.8	1,009.5	954.5	917.5	882.6	849.6	818.3	788.6	760.5	733.8
60-64	2,078.4	1,887.9	1,618.8	1,532.1	1,471.8	1,414.9	1,361.1	1,310.3	1,262.2	1,216.5	1,173.3
65-69	3,186.6	2,980.5	2,680.3	2,551.5	2,449.7	2,353.8	2,263.2	2,177.6	2,096.7	2,020.1	1,947.5
70-74	4,792.8	4,532.9	4,155.2	3,965.0	3,803.0	3,650.4	3,506.5	3,370.8	3,242.6	3,121.5	3,006.9

[Continued]

★ 84 ★

Central Death Rate Projections by Age, Sex, and Alternative, 1985-2080
[Continued]

Alternative, sex, and age group	Calendar year										
	1985	1990	2000	2010	2020	2030	2040	2050	2060	2070	2080
75-79	7,308.7	6,960.9	6,461.3	6,177.6	5,917.8	5,673.5	5,443.6	5,227.0	5,022.9	4,830.3	4,648.4
80-84	10,935.3	10,419.9	9,699.7	9,264.7	8,860.3	8,480.8	8,124.3	7,789.1	7,473.7	7,176.6	6,896.6
85-89	15,749.1	14,995.6	13,961.2	13,316.9	12,714.6	12,150.1	11,620.6	11,123.5	10,656.4	10,217.2	9,803.8
90-94	22,547.1	21,433.4	19,867.4	18,878.2	17,978.1	17,136.1	16,347.8	15,609.3	14,916.7	14,266.7	13,656.2
Alternative III:											
Male:											
0	1,177.6	877.8	593.9	525.4	473.6	429.2	391.1	358.1	329.5	304.4	282.4
1-4	56.8	47.7	35.6	31.8	29.4	27.2	25.3	23.5	21.9	20.4	19.0
5-9	31.3	24.7	16.4	14.6	13.6	12.7	11.8	11.1	10.3	9.7	9.1
10-14	35.2	28.9	20.2	18.1	16.8	15.7	14.7	13.7	12.8	12.0	11.2
15-19	116.4	103.2	82.8	75.4	70.7	66.4	62.3	58.5	55.0	51.7	48.6
20-24	163.6	146.6	119.9	109.4	102.7	96.5	90.7	85.2	80.1	75.3	70.8
25-29	172.5	162.3	145.8	135.5	127.3	119.7	112.5	105.8	99.6	93.7	88.2
30-34	185.6	166.9	138.2	126.3	118.5	111.1	104.3	98.0	92.0	86.5	81.3
35-39	236.5	199.0	146.7	131.5	122.4	114.0	106.3	99.2	92.6	86.6	80.9
40-44	348.1	288.5	207.3	184.0	169.6	156.6	144.7	133.8	123.9	114.8	106.5
45-49	509.0	429.6	322.5	287.8	262.5	239.7	219.1	200.5	183.6	168.4	154.6
50-54	844.7	732.9	580.1	519.9	471.8	428.6	389.7	354.6	323.1	294.7	269.0
55-59	1,316.2	1,141.3	905.4	810.7	733.5	664.2	602.0	546.2	496.0	450.8	410.2
60-64	2,078.4	1,814.6	1,454.6	1,302.8	1,178.1	1,066.3	966.0	876.0	795.1	722.4	657.0
65-69	3,186.6	2,883.8	2,436.7	2,194.7	1,988.9	1,804.2	1,638.3	1,489.2	1,355.1	1,134.4	1,125.7
70-74	4,792.8	4,396.1	3,798.6	3,438.3	3,123.6	2,840.8	2,586.5	2,357.5	2,151.4	1,965.5	1,797.9
75-79	7,308.7	6,757.2	5,922.5	5,392.9	4,915.1	4,484.8	4,097.1	3,747.6	3,432.2	3,147.2	2,889.7
80-84	10,935.5	10,091.0	8,833.9	8,060.1	7,365.4	6,738.9	6,173.4	5,662.7	5,200.9	4,783.0	4,404.4
85-89	15,749.1	14,504.1	12,679.2	11,589.3	10,613.2	9,731.5	8,934.5	8,213.3	7,560.2	6,968.0	6,430.5
90-94	22,547.1	20,751.7	18,096.4	16,522.4	15,139.5	13,889.7	12,759.1	11,735.3	10,807.3	9,965.3	9,200.6
Alternative I:											
Female:											
0	927.0	763.5	575.3	516.3	473.3	435.5	402.4	373.1	347.3	324.4	304.1
1-4	45.1	39.3	31.4	29.0	27.5	26.1	24.9	23.7	22.6	21.6	20.6
5-9	23.0	19.6	14.9	13.8	13.2	12.7	12.2	11.7	11.2	10.8	10.4
10-14	21.4	18.8	15.0	13.9	13.3	12.8	12.3	11.8	11.3	10.9	10.4
15-19	43.0	39.5	34.4	32.4	31.1	29.9	28.7	27.6	26.5	25.5	24.5
20-24	51.4	47.6	42.3	40.1	38.5	37.0	35.6	34.2	32.8	31.6	30.4
25-29	60.2	54.4	46.2	43.4	41.7	40.1	38.6	37.1	35.7	34.3	33.1
30-34	72.1	61.9	48.2	44.8	43.1	41.5	39.9	38.5	37.1	35.7	34.4
35-39	107.5	90.3	67.9	62.8	60.4	58.1	55.9	53.8	51.8	49.9	48.1
40-44	175.7	150.6	116.5	107.9	103.6	99.5	95.7	92.0	88.6	85.2	82.1
45-49	281.8	248.6	200.8	186.6	179.1	172.0	165.3	158.9	152.8	147.0	141.5
50-54	465.8	426.5	368.4	347.2	333.3	320.1	307.6	295.8	284.5	273.8	263.5
55-59	713.2	663.8	592.8	564.7	542.1	520.6	500.2	480.9	462.4	444.9	428.2
60-64	1,146.3	1,090.1	1,014.2	973.3	933.2	895.3	859.3	825.2	792.9	762.1	732.9
65-69	1,700.4	1,640.3	1,568.4	1,510.5	1,446.3	1,385.7	1,328.2	1,273.9	1,222.4	1,173.6	1,127.3
70-74	2,610.8	2,457.8	2,259.4	2,158.2	2,060.7	1,968.9	1,882.4	1,800.9	1,723.9	1,651.1	1,582.3
75-79	4,057.2	3,729.8	3,285.1	3,103.4	2,951.7	2,809.7	2,676.5	2,551.5	2,434.1	2,323.8	2,219.9
80-84	6,644.2	6,060.2	5,241.0	4,906.9	4,647.1	4,405.0	4,179.0	3,967.9	3,770.5	3,585.8	3,412.7

[Continued]

★ 84 ★

Central Death Rate Projections by Age, Sex, and Alternative, 1985-2080
[Continued]

Alternative, sex, and age group	Calendar year										
	1985	1990	2000	2010	2020	2030	2040	2050	2060	2070	2080
85-89	11,545.8	10,592.4	9,218.3	8,596.0	8,116.3	7,670.7	7,256.1	6,869.9	6,509.8	6,173.8	5,860.0
90-94	18,288.9	17,052.4	15,203.3	14,172.1	13,346.3	12,580.7	11,869.6	11,208.4	10,593.3	10,020.4	9,486.4
Alternative II:											
Female:											
0	927.0	827.5	712.3	666.4	634.2	604.3	576.8	551.2	527.6	505.6	485.4
1-4	45.1	41.7	37.4	35.8	34.8	34.0	33.2	32.4	31.6	30.9	30.3
5-9	23.0	20.9	18.1	17.3	17.0	16.7	16.4	16.1	15.8	15.6	15.4
10-14	21.4	19.8	17.6	16.9	16.5	16.2	16.0	15.7	15.4	15.2	14.9
15-19	43.0	40.9	37.9	36.7	36.0	35.3	34.7	34.0	33.4	32.9	32.3
20-24	51.4	49.0	45.9	44.6	43.8	43.0	42.2	41.4	40.7	40.0	39.3
25-29	60.2	56.6	51.8	50.0	49.1	4ö.3	47.4	46.6	45.8	45.1	44.4
30-34	72.1	65.8	57.5	55.1	54.2	53.4	52.6	51.8	51.1	50.3	49.6
35-39	107.5	96.8	83.0	79.4	78.2	77.0	75.9	74.8	73.8	72.8	71.9
40-44	175.7	160.1	139.6	133.6	131.4	129.4	127.5	125.6	123.9	122.2	120.6
45-49	281.8	261.3	233.2	223.9	220.2	216.7	213.5	210.3	207.4	204.5	201.9
50-54	465.8	261.3	233.2	223.9	220.2	216.7	213.5	210.3	207.4	204.5	201.9
55-59	713.2	684.0	644.7	628.6	618.2	608.4	599.0	590.1	581.6	573.6	565.9
60-64	1,146.3	1,123.2	1,104.5	1,087.3	1,068.0	1,049.7	1,032.3	1,015.7	1,000.0	985.1	970.9
65-69	1,700.4	1,694.7	1,723.7	1,704.8	1,671.8	1,640.5	1,610.7	1,582.5	1,555.6	1,530.2	1,505.9
70-74	2,610.8	2,551.0	2,510.0	2,459.9	2,403.3	2,349.7	2,298.8	2,250.5	2,204.8	2,161.4	2,120.2
75-79	4,057.2	3,884.3	3,682.2	3,565.8	3,467.0	3,373.6	3,285.2	3,201.5	3,122.2	3,047.2	2,976.1
80-84	6,644.2	6,320.2	5,913.5	5,679.2	5,497.0	5,325.0	5,162.5	5,008.9	4,863.6	4,726.2	4,596.2
85-89	11,545.8	11,029.6	10,382.5	9,946.2	9,598.7	9,271.1	8,961.7	8,669.3	8,393.1	8,132.0	7,885.2
90-94	18,288.9	17,673.7	16,939.1	16,249.2	15,644.9	15,075.2	14,537.2	14,029.0	13,548.9	13,095.2	12,666.3
Alternative III:											
Female											
0	927.0	705.0	479.6	420.2	376.1	338.5	306.4	278.9	255.1	234.4	216.4
1-4	45.1	37.0	26.5	23.4	21.3	19.5	17.8	16.4	15.0	13.8	12.8
5-9	23.0	18.3	12.3	10.8	9.9	9.1	8.4	7.7	7.1	6.6	6.1
10-14	21.4	17.8	12.9	11.3	10.4	9.5	8.7	8.0	7.4	6.8	6.3
15-19	43.0	38.3	31.4	28.3	26.1	24.0	22.1	20.4	18.8	17.3	16.0
20-24	51.4	46.2	39.3	36.0	33.1	30.4	28.0	25.8	23.8	22.0	20.3
25-29	60.2	52.3	41.6	37.3	34.2	31.4	28.9	26.6	24.5	22.6	20.9
30-34	72.1	58.3	40.6	35.5	32.3	29.4	26.9	24.6	22.5	20.6	18.9
35-39	107.5	84.2	55.7	47.9	43.1	38.8	34.9	31.6	28.6	25.9	23.5
40-44	175.7	141.6	97.3	83.6	74.6	66.7	59.7	53.6	48.2	43.4	39.2
45-49	281.8	236.5	173.2	149.3	132.8	118.3	105.6	94.4	84.6	75.9	68.3
50-54	465.8	412.0	334.6	294.9	261.2	231.7	206.0	183.4	163.6	146.2	131.0
55-59	713.2	644.6	546.0	483.7	428.5	380.2	338.0	301.0	268.6	240.2	215.2
60-64	1,146.3	1,058.3	930.8	832.4	741.0	660.9	590.6	528.8	474.4	426.5	384.2
65-69	1,700.4	1,587.9	1,424.1	1,282.5	1,146.8	1,027.4	922.3	829.5	747.6	675.2	611.0
70-74	2,610.8	2,368.8	2,037.8	1,832.6	1,644.7	1,478.8	1,332.2	1,202.6	1,087.7	985.7	895.1
75-79	4,057.2	3,582.9	2,949.1	2,645.8	2,384.8	2,153.6	1,948.6	1,766.4	1,604.3	1,459.8	1,330.9
80-84	6,644.2	5,821.8	4,676.8	4,180.5	3,776.0	3,416.8	3,097.2	2,812.6	2,558.7	2,331.7	2,128.7

[Continued]

★ 84 ★

Central Death Rate Projections by Age, Sex, and Alternative, 1985-2080

[Continued]

Alternative, sex, and age group	Calendar year										
	1985	1990	2000	2010	2020	2030	2040	2050	2060	2070	2080
85-89	11,545.8	10,174.8	8,232.7	7,355.4	6,659.0	6,039.2	5,486.4	4,992.6	4,550.8	4,155.0	3,799.8
90-94	18,288.9	16,455.4	13,697.0	12,255.8	11,106.3	10,081.2	9,165.1	8,345.2	7,610.4	6,950.8	6,357.9

Source: "Social Security Area Population Projections," Alice H. Wade (Office of the Actuary, Social Security Administration), *Social Security Bulletin* 51, No. 2, February, 1988, pp. 14-15. *Note:* OASDI stands for Old Age, Survivors, and Disability Insurance.

★ 85 ★

Mortality

Suicide: Death by Suicide

The elderly, from age 65 through 85 and older, commit 21 percent of all suicides but represent only 12.6 percent of the total population.

	Percentage
24 and under	17
25-44	39
45-64	23
65-84	19
85 and over	2

Source: USA TODAY, February 24, 1993, p. 1. Primary source: National Center for Health Statistics.

★ 86 ★

Mortality

Suicide: Death Rates for Suicide, According to Sex, Race, and Age: United States, Selected Years 1960-89

Data are based on the National Vital Statistics System.

[Deaths per 100,000 resident population]

Sex, race, and age	1960[1]	1970	1980	1981	1982	1983	1984	1985	1986	1987	1988	1989
ALL RACES												
All ages, age adjusted	10.6	11.8	11.4	11.5	11.6	11.4	11.6	11.5	11.9	11.7	11.4	11.3
All ages, crude	10.6	11.6	11.9	12.0	12.2	12.1	12.4	12.3	12.8	12.7	12.4	12.2
55-64 years	23.7	21.4	15.9	16.4	16.9	16.5	17.3	16.7	17.0	16.6	15.6	15.5
65-74 years	23.0	20.8	16.9	16.2	17.4	17.7	18.8	18.5	19.7	19.4	18.4	18.0
75-84 years	27.9	21.2	19.1	18.6	20.3	22.3	22.0	24.1	25.2	25.8	25.9	23.1

[Continued]

★ 86 ★

Suicide: Death Rates for Suicide, According to Sex, Race, and Age: United States, Selected Years 1960-89
[Continued]

Sex, race, and age	1960[1]	1970	1980	1981	1982	1983	1984	1985	1986	1987	1988	1989
85 years and over	26.0	19.0	19.2	17.7	17.6	19.0	18.4	19.1	20.8	22.1	20.5	22.8
WHITE MALE												
All ages, age adjusted	17.5	18.2	18.9	18.9	19.4	19.3	19.7	19.9	20.5	20.1	19.8	19.6
All ages, crude	17.6	18.0	19.9	20.0	20.7	20.6	21.3	21.5	22.3	22.1	21.7	21.4
55-64 years	40.2	35.0	25.8	26.3	27.9	27.4	28.8	28.6	28.7	28.7	27.0	26.6
65-74 years	42.0	38.7	32.5	30.3	33.1	33.2	35.6	35.3	37.6	36.8	35.4	35.1
75-84 years	55.7	45.5	45.5	43.8	48.5	52.5	52.0	57.1	58.9	60.9	61.5	55.3
85 years and over	61.3	45.8	52.8	53.6	53.9	56.8	55.8	60.3	66.3	71.9	65.8	71.9
BLACK MALE												
All ages, age adjusted	7.8	9.9	11.1	11.0	10.8	10.5	11.2	11.3	11.5	12.0	11.8	12.5
All ages, crude	6.4	8.0	10.3	10.2	10.1	9.9	10.6	10.8	11.1	11.6	11.5	12.2
55-64 years	16.2	10.6	11.7	12.5	11.9	11.6	13.4	11.5	9.9	10.3	10.6	10.4
65-74 years	11.3	8.7	11.1	9.7	12.1	13.6	13.8	15.8	16.1	17.6	12.9	15.4
75-84 years	6.6	8.9	10.5	18.0	12.2	15.8	15.1	15.6	16.0	20.9	17.6	14.7
85 years and over	6.9	8.7	18.9	12.7	16.1	12.7	11.1	7.7	17.9	13.0	10.0	22.2
WHITE FEMALE												
All ages, age adjusted	5.3	7.2	5.7	6.0	5.8	5.6	5.6	5.3	5.4	5.3	5.1	4.8
All ages, crude	5.3	7.1	5.9	6.2	6.1	5.9	5.9	5.6	5.9	5.7	5.5	5.2
55-64 years	10.9	12.3	9.1	9.4	9.5	9.1	9.1	8.4	9.0	8.4	7.9	7.9
65-74 years	8.8	9.6	7.0	7.3	7.4	7.9	7.8	7.3	7.7	7.6	7.3	6.4
75-84 years	9.2	7.2	5.7	5.5	6.1	6.6	6.8	7.0	8.0	7.5	7.4	6.3
85 years and over	6.1	5.8	5.8	3.7	3.9	5.3	5.1	4.7	5.0	4.8	5.3	6.2
BLACK FEMALE												
All ages, age adjusted	1.9	2.9	2.4	2.5	2.2	2.1	2.3	2.1	2.4	2.1	2.4	2.4
All ages, crude	1.6	2.6	2.2	2.4	2.1	2.0	2.2	2.1	2.3	2.1	2.4	2.4
55-64 years	3.0	2.0	2.3	2.9	2.2	1.7	3.1	2.2	4.2	1.8	2.5	2.5
65-74 years	2.3	2.9	1.7	3.0	2.1	1.3	2.5	2.0	2.8	2.5	2.0	2.1
75-84 years	1.3	1.7	1.4	1.0	1.3	1.3	0.5	4.5	2.6	2.3	1.3	1.7
85 years and over	-	2.8	-	1.8	0.9	2.3	0.8	1.4	-	-	-	0.6

Source: U.S. Department of Commerce, Economics and Statistics Administration, *National Economic, Social, and Environmental Data Bank, CD-ROM,* November 1992. Primary source: National Center for Health Statistics: *Vital Statistics of the United States, Vol. II, Mortality, Part A, 1950-89.* Public Health Service. Washington. U.S. Government Printing Office; Data computed by the Division of Analysis from data compiled by the Division of Vital Statistics and from table 1 in the original source. *Notes:* For data years shown, the code numbers for cause of death are based on the then current International Classification of Diseases, which is described in the original source. 1. Includes deaths of nonresidents of the United States.

★ 87 ★

Mortality

Suicide: Rates for Persons Aged 65+, by Race, 1987

Across all age groups, white men are the most likely to take their own lives and black women are the least likely.

[Rate per 100,000 people in specified group]

Sex and Race	Age		
	65 to 74	75 to 84	85+
Men			
White	37	61	72
Black	18	21	13
Women			
White	8	8	5
Black	3	2	0

Source: Aging America, Trends and Projections, prepared by the U.S. Senate Special Committee on Aging, the American Association of Retired Persons, the Federal Council on the Aging, and the U.S. Administration on Aging, 1991, Washington, D.C., p. 117. Primary source: National Center for Health Statistics, *Health, United States, 1989*, DHHS Pub. No. (PHS) 90-1232, Washington: Department of Health and Human Services, March 1990.

★ 88 ★

Mortality

Suicide: Rates for Selected Countries, by Sex and Age Group - Part I

Data include deaths resulting indirectly from self-inflicted injuries.

[Rate per 100,000 population]

Sex and age	United States 1988	Australia 1988	Austria 1989	Canada 1988	Denmark 1988	France 1988	Italy 1987
Male							
Total[2]	20.1	21.0	36.1	21.4	33.3	30.2	11.7
15 to 24 years old	21.9	27.8	27.1	26.9	15.9	13.9	5.1
25 to 34 years old	25.0	28.2	35.6	29.2	33.6	32.5	10.3
35 to 44 years old	22.9	26.0	38.2	26.1	44.7	38.2	10.0
45 to 54 years old	21.7	24.4	45.1	24.2	50.5	40.0	14.1
55 to 64 years old	25.0	23.8	52.4	28.0	52.6	41.2	18.5
65 to 74 years old	33.0	27.7	71.6	26.2	47.2	47.5	29.1
75 years old and over	57.8	39.8	96.0	30.6	69.2	109.0	47.1
Female							
Total[2]	5.0	5.6	14.7	5.9	19.0	11.7	4.2
15 to 24 years old	4.2	4.5	8.3	4.9	5.5	4.2	1.4
25 to 34 years old	5.7	7.2	10.6	7.1	12.0	9.0	2.4

[Continued]

★ 88 ★

Suicide: Rates for Selected Countries, by Sex and Age Group - Part I

[Continued]

Sex and age	United States 1988	Australia 1988	Austria 1989	Canada 1988	Denmark 1988	France 1988	Italy 1987
35 to 44 years old	6.9	7.5	13.2	9.8	20.6	12.7	3.6
45 to 54 years old	7.9	8.2	19.0	9.9	33.2	19.8	5.6
55 to 64 years old	7.2	8.7	20.0	6.9	33.2	17.6	7.5
65 to 74 years old	6.8	7.4	25.2	6.1	36.0	22.9	9.0
75 years old and over	6.4	10.0	36.2	6.2	33.1	25.3	11.7

Source: U.S. Bureau of the Census, *Statistical Abstract of the United States: 1992* (112th edition.) Washington, DC, 1992, p. 829. Primary source: World Health Organization. Geneva, Switzerland, *1990 World Health Statistics Annual. Notes:* 1. England and Wales only. 2. Includes under 15 years old not shown separately.

★ 89 ★

Mortality

Suicide: Rates for Selected Countries, by Sex and Age Group - Part II

Data includes deaths resulting indirectly from self-inflicted injuries.

[Rate per 100,000 population]

Sex and age	United States 1988	Japan 1988	Netherlands 1988	Poland 1989	Sweden 1987	United Kingdom[1] 1988	West Germany 1988
Male							
Total[2]	20.1	21.5	13.2	19.3	26.0	11.2	25.0
15 to 24 years old	21.9	9.7	8.2	14.5	16.9	10.3	15.8
25 to 34 years old	25.0	19.9	16.1	26.4	30.0	14.7	22.7
35 to 44 years old	22.9	23.8	14.3	29.5	30.2	16.0	24.4
45 to 54 years old	21.7	33.2	17.2	33.2	41.9	14.1	33.0
55 to 64 years old	25.0	33.7	20.0	30.3	29.7	13.0	35.5
65 to 74 years old	33.0	38.7	21.2	25.8	39.4	13.3	41.3
75 years old and over	57.8	68.0	41.3	29.6	50.2	20.4	77.8
Female							
Total[2]	5.0	13.1	7.5	3.7	10.9	3.7	10.8
15 to 24 years old	4.2	5.3	2.4	2.8	5.6	1.9	4.7
25 to 34 years old	5.7	9.4	8.3	3.6	10.3	3.5	7.7
35 to 44 years old	6.9	10.5	9.3	5.0	14.8	3.6	9.5
45 to 54 years old	7.9	14.8	11.2	5.9	20.1	5.8	13.6
55 to 64 years old	7.2	18.2	14.0	6.5	13.2	6.0	14.6

[Continued]

★ 89 ★

Suicide: Rates for Selected Countries, by Sex and Age Group - Part II

[Continued]

Sex and age	United States 1988	Japan 1988	Netherlands 1988	Poland 1989	Sweden 1987	United Kingdom[1] 1988	West Germany 1988
65 to 74 years old	6.8	29.4	13.1	6.0	12.6	5.5	19.5
75 years old and over	6.4	51.6	10.7	7.2	18.3	7.1	24.1

Source: U.S. Bureau of the Census, *Statistical Abstract of the United States: 1992* (112th edition.) Washington, DC, 1992, p. 829. Primary source: World Health Organization. Geneva, Switzerland, *1990 World Health Statistics Annual. Notes:* 1. England and Wales only. 2. Includes under 15 years old not shown separately.

★ 90 ★

Mortality

Death Rates: 1950-1989 by Sex and Race

Black males have not fared as well as the rest of the population in terms of death rates. While the rates of other groups shown here have dropped dramatically, death rates for black males, aged 75+, have actually gone up.

[Deaths per 1,000 resident population]

Age, sex, and race	1950[1]	1960[1]	1970	1980	1989 Death rate[2]	1989 % change since 1960[3]
All races, both sexes						
65 to 74	40.7	38.2	35.8	29.9	26.3	-31.15
75 to 84	93.3	87.5	80.0	66.9	61.7	-29.49
85+	202.0	198.6	163.4	159.8	150.8	-24.07
All races, men						
65 to 74	49.3	49.1	48.7	41.1	34.1	-30.55
75 to 84	104.3	101.8	100.1	88.2	79.5	-21.91
85+	216.4	211.9	178.2	188.0	177.0	-16.47
All races, women						
65 to 74	33.3	28.7	25.8	21.4	20.0	-30.31
75 to 84	84.0	76.3	66.8	54.4	50.8	-33.42
85+	191.9	190.1	155.2	147.5	140.7	-25.99
White, men						
65 to 74	48.6	48.5	48.1	40.4	33.5	-30.93
75 to 84	105.3	103.0	101.0	88.3	79.4	-22.91
85+	221.2	217.5	185.5	191.0	181.1	-16.74
White, women						
65 to 74	32.4	27.8	24.7	20.7	19.5	-29.86
75 to 84	84.8	77.0	67.0	54.0	50.7	-34.16
85+	196.8	194.8	159.8	149.8	143.2	-26.49
Black men						
65 to 74	53.1	58.0	58.0	51.3	45.2	-22.07
75 to 84	101.0[4]	86.1	94.5	92.3	89.0	3.37

[Continued]

★ 90 ★

Death Rates: 1950-1989 by Sex and Race
[Continued]

Age, sex, and race	1950[1]	1960[1]	1970	1980	1989	
					Death rate[2]	% change since 1960[3]
85+	101.0[4]	148.4	122.2	161.0	149.6	0.81
Black women						
65 to 74	40.0	40.6	38.6	30.6	27.4	-32.51
75 to 84	83.5[4]	67.3	66.9	62.1	58.1	-13.67
85+	83.5[4]	130.5	107.1	123.7	122.2	-6.36

Source: Aging America, Trends and Projections, prepared by the U.S. Senate Special Committee on Aging, the American Association of Retired Persons, the Federal Council on the Aging, and the U.S. Administration on Aging, 1991, Washington, D.C., p. 119. Primary source: 1960-1989 data: National Center for Health Statistics, "Annual Summary of Births, Marriages, Divorces, and Deaths: United States, 1989," *Monthly Vital Statistics Report*, Vol. 38, No. 13, August 30, 1990; 1950 race data: National Center for Health Statistics, *Health, United States, 1988*, DHHS Pub. No. (PHS) 89-1232, Washington, Department of Health and human Services, March 1989; 1950 data for all races: "Annual Summary of Births, Marriages, Divorces, and Deaths: United States, 1984," *Monthly Vital Statistics Report*, Vol. 33, No. 13, September 26, 1985. *Notes:* 1. Includes deaths of nonresidents. 2. Provisional data based on 10 percent sample of deaths. 3. Figures are estimates calculated by the editors of SROA. 4. Figure is for people over 75+ within that group.

★ 91 ★

Mortality

Death Rates: Trends, 1980 to 1989

Death rates dropped quite dramatically for Older Americans in the 1980's.

Sex	65 to 74	75 to 84	85+
Men	-30.8	-23.8	-18.2
Women	-39.9	-39.5	-26.7

Source: Aging America, Trends and Projections, prepared by the U.S. Senate Special Committee on Aging, the American Association of Retired Persons, the Federal Council on the Aging, and the U.S. Administration on Aging, 1991, Washington, D.C., p. 118. Primary source: National Center for Health Statistics, "Annual Summary of Births, Marriages, Divorces, and Deaths: United States, 1989," *Monthly Vital Statistics Report*, Vol. 38, No. 13, August 30, 1990 and "Annual Summary of Births, Marriages, Divorces, and Deaths: United States, 1984," *Monthly Vital Statistics Report*, Vol. 33, No. 13, September 26, 1985.

★ 92 ★

Mortality

Death Rates: All Causes, According to Sex, Race, and Age: United States, Selected Years, 1960-89

Death rates for most older American categories show a steady decline throughout this period. Also noteworthy is the similarity in death rates for infants under one year of age to that of some older American groups. Data are based on the National Vital Statistics System.

[Deaths per 100,000 resident population]

Sex, race, and age	1960[1]	1970	1980	1981	1982	1983	1984	1985	1986	1987	1988	1989
ALL RACES												
All ages, age adjusted	760.9	714.3	585.8	568.2	553.8	550.5	545.9	546.1	541.7	535.5	535.5	523.0
All ages, crude	954.7	945.3	878.3	862.4	852.0	862.8	862.3	873.9	873.2	872.4	882.0	866.3
Under 1 year	2,696.4	2,142.4	1,288.3	1,207.3	1,164.2	1,107.3	1,085.6	1,067.8	1,032.1	1,018.5	1,008.3	1,005.2
55-64 years	1,735.1	1,658.8	1,346.3	1,322.1	1,297.9	1,299.5	1,287.8	1,282.7	1,255.1	1,241.3	1,235.6	1,204.4
65-74 years	3,822.1	3,582.7	2,994.9	2,922.3	2,885.2	2,874.3	2,848.1	2,838.6	2,801.4	2,751.3	2,729.8	2,646.7
75-84 years	8,745.2	8,004.4	6,692.6	6,429.9	6,329.8	6,441.5	6,399.3	6,445.1	6,348.2	6,282.5	6,321.3	6,138.8
85 years and over	19,857.5	16,344.9	15,980.3	15,379.7	15,048.3	15,168.0	15,223.6	15,480.3	15,398.9	15,320.8	15,594.0	15,034.8
WHITE MALE												
All ages, age adjusted	917.7	893.4	745.3	724.4	706.0	698.4	689.9	688.7	679.8	668.2	664.3	644.2
All ages, crude	1,098.5	1,086.7	983.3	965.1	951.8	957.4	951.1	960.0	954.4	947.8	952.2	930.2
Under 1 year	2,694.1	2,113.2	1,230.3	1,182.0	1,135.5	1,052.9	1,038.4	1,033.9	976.6	942.1	930.5	909.4
55-64 years	2,225.2	2,202.6	1,728.5	1,692.0	1,654.6	1,625.5	1,625.1	1,614.3	1,573.1	1,552.8	1,530.2	1,486.1
65-74 years	4,848.4	4,810.1	4,035.7	3,926.9	3,859.8	3,816.1	3,745.3	3,716.8	3,634.8	3,548.4	3,504.5	3,362.7
75-84 years	10,299.6	10,098.8	8,829.8	8,565.2	8,444.7	8,556.9	8,459.1	8,500.4	8,341.7	8,212.2	8,201.8	7,911.0
85 years and over	21,750.0	18,551.7	19,097.3	18,454.0	18,123.1	18,443.3	18,552.7	18,788.9	18,576.1	18,434.9	18,814.9	17,978.1
BLACK MALE												
All ages, age adjusted	1,246.1	1,318.6	1,112.8	1,067.7	1,035.0	1,019.6	1,011.7	1,024.0	1,026.9	1,023.2	1,037.8	1,032.1
All ages, crude	1,181.7	1,186.6	1,034.1	991.6	960.4	963.3	958.1	976.8	987.7	989.5	1,006.8	1,006.5
Under 1 year	5,306.8	4,298.9	2,586.7	2,164.8	2,168.9	2,243.4	2,136.6	2,134.8	2,181.7	2,211.4	2,167.7	2,179.0
55-64 years	3,316.4	3,256.9	2,873.0	2,804.1	2,758.1	2,713.1	2,658.3	2,623.1	2,545.5	2,464.7	2,477.5	2,439.6
65-74 years	5,798.7	5,803.2	5,131.1	5,046.3	5,040.1	4,949.3	4,874.5	4,888.7	4,789.9	4,737.6	4,695.3	4,621.3
75-84 years	8,605.1	9,454.9	9,231.6	8,635.1	8,477.2	9,100.0	9,023.1	9,298.4	9,290.8	9,240.7	9,419.9	9,064.4
85 years and over	14,844.8	12,222.3	16,098.8	15,396.4	15,117.9	14,155.6	14,642.9	15,046.2	15,488.1	15,226.1	15,454.3	15,355.6
WHITE FEMALE												
All ages, age adjusted	555.0	501.7	411.1	401.4	393.3	392.7	391.3	390.6	387.7	384.1	384.4	374.9
All ages, crude	800.9	812.6	806.1	799.6	797.9	815.3	822.3	837.1	840.7	845.5	860.0	846.0
Under 1 year	2,007.7	1,614.6	962.5	935.4	895.2	837.6	818.5	786.9	759.1	742.9	728.2	716.0
55-64 years	1,078.9	1,014.9	876.2	869.4	859.8	867.8	864.9	864.1	853.3	848.5	850.5	828.4
65-74 years	2,779.3	2,470.7	2,066.6	2,032.8	2,022.9	2,024.7	2,032.5	2,028.3	2,031.8	2,001.8	1,995.9	1,947.5
75-84 years	7,696.6	6,698.7	5,401.7	5,176.3	5,100.7	5,162.2	5,140.0	5,171.4	5,108.7	5,075.2	5,129.3	5,001.7
85 years and over	19,477.7	15,980.2	14,979.6	14,438.2	14,123.9	14,278.3	14,319.6	14,579.4	14,502.9	14,486.9	14,755.9	14,242.8
BLACK FEMALE												
All ages, age adjusted	916.9	814.4	631.1	599.1	581.4	590.4	585.3	589.1	588.2	586.2	593.1	585.6
All ages, crude	905.0	829.2	733.3	707.3	692.4	711.2	712.0	727.7	733.9	737.3	754.5	752.4
Under 1 year	4,162.2	3,368.8	2,123.7	1,823.4	1,760.1	1,818.6	1,789.1	1,756.6	1,731.1	1,791.5	1,821.5	1,863.9
55-64 years	2,510.9	1,986.2	1,561.0	1,527.9	1,498.3	1,526.3	1,489.7	1,501.7	1,469.8	1,445.0	1,465.5	1,424.2
65-74 years	4,064.2	3,860.9	3,057.4	2,929.7	2,863.0	2,930.6	2,907.4	2,925.7	2,892.3	2,874.5	2,874.9	2,854.5
75-84 years	6,730.0	6,691.5	6,212.1	5,822.3	5,708.5	6,064.6	6,184.1	6,252.0	6,148.8	6,145.7	6,255.3	6,211.4
85 years and over	13,052.6	10,706.6	12,367.2	11,933.0	11,660.0	11,329.5	11,439.1	12,154.7	12,510.3	12,313.2	12,694.3	12,526.7

Source: U.S. Department of Commerce, Economics and Statistics Administration, *National Economic, Social, and Environmental Data Bank, CD-ROM,* November 1992. Primary source: National Center for Health Statistics: *Vital Statistics of the United States, Vol. II, Mortality, Part A, 1950-89.* Public Health Service. Washington. U.S. Government Printing Office; Data computed by the Division of Analysis from data compiled by the Division of Vital Statistics and from table 1 in the original source. *Note:* 1. Includes deaths of nonresidents of the United States.

★ 93 ★

Mortality

Death Rates: The Three Leading Causes of Death, by Age: United States, 1988-90

The three leading causes of death include heart disease, malignant neoplasms (cancerous tumors), and cerebrovascular diseases. Data are provisional and are based on a 10-percent sample of death certificates from the National Vital Statistics System.

[Deaths per 100,000 resident population]

Age group	1988		1989		1990	
	Number	%	Number	%	Number	%
All ages, age adjusted	329.8	0.33	318.1	0.32	310.9	0.31
All ages, crude	571.9	0.57	556.0	0.56	548.6	0.55
Under 1 year	25.9	0.03	23.1	0.02	22.6	0.02
1-14 years	5.0	0.01	4.6	0.00	4.4	0.00
15-24 years	8.7	0.01	7.8	0.01	8.0	0.01
25-34 years	20.2	0.02	22.7	0.02	22.2	0.02
35-44 years	84.4	0.08	82.5	0.08	80.0	0.08
45-54 years	309.0	0.31	301.2	0.30	293.3	0.29
55-64 years	914.0	0.91	879.8	0.88	844.4	0.84
65-74 years	1,986.7	1.99	1,901.2	1.90	1,887.6	1.89
75-84 years	4,423.6	4.42	4,281.1	4.28	4,194.5	4.19
85 years and over	10,493.9	10.49	10,030.6	10.03	9,727.4	9.73

Source: U.S. Department of Commerce, Economics and Statistics Administration, *National Economic, Social, and Environmental Data Bank, CD-ROM,* November 1992. Primary source: National Center for Health Statistics: *Annual summary of births, marriages, divorces, and deaths, United States, 1988.* Monthly Vital Statistics Report. Vol. 37, No. 13. DHHS Pub. No. (PHS) 89-1120. July 26, 1989; and *Annual summary of births, marriages, divorces, and deaths, United States, 1990.* Monthly Vital Statistics Report. Vol. 39, No. 13. DHHS Pub. No. (PHS) 91-1120. 1991. Public Health Service. Hyattsville, Md. *Notes:* Includes deaths of nonresidents of the United States. Code numbers for cause of death are based on the International Classification of Diseases, Ninth Revision, described in Appendix II, table V in the primary source.

★ 94 ★

Mortality

Death Rates: Accidents, Homicides, and Suicides for Persons Over 64 Years of Age, 1987-89, According to Race and Hispanic origin: U.S., 1987-89

Data are based on the National Vital Statistics System.

[Deaths per 100,000 resident population]

Age, race, and Hispanic origin	Accidents/adverse effects			Homicides and Suicides		
	1987	1988	1989	1987	1988	1989
All races	2074.6	2066.4	1949.2	1059.8	1067.6	1085.1
White	2087.6	2079.5	1959.9	1054.0	1062.0	1079.0
Black	2179.9	2180.9	2080.6	1231.8	1241.4	1269.8
Hispanic[1]	1352.9	1335.6	1336.0	693.4	665.4	727.3

[Continued]

★ 94 ★

Death Rates: Accidents, Homicides, and Suicides for Persons Over 64 Years of Age, 1987-89, According to Race and Hispanic origin: U.S., 1987-89

[Continued]

Age, race, and Hispanic origin	Accidents/adverse effects			Homicides and Suicides		
	1987	1988	1989	1987	1988	1989
Asian or Pacific Islander	880.9	870.0	831.7	559.5	548.8	561.0
American Indian or Alaskan Native	1144.4	1128.3	1211.4	583.8	606.5	684.2

Primary source: National Center for Health Statistics: *Vital Statistics of the United States, Vol. II, Mortality, Part A.* Public Health Service. Washington. U.S. Government Printing Office; Death rates for Hispanics, Asian or Pacific Islanders, and American Indian or Alaskan Natives were computed by the Office of Analysis and Epidemiology, National Center for Health Statistics. *Notes:* 1. Data shown only for States with an Hispanic-origin item on their death certificates. The race groups include persons of both Hispanic and non-Hispanic origin. Conversely, persons of Hispanic origin may be of any race.

★ 95 ★

Mortality

Death Rates: Black/White Ratios for Acute Myocardial Infarction, 1980

The death rate from acute myocardial infarction is lower for middle-aged and older Black males than for White males. At ages 45 to 54, the death rate is essentially the same for both groups. However, the rate starts to decline steadily at ages 55 to 64 until it is significantly lower for Black males 85 or older (64 percent of the death rate for White males). A different pattern exists for middle-aged and older Black females. Their death rate from acute myocardial infarction is more than twice as great as it is for White females at ages 45 to 54. Then, it drops steadily until the death rate is nearly the same at age 65 to 74. Thereafter, it continues to fall so that the death rate from acute myocardial infarction for Black females 85 or older is 72 percent of that for White females in the same age group.

Age	Black males/ White males	Black females/ White females
25-34	2.00	3.28
35-44	1.28	2.70
45-54	0.98	2.02
55-64	0.84	1.54
65-74	0.71	1.07
75-84	0.66	0.84
85+	0.64	0.72

Source: U.S. Congress, "Profiles in Aging America: Meeting the Health Care Needs of the Nation's Black Elderly," Joint Hearing Before the Special Committee on Aging and the Congressional Black Caucus Health Braintrust, United States Senate, September 28, 1990, 101-29, U.S. Government Printing Office, Washington, D.C., p. 119.

★ 96 ★

Mortality

Death Rates: Black/White Ratios for Other Coronary Heart Diseases, 1980

The black/white death rate for other coronary heart diseases is subtantially higher for black males at ages 45 to 54, significantly higher for black males 55 to 64, slightly higher for black males 65 to 74, and lower for black males after age 75. Black females have a death rate from other coronary heart diseases that is 2 to 3 times as great as for White females in the 45 to 64 age bracket. It is nearly 1.5 times as great for Black females 65 to 74 years old. After age 75, White females have higher death rates from other corona-ry heart disease than black females.

Age	Black males/ White males	Black females/ White females
25-34	2.81	3.33
35-44	1.82	3.27
45-54	1.66	2.83
55-64	1.34	2.22
65-74	1.04	1.46
75-84	0.84	0.95
85+	0.63	0.62

Source: U.S. Congress, "Profiles in Aging America: Meeting the Health Care Needs of the Nation's Black Elderly," Joint Hearing Before the Special Committee on Aging and the Congressional Black Caucus Health Braintrust, United States Senate, September 28, 1990, 101-29, U.S. Government Printing Office, Washington, D.C., p. 120. Primary source: "Report of the Secretary's Task Force on Black and Minority Health, Volume IV: Cardiovascular and Cerebrovascular Disease, Part I," U.S. Dept. of Health and Human Services, Jan. 1986, p. 97.

★ 97 ★

Mortality

Death Rates: Cerebrovascular Diseases for Persons 65 Years and Over, by Age, Sex, and Race: 1988

[Deaths per 100,000 resident population]

Age	Male		Female	
	White	Black	White	Black
65 to 74	164	326	125	265
75 to 84	591	796	513	701
85 and over	1,667	1,303	1,767	1,518

Source: Sixty-Five Plus in America, Cynthia M. Taeuber, U.S. Department of Commerce, Economics and Statistics Administration, Bureau of the Census, U.S. Government Printing Office, Washington, D.C., 1992, p. 3-9. Primary source: National Center for Health Statistics, *Health, United States, 1990,* Hyattsville, MD, Public Health Service, 1991, Table 28.

★ 98 ★

Mortality

Death Rates: Cerebrovascular Diseases, According to Sex, Race, and Age: United States, Selected Years 1960-89

Data are based on the National Vital Statistics System.

[Deaths per 100,000 resident population]

Sex, race, and age	1960[1]	1970	1980	1981	1982	1983	1984	1985	1986	1987	1988	1989
ALL RACES												
All ages, age adjusted	79.7	66.3	40.8	38.1	35.8	34.4	33.4	32.3	31.0	30.3	29.7	28.0
All ages, crude	108.0	101.9	75.1	71.3	68.0	66.5	65.3	64.1	62.1	61.6	61.2	58.6
55-64 years	147.3	115.8	65.2	62.9	58.9	57.6	55.8	54.3	53.0	52.2	51.3	48.8
65-74 years	469.2	384.1	219.5	206.3	193.5	182.2	177.0	171.3	164.1	157.2	154.7	144.7
75-84 years	1,491.3	1,254.2	788.6	715.6	675.1	652.7	626.2	605.8	573.8	562.6	553.6	519.8
85 years and over	3,680.5	3,014.3	2,288.9	2,126.8	2,000.8	1,912.5	1,883.8	1,837.5	1,762.6	1,733.1	1,707.4	1,631.0
WHITE MALE												
All ages, age adjusted	80.3	68.8	41.9	38.9	36.6	35.2	33.9	32.8	31.1	30.3	30.0	28.0
All ages, crude	102.7	93.5	63.3	59.4	56.7	55.5	53.8	52.5	50.5	49.9	50.0	47.5
55-64 years	139.0	119.9	64.2	61.6	57.3	56.5	54.3	54.2	51.4	50.7	50.4	47.4
65-74 years	501.0	420.0	240.4	225.3	211.5	197.1	190.4	183.7	171.4	165.4	163.5	152.2
75-84 years	1,564.8	1,361.6	854.8	775.6	727.3	714.8	671.1	651.1	617.3	601.2	590.8	554.6
85 years and over	3,734.8	3,018.1	2,236.9	2,051.4	1,944.7	1,862.9	1,846.4	1,747.8	1,697.0	1,663.1	1,667.1	1,568.3
BLACK MALE												
All ages, age adjusted	141.2	122.5	77.5	72.7	68.9	64.2	62.8	60.8	58.9	57.1	57.8	54.1
All ages, crude	122.9	108.8	73.1	68.2	64.3	61.3	60.0	58.5	57.1	55.7	56.5	53.2
55-64 years	439.9	343.4	189.8	182.3	174.3	163.8	159.0	151.6	144.3	143.9	146.4	135.6
65-74 years	899.2	780.1	472.8	437.0	428.1	388.0	379.8	358.9	337.8	318.5	325.8	301.8
75-84 years	1,475.2	1,445.7	1,067.6	943.9	881.7	844.1	819.5	817.6	809.9	777.6	796.3	715.5
85 years and over	2,700.0	1,963.1	1,873.2	1,787.3	1,637.5	1,479.4	1,395.2	1,363.1	1,350.7	1,339.1	1,302.9	1,333.3
WHITE FEMALE												
All ages, age adjusted	68.7	56.2	35.2	33.1	31.0	29.6	28.9	27.9	27.1	26.3	25.5	24.1
All ages, crude	110.1	109.8	88.8	85.1	81.7	79.8	79.2	78.1	76.2	75.8	74.9	72.1
55-64 years	103.0	78.1	48.7	47.7	44.0	42.6	42.0	39.7	40.1	38.7	37.0	35.6
65-74 years	383.3	303.2	172.8	163.6	154.2	144.6	140.9	138.0	136.3	129.3	125.3	117.8
75-84 years	1,444.7	1,176.8	730.3	665.4	628.9	602.0	580.9	559.4	530.7	524.0	512.7	479.7
85 years and over	3,795.7	3,167.6	2,367.8	2,206.0	2,074.5	1,986.5	1,962.5	1,923.0	1,837.3	1,807.8	1,767.0	1,695.9
BLACK FEMALE												
All ages, age adjusted	139.5	107.9	61.7	58.1	54.7	53.8	51.8	50.3	47.6	46.7	46.6	44.9
All ages, crude	127.7	112.2	77.9	74.4	70.6	70.5	68.5	68.0	65.0	64.3	65.4	63.5
55-64 years	452.0	272.4	138.7	129.8	127.5	126.0	112.6	111.3	109.4	108.7	105.7	99.5
65-74 years	830.5	673.5	362.2	345.1	305.3	308.4	304.6	281.5	268.5	261.2	264.7	248.1
75-84 years	1,413.1	1,338.3	918.6	828.3	800.8	786.7	803.4	775.4	710.7	685.7	700.7	701.1
85 years and over	2,578.9	2,210.5	1,896.3	1,832.1	1,689.6	1,603.1	1,470.7	1,585.6	1,504.1	1,480.9	1,517.7	1,419.4

Source: U.S. Department of Commerce, Economics and Statistics Administration, *National Economic, Social, and Environmental Data Bank, CD-ROM,* November 1992. Primary source: National Center for Health Statistics: *Vital Statistics of the United States, Vol. II, Mortality, Part A, 1950-89.* Public Health Service. Washington. U.S. Government Printing Office; Data computed by the Division of Analysis from data compiled by the Division of Vital Statistics. *Note:* 1. Includes deaths of nonresidents of the United States.

★ 99 ★

Mortality

Death Rates: Diabetes Mellitus, 1980-86

Data are based on the National Vital Statistics System.

[Number of deaths per 100,000 resident population]

Sex, race, and age	1980	1982	1984	1986
Male, all races[1]				
55-59 years	21.2	20.5	18.8	21.2
60-64 years	34.0	32.0	31.5	32.3
65-69 years	52.2	50.5	48.6	48.6
70-74 years	79.9	74.5	73.2	74.5
75-79 years	115.4	109.9	112.3	105.0
80-84 years	160.0	154.0	161.0	153.0
65 years and over	92.8	87.9	89.4	87.4
75 years and over	147.8	138.3	145.5	138.2
85 years and over	217.3	191.8	213.6	208.7
White male				
55-59 years	18.3	18.5	16.8	18.7
60-64 years	31.2	29.5	27.7	28.8
65-69 years	48.6	47.6	44.1	45.2
70-74 years	76.5	72.3	69.7	69.9
75-79 years	110.8	106.9	108.5	100.9
80-84 years	157.3	151.0	158.0	146.3
65 years and over	89.7	85.5	86.1	83.4
75 years and over	145.1	136.0	143.1	133.9
85 years and over	219.2	191.9	215.9	207.6
Black male				
55-59 years	51.1	41.9	37.6	44.6
60-64 years	64.8	59.4	69.3	67.3
65-69 years	90.6	85.6	94.1	82.2
70-74 years	117.6	100.8	113.3	127.0
75-79 years	171.3	143.5	160.1	152.3
80-84 years	203.9	187.1	209.6	231.4
65 years and over	130.1	118.0	128.1	130.5
75 years and over	187.2	166.6	178.3	187.5
85 years and over	209.4	201.8	185.7	223.9
Female, all races[1]				
55-59 years	19.6	18.8	17.0	18.6
60-64 years	33.9	31.9	31.9	32.4
65-69 years	53.7	48.5	46.9	48.0
70-74 years	80.5	72.8	74.6	72.0
75-79 years	113.7	104.1	105.5	103.2
80-84 years	157.6	157.6	153.1	150.9
65 years and over	102.7	98.1	98.2	97.6
75 years and over	153.6	149.0	148.3	146.4

[Continued]

★ 99 ★

Death Rates: Diabetes Mellitus, 1980-86

[Continued]

Sex, race, and age	1980	1982	1984	1986
85 years and over	223.9	220.7	218.1	216.0
White female				
55-59 years	15.9	15.3	13.6	14.4
60-64 years	28.0	26.1	26.6	26.6
65-69 years	45.5	42.2	40.3	41.5
70-74 years	72.5	66.3	65.2	63.7
75-79 years	106.2	98.3	97.9	95.0
80-84 years	149.8	149.8	143.3	139.6
65 years and over	95.5	92.4	91.2	89.8
75 years and over	146.6	143.3	141.2	136.9
85 years and over	217.9	216.7	213.9	205.6
Black female				
55-59 years	53.7	50.4	47.5	53.5
60-64 years	88.7	90.4	84.6	86.6
65-69 years	131.8	114.0	111.4	112.5
70-74 years	168.3	140.3	174.2	163.5
75-79 years	200.5	170.1	195.1	198.6
80-84 years	267.7	262.3	190.3	303.3
65 years and over	183.5	163.1	178.8	187.1
75 years and over	243.7	220.8	239.9	264.9
85 years and over	311.2	280.0	273.7	351.0

Source: Health Data on Older Americans: United States, 1992, Centers for Disease Control and Prevention/National Center for Health Statistics, Vital and Health Statistics, Series 3: Analytic and Epidemiological Studies, No. 27, pp. 101-102. Primary source: National Center for Health Statistics. *Vital Statistics of the United States, Vol. II, Mortality, Part A,* Washington: Public Health Service, selected years. *Notes:* Diabetes mellitus comprises code 150 of the *International Classification of Diseases, Ninth Revision.* 1. Includes races other than White and Black.

★ 100 ★

Mortality

Death Rates: Diseases of the Heart, According to Sex, Race, and Age: United States, Selected Years 1960-89

Data are based on the National Vital Statistics System.

[Deaths per 100,000 resident population]

Sex, race, and age	1960[1]	1970	1980	1981	1982	1983	1984	1985	1986	1987	1988	1989
ALL RACES												
All ages, age adjusted	286.2	253.6	202.0	195.0	190.5	188.8	183.6	180.5	175.0	169.6	166.3	155.9
All ages, crude	369.0	362.0	336.0	328.7	326.0	329.2	323.5	323.0	317.5	312.4	311.3	295.6
55-64 years	737.9	652.3	494.1	481.5	468.7	463.0	450.3	439.1	424.2	408.8	400.9	376.7
65-74 years	1,740.5	1,558.2	1,218.6	1,175.8	1,156.4	1,139.2	1,102.7	1,080.6	1,043.0	1,007.9	984.1	911.8
75-84 years	4,089.4	3,683.8	2,993.1	2,850.3	2,801.4	2,816.3	2,748.6	2,712.6	2,637.5	2,560.0	2,542.7	2,400.6
85 years and over	9,317.8	7,891.3	7,777.1	7,458.8	7,341.8	7,335.5	7,251.0	7,275.0	7,178.7	7,074.2	7,098.1	6,701.6

[Continued]

★ 100 ★

Death Rates: Diseases of the Heart, According to Sex, Race, and Age: United States, Selected Years 1960-89

[Continued]

Sex, race, and age	1960[1]	1970	1980	1981	1982	1983	1984	1985	1986	1987	1988	1989
WHITE MALE												
All ages, age adjusted	375.4	347.6	277.5	268.8	262.1	257.8	249.5	244.5	234.8	225.9	220.5	205.9
All ages, crude	454.6	438.3	384.0	375.8	371.0	370.9	361.8	358.9	348.6	340.1	336.8	318.3
55-64 years	1,056.0	979.3	730.6	708.7	689.9	674.1	655.5	635.6	610.3	582.7	565.1	531.5
65-74 years	2,297.9	2,177.2	1,729.7	1,669.9	1,636.2	1,603.6	1,533.0	1,501.0	1,440.9	1,378.0	1,348.9	1,243.8
75-84 years	4,839.9	4,617.6	3,883.2	3,751.5	3,674.7	3,664.3	3,579.3	3,532.9	3,405.2	3,291.0	3,257.6	3,066.1
85 years and over	10,135.8	8,818.0	8,958.0	8,596.0	8,442.2	8,503.4	8,416.4	8,396.3	8,138.4	8,030.6	8,072.5	7,549.9
BLACK MALE												
All ages, age adjusted	381.2	375.9	327.3	316.7	309.4	308.2	300.1	301.0	294.3	287.1	286.2	272.6
All ages, crude	330.6	330.3	301.0	289.7	282.3	288.5	282.2	285.0	281.3	276.1	276.3	263.5
55-64 years	1,236.8	1,135.4	987.2	981.5	950.4	928.0	895.9	882.6	864.9	814.7	833.0	795.8
65-74 years	2,281.4	2,237.8	1,847.2	1,812.7	1,822.5	1,804.5	1,734.7	1,738.4	1,673.1	1,659.7	1,616.7	1,531.5
75-84 years	3,533.6	3,783.4	3,578.8	3,302.5	3,245.9	3,457.5	3,375.7	3,450.0	3,407.3	3,371.6	3,435.7	3,157.2
85 years and over	6,037.9	5,367.6	6,819.5	6,394.5	6,378.6	5,907.9	6,015.9	6,098.5	6,268.7	6,050.7	6,165.7	5,837.5
WHITE FEMALE												
All ages, age adjusted	197.1	167.8	134.6	129.8	127.4	126.7	124.0	121.7	119.0	116.3	114.2	106.6
All ages, crude	306.5	313.8	319.2	314.6	315.8	321.5	319.3	320.7	319.0	317.1	318.0	303.0
55-64 years	383.0	317.7	248.1	243.7	237.9	237.5	231.6	225.8	221.4	217.1	213.3	196.1
65-74 years	1,229.8	1,044.0	796.7	769.4	759.6	745.6	735.3	713.7	693.9	675.1	656.2	604.4
75-84 years	3,629.7	3,143.5	2,493.6	2,359.0	2,331.7	2,332.4	2,273.1	2,233.3	2,180.2	2,120.7	2,101.5	1,990.7
85 years and over	9,280.8	7,839.9	7,501.6	7,215.1	7,118.6	7,133.7	7,044.7	7,089.3	7,021.3	6,924.6	6,957.3	6,580.4
BLACK FEMALE												
All ages, age adjusted	292.6	251.7	201.1	191.2	186.3	191.5	186.6	186.8	185.1	180.8	181.1	172.9
All ages, crude	268.5	261.0	249.7	241.1	237.0	248.1	244.6	248.1	250.8	248.3	251.2	242.7
55-64 years	952.3	710.5	530.1	517.2	501.9	517.7	499.6	500.4	479.0	469.9	471.4	453.1
65-74 years	1,680.5	1,553.2	1,210.3	1,152.3	1,124.3	1,159.8	1,127.1	1,133.6	1,108.3	1,090.2	1,060.0	1,024.9
75-84 years	2,926.9	2,964.1	2,707.2	2,509.4	2,445.0	2,660.1	2,618.9	2,606.0	2,623.5	2,566.3	2,625.6	2,492.9
85 years and over	5,650.0	5,003.8	5,796.5	5,583.9	5,491.3	5,298.4	5,315.0	5,441.0	5,698.6	5,627.6	5,648.1	5,469.7

Source: U.S. Department of Commerce, Economics and Statistics Administration, *National Economic, Social, and Environmental Data Bank, CD-ROM,* November 1992. Primary source: National Center for Health Statistics: *Vital Statistics of the United States, Vol. II, Mortality, Part A, 1950-89.* Public Health Service. Washington. U.S. Government Printing Office; Data computed by the Division of Analysis from data compiled by the Division of Vital Statistics. *Notes:* For data years shown, the code numbers for cause of death are based on the then current International Classification of Diseases, which are described in the original source. 1. Includes deaths of nonresidents of the United States.

★ 101 ★

Mortality

Death Rates: Diseases of the Heart, by Age, Race, and Sex: 1960 and 1988

[Deaths per 100,000 resident population]

Age, race, and sex	Deaths		Percent change
	1960[1]	1988	1960 to 1988
65 to 74 years			
White males	2,297.9	1,348.0	-41.34
Black males	2,281.4	1,616.7	-29.14
White females	1,229.8	656.2	-46.64

[Continued]

★ 101 ★

Death Rates: Diseases of the Heart, by Age, Race, and Sex: 1960 and 1988

[Continued]

Age, race, and sex	Deaths		Percent change
	1960[1]	1988	1960 to 1988
Black females	1,680.5	1,060.0	-36.92
75 to 84 years			
White males	4,839.9	3,257.6	-32.69
Black males	3,533.6	3,435.7	-2.77
White females	3,629.7	2,101.5	-42.10
Black females	2,926.9	2,625.6	-10.29
85 years and over			
White males	10,135.8	8,072.5	-20.36
Black males	6,037.9	6,165.7	2.12
White females	9,280.8	6,957.3	-25.04
Black females	5,650.0	5,648.1	-0.03

Source: *Sixty-Five Plus in America*, Cynthia M. Taeuber, U.S. Department of Commerce, Economics and Statistics Administration, Bureau of the Census, U.S. Government Printing Office, Washington, D.C., 1992, p. 3-10. Primary source: National Center for Health Statistics, *Health, United States, 1990*, Hyattsville, MD, Public Health Service, 1991, Table 27. *Note:* 1. Includes deaths of nonresidents of the United States.

★ 102 ★

Mortality

Death Rates: Diseases of the Heart for Persons 65 Years and Over, by Age, Sex, and Race: 1988

[Deaths per 100,000 resident population]

Age	Male		Female	
	White	Black	White	Black
65 to 74	1,348	1,617	656	1,060
75 to 84	3,258	3,436	2,102	2,626
85 and over	8,073	6,166	6,957	5,648

Source: *Sixty-Five Plus in America*, Cynthia M. Taeuber, U.S. Department of Commerce, Economics and Statistics Administration, Bureau of the Census, U.S. Government Printing Office, Washington, D.C., 1992, p. 3-8. Primary source: National Center for Health Statistics, *Health, United States, 1990*, Hyattsville, MD, Public Health Service, 1991, Table 27.

★ 103 ★

Mortality

Death Rates: Homicide and Legal Intervention, According to Sex, Race, and Age: United States, Selected Years 1960-89

Data are based on the National Vital Statistics System.

[Deaths per 100,000 resident population]

Sex, race, and age	1960[1]	1970	1980	1981	1982	1983	1984	1985	1986	1987	1988	1989
ALL RACES												
All ages, age adjusted	5.2	9.1	10.8	10.4	9.7	8.6	8.4	8.3	9.0	8.6	9.0	9.4
All ages, crude	4.7	8.3	10.7	10.3	9.6	8.6	8.4	8.3	9.0	8.7	9.0	9.2
55-64 years	4.2	7.1	7.0	7.1	6.5	6.1	5.8	5.7	5.4	5.5	5.2	5.0
65-74 years	2.8	5.0	5.7	4.8	4.9	4.3	4.2	4.3	4.4	4.3	4.2	4.1
75-84 years	2.4	4.0	5.2	5.3	4.7	4.9	4.4	4.3	4.6	4.8	4.5	4.2
85 years and over	2.4	4.2	5.3	5.3	5.8	5.0	4.3	4.1	4.7	5.1	4.7	4.3
WHITE MALE												
All ages, age adjusted	3.9	7.3	10.9	10.3	9.5	8.4	8.2	8.1	8.4	7.7	7.7	8.1
All ages, crude	3.6	6.8	10.9	10.4	9.6	8.6	8.3	8.2	8.6	7.9	7.9	8.2
55-64 years	4.3	7.7	7.8	7.9	7.1	6.4	6.3	6.3	6.0	6.3	6.0	5.6
65-74 years	3.4	5.6	6.9	5.2	5.0	4.6	4.2	4.5	4.3	4.2	4.1	3.9
75-84 years	2.7	5.1	6.3	5.1	5.2	4.6	4.2	4.5	4.6	4.9	4.3	3.9
85 years and over	2.7	6.4	6.4	7.9	8.2	5.6	5.3	3.9	4.4	5.4	5.1	5.1
BLACK MALE												
All ages, age adjusted	44.9	82.1	71.9	69.2	62.3	53.8	50.8	49.9	55.9	53.8	58.2	61.5
All ages, crude	36.6	67.6	66.6	64.8	59.1	51.4	48.7	48.4	55.0	53.3	58.0	61.1
55-64 years	31.8	59.8	55.6	53.4	49.3	46.7	40.6	37.8	35.4	32.8	29.1	30.2
65-74 years	19.1	40.6	33.9	36.3	36.6	28.1	30.3	27.6	30.0	28.0	26.2	26.3
75-84 years	16.1	19.0	27.6	33.5	24.8	32.4	28.3	21.5	27.9	29.5	30.5	28.4
85 years and over	10.3	19.6	17.0	29.1	19.6	27.0	28.6	16.9	25.4	29.0	31.4	34.7
WHITE FEMALE												
All ages, age adjusted	1.5	2.2	3.2	3.1	3.1	2.8	2.9	2.9	2.9	2.9	2.8	2.8
All ages, crude	1.4	2.1	3.2	3.1	3.1	2.8	2.9	2.9	3.0	3.0	2.9	2.8
55-64 years	1.5	2.0	2.1	2.2	2.2	2.2	2.2	2.3	1.9	1.9	2.0	1.7
65-74 years	1.1	1.7	2.5	2.1	2.4	2.0	1.9	2.2	2.2	2.4	2.3	2.1
75-84 years	1.2	2.5	3.3	3.6	2.9	3.1	2.9	3.1	3.1	3.1	3.0	2.7
85 years and over	1.5	1.9	4.0	3.3	3.9	3.8	2.6	3.2	3.3	3.8	2.9	2.0
BLACK FEMALE												
All ages, age adjusted	11.8	15.0	13.7	12.9	12.0	11.2	11.0	10.8	11.8	12.3	12.7	12.5
All ages, crude	10.4	13.3	13.5	12.7	12.0	11.3	11.2	11.0	12.1	12.6	13.2	12.9
55-64 years	6.8	8.1	8.9	11.2	8.0	6.3	6.7	6.4	6.8	7.6	6.8	8.1
65-74 years	3.3	7.7	8.6	6.6	8.1	7.0	6.8	7.2	8.7	6.9	9.0	8.2

[Continued]

★ 103 ★

Death Rates: Homicide and Legal Intervention, According to Sex, Race, and Age: United States, Selected Years 1960-89

[Continued]

Sex, race, and age	1960[1]	1970	1980	1981	1982	1983	1984	1985	1986	1987	1988	1989
75-84 years	2.5	5.7	6.7	9.2	8.8	11.3	9.8	7.6	8.6	10.4	9.9	9.9
85 years and over	2.6	9.8	8.5	4.5	12.2	8.5	7.5	11.5	13.1	10.5	12.7	15.2

Source: U.S. Department of Commerce, Economics and Statistics Administration, *National Economic, Social, and Environmental Data Bank, CD-ROM,* November 1992. Primary source: National Center for Health Statistics: *Vital Statistics of the United States, Vol. II, Mortality, Part A, 1950-89.* Public Health Service. Washington. U.S. Government Printing Office; Data computed by the Division of Analysis from data compiled by the Division of Vital Statistics and from Table 1, in the original source. *Notes:* For data years shown, the code numbers for cause of death are based on the then current International Classification of Diseases, which is described in the original source. 1. Includes deaths of nonresidents of the United States.

★ 104 ★

Mortality

Death Rates: Human Immunodeficiency Virus (HIV) Infection, According to Sex, Race, and Age: United States, 1987, 1988, and 1989

Data are based on the National Vital Statistics System.

[Deaths per 100,000 resident population]

Race and age	Both sexes			Male			Female		
	1987	1988	1989	1987	1988	1989	1987	1988	1989
ALL RACES									
All ages, age adjusted	5.5	6.6	8.7	10.0	12.0	15.7	1.1	1.4	1.8
All ages, crude	5.5	6.8	8.9	10.2	12.4	16.3	1.1	1.4	1.8
55-64 years	3.5	4.0	5.3	6.7	7.6	10.3	0.5	0.7	0.8
65-74 years	1.3	1.6	1.8	2.3	2.8	3.2	0.5	0.6	0.7
75-84 years	0.8	0.8	0.7	1.2	1.5	1.2	0.6	0.4	0.4
85 years and over	0.5[1]	0.4[1]	0.4[1]	0.7[1]	1.0[1]	0.9[1]	0.3[1]	0.1[1]	0.2[1]
WHITE									
All ages, age adjusted	4.4	5.3	7.0	8.3	9.9	13.1	0.6	0.7	0.9
All ages, crude	4.5	5.4	7.2	8.6	10.3	13.8	0.6	0.7	0.9
55-64 years	3.0	3.4	4.6	5.9	6.5	9.0	0.4	0.5	0.5
65-74 years	1.3	1.5	1.5	2.3	2.5	2.7	0.5	0.6	0.6
75-84 years	0.8	0.8	0.7	1.2	1.4	1.2	0.6	0.4	0.4
85 years and over	0.4[1]	0.4[1]	0.4[1]	0.6[1]	0.9[1]	0.8[1]	0.3[1]	0.2[1]	0.2[1]
BLACK									
All ages, age adjusted	14.2	17.9	22.9	25.4	31.6	40.3	4.7	6.2	8.1
All ages, crude	13.6	17.2	22.2	23.4	29.3	37.6	4.7	6.3	8.2
55-64 years	7.9	9.7	12.6	15.6	18.4	24.5	1.5[1]	2.6	2.8
65-74 years	1.6	3.4	4.8	2.3[1]	6.4	9.2	1.0[1]	1.1[1]	1.6[1]

[Continued]

★ 104 ★

Death Rates: Human Immunodeficiency Virus (HIV) Infection, According to Sex, Race, and Age: United States, 1987, 1988, and 1989

[Continued]

Race and age	Both sexes			Male			Female		
	1987	1988	1989	1987	1988	1989	1987	1988	1989
75-84 years	0.4[1]	1.4[1]	1.3[1]	0.4[1]	2.6[1]	1.4[1]	0.5[1]	0.7[1]	1.3[1]
85 years and over	1.4[1]	0.4[1]	0.4[1]	2.9[1]	1.4[1]	1.4[1]	0.7[1]	-[1]	-[1]

Source: U.S. Department of Commerce, Economics and Statistics Administration, *National Economic, Social, and Environmental Data Bank, CD-ROM,* November 1992. Primary source: National Center for Health Statistics: *Vital Statistics of the United States, Vol. II, Mortality, Part A, for data years 1987-89.* Public Health Service. Washington. U.S. Government Printing Office. *Notes:* Categories for the coding and classification of human immunodeficiency virus infection were introduced in the United States beginning with mortality data for 1987. 1. Based on fewer than 20 deaths.

★ 105 ★

Mortality

Death Rates: Lung Cancer, Rate per 100,000 people, by Age 75

The table shows estimates of death by lung cancer, by age 75, for non-smokers, smokers who quit, and those who still smoke. Estimates assume that smokers began at age 18. Quitting early reduces the risk of death by lung cancer.

	Men		Women	
	Death from lung cancer Number per 100,000 people	Risk[1] (%)	Death from lung cancer Number per 100,000 people	Risk[1] (%)
Never smoked	37.5	3.0	22.0	4.0
Quit at age				
30-39	87.5	7.0	55.0	10.0
40-49	150.0	12.0	82.5	15.0
50-54	237.5	19.0	126.5	23.0
55-59	337.5	27.0	170.5	31.0
60-64	562.5	45.0	269.5	49.0
Current smokers	1,250.0	100.0	550.0	100.0

Source: New York Times, March 21, 1993, p. 15. Primary source: Based on studies conducted at the University of Michigan and published in the *Journal of the National Cancer Institute. Note:* 1. Percentages of risk compare nonsmokers to current smokers.

★ 106 ★
Mortality

Death Rates: Malignant Neoplasms of the Respiratory and Intrathoracic Organs, 1980-86

Data are based on the National Vital Statistics System. Malignant neoplasms are cancerous tumors.

[Number of deaths per 100,000 resident population]

Sex, race, and age	1980	1982	1984	1986
Male, all races[1]				
55-59 years	179.7	181.1	187.2	178.9
60-64 years	275.6	278.5	278.3	282.1
65-69 years	382.3	391.4	380.9	377.2
70-74 years	476.4	480.2	486.9	484.7
75-79 years	517.7	535.9	550.7	562.0
80-84 years	500.3	510.8	559.4	578.8
65 years and over	444.5	457.4	463.7	468.0
75 years and over	487.4	508.9	532.6	550.0
85 years and over	386.3	432.6	442.8	472.9
White male				
55-59 years	170.8	171.1	177.2	172.6
60-64 years	266.7	267.0	265.4	272.1
65-69 years	375.5	384.0	373.3	368.5
70-74 years	477.0	477.3	484.4	481.6
75-79 years	522.3	543.3	554.4	564.7
80-84 years	505.0	517.5	560.5	581.9
65 years and over	443.9	456.3	461.5	465.2
75 years and over	492.1	515.8	535.7	553.3
85 years and over	391.5	439.1	446.8	477.5
Black male				
55-59 years	292.8	310.2	307.0	264.7
60-64 years	397.9	434.9	449.3	419.2
65-69 years	490.4	516.9	502.0	519.2
70-74 years	512.3	570.8	567.1	574.9
75-79 years	516.5	514.9	571.4	610.2
80-84 years	465.2	488.2	586.7	598.8
65 years and over	489.4	520.8	534.9	553.8
75 years and over	469.0	483.4	545.9	576.0
85 years and over	337.7	385.7	423.8	456.7
Female, all races[1]				
55-59 years	63.7	70.8	75.9	78.1
60-64 years	86.6	97.7	104.0	110.8
65-69 years	104.1	118.9	131.4	141.6
70-74 years	108.5	121.9	139.6	164.6
75-79 years	102.7	112.1	132.3	152.9
80-84 years	90.6	103.9	121.4	136.1
65 years and over	102.5	114.0	129.0	145.7

[Continued]

★ 106 ★

Death Rates: Malignant Neoplasms of the Respiratory and Intrathoracic Organs, 1980-86

[Continued]

Sex, race, and age	1980	1982	1984	1986
75 years and over	97.6	105.7	121.1	137.6
85 years and over	96.3	96.2	101.0	113.0
White female				
55-59 years	62.9	70.6	76.0	77.9
60-64 years	87.0	98.0	104.2	111.8
65-69 years	106.4	121.5	135.2	145.0
70-74 years	110.1	126.0	144.0	169.1
75-79 years	105.0	114.7	134.8	156.8
80-84 years	90.5	103.3	122.3	137.1
65 years and over	104.1	116.2	132.0	148.8
75 years and over	98.7	106.7	122.8	139.8
85 years and over	96.8	96.1	102.5	113.8
Black female				
55-59 years	79.0	82.3	85.1	90.6
60-64 years	89.5	104.9	113.3	115.4
65-69 years	89.0	105.7	106.0	126.7
70-74 years	95.5	88.7	106.3	136.2
75-79 years	79.2	90.6	113.7	118.8
80-84 years	84.7	112.3	109.7	132.0
65 years and over	88.6	97.3	106.0	125.8
75 years and over	83.3	96.3	105.9	118.1
85 years and over	90.5	88.7	86.5	102.1

Source: *Health Data on Older Americans: United States, 1992*, Centers for Disease Control and Prevention/National Center for Health Statistics, Vital and Health Statistics, Series 3: Analytic and Epidemiological Studies, No. 27, pp. 97-98. Primary source: National Center for Health Statistics. *Vital Statistics of the United States, Vol. II, Mortality, Part A*, Washington: Public Health Service, selected years. *Notes:* Malignant neoplasms of the respiratory and intrathoracic organs comprise codes 160-165 of the *International Classification of Diseases, Ninth Revision*. 1. Includes races other than White and Black.

★ 107 ★

Mortality

Death Rates: Malignant Neoplasms, According to Sex, Race, and Age: United States, Selected Years 1960-89

[Deaths per 100,000 resident population]

Sex, race, and age	1960[1]	1970	1980	1981	1982	1983	1984	1985	1986	1987	1988	1989
ALL RACES												
All ages, age adjusted	125.8	129.8	132.8	131.6	132.5	132.6	133.5	133.6	133.2	132.9	132.7	133.0
All ages, crude	149.2	162.8	183.9	184.0	187.2	189.3	191.8	193.3	194.7	195.9	197.3	199.9
55-64 years	396.8	423.0	436.1	434.8	439.7	443.0	448.4	450.5	444.4	447.0	447.3	445.1
65-74 years	713.9	751.2	817.9	814.8	824.9	829.3	835.1	838.3	847.0	843.6	842.7	852.6
75-84 years	1,127.4	1,169.2	1,232.3	1,221.8	1,238.7	1,254.7	1,272.3	1,281.0	1,287.3	1,298.4	1,313.3	1,338.1

[Continued]

★ 107 ★

Death Rates: Malignant Neoplasms, According to Sex, Race, and Age: United States, Selected Years 1960-89

[Continued]

Sex, race, and age	1960[1]	1970	1980	1981	1982	1983	1984	1985	1986	1987	1988	1989
85 years and over	1,450.0	1,320.7	1,594.6	1,575.3	1,598.6	1,583.4	1,604.0	1,591.5	1,612.0	1,618.0	1,638.9	1,662.3
WHITE MALE												
All ages, age adjusted	141.6	154.3	160.5	158.3	159.4	158.9	159.0	159.2	158.8	158.4	157.6	157.2
All ages, crude	166.1	185.1	208.7	207.9	211.7	213.8	215.1	217.2	218.8	220.5	221.4	223.3
55-64 years	450.9	498.1	497.4	494.4	497.3	499.5	504.5	508.4	504.3	509.8	508.6	505.7
65-74 years	887.3	997.0	1,070.7	1,060.3	1,067.8	1,063.7	1,064.1	1,061.2	1,063.3	1,061.1	1,050.4	1,054.3
75-84 years	1,413.7	1,592.7	1,779.7	1,749.5	1,790.0	1,805.3	1,806.9	1,820.1	1,827.0	1,826.6	1,839.7	1,853.0
85 years and over	1,791.4	1,772.2	2,375.6	2,358.7	2,413.4	2,416.3	2,438.6	2,424.5	2,462.3	2,475.5	2,533.0	2,566.1
BLACK MALE												
All ages, age adjusted	158.5	198.0	229.9	232.0	235.2	232.2	234.9	231.6	229.0	227.9	227.0	230.6
All ages, crude	136.7	171.6	205.5	206.3	208.2	210.5	214.0	212.2	211.4	212.2	211.7	216.2
55-64 years	579.7	689.2	812.5	814.8	838.2	821.6	841.7	803.3	776.0	767.3	749.8	759.5
65-74 years	938.5	1,168.9	1,417.2	1,462.1	1,477.3	1,457.4	1,444.9	1,448.7	1,455.1	1,453.6	1,434.5	1,460.7
75-84 years	1,053.3	1,624.8	2,029.6	2,010.5	2,048.4	2,196.8	2,226.3	2,238.3	2,249.2	2,329.5	2,344.5	2,410.4
85 years and over	1,155.2	1,387.0	2,393.9	2,383.6	2,566.1	2,219.0	2,471.4	2,507.7	2,620.9	2,659.4	2,720.0	2,787.5
WHITE FEMALE												
All ages, age adjusted	109.5	107.6	107.7	107.2	108.2	108.5	109.9	110.3	110.1	109.7	110.1	110.7
All ages, crude	139.8	149.4	170.3	172.0	175.6	177.9	181.7	183.7	185.6	186.9	189.3	192.9
55-64 years	329.0	338.6	355.5	356.3	361.5	366.8	370.0	374.1	369.4	370.1	372.5	370.9
65-74 years	562.1	554.7	605.2	605.7	618.4	627.4	638.6	645.3	658.7	654.0	660.0	670.8
75-84 years	939.3	903.5	905.4	907.8	913.0	919.5	944.2	949.2	956.4	968.6	984.4	1,013.9
85 years and over	1,304.9	1,126.6	1,266.8	1,257.2	1,270.6	1,265.7	1,284.3	1,270.9	1,283.6	1,291.0	1,300.1	1,322.0
BLACK FEMALE												
All ages, age adjusted	127.8	123.5	129.7	127.1	128.7	129.8	131.0	130.4	132.1	132.0	131.2	130.9
All ages, crude	113.8	117.3	136.5	135.2	137.9	140.7	142.9	143.9	146.7	147.8	148.9	149.6
55-64 years	442.7	404.8	450.4	446.4	455.4	452.9	462.2	465.4	451.6	457.3	454.1	442.3
65-74 years	541.6	615.8	662.4	656.2	674.9	694.2	685.8	694.2	717.5	703.4	728.3	748.1
75-84 years	696.3	763.3	923.9	916.2	944.3	972.4	1,013.7	1,014.6	1,017.9	1,045.5	1,062.6	1,078.7
85 years and over	728.9	791.5	1,159.9	1,133.9	1,129.6	1,132.6	1,154.9	1,228.8	1,254.5	1,256.6	1,288.0	1,282.4

Source: U.S. Department of Commerce, Economics and Statistics Administration, *National Economic, Social, and Environmental Data Bank, CD-ROM,* November 1992. Primary source: National Center for Health Statistics: *Vital Statistics of the United States, Vol. II, Mortality, Part A, 1960-89.* Public Health Service. Washington. U.S. Government Printing Office; Data computed by the Division of Analysis from data compiled by the Division of Vital Statistics. *Notes:* For data years shown, the code numbers for cause of death are based on the then current International Classification of Diseases. 1. Includes deaths of nonresidents of the United States.

★ 108 ★

Mortality

Death Rates: Malignant Neoplasms, by Age, Race, and Sex: 1960 and 1988

[Deaths per 100,000 resident population]

Age, race, and sex	Deaths		Percent change
	1960[1]	1988	1960 to 1988
65 to 74 years			
White males	887.3	1,050.4	18.4
Black males	938.5	1,434.5	52.9
White females	562.1	660.0	17.4
Black females	541.6	728.3	34.5
75 to 84 years			
White males	1,413.7	1,839.7	30.1
Black males	1,053.3	2,344.5	122.6
White females	939.3	984.4	4.8
Black females	696.3	1,062.6	52.6
85 years and over			
White males	1,791.4	2,533.0	41.4
Black males	1,155.2	2,720.0	135.5
White females	1,304.9	1,300.1	-0.4
Black females	728.9	1,288.0	76.7

Source: Sixty-Five Plus in America, Cynthia M. Taeuber, U.S. Department of Commerce, Economics and Statistics Administration, Bureau of the Census, U.S. Government Printing Office, Washington, D.C., 1992, p. 3-11. Primary source: National Center for Health Statistics, *Health, United States, 1990*, Hyattsville, MD, Public Health Service, 1991, Table 29. *Note:* 1. Includes deaths of nonresidents of the United States.

★ 109 ★

Mortality

Death Rates: Malignant Neoplasms for Persons 65 Years and Over, by Age, Sex, and Race: 1988

[Deaths per 100,000 resident population]

Age	Male		Female	
	White	Black	White	Black
65 to 74	1,050	1,435	660	728
75 to 84	1,840	2,345	984	1,063
85 and over	2,533	2,720	1,300	1,288

Source: Sixty-Five Plus in America, Cynthia M. Taeuber, U.S. Department of Commerce, Economics and Statistics Administration, Bureau of the Census, U.S. Government Printing Office, Washington, D.C., 1992, p. 3-8. Primary source: National Center for Health Statistics, *Health, United States, 1990*, Hyattsville, MD, Public Health Service, 1991, Table 29.

★ 110 ★
Mortality

Death Rates: Motor Vehicle Accidents, According to Sex, Race, and Age: United States, Selected Years 1960-89

Data are based on the National Vital Statistics System.

[Deaths per 100,000 resident population]

Sex, race, and age	1960[1]	1970	1980	1981	1982	1983	1984	1985	1986	1987	1988	1989
ALL RACES												
All ages, age adjusted	22.5	27.4	22.9	21.8	19.3	18.5	19.1	18.8	19.4	19.5	19.7	18.9
All ages, crude	21.3	26.9	23.5	22.4	19.8	19.0	19.6	19.2	19.9	19.8	20.0	19.2
55-64 years	25.1	27.9	17.4	17.3	15.2	14.7	15.7	15.5	15.1	15.6	15.7	15.8
65-74 years	31.4	32.8	19.2	19.4	17.5	17.1	18.0	17.7	17.9	18.5	19.2	19.1
75-84 years	41.8	43.5	28.1	27.3	25.2	26.0	28.2	27.6	28.8	29.3	30.2	29.8
85 years and over	37.9	34.2	27.6	25.8	23.7	25.0	25.0	26.1	25.3	27.1	29.1	28.8
WHITE MALE												
All ages, age adjusted	34.0	40.1	34.8	33.4	29.3	27.8	28.4	27.6	28.7	28.4	28.5	26.8
All ages, crude	31.5	39.1	35.9	34.5	30.1	28.5	29.1	28.2	29.2	28.8	28.7	27.0
55-64 years	34.4	39.0	23.9	24.0	20.8	19.9	20.9	20.6	19.9	20.8	20.5	21.0
65-74 years	45.5	46.2	25.8	26.3	23.1	22.5	24.0	21.7	22.4	24.0	24.2	23.5
75-84 years	66.8	69.2	43.6	43.8	39.6	39.8	41.8	41.2	42.9	43.4	43.4	43.1
85 years and over	61.9	65.5	57.3	54.5	48.4	54.7	52.6	56.4	51.6	58.6	59.3	62.0
BLACK MALE												
All ages, age adjusted	38.2	50.1	32.9	30.7	27.2	26.4	27.2	27.7	29.2	28.5	29.6	29.4
All ages, crude	33.1	44.3	31.1	28.8	25.9	25.2	26.4	26.7	28.6	27.7	28.9	28.3
55-64 years	47.3	62.1	40.3	35.6	31.8	31.2	31.5	34.3	31.9	30.1	30.2	32.0
65-74 years	46.1	54.9	41.8	42.4	33.7	29.6	35.5	30.0	27.2	31.2	37.0	30.0
75-84 years	51.8	51.6	46.5	43.9	39.8	41.7	45.0	42.2	53.1	36.2	45.2	43.9
85 years and over	58.6	45.7	34.0	36.4	37.5	28.6	57.1	36.9	62.7	40.6	65.7	48.6
WHITE FEMALE												
All ages, age adjusted	11.1	14.4	12.3	11.7	10.5	10.3	10.9	10.8	11.0	11.4	11.6	11.5
All ages, crude	11.2	14.8	12.8	12.3	11.0	10.8	11.5	11.4	11.5	11.9	12.1	12.1
55-64 years	15.3	16.1	10.5	10.7	9.3	9.3	10.3	9.9	9.6	10.4	10.5	10.1
65-74 years	19.3	22.1	13.4	13.3	12.6	12.6	13.0	14.3	14.4	13.7	14.5	15.3
75-84 years	23.8	28.1	19.0	18.0	17.3	17.9	20.6	19.9	20.5	22.0	22.8	22.4
85 years and over	22.2	18.1	15.3	14.7	13.9	14.0	13.8	15.1	14.7	15.9	17.7	17.3
BLACK FEMALE												
All ages, age adjusted	10.0	13.8	8.4	7.7	7.5	7.5	7.6	8.2	8.5	8.7	9.2	9.1
All ages, crude	9.7	13.4	8.3	7.7	7.6	7.6	7.8	8.3	8.5	8.8	9.3	9.3
55-64 years	14.0	17.0	9.3	9.3	7.9	8.1	8.5	9.5	10.9	8.8	9.7	9.6
65-74 years	14.2	16.3	8.5	10.2	9.1	9.6	9.7	9.6	9.7	11.8	9.6	12.5

[Continued]

★ 110 ★

Death Rates: Motor Vehicle Accidents, According to Sex, Race, and Age: United States, Selected Years 1960-89

[Continued]

Sex, race, and age	1960[1]	1970	1980	1981	1982	1983	1984	1985	1986	1987	1988	1989
75-84 years	8.8	14.4	11.1	11.8	8.5	15.1	13.7	15.0	10.0	10.9	14.1	13.6
85 years and over	21.1	15.4	12.3	6.3	9.6	7.8	9.8	9.4	11.0	7.2	10.8	6.1

Source: U.S. Department of Commerce, Economics and Statistics Administration, *National Economic, Social, and Environmental Data Bank, CD-ROM,* November 1992. Primary source: National Center for Health Statistics: *Vital Statistics of the United States, Vol. II, Mortality, Part A, 1950-89.* Public Health Service. Washington. U.S. Government Printing Office; Data computed by the Division of Analysis from data compiled by the Division of Vital Statistics and from table 1 in the original source. *Notes:* For data years shown, the code numbers for cause of death are based on the then current International Classification of Diseases, which is described in the original source. 1. Includes deaths of nonresidents of the United States.

★ 111 ★

Mortality

Death Rates: Pneumonia and Influenza, 1980-86

Data are based on the National Vital Statistics System.

[Number of deaths per 100,000 resident population]

Sex, race, and age	1980	1982	1984	1986
Male, all races[1]				
55-59 years	19.5	17.9	17.4	17.8
60-64 years	32.8	28.1	30.6	33.5
65-69 years	58.4	49.0	50.9	56.8
70-74 years	107.4	95.0	109.6	115.0
75-79 years	216.3	195.1	222.8	250.3
80-84 years	465.7	401.4	461.4	512.8
65 years and over	212.5	189.0	214.9	241.4
75 years and over	466.3	412.1	471.7	534.2
85 years and over	1,145.4	1,018.4	1,172.1	1,360.9
White male				
55-59 years	16.4	15.4	15.0	15.4
60-64 years	29.2	24.9	27.3	30.5
65-69 years	53.3	46.4	47.6	53.5
70-74 years	104.4	90.9	105.9	111.6
75-79 years	212.2	197.7	220.7	249.4
80-84 years	471.8	409.2	464.7	514.7
65 years and over	212.4	190.7	215.9	242.3
75 years and over	472.4	422.9	479.8	541.5
85 years and over	1,172.7	1,051.6	1,215.3	1,402.7
Black male				
55-59 years	53.9	44.3	41.6	42.7
60-64 years	74.4	63.6	63.5	67.3
65-69 years	112.8	79.3	86.4	98.1
70-74 years	144.5	143.2	154.9	163.5

[Continued]

★ 111 ★

Death Rates: Pneumonia and Influenza, 1980-86
[Continued]

Sex, race, and age	1980	1982	1984	1986
75-79 years	249.8	173.9	255.4	272.7
80-84 years	399.8	341.2	425.3	511.6
65 years and over	215.7	176.9	211.5	245.4
75 years and over	396.8	307.9	398.1	476.6
85 years and over	816.8	642.9	742.9	967.2
Female, all races[1]				
55-59 years	10.2	8.3	8.1	9.4
60-64 years	15.0	13.5	13.3	15.7
65-69 years	26.9	21.6	24.2	27.9
70-74 years	51.0	42.7	50.3	55.3
75-79 years	111.0	87.6	106.8	123.0
80-84 years	260.5	203.8	248.4	276.3
65 years and over	154.9	128.7	158.9	186.0
75 years and over	316.1	257.7	317.6	370.1
85 years and over	772.2	633.7	766.6	902.3
White female				
55-59 years	8.9	7.1	7.3	8.6
60-64 years	14.4	12.6	12.6	14.3
65-69 years	25.5	20.8	23.0	26.6
70-74 years	49.5	41.9	49.2	54.6
75-79 years	109.9	88.3	107.4	123.3
80-84 years	264.7	206.9	249.8	278.4
65 years and over	158.9	132.7	163.5	191.8
75 years and over	324.2	265.5	326.4	380.5
85 years and over	796.7	654.6	793.1	933.7
Black female				
55-59 years	24.1	18.5	15.6	17.1
60-64 years	22.2	22.3	21.2	31.0
65-69 years	41.7	29.6	37.0	41.5
70-74 years	66.1	51.9	63.6	66.9
75-79 years	121.3	81.9	107.6	128.9
80-84 years	215.7	172.6	237.2	269.3
65 years and over	116.4	91.6	117.8	140.0
75 years and over	223.5	172.0	224.2	270.3
85 years and over	459.2	370.4	440.6	541.4

Source: *Health Data on Older Americans: United States, 1992,* Centers for Disease Control and Prevention/National Center for Health Statistics, Vital and Health Statistics, Series 3: Analytic and Epidemiological Studies, No. 27, pp. 103-104. Primary source: National Center for Health Statistics. *Vital Statistics of the United States, vol. II, Mortality, Part A,* Washington: Public Health Service, selected years. *Notes:* Pneumonia and influenza comprise codes 480-487 of the *International Classification of Diseases, Ninth Revision.* 1. Includes races other than White and Black.

★ 112 ★
Mortality

Change in the Death Rate for Cerebrovascular Disease, 1960-86

Comparison of age-adjusted death rates per 100,000 for cerebrovascular disease for persons 65 years of age and over: 1960-86.

Sex and race	1960	1986	Percent change
Both sexes and all races	857.1	332.3	-61.2
White male	900.6	345.7	-61.6
Black male	1,117.5	498.0	-55.4
White female	789.4	304.7	-61.4
Black female	1,048.3	430.2	-59.0

Source: Health Data on Older Americans: United States, 1992, Centers for Disease Control and Prevention/National Center for Health Statistics, Vital and Health Statistics, Series 3: Analytic and Epidemiological Studies, No. 27, p. 84. *Notes:* Adjusted to the 1940 population distribution. For cerebrovascular disease the comparability ratio for seventh to eighth revisions = 0.9905 and for eighth to ninth revisions = 1.0049.

★ 113 ★
Mortality

Change in the Death Rate for Heart Disease, 1960-86

Comparison of age-adjusted death rates per 100,000 for diseases of the heart for persons 65 years of age and over: 1960-86.

Sex and race	1960	1986	Percent change
Both sexes and all races	2,640.2	1,693.9	-35.8
White male	3,257.0	2,207.9	-32.2
Black male	2,749.5	2,297.0	-16.5
White female	2,161.5	1,325.1	-38.7
Black female	2,155.8	1,677.3	-22.2

Source: Health Data on Older Americans: United States, 1992, Centers for Disease Control and Prevention/National Center for Health Statistics, Vital and Health Statistics, Series 3: Analytic and Epidemiological Studies, No. 27, p. 82. *Notes:* Adjusted to the 1940 population distribution. For diseases of the heart the comparability ratio for seventh to eighth revisions = 1.0045 and for eighth to ninth revisions = 1.0126.

★ 114 ★

Mortality

Change in the Death Rate for Respiratory Cancer, 1960-86

Comparison of age-adjusted death rates per 100,000 for respiratory cancer for persons 65 years of age and over: 1960-86.

Sex and race	1960	1986	Percent change
Both sexes and all races	112.2	277.7	+147.7
White male	213.0	458.1	+115.1
Black male	167.0	555.0	+232.3
White female	29.8	152.6	+412.3
Black female	24.7	127.9	+418.4

Source: Health Data on Older Americans: United States, 1992, Centers for Disease Control and Prevention/National Center for Health Statistics, Vital and Health Statistics, Series 3: Analytic and Epidemiological Studies, No. 27, p. 84. *Notes:* Adjusted to the 1940 population distribution. For respiratory cancer the comparability ratio for seventh to eighth revisions = 1.0316 and for eighth to ninth revisions = 1.0007.

★ 115 ★

Mortality

Military Mortality Experience: Enlisted Personnel

Mortality rates are shown for persons covered by Servicemen's Group Life Insurance (SGLI), which, by law, provides insurance to members on active duty in the uniformed services listed in this table. Data shown for three calendar years, 1989-91.

[Annual death rate per 1,000.]

Age group	Total	Accidental	No. of deaths
Total, all Services			
17-19	0.78	0.70	450
20-24	0.82	0.74	1,700
25-29	0.55	0.46	717
30-34	0.58	0.40	483
35-39	0.58	0.34	318
40-44	0.90	0.35	199
45-49	1.36	0.47	64
50 and over	7.09	1.15	43
Total, all ages	0.71	0.56	3,974
Army			
17-19	0.77	0.67	163
20-24	0.90	0.82	668
25-29	0.65	0.53	286
30-34	0.64	0.42	183

[Continued]

★ 115 ★

Military Mortality Experience: Enlisted Personnel
[Continued]

Age group	Total	Accidental	No. of deaths
35-39	0.71	0.42	132
40-44	0.97	0.41	73
45-49	1.34	0.33	24
50 and over	10.85	1.61	27
Total, all ages	0.79	0.62	1,556
Navy			
17-19	0.85	0.78	162
20-24	0.84	0.75	535
25-29	0.56	0.46	207
30-34	0.60	0.43	140
35-39	0.53	0.30	80
40-44	1.04	0.36	64
45-49	1.33	0.28	19
50 and over	2.89	0.83	7
Total, all ages	0.73	0.58	1,214
Air Force			
17-19	0.52	0.43	44
20-24	0.48	0.44	207
25-29	0.39	0.34	150
30-34	0.52	0.35	130
35-39	0.49	0.29	91
40-44	0.67	0.23	49
45-49	1.54	0.81	19
50 and over	10.59	1.18	9
Total, all ages	0.49	0.37	699
Marine Corps			
17-19	0.90	0.86	81
20-24	1.06	0.97	290
25-29	0.71	0.60	74
30-34	0.53	0.43	30
35-39	0.49	0.30	15
40-44	1.18	0.63	13
45-49	0.83	0.83	2
50 and over	0.00	0.00	0
Total, all ages	0.89	0.79	505

Source: Veterans Benefits Administration, Department of Veterans Affairs, *Servicemen's and Veterans' Group Life Insurance Programs: Twenty-Seventh Annual Report, Year Ending June 30, 1992,* pp. 14-15. *Note:* All exposure and deaths for post-separation period excluded.

★ 116 ★
Mortality

Military Mortality Experience: Officers and Warrant Officers

Mortality rates are shown for persons covered by Servicemen's Group Life Insurance (SGLI), which, by law, provides insurance to members on active duty in the uniformed services listed in this table. Data shown for three calendar years, 1989-91.

[Annual death rate per 1,000 population]

Age group	Total	Accidental	No. of deaths
Total, all Services			
17-19	0.00	0.00	0
20-24	0.80	0.68	69
25-29	0.72	0.67	169
30-34	0.52	0.43	110
35-39	0.51	0.38	95
40-44	0.56	0.34	85
45-49	0.93	0.24	55
50 and over	1.76	0.39	36
Total, all ages	0.65	0.47	619
Army			
17-19	0.00	0.00	0
20-24	0.80	0.70	24
25-29	0.66	0.57	51
30-34	0.44	0.32	33
35-39	0.46	0.36	29
40-44	0.75	0.43	38
45-49	1.28	0.35	26
50 and over	1.83	0.39	14
Total, all ages	0.66	0.44	215
Navy			
17-19	0.00	0.00	0
20-24	1.08	0.81	28
25-29	0.86	0.81	52
30-34	0.66	0.48	32
35-39	0.49	0.36	22
40-44	0.53	0.39	19
45-49	0.85	0.13	13
50 and over	2.55	0.48	16
Total, all ages	0.77	0.54	182
Air Force			
17-19	0.00	0.00	0
20-24	0.48	0.48	11
25-29	0.48	0.47	38
30-34	0.47	0.45	35
35-39	0.57	0.39	37
40-44	0.43	0.23	24
45-49	0.67	0.19	14
50 and over	0.86	0.17	5
Total, all ages	0.51	0.38	164

[Continued]

★116★

Military Mortality Experience: Officers and Warrant Officers
[Continued]

Age group	Total	Accidental	No. of deaths
Marine Corps			
17-19	0.00	0.00	0
20-24	0.84	0.84	6
25-29	1.58	1.52	28
30-34	0.68	0.68	10
35-39	0.58	0.50	7
40-44	0.46	0.23	4
45-49	0.73	0.36	2
50 and over	1.36	1.36	1
Total, all ages	0.91	0.83	58

Source: Veterans Benefits Administration, Department of Veterans Affairs, *Servicemen's and Veterans' Group Life Insurance Programs: Twenty-Seventh Annual Report, Year Ending June 30, 1992*, pp. 12-13. *Note:* All exposure and deaths for post-separation period excluded.

★117★
Mortality

Military Mortality Experience: Service Personnel

Mortality rates are shown for persons covered by Servicemen's Group Life Insurance (SGLI), which, by law, provides insurance to members on active duty in the uniformed services listed in this table. Data shown for three calendar years, 1989-91.

[Annual death rate per 1,000 population]

Age group	Total	Accidental	No. of deaths
Total, all Services			
17-19	0.79	0.71	457
20-24	0.82	0.73	1,790
25-29	0.58	0.50	906
30-34	0.56	0.40	601
35-39	0.56	0.35	421
40-44	0.76	0.34	291
45-49	1.10	0.34	123
50 and over	2.88	0.60	86
Total, all ages	2.88	0.60	86
Army			
17-19	0.77	0.67	163
20-24	0.90	0.81	692
25-29	0.65	0.54	337
30-34	0.60	0.40	216
35-39	0.65	0.41	161
40-44	0.88	0.42	111
45-49	1.31	0.34	50

[Continued]

★ 117 ★

Military Mortality Experience: Service Personnel
[Continued]

Age group	Total	Accidental	No. of deaths
50 and over	4.04	0.69	41
Total, all ages	0.77	0.60	1,771
Navy			
17-19	0.85	0.78	162
20-24	0.85	0.75	563
25-29	0.60	0.51	259
30-34	0.61	0.44	172
35-39	0.52	0.31	102
40-44	0.85	0.37	83
45-49	1.08	0.20	32
50 and over	2.65	0.58	23
Total, all ages	0.74	0.58	1,396
Coast Guard			
17-19	1.21	1.21	7
20-24	0.72	0.66	21
25-29	0.65	0.62	20
30-34	0.30	0.21	7
35-39	0.41	0.41	6
40-44	0.62	0.25	5
45-49	1.16	0.39	3
50 and over	3.31	0.00	3
Total, all ages	0.63	0.51	72
Public Health and National Oceanic and Atmospheric Administration			
17-19	0.00	0.00	0
20-24	0.00	0.00	0
25-29	0.00	0.00	0
30-34	0.35	0.00	1
35-39	0.49	0.25	2
40-44	0.44	0.22	2
45-49	0.32	0.32	1
50 and over	1.65	1.24	4
Total, all ages	0.54	0.32	10
Air Force			
17-19	0.52	0.43	44
20-24	0.48	0.44	218
25-29	0.41	0.36	188
30-34	0.51	0.37	165
35-39	0.51	0.32	128
40-44	0.57	0.23	73
45-49	0.99	0.42	33
50 and over	2.10	0.30	14
Total, all ages	0.49	0.37	863
Marine Corps			
17-19	0.90	0.86	81

[Continued]

★117★

Military Mortality Experience: Service Personnel
[Continued]

Age group	Total	Accidental	No. of deaths
20-24	1.05	0.96	296
25-29	0.83	0.74	102
30-34	0.56	0.48	40
35-39	0.52	0.35	22
40-44	0.86	0.45	17
45-49	0.78	0.58	4
50 and over	0.95	0.95	1
Total, all ages	0.89	0.79	563

Source: Veterans Benefits Administration, Department of Veterans Affairs, *Servicemen's and Veterans' Group Life Insurance Programs: Twenty-Seventh Annual Report, Year Ending June 30, 1992*, pp. 10-11. *Note:* All exposure and deaths for post-separation period excluded.

★118★

Mortality

Motor Vehicle Accidents

Motor vehicle accidents are the most common cause of accidental death among the 65 to 74 age group, and the second most common cause among older people in general.

People over age 65 make up about 12 percent of the population and suffer 27 percent of all accidental deaths. The National Safety Council reports that each year about 27,000 persons over age 65 die from accidental injuries and thousands of others are severely injured.

Source: U.S. Department of Health and Human Services, National Institute on Aging, *Bound for Good Health: A Collection of Age Pages.*

★ 119 ★

Mortality

Number of Deaths and Fatality Rate of Patients Discharged from Short-Stay Hospitals, by Sex and Age of Patient, 1988

From the source: "In 1988, 96.2 percent of patients (excluding newborn infants) discharged from short-stay hospitals were discharged alive, 3.0 percent were discharged dead, and for 0.7 percent a discharge status was not ascribed. Of the 947,000 patients who died, 50.8 percent were male and 49.2 percent were female. As expected, patients 65 years of age and over accounted for the majority of hospital deaths—73.4 percent."

Age	Number in thousands			Rate per 100 discharges		
	Both sexes	Male	Female	Both sexes	Male	Female
All ages	947	481	466	3.0	3.8	2.5
Under 65 years	252	143	108	1.2	1.7	0.8
Under 15 years	21	12	9[1]	0.8	0.8	0.8[1]
15-44 years	56	37	19	0.5	1.0	0.2
45-64 years	175	95	81	2.7	2.9	2.5
65 years and over	695	338	358	6.9	7.6	6.3

Source: U.S. Department of Health and Human Services, National Center for Health Statistics, *National Hospital Discharge Survey: Annual Summary, 1988*, Series 13, No. 106, p. 17. *Notes:* 1. Figure does not meet standard of reliability or precision (more than 30-percent relative standard error).

★ 120 ★

Mortality

Proportionate Mortality for Coronary Heart Disease (CHD) for Black Males and Females in the U.S., 1980

The Task Force debunked several myths about coronary heart disease and its impact on Blacks. For example, there is a widely held belief that coronary heart disease (CHD) is uncommon among Blacks. However, CHD is the leading cause of death among Black males 65 years of age or older.

Age	Males			Females		
	Deaths all causes	Deaths CHD	Percent CHD	Deaths all causes	Deaths CHD	Percent CHD
65-74	29,095	6,561	22.6	23,728	5,662	23.9
75-84	21,046	5,172	24.6	22,371	6,031	27.0
85+	8,534	2,373	27.8	13,115	3,767	28.7

Source: U.S. Congress, "Profiles in Aging America: Meeting the Health Care Needs of the Nation's Black Elderly," Joint Hearing Before the Special Committee on Aging and the Congressional Black Caucus Health Braintrust, United States Senate, September 28, 1990, 101-29, U.S. Government Printing Office, Washington, D.C., p. 120. Primary source: "Report of the Secretary's Task Force on Black and Minority Health, Volume IV: Cardiovascular and Cerebrovascular Disease, Part I," U.S. Dept. of Health and Human Services, Jan. 1986, p. 98.

★ 121 ★

Mortality

Ratio of Stroke Mortality by Age, 1980: Black and White

If the relative death rate is greater than 1.0, the rate is proportionately greater for Blacks than Whites. A value of 1.0 indicates that the Black death rate is the same as·the White death rate. A value less than 1.0 shows that the death rate for Blacks is less than for Whites.

Age	Black males/ White males	Black females/ White females
25-34	3.5	3.5
35-44	4.5	3.2
45-54	3.8	3.3
55-64	3.0	2.8
65-74	2.0	2.1
75-84	1.1	1.3
85+	0.8	0.8
Total	1.8	1.8

Source: U.S. Congress, "Profiles in Aging America: Meeting the Health Care Needs of the Nation's Black Elderly," Joint Hearing Before the Special Committee on Aging and the Congressional Black Caucus Health Braintrust, United States Senate, September 28, 1990, 101-29, U.S. Government Printing Office, Washington, D.C., p. 118. Primary source: "Report of the Secretary's Task Force on Black and Minority Health, Volume IV: Cardiovascular and Cerebrovascular Disease, Part I," U.S. Dept. of Health and Human Services, January 1986, p. 106.

★ 122 ★

Mortality

Death From Various Causes in Selected Countries

Country	Year[1]	Cause of death			
		Diseases of the heart	Cerebro- vascular disease	Cancer	All other causes
Australia	1983	43.3	14.3	20.8	21.6
Belgium	1984	34.3	13.1	21.8	30.8
Canada	1984	41.6	9.9	23.2	25.3
Denmark	1984	36.6	10.7	23.8	28.9
England and Wales	1983	38.1	13.4	20.2	28.3
Federal Republic of Germany	1984	40.9	15.9	20.6	22.7
France	1983	28.1	13.9	20.2	37.8
Greece	1983	28.2	22.9	16.2	32.7
Hong Kong	1984	19.5	15.4	23.1	42.0
Israel	1983	35.7	13.5	17.1	33.7
Italy	1981	37.6	16.1	19.3	27.0
Japan	1984	24.4	22.1	21.0	32.5

[Continued]

★ 122 ★

Death From Various Causes in Selected Countries
[Continued]

Country	Year[1]	Diseases of the heart	Cerebro-vascular disease	Cancer	All other causes
Netherlands	1984	36.9	11.9	24.9	26.3
Norway	1984	33.3	15.0	20.2	31.5
Sweden	1984	42.2	11.7	19.7	26.4
Switzerland	1984	36.6	12.6	25.0	25.8
United States	1986	41.5	8.7	21.0	28.8

Source: Health Data on Older Americans: United States, 1992, Centers for Disease Control and Prevention/ National Center for Health Statistics, Vital and Health Statistics, Series 3: Analytic and Epidemiological Studies, No. 27, p. 295. Primary source: United Nations: *Demographics Yearbook,* 1985, Pub. No. ST/ ESA/STAT/SER.R/15. New York, 1987; U.S. data from National Center for Health Statistics: Vital statistics of the United States, vol II, mortality, part A. Washington: Public Health Service, 1988. *Note:* 1. Data closest to the 1984 reference period are presented.

Geographical Mobility

★ 123 ★

General Mobility, by Race and Hispanic Origin, Sex, and Age

Mobility data are from March 1989 to March 1990.

[Numbers are shown in thousands]

Characteristic	Total	Same house (non-movers)	Different house in the United States									Movers from abroad
			Total	Same county	Different county							
					Total	Same state	Different state				Different region	
							Total	Same region				
								Total	Same division	Different division		
All races												
Both sexes												
55 to 59 years	10,549	9,678	841	477	364	171	194	108	87	21	86	29
60 to 64 years	10,683	9,941	700	355	345	189	155	70	54	16	85	42
60 and 61 years	4,342	4,064	261	121	139	68	71	33	29	4	38	17
62 to 64 years	6,341	5,877	439	234	205	121	84	37	25	12	47	25
65 to 69 years	10,126	9,543	567	314	253	141	112	71	53	18	42	16
70 to 74 years	7,853	7,519	328	187	141	79	62	31	17	14	30	6
75 to 79 years	5,791	5,455	327	178	149	80	69	44	30	13	25	9
80 to 84 years	3,563	3,346	212	114	97	44	54	32	22	10	21	6
85 years and over	2,233	2,090	137	76	61	39	23	19	19	-	4	6
Median age	33.2	35.7	26.6	26.1	27.3	27.3	27.4	27.3	27.4	27.2	27.4	25.3

[Continued]

★ 123 ★

General Mobility, by Race and Hispanic Origin, Sex, and Age
[Continued]

Characteristic	Total	Same house (non-movers)	Different house in the United States									Movers from abroad
			Total	Same county	Different county							
					Total	Same state	Different state					
							Total	Same region			Different region	
								Total	Same division	Different division		
Male												
55 to 59 years	5,012	4,609	392	226	166	75	92	48	40	8	43	10
60 to 64 years	4,991	4,643	326	171	155	84	70	33	27	5	38	22
60 and 61 years	2,074	1,946	119	55	64	36	28	18	18	-	10	9
62 to 64 years	2,917	2,697	207	116	91	49	42	14	9	5	28	13
65 to 69 years	4,598	4,332	259	137	122	79	43	23	18	5	20	7
70 to 74 years	3,416	3,285	131	76	55	35	20	12	7	6	8	-
75 to 79 years	2,298	2,176	121	69	52	28	24	13	9	4	10	1
80 to 84 years	1,264	1,196	64	37	27	16	11	3	1	2	8	4
85 years and over	758	701	55	26	29	20	9	9	9	-	-	2
Median age	32.3	34.5	26.7	26.3	27.3	27.4	27.1	27.1	26.8	27.6	27.2	25.3
Female												
55 to 59 years	5,537	5,069	449	251	198	96	102	60	47	13	42	19
60 to 64 years	5,692	5,298	374	184	190	105	85	38	27	11	47	20
60 and 61 years	2,268	2,118	142	67	75	32	43	15	10	4	29	7
62 to 64 years	3,424	3,180	232	117	115	73	42	23	16	7	19	12
65 to 69 years	5,529	5,212	308	177	131	61	69	47	35	13	22	9
70 to 74 years	4,437	4,234	197	112	86	44	42	19	11	8	23	6
75 to 79 years	3,492	3,278	206	109	97	52	45	30	21	9	15	8
80 to 84 years	2,299	2,150	147	77	71	28	42	29	21	8	13	2
85 years and over	1,475	1,389	83	50	33	18	14	11	11	-	4	3
Median age	34.2	36.8	26.5	26.0	27.4	27.2	27.6	27.6	28.0	26.9	27.6	25.4
White												
Both sexes												
55 to 59 years	9,173	8,434	718	388	329	155	175	92	71	21	83	21
60 to 64 years	9,404	8,763	605	305	300	167	134	62	48	14	72	37
60 and 61 years	3,780	3,542	224	104	121	60	60	26	23	3	35	14
62 to 64 years	5,624	5,220	381	202	180	106	73	36	25	10	37	22
65 to 69 years	8,959	8,445	500	272	228	124	104	66	49	17	36	14
70 to 74 years	7,090	6,790	297	166	131	75	56	28	17	11	28	3
75 to 79 years	5,221	4,908	304	163	141	79	62	44	30	13	18	9
80 to 84 years	3,220	3,033	184	101	83	37	46	25	15	10	21	3
85 years and over	1,990	1,873	111	62	49	33	17	13	13	-	4	5
Median age	34.1	36.6	26.9	26.4	27.5	27.5	27.5	27.7	27.8	27.6	27.3	25.2
Male												
55 to 59 years	4,404	4,066	331	184	147	66	81	41	33	8	40	7
60 to 64 years	4,426	4,117	290	151	139	75	64	29	24	5	35	19
60 and 61 years	1,835	1,718	111	53	58	34	24	15	15	-	9	7

[Continued]

★ 123 ★

General Mobility, by Race and Hispanic Origin, Sex, and Age

[Continued]

Characteristic	Total	Same house (non-movers)	Different house in the United States									Movers from abroad
			Total	Same county	Different county							
					Total	Same state	Different state					
							Total	Same region			Different region	
								Total	Same division	Different division		
62 to 64 years	2,591	2,399	179	98	81	42	40	14	9	5	25	13
65 to 69 years	4,090	3,862	221	114	107	69	38	22	18	4	16	7
70 to 74 years	3,092	2,974	118	65	53	33	20	12	7	6	8	-
75 to 79 years	2,064	1,950	113	64	49	28	21	13	9	4	8	1
80 to 84 years	1,131	1,075	55	32	23	12	11	3	1	2	8	1
85 years and over	658	618	38	22	17	14	3	3	3	-	-	2
Median age	33.2	35.4	27.0	26.7	27.4	27.6	27.3	27.3	27.2	27.5	27.2	25.0
Female												
55 to 59 years	4,769	4,368	387	205	183	89	94	51	38	13	42	15
60 to 64 years	4,979	4,646	315	155	161	91	69	32	24	8	37	17
60 and 61 years	1,945	1,824	114	51	63	27	36	11	7	3	25	7
62 to 64 years	3,033	2,822	202	104	98	65	33	21	16	5	12	10
65 to 69 years	4,869	4,583	279	158	121	55	66	44	31	13	22	7
70 to 74 years	3,998	3,816	179	101	78	42	36	16	11	5	20	3
75 to 79 years	3,156	2,958	191	99	92	51	41	30	21	9	10	8
80 to 84 years	2,089	1,958	129	69	60	25	35	22	14	8	13	2
85 years and over	1,332	1,255	73	40	33	18	14	11	11	-	4	3
Median age	35.0	37.8	26.8	26.2	27.6	27.4	27.8	28.1	28.3	27.7	27.4	25.3
Black												
Both sexes												
55 to 59 years	1,079	997	83	63	19	8	12	10	10	-	2	-
60 to 64 years	1,027	964	63	29	34	19	15	6	4	2	9	-
60 and 61 years	457	433	24	9	16	8	8	4	4	-	4	-
62 to 64 years	570	531	39	21	18	11	7	2	-	2	5	-
65 to 69 years	896	845	51	35	16	12	4	-	-	-	4	-
70 to 74 years	612	593	19	12	7	3	3	3	-	3	-	-
75 to 79 years	481	467	15	15	-	-	-	-	-	-	-	-
80 to 84 years	293	272	21		11	7	4	4	4	-	-	-
85 years and over	205	179	26	14	12	6	6	6	6	-	-	-
Median age	28.4	30.3	24.7	24.2	25.6	25.3	25.8	25.5	26.0	24.4	26.4	26.9
Male												
55 to 59 years	474	432	42	28	14	6	8	6	6	-	2	-
60 to 64 years	463	438	25	12	13	9	4	1	1	-	3	-
60 and 61 years	193	188	6	2	4	2	2	1	1	-	-	-
62 to 64 years	269	250	19	10	9	6	2	-	-	-	2	-
65 to 69 years	373	343	30	20	10	6	4	-	-	-	4	-
70 to 74 years	253	244	10	8	1	1	-	-	-	-	-	-
75 to 79 years	195	191	4	4	-	-	-	-	-	-	-	-

[Continued]

★ 123 ★

General Mobility, by Race and Hispanic Origin, Sex, and Age
[Continued]

Characteristic	Total	Same house (non-movers)	Different house in the United States										Movers from abroad
			Total	Same county	Different county								
					Total	Same state	Different state					
							Total	Same region			Different region	
								Total	Same division	Different division		
80 to 84 years	107	101	6	2	4	4	-	-	-	-	-	-
85 years and over	75	59	16	4	12	6	6	6	6	-	-	-
Median age	27.0	28.1	24.8	23.9	26.2	26.0	26.4	26.4	26.0	(B)	26.5	(B)
Female												
55 to 59 years	605	565	41	35	6	2	4	4	4	-	-	-
60 to 64 years	564	526	38	17	21	10	11	5	3	2	6	-
60 and 61 years	264	245	19	7	12	6	6	3	3	-	3	-
62 to 64 years	301	281	19	10	9	4	5	2	-	2	3	-
65 to 69 years	523	502	21	15	6	6	-	-	-	-	-	-
70 to 74 years	359	349	9	4	5	2	3	3	-	3	-	-
75 to 79 years	286	276	10	10	-	-	-	-	-	-	-	-
80 to 84 years	185	171	15	8	7	3	4	4	4	-	-	-
85 years and over	130	120	10	10	-	-	-	-	-	-	-	-
Median age	29.7	31.9	24.6	24.5	24.9	24.6	25.2	24.7	25.9	(B)	26.2	(B)
Hispanic[1]												
Both sexes												
55 to 59 years	638	579	54	32	21	20	1	1	1	-	-	5
60 to 64 years	569	511	52	40	13	4	9	3	2	1	6	6
60 and 61 years	244	216	24	20	4	2	2	2	2	-	-	4
62 to 64 years	326	295	28	20	9	2	7	1	-	1	6	2
65 to 69 years	429	403	20	11	10	8	2	2	1	1	-	5
70 to 74 years	284	273	9	5	4	3	2	-	-	-	2	3
75 to 79 years	162	151	10	6	4	3	1	1	1	-	-	1
80 to 84 years	92	88	2	2	1	-	-	-	-	-	-	1
85 years and over	56	55	2	2	-	-	-	-	-	-	-	-
Median age	26.6	28.2	23.9	23.6	24.8	25.5	23.9	23.6	24.3	22.4	24.4	23.4
Male												
55 to 59 years	289	263	24	15	9	8	1	-	-	-	-	2
60 to 64 years	248	222	22	18	4	2	2	2	2	-	-	4
60 and 61 years	117	99	16	14	2	-	2	2	2	-	-	2
62 to 64 years	131	122	7	5	2	2	-	-	-	-	-	2
65 to 69 years	215	203	10	5	5	4	1	1	-	1	-	2
70 to 74 years	125	123	2	-	2	1	1	-	-	-	1	-
75 to 79 years	66	62	3	2	1	1	-	-	-	-	-	1
80 to 84 years	35	33	-	-	-	-	-	-	-	-	-	1
85 years and over	26	26	-	-	-	-	-	-	-	-	-	-
Median age	26.0	27.2	24.2	24.0	24.9	25.7	23.7	23.6	23.9	(B)	23.9	(B)

[Continued]

★ 123 ★

General Mobility, by Race and Hispanic Origin, Sex, and Age

[Continued]

Characteristic	Total	Same house (non-movers)	Different house in the United States										Movers from abroad
			Total	Same county	Different county								
					Total	Same state	Different state					
							Total	Same region			Different region	
								Total	Same division	Different division		
Female													
55 to 59 years	348	316	30	17	12	12	-	-	-	-	-	-	3
60 to 64 years	322	289	30	21	9	2	7	1	-	1	6		2
60 and 61 years	127	116	8	6	2	2	-	-	-	-	-		2
62 to 64 years	195	173	22	15	7	-	7	1	-	1	6		-
65 to 69 years	214	201	10	5	5	4	1	1	1	-	-		3
70 to 74 years	159	149	7	5	3	2	1	-	-	-	1		3
75 to 79 years	96	89	7	4	3	3	1	1	1	-	-		-
80 to 84 years	57	55	2	2	1	-	-	-	-	-	-		-
85 years and over	30	28	2	2	-	-	-	-	-	-	-		-
Median age	27.3	29.3	23.5	23.1	24.6	25.1	24.1	23.6	(B)	(B)	24.9		(B)

Source: U.S. Department of Commerce, Bureau of the Census, *Geographical Mobility: March 1987 to March 1990,* Current Population Reports, Population Characteristics, Series P-20, No. 456, pp. 15-18. *Notes:* (B) stands for "Base population is less than 75,000". 1. Persons of Hispanic origin may be of any race.

★ 124 ★

Geographical Mobility

General Mobility, by Race and Hispanic Origin, Age, and Years of School Completed

Mobility data are from March 1989 to March 1990.

[Numbers are shown in thousands]

Characteristic	Total	Same house (non-movers)	Different house in the United States										Movers from abroad
			Total	Same county	Different county								
					Total	Same state	Different state					
							Total	Same region			Different region	
								Total	Same division	Different division		
All races													
Persons 65 years and over	29,566	27,953	1,571	870	701	382	319	197	142	55	122		42
Elementary: 0 to 8 years	8,432	7,983	430	260	169	98	71	49	33	15	22		19
High school: 1 to 3 years	4,758	4,471	286	160	127	77	50	36	26	10	14		1
4 years	9,717	9,218	486	246	240	128	112	69	49	20	43		13
College: 1 to 3 years	3,232	3,038	189	102	87	52	35	27	20	7	8		4
4 years	1,964	1,863	100	55	45	17	28	9	6	3	19		-
5 or more years	1,464	1,380	80	46	34	10	24	8	8	-	16		5
Median years of school completed	12.2	12.2	12.1	12.1	12.2	12.1	12.4	12.2	12.3	(B)	12.6		(B)
White													
Persons 65 years and over	26,479	25,049	1,396	764	633	348	284	176	125	51	109		33
Elementary: 0 to 8 years	6,810	6,450	342	200	142	78	64	45	33	12	19		17
High school: 1 to 3 years	4,239	3,987	251	138	113	68	45	32	22	10	13		1
4 years	9,114	8,652	455	230	226	126	100	61	41	20	39		7

[Continued]

★ 124 ★

General Mobility, by Race and Hispanic Origin, Age, and Years of School Completed
[Continued]

Characteristic	Total	Same house (non-movers)	Different house in the United States										Movers from abroad
			Total	Same county	Different county								
					Total	Same state	Different state					Different region	
							Total	Same region					
								Total	Same division	Different division			
College: 1 to 3 years	3,052	2,870	178	95	83	51	32	24	18	6	8	4
4 years	1,860	1,770	90	55	35	15	20	5	3	3	15	-
5 or more years	1,404	1,320	80	46	34	10	24	8	8	-	16	5
Median years of school completed	12.2	12.2	12.2	12.2	12.3	12.2	12.3	12.2	12.2	(B)	12.6	(B)
Black												
Persons 65 years and over	2,467	2,356	131	86	45	28	17	13	10	3	4	-
Elementary: 0 to 8 years	1,369	1,291	78	56	22	19	3	3	-	3	-	-
High school: 1 to 3 years	450	427	22	11	12	8	4	4	4	-	-	-
4 years	448	425	22	12	10	-	10	6	6	-	4	-
College: 1 to 3 years	131	124	7	7	-	-	-	-	-	-	-	-
4 years	50	48	2	-	2	2	-	-	-	-	-	-
5 or more years	40	40	-	-	-	-	-	-	-	-	-	-
Median years of school completed	8.6	8.7	8.0	7.6	(B)	(B)	(B)	(B)	(B)	(B)	(B)	(B)
Hispanic[1]												
Persons 65 years and over	1,024	971	43	25	19	14	5	3	2	1	2	10
Elementary: 0 to 8 years	642	609	28	20	8	7	1	-	-	-	1	5
High school: 1 to 3 years	105	102	3	-	3	3	-	-	-	-	-	-
4 years	160	151	9	2	6	4	2	1	1	-	1	1
College: 1 to 3 years	52	47	1	-	1	-	1	1	1	-	-	4
4 years	29	29	1	-	1	1	-	-	-	-	-	-
5 or more years	35	33	2	2	-	-	-	-	-	-	-	-
Median years of school completed	7.9	7.9	(B)	(B)	(B)	(B)	(B)	(B)	(B)	(B)	(B)	(B)

Source: U.S. Department of Commerce, Bureau of the Census, *Geographical Mobility: March 1987 to March 1990*, Current Population Reports, Population Characteristics, Series P-20, No. 456, pp. 21-23. *Notes:* 1. Persons of Hispanic origin may be of any race. B= Base population is less than 75,000.

★ 125 ★
Geographical Mobility

Age of Persons, by Mobility Status and Type of Move: 1989-1990
[Number of persons]

Age	Total 1 year and older	Different house in the United States						Movers from abroad
		Total movers	Total	Local movement (same county)	Long-distance (different county)			
					Total	Same state	Different state	
Number								
All persons	242,208	43,381	41,821	25,726	16,094	8,061	8,033	1,560
Age								
1-4 years	14,948	3,553	3,474	2,275	1,199	555	644	79
5-9 years	18,300	3,480	3,373	2,238	1,135	545	590	107
10-14 years	17,168	2,559	2,452	1,559	892	398	494	107
15-19 years	17,266	3,068	2,874	1,789	1,085	557	528	194

[Continued]

★ 125 ★

Age of Persons, by Mobility Status and Type of Move: 1989-1990
[Continued]

| Age | Total 1 year and older | Different house in the United States | | | | | | |
| | | Total movers | Total | Local movement (same county) | Long-distance (different county) | | | |
					Total	Same state	Different state	Movers from abroad
20-24 years	17,988	6,810	6,532	4,046	2,486	1,340	1,146	278
25-29 years	21,200	7,080	6,861	4,172	2,689	1,386	1,303	219
30-34 years	22,040	5,116	4,953	3,023	1,929	931	999	163
35-39 years	19,891	3,572	3,433	2,077	1,355	621	734	139
40-44 years	17,304	2,421	2,342	1,406	936	466	470	79
45-49 years	13,860	1,456	1,408	813	595	339	256	48
50-54 years	11,444	1,041	1,008	625	383	182	201	33
55-59 years	10,549	870	841	477	364	171	194	29
60-64 years	10,683	742	700	355	345	189	155	42
65-69 years	10,126	583	567	314	253	141	112	16
70-74 years	7,853	334	328	187	141	79	62	6
75-79 years	5,791	336	327	178	149	80	69	9
80-84 years	3,563	218	212	114	97	44	54	6
85 years and over	2,233	143	137	76	61	39	23	6
Median age	33.2	26.5	26.6	26.1	27.3	27.3	27.4	25.3

Source: U.S. Department of Commerce, Bureau of the Census, *Geographical Mobility: March 1987 to March 1990*, Current Population Reports, Population Characteristics, Series P-20, No. 456, p. 8.

★ 126 ★

Geographical Mobility

Age Distribution of Persons, by Mobility Status and Type of Move: 1989-1990
[In percent]

| Age | Total 1 year and older | Different house in the United States | | | | | | |
| | | Total movers | Total | Local movement (same county) | Long-distance (different county) | | | |
					Total	Same state	Different state	Movers from abroad
Percent								
All persons	100.0	17.9	17.3	10.6	6.6	3.3	3.3	0.6
Age:								
1-4 years	100.0	23.8	23.2	15.2	8.0	3.7	4.3	0.5
5-9 years	100.0	19.0	18.4	12.2	6.2	3.0	3.2	0.6
10-14 years	100.0	14.9	14.3	9.1	5.2	2.3	2.9	0.6
15-19 years	100.0	17.8	16.6	10.4	6.3	3.2	3.1	1.1
20-24 years	100.0	37.9	36.3	22.5	13.8	7.4	6.4	1.5
25-29 years	100.0	33.4	32.4	19.7	12.7	6.5	6.1	1.0
30-34 years	100.0	23.2	22.5	13.7	8.8	4.2	4.5	0.7

[Continued]

★ 126 ★

Age Distribution of Persons, by Mobility Status and Type of Move: 1989-1990

[Continued]

| Age | Total 1 year and older | Different house in the United States | | | | | | |
| | | Total movers | Total | Local movement (same county) | Long-distance (different county) | | | |
					Total	Same state	Different state	Movers from abroad
35-39 years	100.0	18.0	17.3	10.4	6.8	3.1	3.7	0.7
40-44 years	100.0	14.0	13.5	8.1	5.4	2.7	2.7	0.5
45-49 years	100.0	10.5	10.2	5.9	4.3	2.4	1.8	0.3
50-54 years	100.0	9.1	8.8	5.5	3.3	1.6	1.8	0.3
55-59 years	100.0	8.2	8.0	4.5	3.5	1.6	1.8	0.3
60-64 years	100.0	6.9	6.6	3.3	3.2	1.8	1.5	0.4
65-69 years	100.0	5.8	5.6	3.1	2.5	1.4	1.1	0.2
70-74 years	100.0	4.3	4.2	2.4	1.8	1.0	0.8	0.1
75-79 years	100.0	5.8	5.6	3.1	2.6	1.4	1.2	0.2
80-84 years	100.0	6.1	6.0	3.2	2.7	1.2	1.5	0.2
85 years and older	100.0	6.4	6.1	3.4	2.7	1.7	1.0	0.3

Source: U.S. Department of Commerce, Bureau of the Census, Geographical Mobility: March 1987 to March 1990, Current Population Reports, Population Characteristics, Series P-20, No. 456, p. 9.

Chapter 3
EDUCATION

The educational attainment of older Americans is profiled in this chapter in the section on Attainment. The second part of the chapter, headed Characteristics by Attainment, provides information on household characteristics as these relate to educational attainment of the household members.

The second section, Characteristics by Attainment, provides economic and housing information. These subjects are covered much more extensively in the chapters on *Income, Assets, and Spending* and *Housing*.

Attainment

★ 127 ★

Educational Attainment for People Aged 25+ and 65+, 1950-1989

Data exclude people in institutions.

Year and age group	Median years of school	Percent with...	
		High school education	Four or more years of college
1989			
25+ years	12.7	76.9	21.1
65+ years	12.1	54.9	11.1
1980			
25+ years	12.5	66.5	16.2
65+ years	10.0	38.8	8.2
1970			
25+ years	12.1	52.3	10.7
65+ years	8.7	27.1	5.5

[Continued]

★ 127 ★

Educational Attainment for People Aged 25+ and 65+, 1950-1989

[Continued]

Year and age group	Median years of school	Percent with...	
		High school education	Four or more years of college
1960			
25+ years	10.5	41.1	7.7
65+ years	8.3	19.1	3.7
1950			
25+ years	9.3	33.4	6.0
65+ years	8.3	17.0	3.4

Source: Aging America, Trends and Projections, prepared by the U.S. Senate Special Committee on Aging, the American Association of Retired Persons, the Federal Council on the Aging, and the U.S. Administration on Aging, 1991, Washington, D.C., p. 189. Primary source: U.S. Bureau of the Census. Unpublished data from the March 1989 Current Population Survey; "Detailed Population Characteristics," 1980 Census of Population, PC80-1-D1, United States Summary, March 1984; "Detailed Characteristics," 1970 Census of Population PC(1)- D1, United States Summary, February 1973; "Characteristics of the Population," 1960 Census of Population, Vol. 1, Part 1, United States Summary, Chapter D, 1964.

★ 128 ★

Attainment

Educational Attainment by Age, 1990

From the source: "Data for this study are from the interview component of the 1990 Consumer Expenditure Survey (CE), conducted by the Bureau of the Census for the Bureau of Labor Statistics. The CE is an ongoing survey that collects data on household expenditures, income, and major socioeconomic and demographic characteristics."

[Data are shown in percent]

Level attained	<65 years	65 years or older
8th grade or less	6	29
Some high school	11	19
High school graduate	31	27
Any college	52	25

Source: Family Economics Review, 1992, Vol. 5, No. 4, p. 3. Primary source: 1990 Consumer Expenditure Survey, interview component, Bureau of the Census, Bureau of Labor Statistics.

★ 129 ★

Attainment

Educational Attainment, by Age Group, Sex, Race, and Hispanic Origin, March 1989

Data exclude people in institutions.

Measure of educational attainment and age	Sex			Race and Hispanic origin								
	Total	Men	Women	White			Black			Hispanic origin[1]		
				Total	Men	Women	Total	Men	Women	Total	Men	Women
Median years of school completed												
25+	12.7	12.8	12.6	12.7	12.8	12.7	12.4	12.4	12.4	12.0	12.0	12.0
60 to 64	12.4	12.5	12.4	12.5	12.5	12.4	10.7	10.6	10.7	9.3	9.6	8.9
65+	12.1	12.1	12.2	12.2	12.2	12.2	8.5	8.1	8.7	8.0	8.1	8.0
65 to 69	12.3	12.3	12.3	12.4	12.4	12.4	9.5	9.1	9.8	8.4	8.5	8.3
70 to 74	12.2	12.2	12.2	12.3	12.3	12.3	8.4	8.2	8.6	8.0	8.1	7.9
75+	10.9	10.5	11.3	11.6	11.1	11.9	7.8	7.0	8.2	7.1	7.0	7.1
Percent with a high school education												
25+	77	77	77	78	79	78	65	64	65	51	51	51
60 to 64	66	65	67	69	68	71	39	43	37	34	37	31
65+	55	54	56	58	57	59	25	22	26	28	26	29
65 to 69	63	61	65	67	65	68	31	28	33	33	31	35
70 to 74	57	56	58	60	59	62	21	20	22	25	21	29
75+	46	44	48	49	47	50	21	18	23	23	21	24
Percent with four or more years of college												
25+	21	25	18	22	25	19	12	12	12	10	11	9
60 to 64	14	19	10	15	21	10	5	7	4	6	5	7
65+	11	14	9	12	15	10	5	4	5	6	7	5
65 to 69	13	16	10	13	17	10	5	3	6	9	9	9
70 to 74	11	13	9	11	13	10	3	3	3	3	3	3
75+	10	12	9	11	13	9	6	4	6	4	7	3

Source: Aging America, Trends and Projections, prepared by the U.S. Senate Special Committee on Aging, the American Association of Retired Persons, the Federal Council on the Aging, and the U.S. Administration on Aging, 1991, Washington, D.C., p. 192. Primary source: U.S. Bureau of the Census. Unpublished data from the March 1989, *Current Population Survey. Note:* 1. People of Hispanic origin may be of any race.

★ 130 ★

Attainment

Years of School Completed, by Poverty Status and Selected Characteristics, 1991

[Numbers in thousands]

Characteristic	All races			White			Black			Hispanic origin[1]		
	Total	Below poverty		Total	Below poverty		Total	Below poverty		Total	Below poverty	
		No.	% of total		No.	% of total		No.	% of total		No.	% of total
ALL EDUCATION LEVELS												
Both sexes												
Total	160,827	17,247	10.7	137,646	12,109	8.8	17,445	4,364	25.0	11,623	2,475	21.3
55 to 64 years	21,150	2,139	10.1	18,280	1,511	8.3	2,166	524	24.2	1,250	228	18.2
65 years and over	30,590	3,781	12.4	27,297	2,802	10.3	2,606	880	33.8	1,143	237	20.8
65 to 74 years	18,441	1,961	10.6	16,315	1,345	8.2	1,665	547	32.9	732	137	18.8
75 years and over	12,149	1,820	15.0	10,983	1,457	13.3	941	333	35.3	411	100	24.3
Male												
Total	76,579	6,244	8.2	66,063	4,491	6.8	7,803	1,421	18.2	5,744	996	17.3
55 to 64 years	10,036	793	7.9	8,731	564	6.5	978	182	18.6	597	102	17.1
65 years and over	12,800	1,015	7.9	11,431	693	6.1	1,058	271	25.6	466	72	15.4
65 to 74 years	8,266	632	7.6	7,323	407	5.6	739	193	26.1	310	42	13.4
75 years and over	4,533	383	8.5	4,108	286	7.0	319	78	24.6	157	30	19.3
Female												
Total	84,248	11,003	13.1	71,583	7,618	10.6	9,641	2,943	30.5	5,878	1,479	25.2
55 to 64 years	11,114	1,346	12.1	9,549	947	9.9	1,188	342	28.7	654	126	19.3
65 years and over	17,790	2,766	15.5	15,866	2,109	13.3	1,549	609	39.3	677	166	24.5
65 to 74 years	10,174	1,329	13.1	8,992	939	10.4	926	355	38.3	422	96	22.7
75 years and over	7,616	1,436	18.9	6,874	1,171	17.0	623	254	40.8	255	70	27.4
NO HIGH SCHOOL DIPLOMA												
Both sexes												
Total	33,110	8,340	25.2	26,337	5,749	21.8	5,642	2,276	40.3	5,510	1,761	32.0
55 to 64 years	5,677	1,230	21.7	4,385	796	18.1	1,075	365	34.0	710	185	26.1
65 years and over	12,328	2,587	21.0	10,182	1,774	17.4	1,842	750	40.7	850	213	25.0
65 to 74 years	6,449	1,266	19.6	5,174	772	14.9	1,083	449	41.5	531	124	23.3
75 years and over	5,879	1,321	22.5	5,008	1,002	20.0	759	300	39.6	319	89	27.9
Male												
Total	15,547	2,955	19.0	12,498	2,071	16.6	2,574	745	28.9	2,660	697	26.2
55 to 64 years	2,797	474	16.9	2,176	304	14.0	527	141	26.8	328	82	25.0
65 years and over	5,189	740	14.3	4,284	464	10.8	783	240	30.6	335	63	18.8
65 to 74 years	2,991	440	14.7	2,409	248	10.3	509	168	32.9	217	36	16.7
75 years and over	2,198	300	13.6	1,875	216	11.5	274	72	26.3	117	27	22.7
Female												
Total	17,563	5,386	30.7	13,839	3,678	26.6	3,068	1,531	49.9	2,850	1,065	37.4
55 to 64 years	2,880	757	26.3	2,210	491	22.2	548	224	40.9	382	103	27.0
65 years and over	7,138	1,847	25.9	5,898	1,310	22.2	1,060	510	48.1	515	150	29.1
65 to 74 years	3,458	826	23.9	2,764	524	19.0	574	282	49.0	313	87	27.9
75 years and over	3,680	1,021	27.8	3,134	786	25.1	485	229	47.1	202	62	30.9
HIGH SCHOOL DIPLOMA, NO COLLEGE												
Both sexes												
Total	57,860	5,541	9.6	50,045	3,883	7.8	6,220	1,467	23.6	3,176	481	15.2
55 to 64 years	8,031	600	7.5	7,133	474	6.6	666	113	17.0	317	32	10.0
65 years and over	10,367	842	8.1	9,720	707	7.3	441	108	24.5	157	15	9.3

[Continued]

★ 130 ★

Years of School Completed, by Poverty Status and Selected Characteristics, 1991
[Continued]

Characteristic	All races			White			Black			Hispanic origin[1]		
	Total	Below poverty		Total	Below poverty		Total	Below poverty		Total	Below poverty	
		No.	% of total		No.	% of total		No.	% of total		No.	% of total
65 to 74 years	6,852	503	7.3	6,360	398	6.3	346	87	25.1	106	9	8.7
75 years and over	3,515	338	9.6	3,361	310	9.2	95	21	22.4	52	6	(B)
Male												
Total	25,774	1,917	7.4	22,261	1,397	6.3	2,842	460	16.2	1,557	210	13.5
55 to 64 years	3,244	195	6.0	2,889	157	5.4	272	29	10.8	135	14	10.1
65 years and over	3,746	178	4.7	3,516	144	4.1	135	25	18.7	62	6	(B)
65 to 74 years	2,584	131	5.1	2,401	101	4.2	116	24	20.9	42	4	(B)
75 years and over	1,161	47	4.0	1,115	43	3.9	19	1	(B)	20	2	(B)
Female												
Total	32,086	3,624	11.3	27,784	2,486	8.9	3,379	1,007	29.8	1,618	271	16.8
55 to 64 years	4,786	405	8.5	4,244	317	7.5	394	84	21.3	182	18	9.9
65 years and over	6,622	664	10.0	6,205	563	9.1	306	83	27.1	95	9	9.5
65 to 74 years	4,268	373	8.7	3,959	297	7.5	230	63	27.2	63	5	(B)
75 years and over	2,354	291	12.4	2,246	266	11.9	76	20	26.6	32	4	(B)
BACHELOR'S DEGREE OR MORE												
Both sexes												
Total	34,337	1,058	3.1	30,352	790	2.6	2,080	109	5.2	1,084	68	6.3
55 to 64 years	3,741	103	2.8	3,404	84	2.5	173	6	3.3	101	4	3.5
65 years and over	3,591	137	3.8	3,365	123	3.7	143	10	7.0	67	5	(B)
65 to 74 years	2,356	70	3.0	2,204	66	3.0	90	3	3.7	43	1	(B)
75 years and over	1,235	67	5.5	1,161	57	4.9	53	7	(B)	23	4	(B)
Male												
Total	18,628	531	2.9	16,651	379	2.3	926	59	6.3	583	27	4.7
55 to 64 years	2,262	49	2.1	2,078	40	1.9	80	1	1.7	68	2	(B)
65 years and over	2,048	51	2.5	1,943	43	2.2	52	5	(B)	40	1	(B)
65 to 74 years	1,464	27	1.9	1,387	27	2.0	39	-	(B)	12	1	(B)
75 years and over	584	24	4.1	556	15	2.8	14	5	(B)	12	1	(B)
Female												
Total	15,709	526	3.4	13,701	411	3.0	1,154	50	4.3	500	41	8.2
55 to 64 years	1,479	54	3.7	1,327	44	3.3	93	4	4.8	33	2	(B)
65 years and over	1,543	86	5.6	1,422	81	5.7	91	5	6.0	27	4	(B)
65 to 74 years	892	43	4.8	818	39	4.8	51	3	(B)	15	1	(B)
75 years and over	651	44	6.7	604	41	6.9	39	2	(B)	11	3	(B)

Source: Poverty in the United States: 1991, Current Population Reports, Series P-60, No. 181, U.S. Department of Commerce, Bureau of the Census, August 1992, pp. 70-72. *Notes:* A (B) stands for base is less than 75,000 and is too small to show derived measures; or not applicable. A dash (-) represents zero or rounds to zero. 1. Persons of Hispanic origin may be of any race.

★ 131 ★

Attainment

Years of School Completed, by Age: 1991

[For persons, 25 years old and over. As of March]

Age	Population (1,000)	Percent of population with:		
		4 years of high school or more	1 or more years of college	4 or more years of college
Total persons	158,694	78.4	39.8	21.4
25 to 34 years old	42,905	86.1	45.3	23.7
35 to 44 years old	38,665	87.7	50.2	27.5
45 to 54 years old	25,686	81.2	41.1	23.2
55 to 64 years old	21,346	71.9	31.4	16.9
65 to 74 years old	18,237	63.5	25.3	13.2
75 years old or over	11,855	49.0	20.8	10.5

Source: U.S. Bureau of the Census, *Statistical Abstract of the United States: 1992* (112th edition.) Washington, DC, 1992, p. 144. Primary source: U.S. Bureau of the Census, Current *Population Reports*, series P-20, No. 462.

★ 132 ★

Attainment

Secondary School Completion

From the source: "Throughout the world, average levels of educational attainment for the elderly populations are well below those of younger populations. Differences at the primary level, however, are narrowing with time." Data show percentage of persons in each age cohort who have completed secondary school.

Country	Male		Female	
	25-44 years	65+ years	25-44 years	65+ years
United States, 1991	86.5	57.0	87.3	58.4
Canada, 1986	72.2	32.2	69.5	31.9
Denmark, 1983	62.7	43.2	54.0	27.0
Mexico, 1990	23.4	5.6	18.1	3.5
Turkey, 1985	20.4	4.8	9.8	1.6

Source: U.S. Department of Commerce, Economics and Statistics Administration, Bureau of the Census, International Population Reports P95/92-3: *An Aging World II*, by Kevin Kinsella and Cynthia M. Taeuber, February 1993, p. 66. Primary source: U.S. Bureau of the Census, Center for International Research, International Data Base on Aging.

★ 133 ★

Attainment

Highest Degree Earned, by Age: 1987

[In thousands, for persons 18 years old and older]

Age	Total persons	Level of degree								
		Not a high school graduate	High school graduate only	Some college, no degree	Vocational	Associate	Bachelor's	Master's	Professional	Doctorate
All persons	176,405	39,679	64,636	31,045	3,743	7,393	21,018	6,192	1,723	977
18 to 24 years old	26,148	4,203	10,596	8,043	389	928	1,912	77	-	-
25 to 34 years old	42,858	5,032	16,202	8,248	987	2,574	7,623	1,575	499	117
35 to 44 years old	34,352	4,921	12,101	5,931	862	2,208	5,359	2,114	509	347
45 to 54 years old	23,052	5,394	9,048	3,208	478	763	2,508	1,211	232	210
55 to 64 years old	21,726	6,668	8,364	2,690	457	473	1,928	656	285	205
65 years old and over	28,268	13,462	8,324	2,924	571	446	1,687	558	198	98

Source: U.S. Bureau of the Census, *Statistical Abstract of the United States: 1992* (112th edition.) Washington, DC, 1992, p. 145. Primary source: U.S. Bureau of the Census, *Current Population Reports*, series P-70, No. 21. *Note:* (-) A dash indicates less than .05 percent.

★ 134 ★

Attainment

Persons 100 Years and Over, by Age, Sex, Educational Attainment, and Age: 1980

Age	Total	Elementary 0-8	High school		College	
			1-3	4	1-3	4+
Total persons[1]	22,012	13,573	2,434	3,456	1,319	1,230
100-104	18,015	11,291	1,941	2,762	993	1,028
105-109	3,158	1,775	393	543	254	193
110+	839	507	100	151	72	9
Total male	6,367	4,416	548	677	370	356
100-104	4,934	3,563	404	435	238	294
105-109	1,095	643	104	199	90	59
110+	338	210	40	43	42	3
Total female	15,645	9,157	1,886	2,779	949	874
100-104	13,081	7,728	1,537	2,327	755	734
105-109	2,063	1,132	289	344	164	134
110+	501	297	60	108	30	6

Source: Gregory Spencer, Arnold A. Goldstein, and Cynthia M. Taeuber, *America's Centenarians: Data from the 1980 Census*, National Institute on Aging, Washington, DC, June 1987, p. B2. *Notes:* 1. A problem with 1980 Census allocation procedures resulted in an inflation of the count of the centenarian population by about one-fourth. This data reflects unallocated age data only and therefore may be subject to sampling error due to incorrect reporting, overreporting by respondents, or incomplete documentation.

Characteristics by Attainment

★ 135 ★

Characteristics of Households Headed by Adults 65 Years or Older, by Educational Level, 1990: Before-Tax Household Income

Figures in this table reflect a correlation between education and higher income, with 57% of those with an 8th grade education or less earning less than $10,000 per year and 30% of those with a college education earning $30,000 per year or more. From the source: "Data for this study are from the interview component of the 1990 Consumer Expenditures Survey (CE), conducted by the Bureau of the Census for the Bureau of Labor Statistics.... Findings are based on responses from 3,715 consumer units[1] with reference persons 65 years and older."

[Data are shown in percent]

Characteristic	All 65 +	8th grade or less	Some high school	High school graduate	Any college
Number of households (weighted, in thousands)	17,850	5,156	3,429	4,841	4,423
Under $10,000	36.7	56.8	33.0	34.2	18.8
$10,000-$14,999	19.6	18.5	23.8	19.8	17.3
$15,000-$19,999	12.4	10.8	16.1	13.0	10.6
$20,000-$29,999	16.2	8.7	17.1	17.6	22.8
$30,000 and over	15.1	5.2	10.0	15.4	30.5

Source: "A Comparison of Income, Income Sources, and Expenditures of Older Adults by Educational Attainment", *Family Economics Review*, 1992, Vol. 5, No. 4, pp. 2-8. *Notes:* 1. A consumer unit consists of either: (1) all members of a particular household who are related by blood, marriage, adoption, or other legal arrangement; (2) two or more people living together who pool their incomes to make joint expenditure decisions; (3) a person living alone or sharing a household with others or living as a roomer in a private home or lodging house or in permanent living quarters in a hotel or motel, but who is financially independent. To be considered financially independent, at least two of the three major expense categories (housing, food, and other living expenses) have to be provided by the respondent.

★ 136 ★

Characteristics by Attainment

Characteristics of Households Headed by Adults 65 Years or Older, by Educational Level, 1990: Location and Housing Tenure

This table shows that most older adults are homeowners without mortgages and live in urban areas. Persons with less education tend to rent and the majority live in rural areas. From the source: "Data for this study are from the interview component of the 1990 Consumer Expenditures Survey (CE), conducted by the Bureau of the Census for the Bureau of Labor Statistics.... Findings are based on responses from 3,715 consumer units[1] with reference persons 65 years and older."

[Data are shown in percent]

Characteristic	All 65+	8th grade or less	Some high school	High school graduate	Any college
Number of households (weighted, in thousands)	17,850	5,156	3,429	4,841	4,423
Geographical location					
Urban	83.4	78.7	81.1	87.3	86.5
Rural	16.6	21.3	18.9	12.7	13.5
Housing tenure					
Homeowner without mortgage	62.7	63.0	64.6	61.8	62.0
Homeowner with mortgage	15.1	8.6	15.9	14.9	22.2
Renter	22.2	28.4	19.5	23.3	15.8

Source: "A Comparison of Income, Income Sources, and Expenditures of Older Adults by Educational Attainment", *Family Economics Review*, 1992, Vol. 5, No. 4, pp. 2-8. *Notes:* 1. A consumer unit consists of either: (1) all members of a particular household who are related by blood, marriage, adoption, or other legal arrangement; (2) two or more people living together who pool their incomes to make joint expenditure decisions; (3) a person living alone or sharing a household with others or living as a roomer in a private home or lodging house or in permanent living quarters in a hotel or motel, but who is financially independent. To be considered financially independent, at least two of the three major expense categories (housing, food, and other living expenses) have to be provided by the respondent.

★ 137 ★

Characteristics by Attainment

Characteristics of Households Headed by Adults 65 Years or Older, by Educational Level and Race/Ethnicity, 1990

Data in this table show overrepresentation of minorities among persons with lower educational attainment levels. From the source: "Data for this study are from the interview component of the 1990 Consumer Expenditures Survey (CE), conducted by the Bureau of the Census for the Bureau of Labor Statistics.... Findings are based on responses from 3,715 consumer units[1] with reference persons 65 years and older.

[Data are shown in percent]

Race/ethnicity	All 65 +	8th grade or less	Some high school	High school graduate	Any college
Number of households (weighted, in thousands)	17,850	5,156	3,429	4,841	4,423
Non-Hispanic White and other	88.0	77.7	86.6	93.2	95.3
Non-Hispanic Black	9.1	15.4	11.9	5.6	3.3
Hispanic	2.9	6.9	1.5	1.2	1.4

Source: "A Comparison of Income, Income Sources, and Expenditures of Older Adults by Educational Attainment", *Family Economics Review*, 1992, Vol. 5, No. 4, pp. 2-8. *Notes:* 1. A consumer unit consists of either: (1) all members of a particular household who are related by blood, marriage, adoption, or other legal arrangement; (2) two or more people living together who pool their incomes to make joint expenditure decisions; (3) a person living alone or sharing a household with others or living as a roomer in a private home or lodging house or in permanent living quarters in a hotel or motel, but who is financially independent. To be considered financially independent, at least two of the three major expense categories (housing, food, and other living expenses) have to be provided by the respondent.

★ 138 ★

Characteristics by Attainment

Characteristics of Households Headed by Adults 65 Years or Older, by Educational Level and Age, 1990

Data in this table show that persons over the age of 80 were less likely to have completed high school than younger age cohorts. The source suggests that this may be due to difficulty in continuing education during the Depression. From the source: "Data for this study are from the interview component of the 1990 Consumer Expenditures Survey (CE), conducted by the Bureau of the Census for the Bureau of Labor Statistics.... Findings are based on responses from 3,715 consumer units[1] with reference persons 65 years and older.

[Data are shown in percent]

Age group	All 65 +	8th grade or less	Some high school	High school graduate	Any college
Number of households (weighted, in thousands)	17,850	5,156	3,429	4,841	4,423
65-69	29.1	18.9	29.9	33.8	35.0
70-74	26.9	21.8	29.2	31.4	26.2
75-79	22.0	25.2	20.4	21.9	19.6
80 and older	22.0	34.1	20.5	12.9	19.2

Source: "A Comparison of Income, Income Sources, and Expenditures of Older Adults by Educational Attainment", *Family Economics Review*, 1992, Vol. 5, No. 4, pp. 2-8. *Notes:* 1. A consumer unit consists of either: (1) all members of a particular household who are related by blood, marriage, adoption, or other legal arrangement; (2) two or more people living together who pool their incomes to make joint expenditure decisions; (3) a person living alone or sharing a household with others or living as a roomer in a private home or lodging house or in permanent living quarters in a hotel or motel, but who is financially independent. To be considered financially independent, at least two of the three major expense categories (housing, food, and other living expenses) have to be provided by the respondent.

Characteristics of Households Headed by Adults 65 Years or Older, by Educational Level and Marital Status, 1990

From the source: "Data for this study are from the interview component of the 1990 Consumer Expenditures Survey (CE), conducted by the Bureau of the Census for the Bureau of Labor Statistics.... Findings are based on responses from 3,715 consumer units[1] with reference persons 65 years and older.

[Data are shown in percent]

Marital status	All 65+	8th grade or less	Some high school	High school graduate	Any college
Number of households (weighted, in thousands)	17,850	5,156	3,429	4,841	4,423
Marital status					
Married	45.9	41.4	48.5	44.1	50.9
Widowed	40.3	46.1	35.9	43.9	32.9
Divorced/separated	9.7	8.8	11.2	9.0	10.6
Never married	4.1	3.7	4.4	3.0	5.6

Source: "A Comparison of Income, Income Sources, and Expenditures of Older Adults by Educational Attainment", *Family Economics Review*, 1992, Vol. 5, No. 4, pp. 2-8. *Notes:* 1. A consumer unit consists of either: (1) all members of a particular household who are related by blood, marriage, adoption, or other legal arrangement; (2) two or more people living together who pool their incomes to make joint expenditure decisions; (3) a person living alone or sharing a household with others or living as a roomer in a private home or lodging house or in permanent living quarters in a hotel or motel, but who is financially independent. To be considered financially independent, at least two of the three major expense categories (housing, food, and other living expenses) have to be provided by the respondent.

★ 140 ★
Characteristics by Attainment

Characteristics of Households Headed by Adults 65 Years or Older, by Educational Level and Family Type, 1990

This table shows that older adults with some college education were more likely to be living with a spouse than were persons with less than an 8th grade education. From the source: "Data for this study are from the interview component of the 1990 Consumer Expenditures Survey (CE), conducted by the Bureau of the Census for the Bureau of Labor Statistics.... Findings are based on responses from 3,715 consumer units[1] with reference persons 65 years and older.

[Data are shown in percent]

Characteristic	All 65+	8th grade or less	Some high school	High school graduate	Any college
Number of households (weighted, in thousands)	17,850	5,156	3,429	4,841	4,423
Family type					
Husband/wife families	44.1	38.8	47.5	43.3	48.6
Other families	10.9	11.5	14.8	8.4	9.9
Single males	10.2	15.4	7.6	8.3	8.2
Single females	34.8	34.3	30.1	40.0	33.3

Source: "A Comparison of Income, Income Sources, and Expenditures of Older Adults by Educational Attainment", *Family Economics Review*, 1992, Vol. 5, No. 4, pp. 2-8. *Notes:* 1. A consumer unit consists of either: (1) all members of a particular household who are related by blood, marriage, adoption, or other legal arrangement; (2) two or more people living together who pool their incomes to make joint expenditure decisions; (3) a person living alone or sharing a household with others or living as a roomer in a private home or lodging house or in permanent living quarters in a hotel or motel, but who is financially independent. To be considered financially independent, at least two of the three major expense categories (housing, food, and other living expenses) have to be provided by the respondent.

★ 141 ★

Characteristics by Attainment

Characteristics of Households Headed by Adults 65 Years or Older, by Educational Level, 1990: Employment Status

This table shows a correlation between educational attainment and employment. From the source: "Data for this study are from the interview component of the 1990 Consumer Expenditures Survey (CE), conducted by the Bureau of the Census for the Bureau of Labor Statistics. Findings are based on responses from 3,715 consumer units[1] with reference persons 65 years and older."

[Data are shown in percent]

Characteristic	All 65+	8th grade or less	Some high school	High school graduate	Any college
Number of households (weighted, in thousands)	17,850	5,156	3,429	4,841	4,423
Reference person employed	17.5	11.0	13.6	22.1	23.1
Others only employed	13.0	13.6	16.9	11.1	11.5
No earner	69.5	75.4	69.5	66.8	65.4

Source: "A Comparison of Income, Income Sources, and Expenditures of Older Adults by Educational Attainment", *Family Economics Review*, 1992, Vol. 5, No. 4, pp. 2-8. *Notes:* 1. A consumer unit consists of either: (1) all members of a particular household who are related by blood, marriage, adoption, or other legal arrangement; (2) two or more people living together who pool their incomes to make joint expenditure decisions; (3) a person living alone or sharing a household with others or living as a roomer in a private home or lodging house or in permanent living quarters in a hotel or motel, but who is financially independent. To be considered financially independent, at least two of the three major expense categories (housing, food, and other living expenses) have to be provided by the respondent.

Chapter 4
FAMILIES

The family structure and characteristics of elderly Americans are portrayed in this chapter under the headings of Family Status, Household Characteristics, Living Arrangements, Marital Status, Contact with Children, and Relationships. For most headings, breakouts by race and Hispanic origin are shown and regional data are included.

Related information may be found in the chapters on *Demographics*, *Education*, and *Housing*. A number of other chapters also present tables on families or "households" but were placed in those chapters to keep information on subject matter (e.g., Income or Pensions) in the same place.

Family Status

★ 142 ★

Family Status, All Races, by Selected Age Groups, March 1990

Gender and characteristics	Total 15 years and over	55 to 64	65 to 74	75 to 84	85 years and over
Male	91,955	10,002	8,013	3,562	758
In family groups	75,746	8,609	6,793	2,802	516
In families	75,590	8,605	6,790	2,799	514
Householder	51,323	7,732	6,074	2,442	346
Married, spouse present	48,439	7,403	5,845	2,340	319
Other	2,884	328	228	103	27
Spouse of householder	3,878	468	350	159	25
In related subfamilies	1,112	81	67	36	9
Child of householder	372	8	2	-	-
Married, spouse present	871	81	67	36	9

[Continued]

147

★ 142 ★

Family Status, All Races, by Selected Age Groups, March 1990
[Continued]

Gender and characteristics	Total 15 years and over	55 to 64	65 to 74	75 to 84	85 years and over
Parent, no spouse present	153	-	-	-	-
Child of reference person	87	-	-	-	-
Child of householder, not in related subfamily	16,350	145	37	3	-
Other, not in related subfamily	2,927	180	263	158	134
In unrelated subfamilies	156	4	3	3	3
Married, spouse present	68	1	3	3	3
Parent, no spouse present	45	3	-	-	-
Child of reference person	43	-	-	-	-
Not in family groups	16,209	1,394	1,220	761	242
Nonfamily householder	11,606	1,125	1,122	712	219
Other unrelated persons in household	4,401	260	95	45	19
In group quarters	202	9	3	3	4
Female	99,838	11,230	9,966	5,792	1,475
In family groups	80,862	8,940	6,490	2,581	556
In families	80,341	8,937	6,489	2,578	556
Householder	14,767	1,520	1,154	572	7
Married, spouse present	3,878	440	298	89	7
Other	10,890	1,079	856	483	132
Spouse of householder	48,439	6,911	4,745	1,486	138
In related subfamilies	2,325	82	44	31	4
Child of householder	1,390	9	3	-	-
Married, spouse present	871	72	44	30	4
Parent, no spouse present	1,378	10	-	1	-
Child of reference person	76	-	-	-	-
Child of householder, not in related subfamily	11,874	85	19	3	-
Other, not in related subfamily	2,926	339	526	487	275
In unrelated subfamilies	521	3	2	3	-
Married, spouse present	68	3	2	3	-
Parent, no spouse present	421	1	-	-	-
Child of reference person	32	-	-	-	-
Not in family groups	18,976	2,289	3,476	3,211	919
Nonfamily householder	15,651	2,153	3,383	3,130	864

[Continued]

★ 142 ★

Family Status, All Races, by Selected Age Groups, March 1990
[Continued]

Gender and characteristics	Total 15 years and over	55 to 64	65 to 74	75 to 84	85 years and over
Other unrelated persons in household	3,127	109	67	52	19
In group quarters	198	27	26	29	36

Source: *Marital Status and Living Arrangements: March 1990,* Current Population Reports, Series P-20, No. 450, May 1991, U.S. Bureau of the Census.

★ 143 ★

Family Status

Family Status, Whites, by Selected Age Groups, March 1990

Gender and characteristics	Total 15 years and over	55 to 64	65 to 74	75 to 84	85 years and over
Male	78,908	8,830	7,182	3,195	658
In family groups	65,387	7,711	6,147	2,525	440
In families	65,274	7,711	6,147	2,522	437
Householder	46,095	7,015	5,602	2,235	309
Married, spouse present	43,792	6,744	5,432	2,158	286
Other	2,303	271	170	78	23
Spouse of householder	3,169	408	296	140	25
In related subfamilies	853	58	41	27	7
Child of householder	289	7	2	-	-
Married, spouse present	686	58	41	27	7
Parent, no spouse present	105	-	-	-	-
Child of reference person	62	-	-	-	-
Child of householder, not in related subfamily	13,159	114	28	3	-
Other, not in related subfamily	1,997	116	180	118	96
In unrelated subfamilies	114	1	-	3	3
Married, spouse present	52	1	-	3	3
Parent, no spouse present	34	-	-	-	-
Child of reference person	27	-	-	-	-
Not in family groups	13,521	1,118	1,035	671	218
Nonfamily householder	9,951	925	966	635	202
Other unrelated persons in household	3,409	185	66	32	12
In group quarters	161	9	3	3	4

[Continued]

★ 143 ★

Family Status, Whites, by Selected Age Groups, March 1990
[Continued]

Gender and characteristics	Total 15 years and over	55 to 64	65 to 74	75 to 84	85 years and over
Female	84,508	9,748	8,867	5,245	1,332
In family groups	68,037	7,828	5,784	2,284	476
In families	67,627	7,828	5,782	2,282	476
Householder	10,495	1,127	908	477	111
Married, spouse present	3,189	373	270	82	5
Other	7,306	755	638	396	106
Spouse of householder	43,703	6,351	4,419	1,380	129
In related subfamilies	1,521	60	30	20	4
Child of householder	888	8	3	-	-
Married, spouse present	693	53	30	19	4
Parent, no spouse present	779	7	-	1	-
Child of reference person	49	-	-	-	-
Child of householder, not in related subfamily	9,701	63	16	-	-
Other, not in related subfamily	2,208	227	409	404	232
In unrelated subfamilies	410	-	2	3	-
Married, spouse present	52	-	2	3	-
Parent, no spouse present	332	-	-	-	-
Child of reference person	27	-	-	-	-
Not in family groups	16,471	1,920	3,083	2,961	856
Nonfamily householder	13,622	1,795	3,001	2,896	801
Other unrelated persons in household	2,669	98	57	35	19
In group quarters	181	27	26	29	36

Source: *Marital Status and Living Arrangements: March 1990*, Current Population Reports, Series P-20, No. 450, May 1991, U.S. Bureau of the Census.

★ 144 ★

Family Status

Family Status, Blacks, by Selected Age Groups, March 1990

Gender and characteristics	Total 15 years and over	55 to 64	65 to 74	75 to 84	85 years and over
Male	9,948	937	626	302	75
In family groups	7,793	695	475	219	55
In families	7,759	692	475	219	55
Householder	3,663	555	346	169	29
Married, spouse present	3,217	508	297	150	26
Other	446	47	50	20	2
Spouse of householder	560	45	48	18	-
In related subfamilies	136	11	3	1	-
Child of householder	61	-	-	-	-
Married, spouse present	75	11	3	1	-
Parent, no spouse present	39	-	-	-	-
Child of reference person	22	-	-	-	-
Child of householder, not in related subfamily	2,675	29	8	1	-
Other, not in related subfamily	725	53	70	29	26
In unrelated subfamilies	34	3	-	-	-
Married, spouse present	10	-	-	-	-
Parent, no spouse present	9	3	-	-	-
Child of reference person	15	-	-	-	-
Not in family groups	2,155	241	151	84	20
Nonfamily householder	1,313	174	129	71	13
Other unrelated persons in household	813	68	22	13	7
In group quarters	30	-	-	-	-
Female	11,966	1,170	882	472	130
In family groups	9,941	847	546	244	73
In families	9,858	847	546	244	73
Householder	3,808	350	222	87	26
Married, spouse present	533	58	26	7	2
Other	3,275	291	196	81	24
Spouse of householder	3,144	405	235	94	9
In related subfamilies	649	7	-	3	-
Child of householder	459	-	-	-	-
Married, spouse present	70	5	-	3	-
Parent, no spouse present	557	2	-	-	-
Child of reference person	23	-	-	-	-
Child of householder, not in related subfamily	1,740	20	4	3	-
Other, not in related subfamily	517	65	85	57	38

[Continued]

★ 144 ★

Family Status, Blacks, by Selected Age Groups, March 1990
[Continued]

Gender and characteristics	Total 15 years and over	55 to 64	65 to 74	75 to 84	85 years and over
In unrelated subfamilies	84	1	-	-	-
Married, spouse present	11	-	-	-	-
Parent, no spouse present	71	1	-	-	-
Child of reference person	3	-	-	-	-
Not in family groups	2,024	322	336	227	57
Nonfamily householder	1,702	318	330	215	57
Other unrelated persons in household	313	5	6	12	-
In group quarters	10	-	-	-	-

Source: *Marital Status and Living Arrangements: March 1990*, Current Population Reports, Series P-20, No. 450, May 1991, U.S. Bureau of the Census.

★ 145 ★

Family Status

Family Status, Hispanics, by Selected Age Groups, March 1990

Gender and characteristics	Total 15 years and over	55 to 64	65 to 74	75 to 84	85 years and over
Male	7,254	537	340	101	26
In family groups	5,985	460	285	76	17
In families	5,955	460	285	75	17
Householder	3,356	399	261	60	12
Married, spouse present	3,027	373	246	55	11
Other	329	26	16	5	2
Spouse of householder	371	24	9	2	-
In related subfamilies	211	14	9	10	1
Child of householder	45	-	-	-	-
Married, spouse present	182	14	9	10	1
Parent, no spouse present	16	-	-	-	-
Child of reference person	14	-	-	-	-
Child of householder, not in related subfamily	1,353	3	-	-	-
Other, not in related subfamily	664	19	6	4	3
In unrelated subfamilies	30	-	-	1	-

[Continued]

★ 145 ★

Family Status, Hispanics, by Selected Age Groups, March 1990
[Continued]

Gender and characteristics	Total 15 years and over	55 to 64	65 to 74	75 to 84	85 years and over
Married, spouse present	25	-	-	1	-
Parent, no spouse present	4	-	-	-	-
Child of reference person	1	-	-	-	-
Not in family groups	1,269	77	55	24	10
Nonfamily householder	587	57	54	23	9
Other unrelated persons in household	588	12	1	-	1
In group quarters	94	8	-	1	-
Female	7,323	670	373	154	30
In family groups	6,547	576	284	96	18
In families	6,466	576	284	96	18
Householder	1,485	120	62	31	7
Married, spouse present	369	24	8	1	-
Other	1,116	96	54	30	7
Spouse of householder	3,173	371	163	36	2
In related subfamilies	403	27	9	4	-
Child of householder	178	2	-	-	-
Married, spouse present	189	24	9	4	-
Parent, no spouse present	207	4	-	-	-
Child of reference person	7	-	-	-	-
Child of householder, not in related subfamily	1,025	-	-	-	-
Other, not in related subfamily	379	57	50	25	9
In unrelated subfamilies	81	-	-	-	-
Married, spouse present	26	-	-	-	-
Parent, no spouse present	51	-	-	-	-
Child of reference person	4	-	-	-	-
Not in family groups	776	94	89	57	12
Nonfamily householder	506	88	85	53	12
Other unrelated persons in household	256	6	4	4	-
In group quarters	14	-	-	-	-

Source: *Marital Status and Living Arrangements: March 1990*, Current Population Reports, Series P-20, No. 450, May 1991, U.S. Bureau of the Census.

★ 146 ★

Family Status

Family Status, All Races, Metropolitan, by Selected Age Groups, March 1990

Gender and characteristics	Total 15 years and over	55 to 64	65 to 74	75 to 84	85 years and over
Male	71,601	7,457	5,926	2,540	561
In family groups	58,129	6,340	4,991	1,967	364
In families	57,988	6,336	4,988	1,964	364
Householder	38,617	5,645	4,416	1,701	227
Married, spouse present	36,300	5,408	4,228	1,622	212
Other	2,317	236	188	78	15
Spouse of householder	3,209	383	269	116	18
In related subfamilies	919	65	59	32	8
Child of householder	300	8	-	-	-
Married, spouse present	725	65	59	32	8
Parent, no spouse present	128	-	-	-	-
Child of reference person	65	-	-	-	-
Child of householder, not in related subfamily	12,792	98	27	3	-
Other, not in related subfamily	2,452	146	217	112	111
In unrelated subfamilies	141	4	3	3	-
Married, spouse present	65	1	3	3	-
Parent, no spouse present	40	3	-	-	-
Child of reference person	36	-	-	-	-
Not in family groups	13,472	1,117	935	573	197
Nonfamily householder	9,459	878	857	537	174
Other unrelated persons in household	3,836	230	75	33	19
In group quarters	177	8	3	3	4
Female	77,715	8,491	7,370	4,246	1,035
In family groups	62,608	6,712	4,799	1,899	436
In families	62,198	6,709	4,797	1,899	436
Householder	12,002	1,235	911	426	108
Married, spouse present	3,209	353	234	61	5
Other	8,793	883	677	365	103
Spouse of householder	36,300	5,045	3,406	1,027	100
In related subfamilies	1,873	66	44	25	3
Child of householder	1,105	7	3	-	-
Married, spouse present	725	56	44	24	3
Parent, no spouse present	1,093	10	-	1	-
Child of reference person	54	-	-	-	-
Child of householder, not in related subfamily	9,523	66	15	3	-

[Continued]

★ 146 ★

Family Status, All Races, Metropolitan, by Selected Age Groups, March 1990

[Continued]

Gender and characteristics	Total 15 years and over	55 to 64	65 to 74	75 to 84	85 years and over
Other, not in related subfamily	2,500	296	422	418	225
In unrelated subfamilies	409	3	2	-	-
Married, spouse present	65	3	2	-	-
Parent, no spouse present	319	1	-	-	-
Child of reference person	25	-	-	-	-
Not in family groups	15,107	1,779	2,571	2,347	599
Nonfamily householder	12,253	1,666	2,497	2,281	552
Other unrelated persons in household	2,679	86	55	41	15
In group quarters	175	27	19	25	32

Source: *Marital Status and Living Arrangements: March 1990*, Current Population Reports, Series P-20, No. 450, May 1991, U.S. Bureau of the Census.

★ 147 ★

Family Status

Family Status, All Races, Northeast, by Selected Age Groups, March 1990

Gender and characteristics	Total 15 years and over	55 to 64	65 to 74	75 to 84	85 years and over
Male	19,222	2,153	1,802	775	175
In family groups	15,955	1,833	1,493	586	122
In families	15,926	1,832	1,493	585	122
Householder	10,263	1,616	1,327	482	70
Married, spouse present	9,719	1,543	1,270	464	64
Other	544	72	57	17	6
Spouse of householder	866	113	69	40	7
In related subfamilies	241	19	14	12	5
Child of householder	62	3	2	-	-
Married, spouse present	206	19	14	12	5
Parent, no spouse present	22	-	-	-	-
Child of reference person	13	-	-	-	-

[Continued]

★ 147 ★

Family Status, All Races, Northeast, by Selected Age Groups, March 1990

[Continued]

Gender and characteristics	Total 15 years and over	55 to 64	65 to 74	75 to 84	85 years and over
Child of householder, not in related subfamily	3,887	27	6	-	-
Other, not in related subfamily	670	58	78	51	41
In unrelated subfamilies	39	1	-	1	-
Married, spouse present	16	1	-	1	-
Parent, no spouse present	4	-	-	-	-
Child of reference person	8	-	-	-	-
Not in family groups	3,267	320	309	189	53
Nonfamily householder	2,353	257	268	177	49
Other unrelated persons in household	868	60	41	12	-
In group quarters	46	3	-	-	4
Female	20,930	2,448	2,229	1,317	379
In family groups	16,979	1,946	1,491	597	146
In families	16,901	1,946	1,491	597	146
Householder	3,231	356	296	143	34
Married, spouse present	866	95	86	16	-
Other	2,365	261	210	126	34
Spouse of householder	9,719	1,470	1,025	297	32
In related subfamilies	459	16	17	10	3
Child of householder	254	1	-	-	-
Married, spouse present	206	12	17	9	3
Parent, no spouse present	232	4	-	1	-
Child of reference person	20	-	-	-	-
Child of householder, not in related subfamily	2,780	27	6	-	-
Other, not in related subfamily	712	79	148	147	77
In unrelated subfamilies	78	-	-	-	-
Married, spouse present	16	-	-	-	-
Parent, no spouse present	56	-	-	-	-
Child of reference person	6	-	-	-	-
Not in family groups	3,951	501	739	720	233
Nonfamily householder	3,280	475	720	691	196

[Continued]

★ 147 ★

Family Status, All Races, Northeast, by Selected Age Groups, March 1990

[Continued]

Gender and characteristics	Total 15 years and over	55 to 64	65 to 74	75 to 84	85 years and over
Other unrelated persons in household	602	18	16	14	17
In group quarters	68	8	2	15	30

Source: *Marital Status and Living Arrangements: March 1990,* Current Population Reports, Series P-20, No. 450, May 1991, U.S. Bureau of the Census.

★ 148 ★

Family Status

Family Status, All Races, Midwest, by Selected Age Groups, March 1990

Gender and characteristics	Total 15 years and over	55 to 64	65 to 74	75 to 84	85 years and over
Male	22,227	2,451	1,956	856	169
In family groups	18,496	2,167	1,675	668	107
In families	18,458	2,167	1,675	667	107
Householder	12,836	1,959	1,515	599	92
Married, spouse present	12,145	1,851	1,468	577	87
Other	691	108	47	21	4
Spouse of householder	813	118	76	38	2
In related subfamilies	156	11	10	8	-
Child of householder	66	-	-	-	-
Married, spouse present	112	11	10	8	-
Parent, no spouse present	34	-	-	-	-
Child of reference person	10	-	-	-	-
Child of householder, not in related subfamily	4,140	42	21	-	-
Other, not in related subfamily	514	37	52	22	12
In unrelated subfamilies	37	-	-	2	-
Married, spouse present	7	-	-	2	-
Parent, no spouse present	12	-	-	-	-
Child of reference person	18	-	-	-	-
Not in family groups	3,732	284	281	188	62

[Continued]

★ 148 ★

Family Status, All Races, Midwest, by Selected Age Groups, March 1990

[Continued]

Gender and characteristics	Total 15 years and over	55 to 64	65 to 74	75 to 84	85 years and over
Nonfamily householder	2,779	239	263	173	54
Other unrelated persons in household	920	46	14	12	8
In group quarters	33	-	3	3	-
Female	24,100	2,712	2,393	1,554	392
In family groups	19,433	2,176	1,536	695	115
In families	19,302	2,176	1,534	695	115
Householder	3,223	332	237	130	31
Married, spouse present	813	113	64	19	-
Other	2,410	218	172	110	31
Spouse of householder	12,145	1,747	1,175	432	32
In related subfamilies	391	14	6	3	-
Child of householder	263	2	3	-	-
Married, spouse present	112	12	6	3	-
Parent, no spouse present	268	2	-	-	-
Child of reference person	10	-	-	-	-
Child of householder, not in related subfamily	2,959	16	5	-	-
Other, not in related subfamily	584	67	111	131	51
In unrelated subfamilies	132	-	2	-	-
Married, spouse present	7	-	2	-	-
Parent, no spouse present	119	-	-	-	-
Child of reference person	6	-	-	-	-
Not in family groups	4,666	536	858	859	277
Nonfamily householder	3,923	496	823	841	264
Other unrelated persons in household	665	25	13	3	7
In group quarters	79	15	22	14	6

Source: Marital Status and Living Arrangements: March 1990, Current Population Reports, Series P-20, No. 450, May 1991, U.S. Bureau of the Census.

★ 149 ★
Family Status

Family Status, All Races, South, by Selected Age Groups, March 1990

Gender and characteristics	Total 15 years and over	55 to 64	65 to 74	75 to 84	85 years and over
Male	31,081	3,498	2,631	1,267	267
In family groups	26,045	3,018	2,274	1,011	183
In families	26,006	3,018	2,274	1,011	180
Householder	18,023	2,735	2,058	905	123
Married, spouse present	17,096	2,639	1,978	867	113
Other	926	96	80	38	10
Spouse of householder	1,195	127	117	43	9
In related subfamilies	373	26	15	9	1
Child of householder	133	4	-	-	-
Married, spouse present	280	26	15	9	1
Parent, no spouse present	49	-	-	-	-
Child of reference person	44	-	-	-	-
Child of householder, not in related subfamily	5,500	70	10	3	-
Other, not in related subfamily	915	61	75	50	47
In unrelated subfamilies	40	-	-	-	3
Married, spouse present	19	-	-	-	3
Parent, no spouse present	10	-	-	-	-
Child of reference person	10	-	-	-	-
Not in family groups	5,036	480	357	256	84
Nonfamily householder	3,694	371	341	238	73
Other unrelated persons in household	1,284	108	16	17	11
In group quarters	58	1	-	1	-
Female	34,573	3,912	3,509	1,970	442
In family groups	28,299	3,103	2,261	874	189
In families	28,128	3,103	2,261	871	189
Householder	5,222	543	416	37	48
Married, spouse present	1,195	133	74	37	4
Other	4,027	410	342	190	43
Spouse of householder	17,096	2,394	1,646	490	45
In related subfamilies	911	23	7	9	1
Child of householder	594	-	-	-	-
Married, spouse present	280	23	7	9	1
Parent, no spouse present	606	-	-	-	-
Child of reference person	25	-	-	-	-
Child of householder, not in related subfamily	3,926	32	8	3	-

[Continued]

★ 149 ★

Family Status, All Races, South, by Selected Age Groups, March 1990

[Continued]

Gender and characteristics	Total 15 years and over	55 to 64	65 to 74	75 to 84	85 years and over
Other, not in related subfamily	973	110	184	143	95
In unrelated subfamilies	171	1	-	3	-
Married, spouse present	19	-	-	3	-
Parent, no spouse present	142	1	-	-	-
Child of reference person	10	-	-	-	-
Not in family groups	6,274	809	1,248	1,096	254
Nonfamily householder	5,324	778	1,228	1,073	252
Other unrelated persons in household	925	30	19	23	2
In group quarters	25	2	-	-	-

Source: *Marital Status and Living Arrangements: March 1990*, Current Population Reports, Series P-20, No. 450, May 1991, U.S. Bureau of the Census.

★ 150 ★

Family Status

Family Status, All Races, West, by Selected Age Groups, March 1990

Gender and characteristics	Total 15 years and over	55 to 64	65 to 74	75 to 84	85 years and over
Male	19,425	1,900	1,625	664	147
In family groups	15,250	1,590	1,350	536	104
In families	15,200	1,587	1,348	536	104
Householder	10,202	1,422	1,174	457	62
Married, spouse present	9,479	1,370	1,129	431	55
Other	722	52	45	26	7
Spouse of householder	1,004	109	88	38	6
In related subfamilies	342	25	28	6	3
Child of householder	111	1	-	-	-
Married, spouse present	273	25	28	6	3
Parent, no spouse present	49	-	-	-	-
Child of reference person	20	-	-	-	-

[Continued]

★ 150 ★

Family Status, All Races, West, by Selected Age Groups, March 1990
[Continued]

Gender and characteristics	Total 15 years and over	55 to 64	65 to 74	75 to 84	85 years and over
Child of householder, not in related subfamily	2,824	6	-	-	-
Other, not in related subfamily	828	25	58	35	34
In unrelated subfamilies	50	3	3	-	-
Married, spouse present	26	-	3	-	-
Parent, no spouse present	18	3	-	-	-
Child of reference person	6	-	-	-	-
Not in family groups	4,175	310	274	128	43
Nonfamily householder	2,780	259	249	124	43
Other unrelated persons in household	1,329	47	25	4	-
In group quarters	65	4	-	-	-
Female	20,235	2,158	1,834	951	261
In family groups	16,151	1,714	1,203	415	107
In families	16,011	1,712	1,203	415	107
Householder	3,091	289	206	73	26
Married, spouse present	1,004	99	75	16	3
Other	2,087	190	132	57	23
Spouse of householder	9,479	1,300	899	268	29
In related subfamilies	565	29	13	10	-
Child of householder	279	6	-	-	-
Married, spouse present	273	25	13	10	-
Parent, no spouse present	272	4	-	-	-
Child of reference person	20	-	-	-	-
Child of householder, not in related subfamily	2,209	10	-	-	-
Other, not in related subfamily	667	83	83	66	52
In unrelated subfamilies	140	3	-	-	-
Married, spouse present	26	3	-	-	-
Parent, no spouse present	104	-	-	-	-
Child of reference person	10	-	-	-	-
Not in family groups	4,085	443	631	536	155
Nonfamily householder	3,124	404	611	524	152

[Continued]

★ 150 ★

Family Status, All Races, West, by Selected Age Groups, March 1990
[Continued]

Gender and characteristics	Total 15 years and over	55 to 64	65 to 74	75 to 84	85 years and over
Other unrelated persons in household	934	36	18	12	3
In group quarters	26	3	2	-	-

Source: Marital Status and Living Arrangements: March 1990, Current Population Reports, Series P-20, No. 450, May 1991, U.S. Bureau of the Census.

★ 151 ★

Family Status

Persons in Families, by Poverty Status and Selected Characteristics, 1991

Data are shown for persons, families, and unrelated individuals as of March of the following year.

[Numbers in thousands]

Characteristic	All races			White			Black			Hispanic origin[1]		
	Total	Below poverty		Total	Below poverty		Total	Below poverty		Total	Below poverty	
		No.	% of total		No.	% of total		No.	% of total		No.	% of total
ALL PERSONS												
Both Sexes												
Total	251,179	35,708	14.2	210,121	23,747	11.3	31,312	10,242	32.7	22,068	6,339	28.7
55 to 59 years	10,620	1,019	9.6	9,083	716	7.9	1,155	246	21.3	662	113	17.0
60 to 64 years	10,530	1,120	10.6	9,196	796	8.7	1,011	278	27.5	589	115	19.6
65 years and over	30,590	3,781	12.4	27,297	2,802	10.3	2,606	880	33.8	1,143	237	20.8
65 to 74 years	18,441	1,961	10.6	16,315	1,345	8.2	1,665	547	32.9	732	137	18.8
75 years and over	12,149	1,820	15.0	10,983	1,457	13.3	941	333	35.3	411	100	24.3
Male												
Total	122,418	15,082	12.3	102,907	10,079	9.8	14,731	4,197	28.5	11,051	2,900	26.2
55 to 59 years	5,108	387	7.6	4,373	271	6.2	538	87	16.2	334	60	17.8
60 to 64 years	4,928	406	8.2	4,357	293	6.7	439	95	21.6	263	42	16.2
65 years and over	12,800	1,015	7.9	11,431	693	6.1	1,058	271	25.6	466	72	15.4
65 to 74 years	8,266	632	7.6	7,323	407	5.6	739	193	26.1	310	42	13.4
75 years and over	4,533	383	8.5	4,108	286	7.0	319	78	24.6	157	30	19.3
Female												
Total	128,761	20,626	16.0	107.214	13,668	12.7	16,581	6,044	36.5	11,017	3,439	31.2
55 to 59 years	5,511	632	11.5	4,710	444	9.4	616	159	25.8	327	53	16.2
60 to 64 years	5,603	714	12.7	4,839	503	10.4	572	183	32.0	326	73	22.3
65 years and over	17,790	2,766	15.5	15,866	2,109	13.3	1,549	609	39.3	677	166	24.5
65 to 74 years	10,174	1,329	13.1	8,992	939	10.4	926	355	38.3	422	96	22.7
75 years and over	7,616	1,436	18.9	6,874	1,171	17.0	623	254	40.8	255	70	27.4

[Continued]

★ 151 ★

Persons in Families, by Poverty Status and Selected Characteristics, 1991

[Continued]

Characteristic	All races			White			Black			Hispanic origin[1]		
	Total	Below poverty		Total	Below poverty		Total	Below poverty		Total	Below poverty	
		No.	% of total		No.	% of total		No.	% of total		No.	% of total
PERSONS IN FAMILIES												
Both sexes												
Total	212,716	27,143	12.8	177,613	17,268	9.7	26,564	8,504	32.0	19,657	5,541	28.2
55 to 59 years	8,935	641	7.2	7,701	428	5.6	896	171	19.1	560	79	14.2
60 to 64 years	8,600	626	7.3	7,649	448	5.9	682	142	20.8	506	79	15.6
65 years and over	20,341	1,228	6.0	18,212	829	4.5	1,593	348	21.9	891	124	13.9
65 to 74 years	13,440	762	5.7	12,029	504	4.2	1,047	224	21.4	590	79	13.4
75 years and over	6,901	466	6.8	6,184	325	5.3	546	124	22.8	301	45	14.8
Male												
Total	104,431	11,781	11.3	88,091	7,724	8.8	12,240	3,438	28.1	9,654	2,527	26.2
55 to 59 years	4,361	259	5.9	3,781	182	4.8	403	57	14.2	271	40	14.8
60 to 64 years	4,203	272	6.5	3,821	207	5.4	272	49	18.1	237	33	13.7
65 years and over	10,339	560	5.4	9,384	411	4.4	695	115	16.5	404	52	12.9
65 to 74 years	6,888	353	5.1	6,225	259	4.2	494	73	14.9	272	30	11.1
75 years and over	3,452	208	6.0	3,158	153	4.8	202	42	20.7	132	22	16.8
Female												
Total	108,285	15,362	14.2	89,523	9,544	10.7	14,324	5,066	35.4	10,003	3,014	30.1
55 to 59 years	4,574	382	8.3	3,920	246	6.3	492	114	23.1	289	39	13.6
60 to 64 years	4,397	354	8.1	3,828	241	6.3	410	93	22.7	269	46	17.2
65 years and over	10,001	668	6.7	8,828	417	4.7	897	233	26.0	487	71	14.7
65 to 74 years	6,552	410	6.3	5,803	245	4.2	553	151	27.2	318	49	15.4
75 years and over	3,449	258	7.5	3,025	172	5.7	344	83	24.0	169	23	13.3

Source: *Poverty in the United States: 1991*, Current Population Reports, Series P-60, No. 181, U.S. Department of Commerce, Bureau of the Census, August 1992, p. 10. *Note:* 1. Persons of Hispanic origin may be of any race.

Household Characteristics

★ 152 ★

Distribution of Households by Household Type and Age of Head, 1985 and 2010

The table below provides the projected changes in the distribution of households by type. The number of households headed by a person under age 35 is expected to decline significantly when the baby boom age cohort enters a higher age bracket, creating a 9 percent increase in the 45-64 age group. The projected rise in the percentage of households headed by persons 75 years of age or older is substantial; it compensates for decreases in the age group 65-74; and this type of household will likely comprise 12 percent of all households by 2010.

[Numbers in percent]

	1985	2010
Household type		
Husband-wife	58.0	50.1
Male-headed families	2.6	3.4
Female-headed families	11.7	12.0
Male individual	12.3	16.6
Female individual	15.5	17.9
Age of household head		
Under 35	29.2	18.9
35-44	20.1	21.1
45-64	29.7	38.7
65-74	12.6	9.3
75+	8.5	12.0

Source: "Projected Changes in the Characteristics and Housing Situation of the Elderly Population if Current Policies Continue," Harold M. Katsura, Raymond J. Struyk, and Sandra J. Newman, *Housing for the Elderly in 2010: Projections and Policy Options*, Urban Institute Report 89-4. Washington, D.C.: The Urban Institute Press, 1989, p. 16.

★ 153 ★

Household Characteristics

Age of Householders, 1990-2000

From the source: "Between now and 2000, the market will shift to older buyers as the number of households headed by 35- to 44-year olds jumps 16% to 24.4 million while younger households decline 16.9% to 16.8 million. Yet how many of those aging baby-boom households buy new homes will depend on local affordability and competition from existing stock."

[Numbers in thousands]

Age of householder	1990	1995	2000
Under 25	4,573	4,151	4,375
25-34	20,693	19,114	16,782
35-44	21,028	23,416	24,356
45-64	27,143	30,946	36,496
65+	20,621	22,548	23,619

Source: "Starter Homes," Brad German, *Builder* 15, No. 1, January, 1992, p. 266. Primary source: Joint Center for Housing Studies.

★ 154 ★

Household Characteristics

Census Household Projections by Age of Head and Household Type, 2000-2010

Projections by household type to the year 2000 are shown in the top section of the table. The assumed annual rates of growth for the period 2000-2010 are shown in the next panel. These rates were used in calculating the percentage distribution of households by age of the head. This distribution is shown in the third section. Assuming that this distribution, as well as the targeted growth rates by type of household, are specifically achieved in 2010, the final projection of the number of households by type and age of head may be calculated as shown in the bottom panel.

[Numbers in thousands of households]

	Husband/ Wife	Female head	Male head	Female prime	Male prime	Total	Calculated total
All households	56,294	12,701	3,282	18,204	15,452	105,933	105,933
Under 25	1,064	813	232	1,077	1,256	4,442	4,442
25-29	3,251	1,132	259	1,148	2,011	7,801	7,801
30-34	5,010	1,474	423	1,341	1,955	10,203	10,203
35-44	14,947	3,632	934	1,806	4,020	25,339	25,339
45-54	13,557	2,958	768	1,930	2,390	21,603	21,603
55-64	8,805	1,124	358	2,198	1,417	13,903	13,902
65-74	5,922	718	165	3,581	1,129	11,516	11,515
75+	3,739	849	141	5,123	1,274	11,126	11,126
Calculated total	56,295	12,700	3,280	18,204	15,452	105,933	105,931

[Continued]

★ 154 ★

Census Household Projections by Age of Head and Household Type, 2000-2010

[Continued]

	Husband/ Wife	Female head	Male head	Female prime	Male prime	Total	Calculated total
Assumed Annual Rate of Growth 2000-2010							
All households	.0050	.0110	.0210	.0150	.0240	.0110	
Under 25	-.0065	.0370	.0498	.0416	.0320	.0266	
25-29	-.0475	-.0165	-.0115	-.0095	-.0108	-.0271	
30-34	-.0259	-.0054	.0120	.0167	.0093	-.0091	
35-44	-.0074	.0006	.0141	.0135	.0276	.0015	
45-54	.0323	.0438	.0463	.0416	.0580	.0380	
55-64	.0281	.0227	.0317	.0233	.0411	.0284	
65-74	-.0072	.0205	-.0179	-.0100	.0018	-.0081	
75+	.0205	.0107	.0000	.0236	.0258	.0215	
Percentage Distribution of Projected Households in 2010 by Age of Head							
All households	.501	.120	.034	.179	.166	1.000	
Under 25	.016	.080	.091	.075	.086		
25-29	.033	.065	.056	.048	.090		
30-34	.063	.095	.115	.073	.107		
35-44	.227	.249	.260	.095	.263		
45-54	.305	.310	.292	.134	.209		
55-64	.190	.096	.118	.128	.106		
65-74	.090	.040	.033	.149	.057		
75+	.075	.064	.034	.298	.082		
Total	1.000	1.000	1.000	1.000	1.000		
Final Projection: Households in 2010 by Age of Head and Type							
All households	59,233	14,187	4,020	21,163	19,626	118,229	118,229
Under 25	967	1,132	367	1,580	1,684		5,730
25-29	1,939	928	224	1,019	1,765		5,875
30-34	3,739	1,352	463	1,544	2,098		9,197
35-44	13,464	3,537	1,045	2,015	5,164		25,224
45-54	18,068	4,396	1,174	2,830	4,109		30,577
55-64	11,272	1,363	476	2,700	2,075		17,886
65-74	5,343	565	134	3,162	1,124		10,329
⁻ +	4,441	915	137	6,312	1,607		13,413
'ated total	59,233	14,187	4,020	21,163	19,626		118,229

ⱸ: "Appendix C," Harold M. Katsura, Raymond J. Struyk, and Sandra J. Newman, *Housing for the Elderly in 2010: Projections and Policy .ons*, Urban Institute Report 89-4. Washington, D.C.: The Urban Institute Press, 1989, pp. 145-46.

★ 155 ★

Household Characteristics

Annual Household Growth Due to Aging[1]

The effects "on household growth of the aging of the baby boom and baby bust generations can be seen in [the table below] where calculations of trends and projections in the age structure factor in household growth are presented. The 1980-85 period was when the age structure factor exercised its biggest influence. Between 1990 and 1995 the effects of aging will decrease dramatically, and by the last five years of the century the age structure factor should account for almost 500,000 fewer households annually than in 1980-85. Total household growth from all factors (age structure, migration and hardship) should fall to an average of just over one million per year by the end of the century, down from 1.7 million in the 1970s and 1.4 million per year in the 1980s."

[Numbers in millions of households]

Period	Millions
1970-80	1.054
1980-85	1.243
1985-90	1.164
1990-95	0.964
1995-2000	0.843

Source: Working Paper W89-1 for the Joint Center for Housing Studies of Harvard University, *U.S. Household Trends: The 1980s and Beyond*, George S. Masnick, 1989. Primary source: George Masnick, "New Projections of Population and Households for States and Regions," Joint Center for Housing Studies, August 1989. *Note:* 1. Includes aging of previous migrants.

★ 156 ★

Household Characteristics

Size of Households for Householders 65 Years and Over, by Age, Race, and Hispanic Origin, March 1990

[Data are in thousands; noninstitutional populations]

Size of household	All ages	Number				Percent			
		65 years and over	65 to 74 years	75 to 84 years	85 years and over	65 years and over	65 to 74 years	75 to 84 years	85 years and over
All races									
All households	93,347	20,156	11,733	6,856	1,567	100.0	100.0	100.0	100.0
One-person household	22,999	9,175	4,350	3,774	1,051	45.5	37.1	55.0	67.1
Two-person households	30,114	8,927	5,847	2,641	439	44.3	49.8	38.5	28.0
Three-person households	16,128	1,328	971	310	47	6.6	8.3	4.5	3.0
Four-or-more-person households	24,107	728	566	131	31	3.6	4.8	1.9	2.0
Persons per household	2.63	1.75	1.89	1.57	1.44	(X)	(X)	(X)	(X)
White									
All households	80,163	18,144	10,477	6,244	1,423	100.0	100.0	100.0	100.0
One-person household	19,879	8,290	3,841	3,475	974	45.7	36.7	55.7	68.4
Two-person households	26,714	8,235	5,411	2,431	393	45.4	51.6	38.9	27.6

[Continued]

★ 156 ★

Size of Households for Householders 65 Years and Over, by Age, Race, and Hispanic Origin, March 1990
[Continued]

Size of household	All ages	Number				Percent			
		65 years and over	65 to 74 years	75 to 84 years	85 years and over	65 years and over	65 to 74 years	75 to 84 years	85 years and over
Three-person households	13,585	1,108	809	261	38	6.1	7.7	4.2	2.7
Four-or-more-person households	19,985	511	417	77	17	2.8	4.0	1.2	1.2
Persons per household	2.58	1.71	1.85	1.54	1.4	(X)	(X)	(X)	(X)
Black									
All households	10,486	1,696	1,028	543	125	100.0	100.0	100.0	100.0
One-person household	2,610	776	435	274	67	45.8	42.3	50.5	53.6
Two-person households	2,721	559	335	183	41	33.0	32.6	33.7	32.8
Three-person households	2,043	179	130	41	8	10.6	12.6	7.6	6.4
Four-or-more-person households	3,113	182	129	45	8	10.7	12.5	8.3	6.4
Persons per household	2.88	2.08	2.24	1.86	1.78	(X)	(X)	(X)	(X)
Hispanic origin[1]									
All households	5,933	671	463	168	40	100.0	100.0	100.0	(B)
One-person household	856	222	125	76	21	33.1	27.0	45.2	(B)
Two-person households	1,292	278	204	64	10	41.4	44.1	38.1	(B)
Three-person households	1,139	84	67	13	4	12.5	14.5	7.7	(B)
Four-or-more-person households	2,646	88	68	14	6	13.1	14.7	8.3	(B)
Persons per household	3.47	2.21	2.32	1.95	(B)	(X)	(X)	(X)	(X)

Source: Sixty-Five Plus in America, Cynthia M. Taeuber, U.S. Department of Commerce, Economics and Statistics Administration, Bureau of the Census, U.S. Government Printing Office, Washington, D.C., 1992, p. 6-10. Primary source: Steve Rawlings, U.S. Bureau of the Census, Household and Family Characteristics: March 1990 and 1989, Current Population Reports, Series P- 20, No. 447, U.S. Government Printing Office, Washington, D.C., 1990, Table 17. Notes: (B) means Base is less than 75,000. An (X) means not applicable. 1. Hispanic origin may be of any race.

Living Arrangements

★ 157 ★

Living Arrangements of Older Americans, by Age Group, 1989

Almost half of the men over 85 years old live with their spouses, compared to just 9.1% of the women. This is probably due, in part, to the fact that men in this age group are outnumbered by women by more than 2 to 1. Data are shown for the non-institutional population.

Living arrangement and age	Number (thousands)			Percent distribution		
	Total	Men	Women	Total	Men	Women
65+	29,022	12,078	16,944	100.0	100.0	100.0
Living--						
Alone	8,851	1,916	6,935	30.5	15.9	40.9
With spouse	15,773	8,977	6,796	54.3	74.3	40.1
With other relatives	3,797	927	2,870	13.1	7.7	16.9
With nonrelatives only	601	258	343	2.1	2.1	2.0
65 to 74 years	17,747	7,880	9,867	100.1	100.0	100.0
Living--						
Alone	4,355	1,045	3,310	24.5	13.3	33.5
With spouse	11,252	6,176	5,075	63.4	78.4	51.4
With other relatives	1,832	502	1,331	10.3	6.4	13.5
With nonrelatives only	308	157	151	1.7	2.0	1.5
75 to 84 years	9,175	3,506	5,669	100.0	100.0	100.0
Living--						
Alone	3,509	645	2,864	38.2	18.4	50.5
With spouse	4,060	2,468	1,593	44.3	70.4	28.1
With other relatives	1,386	305	1,080	15.1	8.7	19.1
With nonrelatives only	220	88	132	2.4	2.5	2.3
85+	2,101	693	1,408	100.0	100.0	100.0
Living--						
Alone	987	226	760	47.0	32.6	54.0
With spouse	462	334	128	22.0	48.2	9.1
With other relatives	579	121	459	27.6	17.5	32.6
With nonrelatives only	73	12	61	3.5	1.7	4.3

Source: *Aging America, Trends and Projections*, prepared by the U.S. Senate Special Committee on Aging, the American Association of Retired Persons, the Federal Council on the Aging, and the U.S. Administration on Aging, 1991, Washington, D.C., p. 211. Primary source: U.S. Bureau of the Census, "Marital Status and Living Arrangements: March 1989," *Current Population Reports*, Series P-20, No. 445, June 1990. *Note:* Numbers and percentages may not add to totals due to rounding.

★ 158 ★
Living Arrangements

Living Arrangements of Older Americans, by Age, Sex, Race, and Hispanic Origin, March 1989

Data exclude persons in institutions.

Living arrangements	65 +		65 to 74		75 to 84		85 +	
	Men	Women	Men	Women	Men	Women	Men	Women
All races								
Total (thousands)	12,078	16,944	7,880	9,867	3,506	5,669	693	1,408
Percent[1]	100.0	100.0	100.0	100.0	100.0	100.0	100.0	100.0
Living with spouse	74.3	40.1	78.4	51.4	70.4	28.1	48.2	9.1
Living with other relatives	7.7	16.9	6.4	13.5	8.7	19.1	17.3	32.6
Living alone	15.9	40.9	13.3	33.5	18.4	50.5	32.6	54.0
Living with nonrelatives	2.1	2.0	2.0	1.5	2.5	2.3	1.7	4.3
White								
Total (thousands)	10,798	15,204	7,050	8,767	3,136	5,174	612	1,263
Percent[1]	100.0	100.0	100.0	100.0	100.0	100.0	100.0	100.0
Living with spouse	76.3	41.2	80.6	53.3	72.3	28.7	47.9	8.8
Living with other relatives	6.6	15.4	5.3	11.8	7.7	17.5	16.8	31.1
Living alone	15.3	41.4	12.5	33.5	17.9	51.5	33.7	55.5
Living with nonrelatives	1.8	2.0	1.7	1.4	2.0	2.3	1.6	4.6
Black								
Total (thousands)	981	1,455	619	913	300	416	62	126
Percent[1]	100.0	100.0	100.0	100.0	100.0	100.0	100.0	100.0
Living with spouse	56.1	27.9	58.6	33.4	51.0	20.7	(B)	11.9
Living with other relatives	15.6	29.7	15.0	26.4	17.0	32.2	(B)	45.2
Living alone	23.9	39.8	22.8	37.7	24.7	43.5	(B)	42.9
Living with nonrelatives	4.6	2.6	3.7	2.5	7.3	3.6	(B)	0.0
Hispanic origin[2]								
Total (thousands)	447	557	301	350	120	176	26	31
Percent[1]	100.0	100.0	100.0	100.0	100.0	100.0	100.0	100.0
Living with spouse	65.5	37.7	69.8	47.4	62.5	23.3	(B)	(B)
Living with other relatives	15.2	35.5	12.6	30.0	18.3	43.2	(B)	(B)
Living alone	17.4	25.7	15.0	21.1	19.2	33.5	(B)	(B)
Living with nonrelatives	1.8	1.4	2.7	1.4	0.0	0.6	(B)	(B)

Source: *Aging America, Trends and Projections*, prepared by the U.S. Senate Special Committee on Aging, the American Association of Retired Persons, the Federal Council on the Aging, and the U.S. Administration on Aging, 1991, Washington, D.C., p. 187. Primary source: U.S. Bureau of the Census, "Marital Status and Living Arrangements: March 1989," *Current Population Reports*, Series P-20, No. 445, June 1990. *Notes:* (B) indicates that the base population was less than 75,000 and is too small to show derived measures. 1. Percentage distributions may not add to 100.0 due to rounding. 2. People of Hispanic origin may be of any race.

★ 159 ★

Living Arrangements

Living Arrangements of People 65+, 1989

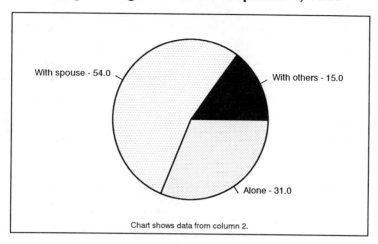

With spouse - 54.0

With others - 15.0

Alone - 31.0

Chart shows data from column 2.

The majority of older Americans live with a spouse, but there are a substantial number who live alone.

[Numbers in millions]

	Number	Percent
With spouse	15.8	54.0
Alone	8.9	31.0
With others	4.4	15.0

Source: Aging America, Trends and Projections, prepared by the U.S. Senate Special Committee on Aging, the American Association of Retired Persons, the Federal Council on the Aging, and the U.S. Administration on Aging, 1991, Washington, D.C., p. 209. Primary source: U.S. Bureau of the Census, "Marital Status and Living Arrangements: March 1989," *Current Population Reports,* Series P-20, No. 445, June 1990.

★ 160 ★

Living Arrangements

Alone: Older Americans Living Alone

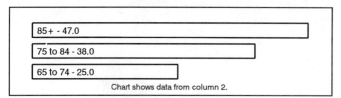

85+ - 47.0

75 to 84 - 38.0

65 to 74 - 25.0

Chart shows data from column 2.

[Numbers in millions]

Age group	Number	Percent
65 to 74	4.4	25.0
75 to 84	3.5	38.0
85+	1.0	47.0

Source: Aging America, Trends and Projections, prepared by the U.S. Senate Special Committee on Aging, the American Association of Retired Persons, the Federal Council on the Aging, and the U.S. Administration on Aging, 1991, Washington, D.C., p. 212. Primary source: U.S. Bureau of the Census, "Marital Status and Living Arrangements: March 1989," *Current Population Reports*, Series P-20, No 445, June 1990.

★ 161 ★

Living Arrangements

Alone: Older Americans Living Alone, by Age and Sex, 1989

[Numbers in percent]

Age group	Men	Women
65 to 74	13.3	33.5
75 to 84	18.4	50.5
85+	32.6	54.0

Source: Aging America, Trends and Projections, prepared by the U.S. Senate Special Committee on Aging, the American Association of Retired Persons, the Federal Council on the Aging, and the U.S. Administration on Aging, 1991, Washington, D.C., p. 214. Primary source: U.S. Bureau of the Census, "Marital Status and Living Arrangements: March 1989," *Current Population Reports*, Series P-20, No. 445, June 1990.

★ 162 ★

Living Arrangements

Alone: Older Americans Living Alone, by Race and Hispanic Origin, 1989

Black - 33.0	
White - 31.0	
Hispanic - 22.0	

From the source: "Whereas white and black people age 65+ are about equally likely to live alone, a smaller proportion of older Hispanics live alone... The number of elderly black and Hispanic people who live alone is relatively small—approximately 813,00 blacks and some 221,000 Hispanics. About 8.0 million older whites live alone."

Characteristic	Percent
Black	33.0
White	31.0
Hispanic	22.0

Source: Aging America, Trends and Projections, prepared by the U.S. Senate Special Committee on Aging, the American Association of Retired Persons, the Federal Council on the Aging, and the U.S. Administration on Aging, 1991, Washington, D.C., p. 215. Primary source: U.S. Bureau of the Census, "Marital Status and Living Arrangements: March 1989," *Current Population Reports,* Series P-20, No. 445, June 1990.

★ 163 ★

Living Arrangements

Alone: Percentage of Persons 65 Years and Over Living Alone: 1990

State	Number	Percent
United States	8,824,845	28.2
Alabama	154,191	29.5
Alaska	5,737	25.6
Arizona	119,287	24.9
Arkansas	103,386	29.5
California	818,520	26.1
Colorado	95,849	29.1
Connecticut	121,918	27.3
Delaware	21,566	26.7
District of Columbia	27,237	35.0
Florida	591,468	25.0
Georgia	185,027	28.3

[Continued]

★ 163 ★

Alone: Percentage of Persons 65 Years and Over Living Alone: 1990
[Continued]

State	Number	Percent
Hawaii	20,933	16.7
Idaho	32,939	27.2
Illinois	423,740	29.5
Indiana	208,437	29.9
Iowa	130,964	30.7
Kansas	104,297	30.4
Kentucky	142,045	30.4
Louisiana	137,596	29.3
Maine	48,257	29.5
Maryland	135,318	26.1
Massachusetts	243,334	29.7
Michigan	317,659	28.7
Minnesota	167,001	30.5
Mississippi	98,180	30.6
Missouri	221,516	30.9
Montana	32,208	30.2
Nebraska	69,640	31.2
Nevada	33,244	26.0
New Hampshire	34,522	27.6
New Jersey	273,736	26.5
New Mexico	42,964	26.3
New York	700,016	29.6
North Carolina	226,384	28.1
North Dakota	28,021	30.8
Ohio	416,352	29.6
Oklahoma	131,237	30.9
Oregon	108,579	27.7
Pennsylvania	526,264	28.8
Rhode Island	44,627	29.6
South Carolina	109,012	27.5
South Dakota	31,560	30.8
Tennessee	178,077	28.8
Texas	472,029	27.5
Utah	38,320	25.6
Vermont	19,648	29.7
Virginia	178,575	26.9
Washington	162,520	28.3
West Virginia	84,405	31.4

[Continued]

★ 163 ★

Alone: Percentage of Persons 65 Years and Over Living Alone: 1990

[Continued]

State	Number	Percent
Wisconsin	192,072	29.5
Wyoming	14,431	30.6

Source: U.S. Bureau of the Census, 1990 Census of Population and Housing, Summary Tape File 1A.

★ 164 ★

Living Arrangements

Alone: Older Americans Aged 65+ Who Live Alone and Do Not Have Any Living Children, by Race and Hispanic Origin, 1990

Black - 36.0
White - 26.0
Hispanic - 16.0

From the source: "With increasing age, a growing proportion of elderly people who live alone have neither a living child nor a living sibling... For example, among elderly people age 65 to 74 who live alone, just 5 percent have no living child or sibling; by age 85 the proportion increases to 12 percent. Such people are at the greatest risk of needing community services to assist them as the grow increasingly frail."

[Numbers in percent]

Race/ethnicity	Percent
Black	36.0
White	26.0
Hispanic	16.0

Source: Aging America, Trends and Projections, prepared by the U.S. Senate Special Committee on Aging, the American Association of Retired Persons, the Federal Council on the Aging, and the U.S. Administration on Aging, 1991, Washington, D.C., p. 234. Primary source: Lewin/ICF estimates based on data from the 1984 *Supplement on Aging* and the Brookings/ICF Long-Term Care Financing Model, 1990.

★ 165 ★

Living Arrangements

Alone: Older Americans Living Alone, with No Living Sibling or Child, by Age Group, 1990

| 85+ - 12.0 |
| 75 to 84 - 9.0 |
| 65 to 74 - 5.0 |

Data are shown for persons aged 65+.

Age	Percent
65 to 74	5.0
75 to 84	9.0
85+	12.0

Source: Aging America, Trends and Projections, prepared by the U.S. Senate Special Committee on Aging, the American Association of Retired Persons, the Federal Council on the Aging, and the U.S. Administration on Aging, 1991, Washington, D.C., p. 235. Primary source: Lewin/ICF estimates based on data from the 1984 *Supplement on Aging* and the Brookings/ICF Long-Term Care Financing Model, 1990.

★ 166 ★

Living Arrangements

Alone: Older Americans Who Live Alone and Have a Child Who Lives Nearby, by Race and Hispanic Origin, 1990

| Hispanic - 68.0 |
| White - 58.0 |
| Black - 48.0 |

Race/ethnicity	Percent
Hispanic	68.0
White	58.0
Black	48.0

Source: Aging America, Trends and Projections, prepared by the U.S. Senate Special Committee on Aging, the American Association of Retired Persons, the Federal Council on the Aging, and the U.S. Administration on Aging, 1991, Washington, D.C., p. 233. Primary source: Lewin/ICF estimates based on data from the 1984 *Supplement on Aging* and the Brookings/ICF Long-Term Care Financing Model, 1990.

★ 167 ★

Living Arrangements

Alone: Projected Growth in Number of Minority Elderly People Living Alone, 1990-2020

[Numbers in thousands]

Characteristic	1990	2005	2020
Black	925	1,365	2,381
Hispanic	221	482	930

Source: Aging America, Trends and Projections, prepared by the U.S. Senate Special Committee on Aging, the American Association of Retired Persons, the Federal Council on the Aging, and the U.S. Administration on Aging, 1991, Washington, D.C., p. 216. Primary source: Lewin/ICF estimates based on data from the *Current Population Survey* and the Brookings/ICF Long-Term Care Financing Model, 1990.

★ 168 ★

Living Arrangements

Alone: Projected Increase in Number of Elderly People Living Alone, by Age Group, 1990-2020

[Numbers in millions]

Age	1990	2005	2020
65 to 74	4.4	4.5	7.7
75 to 84	3.6	4.5	5.2
85+	1.1	1.9	2.3

Source: Aging America, Trends and Projections, prepared by the U.S. Senate Special Committee on Aging, the American Association of Retired Persons, the Federal Council on the Aging, and the U.S. Administration on Aging, 1991, Washington, D.C., p. 213. Primary source: Lewin/ICF estimates based on data from the *Current Population Survey* and the Brookings/ICF Long-Term Care Financing Model, 1990.

★ 169 ★

Living Arrangements

Alone: Projected Increase in Number of People 65+ Living Alone, 1990-2020

```
2020 - 15.2
2005 - 10.9
1990 - 9.2
```

The number of Older Americans who live alone is expected to rise, almost doubling by the year 2020.

Year	Millions
1990	9.2
2005	10.9
2020	15.2

Source: Aging America, Trends and Projections, prepared by the U.S. Senate Special Committee on Aging, the American Association of Retired Persons, the Federal Council on the Aging, and the U.S. Administration on Aging, 1991, Washington, D.C., p. 210. Primary source: Lewin/ICF estimates based on data from the *Current Population Survey* and the Brookings/ICF Long-Term Care Financing Model, 1990.

★ 170 ★

Living Arrangements

Alone: Projections of People 65+ Living Alone Who Will Report Fair or Poor Health, 1990-2020

From the source: "In the future, it is projected that the health status of low-income white people who live alone will improve. Whereas the number of such people who report fair or poor health totaled some 655,000 individuals in 1990, that number is projected to decline to 312,00 people by 2020...The number of low-income minorities who live alone and report poor health, however, is expected to increase. The number of poor blacks in poor or fair health who live alone is projected to grow from 268,000 to 349,000 people, over the next 30 years. Among low-income Hispanics who live alone, the number in poor health is projected to nearly double, from 40,000 to 73,000 by 2020."

[Numbers in thousands]

Characteristic	1990	2005	2020
Black	268	300	349
White	655	486	312
Hispanic	40	60	73

Source: Aging America, Trends and Projections, prepared by the U.S. Senate Special Committee on Aging, the American Association of Retired Persons, the Federal Council on the Aging, and the U.S. Administration on Aging, 1991, Washington, D.C., p. 225. Primary source: Lewin/ICF estimates based on data from the 1984 *Supplement on Aging*, and the Brookings/ICF Long-Term Care Financing Model, 1990.

★ 171 ★

Living Arrangements

Alone: Proportion of People 65+ Living Alone Who Are in Fair or Poor Health, by Poverty Status, 1990

From the source: "Many elderly people who live alone report their health to be poor or fair. Among those who are poor, greater proportions report poor health status and poor black people are at greater risk of having poor health... For example, 22 percent of non-poor whites who live alone report fair of poor health status, whereas among poor blacks who live alone, 56 percent report poor health."

Characteristic	Below poverty	Above poverty
Hispanic	38.0	34.0
Black	56.0	28.0
White	39.0	22.0

Source: Aging America, Trends and Projections, prepared by the U.S. Senate Special Committee on Aging, the American Association of Retired Persons, the Federal Council on the Aging, and the U.S. Administration on Aging, 1991, Washington, D.C., p. 224. Primary source: Lewin/ICF estimates based on data from the 1984 *Supplement on Aging*, and the Brookings/ICF Long-Term Care Financing Model, 1990.

★ 172 ★

Living Arrangements

Sources of Help for Elderly People, by Living Arrangement, 1990

Living arrangement	Relative in home	Relative outside	Unrelated person	Don't know/ none
Living alone	1.0	63.0	12.0	24.0
Living with others	65.0	18.0	7.0	10.0
Couples	78.0	15.0	2.0	5.0

Source: Aging America, Trends and Projections, prepared by the U.S. Senate Special Committee on Aging, the American Association of Retired Persons, the Federal Council on the Aging, and the U.S. Administration on Aging, 1991, Washington, D.C., p. 232. Primary source: Lewin/ICF estimates based on data from the *Current Population Survey* and the Brookings/ICF Long-Term Care Financing Model, 1990.

Marital Status

★ 173 ★

Marital Status of the Elderly

The table shows people of 65 years or older by marital status. Females show a much higher likelihood of being widows because women live an average of seven years longer than men.

	Male	Female
Total	12,547,000	17,546,000
Percent	100.0	100.0
Never married	4.3	5.1
Married	74.3	39.7
Separated[1]/divorced	6.8	6.9
Widowed	14.7	48.2

Source: American Demographics, December 1992, p. 46. Primary source: Bureau of the Census, Current Population Reports, Series p. 20, No. 461. *Notes:* 1. Includes married, spouse absent for reasons other than marital discord.

★ 174 ★
Marital Status

Marital Status of Older Americans, by Selected Characteristics, March 1989

Data exclude persons in institutions.

Marital status	65+		65 to 74		75 to 84		85+	
	Men	Women	Men	Women	Men	Women	Men	Women
All races								
Total (thousands)	12,078	16,944	7,880	9,867	3,506	5,669	693	1,408
Percent[1]	100.0	100.0	100.0	100.0	100.0	100.0	100.0	100.0
Never married	4.7	5.0	4.9	4.5	4.6	5.8	3.2	5.6
Married, spouse present	74.3	40.1	78.4	51.4	70.4	28.1	48.2	9.1
Married, spouse absent	2.7	1.6	2.7	1.8	2.3	1.5	4.4	0.9
Widowed	14.0	48.7	8.9	36.6	19.7	61.5	42.1	82.3
Divorced	4.3	4.5	5.1	5.7	2.9	3.0	2.1	2.1
White								
Total (thousands)	10,798	15,204	7,050	8,767	3,136	5,174	612	1,263
Percent[1]	100.0	100.0	100.0	100.0	100.0	100.0	100.0	100.0
Never married	4.6	5.1	4.8	4.5	4.5	6.0	3.1	5.7
Married, spouse present	76.3	41.2	80.6	53.3	72.3	28.7	47.9	8.8
Married, spouse absent	2.1	1.2	2.0	1.3	1.6	1.1	4.8	0.6
Widowed	13.2	48.1	8.1	35.5	19.2	61.0	41.8	82.7
Divorced	3.8	4.4	4.5	5.4	2.4	3.2	2.4	2.2
Black								
Total (thousands)	981	1,455	619	913	300	416	62	126
Percent[1]	100.0	100.0	100.0	100.0	100.0	100.0	100.0	100.0
Never married	4.5	4.5	4.0	4.3	6.0	4.6	(B)	5.7
Married, spouse present	56.0	27.9	58.6	33.4	50.9	20.8	(B)	12.2
Married, spouse absent	8.3	5.8	8.6	6.0	9.2	5.9	(B)	4.2
Widowed	21.4	55.3	17.6	47.1	24.7	66.9	(B)	76.3
Divorced	9.8	6.5	11.1	9.2	9.2	1.9	(B)	1.6
Hispanic origin[2]								
Total (thousands)	447	558	301	350	120	176	26	31
Percent[1]	100.0	100.0	100.0	100.0	100.0	100.0	100.0	100.0
Never married	6.6	8.2	6.4	6.8	6.0	11.0	(B)	(B)
Married, spouse present	65.6	37.6	69.7	47.5	62.8	23.1	(B)	(B)
Married, spouse absent	7.7	2.5	8.5	2.4	6.6	2.9	(B)	(B)
Widowed	15.1	43.6	9.3	33.6	21.4	57.8	(B)	(B)
Divorced	5.0	8.1	6.1	9.7	3.2	5.2	(B)	(B)

Source: Aging America, Trends and Projections, prepared by the U.S. Senate Special Committee on Aging, the American Association of Retired Persons, the Federal Council on the Aging, and the U.S. Administration on Aging, 1991, Washington, D.C., p. 184. Primary source: U.S. Bureau of the Census, "Marital Status and Living Arrangements: March 1989," *Current Population Reports,* Series P-20, No. 445, June 1990. *Notes:* (B) indicates that the base population was less than 75,000 and is too small to show derived measures. 1. Percentage distributions may not add to 100.0 due to rounding. 2. People of Hispanic origin may be of any race.

★ 175 ★

Marital Status

Marital Status, All Races, Both Sexes, by Selected Age Groups, March 1990

[Values in thousands and percent]

	Total 65 years and over	Total 18 years and over	55 to 64	65 to 74	75 to 84	85 years and over
Number (000)						
Total	29,566	181,849	21,232	17,979	9,354	2,233
Never married	1,373	40,361	1,019	836	418	119
Married, spouse present	16,003	106,441	15,379	11,353	4,145	505
Married, spouse absent	585	6,111	648	369	178	38
Separated	363	4,662	483	255	96	13
Other	222	1,449	165	114	82	26
Widowed	10,122	13,810	2,265	4,330	4,286	1,506
Divorced	1,483	15,125	1,921	1,091	328	65
Percent						
Total	100.0	100.0	100.0	100.0	100.0	100.0
Never married	4.6	22.2	4.8	4.7	4.5	5.3
Married, spouse present	54.1	58.5	72.4	63.1	44.3	22.6
Married, spouse absent	2.0	3.4	3.0	2.1	1.9	1.7
Separated	1.2	2.6	2.3	1.4	1.0	.6
Other	.8	.8	.8	.6	.9	1.2
Widowed	34.2	7.6	10.7	24.1	45.8	67.4
Divorced	5.0	8.3	9.0	6.1	3.5	2.9

Source: Marital Status and Living Arrangements: March 1990, Current Population Reports, Series P-20, No. 450, May 1991, U.S. Bureau of the Census.

★ 176 ★

Marital Status

Marital Status, All Races, Both Sexes, Metropolitan, by Selected Age Groups, March 1990

[Values in thousands and percent]

	Total 65 years and over	Total 18 years and over	55 to 64	65 to 74	75 to 84	85 years and over
	Number (000)					
Total	21,678	141,789	15,948	13,296	6,786	1,596
Never married	1,080	33,800	847	658	333	89
Married, spouse present	11,474	80,551	11,313	8,243	2,884	346
Married, spouse absent	451	4,971	514	288	136	27
Separated	295	3,785	396	207	78	10
Other	156	1,185	118	81	58	17
Widowed	7,510	10,364	1,728	3,257	3,174	1,079
Divorced	1,163	12,103	1,546	850	259	55
	Percent					
Total	100.0	100.0	100.0	100.0	100.0	100.0
Never married	5.0	23.8	5.3	4.9	4.9	5.6
Married, spouse present	52.9	56.8	70.9	62.0	42.5	21.7
Married, spouse absent	2.1	3.5	3.2	2.2	2.0	1.7
Separated	1.4	2.7	2.5	1.6	1.1	.6
Other	.7	.8	.7	.6	.9	1.0
Widowed	34.6	7.3	10.8	24.5	46.8	67.6
Divorced	5.4	8.5	9.7	6.4	3.8	3.4

Source: Marital Status and Living Arrangements: March 1990, Current Population Reports, Series P-20, No. 450, May 1991, U.S. Bureau of the Census.

★ 177 ★

Marital Status

Marital Status, All Races, Both Sexes, Midwest, by Selected Age Groups, March 1990

[Values in thousands and percent]

	Total 65 years and over	Total 18 years and over	55 to 64	65 to 74	75 to 84	85 years and over
			Number (000)			
Total	7,321	43,809	5,164	4,349	2,410	561
Never married	359	9,671	259	218	115	26
Married, spouse present	4,004	26,134	3,853	2,802	1,080	122
Married, spouse absent	122	1,031	103	66	48	8
Separated	64	819	83	39	23	3
Other	58	211	21	27	25	6
Widowed	2,504	3,344	541	1,024	1,091	389
Divorced	331	3,630	407	239	76	16
			Percent			
Total	100.0	100.0	100.0	100.0	100.0	100.0
Never married	4.9	22.1	5.0	5.0	4.8	4.6
Married, spouse present	54.7	59.7	74.6	64.4	44.8	21.7
Married, spouse absent	1.7	2.4	2.0	1.5	2.0	1.5
Separated	.9	1.9	1.6	.9	1.0	.5
Other	.8	.5	.4	.6	1.0	1.0
Widowed	34.2	7.6	10.5	23.5	45.3	69.3
Divorced	4.5	8.3	7.9	5.5	3.2	2.8

Source: Marital Status and Living Arrangements: March 1990, Current Population Reports, Series P-20, No. 450, May 1991, U.S. Bureau of the Census.

★ 178 ★
Marital Status

Marital Status, All Races, Both Sexes, Northeast, by Selected Age Groups, March 1990

[Values in thousands and percent]

	Total 65 years and over	Total 18 years and over	55 to 64	65 to 74	75 to 84	85 years and over
Number (000)						
Total	6,678	38,256	4,600	4,031	2,092	555
Never married	530	9,744	308	318	166	46
Married, spouse present	3,429	21,611	3,252	2,479	839	111
Married, spouse absent	135	1,335	179	89	37	9
Separated	87	1,023	139	67	16	4
Other	48	311	40	22	21	5
Widowed	2,337	3,162	513	960	1,002	375
Divorced	247	2,405	348	185	48	13
Percent						
Total	100.0	100.0	100.0	100.0	100.0	100.0
Never married	7.9	25.5	6.7	7.9	7.9	8.3
Married, spouse present	51.4	56.5	70.7	61.5	40.1	20.0
Married, spouse absent	2.0	3.5	3.9	2.2	1.7	1.7
Separated	1.3	2.7	3.0	1.7	.8	.8
Other	.7	.8	.9	.5	1.0	.9
Widowed	35.0	8.3	11.2	23.8	47.9	67.7
Divorced	3.7	6.3	7.6	4.6	2.3	2.4

Source: *Marital Status and Living Arrangements: March 1990*, Current Population Reports, Series P-20, No. 450, May 1991, U.S. Bureau of the Census.

★ 179 ★

Marital Status

Marital Status, All Races, Both Sexes, South, by Selected Age Groups, March 1990

[Values in thousands and percent]

	Total 65 years and over	Total 18 years and over	55 to 64	65 to 74	75 to 84	85 years and over
Number (000)						
Total	10,085	62,129	7,410	6,140	3,237	709
Never married	288	12,342	312	166	97	26
Married, spouse present	5,470	37,150	5,342	3,836	1,458	177
Married, spouse absent	208	2,328	239	135	61	11
Separated	139	1,858	188	103	31	5
Other	69	469	51	32	31	7
Widowed	3,587	4,942	841	1,605	1,505	477
Divorced	532	5,368	676	398	116	19
Percent						
Total	100.0	100.0	100.0	100.0	100.0	100.0
Never married	2.9	19.9	4.2	2.7	3.0	3.6
Married, spouse present	54.2	59.8	72.1	62.5	45.0	24.9
Married, spouse absent	2.1	3.7	3.2	2.2	1.9	1.6
Separated	1.4	3.0	2.5	1.7	.9	.7
Other	.7	.8	.7	.5	.9	.9
Widowed	35.6	8.0	11.3	26.1	46.5	67.3
Divorced	5.3	8.6	9.1	6.5	3.6	2.6

Source: Marital Status and Living Arrangements: March 1990, Current Population Reports, Series P-20, No. 450, May 1991, U.S. Bureau of the Census.

★ 180 ★

Marital Status

Marital Status, All Races, Both Sexes, West, by Selected Age Groups, March 1990

[Values in thousands and percent]

	Total 65 years and over	Total 18 years and over	55 to 64	65 to 74	75 to 84	85 years and over
Number (000)						
Total	5,483	37,654	4,058	3,459	1,616	408
Never married	195	8,605	141	134	40	22
Married, spouse present	3,099	21,547	2,932	2,236	768	96
Married, spouse absent	121	1,418	126	79	32	10
Separated	73	961	73	46	27	1
Other	47	457	53	34	5	9
Widowed	1,694	2,362	370	741	689	265
Divorced	373	3,722	490	269	87	17
Percent						
Total	100.0	100.0	100.0	100.0	100.0	100.0
Never married	3.6	22.9	3.5	3.9	2.5	5.3
Married, spouse present	56.5	57.2	72.2	64.6	47.5	23.4
Married, spouse absent	2.2	3.8	3.1	2.3	2.0	2.4
Separated	1.3	2.6	1.8	1.3	1.7	.2
Other	.9	1.2	1.3	1.0	.3	2.1
Widowed	30.9	6.3	9.1	21.4	42.6	64.8
Divorced	6.8	9.9	12.1	7.8	5.4	4.2

Source: Marital Status and Living Arrangements: March 1990, Current Population Reports, Series P-20, No. 450, May 1991, U.S. Bureau of the Census.

★ 181 ★

Marital Status

Marital Status, All Races, Females, by Selected Age Groups, March 1990

[Values in thousands and percent]

	Total 65 years and over	Total 18 years and over	55 to 64	65 to 74	75 to 84	85 years and over
Number (000)						
Total	17,232	94,977	11,230	9,966	5,792	1,475
Never married	850	17,927	443	460	299	92
Married, spouse present	6,845	53,193	7,426	5,089	1,607	150
Married, spouse absent	298	3,535	321	208	83	7
Separated	180	2,843	253	137	39	5
Other	118	692	68	71	45	2
Widowed	8,367	11,477	1,931	3,597	3,593	1,177
Divorced	872	8,844	1,107	613	209	50
Percent						
Total	100.0	100.0	100.0	100.0	100.0	100.0
Never married	4.9	18.9	3.9	4.6	5.2	6.2
Married, spouse present	39.7	56.0	66.1	51.1	27.7	10.1
Married, spouse absent	1.7	3.7	2.9	2.1	1.4	.5
Separated	1.0	3.0	2.3	1.4	.7	.3
Other	.7	.7	.6	.7	.8	.2
Widowed	48.6	12.1	17.2	36.1	62.0	79.8
Divorced	5.1	9.3	9.9	6.2	3.6	3.4

Source: Marital Status and Living Arrangements: March 1990, Current Population Reports, Series P-20, No. 450, May 1991, U.S. Bureau of the Census.

★ 182 ★

Marital Status

Marital Status, All Races, Males, by Selected Age Groups, March 1990

[Values in thousands and percent]

	Total 65 years and over	Total 18 years and over	55 to 64	65 to 74	75 to 84	85 years and over
Number (000)						
Total	12,334	86,872	10,002	8,013	3,562	758
Never married	522	22,434	576	376	119	27
Married, spouse present	9,158	53,249	7,953	6,265	2,537	356
Married, spouse absent	287	2,576	326	161	94	32
Separated	183	1,819	230	118	58	8
Other	104	756	97	43	37	24
Widowed	1,755	2,333	334	733	693	329
Divorced	611	6,281	813	478	118	15
Percent						
Total	100.0	100.0	100.0	100.0	100.0	100.0
Never married	4.2	25.8	5.8	4.7	3.3	3.5
Married, spouse present	74.2	61.3	79.5	78.2	71.2	46.9
Married, spouse absent	2.3	3.0	3.3	2.0	2.6	4.2
Separated	1.5	2.1	2.3	1.5	1.6	1.0
Other	.8	.9	1.0	.5	1.0	3.1
Widowed	14.2	2.7	3.3	9.2	19.5	43.4
Divorced	5.0	7.2	8.1	6.0	3.3	2.0

Source: Marital Status and Living Arrangements: March 1990, Current Population Reports, Series P-20, No. 450, May 1991, U.S. Bureau of the Census.

★ 183 ★

Marital Status

Marital Status, Blacks, Both Sexes, by Selected Age Groups, March 1990

[Values in thousands and percent]

	Total 65 years and over	Total 18 years and over	55 to 64	65 to 74	75 to 84	85 years and over
			Number (000)			
Total	2,487	20,320	2,106	1,508	774	205
Never married	137	7,141	185	91	34	11
Married, spouse present	920	7,619	1,032	609	273	38
Married, spouse absent	177	1,683	211	112	61	4
Separated	154	1,471	188	96	55	2
Other	23	212	24	16	6	2
Widowed	1,032	1,730	394	522	359	151
Divorced	221	2,146	284	174	46	1
			Percent			
Total	100.0	100.0	100.0	100.0	100.0	100.0
Never married	5.5	35.1	8.8	6.0	4.4	5.6
Married, spouse present	37.0	37.5	49.0	40.4	35.3	18.3
Married, spouse absent	7.1	8.3	10.0	7.4	7.9	1.8
Separated	6.2	7.2	8.9	6.4	7.2	.9
Other	.9	1.0	1.1	1.0	.7	.9
Widowed	41.5	8.5	18.7	34.6	46.4	73.8
Divorced	8.9	10.6	13.5	11.6	5.9	.6

Source: Marital Status and Living Arrangements: March 1990, Current Population Reports, Series P-20, No. 450, May 1991, U.S. Bureau of the Census.

★ 184 ★

Marital Status

Marital Status, Blacks, Females, by Selected Age Groups, March 1990

[Values in thousands and percent]

	Total 65 years and over	Total 18 years and over	55 to 64	65 to 74	75 to 84	85 years and over
Number (000)						
Total	1,484	11,183	1,170	882	472	130
Never married	79	3,634	79	51	23	5
Married, spouse present	376	3,757	468	261	104	11
Married, spouse absent	93	1,056	125	65	26	2
Separated	88	939	115	60	26	2
Other	5	117	10	5	-	-
Widowed	797	1,392	336	398	288	111
Divorced	138	1,344	162	106	31	1
Percent						
Total	100.0	100.0	100.0	100.0	100.0	100.0
Never married	5.3	32.5	6.8	5.8	4.9	3.5
Married, spouse present	25.3	33.6	40.0	29.6	22.0	8.6
Married, spouse absent	6.3	9.4	10.6	7.4	5.6	1.4
Separated	5.9	8.4	9.8	6.8	5.6	1.4
Other	.3	1.0	.8	.5	-	-
Widowed	53.7	12.4	28.7	45.1	61.0	85.6
Divorced	9.3	12.0	13.8	12.1	6.5	.9

Source: Marital Status and Living Arrangements: March 1990, Current Population Reports, Series P-20, No. 450, May 1991, U.S. Bureau of the Census.

★ 185 ★
Marital Status

Marital Status, Blacks, Males, by Selected Age Groups, March 1990

[Values in thousands and percent]

	Total 65 years and over	Total 18 years and over	55 to 64	65 to 74	75 to 84	85 years and over
Number (000)						
Total	1,003	9,137	937	626	302	75
Never married	57	3,508	106	39	11	7
Married, spouse present	544	3,862	563	348	170	26
Married, spouse absent	84	627	87	47	35	2
Separated	65	533	73	36	29	-
Other	19	95	14	11	6	2
Widowed	235	338	58	124	71	40
Divorced	83	802	122	68	15	-
Percent						
Total	100.0	100.0	100.0	100.0	100.0	(B)
Never married	5.7	38.4	11.3	6.3	3.7	(B)
Married, spouse present	54.2	42.3	60.2	55.5	56.1	(B)
Married, spouse absent	8.4	6.9	9.3	7.5	11.5	(B)
Separated	6.5	5.8	7.8	5.8	9.6	(B)
Other	1.8	1.0	1.5	1.8	1.9	(B)
Widowed	23.4	3.7	6.2	19.8	23.6	(B)
Divorced	8.3	8.8	13.0	10.9	5.0	(B)

Source: Marital Status and Living Arrangements: March 1990, Current Population Reports, Series P-20, No. 450, May 1991, U.S. Bureau of the Census. *Note:* (B) means base population is less than 75,000 and is too small to show derived measures.

★ 186 ★

Marital Status

Marital Status, Hispanics, Both Sexes, by Selected Age Groups, March 1990

[Values in thousands and percent]

	Total 65 years and over	Total 18 years and over	55 to 64	65 to 74	75 to 84	85 years and over
Number (000)						
Total	1,024	13,560	1,207	713	254	56
Never married	42	3,694	63	26	12	4
Married, spouse present	566	7,344	830	443	108	14
Married, spouse absent	55	1,021	84	42	12	1
Separated	41	578	47	30	11	-
Other	14	443	37	12	1	1
Widowed	294	548	138	144	112	37
Divorced	68	952	92	58	9	1
Percent						
Total	100.0	100.0	100.0	100.0	100.0	(B)
Never married	4.1	27.2	5.2	3.7	4.8	(B)
Married, spouse present	55.2	54.2	68.8	62.1	42.5	(B)
Married, spouse absent	5.4	7.5	6.9	5.9	4.9	(B)
Separated	4.0	4.3	3.9	4.1	4.4	(B)
Other	1.4	3.3	3.1	1.7	.5	(B)
Widowed	28.7	4.0	11.4	20.2	44.2	(B)
Divorced	6.6	7.0	7.6	8.1	3.6	(B)

Source: Marital Status and Living Arrangements: March 1990, Current Population Reports, Series P-20, No. 450, May 1991, U.S. Bureau of the Census. *Note:* (B) means base population is less than 75,000 and is too small to show derived measures.

★ 187 ★

Marital Status

Marital Status, Hispanics, Females, by Selected Age Groups, March 1990

[Values in thousands and percent]

	Total 65 years and over	Total 18 years and over	55 to 64	65 to 74	75 to 84	85 years and over
Number (000)						
Total	557	6,819	670	373	154	30
Never married	30	1,532	31	19	8	3
Married, spouse present	223	3,739	419	180	40	2
Married, spouse absent	21	520	51	15	7	-
Separated	16	393	32	11	6	-
Other	5	127	19	4	1	-
Widowed	235	445	118	118	94	24
Divorced	48	582	51	42	5	1
Percent						
Total	100.0	100.0	100.0	100.0	100.0	(B)
Never married	5.4	22.5	4.7	5.0	5.3	(B)
Married, spouse present	40.0	54.8	62.6	48.2	26.3	(B)
Married, spouse absent	3.8	7.6	7.6	3.9	4.4	(B)
Separated	2.9	5.8	4.7	2.9	3.6	(B)
Other	.9	1.9	2.8	1.0	.8	(B)
Widowed	42.2	6.5	17.6	31.5	60.9	(B)
Divorced	8.6	8.5	7.6	11.3	3.1	(B)

Source: Marital Status and Living Arrangements: March 1990, Current Population Reports, Series P-20, No. 450, May 1991, U.S. Bureau of the Census. *Note:* (B) means base population is less than 75,000 and is too small to show derived measures.

★ 188 ★

Marital Status

Marital Status, Hispanics, Males, by Selected Age Groups, March 1990

[Values in thousands and percent]

	Total 65 years and over	Total 18 years and over	55 to 64	65 to 74	75 to 84	85 years and over
Number (000)						
Total	467	6,741	537	340	101	26
Never married	12	2,162	32	8	4	1
Married, spouse present	343	3,605	411	263	68	12
Married, spouse absent	34	501	33	27	6	1
Separated	25	185	15	19	6	-
Other	9	316	18	8	-	1
Widowed	59	103	20	27	19	13
Divorced	20	370	40	15	5	-
Percent						
Total	100.0	100.0	100.0	100.0	100.0	(B)
Never married	2.6	32.1	6.0	2.2	3.9	(B)
Married, spouse present	73.3	53.5	76.6	77.4	67.2	(B)
Married, spouse absent	7.2	7.4	6.1	8.0	5.6	(B)
Separated	5.2	2.7	2.8	5.5	5.6	(B)
Other	2.0	4.7	3.4	2.5	-	(B)
Widowed	12.6	1.5	3.8	7.9	18.8	(B)
Divorced	4.3	5.5	7.5	4.5	4.5	(B)

Source: Marital Status and Living Arrangements: March 1990, Current Population Reports, Series P-20, No. 450, May 1991, U.S. Bureau of the Census. *Note:* (B) means base population is less than 75,000 and is too small to show derived measures.

★ 189 ★

Marital Status

Marital Status, Whites, Both Sexes, by Selected Age Groups, March 1990

[Values in thousands and percent]

	Total 65 years and over	Total 18 years and over	55 to 64	65 to 74	75 to 84	85 years and over
Number (000)						
Total	26,479	155,454	18,578	16,049	8,440	1,990
Never Married	1,201	31,633	810	715	381	106
Married, spouse present	14,758	95,267	13,988	10,490	3,810	458
Married, spouse absent	382	4,183	406	242	108	32
Separated	199	3,069	285	152	37	11
Other	183	1,114	121	90	71	22
Widowed	8,896	11,730	1,776	3,705	3,862	1,330
Divorced	1,241	12,640	1,597	897	280	64
Percent						
Total	100.0	100.0	100.0	100.0	100.0	100.0
Never Married	4.5	20.3	4.4	4.5	4.5	5.3
Married, spouse present	55.7	61.3	75.3	65.4	45.1	23.0
Married, spouse absent	1.4	2.7	2.2	1.5	1.3	1.6
Separated	.8	2.0	1.5	.9	.4	.5
Other	.7	.7	.7	.6	.8	1.1
Widowed	33.6	7.5	9.6	23.1	45.8	66.8
Divorced	4.7	8.1	8.6	5.6	3.3	3.2

Source: Marital Status and Living Arrangements: March 1990, Current Population Reports, Series P-20, No. 450, May 1991, U.S. Bureau of the Census.

★ 190 ★

Marital Status

Marital Status, Whites, Females, by Selected Age Groups, March 1990

[Values in thousands and percent]

	Total 65 years and over	Total 18 years and over	55 to 64	65 to 74	75 to 84	85 years and over
Number (000)						
Total	15,444	80,624	9,748	8,867	5,245	1,332
Never married	757	13,622	352	394	275	87
Married, spouse present	6,342	47,575	6,777	4,721	1,483	138
Married, spouse absent	199	2,343	182	140	54	5
Separated	91	1,823	132	77	11	3
Other	109	520	49	63	43	2
Widowed	7,423	9,800	1,512	3,115	3,255	1,053
Divorced	722	7,284	925	497	177	48
Percent						
Total	100.0	100.0	100.0	100.0	100.0	100.0
Never married	4.9	16.9	3.6	4.4	5.2	6.6
Married, spouse present	41.1	59.0	69.5	53.2	28.3	10.3
Married, spouse absent	1.3	2.9	1.9	1.6	1.0	.4
Separated	.6	2.3	1.4	.9	.2	.2
Other	.7	.6	.5	.7	.8	.2
Widowed	48.1	12.2	15.5	35.1	62.1	79.1
Divorced	4.7	9.0	9.5	5.6	3.4	3.6

Source: Marital Status and Living Arrangements: March 1990, Current Population Reports, Series P-20, No. 450, May 1991, U.S. Bureau of the Census.

★ 191 ★

Marital Status

Marital Status, Whites, Males, by Selected Age Groups, March 1990

[Values in thousands and percent]

	Total 65 years and over	Total 18 years and over	55 to 64	65 to 74	75 to 84	85 years and over
	Number (000)					
Total	11,035	74,830	8,830	7,182	3,195	658
Never married	445	18,011	458	321	105	18
Married, spouse present	8,416	47,692	7,211	5,768	2,327	321
Married, spouse absent	183	1,840	225	102	53	27
Separated	109	1,246	153	75	25	8
Other	74	594	72	27	28	19
Widowed	1,473	1,930	264	590	607	277
Divorced	519	5,356	673	400	103	15
	Percent					
Total	100.0	100.0	100.0	100.0	100.0	100.0
Never married	4.0	24.1	5.2	4.5	3.3	2.8
Married, spouse present	76.3	63.7	81.7	80.3	72.8	48.7
Married, spouse absent	1.7	2.5	2.5	1.4	1.7	4.1
Separated	1.0	1.7	1.7	1.0	.8	1.2
Other	.7	.8	.8	.4	.9	2.9
Widowed	13.3	2.6	3.0	8.2	19.0	42.0
Divorced	4.7	7.2	7.6	5.6	3.2	2.3

Source: *Marital Status and Living Arrangements: March 1990,* Current Population Reports, Series P-20, No. 450, May 1991, U.S. Bureau of the Census.

★ 192 ★

Marital Status

Persons 100 Years and Over, by Age, Marital Status, and Age Allocation: 1980

Age	Total	Never married	Now married	Separated	Widowed	Divorced
Total persons[1]	22,012	3,410	2,270	151	15,803	378
100-104	18,015	2,271	1,759	105	13,574	306
105-109	3,158	814	401	42	1,837	64
110+	839	325	110	4	392	8

Source: Gregory Spencer, Arnold A. Goldstein, and Cynthia M. Taeuber, *America's Centenarians: Data from the 1980 Census*, National Institute on Aging, Washington, DC, June 1987, p. B2. *Notes:* 1. A problem with 1980 Census allocation procedures resulted in an inflation of the count of the centenarian population by about one-fourth. This data reflects unallocated age data only and therefore may be subject to sampling error due to incorrect reporting, overreporting by respondents, or incomplete documentation.

Contact with Children

★ 193 ★

Number of Living Children of Noninstitutionalized Men, by Race and Age

From the source: "Tables from this paper have been generated in the process of editing and 'cleansing' the study's data tape, which is a continuing process. As a consequence, tables should not be considered final versions. The original authors, however, are confident that while tables generated by the final data tape may show minor differences, the overall conclusions will not be substantially altered."

[Percentage distributions]

Number of children	All races			Blacks		
	Total age	69-74	75-84	Total age	69-74	75-84
n[1]	2,066	1,123	943	481	270	211
Total percent[2]	100	100	100	100	100	100
None	12	11	14	15	15	16
1	16	13	19	16	13	19
2	25	24	27	15	16	15

[Continued]

★ 193 ★

Number of Living Children of Noninstitutionalized Men, by Race and Age

[Continued]

Number of children	All races			Blacks		
	Total age	69-74	75-84	Total age	69-74	75-84
3-5	36	39	32	32	33	31
6+	11	14	8	22	24	20

Source: Herbert S. Parnes, Thomas N. Chirikos, Elizabeth G. Menaghan, Frank L. Mott, Gilbert Nestel, Lois B. Shaw, David G. Sommers, *The NLS Older Male Sample Revisited: A Unique Data Base for Gerontological Research*, Center for Human Resource Research, The Ohio State University, 1993, p. 53, reprinted with permission. *Notes:* 1. Number of sample cases on which weighted percentages are based. 2. Percentages may not add to 100 because of rounding.

★ 194 ★

Contact with Children

Proximity of Nearest Child to Respondent's Residence, by Race and Age: Noninstitutionalized Men with Children

[Percentage distributions]

Proximity of nearest child	All races			Blacks		
	Total age	69-74	75-84	Total age	69-74	75-84
n[1]	1,684	934	750	372	206	166
Total percent[2]	100	100	100	100	100	100
Lives at home	11	13	12	25	28	21
None at home	89	87	88	76	73	79
<1 hour	63	60	61	52	53	52
1-4 hours	16	17	17	15	12	20
5-9 hours	5	5	5	3	3	4
10-23 hours	2	2	2	1	1	1
1 day	2	2	2	2	2	2
2+ days	1	1	1	2	3	2

Source: Herbert S. Parnes, Thomas N. Chirikos, Elizabeth G. Menaghan, Frank L. Mott, Gilbert Nestel, Lois B. Shaw, David G. Sommers, *The NLS Older Male Sample Revisited: A Unique Data Base for Gerontological Research*, Center for Human Resource Research, The Ohio State University, 1993, p. 54, reprinted with permission. *Notes:* 1. Number of sample cases on which weighted percentages are based. 2. Percentages may not add to 100 because of rounding.

★ 195 ★

Contact with Children

Frequency of Face-to-Face Contact with Child(ren) Living Away from Home, by Race and Age: Noninstitutionalized Men with Nonresident Children[1]

[Percentage distributions]

Frequency of contact	All races			Blacks		
	Total age	69-74	75-84	Total age	69-74	75-84
n[2]	1,745	968	777	388	224	164
Total percent[3]	100	100	100	100	100	100
Daily	4	3	4	5	6	6
Weekly	18	15	22	17	19	15
Monthly	16	17	16	13	18	6
Several times a year	30	32	28	25	22	30
Once a year	16	17	15	14	12	17
Less than once a year	11	12	9	15	15	15
Not at all	5	5	6	11	10	12

Source: Herbert S. Parnes, Thomas N. Chirikos, Elizabeth G. Menaghan, Frank L. Mott, Gilbert Nestel, Lois B. Shaw, David G. Sommers, *The NLS Older Male Sample Revisited: A Unique Data Base for Gerontological Research,* Center for Human Resource Research, The Ohio State University, 1993, p. 55, reprinted with permission. *Notes:* 1. If more than one child, the most frequent contact is tabulated. 2. Number of sample cases on which weighted percentages are based. 3. Percentages may not add to 100 because of rounding.

★ 196 ★

Contact with Children

Frequency of Telephone Contact with Child(ren) Living Away from Home, by Race and Age: Noninstitutionalized Men with Nonresidential Children[1]

[Percentage distributions]

Frequency of contact	All races			Blacks		
	Total age	69-74	75-84	Total age	69-74	75-84
n[2]	1,731	961	770	383	223	160
Total percent[3]	100	100	100	100	100	100
Daily	10	8	11	13	16	8
Weekly	34	34	35	23	26	18
Monthly	25	28	22	21	17	27
Several times a year	17	16	17	17	16	19
Once a year	2	3	2	4	3	6

[Continued]

★ 196 ★

Frequency of Telephone Contact with Child(ren) Living Away from Home, by Race and Age: Noninstitutionalized Men with Nonresidential Children

[Continued]

Frequency of contact	All races			Blacks		
	Total age	69-74	75-84	Total age	69-74	75-84
Less than once a year	3	2	3	5	7	3
Not at all	10	9	10	16	15	19

Source: Herbert S. Parnes, Thomas N. Chirikos, Elizabeth G. Menaghan, Frank L. Mott, Gilbert Nestel, Lois B. Shaw, David G. Sommers, *The NLS Older Male Sample Revisited: A Unique Data Base for Gerontological Research*, Center for Human Resource Research, The Ohio State University, 1993, p. 56, reprinted with permission. *Notes:* 1. If more than one child, the most frequent contact is tabulated. 2. Number of sample cases on which weighted percentages are based. 3. Percentages may not add to 100 because of rounding.

★ 197 ★

Contact with Children

Frequency of Contact by Mail with Child(ren) Living Away from Home, by Race and Age: Noninstitutionalized Men with Nonresidential Children[1]

[Percentage distributions]

Frequency of contact	All races			Blacks		
	Total age	69-74	75-84	Total age	69-74	75-84
Number[2]	1,669	930	739	358	206	152
Total percent[3]	100	100	100	100	100	100
Daily	3	4	0	0	0	0
Weekly	1	4	1	1	0	1
Monthly	6	6	6	3	3	3
Several times a year	45	47	43	31	32	29
Once a year	12	11	12	13	14	11
Less than once a year	4	4	3	4	5	2
Not at all	34	32	35	50	46	54

Source: Herbert S. Parnes, Thomas N. Chirikos, Elizabeth G. Menaghan, Frank L. Mott, Gilbert Nestel, Lois B. Shaw, David G. Sommers, *The NLS Older Male Sample Revisited: A Unique Data Base for Gerontological Research*, Center for Human Resource Research, The Ohio State University, 1993, p. 57, reprinted with permission. *Notes:* 1. If more than one child, the most frequent contact is tabulated. 2. Number of sample cases on which weighted percentages are based. 3. Percentages may not add to 100 because of rounding. 4. Percentage less than 0.5.

Relationships

★ 198 ★

Patterns of Intimate Friendship, by Race and Age:
Noninstitutionalized Men[1]
[Percentage distributions]

Pattern of friendship	All races			Blacks		
	Total age	69-74	75-84	Total age	69-74	75-84
n[2]	1,877	1,038	839	431	246	185
Total percent[3]	100	100	100	100	100	100
No close friends	7	6	8	10	10	10
Spouse only close friend	9	9	9	9	8	12
Spouse and other close friend(s)	35	37	33	26	28	23
Spouse not close, but other close friend(s)	29	31	27	24	27	20
No spouse, but other close friend(s)	20	17	24	31	27	36

Source: Herbert S. Parnes, Thomas N. Chirikos, Elizabeth G. Menaghan, Frank L. Mott, Gilbert Nestel, Lois B. Shaw, David G. Sommers, *The NLS Older Male Sample Revisited: A Unique Data Base for Gerontological Research*, Center for Human Resource Research, The Ohio State University, 1993, p. 61, reprinted with permission. *Notes:* 1. "Is there any one special person you know that you feel very close and intimate with—someone you share confidences and feelings with, someone you feel you can depend on?" 2. Number of sample cases on which weighted percentages are based. 3. Percentages may not add to 100 because of rounding.

★ 199 ★

Relationships

Marital Status and Living Arrangements of Widows,
by Race and Age: 1990
[Percentage distributions]

Item	All races				Blacks
	Total age	Less than 65	65-74	75 and over	
Marital status					
n[1]	1,244	134	645	465	336
Total percent[3]	100	100	100	100	100
Married	5	10	7	2	3
Widowed	94	87	93	97	96
Other	1	3	1	1	1
Living arrangements[2]					
n[1]	1,164	123	614	427	314
Total percent	100	100	100	100	100

[Continued]

★ 199 ★

Marital Status and Living Arrangements of Widows,
by Race and Age: 1990
[Continued]

Item	All races				Blacks
	Total age	Less than 65	65-74	75 and over	
Alone or with spouse[4]	81	71	79	86	62
With other relative[4]	19	29	21	14	38

Source: Herbert S. Parnes, Thomas N. Chirikos, Elizabeth G. Menaghan, Frank L. Mott, Gilbert Nestel, Lois B. Shaw, David G. Sommers, *The NLS Older Male Sample Revisited: A Unique Data Base for Gerontological Research*, Center for Human Resource Research, The Ohio State University, 1993, p. 93, reprinted with permission. *Notes:* 1. Number of sample cases on which weighted percentages are based. 2. Noninstitutional population only. 3. Percentages may not add to 100 because of rounding. 4. May include children under 14.

Chapter 5
INCOME, ASSETS, AND SPENDING

This chapter pulls together tables on the economic characteristics of older Americans. The Summary section at the beginning presents materials that provide a general overview. After that, sections are arranged to show data on Assets, Net Worth, Earnings, Income, Household Income, Sources of Income, and Debt. Following these "financial statement" headings are placed materials on Financial Planning, Poverty, and Spending, including one table on Charitable Giving and five tables on Legal Costs.

Not all tables of a financial nature could be included in this chapter. Financial tables relating to pensions and retirement, social security, and housing are placed in chapters on those subjects. Similarly, the chapters on *Health and Health Care*, *Health Insurance*, and *Nursing Homes and Resident Care* also hold information related to income and costs.

Summary

★ 200 ★

Median Income of Elderly Men and Women, by Marital Status: 1989

Median income, as used in this and other tables throughout this chapter, means that half of the population had income below the figure and half had income above the figure shown. Median means the midpoint in a range.

[Values are in dollars]

	Women	Men
Married	5,984	13,756
Widowed	8,362	11,200
Divorced	8,147	10,709
Single	10,048	10,080

Source: *Aging America, Trends and Projections*, prepared by the U.S. Senate Special Committee on Aging, the American Association of Retired Persons, the Federal Council on the Aging, and the U.S. Administration on Aging, 1991, Washington, D.C., p. 47. Primary source: March 1990 *Current Population* Survey. Data prepared by the Congressional Research Service.

★ 201 ★

Summary

Median Income of People Age 65+, by Marital Status: 1989

[Values are in dollars]

Marital status	Both sexes	Men	Women
Married	10,073	13,756	5,984
Single	10,066	10,080	10,048
Widowed	8,756	11,200	8,362
Divorced	9,298	10,709	8,147
All people 65+	9,578	13,107	7,655

Source: *Aging America, Trends and Projections*, prepared by the U.S. Senate Special Committee on Aging, the American Association of Retired Persons, the Federal Council on the Aging, and the U.S. Administration on Aging, 1991, Washington, D.C., p. 48. Primary source: Bureau of the Census. Unpublished data from the March 1990 *Current Population* Survey.

★ 202 ★

Summary

Median Income of People Age 65+, by Age, Race, Hispanic Origin, and Sex: 1989

[Values are in dollars]

Race and Hispanic origin	Both sexes			Men			Women		
	65+	65 to 69	70+	65+	65 to 69	70+	65+	65 to 69	70+
All races	9,420	10,722	8,936	13,024	15,273	12,022	7,508	7,584	7,476
White	9,838	11,323	9,305	13,391	15,680	12,410	7,816	7,977	7,756
Black	5,772	6,552	5,517	8,192	10,464	7,224	5,059	5,235	5,032
Hispanic[1]	5,978	6,664	5,715	8,469	10,240	6,816	4,992	4,640	5,112

Source: Aging America, Trends and Projections, prepared by the U.S. Senate Special Committee on Aging, the American Association of Retired Persons, the Federal Council on the Aging, and the U.S. Administration on Aging, 1991, Washington, D.C., p. 51. Primary source: Unpublished data from the March 1990 *Current Population Survey. Note:* 1. Hispanic people may be of any race.

★ 203 ★

Summary

Median Income, by Marital Status, Race, and Hispanic Origin, 1990

```
Married couples - 23,352
White - 14,542
Non-married men - 10,893
Non-married women - 8,746
Hispanic - 7,879
Black - 6,987
```

Figures based on a sample of 9,343,000 couples and 13,805,000 single "aged units"[1]. From the source: "Income is highest for married couples - with a median income more than twice that of non-married men and more than 2 1/2 times that of non-married women. Whites have a median income approximately twice as great as Hispanics or blacks."

	Median income ($000)
Married couples	23,352
Non-married men	10,893
Non-married women	8,746
White	14,542

[Continued]

★ 203 ★

Median Income, by Marital Status, Race, and Hispanic Origin, 1990

[Continued]

	Median income ($000)
Black	6,987
Hispanic[2]	7,879

Source: U.S. Department of Health and Human Services, Social Security Administration, *Income of the Aged Chartbook, 1990*, GPO, Washington, D.C., September 1992, p. 2. *Notes:* 1. "Aged unit" does not refer to the household, the family, or unrelated individuals, as used by the Bureau of the Census. The aged unit is either a married couple living together with the husband or wife aged 65 or older (generally measured by the age of the husband), or a person 65 or older who does not live with a spouse. The single person unit may be a widow(er), a divorced or separated person, a person legally married who does not live with a spouse, or a person who never married. 2. Persons of Hispanic origin may be of any race.

★ 204 ★

Summary

Median Income, by Age, 1990

Figures based on a sample of 9,343,000 couples and 13,805,000 single "aged units"[1]. From the source: "In each successively older age group, median income is lower. The striking differences by age shown in the chart are in part due to the disproportionate number of non-married women in older age groups. The table shows that in every age group, non-married women have a lower median income than non-married men or married couples. It also shows that non-married women far outnumber the others in the older age groups."

[Median income and percent of units, by age, sex and marital status]

Sex and marital status	65-69	70-74	75-79	80-84	85 or older
	Median income				
Married couples	26,202	23,954	20,719	17,710	16,964
Non-married men	12,792	11,181	10,224	10,325	9,140
Non-married women	10,111	9,281	8,573	8,379	7,416
	Percent of units				
Total number (000)	6,913	6,165	4,682	3,139	2,250
Total percent	100	100	100	100	100
Married couples	54	44	34	28	17

[Continued]

★ 204 ★

Median Income, by Age, 1990
[Continued]

Sex and marital status	65-69	70-74	75-79	80-84	85 or older
Non-married men	12	14	14	14	18
Non-married women	33	42	51	58	65

Source: U.S. Department of Health and Human Services, Social Security Administration, *Income of the Aged Chartbook, 1990*, GPO, Washington, D.C., September 1992, p. 4. *Notes:* 1. "Aged unit" does not refer to the household, the family, or unrelated individuals, as used by the Bureau of the Census. The aged unit is either a married couple living together with the husband or wife aged 65 or older (generally measured by the age of the husband), or a person 65 or older who does not live with a spouse. The single person unit may be a widow(er), a divorced or separated person, a person legally married who does not live with a spouse, or a person who never married.

★ 205 ★

Summary

Median Income, by Receipt of Earnings and Retirement Benefits, 1990

Figures based on a sample of 9,343,000 couples and 13,805,000 single "aged units".[1] From the source: "About 5% of aged units have no retirement benefits; of these, half have earnings and the highest median income ($32,457), and the other half have no earnings, and the lowest median income ($3,115). In the absence of earnings, median income rises markedly with the number of retirement benefits received, from $8,089 with one retirement benefit to $19,171 with two or more retirement benefits. For units with both earnings and retirement benefits, median incomes are $19,625 for those with one retirement benefit and $30,599 for those with more than one."

	With earnings	Without earnings
	Median income ($000)	
No retirement benefits	32,457	3,115
One retirement benefit	19,625	8,089
Two or more retirement benefits	30,599	19,171

Source: U.S. Department of Health and Human Services, Social Security Administration, *Income of the Aged Chartbook, 1990*, GPO, Washington, D.C., September 1992, p. 12. *Notes:* 1. "Aged unit" does not refer to the household, the family, or unrelated individuals, as used by the Bureau of the Census. The aged unit is either a married couple living together with the husband or wife aged 65 or older (generally measured by the age of the husband), or a person 65 or older who does not live with a spouse. The single person unit may be a widow(er), a divorced or separated person, a person legally married who does not live with a spouse, or a person who never married.

★ 206 ★

Summary

Percent Distribution of Aggregate Income by Source for Units and by Marital Status: 1976-1988

Type of unit and year	All sources	Social Security[1]	Assets	Pensions[1,2]	Earnings	SSI public assitance	Other sources
All units[3]							
1976	100	39	18	14	23	2	2
1978	100	38	19	14	23	2	2
1980	100	39	22	15	19	1	3
1982	100	39	25	14	18	1	2
1984	100	38	28	14	16	1	2
1986	100	38	26	15	17	1	2
1988	100	38	25	18	17	1	2
Married couples							
1976	100	34	18	16	29	1	2
1978	100	34	18	14	30	1	1
1980	100	34	22	17	24	1	1
1982	100	35	24	15	23	0	1
1984	100	34	27	16	21	0	1
1986	100	33	25	17	22	0	1
1988	100	34	24	19	21	0	2
Unmarried individuals							
1976	100	46	19	13	13	4	3
1978	100	46	21	14	12	3	3
1980	100	47	23	13	11	3	2
1982	100	45	27	13	10	2	2
1984	100	44	31	12	8	2	2
1986	100	45	28	14	9	2	2
1988	100	44	26	16	10	2	2

Source: Aging America, Trends and Projections, prepared by the U.S. Senate Special Committee on Aging, the American Association of Retired Persons, the Federal Council on the Aging, and the U.S. Administration on Aging, 1991, Washington, D.C., p. 66. Primary source: Susan Grad, *Income of the Population 55 or Over,* 1988 and earlier reports in this series. U.S. Social Security Administration. *Notes:* 1. For all years except 1988, data for Social Security and pensions exclude the relatively small amounts from these sources received by people who reported receiving both sources because only the combined amount is known. 2. Includes Railroad Retirement, government employee pensions, and private pensions or annuities. 3. Units are married couples living together—at least one of whom is 65+—and unmarried people 65+. Income of aged units does not include income from other household members.

★ 207 ★

Summary

Percent Distribution of Units 65+ by Number and Sources of In-Kind Benefits, Marital Status, and Sex: 1984

Number and source of in-kind benefits	Total	Married couples	Unmarried people	
			Men	Women
All units[3]	100	100	100	100
Number of in-kind benefits[2]				
0	85	94	84	78
1	11	5	13	16
2 or more	4	1	3	6
Source of in-kind benefits[3]				
Energy assistance	7	3	7	10
Food stamps	6	3	7	8
Public housing	4	1	4	6
Rental assistance	2	1	2	3

Source: Aging America, Trends and Projections, prepared by the U.S. Senate Special Committee on Aging, the American Association of Retired Persons, the Federal Council on the Aging, and the U.S. Administration on Aging, 1991, Washington, D.C., p. 70. Primary source: Social Security Administration. *Income and Resources of the Population 65 and Over*. SSA Pub. No. 13-11727, Washington; U.S. DHHS, September 1986. *Notes:* 1. Data on number of in-kind benefits refer only to the four sources specified in table. 2. Percentages not additive. 3]Units are married couples living together—at least one of whom is 65+—and unmarried people 65+. Income of aged units does not include income from other household members.

★ 208 ★

Summary

Projected Income Distribution of Impaired People Age 65+, as a Proportion of the Poverty Level: 1990, 2005, and 2020

"Impaired people" refers both to people living in the community and nursing home residents who have at least one limitation for activities of daily living.

[Numbers in thousands]

Income as proportion of poverty level	1990		2005		2020	
	Number	Percent[1]	Number	Percent[1]	Number	Percent[1]
Total	5,913	100.0	7,540	100.0	9,914	100.0
<100%	1,593	27.0	1,341	18.0	1,153	12.0
100-149%	1,578	27.0	1,734	23.0	1,690	17.0
150-199%	745	13.0	1,067	14.0	1,343	14.0
200%+	1,997	34.0	3,398	45.0	5,728	58.0

Source: Aging America, Trends and Projections, prepared by the U.S. Senate Special Committee on Aging, the American Association of Retired Persons, the Federal Council on the Aging, and the U.S. Administration on Aging, 1991, Washington, D.C., p. 176. Primary source: Lewin/ICF estimates based on data from the *1984 Survey on Aging (SOA)*, and the Brookings/ICF, *Long-Term Care Financing Model*, 1990. *Notes:* Projections assume constant age, sex, and marital status rates of disability for people in the community. Improvements in income are the result of expected growth in pension coverage, increases in real earnings, and a higher rates of female labor force participation by women. 1. Totals may exceed 100 percent due to rounding.

★ 209 ★

Summary

Size of Total Income, 1990

```
$5,000 to 9,999 - 26.0
$10,000 to 14,999 - 18.0
$15,000 to 19,999 - 12.0
Less than $5,000 - 10.0
         $20,000 to 24,999 - 9.0
           $50,000 or more - 7.0
         $25,000 to 29,000 - 6.0
         $30,000 to 34,999 - 5.0
       $35,000 to 39,999 - 3.0
     $40,000 to 44,999 - 2.0
     $45,000 to 49,999 - 2.0
```

Figures based on a sample of 9,343,000 couples and 13,805,000 single "aged units"[1]. From the source: "Median income for all aged units is $13,499, but there are wide differences within the total group. About 10% have an income of under $5,000 (an income level that is about 20% below the 1990 poverty threshold of $6,268 for one person aged 65 or older), and 7% have an income of $50,000 or more."

Income	Percent of units
Less than $5,000	10.0
$5,000 to 9,999	26.0
$10,000 to 14,999	18.0
$15,000 to 19,999	12.0
$20,000 to 24,999	9.0
$25,000 to 29,000	6.0
$30,000 to 34,999	5.0
$35,000 to 39,999	3.0
$40,000 to 44,999	2.0
$45,000 to 49,999	2.0
$50,000 or more	7.0

Source: U.S. Department of Health and Human Services, Social Security Administration, *Income of the Aged Chartbook, 1990*, GPO, Washington, D.C., September 1992, p. 1. *Notes:* 1. "Aged unit" does not refer to the household, the family, or unrelated individuals, as used by the Bureau of the Census. The aged unit is either a married couple living together with the husband or wife aged 65 or older (generally measured by the age of the husband), or a person 65 or older who does not live with a spouse. The single person unit may be a widow(er), a divorced or separated person, a person legally married who does not live with a spouse, or a person who never married.

★ 210 ★

Summary

Size of Income, by Receipt of Asset Income, 1990

Figures based on a sample of 9,343,000 couples and 13,805,000 single "aged units".[1] From the source: "The median income of those with asset income is more than 2 1/2 times as large as the median income of those with no asset income ($18,187, compared with $7,190). Aged units with no asset income are concentrated in the lowest income categories - nearly 70% have a total income below $10,000 and only 2% have an income of $30,000 or more. Among aged units with asset income, nearly 80% have a total income of at least $10,000. About 26% have an income of $30,000 or more."

[Data shown in percent]

Income	With asset income	Without asset income
Less than $10,000	22.0	69.0
$10,000 - 19,999	33.0	23.0
$20,000 - 29,999	19.0	5.0
$30,000 or more	26.0	2.0

Source: U.S. Department of Health and Human Services, Social Security Administration, *Income of the Aged Chartbook, 1990*, GPO, Washington, D.C., September 1992, p. 11. *Notes:* 1. "Aged unit" does not refer to the household, the family, or unrelated individuals, as used by the Bureau of the Census. The aged unit is either a married couple living together with the husband or wife aged 65 or older (generally measured by the age of the husband), or a person 65 or older who does not live with a spouse. The single person unit may be a widow(er), a divorced or separated person, a person legally married who does not live with a spouse, or a person who never married.

★ 211 ★

Summary

Sources of Income, 1990

Social Security - 92.0

Asset income - 69.0

Social Security - 44.0

Earnings - 22.0

Public assistance - 7.0

Veterans' benefits - 5.0

Figures based on a sample of 9,343,000 couples and 13,805,000 single "aged units".[1] From the source: "More than 9 out of 10 aged units received Social Security benefits. Asset income is the next most common source of income and it is received by more than two-thirds of the aged. Less than half (44%) received pensions other than Social Security, and only 22% have earnings. Public assistance is received by 7% and veterans' benefits are received by only 5%."

	Percent of units
Social Security	92.0
Asset income	69.0
Retirement benefits other than Social Security[2]	44.0
Earnings	22.0
Public assistance	7.0
Veterans' benefits	5.0

Source: U.S. Department of Health and Human Services, Social Security Administration, *Income of the Aged Chartbook, 1990*, GPO, Washington, D.C., September 1992, p. 8. *Notes:* 1. "Aged unit" does not refer to the household, the family, or unrelated individuals, as used by the Bureau of the Census. The aged unit is either a married couple living together with the husband or wife aged 65 or older (generally measured by the age of the husband), or a person 65 or older who does not live with a spouse. The single person unit may be a widow(er), a divorced or separated person, a person legally married who does not live with a spouse, or a person who never married. 2. Includes private pensions, government employee pensions, and Railroad Retirement.

★ 212 ★

Summary

Receipt of Income from Earnings and Pensions, by Age, 1990

Figures based on a sample of 9,343,000 couples and 13,805,000 single "aged units".[1] From the source: "Earnings are much more common in the youngest age group than in the oldest group - 40%, compared with 3%. Private pensions and other pensions are also more common among the younger groups than the older groups. For the youngest group, earnings are a more common source of income than are either private or other pensions. Among the older cohorts, private pensions are a more common source of income than are earnings or other pensions."

[Percent of units]

Age	Earnings	Private pensions	Other pensions
65-69	40.0	33.0	19.0
70-74	22.0	34.0	18.0
75-79	12.0	29.0	16.0
80-84	8.0	24.0	15.0
85 or older	3.0	19.0	12.0

Source: U.S. Department of Health and Human Services, Social Security Administration, *Income of the Aged Chartbook, 1990*, GPO, Washington, D.C., September 1992, p. 13. *Notes:* 1. "Aged unit" does not refer to the household, the family, or unrelated individuals, as used by the Bureau of the Census. The aged unit is either a married couple living together with the husband or wife aged 65 or older (generally measured by the age of the husband), or a person 65 or older who does not live with a spouse. The single person unit may be a widow(er), a divorced or separated person, a person legally married who does not live with a spouse, or a person who never married.

★ 213 ★

Summary

Economic Status of People 65+, by Living Arrangement, 1990

[Numbers in percent]

Income level	Living alone	Living with others
Above poverty		
300+% of poverty	19.0	38.0
150-299% of poverty	30.0	34.0
Below poverty		
<100% of poverty	24.0	14.0
100-149% of poverty	27.0	14.0

Source: Aging America, Trends and Projections, prepared by the U.S. Senate Special Committee on Aging, the American Association of Retired Persons, the Federal Council on the Aging, and the U.S. Administration on Aging, 1991, Washington, D.C., p. 217. Primary source: Lewin/ICF estimates based on data from the *Current Population Survey*, and the Brookings/ICF Long-Term Financing Model, 1990.

★ 214 ★

Summary

Young, Elderly, and Total Support Ratios: 1900-2050[1]

This table shows the number of people in each of the age groups (65+ and less than 18) for every 100 persons aged 18 through 64. The underlying assumption is that the 18-64 group supports the 65+ and the under 18 group. In 1980, 100 people supported 19 elderly persons and 46 young people under 18. Since both young and old must be supported, the mix of these age groups produces the total "support ratio." It was very high in 1900—because the population had proportionally many more children—and will rise in the 21st century because the elderly are increasing as a proportion of population.

Year	65+	Under 18	Total
Estimates			
1900	7	76	84
1920	8	68	76
1940	11	52	63
1960	17	65	82
1980	19	46	65
Projections			
1990	20	41	62
2000	21	39	60
2010	22	35	57
2020	29	35	64
2030	38	36	74

[Continued]

★ 214 ★

Young, Elderly, and Total Support Ratios: 1900-2050
[Continued]

Year	65 +	Under 18	Total
2040	39	35	74
2050	40	35	75

Source: Aging America, Trends and Projections, prepared by the U.S. Senate Special Committee on Aging, the American Association of Retired Persons, the Federal Council on the Aging, and the U.S. Administration on Aging, 1991, Washington, D.C., p. 18. Primary source: U.S. Bureau of the Census, *Current Population Reports*, Series P-23, No. 128, (September 1983), and P-25 No. 1018 (January 1989). *Note:* 1. Number of people of specified age per 100 people age 18 to 64.

Assets

★ 215 ★

Financial Strength of the Elderly

The financial clout of the 50-plus population in the United States is absolutely staggering. With customers over 50 accounting for a minimum of 60 percent of commercial banking deposits nationwide. They also control:
- 80 percent of all money in S&Ls
- 77 percent of all assets in the U.S.
- 68 percent of MMIA balances
- 66 percent of all investment portfolios $25,000 and larger
- 50 percent of all corporate stocks
- 42 percent of all after-tax income.

Given these figures, it is obvious that serving seniors is a crucial aspect of successful banking.

Source: Phillip Berman, "Make Positive Images of Aging Pay Off for You", *Bank Marketing*, February 1993, p. 23.

★ 216 ★

Assets

Financial Assets Held by Families: 1989

As used in the tables in this section, the term "assets" generally means properties and financial resources owned by a person or institution. Assets differ from "net worth" in that net worth is assets minus the liabilities (indebtedness and similar obligations) of the assets' owner.

[Percent of families owning asset]

Age of family head[1]	Total[2]	Checking accounts	Savings accounts	Money market accounts	Certificates of deposit	Retirement accounts	Stocks	Bonds	Non-taxable bonds
Total, all ages	87.5	75.4	43.5	22.2	19.6	33.3	19.0	4.4	4.4
Under 35 years old	82.2	68.4	45.0	14.9	8.5	23.0	11.4	0.8	0.9
35 to 44 years old	88.4	76.1	50.0	20.4	15.5	44.0	21.2	3.4	3.5
45 to 54 years old	90.4	78.9	44.6	27.0	21.1	45.5	23.1	3.5	4.3
55 to 64 years old	87.5	76.7	38.9	23.0	20.9	42.6	22.0	5.9	7.5
65 to 74 years old	91.5	79.9	37.7	28.3	31.6	30.0	20.8	9.1	9.4
75 years old and over	90.6	79.3	36.2	30.5	39.4	6.6	21.3	9.6	4.9

Source: U.S. Bureau of the Census, *Statistical Abstract of the United States: 1992* (112th edition.) Washington, DC, 1992, p. 493. Primary source: Board of Governors of the Federal Reserve System, *Federal Reserve Bulletin*, January 1992. *Notes:* 1. Families include one person units. 2. Includes other types of financial assets, not shown separately.

★ 217 ★

Assets

Top 20 Areas with the Largest Number of Affluent Elderly

Top ranked counties or county-equivalent places arranged by percent of elderly (ages 55 or older) earning $50,000 or more in 1989. Data exclude counties with fewer than 10,000 inhabitants. In the nation as a whole, the percent of affluent householders in this age group is 17.8.

County (metropolitan area)	All householders age 55 and older	Percent affluent
Fairfax, VA[1] (Washington)	70,125	57.4
Los Alamos, NM (Santa Fe)	2,223	53.3
Montgomery, MD (Washington)	83,446	50.4
Morris, NJ (Newark)	48,269	45.3
Nassau, NY (Nassau-Suffolk)	189,154	45.0
Pitkin, CO	882	44.7
Prince William, VA[2] (Washington)	11,552	42.3
Rockland, NY (New York)	29,603	43.2
Howard, MD (Baltimore)	13,883	41.9
Somerset, NJ (Middlesex-Somersert-	28,155	41.9

[Continued]

★ 217 ★

Top 20 Areas with the Largest Number of Affluent Elderly

[Continued]

County (metropolitan area)	All householders age 55 and older	Percent affluent
Hunterdon)		
Arlington, VA (Washington)	20,705	41.2
Marin, CA (San Francisco)	31,419	41.1
Anchorage, AK (Anchorage)	12,434	40.3
Honolulu, HI (Honolulu)	90,035	39.7
Loudoun, VA (Washington)	6,512	39.3
Westchester, NY (New York)	129,652	39.0
Bergen, NJ (Bergen-Passaic)	130,634	38.7
Fairfield, CT (Bridgeport-Stamford-Norwalk-Danbury)	114,791	38.0
Prince George's, MD (Washington)	61,993	37.9
Alexandria city, VA (Washington)	12,343	37.7

Source: American Demographics, December 1992, p. 42. Primary source: 1990 Census *Notes:* 1. Includes the independent cities of Fairfax and Falls Church. 2. Includes the independent cities of Manassas and Manassas Park.

★ 218 ★

Assets

Projected Asset Distribution of Impaired People Age 65+: 1990, 2005, and 2020

"Impaired people" refers both to people living in the community and nursing home residents who have at least one limitation for activities of daily living.

[Numbers in thousands; assets in non-housing 1989 dollars]

Financial assets	1990		2005		2020	
	Number	Percent	Number	Percent	Number	Percent
Total	5,913	100.0	7,540	100.0	9,914	100.0
Less than $25,000	3,548	60.0	4,222	56.0	5,155	52.0
More than $25,000	2,365	40.0	3,318	44.0	4,759	48.0

Source: Aging America, Trends and Projections, prepared by the U.S. Senate Special Committee on Aging, the American Association of Retired Persons, the Federal Council on the Aging, and the U.S. Administration on Aging, 1991, Washington, D.C., p. 178. Primary source: Lewin/ICF estimates based on data from the *1984 Survey on Aging (SOA)* and Brookings/ICF *Long-Term Care Financing Model,* 1990. *Notes:* Projections assume constant age, sex, and marital status rates of disability for people in the community.

Net Worth

★ 219 ★

Median Net Worth, by Age Group: 1988

The phrase "net worth" as used in the tables in this section means the value of properties, cash, financial instruments, loans to others, etc. held by the individual less liabilities (debt and similar obligations). The "median" represents the middle of a range. Therefore half of those in the population have lower and half have higher values than shown.

Age of householder	Net worth in dollars	
	Total	Less home equity
Under 35	6,078	3,258
35-44	33,183	8,993
45-54	57,466	15,542
55-64	80,032	26,396
65-69	83,478	27,482
70-74	82,111	28,172
75+	61,491	18,819

Source: Aging America, Trends and Projections, prepared by the U.S. Senate Special Committee on Aging, the American Association of Retired Persons, the Federal Council on the Aging, and the U.S. Administration on Aging, 1991, Washington, D.C., p. 72. Primary source: U.S. Bureau of the Census. "Household Wealth and Asset Ownership, 1988." *Current Population Reports* Series P-70, No. 22, December 1990.

★ 220 ★
Net Worth

Median Net Worth of Households, by Age of Householder, 1988

[Data are shown in dollars]

Age of householder	Total	Excluding home equity
All ages	35,752	9,840
Under 35	6,078	3,258
35-44	33,183	8,993
45-54	57,466	15,542
55-64	80,032	26,396
65 or older	73,471	23,856
65-69	83,478	27,482

[Continued]

★ 220 ★

Median Net Worth of Households, by Age of Householder, 1988

[Continued]

Age of householder	Total	Excluding home equity
70-74	82,111	28,172
75 or older	61,491	18,819

Source: *Social Security Bulletin*, Vol. 55, No. 3, Fall 1992, Table 4, p. 13. Primary source: Bureau of the Census (1990), Table E.

★ 221 ★

Net Worth

Distribution of Households, by Age and Net Worth: 1988[1]

Older Americans (65 and older) are relatively wealthy. 61.4 percent have a net worth of $50,000 or greater; only one age group, the 55 to 64 range, has a higher percentage (63.6) in the $50,000 or greater range.

Age of householder	All house-holds	Percent distribution by net worth								
		Zero or nega-tive	$1 to 4,999	$5,000 to 9,999	$10,000 to 24,999	$25,000 to 49,999	$50,000 to 99,999	$100,000 to 249,000	$250,000 to 499,000	$500,000 or more
Total	100.0	11.1	15.1	6.2	11.5	13.0	16.7	17.5	6.0	2.8
Less than 35	100.0	19.4	27.6	11.4	16.2	11.1	8.0	4.8	1.2	0.3
35 to 44	100.0	11.3	13.3	6.4	13.4	15.3	18.2	15.8	4.5	2.0
45 to 54	100.0	8.2	10.5	4.5	9.0	13.7	21.1	21.9	7.5	3.6
55 to 64	100.0	6.4	7.5	2.5	7.4	12.6	20.5	27.5	10.0	5.6
65 +	100.0	5.2	8.9	3.1	8.1	13.2	20.9	26.1	10.0	4.4
65 to 69	100.0	5.1	7.6	2.8	7.5	12.3	19.9	27.6	12.2	5.0
70 to 74	100.0	4.2	8.0	2.5	7.3	12.1	22.4	27.3	10.6	5.6
75 +	100.0	6.0	10.6	3.6	9.0	14.6	20.8	24.2	8.0	3.1

Source: *Aging America, Trends and Projections*, prepared by the U.S. Senate Special Committee on Aging, the American Association of Retired Persons, the Federal Council on the Aging, and the U.S. Administration on Aging, 1991, Washington, D.C., p. 73. Primary source: U.S. Bureau of the Census. "Household Wealth and Asset Ownership: 1988." *Current Population Reports* Series P-70, No. 22, December 1990. *Note:* 1. Excludes group quarters.

★ 222 ★
Net Worth

Distribution of Net Worth, by Age of Householder and Type of Asset: 1988[1]

Households of older Americans (65 and older) differ from all households in having substantially more of their assets in savings accounts and in interest-earning assets at financial institutions. They also have the lowest percentage of unsecured liabilities.

[Values are in percent]

Type of asset	All households	Less than 35 years	35 to 44 years	45 to 54 years	55 to 64 years	65+ years
Total net worth	100.0	100.0	100.0	100.0	100.0	100.0
Own home	43.1	45.1	49.2	43.2	41.0	40.4
Savings and checking accounts	18.9	14.8	12.1	12.6	16.2	29.7
Interest-earning assets at financial institutions[2]	14.1	10.8	9.0	9.4	12.0	22.4
Other interest-earning assets[3]	4.2	2.8	2.5	2.7	3.7	6.8
Checking accounts	0.6	1.2	0.6	0.5	0.5	0.5
Financial investments	11.3	8.2	9.9	9.8	14.2	11.6
Stocks and mutual fund shares	6.5	4.3	5.3	5.2	7.0	8.2
U.S. savings bonds	0.6	0.5	0.4	0.4	0.8	0.6
IRA and KEOGH accounts	4.2	3.4	4.2	4.2	6.4	2.8
Real estate (except own home)	12.2	12.0	11.9	16.2	13.0	9.3
Rental property	7.9	6.8	6.7	11.3	8.0	6.7
Other real estate	4.3	5.2	5.2	4.9	5.0	2.6
Business or profession	8.8	14.6	12.0	11.9	9.4	3.0
Other	5.9	5.3	5.0	6.4	6.1	6.1
Motor vehicles	5.8	15.6	7.6	5.7	4.7	3.1
Other investments[4]	3.0	1.5	1.7	3.9	3.1	3.5
Unsecured liabilities	-2.9	-11.8	-4.3	-3.2	-1.7	-0.5

Source: Aging America, Trends and Projections, prepared by the U.S. Senate Special Committee on Aging, the American Association of Retired Persons, the Federal Council on the Aging, and the U.S. Administration on Aging, 1991, Washington, D.C., p. 75. Primary source: U.S. Bureau of the Census. "Household Wealth and Asset Ownership: 1988." *Current Population Reports* Series P-70, No. 22, December 1990. *Notes:* 1. Excludes group quarters. 2. Passbook savings accounts, money market deposit accounts, certificates of deposit, and interest-earning checking accounts. 3. Money market funds, U.S. Government securities, municipal and corporate bonds, and other assets. 4. Mortgages held from sale of real estate, amount due from sale of business, unit trusts, and other financial investments.

★ 223 ★
Net Worth

Net Worth of People Aged 65 to 75

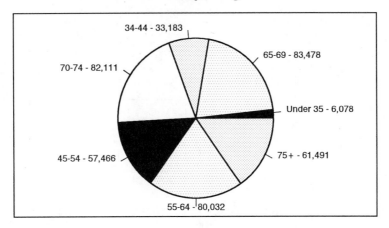

Data show net worth by age bracket. The highest net worth is shown for people aged 65 to 75.

	Net worth $
Under 35	6,078
34-44	33,183
45-54	57,466
55-64	80,032
65-69	83,478
70-74	82,111
75 +	61,491

Source: Detroit News, March 14, 1993, p. 6B. Primary source: U.S. Bureau of the Census.

★ 224 ★
Net Worth

Median Net Worth, by Age of Householder and Monthly Household Income Quintile: 1988

[Data exclude group quarters]

Monthly household income	Total	Age							
		Under 35 years	35 to 44 years	45 to 54 years	55 to 64 years	65 years and over			
						Total	65 to 69 years	70 to 74 years	75 years and over
All households (thousands)	91,554	25,379	19,916	13,613	13,090	19,556	6,331	5,184	8,041
Median income	1,983	2,000	2,500	2,604	2,071	1,211	1,497	1,330	977
Median net worth	35,752	6,078	33,183	57,466	80,032	73,471	83,478	82,111	61,491
Excluding home equity	9,840	3,258	8,993	15,542	26,396	23,856	27,482	28,172	18,819

[Continued]

★ 224 ★

Median Net Worth, by Age of Householder and Monthly Household Income Quintile: 1988

[Continued]

Monthly household income	Total	Age							
		Under 35 years	35 to 44 years	45 to 54 years	55 to 64 years	65 years and over			
						Total	65 to 69 years	70 to 74 years	75 years and over
Net worth by income quintile[1]									
Lowest quintile									
Households (thousands)	18,299	4,642	2,270	1,630	2,467	7,290	1,800	1,647	3,842
Median net worth	4,324	652	848	2,803	16,545	25,220	23,679	28,880	25,291
Excluding home equity	1,152	448	441	897	1,541	3,536	3,055	3,058	4,474
Second quintile									
Households (thousands)	18,253	5,460	3,112	1,894	2,407	5,380	1,615	1,534	2,230
Median net worth	19,694	2,551	7,536	17,159	51,641	76,050	73,712	77,355	76,253
Excluding home equity	5,454	1,823	2,345	4,046	13,319	28,168	25,962	26,958	31,853
Third quintile									
Households (thousands)	18,378	6,186	4,007	2,325	2,480	3,380	1,356	924	1,100
Median net worth	28,044	6,440	20,008	38,295	84,627	141,811	122,848	142,501	159,032
Excluding home equity	8,418	3,393	5,045	9,082	27,627	57,026	47,032	57,022	77,922
Fourth quintile									
Households (thousands)	18,310	5,694	5,025	3,049	2,583	1,959	850	578	530
Median net worth	46,235	15,420	39,983	65,794	96,066	201,562	180,802	217,572	222,320
Excluding home equity	14,376	6,933	11,539	18,809	36,531	100,480	86,319	121,341	121,816
Highest quintile									
Households (thousands)	18,314	3,397	5,502	4,715	3,152	1,548	710	500	338
Median net worth	111,770	37,817	88,293	130,867	198,987	343,015	301,719	370,695	390,649
Excluding home equity	40,688	16,572	30,766	45,799	91,888	208,789	171,183	245,396	252,058

Source: Sixty-Five Plus in America, Cynthia M. Taeuber, U.S. Department of Commerce, Economics and Statistics Administration, Bureau of the Census, U.S. Government Printing Office, Washington, D.C., 1992, p. 4-19. Primary source: Judith Eargle, U.S. Bureau of the Census, Household Wealth and Asset Ownership: 1988, Current Population Reports, Series P-70, No. 22, U.S. Government Printing Office, Washington, D.C., 1990, Table E. Notes: 1. Quintile upper limits for 1988 were: lowest quintile—$939; second quintile—$1,699; third quintile—$2,568; fourth quintile—$3,883.

★ 225 ★

Net Worth

Distribution of Net Worth, by Age of Householder and Asset Type: 1988

[Data exclude group quarters]

Type of asset	Total	Under 35 years	35 to 44 years	45 to 54 years	55 to 64 years	65 years and over
Total net worth	100.0	100.0	100.0	100.0	100.0	100.0
Interest earning assets at financial institutions	14.1	10.8	9.0	9.4	12.0	22.4
Other interest earning assets	4.2	2.8	2.5	2.7	3.7	6.8
Checking accounts	0.6	1.2	0.6	0.5	0.5	0.5

[Continued]

★ 225 ★

Distribution of Net Worth, by Age of Householder and Asset Type:
1988
[Continued]

Type of asset	Total	Under 35 years	35 to 44 years	45 to 54 years	55 to 64 years	65 years and over
Stocks and mutual fund shares	6.5	4.3	5.3	5.2	7.0	8.2
Own home	43.1	45.1	49.2	43.2	41.0	40.4
Rental property	7.9	6.8	6.7	11.3	8.0	6.7
Other real estate	4.3	5.2	5.2	4.9	5.0	2.6
Vehicles	5.8	15.6	7.6	5.7	4.7	3.1
Business or profession	8.8	14.6	12.0	11.9	9.4	3.0
U.S. savings bonds	0.6	0.5	0.4	0.4	0.8	0.6
IRA or KEOGH accounts	4.2	3.4	4.2	4.2	6.4	2.8
Other financial investments[1]	3.0	1.5	1.7	3.9	3.1	3.5
Unsecured liabilities[2]	-2.9	-11.8	-4.3	-3.2	1.7	-0.5

Source: Sixty-Five Plus in America, Cynthia M. Taeuber, U.S. Department of Commerce, Economics and Statistics Administration, Bureau of the Census, U.S. Government Printing Office, Washington, D.C., 1992, p. 4-20. Primary source: Judith Eargle, U.S. Bureau of the Census, *Household Wealth and Asset Ownership: 1988*, Current Population Reports, Series P-70, No. 22, U.S. Government Printing Office, Washington, D.C., 1990, Table G. *Notes:* IRAs are Individual Retirement Accounts; KEOGHs are retirement accounts for selfemployed individuals. 1. Includes mortgages held from sales of real estate, amount due from sale of business, unit trusts, and other financial investments. 2. Since net worth is the value of assets less liabilities, unsecured liabilities are subtracted from the distribution of net worth and are shown as negative.

★ 226 ★

Net Worth

Savings and Investments of Older Americans

[Numbers are shown in thousands for 1989.]

Characteristic	Total occupied units	Tenure		Housing unit characteristics				Household characteristics			
		Owner	Renter	New construction 4 yrs.	Mobile homes	Physical problems		Black	Hispanic	Moved in past year	Below poverty level
						Severe	Moderate				
Income of $25,000 or less	15,221	10,983	4,237	405	1,094	583	791	1,593	552	692	3,766
No savings or investments	4,568	2,643	1,925	105	377	232	494	1,058	314	290	1,873
$25,000 or less	6,540	4,989	1,551	144	486	227	207	428	157	234	1,359
More than $25,000	2,728	2,311	418	121	169	89	49	29	52	106	271
Not reported	1,384	1,040	344	35	62	34	40	77	28	62	263

Source: U.S. Department of Commerce and U.S. Department of Housing and Urban Development, Current Housing Reports, H150/89, *American Housing Survey for the United States in 1989*, July 1991, p. 334.

Earnings

★ 227 ★

Median Weekly Earnings of Full-Time Wage and Salary Workers by Gender, Age, and Country of Birth, November 1989

[Number of workers is in thousands]

Gender and age	U.S. born		Foreign born	
	Number of workers	Median weekly earnings ($)	Number of workers	Median weekly earnings ($)
Men				
16 years and older	42,861	486	4,157	377
55 to 64 years	3,966	539	448	481
65 years and older	424	480	68	398
Women				
16 years and older	31,998	346	2,590	296
55 to 64 years	2,751	360	241	310
65 years and older	421	283	46	386

Source: Meisenheimer, Joseph R. III, "How do immigrants fare in the U.S. labor market?", *Monthly Labor Review*, December 1992, p. 16.

★ 228 ★

Earnings

Median Weekly Earnings of Foreign-Born, Full-Time Wage and Salary Workers by Gender, Age, and Year of Immigration, November 1989

[Number of workers is in thousands]

Gender and age	Year of immigration					
	1982-89		1975-81		Before 1975	
	Number of workers	Median weekly earnings ($)	Number of workers	Median weekly earnings ($)	Number of workers	Median weekly earnings ($)
Men						
16 years and older	1,310	281	1,151	352	1,531	499
55 to 64 years	38	297	25	367	379	499
65 years and older	13	281	10	349	45	943
Women						
16 years and older	559	232	753	273	1,145	379
55 to 64 years	11	99	18	207	197	353
65 years and older	-	-	-	-	43	391

Source: Meisenheimer, Joseph R. III, "How do immigrants fare in the U.S. labor market?", *Monthly Labor Review*, December 1992, p. 16. *Note:* A dash indicates that no cases were found in the sample.

★ 229 ★
Earnings

Median Weekly Earnings of Foreign-Born, Full-Time Wage and Salary Workers, November 1989

[Number of workers is in thousands]

Gender and age	Speak only English at home		Speak other language at home			
			Speak English very well or well		Speak English not well or not at all	
	Number of workers	Median weekly earnings ($)	Number of workers	Median weekly earnings ($)	Number of workers	Median weekly earnings ($)
Men						
16 years and older	833	584	1,889	449	1,399	233
55 to 64 years	122	659	187	480	131	356
65 years and older	23	971	23	400	22	353
Women						
16 years and older	646	411	1,229	310	699	228
55 to 64 years	76	396	87	301	74	247
65 years and older	10	527	28	367	8	399

Source: Meisenheimer, Joseph R. III, "How do immigrants fare in the U.S. labor market?", *Monthly Labor Review*, December 1992, p. 17.

Income

★ 230 ★

Income Distribution of People Age 65+, by Impairment Status, 1990

Elderly persons with 1 or more limitation for activities of daily of living are considered impaired. Single persons with income less than $6,234 are considered 100% below poverty.

Percent above/ below poverty	All elderly	Impaired elderly
Above		
150% poverty	65.0	51.0
125-149% poverty	9.0	8.0
100-124% poverty	9.0	14.0

[Continued]

★ 230 ★

Income Distribution of People Age 65+, by Impairment Status, 1990
[Continued]

Percent above/below poverty	All elderly	Impaired elderly
Below <100% poverty	17.0	27.0

Source: Aging America, Trends and Projections, prepared by the U.S. Senate Special Committee on Aging, the American Association of Retired Persons, the Federal Council on the Aging, and the U.S. Administration on Aging, 1991, Washington, D.C., p. 148. Primary source: Lewin/ICF estimates based on 1984 *SOA, CPS*, Brookings/ICF *LTC Financing Model*.

★ 231 ★

Income

Composition of Gross Income of Elderly Families, by Age of Head and Income Type in Selected Countries, 1979-1981

The phrase "means tested" refers to government programs that are available to those individuals/families that meet a certain test, e.g., less than a specified level of income. The phrase "transfers" refers to payments made; private "transfers" are payments by private organizations or individuals.

[Numbers in percent]

Country	Year	Percent distribution						
		Total income	Social insurance	Pensions	Earnings	Property income	Means-tested transfers	Private transfers
Age 65 to 74								
United States	1979	100.0	35.0	13.0	32.0	18.0	2.0	0.0
West Germany	1981	100.0	67.0	12.0	17.0	2.0	1.0	0.0
Norway	1979	100.0	45.0	7.0	41.0	6.0	0.0	1.0
Sweden	1979	100.0	76.0	(-)	12.0	9.0	3.0	(-)
United Kingdom	1979	100.0	46.0	15.0	26.0	10.0	3.0	0.0
Canada	1981	100.0	35.0	12.0	28.0	22.0	2.0	0.0
Age 75+								
United States	1979	100.0	45.0	12.0	17.0	24.0	2.0	0.0
West Germany	1981	100.0	75.0	12.0	8.0	4.0	1.0	(-)
Norway	1979	100.0	75.0	10.0	6.0	8.0	1.0	(-)
Sweden	1979	100.0	78.0	(-)	2.0	13.0	7.0	(-)
United Kingdom	1979	100.0	54.0	12.0	17.0	10.0	7.0	0.0
Canada	1981	100.0	45.0	8.0	13.0	30.0	2.0	(-)

Source: Aging America, Trends and Projections, prepared by the U.S. Senate Special Committee on Aging, the American Association of Retired Persons, the Federal Council on the Aging, and the U.S. Administration on Aging, 1991, Washington, D.C., p. 263. Primary source: Data from the Luxembourg Income Study as reported in U.S. Bureau of the Census, "An Aging World," by Barbara Boyle Torrey, Kevin Kinsella, and Cynthia M. Taeuber. *International Population Reports*, Series P-95, No. 78, September 1987. *Note:* A dash (-) stands for not available.

★ 232 ★

Income

Total Money Income in 1989 of Married-Couple Households with White Householders 65 Years and Over: March 1990

[Data are in percent]

Under $10,000	9.0 to 10.4
$10,000 to $14,999	14.8 to 16.6
$15,000 to $19,999	13.8 to 15.6
$20,000 to $24,999	12.1 to 13.7
$25,000 to $34,999	16.2 to 18.2
$35,000 to $49,999	12.9 to 14.7
$50,000 and over	15.1 to 16.9

Source: U.S. Bureau of the Census, Housing and Household Economic Statistics Division, Income Branch, unpublished tabulations from March 1990 Current Population Survey. *Note:* The higher value represents the 90% confidence level.

★ 233 ★

Income

Total Money Income in 1989 of Married-Couple Households with Black Householders 65 Years and Over: March 1990

[Data are in percent]

Under $10,000	19.6 to 28.8
$10,000 to $14,999	17.5 to 26.3
$15,000 to $19,999	10.8 to 18.4
$20,000 to $24,999	9.6 to 16.8
$25,000 to $34,999	10.1 to 17.5
$35,000 to $49,999	3.4 to 8.4
$50,000 and over	3.9 to 9.1

Source: U.S. Bureau of the Census, Housing and Household Economic Statistics Division, Income Branch, unpublished tabulations from March 1990 Current Population Survey. *Note:* The higher value represents the 90% confidence level.

★ 234 ★

Income

Total Money Income in 1989 of Married-Couple Households with White Householders 65 to 74 Years: March 1990

[Data are in percent]

Under $10,000	7.3 to 8.9
$10,000 to $14,999	12.4 to 14.4
$15,000 to $19,999	12.8 to 14.8
$20,000 to $24,999	11.4 to 13.4
$25,000 to $34,999	17.2 to 19.6
$35,000 to $49,999	14.2 to 16.4
$50,000 and over	17.4 to 19.8

Source: U.S. Bureau of the Census, Housing and Household Economic Statistics Division, Income Branch, unpublished tabulations from March 1990 Current Population Survey. *Note:* The higher value represents the 90% confidence level.

★ 235 ★

Income

Total Money Income in 1989 of Married-Couple Households with Black Householders 65 to 74 Years: March 1990

[Data are in percent]

Under $10,000	15.0 to 25.8
$10,000 to $14,999	12.5 to 22.7
$15,000 to $19,999	11.5 to 21.3
$20,000 to $24,999	5.7 to 13.5
$25,000 to $34,999	12.3 to 22.3
$35,000 to $49,999	5.2 to 12.8
$50,000 and over	5.7 to 13.5

Source: U.S. Bureau of the Census, Housing and Household Economic Statistics Division, Income Branch, unpublished tabulations from March 1990 Current Population Survey. *Note:* The higher value represents the 90% confidence level.

★ 236 ★

Income

Total Money Income in 1989 of Married-Couple Households with White Householders 75 Years and Over: March 1990

[Data are in percent]

Under $10,000	11.8 to 15.0
$10,000 to $14,999	19.1 to 22.9
$15,000 to $19,999	15.0 to 18.4
$20,000 to $24,999	12.2 to 15.4
$25,000 to $34,999	12.9 to 16.1
$35,000 to $49,999	9.1 to 11.9
$50,000 and over	8.7 to 11.5

Source: U.S. Bureau of the Census, Housing and Household Economic Statistics Division, Income Branch, unpublished tabulations from March 1990 Current Population Survey. *Note:* The higher value represents the 90% confidence level.

★ 237 ★

Income

Total Money Income in 1989 of Married-Couple Households with Black Householders 75 Years and Over: March 1990

[Data are in percent]

Under $10,000	22.9 to 39.3
$10,000 to $14,999	21.0 to 37.0
$15,000 to $19,999	5.8 to 17.2
$20,000 to $24,999	12.7 to 26.7
$25,000 to $34,999	2.6 to 11.6
$35,000 to $49,999	(C)[1]
$50,000 and over	(C)[1]

Source: U.S. Bureau of the Census, Housing and Household Economic Statistics Division, Income Branch, unpublished tabulations from March 1990 Current Population Survey. *Notes:* The higher value represents the 90% confidence level. 1. Confidence interval (includes zero).

★ 238 ★
Income

Money Income From Earnings and Other Sources for Aged Families, 1991
[Based on Current Population Survey (CPS)]

Type of money income received during year[1]	Aged family units					
	Individuals aged 65 or older living alone or with nonrelatives only			Multiperson families with householder aged 65 or older		
	Total	Non-poor	Poor[2]	Total	Non-poor	Poor[2]
Percent receiving income of specified type[3]						
Earnings	13	16	5	43	44	18
Public program payments						
Social Security[4]	92	93	87	93	94	79
Supplemental Security Income	9	3	26	6	4	21
Other public assistance	4	4	3	6	6	16
Other programs[5]	4	5	4	12	12	6
Other sources						
Dividends, interest, rent	65	76	33	77	80	32
Employment-related pensions, alimony, annuities, etc.	40	51	9	56	59	14
Percentage distribution of income by type						
Total percent	100.0	100.0	100.0	100.0	100.0	100.0
Earnings	10	11	1	28	28	9
Public payments						
Social Security[4]	44	41	79	30	30	64
Supplemental Security Income	1	1	12	1	[6]	9
Other public assistance	1	1	1	1	1	5
Other programs[5]	1	1	1	2	2	3
Other sources						
Dividends, interest, rent	22	24	4	20	20	3
Employment-related pensions, alimony, annuities, etc.	20	22	3	18	19	7
Median income (dollars)	10,275	12,848	5,491	4,891	6,198	6,038

Source: Annual Statistical Supplement, 1992 to the Social Security Bulletin, U.S. Department of Health and Human Services, Social Security Administration, January 1993, p. 139. Primary source: Public use file of the March 1992 Income Supplement, Current Population Survey, Bureau of the Census. For a discussion of standard errors of estimated numbers and percentages, see Bureau of the Census, Current Population Reports, P-60 series. *Notes:* 1. Household surveys tend to underestimate the number of income recipients and income sources such as interest, dividends, rents, veterans' payments, unemployment compensation, and workers' compensation. 2. Poverty status based on money income of all family members after receipt of Old-Age, Survivors, and Disability Insurance (OASDI) and any other cash transfer payments. 3. Received by individuals or any family member at any time during 1991. Most individuals or families received more than one type of income during the year. 4. Social Security may include any Railroad Retirement payments. 5. Unemployment insurance, workers' compensation, or veterans' payments. 6. Less than 0.05 percent.

★ 239 ★
Income

Median Annual Earnings of Older Americans, by Sex, 1937-90

Year	Total	Age group					
		55-59	60-61	62-64	65-69	70-71	72+
Both sexes							
1937	761	1,020	1,010	927	512	...	...
1940	746	1,018	978	963	874	924	788
1945	1,159	1,821	1,782	1,739	1,482	1,341	1,307
1950	1,926	2,394	2,492	2,252	1,973	1,916	1,589
1955	2,438	2,728	2,525	2,427	1,736	1,279	1,149
1960	2,894	3,452	3,166	3,052	1,590	1,140	1,252
1965	3,414	4,304	4,087	3,767	1,791	1,171	1,326
1970	4,375	5,831	5,473	5,047	2,099	1,578	1,683
1975	5,803	8,299	7,779	6,620	2,524	2,105	2,137
1980	8,549	12,309	11,606	9,651	4,451	3,306	3,140
1985	11,265	15,831	14,724	11,907	5,974	4,330	3,729
1986	11,831	16,444	15,288	12,095	6,267	4,553	3,869
1987	12,327	17,093	15,780	12,205	6,376	4,736	4,161
1988[1]	12,824	17,699	16,150	12,354	6,549	5,061	4,334
1989[1]	13,392	18,272	16,833	12,728	6,822	5,218	4,446
1990[1]	13,910	18,806	17,264	13,163	6,860	5,355	4,532
Men							
1937	945	1,137	1,131	1,008	563	...	...
1940	935	1,153	1,088	1,058	950	917	899
1945	1,654	2,170	2,106	2,000	1,666	1,462	1,390
1950	2,532	2,959	2,812	2,618	2,317	2,049	1,707
1955	3,315	3,512	3,201	3,044	2,164	1,498	1,292
1960	3,879	4,416	3,982	3,812	2,112	1,207	1,340
1965	4,685	5,581	4,993	4,784	2,628	1,246	1,443
1970	6,180	7,675	7,051	6,456	2,927	1,662	1,863
1975	8,250	11,290	10,398	8,700	2,895	2,276	2,371
1980	11,963	17,585	15,939	13,201	4,902	3,658	3,529
1985	14,959	22,117	19,953	16,532	6,760	4,977	4,351
1986	15,579	23,084	20,512	16,709	7,134	5,323	4,509
1987	16,073	23,924	21,375	16,911	7,169	5,420	4,834
1988[1]	16,626	24,898	22,021	17,131	7,454	5,977	5,016
1989[1]	17,180	25,537	22,914	17,506	7,684	5,882	5,046
1990[1]	17,690	25,967	23,396	17,626	7,812	6,160	5,093
Women							
1937	484	563	585	582	366	...	...
1940	472	562	499	577	607	999	424
1945	770	955	946	899	832	766	928

[Continued]

★ 239 ★

Median Annual Earnings of Older Americans, by Sex, 1937-90

[Continued]

Year	Total	Age group					
		55-59	60-61	62-64	65-69	70-71	72+
1950	1,124	1,416	1,370	1,349	1,176	1,399	1,232
1955	1,351	1,622	1,542	1,445	1,057	949	802
1960	1,679	2,221	2,040	1,783	1,142	1,007	1,036
1965	1,984	2,764	2,678	2,372	1,208	1,054	1,093
1970	2,735	3,747	3,729	3,236	1,674	1,344	1,375
1975	3,730	5,300	5,020	4,055	2,189	1,895	1,715
1980	6,012	7,966	7,756	6,044	3,589	2,853	2,569
1985	8,293	10,714	10,133	7,728	4,959	3,671	3,067
1986	8,796	11,058	10,541	7,787	5,181	3,616	3,154
1987	9,261	11,650	10,932	7,736	5,432	3,968	3,495
1988[1]	9,746	12,080	11,397	8,241	5,505	4,251	3,601
1989[1]	10,291	12,691	11,775	8,414	5,837	4,357	3,785
1990[1]	10,797	13,117	12,223	9,191	5,879	4,386	3,847

Source: *Annual Statistical Supplement, 1992 to the Social Security Bulletin*, U.S. Department of Health and Human Services, Social Security Administration, January 1993, p. 155. *Notes:* Three dots (...) stands for not applicable. 1. Preliminary data.

★ 240 ★

Income

Change in Median Income Since 1962

Figures based on a sample of 9,343,000 couples and 13,805,000 single "aged units".[1] From the source: "Between 1962 and 1990, the income of the aged increased by about 88%, even after adjusting for inflation, for both married couples and non-married persons. The table shows that between 1967 and 1990, the income of both groups increased by about 78%. Since 1967, there were disproportionate increases by race. For whites, income increased by 95%; for blacks, it increased by 32%."

[Median income in 1990 dollars]

Year	Marital status		Race	
	Married couples	Non-married persons	White	Black
1962	12,401	4,874	[2]	[2]
1967	13,199	5,111	7,433	5,259
1971	17,291	6,612	10,475	6,109
1976	18,123	7,718	11,347	6,868
1978	18,964	7,838	11,947	6,515
1980	19,066	7,582	11,769	6,440

[Continued]

★ 240 ★

Change in Median Income Since 1962

[Continued]

Year	Marital status		Race	
	Married couples	Non-married persons	White	Black
1982	20,492	7,964	12,799	6,474
1984	21,699	8,416	13,787	6,881
1986	22,527	8,562	14,048	7,095
1988	22,433	8,759	11,492	6,964
1990	23,352	9,147	14,542	6,987

Source: U.S. Department of Health and Human Services, Social Security Administration, *Income of the Aged Chartbook, 1990,* GPO, Washington, D.C., September 1992, p. 18. *Notes:* 1. "Aged unit" does not refer to the household, the family, or unrelated individuals, as used by the Bureau of the Census. The aged unit is either a married couple living together with the husband or wife aged 65 or older (generally measured by the age of the husband), or a person 65 or older who does not live with a spouse. The single person unit may be a widow(er), a divorced or separated person, a person legally married who does not live with a spouse, or a person who never married. 2. Not available.

★ 241 ★

Income

Income of Widows in 1989 and Ability to Make Ends Meet, 1990, by Race and Age[1]

From the source: "Tables from this paper have been generated in the process of editing and 'cleansing' the study's data tape, which is a continuing process. As a consequence, tables should not be considered final versions. The original authors, however, are confident that while tables generated by the final data tape may show minor differences, the overall conclusions will not be substantially altered."

[Percentage distributions]

Item	All races				Blacks
	Total age	Less than 65	65-74	75 and over	
Income					
n[2]	1,060	120	542	398	301
Total percent[3]	100	100	100	100	100
Less than $5,000	10	17	8	12	29
$5,000-$9,999	35	31	34	38	42
$10,000-$19,999	36	35	39	33	19
$20,000-$29,999	11	11	12	10	7
$30,000 or over	7	6	6	7	3
Ability to make ends meet					
n[2]	1,142	124	600	418	312
Total percent[3]	100	100	100	100	100
Always money left over	20	13	20	22	7
A little extra sometimes	31	23	34	30	18

[Continued]

★ 241 ★

Income of Widows in 1989 and Ability to Make Ends Meet, 1990, by Race and Age

[Continued]

Item	All races				Blacks
	Total age	Less than 65	65-74	75 and over	
Just enough, no more	35	36	34	36	51
Can't make ends meet	13	28	12	12	25

Source: Herbert S. Parnes, Thomas N. Chirikos, Elizabeth G. Menaghan, Frank L. Mott, Gilbert Nestel, Lois B. Shaw, David G. Sommers, *The NLS Older Male Sample Revisited: A Unique Data Base for Gerontological Research*, Center for Human Resource Research, The Ohio State University, 1993, p. 95, reprinted with permission. *Notes:* 1. Income is measured by the "global" income variable. 2. Number of sample cases on which weighted percentages are based. 3. Percentages may not add to 100 because of rounding.

★ 242 ★

Income

Total Net Assets, Including and Excluding Net Value of Home, by Race and Age, 1990[1]

[Percentage distributions]

	All races				Blacks
	Total age	Less than 65	65-74	75 and over	
Assets, including home					
n[2]	571	71	303	197	155
Total percent[3]	100	100	100	100	100
Less than $10,000	27	40	24	27	45
$10,000-$49,999	21	24	21	20	35
$50,000-$99,999	22	27	22	21	14
$100,000 or over	30	9	33	32	6
Median ($)	53,000	21,000	60,000	54,900	15,100
Assets, excluding home					
Total percent	100	100	100	100	100
Less than $10,000	46	64	44	44	84
$10,000-49,999	27	27	28	26	13
$50,000-99,999	13	8	12	14	0
$100,000 or over	14	0	15	16	2
Median ($)	11,900	3,500	13,000	14,000	1,000

Source: Herbert S. Parnes, Thomas N. Chirikos, Elizabeth G. Menaghan, Frank L. Mott, Gilbert Nestel, Lois B. Shaw, David G. Sommers, *The NLS Older Male Sample Revisited: A Unique Data Base for Gerontological Research*, Center for Human Resource Research, The Ohio State University, 1993, p. 96, reprinted with permission. *Notes:* 1. As measured by the "key" asset variable. 2. Number of sample cases on which weighted percentages are based. 3. Percentages may not add to 100 because of rounding.

★ 243 ★
Income

Comparison of Widow's Financial Situation in 1990 with Situation Prior to Death of Spouse, by Race and Age[1]

[Percentage distributions]

Financial situation in 1990	All races				Blacks
	Total age	Less than 65	65-74	75 and over	
n[2]	1,155	124	607	424	312
Total percent[3]	100	100	100	100	100
Better off	20	18	19	20	17
About the same	39	30	39	41	39
Worse off	41	51	41	39	44

Source: Herbert S. Parnes, Thomas N. Chirikos, Elizabeth G. Menaghan, Frank L. Mott, Gilbert Nestel, Lois B. Shaw, David G. Sommers, *The NLS Older Male Sample Revisited: A Unique Data Base for Gerontological Research*, Center for Human Resource Research, The Ohio State University, 1993, p. 97, reprinted with permission. *Notes:* 1. "Considering all aspects of your financial situation, would you say that you are better off, worse off, or about the same as you were when your husband was last interviewed in—?" 2. Number of sample cases on which weighted percentages are based. 3. Percentages may not add to 100 because of rounding.

★ 244 ★
Income

Reasons for Deterioration of Financial Situation, by Race and Age: Widows Reporting Being Worse Off in 1990 than Prior to Husband's Death

[Percentages[1]]

Reason	All races				Blacks
	Total age	Less than 65	65-74	75 and over	
n[2]	486	64	250	172	142
No longer working[3]	27	25	29	24	31
Government benefits stopped or decreased	19	22	16	21	25
Pension stopped or decreased	21	22	22	19	11
Medical expenses increased	29	26	27	32	30
Medical, housing, or other expenses increased[4]	56	55	55	59	58

Source: Herbert S. Parnes, Thomas N. Chirikos, Elizabeth G. Menaghan, Frank L. Mott, Gilbert Nestel, Lois B. Shaw, David G. Sommers, *The NLS Older Male Sample Revisited: A Unique Data Base for Gerontological Research*, Center for Human Resource Research, The Ohio State University, 1993, p. 98, reprinted with permission. *Notes:* 1. Includes multiple responses. 2. Number of sample cases on which weighted percentages are based. 3. Includes a few cases working at a worse job. 4. Includes preceding category.

★ 245 ★

Income

Whether Widow Received Any Payment from Husband's Pension, and Type Received, by Race and Age

Item	All races				Blacks
	Total age	Less than 65	65-74	75 and over	
Whether received payment					
n[1]	1,293	136	636	467	337
Percent[2]	32	31	36	26	24
Percentage distributions					
Kind of payment					
n[1]	353	35	212	106	71
Total percent	100	100	100	100	100
Lump sum	15	20	14	14	12
Life-time payments	74	61	77	73	84
Fixed period payments	11	19	9	13	4

Source: Herbert S. Parnes, Thomas N. Chirikos, Elizabeth G. Menaghan, Frank L. Mott, Gilbert Nestel, Lois B. Shaw, David G. Sommers, *The NLS Older Male Sample Revisited: A Unique Data Base for Gerontological Research*, Center for Human Resource Research, The Ohio State University, 1993, p. 99, reprinted with permission. *Notes:* 1. Number of sample cases on which weighted percentages are based. 2. Percentages may not add to 100 because of rounding.

★ 246 ★

Income

Hired Farmworkers - Workers and Weekly Earnings: 1990

Data show average number of persons 15 years old and over in the civilian noninstitutional population who were employed at hired farmwork at any time during the year.

Age	Workers (1,000)	Median weekly earnings[1]
All workers	886	$200
15 to 19 years old	144	100
20 to 24 years old	135	206
25 to 34 years old	251	240
35 to 44 years old	170	250

[Continued]

★ 246 ★

Hired Farmworkers - Workers and Weekly Earnings: 1990
[Continued]

Age	Workers (1,000)	Median weekly earnings[1]
45 to 54 years old	90	200
55 years old and over	95	200

Source: U.S. Bureau of the Census, *Statistical Abstract of the United States: 1992* (112th edition.) Washington, DC, 1992, p. 657. Primary source: U.S. Dept. of Agriculture, Economic Research Service, unpublished data. *Notes:* 1. The weekly earnings the farmworker usually earns at his farmwork job before deductions and including any overtime pay or commissions.

★ 247 ★

Income

Persons 100 Years and Over with Income, by Age, Sex, Income in 1979, and Age: 1980

Age	Total	$1-$1,999 or less	$2,000-$3,999	$4,000-$5,999	$6,000-$9,999	$10,000-19,999	$20,000 or more
Total persons[1]	18,179	5,458	7,885	2,073	1,480	896	387
100-104	14,868	4,732	6,328	1,626	1,220	666	296
105-109	2,590	613	1,207	330	199	162	79
110+	721	113	350	117	61	68	12
Total male	5,566	1,211	2,226	804	707	353	265
100-104	4,311	945	1,738	627	560	219	222
105-109	949	204	367	134	122	86	36
110+	306	62	121	43	25	48	7
Total female	12,613	4,247	5,659	1,269	773	543	122
100-104	10,557	3,787	4,590	999	660	447	74
105-109	1,641	409	840	196	77	76	43
110+	415	51	229	74	36	20	5

Source: Gregory Spencer, Arnold A. Goldstein, and Cynthia M. Taeuber, *America's Centenarians: Data from the 1980 Census*, National Institute on Aging, Washington, DC, June 1987, p. B3. *Notes:* 1. A problem with 1980 Census allocation procedures resulted in an inflation of the count of the centenarian population by about one-fourth. This data reflects unallocated age data only and therefore may be subject to sampling error due to incorrect reporting, overreporting by respondents, or incomplete documentation.

Household Income

★ 248 ★

Median Income of Families and Unrelated Individuals: 1989

The term "median" in this and other tables indicates the midpoint of a range. Half of the population has values lower than shown and half has values higher than shown.

[Values are in dollars]

Type of unit and age	Median income
Families	
Head 25 to 64	36,058
Head 65+	22,806
65 to 74	24,868
75 to 84	18,520
85+	17,600
Unrelated individuals	
25 to 64	20,277
65+	9,422
65 to 74	10,821
75 to 84	8,684
85+	7,947

Source: *Aging America, Trends and Projections*, prepared by the U.S. Senate Special Committee on Aging, the American Association of Retired Persons, the Federal Council on the Aging, and the U.S. Administration on Aging, 1991, Washington, D.C., p. 39. Primary source: U.S. Bureau of the Census and unpublished data from the March 1990 Current Population Survey.

★ 249 ★

Household Income

Median Income of Older Families and Unrelated Individuals, by Age Group: 1989

[Values are in dollars]

	Families	Unrelated individual
65 to 74	24,868	10,821
75 to 84	19,520	8,684
85+	17,600	7,947

Source: *Aging America, Trends and Projections*, prepared by the U.S. Senate Special Committee on Aging, the American Association of Retired Persons, the Federal Council on the Aging, and the U.S. Administration on Aging, 1991, Washington, D.C., p. 43. Primary source: March 1990 *Current Population* Survey. Data prepared by the Congressional Research Service.

★ 250 ★

Household Income

Median Family Income of Elderly and Nonelderly Families: 1965-1989

Median family income is stated both in inflation-adjusted 1989 dollars and in current dollars. Current dollars are actual values measured in the given year.

Year	Median family income				CPI (1982-1984 = 100)
	1989 dollars		Current dollars		
	Head 25 to 64	Head 65+	Head 25 to 64	Head 65+	
1965	29,669	13,620	7,537	3,460	31.5
1966	31,176	13,950	8,146	3,645	32.4
1967	32,496	14,583	8,753	3,928	33.4
1968	33,890	16,362	9,511	4,592	34.8
1969	35,267	16,228	10,438	4,803	36.7
1970	34,768	16,149	10,879	5,053	38.8
1971	34,922	16,696	11,406	5,453	40.5
1972	37,725	17,704	12,717	5,968	41.8
1973	37,692	17,946	13,496	6,426	44.4
1974	36,169	18,877	14,380	7,505	49.3
1975	35,335	18,570	15,331	8,057	53.8
1976	36,228	19,005	16,624	8,721	56.9
1977	36,750	18,641	17,960	9,110	60.6
1978	37,588	19,287	19,764	10,141	65.2
1979	37,875	19,331	22,175	11,318	72.6
1980	35,202	19,384	23,392	12,881	82.4
1981	34,292	19,555	25,138	14,335	90.9
1982	33,413	20,711	26,003	16,118	96.5
1983	33,917	20,993	27,243	16,862	99.6
1984	34,959	21,739	29,292	18,215	103.9

[Continued]

★ 250 ★

Median Family Income of Elderly and Nonelderly Families: 1965-1989
[Continued]

| Year | Median family income | | | | CPI (1982-1984 = 100) |
| | 1989 dollars | | Current dollars | | |
	Head 25 to 64	Head 65 +	Head 25 to 64	Head 65 +	
1985	35,153	22,031	30,504	19,117	107.6
1986	36,621	22,551	32,368	19,932	109.6
1987	37,483	22,718	34,339	20,813	113.6
1988	37,633	22,751	35,903	21,705	118.3
1989	36,058	22,806	36,058	22,806	124.0

Source: *Aging America, Trends and Projections*, prepared by the U.S. Senate Special Committee on Aging, the American Association of Retired Persons, the Federal Council on the Aging, and the U.S. Administration on Aging, 1991, Washington, D.C., p. 60. Primary source: U.S. Bureau of the Census. *Current Population Reports*, various reports in Series P-60. *Notes:* CPI (Consumer Price Index) figures establish a baseline (100) of the cost of goods and services in 1982-1984, against which price increases and decreases can be measured.

★ 251 ★
Household Income

Median Net Worth and Monthly Household Income, by Age of Householder: 1988[1]
[Households are in thousands; other data are in dollars]

| Age of householder | Number of households (thousands) | Median monthly household income | Median net worth | |
			Total	Excluding home equity
Total	91,554	1,983	35,752	9,840
Less than 35 years	25,379	2,000	6,078	3,258
35 to 44 years	19,916	2,500	33,183	8,993
45 to 54 years	13,613	2,604	57,466	15,542
55 to 64 years	13,090	2,071	80,032	26,396
65 +	19,556	1,211	73,471	23,856
65 to 69 years	6,331	1,497	83,478	27,482
70 to 74 years	5,184	1,330	82,111	28,172
75 +	8,041	977	61,491	18,819

Source: *Aging America, Trends and Projections*, prepared by the U.S. Senate Special Committee on Aging, the American Association of Retired Persons, the Federal Council on the Aging, and the U.S. Administration on Aging, 1991, Washington, D.C., p. 71. Primary source: U.S. Bureau of the Census. "Household Wealth and Asset Ownership: 1988." *Current Population Reports* Series P-70, No. 22, December 1990. *Note:* 1. Excludes group quarters.

★ 252 ★

Household Income

Income in 1989 of Married-Couple Households, by Age of Householder: March 1990

[Data are in percent]

Amount	65 to 69	70 to 74	75 and older
Less than $20,000	27.3	34.9	48.5
$20,000 to $34,999	32.5	33.8	28.4
$35,000 or more	40.1	31.3	23.0

Source: Sixty-Five Plus in America, Cynthia M. Taeuber, U.S. Department of Commerce, Economics and Statistics Administration, Bureau of the Census, U.S. Government Printing Office, Washington, D.C., 1992, p. 4-10. Primary source: C. DeNavas and Ed Welniak, U.S. Bureau of the Census, *Money Income of Households, Families, and Persons in the United States: 1990*, Current Population Reports, Series P-60, No. 174, U.S. Government Printing Office, Washington, D.C., July, 1991, Table 8.

★ 253 ★

Household Income

Income in 1989 of Elderly Householders Living Alone, by Age and Sex: March 1990

[Data are in percent]

Amount	Male		Female	
	65 to 74	75 and older	65 to 74	75 and older
Less than $10,000	33.8	41.9	47.8	58.0
$10,000 to $19,999	34.3	36.1	33.7	27.7
$20,000 to $34,999	21.1	13.8	13.0	10.9
$35,000 or more	10.9	8.2	5.5	3.4

Source: Sixty-Five Plus in America, Cynthia M. Taeuber, U.S. Department of Commerce, Economics and Statistics Administration, Bureau of the Census, U.S. Government Printing Office, Washington, D.C., 1992, p. 4-10. Primary source: C. DeNavas and Ed Welniak, U.S. Bureau of the Census, *Money Income of Households, Families, and Persons in the United States: 1990*, Current Population Reports, Series P-60, No. 174, U.S. Government Printing Office, Washington, D.C., July, 1991, Table 8.

★ 254 ★

Household Income

Household Income, Pension, and Spouse's Employment Status

[Numbers are in percent]

Characteristic	Working in career job	Working in bridge job	Not working
Spouse working	50.1	49.3	43.1
Pension			
Receives benefits	2.7	18.8	34.2
Covered by pension plan in current job	74.0	48.5	-
1988 household income (in thousands of dollars)			
<15	9.1	14.1	25.9
15-35	34.7	35.8	36.8
35-50	24.2	22.7	15.2
>50	27.4	22.9	14.0
Not reported	4.6	4.6	8.1

Source: Ruhm, Christopher J., "Bridge Employment and Job Stopping in the 1980s," *The Commonwealth Fund, Americans Over 55 at Work Program,* May 1991, p. 18. *Notes:* Data are based on a survey of 3,509 Americans aged 50 to 64 conducted by Louis Harris Associates for The Commonwealth Fund between March and September 1989. The survey is a national cross section but excludes Alaska and Hawaii and people in prisons, hospitals, nursing homes, or religious and educational institutions.

★ 255 ★

Household Income

Income and Income Sources of Households Headed by Adults 65 Years or Older, by Educational Level, 1990

This table shows that while all older adults cited Social Security as a major income source, dependency on Social Security decreased as educational attainment increased. The source points out that persons with higher education are more likely to have jobs which provide alternative retirement income possibilities, such as pensions, annuities, etc. From the source: "Data for this study are from the interview component of the 1990 Consumer Expenditures Survey (CE), conducted by the Bureau of the Census for the Bureau of Labor Statistics.... Findings are based on responses from 3,715 consumer units[1] with reference persons 65 years or older.

Income sources	Average income ($)					Percent of income from sources				
	All 65+	8th grade or less	Some high school	High school graduate	Any college	All 65+	8th grade or less	Some high school	High school graduate	Any college
Before-tax income	18,646	12,128	16,276	18,072	28,712					
After-tax income	17,517	11,865	15,624	17,048	26,089					
Social Security and Railroad Retirement	8,357	7,496	8,652	8,370	9,118	45	62	53	46	32
Earnings[2]	4,308	2,298	3,424	3,975	7,702	23	19	21	22	27
Pensions and annuities[3]	3,294	1,186	2,488	3,168	6,514	18	10	15	18	23
Interest and dividends[4]	2,255	641	1,464	2,176	4,837	12	5	9	12	17
Other[5]	432	507	248	383	541	2	4	2	2	1

Source: "A Comparison of Income, Income Sources, and Expenditures of Older Adults by Educational Attainment", Family Economics Review, 1992, Vol. 5, No. 4, pp. 2-8. Notes: 1. Units are married couples living together—at least one of whom is 65+—and unmarried people 65+. Income of aged units does not include income from other household members. 2. Includes wages and salary income; income (or loss) from nonfarm business, farm, and roomers, boarders, rental units. 3. From private companies, the military, or government. 4. Includes royalties, estates, and trusts. 5. Includes supplemental security income, unemployment compensation, workers' compensation, veterans' benefits, public assistance or welfare, value of food stamps, regular contributions received.

★ 256 ★

Household Income

Median Homeowner Incomes, by Age and Race

| 65-74 years - 19,715 |
| 75-84 years - 13,680 |
| 85/85+ years - 10,704 |

Chart shows data from column 1.

[Values in dollars per year]

Age	White	Black	Hispanic
65-74 years	19,715	12,966	16,810
75-84 years	13,680	7,803	11,762
85/85+ years	10,704	6,330	7,979

Source: Elderly Households, a Profile, Senate Select Committee on Aging, Comm. Pub. No. 102-912, 1992, p. 39. Primary source: The American Housing Survey, 1989, Data on C-D ROM US Dept. of Housing and Urban Development & Bureau of the Census.

Sources of Income

★ 257 ★

Income Sources of Units Age 65+: 1988[1]

This table shows the percentage breakdown of income, by source, for people of all categories aged 65 and older.

	Percent
Social Security	38.0
Assets	25.0
Pensions	18.0
Earnings	17.0
Other	3.0

Source: Aging America, Trends and Projections, prepared by the U.S. Senate Special Committee on Aging, the American Association of Retired Persons, the Federal Council on the Aging, and the U.S. Administration on Aging, 1991, Washington, D.C., p. 63. Primary source: Susan Grad, *Income of the Population 65 or Over, 1988*, Pub. No. 13-11871, Washington: U.S. Social Security Administration, June 1990. *Notes:* 1. Units are married couples living together—at least one of whom is 65+—and unmarried people 65+. Income of aged units does not include income from other household members.

★ 258 ★

Sources of Income

Sources of Retirement Income

In the year 1988, persons 65 and older derived their income from the sources shown below. Only those with at least $20,000 a year in income are included.

	Percent of income
Earned income	24.0
Investment/savings	32.0
Social Security	23.0
Pension	19.0
Other	2.0

Source: Detroit News, November 30, 1992, p. 10F. Primary source: T. Rowe Price Associates, IRS, Social Security Administration.

★ 259 ★

Sources of Income

Sources of Income for Older Americans, 1990

Source of income	Total	Men					Women				
		Total	62-64	65-69	70-74	75+	Total	62-64	65-69	70-74	75+
Number (in thousands)	23,348	12,454	1,331	3,787	3,132	4,203	10,894	1,111	2,982	2,532	4,269
Percent receiving money from:											
Earnings	12.1	14.2	23.9	20.8	11.8	7.0	9.7	17.1	16.4	9.1	3.5
Assets	77.6	77.2	70.8	77.2	80.1	77.1	78.0	80.6	78.5	78.0	76.9
Employer pensions	45.2	53.9	58.7	56.2	55.2	49.4	35.3	30.7	38.9	39.0	31.7
Private pensions	33.4	41.5	44.7	42.8	42.8	38.3	24.0	20.8	27.7	28.5	19.7
Public pensions	12.8	13.4	14.9	14.4	13.7	11.7	12.1	10.5	12.4	11.1	12.8
Railroad retirement	.8	.5	.2	.4	.2	.8	1.1	.3	.4	.4	2.1
Federal Government	3.0	3.5	2.1	3.1	5.1	3.0	2.5	1.1	1.9	2.6	3.3
Military	1.7	2.9	4.5	3.2	3.7	1.6	.3	1	.6	1	.4
State government	5.9	5.1	6.4	5.7	4.0	4.9	6.7	7.3	7.2	6.4	6.5
Local government	2.0	2.3	2.0	2.9	2.3	1.9	1.7	1.8	2.4	1.7	1.3
Other pensions or annuities	4.8	4.9	5.5	4.8	4.0	5.6	4.6	4.0	3.8	3.3	6.1
Vets.' compensation or pension	4.4	7.3	10.0	9.3	8.5	3.9	1.1	.4	.9	.9	1.5
Public assistance	3.7	2.3	.2	1.9	2.4	3.1	5.3	.6	5.5	5.4	6.4
Supplemental Security Income	3.5	2.2	.2	1.8	2.4	3.1	5.1	.3	5.1	5.4	6.1
Other	5.3	5.5	9.2	5.7	6.3	3.7	5.1	6.5	5.4	5.7	4.1

Source: Annual Statistical Supplement, 1992 to the Social Security Bulletin, U.S. Department of Health and Human Services, Social Security Administration, January 1993, p. 184. Primary source: Restricted use file, Survey of Income and Program Participation. *Notes:* Based of the Survey of Income and Program Participation (SIPP). 1. Less than 0.05 percent.

★ 260 ★

Sources of Income

Share of Income from Sources, by Income Level, 1990

Figures based on a sample of 9,343,000 couples and 13,805,000 single "aged units".[1] From the source: "Aged units are ranked by total income and divided into five groups of equal size - called quintiles. In this chart, shares of income of the quintile with the lowest income are compared with those of the quintile with the highest. Social Security benefits provide 79% of the total income for those in the lowest income quintile, and public assistance provides the second largest share (11%). For those in the highest income quintile, asset income is the most important share (33%), and earnings are the next most important (27%). Social Security and pensions are about equally important (18% and 20% respectively)."

[Shares of income by quintiles of total income]

Sources	Lowest	Second	Third	Fourth	Highest
Social Security	79.0	76.0	58.0	41.0	18.0
Pensions	3.0	8.0	16.0	22.0	20.0
Asset income	4.0	8.0	15.0	21.0	33.0
Earnings	1.0	3.0	7.0	12.0	27.0

[Continued]

★ 260 ★

Share of Income from Sources, by Income Level, 1990
[Continued]

Sources	Lowest	Second	Third	Fourth	Highest
Public assistance	11.0	2.0	1.0	_2	_2
Other income	2.0	2.0	2.0	2.0	2.0

Source: U.S. Department of Health and Human Services, Social Security Administration, *Income of the Aged Chartbook, 1990,* GPO, Washington, D.C., September 1992, p. 16. *Notes:* 1. "Aged unit" does not refer to the household, the family, or unrelated individuals, as used by the Bureau of the Census. The aged unit is either a married couple living together with the husband or wife aged 65 or older (generally measured by the age of the husband), or a person 65 or older who does not live with a spouse. The single person unit may be a widow(er), a divorced or separated person, a person legally married who does not live with a spouse, or a person who never married. 2. Less than 0.5%.

★ 261 ★

Sources of Income

Change in Income Sources Since 1962

Figures based on a sample of 9,343,000 couples and 13,805,000 single "aged units".[1] From the source: "In 1962, Social Security was received by 69% of the aged; in 1990, by 92%. As shown in the table, ... most of the increase occurred in the 1960's. Receipt of other pension income more than doubled since 1962, with most of the increase occurring since the early 1970s. The proportion of aged units with asset income grew from just over one-half to more than two-thirds, and the proportion with earnings declined from less than two-fifths to about one-fifth. The proportion receiving public assistance also declined substantially to only half its 1962 level."

[Sources of income, in percent]

Year	Social Security	Asset income	Pensions[2]	Earnings	Public assistance
1962	69.0	54.0	18.0	36.0	14.0
1967	86.0	50.0	22.0	27.0	12.0
1971	87.0	49.0	23.0	31.0	10.0
1976	89.0	56.0	31.0	25.0	11.0
1978	90.0	62.0	32.0	25.0	9.0
1980	90.0	66.0	34.0	23.0	10.0
1982	90.0	68.0	35.0	22.0	8.0
1984	91.0	68.0	38.0	21.0	9.0
1986	91.0	67.0	40.0	20.0	7.0

[Continued]

★ 261 ★

Change in Income Sources Since 1962
[Continued]

Year	Social Security	Asset income	Pensions[2]	Earnings	Public assistance
1988	92.0	68.0	42.0	22.0	7.0
1990	92.0	69.0	44.0	22.0	7.0

Source: U.S. Department of Health and Human Services, Social Security Administration, *Income of the Aged Chartbook, 1990*, GPO, Washington, D.C., September 1992, p. 20. *Notes:* 1. "Aged unit" does not refer to the household, the family, or unrelated individuals, as used by the Bureau of the Census. The aged unit is either a married couple living together with the husband or wife aged 65 or older (generally measured by the age of the husband), or a person 65 or older who does not live with a spouse. The single person unit may be a widow(er), a divorced or separated person, a person legally married who does not live with a spouse, or a person who never married. 2. Includes private pensions, government employee pensions, Railroad Retirement.

★ 262 ★

Sources of Income

Food Stamp Use in Elderly Households
[Numbers are shown in thousands for 1989]

Characteristic	Total occupied units	Tenure		Housing unit characteristics				Household characteristics			
		Owner	Renter	New construction 4 yrs.	Mobile homes	Physical problems		Black	Hispanic	Moved in past year	Below poverty level
						Severe	Moderate				
Income of $25,000 or less	15,221	10,983	4,237	405	1,094	583	791	1,593	552	692	3,766
Family members received food stamps	997	433	565	19	69	65	171	342	81	91	761
Did not receive food stamps	13,642	10,094	3,549	371	1,001	504	595	1,199	451	569	2,891
Not reported	581	457	124	16	24	13	25	51	21	32	113

Source: U.S. Department of Commerce and U.S. Department of Housing and Urban Development, Current Housing Reports, H150/89, *American Housing Survey for the United States in 1989*, July 1991, p. 334.

Indebtedness

★ 263 ★

Financial Debt Held by Families, by Type: 1989

[Percent of families carrying debt]

Age of family head[1]	Total[2]	Home mortgage	Investment real estate	Home equity lines	Other lines of credit	Credit cards	Car loans
Total, all ages	72.7	38.7	7.0	3.3	3.3	39.9	35.1
Under 35 years old	79.5	32.8	2.6	1.0	4.5	44.0	37.4
35 to 44 years old	89.6	57.7	10.2	4.3	4.7	52.4	51.5
45 to 54 years old	85.9	56.3	12.3	6.3	4.0	50.0	48.7
55 to 64 years old	74.0	37.5	10.7	6.1	1.9	34.1	29.3
65 to 74 years old	47.9	19.9	3.9	1.0	0.6	25.4	14.0
75 years old and over	23.8	8.6	1.4	(B)	(B)	10.6	5.3

Source: U.S. Bureau of the Census, *Statistical Abstract of the United States: 1992* (112th edition.) Washington, DC, 1992, p. 493. Primary source: Board of Governors of the Federal Reserve System, *Federal Reserve Bulletin*, January 1992. *Notes:* (B) Base figure too small. 1. Families include one person units. 2. Includes other types of debt, not shown separately.

Services

★ 264 ★

Financial Activity Assistance

As many as 10% of all senior citizens require assistance in performing basic financial tasks. The need increases as people age. A National Institutes of Health study shows that 24% of people 85 and older need help managing their money—and this age group is growing faster than any other.

Source: Business Week, April 12, 1993, p. 95. Primary source: Desert State Life Management Services Inc.

Poverty

★ 265 ★

Poverty Population: Composition in 1980 and 1988

[Numbers are shown in thousands]

Family type	All persons				Poverty rate		Poor persons			
	1980		1988		1980	1988	1980		1988	
	Number	%	Number	%	%	%	Number	%	Number	%
Elderly heads of family	29,355	(13.0)	34,339	(14.1)	15.7	12.0	4,620	(15.8)	4,116	(13.0)
Disabled heads of family	9,834	(4.4)	10,380	(4.3)	39.6	41.1	3,894	(13.3)	4,263	(13.4)
Single-parent families with children under 18	20,421	(9.1)	25,035	(10.3)	41.8	42.6	8,539	(29.2)	10,673	(33.6)
Married-couple families with children under 18	103,877	(46.2)	101,625	(41.7)	7.6	7.3	7,914	(27.0)	7,456	(23.5)
Unrelated individuals (singles)	17,684	(7.9)	23,012	(9.4)	16.4	15.9	2,902	(9.9)	3,667	(11.6)
Families without children under 18	43,857	(19.5)	49,138	(20.1)	3.2	3.2	1,413	(4.8)	1,570	(4.9)
Total	225,027	(100.0)	243,530	(100.0)	13.0	13.0	29,282	(100.0)	31,745	(100.0)

Source: U.S. General Accounting Office, *Poverty Trends 1980-88: Changes in Family Composition and Income Sources Among the Poor*, GAO/PEMD-92-34, September 1992, p. 106. *Note:* Numbers and percentages may not add to totals shown due to rounding.

★ 266 ★

Poverty

Poverty Population: Composition in 1980 and 1988 Using Adjusted Definition of Income[1]

From the source: "The overall poverty rate for U.S. families in 1988 differed little from the rate in 1980, declining from 14.4 percent to 14.1 percent. However, classifying families by their presumed ability to support themselves through earnings uncovered some small but important shifts in the composition of the poor. In 1988, families headed by an elderly person and married-couple families with children had declined as a proportion of the poor. Instead, poor families were more likely to be headed by a single parent or to consist of a nonelderly, nondisabled, single adult, compared with 1980."

Family type	All families[2]		Poverty rate		Poor families[2]	
	1980	1988	1980	1988	1980	1988
Elderly head of family	17,178	20,080		2,845	2,447	
Percent	(19.6)	(20.0)	16.6	12.2[3]	(24.6)	(18.6)
Disabled head of family	4,044	4,562			1,425	1,750

[Continued]

★ 266 ★

Poverty Population: Composition in 1980 and 1988 Using Adjusted Definition of Income

[Continued]

Family type	All families[2]		Poverty rate		Poor families[2]	
	1980	1988	1980	1988	1980	1988
Percent	(4.6)	(4.5)	35.2	38.4	(12.3)	(13.3)
Single-parent families with children under 18	6,466	8,117			2,076	2,809
Percent	(7.4)	(8.1)	32.1	34.6	(17.9)	(21.3)
Married-couple families with children under 18	24,539	24,599			1,566	1,547
Percent	(27.9)	(24.4)	6.4	6.3	(13.5)	(11.7)
Unrelated individuals (singles)	17,684	23,012			3,074	3,931
Percent	(20.1)	(22.9)	17.4	17.1	(26.5)	(29.8)
Families without children under 18	17,923	20,281			593	707
Percent	(20.4)	(20.1)	3.3	3.5	(5.1)	(5.3)
Total	87,834	100,649			11,579	13,191
Percent	(100.0)	(100.0)	13.2	13.1	(100.0)	(100.0)

Source: U.S. General Accounting Office, *Poverty Trends 1980-88: Changes in Family Composition and Income Sources Among the Poor*, GAO/PEMD-92-34, September 1992, p. 33. *Notes:* 1. Here family income includes the estimated market value of food and housing benefits received and federal income taxes paid. 2. Numbers in thousands. Numbers and percentages may not add to totals shown due to rounding. 3. p > 0.01.

★ 267 ★

Poverty

Poverty Population: Older People Below and Near Poverty Level, by Age Group: 1989

[Values are in percent]

Age	Below poverty	100 to 124% of poverty	Percent total
65 to 74	9.0	6.3	15.3
75 to 84	15.0	9.1	24.1
85 +	18.0	10.9	28.9

Source: *Aging America, Trends and Projections*, prepared by the U.S. Senate Special Committee on Aging, the American Association of Retired Persons, the Federal Council on the Aging, and the U.S. Administration on Aging, 1991, Washington, D.C., p. 44. Primary source: March 1990 *Current Population* Survey. Data prepared by the Congressional Research Service.

★ 268 ★

Poverty

Poverty Population: Percent of Elderly Below the Poverty Level, by Selected Characteristics: 1989

Unless otherwise noted, data are for age 65+. Data are arranged by increasing level of poverty. Black women, living alone, experience the greatest degree of poverty among the elderly.

	Percent
All people	11.4
Central city	13.8
Women	14.0
Nonmetropolitan	15.4
All people 85+	18.5
Hispanics	20.6
Not completed high school	20.7
Living alone	22.0
Women living alone	23.3
Black	30.8
Black women living alone	60.6

Source: Aging America, Trends and Projections, prepared by the U.S. Senate Special Committee on Aging, the American Association of Retired Persons, the Federal Council on the Aging, and the U.S. Administration on Aging, 1991, Washington, D.C., p. 55. Primary source: U.S. Bureau of the Census, "Money Income and Poverty Status in the United States: 1989." *Current Population Report* Series P-60, No. 168, September 1990, and unpublished data from the March 1990 *Current Population Survey.*

★ 269 ★

Poverty

Poverty Population: Percentage of Persons Poor or Near Poor, by Age, 1990

Age of person	Percentage of age group below -		
	Poverty threshold	125 percent of poverty threshold	150 percent of poverty threshold
All ages	13.5	18.0	22.7
Under 65	13.7	17.9	22.2
65 or older	12.2	19.0	26.3
Under 5	24.0	29.5	35.0
5-9	21.3	27.0	32.8
10-14	18.7	24.1	29.1
15-19	16.4	21.3	26.0

[Continued]

★ 269 ★

Poverty Population: Percentage of Persons Poor or Near Poor, by Age, 1990
[Continued]

Age of person	Percentage of age group below -		
	Poverty threshold	125 percent of poverty threshold	150 percent of poverty threshold
20-24	15.8	21.0	26.6
25-29	12.8	17.2	21.8
30-34	11.4	15.5	19.6
35-39	9.1	12.3	15.8
40-44	7.7	10.4	13.4
45-49	7.3	9.7	12.3
50-54	8.4	10.8	13.4
55-59	9.0	12.1	15.4
60-64	10.3	14.8	18.9
65-69	8.4	13.4	18.7
70-74	11.3	17.3	24.3
75-79	13.3	21.5	30.0
80-84	17.5	26.8	36.9
85 or older	20.2	30.4	39.8

Source: Social Security Bulletin, Vol. 55, No. 3, Fall 1992, Table 5, p. 14. Primary source: Tabulations from the March 1991 Current Population Survey.

★ 270 ★
Poverty

Poverty Rates: 1966 to 1989, Elderly and Nonelderly Adults

Year	Poverty rate	
	18 to 64	65 +
1966	10.5	28.5
1967	10.0	29.5
1968	9.0	25.0
1969	8.7	25.3
1970	9.0	24.6
1971	9.3	21.6
1972	8.8	18.6
1973	8.3	16.3
1974	8.3	14.6
1975	9.2	15.3
1976	9.0	15.0
1977	8.8	14.1
1978	8.7	14.0
1979	8.9	15.2

[Continued]

★ 270 ★

Poverty Rates: 1966 to 1989, Elderly and Nonelderly Adults
[Continued]

Year	Poverty rate	
	18 to 64	65 +
1980	10.1	15.7
1981	11.1	15.3
1982	12.0	14.6
1983	12.4	13.8
1984	11.7	12.4
1985	11.3	12.6
1986	10.8	12.4
1987	10.6	12.5
1988	10.5	12.0
1989	10.2	11.4

Source: *Aging America, Trends and Projections*, prepared by the U.S. Senate Special Committee on Aging, the American Association of Retired Persons, the Federal Council on the Aging, and the U.S. Administration on Aging, 1991, Washington, D.C., p. 58. Primary source: U.S. Bureau of the Census. "Money Income and Poverty Status in the United States: 1989." *Current Population Reports* Series P-60, No. 168, September 1990.

★ 271 ★
Poverty

Poverty Rates: 1981 to 1990, Persons 85 Years and Over
[Percent of poor are shown in 90-percent confidence intervals]

Year	White males	White females	Black females[1]
1981	8.3 to 16.1	21.0 to 28.0	35.4 to 63.6
1982	9.3 to 17.9	18.0 to 25.4	30.1 to 59.9
1983	8.0 to 16.2	18.9 to 26.1	30.6 to 61.0
1984	8.0 to 16.0	14.3 to 20.9	32.8 to 60.4
1985	10.1 to 18.9	14.0 to 20.4	31.1 to 56.5
1986	9.2 to 16.8	14.6 to 20.6	29.8 to 57.8
1987	7.8 to 15.2	15.5 to 21.7	41.5 to 67.7
1988	5.3 to 19.1	11.9 to 22.9	16.3 to 61.5
1989	4.1 to 15.5	14.4 to 25.2	24.2 to 67.2
1990	4.3 to 15.3	17.4 to 28.4	15.2 to 55.6

Source: *Sixty-Five Plus in America*, Cynthia M. Taeuber, U.S. Department of Commerce, Economics and Statistics Administration, Bureau of the Census, U.S. Government Printing Office, Washington, D.C., 1992, p. 4-14. Primary source: U.S. Bureau of the Census, unpublished data from March 1982 to 1991, Current Population Survey, available from Mark Littman, Housing and Household Economic Statistics. *Notes:* 1. There are not enough Black males 85 years and over in the survey to show statistically reliable data.

★ 272 ★

Poverty

Poverty Rates: Disabled and Nondisabled Heads of Families, by Age, Sex, and Race: 1988

From the source: "Although poverty tends to decrease with age..., because disabled family heads were so concentrated among the oldest nonelderly group (ages 55 to 64), disability accounted for almost half of the poverty for all family heads in that age group."

[Numbers in thousands]

Characteristic	Disabled					Nondisabled				
	In poverty		Total		Poverty rate	In poverty		Total		Poverty rate
	Number	%	Number	%	%	Number	%	Number	%	%
Age										
15 to 24	108	(5)	144	(3)	75.0	2,389	(26)	7,671	(10)	31.1[1]
25 to 34	263	(13)	478	(10)	55.0	3,187	(35)	23,323	(31)	13.7[1]
35 to 44	364	(18)	855	(19)	42.6	1,846	(20)	20,355	(27)	9.1[1]
45 to 54	514	(25)	1,051	(23)	48.9	880	(10)	13,524	(18)	6.5[1]
55 to 64	794	(39)	2,033	(45)	39.1	876	(10)	11,136	(15)	7.9[1]
Sex										
Male	916	(45)	2,705	(59)	33.9	4,038	(44)	54,037	(71)	7.5[1]
Female	1,126	(55)	1,856	(41)	60.5	5,141	(56)	21,972	(29)	23.4[1]
Race										
White	1,243	(61)	3,272	(72)	38.0	6,464	(70)	64,866	(85)	10.0[1]
Black	739	(36)	1,157	(25)	63.9	2,279	(25)	8,698	(11)	26.2[1]
Other	61	(3)	133	(3)	45.9	434	(5)	2,446	(3)	17.7[1]
Total	2,042	(100)	4,562	(100)	44.8	9,178	(100)	76,008	(100)	12.1[1]

Source: U.S. General Accounting Office, *Poverty Trends 1980-88: Changes in Family Composition and Income Sources Among the Poor*, GAO/ PEMD-92-34, September 1992, p. 81. *Notes:* Numbers and percentages may not add to totals shown due to rounding. 1. p > 0.01.

★ 273 ★
Poverty

Poverty Rates: Elderly and Nonelderly People, by Ratio of Income to Poverty: 1989

Ratio of income to poverty level	Number (in thousands)		Percent	
	Under 65	65+	Under 65	65+
Below poverty	28,165	3,369	13.0	11.4
100 to 124 percent of poverty level	8,845	2,280	4.1	7.7
125 to 149 percent of poverty level	8,979	2,404	4.1	8.1
Total below 150 percent of poverty level	45,989	8,053	21.2	27.2

Source: *Aging America, Trends and Projections,* prepared by the U.S. Senate Special Committee on Aging, the American Association of Retired Persons, the Federal Council on the Aging, and the U.S. Administration on Aging, 1991, Washington, D.C., p. 41. Primary source: U.S. Bureau of the Census, "Money Income and Poverty Status in the United States: 1989," *Current Population Reports* Series P-60, No. 168, September 1990.

★ 274 ★
Poverty

Poverty Rates: Female-Headed, Single-Parent Families Living Alone, by Age: 1980 and 1988

[Numbers in thousands]

Age group of family head	1980					1988				
	In poverty		Total		Poverty rate	In poverty		Total		Poverty rate
	Number	%	Number	%	%	Number	%	Number	%	%
With young children										
15 to 24	391	(34)	527	(28)	74.0	456	(32)	588	(26)	77.6
25 to 34	559	(48)	963	(52)	58.1	753	(54)	1,273	(57)	59.2
35 to 44	155	(13)	250	(13)	62.0	167	(12)	323	(14)	51.7
45 to 64[1]	54	(5)	120	(6)	45.0	25	(2)	46	(2)	54.3
Total	1,159	(100)	1,862	(100)	62.3	1,400	(100)	2,230	(100)	62.8
Without young children										
15 to 34[1]	405	(46)	1,108	(35)	36.6	444	(45)	997	(31)	44.5
35 to 44	319	(36)	1,272	(41)	25.1	389	(39)	1,597	(50)	24.4
45 to 54	127	(14)	577	(18)	22.0	109	(11)	500	(16)	21.8
55 to 64	38	(4)	169	(5)	22.5	50	(5)	115	(4)	43.5
Total	888	(100)	3,126	(100)	28.4	994	(100)	3,209	(100)	31.0

Source: U.S. General Accounting Office, *Poverty Trends 1980-88: Changes in Family Composition and Income Sources Among the Poor,* GAO/PEMD-92-34, September 1992, p. 45. *Notes:* Numbers and percentages may not add to totals shown due to rounding. 1. Age groups combined due to small sample size.

★ 275 ★

Poverty

Poverty Rates: Percent Elderly Poor in 1990, by Age, Sex, Race, and Hispanic Origin: March 1991

Age	Male			Female		
	White	Black	Hispanic origin[1]	White	Black	Hispanic origin[1]
65 to 74	4.5	24.6	18.0	10.2	33.6	22.7
75 and over	7.8	34.4	20.1	17.3	43.9	30.1

Source: Mark Littman, U.S. Bureau of the Census, *Poverty in the United States: 1990*, Current Population Reports, Series P-60, No. 175, U.S. Government Printing Office, Washington, D.C., 1991, Table 5. *Note:* 1. Hispanic origin may be of any race.

★ 276 ★

Poverty

Poverty Rates: Percent of Elderly and Nonelderly Below and Near Poverty: 1989

Age group	125-150% of poverty	100-124% of poverty	Below poverty	Total
Under age 65	4.2	4.0	13.0	21.2
65+	8.2	7.0	12.0	27.2

Source: Aging America, Trends and Projections, prepared by the U.S. Senate Special Committee on Aging, the American Association of Retired Persons, the Federal Council on the Aging, and the U.S. Administration on Aging, 1991, Washington, D.C., p. 42. Primary source: U.S. Bureau of the Census, "Money, Income and Poverty Status in the United States: 1989." *Current Population Reports* Series P-60, No. 168, September 1990.

★ 277 ★
Poverty

Poverty Rates: Percent of Older People, by Ratio of Income to Poverty Level, by Age and Sex: 1989

Ratio of income to poverty level	Age			
	65 to 74	75 to 84	85+	Total 65+
Both sexes				
Below poverty level	8.8	14.7	18.4	11.4
100 to 124 percent of poverty level	6.5	9.4	10.5	7.7
Men				
Below poverty level	6.6	9.8	11.3	7.8
100 to 124 percent of poverty level	5.6	7.0	8.4	6.2
Women				
Below poverty level	10.6	17.7	22.1	14.0
100 to 124 percent of poverty level	7.2	10.9	11.5	8.8

Source: Aging America, Trends and Projections, prepared by the U.S. Senate Special Committee on Aging, the American Association of Retired Persons, the Federal Council on the Aging, and the U.S. Administration on Aging, 1991, Washington, D.C., p. 46. Primary source: Bureau of the Census. Unpublished data from the March 1990 *Current Population* Survey.

★ 278 ★
Poverty

Poverty Rates: Percent of Total Unit Income from Various Sources, by the Ratio of Total Income to the Poverty Threshold, for Units Age 65+: 1989[1]

This table only includes couples/people who had income. The poverty threshold is that defined by the Bureau of the Census. A ratio of 1.50 means that the percentage of couples/people who fall into that range have 1.5 times as much income as the poverty level, i.e., 50 percent more. A ratio of 5.00 means that they have 5 times the poverty level income.

Source of income	Ratio of total unit income to poverty threshold								
	0 to 0.99	1.00 to 1.24	1.25 to 1.49	1.50 to 1.99	2.00 to 2.99	3.00 to 4.99	5.00 and over	1.00 and over	Total
Total	100.0	100.0	100.0	100.0	100.0	100.0	100.0	100.0	100.0
Earnings	0.1	1.8	3.2	3.9	7.1	12.7	25.3	11.7	15.4
OASDI, railroad retirement	79.3	79.9	76.4	67.8	53.1	37.0	17.0	36.4	37.8
Pensions	3.7	5.1	7.1	12.8	20.1	23.8	19.2	19.0	18.5
Unemployment compensation, veterans payments	1.2	2.9	1.3	1.4	1.2	1.1	0.6	1.0	1.0
AFDC, SSI, general assistance	11.6	4.5	3.8	1.6	0.5	0.2	0.1	0.1	0.9
Child support, alimony	0.1	0.1	0.0	0.1	0.1	0.1	0.1	0.1	0.1

[Continued]

★ 278 ★

Poverty Rates: Percent of Total Unit Income from Various Sources, by the Ratio of Total Income to the Poverty Threshold, for Units Age 65+: 1989

[Continued]

Source of income	Ratio of total unit income to poverty threshold								
	0 to 0.99	1.00 to 1.24	1.25 to 1.49	1.50 to 1.99	2.00 to 2.99	3.00 to 4.99	5.00 and over	1.00 and over	Total
Interest, dividends	3.7	4.6	6.7	10.0	14.8	21.7	32.3	23.1	22.5
Other income	0.3	1.1	1.5	2.4	3.1	3.4	5.4	8.6	3.8

Source: *Aging America, Trends and Projections*, prepared by the U.S. Senate Special Committee on Aging, the American Association of Retired Persons, the Federal Council on the Aging, and the U.S. Administration on Aging, 1991, Washington, D.C., p. 68. Primary source: U.S. Bureau of the Census. Unpublished data from the March 1990 Current Population Survey. *Notes:* OASDI stands for Old-Age, Survivors, and Disability Insurance; AFDC is Aid to Families with Dependent Children; SSI is Supplemental Security Income. 1. Units are married couples living together—at least one of whom is 65+—and unmarried people 65+. Income of aged units does not include income from other household members.

★ 279 ★

Poverty

Poverty Status: 1959 to 1990, by Age, Race, and Hispanic Origin

[Numbers are in thousands. Persons counted as of March of the following year]

Year and race	All persons below poverty		Persons under 18 years below poverty		Persons 65 years and over below poverty	
	Number	Percent	Number	Percent	Number	Percent
All races						
1959	39,490	22.4	17,552	27.3	5,481	35.2
1966	28,510	14.7	12,389	17.6	5,114	28.5
1970	25,420	12.6	10,440	15.1	4,793	24.6
1975	25,877	12.3	11,104	17.1	3,317	15.3
1980	29,272	13.0	11,543	18.3	3,871	15.7
1985	33,064	14.0	13,110	20.7	3,456	12.6
1990	33,585	13.5	13,431	20.6	3,658	12.2
White						
1959	28,484	18.1	(NA)	(NA)	4,744	33.1
1966	19,290	11.3	(NA)	(NA)	4,357	26.4
1970	17,484	9.9	(NA)	(NA)	4,011	22.6
1975	17,770	9.7	6,927	12.7	2,634	13.4
1980	19,699	10.2	7,181	13.9	3,042	13.6
1985	22,860	11.4	8,253	16.2	2,698	11.0
1990	22,326	10.7	8,232	15.9	2,707	10.1
Black						
1959	9,927	55.1	(NA)	(NA)	711	62.5
1966	8,867	41.8	(NA)	(NA)	722	55.1
1970	7,548	33.5	(NA0	(NA)	683	48.0
1975	7,545	31.3	3,925	41.7	652	36.3
1980	8,579	32.5	3,961	42.3	783	38.1

[Continued]

★ 279 ★

Poverty Status: 1959 to 1990, by Age, Race, and Hispanic Origin

[Continued]

Year and race	All persons below poverty		Persons under 18 years below poverty		Persons 65 years and over below poverty	
	Number	Percent	Number	Percent	Number	Percent
1985	8,926	31.3	4,157	43.6	717	31.5
1990	9,837	31.9	4,550	44.8	860	33.8
Hispanic origin[1]						
1959	(NA)	(NA)	(NA)	(NA)	(NA)	(NA)
1966	(NA)	(NA)	(NA)	(NA)	(NA)	(NA)
1970	(NA)	(NA)	(NA)	(NA)	(NA)	(NA)
1975	2,991	26.9	(NA)	(NA)	137	32.6
1980	3,491	25.7	1,749	33.2	179	30.8
1985	5,236	29.0	2,606	40.3	219	23.9
1990	6,006	28.1	2,865	38.4	245	22.5

Source: Sixty-Five Plus in America, Cynthia M. Taeuber, U.S. Department of Commerce, Economics and Statistics Administration, Bureau of the Census, U.S. Government Printing Office, Washington, D.C., 1992, p. 4-13. Primary source: Mark Littman, U.S. Bureau of the Census, Poverty in the United States: 1990, Current Population Reports, Series P-60, No. 175, U.S. Government Printing Office, Washington, D.C., 1991, Tables 2 and 3. Notes: NA stands for not available. 1. Hispanic origin may be of any race.

★ 280 ★

Poverty

Poverty Status: 1988, Among Persons 65 or Older

[In thousands]

	Total	White	Black
Number of persons	29,022	26,001	2,436
Number of poor persons	3,482	2,595	785
Percent poor	12.0	10.0	32.2

Source: U.S. Congress, "Profiles in Aging America: Meeting the Health Care Needs of the Nation's Black Elderly," Joint Hearing Before the Special Committee on Aging and the Congressional Black Caucus Health Braintrust, United States Senate, September 28, 1990, 101-29, U.S. Government Printing Office, Washington, D.C., p. 125. Primary source: "Money, Income and Poverty Status in the United States: 1988," Current Population Reports, Consumer Income, Series P-60, No. 166, Oct. 1989, p. 66.

★ 281 ★

Poverty

Poverty Status: 1990, by Age

Figures based on a sample of 9,343,000 couples and 13,805,000 single "aged units".[1,2] From the source: "In addition to the lower median income of older age groups, poverty rates are higher for those who are older. As with income, the large proportion of non-married women in the older age groups contributes to the difference in poverty rates by age."

Age	Married couples	Non-married men	Non-married women
Percent poor			
65-69	4.0	15.0	20.0
70-74	5.0	14.0	22.0
75-79	6.0	14.0	22.0
80-84	8.0	18.0	23.0
85 or older	11.0	14.0	26.0
Percent poor or near poor[3]			
65-69	7.0	24.0	29.0
70-74	9.0	22.0	31.0
75-79	10.0	22.0	35.0
80-84	14.0	27.0	36.0
85 or older	18.0	22.0	38.0

Source: U.S. Department of Health and Human Services, Social Security Administration, *Income of the Aged Chartbook, 1990,* GPO, Washington, D.C., September 1992, p. 6. *Notes:* 1. "Aged unit" does not refer to the household, the family, or unrelated individuals, as used by the Bureau of the Census. The aged unit is either a married couple living together with the husband or wife aged 65 or older (generally measured by the age of the husband), or a person 65 or older who does not live with a spouse. The single person unit may be a widow(er), a divorced or separated person, a person legally married who does not live with a spouse, or a person who never married. 2. The information in the table is based on family income. 3. The near poor are defined as having income between the poverty line and 125% of the poverty line.

★ 282 ★

Poverty

Poverty Status: 1990, by Marital Status, Race, and Hispanic Origin

Figures based on a sample of 9,343,000 couples and 13,805,000 single "aged units"[1]. From the source: "The variations in income by marital status and by race are reflected in the poverty rates[2] for these subgroups of the aged. Non-married men, non-married women, and minorities have the highest poverty rates, ranging from 15% to 36%. When the near poor[3] are included, the rates for the nonmarried and nonwhites range from 23% to 48%."

	Percent of units	
	Near poor[2]	Poor
Married couples	4	5
Non-married men	8	15
Non-married women	11	22
White	7	12
Black	12	36
Hispanic[4]	12	25

Source: U.S. Department of Health and Human Services, Social Security Administration, *Income of the Aged Chartbook, 1990*, GPO, Washington, D.C., September 1992, p. 3. *Notes:* 1. "Aged unit" does not refer to the household, the family, or unrelated individuals, as used by the Bureau of the Census. The aged unit is either a married couple living together with the husband or wife aged 65 or older (generally measured by the age of the husband), or a person 65 or older who does not live with a spouse. The single person unit may be a widow(er), a divorced or separated person, a person legally married who does not live with a spouse, or a person who never married. 2. Based on family income rather than aged unit income to conform with official measures of poverty. 3. The near poor are defined as having income between the poverty line and 125% of the poverty line. 4. Persons of Hispanic origin may be of any race.

★ 283 ★

Poverty

Poverty Status: Number and Percent of Elderly Below Poverty, by Race, Hispanic Origin, Sex, and Living Arrangement: 1989

Race & Hispanic origin	Number (thousands)				Percent			
	Total	Alone	With spouse	With others	Total	Alone	With spouse	With others
All races								
Men	965	339	525	101	7.8	17.4	5.6	10.4
Women	2,404	1,705	390	310	14.0	23.3	5.2	12.7
Total	3,369	2,044	915	411	11.4	22.0	5.4	12.0
White								
Men	723	240	431	52	6.6	13.9	5.0	7.2
Women	1,819	1,339	318	162	11.8	20.0	4.6	8.5

[Continued]

263

★ 283 ★

Poverty Status: Number and Percent of Elderly Below Poverty, by Race, Hispanic Origin, Sex, and Living Arrangement: 1989

[Continued]

Race & Hispanic origin	Number (thousands)				Percent			
	Total	Alone	With spouse	With others	Total	Alone	With spouse	With others
Total	2,542	1,579	748	214	9.6	18.8	4.8	8.1
Black								
Men	221	96	80	46	22.1	48.2	13.7	21.0
Women	544	350	57	138	36.7	60.6	13.0	29.6
Total	766	445	137	183	30.8	57.3	13.4	26.6
Hispanic[1]								
Men	87	26	53	8	18.6	34.7	15.1	19.5
Women	124	62	33	29	22.4	41.9	12.4	20.4
Total	211	88	86	37	20.6	39.5	13.9	20.2

Source: Aging America, Trends and Projections, prepared by the U.S. Senate Special Committee on Aging, the American Association of Retired Persons, the Federal Council on the Aging, and the U.S. Administration on Aging, 1991, Washington, D.C., p. 53. Primary source: Unpublished data from the March 1990 Current Population Survey. Notes: Details may not add to total due to rounding. 1. Hispanic people may be of any race.

★ 284 ★

Poverty

Poverty Status: Older Americans Living Alone and Below Poverty or Near-Poverty Levels, 1989

Nearly 1 in 5 persons, 65 to 74 years old, who lives alone also has an income that is below the federal poverty level. For persons over 75 years old, the ratios are even greater.

[Numbers in percent]

Age	Below 100% of poverty	100-125% of poverty
65 to 74	18.0	12.0
75 to 84	24.0	15.0
85 +	28.0	17.0

Source: Aging America, Trends and Projections, prepared by the U.S. Senate Special Committee on Aging, the American Association of Retired Persons, the Federal Council on the Aging, and the U.S. Administration on Aging, 1991, Washington, D.C., p. 220. Primary source: Bureau of the Census, 1990. Unpublished data prepared by Fu Associates.

★ 285 ★

Poverty

Poverty Status: Older Americans Living Alone and Below Poverty or Near-Poverty Levels, by Race, 1989

From the source: "More than half of older blacks (57 percent) and two-fifths of older Hispanics (40 percent) who live alone have incomes below the federal poverty threshold... By contrast, just 19 percent of older whites who live alone are poor. Moreover, most older minorities who live alone are near-poor, with incomes below 125 percent of poverty."

[Numbers in percent]

Race/ ethnicity	Below poverty	Below 125% of poverty
Black	57.0	72.0
Hispanic	40.0	60.0
White	19.0	32.0

Source: Aging America, Trends and Projections, prepared by the U.S. Senate Special Committee on Aging, the American Association of Retired Persons, the Federal Council on the Aging, and the U.S. Administration on Aging, 1991, Washington, D.C., p. 221.

★ 286 ★
Poverty

Poverty Status: Older Americans Living Alone and Below Poverty or Near-Poverty Levels, by Type of Residence, 1989

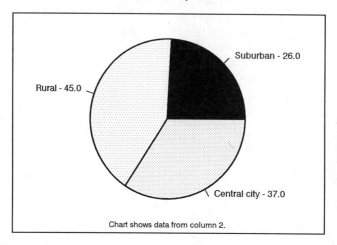

Chart shows data from column 2.

Nearly 1 in 3 Older Americans over 65 years old who lives alone also lives below the federal government's poverty threshold. Most of these people live in inner cities or in rural areas.

[Numbers in percent]

Type of residence	Below 100% of poverty	Below 125% of poverty
Rural	29.0	45.0
Central city	24.0	37.0
Suburban	15.0	26.0

Source: Aging America, Trends and Projections, prepared by the U.S. Senate Special Committee on Aging, the American Association of Retired Persons, the Federal Council on the Aging, and the U.S. Administration on Aging, 1991, Washington, D.C., p. 222. Primary source: Bureau of the Census, 1990. Unpublished data prepared by Fu Associates. *Notes:* Type of residence is based on metropolitan statistical areas (MSAs) as defined by the U.S. Office of Management and Budget. "Suburban" refers to those portions of MSAs outside central cities, and "rural" refers to nonmetropolitan areas.

★ 287 ★

Poverty

Poverty Status: Older Americans Who Live Alone and Use Community Services, by Age Group and Poverty Status, 1990

Data are shown for persons aged 65+.

Age group	Non-poor	Poor
65 to 74	26.0	37.0
75+	32.0	48.0

Source: Aging America, Trends and Projections, prepared by the U.S. Senate Special Committee on Aging, the American Association of Retired Persons, the Federal Council on the Aging, and the U.S. Administration on Aging, 1991, Washington, D.C., p. 236. Primary source: Lewin/ICF estimates based on data from the *Current Population Survey* and the Brookings/ICF Long-Term Care Financing Model, 1990.

★ 288 ★

Poverty

Poverty Status: Persons, by Age and Race: All Races

[Numbers in thousands]

Year	18 to 64 years			65 years and over		
	Total	Below poverty		Total	Below poverty	
		Number	Percent		Number	Percent
1980	137,428	13,858	10.1	24,686	3,871	15.7
1981	139,477	15,464	11.1	25,231	3,853	15.3
1982	141,328	17,000	12.0	25,738	3,751	14.6
1983	143,052	17,767	12.4	26,313	3,625	13.8
1984	144,551	16,952	11.7	26,818	3,330	12.4
1985	146,396	16,598	11.3	27,322	3,456	12.6
1986	147,631	16,017	10.8	27,975	3,477	12.4
1987[1]	149,201	15,815	10.6	28,487	3,563	12.5
1988[1]	150,761	15,809	10.5	29,022	3,481	12.0
1989	152,282	15,575	10.2	29,566	3,363	11.4
1990	153,502	16,496	10.7	30,093	3,658	12.2
1991	154,671	17,585	11.4	30,590	3,781	12.4

Source: Poverty in the United States: 1991, Current Population Reports, Series P-60, No. 181, U.S. Department of Commerce, Bureau of the Census, August 1992, p. 4. *Notes:* 1. Figures are based on new processing procedures. The 1987 and 1988 figures are also revised to reflect corrections to files after publication of the 1988 advance report, *Money, Income, and Poverty Status in the United States: 1988,* P-60, No. 166.

★ 289 ★

Poverty

Poverty Status: Persons, by Age and Race: Black

[Numbers in thousands]

Year	18 to 64 years			65 years and over		
	Total	Below poverty		Total	Below poverty	
		Number	Percent		Number	Percent
1980	14,987	3,835	25.6	2,054	783	38.1
1981	15,358	4,117	26.8	2,102	820	39.0
1982	15,692	4,415	28.1	2,124	811	38.2
1983	16,065	4,694	29.2	2,197	791	36.0
1984	16,369	4,368	26.7	2,238	710	31.7
1985	16,667	4,052	24.3	2,273	717	31.5
1986	16,911	4,113	24.3	2,331	722	31.0
1987[1]	17,245	4,361	25.3	2,387	774	32.4
1988[1]	17,548	4,275	24.4	2,436	785	32.2
1989	17,833	4,164	23.3	2,487	763	30.7
1990	18,097	4,427	24.5	2,547	860	33.8
1991	18,355	4,607	25.1	2,606	880	33.8

Source: Poverty in the United States: 1991, Current Population Reports, Series P-60, No. 181, U.S. Department of Commerce, Bureau of the Census, August 1992, p. 5. *Notes:* 1. Figures are based on new processing procedures. The 1987 and 1988 figures are also revised to reflect corrections to files after publication of the 1988 advance report, *Money, Income, and Poverty Status in the United States: 1988*, P-60, No. 166.

★ 290 ★

Poverty

Poverty Status: Persons, by Age and Race: Hispanic Origin

[Numbers in thousands]

Year	18 to 64 years			65 years and over		
	Total	Below poverty		Total	Below poverty	
		Number	Percent		Number	Percent
1980	7,740	1,563	20.2	582	179	30.8
1981	8,084	1,642	20.3	568	146	25.7
1982	8,262	1,963	23.8	596	159	26.6
1983	9,697	2,148	22.5	782	173	22.1
1984	10,029	2,254	22.5	819	176	21.5
1985	10,685	2,411	22.6	915	219	23.9
1986	11,206	2,406	21.5	906	204	22.5
1987[1]	11,718	2,509	21.4	885	243	27.5
1988[1]	12,056	2,501	20.7	1,005	225	22.4
1989	12,536	2,616	20.9	1,024	211	20.6

[Continued]

★ 290 ★

Poverty Status: Persons, by Age and Race: Hispanic Origin
[Continued]

Year	18 to 64 years			65 years and over		
	Total	Below poverty		Total	Below poverty	
		Number	Percent		Number	Percent
1990	12,857	2,896	22.5	1,091	245	22.5
1991	13,279	3,009	22.7	1,143	237	20.8

Source: *Poverty in the United States: 1991*, Current Population Reports, Series P-60, No. 181, U.S. Department of Commerce, Bureau of the Census, August 1992, p. 5. *Notes:* Persons of Hispanic origin may be of any race. 1. Figures are based on new processing procedures. The 1987 and 1988 figures are also revised to reflect corrections to files after publication of the 1988 advance report, *Money, Income, and Poverty Status in the United States: 1988, P-60*, No. 166.

★ 291 ★

Poverty

Poverty Status: Persons, by Age and Race: White
[Numbers in thousands]

Year	18 to 64 years			65 years and over		
	Total	Below poverty		Total	Below poverty	
		Number	Percent		Number	Percent
1980	118,935	9,478	8.0	22,325	3,042	13.6
1981	120,574	10,790	8.9	22,791	2,978	13.1
1982	121,766	11,971	9.8	23,234	2,870	12.4
1983	123,014	12,347	10.0	23,754	2,776	11.7
1984	123,922	11,904	9.6	24,206	2,579	10.7
1985	125,258	11,909	9.5	24,629	2,698	11.0
1986	125,998	11,285	9.0	25,173	2,689	10.7
1987[1]	126,991	10,703	8.4	25,602	2,704	10.6
1988[1]	128,031	10,687	8.3	26,001	2,593	10.0
1989	128,974	10,647	8.3	26,479	2,539	9.6
1990	129,784	11,387	8.8	26,898	2,707	10.1
1991	130,300	12,098	9.3	27,297	2,802	10.3

Source: *Poverty in the United States: 1991*, Current Population Reports, Series P-60, No. 181, U.S. Department of Commerce, Bureau of the Census, August 1992, p. 4. *Notes:* 1. Figures are based on new processing procedures. The 1987 and 1988 figures are also revised to reflect corrections to files after publication of the 1988 advance report, *Money, Income, and Poverty Status in the United States: 1988*, P-60, No. 166.

★ 292 ★

Poverty

Poverty Status: Poverty Thresholds in 1991, by Size of Family and Number of Related Children Under 18 Years

Size of family unit	Weighted average thresholds ($)	Related children under 18 years								
		None	One	Two	Three	Four	Five	Six	Seven	Eight or more
One person (unrelated individual)	6,932	-	-	-	-	-	-	-	-	-
Under 65 years	7,086	7,086	-	-	-	-	-	-	-	-
65 years and over	6,532	6,532	-	-	-	-	-	-	-	-
Two persons	8,865	-	-	-	-	-	-	-	-	-
Householder under 65 years	9,165	9,120	9,388	-	-	-	-	-	-	-
Householder 65 years and over	8,241	8,233	9,352	-	-	-	-	-	-	-
Three persons	10,860	10,654	10,963	10,973	-	-	-	-	-	-
Four persons	13,924	14,048	14,278	13,812	13,860	-	-	-	-	-
Five persons	16,456	16,941	17,188	16,662	16,254	16,006	-	-	-	-
Six persons	18,587	19,486	19,563	19,160	18,773	18,199	17,859	-	-	-
Seven persons	21,058	22,421	22,561	22,078	21,742	21,115	20,384	19,582	-	-
Eight persons	23,605	25,076	25,297	24,842	24,443	23,877	23,158	22,410	22,220	-
Nine persons or more	27,942	30,165	30,311	29,908	29,569	29,014	28,249	27,558	27,386	26,331

Source: Poverty in the United States: 1991, Current Population Reports, Series P-60, No. 181, U.S. Department of Commerce, Bureau of the Census, August 1992, p. A-8.

★ 293 ★

Poverty

Program Participation Status of Households, by Poverty Status of Persons in 1991

About 50.2 percent of older Americans who live in poverty depend on some form of government assistance.

[Numbers in thousands]

Characteristic	All income levels		Below poverty level	
	Total	65 years and over	Total	65 years and over
Total	251,179	30,590	35,708	3,781
In household that received means-tested assistance				
Number	57,925	5,498	26,034	1,897
Percent	23.1	18.0	72.9	50.2

[Continued]

★ 293 ★

Program Participation Status of Households, by Poverty Status of Persons in 1991

[Continued]

Characteristic	All income levels		Below poverty level	
	Total	65 years and over	Total	65 years and over
In household that received means-tested assistance excluding school lunches				
Number	46,977	5,421	23,359	1,874
Percent	18.7	17.7	65.4	49.6
In household that received means-tested cash assistance				
Number	27,184	2,961	15,566	1,113
Percent	10.8	9.7	43.6	29.4
In household that received food stamps				
Number	25,697	1,416	17,920	879
Percent	10.2	4.6	50.2	23.2
In household in which one or more persons covered by Medicaid				
Number	37,117	3,655	19,824	1,328
Percent	14.8	11.9	55.5	35.1
Live in public or subsidized housing				
Number	10,873	1,537	7,183	736
Percent	4.3	5.0	20.1	19.5

Source: *Poverty in the United States: 1991*, Current Population Reports, Series P-60, No. 181, U.S. Department of Commerce, Bureau of the Census, August 1992, p. xvii.

★ 294 ★

Poverty

Income: Household Income Under $5,000 &
Household Composition and Age

Household composition	Income under $5,000 (in 000s)	As % of households <$5,000	As % of HH age/ composition group
Married couples only			
Age 65-74 years	215.2	9.4	4.2
Age 75-84 years	133.9	5.8	5.8
Age 85/85+ years	29.3	1.3	8.1
Married couple, others present			
Age 65-74 years	27.0	1.2	2.3
Age 75-84 years	6.9	0.3	2.8
Age 85/85+ years	2.2	0.1	8.7
Single male head, others present			
Age 65-74 years	36.2	1.6	7.3
Age 75-84 years	18.7	0.8	8.9
Age 85/85+ years	2.4	0.1	6.5
Single female head, others present			
Age 65-74 years	71.4	3.1	7.3
Age 75-84 years	57.1	2.5	9.1
Age 85/85+ years	24.8	1.1	10.8
One person male household			
Age 65-74 years	129.3	5.6	12.7
Age 75-84 years	91.0	4.0	14.6
Age 85/85+ years	30.2	1.3	15.6
One person female household			
Age 65-74 years	620.7	27.0	19.6
Age 75-84 years	601.1	26.2	21.0
Age 85/85+ years	199.1	8.7	22.7
Total	2,296.5	100.0	

Source: Elderly Households, a Profile, Senate Select Committee on Aging, Comm. Pub. No. 102-912, 1992, p. 32. Primary source: The American Housing Survey, 1989, Data on C-D ROM. US Dept. of Housing and Urban Development & Bureau of the Census.

★ 295 ★

Poverty

Income: Household Income $5,000 to $9,999 & Household Composition and Age

Household composition	Income $5,000 - $9,999 (in 000s)	As % of households $5K-$9,999	As % of HH age/ composition group
Married couples only			
Age 65-74 years	465.1	9.4	9.1
Age 75-84 years	335.8	6.8	14.6
Age 85/85+ years	85.9	1.7	23.7
Married couple, others present			
Age 65-74 years	68.0	1.4	5.7
Age 75-84 years	15.8	0.3	6.4
Age 85/85+ years	7.7	0.2	30.7
Single male head, others present			
Age 65-74 years	78.4	1.6	15.8
Age 75-84 years	34.6	0.7	16.4
Age 85/85+ years	8.9	0.2	23.9
Single female head, others present			
Age 65-74 years	180.1	3.6	18.3
Age 75-84 years	132.8	2.7	21.2
Age 85/85+ years	74.0	1.5	32.1
One person male household			
Age 65-74 years	349.9	7.1	34.5
Age 75-84 years	216.9	4.4	34.8
Age 85/85+ years	80.2	1.6	41.4
One person female household			
Age 65-74 years	1,127.0	22.9	35.5
Age 75-84 years	1,233.6	25.0	43.1
Age 85/85+ years	436.7	8.9	48.6
Total	4,931.5	100.0	

Source: Elderly Households, a Profile, Senate Select Committee on Aging, Comm. Pub. No. 102-912, 1992, p. 33. Primary source: The American Housing Survey, 1989, Data on C-D ROM. US Dept. of Housing and Urban Development & Bureau of the Census.

★ 296 ★
Poverty

Income: Incidence of Low Incomes Among Elderly Population Groups

The table summarizes the incidence of low incomes by age and population group. While very few elderly, as a whole, have extremely low incomes, the incidence is significant for all except the whites who are in the 65-74 group.

[Data are in percent]

	Under $5,000	$5,000 to $9,999	Total under $10,000
All elderly households	11.2	24.0	35.2
Whites			
Age 65-74 years	7.7	17.7	25.4
Age 75-84 years	11.4	28.0	39.4
Age 85/85+ years	14.8	39.0	53.8
Blacks			
Age 65-74 years	21.9	30.2	52.1
Age 75-84 years	32.2	34.6	66.8
Age 85/85+ years	34.5	46.8	81.3
Hispanics			
Age 65-74 years	9.2	24.4	33.6
Age 75-84 years	21.8	29.6	51.4
Age 85/85+ years	30.1	46.1	76.2

Source: Elderly Households, a Profile, Senate Select Committee on Aging, Comm. Pub. No. 102-912, 1992, p. 30. Primary source: The American Housing Survey, 1989, Data on C-D ROM. US Dept. of Housing and Urban Development & Bureau of the Census.

★ 297 ★

Poverty

Income: Low Annual Earnings of Year-Round, Full-Time Workers, by Age and Sex: 1979, 1984, and 1990

This table shows that the likelihood of receiving low annual earnings has increased for all persons between the ages of 18 and 64, but has decreased over the last decade for persons age 65 and older. From the source: "[Year-round, full-time workers include] people who spent at least 50 weeks during the year at work or looking for work and who either worked 35 hours a week or more or worked fewer hours for nonvoluntary reasons. Within each of these categories, workers are classified as having low earnings if their annual earnings are less than the poverty level for a four-person family."

Characteristics	Percent		
	1979	1984	1990
Both sexes (years)			
18-64	11.6	14.2	17.8
35-54	9.9	11.4	13.2
55-64	12.0	13.6	16.4
65 and over	28.9	32.1	28.8
Males			
18-64	7.3	10.1	13.6
35-54	5.3	7.0	8.9
55-64	7.3	8.9	11.7
65 and over	25.5	26.5	26.5
Females			
18-64	20.0	21.0	24.1
35-54	19.5	19.1	19.6
55-64	21.7	22.3	24.8
65 and over	36.8	45.4	33.2

Source: "Workers With Low Earnings: 1964 to 1990," *Family Economics Review*, 1992, Vol. 5, No. 4, pp. 32-33. Primary source: U.S. Department of Commerce, Bureau of the Census, 1992. *Workers With Low Earnings: 1964 to 1990. Current Population Reports, Consumer Income*, Series P-60, No. 178.

★ 298 ★

Poverty

Disabled: Age Distribution of Disabled Heads of Families, 1980 and 1988

From the source: "The age distribution of disabled family heads changed considerably between 1980 and 1988. Numerically, about 60 percent of the increase in the disabled population occurred among 15 to 44 year olds. Conversely, those aged 45 to 54 declined as a percentage of the total, and those in the oldest age group showed a decline in percentage *and* a decline in numbers."

[Numbers in thousands]

Age group	1980		1988	
	Number	Percent of total	Number	Percent of total
15 to 24	109	2.7	144	3.2
25 to 34	366	9.1	478	10.5
35 to 44	544	13.5	855	18.7
45 to 54	959	23.7	1,051	23.0
55 to 64	2,065	51.1	2,033	44.6
Total	4,044	100.0	4,562	100.0

Source: U.S. General Accounting Office, *Poverty Trends 1980-88: Changes in Family Composition and Income Sources Among the Poor*, GAO/PEMD-92-34, September 1992, p. 85. *Note:* Numbers and percentages may not add to totals shown due to rounding.

★ 299 ★

Poverty

Single Mothers: Characteristics in 1980 and 1988

Data show change in characteristics of never-married, female-headed, single-parent families living alone, 1980 to 1988. From the source: "In 1980, thirty-seven percent of these women were under 25, and 84 percent were under 35. By 1988, however, this group tended to be older.... This shift may reflect changes in the age distribution of the general population, as well as the overall trend of women postponing having children."

[Numbers in thousands]

Characteristic	1980		1988	
	Number	Percent of total	Number	Percent of total
Age group				
15 to 24	315	37.4	423	29.8
25 to 34	396	47.1	720	50.6
35 to 64	130	15.5	279	19.6
Total	841	100.0	1,422	100.0
Education level				
Did not complete high school	329	39.1	482	33.9

[Continued]

★ 299 ★

Single Mothers: Characteristics in 1980 and 1988

[Continued]

Characteristic	1980		1988	
	Number	Percent of total	Number	Percent of total
Completed high school	362	43.0	659	46.3
Some college (including graduates)	149	17.7	281	19.8
Total	841	100.0	1,422	100.0
Teenage motherhood				
Not a teenage mother	444	52.8	845	59.4
Teenage mother	397	47.2	578	40.6
Total	841	100.0	1,422	100.0

Source: U.S. General Accounting Office, *Poverty Trends 1980-88: Changes in Family Composition and Income Sources Among the Poor*, GAO/PEMD-92-34, September 1992, p. 41. *Note:* Numbers and percentages may not add to totals shown due to rounding.

Spending

★ 300 ★

Average Annual Expenditures of Consumers by Type of Expenditure and Age of Reference Person: 1989

Type of expenditure	Amount expended ($)				Percent distribution			
	Under 65	65+			Under 65	65+		
		Total	65 to 74	75+		Total	65 to 74	75+
Total	30,191	18,967	21,152	15,919	100.0	100.0	100.0	100.0
Housing, exc. utilities	7,394	4,475	4,960	3,795	24.5	23.6	23.4	23.8
Shelter	5,332	2,988	3,283	2,574	17.7	15.8	15.5	16.2
Operations, supplies, and furnishings	2,062	1,487	1,677	1,221	6.8	7.8	7.9	7.7
Transportation	5,751	3,092	3,695	2,248	19.0	16.3	17.5	14.1
Food	4,486	2,912	3,205	2,505	14.9	15.4	15.2	15.7
At home	2,520	1,907	2,048	1,713	8.3	10.1	9.7	10.8
Away from home	1,966	1,004	1,157	792	6.5	5.3	5.5	5.0
Health care	1,211	2,135	1,981	2,351	4.0	11.3	9.4	14.8
Utilities, fuels, public service	1,873	1,694	1,813	1,528	6.2	8.9	8.6	9.6
Cash contributions	849	1,091	1,022	1,187	2.8	5.8	4.8	7.5
Clothing	1,765	902	1,138	576	5.8	4.8	5.4	3.6
Personal insurance and pensions	2,938	740	1,059	295	9.7	3.9	5.0	1.9

[Continued]

★ 300 ★

Average Annual Expenditures of Consumers by Type of Expenditure and Age of Reference Person: 1989
[Continued]

Type of expenditure	Amount expended ($)				Percent distribution			
	Under 65	65+			Under 65	65+		
		Total	65 to 74	75+		Total	65 to 74	75+
Entertainment	1,614	719	843	546	5.3	3.8	4.0	3.4
Other[1]	2,312	1,207	1,436	888	7.7	6.4	6.8	5.6

Source: Aging America, Trends and Projections, prepared by the U.S. Senate Special Committee on Aging, the American Association of Retired Persons, the Federal Council on the Aging, and the U.S. Administration on Aging, 1991, Washington, D.C., p. 79. Primary source: U.S. Department of Labor, Bureau of Labor Statistics. "Consumer Expenditures in 1989." Press Release USDL: 90-616, November 30, 1990. Notes: 1. Includes tobacco products, alcoholic beverages, personal care products and services, reading, education, and miscellaneous expenditures.

★ 301 ★

Spending

Health Care Expenditures of Consumer by Type of Expenditure and Age Reference of Person: 1989

Type of expenditure	Age of reference person			
	Under 65	65+	65-74	75+
Number of consuming units (000)	75,496	20,322	11,848	8,474
Amount of expenditures ($)				
Health care, total	1,211	2,135	1,981	2,351
Health insurance	428	943	939	950
Medical services	518	632	555	738
Drugs and supplies	264	560	487	662
Drugs	189	428	402	465
Medical supplies	75	132	85	197
Percent distribution				
Health care, total	100.0	100.0	100.0	100.0
Health insurance	35.3	44.2	47.4	40.4
Medical services	42.8	29.6	28.0	31.4
Drugs and supplies	21.8	26.2	24.6	28.2
Drugs	15.6	20.1	20.3	19.8
Medical supplies	6.2	6.2	4.3	8.4

Source: Aging America, Trends and Projections, prepared by the U.S. Senate Special Committee on Aging, the American Association of Retired Persons, the Federal Council on the Aging, and the U.S. Administration on Aging, 1991, Washington, D.C., p. 83. Primary source: U.S. Department of Labor, Bureau of Labor Statistics. "Consumer Expenditures in 1989." Press Release USDL: 90-616, November 20, 1990. Also unpublished data from the 1989 Consumer Expenditure Survey.

★ 302 ★

Spending

Anticipated Apparel Spending, 1990-2000

The table shows the percent of total expenditures devoted to apparel for the years 1990 and 2000 for ten population groups. These divisions, determined by a study conducted by DuPont and Management Horizons, segment the consuming public by common values set during the ages of 7-21. McAllister Isaacs III projects that "women's apparel spending will increase (in today's dollars) from $120-billion in 1990 to $215-billion in 2000," and that "men's apparel spending will increase from $58-billion in 1990 to $105-billion in 2000." The term "busters" is a play on words meaning the age cohorts born after the baby "boom" generation.

Cohort (Birth)	1990			2000		
	Age span	Percent of U.S. population	Percent of apparel spending	Age span	Percent of U.S. population	Percent of apparel spending
World War I Babies (1910-1919)	71-80	5.3	4.0	81-90	2.6	0.7
Roaring 20's Babies (1920-1929)	61-70	8.2	8.1	71-80	5.7	3.8
Depression Babies (1930-1939)	51-60	8.8	9.5	61-70	7.3	6.7
World War II Babies (1940-1945)	45-50	6.5	6.2	55-60	5.9	6.1
Mature Boomers (1946-1950)	40-44	7.1	8.6	50-54	6.5	6.8
Mid-Boomers (1951-1957)	33-39	11.6	13.8	43-49	10.7	10.0
Young Boomers (1958-1964)	26-32	12.4	13.1	36-42	11.6	14.1
Mature Busters (1965-1970)	20-25	9.1	9.6	30-35	8.8	11.3
Young Busters (1971-1976)	14-19	8.3	10.7	24-29	7.9	9.7
Mature Boomlets (1977-1982)	8-13	8.5	6.7	18-23	8.2	9.1

Source: "Focus on Everybody's Customer—The Consumer," McAllister Isaacs III, *Textile World* 139, No. 11, November, 1989, p. 74.

★ 303 ★

Spending

Spending on Household Appliances, 1990 and 2000

Appliance and age range	1990		2000		Growth/ decline (%)
	Expenditures ($ mil.)	Market share (%)	Expenditures ($ mil.)	Market share (%)	
Washing machines	3,191	100	4,362	100	36.7
18-34	786	24.6	1,085	24.9	38.0
35-64	1,573	49.3	2,106	48.3	33.9
65+	832	26.1	1,171	26.8	40.7
Clothes dryers	1,847	100	2,551	100	38.1
18-34	404	21.9	525	20.6	30.0
35-64	975	52.8	1,319	51.7	35.3
65+	468	25.3	707	27.7	51.1

[Continued]

★ 303 ★

Spending on Household Appliances, 1990 and 2000
[Continued]

Appliance and age range	1990		2000			Growth/ decline (%)
	Expenditures ($ mil.)	Market share (%)	Expenditures ($ mil.)	Market share (%)		
Electric floor cleaners	1,384	100	2,073		100	49.8
18-34	384	27.7	571		27.5	48.7
35-64	812	58.7	1,216		58.7	49.8
65+	188	13.6	286		13.8	52.1
Sewing machines	721	100	998		100	38.4
18-34	130	1	8	126	1	2.6	-	3.1
35-64	401	5	5.6	597	5	9.8	4	8.9
65+	190	2	6.4	274	2	7.5	4	4.2
Room airconditioners	1,715	1	00	2,275	1	00	3	2.7
18-34	232	1	3.5	212	9	.3	-	8.6
35-64	767	4	4.7	1,057	4	6.5	3	7.8
65+	716	4	1.7	1,006	4	4.2	4	0.5

Source: "Projected Consumer Spending in the 90s," James Stevens, *Appliances* 47, No. 12, December, 1990, p. 13. Primary source: A *Preventive Magazine* report based on information from the U.S. Bureau of Labor Statistics. Numbers may not add perfectly because of rounding.

★ 304 ★

Spending

Supermarket Beer Purchases by Grade, 2000

The elderly population (55 and over) uses beer much less than the average. As this population increases, it affects the consumption of beer in future years.

Beer Base = Adults	Percent who use (1988)	Use by Age (vs. average) by percentage						Growth in users (vs. 1988, in %)	
		18-24	25-34	35-44	45-54	55-64	65+	1955	2000
Beer, Domestic, regular (HU)[1]	12.8	+42	+21	-2	-16	-20	-41	+3.0	+6.2
Beer, Domestic, low calorie	16.6	+41	+36	+7	-7	-42	-64	+3.2	+5.8
Ale	3.6	+46	+33	-1	-31	-33	-42	+2.2	+4.4
Beer, low alcohol	1.2	-3	+48	-16	-49	-15	-	+2.2	+3.6
Beer, Imported	14.4	+65	+43	-5	-25	-43	-68	+1.4	+3.3
Malt liquor	2.3	+65	+50	-3	-35	-47	-70	+0.9	+2.3

Source: "Looking Toward the 1990s," Robert Dietrich, *Supermarket Business* 44, No. 3, March, 1989, p. 42-3. *Note:* 1. HU stands for Heavy Users.

★ 305 ★
Spending

Supermarket Breakfast Foods Purchases, by Type, 2000

Breakfast Foods	Percent who use (1988)	Use by age (vs. average) by percentage						Growth in users (vs. 1988, in %)	
		18-24	25-34	35-44	45-54	55-64	65+	1955	2000
Jams, jellies (HU)[1]	11.0	-52	-	-4	+16	+11	+8	+8.7	+14.0
Honey	32.5	-25	+3	_4	+4	+9	+3	+7.7	+12.5
Pancake, waffle mix	44.9	+1	+8	+9	+6	-8	-21	+7.6	+12.0
Peanut butter (HU)	7.1	+11	+12	+19	+9	-15	-38	+7.6	+11.9
Cold breakfast cereals (HU)	22.6	-32	+18	+30	-6	-6	-31	+7.8	+11.7
Hot breakfast cereals (HU)	11.0	-35	-2	-22	-24	+35	+36	+6.4*	+11.0
Breakfast, snack, and nutritional bars	21.6	+9	+41	+22	-1	-30	-59	+7.1	+9.9
Table syrup/Molasses (HU)	4.8	-26	+31	+5	-16	-2	-20	+6.3	+9.5
Toaster products (HU)	6.3	+38	+37	+32	-13	-47	-59	+6.3	+8.7

Source: "Looking Toward the 1990s," Robert Dietrich, *Supermarket Business* 44, No. 3, March, 1989, p. 43. *Note:* 1. HU stands for Heavy Users.

★ 306 ★
Spending

Supermarket Pet Products Purchases, by Type, 2000

The 65 and older age group expends significantly less money on pet food, on average, than the rest of the population.

Pet products	Percent who use (1988)	Use by age (vs. average) by percentage						Growth in users (vs. 1988, in %)	
		18-24	25-34	35-44	45-54	55-64	65+	1955	2000
Dog food, canned	14.4	-33	-11	+22	+28	+2	-16	+9.8	+15.7
Dog food, moist	6.1	-30	-12	+23	+12	+20	-18	+8.9	+14.6
Dog biscuits/treats	18.9	-24	-	+26	+16	+4	-31	+8.8	+14.0
Flea/tick care products for dogs/cats	24.1	-15	+4	+32	+13	+3	-45	+8.4	+13.3
Dog food, dry	28.7	-17	+10	+33	+15	-7	-48	+8.5	+13.1
Cat food, canned	13.9	-3	+3	+23	+12	-13	-28	+8.4	+13.1
Cat food, moist	7.8	+2	+3	+20	+8	-7	-28	+8.0	+12.7
Cat food, dry	20.6	+3	+14	+34	-4	-20	-38	+7.7	+11.5
Cat litter	15.9	+22	+20	+22	+7	-23	-50	+7.3	+11.1
Cat treats	6.8	+61	+10	+9	-9	-6	-41	+5.8	+9.8

Source: "Looking Toward the 1990s," Robert Dietrich, *Supermarket Business* 44, No. 3, March, 1989, p. 56.

★ 307 ★

Spending

Expenditures of Elderly Households, by Educational Level, 1990

Expenditures	Average expenditures ($)					Percent of total expenditures (%)				
	All 65+	8th grade or less	Some high school	High school graduate	Any college	All 65+	8th grade or less	Some high school	High school graduate	Any college
Total expenditures	16,977	11,777	13,873	17,137	25,270					
Housing	5,627	4,215	4,509	5,765	7,991	33	36	33	34	31
Food	3,184	2,456	3,011	3,189	4,161	19	21	22	18	16
Transportation	2,793	1,510	2,168	3,006	4,538	16	13	16	17	18
Health care	2,092	1,922	1,678	2,008	2,702	12	16	12	12	11
Entertainment	650	278	513	647	1,193	4	2	4	4	5
Apparel and services	603	327	452	687	949	4	3	3	4	4
Retirement	499	201	285	493	1,020	3	2	2	3	4
Cash contributions	267	127	135	159	649	2	1	1	1	3
Life insurance	259	173	195	278	390	1	1	1	2	2
Other	1,003	568	927	905	1,677	6	5	6	5	6

Source: *Family Economics Review*, 1992, Vol. 5, No. 4, p. 7.

★ 308 ★

Spending

Expenditures of Households Headed by Adults 65 Years or Older, by Educational Levels, 1990

This table shows that the majority of elderly household expenditures fall into the categories of housing, food, transportation, and health care. In general, spending increases as the level of educational attainment increases. From the source: "Data for this study are from the interview component of the 1990 Consumer Expenditures Survey (CE), conducted by the Bureau of the Census for the Bureau of Labor Statistics.... Findings are based on responses from 3,715 consumer units[1] with reference persons 65 years and older.

Expenditures	Average expenditures ($)					Percent of total expenditures				
	All 65+	8th grade or less	Some high school	High school graduate	Any college	All 65+	8th grade or less	Some high school	High school graduate	Any college
Total expenditures	16,977	11,777	13,873	17,137	25,270					
Housing	5,627	4,215	4,509	5,765	7,991	33	36	33	34	31
Food	3,184	2,456	3,011	3,189	4,161	19	21	22	18	16
Transportation	2,793	1,510	2,168	3,006	4,538	16	13	16	17	18
Health care	2,092	1,922	1,678	2,008	2,702	12	16	12	12	11
Entertainment	650	278	513	647	1,193	4	2	4	4	5
Apparel and services	603	327	452	687	949	4	3	3	4	4
Retirement	499	201	285	493	1,020	3	2	2	3	4

[Continued]

★ 308 ★

Expenditures of Households Headed by Adults 65 Years or Older, by Educational Levels, 1990

[Continued]

Expenditures	Average expenditures ($)					Percent of total expenditures				
	All 65+	8th grade or less	Some high school	High school graduate	Any college	All 65+	8th grade or less	Some high school	High school graduate	Any college
Cash contributions	267	127	135	159	649	2	1	1	1	3
Life insurance	259	173	195	278	390	1	1	1	2	2
Other	1,003	568	927	905	1,677	6	5	6	5	6

Source: "A Comparison of Income, Income Sources, and Expenditures of Older Adults by Educational Attainment", *Family Economics Review*, 1992, Vol. 5, No. 4, pp. 2-8. *Notes:* 1. A consumer unit consists of either: (1) all members of a particular household who are related by blood, marriage, adoption, or other legal arrangement; (2) two or more people living together who pool their incomes to make joint expenditure decisions; (3) a person living alone or sharing a household with others or living as a roomer in a private home or lodging house or in permanent living quarters in a hotel or motel, but who is financially independent. To be considered financially independent, at least two of the three major expense categories (housing, food, and other living expenses) have to be provided by the respondent.

★ 309 ★

Spending

Cost of Food at Home

The cost of food is estimated for food plans at four cost levels, September 1992, U.S. average[1].

Sex-age group	Cost for 1 week				Cost for 1 month			
	Thrifty plan	Low-cost plan	Moderate-cost plan	Liberal plan	Thrifty plan	Low-cost plan	Moderate-cost plan	Liberal plan
Families								
Family of 2[2]								
20-50 years	49.60	62.50	76.90	95.40	214.70	270.70	333.10	413.40
51 years and over	47.00	60.00	73.80	88.30	203.20	259.90	320.00	382.50
Family of 4								
Couple 20-50 years and children								
1-2 and 3-5 years	72.40	90.20	110.10	135.00	313.40	391.00	476.70	585.20
6-8 and 9-11 years	83.00	106.10	132.30	159.20	359.20	459.60	573.20	689.70
Individuals[3]								
Child								
1-2 years	13.20	16.00	18.70	22.60	57.00	69.40	80.90	98.00
3-5 years	14.10	17.40	21.50	25.70	61.20	75.50	93.00	111.40
6-8 years	17.30	23.10	28.80	33.60	74.90	99.90	124.90	145.40
9-11 years	20.60	26.20	33.60	38.90	89.10	113.60	145.50	168.50
Male								
12-14 years	21.30	29.60	37.00	43.30	92.40	128.50	160.10	187.80
15-19 years	22.10	30.60	38.00	44.00	95.90	132.60	164.70	190.80
20-50 years	23.70	30.30	37.70	45.60	102.60	131.20	163.40	197.80
51 years and over	21.50	28.70	35.30	42.30	93.00	124.50	153.10	183.30

[Continued]

★ 309 ★

Cost of Food at Home
[Continued]

Sex-age group	Cost for 1 week				Cost for 1 month			
	Thrifty plan	Low-cost plan	Moderate-cost plan	Liberal plan	Thrifty plan	Low-cost plan	Moderate-cost plan	Liberal plan
Female								
12-19 years	21.50	25.60	31.00	37.50	93.10	111.10	134.50	162.50
20-50 years	21.40	26.50	32.20	41.10	92.60	114.90	139.40	178.00
51 years and over	21.10	25.80	31.80	38.00	91.70	111.80	137.80	164.40

Source: "Cost of Food at Home," *Family Economics Review*, 1992, Vol. 5, No. 4, p. 39. Primary source: USDA. *Notes:* 1. Assumes that food for all meals and snacks is purchased at the store and prepared at home. Estimates for the thrifty food plan were computed from quantities of foods published in *Family Economics Review* 1984(1). Estimates for the other plans were computed from quantities of food published in *Family Economics Review* 1983 (2). The costs of the food plans are estimated by updating prices paid by households surveyed in 1977-78 in USDA's Nationwide Food Consumption Survey. USDA updates these survey prices using information from the Bureau of Labor Statistics, *CPI Detailed Report*, table 4, to estimate the costs for the food plans. 2. Ten percent added for family size adjustment. 3. The costs given are for individuals in 4-person families. For individuals in other size families, the following adjustments are suggested: 1-person—add 20 percent; 2-person—add 10 percent; 3-person—add 5 percent; 5- or 6-person—subtract 5 percent; 7- or more-person—subtract 10 percent.

Charitable Giving

★ 310 ★

Donations to the Arts and Humanities, by Age

A total of 41% of the U.S. population contributes to the arts and humanities. Percent contributing in each age group is shown.

Age	Percent
18-34	39.0
35-55	51.0
56 and over	31.0

Source: "Who Gives to the Arts and Humanities," *The Chronicle of Philanthropy*, p. 15. Primary source: National Cultural Alliance.

Legal Costs

★ 311 ★

Price Range for Drafting a Will

A standard will costs between $50 and $200. The price may vary from place to place, but generally, the cost of writing a will is less than it is for writing a living trust. Thirty lawyers in each of three cities—San Diego, CA; Milwaukee, WI; and Wilmington, DE provided their price quotes for wills and living trusts.

	San Diego ($)	Milwaukee ($)	Wilmington ($)
Low	50	75	70
Average	173	149	143
High	500	300	400

Source: U.S. Congress, "Consumer Fraud and the Elderly: Easy Prey?," Hearing before the Special Committee on Aging, United States Senate, September 24, 1992, 102-25, U.S. Government Printing Office, Washington, D.C., p. 106. *Notes:* Lawyers who were surveyed by phone were selected at random from among all lawyers who listed "probate," "wills," "trusts and estates," or "estate planning" as areas of expertise in the Yellow Pages and Martindale-Hubbell directories.

★ 312 ★

Legal Costs

Average Price of Will and Probate for an $80,000 Estate

The price of handling probate may depend on whether the attorney charges by the hour or charges a percentage of the estate's value.

	San Diego ($)	Milwaukee ($)	Wilmington ($)
Will	173	149	143
Probate	1,798	1,505	1,358
Total	1,971	1,654	1,501

Source: U.S. Congress, "Consumer Fraud and the Elderly: Easy Prey?," Hearing before the Special Committee on Aging, United States Senate, September 24, 1992, 102-25, U.S. Government Printing Office, Washington, D.C., p. 107. Primary source: AARP study entitled "A Report on Probate: Consumer Perspectives and Concerns." *Notes:* These averages are based on fees for actual probate cases in San Diego, Milwaukee, and Wilmington that were opened in 1985 and closed by mid-1989. Since they reflect attorney fees from a few years ago, the average fees reported may be lower than the current average fees. These fees are best used as guidelines to compare the cost of probate and living trusts.

★ 313 ★

Legal Costs

Price Range of Will and Probate for a 77-Year-Old with $80,000

On average, living trusts cost about $400 more than wills.

	San Diego ($)	Milwaukee ($)	Wilmington ($)
Low	1,848	1,580	1,428
Average	1,971	1,654	1,501
High	2,298	1,805	1,758

Source: U.S. Congress, "Consumer Fraud and the Elderly: Easy Prey?," Hearing before the Special Committee on Aging, United States Senate, September 24, 1992, 102-25, U.S. Government Printing Office, Washington, D.C., p. 110.

★ 314 ★

Legal Costs

Cost of Living Trust for a 77-Year-Old with $80,000

On average, living trusts cost about $400 more than wills.

	San Diego ($)	Milwaukee ($)	Wilmington ($)
Low	300	300	150
Average	598	540	350
High	850	1,000	600

Source: U.S. Congress, "Consumer Fraud and the Elderly: Easy Prey?," Hearing before the Special Committee on Aging, United States Senate, September 24, 1992, 102-25, U.S. Government Printing Office, Washington, D.C., p. 110. *Notes:* In the long run, a living trust is likely to cost much less than the combined cost of a will and a typical probate proceeding. When a lawyer's probate fee is added to the cost of a will, the living trust starts to look more like a bargain.

★ 315 ★

Legal Costs

Price Range of Living Trust for a Couple with a $150,000 Home and $50,000 in Stocks

Married couples with trusts could see sizable savings, although attorneys apparently charge more to draft living trusts for couples than for single persons.

	San Diego ($)	Milwaukee ($)	Wilmington ($)
Low	495	350	250
Average	956	795	565
High	1,600	1,500	1,850

Source: U.S. Congress, "Consumer Fraud and the Elderly: Easy Prey?," Hearing before the Special Committee on Aging, United States Senate, September 24, 1992, 102-25, U.S. Government Printing Office, Washington, D.C., p. 111.

Chapter 6
PENSIONS AND RETIREMENT

Data on pensions and retirement are divided into two chapters. This chapter deals with public and private pension or retirement plans. The next chapter covers the largest single pension plan of all—Social Security.

The chapters on *Income, Assets, and Spending*, *Health and Health Care*, *Health Insurance*, and *Nursing Homes and Resident Care* present information on income and costs that are related to the subject of pensions and retirement.

Pensions

★ 316 ★

Public Plans: Full-Time State and Local Government Workers with Pension Coverage for 10 Largest States, 1983 and 1988

[Thousands unless percent]

State	Number of workers		Number with pension coverage		Percentage of workers covered	
	1983	1988	1983	1988	1983	1988
Total, all states	10,652	11,959	8,605	10,201	81	85
California	1,046	1,370	806	1,223	77	89
New York	886	1,066	765	954	86	89
Texas	644	850	477	773	94	91
Florida	422	565	284	454	67	80
Pennsylvania	413	463	335	400	81	86
Illinois	605	423	532	371	88	88
Ohio	523	471	458	416	88	88
Michigan	342	367	300	304	88	83

[Continued]

★ 316 ★

Public Plans: Full-Time State and Local Government Workers with Pension Coverage for 10 Largest States, 1983 and 1988
[Continued]

State	Number of workers		Number with pension coverage		Percentage of workers covered	
	1983	1988	1983	1988	1983	1988
New Jersey	403	434	318	369	79	85
North Carolina	322	338	276	297	86	88

Source: Kristen Philips, "State and Local Government Pension Benefits," in *Trends in Pensions 1992*, U.S. Department of Labor, Pension and Welfare Benefits Administration, U.S. Government Printing Office, Washington, DC, 1992, p. 358. Primary source: Pension supplements to the May 1983 and 1988 Current Population Surveys.

★ 317 ★
Pensions

Public Plans: Number of Public Pension Recipients and Annual Pension Benefit by Age of Initial Benefit Receipt, December 1989

From the source: "[This table] shows the number of recipients and median annual pension benefit by age of initial benefit receipt. Out of 2.9 million public pension recipients, 1.2 million (41 percent) are age 60 to 64 when they first receive pension benefits, while there are 870,000 recipients (30 percent) over age 65 at first receipt. These older recipients receive the lowest benefits of any retirement age group, with median benefits of about $6,000 in both state and local governments."

Age of initial benefit receipt	Number of pension recipients	Median benefit ($)	Mean benefit ($)
	Total employees		
Total	2,905,799	7,200	9,318
30-49	162,790	11,880	12,300
50-54	188,376	11,436	12,514
55-59	516,945	10,656	12,498
60-64	1,165,505	6,000	8,231
65 or older	872,182	6,000	7,379
	State		
Total	920,515	7,200	9,232
30-49	47,213	[1]	[1]
50-54	64,862	[1]	[1]
55-59	142,507	12,000	14,741
60-64	381,484	6,012	7,951
65 or older	284,450	5,400	6,828

[Continued]

★ 317 ★

Public Plans: Number of Public Pension Recipients and Annual Pension Benefit by Age of Initial Benefit Receipt, December 1989

[Continued]

Age of initial benefit receipt	Number of pension recipients	Median benefit ($)	Mean benefit ($)
	Local		
Total	1,985,284	7,200	9,358
30-49	115,577	11,880	12,310
50-54	123,515	11,436	12,693
55-59	374,439	9,900	11,684
60-64	784,021	6,000	8,364
65 or older	587,732	6,000	7,661

Source: Kristen Philips, "State and Local Government Pension Benefits," in *Trends in Pensions 1992*, U.S. Department of Labor, Pension and Welfare Benefits Administration, U.S. Government Printing Office, Washington, DC, 1992, p. 367. Primary source: Pension supplement to the December Current Population Survey. *Note:* 1. Not computed where base is less than 75,000.

★ 318 ★

Pensions

Public Plans: Number of Public Pension Recipients and Annual Pension Benefit in Ten Largest States by Population, December 1989

From the source: "Among the 10 most populous states, average annual benefits differ greatly....Tabulations of benefits by state and region are based on the states where recipients reside, which may differ from states providing the benefits. To the extent that retirees migrate to sunbelt states, the benefit amounts in those states reflect benefits received in other states. If higher income retirees are more likely to migrate, this would raise average benefits in sunbelt states and lower average benefits elsewhere."

State	Number of pension recipients	Median benefit ($)	Mean benefit ($)
California	358,085	9,600	10,918
New York	245,416	8,400	11,084
Texas	149,896	6,720	8,119
Florida	199,844	6,000	7,323
Pennsylvania	191,531	5,700	7,534
Illinois	91,478	7,476	8,938
Ohio	149,394	8,400	10,587
Michigan	97,791	9,360	11,384

[Continued]

★ 318 ★

Public Plans: Number of Public Pension Recipients and Annual Pension Benefit in Ten Largest States by Population, December 1989

[Continued]

State	Number of pension recipients	Median benefit ($)	Mean benefit ($)
New Jersey	73,706	7,200	10,309
North Carolina	88,617	6,000	9,242

Source: Kristen Philips, "State and Local Government Pension Benefits," in *Trends in Pensions 1992*, U.S. Department of Labor, Pension and Welfare Benefits Administration, U.S. Government Printing Office, Washington, DC, 1992, p. 362. Primary source: Pension supplement to the December Current Population Survey.

★ 319 ★

Pensions

Private Plans: Demographic Characteristics of Wage-and-Salary Workers Offered an Employer or Union Pension Plan by Employment Size of Firm, 1988

From the source: "Small firms are significantly less likely to offer pensions to their workers than large firms. Only 16 percent of firms with less than 500 employees have a pension or 401(k) plan, compared with 79 percent of firms with 500 or more employees....Workers more likely to be employed in small firms which do not offer pension plans...include young workers, old workers, minorities (particularly Hispanics), and single workers. These workers are more likely to live in the West or South and outside metropolitan areas."

[Data are shown in percent]

Demographic characteristic	All firms	Employment size of firm						
		1-24	25-99	100-499	500+	Under 100	100+	Under 500
Total	57.6	17.0	44.2	62.9	84.0	26.3	79.2	35.3
Age								
16-24	43.1	10.5	32.5	59.1	69.4	17.5	67.1	25.6
25-44	61.0	18.7	45.8	63.8	86.2	28.5	81.1	37.9
45-64	61.5	19.5	48.9	63.9	88.1	29.4	82.9	37.9
65+	39.2	15.2[1]	54.8[1]	51.5	73.7	25.2	66.3	29.1
Gender								
Men	59.6	18.0	46.3	64.3	86.2	27.9	81.5	36.6
Women	55.0	15.8	41.2	61.1	81.0	24.3	76.3	33.5
Marital status								
Married, spouse present	60.9	20.1	49.5	62.5	86.3	30.2	81.0	38.4
Other	52.4	12.7	36.8	63.4	80.2	21.0	76.4	30.7
Race								
White	57.6	17.5	45.9	63.8	84.5	27.0	79.8	35.8
Black	59.3	11.9[1]	32.2[1]	55.4	79.8	19.7	74.9	31.8
Other	52.6	58.4[1]	25.7[1]	58.4	84.2[1]	18.1	79.3	26.1

[Continued]

★ 319 ★

Private Plans: Demographic Characteristics of Wage-and-Salary Workers Offered an Employer or Union Pension Plan by Employment Size of Firm, 1988

[Continued]

Demographic characteristic	All firms	Employment size of firm						
		1-24	25-99	100-499	500+	Under 100	100+	Under 500
Origin								
Hispanic	43.5	8.3[1]	31.0[1]	59.4	72.0	15.8	69.1	24.5
Non-Hispanic	58.5	17.7	45.2	63.1	84.7	27.2	79.8	36.1
Years of education								
<12	41.5	8.3	32.1	51.8	69.5	16.4	64.9	24.1
12-15	57.5	16.5	44.1	63.1	84.2	25.7	79.5	34.7
>16	69.2	27.9	54.7	70.1	91.2	38.0	86.7	46.8
Region								
Northeast	61.8	19.4	46.8	70.1	88.7	29.6	83.9	40.6
Midwest	62.1	20.8	46.4	68.6	85.3	29.9	81.7	40.2
South	53.5	13.0	41.3	57.1	80.9	21.9	75.8	30.0
West	53.9	54.7	82.4	54.7	82.4	26.2	76.4	32.2
Area								
Metropolitan	59.1	17.7	44.6	64.0	84.6	27.1	80.1	36.3
Non-metropolitan	50.9	14.8	42.6	58.2	80.7	23.4	74.8	31.4
Central city	56.8	17.3	42.5	63.3	81.8	26.3	77.7	35.4
Non-central city	60.4	17.9	45.8	64.4	86.1	27.6	81.5	36.7

Source: Jules H. Lichtenstein, Ph.D., "Pension Availability and Coverage in Small and Large Firms", in *Trends in Pensions 1992*, U.S. Department of Labor, Pension and Welfare Benefits Administration, U.S. Government Printing Office, Washington, DC, 1992, pp. 105-106. Primary source: U.S. Small Business Administration, Office of Advocacy. Tabulations by Sheldon Haber of unpublished data from the U.S. Department of Commerce, Bureau of the Census, *Current Population Survey*, May 1988. *Note:* 1. Less than 50 observations.

★ 320 ★

Pensions

Private Plans: Female/Male Pension Coverage and Earnings Ratios for Full-Time Private Sector Wage and Salary Workers, 1972-88

From the source: "The pension gap between men and women has closed more rapidly than the earnings gap. Between 1972 and 1988, median weekly earnings of female full-time wage and salary workers grew from 62 percent to 70 percent of those of men, for an increase of 8 percentage points. In contrast, pension coverage among women increased from 70 percent to 88 percent of men's coverage, for an increase of 18 percentage points."

[Data are in percent]

Year	Ratio of women's pension coverage to men's	Ratio of women's earnings to men's[1]
1972	70	62
1979	73	62
1983	81	67
1988	88	70

Source: Sophie M. Korczyk, "Gender and Pension Coverage", in *Trends in Pensions 1992*, U.S. Department of Labor, Pension and Welfare Benefits Administration, U.S. Government Printing Office, Washington, DC, 1992, p. 128. Primary source: Table 6.4 of original source and U.S. Bureau of Labor Statistics, *Employment and Earnings*, various issues. *Note:* 1. Median weekly earnings.

★ 321 ★

Pensions

Private Plans: Number and Percentage of Former Private Pension Plan Participants Ages 40 and Over with Pension Benefits by Age, 1989

From the source: "A total of 20.9 million individuals ages 40 and over were covered under a private pension plan of a former employer. Seventy-two percent of those with prior coverage have or expect to receive some pension benefits. For males with previous pension coverage, 74 percent have or expect to receive benefits, compared to 69 percent of females."

[Individuals are shown in thousands]

Age	Covered under plan of former employer	Currently receiving annuity[1]	Percent currently receiving annuity	Received lump sum distribution only	Percent who received lump sum distribution	Expect to receive retirement benefits	Percent expecting to receive retirement benefits
Total							
Total	20,948	7,517	36	5,067	24	2,469	12
40-54	8,652	198	2	2,912	34	1,692	20
55-59	2,268	501	22	575	25	443	20
60-64	2,869	1,455	51	585	20	245	9
65-69	2,812	1,992	71	429	15	67	2
70-74	2,056	1,548	75	322	16	13	1
75-79	1,271	999	79	147	12	6	1
80 and older	1,020	824	81	98	10	3	0
55 and older	12,296	7,319	60	2,154	18	777	6
65 and older	7,159	5,363	75	994	14	89	1
Men							
Total	13,181	5,299	40	2,734	21	1,690	13
40-54	5,213	145	3	1,604	31	1,171	22
55-59	1,478	387	26	312	21	318	22
60-64	1,790	1,025	57	297	17	149	8
65-69	1,849	1,400	76	223	12	45	2
70-74	1,352	1,096	81	157	12	5	0
75-79	828	682	82	88	11	2	0
80 and older	670	563	84	53	8	0	0
55 and older	7,967	5,153	65	1,130	14	519	7
65 and older	4,699	3,741	80	521	11	52	1
Women							
Total	7,767	2,218	29	2,333	30	778	10
40-54	3,439	53	2	1,308	38	521	15
55-59	790	113	14	263	33	125	16
60-64	1,079	430	40	288	27	96	9
65-69	963	592	61	206	21	22	2
70-74	704	452	64	165	23	8	1
75-79	443	316	71	59	13	4	1
80 and older	349	261	75	45	13	2	1

[Continued]

★ 321 ★

Private Plans: Number and Percentage of Former Private Pension Plan Participants Ages 40 and Over with Pension Benefits by Age, 1989

[Continued]

Age	Covered under plan of former employer	Currently receiving annuity[1]	Percent currently receiving annuity	Received lump sum distribution only	Percent who received lump sum distribution	Expect to receive retirement benefits	Percent expecting to receive retirement benefits
55 and older	4,328	2,162	50	1,026	24	257	6
65 and older	2,459	1,619	66	475	19	36	1

Source: David J. Beller and David D. McCarthy, "Private Pension Benefits," in *Trends in Pensions 1992*, U.S. Department of Labor, Pension and Welfare Benefits Administration, U.S. Government Printing Office, Washington, DC, 1992, pp. 239-240. Primary source: Pension benefit amount supplement to the December 1989 Current Population Survey. *Note:* 1. Includes some individuals who also received lump sum distribution.

★ 322 ★

Pensions

Private Plans: Number and Percentage of Private Pension Plan Participants by Age and Type of Benefit, 1989

From the source: "The majority of pension recipients ages 40 and over (52 percent) receive only an annuity, with eight percent receiving an annuity and a prior lump sum benefit. Two-thirds of male pensioners receive at least some of their benefits as annuities, compared to about half of female pensioners."

[Recipients are shown in thousands]

Age	Total		Annuity and lump sum[1]		Annuity only		Lump sum only	
	Number	Percent	Number	Percent	Number	Percent	Number	Percent
Total								
Total	12,584	100	969	8	6,548	52	5,067	40
40-54	3,110	100	41	1	157	5	2,912	94
55-59	1,075	100	83	8	418	39	575	53
60-64	2,039	100	236	12	1,218	60	585	29
65-69	2,421	100	302	12	1,690	70	429	18
70-74	1,870	100	196	10	1,353	72	322	17
75-79	1,146	100	81	7	917	80	147	13
80 and older	923	100	31	3	794	86	98	11
55 and older	9,474	100	929	10	6,390	67	2,156	23
65 and older	6,360	100	610	10	4,754	75	996	16
Men								
Total	8,032	100	682	8	4,616	57	2,734	34
40-54	1,749	100	25	1	119	7	1,604	92
55-59	699	100	74	11	313	45	312	45
60-64	1,321	100	166	13	859	65	297	22

[Continued]

★ 322 ★

Private Plans: Number and Percentage of Private Pension Plan Participants by Age and Type of Benefit, 1989
[Continued]

Age	Type of pension benefit							
	Total		Annuity and lump sum[1]		Annuity only		Lump sum only	
	Number	Percent	Number	Percent	Number	Percent	Number	Percent
65-69	1,623	100	203	13	1,196	74	223	14
70-74	1,253	100	144	11	952	76	157	13
75-79	770	100	52	7	630	82	88	11
80 and older	616	100	17	3	547	89	53	9
55 and older	6,282	100	656	10	4,497	72	1,130	18
65 and older	4,262	100	416	10	3,325	78	521	12
Women								
Total	4,552	100	287	6	1,931	42	2,333	51
40-54	1,361	100	15	1	38	3	1,308	96
55-59	376	100	8	2	105	28	263	70
60-64	718	100	70	10	360	50	288	40
65-69	798	100	98	12	494	62	206	26
70-74	617	100	52	8	400	65	165	27
75-79	376	100	29	8	288	77	59	16
80 and older	306	100	14	5	247	81	45	15
55 and older	3,191	100	271	8	1,894	59	1,028	32
65 and older	2,097	100	193	9	1,429	68	477	23

Source: David J. Beller and David D. McCarthy, "Private Pension Benefits," in *Trends in Pensions 1992,* U.S. Department of Labor, Pension and Welfare Benefits Administration, U.S. Government Printing Office, Washington, DC, 1992, p. 241. Primary source: Pension benefit amount supplement to the December 1989 Current Population Survey. *Notes:* 1. The year of initial receipt used is based on the year when the annuity began.

★ 323 ★
Pensions

Private Plans: Percentage of Workers Receiving Pension Annuities from Pension Plans Sponsored by a Former Employer, 1989[1]

From the source: "One-third of private sector retirees ages 55 and over currently receive annuities based on former employment. Among retirees ages 55 and over, 47 percent of men receive annuities, compared to only 20 percent of women."

[Data are in thousands]

Age	Total	Presently working[2]			Retired or not presently working			
		Total	Private sector	Public sector	Total	Private sector[3]	Public sector[4]	Employment sector not determinable
Total								
Total	14	5	5	5	35	29	63	20
40-54	2	2	2	3	6	3	22	3
55-59	9	6	6	8	23	17	48	19
60-64	22	11	11	12	41	35	68	22
65-69	32	21	20	28	45	38	72	30
70-74	33	23	22	33	44	37	70	24
75-79	28	23	23	5	39	31	71	24
80 and older	24	22	20	5	36	29	68	16
55 and older	24	11	11	13	40	33	68	23
65 and older	30	22	21	29	42	34	71	24
Men								
Total	20	7	6	9	48	42	74	29
40-54	4	3	3	5	13	5	44	6
55-59	15	9	8	14	38	31	65	5
60-64	32	15	14	22	55	50	76	34
65-69	46	27	26	37	56	51	79	42
70-74	50	31	29	5	56	50	81	31
75-79	44	28	27	5	50	44	81	30
80 and older	39	22	20	5	45	41	74	24
55 and older	36	15	14	21	52	47	78	31
65 and older	46	28	27	40	53	47	79	32
Women								
Total	9	2	2	2	24	17	53	12
40-54	1	1	1	1	2	1	7	-
55-59	4	3	3	3	11	7	30	5
60-64	13	6	7	4	27	20	58	5
65-69	20	12	11	17	33	25	65	18
70-74	19	13	11	5	31	22	60	17
75-79	18	15	16	5	29	19	64	17

[Continued]

★ 323 ★

Private Plans: Percentage of Workers Receiving Pension Annuities from Pension Plans Sponsored by a Former Employer, 1989

[Continued]

Age	Total	Presently working[2]			Retired or not presently working			
		Total	Private sector	Public sector	Total	Private sector[3]	Public sector[4]	Employment sector not determinable
80 and older	15	5	5	5	28	18	64	11
55 and older	14	6	6	6	28	20	61	14
65 and older	18	13	12	18	31	21	65	16

Source: David J. Beller and David D. McCarthy, "Private Pension Benefits," in *Trends in Pensions 1992*, U.S. Department of Labor, Pension and Welfare Benefits Administration, U.S. Government Printing Office, Washington, DC, 1992, pp. 235-236. Primary source: Pension benefit amount supplement to the December 1989 Current Population Survey. *Notes:* 1. A worker is defined here as someone who is either currently employed or was formerly employed for a period of at least 5 years. An annuity is defined as a lifetime retirement benefit paid out at regular intervals, generally monthly. 2. Sector from which pension annuity received may not be sector in which worker is currently employed. 3. Job with pension coverage or longest job was in private sector. 4. Job with pension coverage or longest job was in public sector. 5. Not calculated where base is less than 75,000.

★ 324 ★

Pensions

Private Plans: Wage-and-Salary Workers Offered an Employer or Union Pension Plan by Small Firms: 1988

From the source: "Workers more commonly employed in small firms are less likely to be covered by a union contract and are more likely to be part-time, lower-wage workers and to more frequently change jobs. Employer plans are less likely to provide significant retirement benefits to intermittent workers, workers who change jobs frequently, have short careers, or work part-time or for very low pay."

[Data are shown in percent]

Demographic characteristic	All firms	Employment size of firm					
		1-9	10-24	25-49	50-99	Under 100	100+
Total	57.6	12.6	25.8	40.6	50.6	26.3	79.2
Age							
16-24	43.1	6.3	18.1	23.0	46.4	17.5	67.1
25-44	61.0	12.7	28.1	42.1	50.8	28.5	81.1
45-64	61.5	15.9	26.5	47.3	50.9	29.4	82.9
65+	39.2	9.5	28.4	51.3	58.2	25.2	66.3
Gender							
Men	59.6	12.5	27.2	43.0	50.8	27.9	81.5
Women	55.0	11.4	23.7	34.8	49.5	24.3	76.3
Marital status							
Married, spouse present	60.9	15.4	28.1	46.6	53.3	30.2	81.0
Other	52.4	7.2	22.3	29.8	46.0	21.0	76.4

[Continued]

★ 324 ★

Private Plans: Wage-and-Salary Workers Offered an Employer or Union Pension Plan by Small Firms: 1988
[Continued]

Demographic characteristic	All firms	Employment size of firm					
		1-9	10-24	25-49	50-99	Under 100	100+
Race							
White	57.6	12.2	26.7	41.5	51.7	27.0	79.8
Black	59.3	8.6	16.9	25.8	39.6	19.7	74.9
Other	57.6	12.7	9.9	23.2	31.7	18.1	79.3
Origin							
Hispanic	43.5	5.4[1]	11.9[1]	28.2[1]	40.0[1]	15.8	69.1
Non-Hispanic	58.5	12.4	27.0	40.7	50.9	27.2	79.8
Years of education							
<12	41.5	5.9	12.6	28.4	37.9	16.4	64.9
12-15	57.5	11.2	25.5	38.8	51.0	25.7	79.5
>16	69.2	21.3	37.8	52.2	57.9	38.0	86.7
Region							
Northeast	61.8	13.7	29.9	44.5	50.1	29.6	83.9
Midwest	62.1	14.2	30.9	44.8	52.0	29.9	81.7
South	53.5	9.4	19.8	37.0	46.7	21.9	75.8
West	53.9	12.4	25.0	35.5	53.6	26.2	76.4
Area							
Metropolitan	59.1	12.3	26.3	39.7	51.2	27.1	80.1
Non-metropolitan	50.9	10.8	23.0	38.8	46.6	23.4	74.8
Central city	56.8	11.5	26.6	36.5	51.6	26.3	77.7
Non-central city	60.4	12.8	26.2	41.7	51.0	27.6	81.5

Source: Jules H. Lichtenstein, Ph.D., "Pension Availability and Coverage in Small and Large Firms", in *Trends in Pensions 1992*, U.S. Department of Labor, Pension and Welfare Benefits Administration, U.S. Government Printing Office, Washington, DC, 1992, pp. 106-107. Primary source: U.S. Small Business Administration, Office of Advocacy. Tabulations by Sheldon Haber of unpublished data from the U.S. Department of Commerce, Bureau of the Census, *Current Population Survey*, May 1988. *Note:* 1. Less than 50 observations.

★ 325 ★

Pensions

Pension Coverage: Earnings Distribution and Pension Coverage Rates Among Full-Time Private Sector Workers, by Gender 1988

From the source: "Pension coverage rates rise with earnings among both women and men. Women's coverage rates are not significantly different from those of men with equal earnings. Only among workers earning $10,000 to $19,999 does women's coverage rate differ from that of men by more than 2 percentage points."

[Data are in percent]

Earnings	Women	Men
Earnings distribution		
Total	100	100
Less than $10,000	23	10
$10,000 to $19,999	47	31
$20,000 to $29,999	21	25
$30,000 to $49,999	9	27
$50,000 and over	1	8
Pension coverage rate		
All earnings	43	50
Less than $10,000	13	13
$10,000 to $19,999	46	36
$20,000 to $29,999	64	63
$30,000 to $49,999	75	74
$50,000 and over	77	79

Source: Sophie M. Korczyk, "Gender and Pension Coverage", in *Trends in Pensions 1992*, U.S. Department of Labor, Pension and Welfare Benefits Administration, U.S. Government Printing Office, Washington, DC, 1992, p. 128. Primary source: Author's calculations based on Employee Benefit Research Institute tabulations of May, 1988 Current Population Survey.

★ 326 ★
Pensions

Pension Coverage: Full-Time Private Sector Workers, by Occupation and Gender, 1988

From the source: "Both men and women have the lowest pension coverage rates—40 percent for each—in female-dominated occupations. However, women have similar coverage rates in both male-dominated and gender-balanced occupations. For men, pensions coverage rates are the highest—at 57 percent—in gender-balanced occupations."

[Data are in percent]

Occupation	Women	Men
Male-dominated occupations		
Nonfarm laborers	34	37
Craftsmen	55	52
Transportation equipment operators	40	44
Other	12	13
Total	43	46
Female-dominated occupations		
Administrative support, including clerical	50	56
Service workers	19	26
Total	40	40
Gender-balanced occupations		
Professional and technical	52	64
Managers and officials	51	59
Sales	34	44
Operatives	46	58
Total	46	57

Source: Sophie M. Korczyk, "Gender and Pension Coverage", in *Trends in Pensions 1992*, U.S. Department of Labor, Pension and Welfare Benefits Administration, U.S. Government Printing Office, Washington, DC, 1992, p. 132. Primary source: Author's calculations based on Employee Benefit Research Institute tabulations of May, 1988 Current Population Survey.

★ 327 ★
Pensions

Pension Coverage: Full-Time Private Wage and Salary Workers by Sex and Age, May 1988

Age	Number (thousands)	Percent distribution			
		Total	Covered[1]	Not covered	Don't know
Total					
Total	72,487	100	48	47	5
Under 25	11,265	100	22	67	11
25-29	12,793	100	44	52	5
30-34	11,684	100	50	46	4
35-39	9,659	100	56	41	3
40-44	8,129	100	58	38	3
45-49	6,415	100	59	38	3
50-54	5,058	100	59	38	2
55-59	4,040	100	58	38	4
60-64	2,385	100	55	43	2
65 and older	1,060	100	33	62	5
Men					
Total	43,487	100	51	45	4
Under 25	6,364	100	22	68	10
25-29	7,363	100	44	50	5
30-34	7,226	100	50	46	3
35-39	5,959	100	59	38	3
40-44	4,885	100	63	35	3
45-49	3,784	100	64	34	2
50-54	3,146	100	65	33	2
55-59	2,556	100	63	32	4
60-64	1,542	100	60	39	2
65 and older	663	100	34	59	7
Women					
Total	29,000	100	44	51	5
Under 25	4,901	100	23	66	11
25-29	5,430	100	43	53	4
30-34	4,457	100	49	46	5
35-39	3,700	100	50	46	3
40-44	3,244	100	52	44	4
45-49	2,631	100	51	45	4
50-54	1,911	100	50	48	2
55-59	1,485	100	49	48	3

[Continued]

★ 327 ★

Pension Coverage: Full-Time Private Wage and Salary Workers by Sex and Age, May 1988

[Continued]

Age	Number (thousands)	Percent distribution			
		Total	Covered[1]	Not covered	Don't know
60-64	843	100	48	51	2
65 and older	397	100	31	66	3

Source: U.S. Department of Labor, Pension and Welfare Benefits Administration, *Trends in Pensions 1992*, U.S. Government Printing Office, Washington, DC, 1992, Table B3, p. 622. Primary source: Pension supplement to the May 1988 Current Population Survey. *Notes:* 1. Covered workers include about one percent of workers who are in plans financed entirely by employee contributions.

★ 328 ★

Pensions

Pension Coverage: Percentage of Population 40 and Over with Pension Plan Benefits, by Age and Currently Employed or Retired Status, 1989[1]

From the source: "Workers who accrue five or more years of credited service under a pension plan generally have a vested right to benefits even if they terminate employment before reaching retirement age. Depending upon individual plan provisions, such workers will either receive pension benefits upon reaching the retirement age specified by their plan or may receive an immediate lump sum benefit. If vested workers not yet receiving benefits and those who received lump sum benefits are included as pension recipients, the rate of pension receipt for private sector retirees ages 55 and over increases to 41 percent. For those ages 65 and over, the rate of pension receipt is also 41 percent."

	Age	Total	Presently working[2]			Retired or not presently working		
			Total	Private sector	Public sector	Total	Private sector[3]	Public sector[4]
Total								
Total	25	20	20	20	44	38	73	24
40-54	18	18	18	19	27	21	60	8
55-59	22	21	21	22	39	32	68	28
60-64	32	25	25	24	50	45	77	27
65-69	38	32	30	42	53	46	79	35
70-74	38	30	29	36	50	44	74	27
75-79	32	27	26	[5]	43	36	76	25
80 and older	26	27	24	[5]	39	33	70	16
55 and older	31	24	24	26	47	41	75	27
65 and older	35	31	29	40	47	41	75	27
Men								
Total	33	23	23	24	56	51	81	33
40-54	21	21	21	21	35	26	74	14
55-59	30	25	25	26	52	47	75	[5]
60-64	43	30	29	34	63	59	82	38
65-69	54	38	37	50	63	58	84	45

[Continued]

★ 328 ★

Pension Coverage: Percentage of Population 40 and Over with Pension Plan Benefits, by Age and Currently Employed or Retired Status, 1989

[Continued]

	Age	Total	Presently working[2]			Retired or not presently working		
			Total	Private sector	Public sector	Total	Private sector[3]	Public sector[4]
70-74	55	39	38	[5]	61	57	82	34
75-79	48	32	30	[5]	54	49	83	31
80 and older	43	30	25	[5]	48	45	75	24
55 and older	45	29	29	33	58	53	81	36
65 and older	51	37	36	51	58	53	82	35
Women								
Total	18	16	16	17	34	26	67	15
40-54	14	16	16	16	23	18	51	3
55-59	15	15	14	18	28	22	61	[5]
60-64	22	18	19	16	39	32	70	15
65-69	26	22	20	32	42	33	74	25
70-74	24	18	16	[5]	39	31	65	20
75-79	21	19	20	[5]	34	23	71	18
80 and older	17	[5]	[5]	[5]	31	21	68	11
55 and older	21	17	17	19	37	28	69	18
65 and older	23	21	19	29	37	28	70	19

Source: David J. Beller and David D. McCarthy, "Private Pension Benefits," in Trends in Pensions 1992, U.S. Department of Labor, Pension and Welfare Benefits Administration, U.S. Government Printing Office, Washington, DC, 1992, pp. 236-237. Primary source: Pension benefit amount supplement to the December 1989 Current Population Survey. Notes: 1. Includes those who are currently receiving annuities, those who received lump sum distributions, and those who expect to receive either annuities or lump sums based on former pension covered job. 2. Sector from which pension benefit received or expected to be received may not be sector in which worker is currently employed. 3. Job with pension coverage or longest job was in private sector. 4. Job with pension coverage or longest job was in public sector. 5. Not calculated where base is less than 75,000.

★ 329 ★
Pensions

Pension Coverage: Private Pension Plan Coverage Rates, Selected Years, 1940-87

From the source: "The development of the private pension system can be divided into two stages. In the first stage, lasting from the late 1930s through the 1960s, coverage grew at a phenomenal rate, increasing from 17 percent of full-time workers in 1940 to 52 percent in 1970.... The second stage of development began in the early 1970s and continues today. This stage is characterized by a flat or declining rate of plan coverage, a shift in basic coverage from defined benefit to defined contribution plans, and an increase in the establishment of defined contribution plans to provide supplemental coverage to employees already participating in defined benefit plans."

[Workers in thousands]

Year	Private wage and salary workers[1]	Workers covered by private pension plans[2]	Percent of workers covered by pensions	Percent of full-time workers covered by pensions
1940	28,159	4,100	15	17
1945	34,431	6,400	19	21
1950	39,170	9,800	25	29
1955	43,727	14,200	32	37
1960	45,836	18,700	41	47
1965	50,689	21,800	43	49
1970	58,325	26,300	45	52
1975	68,104	30,738	45	52
1976	71,117	31,710	45	51
1977	73,254	32,796	45	51
1978	75,939	34,037	45	51
1979	78,058	34,798	45	51
1980	78,349	35,939	46	53
1981	80,282	36,912	46	53
1982	82,318	37,481	46	52
1983	84,410	38,971	46	53
1984	86,732	39,713	46	53
1985	88,293	40,444	46	53

[Continued]

★ 329 ★

Pension Coverage: Private Pension Plan Coverage Rates, Selected Years, 1940-87
[Continued]

Year	Private wage and salary workers[1]	Workers covered by private pension plans[2]	Percent of workers covered by pensions	Percent of full-time workers covered by pensions
1986	90,267	41,209	46	52
1987	91,559	41,784	46	52

Source: Daniel Beller and Helen H. Lawrence, "Trends in Private Pension Coverage", in *Trends in Pensions 1992*, U.S. Department of Labor, Pension and Welfare Benefits Administration, U.S. Government Printing Office, Washington, DC, 1992, p. 75. *Notes:* 1. Source: Employment and Earnings, U.S. Department of Labor, Bureau of Labor Statistics. Data for 1940-70 include employed nonagriculture private wage and salary workers. Data for 1975-87 include both employed and unemployed private wage and salary workers in agriculture and nonagriculture industries. 2. Source: Data for 1940-1970 are from Alfred M. Skolnik, "Private Pension Plans, 1950-74", Social Security Bulletin, Vol. 39 (June, 1976), p. 4. Data for 1975-87 are based on an annual Form 5500 financial reports filed with the Internal Revenue Service.

★ 330 ★
Pensions

Pension Coverage: Rates Among Full-Time Private Sector Wage and Salary Workers, by Age and Gender, 1972-88

From the source: "Women are reaching parity in pension coverage with men. Women's relative position is improving in part because their coverage is increasing and in part because men's coverage is declining. Coverage among men dropped from 54 percent to 49 percent of full-time wage and salary workers between 1972 and 1988."

[Data are shown in percent]

Year	Women				Men			
	Total	45-49	50-54	55-59	Total	45-49	50-54	55-59
1972	38	44	45	42	54	63	64	59
1979	40	50	56	50	55	66	69	69
1983	42	49	55	55	52	63	63	66
1988[1]	43	49	49	49	49	61	63	60

Source: Sophie M. Korczyk, "Gender and Pension Coverage", in *Trends in Pensions 1992*, U.S. Department of Labor, Pension and Welfare Benefits Administration, U.S. Government Printing Office, Washington, DC, 1992, p. 127. Primary source: John R. Woods, "Pension Coverage Among Private Wage and Salary Workers: Preliminary Findings from the 1988 Survey of Employee Benefits," *Social Security Bulletin* 52 (October 1989): 2-19. *Notes:* 1. Coverage rates for 1988 reported in this table differ slightly from those reported in other tables in this report for two reasons. First, this table uses a more restrictive definition of full-time workers than is used in derivation of the other tables. The more restrictive definition is used in this table to permit comparisons with prior years. Second, this table does not consider as covered those wage and salary workers who are not covered on their primary job but have coverage from a secondary self-employed job. This group is very small.

★ 331 ★

Pensions

Pension Coverage: Rates Among Full-Time Private Sector Workers, by Age and Gender, 1988

From the source: "Coverage rates rose with age among both men and women. Coverage rates did not differ significantly by gender among workers under age 35. After that age, men had a significant advantage over women. This advantage reached its maximum among workers age 55 to 59. In this group, men's coverage rates were 15 percentage points higher than those of women."

[Data are in percent]

Age	Women	Men
16 to 20	11	12
21 to 24	27	25
25 to 34	45	47
35 to 44	51	60
45 to 54	50	64
55 to 59	48	63
60 to 64	48	60

Source: Sophie M. Korczyk, "Gender and Pension Coverage", in *Trends in Pensions 1992*, U.S. Department of Labor, Pension and Welfare Benefits Administration, U.S. Government Printing Office, Washington, DC, 1992, p. 126. Primary source: Author's calculations based on Employee Benefit Research Institute tabulations of May, 1988 Current Population Survey.

★ 332 ★

Pensions

Pension Coverage: Rates for Full-Time Private Sector Workers, by Industry and Gender, 1988

From the source: "Economic segregation may not always be harmful to women's economic prospects. While women's pension coverage rates are highest in male-dominated industries, they are more likely to gain coverage in in female-dominated industries than in gender-balanced sectors."

[Data are in percent]

Industry	Women	Men
Male-dominated industries		
Agriculture	15	13
Manufacturing, durable goods	64	68
Trade, wholesale	38	52
Transportation and public utilities	65	60
Construction	25	32
Mining	-	-
Total	56	54

[Continued]

★ 332 ★

Pension Coverage: Rates for Full-Time Private Sector Workers, by Industry and Gender, 1988
[Continued]

Industry	Women	Men
Female-dominated industries		
Finance, insurance, and real estate	59	59
Services, professional	43	55
Total	49	57
Gender-balanced industries		
Services, business and personal	19	30
Manufacturing, nondurable goods	50	66
Trade, retail	28	31
Total	32	43

Source: Sophie M. Korczyk, "Gender and Pension Coverage", in *Trends in Pensions 1992*, U.S. Department of Labor, Pension and Welfare Benefits Administration, U.S. Government Printing Office, Washington, DC, 1992, p. 130. Primary source: Author's calculations based on Employee Benefit Research Institute tabulations of May, 1988 Current Population Survey.

★ 333 ★
Pensions

Pension Coverage: Rates for Full-Time Private Wage and Salary Workers by Industry, Selected Years, 1972-88

From the source: "The two industries experiencing the highest rate of employment growth from 1979 to 1988 were the service sector and the finance, insurance, and real estate sector.... The pension coverage rate also increased most rapidly in these two groups, with coverage increasing from 30 to 38 percent among service industry workers and from 54 to 59 percent among finance, insurance, and real estate industry workers."

[Data are in percent]

Industry	1972	1979	1983	1988
	Total			
Total	49	50	47	48
Mining	73	69	69	64
Construction	36	39	32	32
Manufacturing				
Durable goods	64	68	67	67
Nondurable goods	58	61	59	61
Transportation	48	56	53	46
Communications and public utilities	84	82	81	78
Trade				
Wholesale	49	50	47	49
Retail	33	30	28	30

[Continued]

★ 333 ★

Pension Coverage: Rates for Full-Time Private Wage and Salary Workers by Industry, Selected Years, 1972-88

[Continued]

Industry	1972	1979	1983	1988
Finance, insurance and real estate	54	52	54	59
Services	30	36	35	38
Men				
Total	54	55	51	51
Mining	74	70	70	62
Construction	37	40	32	33
Manufacturing				
Durable goods	67	71	68	68
Nondurable goods	67	72	65	68
Transportation	49	59	55	48
Communications and public utilities	84	87	83	78
Trade				
Wholesale	53	54	51	52
Retail	36	33	31	31
Finance, insurance and real estate	62	56	58	59
Services	37	42	40	41
Women				
Total	37	40	41	44
Mining	1	1	1	1
Construction	1	26	35	24
Manufacturing				
Durable goods	54	58	63	64
Nondurable goods	44	44	49	51
Transportation	35	45	46	40
Communications and public utilities	81	72	77	79
Trade				
Wholesale	34	41	36	39
Retail	26	24	25	28
Finance, insurance and real estate	46	48	52	60
Services	25	32	32	35

Source: Daniel Beller and Helen H. Lawrence, "Trends in Private Pension Coverage", in *Trends in Pensions 1992*, U.S. Department of Labor, Pension and Welfare Benefits Administration, U.S. Government Printing Office, Washington, DC, 1992, p. 78. Primary source: Pension supplements to the Current Population Survey. *Notes:* Coverage status totals include workers in agriculture, not shown separately. 1. Not calculated where base is less than 150,000.

★ 334 ★
Pensions

Minimum Age and Service Requirements for Normal Retirement: Defined Benefit Pension Plans, 1980-89[1]

From the source: "In most defined benefit plans, the modal retirement age is 65, unchanged since 1980. However, what has changed is that many workers can retire before the normal age and receive unreduced benefits.... Moreover, service requirements for normal retirements are declining. These patterns are in line with findings from other studies indicating that many pension plans have encouraged earlier retirement over time."

Type of retirement	Percent of full-time participants									
	1980	1981	1982	1983	1984	1985	1986	1988[3]	1988	1989
Service requirements alone	11	14	13	17	17	14	13	9	7	8
30 years required	11	14	13	16	16	14	13	9	7	7
Age requirements alone	45	46	43	38	40	37	40	35	42	43
Age 60	2	2	2	4	3	4	4	4	3	4
Age 62	4	4	4	2	4	4	4	4	6	6
Age 65	39	39	36	31	33	29	32	27	33	33
Age & service requirements	37	33	36	36	34	39	36	41	39	37
Age 55 and 20 years	NA	2	2	2	2	1	2	1	1	1
Age 55 and 30 years	NA	2	2	2	2	2	1	1	1	1
Age 60 and 1-5 years	NA	-	-	-	2	-	3	2	2	2
Age 60 and 10 years	NA	2	2	2	2	4	3	3	2	2
Age 60 and 15-20 years	NA	1[2]	2[2]	3[2]	2	1	1	3	3	1
Age 60 and 30 years	NA	2	2	4	3	3	3	2	1	3
Age 62 and 1-5 years	NA	1	1	1	1	1	1	4	-	2
Age 62 and 15-20 years	NA	2[2]	2[2]	2[2]	2	4	4	2	2	2
Age 62 and 30 years	NA	2	2	3	1	2	1	3	2	2
Age 65 and 5 years	2	1	1	1	1	1	2	1	3	2
Age 65 and 10 years	NA	3	5	5	3	2	2	2	5	2
Age plus service sum	6	7	8	9	9	10	11	15	12	12
Equals 80	1	-	1	1	1	1	1	1	1	1
Equals 85	3	3	3	4	4	4	5	6	5	6
Equals 90+	1	1	2	2	2	3	4	5	4	4

Source: Olivia S. Mitchell, "Trends in Pension Benefit Formulas and Retirement Provisions", in *Trends in Pensions 1992*, U.S. Department of Labor, Pension and Welfare Benefits Administration, U.S. Government Printing Office, Washington, DC, 1992, p. 199. Primary source: U.S. Department of Labor, Bureau of Labor Statistics, "Employee Benefits in Medium and Large Firms, 1980-1989." *Notes:* Data exclude supplemental pension plans. Sums may not equal totals because of rounding. NA means data not available, and "-" means less than 0.5 percent. A comparable Employee Benefits Survey (EBS) was not conducted in 1987. The EBS sampling frame changed in 1988 to include smaller firms and more industries than before, so data for 1988 and 1989 are not precisely comparable with previous years' tabulations. 1. At normal retirement a participant can retire and receive unreduced benefits immediately. 2. Data available for 15 years' service only instead of 15-20. 3. In a few cases the Bureau of Labor Statistics tabulated 1988 results using a sampling frame similar to that employed in previous years. For comparability purposes these figures have been presented where available, under columns headed "1988", whereas tabulations from 1988 and 1989 otherwise employ the new, larger sampling frame.

★ 335 ★

Pensions

Provisions for Adjusting Accrued Benefits for Service Beyond Age 65: Defined Benefit Pension Plans, 1981-89

From the source: "In the past, many defined benefit pension plans provided no credit for work after age 65, a policy intended to discourage work after the normal retirement age.... In 1986, however, the Omnibus Budget Reconciliation Act mandated that benefit accruals be continued for work beyond the plan's normal retirement age (subject to any plan maximum credited service provisions), beginning in 1988 for most plans."

Type of provision	Percent of full-time participants							
	1981	1982	1983	1984	1985	1986	1988[2]	1988
Credit for service after age 65	42	42	47	44	38	41	49	49[1]
All service credited	26	25	30	26	19	23	NA	NA
Service credited to maximum age	15	16	18	17	19	18	NA	NA
Service credited to maximum years	1	1	-	-	1	-	NA	NA
No credit service after age 65	58	58	53	56	61	59	49	49[1]
Pension deferred with no change in amount	51	52	45	49	54	51	42	40
Pension deferred, increased actuarially	4	4	4	5	5	5	7	9
Pension deferred, increased by percent	2	2	3	2	2	2		
Pension begins at age 65	1	1	-	1	-	1		-

Source: Olivia S. Mitchell, "Trends in Pension Benefit Formulas and Retirement Provisions", in *Trends in Pensions 1992*, U.S. Department of Labor, Pension and Welfare Benefits Administration, U.S. Government Printing Office, Washington, DC, 1992, p. 200. Primary source: U.S. Department of Labor Statistics, "Employee Benefits in Medium and Large Firms, 1981-1989" and unpublished data from the BLS for 1988 figures. A comparable Employee Benefits Survey (EBS) was not conducted in 1987. The EBS sampling frame changed in 1988 to include smaller firms and more industries than before, so data for 1988 and 1989 are not precisely comparable with previous years' tabulations. *Notes:* Data exclude supplemental pension plans. Sums may not equal totals because of rounding. NA means data not available, and "-" means less than 0.5 percent. 1. The Omnibus Reconciliation Act of 1986 required that benefit accruals be continued for service beyond the plan's normal retirement age. This took effect in January of 1988 for noncollectively bargained plans and later for negotiated plans. Data for 1989 are not comparable, for this reason. 2. In a few cases the Bureau of Labor Statistics tabulated 1988 results using a sampling frame similar to that employed in previous years. For comparability purposes these figures have been presented, where available, under columns headed "1988", whereas tabulations from 1988 and 1989 otherwise employ the new, larger survey sampling frame.

Pensions: Worldwide

★ 336 ★

Active Participants in Private Pension Plans, 1970-89

From the source: "Because of its large labor force, the United States has a major share of the world's private pension participants. Its 42 million worker participants in private pension plans are 43 percent of the nearly 100 million workers participating in pension plans in the nine countries [shown]. This percentage is higher than the United States' 39 percent share of the working age population in these countries."

[Thousands]

Year	Australia	Canada	France	Germany (FRG)[1]	Japan	Netherlands	Switzerland	United Kingdom	United States
1970	-	1,552	10,583	-	5,905[2]	1,592	1,102	7,125[3]	26,100
1975	-	2,046[4]	15,183	-	9,424[5]	1,729	1,207	6,000	30,738
1980	-	2,505	16,502	-	11,200	2,109	1,311	6,025[6]	35,939
1981	-	-	16,494	-	11,810	2,106	1,365	-	36,912
1982	-	2,682	16,414	-	12,440	2,063	1,434	-	37,481
1983	-	-	16,407	-	12,830	2,059	1,518	5,800	38,971
1984	-	2,536	15,823	9,000	13,430	2,083	1,543	-	39,713
1985	1,014	-	15,509	-	14,030	2,137	-	-	40,444
1986	1,160	2,582	15,324	-	14,620	2,205	-	-	41,209
1987	1,261	-	15,429	9,200	15,150	2,232	2,331	5,800	41,784
1988	1,572	2,673	15,730	-	15,850	2,292	-	-	42,300[7]
1989	1,742	2,754	16,000	-	16,720	2,423	-	-	-

Source: Lorna M. Daily and John A. Turner, "U.S. Private Pensions in World Perspective: 1970-89," in *Trends in Pensions 1992*, U.S. Department of Labor, Pension and Welfare Benefits Administration, U.S. Government Printing Office, Washington, DC, 1992, p. 18. *Notes:* - stands for data not available. 1. Federal Republic of Germany (West Germany). 2. Interpolated by the author from data for 1967 and 1972. 3. Interpolated by the author from data for 1967 and 1971. 4. Interpolated by the author from data for 1974 and 1976. 5. Interpolated by the author from data for 1972 and 1977. 6. Interpolated by the author from data for 1979 and 1983. 7. Preliminary.

★ 337 ★

Pensions: Worldwide

Average Annual Retirement Pension From Private Pension Plans, 1970-89

From the source: "Private pension benefits in the United States are high by world standards. They were estimated to be $6,359 per year in 1989, a large increase over the $4,950 [in benefits] in 1986."

[U.S. dollars]

Year	Australia	Canada	France	Germany (FRG)[1]	Japan	Netherlands	Switzerland	United Kingdom	United States
1970	-	-	-	-	-	387	896	-	1,767
1975	-	-	-	-	-	935	1,995	-	2,421
1980	-	-	2,308	-	520	1,834	3,954	-	3,470
1981	-	3,764	2,075	-	614	1,586	3,512	-	3,810
1982	-	3,989	1,908	1,484	658	1,616	3,612	-	4,080
1983	-	4,356	1,775	-	740	1,629	3,624	1,735	4,310
1984	-	4,511	1,722	-	834	1,537	3,434	-	4,530
1985	-	4,510	1,684	-	931	1,725	-	-	4,700
1986	-	4,597	2,381	-	1,490	2,512	-	-	4,950
1987	-	5,100	2,986	-	1,867	3,178	6,326	-	-
1988	-	5,859	3,203	2,940	2,292	3,505	-	-	-
1989	-	-	3,226	-	2,304	3,450	-	-	6,359

Source: Lorna M. Daily and John A. Turner, "U.S. Private Pensions in World Perspective: 1970-89," in *Trends in Pensions 1992*, U.S. Department of Labor, Pension and Welfare Benefits Administration, U.S. Government Printing Office, Washington, DC, 1992, p. 23. *Notes:* - stands for data not available. Statistics for Canada include both private pension plans and plans for government employees. 1. Federal Republic of Germany (former West Germany).

★ 338 ★

Pensions: Worldwide

Average Assets Per Participant, 1970-89

From the source: "Average pension assets per participant provide [an] indication of funding. That figure is low when benefits provided by the system are low or when the system is underfunded."

[Thousands of U.S. dollars]

Year	Australia	Canada	France	Germany (FRG)[1]	Japan	Netherlands	Switzerland	United Kingdom	United States
1970	-	-	-	-	-	2.7	3.8	1.3	5.1
1975	-	-	0.2	-	-	8.6	10.5	3.0	8.2
1980	-	-	0.4	-	2.4	17.5	22.6	10.6	14.8
1981	-	-	0.4	-	2.9	15.6	20.2	-	15.2
1982	-	15.6	0.4	-	3.0	16.8	20.2	-	17.5
1983	-	-	0.4	-	3.7	17.7	20.4	13.4	19.7
1984	-	20.3	0.4	-	4.2	17.2	18.9	-	20.6
1985	14.8	-	0.4	-	4.7	17.8	-	-	24.3

[Continued]

★ 338 ★

Average Assets Per Participant, 1970-89
[Continued]

Year	Australia	Canada	France	Germany (FRG)[1]	Japan	Netherlands	Switzerland	United Kingdom	United States
1986	14.5	24.0	0.6	-	7.5	25.3	-	-	26.9
1987	-	-	0.7	-	9.8	31.7	30.0	27.0	24.9
1988	-	29.1	0.7	-	12.1	34.3	-	-	28.8
1989	-	-	0.7	-	12.1	33.1	-	-	-

Source: Lorna M. Daily and John A. Turner, "U.S. Private Pensions in World Perspective: 1970-89," in *Trends in Pensions 1992*, U.S. Department of Labor, Pension and Welfare Benefits Administration, U.S. Government Printing Office, Washington, DC, 1992, p. 29. *Notes:* - stands for data not available. Participant is the total of active participants and beneficiaries. 1. Federal Republic of Germany (former West Germany).

★ 339 ★

Pensions: Worldwide

Beneficiaries Receiving a Retirement Pension From a Private Pension Plan, 1970-89

From the source: "The United States experienced a rapid increase in pension beneficiaries during the 1980s, growing 49 percent between 1980 and 1989. Growth was even more rapid in Japan, where beneficiaries in funded private pension plans increased 144 percent over that period. Canada, France, and the Netherlands also had large percentage increases in beneficiaries (61 percent, 46 percent, and 31 percent). In spite of rapid growth in beneficiaries, however, only 22.5 million beneficiaries are counted in the statistics for the nine countries [shown], with 9.0 million of them in the United States."

[Thousands]

Year	Australia	Canada	France	Germany (FRG)[1]	Japan	Netherlands	Switzerland	United Kingdom	United States
1970	-	-	-	-	-	292	127	1,025[2]	3,230
1975	-	-	2,324	-	-	364	167	1,100	4,600
1980	-	-	3,455	-	551	449	208	1,350[3]	6,030
1981	-	610[4]	3,569	-	616	467	218	-	6,370
1982	-	640	3,660	-	687	483	225	-	6,750
1983	-	671	3,741	-	766	497	237	1,800	7,160
1984	-	700	3,932	-	850	515	244	-	7,600
1985	25	752	4,242	-	943	535	-	-	8,000
1986	22	828	4,575	-	1,031	559	-	-	8,500
1987	-	904	4,764	-	1,142	581	274	2,300	-
1988	-	981	4,953	3,000	1,239	578	-	-	-
1989	-	-	5,047	-	1,342	590	-	-	9,000

Source: Lorna M. Daily and John A. Turner, "U.S. Private Pensions in World Perspective: 1970-89," in *Trends in Pensions 1992*, U.S. Department of Labor, Pension and Welfare Benefits Administration, U.S. Government Printing Office, Washington, DC, 1992, p. 20. *Notes:* - stands for data not available. 1. Federal Republic of Germany (former West Germany). 2. Interpolated by the author from data for 1967 and 1972. 3. Interpolated by the author from data for 1979 and 1983. 4. Data for all years for Canada include retirees from pension plans for government workers.

★ 340 ★

Pensions: Worldwide

Total Assets of Private Pension Plans, 1970-89

From the source: "Reflecting both its large economy and the requirement that its pensions be funded, the United States had 68 percent of the $2.6 trillion in world pension assets in the late 1980s.... The difference between the U.S. share of world private pension assets (68 percent) and its share of participants (43 percent) is due partly to low private pension assets in France, which uses pay-as-you-go finances."

[Millions of U.S. dollars]

Year	Australia	Canada	France	Germany (FRG)[1]	Japan	Netherlands	Switzerland	United Kingdom	United States
1970	-	-	1,244	-	-	5,032[2]	4,617	10,704	149,500
1975	-	-	3,782	14,681[3]	6,739[4]	18,070[2]	14,478	21,422	289,600
1980	-	42,066	8,866	31,468	28,563	44,738	34,288	78,000	621,800
1981	-	44,286	7,948	29,646	36,168	40,225	31,935	79,635	659,200
1982	-	51,761	7,443	30,248	39,639	42,842	33,530	90,695	781,600
1983	-	63,371	7,252	31,528	50,278	45,114	35,728	102,071	923,200
1984	-	65,816	7,411	-	60,059	44,684	33,857	108,223	994,100
1985	15,362	74,173	8,238	-	70,805	47,548	-	130,980	1,186,000
1986	17,158	81,927	11,859	-	117,412	70,038	-	178,954	1,339,600
1987	-	89,741	14,022	55,636	159,219	89,183	78,222	218,579	1,436,000
1988	-	106,246	14,755	-	207,434	98,529	-	245,844	1,745,600
1989	-	124,432	14,486	-	218,681	99,710	-	216,973	-

Source: Lorna M. Daily and John A. Turner, "U.S. Private Pensions in World Perspective: 1970-89," in *Trends in Pensions 1992*, U.S. Department of Labor, Pension and Welfare Benefits Administration, U.S. Government Printing Office, Washington, DC, 1992, p. 25. *Notes:* - stands for data not available. Assets for the Netherlands and for the United Kingdom include only non-insured private pension plans. Assets for Germany include support funds, pensionskassen and direct insurance. Book reserves are not included for Germany and Japan. 1. Federal Republic of Germany (former West Germany). 2. Data are partially estimated by the author. 3. Interpolated by the author from data for 1973 and 1978. 4. Data are partially estimated by the author for this year from data available for 1976.

Retirement

★ 341 ★

After-Tax Earnings of the Elderly

From the source: "This table assumes a married couple in their late sixties who receive $25,000 in pension and investment income and $18,000 in social security benefits. The couple files jointly and claims the standard deduction; the state income tax rate is 7.5%."

Earnings from a job	$10,000	$20,000	$30,000
Less			
Federal, state and social security tax	2,872	5,888	9,796
Social security benefits lost to earnings test	0	3,147	6,480
Additional federal tax on benefits	750	1,384	1,333
What you get to keep	6,378	9,581	12,391
Percent of earnings you keep	63.8	47.9	41.3

Source: Melynda Dovel Wilcox, "The High Cost of Working in Retirement," *Kiplinger's Personal Finance Magazine*, August 1993, p. 92. Primary source: Coopers & Lybrand Personal Financial Services.

★ 342 ★

Retirement

Age at Which Wage and Salary Workers Aged 50 to 66+ Are Planning to Stop Work, by Health Coverage After Retirement

[Numbers are in percent]

Age planning to stop working	Health coverage after retirement	
	Yes	No
Men		
50-59	6	2
60-64	51	42
65	27	31
66+	16	25
Women		
50-59	22	12
60-64	44	43

[Continued]

★ 342 ★

Age at Which Wage and Salary Workers Aged 50 to 66+ Are Planning to Stop Work, by Health Coverage After Retirement

[Continued]

Age planning to stop working	Health coverage after retirement	
	Yes	No
65	27	32
66+	6	13

Source: Quinn, Joseph F. and Richard V. Berkhauser, "Retirement Preferences and Plans of Older American Workers," *The Commonwealth Fund, Americans Over 55 at Work Program,* October 1990, p. 18. *Notes:* Data are based on a survey of about 2,000 employed Americans, part of a larger survey conducted by Louis Harris and Associates, March-September 1989, for The Commonwealth Fund.

★ 343 ★

Retirement

Minimum Age and Service Requirements for Early Retirement: Defined Benefit Pension Plans, 1980-89

From the source: "Defined benefit plans generally specify age and/or service criteria under which a worker can receive 'early retirement' benefits.... Rule changes have made early retirement more accessible. Two thirds of all participants [surveyed] could retire at age 55 in 1989, up from 60 percent 10 years earlier."

Type of retirement	Percent of full-time participants								
	1980	1981	1982	1983	1984	1985	1986	1988	1989
Plans permitting early retirement[1]	98	98	97	97	97	97	98	98	97
Service requirements alone	10	5	5	6	5	4	5	7	6
30 years required	9	5	5	6	5	4	5	6	5
Age requirements alone	9	10	9	10	10	9	10	10	6
Age 55	8	9	9	10	9	9	10	10	6
Age and service requirements									
Age 55 and 5 years	3	4	4	3	4	3	3	4	9
Age 55 and 10 years	NA	36	35	35	39	43	41	44	43
Age 55 and 15 years	NA	11	10	9	7	8	7	10	8
Age 60 and 10 years	NA	4	4	5	5	4	4	5	4
Age plus service sum	5	9	10	9	10	10	9	4	4
Sum equals 80 or less	NA	NA	NA	6	6	5	5	2	1
Sum equals 85 or more	3	6	5	5	5	4	4	1	-

[Continued]

★ 343 ★

Minimum Age and Service Requirements for Early Retirement:
Defined Benefit Pension Plans, 1980-89
[Continued]

Type of retirement	Percent of full-time participants								
	1980	1981	1982	1983	1984	1985	1986	1988	1989
Plans not permitting early retirement	2	2	3	3	3	3	2	2	3

Source: Olivia S. Mitchell, "Trends in Pension Benefit Formulas and Retirement Provisions", in *Trends in Pensions 1992*, U.S. Department of Labor, Pension and Welfare Benefits Administration, U.S. Government Printing Office, Washington, DC, 1992, p. 198. Primary source: U.S. Department of Labor, Bureau of Labor Statistics, "Employee Benefits in Medium and Large Firms, 1980-1989." *Notes:* NA means data not available, and "-" means less than 0.5 percent. Data exclude supplemental pension plans. Sums may not equal totals because of rounding. A comparable Employee Benefits Survey (EBS) was not conducted in 1987. The EBS sampling frame changed in 1988 to include smaller firms and more industries than before, so data for 1988 and 1989 are not precisely comparable with previous years tabulations. 1. Early retirement is defined as the point when a worker can retire and immediately receive accrued benefits based on service and earnings; benefits are reduced for years prior to the normal age.

★ 344 ★

Retirement

Number of Post-Retirement Benefit Increases, 1981-85

From the source: "[This table] illustrates the percentage of participants in plans awarding at least one increase between 1981 and 1985 by the number of increases received during the period. Approximately half of all the participants receiving an increase were in plans that awarded only one increase during the five years, while 22 percent of the sample received four or five increases. Given that they were in plans that gave an increase, production workers were more frequently in plans that gave multiple adjustments than professional/administrative and technical/clerical workers."

Plan characteristics	Percentage of participants in plans with at least one PRA[1]	Percentage of participants in plans with at least one PRA having the designated number of PRAs				
		One	Two	Three	Four	Five
All participants	34.7	45.6	23.9	8.6	18.4	3.5
Operational group						
Professional and administrative	32.2	55.5	24.5	9.9	6.8	3.3
Technical and clerical	29.5	58.7	20.9	8.3	10.3	1.8
Production	39.1	35.1	24.8	8.2	27.7	4.3
Industry						
Mining	42.2	22.4	9.1	68.5	0.0	0.0
Construction	0.0	0.0	0.0	0.0	0.0	0.0
Manufacturing	38.4	38.8	29.2	7.8	18.4	5.8
Transportation	47.8	37.4	18.5	7.0	37.1	0.0
Wholesale trade	19.2	38.3	41.0	20.7	0.0	0.0
Retail trade	24.6	96.4	3.6	0.0	0.0	0.0
Finance, insurance, real estate	19.3	88.2	7.2	4.5	0.0	0.0
Services	15.6	49.7	50.3	0.0	0.0	0.0
Size						
1-99	22.6	78.3	21.7	0.0	0.0	0.0
100-249	18.7	62.1	34.1	0.0	3.7	0.0

[Continued]

★ 344 ★

Number of Post-Retirement Benefit Increases, 1981-85

[Continued]

Plan characteristics	Percentage of participants in plans with at least one PRA[1]	Percentage of participants in plans with at least one PRA having the designated number of PRAs				
		One	Two	Three	Four	Five
250-499	23.1	49.3	26.7	14.0	10.0	0.0
500-999	24.6	77.4	13.4	1.5	6.3	1.4
1,000-2,499	36.3	52.0	34.6	12.7	0.7	0.0
2,500 and over	49.4	31.0	20.7	8.6	32.9	6.7
Region						
Northeast	31.9	65.6	15.0	4.5	14.0	0.9
South	32.7	52.1	38.6	5.5	3.8	0.0
North Central	42.9	23.1	18.5	14.8	34.5	9.2
West	28.2	59.8	21.4	5.3	13.5	0.0

Source: Steven G. Allen, Robert L. Clark, Ann A. McDermed, "Post-Retirement Benefits Increases in the 1980s," in *Trends in Pensions 1992*, U.S. Department of Labor, Pension and Welfare Benefits Administration, U.S. Government Printing Office, Washington, DC, 1992, p. 336. Primary source: Employee Benefit Survey, 1986. *Note:* 1. Post-retirement adjustment in pension benefits.

★ 345 ★

Retirement

Post-Retirement Increases, 1981-85 as a Percentage of 1980 Pension by Years of Service, Year of Retirement, and 1980 Monthly Benefit

From the source: "[This table] reports the size of post-retirement increases for 1981-85.... The cumulative increase for the period 1981 to 1985 indicates the average increase for all persons who received at least one increase during the period. These calculations clearly reveal three important points concerning post-retirement increases: (1) retirees with more years of service receive larger post-retirement increases; (2) retirees with larger pension benefits receive smaller post-retirement increases; and (3) persons who have been retired longer receive larger increases."

Years of service	Year of retirement			
	1965	1970	1975	1980
1980 pension = $250				
10	19.3	20.6	17.3	11.0
20	22.2	23.6	20.3	14.1
30	24.8	26.3	22.9	16.9
1980 pension = $500				
10	17.0	18.5	15.3	9.0
20	18.4	20.0	16.8	10.6
30	19.9	21.4	18.2	12.1

[Continued]

★ 345 ★

Post-Retirement Increases, 1981-85 as a Percentage of 1980 Pension by Years of Service, Year of Retirement, and 1980 Monthly Benefit
[Continued]

Years of service	Year of retirement			
	1965	1970	1975	1980
1980 pension = $1,000				
10	15.8	17.3	14.3	8.1
20	16.5	18.1	15.1	8.9
30	17.3	18.8	15.8	9.6

Source: Steven G. Allen, Robert L. Clark, Ann A. McDermed, "Post-Retirement Benefits Increases in the 1980s," in *Trends in Pensions 1992*, U.S. Department of Labor, Pension and Welfare Benefits Administration, U.S. Government Printing Office, Washington, DC, 1992, p. 337. Primary source: Employee Benefit Survey, 1986.

★ 346 ★

Retirement

Retirement Plan Coverage, by Firm Size, 1990
[Percentage of employees covered, by firm size]

	All firms by category	Number of employees			
		1-24	25-99	100-499	500+
Mining, construction, transportation, communications, and public utilities	52.8	12.2	34.8	52.8	70.8
Trade	28.8	8.3	32.1	27.9	44.8
Finance, insurance, and real estate	82.1	18.7	47.3	57.5	88.5
Services	33.5	20.5	33.6	31.4	45.5
All firms	41.8	12.8	34.5	41.1	81.8

Source: Roger Thompson, "A Decline in Covered Workers," *Nations Business*, March 1993, p. 57. Primary source: U.S. Small Business Administration.

★ 347 ★

Retirement

Retirement Plans

Don't know - 28.0	
Children - 26.0	
Government - 12.0	
Nursing home - 12.0	
Family - 8.0	
Own income - 8.0	
	Spouse - 5.0
Other - 5.0	
	Insurance - 1.0

Data show how older Americans expect to be cared for if unable to care for themselves. Responses are given for a sample of 1,500 persons.

	Percent
Children	26.0
Government	12.0
Nursing home	12.0
Own income	8.0
Family	8.0
Spouse	5.0
Insurance	1.0
Don't know	28.0
Other	5.0

Source: Brenda Intindola, "75 Million Dangerously Weak Savers", *National Underwriter*, April 5, 1993, p. 3. Primary source: Phoenix Home Life.

★ 348 ★

Retirement

Retirement Preferences and Plans of Wage and Salary Men Aged 50-70+

Age	Percent who would like to stop working	Percent who will probably stop working
50-55	2.0	1.0
56-59	9.0	4.0
60-61	13.0	10.0
62-64	35.0	37.0

[Continued]

★ 348 ★

Retirement Preferences and Plans of Wage and Salary Men Aged 50-70+
[Continued]

Age	Percent who would like to stop working	Percent who will probably stop working
65	23.0	29.0
66-69	2.0	3.0
70+	15.0	17.0

Source: Quinn, Joseph F. and Richard V. Berkhauser, "Retirement Preferences and Plans of Older American Workers," *The Commonwealth Fund, Americans Over 55 at Work Program,* October 1990, p. 5. *Notes:* Data are based on a survey of about 2,000 employed Americans, part of a larger survey conducted by Louis Harris and Associates, March-September 1989, for The Commonwealth Fund.

★ 349 ★

Retirement

Retirement Preferences and Plans of Wage and Salary Men Aged 50-98

Age	Percent who would like to stop working	Percent who will probably stop working
50-55	2.0	8.0
56-59	9.0	8.0
60-61	13.0	17.0
62-64	23.0	27.0
65	19.0	29.0
66-69	1.0	1.0
70-98	10.0	10.0

Source: Quinn, Joseph F. and Richard V. Berkhauser, "Retirement Preferences and Plans of Older American Workers," *The Commonwealth Fund, Americans Over 55 at Work Program,* October 1990, p. 6. *Notes:* Data are based on a survey of about 2,000 employed Americans, part of a larger survey conducted by Louis Harris and Associates, March-September 1989, for The Commonwealth Fund.

Chapter 7
SOCIAL SECURITY

This chapter presents information on the Social Security system in the United States. Information on private and public pension and retirement plans other than Social Security are in the chapter on *Pensions and Retirement*.

Tables in this chapter begin with a section headed Summary that provides data for overview. Thereafter, information is presented under headings of Costs (at the national level), Benefits (to individuals or households), Benefits by states, Supplemental Security Income (SSI), and five tables that provide information on social security systems in other countries.

The chapters on *Income, Assets, and Spending, Health and Health Care, Health Insurance,* and *Nursing Homes and Resident Care* contain materials on income and costs useful in placing data on Social Security into full context.

Summary

★ 350 ★

Social Security as Percent of Income

Elderly people (65 or older) are shown by income bracket with an indication of the percentage of their income derived from Social Security.

Income bracket	Percent in bracket	Percent of income from Social Security
Under 10,000	27.6	74.5
10,000 to 19,999	32.3	59.9
20,000 to 29,999	17.6	72.3
30,000 to 49,999	14.3	29.5

[Continued]

★ 350 ★

Social Security as Percent of Income
[Continued]

Income bracket	Percent in bracket	Percent of income from Social Security
50,000 t0 74,999	4.5	19.8
Over 75,000	3.7	10.1

Source: New York Times, February 11, 1993, p. A17. Primary source: House Ways and Means Committee, U.S. House of Representatives.

★ 351 ★

Summary

How Long Does It Take to Recover Social Security Contributions?

A letter to the editor aimed to dispel the notion that most recipients of Social Security recover their contribution far sooner than they die—which is the apparent message of several other tables in this section.

Let us examine the history of a hypothetical taxpayer who entered the system in 1948 at the age of 20 and retired and started to receive benefits at the end of 1992 at the age of 65. In each year, he earned the maximum taxable income, which when he first joined was $3,600 with a tax rate of 4.5 percent. At the end of his earnings history, the maximum taxable income was $55,500 with a tax rate of 12.4 percent. (For purposes of this computation the Medicare portion—2.9 percent—was not included.)

His total contributions amounted to $84,365, paid in equal amounts by himself and his employer. (The employer's share was factored into the prices of goods and services purchased by the employee and so was indirectly paid by him.) In addition to these contributions must be added the time value of money (Mr. Dunton's interest) earned by these funds during the 45 years of participation.

I used the minimum yield on long-term Treasury bonds as a guide; the rate varied from 6 percent to 7.8 percent during this period. Adding this to the actual amounts paid into the fund, the total value at the end of 1992 amounted to $223,608.

For the year 1993, the first year after the individual's retirement, the maximum benefit is $13,536 and I am assuming that this is what he would receive. I further assumed that this amount would increase at the rate of 3 percent per year for cost-of-living adjustments.

[Continued]

★ 351 ★

How Long Does It Take to Recover Social Security Contributions?
[Continued]

On this basis, and further assuming that the time value of the balance of the fund would continue to grow at the rate of 7.8 percent a year, after 24.5 years the retirement fund would still be approximately what it was when retirement began and the recipient would then be almost 90 years old.

The fund would not be consumed until he or his surviving spouse reached 100.

Source: New York Times, March 14, 1993, p. 13. Primary source: Letter to the editor from Stephan Zneimer, C.P.A., Dallas, PA., dated March 1, 1993.

★ 352 ★
Summary

Family Income of Social Security Recipients, 1991

The table shows the family income ranges of Social Security recipients in 1991. The average family income in 1991 was $36,000.

	Percent in income range
Under $10,000	21.8
$10,000 to $29,999	41.5
$30,000 to $49,999	19.6
$50,000 to $100,000	12.9
More than $100,000	3.7

Source: New York Times, August 20, 1992, p. 4. Primary source: Congressional Budget Office; Bureau of Labor Statistics.

★ 353 ★
Summary

Social Security Beneficiaries, 1992

Beneficiaries	Million
Number of beneficiaries	41.2
Retired workers, spouses, and children	29.1
Retired workers	25.6
Survivors of deceased workers	7.3
Disabled workers, spouses, and children	4.8

[Continued]

★ 353 ★

Social Security Beneficiaries, 1992
[Continued]

Beneficiaries	Million
Disabled workers	3.4
Age 65 or older	30.2

Source: Social Security Bulletin, Vol. 55, No. 3, Fall 1992, (inside page of back cover).

★ 354 ★
Summary

Average Monthly Social Security Benefits, 1992
[Dollars per month]

Average monthly benefit for	Benefits	Awards
Retired workers	632	601
Disabled workers	608	600
Nondisabled widow(er)s	588	584
Children of deceased workers	419	401

Source: Social Security Bulletin, Vol. 55, No. 3, Fall 1992, (inside page of back cover).

★ 355 ★
Summary

Eligibility and Taxable Earnings for Social Security, 1992

From the source: "To become elegible for his or her benefit and benefits for family members or survivors, a worker must earn a certain number of credits based on work in covered employment or self-employment. These credits are measured in terms of quarters of coverage (QC). In 1993, a QC is acquired for each $590 in annual covered earnings up to a maximum of four [quarters of coverage] for the year based on earnings of $2,360 or more." For the section labeled "Earnings test exempt amounts" the beneficiary earns $1 less for each $3 dollars over the amount shown.

Characteristic	Dollars
Maximum taxable earnings	
Social Security	55,500
Medicare	130,200
Earnings required for work credits (quarter of coverage)	
One work credit	570

[Continued]

★ 355 ★

Eligibility and Taxable Earnings for Social Security, 1992
[Continued]

Characteristic	Dollars
Maximum of four work credits per year	2,280
Earnings test exempt amounts	
Under age 65	7,440 (620 monthly)
Age 65-69	10,200 (850 monthly)

Source: Social Security Bulletin, Vol. 55, No. 3, Fall 1992, (inside page of back cover).

★ 356 ★
Summary

Average Monthly Social Security Benefits for Beneficiaries Aged 60 or Older, by Type of Benefit, Race, Age, and Sex, 1991

Social Security benefits vary based on income, the amount contributed throughout the work history of the individual and his or her spouse, and the age at which the individual retires.

Type of benefit	Total[1]	Age group								
		60-61	62-64	65-69	70-74	75-79	80-84	85-89	90-94	95 or older
Both sexes[2]	594.30	579.30	524.50	569.80	602.60	656.80	619.70	596.60	564.10	511.90
Retired workers	629.30	...	540.70	603.50	636.90	703.30	653.40	620.80	576.70	522.00
Widows, widowers, mothers, and fathers	581.4	520.10	545.60	590.10	604.40	594.50	586.70	572.30	552.80	518.70
Wives and husbands	325.50	239.60	298.20	318.60	338.20	343.80	331.70	324.10	316.80	307.30
Disabled workers	634.60	632.10	636.10	...	...	...	...	...	...	...
Disabled children	357.70	374.30	371.20	360.90	347.10	329.30	313.30	305.20	[3]	[3]
Men[2]	707.30	706.00	664.40	629.40	708.10	782.90	705.00	666.20	624.50	584.00
Retired workers	709.30	...	651.30	694.40	710.10	785.90	708.30	669.10	626.90	589.70
Widowers and fathers	422.80	357.50	458.90	461.80	464.90	395.90	405.50	363.00	420.60	...
Husbands	202.40	...	164.20	178.20	198.00	211.30	221.40	220.90	218.00	...
Disabled workers	729.50	728.40	730.20	...	...	...	...	[3]	[3]	...
Disabled children	357.10	378.20	367.20	358.50	341.30	326.80	312.50		[3]	[3]
Women[2]	517.90	492.00	418.90	473.00	523.30	574.10	573.90	567.10	544.30	494.00
Retired workers	541.60	...	411.40	487.70	548.00	616.20	604.40	585.50	546.60	489.00
Widows and mothers	582.50	525.90	547.40	590.90	605.00	595.30	587.50	573.10	553.20	519.00
Wives	326.80	240.80	298.70	319.50	339.40	345.80	334.60	327.30	321.60	319.00
Disabled workers	462.30	460.80	463.20	...	...	...	...	[3]	[3]	[3]
Disabled children	358.20	370.20	374.30	362.90	351.50	331.00	313.80	[3]	[3]	[3]

Source: Annual Statistical Supplement, 1992 to the Social Security Bulletin, U.S. Department of Health and Human Services, Social Security Administration, January 1993, p. 183. Notes: Three dots (...) signifies the category does not apply. 1. The sum of the individual categories may not equal total because of independent rounding. 2. Includes parents and special age-72 beneficiaries. 3. Fewer than 500 beneficiaries in the sample.

★ 357 ★

Summary

Percentage of Older Americans Who Receive Some Form of Non-Cash Social Security Benefit, by Type of Benefit, 1990

Source of non-cash benefit	Total	Men					Women				
		Total	62-64	65-69	70-74	75+	Total	62-64	65-69	70-74	75+
Percent receiving benefits from:[1]											
Total	100.0	100.0	100.0	100.0	100.0	100.0	100.0	100.0	100.0	100.0	100.0
Medicare	89.5	89.3	[2]	99.9	100.0	100.0	89.7	[2]	99.9	99.8	100.0
Medicaid	5.2	3.7	.7	3.1	3.6	5.2	6.8	1.0	6.5	8.4	7.6
Food Stamps	2.8	2.0	1.3	1.2	1.4	3.4	3.7	1.7	2.7	4.1	4.7
Free or subsidized school meals	.7	.7	.3	.8	1.0	.7	.6	.3	.8	.9	.5
Public or subsidized rental housing	4.6	2.8	.6	2.8	3.0	3.5	6.5	1.3	4.6	6.1	9.5
Energy assistance	.7	.4	[2]	.6	.6	.4	1.1	[2]	1.4	.7	1.3
Number of non-cash benefits received:											
0	10.2	10.4	97.3	.1	[2]	[2]	9.9	96.7	.1	[2]	[2]
1	80.3	82.6	2.5	94.0	92.9	90.1	77.7	2.4	90.3	87.1	82.9
3 or more	3.2	2.0	[2]	1.8	1.9	3.0	4.4	.3	4.8	4.7	5.1
Percent in households with means-tested benefits[3]	13.1	10.8	7.9	9.3	10.5	13.2	15.8	7.6	12.2	16.0	20.3

Source: Annual Statistical Supplement, 1992 to the Social Security Bulletin, U.S. Department of Health and Human Services, Social Security Administration, January 1993, p. 184. Primary source: Restricted use file, Survey of Income and Program Participation (SIPP). The Old-Age, Survivors, and Disability Insurance (OASDI) benefit classification is based on Social Security program information that was matched to SIPP public use files and edited to be consistent with survey variables on Social Security benefit receipt, Medicare coverage, age, sex, and marital status. The file was developed as part of a joint statistical project between the Social Security Administration and the Bureau of the Census under the aegis of the agencies' 1967 Memorandum of Agreement on the Exchange of Statistical Information and Service. *Notes:* Based of the Survey of Income and Program Participation (SIPP). 1. Medicare, Medicaid, and Food Stamp receipts are for individuals; other non-cash benefits are for households. 2. Less than 0.05 percent. 3. Includes Supplemental Security Insurance (SSI), veterans' pensions, Aid to Families with Dependent Children (AFDC), general assistance, Indian, Cuban or refugee assistance, other cash welfare benefits, food stamps, Women, Infants, and Children supplemental food program (WIC), energy assistance, Medicaid, free or subsidized school meals, and public or subsidized rental housing.

★ 358 ★

Summary

Age Distribution, Average Age, and Number of Social Security Beneficiaries, 1940-91

For men, the average age of Social Security beneficiaries has remained fairly steady since 1950. For women, it has increased by about 2 years.

Year and sex	Total number (in thous.)	Average age	Percentage distribution, by age						
			Total	62-64	65-69	70-74	75-79	80-84	85 or older
Men									
1940	99	68.8	100.0	...	74.4	17.4	6.4	1.6	0.2
1945	447	71.7	100.0	...	39.9	40.2	15.1	4.0	.7
1950	1,469	72.2	100.0	...	39.1	33.7	20.2	5.9	1.2
1955	3,252	72.7	100.0	...	35.7	34.8	20.0	7.6	1.9

[Continued]

★ 358 ★

Age Distribution, Average Age, and Number of Social Security Beneficiaries, 1940-91

[Continued]

Year and sex	Total number (in thous.)	Average age	Percentage distribution, by age						
			Total	62-64	65-69	70-74	75-79	80-84	85 or older
1960	5,217	73.2	100.0	...	33.8	33.1	21.1	9.0	3.1
1965	6,825	72.9	100.0	6.9	29.7	29.5	19.9	9.9	4.1
1970	7,688	72.6	100.0	7.5	30.1	26.9	19.6	10.6	5.3
1975	9,163	72.3	100.0	9.3	32.2	25.6	17.1	10.1	5.7
1980	10,461	72.2	100.0	9.5	32.1	25.8	16.9	9.5	6.1
1985	11,817	72.3	100.0	10.9	30.2	25.9	17.3	9.6	6.1
1990[1]	12,985	72.5	100.0	10.3	30.0	25.3	17.8	10.2	6.4
1991[1]	13,227	72.6	100.0	10.2	29.5	25.7	17.9	10.3	6.4
Women									
1940	13	68.1	100.0	...	82.6	12.8	3.9	0.6	[2]
1945	71	70.8	100.0	...	47.1	40.0	10.2	2.3	0.3
1950	302	71.1	100.0	...	48.4	32.9	15.0	3.2	.5
1955	1,222	71.3	100.0	...	47.8	32.3	14.6	4.4	.8
1960	2,845	71.0	100.0	12.6	36.3	29.0	15.0	5.6	1.6
1965	4,276	71.8	100.0	12.2	31.6	28.1	17.6	7.7	2.8
1970	5,661	72.0	100.0	11.5	30.1	25.4	18.7	10.0	4.4
1975	7,424	72.2	100.0	11.8	30.4	24.2	16.9	10.6	6.1
1980	9,101	72.6	100.0	11.2	29.2	24.2	17.1	10.6	7.7
1985	10,615	73.3	100.0	11.0	26.9	23.9	17.9	11.4	8.8
1990[1]	11,842	73.7	100.0	9.9	25.9	23.0	18.5	12.5	10.2
1991[1]	12,048	73.9	100.0	9.5	25.4	23.2	18.6	12.7	10.5

Source: *Annual Statistical Supplement, 1992 to the Social Security Bulletin*, U.S. Department of Health and Human Services, Social Security Administration, January 1993, p. 194. *Notes:* Three dots (...) means not applicable. 1. Based on 10-percent sample. 2. Less than 0.05 percent.

★ 359 ★

Summary

Social Security (OASDI)

The Old-Age, Survivors, and Disability Insurance (OASDI) program provides monthly benefits to retired and disabled workers and their dependents and to survivors of insured workers. Benefits are paid as a matter of earned right to workers who gain insured status and to their eligible spouses and children and survivors. Retirement benefits were provided by the original Social Security Act of 1935, benefits for dependents and survivors by the 1939 amendments, benefits for the disabled by the 1956 amendments, and benefits for the dependents of disabled workers by the 1958 amendments.

[Continued]

★ 359 ★

Social Security (OASDI)
[Continued]

In 1991, about 132 million persons worked in employment or self-employment covered under the OASDI program. In recent years, coverage has become nearly universal for work performed in the United States (including American Samoa, Guam, the Northern Mariana Islands, Puerto Rico, and the Virgin Islands). About 95 percent of all jobs in the United States are covered. Coverage generally applies to persons irrespective of their age, sex, or citizenship.

Source: Annual Statistical Supplement, 1992 to the Social Security Bulletin, U.S. Department of Health and Human Services, Social Security Administration, January 1993, pp. 7-9.

★ 360 ★

Summary

Supplemental Security Income (SSI)

The Supplemental Security Income (SSI) program provides income support to persons aged 65 or older, blind or disabled adults, and blind or disabled children. Eligibility requirements and Federal payment standards are nationally uniform. The program is administered by SSA. The 1993 Federal SSI benefit rate for an individual living in his or her own household and with no other countable income is $434 monthly; for a couple (with both husband and wife eligible), the SSI benefit rate is $652 monthly.

The federally administered Supplemental Security Income (SSI) program was established by Congress in 1972, with payments beginning in January 1974. It replaced the former Federal-State programs of Old-Age Assistance (OAA), Aid to the Blind (AB), and Aid to the Permanently and Totally Disabled (APTD) in the 50 States and the District of Columbia. Residents of the Northern Mariana Islands became eligible for SSI in January 1978.

Under the SSI program, each eligible person living in his or her own household and having no other income is provided, as of January 1993, a monthly cash payment of $434 ($652 for a couple if both members are eligible).

Cost-of-living increases in SSI continue to be based on changes in the Consumer Price Index.

Source: Annual Statistical Supplement, 1992 to the Social Security Bulletin, U.S. Department of Health and Human Services, Social Security Administration, January 1993, p. 51.

★ 361 ★

Summary

Social Security Numbers Issued, 1937 to 1992

Since the Social Security program began, 351 million Social Security numbers have been issued, although some individuals have been issued more than one number.

Year	Social Security numbers issued[1] (in mil.)	Year	Social Security numbers issued[1] (in mil.)
1937	37.139	1965	6.131
1938	6.304	1966	6.506
1939	5.555	1967	5.920
1940	5.227	1968	5.862
1941	6.678	1969	6.289
1942	7.637	1970	6.132
1943	7.426	1971	6.401
1944	4.537	1972	9.564
1945	3.321	1973	10.038
1946	3.022	1974	7.998
1947	2,278	1975	8.164
1948	2.720	1976	9.043
1949	2.340	1977	7.724
1950	2.891	1978	5.260
1951	4.927	1979	5.213
1952	4.363	1980	5.984
1953	3.464	1981	5.581
1954	2.743	1982	5.362
1955	4.323	1983	6.699
1956	4.376	1984	5.980
1957	3.639	1985	5.720
1958	2.290	1986	5.711
1959	3.388	1987	11.621
1960	3.415	1988[2]	11.370
1961	3.370	1989[2]	8.049
1962	4.519	1990[3]	9.054
1963	8.617	1991	7.509
1964	5.623	1992	na

Source: Annual Statistical Supplement, 1992 to the Social Security Bulletin, U.S. Department of Health and Human Services, Social Security Administration, January 1993, p. 150. *Notes:* (na) means not available. 1. Excludes railroad account numbers. 2. Preliminary data. 3. Taxable earnings are preliminary estimates based on Social Security data; employment and total covered earnings are preliminary estimates based on data from Bureau of Labor Statistics and the National Income and Product Accounts.

★ 362 ★
Summary

Percent of Income from Social Security, 1990

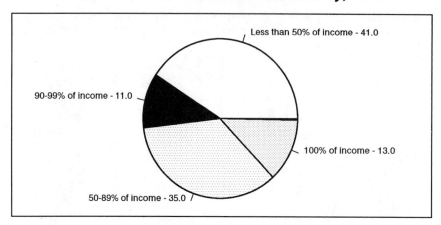

Figures based on a sample of 9,343,000 couples and 13,805,000 single "aged units".[1] From the source: "Social Security pays benefits to more than 90% of those aged 65 or older. It is the major source of income (providing 50% or more of total income) for 59% of the beneficiaries. It contributes 90% or more of income for about one-fourth of the beneficiaries, and is the only source of income for 13% of them."

	Percent of beneficiaries
Less than 50% of income	41.0
50-89% of income	35.0
90-99% of income	11.0
100% of income	13.0

Source: U.S. Department of Health and Human Services, Social Security Administration, *Income of the Aged Chartbook, 1990*, GPO, Washington, D.C., September 1992, p. 9. *Notes:* 1. "Aged unit" does not refer to the household, the family, or unrelated individuals, as used by the Bureau of the Census. The aged unit is either a married couple living together with the husband or wife aged 65 or older (generally measured by the age of the husband), or a person 65 or older who does not live with a spouse. The single person unit may be a widow(er), a divorced or separated person, a person legally married who does not live with a spouse, or a person who never married.

★ 363 ★

Summary

Receipt of Income from Sources, by Race and Hispanic Origin, 1990

Figures based on a sample of 9,343,000 couples and 13,805,000 single "aged units".[1] From the source: "Among the aged, whites are somewhat more likely than blacks or Hispanics to receive Social Security. They are much more likely to receive income from assets and from pensions. The groups are about equally likely to have earnings. Supplemental Security Income (SSI) is received much more often by the minority aged than by whites."

	White	Black	Hispanic[3]
Social Security	93	87	80
Asset income	74	29	38
Pensions[2]	46	28	24
Earnings	22	20	20
Social Security Income	5	20	23

Source: U.S. Department of Health and Human Services, Social Security Administration, *Income of the Aged Chartbook, 1990*, GPO, Washington, D.C., September 1992, p. 14. *Notes:* 1. "Aged unit" does not refer to the household, the family, or unrelated individuals, as used by the Bureau of the Census. The aged unit is either a married couple living together with the husband or wife aged 65 or older (generally measured by the age of the husband), or a person 65 or older who does not live with a spouse. The single person unit may be a widow(er), a divorced or separated person, a person legally married who does not live with a spouse, or a person who never married. 2. Persons of Hispanic origin may be of any race. 3. Includes private pensions, government employee pensions, and Railroad Retirement.

★ 364 ★

Summary

Share of Income from Sources, 1990

Figures based on a sample of 9,343,000 couples and 13,805,000 single "aged units".[1] From the source: "Money income for the population 65 or older comes largely from four sources. Social Security provides the largest portion - 36%. Asset income provides the next largest proportion - 24%. These two sources together account for 60% of the aged units' total income. Smaller, but still important shares come from earnings and from pensions other than Social Security. Only 3% of the aged units' income comes from other sources."

	Percent
Earnings	18.0
Social Security	36.0
Pensions[2]	18.0
Asset income	24.0
Other	3.0

Source: U.S. Department of Health and Human Services, Social Security Administration, *Income of the Aged Chartbook, 1990*, GPO, Washington, D.C., September 1992, p. 15. *Notes:* 1. "Aged unit" does not refer to the household, the family, or unrelated individuals, as used by the Bureau of the Census. The aged unit is either a married couple living together with the husband or wife aged 65 or older (generally measured by the age of the husband), or a person 65 or older who does not live with a spouse. The single person unit may be a widow(er), a divorced or separated person, a person legally married who does not live with a spouse, or a person who never married. 2. Includes private pensions, government employee pensions, and Railroad Retirement.

★ 365 ★

Summary

Social Security Benefits - Part I

Region, division, and state	Recipients (Dec. 31)					Payments (Mil. dol.)			
	1988				1980, total (1,000)	1988			1980
	Number (1,000)			Percent of population		Total[1]	Retired workers and dependents	Survivors	
	Total[1]	Retired workers[2]	Widows, widowers						
United States	37,706	23,467	5,217	15.3	34,682	213,863	148,668	44,120	118,524
Northeast	8,291	5,491	1,112	16.4	8,078	50,091	36,069	9,710	29,641
New England	2,090	1,422	261	16.1	1,996	12,270	9,013	2,248	7,138
Maine	209	133	28	17.3	198	1,106	772	221	633
New Hampshire	155	107	18	14.3	141	896	662	160	493
Vermont	85	54	11	15.2	81	475	334	95	270
Massachusetts	951	644	122	16.1	927	5,540	4,041	1,037	3,309
Rhode Island	178	124	21	17.9	170	1,030	760	176	600
Connecticut	512	360	61	15.8	479	3,223	2,444	559	1,833
Middle Atlantic	6,201	4,069	852	16.5	6,083	37,821	27,056	7,462	22,503
New York	2,800	1,848	362	15.6	2,873	17,191	12,358	3,236	10,715

[Continued]

★ 365 ★

Social Security Benefits - Part I
[Continued]

Region, division, and state	Recipients (Dec. 31)					Payments (Mil. dol.)			
	1988				1980, total (1,000)	1988			1980
	Number (1,000)			Percent of population		Total[1]	Retired workers and dependents	Survivors	
	Total[1]	Retired workers[2]	Widows, widowers						
New Jersey	1,205	817	156	15.6	1,138	7,562	5,524	1,413	4,321
Pennsylvania	2,196	1,404	333	18.3	2,072	13,068	9,174	2,813	7,467
Midwest	9,622	5,960	1,387	16.1	9,048	56,178	38,908	11,999	31,826
East North Central	6,654	4,092	964	15.8	6,215	39,638	27,175	8,541	22,383
Ohio	1,764	1,037	278	16.2	1,625	10,290	6,830	2,388	5,759
Indiana	891	550	125	16.0	822	5,283	3,624	1,117	2,941
Illinois	1,725	1,099	244	14.9	1,639	10,468	7,361	2,193	6,018
Michigan	1,453	878	208	15.7	1,359	8,806	5,938	1,905	4,969
Wisconsin	821	528	109	17.0	770	4,791	3,422	938	2,696
West North Central	2,968	1,869	423	16.7	2,833	16,540	11,733	3,458	9,443
Minnesota	654	422	90	15.2	617	3,632	2,625	740	2,045
Iowa	517	325	76	18.3	494	2,946	2,106	622	1,689
Missouri	895	553	126	17.4	863	4,950	3,406	1,037	2,855
North Dakota	111	65	17	16.6	105	580	406	133	330
South Dakota	126	76	19	17.6	120	646	454	142	371
Nebraska	264	169	37	16.5	256	1,475	1,066	307	853
Kansas	401	257	57	16.1	378	2,311	1,670	477	1,299
South	13,089	7,723	1,908	15.5	11,749	69,360	46,260	15,256	36,846
South Atlantic	6,825	4,259	920	16.1	5,987	37,073	25,626	7,459	19,420
Delaware	100	64	13	15.2	87	593	418	116	312
Maryland	591	378	85	12.8	531	3,407	2,370	736	1,861
District of Columbia	79	51	11	12.9	87	396	275	83	269
Virginia	801	480	118	13.3	721	4,255	2,824	938	2,280
West Virginia	365	183	66	19.5	360	1,994	1,172	523	1,162
North Carolina	1,023	623	141	15.8	900	5,303	3,561	1,084	2,730
South Carolina	517	302	70	14.9	450	2,666	1,727	564	1,351
Georgia	845	479	122	13.3	771	4,340	2,741	983	2,315
Florida	2,504	1,699	295	20.3	2,080	14,119	10,538	2,432	7,140
East South Central	2,556	1,383	402	16.7	2,417	12,847	7,977	3,047	7,093
Kentucky	630	329	104	16.9	602	3,191	1,926	781	1,793
Tennessee	797	455	121	16.3	740	4,102	2,652	921	2,230
Alabama	687	369	112	16.7	642	3,477	2,149	854	1,912
Mississippi	442	231	66	16.9	433	2,077	1,250	491	1,158
West South Central	3,708	2,081	586	13.8	3,345	19,440	12,657	4,750	10,333
Arkansas	458	259	67	19.1	444	2,268	1,462	494	1,276
Louisiana	632	308	111	14.3	588	3,213	1,872	883	1,750
Oklahoma	518	312	79	16.0	482	2,770	1,891	627	1,532
Texas	2,100	1,202	329	12.5	1,831	11,189	7,432	2,746	5,776

[Continued]

★ 365 ★

Social Security Benefits - Part I
[Continued]

Region, division, and state	Recipients (Dec. 31)				Payments (Mil. dol.)			
	1988			1980, total (1,000)	1988			1980
	Number (1,000)				Total[1]	Retired workers and dependents	Survivors	
	Total[1]	Retired workers[2]	Widows, widowers	Percent of population				
West	6,707	4,292	810	13.2	5,807	38,234	27,431	7,155	20,211
Mountain	1,824	1,139	222	13.7	1,482	10,068	7,113	1,961	4,968
Montana	133	80	17	16.5	119	729	501	151	398
Idaho	151	96	18	15.1	133	827	595	160	437
Wyoming	59	37	8	12.3	50	332	233	70	171
Colorado	397	242	53	12.0	332	2,182	1,500	456	1,115
New Mexico	206	116	27	13.6	176	1,052	700	229	531
Arizona	552	357	62	15.8	426	3,115	2,262	552	1,462
Utah	180	113	21	10.6	149	1,009	725	204	512
Nevada	146	98	15	13.9	96	822	597	139	341
Pacific	4,883	3,153	588	13.1	4,325	28,166	20,318	5,194	15,243
Washington	684	447	82	14.7	580	4,012	2,920	728	2,080
Oregon	473	315	56	17.1	412	2,737	2,015	492	1,452
California	3,553	2,278	432	12.5	3,198	20,481	14,685	3,812	11,269
Alaska	31	17	3	5.9	21	166	106	40	72
Hawaii	142	96	14	13.0	114	770	592	122	371

Source: U.S. Department of Commerce, Bureau of the Census, *State and Metropolitan Area Data Book 1991*, August 1991, p. 229. *Notes:* 1. Includes dependents of retired and disabled workers and other types of beneficiaries, not shown separately. 2. Excludes dependents.

★ 366 ★
Summary

Social Security Benefits - Part II

Region, division, and state	Supplemental Security Program[1]			
	Recipients (June) (1,000)		Payments for calendar year (Mil. dol.)	
	1989, total	1980, total	1988, total	1980, total
United States	4,514.4[2]	4,155.36[3]	13,403	7,690
Northeast	859.8	824.3	2,732	1,615
New England	199.3	202.5	569	356
Maine	22.9	22.0	50	29
New Hampshire	6.5	5.3	16	8
Vermont	9.7	9.0	27	16
Massachusetts	113.7	127.7	349	241
Rhode Island	16.6	15.1	46	25
Connecticut	29.9	23.4	81	39

[Continued]

★ 366 ★

Social Security Benefits - Part II
[Continued]

Region, division, and state	Supplemental Security Program[1]			
	Recipients (June) (1,000)		Payments for calendar year (Mil. dol.)	
	1989, total	1980, total	1988, total	1980, total
Middle Atlantic	660.5	621.8	2,163	1,259
New York	384.0	374.5	1,326	791
New Jersey	98.6	85.3	299	156
Pennsylvania	177.9	165.0	538	312
Midwest	780.3	661.7	2,141	1,097
East North Central	575.2	469.2	1,654	827
Ohio	144.1	119.4	397	200
Indiana	55.6	41.3	141	60
Illinois	160.6	123.1	466	207
Michigan	133.4	117.0	404	237
Wisconsin	81.5	68.4	245	124
West North Central	205.2	192.5	487	270
Minnesota	37.5	32.4	87	42
Iowa	31.3	25.7	72	34
Missouri	81.6	85.4	202	128
North Dakota	7.4	6.4	16	9
South Dakota	9.6	8.0	21	10
Nebraska	14.8	13.7	35	19
Kansas	23.0	20.8	54	28
South	1,834.3	1,765.7	4,464	2,682
South Atlantic	809.6	741.8	2,023	1,173
Delaware	7.7	7.2	20	11
Maryland	56.9	48.4	156	82
District of Columbia	16.2	15.1	51	31
Virginia	90.8	80.5	218	120
West Virginia	45.1	41.2	126	72
North Carolina	143.3	141.2	337	210
South Carolina	88.4	83.7	207	124
Georgia	155.4	155.3	366	233
Florida	205.9	169.3	543	291
East South Central	485.3	475.2	1,180	716
Kentucky	108.3	94.8	278	151
Tennessee	134.7	131.7	327	199
Alabama	130.2	136.1	307	195
Mississippi	112.1	112.6	268	171

[Continued]

★ 366 ★

Social Security Benefits - Part II
[Continued]

Region, division, and state	Supplemental Security Program[1]			
	Recipients (June) (1,000)		Payments for calendar year (Mil. dol.)	
	1989, total	1980, total	1988, total	1980, total
West South Central	539.4	548.6	1,261	793
Arkansas	73.9	79.2	161	107
Louisiana	129.3	138.1	330	221
Oklahoma	58.6	68.2	137	100
Texas	277.5	263.1	632	365
West	1,039.6	903.6	4,066	2,296
Mountain	146.1	116.5	383	188
Montana	9.1	7.0	23	11
Idaho	9.5	7.4	23	11
Wyoming	3.0	1.8	7	3
Colorado	34.9	31.0	88	46
New Mexico	29.0	25.5	73	41
Arizona	39.6	29.4	109	53
Utah	10.9	7.8	35	11
Nevada	10.1	6.6	25	11
Pacific	893.5	787.2	3,683	2,108
Washington	55.8	46.3	165	85
Oregon	29.4	22.2	76	35
California	791.2	705.5	3,391	1,962
Alaska	4.2	3.1	11	6
Hawaii	13.0	10.1	40	20

Source: U.S. Department of Commerce, Bureau of the Census, *State and Metropolitan Area Data Book 1991*, August 1991, p. 229. *Notes:* 1. Includes the children and one or both parents, or one caretaker relative other than a parent, in families where the needs of such adults were considered in determining the amount of assistance. 2. Includes unknown. 3. Includes data not distributed by state.

Costs

★ 367 ★

Social Security as a Percent of U.S. Budget

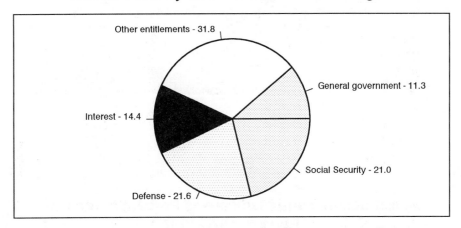

Social Security represents 21.0% of the U.S. budget in 1993. Combined with other difficult-to-control categories (Interest - 14.4%, Other Entitlements - 31.8%) the ability of Congress to manage the budget is seriously curtailed.

	Percent of U.S. budget 1993
Social Security	21.0
Other entitlements	31.8
Interest	14.4
Defense	21.6
General government	11.3

Source: Wall Street Journal, February 15, 1993, p. A12.

★ 368 ★

Costs

Social Security as a Percent of the U.S. Budget, 1953, 1973, and 1993

In the last 20 years, Social Security has remained at about the same percentage relative to the total budget of the United States. The big increase in the budgetary role of Social Security took place in the 1953-1973 period.

	1953	1973	1993
Defense	69	31	20
Social Security	4	20	21
Other	27	49	59

Source: Detroit Free Press, April 4, 1993, p. 4F. Primary source: Office of Management and Budget; Congressional Budget Office.

★ 369 ★

Costs

Social Security and Medicare as Percent of the U.S. Budget, 1970-1997

Social Security and Medicare, combined, are expected to rise from 29.4 percent of the U.S. budget in 1993 to 34.4 percent by 1997.

	Percent of U.S. budget		
	Social Security	Medicare	Both
1970	15.3	3.6	18.9
1975	19.3	4.2	23.5
1980	19.8	5.8	25.5
1985	19.7	7.4	27.1
1990	19.7	8.5	28.3
1991	20.2	8.6	28.8
1992	19.6	8.8	28.4
1993	19.9	9.5	29.4
1994	20.8	10.4	31.2
1995	21.7	11.5	33.2
1996	22.1	12.4	34.5
1997	21.7	12.7	34.4

Source: New York Times, August 20, 1992, p. 4. Primary source: Congressional Budget Office.

★ 370 ★

Costs

Social Security Trust Fund Balance, 2000, 2010, and 2020

Demographic factors indicate that as the Baby Boom generation retires and fewer people pay Social Security taxes, the Social Security Trust Fund will show a deficit by 2020. The data exclude interest earnings of Social Security trust fund reserves.

	In billions ($)
2000	55
2010	81
2020	-157

Source: Detroit Free Press, April 4, 1993, p. 4F. Primary source: Social Security Administration.

★ 371 ★

Costs

Number of Workers Paying into Social Security for Each Person Getting Benefits, 1970-2040

```
┌─────────────────────────────────────────────────┐
│  ┌──────────────────────────────────────────┐    │
│  │ 1970 - 3.7                               │    │
│  ├───────────────────────────────────┐      │    │
│  │ 1980 - 3.2                        │      │    │
│  ├───────────────────────────────────┐      │    │
│  │ 1990 - 3.4                        │      │    │
│  ├───────────────────────────────────┐      │    │
│  │ 2000 - 3.2                        │      │    │
│  ├───────────────────────────────────┐      │    │
│  │ 2010 - 2.9                        │      │    │
│  ├─────────────────────────┐                │    │
│  │ 2020 - 2.4              │                │    │
│  ├─────────────────────────┐                │    │
│  │ 2030 - 2.0              │                │    │
│  ├─────────────────────────┐                │    │
│  │ 2040 - 2.0              │                │    │
│  └─────────────────────────┘                     │
└─────────────────────────────────────────────────┘
```

The table shows the number of workers making Social Security payments for each person receiving benefits. In 1970, nearly four people (3.7) worked for each retiree; in 2040, the "support ratio" will be two for one.

	Worker per retiree
1970	3.7
1980	3.2
1990	3.4
2000	3.2
2010	2.9
2020	2.4

[Continued]

★ 371 ★

Number of Workers Paying into Social Security for Each Person Getting Benefits, 1970-2040
[Continued]

	Worker per retiree
2030	2.0
2040	2.0

Source: New York Times, August 30, 1992, p. 4E. Primary source: Social Security Administration.

★ 372 ★

Costs

Support Ratios of Elderly Persons, by Age, Race, and Hispanic Origin: 1990 and 2050
[Number of persons of given age per 100 persons aged 20 to 64]

	1990		2050	
	65 to 74 years	75 years and older	65 to 74 years	75 years and older
Total	12.4	8.9	19.2	22.4
White	13.1	9.6	19.7	24.0
Black	8.8	5.9	18.6	18.2
Other races	6.5	3.4	16.3	17.1
Hispanic origin[1]	5.7	3.5	13.5	13.7

Source: Sixty-Five Plus in America, Cynthia M. Taeuber, U.S. Department of Commerce, Economics and Statistics Administration, Bureau of the Census, U.S. Government Printing Office, Washington, D.C., 1992, p. 2-20. Primary source: U.S. Bureau of the Census, 1990 from 1990 Census of Population and Housing, Series CPH-L-74, *Modified and Actual Age, Sex, Race, and Hispanic Origin Data*; 2050 from *Projections of the Population of the United States, by Age, Sex, and Race: 1988 to 2080*, Current Population Reports, Series P-25, No. 1018. U.S. Government Printing Office, Washington, D.C., 1989 (middle series projections), Hispanic from *Projections of the Hispanic Population: 1983 to 2080*, Current Population Reports, Series P-25, No. 995, U.S. Government Printing Office, Washington, D.C., 1988 (middle series projections). *Note:* 1. Hispanic origin may be of any race.

★ 373 ★

Costs

Federal Outlays Benefiting the Elderly, 1990 and 1991

[Numbers in millions of dollars]

Type of outlay	Fiscal year	
	1990	1991
Medicare	93,510	101,949
Medicaid	14,862	16,975
Other federal health	5,927	6,698
Health subtotal	114,299	125,622
Social Security	194,073	207,329
Supplemental Security Income (SSI)	4,606	5,345
Veterans compensation-pensions	4,809	5,313
Other retired, disabled, and survivors benefits	29,389	30,506
Retirement/disability subtotal	232,877	248,493
Older American volunteer programs	119	121
Senior community service employment	346	359
Subsidized housing	5,778	6,078
Section 202 elderly housing loans	390	401
Farmers Home Administration housing	596	633
Food stamps	1,292	1,385
Older Americans Act	730	819
Social Services (Title XX)	581	588
Low-income home energy assistance	436	468
Other miscellaneous	1,055	2,375
Other subtotal	11,323	13,227
Total elderly outlays	358,499	387,342
Percentage of total federal outlays	30.0	30.0

Source: Aging America, Trends and Projections, prepared by the U.S. Senate Special Committee on Aging, the American Association of Retired Persons, the Federal Council on the Aging, and the U.S. Administration on Aging, 1991, Washington, D.C., p. 239. Primary source: Calculated by Chambers and Associates for the American Association of Retired Persons.

★ 374 ★

Costs

Social Security Contributions: Maximum Annual Amounts for Employed Persons, 1937-93

Contributions to Social Security vary based on income. The maximum contributions for an employed person are shown here. At the time this report was published, the maximum annual amount of earnings, that were taxable to Social Security, was expected to be around $57,000 for OASI/DI and $135,000 for HI in 1993. "Old Age and Survivors Insurance" (Social Security) is for monthly Social Security benefits payable to a fully insured worker over 62 years old and older. "Disability Insurance" serves persons who are physically or mentally disabled and have been "unable to engage in substantial gainful activity" for a certain length of time. "Health Insurance" includes contributions for Medicare and Supplemental Medical Insurance (SMI), but not Medicaid. For further explanations see the summary section at the beginning of the chapter.

[Numbers in dollars]

Beginning	Total		Old Age and Survivors Insurance (OASI)	Disability Insurance (DI)	Health Insurance (HI)
	$	% of income			
1937	30.00	1.0	30.00	...	...
1950	45.00	1.5	45.00	...	...
1960	144.00	3.0	132.00	12.00	...
1966	277.20	4.2	231.00	23.10	23.10
1971	405.60	5.2	315.90	42.90	46.80
1975	824.85	5.85	616.875	81.075	126.90
1980	1,587.67	6.13	1,170.680	145.040	271.95
1981	1,975.05	6.65	1,395.900	193.050	386.10
1982	2,170.80	6.7	1,482.300	267.300	421.20
1983	2,391.90	6.7	1,704.675	223.125	464.10
1984[1]	2,646.00	7.0	1,965.600	189.000	491.40
1985[1]	2,791.80	7.05	2,059.200	198.000	534.60
1986[1]	3,003.00	7.15	2,184.000	210.000	609.00
1987[1]	3,131.70	7.15	2,277.600	219.000	635.10
1988[1]	3,379.50	7.51	2,488.500	238.500	652.50
1989[1]	3,604.80	7.51	2,654.400	254.400	696.00
1990	3,924.45	7.65	2,872.800	307.800	743.85
1991	5,123.30	7.65	2,990.400	320.400	1,812.50
1992	5,328.90	7.65	3,108.000	333.000	1,887.90
1993	5,528.70	7.65	3,225.600	345.600	1,957.50

Source: Annual Statistical Supplement, 1992 to the Social Security Bulletin, U.S. Department of Health and Human Services, Social Security Administration, January 1993, p. 15. *Notes:* Three dots (...) means not applicable. 1. Includes tax credit.

★ 375 ★

Costs

Social Security Contributions: Maximum Annual Amounts for Self-Employed Persons, 1937-93

For explanations, see previous table.

[Numbers in dollars]

Beginning	Total		Old Age and Survivors Insurance (OASI)	Disability Insurance (DI)	Health Insurance (HI)
	$	% of income			
1937	...	...	...	...	...
1950	...	...	...	...	...
1960	216.00	4.5	198.00	18.00	...
1966	405.90	6.15	348.15	34.65	23.10
1971	585.00	7.5	473.85	64.35	46.80
1975	1,113.90	7.9	872.08	144.91	126.90
1980	2,097.90	8.1	1,624.58	201.37	271.95
1981	2,762.10	9.3	2,086.43	289.57	386.10
1982	3,029.40	9.35	2,207.25	400.95	421.20
1983	3,337.95	9.35	2,539.16	334.68	464.10
1984[1]	5,292.00	14.0	3,931.20	378.00	982.80
1985[1]	5,583.60	14.1	4,118.40	396.00	1,069.20
1986[1]	6,006.00	14.3	4,368.00	420.00	1,218.00
1987[1]	6,263.40	14.3	4,555.20	438.00	1,270.20
1988[1]	6,759.00	15.02	4,977.00	477.00	1,305.00
1989[1]	7,209.60	15.02	5,308.80	508.80	1,392.00
1990	7,848.90	15.3	5,745.60	615.60	1,487.70
1991	10,246.60	15.3	5,980.80	640.80	3,625.00
1992	10,657.80	15.3	6,216.00	666.00	3,775.80
1993	11,057.40	15.3	6,451.20	691.20	3,915.00

Source: Annual Statistical Supplement, 1992 to the Social Security Bulletin, U.S. Department of Health and Human Services, Social Security Administration, January 1993, p. 15. *Notes:* Three dots (...) means not applicable. 1. Includes tax credit.

★ 376 ★

Costs

Social Security as a Percent of the Total Retirement Income

Social Security is a large percentage of the retirement income of the poor (not further defined); however, Social Security receipts are also a significant proportion of the income of the "non-poor"—nearly 40 percent.

	Poor	Non-poor
Social Security	71.0	39.0
Interest dividends	4.0	28.0
Pensions	-	18.0
Welfare	19.0	-
Other	6.0	15.0

Source: Detroit Free Press, April 4, 1993, p. 4F. Primary source: House Ways and Means Committee, U.S. House of Representatives.

Benefits

★ 377 ★

Sources of Income for Older American Men, 1990

Components of retirement status	Age										
	55	60	61	62	63	64	65	66-69	70-74	75-79	80+
Number (in thousands)	1,084	987	975	925	1,088	926	1,010	3,492	3,328	2,333	2,092
Social Security benefits											
Aged[1]	[2]	[2]	[2]	34.7	48.0	52.7	79.1	85.6	94.7	97.2	93.3
Nonaged[3]	3.2	7.7	11.2	8.5	15.5	15.8	[2]	.1	[2]	[2]	[2]
Unspecified	[2]	.6	.4	.5	[2]	[2]	[2]	[2]	[2]	[2]	[2]
No benefits	96.8	91.7	88.3	56.4	36.5	31.5	20.9	14.3	5.3	2.8	6.7
Total percent	100.0	100.0	100.0	100.0	100.0	100.0	100.0	100.0	100.0	100.0	100.0
Employer pensions											
Pensions	14.9	27.1	30.4	42.5	39.0	47.9	54.7	53.1	56.0	55.1	46.2
No pensions	85.1	72.9	69.6	57.5	61.0	52.1	45.3	46.9	44.0	44.9	53.8
Total percent	100.0	100.0	100.0	100.0	100.0	100.0	100.0	100.0	100.0	100.0	100.0
Work status											
With job	87.6	70.1	62.0	58.7	47.8	42.4	35.0	29.7	13.5	10.4	5.6
No job	12.4	29.9	38.0	41.3	52.2	57.6	65.0	70.3	86.5	89.6	94.4
Total percent	100.0	100.0	100.0	100.0	100.0	100.0	100.0	100.0	100.0	100.0	100.0

[Continued]

★ 377 ★

Sources of Income for Older American Men, 1990

[Continued]

Components of retirement status	Age										
	55	60	61	62	63	64	65	66-69	70-74	75-79	80+
Aged Social Security benefits:											
Employer pensions											
With job	2	2	2	4.9	7.6	3.9	8.6	10.3	3.7	4.0	2.3
No job	2	2	2	18.0	19.1	26.3	37.4	37.3	48.5	49.1	38.5
No employer pensions											
With job	2	2	2	5.0	6.2	10.6	11.1	10.6	9.5	6.3	3.1
No job	2	2	2	6.8	15.0	11.9	22.0	27.4	33.0	37.9	49.6
No Social Security benefits											
Employer pensions											
With job	8.8	12.1	8.5	8.6	5.3	3.9	4.0	1.9	.1	2	2
No job	6.1	13.5	18.0	6.5	2.0	3.6	4.6	3.5	3.7	2.1	5.5
No employer pensions											
With job	77.8	57.8	52.0	39.3	27.1	22.8	11.3	6.8	.2	.1	.2
No job	4.2	8.4	9.9	2.0	2.1	1.2	1.0	2.0	1.3	.5	1.0

Source: Annual Statistical Supplement, 1992 to the Social Security Bulletin, U.S. Department of Health and Human Services, Social Security Administration, January 1993, pp. 133-134. Primary source: Restricted use file, Survey of Income and Program Participation. The OASDI benefit classification is based on Social Security program information that was matched to SIPP public use files and edited to be consistent with survey variables on Social Security benefit receipt, Medicare coverage, age, sex, and marital status. The file was developed as part of a joint statistical project between the Social Security Security Administration and the Bureau of the Census under the aegis of the agencies' 1967 Memorandum of Agreement on the Exchange of Statistical Information and Service. *Notes:* 1. Includes those 62 or older with retired-worker benefits or spouse benefits based on age, and those aged 60 or older with widow(er) benefits based on age, 2. Less than 0.05 percent. 3. Includes those with disabled-worker benefits, spouse or widow(er) benefits based on the case of a minor child, disabled-widow benefits, and children's benefits of students and adults disabled in childhood.

★ 378 ★

Benefits

Sources of Income for Older American Women, 1990

Components of retirement status	Age										
	55	60	61	62	63	64	65	66-69	70-74	75-79	80 or older
Number (in thousands)	1,064	1,115	1,156	1,080	1,005	1,249	1,195	4,351	4,416	3,467	3,927
Social Security benefits											
Aged[1]	2	6.7	9.1	49.5	57.7	67.9	87.9	91.2	95.3	96.2	92.2
Nonaged[3]	2.9	4.4	6.5	9.8	7.6	8.4	2	.1	2	2	2
Unspecified	.4	2	1.6	.5	1.4	1.8	2	.1	.1	.1	.3
No benefits	96.7	88.9	82.8	40.3	33.4	21.9	12.1	8.6	4.6	3.7	7.5
Total percent	100.0	100.0	100.0	100.0	100.0	100.0	100.0	100.0	100.0	100.0	100.0
Employer pensions											
Pensions	5.6	10.7	20.1	22.3	20.9	22.3	27.9	30.2	32.2	30.0	22.7
No pensions	94.4	89.3	79.9	77.7	79.1	77.7	72.1	69.8	67.8	70.0	77.3
Total percent	100.0	100.0	100.0	100.0	100.0	100.0	100.0	100.0	100.0	100.0	100.0
Work status											
With job	61.9	47.5	38.0	28.9	25.7	27.0	19.5	16.3	10.5	3.1	2.3
No job	38.1	52.5	62.0	71.1	74.3	73.0	80.5	83.7	89.5	96.9	97.7

[Continued]

★ 378 ★

Sources of Income for Older American Women, 1990

[Continued]

Components of retirement status	Age										
	55	60	61	62	63	64	65	66-69	70-74	75-79	80 or older
Total percent	100.0	100.0	100.0	100.0	100.0	100.0	100.0	100.0	100.0	100.0	100.0
Aged Social Security benefits:											
Employer pensions											
With job	[2]	.4	.6	1.6	3.4	2.7	2.8	2.8	2.5	.6	.8
No job	[2]	3.5	2.5	12.6	12.5	13.9	22.9	25.7	28.0	27.8	19.2
No employer pensions											
With job	[2]	1.5	2.1	7.2	4.7	10.7	9.3	10.1	7.4	2.2	1.4
No job	[2]	1.3	3.9	28.0	37.0	40.5	52.8	52.6	57.5	65.6	70.9
No Social Security benefits											
Employer pensions											
With job	2.6	4.5	6.2	1.1	1.2	.6	.5	.1	.2	.2	[2]
No job	2.3	1.5	7.8	5.2	2.3	1.3	1.7	1.5	1.5	1.3	2.8
No employer pensions											
With job	58.5	41.2	29.1	19.0	16.4	11.8	6.9	3.3	.5	.1	.1
No job	33.3	41.8	39.6	15.0	13.4	8.2	3.1	3.7	2.4	2.1	4.6

Source: Annual Statistical Supplement, 1992 to the Social Security Bulletin, U.S. Department of Health and Human Services, Social Security Administration, January 1993, pp. 135-136. Primary source: Restricted use file, Survey of Income and Program Participation. The OASDI benefit classification is based on Social Security program information that was matched to SIPP public use files and edited to be consistent with survey variables on Social Security benefit receipt, Medicare coverage, age, sex, and marital status. The file was developed as part of a joint statistical project between the Social Security Security Administration and the Bureau of the Census under the aegis of the agencies' 1967 Memorandum of Agreement on the Exchange of Statistical Information and Service. Notes: 1. Includes those 62 or older with retired-worker benefits or spouse benefits based on age, and those aged 60 or older with widow(er) benefits based on age. 2. Less than 0.05 percent. 3. Includes those with disabled-worker benefits, spouse or widow(er) benefits based on the case of a minor child, disabled-widow benefits, and children's benefits of students and adults disabled in childhood.

★ 379 ★

Benefits

Average Monthly Amounts for Social Security and Supplemental Security Income, 1950-1991

Data are shown in current and 1991 dollars.

Period	Consumer Price Index all items[1] (1982-84 = 100)	Retired workers[2]		Widowed mother or father and 2 children		Supplemental Security Income/ Old-Age Assistance[3]	
		Current ($)	1991 ($)	Current ($)	1991 ($)	Current ($)	1991 ($)
1950	25.0	43.86	241.93	93.90	517.95	43.05	237.46
1955	26.8	61.90	318.51	135.40	696.70	50.05	257.53
1960	29.8	74.04	342.62	188.00	869.97	58.90	272.56
1965	31.8	83.92	363.92	219.80	953.16	63.10	273.63
1970	39.8	118.10	409.20	291.10	1,008.61	77.65	269.04
1975	55.5	207.18	514.78	468.60	1,164.32	90.93	225.93

[Continued]

★ 379 ★

Average Monthly Amounts for Social Security and Supplemental Security Income, 1950-1991

[Continued]

Period	Consumer Price Index all items[1] (1982-84=100)	Retired workers[2]		Widowed mother or father and 2 children		Supplemental Security Income/ Old-Age Assistance[3]	
		Current ($)	1991 ($)	Current ($)	1991 ($)	Current ($)	1991 ($)
1980	86.3	341.40	545.53	759.20	1,213.14	128.20	204.85
1981	94.0	385.97	566.23	858.00	1,258.70	137.81	202.17
1982	97.6	419.30	592.43	885.50	1,251.13	145.69	205.85
1983	101.3	440.77	600.02	923.00	1,256.48	157.89	214.94
1984	105.3	460.57	603.16	948.30	1,241.89	157.88	206.76
1985	109.3	478.62	603.86	981.50	1,238.32	164.26	207.24
1986	110.5	488.44	609.56	994.00	1,240.48	173.66	216.72
1987	115.4	512.65	612.60	1,032.30	1,233.57	180.64	215.86
1988	120.5	536.77	614.28	1,070.40	1,224.96	188.23	215.41
1989	126.1	566.85	619.89	1,120.04	1,224.85	198.81	217.41
1990	133.8	602.56	621.02	1,177.70	1,213.79	212.66	219.18
1991	137.9	629.32	629.32	1,216.76	1,216.76	221.30	221.30

Source: Annual Statistical Supplement, 1992 to the Social Security Bulletin, U.S. Department of Health and Human Services, Social Security Administration, January 1993, p. 125. *Notes:* 1. Data from Bureau of Labor Statistics, Consumer Price Index for All Urban Consumers. 2. Average monthly Social Security amount in current payment status. 3. Beginning in 1974, represents payments to the aged under the SSI program.

★ 380 ★

Benefits

Average Monthly Social Security Benefits, by Amount of Benefit and Age of Beneficiary, 1991

[Data are based on a 10-percent sample]

Monthly benefit	Total	Age attained during 1991						
		62-64	65-69	70-74	75-79	80-84	85-89	90 or older
Total								
Total number (in thous.)	25,275	2,496	6,958	6,193	4,602	2,901	1,458	666
Average benefit ($)	629.30	540.70	603.50	636.90	703.30	653.40	620.80	564.70
Total percent	100.0	100.0	100.0	100.0	100.0	100.0	100.0	100.0
Less than $200.00	2.1	5.3	3.7	2.3	[1]	[1]	[1]	.1
$200.00-$249.90	2.7	2.7	1.9	2.4	3.3	3.6	4.0	4.4
$250.00-$299.90	3.9	4.6	3.6	3.6	3.7	3.7	4.6	7.7
$300.00-$349.90	5.4	8.4	6.2	5.1	4.5	4.4	3.9	4.2
$350.00-$399.90	7.5	12.4	8.9	7.0	5.2	5.3	5.7	6.8

[Continued]

★ 380 ★

Average Monthly Social Security Benefits, by Amount of Benefit and Age of Beneficiary, 1991

[Continued]

Monthly benefit	Total	Age attained during 1991						
		62-64	65-69	70-74	75-79	80-84	85-89	90 or older
$400.00-$449.90	6.5	8.5	7.1	6.5	5.3	5.3	5.8	7.2
$450.00-$499.90	5.9	5.7	6.3	5.8	5.2	5.6	6.0	7.4
$500.00-$549.90	5.6	5.2	5.5	5.5	5.2	6.0	6.5	7.7
$550.00-$599.90	6.0	5.2	5.4	5.7	5.8	7.2	8.6	9.9
$600.00-$649.90	6.9	5.3	5.7	6.4	6.9	9.6	10.6	11.8
$650.00-$699.90	7.9	5.6	6.4	8.0	7.7	10.0	11.2	16.3
$700.00-$749.90	8.2	6.2	8.2	9.4	7.3	8.3	10.4	5.6
$750.00-$799.90	7.7	9.2	9.3	6.5	6.5	7.6	8.4	2.8
$800.00-$849.90	6.3	11.3	6.2	5.7	5.6	6.5	4.1	1.8
$580.00-$899.90	4.1	2.7	4.4	5.0	4.2	4.3	2.3	1.2
$900.00-$949.90	3.4	1.2	4.1	4.6	3.4	2.9	1.3	.9
$950.00-$999.90	2.8	.5	3.5	3.5	3.4	2.1	1.1	.7
$1,000.00 or more	7.0	.1	3.7	6.9	16.7	7.7	5.5	3.6
Men								
Total number (in thous.)	13,227	1,345	3,896	3,396	2,363	1,368	616	242
Average benefit ($)	709.30	651.30	694.40	710.10	785.90	708.30	669.10	619.60
Total percent	100.0	100.0	100.0	100.0	100.0	100.0	100.0	100.0
Less than $200.00	1.6	3.1	2.7	2.0	.1	[1]	[1]	[1]
$200.00-$249.90	1.9	1.5	1.2	1.8	2.6	2.8	3.0	2.8
$250.00-$299.90	2.5	2.1	2.0	2.3	2.8	3.1	3.9	6.0
$300.00-$349.90	2.8	3.5	2.8	2.6	2.6	3.1	3.0	3.2
$350.00-$399.90	3.5	3.8	3.4	3.2	3.1	3.9	4.5	5.2
$400.00-$449.90	3.7	4.0	3.6	3.3	3.2	4.0	4.7	5.8
$450.00-$499.90	4.0	4.5	4.0	3.8	3.5	4.3	4.8	5.8
$500.00-$549.90	4.4	5.1	4.3	4.3	3.8	4.8	5.3	6.3
$550.00-$599.90	5.4	5.8	5.0	5.1	4.9	6.1	7.6	8.8
$600.00-$649.90	6.9	6.6	6.0	6.4	6.4	9.6	9.6	11.5
$650.00-$699.90	8.7	7.8	7.6	9.6	7.6	9.6	10.0	20.5
$700.00-$749.90	10.4	9.5	11.1	12.5	7.6	8.4	13.0	7.8
$750.00-$799.90	10.4	15.3	13.7	8.1	7.0	8.7	11.7	3.8
$800.00-$849.90	8.8	19.8	9.1	7.2	6.4	8.3	4.8	2.5
$580.00-$899.90	5.7	4.6	6.3	6.8	4.9	5.7	2.8	1.7
$900.00-$949.90	4.9	2.0	6.2	6.5	4.3	3.9	1.7	1.2
$950.00-$999.90	4.1	.8	5.4	5.0	4.5	2.9	1.3	1.0
$1,000.00 or more	10.2	.2	5.7	9.5	24.6	10.9	8.2	6.1

[Continued]

★ 380 ★

Average Monthly Social Security Benefits, by Amount of Benefit and Age of Beneficiary, 1991
[Continued]

Monthly benefit	Total	Age attained during 1991						
		62-64	65-69	70-74	75-79	80-84	85-89	90 or older
Women								
Total number (in thous.)	12,048	1,150	3,062	2,798	2,239	1,533	842	423
Average benefit ($)	541.60	411.40	487.70	548.00	616.20	604.40	585.50	533.30
Total percent	100.0	100.0	100.0	100.0	100.0	100.0	100.0	100.0
Less than $200.00	2.7	7.9	5.0	2.7	[1]	[1]	[1]	.1
$200.00-$249.90	3.7	4.2	2.9	3.0	4.1	4.4	4.6	5.4
$250.00-$299.90	5.4	7.4	5.7	5.2	4.7	4.2	5.1	8.6
$300.00-$349.90	8.3	14.0	10.5	8.2	6.4	5.5	4.6	4.8
$350.00-$399.90	11.8	22.5	15.9	11.6	7.5	6.6	6.5	7.7
$400.00-$449.90	9.6	13.8	11.6	10.3	7.5	6.5	6.6	8.0
$450.00-$499.90	7.9	7.1	9.3	8.3	7.0	6.7	6.9	8.2
$500.00-$549.90	6.8	5.4	6.9	6.9	6.6	7.0	7.3	8.5
$550.00-$599.90	6.7	4.4	5.8	6.4	6.8	8.1	9.4	10.5
$600.00-$649.90	7.0	3.7	5.3	6.3	7.4	9.6	11.4	12.0
$650.00-$699.90	7.0	3.0	4.8	6.2	7.8	10.2	12.1	13.8
$700.00-$749.90	5.8	2.3	4.4	5.7	7.0	8.2	8.5	4.4
$750.00-$799.90	4.6	2.0	3.6	4.6	5.9	6.7	6.0	2.2
$800.00-$849.90	3.5	1.3	2.6	3.8	4.8	4.9	3.7	1.4
$580.00-$899.90	2.4	.5	1.9	2.9	3.5	3.1	1.9	.9
$900.00-$949.90	1.8	.2	1.5	2.3	2.6	2.0	1.1	.7
$950.00-$999.90	1.4	.1	1.1	1.7	2.2	1.4	.8	.6
$1,000.00 or more	3.6	.1	1.1	3.8	8.3	4.8	3.5	2.1

Source: Annual Statistical Supplement, 1992 to the Social Security Bulletin, U.S. Department of Health and Human Services, Social Security Administration, January 1993, p. 198. Note: 1. Less than 0.05 percent.

★ 381 ★

Benefits

Average Monthly Social Security Benefits for Women Aged 65 or Older, by Type of Benefit and Dual Entitlement Status, 1991

Widows tend to fare much better than retired women who are only entitled as workers, averaging over $150.00 a month more.

Type of benefit	Total	65-69	70-74	75-79	80-84	85-89	90 or older
				Number of women			
Total[1]	17,902,600	4,951,100	4,567,600	3,604,400	2,540,900	1,462,100	776,500
Entitled as retired worker	10,896,800	3,047,200	2,813,600	2,232,000	1,526,300	855,900	421,800
Worker only	6,465,900	1,895,900	1,593,500	1,331,100	876,300	504,300	264,800
Dually entitled	4,430,900	1,151,300	1,220,100	900,900	650,000	351,600	157,000
Wife's benefit	1,764,900	795,400	594,800	249,600	97,000	23,600	4,500
Widow's benefit	2,666,000	355,900	625,300	651,300	553,000	328,000	152,500
Entitled as wife or widow only	7,005,800	1,903,900	1,754,000	1,372,400	1,014,600	606,200	354,700
Wife's benefit	2,578,700	983,900	794,700	482,600	221,200	80,200	16,100
Widow's benefit	4,427,100	920,000	959,300	889,800	793,400	526,000	338,600
				Average monthly benefit			
Total[1]	531.80	474.10	523.60	574.50	578.50	566.00	532.90
Entitled as retired worker	555.60	488.40	548.10	615.80	606.10	584.30	531.20
Worker only	542.90	492.50	532.10	605.10	581.90	557.60	498.60
Dually entitled	574.10	481.60	568.90	631.60	638.70	622.70	586.30
Wife's benefit	382.70	371.40	388.40	397.20	398.50	397.50	397.80
Widow's benefit	700.80	727.80	740.60	721.40	680.80	638.90	591.90
Entitled as wife or widow only	494.80	451.30	484.20	507.20	537.00	540.10	534.90
Wife's benefit	333.80	319.90	341.50	347.80	337.50	335.10	321.70
Widow's benefit	588.60	391.70	602.50	593.70	592.70	571.40	545.00

Source: Annual Statistical Supplement, 1992 to the Social Security Bulletin, U.S. Department of Health and Human Services, Social Security Administration, January 1993, p. 189. *Notes:* Based on 1 percent sample. 1. Excludes parents, special age-72 beneficiaries, and adults receiving benefits because of childhood disability.

★ 382 ★
Benefits

Number and Average Monthly Social Security Benefits for Older American Widows and Widowers, 1991

Age and Sex	Total		White[1]		Black[1]		Other	
	Number	Average monthly benefit	Number	Average monthly benefit	Number	Average monthly benefit	Number	Average monthly benefit
Total	5,028,830	583.60	4,549,260	595.80	399,070	463.50	80,500	491.20
Widowers	34,410	428.40	28,670	435.80	4,310	396.90	1,430	375.80
60-61	5,790	368.90	5,090	370.60	540	353.50	160	364.90
62-64	8,520	470.20	7,100	480.30	980	429.10	440	399.80
65-69	5,690	461.80	4,440	479.60	900	413.00	350	362.00
70-74	4,050	464.80	3,300	481.00	580	403.20	170	362.10
75-79	3,580	395.90	2,990	404.90	440	351.10	150	347.90
80-84	3,580	405.50	3,010	401.00	480	432.40	90	410.60
85-89	2,080	363.00	1,780	367.90	230	323.90	70	367.40
90 or older	1,120	416.30	960	426.20	160	357.20	...	...
Widows	4,994,420	584.70	4,520,590	596.80	394,760	464.20	79,070	493.20
60-61	156,860	544.60	136,930	558.10	16,630	455.30	3,300	436.70
60	62,890	544.10	55,130	557.70	6,480	448.60	1,280	438.40
61	93,970	545.00	81,800	558.30	10,150	459.60	2,020	435.70
62-64	407,320	560.20	352,320	575.40	45,150	463.70	9,850	458.80
62	119,020	554.20	101,980	570.50	14,080	454.70	2,960	464.40
63	137,700	560.10	119,190	575.00	15,320	467.50	3,190	447.30
64	150,600	564.90	131,150	579.40	15,750	467.90	3,700	464.30
65-69	907,570	590.90	799,100	605.20	88,610	478.10	19,860	517.50
65	168,510	584.10	146,290	599.20	18,110	477.80	4,110	516.00
66	173,180	591.00	151,350	605.90	17,710	482.30	4,120	509.50
67	185,120	590.60	163,590	604.50	17,350	476.20	4,180	523.80
68	187,290	593.00	166,180	607.10	17,400	474.50	3,710	519.30
69	193,470	594.80	171,690	608.60	18,040	479.70	3,740	518.80
70-74	949,720	605.00	855,730	618.10	78,240	480.00	15,750	515.50
70	204,600	599.70	183,730	613.00	17,350	475.80	3,520	518.80
71	200,620	603.90	180,480	616.90	16,410	480.40	3,730	519.30
72	183,630	603.80	164,780	617.10	15,730	482.10	3,120	511.50
73	184,090	609.10	166,680	621.70	14,670	481.10	2,740	524.20
74	176,780	609.40	160,060	622.40	14,080	481.10	2,640	501.60
75-79	891,830	595.30	811,660	607.90	66,800	462.50	13,370	495.10
75	177,730	599.00	160,450	612.30	14,590	472.40	2,690	488.30
76	177,570	599.00	161,570	611.30	13,430	467.00	2,570	515.10
77	179,230	595.30	163,280	607.70	13,230	463.20	2,720	492.70
78	180,020	593.80	164,070	606.50	13,100	453.80	2,850	507.40
79	177,280	589.50	162,290	601.70	12,450	454.60	2,540	470.60
80-84	789,330	587.50	730,550	597.70	49,690	456.20	9,090	482.80
80	169,770	589.70	156,830	600.20	10,670	455.50	2,270	489.80
81	166,610	588.80	154,170	598.90	10,610	463.50	1,830	468.00
82	157,770	584.80	145,180	595.50	10,710	454.10	1,880	500.60

[Continued]

★ 382 ★

Number and Average Monthly Social Security Benefits for Older American Widows and Widowers, 1991

[Continued]

Age and Sex	Total		White[1]		Black[1]		Other	
	Number	Average monthly benefit	Number	Average monthly benefit	Number	Average monthly benefit	Number	Average monthly benefit
83	152,540	589.40	142,190	599.00	8,860	454.90	1,490	477.60
84	142,640	584.30	132,180	594.50	8,840	452.10	1,620	473.60
85-89	545,770	573.10	509,800	582.50	30,900	440.30	5,070	464.90
85	129,980	579.10	121,090	588.40	7,530	449.10	1,360	465.00
86	122,960	575.10	114,600	584.10	7,350	451.40	1,010	455.50
87	107,490	574.00	100,640	583.40	6,010	429.30	840	486.60
88	98,000	569.00	91,810	578.00	5,200	432.30	990	452.30
89	87,340	564.90	81,660	573.70	4,810	431.70	870	469.20
90-94	256,370	553.20	240,700	561.60	13,510	418.00	2,160	466.80
95 or older	89,650	519.00	83,800	527.90	5,230	386.20	620	436.50

Source: Annual Statistical Supplement, 1992 to the Social Security Bulletin, U.S. Department of Health and Human Services, Social Security Administration, January 1993, pp. 175-176. *Notes:* Three dots (...) stands for not applicable. 1. For dependents and survivors, race is assumed to be same as that shown on the Social Security application of the wage earner on whose work record the benefit is based.

★ 383 ★

Benefits

Number and Average Monthly Social Security Benefit, by Race and Age, 1991: Both Sexes

[Data are based on a 10-percent sample]

Age and sex	Total		White[1]		Black[1]		Other[1]	
	Number	Average monthly benefit ($)	Number	Average monthly benefit ($)	Number	Average monthly benefit ($)	Number	Average monthly benefit ($)
All ages								
Old Age and Survivors Insurance	36,057,360	579.60	31,998,410	592.50	3,763,190	473.40	1,071,250	490.90
Disability Insurance	4,513,930	479.60	3,394,610	499.70	775,880	421.60	343,440	412.30
Total	40,571,290	568.50	35,393,410	583.60	3,763,190	462.70	1,414,690	471.80
Both sexes, by age								
Total, aged 62+	25,274,870	629.30	22,671,940	639.60	1,905,700	529.30	697,230	568.20
62-64	2,495,620	540.70	2,242,230	548.90	169,950	465.10	83,440	475.70
62	645,650	519.70	593,070	526.00	34,680	440.20	17,900	463.20
63	875,920	540.50	784,270	548.90	62,890	466.90	28,760	474.90
64	974,050	554.90	864,890	564.60	72,380	475.50	36,780	482.40

[Continued]

★ 383 ★

Number and Average Monthly Social Security Benefit, by Race and Age, 1991: Both Sexes
[Continued]

Age and sex	Total		White[1]		Black[1]		Other[1]	
	Number	Average monthly benefit ($)	Number	Average monthly benefit ($)	Number	Average monthly benefit ($)	Number	Average monthly benefit ($)
65-69	6,958,330	603.50	6,112,820	613.10	542,560	517.50	302,950	562.90
65	1,347,120	590.00	1,182,840	599.70	103,330	504.10	60,950	545.40
66	1,421,060	611.70	1,240,210	622.20	111,430	523.40	69,420	567.00
67	1,440,770	606.30	1,263,050	616.20	112,640	519.40	65,080	564.50
68	1,390,230	603.30	1,227,020	612.20	106,550	519.00	56,660	568.90
69	1,359,150	605.40	1,199,700	614.50	108,610	520.90	50,840	569.30
70-74	6,193,480	636.90	5,572,290	646.60	469,470	539.00	151,720	580.90
70	1,411,920	615.60	1,262,730	625.00	106,390	520.50	42,800	573.50
71	1,318,730	613.40	1,183,960	623.00	101,490	517.80	33,280	566.40
72	1,188,950	625.60	1,065,250	635.10	95,960	536.00	27,740	570.00
73	1,177,740	658.20	1,066,660	667.90	85,760	558.40	25,320	588.00
74	1,096,140	681.70	993,690	691.70	79,870	573.50	22,580	621.90
75-79	4,602,260	703.30	4,167,880	714.20	344,010	587.80	90,370	642.10
75	1,033,470	724.50	934,840	735.00	77,090	613.60	21,540	662.30
76	982,400	713.80	891,550	724.40	70,120	597.60	20,730	649.30
77	938,100	702.90	848,810	714.80	71,470	579.50	17,820	633.90
78	856,290	691.80	774,810	702.40	65,080	579.10	16,400	638.50
79	792,000	675.70	717,870	686.40	60,250	562.40	13,880	614.80
80-84	2,901,150	653.40	2,644,600	664.00	214,780	534.50	41,770	594.10
80	705,420	667.30	643,950	677.20	50,560	553.20	10,910	611.40
81	638,070	655.00	580,690	666.70	48,200	529.70	9,180	576.00
82	576,510	650.30	524,820	660.50	43,380	536.00	8,310	600.60
83	520,110	646.80	475,420	657.30	37,550	526.40	7,140	576.80
84	461,040	641.30	419,720	651.90	35,090	520.60	6,230	601.60
85-89	1,458,490	620.80	1,328,110	631.90	110,860	496.70	19,520	573.20
85	388,700	637.60	354,290	648.50	29,040	511.90	5,370	596.30
86	340,200	625.10	309,070	636.30	26,890	504.90	4,240	567.40
87	285,410	618.40	260,030	629.70	21,670	489.50	3,710	580.70
88	241,950	607.3	220,270	618.20	18,220	485.10	3,460	559.20
89	202,230	600.80	184,450	611.70	15,040	477.40	2,740	544.70
90-94	520,170	576.70	473,400	588.20	40,880	449.70	5,890	533.90
95 or older	145,370	522.00	130,610	534.90	13,190	405.60	1,570	423.60

Source: Annual Statistical Supplement, 1992 to the Social Security Bulletin, U.S. Department of Health and Human Services, Social Security Administration, January 1993, pp. 166-176. *Notes:* 1. For dependents and survivors, race assumed to be same as that shown on the Social Security application of wage earner on whose work record the benefit is based.

★ 384 ★

Benefits

Number and Average Monthly Social Security Benefit, by Race and Age, 1991: Men

[Data are based on a 10-percent sample]

Age and sex	Total		White[1]		Black[1]		Other[1]	
	Number[2]	Average monthly benefit ($)	Number	Average monthly benefit ($)	Number	Average monthly benefit ($)	Number	Average monthly benefit ($)
Total	13,226,940	709.30	11,925,950	721.50	951,150	588.00	349,840	623.60
62-64	1,345,320	651.30	1,209,890	664.20	93,360	532.50	42,070	544.10
62	345,280	631.70	316,520	642.00	19,310	508.40	9,450	538.50
63	474,050	651.50	425,270	664.30	34,580	536.50	14,200	548.80
64	525,990	664.10	468,100	679.20	39,470	540.80	18,420	543.30
65-69	3,896,210	694.40	3,462,410	707.00	295,950	578.30	137,850	627.50
65	755,010	690.50	670,100	704.00	57,310	570.80	27,600	611.50
66	795,150	710.20	703,300	723.90	61,170	586.60	30,680	643.60
67	805,020	698.80	714,690	711.30	60,830	583.40	29,500	634.60
68	779,530	687.80	695,790	699.60	57,560	574.80	26,180	622.40
69	761,500	683.90	678,530	695.50	59,080	574.90	23,890	622.40
70-74	3,395,950	710.10	3,075,080	721.40	242,560	592.60	78,310	627.30
70	791,780	691.50	713,770	702.70	56,710	574.30	21,300	627.70
71	737,090	681.90	665,960	692.90	53,460	565.40	17,670	617.20
72	651,430	694.40	587,170	705.50	49,990	587.70	14,270	610.10
73	632,280	733.40	575,590	744.70	43,530	615.90	13,160	626.60
74	583,370	763.20	532,590	774.70	38,870	636.90	11,910	663.20
75-79	2,363,140	785.90	2,154,320	797.50	161,470	656.80	47,350	696.40
75	543,230	814.50	495,570	826.00	36,970	685.60	10,690	726.70
76	509,330	801.40	465,670	812.80	33,240	668.10	10,420	715.80
77	482,280	784.40	439,080	796.90	33,500	650.20	9,700	682.60
78	434,210	769.70	395,090	780.90	30,330	647.50	8,790	687.40
79	394,090	745.90	358,910	757.30	27,430	622.70	7,750	656.30
80-84	1,368,040	708.30	1,246,650	719.70	94,360	584.90	27,030	614.30
80	344,610	729.80	315,060	740.40	22,910	612.00	6,640	632.00
81	305,330	710.80	278,240	723.40	21,300	578.00	5,790	597.00
82	272,480	700.80	247,830	712.10	19,360	579.40	5,290	618.90
83	236,940	697.30	216,220	708.90	15,870	570.40	4,850	595.80
84	208,680	691.30	189,300	701.90	14,920	575.60	4,460	625.40
85-89	616,110	669.10	558,960	680.60	44,200	544.40	12,950	595.70
85	170,630	686.50	155,010	697.20	11,950	568.80	3,670	616.30
86	146,080	671.00	131,950	683.20	11,310	550.40	2,820	584.30
87	119,310	667.10	108,260	678.40	8,480	538.60	2,570	614.50
88	99,180	653.60	89,930	666.10	7,080	516.40	2,170	585.60
89	80,910	650.70	73,810	662.20	5,380	523.90	1,720	554.70

[Continued]

★ 384 ★

Number and Average Monthly Social Security Benefit, by Race and Age, 1991: Men
[Continued]

Age and sex	Total		White[1]		Black[1]		Other[1]	
	Number[2]	Average monthly benefit ($)	Number	Average monthly benefit ($)	Number	Average monthly benefit ($)	Number	Average monthly benefit ($)
90-94	194,620	626.90	176,310	638.80	14,760	498.70	3,550	570.90
95 or older	47,550	589.70	42,330	606.00	4,490	459.10	730	450.10

Source: Annual Statistical Supplement, 1992 to the Social Security Bulletin, U.S. Department of Health and Human Services, Social Security Administration, January 1993, pp. 166-176. *Notes:* 1. For dependents and survivors, race assumed to be same as that shown on the Social Security application of wage earner on whose work record the benefit is based. 2. See OASDI program summary section in the original source for "Special Provisions for Railroad Retirement Beneficiaries".

★ 385 ★

Benefits

Number and Average Monthly Social Security Benefit, by Race and Age, 1991: Women

[Data are based on a 10-percent sample]

Age and sex	Total		White[1]		Black[1]		Other[1]	
	Number[2]	Average monthly benefit ($)	Number	Average monthly benefit ($)	Number	Average monthly benefit ($)	Number	Average monthly benefit ($)
Total	12,047,930	541.60	10,745,990	548.80	954,550	470.80	347,390	512.50
62-64	1,150,300	411.40	1,032,340	413.70	76,590	383.00	41,370	406.20
62	300,370	390.90	276,550	393.30	15,370	354.50	8,450	379.00
63	401,870	409.70	359,000	412.10	28,310	381.90	14,560	402.90
64	448,060	426.70	396,790	429.40	32,910	397.30	18,360	421.30
65-69	3,062,120	487.70	2,650,410	490.40	246,610	444.60	165,100	508.90
65	592,110	461.70	512,740	463.50	46,020	421.00	33,350	490.80
66	625,910	486.50	536,910	488.90	50,260	446.40	38,740	506.40
67	635,750	489.20	548,360	492.40	51,810	444.30	35,580	506.40
68	610,700	495.40	531,230	497.70	48,990	453.40	30,480	522.90
69	597,650	505.40	521,170	509.10	49,530	456.50	26,950	522.30
70-74	2,797,530	548.00	2,497,210	554.50	226,910	481.80	73,410	531.40
70	620,140	518.70	548,960	524.00	49,680	459.20	21,500	519.70
71	581,640	526.70	518,000	533.00	48,030	464.70	15,610	508.90
72	537,520	542.20	478,080	548.70	45,970	479.80	13,470	527.50
73	545,460	571.10	491,070	577.90	42,230	499.20	12,160	546.30
74	512,770	589.00	461,100	596.00	41,000	513.50	10,670	575.80
75-79	2,239,120	616.20	2,013,560	625.10	182,540	526.70	43,020	582.30
75	490,240	624.70	439,270	632.40	40,120	547.20	10,850	598.90
76	473,070	619.50	425,880	627.80	36,880	534.10	10,310	582.10
77	455,820	616.80	409,730	626.80	37,970	517.10	8,120	575.70

[Continued]

★ 385 ★

Number and Average Monthly Social Security Benefit, by Race and Age, 1991: Women

[Continued]

Age and sex	Total		White[1]		Black[1]		Other[1]	
	Number[2]	Average monthly benefit ($)	Number	Average monthly benefit ($)	Number	Average monthly benefit ($)	Number	Average monthly benefit ($)
78	422,080	611.80	379,720	620.80	34,750	519.40	7,610	582.00
79	397,910	606.10	358,960	615.50	32,820	511.90	6,130	562.30
80-84	1,533,110	604.40	1,397,950	614.30	120,420	495.00	14,740	556.90
80	360,810	607.60	328,890	616.60	27,650	504.50	4,270	579.30
81	332,740	603.80	302,450	614.50	26,900	491.50	3,390	540.00
82	304,030	604.90	276,990	614.30	24,020	501.10	3,020	568.50
83	283,170	604.40	259,200	614.20	21,680	494.20	2,290	536.50
84	252,360	599.90	230,420	610.90	20,170	479.90	1,770	541.60
85-89	842,380	585.50	769,150	596.40	66,660	465.10	6,570	529.00
85	218,070	599.30	199,280	610.60	17,090	472.10	1,700	553.20
86	194,120	590.50	177,120	601.40	15,580	471.90	1,420	533.80
87	166,100	583.40	151,770	594.90	13,190	457.90	1,140	504.40
88	142,770	575.20	130,340	585.20	11,140	465.10	1,290	514.60
89	121,320	567.50	110,640	578.00	9,660	451.50	1,020	527.90
90-94	325,550	546.60	297,090	558.10	26,120	422.00	2,340	477.90
95 or older	97,820	489.00	88,280	500.80	8,700	377.90	840	400.70

Source: Annual Statistical Supplement, 1992 to the Social Security Bulletin, U.S. Department of Health and Human Services, Social Security Administration, January 1993, pp. 166-176. *Notes:* 1. For dependents and survivors, race assumed to be same as that shown on the Social Security application of wage earner on whose work record the benefit is based. 2. See OASDI program summary section in the original source for "Special Provisions for Railroad Retirement Beneficiaries".

★ 386 ★

Benefits

Number and Average Monthly Social Security Benefit, with Reduction for Early Retirement, by Race, Age, and Sex, 1991

Benefits vary based on income, the amount contributed throughout the work history of the individual and his or her spouse, and the age at which the individual retires. Of the groups shown here, black women have the lowest average Social Security benefits.

[Based on 10-percent sample]

Age and sex	Total		White		Black		Other	
	Number	Average monthly benefit ($)	Number	Average monthly benefit ($)	Number	Average monthly benefit ($)	Number	Average monthly benefit ($)
Both Sexes	17,340,200	562.10	15,676,430	570.60	1,235,710	475.30	428,060	502.00
62-64	2,495,620	540.70	2,242,230	548.90	169,950	465.10	83,440	475.70
65-69	5,136,760	562.40	4,579,110	571.30	370,110	481.90	187,540	505.10
70-74	4,072,990	563.90	3,717,220	571.70	281,750	479.30	74,020	495.90
75-79	2,853,170	596.90	2,604,200	604.70	199,760	506.20	49,210	551.20
80-84	1,703,090	555.30	1,554,380	564.10	127,410	456.50	21,300	500.00
85-89	771,730	531.20	701,390	541.40	61,110	421.80	9,230	483.40
90-94	265,220	502.80	239,990	513.90	22,320	388.70	2,910	465.50
95 or older	41,620	465.00	37,910	475.00	3,300	358.30	410	397.90
Men	8,893,440	638.80	7,794,350	649.10	594,260	532.60	204,830	556.10
62-64	1,345,320	651.30	1,209,890	664.20	93,360	532.50	42,070	544.10
65-69	2,754,980	655.30	2,746,150	667.00	197,930	543.50	80,900	568.90
70-74	2,089,990	632.00	1,914,200	641.00	139,100	531.80	36,690	542.70
75-79	1,355,200	662.10	1,242,560	670.10	87,890	567.50	24,750	596.80
80-84	708,130	580.90	646,250	589.30	48,620	487.70	13,260	515.60
85-89	263,980	534.10	238,120	543.50	20,170	436.20	5,690	490.60
90 or older	75,840	495.90	67,180	506.90	7,190	399.30	1,470	464.10
Women	8,746,760	486.70	7,882,080	492.90	641,450	422.20	223,230	452.30
62-64	1,150,300	411.40	1,032,340	413.70	76,590	383.00	41,370	406.20
65-69	2,381,780	455.00	2,102,960	458.50	172,180	411.20	106,640	456.60
70-74	1,983,000	492.10	1,803,020	498.00	142,650	428.00	37,330	449.90
75-79	1,497,970	537.90	1,361,640	545.10	111,870	458.00	24,460	505.10
80-84	994,960	537.00	908,130	546.20	78,790	437.20	8,040	474.20
85-89	507,750	529.70	463,270	540.30	40,940	414.70	3,540	471.70
90-94	190,650	505.10	173,890	516.20	15,270	383.20	1,490	463.10
95 or older	40,350	465.90	36,830	475.60	3,160	359.30	360	404.10

Source: Annual Statistical Supplement, 1992 to the Social Security Bulletin, U.S. Department of Health and Human Services, Social Security Administration, January 1993, pp. 177-180.

★ 387 ★

Benefits

Number of Social Security Benefits Awarded, by Type of Award, 1990

An award is the action following the determination that an individual is entitled to a specified type of Social Security benefit. The action adds the individual to the Social Security benefit rolls maintained for that type of benefit and is counted as an award in a particular month. Award actions are processed not only for new entrants to the benefit rolls but also for persons already on the rolls whose benefits in one category are terminated but who become entitled to another type of benefit. These actions are called conversions.

Type of benefit sex, and age in month of award	Total[1]		White		Black		Other	
	Number	Average monthly benefit[2]	Number	Average monthly benefit[2]	Number	Average monthly benefit[2]	Number	Average monthly Benefit[2]
				Retired workers				
Total	1,642,300	581.30	1,399,200	591.90	129,000	495.00	96,000	533.80
62-64	1,131,900	539.80	992,100	550.20	84,000	461.70	47,600	478.20
65-69	488,600	673.80	394,200	694.10	42,100	552.10	43,100	586.60
70 or older	21,800	658.60	12,900	671.80	2,900	631.70	5,300	603.80
Men	963,600	687.00	832,600	701.30	73,700	567.40	46,100	603.70
62-64	637,100	651.30	563,600	665.40	47,000	537.10	23,000	553.40
65-69	314,800	760.50	261,500	779.30	25,500	620.30	20,800	670.10
70 or older	11,700	654.40	7,500	676.20	1,200	634.10	2,300	506.10
Women	678,700	431.20	566,600	431.10	55,300	398.50	49,900	469.30
62-64	494,800	396.30	428,500	398.70	37,000	365.90	24,600	408.00
65-69	173,800	516.90	132,700	526.30	16,600	447.50	22,300	508.80
70 or older	10,100	663.60	5,400	665.70	1,700	630.10	3,000	678.70
				Disabled workers				
Total	461,800	594.20	333,800	616.00	71,100	537.10	50,800	532.80
Under 30	46,400	413.60	30,900	422.80	8,600	403.30	6,200	370.60
30-39	77,200	546.90	53,200	558.80	14,000	527.10	7,600	499.60
40-49	94,000	594.50	65,300	604.80	15,200	592.40	11,900	534.40
50-54	63,400	627.00	47,300	646.80	9,300	558.50	6,500	579.80
55-59	97,800	637.60	74,200	662.00	14,100	545.00	8,900	586.70
60 or older	83,000	662.50	62,900	693.60	9,900	551.30	9,700	579.50
Men	293,300	667.90	216,600	690.60	43,200	588.90	29,500	619.70
Under 30	32,000	421.20	21,700	427.70	6,200	409.20	3,600	383.90
30-39	49,700	574.00	33,700	586.10	9,600	548.00	4,900	537.10
40-49	55,400	681.50	38,400	696.10	9,300	656.10	6,700	613.90
50-54	39,500	729.70	30,200	748.80	5,200	660.10	3,800	680.00
55-59	60,200	743.00	47,200	766.80	7,300	605.80	5,200	737.40
60 or older	56,500	753.60	45,400	771.10	5,600	658.00	5,300	704.70
Women	168,500	465.80	117,200	478.20	27,900	456.90	21,300	412.40
Under 30	14,400	396.60	9,200	411.00	2,400	388.10	2,600	352.10
30-39	27,500	497.90	19,500	511.60	4,400	481.60	2,700	431.50
40-49	38,600	469.60	26,900	474.60	5,900	491.90	5,200	431.90
50-59	37,600	468.90	27,000	478.70	6,800	479.70	3,700	374.90
60 or older	26,500	468.20	17,500	492.60	4,300	412.20	4,400	428.60
				Wives				
Total	349,800	269.70	302,700	278.20	25,200	202.50	18,400	211.90

[Continued]

★ 387 ★

Number of Social Security Benefits Awarded, by Type of Award, 1990
[Continued]

Type of benefit sex, and age in month of award	Total[1]		White		Black		Other	
	Number	Average monthly benefit[2]	Number	Average monthly benefit[2]	Number	Average monthly benefit[2]	Number	Average monthly Benefit[2]
Wives of retired workers	287,300	295.20	253,300	300.90	17,800	232.80	13,000	256.80
Entitlement based on care of children	19,000	185.40	14,700	200.10	2,600	134.80	1,200	103.80
Entitlement based on age	268,300	303.00	238,600	307.10	15,200	249.50	11,800	272.40
62-64	208,700	297.90	188,700	303.20	10,800	238.90	7,600	244.50
65-69	51,800	329.20	43,400	331.30	3,600	270.20	3,800	329.00
70 or older	7,800	265.80	6,500	259.70	800	299.20	400	[4]
Wives of disabled workers	62,500	152.50	49,400	161.30	7,400	129.70	5,400	103.90
Entitlement based on care of children	36,400	115.40	26,500	120.90	5,500	112.20	4,100	82.20
Entitlement based on age	26,100	204.30	22,900	208.10	1,900	180.40	1,300	172.10
Husbands								
Total	12,000	165.20	8,500	170.50	1,200	180.70	2,200	132.20
Husbands of retired workers	10,600	172.10	7,700	766.80	900	153.40	1,900	144.20
Husbands of disabled workers	1,400	112.80	800	77.60	300	[4]	300	[4]
Children								
Total	656,800	...	435,800	...	137,800	...	73,200	...
Children of retired workers	104,500	245.30	74,200	263.10	18,500	210.00	10,300	180.50
Children of deceased workers	294,900	394.50	194,500	427.80	65,300	336.90	30,300	306.40
Children of disabled workers	257,400	151.10	167,100	164.10	54,000	140.60	32,600	104.40
Under age 18	447,000	237.00	287,200	255.00	95,000	218.00	57,200	175.80
Disabled, aged 18 or older	36,400	274.90	27,000	300.10	4,500	206.50	4,600	197.00
Students, aged 18-19	173,400	374.40	121,600	401.30	38,300	309.20	11,400	314.10
Widowed mothers and fathers								
Total	55,200	389.30	38,800	418.70	8,900	324.80	6,000	279.70
Under 30	9,000	321.10	5,500	353.60	2,100	275.70	800	199.90
30-39	19,900	383.10	14,700	408.30	2,800	284.90	1,800	300.70
40-49	18,400	419.10	12,500	457.30	2,700	346.30	2,900	300.80
50-59	6,300	402.10	4,800	411.20	1,000	454.50	500	209.30
60 or older	1,600	457.20	1,300	466.90	300	[4]	...	...
Widowed mothers	49,800	400.70	34,600	435.50	8,400	326.60	5,400	276.80
Widowed fathers	5,400	283.60	4,200	279.80	500	294.50	600	305.80
Nondisabled widows and widowers								
Total	393,400	594.90	339,600	610.00	38,500	488.20	11,100	517.10
60-64	187,800	539.10	155,200	554.10	24,600	462.90	6,000	478.40
65-69	77,500	630.10	66,300	642.90	7,100	532.40	3,000	579.70
70-74	46,300	668.30	41,000	676.10	3,600	600.10	1,200	573.50
75 or older	81,800	648.20	77,100	659.10	3,200	459.20	900	491.00
Widows	380,300	602.50	328,900	618.00	37,400	486.60	10,000	536.40
Widowers	13,100	375.90	10,700	362.80	1,100	542.00	1,100	341.80
Disabled widows and widowers								
Total	13,300	383.80	8,500	424.00	3,600	320.30	900	285.80
50-54	4,700	402.10	3,100	440.30	[3]	...	[3]	...
55-59	6,900	374.40	4,400	412.70	[3]	...	[3]	...

[Continued]

★ 387 ★

Number of Social Security Benefits Awarded, by Type of Award, 1990

[Continued]

Type of benefit sex, and age in month of award	Total[1]		White		Black		Other	
	Number	Average monthly benefit[2]	Number	Average monthly benefit[2]	Number	Average monthly benefit[2]	Number	Average monthly Benefit[2]
60 or older	1,700	371.10	1,000	423.00	3	...	3	...
Widows	12,500	386.40	7,800	431.30	3,500	319.60	900	285.80
Widowers	800	342.50	700	342.00	100	4	...	...

Source: Annual Statistical Supplement, 1992 to the Social Security Bulletin, U.S. Department of Health and Human Services, Social Security Administration, January 1993, pp. 239-240. *Notes:* Three dots (...) means not applicable. 1. Includes persons with unknown race. 2. Benefits awarded before the December increase are converted to the December rates before computation of the averages. 3. Base figure too small to meet statistical standards for reliability of derived figure. 4. Average benefit not shown for groups with fewer than 500 beneficiaries.

★ 388 ★

Benefits

Aged Families Receiving Social Security Benefits, by Share of Income from Benefits and Race, 1991

Based on data from the Current Population Survey (CPS) for the civilian noninstitutionalized population.

Social Security share of money income for year[1]	Individuals aged 65 or older living alone or with nonrelatives only				Multiperson families with householder 65 or older			
	Total	Nonpoor	Poor	Percent poor	Total	Nonpoor	Poor	Percent poor
All races[2]								
Total number (in millions)	10.2	7.7	2.6	...	11.1	10.4	0.7	...
Total percent	100	100	100	25	100	100	100	7
No Social Security benefits	8	7	13	40	7	6	21	19
Some Social Security benefits	92	93	87	24	93	94	79	6
Less than one-fourth of income	9	12	1	3	23	24	5	1
One-fourth up to one-half of income	22	27	5	6	29	30	9	2
One-half up to three-fourths of income	21	23	14	17	22	22	18	5
Three-fourths or more of income	40	31	67	41	18	17	46	16
White								
Total number (in millions)	9.1	7.1	2.0	...	9.9	9.5	.5	...
Total percent	100	100	100	25	100	100	100	7
No Social Security benefits	8	6	12	34	7	6	23	15
Some Social Security benefits	92	94	88	21	93	94	77	4
Less than one-fourth of income	9	12	1	2	23	24	5	1
One-fourth up to one-half of income	22	27	5	4	29	30	9	1
One-half up to three-fourths of income	21	24	14	14	23	23	15	3
Three-fourths or more of income	39	31	69	38	18	16	48	13

[Continued]

★ 388 ★

Aged Families Receiving Social Security Benefits, by Share of Income from Benefits and Race, 1991

[Continued]

Social Security share of money income for year[1]	Individuals aged 65 or older living alone or with nonrelatives only				Multiperson families with householder 65 or older			
	Total	Nonpoor	Poor	Percent poor	Total	Nonpoor	Poor	Percent poor
Black								
Total number (in millions)	1.0	.5	.5	...	1.0	.7	.2	...
Total percent	100	100	100	25	100	100	100	7
No Social Security benefits	13	8	17	70	10	7	19	45
Some Social Security benefits	87	92	83	50	90	93	81	21
Less than one-fourth of income	5	10	1	6	20	25	6	7
One-fourth up to one-half of income	16	27	7	22	27	32	11	10
One-half up to three-fourths of income	20	22	18	47	18	16	25	32
Three-fourths or more of income	46	33	58	66	25	20	40	38

Source: *Annual Statistical Supplement, 1992 to the Social Security Bulletin*, U.S. Department of Health and Human Services, Social Security Administration, January 1993, p. 141. Primary source: Public use file of the March 1992 Income Supplement, Current Population Survey, Bureau of the Census. For a discussion of standard errors of estimated numbers and percentages, see Bureau of the Census, Current Population Reports, P-60 series. *Notes:* Three dots (...) means not applicable. 1. Payments under Old-Age Survivors, and Disability Insurance program any time in 1991 to any family member as reported in the March 1992 Current Population Survey. For 1987, according to program records, receipt of Social Security benefits reported by survey respondents represented 92 percent of aggregate Social Security payments. 2. Includes other races not shown below.

★ 389 ★

Benefits

Percentage of Total Income Which Comes From Social Security, by Selected Population Characteristics, 1990

About half of the income of older Americans is in some form of Social Security.

Characteristic	Number (in thous.)	Median monthly family amount		
		Social Security benefit	Total money income	% of income from Social Security
Total	23,348	782	1,676	.51
Men	12,454	837	1,858	.48
Women	10,894	703	1,467	.55
Age of beneficiary				
Men				
62-64	1,331	695	2,054	.37
65-69	3,787	826	2,086	.42
70-74	3,132	955	1,931	.51
75 or older	4,203	866	1,537	.60
Women				
62-64	1,111	832	2,206	.39
65-69	2,982	797	1,834	.47

[Continued]

★ 389 ★

Percentage of Total Income Which Comes From Social Security, by Selected Population Characteristics, 1990

[Continued]

Characteristic	Number (in thous.)	Median monthly family amount		
		Social Security benefit	Total money income	% of income from Social Security
70-74	2,532	752	1,464	.58
75 or older	4,269	620	1,094	.66
Marital status[1]				
Men				
Married	9,399	943	2,070	.47
Widowed	1,690	620	1,267	.53
Divorced	550	594	993	.55
Never married	510	635	1,187	.61
Women				
Married	4,891	1,017	2,051	.50
Widowed	4,205	563	983	.62
Divorced	816	485	978	.59
Never married	812	567	1,174	.51
Size of family				
1 person	6,990	556	894	.65
2 persons	13,261	962	1,939	.51
3 persons or more	3,098	826	3,001	.29
Monthly family income				
Less than $500	1,199	344	406	.95
$500-$999	4,539	587	758	.84
$1,000-$1,499	4,551	815	1,247	.67
$1,500-$1,999	3,639	937	1,769	.53
$2,000-$2,499	2,645	979	2,218	.45
$2,500-$2,999	1,961	1,048	2,729	.38
$3,000 or more	4,812	961	4,150	.21
Family source of income				
Earnings				
Yes	6,468	743	2,692	.30
No	16,881	800	1,398	.61
Assets				
Yes	18,841	826	1,903	.47
No	4,508	620	902	.75
Means-tested cash benefits[2]				
Yes	1,476	461	934	.60
No	21,873	802	1,738	.50

[Continued]

★ 389 ★

Percentage of Total Income Which Comes From Social Security, by Selected Population Characteristics, 1990
[Continued]

Characteristic	Number (in thous.)	Median monthly family amount		
		Social Security benefit	Total money income	% of income from Social Security
Other cash income[3]				
Yes	15,136	858	1,994	.45
No	8,213	669	1,085	.72

Source: *Annual Statistical Supplement, 1992 to the Social Security Bulletin*, U.S. Department of Health and Human Services, Social Security Administration, January 1993, pp. 186-188. Primary source: Restricted use file, Survey of Income and Program Participation. The OASDI benefit classification is based on Social Security program information that was matched to SIPP public use files and edited to be consistent with survey variables on Social Security benefit receipt, Medicare coverage, age, sex, and marital status. The file was developed as part of a joint statistical project between the Social Security Administration and the Bureau of the Census under the aegis of the agencies' 1967 Memorandum of Agreement on the Exchange of Statistical Information and Service. *Notes:* Based on data from the Survey of Income and Program Participation (SIPP). 1. Excludes those who are married, spouse absent, or separated. 2. Includes SSI, veterans' pensions, AFDC, general assistance, Indian, Cuban or refugee assistance, and other cash welfare benefits. 3. Includes: retirement benefits and annuities other than Social Security, veterans' compensation, unemployment compensation, workers' compensation and other sickness and disability benefits, child support, foster child care payments, alimony, money from relatives or friends, assistance from charitable groups, lump-sum payments, income from estates and trusts, income from roomers and boarders, casual earnings, National Guard and Reserve pay, GI education benefits, and other income not elsewhere included.

★ 390 ★
Benefits

Estimated Number and Percent Fully Insured in the Social Security Area, by Age and Sex, 1989-93

The population commonly referred to as "the Social Security area" includes the following: residents of the 50 States, the District of Columbia, Puerto Rico, the Virgin Islands, Guam, American Samoa, Federal civilian employees and persons in the Armed Forces abroad and their dependents, crew members of vessels, and all other U.S. citizens abroad. Eligibility for most types of Social Security benefits requires that workers be fully insured. To become eligible a worker or family member of a worker must earn a certain number of credits based on that worker's amount of experience in covered- or self-employment.

[Numbers in thousands]

Age attained at beginning of year	1989		1990		1991		1992		1993	
	Pop-ulation	% fully insured	Pop-ulation	% fully insured	Pop-ulation	% fully insured	Pop-ulation	% fully insured	Pop-ulation	% fully insured
Both sexes	255,691	82.0[1]	258,241	83.0[1]	260,904	83.0[1]	263,402	84.0[1]	265,972	84.0[1]
55-59	11,084	79.0	10,963	79.0	10,910	80.0	10,917	81.0	11,055	81.0
60-64	11,110	78.0	11,039	78.0	10,976	79.0	10,881	79.0	10,712	79.0
65-69	10,042	78.0	10,231	78.0	10,256	79.0	10,216	79.0	10,212	79.0
70-74	8,028	77.0	8,110	77.0	8,313	77.0	8,525	78.0	8,680	78.0
75 or older	13,035	71.0	13,346	72.0	13,628	73.0	13,915	73.0	14,227	74.0

[Continued]

★ 390 ★

Estimated Number and Percent Fully Insured in the Social Security Area, by Age and Sex, 1989-93
[Continued]

Age attained at beginning of year	1989		1990		1991		1992		1993	
	Pop-ulation	% fully insured	Pop-ulation	% fully insured	Pop-ulation	% fully insured	Pop-ulation	% fully insured	Pop-ulation	% fully insured
Men	125,951	89.0[1]	127,235	90.0[1]	128,571	90.0[1]	129,833	90.0[1]	131,129	90.0[1]
55-59	5,389	90.0	5,333	90.0	5,310	91.0	5,319	91.0	5,391	92.0
60-64	5,254	90.0	5,235	90.0	5,220	91.0	5,185	90.0	5,112	91.0
65-69	4,606	91.0	4,692	91.0	4,698	91.0	4,677	91.0	4,683	92.0
70-74	3,469	92.0	3,519	91.0	3,624	91.0	3,731	91.0	3,805	91.0
75 or older	4,565	93.0	4,686	93.0	4,796	94.0	4,908	94.0	5,034	94.0
Women	129,739	75.0[1]	131,006	76.0[1]	132,333	77.0[1]	133,569	77.0[1]	134,844	78.0[1]
55-59	5,695	68.0	5,630	69.0	5,600	70.0	5,598	70.0	5,664	71.0
60-64	5,856	67.0	5,804	67.0	5,756	68.0	5,696	69.0	5,601	69.0
65-69	5,435	67.0	5,539	68.0	5,557	68.0	5,538	68.0	5,529	69.0
70-74	4,559	66.0	4,591	66.0	4,690	67.0	4,795	67.0	4,874	67.0
75 or older	8,470	59.0	8,660	60.0	8,833	61.0	9,007	62.0	9,193	63.0

Source: *Annual Statistical Supplement, 1992 to the Social Security Bulletin*, U.S. Department of Health and Human Services, Social Security Administration, January 1993, p. 164. *Note:* 1. Percent of population fully insured aged 17 or older.

★ 391 ★
Benefits

Mean Age of Persons Initially Awarded Social Security Retirement Benefits, by Sex, 1950-89

This table shows the decline in the median age of retirement. The source suggests that this decline, combined with an increase in longevity, "raise[s] the economic dependency burden the elderly place on younger cohorts still in the work force. This tends to make increases in per capita income harder to achieve, even as the cost of income transfers to the elderly rise."

Year	Age	
	Men	Women
1950	68.7	68.0
1955	68.4	67.8
1960	66.8	65.2
1965	65.8	66.2
1970	64.4	63.9
1975	64.0	63.7
1980	63.9	63.5

[Continued]

★ 391 ★

Mean Age of Persons Initially Awarded Social Security Retirement Benefits, by Sex, 1950-89

[Continued]

Year	Age	
	Men	Women
1985	63.7	63.4
1989	63.7	63.4

Source: "Age at Retirement," *Family Economics Review*, 1992, Vol. 5., No.4, pp. 28-30. Primary source: Social Security Bulletin, *Annual Statistical Supplement, 1990*, Social Security Administration, 1990, p. 236, table 6B5.

★ 392 ★

Benefits

Social Security Benefits and Benefits Withheld Due to Other Earnings, for Initial Awards, 1991

An award is the action following the determination that an individual is entitled to a specified type of Social Security benefit. The action adds the individual to the Social Security benefit rolls maintained for that type of benefit and is counted as an award in a particular month. Award actions are processed not only for new entrants to the benefit rolls but also for persons already on the rolls whose benefits in one category are terminated but who become entitled to another type of benefit. These actions are called conversions.

Age in month of award and sex	Number of beneficiaries					Percentage distribution				
	All initial awards[1]	Benefits received for all entitlement months[2]	Benefits withheld due to earnings			All initial awards[1]	Benefits received for all entitlement months[2]	Benefits withheld due to earnings		
			All entitlement months	One-half or more of entitlement months	Less than on-half of entitlement months			All entitlement months	One-half or more of entitlement months	Less than one-half of entitlement months
Total	1,492,200	1,213,700	108,300	108,700	55,900	100.0	100.0	100.0	100.0	100.0
62-64	1,128,900	1,019,900	16,500	61,900	27,800	75.7	84.0	15.2	56.9	49.7
62	837,500	792,700	7,600	25,300	10,200	56.1	65.3	7.0	23.3	18.2
63	128,100	111,600	2,700	9,800	3,700	8.6	9.2	2.5	9.0	6.6
64	163,300	115,600	6,200	26,800	13,900	10.9	9.5	5.7	24.7	24.9
65	267,600	128,500	82,400	33,800	21,700	17.9	10.6	76.1	31.1	38.8
Reduced[3]	49,600	33,900	3,100	7,400	4,900	3.3	2.8	2.9	6.8	8.8
Unreduced	218,000	94,600	79,300	26,400	16,800	14.6	7.8	73.2	24.3	30.1
66-69	76,100	46,100	9,400	13,000	6,400	5.1	3.8	8.7	12.0	11.4
70 or older	19,600	19,200	...	...	...	1.3	1.6	...	...	...
Men	873,300	686,700	77,000	71,400	35,300	100.0	100.0	100.0	100.0	100.0
62-64	639,800	570,000	11,200	39,800	17,300	73.3	83.0	14.5	55.7	49.0
62	457,900	431,200	4,800	15,300	5,800	52.4	62.8	6.2	21.4	16.4
63	80,400	69,500	1,800	6,400	2,600	9.2	10.1	2.3	9.0	7.4
64	101,500	69,300	4,600	18,100	8,900	11.6	10.1	6.0	25.4	25.2
65	172,200	75,900	58,800	22,900	14,100	19.7	11.1	76.4	32.1	39.9
Reduced[3]	29,300	20,500	1,800	4,300	2,700	3.4	3.0	2.3	6.0	7.6
Unreduced	142,900	55,400	57,000	18,600	11,400	16.4	8.1	74.0	26.1	32.3
66-69	50,100	29,700	7,000	8,700	3,900	5.7	4.3	9.1	12.2	11.0
70 or older	11,200	11,100	...	...	...	1.3	1.6	...	...	...
Women	618,900	527,000	31,300	37,300	20,600	100.0	100.0	100.0	100.0	100.0
62-64	489,100	449,900	5,300	22,100	10,500	79.0	85.4	16.9	59.2	51.0
62	379,600	361,500	2,800	10,000	4,400	61.3	68.6	8.9	26.8	21.4
63	47,700	42,100	900	3,400	1,100	7.7	8.0	2.9	9.1	5.3
64	61,800	46,300	1,600	8,700	5,000	10.0	8.8	5.1	23.3	24.3
65	95,400	52,600	23,600	10,900	7,600	15.4	10.0	75.4	29.2	36.9
Reduced[3]	20,300	13,400	1,300	3,100	2,200	3.3	2.5	4.2	8.3	10.7
Unreduced	75,100	39,200	22,300	7,800	5,400	12.1	7.4	71.2	20.9	26.2

[Continued]

★ 392 ★

Social Security Benefits and Benefits Withheld Due to Other Earnings, for Initial Awards, 1991

[Continued]

Age in month of award and sex	Number of beneficiaries					Percentage distribution				
	All initial awards[1]	Benefits received for all entitlement months[2]	Benefits withheld due to earnings			All initial awards[1]	Benefits received for all entitlement months[2]	Benefits withheld due to earnings		
			All entitlement months	One-half or more of entitlement months	Less than on-half of entitlement months			All entitlement months	One-half or more of entitlement months	Less than one-half of entitlement months
66-69	26,000	16,400	2,400	4,300	2,500	4.2	3.1	7.7	11.5	12.1
70 or older	8,400	8,100	...	...	...	1.4	1.5	...	...	...

Source: Annual Statistical Supplement, 1992 to the Social Security Bulletin, U.S. Department of Health and Human Services, Social Security Administration, January 1993, p. 243. *Notes:* Excludes persons whose benefits were converted from disabled worker to retired worker in 1991. Problems in processing award data resulted in a difference of 14,500 awards. Three dots (...) stands for not applicable. 1. Includes 5,600 awards for which benefits were withheld for reasons other than earnings. 2. Months of entitlement begin with the month of award and end either in December 1991 or the month before the retired-worker benefit is terminated. 3. Includes awards to retired workers aged 65 at time of award, when the first month of entitlement to benefits preceded the attainment of age 65.

★ 393 ★

Benefits

Social Security's Role in Reducing Poverty, by Marital Status and Race, 1990

Figures based on a sample of 9,343,000 couples and 13,805,000 single "aged units".[1] From the source: "Although there are aged beneficiaries with family income below the poverty line[2], the poverty rate would be much higher if they did not have their Social Security benefits. Fourteen percent of the aged are poor, and 36% are kept out of poverty by their Social Security benefits—so that the total poverty rate without Social Security would be about 50%. Although poverty rates vary considerably by marital status and race, the proportion kept out of poverty by their Social Security benefits is close to one-third for all groups."

[Percent of units.]

	Kept out of poverty by Social Security	Poor with Social Security
Total beneficiaries	36.0	14.0
Married	32.0	5.0
Non-married	38.0	20.0
White	36.0	11.0
Black	34.0	35.0

Source: U.S. Department of Health and Human Services, Social Security Administration, *Income of the Aged Chartbook, 1990,* GPO, Washington, D.C., September 1992, p. 10. *Notes:* 1. "Aged unit" does not refer to the household, the family, or unrelated individuals, as used by the Bureau of the Census. The aged unit is either a married couple living together with the husband or wife aged 65 or older (generally measured by the age of the husband), or a person 65 or older who does not live with a spouse. The single person unit may be a widow(er), a divorced or separated person, a person legally married who does not live with a spouse, or a person who never married. 2. Based on family income rather than aged unit income to conform with official measures of poverty.

★ 394 ★
Benefits

Time Required to Recapture Social Security Contributions

Based on Congressional Research Service data, more people collect more in Social Security benefits than they paid in because life expectancy has increased more rapidly than Social Security contributions.

Retirement year	Age at which contributions are recovered	Life expectancy[1]
1940	65.5	77
1980	67.0	81
2000	73.0	82
2030	76.0	84

Source: Detroit Free Press, April 4, 1993, p. 4F. Primary source: Congressional Research Service. *Note:* 1. Benefits continue until death.

Benefits: Geographic Data

★ 395 ★

Total Social Security Benefits Paid, by State and Outlying Area, 1991

[Numbers in millions of dollars]

State and Area	Total	Retirement program Number	Rank	Survivor program	Disability program
Total	$268,098	$185,545	-	$54,891	$27,662
Alabama	4,358	2,706	23	1,046	605
Alaska	228	147	53	52	28
Arizona	4,066	2,939	21	702	425
Arkansas	2,791	1,784	32	604	403
California	25,199	17,948	1	4,713	2,539
Colorado	2,802	1,915	31	571	317
Connecticut	3,938	2,993	20	664	281
Delaware	755	538	48	145	73
District of Columbia	456	312	51	99	45
Florida	18,171	13,532	3	3,143	1,495
Georgia	5,550	3,519	17	1,215	816
Hawaii	971	753	44	150	68

[Continued]

★ 395 ★

Total Social Security Benefits Paid, by State and Outlying Area, 1991
[Continued]

State and Area	Total	Retirement program Number	Retirement program Rank	Survivor program	Disability program
Idaho	1,035	733	45	202	100
Illinois	12,591	8,837	6	2,622	1,132
Indiana	6,386	4,397	12	1,335	655
Iowa	3,523	2,505	25	734	283
Kansas	2,817	2,032	30	574	210
Kentucky	3,963	2,365	26	951	647
Louisiana	3,990	2,304	28	1,085	600
Maine	1,344	932	38	265	148
Maryland	4,204	2,933	22	894	377
Massachusetts	6,719	4,851	10	1,246	622
Michigan	10,793	7,317	8	2,297	1,179
Minnesota	4,424	3,172	19	908	344
Mississippi	2,577	1,559	33	588	430
Missouri	6,012	4,117	14	1,244	651
Montana	915	617	46	185	113
Nebraska	1,786	1,274	35	377	135
Nevada	1,193	869	42	199	125
New Hampshire	1,127	830	43	199	98
New Jersey	9,124	6,706	9	1,677	742
New Mexico	1,364	907	41	292	165
New York	20,452	14,648	2	3,828	1,975
North Carolina	6,858	4,599	11	1,361	898
North Dakota	697	485	49	159	54
Ohio	12,501	8,340	7	2,872	1,289
Oklahoma	3,410	2,312	27	761	337
Oregon	3,437	2,530	24	610	297
Pennsylvania	15,745	11,099	4	3,368	1,277
Rhode Island	1,241	920	40	210	110
South Carolina	3,416	2,245	29	678	492
South Dakota	793	551	47	175	68
Tennessee	5,188	3,343	18	1,143	703
Texas	14,199	9,415	5	3,414	1,370
Utah	1,289	924	39	248	116
Vermont	586	407	50	117	62
Virginia	5,387	3,607	16	1,149	631
Washington	5,021	3,638	15	906	477
West Virginia	2,409	1,422	34	616	371
Wisconsin	5,825	4,160	13	1,127	537
Wyoming	426	299	52	86	41
Outlying areas					
American Samoa	13	5	56	5	3
Guam	24	12	55	9	3
Puerto Rico	2,335	1,203	36	526	606

[Continued]

★ 395 ★

Total Social Security Benefits Paid, by State and Outlying Area, 1991
[Continued]

State and Area	Total	Retirement program		Survivor program	Disability program
		Number	Rank		
Virgin Islands	52	33	54	13	6
Foreign countries	1,625	1,005	37	534	85

Source: *Annual Statistical Supplement, 1992 to the Social Security Bulletin*, U.S. Department of Health and Human Services, Social Security Administration, January 1993, p. 224.

★ 396 ★

Benefits: Geographic Data

Estimated Number of Benefits Paid, by State, Age, and Race, 1991
[Data are based on a 10-percent sample]

State	Total	Age					Race		
		17 or under	18-64	65-69	70-74	75 or older	White	Black	Other
Total	40,571,290	2,559,820	8,100,840	8,882,580	7,958,350	13,069,700	35,393,410	3,763,190	1,414,690
Alabama	722,030	62,690	171,120	146,690	128,800	212,730	543,990	165,980	12,060
Alaska	35,470	4,720	8,390	8,500	6,700	7,160	26,960	990	7,520
Arizona	608,920	37,260	118,490	139,940	125,860	187,370	564,360	12,830	31,730
Arkansas	472,940	36,790	106,540	95,660	86,270	147,680	402,340	62,670	7,930
California	3,737,710	234,370	698,420	833,400	765,440	1,206,080	3,218,410	236,630	282,670
Colorado	434,310	27,680	91,000	97,890	84,380	133,360	407,600	11,620	15,090
Connecticut	534,460	21,990	86,290	121,320	116,100	188,760	498,670	25,600	10,190
Delaware	108,450	5,680	22,770	25,200	22,250	32,550	92,660	13,680	2,110
D.C.	78,480	5,170	12,690	15,430	16,080	29,110	21,570	54,090	2,820
Florida	2,727,810	131,370	474,990	612,810	573,540	935,100	2,467,040	204,570	56,200
Georgia	905,320	80,360	215,370	188,030	163,530	258,030	679,640	208,230	17,450
Hawaii	151,390	9,970	27,210	37,950	31,930	44,330	41,580	1,060	108,750
Idaho	161,060	10,700	30,610	34,810	32,240	52,700	156,440	300	4,320
Illinois	1,771,680	102,610	324,650	385,900	353,750	604,770	1,532,790	197,120	41,770
Indiana	919,360	56,950	189,420	204,110	176,840	292,040	841,710	62,110	15,540
Iowa	526,840	22,330	93,000	112,910	103,470	195,130	512,200	6,620	8,020
Kansas	413,700	21,500	68,250	87,510	81,820	154,620	387,610	16,950	9,140
Kentucky	658,300	54,840	163,590	132,520	115,960	191,390	604,930	40,150	13,220
Louisiana	662,860	70,010	161,730	134,680	114,910	181,530	470,340	178,490	14,030
Maine	218,170	11,260	45,900	48,540	41,270	71,200	213,830	430	3,910
Maryland	624,800	36,740	117,960	146,220	129,040	194,840	498,880	111,380	14,540
Massachusetts	989,250	43,700	173,880	213,670	205,790	352,210	936,890	27,940	24,420
Michigan	1,514,690	94,200	322,580	338,970	295,710	463,210	1,313,070	172,670	28,950
Minnesota	676,750	30,180	119,520	145,070	131,910	250,070	657,300	7,450	12,000
Mississippi	459,290	48,920	112,990	87,200	75,860	134,320	311,700	138,440	9,150
Missouri	922,240	56,170	186,090	194,190	171,680	314,110	831,520	76,140	14,580
Montana	142,060	9,960	29,680	28,850	27,810	45,760	136,130	270	5,660
Nebraska	271,560	13,110	46,230	57,740	51,850	102,630	261,030	6,330	4,200
Nevada	177,890	10,850	36,610	47,150	38,220	45,060	162,970	7,350	7,570
New Hampshire	166,940	8,730	32,240	37,910	32,760	55,300	163,850	430	2,660

[Continued]

★ 396 ★

Estimated Number of Benefits Paid, by State, Age, and Race, 1991
[Continued]

State	Total	Age					Race		
		17 or under	18-64	65-69	70-74	75 or older	White	Black	Other
New Jersey	1,242,420	58,190	215,960	282,550	265,400	420,320	1,096,570	112,990	32,860
New Mexico	226,510	21,700	49,650	49,510	41,860	63,790	202,270	3,720	20,520
New York	2,867,590	156,690	548,710	617,410	566,800	977,980	2,470,160	282,470	114,960
North Carolina	1,111,110	75,530	254,280	246,890	212,460	321,950	874,480	209,760	26,870
North Dakota	112,320	4,650	19,540	23,210	22,260	42,660	109,490	300	2,530
Ohio	1,827,270	103,260	375,750	414,160	361,580	572,520	1,641,190	160,560	25,520
Oklahoma	538,560	33,470	106,000	114,060	103,630	181,400	490,010	29,070	19,480
Oregon	508,530	26,770	93,680	114,550	103,870	169,660	489,150	5,810	13,570
Pennsylvania	2,264,790	95,730	420,130	521,240	466,960	760,730	2,070,460	150,740	43,590
Rhode Island	184,110	8,260	33,120	41,660	37,830	63,240	175,820	4,210	4,080
South Carolina	558,410	46,450	134,900	123,610	104,290	149,160	403,650	143,840	10,920
South Dakota	130,490	7,770	22,870	26,260	25,390	48,200	124,420	240	5,830
Tennessee	845,500	61,400	193,850	179,540	154,960	255,750	722,140	106,210	17,150
Texas	2,249,080	184,060	460,760	494,820	422,850	686,590	1,937,490	235,680	75,910
Utah	197,540	17,020	37,110	43,090	37,760	62,560	189,650	1,050	6,840
Vermont	89,770	5,120	18,250	19,400	17,100	29,900	87,590	150	2,030
Virginia	856,650	51,860	184,210	192,660	169,720	258,200	684,390	152,740	19,520
Washington	728,360	39,040	136,960	164,020	150,310	238,030	686,030	14,100	28,230
West Virginia	373,050	27,820	93,470	77,580	65,560	108,620	353,690	12,050	7,310
Wisconsin	849,870	42,270	167,140	182,340	163,890	294,230	809,690	26,580	13,600
Wyoming	64,160	4,760	13,010	14,150	12,420	19,820	61,770	330	2,060
Outlying areas									
American Samoa	3,960	1,590	1,230	380	370	390	210	...	3,750
Guam	5,680	1,540	1,480	1,210	820	630	1,020	80	4,580
Puerto Rico	569,940	87,200	170,530	97,320	81,300	133,590	454,030	44,110	71,800
Virgin Islands	9,930	1,780	2,350	2,070	1,530	2,200	2,330	6,950	650
Foreign countries	345,640	29,000	52,160	75,410	65,140	123,930	287,890	8,770	48,980
Unknown[1]	15,320	6,060	5,530	2,710	520	500	9,810	2,160	3,350

Source: Annual Statistical Supplement, 1992 to the Social Security Bulletin, U.S. Department of Health and Human Services, Social Security Administration, January 1993, p. 228. Notes: Three dots (...) stands for not applicable. 1. State code unknown.

★ 397 ★

Benefits: Geographic Data

Average Monthly Benefit for Retired Workers, by State, Area, and Benefit Amount, 1991

Data are based on a 10-percent sample.

| State | Ave. monthly benefit | Number | \multicolumn{10}{c}{Percentage distribution of beneficiaries receiving--} |
			Less than $300.00	$300.0 - $349.90	$350.00 - $399.90	$400.00 - $449.90	$450.00 - $499.90	$500.00 - $599.90	$600.00 - $699.90	$700.00 - $799.90	$800.00 - $899.90	$900.00 or more
Total	$629.30	25,274,870	8.8	5.4	7.5	6.5	5.9	11.6	14.8	15.9	10.4	13.3
Alabama	580.90	393,820	12.3	6.6	8.3	7.5	7.0	13.3	13.8	13.3	8.1	9.9
Alaska	626.30	20,420	9.9	5.8	8.4	6.0	5.9	11.9	13.3	13.7	9.8	15.2
Arizona	636.90	397,080	7.5	5.4	7.0	6.0	5.4	11.3	16.1	17.8	10.7	12.8
Arkansas	565.20	268,410	11.5	7.0	9.2	8.3	7.8	14.4	14.1	12.5	7.2	7.8
California	642.50	2,388,930	9.2	5.3	6.9	6.1	5.7	11.0	14.3	15.3	10.4	15.7
Colorado	613.30	265,860	10.6	5.8	7.6	6.6	6.2	11.7	13.7	15.3	10.1	12.5
Connecticut	690.90	378,820	4.7	3.7	6.4	5.5	5.0	10.1	14.9	17.9	13.0	18.8
Delaware	656.00	70,940	5.9	4.9	7.1	6.1	5.0	10.9	14.4	18.8	12.5	14.2
D.C.	536.60	50,640	21.4	8.1	8.6	8.4	7.6	12.2	10.0	7.8	5.5	10.5
Florida	628.20	1,863,310	7.8	5.8	7.6	6.5	5.7	12.1	15.9	16.0	9.9	12.6
Georgia	587.10	516,870	11.0	6.3	8.4	7.9	7.3	14.1	13.7	12.4	8.5	10.4
Hawaii	618.80	105,340	9.7	5.2	7.0	6.7	5.6	12.5	16.1	16.2	9.3	11.7
Idaho	611.20	101,790	7.9	6.3	7.9	6.7	6.1	13.1	15.5	16.4	9.8	10.1
Illinois	667.80	1,139,860	6.9	4.5	6.8	5.9	5.3	10.1	14.2	17.0	12.1	17.2
Indiana	654.90	576,880	5.5	4.8	6.9	5.9	5.0	10.8	16.5	19.3	12.0	13.2
Iowa	631.10	333,990	6.9	5.4	7.5	6.5	5.9	12.3	16.4	16.9	10.3	12.0
Kansas	645.00	257,760	7.1	5.4	7.3	6.4	5.9	11.9	14.8	15.6	10.8	14.9
Kentucky	579.10	343,510	12.1	6.9	8.4	7.4	6.7	12.8	14.1	14.2	8.4	9.1
Louisiana	583.80	325,880	14.1	6.7	8.0	7.2	6.4	11.8	12.4	13.5	8.7	11.1
Maine	578.10	137,940	10.6	6.7	8.0	7.1	7.2	15.0	15.5	14.0	8.0	7.9
Maryland	628.30	403,190	10.5	5.2	7.2	6.5	5.7	11.1	13.8	15.1	10.6	14.3
Massachusetts	632.20	668,040	9.2	5.1	7.4	6.7	6.0	11.3	14.5	14.9	10.7	14.2
Michigan	672.10	929,520	4.8	4.2	6.7	5.2	4.2	9.5	18.0	20.0	12.7	14.6
Minnesota	613.80	439,350	9.2	6.1	8.0	7.0	5.9	11.6	14.5	15.7	10.6	11.5
Mississippi	546.30	244,140	14.6	7.5	9.4	8.6	7.8	14.3	12.6	10.5	6.8	7.8
Missouri	615.30	573,590	8.6	5.6	8.0	7.1	6.4	12.4	15.2	15.4	9.8	11.5
Montana	611.10	85,480	8.7	6.0	7.6	6.9	6.4	12.2	16.5	15.6	9.7	10.5
Nebraska	620.90	173,890	7.9	5.7	7.6	6.8	6.7	13.3	15.6	14.4	9.9	12.2
Nevada	631.20	121,340	8.2	5.7	7.5	6.6	6.2	11.8	14.7	15.4	10.3	13.8
New Hampshire	632.20	114,700	7.1	4.8	7.1	6.3	6.0	13.5	16.3	16.6	10.0	12.2
New Jersey	689.40	854,030	5.5	4.0	6.6	5.8	4.9	9.7	14.3	16.6	12.9	19.7
New Mexico	592.40	128,860	11.9	6.6	7.4	7.0	6.4	12.7	14.6	13.7	9.0	10.7
New York	673.10	1,895,000	6.3	4.4	6.5	5.7	5.3	11.0	15.3	16.7	11.8	17.1
North Carolina	587.80	680,400	9.6	6.0	8.0	7.8	7.6	15.3	15.2	13.1	8.1	9.2
North Dakota	592.70	66,970	10.0	6.3	8.3	7.3	7.8	14.4	14.3	12.5	8.5	10.6
Ohio	644.60	1,091,700	8.2	5.0	7.1	5.8	4.8	9.6	14.9	19.1	12.0	13.5
Oklahoma	599.50	327,580	10.4	6.2	8.1	6.9	6.5	13.1	15.0	14.5	8.8	10.6
Oregon	640.60	338,840	6.6	5.0	7.4	6.1	5.3	11.1	16.3	18.6	11.4	12.1
Pennsylvania	647.80	1,469,150	6.4	4.8	7.3	6.0	5.3	10.8	15.9	18.8	11.7	13.0
Rhode Island	628.50	129,220	7.3	5.2	7.2	6.4	6.6	12.6	16.9	15.4	9.9	12.4
South Carolina	587.80	331,830	10.1	5.9	8.1	7.6	7.5	14.9	15.1	13.1	8.2	9.4
South Dakota	582.30	79,190	10.4	6.4	9.3	7.3	7.5	14.1	14.2	13.5	8.4	8.8
Tennessee	587.80	485,970	11.1	6.4	8.6	7.7	7.1	13.1	13.8	13.6	8.4	10.2
Texas	609.90	1,298,640	11.1	6.1	7.9	7.0	6.4	12.2	12.9	14.0	9.3	13.0
Utah	635.00	123,400	9.6	5.6	7.6	6.4	5.0	9.8	13.3	16.5	11.5	14.7
Vermont	617.40	57,070	7.5	5.4	7.2	6.5	6.8	14.1	16.4	15.7	10.0	10.3
Virginia	595.10	522,050	11.7	6.2	7.8	7.0	6.8	12.9	14.0	13.6	8.9	11.3
Washington	652.80	477,310	6.6	5.0	7.0	5.9	5.1	10.6	15.3	18.3	12.1	14.1
West Virginia	621.70	189,730	8.0	5.3	7.4	6.0	5.8	11.7	16.6	18.8	10.3	10.1
Wisconsin	646.00	551,380	5.7	5.0	7.8	6.2	5.2	10.6	15.9	19.0	12.1	12.5
Wyoming	628.00	40,690	8.2	5.8	7.5	7.0	6.3	11.4	14.4	15.9	10.3	13.2
Outlying areas												
American Samoa	393.40	910	37.4	14.3	13.2	3.3	7.7	12.1	3.3	3.3	2.2	3.3
Guam	450.00	2,190	29.7	14.6	11.4	12.8	7.3	5.0	2.7	5.5	2.7	8.2
Puerto Rico	402.20	240,880	35.6	11.1	11.2	9.4	7.1	10.9	6.5	4.0	2.0	2.1
Virgin Islands	530.50	5,350	13.5	10.3	10.3	8.8	9.9	12.9	14.8	7.1	3.7	8.8

[Continued]

★ 397 ★

Average Monthly Benefit for Retired Workers, by State, Area, and Benefit Amount, 1991
[Continued]

State	Ave. monthly benefit	Number	Percentage distribution of beneficiaries receiving--									
			Less than $300.00	$300.0 - $349.90	$350.00 - $399.90	$400.00 - $449.90	$450.00 - $499.90	$500.00 - $599.90	$600.00 - $699.90	$700.00 - $799.90	$800.00 - $899.90	$900.00 or more
Foreign countries	445.60	182,740	25.9	9.8	11.2	9.4	7.9	12.3	10.0	6.8	3.2	3.6
Unknown[1]	603.30	2,500	14.8	6.4	7.6	6.0	6.0	8.4	10.8	14.8	9.6	15.6

Source: *Annual Statistical Supplement, 1992 to the Social Security Bulletin*, U.S. Department of Health and Human Services, Social Security Administration, January 1993, p. 229. *Note:* 1. State code unknown.

★ 398 ★

Benefits: Geographic Data

State Ranking of Persons Aged 65+ Receiving OASDI (Social Security) Benefits, and SSI (Supplemental Security Income) Payments, 1940-1991

Vermont ranks first in the nation for Social Security (OASDI) benefits, where only 5 in 1,000 do not receive any benefit. In Florida, 126 out of 1,000 do not get any Social Security (OASDI) benefits.

State	Population aged 65 or older receiving--						Persons receiving both OASDI and SSI as percent of--	
	OASDI		SSI[1]		OASDI and SSI, number per 1,000	OASDI or SSI both, number per 1,000		
	Number per 1,000	State rank	Number per 1,000	State rank			OASDI beneficiaries	SSI recipients
Alabama	925	37	122	3	102	945	11.0	83.5
Alaska	890	46	67	15	27	930	3.1	40.5
Arizona	914	43	35	35	24	925	2.6	68.2
Arkansas	939	24	106	6	91	953	9.7	86.4
California	883	49	142	2	83	941	9.4	58.7
Colorado	931	32	37	30	25	944	2.7	66.7
Connecticut	947	16	24	45	12	959	1.3	51.6
Delaware	951	14	33	37	24	959	2.6	74.8
D.C.	770	51	80	13	56	794	7.3	69.7
Florida	874	50	48	24	26	897	2.9	52.9
Georgia	919	39	110	5	90	939	9.8	81.3
Hawaii	887	48	55	22	21	921	2.3	37.5
Idaho	966	6	24	43	20	969	2.1	84.4
Illinois	928	34	36	32	18	945	2.0	50.8
Indiana	956	10	22	46	17	961	1.8	78.3
Iowa	959	9	24	44	19	964	1.9	78.9
Kansas	940	23	22	48	16	946	1.7	73.7
Kentucky	933	29	91	9	75	949	8.0	82.2
Louisiana	910	44	120	4	92	938	10.1	77.0
Maine	971	4	57	21	52	977	5.4	90.6
Maryland	890	47	43	28	25	908	2.8	58.1
Massachusetts	934	26	62	17	45	951	4.8	72.2

[Continued]

★ 398 ★

State Ranking of Persons Aged 65+ Receiving OASDI (Social Security) Benefits, and SSI (Supplemental Security Income) Payments, 1940-1991
[Continued]

State	Population aged 65 or older receiving--						Persons receiving both OASDI and SSI as percent of--	
	OASDI		SSI[1]		OASDI and SSI, number per 1,000	OASDI or SSI both, number per 1,000		
	Number per 1,000	State rank	Number per 1,000	State rank			OASDI beneficiaries	SSI recipients
Michigan	970	5	38	29	27	980	2.8	73.3
Minnesota	953	11	26	40	18	960	1.9	71.4
Mississippi	916	41	175	1	149	942	16.3	85.5
Missouri	943	19	43	26	34	953	3.6	78.5
Montana	944	17	26	41	21	949	2.2	81.1
Nebraska	941	21	22	47	18	946	1.9	80.8
Nevada	950	15	35	33	24	961	2.6	69.2
New Hampshire	982	2	16	51	11	987	1.1	70.5
New Jersey	934	27	43	27	21	956	2.3	49.6
New Mexico	922	38	86	12	65	943	7.0	75.7
New York	917	40	78	14	42	953	4.5	53.1
North Carolina	944	18	86	11	74	957	7.9	85.8
North Dakota	953	12	34	36	28	960	2.9	81.4
Ohio	942	20	28	39	19	950	2.1	69.6
Oklahoma	929	33	64	16	51	943	5.4	78.4
Oregon	963	8	25	42	18	970	1.8	71.1
Pennsylvania	941	22	35	34	25	952	2.6	70.1
Rhode Island	933	30	49	23	34	948	3.6	69.2
South Carolina	926	36	103	7	87	942	9.4	84.9
South Dakota	964	7	36	31	29	971	3.0	80.1
Tennessee	937	25	96	8	81	951	8.7	84.8
Texas	916	42	89	10	65	940	7.1	73.4
Utah	928	35	19	50	12	936	1.3	61.6
Vermont	995	1	57	20	51	1,002	5.1	89.0
Virginia	908	45	62	18	46	924	5.0	74.2
Washington	953	13	32	38	18	967	1.9	56.3
West Virginia	932	31	58	19	45	945	4.9	77.9
Wisconsin	972	3	45	25	38	978	3.9	85.9
Wyoming	934	28	21	49	17	938	1.8	80.0

Source: Annual Statistical Supplement, 1992 to the Social Security Bulletin, U.S. Department of Health and Human Services, Social Security Administration, January 1993, p. 126. *Notes:* OASDI stands for Old-Age, Survivors, and Disability Insurance. 1. For 1940-73, data refer to Old-Age Assistance program. Beginning in January 1974, the Supplemental Security Income program superseded the Old-Age Assistance program in the 50 States and the District of Columbia.

Supplemental Security Income (SSI)

★ 399 ★

Supplemental Security Income (SSI): Federally Administered Payments, by State, 1991

The SSI program provides income support to persons aged 65 or older, blind or disabled adults, and blind or disabled children. It is mainly intended to aid individuals with little or no other income resources. Some states also contribute additional funds to SSI for residents in their own states, but, only federal contributions are shown here. Federal contributions for individuals are reduced if that individual has other sources of income.

State	Number receiving benefits, December[1]					Amount of payments during year[3] (in thousands of dollars)				
	Total	Aged		Blind[2]	Disabled[2]	Total	Aged		Blind	Disabled
		Number	%				Amount	%		
Total	5,118,470	1,464,684	28.62	84,549	3,569,237	17,995,639	3,690,333	20.51	340,577	13,964,729
Alabama[4]	137,114	46,614	34.00	1,627	88,873	387,247	81,317	21.00	5,130	300,800
Alaska[4]	4,974	1,173	23.58	98	3,703	16,002	2,422	15.14	317	13,262
Arizona[4]	49,761	11,924	23.96	706	37,131	162,452	25,318	15.58	2,490	134,643
Arkansas	79,339	26,066	32.85	1,212	52,061	210,990	40,709	19.29	3,795	166,486
California	920,248	334,324	36.33	22,208	563,716	4,536,902	1,345,741	29.66	125,089	3,066,072
Colorado[4]	41,671	8,856	21.25	472	32,343	130,555	17,923	13.73	1,560	111,072
Connecticut[4]	34,424	7,054	20.49	522	26,848	111,529	15,782	14.15	1,747	94,000
Delaware	8,383	1,692	20.18	124	6,567	24,800	2,974	11.99	385	21,441
D.C.	16,914	3,492	20.65	205	13,217	59,037	7,000	11.86	735	51,302
Florida	241,371	86,859	35.99	3,244	151,268	750,603	216,716	28.87	11,032	522,855
Georgia	166,372	49,402	29.69	2,670	114,300	461,586	83,089	18.00	8,657	369,840
Hawaii	14,443	5,815	40.26	178	8,450	56,207	18,710	33.29	686	36,811
Idaho[4]	11,414	1,906	16.70	154	9,354	34,565	2,875	8.32	521	31,169
Illinois[4]	192,254	32,277	16.79	2,433	157,544	688,221	76,822	11.16	8,691	602,708
Indiana[4]	65,515	10,373	15.83	1,190	53,952	203,810	16,657	8.17	3,916	183,237
Iowa	34,473	7,304	21.19	1,032	26,137	95,841	10,841	11.31	3,131	81,869
Kansas	26,199	4,927	18.81	376	20,896	75,581	8,164	10.80	1,240	66,177
Kentucky[4]	121,591	28,327	23.30	1,932	91,332	382,372	50,089	13.10	6,840	325,443
Louisiana	139,965	38,930	27.81	2,268	98,767	427,942	71,677	16.75	7,523	348,742
Maine	24,318	6,563	26.99	266	17,489	61,764	8,047	13.03	849	52,869
Maryland	63,326	15,135	23.90	790	47,401	209,452	31,899	15.23	2,752	174,801
Massachusetts	127,014	46,735	36.80	4,386	75,893	449,568	118,445	26.35	17,707	313,416
Michigan	151,276	26,020	17.20	2,194	123,062	538,116	54,341	10.10	8,242	475,533
Minnesota[4]	43,781	10,124	23.12	705	32,952	129,443	18,293	14.13	2,171	108,979
Mississippi	118,228	39,593	33.49	1,636	76,999	336,578	68,328	20.30	5,153	263,097
Missouri[4]	90,062	20,426	22.68	1,150	68,486	268,776	34,340	12.78	3,687	230,750
Montana	10,753	1,797	16.71	121	8,835	33,290	2,705	8.13	401	30,185
Nebraska[4]	16,780	3,449	20.55	244	13,087	48,411	4,952	10.23	782	42,677
Nevada	12,615	4,588	36.37	527	7,500	38,873	10,103	25.99	1,906	26,864
New Hampshire[4]	7,489	1,382	18.45	100	6,007	22,104	2,201	9.96	310	19,593
New Jersey	111,806	31,699	28.35	1,181	78,926	386,762	82,869	21.43	4,221	299,672
New Mexico[4]	33,874	9,604	28.35	604	23,666	101,905	17,921	17.59	2,042	81,943
New York	444,559	126,077	28.36	4,042	314,440	1,762,371	373,929	21.22	15,822	1,372,620
North Carolina[4]	156,973	47,677	30.37	2,653	106,643	444,010	81,324	18.32	8,351	354,336
North Dakota[5]	7,941	2,207	27.79	95	5,639	20,335	3,416	16.80	328	16,591
Ohio	169,098	23,201	13.72	2,564	143,333	563,644	41,886	7.43	8,657	513,101
Oklahoma[4]	62,390	18,718	30.00	964	42,708	173,996	31,666	18.20	3,221	139,109
Oregon[4]	34,390	6,575	19.12	598	27,217	110,445	12,125	10.98	1,955	96,365
Pennsylvania	202,013	41,567	20.58	2,853	157,593	716,568	89,454	12.48	10,422	616,692

[Continued]

★ 399 ★

Supplemental Security Income (SSI): Federally Administered Payments, by State, 1991

[Continued]

State	Number receiving benefits, December[1]					Amount of payments during year[3] (in thousands of dollars)				
	Total	Aged		Blind[2]	Disabled[2]	Total	Aged		Blind	Disabled
		Number	%				Amount	%		
Rhode Island	18,374	5,035	27.40	208	13,131	59,327	10,743	18.11	742	47,842
South Carolina[4]	93,082	27,915	29.99	1,783	63,384	257,252	46,916	18.24	5,908	204,429
South Dakota	10,783	2,705	25.09	140	7,938	30,322	4,138	13.65	464	25,719
Tennessee	147,388	39,899	27.07	1,985	105,504	432,994	65,242	15.07	6,618	361,134
Texas[5]	314,657	121,998	38.77	5,327	187,332	865,347	229,019	26.47	17,468	618,860
Vermont	10,696	2,477	23.16	123	8,096	35,000	4,452	12.72	470	30,078
Virginia[4]	101,371	29,215	28.82	1,569	70,587	289,542	53,601	18.51	5,092	230,849
Washington	67,377	11,762	17.46	847	54,768	242,376	28,910	11.93	2,989	210,476
West Virginia[5]	50,212	8,836	17.60	690	40,686	165,390	15,360	9.29	2,400	147,630
Wisconsin	90,880	21,468	23.62	1,184	68,228	326,173	42,768	13.11	4,647	278,758
Wyoming[4]	3,895	724	18.59	54	3,117	11,241	1,053	9.37	172	10,017
Other: Northern Mariana Islands[5]	522	239	45.79	17	266	1,954	825	42.22	75	1,054

Source: Annual Statistical Supplement, 1992 to the Social Security Bulletin, U.S. Department of Health and Human Services, Social Security Administration, January 1993, pp. 275. *Notes:* 1. Includes persons with Federal SSI payments and/or federally administered State supplementation, unless otherwise indicated. 2. Includes approximately 22,100 blind and 593,000 disabled persons aged 65 or older. 3. Federal SSI payments and federally administered State supplementation. 4. Federal SSI payments only. State has State administered supplementation. 5. Federal SSI payments only. State supplementary payments not made.

★ 400 ★

Supplemental Security Income (SSI)

Supplemental Security Income (SSI): State Administered Payments, 1991

The SSI program provides income support to persons aged 65 or older, blind or disabled adults, and blind or disabled children. It is mainly intended to aid individuals with little or no other income resources. Though the federal government is a large contributor to SSI, some states also contribute additional funds for their residents. Eligibility usually depends on other sources of income available to individuals.

State	Number of persons					Amount of payments during year (in thousands of dollars)				
	Total	Aged		Blind	Disabled	Total	Aged		Blind	Disabled
		Number	%				Amount	%		
Total	307,891	119,960	38.96	3,595	182,990	528,590[2]	200,079	37.85	6,251	303,463
Alabama	8,657	4,692	54.20	91	3,874	6,182	3,306	53.48	64	2,812
Alaska[3]	4,726	1,744	36.90	62	2,920	12,970	4,761	36.71	174	8,035
Arizona[3]	4,021	81	2.01	2	3,938	3,184	77	2.42	2	3,105
Colorado	30,153	22,893	75.92	52	7,208	51,673	35,964	69.60	69	15,640
Connecticut	26,727	8,838	33.07	157	17,732	99,958	29,126	29.14	491	70,341
Florida	13,584[1]	6,546	48.19	4	7,104[5]	18,872	8,172	43.30	4	10,700[5]
Idaho[3]	2,985	970	32.50	21	1,994	4,205	1,153	27.42	20	3,032
Illinois	58,535	6,036	10.31	201	52,298	68,066	4,736	6.96	244	63,086
Indiana	1,009	535	53.02	5	469	3,439	1,453	42.25	25	1,961

[Continued]

★ 400 ★

Supplemental Security Income (SSI): State Administered Payments, 1991

[Continued]

State	Number of persons					Amount of payments during year (in thousands of dollars)				
	Total	Aged		Blind	Disabled	Total	Aged		Blind	Disabled
		Number	%				Amount	%		
Kentucky	6,573	3,314	50.42	79	3,180	15,190	7,729	50.88	103	7,358
Maryland	1,057[2]	[4]	[4]	[4]	[4]	6,461[2]	[4]	[4]	[4]	[4]
Minnesota	19,643	4,825	24.56	129	14,689	50,655	7,567	14.94	367	42,721
Missouri	12,395	6,513	52.55	899	4,983	14,392	7,032	48.86	1,522	5,838
Nebraska	6,440	1,720	26.71	68	4,652	5,288	1,037	19.61	43	4,208
New Hampshire	5,202	1,442	27.72	204	3,556	7,857	1,492	18.99	428	5,937
New Mexico	289[2]	[4]	[4]	[4]	[4]	327	[4]	[4]	[4]	[4]
North Carolina	16,693	9,998	59.89	231	6,464	74,188	43,388	58.48	1,210	29,590
Oklahoma	60,155	29,563	49.14	614	29,978	35,395	16,511	46.65	396	18,488
Oregon[3]	16,743	4,552	27.19	693	11,498	18,963	11,172	58.91	894	6,897
South Carolina	4,032	2,319	57.51	23	1,690	12,157	6,856	56.40	81	5,220
South Dakota	273	178	65.20	2	93	610	437	71.64	3	170
Virginia	6,286	3,097	49.27	33	3,156	16,879	8,084	47.89	109	8,686
Wyoming	1,712	104	6.07	29	1,579	368	26	7.07	6	336

Source: Annual Statistical Supplement, 1992 to the Social Security Bulletin, U.S. Department of Health and Human Services, Social Security Administration, January 1993, p. 276. Notes: 1. Excludes data for Iowa, North Dakota, and Ohio. 2. Includes data not distributed by category. 3. Data partly estimated. 4. Data not available. 5. Includes data for the blind.

★ 401 ★

Supplemental Security Income (SSI)

Persons Receiving Federally Administered Supplemental Security Income (SSI) Payments, 1991

From the source: "The Supplemental Security Income (SSI) program provides income support to persons aged 65 or older, blind or disabled adults, and blind or disabled children. Eligibility requirements and Federal payment standards are nationally uniform. The program is administered by SSA. The 1993 Federal SSI benefit rate for an individual living in his or her own household and with no other countable income is $434 monthly; for a couple (with both husband and wife eligible), the SSI benefit rate is $652 monthly." Both federal and state contributions are shown here.

Source of payment	Total	Aged	Blind	Disabled
Number of persons with--				
Federally administered payments[1]	5,118,470	1,464,684	84,549[2]	3,569,237[3]
Federal SSI payments only	2,914,141	799,278	43,226	2,071,637
Both Federal payment and State supplementation	1,815,498	479,396	32,917	1,303,185
State supplementation only	388,831	186,010	8,406	194,415
Total with--				
Federal payment[4]	4,729,639	1,278,674	76,143	3,374,822
State supplementation[5]	2,204,329	665,406	41,323	1,497,600

[Continued]

★ 401 ★

Persons Receiving Federally Administered Supplemental Security Income (SSI) Payments, 1991

[Continued]

Source of payment	Total	Aged	Blind	Disabled
Amount of payments (in thousands)				
Total	$1,640,611	$324,135	$29,674	$1,286,801
Federal payments	1,352,826	235,927	22,140	1,094,758
State supplementation	287,785	88,208	7,534	192,043
Average monthly amount				
Total	$320.53	$221.30	$350.97	$360.53
Federal payments	286.30	184.51	290.77	324.39
State supplementation	130.55	132.56	182.31	128.23

Source: *Annual Statistical Supplement, 1992 to the Social Security Bulletin*, U.S. Department of Health and Human Services, Social Security Administration, January 1993, p. 269. *Notes:* SSA stands for Social Security Administration. 1. All persons with a Federal SSI payment and\or federally administered state supplementation. 2. Includes approximately 22,100 persons aged 65 or older. 3. Includes approximately 593,000 persons aged 65 or older. 4. All persons with a Federal SSI payment whether receiving a Federal payment only or both a Federal payment and State supplementation. 5. All persons with federally administered State supplementation whether receiving State supplementation only or both a Federal SSI payment and State supplementation.

★ 402 ★

Supplemental Security Income (SSI)

Characteristics of Supplemental Security Income (SSI) Recipients, 1990

[Numbers show percentages, unless otherwise indicated]

Characteristic	Aged 65 or older				
	Total	Sex		Age	
		Men	Women	65-74	75 or older
Total number (in thousands)	1,647	397	1,251	830	817
Sex					
Men	24.1	100.0	...	25.9	22.2
Women	75.9	...	100.0	74.1	77.8
Race					
White	64.7	62.0	65.6	60.5	69.1
Black	29.8	24.3	31.5	33.0	26.5
Other	5.5	13.7	2.9	6.5	4.4
Hispanic origin[1]	16.5	17.2	16.2	19.4	13.5
Years of education					
0-8	63.2	58.6	64.6	55.9	70.6
9-11	13.8	12.1	14.3	16.7	10.8

[Continued]

★ 402 ★

Characteristics of Supplemental Security Income
(SSI) Recipients, 1990
[Continued]

Characteristic	Aged 65 or older				
	Total	Sex		Age	
		Men	Women	65-74	75 or older
12	15.4	17.3	14.8	18.2	12.7
13-15	5.3	6.7	4.8	6.6	3.9
16 or more	2.4	5.2	1.5	2.6	2.1
Marital status					
Married	20.5	54.0	9.9	26.2	14.8
Widowed	48.9	18.9	58.4	32.8	65.2
Divorced or separated	20.1	15.8	21.4	27.0	13.0
Never married	10.5	11.3	10.2	14.0	7.0
Size of household					
1 person	49.0	28.2	55.6	47.2	50.9
2 persons	25.0	36.0	21.5	23.9	26.2
3-4 persons	16.2	18.4	15.5	18.0	14.4
5 persons or more	9.7	17.4	7.3	10.9	8.5
Housing status					
Owning or buying	49.4	49.4	49.5	44.3	54.6
Renting	46.1	48.9	45.2	52.2	39.9
Other	4.5	1.7	5.3	3.5	5.5
Recipient's monthly total income					
Less than $300	9.9	10.1	9.8	13.0	6.8
$300-$399	17.8	23.7	16.0	15.4	20.3
$400-$499	39.3	20.8	45.1	36.6	41.9
$500 or more	33.0	45.3	29.1	34.9	31.0
Median	457	478	454	459	455
Recipients monthly SSI payment					
Less than $100	31.2	29.0	31.9	28.1	34.3
$100-$199	24.5	25.4	24.2	21.3	27.8
$200-$299	15.0	17.6	14.2	18.7	11.3
$300-$399	15.6	14.0	16.1	16.8	14.4
$400-$499	7.2	5.1	7.9	6.6	7.8

[Continued]

★ 402 ★

Characteristics of Supplemental Security Income (SSI) Recipients, 1990
[Continued]

Characteristic	Aged 65 or older				
	Total	Sex		Age	
		Men	Women	65-74	75 or older
$500 or more	6.5	8.7	5.7	8.5	4.3
Median	171	178	170	197	153

Source: Annual Statistical Supplement, 1992 to the Social Security Bulletin, U.S. Department of Health and Human Services, Social Security Administration, January 1993, p. 273. Primary source: Public use file of the Survey of Income and Program Participation, Bureau of the Census. Notes: Three dots (...) stands for not applicable. 1. Persons of Hispanic origin may be of any race.

Social Security: Worldwide

★ 403 ★

Support Ratios for Selected Countries, 1990[1]

Data show the number of people in the dependent age group per 100 people in the supporting age group.

Country	Total ratio ([0 to 19] + 65+)/(20 to 64)	Elderly ratio (65+)/ (20 to 64)
Canada	64.9	19.0
France	71.2	24.1
Germany	58.0	23.7
Italy	63.3	24.0
Japan	62.4	19.2
Sweden	73.1	31.0
United Kingdom	70.5	26.7
United States	69.9	21.4

Source: Aging America, Trends and Projections, prepared by the U.S. Senate Special Committee on Aging, the American Association of Retired Persons, the Federal Council on the Aging, and the U.S. Administration on Aging, 1991, Washington, D.C., p. 265. Primary source: U.S. Bureau of the Census. International Data Base.

★ 404 ★

Social Security: Worldwide

Social Expenditures as a Percentage of Gross Domestic Product for Selected Countries, by Type of Expenditure, 1980

Country	Government expenditures only				Government and private expenditures			
	Total	Pensions	Medical care	Other	Total	Pensions	Medical care	Other
United States	17.7	6.3	4.5	6.9	28.2	8.1	9.5	10.6
France	31.0	10.0	6.7	14.3	33.9	10.0	8.0	15.9
West Germany	31.1	13.3	6.1	11.7	33.9	13.3	8.7	11.9
Italy	25.0	12.1	5.9	7.0	25.9	12.1	6.8	7.0
United Kingdom	22.9	5.8	5.8	11.3	27.1	9.0	5.8	12.3
Canada	20.3.	3.5	5.6	11.2	24.4	4.8	7.5	12.1
Japan	15.4	4.2	4.8	6.4	16.8	4.2	5.0	7.6

Source: Aging America, Trends and Projections, prepared by the U.S. Senate Special Committee on Aging, the American Association of Retired Persons, the Federal Council on the Aging, and the U.S. Administration on Aging, 1991, Washington, D.C., p. 266. Primary source: International Monetary Fund (IMF), *Aging and Social Expenditure in the Major Industrial Countries, 1980-2025,* by Peter S. Heller, Richard Hemming, Peter W. Kohnert, and IMF staff. Occasional Paper 47, September 1986.

★ 405 ★

Social Security: Worldwide

Annual Growth Rate in Real Government Pension Expenditures for Selected Countries, 1960-1980 and 1980-2025

From the source: "The historical and projected pension cost growth rates for the United States are a bit lower than average for the developed world. Between 1960 and 1980, real (i.e., inflation-adjusted) U.S. government pension costs grew by an average of 6.2 percent per year. Between 1980 and 2025, these costs are projected to grow at an average real rate of 2.5 percent... A similar slowdown in growth can be seen in other developed countries."

[Percent growth per year]

Country	1960-1980	1980-2025
United States	6.2	2.5
France	8.2	2.7
West Germany	4.9	2.5
Italy	8.5	3.6
United Kingdom	4.8	2.4

[Continued]

★ 405 ★

Annual Growth Rate in Real Government Pension Expenditures for Selected Countries, 1960-1980 and 1980-2025
[Continued]

Country	1960-1980	1980-2025
Canada	7.2	2.6
Japan	14.1	5.9

Source: *Aging America, Trends and Projections*, prepared by the U.S. Senate Special Committee on Aging, the American Association of Retired Persons, the Federal Council on the Aging, and the U.S. Administration on Aging, 1991, Washington, D.C., p. 268. Primary source: International Monetary Fund (IMF), *Aging and Social Expenditure in the Major Industrial Countries, 1980-2025*, by Peter S. Heller, Richard W. Kohnert, and IMF staff. Occasional Paper 47, September 1986.

★ 406 ★

Social Security: Worldwide

Shared Social Security Agreements

The United States currently has social security agreements in effect with the 14 countries shown here. Additionally, agreements with Luxembourg and Ireland were signed in 1992.

Country	Effective in
Austria	1991
Belgium	1984
Canada	1984
Federal Republic of Germany (former)	1979
Finland	1992
France	1988
Italy	1973
Netherlands	1990
Norway	1984
Portugal	1989
Spain	1988
Sweden	1987
Switzerland	1980
United Kingdom	1985

Source: *Annual Statistical Supplement, 1992 to the Social Security Bulletin*, U.S. Department of Health and Human Services, Social Security Administration, January 1993, p. 10.

★ 407 ★

Social Security: Worldwide

Employee-Employer Payroll Tax Rates for Social Security Programs, Selected Countries: 1981 to 1989

Data cover old-age, disability and survivors insurance, public health or sickness insurance, workers' compensation, unemployment insurance, and family allowance programs.

[In percent]

Country	All social security programs					Old-age, disability and survivors insurance				
	1981, total	1985, total	1989			1981, total	1985, total	1989		
			Total	Employer	Employee			Total	Employer	Employee
United States	17.60	18.90	19.72	12.21	7.51	10.70	11.40	12.12	6.06	6.06
Austria	35.80	39.90	42.40	24.20	18.20	21.10	22.78	22.80	12.55	10.25
Belgium	34.70	39.71	52.94	40.24	12.70	15.11	16.36	16.36	8.86	7.50
Canada	7.92[1]	9.24[1]	8.88[1]	4.83[1]	4.05	3.60	3.60	4.20	2.10	2.10
France	47.55	51.23	53.03	36.96	16.07	13.00[2]	14.00[2]	15.90[2]	8.20[2]	7.70[2]
Ireland	14.95	23.60	21.76	14.01	7.75	12.00	20.7	18.83	12.33	6.50
Italy	54.30	55.91	53.11	45.16	8.05	24.46	24.36	25.21	18.06	7.15
Japan	21.41[3]	21.61[3]	23.40[3]	12.45[3]	10.95	10.60[4]	10.60[4]	12.40[4]	6.20[4]	6.20[4]
Luxembourg	34.25	34.30	30.20	18.00	12.20	16.00	16.00	16.00	8.00	8.00
Netherlands	54.85	51.18	43.03	21.93	21.10	32.45	24.63	21.90	6.20	15.70
Sweden	32.65	30.45	34.11	34.11	-	21.15	19.95	20.95	20.95	-
Switzerland	11.9	12.0	12.2	7.1	5.1	9.40	9.4	9.60	4.80	4.80
United Kingdom	21.45	19.45	19.45	10.45	9.00	(NA)	(NA)	(NA)	(NA)	(NA)
West Germany	34.80	34.30	36.18	18.73	17.40	18.50	18.70	18.70	9.35	9.35

Source: U.S. Bureau of the Census, *Statistical Abstract of the United States: 1992* (112th edition.) Washington, DC, 1992, p. 837. Primary source: U.S. Social Security Administration, Office of International Policy, unpublished data. *Notes:* (-) A dash represents zero. (NA) stands for Not available. 1. Excludes work-injury compensation program. 2. Disability and survivors benefits financed through sickness insurance. 3. Rate refers to male employees and contributions for employee pension and health insurance only. 4. Rate refers to male employees and contributions for employee pension insurance only.

Chapter 8
LABOR AND EMPLOYMENT

This chapter presents statistics on multiple aspects of labor and employment under ten headings: Labor Force, Employment Status, Job Tenure, Bridge Jobs, Unemployment, Work Preferences, Immigration, Unions, Age Discrimination, and Disability Status. The general logic of arrangement is to present general statistics on labor and employment first followed by unemployment statistics. Other topics of a more special nature follow.

Information on earnings from work will be found in the chapter on *Income, Assets, and Spending.* Information related to the section on Disability Status will be found in the chapter on *Health and Health Care.*

Labor Force

★ 408 ★

The Aging Labor Force, 1970-2000

From the source: "The age of the labor force will closely track the population, rising from a median of 35 years in 1984 to about 39 in 2000. All of the gains will come in the middle years of worklife, while the numbers at the two extremes decline. The number of workers age 35-54 will rise by more than 25 million, approximately equal to the total increase in the workforce."

Age	1970	1985	2000
Total	82,900,000	115,460,000	140,460,000
	Percent of total		
16-34	42.0	50.0	38.0
35-54	40.0	38.0	51.0
55+	18.0	13.0	11.0

Source: Workforce 2000: Work and Workers for the Twenty-First Century, Hudson Institute, Indianapolis, Indiana, 1987, p. 81.

★ 409 ★

Labor Force

The Aging of the Work Force through 2010

The rapid growth of the U.S. labor force has been pushed by the baby boomers who have now matured into working-age adults. Between 1990 and 2000, the number of people between 35 and 44 will jump by 16%, and those between the ages of 45 and 54 will increase by 46%, compared with an overall expected population growth of 7.1%.

Source: "Future Work," Joseph F. Coates, Jennifer Jarratt, and John B. Mahaffie, *The Futurist* 25, No. 3, May-June, 1991 p. 10.

★ 410 ★

Labor Force

Growth Projections of the Labor Force, 2000

Projections are based on moderate growth assumptions for the civilian labor force.

[Numbers in thousands]

Age and sex	Projections for 2000	Change, 1988 to 2000	
		Number	Percent
Total 16+	141,134	19,465	16.0
Men			
16+	74,324	7,397	11.1
16 to 24	11,352	-401	-3.4
25 to 54	53,155	6,773	14.6
55+	9,817	1,026	11.7
65+	2,021	61	3.1
Women			
16+	66,810	12,068	22.0
16 to 24	11,104	322	3.0
25 to 54	48,112	10,453	27.8
55+	7,594	1,293	20.5
65+	1,454	130	9.8

Source: Aging America, Trends and Projections, prepared by the U.S. Senate Special Committee on Aging, the American Association of Retired Persons, the Federal Council on the Aging, and the U.S. Administration on Aging, 1991, Washington, D.C., p. 97. Primary source: Howard N. Fullerton, "New Labor Force Projections, Spanning 1988 to 2000," *Monthly Labor Review,* Vol. 112, No. 11, November 1989.

★ 411 ★

Labor Force

Labor Force Participation: Percent of Older Men and Women in the Labor Force, by Age: 1989

Age	Men	Women
50 to 54	89.3	65.9
55 to 59	79.5	54.8
60 to 64	54.8	35.5
65 to 69	26.1	16.4
70+	10.9	4.6

Source: *Aging America, Trends and Projections*, prepared by the U.S. Senate Special Committee on Aging, the American Association of Retired Persons, the Federal Council on the Aging, and the U.S. Administration on Aging, 1991, Washington, D.C., p. 93. Primary source: U.S. Department of Labor, Bureau of Labor Statistics, *Employment and Earnings* Vol. 37, No. 1, January 1990.

★ 412 ★

Labor Force

Labor Force Participation: Percentage of Civilian Noninstitutional Population in the Labor Force, by Age and Sex: 1950 and 1990

Age	Male		Female	
	1950	1990	1950	1990
55 and over	68.6	39.3	18.9	23.0
65 and over	45.8	16.4	9.7	8.7

Source: *Sixty-Five Plus in America*, Cynthia M. Taeuber, U.S. Department of Commerce, Economics and Statistics Administration, Bureau of the Census, U.S. Government Printing Office, Washington, D.C., 1992, p. 4-1. Primary source: U.S. Bureau of Labor Statistics, data for 1990, *Employment and Earnings*, Vol. 38, No. 1, January 1991, Table 3; data for 1950, unpublished tabulations from 1950 Current Population Survey, available from the Bureau of Labor Statistics.

★ 413 ★
Labor Force

Labor Force Participation: Percent Change, Men 55 Years and Over, by Age: 1970 to 2005

Period	55 years and over	55 to 59 years	60 to 64 years	65 to 69 years	70 to 74 years
Historical					
1970 to 1975	-6.4	-5.1	-9.5	-9.9	-5.9
1975 to 1980	-3.7	-2.7	-4.7	-3.2	-2.9
1980 to 1985	-4.6	-2.1	-5.2	-4.1	-3.3
1985 to 1990	-1.7	0.2	-0.1	1.6	0.6
Projected					
1990 to 1995	-0.9	-0.3	-0.8	0.6	0.0
1995 to 2000	1.2	-0.3	-0.5	0.7	0.2
2000 to 2005	2.2	-0.4	-0.9	0.6	0.1

Source: Howard Fullerton, Jr., Bureau of Labor Statistics, "Labor Force Projections: The Baby Boom Moves On," *Monthly Labor Review*, Vol. 114, No. 11, November 1991, pp. 37-38.

★ 414 ★
Labor Force

Labor Force Participation: Population Aged 25 and Older by Gender, Country of Birth, Age, and Years of School Completed, November 1989

Gender, country of birth, and age	Total	Years of school completed				
		8 years or less	9-11 years	12 years	1 to 3 years of college	4 years of college or more
Men						
U.S. born, 25 years and older	77.3	37.7	65.2	80.5	84.9	87.9
55 years and older	39.1	22.4	32.0	42.5	44.8	55.5
55 to 64 years	66.9	51.4	59.0	68.1	68.3	80.8
65 years and older	16.3	9.2	12.1	17.0	21.4	29.0
Foreign born, 25 years and older	79.9	72.9	77.9	80.7	83.5	84.9
55 years and older	42.7	34.8	30.3	46.0	46.0	55.2
55 to 64 years	78.8	69.9	-	84.3	80.7	84.6
65 years and older	14.0	9.5	-	16.5	-	26.9
Women						
U.S. born, 25 years and older	57.7	18.2	37.5	59.5	68.7	75.2
55 years and older	23.5	10.8	17.1	27.4	31.3	34.8
55 to 64 years	46.2	31.4	34.5	47.8	55.5	59.9
65 years and older	8.8	4.6	7.0	10.3	11.7	13.8
Foreign born, 25 years and older	52.1	34.2	46.4	53.6	69.4	69.4

[Continued]

★ 414 ★

Labor Force Participation: Population Aged 25 and Older by Gender, Country of Birth, Age, and Years of School Completed, November 1989

[Continued]

Gender, country of birth, and age	Total	Years of school completed				
		8 years or less	9-11 years	12 years	1 to 3 years of college	4 years of college or more
55 years and older	25.1	15.5	25.8	28.6	42.6	41.4
55 to 64 years	48.8	34.4	-	52.6	65.2	60.8
65 years and older	7.7	5.3	8.5	7.0	12.9	19.8

Source: Meisenheimer, Joseph R. III, "How do immigrants fare in the U.S. labor market?," *Monthly Labor Review*, December 1992, p. 10.
Note: Data are not shown where there are fewer than 75,000 in the population.

★ 415 ★

Labor Force

Labor Force Participation: All Ages, 1950-1988, and Projections for 2000

Projections are based on moderate growth assumptions for the civilian labor force.

[Numbers in percent]

Age and sex	Actual					Projected
	1950	1960	1970	1980	1988	2000
Total 16+	59.2	59.4	60.4	63.8	65.9	69.0
Men						
16+	86.4	83.3	79.7	77.4	76.2	75.9
16 to 24	77.3	71.7	69.4	74.4	72.4	73.2
25 to 54	96.5	97.0	95.8	94.2	93.6	93.0
55+	68.6	60.96	55.7	45.6	39.9	38.9
55 to 64	86.9	86.8	83.0	72.1	67.0	68.1
65+	45.8	33.1	26.8	19.0	16.5	14.7
Women						
16+	33.9	37.7	43.3	51.5	56.6	62.6
16 to 24	43.9	42.8	51.3	61.9	64.5	69.4
25 to 54	36.8	42.9	50.1	64	72.7	81.4
55+	18.9	23.6	25.3	22.8	22.3	24.0
55 to 64	27.0	37.2	43.0	41.3	43.5	49.0
65+	9.7	10.8	9.7	8.1	7.9	7.6

Source: Aging America, Trends and Projections, prepared by the U.S. Senate Special Committee on Aging, the American Association of Retired Persons, the Federal Council on the Aging, and the U.S. Administration on Aging, 1991, Washington, D.C., p. 97. Primary source: Howard N. Fullerton, "New Labor Force Projections, Spanning 1988 to 2000," *Monthly Labor Review*, Vol. 112, No. 11, November 1989.

★ 416 ★
Labor Force

Labor Force Participation: Older Americans, by Sex, 1950-1989

The U.S. labor force includes workers who are employed or unemployed but actively seeking employment. The participation rate is the percentage of individuals in a given group who are in the civilian labor force.

[Numbers in percent]

Year	Men		Women		Total	
	55 to 64	65+	55 to 64	65+	55 to 64	65+
1950	86.9	45.8	27.0	9.7	56.7	26.7
1955	87.9	39.6	32.5	10.6	59.5	24.1
1960	86.8	33.1	37.2	10.8	60.9	20.8
1965	84.6	27.9	41.1	10.0	61.9	17.8
1970	83.0	26.8	43.0	9.7	61.8	17.0
1975	75.6	21.6	40.9	8.2	57.2	13.7
1980	72.1	19.0	41.3	8.1	55.7	12.5
1985	67.9	15.8	42.0	7.3	54.2	10.8
1989	67.2	16.6	45.0	8.4	55.5	11.8

Source: *Aging America, Trends and Projections*, prepared by the U.S. Senate Special Committee on Aging, the American Association of Retired Persons, the Federal Council on the Aging, and the U.S. Administration on Aging, 1991, Washington, D.C., p. 95. Primary source: 1950-1980 data: U.S. Department of Labor, Bureau of Labor Statistics, *Handbook of Labor Statistics*, Bulletin 2217, June 1985; 1985 data, *Employment and Earnings*, Vol. 33, No. 1, January 1986; 1989 data, *Employment and Earnings*, Vol. 37, No 1.

★ 417 ★
Labor Force

Labor Force Participation: Older Men and Women in Selected Countries, 1988

From the source: "If any trend characterizes the developed nations of the twentieth century, it has been the decline in the labor force participation of the elderly. With few exceptions, older people in the developed world are neither working nor looking for work, and in many countries, labor force withdrawal is occurring well before workers reach age 65. This is as true of the United States as it is of other developed nations."

[Numbers in percent]

Country	Men		Women	
	60 to 64	65+	60 to 64	65+
United States	54.2	16.0	35.3	7.8
France	24.1	4.4	17.7	1.9
West Germany[1]	36.5	5.4	11.8	2.0
Italy	35.2	7.9	9.8	2.2
Sweden	62.7	14.2	50.6	5.8

[Continued]

★ 417 ★

Labor Force Participation: Older Men and Women in Selected Countries, 1988
[Continued]

Country	Men		Women	
	60 to 64	65+	60 to 64	65+
United Kingdom	53.5	8.8	22.3	3.3
Canada	-	11.0	-	4.0
Japan	71.4	35.8	39.2	15.8

Source: *Aging America, Trends and Projections*, prepared by the U.S. Senate Special Committee on Aging, the American Association of Retired Persons, the Federal Council on the Aging, and the U.S. Administration on Aging, 1991, Washington, D.C., p. 260. Primary source: Organization for Economic Co-operation and Development (OECD) Labor Force Statistics, 1988. Paris: OECD, 1990. *Notes:* A dash (-) indicates that data were not given in the original source. 1. Rates for West Germany are for 1987.

★ 418 ★
Labor Force

Labor Force Participation: Older People, by Age and Sex: 1989[1]

Labor force status	55 to 59			60 to 64			65+		
	Total	Men	Women	Total	Men	Women	Total	Men	Women
Civilian labor force (000)	7,088	4,033	3,055	4,789	2,750	2,039	3,446	2,017	1,429
Labor force participation rate (percent)	66.6	79.5	54.8	44.5	54.8	35.5	11.8	16.6	8.4
Number employed (000)	6,854	3,890	2,964	4,644	2,658	1,986	3,355	1,968	1,388

Source: *Aging America, Trends and Projections*, prepared by the U.S. Senate Special Committee on Aging, the American Association of Retired Persons, the Federal Council on the Aging, and the U.S. Administration on Aging, 1991, Washington, D.C., p. 91. Primary source: U.S. Department of Labor, Bureau of Labor Statistics, *Employment and Earnings* Vol. 37, No. 1, January 1990. *Notes:* The U.S. labor force includes workers who are employed or unemployed but actively seeking employment. The participation rate is the percentage of individuals in a given group (e.g., age group) who are in the labor force. 1. Annual averages.

★ 419 ★
Labor Force

Labor Force Participation: Older People, by Age, Sex, and Race: 1989[1]

Sex and race	50 to 54 years	55 to 59 years	60 to 64 years	65 to 69 years	70+ years
Total					
Women	65.9	54.8	35.5	16.4	4.6
Men	89.3	79.5	54.8	26.1	10.9
White					
Women	65.6	55.1	35.7	16.4	4.5
Men	90.4	81.0	55.7	26.6	11.0
Black					
Women	68.2	51.5	32.7	16.4	5.9
Men	79.9	66.4	43.6	20.7	10.3

Source: *Aging America, Trends and Projections*, prepared by the U.S. Senate Special Committee on Aging, the American Association of Retired Persons, the Federal Council on the Aging, and the U.S. Administration on Aging, 1991, Washington, D.C., p. 91. Primary source: U.S. Department of Labor, Bureau of Labor Statistics, *Employment and Earnings* Vol. 37, No. 1, January 1990. *Notes:* The U.S. labor force includes workers who are employed or unemployed but actively seeking employment. The participation rate is the percentage of individuals in a given group (e.g., age group) who are in the labor force. 1. Annual averages in percent.

★ 420 ★
Labor Force

Labor Force Participation: Selected Countries: 1980 and 1990

[Percent of population of each specified group in labor force]

Country and sex	15 to 19 years old		20 to 24 years old		25 to 54 years old		55 to 64 years old		65 years and over	
	1980	1990	1980	1990	1980	1990	1980	1990	1980	1990
United States:										
Total	56.5[1]	53.9	77.5	77.9	78.4	83.2	55.1	55.4	11.9	11.2
Male	60.5[1]	55.9	85.7	84.0	93.4	92.6	71.2	67.1	18.3	15.8
Female	52.4[1]	51.7	69.1	71.6	63.8	73.9	41.0	45.0	7.6	8.1
Canada:										
Total	55.1	57.5	79.6	79.7	77.4	84.3	53.9	49.9	8.9	7.1
Male	57.9	58.9	86.3	82.8	94.8	93.3	76.2	64.9	14.8	11.4
Female	52.2	55.9	73.0	76.5	60.1	75.6	33.6	35.7	4.4	3.9
France:										
Total	22.0	11.4	73.7	61.3	79.8	81.3	53.4	38.2	5.0	2.4

[Continued]

★ 420 ★

Labor Force Participation: Selected Countries: 1980 and 1990
[Continued]

Country and sex	15 to 19 years old		20 to 24 years old		25 to 54 years old		55 to 64 years old		65 years and over	
	1980	1990	1980	1990	1980	1990	1980	1990	1980	1990
Male	25.7	14.5	80.2	65.1	96.4	90.1	68.5	45.8	7.5	3.7
Female	18.3	8.1	67.5	57.4	63.0	72.6	39.7	31.3	3.3	1.5
Germany:[2]										
Total	43.9	(NA)	73.8	(NA)	74.0	(NA)	42.8	(NA)	4.5	(NA)
Male	47.0	(NA)	79.2	(NA)	93.6	(NA)	65.5	(NA)	7.0	(NA)
Female	40.5	(NA)	68.0	(NA)	53.6	(NA)	27.2	(NA)	3.1	(NA)
Italy:										
Total	31.1	23.1	65.1	66.5	65.9[3]	69.5	24.5[4]	22.3	7.5	4.6
Male	33.3	24.7	72.5	70.2	93.1[3]	90.7	39.6[4]	35.9	12.6	8.0
Female	28.9	21.4	57.9	62.8	39.9[3]	49.0	11.0[4]	10.1	3.5	2.2
Japan:										
Total	17.9	18.1	69.8	73.4	76.8	80.9	63.0	64.7	26.3	24.3
Male	17.4	18.3	69.6	71.7	97.0	97.5	85.4	83.3	41.0	36.5
Female	18.5	17.8	70.0	75.1	56.7	64.2	45.3	47.2	15.5	16.2
Sweden:										
Total	55.6	49.1	83.1	82.7	89.3	93.1	66.8	70.7	8.6	8.5
Male	55.3	47.7	84.5	84.7	95.4	94.9	78.7	75.4	14.2	12.3
Female	55.8	50.6	81.6	80.6	82.9	91.3	55.3	66.3	3.7	5.1
United Kingdom:										
Total	74.4	72.5	77.1	80.7	79.5	83.4	59.4	53.1	6.2	5.4
Male	73.6	74.2	86.0	86.3	95.4	93.6	81.6	68.1	10.3	8.6
Female	75.3	70.7	67.9	74.8	63.4	73.0	39.1	38.9	3.6	3.3

Source: U.S. Bureau of the Census, *Statistical Abstract of the United States: 1992* (112th edition.) Washington, DC, 1992, p. 839. Primary source: Organization for Economic Cooperation and Development, Paris, France, *Labour Force Statistics*, annual. *Notes:* (NA) stands for not available. 1. Persons 16 to 19 years old. 2. Former West Germany (prior to unification). 3. Persons 25 to 59 years old. 4. Persons 60 to 64 years old.

★ 421 ★

Labor Force

Farm Operators, by Age: 1982 and 1987

[In thousands]

Age	All farms		Farms with sales of $10,000 and over	
	1982	1987	1982	1987
Total operators	2,241	2,088	1,143	1,060
Under 25 years old	62	36	39	21
25 to 34 years old	294	243	173	147
35 to 44 years old	443	411	223	212
45 to 54 years old	505	455	264	228
55 to 64 years old	536	496	288	263
65 years old and over	400	447	156	188
Average age (years)	50.5	52.0	49.1	50.6

Source: U.S. Bureau of the Census, *Statistical Abstract of the United States: 1992* (112th edition.) Washington, DC, 1992, p. 645. Primary source: U.S. Bureau of the Census, *Census of Agriculture: 1974*, vol. II; 1982, vol. 1.

★ 422 ★

Labor Force

Farm Operator Off-Farm Employment, by Age of Operator: 1988

Based on a sample survey of 44,125 farm operators conducted as part of the Agricultural Economics and Land Ownership Survey.

Type of off-farm employment	Number (1,000)				Percent distribution			
	All farms	Under 35 years	35 to 64 years	65 years and over	All farms	Under 35 years	35 to 64 years	65 years and over
Total	1,879.6	245.2	1,224.2	410.1	100.0	100.0	100.0	100.0
Farm reporting off-farm work	924.7	149.7	700.2	74.8	49.2	61.0	57.2	18.2
Only operator	336.3	55.7	246.1	34.4	17.9	22.7	20.1	8.4
Only spouse	69.7	8.5	49.5	11.6	3.7	3.5	4.0	2.8
Both operator and spouse	518.7	85.4	404.6	28.7	27.6	34.8	33.0	7.0
Farms reporting no off-farm work	586.8	60.3	322.2	204.3	31.2	24.6	26.3	49.8
Farms not responding	368.1	35.2	201.8	131.1	19.6	14.3	16.5	32.0
Operators reporting off-farm work	855.0	141.2	650.7	63.1	100.0	100.0	100.0	100.0
Employee of another farm	54.9	10.2	35.2	9.5	6.4	7.2	5.4	15.1
Employee of private business	349.7	70.3	263.8	15.6	40.9	49.8	40.5	24.7
Government employee	135.3	14.5	112.9	7.9	15.8	10.3	17.3	12.5

[Continued]

★ 422 ★

Farm Operator Off-Farm Employment, by Age of Operator: 1988
[Continued]

Type of off-farm employment	Number (1,000)				Percent distribution			
	All farms	Under 35 years	35 to 64 years	65 years and over	All farms	Under 35 years	35 to 64 years	65 years and over
Self-employed:								
Farm related business	75.0	15.1	52.4	7.5	8.8	10.7	8.1	11.8
Nonfarm related								
business or profession	94.5	11.7	73.2	9.6	11.1	8.3	11.2	15.2
Type of employment not reported	145.6	19.4	113.2	13.0	17.0	13.7	17.4	20.7
Spouses reporting off-farm work	588.4	93.9	454.1	40.4	100.0	100.0	100.0	100.0
Employee of another farm	17.1	1.1	13.4	2.6	2.9	1.2	2.9	6.4
Employee of private business	267.4	49.5	200.9	17.1	45.4	52.7	44.2	42.2
Government employee	140.0	19.4	112.8	7.8	23.8	20.7	24.8	19.4
Self-employed:								
Farm related business	18.3	3.1	13.3	2.0	3.1	3.3	2.9	4.9
Nonfarm related								
business or profession	48.3	5.8	36.6	5.8	8.2	6.2	8.1	14.4
Type of employment not reported	97.2	15.0	77.1	5.1	16.5	16.0	17.0	12.5

Source: U.S. Bureau of the Census, *Statistical Abstract of the United States: 1992* (112th edition.) Washington, DC, 1992, p. 643 Primary source: U.S. Bureau of the Census, *1987 Census of Agriculture, Vol. 3, Related Surveys,* Part 2, *Agriculture Economics and Land Ownership Survey (1988).*

Employment Status

★ 423 ★

Employed Older American Workers, by Occupation Group, 1989

The largest occupation groups for older Americans are the managerial and professional specialty; technical, sales, and administrative support; and operators, fabricators, and laborers occupations. These percent distributions remain somewhat stable even after the age of 65.

[Numbers in thousands]

Occupation	55 to 59		60 to 64		65+	
	Number[1]	%	Number[1]	%	Number[1]	%
Total	6,854	100.0	4,644	100.0	3,355	100.0
Managerial and professional specialty	1,919	28.0	1,254	27.0	872	26.0
Technical, sales, administrative support	1,919	28.0	1,393	30.0	1,007	30.0
Service	891	13.0	650	14.0	604	18.0
Precision production, craft, repair	822	12.0	511	11.0	235	7.0

[Continued]

★ 423 ★

Employed Older American Workers, by Occupation Group, 1989

[Continued]

Occupation	55 to 59		60 to 64		65 +	
	Number[1]	%	Number[1]	%	Number[1]	%
Operators, fabricators, laborers	1,028	15.0	650	14.0	336	10.0
Farming, forestry, fishing	206	3.0	232	5.0	302	9.0

Source: Aging America, Trends and Projections, prepared by the U.S. Senate Special Committee on Aging, the American Association of Retired Persons, the Federal Council on the Aging, and the U.S. Administration on Aging, 1991, Washington, D.C., p. 99. Primary source: U.S. Department of Labor, Bureau of Labor Statistics, Unpublished data from the 1989 Current Population Survey. *Notes:* Data are based on annual averages. 1. Percent figures have been rounded, and the industry numbers were extrapolated from these figures by the editors; therefore, the figures shown are estimates.

★ 424 ★

Employment Status

Employment of Older American Workers, by Industry, 1989

The largest employers of Older Americans are the services, durable manufacturers, and wholesale/retail trade industries; but after the age of 65, there is a sharp drop in services and manufacturing industry employment, and the wholesale/retail-trade industries become the largest employers of Older Americans.

[Numbers in thousands]

Industry	55 to 59		60 to 64		65 +	
	Number	%	Number	%	Number	%
Total	6,854	100.0	4,644	100.0	3,355	100.0
Agriculture	206	3.0	232	5.0	302	9.0
Mining	69	1.0	0	0.0	0	0.0
Construction	411	6.0	279	6.0	134	4.0
Manufacturing--durables	822	12.0	511	11.0	201	6.0
Manufacturing--nondurables	617	9.0	325	7.0	168	5.0
Transportation/public utilities	480	7.0	279	6.0	101	3.0
Trade-wholesale and retail	1,097	16.0	836	18.0	705	21.0
Finance, insurance, and real estate	480	7.0	325	7.0	268	8.0
Services	2,330	34.0	1,625	35.0	268	8.0
Public administration	343	5.0	232	5.0	134	4.0

Source: Aging America, Trends and Projections, prepared by the U.S. Senate Special Committee on Aging, the American Association of Retired Persons, the Federal Council on the Aging, and the U.S. Administration on Aging, 1991, Washington, D.C., p. 98. Primary source: U.S. Department of Labor, Bureau of Labor Statistics, Unpublished data from the 1989 Current Population Survey. *Notes:* Percent figures have been rounded, and the industry numbers were extrapolated from these figures by the editors; therefore, the figures shown are estimates. Data are based on annual averages.

★ 425 ★

Employment Status

Employment Status, by Health

Health status is derived from a set of questions on activity limitations (e.g., difficulty walking a mile or reading the phone book) and previous health problems (e.g., lung disease or heart trouble). Numbers are in percent.

Health status	Working in career job	Working in bridge job	Not working
Poor health	14.0	16.9	37.9
Average health	54.8	56.2	43.1
Good health	31.2	26.9	19.0

Source: Ruhm, Christopher J., "Bridge Employment and Job Stopping in the 1980s," *The Commonwealth Fund, Americans Over 55 at Work Program*, May 1991, p. 16. *Notes:* Data are based on a survey of 3,509 Americans aged 50 to 64 conducted by Louis Harris Associates for The Commonwealth Fund between March and September 1989. The survey is a national cross section but excludes Alaska and Hawaii and people in prisons, hospitals, nursing homes, or religious and educational institutions.

★ 426 ★

Employment Status

Full- or Part-Time Status of Workers 45+ in Nonagricultural Industries, 1960 to 1989

Since 1960, the ratio of full- and part-time workers has remained fairly steady for both men and women aged 45 to 64. For workers over 65, full-time employment has dropped significantly for both sexes.

[Numbers in percent]

Sex and age	1960		1970		1982		1989	
	Full-time	Part-time	Full-time	Part-time	Full-time	Part-time	Full-time	Part-time
Men								
45 to 64	94	6	96	4	93	7	93	7
65+	70	30	62	38	52	48	52	48
Women								
45 to 64	78	22	77	23	74	26	76	24
65+	56	44	50	50	40	61	41	59

Source: Aging America, Trends and Projections, prepared by the U.S. Senate Special Committee on Aging, the American Association of Retired Persons, the Federal Council on the Aging, and the U.S. Administration on Aging, 1991, Washington, D.C., p. 102. Primary source: U.S. Department of Labor, Bureau of Labor Statistics, *Employment and Earnings*, Vol. 37, No. 1, January 1990; Vol. 30, No. 1, January 1983; Vol. 17, No. 7, January 1971; and *Labor Force and Employment in 1960*, Special Labor Force Report No. 14 (April 1961).

★ 427 ★

Employment Status

Full-Time Private Sector Workers, By Industry and Gender, 1988

From the source: "Women constitute nearly 40 percent of private full-time wage and salary workers, but their share of employment by industry differs widely.... Nearly 63 percent of full-time private sector workers work in either male- or female-dominated industries. The remainder, including 41 percent of women and 35 percent of men, work in industries whose gender composition closely reflects that of the private work force."

[Data are in percent]

Industry[1]	Women	Men
Total (percent)	100	100
Male-dominated industries		
Agriculture (80)	1	2
Manufacturing, durable goods (74)	11	20
Trade, wholesale (74)	4	7
Transportation and public utilities (73)	5	10
Construction (92)	1	11
Mining (86)	[2]	1
Total	22	51
Female-dominated industries		
Finance, insurance, and real estate (37)	14	6
Services, professional (35)	23	8
Total	37	14
Gender-balanced industries		
Services, business and personal (54)	11	9
Manufacturing, nondurable goods (61)	12	12
Trade, retail (54)	18	14
Total	41	35

Source: Sophie M. Korczyk, "Gender and Pension Coverage", in *Trends in Pensions 1992,* U.S. Department of Labor, Pension and Welfare Benefits Administration, U.S. Government Printing Office, Washington, DC, 1992, p. 129. Primary source: Employee Benefit Research Institute tabulations of May, 1988 Current Population Survey. *Notes:* 1. Percent male in parentheses. 2. Less than 1 percent.

★ 428 ★

Employment Status

Full-Time Private Sector Workers, by Occupation and Gender, 1988

From the source: "Women are more concentrated by occupation than by industry. Nearly half of both men and women work in occupations whose gender makeup closely resembles that of the full-time private work force. Most of the remainder, however, are sharply split along occupational lines. Among full-time women wage and salary workers, 45 percent worked in female-dominated occupations in 1988. Among men, in turn, 40 percent worked in male-dominated occupations."

[Data are in percent]

Occupation[1]	Women	Men
Total	100	100
Male-dominated occupations		
Nonfarm laborers (82)	2	6
Craftsmen (92)	3	23
Transportation equipment operators (95)	1	8
Other (87)	1	3
Total	7	40
Female-dominated occupations		
Administrative support, including clerical (20)	31	5
Service workers (39)	14	6
Total	45	11
Gender-balanced occupations		
Professional and technical (60)	13	13
Managers and officials (59)	14	14
Sales (60)	12	12
Operatives (61)	10	10
Total	49	49

Source: Sophie M. Korczyk, "Gender and Pension Coverage", in *Trends in Pensions 1992*, U.S. Department of Labor, Pension and Welfare Benefits Administration, U.S. Government Printing Office, Washington, DC, 1992, p. 131. Primary source: Author's calculations based on Employee Benefit Research Institute tabulations of May, 1988 Current Population Survey. *Notes:* Because of rounding, sums of individual items may not equal totals. 1. Percent male in parentheses.

★ 429 ★

Employment Status

Labor Force and Employment Status of Widows in Survey Week, by Race and Age[1]

[Percentage distributions]

Employment status	All races				Blacks
	Total age	Less than 65	65-74	75 and over	
n[2]	1,184	126	626	432	319
Total percent	100	100	100	100	100
Employed	11	34	13	3	15
Keeping house	30	26	27	34	30
Unable to work	5	4	4	7	11
Retired	50	31	51	52	41
Other[4]	5	6	5	4	3

Source: Herbert S. Parnes, Thomas N. Chirikos, Elizabeth G. Menaghan, Frank L. Mott, Gilbert Nestel, Lois B. Shaw, David G. Sommers, *The NLS Older Male Sample Revisited: A Unique Data Base for Gerontological Research*, Center for Human Resource Research, The Ohio State University, 1993, p. 94, reprinted with permission. *Notes:* 1. Noninstitutionalized population only. 2. Number of sample cases on which weighted percentages are based. 3. Percentages may not add to 100 because of rounding. 4. Includes 1 percent or less who were unemployed.

★ 430 ★

Employment Status

Number of Self-Employed Older American Workers, by Age and Sex, 1951-90

[Number in thousands]

Year	Total	Age group					
		55-59	60-61	62-64	65-69	70-71	72+
Both sexes							
1951	4,190	462	164	215	237	55	117
1955	6,810	737	290	441	497	143	322
1960	6,870	846	316	452	414	101	286
1965	6,550	885	328	411	388	92	267
1970	6,270	839	327	407	388	94	244
1975	7,000	823	317	382	393	95	248
1980	8,200	852	307	381	419	112	280
1985	10,600	929	368	434	455	124	321
1990[1]	12,900	1,046	414	543	638	170	442
Men							
1951	3,620	393	139	179	204	47	97
1955	5,980	631	247	373	420	122	265
1960	5,990	709	260	386	348	83	230
1965	5,640	742	272	339	326	75	217

[Continued]

★ 430 ★

Number of Self-Employed Older American Workers, by Age and Sex, 1951-90

[Continued]

Year	Total	Age group					
		55-59	60-61	62-64	65-69	70-71	72+
1970	5,370	695	268	324	320	77	201
1975	5,790	672	255	309	326	78	201
1980	6,407	668	244	301	333	92	226
1985	7,623	686	278	328	351	97	249
1990[1]	8,705	736	293	395	476	131	337
Women							
1951	570	69	25	36	33	8	20
1955	830	106	43	68	77	21	57
1960	880	137	56	66	67	18	55
1965	910	143	56	72	62	17	50
1970	900	144	59	65	68	17	43
1975	1,210	151	62	73	67	17	47
1980	1,793	184	63	80	86	20	54
1985	2,977	243	90	106	104	27	72
1990[1]	4,195	310	122	148	162	40	106

Source: *Annual Statistical Supplement, 1992 to the Social Security Bulletin*, U.S. Department of Health and Human Services, Social Security Administration, January 1993, p. 157. *Note:* 1. Preliminary data.

★ 431 ★

Employment Status

Survey Date Employment Status of Respondents, by Marital Status, Age, and Gender

[Numbers are in percent]

Age, marital status, gender	Working in career job	Working in bridge job	Not working
All respondents	32.6	28.4	39.0
Marital status			
Married	31.4	28.2	40.4
Unmarried	36.3	28.0	35.7
Age (in years)			
Men			
55-59	42.1	36.8	21.2
60-61	33.3	31.3	35.4
62-64	21.5	21.0	57.5

[Continued]

★ 431 ★

Survey Date Employment Status of Respondents, by Marital Status, Age, and Gender
[Continued]

Age, marital status, gender	Working in career job	Working in bridge job	Not working
Women			
50-54	41.6	26.7	31.7
55-59	33.9	24.1	42.1

Source: Ruhm, Christopher J., "Bridge Employment and Job Stopping in the 1980s," *The Commonwealth Fund, Americans Over 55 at Work Program*, May 1991, p. 4. *Notes:* Data are based on a survey of 3,509 Americans aged 50 to 64 conducted by Louis Harris Associates for The Commonwealth Fund between March and September 1989. The survey is a national cross section but excludes Alaska and Hawaii and people in prisons, hospitals, nursing homes, or religious and educational institutions.

★ 432 ★

Employment Status

Work Experience and Mean Earnings

Noninstitutional persons as of March 1988.

	Age 55 to 64		
	Both sexes	Male	Female
With a work disability			
All workers			
Number (thous.)	1,111	646	465
Mean earnings			
Value (dol.)	12,074	15,187	7,747
Standard error (dol.)	557	798	630
Year-round full-time			
Number (thous.)	332	239	93
Mean earnings			
Value (dol.)	21,056	22,601	17,078
Standard error (dol.)	1,098	1,324	1,816
With no work disability			
All workers			
Number (thous.)	11,872	6,778	5,095
Mean earnings			
Value (dol.)	22,236	28,899	13,372
Standard error (dol.)	292	441	250
Year-round full-time			
Number (thous.)	7,994	5,159	2,835

[Continued]

★ 432 ★

Work Experience and Mean Earnings
[Continued]

	Age 55 to 64		
	Both sexes	Male	Female
Mean earnings			
Value (dol.)	27,950	33,116	18,547
Standard error (dol.)	368	507	357

Source: U.S. Department of Commerce, Bureau of the Census, Current Population Reports, Special Studies, Series P-23, No. 160, *Labor Force Status and Other Characteristics of Persons With a Work Disability: 1981 to 1988*, U.S. Government Printing Office, Washington, DC, 1989, pp. 52-57.

★ 433 ★
Employment Status

Work Status of Population Ages 40 and Over, 1989
[Data are in thousands]

Age	Total	Presently working			Retired or not presently working				Never or less than 5 years total
		Total	Private sector	Public sector	Total	Private sector[1]	Public sector[2]	Sector not deter-mined	
					Total				
Total	92,875	48,714	38,989	9,724	30,260	22,706	6,155	1,399	13,901
40-54	42,106	33,709	26,699	7,010	4,300	3,341	743	216	4,098
55-59	10,594	6,923	5,484	1,440	2,261	1,730	435	96	1,409
60-64	10,699	4,712	3,888	825	4,415	3,337	886	192	1,572
65-69	10,152	2,044	1,736	308	6,201	4,556	1,370	274	1,907
70-74	7,854	840	751	90	5,378	3,915	1,221	242	1,637
75-79	5,845	327	295	32	4,068	3,065	824	180	1,450
80 and older	5,623	157	137	19	3,638	2,763	675	200	1,829
55 and older	50,767	15,005	12,290	2,714	25,960	19,365	5,412	1,183	9,804
65 and older	29,474	3,370	2,918	449	19,399	14,298	4,091	895	6,822
					Men				
Total	42,756	26,775	22,184	4,591	14,318	10,751	2,876	691	1,662
40-54	20,452	18,287	15,002	3,285	1,609	1,209	306	94	556
55-59	5,056	3,884	3,191	693	1,009	735	219	55	163
60-64	4,988	2,630	2,248	382	2,153	1,591	462	100	205
65-69	4,609	1,199	1,031	168	3,203	2,369	694	140	206
70-74	3,399	474	441	32	2,757	2,031	603	124	168
75-79	2,289	198	182	17	1,920	1,475	344	100	171
80 and older	1,962	103	90	13	1,667	1,342	247	78	192

[Continued]

★ 433 ★

Work Status of Population Ages 40 and Over, 1989

[Continued]

Age	Total	Presently working			Retired or not presently working				Never or less than 5 years total
		Total	Private sector	Public sector	Total	Private sector[1]	Public sector[2]	Sector not deter-mined	
55 and older	22,304	8,488	7,182	1,306	12,709	9,542	2,570	597	1,106
65 and older	12,260	1,974	1,743	231	9,547	7,216	1,889	442	738
Women									
Total	50,119	21,938	16,805	5,133	15,942	11,955	3,279	708	12,239
40-54	21,655	15,422	11,697	3,725	2,691	2,133	437	122	3,541
55-59	5,538	3,039	2,292	747	1,252	995	216	41	1,246
60-64	5,711	2,082	1,640	442	2,262	1,746	424	91	1,367
65-69	5,543	845	706	140	2,998	2,187	676	134	1,701
70-74	4,455	367	309	57	2,620	1,884	619	118	1,468
75-79	3,556	129	114	15	2,148	1,589	479	79	1,279
80 and older	3,661	53	47	6	1,971	1,421	428	122	1,637
55 and older	28,464	6,516	5,708	1,408	13,251	9,822	2,842	586	8,698
65 and older	17,215	1,395	1,176	219	9,737	7,018	2,202	454	6,085

Source: David J. Beller and David D. McCarthy, "Private Pension Benefits," in *Trends in Pensions 1992*, U.S. Department of Labor, Pension and Welfare Benefits Administration, U.S. Government Printing Office, Washington, DC, 1992, pp. 233-234. Primary source: Pension benefit amount supplement to the December 1989 Current Population Survey. *Notes:* 1. Job with pension coverage or longest job was in private sector. 2. Job with pension coverage or longest job was in public sector.

Job Tenure

★ 434 ★

Job Tenure and Pension Coverage of Full-Time Private Sector Workers, by Gender, 1988

From the source: "Women's pension prospects depend in large part on their mobility among jobs, industries, and professions. The interactions between mobility and pension coverage are complex. Long-tenured employees are more likely to have pension coverage. Pension coverage, in turn, may reduce mobility for some employees. For others, it may have the reverse effect."

[Data are in percent]

Years with primary employer	Women	Men
Job tenure		
All tenures	100	100
Less than 1 year	19	17
1 to 4 years	37	33
5 to 9 years	18	17
10 to 14 years	10	11
15 to 19 years	6	7
20 years or more	5	11
Pension coverage		
All tenures	43	50
Less than 1 year	13	18
1 to 4 years	37	39
5 to 9 years	63	62
10 to 14 years	70	73
15 to 19 years	72	77
20 years or more	75	82

Source: Sophie M. Korczyk, "Gender and Pension Coverage", in *Trends in Pensions 1992*, U.S. Department of Labor, Pension and Welfare Benefits Administration, U.S. Government Printing Office, Washington, DC, 1992, p. 133. Primary source: Author's calculations based on Employee Benefit Research Institute tabulations of May, 1988 Current Population Survey.

Bridge Jobs

★ 435 ★

Characteristics of Career and Bridge Jobs

[Numbers are in percent]

Employment, hours, and occupation	Career job character- istics	Bridge job character- istics
Type of employment		
Salary	46.5	36.4
Hourly wage	38.3	39.9
Self-employed	14.1	22.1
Hours		
Full-time	86.5	76.1
Part-time	13.5	23.9
Occupation		
Professional/managerial	26.9	28.2
Technical/sales	12.5	15.1
Clerical/service	27.0	27.9
Agricultural	2.9	3.3
Production	18.3	13.5
Transport/laborer	11.4	11.4

Source: Ruhm, Christopher J., "Bridge Employment and Job Stopping in the 1980s," *The Commonwealth Fund, Americans Over 55 at Work Program*, May 1991, p. 7. *Notes:* Data are based on a survey of 3,509 Americans aged 50 to 64 conducted by Louis Harris Associates for The Commonwealth Fund between March and September 1989. The survey is a national cross section but excludes Alaska and Hawaii and people in prisons, hospitals, nursing homes, or religious and educational institutions.

★ 436 ★

Bridge Jobs

Number of Bridge Jobs Held by Respondents

[Numbers are in percent]

Number of bridge jobs held	Currently working in bridge job	Previously worked in bridge job
1	44.9	45.7
2	19.7	21.3
3	13.7	11.5
4 or greater	21.7	21.5
Average No.	2.2	2.1

Source: Ruhm, Christopher J., ''Bridge Employment and Job Stopping in the 1980s,'' *The Commonwealth Fund, Americans Over 55 at Work Program*, May 1991, p. 6. *Notes:* Data are based on a survey of 3,509 Americans aged 50 to 64 conducted by Louis Harris Associates for The Commonwealth Fund between March and September 1989. The survey is a national cross section but excludes Alaska and Hawaii and people in prisons, hospitals, nursing homes, or religious and educational institutions.

Unemployment

★ 437 ★

Unemployment of Older Americans, 1989

Characteristic	60 to 64			65 +		
	Total	Men	Women	Total	Men	Women
Number unemployed (in thousands)	145	92	53	91	49	41
Unemployment rate (percent)	3.0	3.3	2.6	2.6	2.4	2.9

Source: Aging America, Trends and Projections, prepared by the U.S. Senate Special Committee on Aging, the American Association of Retired Persons, the Federal Council on the Aging, and the U.S. Administration on Aging, 1991, Washington, D.C., p. 104. Primary source: U.S. Department of Labor, Bureau of Labor Statistics, *Employment and Earnings*, Vol. 37, No. 1, January 1990. *Note:* Data are based on annual averages.

★ 438 ★

Unemployment

Employment Status of Displaced Workers, by Age: January 1990

Displaced workers were defined in the original source as being workers "20+ with three or more years of job tenure who lost their jobs in the preceding five years as a result of plant closings or moves, slack work, or the abolition of their positions or shifts." Displaced older Americans are less likely to search for new jobs, often going directly into retirement. For those older Americans who are still too young to retire, displacement is often very difficult. "In fact, people age 55 to 64 have the longest duration of unemployment of any group in the country. Unemployed workers age 55 to 64 in 1989 had an average of 18 weeks of unemployment, compared with 9 weeks for workers age 20 to 24."

Labor characteristic	20 to 24	25 to 54	55 to 64	65+
Not in labor force	13.9	8.1	31.5	61.5
Employed	76.3	77.9	52.7	28.4
Unemployed	9.9	14.0	15.8	10.1

Source: Aging America, Trends and Projections, prepared by the U.S. Senate Special Committee on Aging, the American Association of Retired Persons, the Federal Council on the Aging, and the U.S. Administration on Aging, 1991, Washington, D.C., p. 106. Primary source: U.S. Department of Labor, Bureau of Labor Statistics "Worker Displacement Continues to Decline," Press Release USDL 90-364, July 17, 1990.

★ 439 ★

Unemployment

Status of Unemployed Jobseekers in Second Sample Month, by Age of All Jobseekers and of Those Using Public Employment Agencies in the First Sample Month, 1991

Age group	Total jobseekers in first month	Labor force status in second month (percent distribution)				
		Total	Employed	Unemployed		Not in labor force
				Still searching	On layoff	
Unemployed jobseekers	32,058	100.0	22.5	53.9	2.4	21.2
16-19 years	5,689	100.0	23.9	43.0	0.6	32.5
20-24 years	5,602	100.0	26.8	49.9	1.5	21.8
25-34 years	8,595	100.0	23.2	55.8	2.9	18.1
35-44 years	6,349	100.0	20.5	60.0	3.2	16.3
45-54 years	3,526	100.0	20.3	60.5	3.1	16.1
55-64 years	1,832	100.0	15.7	58.5	3.8	22.0
65 years and over	465	100.0	11.8	50.3	2.6	35.3

[Continued]

★ 439 ★

Status of Unemployed Jobseekers in Second Sample Month, by Age of All Jobseekers and of Those Using Public Employment Agencies in the First Sample Month, 1991

[Continued]

Age group	Total jobseekers in first month	Labor force status in second month (percent distribution)				
		Total	Employed	Unemployed		Not in labor force
				Still searching	On layoff	
Public employment agency[1]	8,178	100.0	21.6	61.3	2.4	14.7
16-19 years	791	100.0	25.2	50.6	1.4	22.9
20-24 years	1,512	100.0	24.9	56.8	1.3	17.1
25-34 years	2,467	100.0	22.2	62.1	2.6	13.1
35-44 years	1,920	100.0	19.7	65.4	3.2	11.7
45-54 years	985	100.0	18.9	64.9	3.1	13.1
55-64 years	422	100.0	15.9	65.4	2.8	15.9
65 years and over	81	100.0	12.3	61.7	2.5	23.5

Source: Bortnick, Steven M. and Ports, Michelle Harrison, "Job search methods and results: tracking the unemployed, 1991," *Monthly Labor Review*, December 1992, p. 33. *Notes:* 1. The remaining methods of job search are excluded because the results, by age, are quite similar to those for all jobseekers.

Work Preferences

★ 440 ★

Preferred Hours of Work

[Numbers are in percent]

Preference	Working in career job	Working in bridge job	Not working
Prefer full-time job	66.8	61.2	44.1
Prefer part-time job	31.5	37.5	53.6
Currently work full time			
Prefer full time	75.3	75.3	
Prefer part time	24.7	24.7	
Currently work part time			
Prefer full time	22.7	21.0	
Prefer part time	77.3	79.0	

Source: Ruhm, Christopher J., "Bridge Employment and Job Stopping in the 1980s," *The Commonwealth Fund, Americans Over 55 at Work Program*, May 1991, p. 8. *Notes:* Data are based on a survey of 3,509 Americans aged 50 to 64 conducted by Louis Harris Associates for The Commonwealth Fund between March and September 1989. The survey is a national cross section but excludes Alaska and Hawaii and people in prisons, hospitals, nursing homes, or religious and educational institutions.

★ 441 ★

Work Preferences

Actual and Preferred Work Schedules: Wage and Salary Men and Women

[Numbers are in percent]

Actual schedule	Prefer full time	Prefer part time	Don't know	Percentage
Men				
Working FT	80.0	18.0	2.0	93.0
Working PT	33.0	67.0	0.0	6.0
Don't know	-	-	-	1.0
Total	77.0	21.0	2.0	100.0
Women				
Working FT	66.0	33.0	1.0	80.0
Working PT	17.0	82.0	1.0	19.0
Don't know	-	-	-	1.0
Total	56.0	43.0	1.0	100.0

Source: Quinn, Joseph F. and Richard V. Berkhauser, "Retirement Preferences and Plans of Older American Workers," *The Commonwealth Fund, Americans Over 55 at Work Program,* October 1990, p. 9. *Notes:* Data are based on a survey of about 2,000 employed Americans, part of a larger survey conducted by Louis Harris and Associates, March-September 1989, for The Commonwealth Fund.

★ 442 ★

Work Preferences

Actual and Preferred Work Schedules, by Age of Worker

Age	Percent who work part time	Percent who would like to work part time
Men		
55-57	5.0	17.0
58-59	4.0	19.0
60-61	8.0	26.0
62-64	13.0	28.0
Women		
50-52	17.0	44.0
53-54	20.0	43.0

[Continued]

★ 442 ★

Actual and Preferred Work Schedules, by Age of Worker

[Continued]

Age	Percent who work part time	Percent who would like to work part time
55-57	19.0	40.0
58-59	20.0	45.0

Source: Quinn, Joseph F. and Richard V. Berkhauser, "Retirement Preferences and Plans of Older American Workers," *The Commonwealth Fund, Americans Over 55 at Work Program,* October 1990, p. 10. *Notes:* Data are based on a survey of about 2,000 employed Americans, part of a larger survey conducted by Louis Harris and Associates, March-September 1989, for The Commonwealth Fund.

★ 443 ★

Work Preferences

Wage and Salary Workers Aged 50 to 64 Who Would Extend Their Working Careers, by Program Option

[Numbers are in millions and percent]

Response	Men aged 55-64		Women aged 50-59		Total
	Number	Percent	Number	Percent	
Would work longer than now planned if employer pension contributions continued past age 65	1.15	26.0	1.23	24.0	2.38
Would work longer than now planned if offered fewer hours and responsibilities and somewhat lower pay	1.37	31.0	1.56	30.0	2.93
Would accept training for job with different responsibilities but same hours and pay	1.41	2.0	2.13	42.0	3.54
Answered yes to at least one of the three questions above	2.33	53.0	2.94	57.0	5.27

Source: Quinn, Joseph F. and Richard V. Berkhauser, "Retirement Preferences and Plans of Older American Workers," *The Commonwealth Fund, Americans Over 55 at Work Program,* October 1990, p. 11. *Notes:* Data are based on a survey of about 2,000 employed Americans, part of a larger survey conducted by Louis Harris and Associates, March-September 1989, for The Commonwealth Fund.

★ 444 ★

Work Preferences

Most Important Reason for Working

[Numbers are in percent]

Reason	Men aged 55-64	Women aged 50-59
Need a job	59	62
I need the money	54	54
I need health insurance	5	6
I have medical bills to pay	1	1
Want a job	41	38
I enjoy my work	11	13
I would be bored otherwise	10	10
I want to do something useful	8	7
My work is challenging	6	6
Working makes me feel younger	3	2
Other	2	1

Source: Quinn, Joseph F. and Richard V. Berkhauser, "Retirement Preferences and Plans of Older American Workers," *The Commonwealth Fund, Americans Over 55 at Work Program,* October 1990, p. 14. *Notes:* Data are based on a survey of about 2,000 employed Americans, part of a larger survey conducted by Louis Harris and Associates, March-September 1989, for The Commonwealth Fund. 1. Fewer than 0.5%.

★ 445 ★

Work Preferences

Most Important Reason for Working, by Age and Sex

[Numbers are in percent]

Age	Need a job[1]	Want a job[1]
Men		
55-57	62	38
58-59	62	38
60-61	58	42
62-64	48	52
Women		
50-52	57	43
53-54	58	42

[Continued]

★ 445 ★

Most Important Reason for Working, by Age and Sex
[Continued]

Age	Need a job[1]	Want a job[1]
55-57	64	36
58-59	67	33

Source: Quinn, Joseph F. and Richard V. Berkhauser, "Retirement Preferences and Plans of Older American Workers," *The Commonwealth Fund, Americans Over 55 at Work Program,* October 1990, p. 14. *Notes:* Data are based on a survey of about 2,000 employed Americans, part of a larger survey conducted by Louis Harris and Associates, March-September 1989, for The Commonwealth Fund. 1. Fewer than 0.5%.

Immigrants

★ 446 ★

Labor Force Participation Rates by Gender, Age, and Year of Immigration, November 1989

Gender and age	All years	1982-89			1975-81	1965-74	1960-64	Before 1960
		Total	1987-89	1982-86				
Men								
16 years and older	78.3	81.4	75.7	85.2	87.6	85.4	81.7	48.6
55 years and older	42.7	48.7	[1]	[1]	59.3	56.0	55.3	33.7
55 to 64 years	78.8	[1]	[1]	[1]	75.5	77.6	79.4	80.4
65 years and older	14.0	[1]	[1]	[1]	[1]	22.7	[1]	10.6
Women								
16 years and older	52.2	49.0	40.5	54.5	60.2	62.6	60.8	34.3
55 years and older	25.1	20.7	[1]	23.0	30.0	34.1	37.5	20.3
55 to 64 years	48.8	37.0	[1]	[1]	49.3	53.5	52.1	47.3
65 years and older	7.7	[1]	[1]	[1]	8.0	7.7	[1]	7.2

Source: Meisenheimer, Joseph R. III, "How do immigrants fare in the U.S. labor market?," *Monthly Labor Review,* December 1992, p. 7. *Notes:* 1. Data are not shown where there are fewer than 75,000 in the population.

★ 447 ★

Immigrants

Labor Force Status by Country of Birth and Age, November 1989

[Numbers in thousands]

Gender, country of birth and age	Population	Labor force	Labor force participation rate	Employed	Employment-population ratio	Unemployed	Unemployment rate
Men							
U.S. born, 16 years and older	77,763	59,326	76.3	56,263	72.4	3,063	5.2
55 years and older	19,609	7,661	39.1	7,395	37.7	265	3.5
55 to 64 years	8,832	5,908	66.9	5,705	64.6	203	3.4
65 years and older	10,777	1,753	16.3	1,691	15.7	63	3.6
Foreign born, 16 years and older	7,173	5,615	78.3	5,297	73.8	318	5.7
55 years and older	1,533	654	42.7	626	40.8	28	4.3
55 to 64 years	678	534	78.8	513	75.6	22	4.1
65 years and older	855	120	14.0	113	13.2	7	5.6
Women							
U.S. born, 16 years and older	85,811	50,529	58.9	47,923	55.8	2,607	5.2
55 years and older	24,893	5,858	23.5	5,690	22.9	168	2.9
55 to 64 years	9,811	4,536	46.2	4,401	44.9	135	3.0
65 years and older	15,082	1,323	8.8	1,289	8.5	33	2.5
Foreign born, 16 years and older	7,701	4,020	52.2	3,791	49.2	229	5.7
55 years and older	2,098	527	25.1	503	24.0	24	4.6
55 to 64 years	891	435	48.8	414	46.5	20	4.7
65 years and older	1,207	93	7.7	89	7.4	4	4.0

Source: Meisenheimer, Joseph R. III, "How do immigrants fare in the U.S. labor market?," *Monthly Labor Review*, December 1992, p. 6.

★ 448 ★

Immigrants

Percent Distribution of Population Aged 25 and Older by Gender, Country of Birth, Age, and Years of School Completed, November 1989

Gender, country of birth, and age	Total		Years of school completed				
	Number (thousands)	Percent	8 years or less	9 to 11 years	12 years	1 to 3 years of college	4 years of college or more
Men							
U.S. born, 25 years and older	63,937	100.0	9.7	10.8	36.6	18.4	24.5
55 years and older	19,609	100.0	22.5	14.7	32.6	12.3	18.0
55 to 64 years	8,832	100.0	15.7	13.8	36.1	13.6	20.8
65 years and older	10,777	100.0	28.0	15.4	29.8	11.2	15.6
Foreign born, 25 years and older	6,004	100.0	27.0	7.9	24.9	13.6	26.6
55 years and older	1,533	100.0	37.1	7.3	24.1	9.8	21.7
55 to 64 years	678	100.0	35.1	5.8	23.7	11.3	24.1
65 years and older	855	100.0	38.7	8.5	24.4	8.5	19.9
Women							
U.S. born, 25 years and older	71,403	100.0	9.1	11.9	42.3	18.5	18.2

[Continued]

★ 448 ★

Percent Distribution of Population Aged 25 and Older by Gender, Country of Birth, Age, and Years of School Completed, November 1989

[Continued]

Gender, country of birth, and age	Total		Years of school completed				
	Number (thousands)	Percent	8 years or less	9 to 11 years	12 years	1 to 3 years of college	4 years of college or more
55 years and older	24,893	100.0	20.2	17.0	40.5	12.2	10.2
55 to 64 years	9,811	100.0	11.8	15.9	46.8	13.8	11.8
65 years and older	15,082	100.0	25.6	17.7	36.4	11.1	9.2
Foreign born, 25 years and older	6,672	100.0	30.3	8.4	29.6	13.0	18.7
55 years and older	2,098	100.0	42.7	9.5	30.1	8.6	9.2
55 to 64 years	891	100.0	35.4	8.2	33.5	11.5	11.4
65 years and older	1,207	100.0	48.1	10.4	27.5	6.5	7.5

Source: Meisenheimer, Joseph R. III, "How do immigrants fare in the U.S. labor market?," *Monthly Labor Review*, December 1992, p. 7.

Unions

★ 449 ★

Union Member Earnings, by Age: 1983 and 1991

Data include employed wage and salary workers, 16 years old and over and exclude self-employed workers whose businesses are incorporated although they technically qualify as wage and salary workers.

[Annual averages of monthly data. Figures in dollars]

Characteristic	Median usual weekly earnings[1]							
	Total		Union members[2]		Represented by unions[3]		Not represented by unions	
	1983	1991	1983	1991	1983	1991	1983	1991
Total	313	430	388	526	383	522	288	404
16 to 24 years old	210	278	281	356	275	347	203	272
25 to 34 years old	321	417	382	496	376	491	304	403
35 to 44 years old	369	499	411	557	407	555	339	479
45 to 54 years old	366	507	404	581	402	580	335	480
55 to 64 years old	346	469	392	534	390	529	316	427
65 years and over	260	381	338	522	330	526	238	348

Source: U.S. Bureau of the Census, *Statistical Abstract of the United States: 1992* (112th edition.) Washington, DC, 1992, p. 422. Primary source: U.S. Bureau of Labor Statistics, *Employment and Earnings*, January issues. *Notes:* 1. For full-time employed wage and salary workers. 2. Members of a labor union or an employee association similar to labor union. 3. Members of a labor union or an employee association similar to a union as well as workers who report no union affiliation but whose jobs are covered by a union or an employee association contract.

★ 450 ★

Unions

Union Membership of Employed Wage and Salary Workers, by Age: 1983 and 1991

Data include employed wage and salary workers, 16 years old and over and exclude self-employed workers whose businesses are incorporated although they technically qualify as wage and salary workers.

[Annual averages of monthly data]

Age	Employed wage and salary workers									
	Total (1,000)		Union members[1] (1,000)		Represented by unions[2] (1,000)		Percent union members		Percent represented by union	
	1983	1991	1983	1991	1983	1991	1983	1991	1983	1991
Total	88,290	102,786	17,717	16,568	20,532	18,734	20.1	16.1	23.3	18.2
16 to 24 years old	19,305	17,340	1,749	1,142	2,145	1,341	9.1	6.6	11.1	7.7
25 to 34 years old	25,978	30,106	5,097	4,228	5,990	4,824	19.6	14.0	23.1	16.0
35 to 44 years old	18,722	27,056	4,648	5,339	5,362	6,040	24.8	19.7	28.6	22.3
45 to 54 years old	13,150	16,863	3,554	3,743	4,014	4,163	27.0	22.2	30.5	24.7
55 to 64 years old	9,201	9,116	2,474	1,919	2,788	2,138	26.9	21.1	30.3	23.5
65 years and over	1,934	2,305	196	198	234	228	10.1	8.6	12.1	9.9

Source: U.S. Bureau of the Census, *Statistical Abstract of the United States: 1992* (112th edition.) Washington, DC, 1992, p. 422. Primary source: U.S. Bureau of Labor Statistics, *Employment and Earnings*, January issues. *Notes:* 1. Members of a labor union or an employee association similar to labor union. 2. Members of a labor union or an employee association similar to a union as well as workers who report no union affiliation but whose jobs are covered by a union or an employee association contract.

Age Discrimination

★ 451 ★

Administrative Enforcement of Age Discrimination Laws

This table shows age discrimination charges[1] handled by the Equal Employment Opportunity Commission (EEOC) and the Fair Employment Practices Agencies (FEPAs).

	EEOC		FEPAs	
	FY1988	FY1989	FY1988	FY1989
Charge receipts to process Resolutions[2]	11,290	11,454	7,343	7,743
Negotiated settlements	2,161	1,927	1,152	2,027
No cause	9,482	9,594	2,868	3,143
Unsuccessful conciliations	569	633	29	18
Administrative closures	4,777	7,296	1,093	974

[Continued]

★ 451 ★

Administrative Enforcement of Age Discrimination Laws
[Continued]

| | EEOC | | FEPAs | |
	FY1988	FY1989	FY1988	FY1989
Subtotal by statute	16,989	19,427	5,142	6,172
Benefits	36,341,000	26,208,000	NA[3]	NA[3]

Source: U.S. Equal Employment Opportunity Commission, *Fiscal Year 1989 Annual Report*, pp. 8-9. *Notes:* 1. Under the Age Discrimination in Employment Act (ADEA). 2. Includes all charges concurrent with Equal Pay Act (EPA) charges. 3. Not applicable.

★ 452 ★

Age Discrimination

Age Discrimination Charge Receipts, by Issue, Fiscal Year 1989

Employment discrimination charges filed with the Equal Employment Opportunity Commission (EEOC) and the Fair Employment Practices Agencies (FEPAs) on the basis of age. From the source: "Employment discrimination charges received by the EEOC and FEPAs can be categorized by the issues and bases raised in each charge. Because there are multiple bases[1] and issues for most charges, the totals show a substantially higher number of issues connected with individual charges than the actual number of charges received. Charge receipt analyses are based on EEOC computer data on charges received by EEOC and on records recorded by FEPAs under contract with the Commission. The total number of charges analyzed... may not equal the total number of charges received by the EEOC and FEPAs in a given year."

Issues	ADEA charges	Total charges	Percent ADEA
Advertising	8	28	28.57
Apprentice	7	56	12.50
Benefits	1,606	3,096	51.87
Demotion	1,014	3,528	28.74
Discharge	11,317	54,597	20.73
Discipline	437	3,658	11.95
Exclusion	39	237	16.46
Harassment	1,350	9,360	14.42
Hiring	3,412	9,113	37.44
Intimidation	269	2,118	12.70
Job classification	116	596	19.46
Layoff	2,068	4,961	41.69
Maternity	9	3,231	0.28
Paternity	12	151	7.95
Promotion	1,322	7,426	17.80
Qualifications	104	262	39.69
Recall	341	874	39.02
Reference unfavorable	46	328	14.02

[Continued]

★ 452 ★

Age Discrimination Charge Receipts, by Issue, Fiscal Year 1989

[Continued]

Issues	ADEA charges	Total charges	Percent ADEA
Referral	93	306	30.39
Reinstatement	135	550	24.55
Retirement, involuntary	755	792	95.33
Segregated faciliy	8	120	6.67
Segregated location	3	26	11.54
Seniority	185	503	36.78
Sex harass	127	5,264	2.41
Suspension	277	2,795	9.91
Tenure	40	181	22.10
Terms of employment	3,130	19,013	16.46
Testing	17	126	13.49
Training	206	1,222	16.86
Union representation	222	1,015	21.87
Wages	1,721	10,253	16.79
Other	1,234	7,112	17.35
Total issues	31,630	0	
Total charges	24,041	106,428	
% total charges	22.6		

Source: U.S. Equal Employment Opportunity Commission, *Fiscal Year 1989 Annual Report*, p. 17. Primary source: Equal Employment Opportunity Commission National Database. *Notes:* 1. Original source includes data on charges for other bases, such as race, religion, etc. [ed.]. 2. Data extrapolated by *SROA* editors.

★ 453 ★

Age Discrimination

Age Discrimination Charge Receipts, by State or Territory

Number of age discrimination charges filed (under any statute and over any issue) with the Equal Employment Opportunity Commission (EEOC) and the Fair Employment Practices Agencies (FEPAs) in fiscal year 1989.

	Charge receipts
Alabama	446
Alaska	43
Arizona	460
Arkansas	212
California	1,210
Colorado	583
Connecticut	393

[Continued]

★ 453 ★

Age Discrimination Charge Receipts, by State or Territory

[Continued]

	Charge receipts
Delaware	51
District of Columbia	219
Florida	1,348
Georgia	694
Hawaii	94
Idaho	53
Illinois	1,379
Indiana	544
Iowa	220
Kansas	357
Kentucky	287
Louisiana	283
Maine	81
Maryland	411
Massachusetts	875
Michigan	827
Minnesota	469
Mississippi	188
Missouri	685
Montana	58
Nebraska	142
Nevada	233
New Hampshire	57
New Jersey	669
New Mexico	251
New York	1,812
North Carolina	686
North Dakota	20
Ohio	1,510
Oklahoma	227
Oregon	268
Pennsylvania	1,598
Rhode Island	134
South Carolina	397
South Dakota	36
Tennessee	643
Texas	1,908
Utah	253
Vermont	31
Virginia	469
Washington	390
West Virginia	139
Wisconsin	465
Wyoming	71

[Continued]

★ 453 ★

Age Discrimination Charge Receipts, by State or Territory

[Continued]

	Charge receipts
Guam	0
Puerto Rico	73
Virgin Islands	2
Total	24,954

Source: U.S. Equal Employment Opportunity Commission, *Fiscal Year 1989 Annual Report*, p. 18.

★ 454 ★

Age Discrimination

EEOC Litigation Activity, FY 1988 and FY 1989

Data show number of substantive lawsuits filed with the EEOC (Equal Employment Opportunity Commission) under fair employment statutes, resolution of those cases, and monetary compensation made.

	FY 1988	FY 1989
Total actions filed	555	598
Direct suits and interventions	438	484
Title VII[1]	299	312
ADEA[2]	106	134
EPA[3]	6	4
Concurrent	27	34
Subpoena enforcement and other	117	114
Total resolutions	540	536
Direct suits and interventions	430	435
Title VII	306	303
ADEA	85	99
EPA	16	6
Concurrent	23	27
Subpoena enforcement and other	110	101
Monetary benefits secured (dollars) through litigation		
Title VII	22,538,000	8,998,000
ADEA	26,214,000	25,015,000
EPA	1,127,000	784,000
Concurrent	5,731,000	590,000
Total	55,609,000	35,387,000

Source: U.S. Equal Employment Opportunity Commission, *Fiscal Year 1989 Annual Report*, p. 11. *Notes:* Data does not include subpoena enforcement actions. 1. Title VII is part of Civil Rights Act of 1964. 2. ADEA stands for Age Discrimination in Employment Act. 3. EPA stands for the Equal Pay Act.

★ 455 ★

Age Discrimination

EEOC Litigation Activity, by District Office, FY 1989[1]

	Recommend-ations received by OGC[2]	Cases submitted to the commission	Cases approved by the commission	Cases filed by EEOC (direct suits and interventions)	Cases resolved direct) suits and intervention)	Monetary Benefits I[3]	Monetary Benefits II[4]
Atlanta, GA	3	3	2	1	5	810,500	0
Baltimore, MD	14	11	7	5	4	15,938	0
Birmingham, AL	13	9	4	4	1	302,000	0
Charlotte, NC	12	12	7	9	5	33,824	0
Chicago, IL	12	18	6	7	3	4,741,786	200,000
Cleveland, OH	3	4	2	2	3	8,634,379	39,209
Dallas, TX	10	10	7	8	3	207,500	5,961
Denver, CO	10	12	10	7	6	216,902	0
Detroit, MI	9	7	2	4	3	93,389	0
Houston, TX	3	6	4	5	1	901	0
Indianapolis, IN	0	0	0	0	2	0	0
Los Angeles, CA	17	18	12	10	5	1,664,000	0
Memphis, TN	4	3	3	4	6	107,956	160,975
Miami, FL	14	12	7	8	6	147,500	0
Milwaukee, WI	13	14	11	10	6	418,206	0
New Orleans, LA	9	10	7	5	2	23,251	0
New York, NY	22	18	9	7	4	15,000	0
Philadelphia, PA	41	42	23	19	19	6,146,898	4,000
Phoenix, AZ	6	6	4	2	3	37,017	0
San Antonio, TX	7	7	4	4	1	2,340	0
St. Louis, MO	10	8	5	7	7	174,360	0
San Francisco, CA	6	4	3	3	2	421,500	18,000
Seattle, WA	8	8	5	3	1	0	0
Systemic Litiga-tion Services	1	1	0	0	1	800,000	1,300,000
Total	248	243	144	134	99	25,015,137	1,728,145

Source: U.S. Equal Employment Opportunity Commission, *Fiscal Year 1989 Annual Report*, pp. 38-41. *Notes:* 1. EEOC stands for Equal Employment Opportunity Commission. 2. OGC stands for Office of General Counsel. 3. Includes actual monetary relief to victims of discrimination. 4. Includes attorney's fees and other non-monetary benefits including training.

Disability Status

★ 456 ★

Persons 55 to 64 Years Old with a Work Disability, by Sex, Race, and Hispanic Origin: 1981 to 1988

Noninstitutional persons as of March of each year.

[Numbers are shown in thousands]

| Year and characteristic | Total | With a work disability | | | | | |
| | | Total | | Not severe | | Severe | |
		Number	Percent of total	Number	Percent of total	Number	Percent of total
All races							
Both sexes							
1981	21,705	5,133	23.6	2,003	9.2	3,130	14.4
1982	21,870	5,273	24.1	2,080	9.5	3,193	14.6
1983	21,985	5,127	23.3	1,891	8.6	3,236	14.7
1984	22,033	5,177	23.5	1,992	9.0	3,186	14.5
1985	22,151	5,247	23.7	2,209	10.0	3,038	13.7
1986	22,061	5,134	23.3	1,960	8.9	3,174	14.4
1987	21,883	4,854	22.2	1,874	8.6	2,980	13.6
1988	21,642	4,825	22.3	1,798	8.3	3,027	14.0
Male							
1981	10,131	2,585	25.5	1,113	11.0	1,472	14.5
1982	10,198	2,674	26.2	1,200	11.8	1,474	14.5
1983	10,253	2,537	24.7	1,029	10.0	1,508	14.7
1984	10,266	2,608	25.4	1,098	10.7	1,510	14.7
1985	10,377	2,566	24.7	1,102	10.6	1,464	14.1
1986	10,350	2,605	25.2	1,040	10.0	1,565	15.1
1987	10,277	2,394	23.3	1,011	9.8	1,384	13.5
1988	10,186	2,285	22.4	884	8.7	1,400	13.7
Female							
1981	11,575	2,548	22.0	891	7.7	1,658	14.3
1982	11,672	2,599	22.3	880	7.5	1,719	14.7
1983	11,732	2,590	22.1	862	7.4	1,728	14.7
1984	11,767	2,569	21.8	893	7.6	1,676	14.2
1985	11,774	2,681	22.8	1,107	9.4	1,574	13.4
1986	11,712	2,529	21.6	920	7.9	1,609	13.7
1987	11,606	2,459	21.2	863	7.4	1,596	13.8
1988	11,456	2,540	22.2	914	8.0	1,626	14.2
White							
Both sexes							
1981	19,464	4,320	22.2	1,803	9.3	2,517	12.9
1982	19,558	4,420	22.6	1,869	9.6	2,551	13.0
1983	19,622	4,352	22.2	1,724	8.8	2,628	13.4
1984	19,701	4,375	22.2	1,813	9.2	2,562	13.0

[Continued]

★ 456 ★

Persons 55 to 64 Years Old with a Work Disability, by Sex, Race, and Hispanic Origin: 1981 to 1988

[Continued]

Year and characteristic	Total	With a work disability					
		Total		Not severe		Severe	
		Number	Percent of total	Number	Percent of total	Number	Percent of total
1985	19,631	4,364	22.2	1,989	10.1	2,375	12.1
1986	19,522	4,204	21.5	1,711	8.8	2,493	12.8
1987	19,307	4,039	20.9	1,684	8.7	2,355	12.2
1988	19,074	3,898	20.4	1,571	8.2	2,327	12.2
Male							
1981	9,136	2,212	24.2	1,007	11.0	1,205	13.2
1982	9,185	2,294	25.0	1,095	11.9	1,199	13.1
1983	9,219	2,193	23.8	962	10.4	1,231	13.4
1984	9,267	2,258	24.4	1,009	10.9	1,249	13.5
1985	9,256	2,173	23.5	998	10.8	1,175	12.7
1986	9,213	2,151	23.3	921	10.0	1,230	13.3
1987	9,123	2,036	22.3	926	10.2	1,110	12.2
1988	9,034	1,870	20.7	776	8.6	1,094	12.1
Female							
1981	10,329	2,108	20.4	796	7.7	1,312	12.7
1982	10,373	2,126	20.5	774	7.5	1,352	13.0
1983	10,403	2,159	20.8	763	7.3	1,396	13.4
1984	10,434	2,117	20.3	804	7.7	1,313	12.6
1985	10,375	2,191	21.1	990	9.5	1,201	11.6
1986	10,309	2,053	19.9	790	7.7	1,263	12.3
1987	10,184	2,003	19.7	758	7.4	1,245	12.2
1988	10,040	2,028	20.2	795	7.9	1,233	12.3
Black							
Both sexes							
1981	1,908	752	39.4	174	9.1	578	30.1
1982	1,928	771	40.0	190	9.9	581	
1983	1,960	697	35.6	148	7.6	549	28.0
1984	1,953	722	37.0	159	8.1	563	28.8
1985	2,047	783	38.3	181	8.8	602	29.4
1986	2,050	812	39.6	200	9.8	612	29.9
1987	2,063	735	35.6	164	7.9	571	27.7
1988	2,074	822	39.6	187	9.0	635	30.6
Male							
1981	843	337	40.0	84	10.0	253	30.0
1982	847	338	40.0	90	10.6	248	29.3
1983	856	305	35.6	59	6.9	246	28.8
1984	836	310	37.1	84	10.0	226	27.1
1985	913	348	38.1	83	9.1	265	29.0
1986	907	389	42.9	94	10.4	295	32.5
1987	911	319	35.0	70	7.7	249	27.3
1988	916	372	40.6	92	10.0	280	30.6

[Continued]

★ 456 ★

Persons 55 to 64 Years Old with a Work Disability, by Sex, Race, and Hispanic Origin: 1981 to 1988
[Continued]

Year and characteristic	Total	With a work disability					
		Total		Not severe		Severe	
		Number	Percent of total	Number	Percent of total	Number	Percent of total
Female							
1981	1,065	414	38.9	89	8.4	325	30.5
1982	1,081	432	40.0	99	9.2	333	30.8
1983	1,103	392	35.6	89	8.1	303	27.4
1984	1,117	412	36.9	76	6.8	336	30.1
1985	1,133	436	38.4	98	8.6	338	29.8
1986	1,142	422	37.0	105	9.2	317	27.7
1987	1,151	416	36.1	94	8.2	322	28.0
1988	1,158	449	38.8	95	8.2	354	30.6
Hispanic origin							
Both sexes							
1981	750	206	27.5	54	7.2	152	20.3
1982	795	226	28.4	62	7.8	164	20.6
1983	771	206	26.7	50	6.5	156	20.2
1984	8.8	208	24.9	45	5.4	163	19.4
1985	1,041	289	27.7	82	7.9	207	19.9
1986	976	263	26.9	60	6.1	203	20.8
1987	1,042	282	27.0	78	7.5	204	19.6
1988	1,142	290	25.4	68	6.0	222	19.5
Male							
1981	332	78	23.4	24	7.2	54	16.2
1982	346	88	25.4	32	9.2	56	16.1
1983	332	76	22.9	20	6.0	56	16.8
1984	371	85	23.0	21	5.7	64	17.4
1985	471	131	27.8	27	5.7	104	22.1
1986	443	120	27.0	34	7.7	86	19.5
1987	472	124	26.4	40	8.5	84	17.8
1988	499	128	25.6	36	7.2	92	18.4
Female							
1981	418	128	30.7	30	7.2	98	23.5
1982	449	138	30.7	30	6.7	108	24.0
1983	438	130	29.6	30	6.8	100	22.8
1984	467	123	26.4	25	5.4	98	21.0
1985	569	157	27.6	54	9.5	103	18.0
1986	533	143	26.8	26	4.9	117	21.9
1987	571	157	27.6	37	6.5	120	21.1
1988	643	163	25.3	33	5.1	130	20.3

Source: U.S. Department of Commerce, Bureau of the Census, Current Population Reports, Special Studies, Series P-23, No. 160, *Labor Force Status and Other Characteristics of Persons With a Work Disability: 1981 to 1988*, U.S. Government Printing Office, Washington, DC, 1989, pp. 13-21.

★ 457 ★

Disability Status

Selected Characteristics of Persons 55 to 64 Years Old with a Work Disability: Age and Years of School Completed

| Characteristic | Total | With a work disability | | | | | |
| | | Total | | Not severe | | Severe | |
		Number	Percent of total	Number	Percent of total	Number	Percent of total
55 to 64 years old	21,642	4,825	22.3	1,798	8.3	3,027	14.0
Elementary:							
Less than 8 years	1,965	834	42.5	188	9.6	647	32.9
8 years	1,671	522	31.3	167	10.0	355	21.2
High school:							
1 to 3 years	3,388	979	28.9	310	9.1	669	19.8
4 years	8,580	1,612	18.8	676	7.9	936	10.9
College:							
1 to 3 years	2,793	532	19.0	255	9.1	277	9.9
4 years or more	3,245	345	10.6	202	6.2	142	4.4

Source: U.S. Department of Commerce, Bureau of the Census, Current Population Reports, Special Studies, Series P-23, No. 160, *Labor Force Status and Other Characteristics of Persons With a Work Disability: 1981 to 1988*, U.S. Government Printing Office, Washington, DC, 1989, p. 22.

★ 458 ★

Disability Status

Work Disability Status of Civilians 55 to 64 Years Old, by Sex: 1988

Noninstitutional persons as of March 1988.

[Numbers are shown in thousands]

| | Age 55 to 64 | | |
	Both sexes	Male	Female
With a work disability			
Number	4,825	2,285	2,540
Percent			
In labor force	16.7	20.7	13.1
Employed			
Total	15.5	18.8	12.6
Full-time	8.6	12.7	5.0
Not in labor force	83.3	79.3	86.9
Unemployment rate	7.0	9.2	3.9
With no work disability			
Number	16,815	7,900	8,916

[Continued]

★ 458 ★

Work Disability Status of Civilians 55 to 64 Years Old, by Sex: 1988

[Continued]

	Age 55 to 64		
	Both sexes	Male	Female
Percent			
In labor force	64.9	80.5	51.1
Employed			
Total	62.8	77.2	50.0
Full-time	52.1	70.8	35.6
Not in labor force	35.1	19.5	48.9
Unemployment rate	3.3	4.1	2.3

Source: U.S. Department of Commerce, Bureau of the Census, Current Population Reports, Special Studies, Series P-23, No. 160, *Labor Force Status and Other Characteristics of Persons With a Work Disability: 1981 to 1988*, U.S. Government Printing Office, Washington, DC, 1989, pp. 28-33.

★ 459 ★

Disability Status

Civilians 55 to 64 Years Old with a Work Disability, 1988

Noninstitutional persons as of March 1988.

[Numbers are shown in thousands]

Characteristic	Both sexes			Male			Female		
	Number	With a work disability		Number	With a work disability		Number	With a work disability	
		Number	Percent of total		Number	Percent of total		Number	Percent of total
55 to 64 years old	11,726	806	6.90	6,833	473	6.9	4,893	333	6.8
Elementary:									
Less than 8 years	772	87	11.13	552	61	11.0	220	27	12.0
8 years	793	76	9.60	524	49	9.4	269	27	10.1
High school:									
1 to 3 years	1,596	122	7.60	910	63	7.0	686	58	8.5
4 years	4,599	288	6.30	2,332	156	6.7	2,266	132	5.8
College:									
1 to 3 years	1,674	121	7.30	932	73	7.8	742	49	6.6
4 years or more	2,291	111	4.80	1,583	71	4.5	708	40	5.6

Source: U.S. Department of Commerce, Bureau of the Census, Current Population Reports, Special Studies, Series P-23, No. 160, *Labor Force Status and Other Characteristics of Persons With a Work Disability: 1981 to 1988*, U.S. Government Printing Office, Washington, DC, 1989, p. 34.

★ 460 ★

Disability Status

Work Disability Status of Civilians 55 to 64 Years Old, by Sex: 1988

Noninstitutional persons as of March 1988.

[Numbers are shown in thousands]

	Age 55 to 64		
	Both sexes	Male	Female
With a work disability			
Number	4,825	2,285	2,540
Percent			
Worked in 1987			
Total	2.0	28.3	18.3
Year-round full-time	6.9	10.5	3.7
Did not work in 1987	77.0	71.7	81.7
Unemployed 4 or more weeks in 1987	5.3	6.4	3.6
With no work disability			
Number	16,815	7,900	8,916
Percent			
Worked in 1987			
Total	70.6	85.8	57.1
Year-round full-time	47.5	65.3	31.8
Did not work in 1987	29.4	14.2	42.9
Unemployed 4 or more weeks in 1987	.7	.7	.8

Source: U.S. Department of Commerce, Bureau of the Census, Current Population Reports, Special Studies, Series P-23, No. 160, *Labor Force Status and Other Characteristics of Persons With a Work Disability: 1981 to 1988*, U.S. Government Printing Office, Washington, DC, 1989, pp. 40-45.

★ 461 ★

Disability Status

Work Disability Status of Civilians 55 to 64 Years Old, by Sex: 1988

Noninstitutional persons as of March 1988.

	Age 55 to 64		
	Both sexes	Male	Female
With a work disability			
Number (thous.)	4,825	2,285	2,540
In families			
Percent of total	76.3	81.2	71.8

[Continued]

★ 461 ★

Work Disability Status of Civilians 55 to 64 Years Old, by Sex: 1988

[Continued]

	Age 55 to 64		
	Both sexes	Male	Female
Mean family income			
Value (dol.)	26,137	25,719	26,562
Standard error (dol.)	539	753	773
Not in families			
Percent of total	23.7	18.8	28.2
Mean income of persons			
Value (dol.)	9,699	10,908	8,974
Standard error (dol.)	534	883	667
With no work disability			
Number (thous.)	16,815	7,900	8,916
In families			
Percent of total	86.4	89.2	84.0
Mean family income			
Value (dol.)	42,627	46,183	39,282
Standard error (dol.)	375	560	495
Not in families			
Percent of total	13.6	10.8	16.0
Mean income of persons			
Value (dol.)	20,324	25,589	17,169
Standard error (dol.)	584	1,184	575

Source: U.S. Department of Commerce, Bureau of the Census, Current Population Reports, Special Studies, Series P-23, No. 160, *Labor Force Status and Other Characteristics of Persons With a Work Disability: 1981 to 1988*, U.S. Government Printing Office, Washington, DC, 1989, pp. 46-50.

★ 462 ★

Disability Status

Persons 65 to 74 Years Old - Work Disability Status

Data are for noninstitutional persons as of March 1988. Numbers are shown in thousands.

	65 to 74 Years Old	
	Male	Female
Number	7,736	9,736
Percent employed	20.8	11.2
With a work disability		
Number	2,104	2,435
Percent employed	8.1	3.5

[Continued]

★ 462 ★

Persons 65 to 74 Years Old - Work Disability Status
[Continued]

	65 to 74 Years Old	
	Male	Female
With no work disability		
Number	5,632	7,301
Percent employed	25.5	13.8

Source: U.S. Department of Commerce, Bureau of the Census, Current Population Reports, Special Studies, Series P-23, No. 160, *Labor Force Status and Other Characteristics of Persons With a Work Disability: 1981 to 1988*, U.S. Government Printing Office, Washington, DC, 1989, pp. 58-59.

★ 463 ★

Disability Status

Persons 65 to 69 Years Old - Work Disability Status

Data are for noninstitutional persons as of March 1988.

[Numbers are shown in thousands]

	65 to 74 Years Old	
	Male	Female
Number	4,460	5,344
Percent employed	25.0	14.5
With a work disability		
Number	1,202	1,284
Percent employed	9.4	4.4
With no work disability		
Number	3,258	4,060
Percent employed	30.8	17.8

Source: U.S. Department of Commerce, Bureau of the Census, Current Population Reports, Special Studies, Series P-23, No. 160, *Labor Force Status and Other Characteristics of Persons With a Work Disability: 1981 to 1988*, U.S. Government Printing Office, Washington, DC, 1989, pp. 60-61.

★ 464 ★

Disability Status

Persons 70 to 74 Years Old - Work Disability Status

Data are for noninstitutional persons as of March 1988.

[Numbers are shown in thousands]

	65 to 74 Years Old	
	Male	Female
Number	3,276	4,392
Percent employed	15.0	7.2
With a work disability		
Number	901	1,151
Percent employed	6.5	2.4
With no work disability		
Number	2,374	3,241
Percent employed	18.2	8.9

Source: U.S. Department of Commerce, Bureau of the Census, Current Population Reports, Special Studies, Series P-23, No. 160, *Labor Force Status and Other Characteristics of Persons With a Work Disability: 1981 to 1988*, U.S. Government Printing Office, Washington, DC, 1989, pp. 62-63.

Chapter 9
HOUSING

This chapter provides statistics under the headings of General Characteristics, Housing Quality, Building Characteristics, Housing Amenities, Homeownership, Housing Costs, Housing Value, Neighborhoods, and a single table on Geographic Mobility. Most of the data in this chapter are based directly or indirectly on the 1989 housing survey, issued in mid-1991.

Additional information on costs may be found in the chapter on *Income, Assets, and Spending*. The chapter on *Criminals and Victims* presents information related to the section on Neighborhoods.

General Characteristics

★ 465 ★

Occupied Units with Elderly Householder, by Race/Ethnicity

[Numbers are shown in thousands for 1989]

Race and origin	Total occupied units	Tenure		Housing unit characteristics				Household characteristics			
		Owner	Renter	New con-struction 4 yrs.	Mobile homes	Physical problems		Black	Hispanic	Moved in past year	Below poverty level
						Severe	Moderate				
White	18,053	14,031	4,022	546	188	563	583	...	594	798	2,952
Non-Hispanic	17,459	13,660	3,799	525	1,159	547	522	...	...	755	2,797
Hispanic	594	371	223	21	29	17	61	...	594	43	154
Black	1,827	1,159	669	10	35	101	287	1,827	38	110	749
Other	220	136	84	7	12	11	15	...	28	14	67
Total Hispanic	661	406	255	21	29	18	71	38	661	48	173

Source: U.S. Department of Commerce and U.S. Department of Housing and Urban Development, Current Housing Reports, H150/89, *American Housing Survey for the United States in 1989*, July 1991, p. 310. *Notes:* ... means not applicable or sample too small. A dash (-) means zero or rounds to zero.

★ 466 ★

General Characteristics

Occupied Units with Elderly Householder: Units in Structure, Cooperatives, and Condominiums

[Numbers are shown in thousands for 1989]

Characteristic	Total occupied units	Tenure		New construction 4 yrs.	Mobile homes	Physical problems		Black	Hispanic	Moved in past year	Below poverty level
		Owner	Renter			Severe	Moderate				
Units in structure											
1, detached	13,314	12,373	941	196	...	426	668	1,117	363	288	2,258
1, attached	972	649	323	85	...	36	26	190	37	92	187
2 to 4	1,643	621	1,022	27	...	56	73	193	72	127	363
5 to 9	574	104	470	25	...	20	17	62	18	50	129
10 to 19	536	75	461	33	...	17	16	55	38	87	87
20 to 49	573	137	436	13	...	21	16	30	20	51	135
50 or more	1,254	219	1,035	78	...	65	30	145	83	157	336
Mobile home or trailer	1,235	1,149	86	107	1,235	35	40	35	29	72	273
Cooperatives and condominiums											
Cooperatives	217	149	68	8	4	7	5	13	9	11	50
Condominiums	775	655	120	58	5	20	2	5	12	83	47

Source: U.S. Department of Commerce and U.S. Department of Housing and Urban Development, Current Housing Reports, H150/89, *American Housing Survey for the United States in 1989*, July 1991, p. 310. *Note:* ... means not applicable. A dash (-) means zero or rounds to zero.

★ 467 ★

General Characteristics

Occupied Units with Elderly Householder: Year Structure Was Built

[Numbers are shown in thousands for 1989]

Year built	Total occupied units	Tenure		New construction 4 yrs.	Mobile homes[1]	Physical problems		Black	Hispanic	Moved in past year	Below poverty level
		Owner	Renter			Severe	Moderate				
1990 to 1994	-	-	-	-	-	-	-	-	-	-	-
1985 to 1989	711	475	236	564	138	15	7	10	23	183	81
1980 to 1984	907	544	363	...	135	17	5	45	16	71	142
1975 to 1979	1,705	1,139	566	...	289	47	32	70	58	175	278
1970 to 1974	1,965	1,318	646	...	352	62	51	142	73	117	418
1960 to 1969	3,278	2,513	764	...	289	94	98	250	106	148	543
1950 to 1959	3,696	3,219	477	...	24	95	132	275	126	83	543
1940 to 1949	2,327	1,886	441	...	8	82	189	323	100	42	468
1930 to 1939	1,535	1,152	383	...	1	64	144	247	67	32	367
1920 to 1929	1,388	1,031	357	...	-	59	76	196	46	35	332
1919 or earlier	2,589	2,049	540	...	-	142	151	269	47	39	597
Median	1956	1955	1962	...	1974	1949	1944	1946	1956	1974	1952

Source: U.S. Department of Commerce and U.S. Department of Housing and Urban Development, Current Housing Reports, H150/89, *American Housing Survey for the United States in 1989*, July 1991, p. 310. *Notes:* ... means not applicable. A dash (-) means zero or rounds to zero. 1. For mobile home, oldest category is 1939 or earlier.

★ 468 ★

General Characteristics

Occupied Units with Elderly Householder, by Geographic Area

[Numbers are shown in thousands for 1989]

Characteristic	Total occupied units	Tenure		Housing unit characteristics				Household characteristics			
		Owner	Renter	New con-struction 4 yrs.	Mobile homes	Physical problems		Black	Hispanic	Moved in past year	Below poverty level
						Severe	Moderate				
Metropolitan/ nonmetropolitan areas											
Inside MSAs[1]	14,669	10,857	3,812	408	726	432	525	1,437	581	691	2,411
In central cities	6,227	4,050	2,177	106	102	214	293	1,094	340	270	1,259
Suburbs	8,442	6,807	1,636	303	624	217	232	343	241	421	1,152
Outside MSAs	5,432	4,470	962	156	509	243	360	391	79	232	1,357
Regions											
Northeast	4,622	3,191	1,431	69	120	142	111	336	132	111	703
Midwest	4,902	3,771	1,131	115	169	156	71	325	54	224	872
South	7,015	5,667	1,348	231	577	265	646	1,054	242	356	1,746
West	3,561	2,698	863	148	369	113	57	113	233	231	447
Urbanized area											
Inside urbanized areas	11,676	8,250	3,425	269	379	344	400	1,293	533	559	1,902
In central cities of PMSAs[2]	6,153	3,996	2,157	103	102	214	293	1,086	340	265	1,253
Urban fringe	5,522	4,255	1,268	166	277	130	106	207	192	294	649
Outside urbanized areas	8,425	7,076	1,349	295	856	331	486	535	128	363	1,866
Other urban	2,965	2,285	680	69	134	71	169	206	77	169	632
Rural	5,460	4,791	669	227	722	260	317	329	51	194	1,234
Place size											
Less than 2,500 persons	1,293	1,066	226	23	96	42	77	49	8	44	321
2,500 to 9,999 persons	2,306	1,846	460	36	131	62	116	108	86	122	432
10,000 to 19,999 persons	2,015	1,539	476	25	68	39	82	141	35	79	316
20,000 to 49,999 persons	2,581	1,930	651	69	86	69	64	169	92	152	396
50,000 to 99,999 persons	1,807	1,272	535	52	56	59	60	113	86	96	270
100,000 to 249,999 persons	1,423	965	459	37	38	28	65	199	69	72	265
250,000 to 499,999 persons	1,004	681	323	4	4	40	25	179	62	36	194
500,000 to 999,999 persons	862	574	288	18	11	30	47	206	42	45	193
1,000,000 persons or more	1,422	729	693	18	7	64	90	347	121	41	332

Source: U.S. Department of Commerce and U.S. Department of Housing and Urban Development, Current Housing Reports, H150/89, *American Housing Survey for the United States in 1989*, July 1991, p. 310. *Notes:* ... means not applicable. A dash (-) means zero or rounds to zero. 1. MSA stands for metropolitan statistical area. 2. PMSA stands for metropolitan primary statistical area.

★ 469 ★

General Characteristics

Housing Tenure, by Marital Status and Race/Ethnicity

[Numbers are shown in thousands for 1989]

Characteristic	Owner occupied	Percent of all occupied	Renter occupied
All households	15,326	76.2	4,774
Family households	9,653	87.4	1,398
Married couple	7,830	89.5	923
With own children under 18	76	89.7	9
White	64	94.0	4
Black	12	71.9	5
Householder of Hispanic origin	2	49.9	2
Male householder, no wife present	527	84.3	98
With own children under 18	9	82.8	2
White	6	78.1	2
Black	2	100.0	-
Householder of Hispanic origin	3	100.0	-
Female householder, no husband present	1,296	77.5	377
With own children under 18	11	71.3	4
White	6	58.4	4
Black	5	100.0	-
Householder of Hispanic origin	-	...	-
Nonfamily households	5,673	62.7	3,376
Living alone			
Male	1,109	60.6	721
Female	4,391	63.3	2,541
Other nonfamily			
Male	56	47.8	62
Female	117	68.8	53

Source: U.S. Department of Commerce and U.S. Department of Housing and Urban Development, Current Housing Reports H151/89, *Supplement to the American Housing Survey for the United States in 1989*, October 1992, pp. 72-73. *Note:* A dash (-) means zero or rounds to zero.

★ 470 ★

General Characteristics

Age of Elderly Householders, by Marital Status and Race/Ethnicity

[Numbers are shown in thousands for 1989]

Characteristic	65 to 74	75 years and over	Median
All households	11,781	8,319	74
Family households	7,411	3,640	72
Married couple	6,116	2,636	72
With own children under 18	73	11	71
White	59	9	71
Black	14	2	...
Householder of Hispanic origin	4	-	...
Male householder, no wife present	407	219	73
With own children under 18	8	2	...
White	6	2	...
Black	2	-	...
Householder of Hispanic origin	3	-	...
Female householder, no husband present	88	785	74
With own children under 18	8	2	...
White	8	2	...
Black	5	-	...
Householder of Hispanic origin	-	-	...
Nonfamily households	4,370	4,680	75+
Living alone			
Male	1,013	817	74
Female	3,173	3,759	75+
Other nonfamily			
Male	88	30	72
Female	96	74	74

Source: U.S. Department of Commerce and U.S. Department of Housing and Urban Development, Current Housing Reports H151/89, *Supplement to the American Housing Survey for the United States in 1989*, October 1992, pp. 72-73. *Notes:* ... means not applicable or sample too small. A dash (-) means zero or rounds to zero.

★ 471 ★

General Characteristics

Low-Income Public Housing Units, by Progress Stage: 1960 to 1988

Housing for the elderly is intended for persons 62 years old or over, disabled or handicapped. Data include Puerto Rico and Virgin Islands and cover units subsidized by HUD under annual contributions contracts.

[In thousands]

Year	Total[1]	Occupied units[2]	Under construction
1960	593.3	478.2	36.4
Elderly	18.9	1.1	4.1
1970	1,155.3	893.5	126.6
Elderly	294.4	143.4	65.7
1980	1,321.1	1,195.6	20.9
Elderly	358.3	317.7	11.5
1985	1,378.0	1,344.6	9.6
Elderly	373.5	361.1	2.1
1987	1,443.0	1,406.4	9.7
Elderly	378.6	374.2	1.3
1988	1,448.8	1,413.3	9.7
Elderly	382.5	374.7	1.4

Source: U.S. Bureau of the Census, *Statistical Abstract of the United States: 1992* (112th edition.) Washington, DC, 1992, p. 724. Primary source: U.S. Department of Housing and Urban Development, unpublished data. *Notes:* 1. Includes units to be constructed or to go directly, "under management" because no rehabilitation needed, not shown separately. 2. Under management or available for occupancy.

★ 472 ★

General Characteristics

Percentage of Homeowners, by Family Status and Age of Householders: 1989

Age	Married-couple families	Female householder living alone
60 to 64	90.5	65.0
65 to 69	90.8	66.7
70 to 74	89.7	63.6
75 and over	86.5	60.4

Source: Robert R. Callis, U.S. Bureau of the Census, *Homeownership Trends in the 1980's*, Series H-121, No. 2, U.S. Government Printing Office, Washington, D.C., December 1990, Table 4.

★ 473 ★

General Characteristics

Percent of Ownership of Homes for Persons 65 Years and Over, by Region of Country: 1989

Region	
Northeast	68.0
Midwest	76.9
South	80.5
West	75.0

Source: Robert R. Callis, U.S. Bureau of the Census, *Homeownership Trends in the 1980's,* Series H-121, No. 2, U.S. Government Printing Office, Washington, D.C., December 1990, Tables 6 through 9.

★ 474 ★

General Characteristics

Veterans Among the Homeless

Data show percentage of veterans among homeless men and percentage of veterans among all men in each age cohort.

Age group	Homeless men who are vets	Male vets in age group
20-29	26.7	7.6
30-34	36.0	14.8
35-44	37.2	36.9
45-54	58.4	44.8
55-64	63.5	69.9
65 +	37.0	33.6

Source: USA TODAY, June 1, 1993, p. 4A. "The Proportion of Veterans Among Homeless Men," by Robert Rosenheck, Linda Frisman and An-Me Chung.

Housing Quality

★ 475 ★

Housing Quality of Elderly Households

[Numbers are shown in thousands for 1989]

Characteristic	Total occupied units	Tenure		Housing unit characteristics				Household characteristics			
		Owner	Renter	New con-struction 4 yrs.	Mobile homes	Physical problems		Black	Hispanic	Moved in past year	Below poverty level
						Severe	Moderate				
Selected physical problems											
Severe physical problems[1]	675	465	210	7	35	675	...	101	18	21	196
Plumbing	609	420	189	5	35	609	...	82	15	21	176
Heating	36	20	16	3	-	36	...	7	3	-	9
Electric	11	9	2	-	-	11	...	2	-	-	7
Upkeep	30	22	8	-	-	30	...	15	3	-	15
Hallways	-	-	-	-	-	-	...	-	-	-	-
Moderate physical problems[1]	885	619	266	7	40	...	885	287	71	35	401
Plumbing	32	15	17	-	2	...	32	12	3	3	14
Heating	568	425	143	-	18	...	568	212	66	14	289
Upkeep	203	130	72	-	13	...	203	67	11	7	89
Hallways	8	-	8	-	-	...	8	5	-	3	3
Kitchen	120	75	45	7	12	...	120	14	-	11	33

Source: U.S. Department of Commerce and U.S. Department of Housing and Urban Development, Current Housing Reports, H150/89, *American Housing Survey for the United States in 1989*, July 1991, p. 322. *Notes:* ... means not applicable. A dash (-) means zero or rounds to zero. 1. Figures may not add to total because more than one category may apply to a unit.

★ 476 ★

Housing Quality

Repairs, Improvements, Alterations in Last 2 Years

[Numbers are shown in thousands for 1989]

Characteristic	Total occupied units	Tenure		Housing unit characteristics				Household characteristics			
		Owner	Renter	New con-struction 4 yrs.	Mobile homes	Physical problems		Black	Hispanic	Moved in past year	Below poverty level
						Severe	Moderate				
Roof replaced (all or part)	2,651	2,651	...	8	153	105	142	294	64	24	397
Mostly done by householder	320	320	...	-	27	13	31	32	10	1	63
Mostly done by others	2,252	2,252	...	8	110	85	106	258	49	18	322
Workers not reported	79	79	...	-	16	7	4	4	5	4	12
Costing $500 or more	1,759	1,759	...	8	79	50	81	186	42	16	218
Costing less than $500	530	530	...	-	50	33	44	65	10	6	120
Cost not reported	362	362	...	-	25	23	17	43	12	2	58
Roof replacement not reported	207	207	...	6	21	2	11	7	17	5	33
Additions built	371	371	...	15	56	13	11	19	12	15	43
Mostly done by household	114	114	...	6	20	11	2	2	5	9	13
Mostly done by others	248	248	...	9	35	2	9	17	7	6	29
Workers not reported	9	9	...	-	-	-	-	-	-	-	-
Costing $500 or more	246	246	...	9	31	8	11	15	8	15	25

[Continued]

★ 476 ★

Repairs, Improvements, Alterations in Last 2 Years
[Continued]

Characteristic	Total occupied units	Tenure		Housing unit characteristics				Household characteristics			
		Owner	Renter	New construction 4 yrs.	Mobile homes	Physical problems		Black	Hispanic	Moved in past year	Below poverty level
						Severe	Moderate				
Costing less than $500	54	54	...	-	16	-	-	-	-	-	9
Cost not reported	71	71	...	6	9	4	-	4	4	-	9
Additions not reported	210	210	...	6	19	5	11	17	20	5	29
Kitchen remodeled or added	608	608	...	10	29	20	11	56	21	28	67
Mostly done by household	170	170	...	5	14	5	2	9	5	5	14
Mostly done by others	417	417	...	5	15	14	9	41	14	21	52
Workers not reported	21	21	...	-	-	2	-	6	2	2	1
Costing $500 or more	399	399	...	3	17	7	7	30	12	26	28
Costing less than $500	110	110	...	5	10	4	4	10	7	-	30
Cost not reported	100	100	...	2	2	9	-	16	2	2	9
Kitchen remodeled or added not reported	206	206	...	6	28	2	11	7	20	5	32
Bathroom remodeled or added	776	776	...	3	29	34	23	100	33	23	88
Mostly done by household	230	230	...	-	11	13	4	24	5	7	24
Mostly done by others	513	513	...	3	18	17	16	65	26	14	60
Workers not reported	34	34	...	-	-	5	3	11	3	2	4
Costing $500 or more	401	401	...	-	16	15	7	28	16	16	24
Costing less than $500	221	221	...	3	13	9	11	32	12	4	41
Cost not reported	155	155	...	-	-	11	5	39	5	2	23
Bathroom remodeled or added not reported	209	209	...	8	22	2	11	8	22	7	31
Siding replaced or added	676	676	...	-	35	38	24	59	9	2	85
Mostly done by household	141	141	...	-	16	2	9	12	4	-	13
Mostly done by others	519	519	...	-	19	33	15	40	5	2	70
Workers not reported	16	16	...	-	-	2	-	7	-	-	3
Costing $500 or more	438	438	...	-	16	18	15	34	2	2	47
Costing less than $500	125	125	...	-	19	11	6	12	4	-	20
Cost not reported	113	113	...	-	-	9	2	13	2	-	18
Siding replaced or added not reported	213	213	...	8	22	2	16	9	20	7	34
Storm doors/windows bought and installed	1,428	1,428	...	23	71	59	46	148	19	17	181
Mostly done by household	338	338	...	8	18	9	14	26	3	2	22
Mostly done by others	1,051	1,051	...	16	52	45	25	118	16	8	148
Workers not reported	39	39	...	-	2	5	6	5	-	6	11
Costing $500 or more	548	548	...	2	14	20	7	56	4	9	58
Costing less than $500	636	636	...	21	50	25	23	64	10	4	78
Cost not reported	244	244	...	-	7	14	16	28	5	4	45
Storm doors/windows bought and installed not reported	202	202	...	6	22	2	11	7	20	5	32
Major equipment replaced or added	1,358	1,358	...	11	98	50	20	69	21	29	140
Mostly done by household	124	124	...	-	7	2	7	2	-	-	9
Mostly done by others	1,187	1,187	...	11	82	45	11	67	16	26	129
Workers not reported	47	47	...	-	10	2	3	-	4	2	3
Costing $500 or more	1,062	1,062	...	11	79	32	11	36	16	26	93
Costing less than $500	152	152	...	-	12	7	10	17	-	-	24
Cost not reported	145	145	...	-	7	11	-	16	5	2	23
Major equipment replaced or added not reported	219	219	...	10	22	2	11	7	20	5	29
Insulation added	666	666	...	2	30	27	22	52	22	15	74
Mostly done by household	186	186	...	-	9	11	5	9	7	9	16
Mostly done by others	438	438	...	2	20	14	17	36	12	4	58
Workers not reported	43	43	...	-	-	2	-	7	2	2	-
Costing $500 or more	133	133	...	-	8	5	-	2	5	4	6

[Continued]

★ 476 ★

Repairs, Improvements, Alterations in Last 2 Years

[Continued]

Characteristic	Total occupied units	Tenure		Housing unit characteristics				Household characteristics			
		Owner	Renter	New construction 4 yrs.	Mobile homes	Physical problems		Black	Hispanic	Moved in past year	Below poverty level
						Severe	Moderate				
Costing less than $500	313	313	...	2	12	13	13	30	10	9	47
Cost not reported	220	220	...	-	10	9	9	20	7	2	20
Insulation added not reported	262	262	...	6	26	5	13	21	24	10	48
Other major work[1]	1,998	1,998	...	36	103	43	48	167	44	79	215
Mostly done by household	321	321	...	8	18	9	12	18	16	13	23
Mostly done by others	1,587	1,587	...	28	79	32	32	138	28	63	188
Workers not reported	91	91	...	-	7	2	4	12	-	2	4
Other major work not reported	236	236	...	6	24	2	15	12	17	5	32

Source: U.S. Department of Commerce and U.S. Department of Housing and Urban Development, Current Housing Reports, H150/89, *American Housing Survey for the United States in 1989*, July 1991, p. 348. Notes: ... means not applicable or sample too small. A dash (-) means zero or rounds to zero.

★ 477 ★

Housing Quality

Housing Quality: Selected Amenities

[Numbers are shown in thousands]

Selected amenities	Porch, deck, balcony, or patio	Not reported	Telephone available	Usable fireplace	Separate dining room	With 2 or more living rooms or recreation rooms, etc.	Garage or carport		Offstreet parking		Garage or carport not reported
							Included with home	Not included	Included	Not reported	
All households	14,951	48	19,410	5,175	8,316	5,889	12,500	7,565	5,485	88	35
Family households	8,734	31	10,795	3,607	5,284	4,091	7,858	3,176	2,357	16	18
Married couple	6,990	29	8,595	3,061	4,237	3,433	6,534	2,205	1,681	5	13
With own children under 18	73	-	82	29	42	45	55	29	20	-	-
White	60	-	68	22	32	40	46	22	15	-	-
Black	14	-	14	7	10	5	9	7	5	-	-
Hispanic origin	4	-	4	-	2	-	2	2	-	-	-
Male householder, no wife present	475	-	597	182	295	208	399	227	162	3	-
With own children under 18	6	-	10	4	5	2	6	4	2	-	-
White	6	-	8	4	2	2	6	2	-	-	-
Black	-	-	2	-	2	-	-	2	2	-	-
Hispanic origin	3	-	3	-	-	-	3	-	-	-	-
Female householder, no husband present	1,270	1	1,603	364	751	450	925	743	514	9	5
With own children under 18	15	-	13	6	7	2	4	9	7	-	2
White	11	-	8	6	4	2	4	4	4	-	2
Black	5	-	5	-	2	-	-	5	2	-	-
Hispanic origin	-	-	-	-	-	-	-	-	-	-	-
Nonfamily households	6,217	17	8,615	1,568	3,032	1,798	4,642	4,389	3,129	71	18
Living alone											
Male	1,150	-	1,639	294	592	304	879	946	676	8	5
Female	4,861	17	6,717	1,226	2,340	1,432	3,615	3,306	2,355	61	11
Other nonfamily											
Male	75	-	102	19	30	25	51	65	47	2	2
Female	131	-	157	30	69	36	98	72	50	-	-

Source: U.S. Department of Commerce and U.S. Department of Housing and Urban Development, Current Housing Reports H151/89, *Supplement to the American Housing Survey for the United States in 1989*, October 1992, pp. 76-77. Note: A dash (-) means zero or rounds to zero.

★ 478 ★

Housing Quality

Housing Quality: Selected Deficiencies

[Numbers are shown in thousands]

Selected deficiencies	Signs of rats in last 3 months	Holes in floors	Open cracks or holes (interior)	Broken plaster or peeling paint (interior)	No electrical wiring	Exposed wiring	Rooms without electric outlets
All households	566	155	679	641	5	362	423
Family households	295	67	312	300	3	156	202
Married couple	176	30	185	168	-	114	128
With own children under 18	15	-	11	2	-	7	2
White	9	-	2	-	-	2	-
Black	7	-	9	2	-	5	2
Hispanic origin	2	-	2	-	-	2	-
Male householder, no wife present	34	6	28	21	-	10	13
With own children under 18	-	-	-	-	-	-	-
White	-	-	-	-	-	-	-
Black	-	-	-	-	-	-	-
Hispanic origin	-	-	-	-	-	-	-
Female householder, no husband present	85	31	99	111	3	31	61
With own children under 18	7	2	5	2	-	2	-
White	7	2	2	2	-	2	-
Black	-	-	2	-	-	-	-
Hispanic	-	-	-	-	-	-	-
Nonfamily households	270	89	367	341	2	207	220
Living alone							
Male	53	17	91	107	-	59	46
Female	198	60	246	218	2	133	160
Other nonfamily							
Male	6	9	23	11	-	8	5
Female	13	2	7	5	-	7	9

Source: U.S. Department of Commerce and U.S. Department of Housing and Urban Development, Current Housing Reports H151/89, *Supplement to the American Housing Survey for the United States in 1989*, October 1992, pp. 76-77. *Note:* A dash (-) means zero or rounds to zero.

Building Characteristics

★ 479 ★

Housing Conditions of the Elderly: External Building Conditions

[Numbers are shown in thousands for 1989]

External building conditions[1]	Total occupied units	Tenure		Housing unit characteristics				Household characteristics			
		Owner	Renter	New con-struction 4 yrs.	Mobile homes	Physical problems		Black	Hispanic	Moved in past year	Below poverty level
						Severe	Moderate				
Sagging roof	3	-	3	-	...	-	-	-	3	-	3
Missing roofing material	5	-	5	-	...	0	0	0	3	-	3
Hole in roof	-	-	-	-	...	-	-	-	-	-	-
Could not see roof	3798	103	276	8	...	15	27	60	45	52	85
Missing bricks, siding, other outside wall material	29	2	28	-	...	4	10	3	11	5	15
Sloping outside walls	-	-	-	-	...	-	-	-	-	-	-
Boarded up windows	10	4	6	-	...	1	3	5	1	4	4
Broken windows	35	-	35	-	...	1	8	19	4	6	6
Bars on windows	54	16	38	-	...	-	10	24	5	5	5
Foundation crumbling or has open crack or hole	32	2	30	-	...	1	2	13	5	1	9
Could not see foundation	119	33	86	-	...	2	10	21	8	15	22
None of the above	2,448	625	1,823	147	...	69	71	270	123	384	589
Could not observe or not reported	1,699	420	1,279	21	...	90	46	144	59	34	357

Source: U.S. Department of Commerce and U.S. Department of Housing and Urban Development, Current Housing Reports, H150/89, *American Housing Survey for the United States in 1989*, July 1991, p. 312. *Notes:* ... means not applicable. A dash (-) means zero or rounds to zero. Figures may not add to total because more than one category may apply. 1. Limited to multiunit structures.

★ 480 ★

Building Characteristics

Number of Rooms in Elderly Households

[Numbers are shown in thousands for 1989]

Number of rooms	Total occupied units	Tenure		Housing unit characteristics				Household characteristics			
		Owner	Renter	New con-struction 4 yrs.	Mobile homes	Physical problems		Black	Hispanic	Moved in past year	Below poverty level
						Severe	Moderate				
Rooms											
1 room	153	13	140	7	9	27	20	15	11	20	52
2 rooms	223	23	200	11	3	20	12	41	20	35	81
3 rooms	2,113	339	1,774	104	71	89	68	256	143	256	713
4 rooms	3,972	2,587	1,385	114	578	161	228	396	143	253	871
5 rooms	5,209	4,430	778	166	376	154	271	444	140	160	963
6 rooms	4,357	4,016	342	83	147	120	168	362	109	111	680
7 rooms	2,334	2,227	107	46	35	57	80	214	66	53	280
8 rooms	1,024	995	29	22	10	26	19	54	17	19	80
9 rooms	400	394	7	11	3	13	7	24	9	12	23
10 rooms or more	315	304	12	-	2	9	11	21	3	2	25
Median	5.2	5.6	3.7	4.8	4.4	4.8	4.9	5.0	4.6	4.1	4.7
Bedrooms											
None	265	18	247	11	9	34	25	41	22	44	94

[Continued]

★ 480 ★

Number of Rooms in Elderly Households
[Continued]

Number of rooms	Total occupied units	Tenure		Housing unit characteristics				Household characteristics			
		Owner	Renter	New construction 4 yrs.	Mobile homes	Physical problems Severe	Moderate	Black	Hispanic	Moved in past year	Below poverty level
1	2,902	770	2,133	113	107	144	101	331	165	300	912
2	7,707	5,920	1,787	292	890	236	394	613	221	378	1,426
3	7,310	6,801	508	138	222	195	312	644	202	163	1,098
4 or more	1,916	1,818	99	10	7	65	54	198	51	38	239
Median	2.4	2.6	1.5	2.0	2.1	2.2	2.3	2.4	2.1	1.8	2.1
Complete bathrooms											
None	178	101	78	3	-	146	2	50	8	4	98
1	11,086	7,152	3,934	189	606	335	695	1,281	446	549	2,750
1 and one-half	3,623	3,262	362	54	168	76	80	280	79	95	479
2 or more	5,213	4,812	400	319	461	118	109	216	128	275	441

Source: U.S. Department of Commerce and U.S. Department of Housing and Urban Development, Current Housing Reports, H150/89, *American Housing Survey for the United States in 1989*, July 1991, p. 314. *Note:* ... means not applicable. A dash (-) means zero or rounds to zero.

★ 481 ★

Building Characteristics

Unit Size and Lot Size of Elderly Households
[Numbers are shown in thousands for 1989]

Characteristic	Total occupied units	Tenure		Housing unit characteristics				Household characteristics			
		Owner	Renter	New construction 4 yrs.	Mobile homes	Physical problems Severe	Moderate	Black	Hispanic	Moved in past year	Below poverty level
Square footage of unit											
Single detached and mobile homes	14,547	13,520	1,028	303	1,233	461	708	1,153	392	360	2,531
Less than 500	213	168	45	6	66	25	13	31	20	18	81
500 to 749	780	614	166	3	250	59	95	140	38	26	284
750 to 999	1,617	1,451	166	60	395	76	172	196	58	49	430
1,000 to 1,499	3,967	3,726	241	81	330	112	192	311	110	105	782
1,500 to 1,999	2,875	2,732	143	52	76	54	93	156	63	49	343
2,000 to 2,499	1,859	1,794	66	36	14	34	39	88	46	33	205
2,500 to 2,999	964	941	23	21	-	28	15	34	8	20	75
3,000 to 3,999	870	845	26	5	5	28	14	43	12	19	88
4,000 or more	503	482	21	10	5	5	18	26	11	14	56
Not reported	900	768	132	28	92	39	56	127	25	28	188
Median	1,543	1,576	1,148	1,416	911	1,226	1,117	1,234	1,305	1,349	1,242
Lot size											
Less than one-eighth acre	1,857	1,720	138	28	313	54	107	200	79	49	335
One-eighth up to one-quarter acre	3,212	3,084	128	77	133	96	113	190	112	60	398
One-quarter up to one-half acre	2,160	2,092	68	42	80	35	67	89	37	46	238
One-half up to one acre	1,167	1,113	55	37	60	24	43	55	15	28	133
1 to 4 acres	1,786	1,679	107	26	159	75	117	148	21	35	391
5 to 9 acres	257	241	15	2	18	17	20	7	3	4	37
10 acres or more	1,128	1,049	79	27	72	64	78	64	2	14	278
Don't know	3,405	2,744	662	105	362	104	174	543	139	173	832
Not reported	545	446	99	45	38	29	16	45	22	44	76
Median	.33	.33	.36	.34	.22	.48	.45	.24	.19	.30	.43

Source: U.S. Department of Commerce and U.S. Department of Housing and Urban Development, Current Housing Reports, H150/89, *American Housing Survey for the United States in 1989*, July 1991, p. 314. *Note:* ... means not applicable. A dash (-) means zero or rounds to zero.

★ 482 ★

Building Characteristics

Space per Person in Elderly Households

[Numbers are shown in thousands for 1989]

Characteristic	Total occupied units	Tenure		Housing unit characteristics				Household characteristics			
		Owner	Renter	New con-struction 4 yrs.	Mobile homes	Physical problems		Black	Hispanic	Moved in past year	Below poverty level
						Severe	Moderate				
Persons per room											
0.50 or less	18,384	14,233	4,151	497	1,123	592	755	1,534	513	804	3,416
0.51 to 1.00	1,642	1,034	608	65	110	78	119	266	144	113	315
1.01 to 1.50	49	42	7	-	2	-	2	17	3	1	18
1.51 or more	25	18	8	2	-	5	8	11	2	4	20
Square feet per person											
Single detached and mobile homes	14,547	13,520	1,028	303	1,233	461	708	1,153	392	360	2,531
Less than 200	160	141	18	6	30	14	17	50	20	5	56
200 to 299	349	299	49	3	54	26	38	66	25	19	77
300 to 399	601	542	59	17	113	29	57	90	27	16	114
400 to 499	874	803	72	17	156	35	73	102	29	15	142
500 to 599	1,022	951	70	21	163	36	58	79	38	18	189
600 to 699	1,280	1,191	89	24	136	45	66	97	42	42	223
700 to 799	1,232	1,146	85	33	178	28	53	106	41	27	193
800 to 899	949	879	69	32	92	23	41	61	28	26	184
900 to 999	990	940	50	24	75	29	54	59	26	30	158
1,000 to 1,499	3,256	3,077	179	70	114	89	99	180	61	94	553
1,500 or more	2,935	2,782	154	28	31	69	96	135	29	40	455
Not reported	900	768	132	28	92	39	56	127	25	28	188
Median	936	945	807	852	641	794	733	727	704	891	897

Source: U.S. Department of Commerce and U.S. Department of Housing and Urban Development, Current Housing Reports, H150/89, *American Housing Survey for the United States in 1989*, July 1991, p. 314. *Note:* ... means not applicable. A dash (-) means zero or rounds to zero.

★ 483 ★

Building Characteristics

Space per Person, by Family Type, in Elderly Households

[Numbers are shown in thousands for 1989]

Characteristic	All households	Family households								Nonfamily households
		Total	Married couple		Male householder No wife present		Female householder No husband present		
			Total	With own children under 18	Total	With own children under 18	Total	With own children under 18	
Persons 65 Years Old and Over									
None	...	...	...	...	...	...	...	...	...
1 person	12,992	4,012	2,345	66	368	10	1,299	15	8,980
2 persons or more	7,109	7,039	6,408	18	258	-	373	-	70

[Continued]

★ 483 ★

Space per Person, by Family Type, in Elderly Households

[Continued]

Characteristic	All households	Family households							Nonfamily households
		Total	Married couple		Male householder No wife present		Female householder No husband present		
			Total	With own children under 18	Total	With own children under 18	Total	With own children under 18	
Persons									
1 person	8,762	...	...	...	...	...	...	...	8,762
2 persons	9,225	8,985	7,370	...	476	4	1,139	4	240
3 persons	1,415	1,377	973	43	106	4	298	5	39
4 persons	371	362	223	17	28	2	111	-	9
5 persons	179	179	107	11	10	-	62	2	-
6 persons	67	67	42	4	-	-	25	2	-
7 persons or more	82	82	37	9	5	-	39	2	-
Median	1.6	2.1	2.1	3.5	2.2	...	2.2	...	1.5-
Rooms									
1 room	153	2	2	-	-	-	-	-	151
2 rooms	223	17	12	-	2	-	2	2	206
3 rooms	2,113	376	283	25	-	-	68	-	1,737
4 rooms	3,972	1,766	1,325	6	113	2	328	-	2,205
5 rooms	5,209	3,021	2,395	14	167	3	460	7	2,187
6 rooms	4,357	2,868	2,296	34	160	6	412	5	1,490
7 rooms	2,334	1,682	1,339	9	83	-	259	-	653
8 rooms	1,024	797	652	12	58	-	87	2	227
9 rooms	400	300	259	5	9	-	31	-	100
10 rooms or more	315	222	189	5	8	-	25	-	93
Median	5.2	5.6	5.7	6.2	5.5	...	5.5	...	4.6
Persons per room									
0.50 or less	18,384	9,544	7,763	35	511	8	1,269	5	8,840
0.51 to 1.00	1,642	1,435	953	42	113	2	368	8	208
1.01 to 1.50	49	49	32	7	-	-	18	-	-
1.51 or more	25	24	4	-	2	-	18	2	2

Source: U.S. Department of Commerce and U.S. Department of Housing and Urban Development, Current Housing Reports H151/89, *Supplement to the American Housing Survey for the United States in 1989,* October 1992, pp. 72-73. *Notes:* ... means not applicable or sample too small. A dash (-) means zero or rounds to zero.

Housing Amenities

★ 484 ★

Heating and Air Conditioning in Elderly Households

[Numbers are shown in thousands for 1989.]

Characteristic	Total occupied units	Tenure		Housing unit characteristics				Household characteristics			
		Owner	Renter	New construction 4 yrs.	Mobile homes	Physical problems Severe	Physical problems Moderate	Black	Hispanic	Moved in past year	Below poverty level
Air conditioning											
Central	7,414	6,065	1,349	444	636	180	110	303	200	434	873
1 room unit	4,231	2,935	1,296	37	211	138	255	458	144	170	978
2 room units	1,651	1,344	307	8	75	42	91	144	42	28	270
3 room units or more	602	562	40	-	10	14	48	47	24	9	55
Main heating equipment											
Warm-air furnace	10,438	8,667	1,770	331	948	261	119	715	222	422	1,578
Steam or hot water system	3,248	2,074	1,173	32	7	114	55	330	103	123	521
Electric heat pump	1,147	938	209	109	79	35	21	28	40	101	80
Built-in electric units	1,403	736	667	80	36	26	12	73	59	151	291
Floor, wall, or other built-in hot air units without ducts	1,087	752	335	-	16	25	26	119	83	49	239
Room heaters with flue	895	666	229	3	36	53	25	179	23	27	345
Room heaters without flue	623	471	153	-	20	55	568	228	69	18	322
Portable electric heaters	153	102	51	3	12	20	19	28	23	16	57
Stoves	631	533	98	2	62	69	32	78	20	9	215
Fireplaces with inserts	93	87	6	3	-	2	2	2	-	-	11
Fireplaces without inserts	41	34	7	-	3	6	-	13	-	-	16
Other	258	198	60	2	15	7	3	31	14	-	67
None	83	68	15	-	2	2	2	3	5	6	26

Source: U.S. Department of Commerce and U.S. Department of Housing and Urban Development, Current Housing Reports, H150/89, *American Housing Survey for the United States in 1989,* July 1991, p. 316. *Note:* ... means not applicable. A dash (-) means zero or rounds to zero.

★ 485 ★

Housing Amenities

Heating Fuel Use in Elderly Households

[Numbers are shown in thousands for 1989]

Fuel type	Total occupied units	Tenure		Housing unit characteristics				Household characteristics			
		Owner	Renter	New construction 4 yrs.	Mobile homes	Physical problems Severe	Physical problems Moderate	Black	Hispanic	Moved in past year	Below poverty level
Main house heating fuel											
Housing units with heating fuel	20,017	15,258	4,759	564	1,233	673	883	1,824	655	916	3,742
Electricity	4,081	2,715	1,366	292	373	113	71	206	168	395	703
Piped gas	10,379	8,176	2,203	198	410	279	503	1,036	362	404	1,772
Bottled gas	983	859	124	47	213	47	168	131	13	31	307
Fuel oil	3,265	2,433	832	19	84	115	50	277	82	67	558
Kerosene or other liquid fuel	282	221	61	3	73	27	48	62	1	6	99

[Continued]

★ 485 ★

Heating Fuel Use in Elderly Households
[Continued]

Fuel type	Total occupied units	Tenure		New con-struction 4 yrs.	Mobile homes	Physical problems		Black	Hispanic	Moved in past year	Below poverty level
		Owner	Renter			Severe	Moderate				
Coal or coke	102	87	15	-	-	14	4	6	3	-	25
Wood	823	714	109	5	60	71	35	94	26	9	254
Solar energy	10	8	2	-	3	-	-	-	-	2	-
Other	91	46	45	-	18	7	2	13	-	3	23
Other house heating fuels											
With other heating fuels[1]	3,513	3,150	364	82	211	126	175	286	106	105	591
Electricity	1,389	1,181	208	22	92	48	109	126	34	32	268
Piped gas	153	120	33	2	6	5	3	23	15	2	31
Bottled gas	147	141	7	-	17	6	10	38	2	-	55
Fuel oil	107	91	16	-	3	-	-	5	4	-	2
Kerosene or other liquid fuel	242	209	33	-	26	16	11	63	-	5	56
Coal or coke	49	39	10	-	2	2	2	5	-	-	19
Wood	1,483	1,420	63	58	55	56	41	45	51	65	174
Solar energy	14	14	-	-	3	-	-	-	2	-	2
Other	67	60	7	-	14	-	2	2	-	2	5
Not reported	119	96	24	2	3	5	2	13	7	-	20

Source: U.S. Department of Commerce and U.S. Department of Housing and Urban Development, Current Housing Reports, H150/89, *American Housing Survey for the United States in 1989*, July 1991, p. 318. *Notes:* ... means not applicable. A dash (-) means zero or rounds to zero. 1. Figures may not add to total because more than one category may apply to a unit.

★ 486 ★

Housing Amenities

Plumbing Facilities in Elderly Households
[Numbers are shown in thousands for 1989]

Characteristic	Total occupied units	Tenure		New con-struction 4 yrs.	Mobile homes	Physical problems		Black	Hispanic	Moved in past year	Below poverty level
		Owner	Renter			Severe	Moderate				
Plumbing											
With all plumbing facilities	19,491	14,906	4,585	559	1,200	66	885	1,745	646	901	3,592
Lacking some plumbing facilities[1]	70	44	26	-	-	70	-	12	3	-	38
No hot piped water	22	17	5	-	-	22	-	3	3	-	13
No bathtub nor shower	52	27	24	-	-	52	-	10	-	-	33
No flush toilet	17	13	4	-	-	17	-	4	-	-	6
No plumbing facilities for exclusive use	539	377	162	5	35	539	-	71	12	21	138
Source of water											
Public system or private company	17,351	12,873	4,478	494	948	494	751	1,655	636	861	3,189
Well serving 1 to 5 units	2,564	2,309	255	65	276	141	124	156	22	59	528
Drilled	2,150	1,957	193	61	224	97	103	106	18	52	406
Dug	332	284	48	4	39	42	17	47	1	7	105
Not reported	82	68	15	-	14	2	4	2	3	-	17
Other	186	145	41	6	11	41	10	16	3	2	52
Means of sewage disposal											
Public sewer	15,293	10,976	4,316	414	662	440	595	1,509	610	805	2,740

[Continued]

★ 486 ★

Plumbing Facilities in Elderly Households
[Continued]

Characteristic	Total occupied units	Tenure		New con-struction 4 yrs.	Mobile homes	Physical problems		Black	Hispanic	Moved in past year	Below poverty level
		Owner	Renter			Severe	Moderate				
Septic tank, cesspool, chemical toilet	4,737	4,311	427	150	573	164	290	288	51	116	986
Other	70	40	31	-	-	70	-	30	-	2	41

Source: U.S. Department of Commerce and U.S. Department of Housing and Urban Development, Current Housing Reports, H150/89, *American Housing Survey for the United States in 1989*, July 1991, p. 316. *Notes:* ... means not applicable. A dash (-) means zero or rounds to zero. 1. Figures may not add to total because more than one category may apply to a unit.

Homeownership

★ 487 ★

Homeownership Rates by Age, Race, and Hispanic Origin

[Data are in percent]

	Age			Total
	65-74	75-84	85/85+	
White	82.2	73.7	67.2	78.0
Black	63.4	65.0	63.3	63.9
Hispanic	68.5	57.3	42.6	62.5
Other	67.1	51.8	72.6	63.3
Total	80.2	72.7	66.9	73.0

Source: Elderly Households, a Profile, Senate Select Committee on Aging, Comm. Pub. No. 102-912, 1992, p. 38.

★ 488 ★

Homeownership

Homeownership Patterns by Age, Race, and Hispanic Origin

[Data are in thousands]

	Age						Total	
	65-74		75-84		85/85+			
	Number	%	Number	%	Number	%	Number	%
White	8,748.9	55.5	4,586.4	29.1	1,076.8	6.8	14,412.1	91.4
Black	743.4	4.7	380.3	2.4	79.9	0.5	1,203.7	7.6
Hispanic	289.0	1.8	115.3	0.7	31.8	0.2	436.1	2.8
Other	100.5	0.6	34.0	0.2	13.0	0.1	147.5	0.9
Total	9,592.8	60.9	5,000.7	31.7	1,169.7	7.4	15,763.2	100.0

Source: Elderly Households, a Profile, Senate Select Committee on Aging, Comm. Pub. No. 102-912, 1992, p.38. Primary source: The American Housing Survey, 1989, Data on CD ROM. US Dept. of Housing and Urban Development & Bureau of the Census. *Note:* Numbers do not add due to rounding.

★ 489 ★

Homeownership

Homeowners at Risk

[Data are in thousands]

Income	Age						Total	
	65-74		75-84		85/85+			
	Number	%	Number	%	Number	%	Number	%
Under $5,000	663.4	6.9	558.3	11.2	156.7	13.4	1,378.4	8.7
$5,000-$9,999	1,512.0	15.8	1,195.2	23.9	418.6	35.8	3,125.9	19.8
$10,000-$14,999	1,543.4	16.1	1,026.3	20.5	174.4	4.9	2,744.1	17.4
$15,000-$19,999	1,234.2	12.9	565.6	11.3	96.2	8.2	1,896.0	12.0
$20,000 and over	4,639.8	48.4	1,655.3	33.1	323.8	27.7	6,618.9	42.0
At Risk	4,953.0	51.6	3,345.4	66.9	845.9	72.3	9,144.3	58.0
Total	9,592.8	100.0	5,000.7	100.0	1,169.7	100.0	15,763.2	100.0

Source: Elderly Households, a Profile, Senate Select Committee on Aging, Comm. Pub. No. 102-912, 1992, p.41. Primary source: The American Housing Survey, 1989, Data on CD ROM. U.S. Department of Housing and Urban Development & Bureau of the Census. *Note:* Numbers do not add due to rounding.

Housing Costs

★ 490 ★

Monthly Housing Costs

[Numbers are shown in thousands]

| Characteristic | All households | Total | Family households | | | | | | | Nonfamily households |
| | | | Married couple | | Male householder no wife present | | Female householder no husband present | | | |
			Total	With own children under 18	Total	With own children under 18	Total	With own children under 18		
Less than $100	1,325	450	301	7	41	-	107	-		876
$100 to $199	6,382	3,195	2,531	16	199	5	464	4		3,187
$200 to $249	2,730	1,618	1,299	2	87	-	232	2		1,112
$250 to $299	1,941	1,148	940	11	49	-	159	-		793
$300 to $349	1,481	867	718	6	46	-	103	-		614
$350 to $399	1,021	598	451	4	27	-	120	2		423
$400 to $449	824	453	345	2	38	-	70	2		372
$450 to $499	645	382	310	-	24	-	49	-		262
$500 to $599	941	583	458	9	22	2	103	-		358
$600 to $699	596	350	274	2	16	-	59	-		246
$700 to $799	343	217	180	-	7	-	29	2		127
$800 to $899	216	154	124	2	6	-	25	-		62
$900 to $999	132	90	78	4	2	-	9	-		42
$1,000 to $1,249	208	158	132	5	8	-	18	-		50
$1,250 to $1,499	96	53	41	-	4	1	8	-		43
$1,500 or more	145	106	81	5	6	2	19	-		39
No cash rent	443	144	103	-	8	-	34	-		299
Mortgage payment not reported	630	485	386	7	34	-	64	2		145
Median (excludes no cash rent)	233	248	250	324	229	...	247	...		211

Source: U.S. Department of Commerce and U.S. Department of Housing and Urban Development, Current Housing Reports H151/89, *Supplement to the American Housing Survey for the United States in 1989*, October 1992, pp. 74-75. *Notes:* ... means not applicable or sample too small. A dash (-) means zero or rounds to zero.

★ 491 ★

Housing Costs

Monthly Housing Costs as Percent of Current Income[1]

[Numbers are shown in thousands for 1989]

| Characteristic | All households | Family households | | | | | | | Nonfamily households |
| | | Total | Married couple | | Male householder no wife present | | Female householder no husband present | | |
			Total	With own children under 18	Total	With own children under 18	Total	With own children under 18	
Less than 5 percent	578	478	363	2	47	-	68	-	100
5 to 9 percent	2,733	2,177	1,760	14	130	3	287	-	556
10 to 14 percent	3,028	2,188	1,796	16	101	-	291	4	840
15 to 19 percent	2,558	1,592	1,284	11	102	2	206	5	966
20 to 24 percent	2,053	1,014	785	9	57	-	172	-	1,039
25 to 29 percent	1,745	665	527	9	26	1	112	-	1,080
30 to 34 percent	1,269	509	371	2	39	2	99	2	760
35 to 39 percent	885	332	265	-	11	-	56	-	554
40 to 49 percent	1,233	436	318	7	26	-	92	-	797
50 to 59 percent	699	226	162	-	7	-	57	-	473
60 to 69 percent	514	143	116	-	4	-	23	-	371
70 to 99 percent	700	228	161	5	16	-	51	-	472
100 percent or more[2]	837	335	272	2	14	2	49	-	502
Zero or negative income	194	99	83	-	3	-	12	2	95
No cash rent	443	144	103	-	8	-	34	-	299
Mortgage payment not reported	630	485	386	7	34	-	64	2	145
Median (excludes 3 previous lines)	21	16	16	18	16	...	18	...	28

Source: U.S. Department of Commerce and U.S. Department of Housing and Urban Development, Current Housing Reports H151/89, *Supplement to the American Housing Survey for the United States in 1989*, October 1992, pp. 74-75. *Notes:* ... means not applicable or sample too small. A dash (-) means zero or rounds to zero. 1. Beginning with 1989 this item uses current income in its calculation. 2. May reflect a temporary situation, living off savings, or response error.

★ 492 ★

Housing Costs

Older Americans Living Alone Who Have Excessive Housing Costs, by Type of Tenure and Sex: 1987

From the source: "Many elderly people who live alone must pay excessive costs for housing. According to the Department of Housing and Urban Development (HUD), renters who spend more than 30 percent of before-tax income on housing have excessive housing costs. HUD defines excess housing expenditures for homeowners as costs in excess of 40 percent of income."

[Numbers in percent]

Type of tenure	Men	Women
Renters	59.0	69.0
Owners	17.0	25.0

Source: Aging America, Trends and Projections, prepared by the U.S. Senate Special Committee on Aging, the American Association of Retired Persons, the Federal Council on the Aging, and the U.S. Administration on Aging, 1991, Washington, D.C., p. 223. Primary source: American Housing Survey, 1987.

★ 493 ★

Housing Costs

Rent Paid by Lodgers to Elderly Households

[Numbers are shown in thousands for 1989]

Characteristic	Total occupied units	Tenure		Housing unit characteristics				Household characteristics			
		Owner	Renter	New con-struction 4 yrs.	Mobile homes	Physical problems		Black	Hispanic	Moved in past year	Below poverty level
						Severe	Moderate				
Lodgers in housing units	42	33	9	-	2	5	7	9	-	2	7
Less than $50 per month	9	7	2	-	-	2	2	-	-	-	2
$50 to $99	2	2	-	-	-	-	-	2	-	-	2
$100 to $149	14	9	4	-	-	-	4	5	-	2	-
$150 to $199	-	-	-	-	-	-	-	-	-	-	-
$200 or more per month	8	6	2	-	-	-	-	2	-	-	-
Not reported	9	9	-	-	2	2	-	-	-	-	-
Median	...	...	...	...	...	...	...	...	...	...	...

Source: U.S. Department of Commerce and U.S. Department of Housing and Urban Development, Current Housing Reports, H150/89, *American Housing Survey for the United States in 1989,* July 1991, p. 336. *Note:* ... means not applicable. A dash (-) means zero or rounds to zero.

★ 494 ★

Housing Costs

Rent Reductions for Elderly Households

[Numbers are shown in thousands for 1989]

Characteristic	Total occupied units	Tenure		Housing unit characteristics				Household characteristics			
		Owner	Renter	New con-struction 4 yrs.	Mobile homes	Severe	Moderate	Black	Hispanic	Moved in past year	Below poverty level
No subsidy or income reporting	3,339	...	3,339	147	77	161	216	376	164	394	788
Rent control	227	...	227	-	-	20	12	17	11	10	42
No rent control	3,105	...	3,105	147	77	142	204	360	152	384	746
Reduced by owner	312	...	312	4	17	15	31	38	23	12	112
Not reduced by owner	2,761	...	2,761	136	60	127	172	319	130	364	627
Owner reduction not reported	32	...	32	6	-	-	-	3	-	8	7
Rent control not reported	7	...	7	-	-	-	-	-	-	-	-
Owned by public housing authority	809	...	809	24	-	25	15	184	54	106	398
Other, federal subsidy	346	...	346	15	4	15	14	68	29	52	143
Other, State or local subsidy	77	...	77	2	-	-	8	11	9	14	28
Other, income verification	133	...	133	10	-	6	5	22	-	11	64
Subsidy or income verification not reported	70	...	70	3	5	2	8	7	-	7	23

Source: U.S. Department of Commerce and U.S. Department of Housing and Urban Development, Current Housing Reports, H150/89, *American Housing Survey for the United States in 1989*, July 1991, p. 334. *Note:* ... means not applicable. A dash (-) means zero or rounds to zero.

★ 495 ★

Housing Costs

Fuel Costs in Elderly Households

[Numbers are shown in thousands for 1989]

Characteristic	Total occupied units	Tenure		Housing unit characteristics				Household characteristics			
		Owner	Renter	New con-struction 4 yrs.	Mobile homes	Severe	Moderate	Black	Hispanic	Moved in past year	Below poverty level
Monthly cost paid for electricity											
Electricity used	20,093	15,319	4,774	564	1,235	668	885	1,827	661	923	3,763
Less than $25	3,448	2,079	1,369	93	213	135	229	384	195	150	917
$25 to $49	7,256	5,871	1,385	194	513	248	343	613	197	306	1,353
$50 to $74	3,891	3,402	489	98	280	113	130	323	78	115	536
$75 to $99	1,744	1,577	166	63	96	50	53	103	50	37	222
$100 to $149	1,081	1,007	74	37	58	21	18	62	24	49	89
$150 to $199	277	265	11	5	3	5	2	27	7	21	20
$200 or more	179	173	7	4	5	2	4	9	2	5	26
Median	44	47	32	45	43	40	37	40	35	41	37
Included in rent, other fee, or obtained free	2,217	944	1,273	70	67	93	105	306	108	240	599
Monthly cost paid for piped gas											
Piped gas used	12,608	9,463	3,144	245	466	371	575	1,308	520	530	2,252
Less than $25	3,194	2,185	1,009	69	175	101	222	307	214	137	649
$25 to $49	4,247	3,667	581	92	195	112	208	359	117	125	664
$50 to $74	1,996	1,787	209	15	34	50	55	218	43	41	316
$75 to $99	625	576	49	7	5	14	11	82	5	16	87
$100 to $149	321	300	21	5	-	7	10	62	22	14	49
$150 to $199	86	83	3	-	-	4	5	17	2	3	9

[Continued]

★ 495 ★

Fuel Costs in Elderly Households
[Continued]

Characteristic	Total occupied units	Tenure		Housing unit characteristics				Household characteristics			
		Owner	Renter	New con-struction 4 yrs.	Mobile homes	Physical problems		Black	Hispanic	Moved in past year	Below poverty level
						Severe	Moderate				
$200 or more	66	62	4	-	-	4	2	12	-	-	9
Median	37	40	25-	32	29	35	29	40	25-	31	34
Included in rent, other fee, or obtained free	2,073	803	1,270	57	58	79	62	253	117	193	469
Average monthly cost paid for fuel oil											
Fuel oil used	3,783	2,758	1,024	26	107	127	78	324	96	89	656
Less than $25	317	262	55	5	23	16	13	29	3	11	62
$25 to $49	794	680	114	7	48	27	6	59	6	9	120
$50 to $74	830	739	91	2	23	15	22	46	14	13	151
$75 to $99	481	434	47	4	2	18	-	16	9	7	42
$100 to $149	401	347	54	-	-	9	7	42	10	2	47
$150 to $199	102	87	14	-	-	2	-	8	5	-	3
$200 or more	70	66	5	-	-	-	-	8	2	-	10
Median	62	62	56	...	38	52	55	59	80	51	56
Included in rent, other fee, or obtained free	789	144	644	8	11	39	29	117	48	47	222

Source: U.S. Department of Commerce and U.S. Department of Housing and Urban Development, Current Housing Reports, H150/89, *American Housing Survey for the United States in 1989*, July 1991, p. 336. *Notes:* ... means not applicable or sample too small. A dash (-) means zero or rounds to zero.

★ 496 ★

Housing Costs

Fuel and Utility Costs in Elderly Households

[Numbers are shown in thousands for 1989]

Characteristic	Total occupied units	Tenure		Housing unit characteristics				Household characteristics			
		Owner	Renter	New con-struction 4 yrs.	Mobile homes	Physical problems		Black	Hispanic	Moved in past year	Below poverty level
						Severe	Moderate				
Water paid separately	10,948	10,172	776	241	393	264	464	876	305	247	1,632
Median	17	17	14	19	15	16	16	16	20	17	14
Trash paid separately	6,581	6,581	-	169	303	145	219	303	182	157	803
Median	10-	10-	...	10-	10-	11	10-	10-	10-	11	10-
Bottled gas paid separately	1,589	1,589	-	52	319	88	167	207	18	32	414
Median	40	40	...	...	38	36	41	44	...	...	40
Other fuel paid separately	2,046	2,046	-	35	192	113	99	185	60	54	378
Median	15	15	...	...	20	21	12	15	16	...	17

Source: U.S. Department of Commerce and U.S. Department of Housing and Urban Development, Current Housing Reports, H150/89, *American Housing Survey for the United States in 1989*, July 1991, p. 338. *Note:* ... means not applicable. A dash (-) means zero or rounds to zero.

★ 497 ★

Housing Costs

Maintenance: Costs in Elderly Households

[Numbers are shown in thousands for 1989]

Characteristic	Total occupied units	Tenure		Housing unit characteristics				Household characteristics			
		Owner	Renter	New con-struction 4 yrs.	Mobile homes	Physical problems		Black	Hispanic	Moved in past year	Below poverty level
						Severe	Moderate				
Less than $25 per month	11,494	11,494	...	308	983	358	515	880	274	267	1,864
$25 to $49	1,530	1,530	...	14	73	45	45	103	43	13	187
$50 to $74	407	407	...	4	18	5	4	40	28	7	36
$75 to $99	421	421	...	7	10	12	5	30	11	19	31
$100 to $149	261	261	...	13	13	5	6	12	11	7	32
$150 to $199	165	165	...	6	8	8	-	2	-	7	16
$200 or more per month	186	186	...	-	5	5	2	9	2	7	13
Not reported	862	862	...	11	40	28	41	83	36	12	146

Source: U.S. Department of Commerce and U.S. Department of Housing and Urban Development, Current Housing Reports, H150/89, *American Housing Survey for the United States in 1989*, July 1991, p. 338. *Note:* ... means not applicable. A dash (-) means zero or rounds to zero.

★ 498 ★

Housing Costs

Maintenance: Government Subsidy for Home Repairs by the Elderly

[Numbers are shown in thousands for 1989]

Characteristic	Total occupied units	Tenure		Housing unit characteristics				Household characteristics			
		Owner	Renter	New con-struction 4 yrs.	Mobile homes	Physical problems		Black	Hispanic	Moved in past year	Below poverty level
						Severe	Moderate				
Units with major repairs the last 2 years	6,590	6,590	...	84	375	203	234	565	142	122	858
Received low-interest loan or grant	127	127	...	-	8	7	5	36	14	3	33
No low-interest loan or grant	6,205	6,205	...	76	347	180	216	509	124	117	795
Not reported	258	258	...	9	21	16	13	21	4	3	30

Source: U.S. Department of Commerce and U.S. Department of Housing and Urban Development, Current Housing Reports, H150/89, *American Housing Survey for the United States in 1989*, July 1991, p. 348. *Notes:* ... means not applicable or sample too small. A dash (-) means zero or rounds to zero.

★ 499 ★

Housing Costs

Property Insurance in Elderly Households

[Numbers are shown in thousands for 1989]

Characteristic	Total occupied units	Tenure		Housing unit characteristics				Household characteristics			
		Owner	Renter	New con-struction 4 yrs.	Mobile homes	Physical problems		Black	Hispanic	Moved in past year	Below poverty level
						Severe	Moderate				
Property insurance paid	16,059	14,233	1,826	455	1,058	425	529	1,054	339	497	2,230
Median per month	23	24	12	21	19	20	21	21	25	20	20

Source: U.S. Department of Commerce and U.S. Department of Housing and Urban Development, Current Housing Reports, H150/89, *American Housing Survey for the United States in 1989*, July 1991, p. 338.

Housing Value

★ 500 ★

Housing Value of Elderly Households, by Family Type

[Numbers are shown in thousands for 1989]

Characteristic	All households	Family households								Nonfamily households
		Total	Married couple		Male householder no wife present		Female householder no husband present			
			Total	With own children under 18	Total	With own children under 18	Total	With own children under 18		
Total	15,326	9,653	7,830	76	527	9	1,296	11		5,673
Value										
Less than $10,000	630	291	209	4	11	-	70	2		339
$10,000 to $19,999	886	465	338	9	37	-	91	-		421
$20,000 to $29,999	1,049	556	430	3	43	-	82	-		493
$30,000 to $39,999	1,369	758	621	9	31	-	106	-		610
$40,000 to $49,999	1,583	922	718	4	31	3	174	4		661
$50,000 to $59,999	1,360	839	685	9	45	-	109	2		521
$60,000 to $69,999	1,322	866	708	4	62	-	96	-		456
$70,000 to $79,999	1,213	732	592	5	53	2	87	-		481
$80,000 to $99,999	1,548	1,121	935	5	53	-	133	2		427
$100,000 to $119,999	856	608	515	2	27	-	66	-		248
$120,000 to $149,999	934	672	553	2	40	1	78	-		262
$150,000 to $199,999	1,106	762	638	5	32	2	93	-		343
$200,000 to $249,999	630	434	360	7	32	-	42	-		196
$250,000 to $299,999	309	225	188	-	5	-	32	-		85

[Continued]

★ 500 ★

Housing Value of Elderly Households, by Family Type
[Continued]

Characteristic	All households	Family households								Nonfamily households
		Total	Married couple		Male householder no wife present		Female householder no husband present			
			Total	With own children under 18	Total	With own children under 18	Total	With own children under 18		
$300,000 or more	531	401	339	8	28	-	35	-		129
Median	65,944	71,765	73,466	60,348	70,909	...	61,623	...		55,987

Source: U.S. Department of Commerce and U.S. Department of Housing and Urban Development, Current Housing Reports H151/89, *Supplement to the American Housing Survey for the United States in 1989,* October 1992, pp. 74-75. *Notes:* ... means not applicable or sample too small. A dash (-) means zero or rounds to zero.

★ 501 ★

Housing Value

Housing Value and Ratio of Value to Current Income[1]
[Numbers are shown in thousands for 1989]

Characteristic	Total occupied units	Tenure		Housing unit characteristics				Household characteristics			
		Owner	Renter	New construction 4 yrs.	Mobile homes	Physical problems		Black	Hispanic	Moved in past year	Below poverty level
						Severe	Moderate				
Value											
Less than $10,000	630	630	...	-	319	48	73	72	23	15	245
$10,000 to $19,999	886	886	...	27	298	44	75	173	17	25	275
$20,000 to $29,999	1,049	1,049	...	47	219	45	76	148	30	22	277
$30,000 to $39,999	1,369	1,369	...	16	145	42	81	152	25	28	293
$40,000 to $49,999	1,583	1,583	...	8	66	55	95	149	38	28	294
$50,000 to $59,999	1,360	1,360	...	22	39	32	57	94	20	19	193
$60,000 to $69,999	1,322	1,322	...	15	15	30	45	74	47	27	162
$70,000 to $79,999	1,213	1,213	...	37	16	22	29	73	10	17	140
$80,000 to $99,999	1,548	1,548	...	38	22	31	33	62	47	36	134
$100,000 to $119,999	856	856	...	32	-	28	13	47	24	26	55
$120,000 to $149,999	934	934	...	58	2	18	4	33	27	34	59
$150,000 to $199,999	1,106	1,106	...	32	7	31	7	38	44	32	96
$200,000 to $249,999	630	630	...	13	-	22	12	22	23	12	48
$250,000 to $299,999	309	309	...	9	-	5	7	15	16	13	23
$300,000 or more	531	531	...	10	-	11	11	5	12	5	30
Median	65,944	65,944	...	85,209	18,563	49,622	40,480	42,205	71,365	73,483	42,456
Ratio of value to current income[1]											
Less than 1.5	2,283	2,283	...	37	566	102	124	243	48	49	184
1.5 to 1.9	1,101	1,101	...	21	130	32	46	86	27	31	69
2.0 to 2.4	1,261	1,261	...	17	127	34	45	102	29	31	103
2.5 to 2.9	1,120	1,120	...	36	77	24	52	56	22	29	42
3.0 to 3.9	1,947	1,947	...	42	74	43	66	142	54	49	135
4.0 to 4.9	1,536	1,536	...	68	60	47	47	101	35	41	131
5.0 or more	5,915	5,915	...	141	98	175	235	416	187	104	1,506

[Continued]

★ 501 ★

Housing Value and Ratio of Value to Current Income
[Continued]

Characteristic	Total occupied units	Tenure		Housing unit characteristics				Household characteristics			
		Owner	Renter	New con-struction 4 yrs.	Mobile homes	Physical problems		Black	Hispanic	Moved in past year	Below poverty level
						Severe	Moderate				
Zero or negative income	164	164	...	3	18	9	5	13	5	6	155
Median	3.9	3.9	...	4.4	1.5-	3.6	3.6	4.6	3.6	5.0+	

Source: U.S. Department of Commerce and U.S. Department of Housing and Urban Development, Current Housing Reports, H150/89, *American Housing Survey for the United States in 1989*, July 1991, p. 342. *Notes:* ... means not applicable. A dash (-) means zero or rounds to zero. 1. Beginning with 1989 this item uses current income in its calculation.

★ 502 ★

Housing Value

Purchase Price of Elderly Housing
[Numbers are shown in thousands for 1989]

Characteristic	Total occupied units	Tenure		Housing unit characteristics				Household characteristics			
		Owner	Renter	New con-struction 4 yrs.	Mobile homes	Physical problems		Black	Hispanic	Moved in past year	Below poverty level
						Severe	Moderate				
Home purchased or built	14,227	14,227	...	355	1,107	410	538	1,059	382	322	2,080
Less than $10,000	3,172	3,172	...	-	347	132	225	374	105	12	738
$10,000 to $19,999	3,437	3,437	...	37	338	91	128	269	89	36	437
$20,000 to $29,999	1,641	1,641	...	41	180	32	24	75	32	33	148
$30,000 to $39,999	1,070	1,070	...	11	71	13	17	59	16	26	74
$40,000 to $49,999	674	674	...	19	45	15	7	32	25	23	45
$50,000 to $59,999	470	470	...	18	11	19	4	18	10	11	34
$60,000 to $69,999	358	358	...	42	9	-	-	2	23	13	13
$70,000 to $79,999	254	254	...	33	3	-	-	5	5	29	13
$80,000 to $99,999	288	288	...	30	3	4	3	5	11	25	15
$100,000 to $119,999	107	107	...	12	-	4	-	-	6	12	2
$120,000 to $149,999	171	171	...	40	-	2	4	5	5	34	5
$150,000 to $199,999	146	146	...	23	3	-	-	-	2	23	3
$200,000 to $249,999	41	41	...	9	-	-	3	-	-	8	5
$250,000 to $299,999	20	20	...	5	-	-	-	-	-	2	-
$300,000 or more	20	20	...	2	-	-	-	-	-	-	-
Not reported	2,358	2,358	...	32	97	98	125	215	53	35	547
Median	18,039	18,039	...	68,407	14,679	12,611	10,000	11,777	16,718	61,654	10,659
Received as inheritance or gift	656	656	...	-	7	42	58	66	5	7	159
Not reported	443	443	...	9	35	13	23	35	19	10	85

Source: U.S. Department of Commerce and U.S. Department of Housing and Urban Development, Current Housing Reports, H150/89, *American Housing Survey for the United States in 1989*, July 1991, p. 342. *Notes:* ... means not applicable or sample too small. A dash (-) means zero or rounds to zero.

Neighborhoods

★ 503 ★

Neighborhood Conditions

[Numbers are shown in thousands]

Characteristic	All households	Family households								Nonfamily households
		Total	Married couple		Male householder no wife present		Female householder no husband present			
			Total	With own children under 18	Total	With own children under 18	Total	With own children under 18		
With neighborhood	19,463	10,782	8,538	77	615	10	1,629	15		8,681
No problems	14,086	7,578	6,050	57	428	8	1,099	5		6,509
With problems[1]	5,297	3,146	2,441	21	180	2	525	11		2,151
Crime	666	331	217	5	21	-	93	-		334
Noise	1,119	646	496	-	34	2	116	2		473
Traffic	989	633	522	3	34	-	77	2		356
Litter or housing deterioration	737	459	360	2	23	-	77	-		277
Poor city or county services	180	115	90	4	-	-	25	-		65
Undesirable commercial, institutional, industrial	268	163	119	-	2	-	41	-		105
People	1,623	895	668	4	62	2	165	7		727
Other	1,300	812	642	7	50	-	120	5		488
Type of problem not reported	91	59	50	-	1	-	7	-		32
Presence of problems not reported	80	58	47	-	6	-	4	-		22

Source: U.S. Department of Commerce and U.S. Department of Housing and Urban Development, Current Housing Reports H151/89, *Supplement to the American Housing Survey for the United States in 1989*, October 1992, pp. 78-79. *Notes:* A dash (-) means zero or rounds to zero. 1. Figures may not add to total because more than one category may apply to a unit.

★ 504 ★

Neighborhoods

Neighborhood Quality

[Numbers are shown in thousands]

Characteristics	Total occupied units	Tenure		Housing unit characteristics				Household characteristics			
		Owner	Renter	New construction 4 yrs.	Mobile homes	Physical problems		Black	Hispanic	Moved in past year	Below poverty level
						Severe	Moderate				
Total	20,100	15,326	4,774	564	1,235	675	885	1,827	661	923	3,768
Condition present as a percent of total[1]											
Street noise or traffic	35.64	33.86	41.37	20.76	24.28	41.84	41.56	43.63	34.57	29.73	39.04
Neighborhood crime	18.07	16.53	23.02	11.78	10.51	24.66	21.37	28.50	15.54	14.51	18.50
Any condition(s)	42.77	40.97	48.53	23.90	29.11	49.94	48.97	51.45	37.14	34.14	44.48
Both conditions present	10.94	9.41	15.86	8.64	5.68	16.56	13.96	20.68	10.96	10.10	13.06
No conditions present	56.24	58.02	50.54	75.71	69.81	49.11	48.91	46.92	59.68	65.33	55.10
Not reported	.99	1.01	.92	.39	1.07	.96	2.12	1.63	1.18	.53	.42

[Continued]

★ 504 ★

Neighborhood Quality

[Continued]

Characteristics	Total occupied units	Tenure		Housing unit characteristics				Household characteristics			
		Owner	Renter	New construction 4 yrs.	Mobile homes	Physical problems		Black	Hispanic	Moved in past year	Below poverty level
						Severe	Moderate				
Condition Bothersome as a percent of total[1]											
Street noise or traffic	12.85	12.64	13.53	8.13	8.81	15.38	15.59	16.95	17.19	8.00	14.18
Neighborhood crime	10.34	9.59	12.72	5.57	5.12	16.10	11.73	16.86	9.77	5.83	10.49
Unsatisfactory neighborhood shopping	17.93	19.17	13.95	14.39	28.92	25.05	30.88	28.54	14.33	14.52	24.21
Unsatisfactory public elementary school	.16	.15	.20	.47	-	.67	.28	.14	.78	.52	.07
Unsatisfactory public transportation	2.15	2.15	2.15	.38	1.15	1.25	2.03	3.37	2.75	1.60	1.69
Any condition(s)	35.00	35.53	33.30	24.05	38.33	45.87	47.82	47.49	34.07	26.19	40.18
Two or more conditions	7.39	7.22	7.94	4.89	5.33	10.93	9.61	14.90	8.45	4.03	8.72
Conditions so objectionable household wants to move as a percent of total[1]											
Street noise or traffic	3.41	3.17	4.18	.36	1.54	3.88	4.56	5.31	5.98	1.76	3.70
Neighborhood crime	2.52	1.99	4.21	1.77	1.41	3.68	3.90	6.01	4.48	2.15	3.16
Unsatisfactory public elementary school	.04	.06	-	-	-	-	-	-	-	-	-
Any condition(s)	4.88	4.38	6.46	1.77	2.71	5.97	6.37	7.93	8.76	3.22	5.14
Two or more conditions	1.09	.82	1.93	.36	.24	1.58	2.09	3.39	1.69	.69	1.72
Incomplete reporting as a percent of total[1]											
Street noise or traffic	1.15	1.15	1.15	.39	1.24	1.32	2.40	1.87	1.18	.53	.47
Neighborhood crime	1.32	1.24	1.58	.39	1.21	.96	2.82	2.03	1.18	.53	.81

Source: U.S. Department of Commerce and U.S. Department of Housing and Urban Development, Current Housing Reports H151/89, *Supplement to the American Housing Survey for the United States in 1989*, October 1992, p. 80. *Notes:* A dash (-) means zero or rounds to zero. 1. Figures may not add to 100%, because more than one condition may apply to a unit or conditions are not reported.

★ 505 ★

Neighborhoods

Building Security of Elderly Households

[Numbers are shown in thousands for 1989]

Characteristic	Total occupied units	Tenure		Housing unit characteristics				Household characteristics			
		Owner	Renter	New construction 4 yrs.	Mobile homes	Physical problems		Black	Hispanic	Moved in past year	Below poverty level
						Severe	Moderate				
Other buildings vandalized or with interior exposed[1]											
None	2,738	704	2,034	145	2	75	104	281	155	415	677
1 building	46	17	29	3	-	3	4	23	5	3	10
More than 1 building	41	2	39	-	-	4	5	20	10	8	11
No buildings within 300 feet	49	12	38	12	-	-	-	6	-	13	11
Not reported	1,706	422	1,284	16	-	96	38	156	62	31	341
Bars on windows of buildings[1]											
With other buildings within 300 feet	2,826	723	2,102	148	2	82	113	323	170	427	698
No bars on windows	2,447	643	1,803	143	-	69	80	211	119	403	594
1 building with bars	65	13	52	-	-	3	3	21	14	8	28

[Continued]

★ 505 ★

Building Security of Elderly Households
[Continued]

Characteristic	Total occupied units	Tenure		Housing unit characteristics				Household characteristics			
		Owner	Renter	New construction 4 yrs.	Mobile homes	Physical problems		Black	Hispanic	Moved in past year	Below poverty level
						Severe	Moderate				
2 or more buildings with bars	293	63	230	4	-	9	31	89	36	15	74
Not reported	21	4	17	-	2	-	-	3	-	-	2

Source: U.S. Department of Commerce and U.S. Department of Housing and Urban Development, Current Housing Reports, H150/89, *American Housing Survey for the United States in 1989,* July 1991, p. 324. *Notes:* A dash (-) means zero or rounds to zero. 1. Limited to multiunit structures.

★ 506 ★

Neighborhoods

Public Transportation in Elderly Neighborhoods
[Percent]

Characteristics	Total occupied units	Tenure		Housing unit characteristics				Household characteristics			
		Owner	Renter	New construction 4 yrs.	Mobile homes	Physical problems		Black	Hispanic	Moved in past year	Below poverty level
						Severe	Moderate				
Public transportation as a percent of the total											
With public transportation	52.15	46.43	70.50	40.27	29.26	46.22	38.90	64.79	68.93	56.94	48.72
Household uses it at least weekly	10.15	6.17	22.93	5.58	2.15	10.31	13.78	25.47	21.96	10.76	13.20
Satisfactory public transportation	9.47	5.58	21.96	5.58	1.69	10.01	12.49	23.44	20.29	10.04	12.57
Unsatisfactory public transportation	.67	.58	.97	-	.46	.31	1.29	2.04	1.67	.72	.57
Not reported	.01	.01	-	-	-	-	-	-	-	-	.06
Household uses it less than weekly	20.53	18.81	26.06	13.02	9.02	20.64	14.36	24.55	22.87	19.30	20.86
Satisfactory public transportation	18.91	17.10	24.74	12.16	8.33	19.71	13.61	22.80	21.43	17.64	19.57
Unsatisfactory public transportation	1.43	1.54	1.08	.38	.69	.60	.75	1.21	1.08	.88	1.12
Not reported	.19	.17	.25	.47	-	.32	-	.53	.36	.77	.17
Household does not use	21.21	21.25	21.09	21.11	17.93	14.93	10.76	14.65	23.74	26.28	14.60
Not reported	.25	.21	.41	.56	.17	.34	-	.12	.35	.60	.06
No public transportation	46.71	52.34	28.65	58.96	69.15	52.79	58.74	33.71	29.89	42.30	50.69
Not reported	1.14	1.23	.86	.77	1.59	.99	2.36	1.50	1.18	.76	.59

Source: U.S. Department of Commerce and U.S. Department of Housing and Urban Development, Current Housing Reports H151/89, *Supplement to the American Housing Survey for the United States in 1989,* October 1992, p. 80. *Notes:* A dash (-) means zero or rounds to zero. 1. Figures may not add to 100%, because more than one condition may apply to a unit or conditions are not reported.

★ 507 ★

Neighborhoods

Shopping in Elderly Neighborhoods

[Percent]

Characteristics	Total occupied units	Tenure		Housing unit characteristics				Household characteristics			
		Owner	Renter	New construction 4 yrs.	Mobile homes	Physical problems		Black	Hispanic	Moved in past year	Below poverty level
						Severe	Moderate				
Neighborhood shopping as a percent of the total											
Satisfactory neighborhood shopping	80.80	79.55	84.83	84.87	69.82	73.99	67.01	69.17	84.15	83.90	75.33
Less than 1 mile	62.46	59.41	72.26	48.92	37.64	53.95	47.46	56.35	71.98	65.98	57.80
1 mile or more	17.44	19.36	11.28	33.72	31.87	17.90	18.57	11.99	11.37	17.00	16.75
Not reported	.90	.78	1.29	2.23	.31	2.14	.98	.83	.81	.92	.78
Unsatisfactory neighborhood shopping	17.93	19.17	13.95	14.39	28.92	25.05	30.88	28.54	14.33	14.52	24.21
Not reported or don't know	1.27	1.29	1.22	.74	1.26	.96	2.12	2.29	1.52	1.58	.47

Source: U.S. Department of Commerce and U.S. Department of Housing and Urban Development, Current Housing Reports H151/89, *Supplement to the American Housing Survey for the United States in 1989*, October 1992, p. 80. *Note:* A dash (-) means zero or rounds to zero.

★ 508 ★

Neighborhoods

Street Conditions of Elderly Neighborhoods

[Numbers are shown in thousands for 1989]

Characteristic	Total occupied units	Tenure		Housing unit characteristics				Household characteristics			
		Owner	Renter	New construction 4 yrs.	Mobile homes	Physical problems		Black	Hispanic	Moved in past year	Below poverty level
						Severe	Moderate				
Condition of streets[1]											
No repairs needed	2,188	601	1,587	136	2	57	76	200	106	354	472
Minor repairs needed	643	113	530	23	-	27	33	126	61	79	223
Major repairs needed	57	13	43	2	-	-	5	12	3	3	14
No streets within 300 feet	40	16	24	2	-	2	2	2	3	6	5
Not reported	1,653	414	1,239	13	-	92	35	145	60	29	336
Trash, litter, or junk on streets or any properties[1]											
None	2,191	594	1,598	140	2	60	60	142	86	335	476
Minor accumulation	683	144	539	19	-	22	51	178	81	101	224
Major accumulation	58	8	50	4	-	3	5	20	4	6	13
Not reported	1,648	412		13	-	92	35	145	60	29	337

Source: U.S. Department of Commerce and U.S. Department of Housing and Urban Development, Current Housing Reports, H150/89, *American Housing Survey for the United States in 1989*, July 1991, p. 324. *Notes:* A dash (-) means zero or rounds to zero. 1. Limited to multiunit structures.

Geographic Mobility

★ 509 ★

Residential Moves of the Elderly, by Cause

[Numbers are shown in thousands for 1989]

Characteristic	Total occupied units	Tenure		Housing unit characteristics				Household characteristics			
		Owner	Renter	New construction 4 yrs.	Mobile homes	Physical problems		Black	Hispanic	Moved in past year	Below poverty level
						Severe	Moderate				
Respondent moved during past year Total	965	379	586	156	74	23	35	115	52	920	231
Reasons for leaving previous unit											
Private displacement	56	8	48	5	2	-	2	15	10	54	14
Owner to move into unit	6	-	6	-	-	-	-	-	-	6	-
To be converted to condominium or cooperative	-	-	-	-	-	-	-	-	-	-	
Closed for repairs	10	-	10	-	-	-	-	10	-	10	5
Other	26	6	20	5	-	-	-	2	8	24	4
Not reported	14	2	12	-	2	-	2	3	2	14	5
Government displacement	9	2	7	2	-	-	-	3	-	9	5
Government wanted building or land	2	2	-	-	-	-	-	-	-	2	-
Unit unfit for occupancy	3	-	3	-	-	-	-	3	-	3	3
Other	-	-	-	-	-	-	-	-	-	-	-
Not reported	4	-	4	2	-	-	-	-	-	4	2
Disaster loss (fire, floods, etc.)	9	4	5	-	-	-	-	-	-	9	2
New job or job transfer	22	8	14	-	2	2	-	-	2	19	3
To be closer to work/school/other	47	22	25	3	5	4	-	-	2	42	11
Other, financial/employment related	24	9	15	-	9	-	-	-	1	22	14
To establish own household	39	4	35	4	7	-	5	8	3	39	14
Needed larger house or apartment	51	21	30	6	3	-	-	12	3	48	12
Married	2	2	-	-	-	-	-	-	-	-	-
Widowed, divorced or separated	81	39	43	18	3	4	4	-	4	76	13
Other, family/person related	232	100	132	36	28	5	12	21	8	212	65
Wanted better home	77	25	52	14	4	-	5	20	3	77	27
Change from owner to renter	56	-	56	7	2	-	-	5	2	56	21
Change from renter to owner	20	20	-	3	-	-	-	5	-	20	8
Wanted lower rent or maintenance	87	25	63	9	2	2	5	15	5	85	29
Other housing related reasons	134	56	78	37	10	2	4	7	2	134	13
Other	265	104	162	34	12	9	7	34	19	259	45
Not reported	39	9	30	6	-	2	3	7	-	37	5

Source: U.S. Department of Commerce and U.S. Department of Housing and Urban Development, Current Housing Reports, H150/89, *American Housing Survey for the United States in 1989*, July 1991, p. 332. *Notes:* A dash (-) means zero or rounds to zero. Figures may not add to total because more than one category may apply to a unit.

Chapter 10
HEALTH AND HEALTH CARE

This chapter covers most aspects of health and health care except *Health Insurance*, covered in a separate chapter.

The chapter begins with a section headed Summary; thereafter, sections on Emotional Health, Exercise and Fitness, Body Weight and Eating Habits, Activities of Daily Living, Risk Behaviors, Drug Use, Self-Assessment of Health, Health Examinations, Doctor Visits, Acute Conditions and Care, Long-Term Conditions and Care, Hospitals, Specific Illnesses, Accidents, Health Costs, Geriatrics Profession, Health: Worldwide, and Dental Health present tables on these subjects.

The presentation is organized to present information on conditions of relative health to conditions of illness, ending with the section on Specific Illnesses. Thereafter, special topics are covered under appropriate headings, including a section on Health Costs.

Chapters holding related information include *Demographics* (section on Mortality), *Health Insurance* (including information on Medicare and Medicaid), and *Income, Assets, and Spending* (related information on expenditures).

Summary

★ 510 ★

Ten Most Prevalent Health Conditions for Persons Aged 65+, by Age Group and Race, 1989

[Number per 1,000 people]

Condition	Age				Race		
	65+	45 to 64	65 to 74	75+	White	Black	Black as % of white
Arthritis	483.0	253.8	437.3	554.5	483.2	522.6	108.0
Hypertension	380.6	229.1	383.8	375.6	367.4	517.7	141.0
Hearing impairment	286.5	127.7	239.4	360.3	297.4	174.5	59.0
Heart disease	278.9	118.9	231.6	353.0	286.5	220.5	77.0
Cataracts	156.8	16.1	107.4	234.3	160.7	139.8	87.0
Deformity or orthopedic impairment	155.2	155.5	141.4	177.0	156.2	150.8	97.0
Chronic sinusitis	153.4	173.5	151.8	155.8	157.1	125.2	80.0
Diabetes	88.2	58.2	89.7	85.7	80.2	165.9	207.0
Visual impairment	81.9	45.1	69.3	101.7	81.1	77.0	95.0
Varicose veins	78.1	57.8	72.6	86.6	80.3	64.0	80.0

Source: Aging America, Trends and Projections, prepared by the U.S. Senate Special Committee on Aging, the American Association of Retired Persons, the Federal Council on the Aging, and the U.S. Administration on Aging, 1991, Washington, D.C., p. 113. Primary source: National Center for Health Statistics, "Current Estimates from the National Health Interview Survey, 1989," *Vital and Health Statistics*, Series 10, No. 176, October 1990.

★ 511 ★

Summary

Expected Growth in Number of People 65+ Living Alone Who Are Unable to Perform One or More Daily Activity, 1990-2020

```
┌─────────────────────────────────────────────────────┐
│  ┌──────────────────────────────────────────────┐    │
│  │ 2020 - 506                                     │    │
│  └──────────────────────────────────────────────┘    │
│  ┌──────────────────────────────────────┐            │
│  │ 2005 - 390                             │            │
│  └──────────────────────────────────────┘            │
│  ┌─────────────────────────────────┐                 │
│  │ 1990 - 291                        │                 │
│  └─────────────────────────────────┘                 │
└─────────────────────────────────────────────────────┘
```

[Numbers in thousands]

Year	Numbers
1990	291
2005	390
2020	506

Source: Aging America, Trends and Projections, prepared by the U.S. Senate Special Committee on Aging, the American Association of Retired Persons, the Federal Council on the Aging, and the U.S. Administration on Aging, 1991, Washington, D.C., p. 230. Primary source: Lewin/ICF estimates based on data from the *Current Population Survey* and Brookings/ICF Long-Term Care Financing Model, 1990.

★ 512 ★

Summary

Percent Distribution of Living Persons 65 Years or Older with Hospital Episodes During 1988

Race	None	One	Two	Three or more
White	83.3	12.3	3.1	1.3
Black	82.1	13.3	3.3	1.3

Source: U.S. Congress, "Profiles in Aging America: Meeting the Health Care Needs of the Nation's Black Elderly," Joint Hearing Before the Special Committee on Aging and the Congressional Black Caucus Health Braintrust, United States Senate, September 28, 1990, 101-29, U.S. Government Printing Office, Washington, D.C., p. 130. Primary source: "Current Estimates from the National Health Interview Survey, 1988," U.S. Dept. of Health and Human Services, Public Health Service, Centers for Disease Control, National Center for Health Statistics, Series 10, No. 173, Oct. 1989, p. 120.

★ 513 ★

Summary

Ethnic Elders' Health Risk Compared to Total Older U.S. Population, 1990

From the source: "[These data illustrate] comparisons of risks of diseases and conditions for ethnic elders. Only conditions which have been found in at least one study to be significantly different for elders in the ethnic categories of interest, compared to the total or white population of U.S. elders, are included."

[- stands for lower than average; + stands for higher than average.]

Type of risk	Am. Indian/ Alaskan Native	Asian/Pacific Islander	Black	Hispanic
Cancer				
Combined	+		Male +	Mexican -
Lung				Mexican male -
				Mexican female +
				Mexican female -
Breast				Puerto Rican +
Liver		Chinese +		Mexican +
Esophageal	+	Chinese +		
		Japanese male +		
Gallbladder	+			
Pancreatic		Chinese female +		Mexican female +
Stomach		Japanese +		Mexican +
Cervical			Female +	Mexican female +
Prostate			Male +	
Cardiac and cardiovascular disease				
Heart disease		Japanese male -	Female +	Puerto Rican female +
Myocardial infarction		XX[1]	Male +	
Hypertension		Japanese female -	+	
		Filipino +		
		Pacific Islander +		
Congestive heart failure			+	
Stroke			+	
Cataracts	+			
Dementia				
Alzheimer's			-	
Multi-infarct		Chinese +	+	
		Japanese +		
		Guamanian +		
Parkinsons				
Diabetes	+	Japanese +	+	Mexican +
		Filipino +		Puerto Rican +
		Pacific Islander +		
		Southeast Asian +		Female +
Depression				
Glaucoma			Male +	
Gout		Filipino +		
Hearing problems	+			
Kidney disease	+			
Liver disease	+			
Obesity		Pacific Islander +	Female +	Mexican +
Osteoporosis		Japanese +		
(Hip fracture)			Female -	Female -
Suicide		Chinese female +	-	

[Continued]

★ 513 ★

Ethnic Elders' Health Risk Compared to Total Older U.S. Population, 1990
[Continued]

Type of risk	Am. Indian/ Alaskan Native	Asian/Pacific Islander	Black	Hispanic
		Japanese +		
Tuberculosis	+			
Undernutrition	+[2]			
Unintentional injury	+			
Vision problems	+			

Source: Yeo, Gwen, Ph.D., "Ethnogeriatric Education: Need and Recommendations," *Shortage of Health Care Professions Caring for the Elderly: Recommendations for Change*, Senate Select Committee on Aging, Comm. Pub. No. 102-915, p. 79. Primary source: SGEC Ethnogeriatric Reviews by J. Cuellar, N. Morioka-Douglas and G. Yeo, and J. Richardson, 1990. *Notes:* 1. Definition not given in original source. 2. Navaho male.

★ 514 ★
Summary

Health Indicators for Hispanic, Black, and White Elders Aged 65 and Over

Data from the National Health Interview Survey, 1978-80, show utilization of services per year. From the source: "Predictors of utilization of health care services in general are related to: income; education; geographic accessibility; and Medicare, Medicaid, and Medigap eligibility and participation. All of these are factors for which ethnic elders tend to be at a greater disadvantage."

	No. of physician visits	Percent hospitali- zation	Percent with dental visits	Percent with limitation of activity
All races	6.4			45.3
White non-Hispanic	6.3	18.3	34.4	44.3
Male	5.7			
Female	6.6			
Black non-Hispanic	6.7	17.3	17.5	57.2
Male	6.3			
Female	7.0			
All Hispanic	8.2			47.5
Mexican American	9.1	18.5	23.3	52.4
Male	9.8			
Female	8.5			
Puerto Rican[1]	6.6	10.5	19.3	52.6
Cuban	10.8	20.3	27.9	42.1
Other Hispanic	6.2	20.8	34.7	44.4

Source: Yeo, Gwen, Ph.D., "Ethnogeriatric Education: Need and Recommendations," *Shortage of Health Care Professions Caring for the Elderly: Recommendations for Change*, Senate Select Committee on Aging, Comm. Pub. No. 102-915, p. 84. Primary source: F.M. Trevino and A.J. Moss. 1984 *Note:* 1. Based on a small sample.

Emotional Health

★ 515 ★

Seeking Help for Personal or Emotional Problems

Percent of persons 18 years of age and over who had sought help for a personal or emotional problem in the past year, by sex, age, and selected characteristics: United States, 1990.

Characteristic	Both sexes 18 years and over	Male					Female				
		Total	18-29 years	30-44 years	45-64 years	65 years and over	Total	18-29 years	30-44 years	45-64 years	65 years and over
All persons[1]	12.5	8.6	9.6	10.7	7.8	3.1	16.0	18.5	21.5	13.3	6.8
Educational level											
Less than 12 years	8.5	5.5	8.8	6.7	5.0	2.3	11.3	14.7	18.1	11.1	6.3
12 years	11.3	7.5	8.2	9.4	6.6	2.7	14.2	17.0	18.7	11.2	6.6
More than 12 years	15.6	10.9	11.4	12.5	10.3	4.5	20.6	21.5	24.6	17.8	8.3
13-15 years	14.9	10.4	10.1	12.0	10.1	4.6	19.0	20.8	22.8	15.9	6.8
16 years or more	16.4	11.4	13.5	12.8	10.4	4.5	22.5	22.9	26.4	19.8	10.3
Income											
Less than $10,000	14.6	11.8	12.6	16.6	15.9	2.8[2]	16.1	18.3	25.7	21.3	6.1
$10,000-$19,999	12.5	8.3	10.8	11.7	6.7	2.8	16.0	18.8	23.8	14.6	7.5
$20,000-$34,999	12.0	8.0	9.1	10.2	6.5	2.6	16.0	18.7	21.6	11.7	4.8
$35,000-$49,999	13.2	9.3	8.3	10.9	8.5	5.2[2]	17.5	17.7	21.4	13.3	7.9
$50,000 or more	14.0	9.1	9.6	10.4	8.5	3.7[2]	19.3	22.6	22.2	15.0	10.6
Race											
White	12.8	8.7	10.1	10.9	8.1	3.0	16.6	20.0	22.4	13.5	6.9
Black	10.2	7.0	6.6	9.0	6.2	3.9[2]	12.7	11.5	17.2	11.8	6.0
Hispanic origin											
Hispanic	10.3	6.2	7.4	6.0	6.3	-[2]	13.9	12.8	16.8	12.6	9.1[2]
Non-Hispanic	12.6	8.7	9.8	11.1	7.9	3.2	16.2	19.3	21.9	13.4	6.7
Geographic region											
Northeast	11.5	8.4	8.5	11.8	6.9	2.8	14.2	18.5	20.3	10.7	5.1
Midwest	13.3	9.0	10.6	10.4	8.4	3.8	17.3	19.9	23.2	14.5	7.1
South	11.2	7.2	8.1	9.1	6.2	3.1	14.7	15.7	19.8	12.6	7.6
West	14.6	10.4	11.5	12.5	10.5	2.5[2]	18.5	21.7	23.2	16.0	7.0
Marital status											
Currently married	10.7	7.0	8.4	8.7	6.6	2.5	14.5	16.5	18.1	11.4	7.1
Formerly married	17.3	14.8	20.6	20.1	14.3	5.8	18.4	29.1	37.0	19.3	6.9
Never married	14.2	10.7	9.8	14.3	11.8	3.2[2]	18.5	19.1	22.6	11.4	3.3[2]
Employment status											
Currently employed	13.1	8.8	9.4	9.9	7.2	2.8[2]	18.2	19.2	21.7	13.3	6.4

[Continued]

★ 515 ★

Seeking Help for Personal or Emotional Problems

[Continued]

Characteristic	Both sexes 18 years and over	Male					Female				
		Total	18-29 years	30-44 years	45-64 years	65 years and over	Total	18-29 years	30-44 years	45-64 years	65 years and over
Unemployed	15.9	11.7	12.6	12.2	10.3^2	2.6^2	20.4	20.0	26.6	11.9^2	2.6^2
Not in labor force	10.8	7.3	9.5	22.0	10.2	3.1	12.6	16.6	20.1	13.4	6.9

Source: *Health Promotion and Disease Prevention: United States, 1990*, National Center for Health Statistics, Vital and Health Statistics, Series 10, No. 185, p. 39.
Notes: Data are based on household interviews of the civilian noninstitutionalized population. The survey design, general qualifications, and information on the reliability of the estimates are given in appendix 1 in the original source. Denominator for each cell excludes unknowns. 1. Includes persons with unknown sociodemographic characteristics. 2. Figure does not meet standard of reliability or precision (more than 30-percent relative standard error in numerator of percent or rate).

Exercise and Fitness

★ 516 ★

Exercise or Sports Play

Percent of persons 18 years of age and over who exercised or played sports regularly, by sex, age, and selected characteristics: United States, 1990.

Characteristic	Both sexes 18 years and over	Male					Female				
		Total	18-29 years	30-44 years	45-64 years	65 years and over	Total	18-29 years	30-44 years	45-64 years	65 years and over
All persons[1]	40.7	44.0	56.1	44.3	35.6	36.9	37.7	44.2	40.1	34.6	29.1
Educational level											
Less than 12 years	25.9	29.3	45.0	23.2	20.6	29.5	22.8	28.1	21.6	22.0	21.1
12 years	37.0	40.3	51.5	37.3	32.0	37.1	34.4	38.5	34.1	33.4	30.5
More than 12 years	52.1	54.3	66.1	53.9	46.6	47.5	49.8	56.7	49.7	45.1	42.3
13-15 years	48.5	50.3	65.2	46.5	37.5	42.2	47.0	53.9	44.8	42.5	42.2
16 years or more	55.8	57.9	67.6	59.5	52.4	51.4	53.2	61.7	54.4	47.8	42.3
Income											
Less than $10,000	32.9	40.4	61.8	28.8	22.0	26.1	28.9	38.3	27.2	21.4	24.8
$10,000-$19,999	32.3	35.3	47.9	33.3	24.3	30.6	29.9	36.5	30.0	24.8	27.5
$20,000-$34,999	40.5	42.6	56.0	40.3	30.9	41.4	38.5	43.7	39.0	34.9	33.4
$35,000-$49,999	46.1	47.2	57.6	49.6	33.3	47.4	44.8	53.2	44.4	38.8	41.3
$50,000 or more	51.7	54.1	62.7	54.8	49.5	49.6	49.1	57.1	50.7	44.5	37.5
Race											
White	41.5	44.1	55.0	45.0	36.3	37.8	39.1	46.4	42.1	35.7	29.9
Black	34.3	42.2	61.7	39.6	28.3	25.1	27.9	32.2	29.4	25.5	19.1

[Continued]

★516★

Exercise or Sports Play
[Continued]

Characteristic	Both sexes 18 years and over	Male					Female				
		Total	18-29 years	30-44 years	45-64 years	65 years and over	Total	18-29 years	30-44 years	45-64 years	65 years and over
Hispanic origin											
Hispanic	34.9	38.4	46.7	38.5	24.4	32.1	31.9	35.1	33.4	27.8	21.2
Non-Hispanic	41.2	44.5	57.3	44.7	36.3	37.1	38.3	45.6	40.7	35.2	29.4
Geographic region											
Northeast	37.4	41.8	53.6	43.5	34.1	31.8	33.5	42.8	36.5	31.1	21.9
Midwest	41.5	43.8	55.5	45.4	36.0	33.3	39.3	46.7	40.2	37.3	30.9
South	39.0	42.8	56.7	42.3	32.1	37.6	35.7	42.6	38.4	31.3	27.7
West	45.9	48.3	58.0	46.8	41.8	45.7	43.5	45.4	46.1	41.1	38.5
Marital status											
Currently married	39.4	40.7	49.0	42.7	35.7	38.0	38.0	40.8	40.0	36.2	31.6
Formerly married	34.3	40.4	48.2	48.1	35.9	32.8	31.8	35.6	39.5	31.7	27.5
Never married	51.3	56.3	61.3	49.7	32.3	33.5	45.0	49.2	42.4	25.0	25.0
Employment status											
Currently employed	43.2	45.6	55.7	45.2	37.0	36.0	40.3	46.0	40.5	34.7	32.4
Unemployed	42.7	43.4	53.5	40.8	28.9	34.6[2]	42.0	46.8	40.6	34.7	34.6[2]
Not in labor force	35.4	38.6	59.7	30.6	30.4	37.1	33.8	39.4	39.0	34.5	28.7

Source: Health Promotion and Disease Prevention: United States, 1990, National Center for Health Statistics, Vital and Health Statistics, Series 10, No. 185, p. 40. *Notes:* Data are based on household interviews of the civilian noninstitutionalized population. The survey design, general qualifications, and information on the reliability of the estimates are given in appendix 1 in the original source. Denominator for each cell excludes unknowns. 1. Includes persons with unknown sociodemographic characteristic. 2. Figure does not meet standard of reliability or precision (more than 30-percent relative standard error in numerator of percent or rate).

★517★
Exercise and Fitness

Walking for Exercise

Percent of persons 18 years of age and over who had walked for exercise in the past 2 weeks, by sex, age, and selected characteristics: United States, 1990.

Characteristic	Both sexes 18 years and over	Male					Female				
		Total	18-29 years	30-44 years	45-64 years	65 years and over	Total	18-29 years	30-44 years	45-64 years	65 years and over
All persons[1]	45.1	40.9	34.2	38.9	44.5	51.6	48.9	50.7	49.7	49.4	44.3
Education level											
Less than 12 years	38.2	37.3	35.2	29.3	36.3	46.2	39.0	40.8	38.6	40.6	37.0
12 years	43.4	37.8	32.0	34.7	41.8	53.1	47.8	48.8	46.6	48.4	47.5
More than 12 years	50.2	45.0	36.1	43.9	50.7	57.9	55.5	56.5	54.9	57.0	52.1
13-15 years	47.8	41.2	34.0	40.8	46.8	57.1	53.8	54.4	52.1	56.8	51.7
16 years or more	52.6	48.4	39.7	46.2	53.2	58.5	57.6	60.4	57.5	57.3	52.6

[Continued]

★517★

Walking for Exercise
[Continued]

Characteristic	Both sexes 18 years and over	Male					Female				
		Total	18-29 years	30-44 years	45-64 years	65 years and over	Total	18-29 years	30-44 years	45-64 years	65 years and over
Income											
Less than $10,000	45.9	44.3	39.4	49.1	51.0	44.5	46.8	50.6	48.4	44.4	42.9
$10,000-$19,999	42.7	40.3	33.5	36.8	42.1	51.4	44.6	45.3	46.3	42.4	44.2
$20,000-$34,999	44.8	41.4	35.7	38.8	44.2	54.6	48.2	50.5	47.3	49.3	43.8
$35,000-$49,999	46.6	40.6	34.3	40.1	41.7	61.7	53.1	54.6	53.4	50.3	56.6
$50,000 or more	48.6	43.1	34.1	39.7	49.0	57.6	54.6	54.6	54.0	56.5	48.2
Race											
White	45.3	40.8	32.9	38.5	44.8	52.4	49.5	51.3	50.0	50.3	44.9
Black	45.0	42.8	42.5	42.4	43.9	42.6	46.8	48.7	49.5	45.1	38.4
Hispanic origin											
Hispanic	36.9	32.5	29.1	32.2	31.6	60.6	40.5	39.9	42.4	38.5	40.6
Non-Hispanic	45.8	41.5	34.8	39.5	45.2	51.4	49.7	52.2	50.3	50.1	44.4
Geographic region											
Northeast	47.7	44.8	39.2	41.9	48.6	54.9	50.3	51.8	52.5	51.3	43.6
Midwest	46.6	41.5	36.2	40.1	43.6	50.9	51.3	54.1	51.0	51.7	47.2
South	43.5	38.9	32.2	37.1	42.1	50.2	47.5	51.7	48.4	46.1	41.6
West	43.4	39.5	30.9	37.4	45.2	51.7	47.1	44.2	47.7	50.1	46.3
Marital status											
Currently married	45.0	41.3	33.6	37.4	44.2	52.1	48.7	48.7	48.7	50.5	44.0
Formerly married	45.5	43.7	30.4	42.6	43.8	49.6	46.2	45.3	50.4	46.4	44.0
Never married	45.0	38.0	34.7	44.3	50.4	50.9	53.5	53.5	56.2	48.6	50.1
Employment status											
Currently employed	43.3	38.0	33.3	37.7	42.6	45.0	49.6	51.2	49.8	48.2	45.4
Unemployed	48.3	44.7	41.1	48.5	45.4	51.3[2]	52.2	52.8	54.2	45.8	59.0[2]
Not in labor force	48.6	50.7	37.5	53.8	53.4	53.2	47.6	49.0	48.6	51.4	44.0

Source: Health Promotion and Disease Prevention: United States, 1990, National Center for Health Statistics, Vital and Health Statistics, Series 10, No. 185, p. 41. *Notes:* Data are based on household interviews of the civilian noninstitutionalized population. The survey design, general qualifications, and information on the reliability of the estimates are given in appendix 1 in the original source. Denominator for each cell excludes unknowns. 1. Includes persons with unknown sociodemographic characteristics. 2. Figure does not meet standard of reliability or precision (more than 30-percent relative standard error in numerator of percent or rate).

★518★
Exercise and Fitness

Physical Activity at Work

Percent of persons 18 years of age and over whose job or main daily activity required at least a moderate amount of physical work, by sex, age, and selected characteristics: United States, 1990.

Characteristic	Both sexes 18 years and over	Male					Female				
		Total	18-29 years	30-44 years	45-64 years	65 years and over	Total	18-29 years	30-44 years	45-64 years	65 years and over
All persons[1]	39.3	43.6	54.2	47.6	39.1	23.3	35.3	36.5	37.4	37.0	27.5
Education level											
Less than 12 years	44.2	49.1	63.6	65.2	52.3	22.9	39.9	46.1	52.1	46.2	25.7
12 years	46.7	56.5	64.8	65.1	49.8	26.1	38.9	39.9	42.7	38.8	30.3
More than 12 years	29.7	30.4	39.1	31.6	23.8	21..3	28.9	29.2	29.5	28.3	26.6
13-15 years	37.8	44.2	50.0	48.8	36.1	22.0	32.0	30.6	34.7	30.6	29.6
16 years or more	21.4	18.3	20.3	18.5	16.0	20.7	25.2	26.8	24.6	26.0	22.4
Income											
Less than $10,000	35.3	37.1	42.1	50.2	30.9	21.1	34.4	35.8	46.6	39.5	23.8
$10,000-$19,999	46.7	50.2	60.2	64.9	45.8	26.4	43.8	46.6	50.0	45.1	34.5
$20,000-$34,999	45.9	53.2	59.3	59.6	53.1	25.1	38.9	36.3	40.7	43.4	31.8
$35,000-$49,999	41.2	46.1	55.8	45.0	43.9	30.5	35.7	33.0	36.0	39.3	29.2
$50,000 or more	29.5	30.5	49.2	28.4	24.9	18.1	28.4	31.0	28.6	28.1	20.5
Race											
White	38.7	43.2	55.3	46.8	38.2	23.6	34.6	36.1	36.2	36.1	27.8
Black	44.1	48.2	52.7	54.8	44.9	22.8	40.8	40.5	43.8	46.4	24.1
Hispanic origin											
Hispanic	45.0	54.3	53.0	60.6	54.6	23.6	37.1	35.5	40.5	38.7	25.2
Non-Hispanic	38.8	42.7	54.4	46.4	38.2	23.3	35.2	36.7	37.2	37.0	27.6
Geographic region											
Northeast	37.9	41.5	51.0	45.3	35.7	27.0	34.6	36.3	37.8	35.7	26.4
Midwest	41.6	45.3	56.8	48.5	41.2	24.9	38.2	40.2	40.4	39.0	30.8
South	39.4	44.1	56.2	49.0	39.2	20.4	35.2	36.0	37.8	38.3	25.1
West	37.6	42.7	50.9	46.3	39.7	22.8	32.7	33.5	33.1	33.7	29.1
Marital status											
Currently married	40.3	42.8	57.1	47.8	39.6	24.7	37.6	39.7	37.6	37.4	35.1
Formerly married	33.2	39.0	65.5	48.6	37.8	18.1	30.8	35.2	39.7	37.0	21.8
Never married	41.3	48.4	51.6	45.6	34.7	19.5	32.6	33.1	32.5	31.8	27.2
Employment status											
Currently employed	43.7	50.2	59.2	49.3	43.8	37.6	35.9	36.7	34.9	36.6	34.3

[Continued]

★ 518 ★

Physical Activity at Work
[Continued]

Characteristic	Both sexes 18 years and over	Male					Female				
		Total	18-29 years	30-44 years	45-64 years	65 years and over	Total	18-29 years	30-44 years	45-64 years	65 years and over
Unemployed	41.3	42.6	48.1	42.5	32.1	43.9[2]	39.9	34.5	45.1	43.4	29.0[2]
Not in labor force	29.8	20.6	23.8	20.3	19.3	20.3	34.2	36.3	44.4	37.4	26.8

Source: Health Promotion and Disease Prevention: United States, 1990, National Center for Health Statistics, Vital and Health Statistics, Series 10, No. 185, p. 43. *Notes:* Data are based on household interviews of the civilian noninstitutionalized population. The survey design, general qualifications, and information on the reliability of the estimates are given in appendix 1 in the original source. Denominator for each cell excludes unknowns. 1. Includes persons with unknown sociodemographic characteristics. 2. Figure does not meet standard of reliability or precision (more than 30-percent relative standard error in numerator of percent or rate).

★ 519 ★

Exercise and Fitness

Knowledge of the Need for Exercise

Percent of persons 18 years of age and over who specified that exercise needs to be performed 3 times per week and maintained 20 minutes per session in order to strengthen the heart and lungs, by sex, age, and selected characteristics: United States, 1990.

Characteristic	Both sexes 18 years and over	Male					Female				
		Total	18-29 years	30-44 years	45-64 years	65 years and over	Total	18-29 years	30-44 years	45-64 years	65 years and over
All persons[1]	5.2	4.9	4.0	6.0	5.3	3.0	5.5	5.2	7.5	5.4	2.8
Education level											
Less than 12 years	2.8	2.4	2.5	3.1	2.0	2.0	3.3	4.6	4.2	3.2	2.1
12 years	4.4	3.3	2.7	4.0	3.8	2.2	5.3	4.8	6.5	5.3	3.6
More than 12 years	7.2	7.3	6.0	8.0	8.4	5.2	7.2	5.8	9.2	7.2	3.0
13-15 years	5.9	6.1	5.0	6.4	7.9	4.9	5.7	4.8	7.2	6.3	2.3[2]
16 years or more	8.6	8.4	7.8	9.2	8.7	5.4	8.9	7.7	11.0	8.1	3.8[2]
Income											
Less than $10,000	3.2	2.5	3.0	3.0[2]	2.1[2]	1.4[2]	3.7	4.2	4.8	4.3	2.2
$10,000-$19,999	3.7	3.2	3.1	3.8	3.1	2.7	4.1	4.2	4.9	4.2	3.3
$20,000-$34,999	5.5	4.5	5.1	5.2	3.3	3.6	6.5	6.7	8.3	5.5	3.7
$35,000-$49,999	6.9	6.4	4.6	7.7	6.2	4.4[2]	7.5	7.0	8.1	7.5	5.2[2]
$50,000 or more	6.9	6.8	3.4	8.0	7.8	4.6[2]	7.1	4.5	9.4	6.2	2.8[2]
Race											
White	5.5	5.2	4.3	6.4	5.6	3.3	5.7	5.4	7.8	5.6	2.9
Black	3.9	3.1	2.9	3.5	4.1	0.5[2]	4.6	4.5	6.2	4.0	2.0[2]
Hispanic origin											
Hispanic	3.4	2.9	2.2[2]	3.5	3.0[2]	3.5	3.9	3.4	4.6	4.7	1.1[2]
Non-Hispanic	5.4	5.0	4.2	6.2	5.5	3.0	5.7	5.4	7.7	5.5	2.9

[Continued]

★ 519 ★

Knowledge of the Need for Exercise
[Continued]

Characteristic	Both sexes 18 years and over	Male					Female				
		Total	18-29 years	30-44 years	45-64 years	65 years and over	Total	18-29 years	30-44 years	45-64 years	65 years and over
Geographic region											
Northeast	5.2	4.7	4.5	5.3	5.8	2.0^2	5.5	4.6	7.7	5.0	4.0
Midwest	6.0	5.8	4.8	7.9	5.5	3.5	6.2	6.5	8.0	5.4	3.6
South	4.5	3.8	2.6	4.8	4.7	2.3	5.1	5.2	6.9	5.4	1.4
West	5.5	5.5	4.9	6.2	5.6	4.7	5.6	4.1	7.8	5.8	2.9
Marital status											
Currently married	5.8	5.2	5.5	5.9	5.6	3.0	6.3	5.7	8.2	5.5	3.2
Formerly married	4.0	3.9	3.5^2	5.0	3.9	2.3^2	4.1	5.2	5.6	5.1	2.5
Never married	4.5	4.1	3.0	7.2	5.1^2	5.2^2	4.9	4.7	5.8	5.8^2	4.0^2
Employment status											
Currently employed	5.9	5.4	4.3	6.1	5.8	4.0	6.4	5.4	7.8	6.1	2.2^2
Unemployed	4.3	3.6	2.1^2	4.6^2	5.2^2	$-^2$	5.0	3.4^2	7.7	3.5^2	6.4^2
Not in labor force	3.9	3.1	3.1	4.4	3.3	2.8	4.3	5.1	6.7	4.5	2.9

Source: *Health Promotion and Disease Prevention: United States, 1990,* National Center for Health Statistics, Vital and Health Statistics, Series 10, No. 185, p. 45. *Notes:* Data are based on household interviews of the civilian noninstitutionalized population. The survey design, general qualifications, and information on the reliability of the estimates are given in appendix 1 in the original source. Denominator for each cell excludes unknowns. 1. Includes persons with unknown sociodemographic characteristics. 2. Figure does not meet standard of reliability or precision (more than 30-percent relative standard error in numerator of percent or rate).

Body Weight and Eating Habits

★ 520 ★

Eating Breakfast

Percent of persons 18 years of age and over who ate breakfast almost everyday, by sex, age, and selected characteristics: United States 1990.

Characteristic	Both sexes 18 years and over	Male					Female				
		Total	18-29 years	30-44 years	45-64 years	65 years and over	Total	18-29 years	30-44 years	45-64 years	65 years and over
All persons[1]	56.4	54.6	45.1	45.1	59.1	86.2	58.0	42.7	49.8	63.5	84.8
Education level											
Less than 12 years	58.6	57.6	48.7	40.3	54.3	84.6	59.5	36.6	37.9	59.1	82.7
12 years	52.6	50.6	43.4	40.1	56.4	85.3	54.2	40.3	42.7	62.1	84.7
More than 12 years	58.8	56.6	47.5	49.7	63.8	89.9	61.0	47.5	58.7	68.3	89.0
13-15 years	53.5	50.6	45.4	43.0	569	88.3	56.1	44.2	51.6	65.7	86.7
16 years or more	64.2	61.9	51.1	54.9	68.2	91.1	67.0	53.6	65.6	70.9	92.1

[Continued]

★ 520 ★

Eating Breakfast
[Continued]

Characteristic	Both sexes 18 years and over	Male					Female				
		Total	18-29 years	30-44 years	45-64 years	65 years and over	Total	18-29 years	30-44 years	45-64 years	65 years and over
Income											
Less than $10,000	54.1	51.5	40.9	40.1	52.6	81.4	55.5	37.2	34.0	58.7	82.8
$10,000-$19,999	56.6	56.1	41.3	43.8	56.3	86.0	56.9	39.0	42.4	59.8	84.8
$20,000-$34,999	55.2	54.2	46.7	42.8	59.6	88.5	56.2	43.2	48.9	62.7	87.3
$35,000-$49,999	53.7	51.3	44.8	47.2	54.2	86.3	56.4	49.2	50.8	64.3	87.6
$50,000 or more	57.2	54.1	44.9	45.5	61.9	89.5	60.5	46.6	58.8	66.2	86.5
Race											
White	57.8	55.6	45.5	45.7	59.4	87.4	59.8	43.9	51.6	64.8	85.8
Black	46.9	47.0	41.6	38.3	53.0	75.8	46.7	37.0	38.7	55.0	73.8
Hispanic origin											
Hispanic	52.5	52.7	50.9	47.2	57.5	80.5	52.2	44.1	47.5	63.6	80.4
Non-Hispanic	56.7	54.8	44.4	44.9	59.2	86.4	58.4	42.5	50.0	63.5	84.9
Geographic region											
Northeast	59.9	57.8	48.7	47.6	63.5	86.6	61.8	45.6	54.8	65.8	84.9
Midwest	55.9	53.8	41.7	44.1	59.2	87.6	57.9	40.9	48.9	63.7	87.8
South	54.5	53.2	42.4	45.1	56.6	84.6	55.7	41.5	46.2	61.4	83.2
West	56.6	55.1	50.3	43.9	58.7	87.1	58.0	44.1	52.0	64.5	83.4
Marital status											
Currently married	57.8	56.9	45.7	45.1	60.2	87.6	58.6	45.6	51.8	65.0	85.6
Formerly married	61.5	54.0	37.2	43.1	51.2	78.7	64.6	37.0	41.2	59.0	83.7
Never married	46.9	47.7	45.0	46.7	61.3	90.7	45.9	40.1	48.2	64.0	90.9
Employment status											
Currently employed	50.5	49.9	45.2	44.9	58.1	84.4	51.3	41.9	49.2	61.4	78.8
Unemployed	46.3	46.5	43.8	49.4	44.3	71.1[2]	46.1	42.6	46.4	46.0	94.9
Not in labor force	69.4	72.1	45.0	45.9	65.3	86.7	68.1	44.7	52.2	67.4	85.5

Source: *Health Promotion and Disease Prevention: United States, 1990*, National Center for Health Statistics, Vital and Health Statistics, Series 10, No. 185, p. 25. Notes: Data are based on household interviews of the civilian noninstitutionalized population. The survey design, general qualifications, and information on the reliability of the estimates are given in appendix 1 in the original source. Denominator for each cell excludes unknowns. 1. Includes persons with unknown sociodemographic characteristics. 2. Figure does not meet standard of reliability or precision (more than 30-percent relative standard error in numerator of percent or rate).

★ 521 ★
Body Weight and Eating Habits

Obesity

Persons 18 years of age and over who were 20 percent or more above desirable body weight, 1990.

Characteristic	Both sexes 18 years and over	Male					Female				
		Total	18-29 years	30-44 years	45-64 years	65 years and over	Total	18-29 years	30-44 years	45-64 years	65 years and over
All persons[1]	27.5	29.6	20.1	32.0	37.8	26.3	25.6	15.9	24.7	34.2	28.2
Education level											
Less than 12 years	32.7	30.0	18.8	30.9	42.9	25.4	35.2	21.7	36.4	47.4	33.0
12 years	28.6	31.2	21.3	35.9	37.6	29.5	26.5	17.9	26.4	33.7	27.5
More than 12 years	23.8	28.2	19.3	29.7	35.3	24.1	19.3	11.6	20.6	25.7	20.4
13-15 years	25.5	30.1	19.2	35.2	39.1	25.1	21.5	13.4	25.5	27.5	21.0
16 years or more	22.0	26.5	19.6	25.5	32.9	23.3	16.6	8.4	16.0	23.9	19.7
Income											
Less than $10,000	29.3	24.0	15.7	31.6	36.5	22.3	32.2	20.7	40.2	49.5	30.1
$10,000-$19,999	28.5	27.5	18.8	32.6	37.3	25.6	29.2	19.1	30.5	40.2	29.1
$20,000-$34,999	28.2	30.2	20.1	32.5	40.1	27.5	26.4	16.0	27.3	36.0	27.7
$35,000-$49,999	27.8	31.3	22.9	32.8	39.1	22.8	23.9	13.0	25.1	31.9	22.4
$50,000 or more	24.9	31.0	21.7	31.3	36.6	25.1	18.4	9.1	15.5	26.7	24.7
Race											
White	26.7	29.7	19.8	32.2	37.8	26.3	24.0	14.7	22.7	32.1	26.6
Black	38.0	35.1	26.5	36.6	46.8	29.5	40.4	25.0	41.9	54.2	47.8
Hispanic origin											
Hispanic	27.6	26.7	13.8	33.4	40.0	25.5	28.4	20.3	30.1	39.0	32.3
Non-Hispanic	27.5	29.9	20.9	31.9	37.7	26.3	25.3	15.3	24.1	33.8	28.1
Geographic region											
Northeast	27.2	30.0	21.7	31.5	37.9	26.3	24.8	14.3	22.3	33.7	28.3
Midwest	29.1	31.4	19.4	33.9	40.3	30.8	27.0	15.8	25.4	36.8	31.0
South	28.2	30.3	22.7	33.9	36.1	25.4	26.4	16.7	27.2	34.2	27.7
West	24.7	26.1	15.2	27.2	37.7	21.5	23.3	16.3	22.2	31.3	25.1
Marital status											
Currently married	29.2	33.3	26.7	33.8	39.3	26.4	25.2	15.5	23.5	32.9	28.0
Formerly married	29.1	26.3	17.1	24.8	30.9	25.3	30.2	21.6	26.3	37.3	29.1
Never married	19.8	19.3	15.6	27.3	30.0	26.9	20.4	15.6	32.0	37.9	18.6
Employment status											
Currently employed	27.3	30.5	21.2	32.1	38.2	26.7	23.4	14.3	23.9	32.0	28.8
Unemployed	26.4	29.5	20.9	34.3	37.5	43.4[2]	23.0	14.5	27.2	35.8	10.8[2]
Not in labor force	28.1	26.4	12.6	29.0	36.3	26.0	28.9	20.2	26.8	37.2	28.2

Source: Health Promotion and Disease Prevention: United States, 1990, National Center for Health Statistics, Vital and Health Statistics, Series 10, No. 185, p. 27. *Notes:* Data are based on household interviews of the civilian noninstitutionalized population. The survey design, general qualifications, and information on the reliability of the estimates are given in appendix 1 in the original source. Denominator for each cell excludes unknowns. 1. Includes persons with unknown sociodemographic characteristics. 2. Figure does not meet standard of reliability or precision (more than 30-percent relative standard error in numerator of percent or rate).

★ 522 ★
Body Weight and Eating Habits
Obese Persons Trying to Lose Weight

Overweight persons 18 years of age and over who were trying to lose weight, 1990.

Characteristic	Both sexes 18 years and over	Male					Female				
		Total	18-29 years	30-44 years	45-64 years	65 years and over	Total	18-29 years	30-44 years	45-64 years	65 years and over
All persons[1]	53.1	44.7	45.6	45.8	44.7	40.1	61.9	65.0	66.9	63.6	48.8
Education level											
Less than 12 years	46.4	35.7	37.9	33.7	36.4	34.8	54.6	62.9	58.6	57.4	46.4
12 years	53.5	43.0	44.7	41.7	43.9	41.9	63.2	62.6	67.1	66.8	49.0
More than 12 years	57.6	50.9	50.3	52.0	51.0	45.6	67.5	70.7	70.1	66.1	56.2
13-15 years	56.3	46.1	48.0	45.8	45.2	46.4	69.0	71.0	70.0	70.1	58.8
16 years or more	59.0	55.8	54.2	58.7	55.5	45.2	65.2	70.0	70.3	61.5	52.3
Income											
Less than $10,000	52.2	44.7	43.3	45.4	53.4	34.1	55.2	57.9	65.6	58.7	43.0
$10,000-$19,999	51.1	41.2	43.9	41.5	36.0	44.3	58.8	67.4	61.0	59.6	50.1
$20,000-$34,999	52.9	42.5	41.9	45.5	42.3	34.5	64.4	67.9	67.1	63.7	55.8
$35,000-$49,999	55.3	49.4	49.0	47.7	51.8	50.8	63.7	62.3	69.6	60.6	40.2
$50,000 or more	58.8	51.2	54.7	49.9	52.4	42.9	72.4	73.8	72.2	74.2	59.7
Race											
White	53.4	44.9	45.9	45.8	45.1	41.0	62.8	67.3	67.4	64.6	50.3
Black	51.6	42.1	41.5	45.9	41.1	33.7	58.2	57.8	63.8	60.4	40.6
Hispanic origin											
Hispanic	53.0	40.5	48.4	40.9	36.3	32.7[2]	63.1	62.0	65.6	65.1	50.0
Non-Hispanic	53.1	45.0	45.4	46.4	45.3	40.4	61.8	65.5	66.9	63.6	48.8
Geographic region											
Northeast	56.0	48.2	50.3	49.7	46.9	44.9	64.2	68.1	68.2	69.1	49.5
Midwest	55.3	45.0	44.3	46.6	44.7	42.5	66.2	72.0	67.8	68.6	56.0
South	48.4	40.4	40.5	42.0	41.9	32.0	56.5	58.4	64.9	55.6	42.6
West	55.8	48.3	53.9	47.9	46.7	47.1	63.6	66.4	68.0	65.1	48.6
Marital status											
Currently married	52.8	44.4	44.5	45.3	44.9	40.7	63.8	61.5	67.7	64.7	52.8
Formerly married	52.8	45.0	47.5[2]	50.4	43.4	39.2	55.5	70.2	65.3	59.6	46.1
Never married	55.4	46.0	47.1	47.0	41.4	34.2[2]	66.2	68.1	64.0	71.1	45.2[2]
Employment status											
Currently employed	52.9	45.1	46.6	45.4	44.1	41.1	64.9	66.4	66.9	63.9	46.0
Unemployed	52.6	46.2	42.1	48.4	49.3	33.3[2]	61.6	75.2	52.5	65.3	25.0[2]
Not in labor force	53.6	42.8	38.3	50.8	46.6	40.0	58.5	61.4	68.7	63.2	49.2

Source: Health Promotion and Disease Prevention: United States, 1990, National Center for Health Statistics, Vital and Health Statistics, Series 10, No. 185, p. 29. *Notes:* Data are based on household interviews of the civilian noninstitutionalized population. The survey design, general qualifications, and information on the reliability of the estimates are given in appendix 1 in the original source. Denominator for each cell excludes unknowns. 1. Includes persons with unknown sociodemographic characteristics. 2. Figure does not meet standard of reliability or precision (more than 30-percent relative standard error in numerator of percent or rate).

Activities of Daily Living

★ 523 ★

Projections for Persons Aged 65+ Who Have Difficulty with Daily Activities, 1990-2020

[Numbers in millions]

Living arrangement	1990	2005	2020
All people	4.4	5.4	7.3
Living alone	1.5	1.8	2.4

Source: Aging America, Trends and Projections, prepared by the U.S. Senate Special Committee on Aging, the American Association of Retired Persons, the Federal Council on the Aging, and the U.S. Administration on Aging, 1991, Washington, D.C., p. 228. Primary source: Lewin/ICF estimates based on data from the 1984, *Supplement on Aging* and the Brookings/ICF Long-Term Care Financing Model, 1990.

★ 524 ★

Activities of Daily Living

Type of Help Received by People Age 65+ with Activity Limitations, by Living Arrangement, 1990

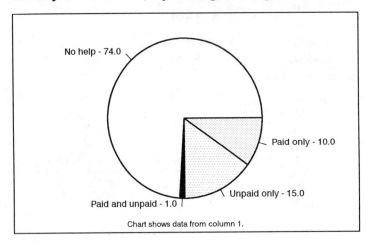

No help - 74.0

Paid only - 10.0

Unpaid only - 15.0

Paid and unpaid - 1.0

Chart shows data from column 1.

Chart refers to the data in column one.

[Numbers in percent]

Type of help	Living alone	Couples
Unpaid only	15.0	54.0
No help	74.0	37.0
Paid only	10.0	5.0
Paid and unpaid	1.0	4.0

Source: Aging America, Trends and Projections, prepared by the U.S. Senate Special Committee on Aging, the American Association of Retired Persons, the Federal Council on the Aging, and the U.S. Administration on Aging, 1991, Washington, D.C., p. 229. Primary source: Lewin/ICF estimates based on data from the 1984, *Supplement on Aging* and the Brookings/ICF Long-Term Care Financing Model, 1990.

★ 525 ★

Activities of Daily Living

Type of Help Received by People Age 65+ Living Alone and Unable to Perform at Least One Daily Activity, 1990

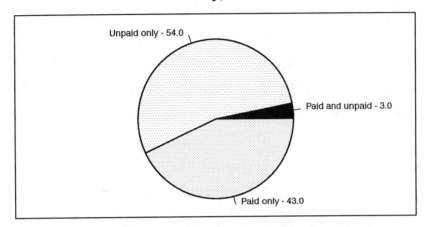

Type of help	Percent
Unpaid only	54.0
Paid only	43.0
Paid and unpaid	3.0

Source: Aging America, Trends and Projections, prepared by the U.S. Senate Special Committee on Aging, the American Association of Retired Persons, the Federal Council on the Aging, and the U.S. Administration on Aging, 1991, Washington, D.C., p. 231. Primary source: Lewin/ICF estimates based on data from the 1984 *Current Population Survey*, and the Brookings/ICF Long-Term Care Financing Model, 1990.

★ 526 ★

Activities of Daily Living

Percentage of Persons Needing Assistance with Everyday Activities, by Age: 1986

Age	
Under 65	2.4
65 to 69	9.3
70 to 74	10.9
75 to 79	18.9

[Continued]

★ 526 ★

Percentage of Persons Needing Assistance with Everyday Activities, by Age: 1986
[Continued]

Age	
80 to 84	23.6
85 and over	45.4

Source: *Sixty-Five Plus in America*, Cynthia M. Taeuber, U.S. Department of Commerce, Economics and Statistics Administration, Bureau of the Census, U.S. Government Printing Office, Washington, D.C., 1992, p. 3-12. Primary source: U.S. Bureau of the Census, *The Need for Personal Assistance With Everyday Activities: Recipients and Caregivers*, Current Population Reports, Series P-70, No. 19, U.S. Government Printing Office, Washington, D.C., 1990, Table B.

★ 527 ★

Activities of Daily Living

Percentage of Persons Needing Assistance with Everyday Activities, by Age and Sex: 1986

age	Male	Female
Under 65	1.7	3.1
65 to 74	7.7	11.7
75 and over	17.2	30.2

Source: *Sixty-Five Plus in America*, Cynthia M. Taeuber, U.S. Department of Commerce, Economics and Statistics Administration, Bureau of the Census, U.S. Government Printing Office, Washington, D.C., 1992, p. 3-13. Primary source: U.S. Bureau of the Census, *The Need for Personal Assistance With Everyday Activities: Recipients and Caregivers*, Current Population Reports, Series P-70, No. 19, U.S. Government Printing Office, Washington, D.C., 1990, Figure 2.

★ 528 ★

Activities of Daily Living

Percentage of Persons 65 Years and Over Needing Assistance with Everyday Activities, by Race and Hispanic Origin: 1986

White	15.4
Black	22.7
Hispanic origin[1]	19.2

Source: Sixty-Five Plus in America, Cynthia M. Taeuber, U.S. Department of Commerce, Economics and Statistics Administration, Bureau of the Census, U.S. Government Printing Office, Washington, D.C., 1992, p. 3-13. Primary source: U.S. Bureau of the Census, *The Need for Personal Assistance With Everyday Activities: Recipients and Caregivers*, Current Population Reports, Series P-70, No. 19, U.S. Government Printing Office, Washington, D.C., 1990, Table B. *Note:* 1. Hispanic origin may be of any race.

★ 529 ★

Activities of Daily Living

Degree of Daily Activity Limitation Due to Illness, 1991

[Percent distribution of persons]

Characteristic	All persons	With no activity limitation	With activity limitation	With limitation in major activity	Unable to carry on major activity	Limited in amount or kind of major activity	Limited, but not in major activity
All persons[1]	100.0	85.7	14.3	9.6	4.3	5.4	4.6
Age							
Under 18 years	100.0	94.2	5.8	4.2	0.5	3.7	1.6
18-44 years	100.0	90.8	9.2	6.4	2.8	3.5	2.9
45-64 years	100.0	77.8	22.2	16.3	8.7	7.6	5.9
65 years and over	100.0	62.1	37.9	22.3	10.6	11.7	15.6
65-69 years	100.0	65.2	34.8	26.9	15.2	11.7	7.9
70 years and over	100.0	60.6	39.4	20.1	8.4	11.7	19.2
Sex and age							
Male							
All ages	100.0	86.1	13.9	9.6	4.7	5.0	4.2
Under 18 years	100.0	93.2	6.8	5.0	0.5	4.5	1.8
18-44 years	100.0	90.6	9.4	6.9	3.3	3.5	2.5
45-64 years	100.0	78.5	21.5	16.9	10.2	6.6	4.6
65-69 years	100.0	64.3	35.7	29.4	18.8	10.5	6.3
70 years and over	100.0	62.0	38.0	15.5	7.4	8.2	22.4

[Continued]

★ 529 ★

Degree of Daily Activity Limitation Due to Illness, 1991
[Continued]

Characteristic	All persons	With no activity limitation	With activity limitation	With limitation in major activity	Unable to carry on major activity	Limited in amount or kind of major activity	Limited, but not in major activity
Female							
All ages	100.0	85.4	14.6	9.6	3.9	5.7	5.0
Under 18 years	100.0	95.3	4.7	3.3	0.5	2.9	1.4
18-44 years	100.0	91.0	9.0	5.9	2.3	3.5	3.2
45-64 years	100.0	77.2	22.8	15.8	7.3	8.6	7.0
65-69 years	100.0	65.9	34.1	24.9	12.2	12.7	9.2
70 years and over	100.0	59.7	40.3	23.2	9.1	14.1	17.1
Race and age							
White							
All ages	100.0	85.5	14.5	9.6	4.1	5.4	4.9
Under 18 years	100.0	94.3	5.7	4.1	0.5	3.6	1.6
18-44 years	100.0	90.6	9.4	6.3	2.7	3.6	3.1
45-64 years	100.0	78.3	21.7	15.7	8.0	7.7	6.0
65-69 years	100.0	65.8	34.2	26.4	14.5	11.9	7.8
70 years and over	100.0	61.2	38.9	19.4	8.0	11.4	19.5
Black							
All ages	100.0	85.6	14.4	11.0	5.5	5.5	3.4
Under 18 years	100.0	93.2	6.8	5.2	0.5	4.7	1.6
18-44 years	100.0	90.7	9.3	7.3	4.0	3.3	2.0
45-64 years	100.0	71.7	28.3	23.2	15.1	8.2	5.0
65-69 years	100.0	57.6	42.4	33.0	22.0	11.0	9.4
70 years and over	100.0	54.0	46.0	28.6	12.9	15.7	17.4
Family income and age							
Under $10,000							
All ages	100.0	73.4	26.6	19.6	10.1	9.6	7.0
Under 18 years	100.0	89.9	10.1	7.7	0.9	6.8	2.4
18-44 years	100.0	83.0	17.0	13.0	7.5	5.6	4.0
45-64 years	100.0	42.2	57.8	48.9	33.6	15.3	8.8
65-69 years	100.0	47.9	52.1	43.7	26.7	17.0	8.5
70 years and over	100.0	51.4	48.6	27.2	9.0	18.1	21.5
$10,000-$19,999							
All ages	100.0	80.2	19.8	13.7	6.4	7.3	6.1
Under 18 years	100.0	92.8	7.2	5.7	0.7	4.9	1.6
18-44 years	100.0	87.6	12.4	9.1	4.3	4.8	3.3
45-64 years	100.0	64.3	35.7	29.1	17.0	12.1	6.7
65-69 years	100.0	60.6	39.4	31.0	18.3	12.6	8.4
70 years and over	100.0	61.3	38.7	17.9	6.8	11.1	20.8
$20,000-$34,999							
All ages	100.0	87.5	12.5	8.2	3.3	5.0	4.2
Under 18 years	100.0	94.7	5.4	3.9	0.4	3.5	1.4

[Continued]

★529★

Degree of Daily Activity Limitation Due to Illness, 1991
[Continued]

Characteristic	All persons	With no activity limitation	With activity limitation	With limitation in major activity	Unable to carry on major activity	Limited in amount or kind of major activity	Limited, but not in major activity
18-44 years	100.0	91.1	8.9	6.0	2.3	3.7	2.9
45-64 years	100.0	79.1	20.9	15.1	7.1	8.0	5.8
65-69 years	100.0	69.4	30.6	22.9	11.5	11.5	7.7
70 years and over	100.0	66.8	33.2	14.9	6.7	8.2	18.4
$35,000 or more							
All ages	100.0	91.3	8.7	5.4	1.8	3.6	3.3
Under 18 years	100.0	95.3	4.7	3.2	0.4	2.8	1.5
18-44 years	100.0	93.4	6.6	4.0	1.3	2.7	2.6
45-64 years	100.0	86.2	13.8	8.6	3.1	5.5	5.2
65-69 years	100.0	77.7	22.3	16.3	7.7	8.6	6.0
70 years and over	100.0	66.7	33.3	16.7	9.2	7.4	16.7
Geographic region							
Northeast	100.0	87.4	12.6	8.5	3.9	4.5	4.1
Midwest	100.0	85.5	14.5	9.7	3.7	6.0	4.7
South	100.0	84.5	15.5	10.8	5.0	5.8	4.7
West	100.0	86.4	13.6	8.8	4.0	4.7	4.9
Place of residence							
MSA[2]	100.0	86.4	13.6	9.2	4.0	5.1	4.4
Central city	100.0	85.3	14.7	10.1	4.6	5.4	4.6
Not central city	100.0	87.2	12.8	8.6	3.6	5.0	4.3
Not MSA[2]	100.0	83.2	16.8	11.2	5.1	6.1	5.6

Source: Current Estimates From the National Health Interview Survey, 1991, National Center for Health Statistics, Vital and Health Statistics, Series 10, No. 184, pp. 106-107. Notes: Data are based on household interviews of the civilian noninstitutionalized population. The survey design, general qualifications, and information on the reliability of the estimates are given in appendix 1 of the original source. 1. Includes other races and unknown family income. 2. MSA is metropolitan statistical area.

★ 530 ★

Activities of Daily Living

Days of Daily Activity Limitation Due to Illness, 1991

[Days restricted due to acute and chronic conditions]

Characteristic	Type of restriction					
	Number of days per person			Number of days in thousands		
	All types	Bed disability	Work or school loss[1]	All types	Bed disability	Work or school loss[1]
All persons[2]	16.1	6.5	5.4	3,996,402	1,612,545	887,025
Age						
Under 5 years	10.9	4.6	...	211,935	89,829	...
5-17 years	9.4	4.1	5.1	432,499	190,601	236,887
18 years and over	18.3	7.3	5.6	3,351,968	1,332,115	650,138
18-24 years	10.2	4.4	4.6	252,184	108,503	74,386
25-44 years	13.4	5.0	5.5	1,088,353	403,591	356,682
45-64 years	20.8	7.9	6.2	981,232	373,470	199,438
65 years and over	34.0	14.7	5.1	1,030,200	446,552	19,633
Sex and age						
Male						
All ages	14.1	5.4	4.9	1,700,766	656,879	426,423
Under 5 years	11.9	5.1	...	118,007	50,449	...
5-17 years	8.7	3.8	4.8	205,082	90,167	113,756
18 years and over	15.8	5.9	4.9	1,377,677	516,262	312,667
18-24 years	8.7	3.6	3.7	105,233	42,979	31,538
25-44 years	11.6	3.8	4.6	461,909	151,030	165,449
45-64 years	18.4	6.6	5.9	415,772	148,881	103,286
65 years and over	31.2	13.7	5.5	394,764	173,371	12,394
Female						
All ages	17.9	7.5	6.1	2,295,636	955,666	460,602
Under 5 years	9.9	4.2	...	93,928	39,380	...
5-17 years	10.1	4.5	5.5	227,417	100,433	123,131
18 years and over	20.6	8.5	6.3	1,974,291	815,853	337,471
18-24 years	11.7	5.2	5.6	146,951	65,524	42,848
25-44 years	15.2	6.1	6.5	626,444	252,560	191,233
45-64 years	23.0	9.2	6.6	565,460	224,589	96,152
65 years and over	36.0	15.5	4.5	635,436	273,180	7,239
Race and age						
White						
All ages	16.1	6.3	5.5	3,343,859	1,312,883	749,485
Under 5 years	11.3	4.4	...	174,861	68,552	...
5-17 years	9.9	4.3	5.4	367,708	161,238	198,564
18 years and over	18.0	7.0	5.5	2,801,290	1,083,093	550,921
18-24 years	10.6	4.4	4.7	210,125	87,118	64,263
25-44 years	13.1	4.6	5.4	892,799	312,415	295,665
45-64 years	20.0	7.3	6.2	813,604	297,957	172,923
65 years and over	32.5	14.2	5.2	884,761	385,603	18,070
Black						
All ages	17.5	8.0	5.9	540,052	245,659	114,366

[Continued]

★ 530 ★

Days of Daily Activity Limitation Due to Illness, 1991
[Continued]

Characteristic	Type of restriction					
	Number of days per person			Number of days in thousands		
	All types	Bed disability	Work or school loss[1]	All types	Bed disability	Work or school loss[1]
Under 5 years	9.6	5.5	...	29,477	16,987	...
5-17 years	7.5	3.4	4.4	54,446	24,366	31,543
18 years and over	22.2	9.9	6.8	456,130	204,305	82,823
18-24 years	9.9	5.3	5.1	34,623	18,523	8,985
25-44 years	16.7	7.7	7.2	160,662	73,983	51,870
45-64 years	28.5	12.1	6.9	138,736	58,927	20,495
65 years and over	47.6	20.6	4.8[4]	122,108	52,871	1,473
Family income and age						
Less than $10,000						
All ages	29.8	12.3	7.6	711,369	294,523	75,753
Under 5 years	12.7	4.9	...	29,310	11,364	...
5-17 years	12.3	5.7	6.9	55,308	25,768	30,934
18 years and over	36.7	15.1	8.3	626,751	257,391	44,819
18-24 years	13.3	5.7	5.4	57,185	24,457	10,541
25-44 years	28.6	12.1	9.9	143,450	60,792	22,033
45-64 years	60.1	23.5	11.4	182,901	71,640	10,522
65 years and over	51.6	21.3	5.9[4]	243,214	100,502	1,723
$10,000-$19,999						
All ages	20.8	8.5	6.6	789,232	323,823	136,032
Under 5 years	13.1	5.9	...	41,794	18,847	...
5-17 years	10.0	4.6	5.9	68,868	31,986	40,419
18 years and over	24.3	9.8	6.9	678,570	272,990	95,614
18-24 years	10.1	3.4	4.9	42,323	14,189	13,582
25-44 years	17.9	7.2	6.7	186,203	74,507	49,213
45-64 years	33.6	13.6	9.8	192,836	77,960	29,274
65 years and over	34.1	14.1	5.0[4]	257,208	106,335	3,544
$20,000-$34,999						
All ages	13.6	5.1	5.9	724,301	269,109	218,005
Under 5 years	10.1	3.7	...	45,354	16,364	...
5-17 years	8.7	3.9	4.9	88,206	39,178	49,696
18 years and over	15.3	5.5	6.3	590,741	213,567	168,309
18-24 years	10.1	4.4	4.9	48,437	21,368	17,327
25-44 years	12.8	4.2	6.2	244,489	81,014	98,636
45-64 years	18.4	7.1	7.2	163,997	62,766	44,778
65 years and over	23.3	8.4	8.7	133,817	48,419	7,568
$35,000 or more						
All ages	11.0	4.2	4.7	983,186	374,261	323,596
Under 5 years	10.7	5.0	...	70,852	32,903	...
5-17 years	9.2	3.8	4.8	161,234	65,982	83,809
18 years and over	11.5	4.2	4.6	751,100	275,376	239,787
18-24 years	8.8	4.0	4.3	61,308	27,434	22,708
25-44 years	10.2	3.5	4.5	346,424	120,035	133,695

[Continued]

★ 530 ★

Days of Daily Activity Limitation Due to Illness, 1991

[Continued]

Characteristic	Type of restriction					
	Number of days per person			Number of days in thousands		
	All types	Bed disability	Work or school loss[1]	All types	Bed disability	Work or school loss[1]
45-64 years	12.9	4.3	5.1	253,547	83,751	79,456
65 years and over	20.4	10.0	4.0[3]	89,821	44,157	3,927
Geographic region						
Northeast	13.1	5.1	5.2	658,053	258,366	170,312
Midwest	15.2	5.5	5.5	906,997	329,830	220,107
South	18.2	8.0	5.5	1,529,302	675,048	300,949
West	16.5	6.4	5.5	902,050	349,301	195,657
Place of residence						
MSA[4]	15.9	6.4	5.4	3,081,071	1,240,553	699,539
Central city	17.6	7.4	5.6	1,350,397	564,930	271,482
Not central city	14.7	5.7	5.3	1,730,674	675,623	428,058
Not MSA[4]	16.7	6.8	5.4	915,331	371,992	187,486

Source: Current Estimates From the National Health Interview Survey, 1991, National Center for Health Statistics, Vital and Health Statistics, Series 10, No. 184, pp. 110-111. *Notes:* Data are based on household interviews of the civilian noninstitutionalized population. The survey design, general qualifications, and information on the reliability of the estimates are given in appendix 1 of the original source. Three dots (...) means the category is not applicable. 1. Sum of school-loss days for children 5-17 years of age and work-loss days for currently employed persons 18 years of age and over. School-loss days are shown for the age group 5-17 years; work-loss days are shown for the age group 18 years and over and each older age group. 2. Includes other races and unknown family income. 3. Figure does not meet standard of reliability or precision. 4. MSA is metropolitan statistical area.

★ 531 ★

Activities of Daily Living

Activities Reported as 'Does Not Do'

Percent who reported "does not do" for instrumental activities of daily living (IADL), by sex and age.

IADL	Male			Female		
	65 years and over	65-74 years	75 years and over	65 years and over	65-74 years	75 years and over
Meal preparation	12.43	11.21	14.81	1.16	0.67	1.86
Shopping	2.79	2.16	4.01	1.21	0.57	2.12
Money management	2.30	2.04	2.81	1.47	1.02	2.11
Telephone use	1.10	0.90	1.49	0.29	0.18	0.46
Light housework	9.14	8.64	10.11	0.86	0.41	1.51
Heavy housework	15.85	14.02	19.39	5.02	3.23	7.56

Source: Health Data on Older Americans: United States, 1992, Centers for Disease Control and Prevention/ National Center for Health Statistics, Vital and Health Statistics, Series 3: Analytic and Epidemiological Studies, No. 27, p. 24.

★ 532 ★

Activities of Daily Living

Daily Activities Reported as Being Difficult

Percent of persons 65 years of age and over with reported difficulty performing activities of daily living (ADL), by race, sex and age: 1986.

Race, sex, and age	Number of persons in thousands Total	ADL with difficulty						
		Eating	Toileting	Dressing	Bathing	Trans-ferring[1]	Walking	Getting outside
Race								
White	24,753	1.9	4.4	5.7	9.5	8.2	17.8	11.3
All other	2,784	1.3	7.0	8.6	14.0	11.6	22.1	15.6
Sex								
Male	11,357	1.7	3.4	5.2	7.1	6.4	14.9	7.5
Female	16,181	1.9	5.6	6.5	12.0	10.1	20.6	14.8
Age								
65-74 years	16,987	1.5	2.8	4.2	6.3	6.2	13.5	7.0
75-84 years	8,552	1.8	6.3	7.3	13.9	11.2	23.4	16.9
65 years and over	27,538	1.8	4.7	6.0	10.0	8.6	18.2	11.7
75 years and over	10,551	2.4	7.7	8.8	16.0	12.3	25.8	19.4
85 years and over	1,999	5.0	14.0	15.1	24.8	17.1	35.9	30.1
Male								
65-74 years	7,490	1.7	2.7	4.5	6.0	5.6	12.6	5.7
75-84 years	3,251	1.1[2]	3.4	5.2	7.8	6.9	17.3	9.2
65 years and over	11,357	1.7	3.4	5.2	7.1	6.4	14.9	7.5
75 years and over	3,866	1.9	4.7	6.4	9.4	8.0	19.2	10.9
85 years and over	615	5.7[2]	11.6	12.7	18.1	14.0	28.9	19.7
Female								
65-74 years	9,496	1.3	2.8	4.0	6.5	6.7	14.2	8.0
75-84 years	5,301	2.3	8.0	8.6	17.6	13.8	27.2	21.6
65 years and over	16,181	1.9	5.6	6.5	12.0	10.1	20.6	14.8
75 years and over	6,685	2.8	9.5	10.2	19.7	14.8	29.6	24.3
85 years and over	1,384	4.7[2]	15.0	16.1	27.8	18.5	39.1	34.7

Source: Health Data on Older Americans: United States, 1992, Centers for Disease Control and Prevention/National Center for Health Statistics, Vital and Health Statistics, Series 3: Analytic and Epidemiological Studies, No. 27, p. 30. Primary source: National Center for Health Statistics: Data from the National Health Interview Survey 1986 Functional Limitations Supplement. *Notes:* Data are based on household interviews of the civilian noninstitutionalized population. Persons reported as not performing an activity of daily living (ADL) were classified with those reported as having difficulty with that activity. 1. Transferring means getting in and out of a bed or chair. 2. Figure does not meet standard of reliability or precision.

★ 533 ★

Activities of Daily Living

Daily Activities Reported as Being Difficult, by Living Arrangement

Percent of persons 65 years of age and over with reported difficulty performing activities of daily living (ADL), by living arrangement, sex, age, and activity: 1986.

Age and ADLs with difficulty	Living arrangement			
	Lives alone		Lives with others[1]	
	Male	Female	Male	Female
65-74 years				
Eating	1.0[3]	1.1	1.8	1.4
Toileting	4.1	2.7	2.5	2.9
Dressing	5.2	3.0	4.4	4.5
Bathing	8.6	6.3	5.6	6.6
Transferring[2]	4.2	7.4	5.8	6.4
Walking	15.8	16.1	12.1	13.1
Getting outside	7.6	8.9	5.4	7.6
75 years and over				
Eating	1.7[3]	1.1	1.9	4.6
Toileting	4.5[3]	7.7	4.7	11.5
Dressing	4.6[3]	7.3	6.9	13.4
Bathing	7.5	16.2	10.0	23.9
Transferring[2]	8.7	13.2	7.8	16.6
Walking	20.4	27.8	18.8	31.7
Getting outside	13.3	20.6	10.2	28.5

Source: Health Data on Older Americans: United States, 1992, Centers for Disease Control and Prevention/National Center for Health Statistics, Vital and Health Statistics, Series 3: Analytic and Epidemilogical Studies, No. 27, p. 37. Primary source: National Center for Health Statistics: Data from the National Health Interview Survey 1986 Functional Limitations Supplement. *Notes:* Persons reported as not performing an activity of daily living (ADL) are included with those reported as having difficulty with that activity. 1. Includes spouse. 2. Transferring means getting in and out of a bed or chair. 3. Figure does not meet standard of reliability or precision.

★ 534 ★

Activities of Daily Living

Daily Activities for Which Help Was Received

Percent of persons 65 years of age and over who reported receiving the help of another person with performing activities of daily living, by race, sex and age: 1986.

Race, sex, and age	Number of persons in thousands Total	Help of another person received for...		ADL with difficulty						
		1 ADL	2 or more ADLs	Eating	Toileting	Dressing	Bathing	Trans-ferring[1]	Walking	Getting outside
Race										
White	24,753	3.6	5.9	1.1	2.3	4.2	5.6	3.0	4.5	6.1
All other	2,784	4.7	8.5	0.6[2]	3.5	6.1	9.4	5.2	5.8	7.8
Sex										
Male	11,357	2.4	4.3	1.0	1.9	3.9	4.3	2.6	3.1	3.8
Female	16,181	4.6	7.5	1.1	2.8	4.7	7.2	3.7	5.8	8.0
Age										
65-74 years	16,987	2.5	3.4	0.8	1.4	2.9	3.2	2.1	2.6	3.2
75-84 years	8,552	4.9	8.6	1.1	3.3	5.4	8.6	4.0	6.4	9.2
65 years +	27,538	3.7	6.2	1.1	2.4	4.4	6.0	3.2	4.6	6.3
75 years +	10,551	5.7	10.6	1.6	4.1	6.8	10.6	5.0	8.0	11.3
85 years +	1,999	9.2	19.6	4.1	7.5	12.6	19.0	9.4	14.8	20.6
Male										
65-74 years	7,490	1.9	3.3	0.9	1.5	3.2	3.3	2.3	2.3	2.7
75-84 years	3,251	2.9	5.1	0.6[2]	1.9	4.2	4.9	2.3	3.7	4.8
65 years +	11,357	2.4	4.3	1.0	1.9	3.9	4.3	2.6	3.1	3.8
75 years +	3,866	3.4	6.3	1.3	2.5	5.2	6.4	3.2	4.5	6.0
85 years +	615	6.0[2]	12.9	4.7[2]	5.9[2]	10.0	14.1	7.8	8.3	12.8
Female										
65-74 years	9,496	2.9	3.5	0.6	1.3	2.6	3.1	2.0	2.8	3.5
75-84 years	5,301	6.1	10.7	1.3	4.1	6.1	10.9	5.0	8.0	11.9
65 years +	16,181	4.6	7.5	1.1	2.8	4.7	7.2	3.7	5.8	8.0
75 years +	6,685	7.0	13.1	1.8	5.0	7.7	13.0	6.1	10.0	14.4
85 years +	1,384	10.5	22.4	3.9[2]	8.3	13.8	21.2	10.1	17.8	24.1

Source: Health Data on Older Americans: United States, 1992, Centers for Disease Control and Prevention/National Center for Health Statistics, Vital and Health Statistics, Series 3: Analytic and Epidemiological Studies, No. 27, pp. 29, 31. Primary source: National Center for Health Statistics: Data from the National Health Interview Survey 1986 Functional Limitations Supplement. *Notes:* Data are based on household interviews of the civilian noninstitutionalized population. Persons reported as not performing an activity of daily living (ADL) were classified with those reported as receiving help with that activity. 1. Transferring means getting in and out of a bed or chair. 2. Figure does not meet standard of reliability or precision.

★ 535 ★

Activities of Daily Living

Instrumental Activities Reported as Being Difficult

Percent of persons 65 years of age and over with reported difficulty performing instrumental activities of daily living (IADL), by race, sex, and age: 1986.

Race, sex, and age	Number of persons in thousands Total	IADL with difficulty					
		Meal preparation	Shopping	Managing money	Using telephone	Light housework	Heavy housework
Race							
White	24,753	6.6	12.1	4.9	4.8	7.5	23.3
All other	2,784	12.8	18.8	8.2	6.7	12.8	28.0
Sex							
Male	11,357	4.5	8.1	4.1	5.1	5.6	13.0
Female	16,181	9.2	16.0	6.0	4.9	9.8	31.3
Age							
65-74 years	16,987	4.0	7.3	2.5	3.2	4.6	18.0
75-84 years	8,552	9.9	18.1	7.3	5.9	11.1	29.5
65 years and over	27,538	7.3	12.8	5.2	5.0	8.1	23.8
75 years and over	10,551	12.5	21.5	9.6	7.8	13.6	33.0
85 years and over	1,999	23.4	36.0	19.5	16.1	24.4	48.0
Male							
65-74 years	7,490	3.1	5.7	2.6	3.4	3.8	10.6
75-84 years	3,251	5.3	10.5	5.7	6.3	6.9	15.2
65 years and over	11,357	4.5	8.1	4.1	5.1	5.6	13.0
75 years and over	3,866	7.3	12.8	7.1	8.4	9.2	17.6
85 years and over	615	17.5	25.2	14.5	19.7	21.5	30.7
Female							
65-74 years	9,496	4.7	8.7	2.4	3.1	5.3	23.9
75-84 years	5,301	12.7	22.8	8.3	5.6	13.7	38.3
65 years and over	16,181	9.2	16.0	6.0	4.9	9.8	31.3
75 years and over	6,685	15.5	26.6	11.1	7.4	16.2	41.9
85 years and over	1,384	26.0	40.8	21.8	14.4	25.7	55.6

Source: Health Data on Older Americans: United States, 1992, Centers for Disease Control and Prevention/National Center for Health Statistics, Vital and Health Statistics, Series 3: Analytic and Epidemiological Studies, No. 27, p. 33. Primary source: National Center for Health Statistics: Data from the National Health Interview Survey 1986 Functional Limitations Supplement. *Notes:* Persons reported as not performing an instrumental activity of daily living (IADL) were not classified with those reported as having difficulty with that activity.

★ 536 ★

Activities of Daily Living

Instrumental Daily Activities for Which Help was Received

Percent of persons 65 years of age and over who reported receiving the help of another person with performing instrumental activities of daily living (IADL), by race, sex, and age: 1986.

Race, sex, and age	Number of persons in thousands Total	IADL for which help of another person received					
		Meal preparation	Shopping	Managing money	Using telephone	Light housework	Heavy housework
Race							
White	24,753	5.9	11.4	4.6	2.9	6.6	18.7
All other	2,784	11.6	17.0	7.4	4.6	10.9	22.6
Sex							
Male	11,357	4.2	7.6	3.9	2.8	5.0	10.0
Female	16,181	8.0	15.1	5.6	3.2	8.4	25.4
Age							
65-74 years	16,987	3.5	6.7	2.1	1.8	3.8	13.7
75-84 years	8,552	8.7	17.1	7.1	3.6	9.7	24.2
65 years and over	27,538	6.5	12.0	4.9	3.0	7.0	19.1
75 years and over	10,551	11.3	20.5	9.4	5.0	12.2	27.8
85 years and over	1,999	22.3	35.1	19.2	10.8	23.1	43.6
Male							
65-74 years	7,490	2.8	5.4	2.4	1.9	3.1	7.9
75-84 years	3,251	5.2	9.5	5.7	3.4	6.4	11.4
65 years and over	11,357	4.2	7.6	3.9	2.8	5.0	10.0
75 years and over	3,866	6.9	11.9	7.0	4.6	8.7	14.2
85 years and over	615	15.9	24.6	13.8	10.7	20.9	28.9
Female							
65-74 years	9,496	4.0	7.8	2.0	1.8	4.3	18.2
75-84 years	5,301	10.9	21.7	7.9	3.7	11.7	32.0
65 years and over	16,181	8.0	15.1	5.6	3.2	8.4	25.4
75 years and over	6,685	13.8	25.4	10.7	5.2	14.2	35.8
85 years and over	1,384	25.2	39.8	21.5	10.8	24.0	50.2

Source: Health Data on Older Americans: United States, 1992, Centers for Disease Control and Prevention/National Center for Health Statistics, Vital and Health Statistics, Series 3: Analytic and Epidemiological Studies, No. 27, p. 34. Primary source: National Center for Health Statistics: Data from the National Health Interview Survey 1986 Functional Limitations Supplement. *Notes:* Persons reported as not performing an instrumental activity of daily living (IADL) were not classified with those reported as receiving help with that activity.

★ 537 ★

Activities of Daily Living

Instrumental Daily Activities Reported as Being Difficult, by Living Arrangement

Percent of persons 65 years of age and over with reported difficulty performing instrumental activities of daily living (IADL), by living arrangement, sex, age, and activity: 1986.

Age and IADLs with difficulty	Living arrangements			
	Lives alone		Lives with others[1]	
	Male	Female	Male	Female
65-74 years				
Meal preparation	4.1	3.1	3.0	5.6
Shopping	9.9	8.8	5.0	8.6
Managing money	4.1[2]	2.0	2.4	2.6
Using telephone	2.8[2]	2.6	3.5	3.3
Light housework	3.3[2]	3.0	3.9	6.5
Heavy housework	15.2	24.6	9.9	23.5
75 years and over				
Meal preparation	11.3	10.1	6.1	21.7
Shopping	15.9	23.4	12.0	30.2
Managing money	8.9	7.8	6.6	14.9
Using telephone	7.2	4.0	8.8	11.4
Light housework	13.8	11.5	8.0	21.6
Heavy housework	20.9	40.1	16.7	43.9

Source: Health Data on Older Americans: United States, 1992, Centers for Disease Control and Prevention/National Center for Health Statistics, Vital and Health Statistics, Series 3: Analytic and Epidemiological Studies, No. 27, p. 39. Primary source: National Center for Health Statistics: Data from the National Health Interview Survey 1986 Functional Limitations Supplement. *Notes:* Data are based on household interviews of the civilian noninstitutionalized population. Persons reported as not performing an instrumental activity of daily living (IADL) are not included with those reported as having difficulty with that activity. 1. Includes spouse. 2. Figure does not meet standard of reliability or precision.

★ 538 ★

Activities of Daily Living

Health of Older Black Americans

Percent distribution of activities of daily living difficulties, by respondent-assessed health status, sex, and race for persons 65 years of age and over: 1986. From the source: "For black males and females, significantly more of those reporting excellent or very good health reported no activity of daily living (ADL) difficulties, compared with those reporting fair or poor health. Fewer elderly black females reported no ADL difficulties than their white counterparts, however, this difference by race did not hold for males."

Sex and respondent-assessed health status	Black		White	
	None	1 or more	None	1 or more
Male				
All health statuses	76.2	23.8	82.5	17.5
Excellent/very good	98.9	1.1[1]	93.6	6.4
Fair/poor	54.4	45.6	60.9	39.1
Female				
All health statuses	67.8	32.2	74.7	25.3
Excellent/very good	86.8	13.2	89.4	10.6
Fair/poor	46.1	53.9	49.4	50.6

Source: *Highlights from Health Data on Older Americans: United States, 1992*, Centers for Disease Control and Prevention/National Center for Health Statistics, Vital and Health Statistics, Series 3: Analytic and Epidemiological Studies, No. 27, p. 231. Primary source: National Center for Health Statistics: Data from the National Health Interview Survey. *Notes:* Percents may not add to 100 because of rounding. 1. Figure does not meet standard of reliability or precision.

★ 539 ★

Activities of Daily Living

Limitation of Activity Caused by Chronic Conditions: United States, 1985 and 1990

Data are based on household interviews of a sample of the civilian noninstitutionalized population.

[Percent of population]

Characteristic	Total with limitation of activity		Limited but not in major activity		Limited in amount or kind of major activity		Unable to carry on major activity	
	1985	1990	1985	1990	1985	1990	1985	1990
Total[1,2]	13.4	12.9	4.2	4.1	5.5	5.0	3.7	3.9
Under 15 years	4.8	4.7	1.2	1.2	3.1	3.1	0.4	0.4
Under 5 years	2.2	2.2	0.6	0.6	1.1	1.0	0.5	0.6
5-14 years	6.2	6.1	1.6	1.6	4.2	4.1	0.4	0.4
15-44 years	8.3	8.5	2.7	2.6	3.6	3.5	1.9	2.4

[Continued]

★ 539 ★

Limitation of Activity Caused by Chronic Conditions: United States, 1985 and 1990
[Continued]

Characteristic	Total with limitation of activity		Limited but not in major activity		Limited in amount or kind of major activity		Unable to carry on major activity	
	1985	1990	1985	1990	1985	1990	1985	1990
45-64 years	23.4	21.8	5.9	5.7	8.8	7.5	8.7	8.6
65 years and over	39.6	37.5	15.5	15.4	13.8	11.9	10.4	10.2
65-74 years	36.7	33.7	14.0	13.2	11.5	9.9	11.2	10.6
75 years and over	44.3	43.3	17.9	18.8	17.3	14.9	9.1	9.6

Source: U.S. Department of Commerce, Economics and Statistics Administration, *National Economic, Social, and Environmental Data Bank, CD-ROM,* November 1992. Primary source: Division of Health Interview Statistics, National Center for Health Statistics: Data from the National Health Interview Survey. *Notes:* 1. Age adjusted. 2. Includes all other races not shown separately and unknown family income.

★ 540 ★
Activities of Daily Living

Causes of Dependence in Home-Dwelling Persons Over Age 75 with Impaired Activities of Daily Living

From the source: "Physical frailty... is epidemic among older persons: Among persons over the age of 75 in the community, 32% (3.7 million) have difficulty climbing 10 steps, 40% (4.5 million) have difficulty walking one-fourth of a mile, and 22% (2.4 million) cannot lift 10 pounds. Such physical impairments are the *sole* cause of difficulty in 40% of persons over 75 living at home with limitations in activities of daily living. Many more have physical disabilities combined with mental or sensory impairments."

	Persons (mil.)
Mental or sensory disabilities with or without physical disabilities	1.9
Physical disabilities only	1.3

Source: National Institute on Aging, *Physical Frailty*: A Reducible Barrier to Independence for Older Americans, Report to Congress, pp. 5-6.

★ 541 ★

Activities of Daily Living

Functional Capabilities, by Race and Age

[Cumulative percentages]

Functional capability[1]	All races			Blacks		
	Total age	69-74	75-84	Total age	67-74	75-84
n[2]	2,057	1,122	935	479	269	210
All market and all nonmarket	38	42	33	35	41	27
Some market and all nonmarket	67	72	62	58	66	48
Some market and some nonmarket	68	73	63	59	67	49
Remaining in home	99	99	98	98	98	97
Cumulative total	100	100	100	100	100	100

Source: Herbert S. Parnes, Thomas N. Chirikos, Elizabeth G. Menaghan, Frank L. Mott, Gilbert Nestel, Lois B. Shaw, David G. Sommers, *The NLS Older Male Sample Revisited: A Unique Data Base for Gerontological Research*, Center for Human Resource Research, The Ohio State University, 1993, p. 23, reprinted with permission. *Notes:* 1. The functional capability categories are defined as follows: 1) All market and all nonmarket; respondent has no limitations on market work activity or on home/leisure activities. 2) Some market and all nonmarket: respondent is limited as to amount or kind of market work he can do; has no limitation on home/leisure activities. 3) Some market and some nonmarket: respondent is limited in amount or kind of market work and has some limitation on home/leisure activity. 4) Remaining in home: respondent is unable to do market work but is not institutionalized. 2. Number of sample cases on which weighted percentages are based.

★ 542 ★

Activities of Daily Living

Prevalence and Severity of Selected Activity Limitations, by Race and Age

[Data are in percentages]

Activity[1]	All races			Blacks		
	Total age	69-74	75-84	Total age	69-74	75-84
n[2]	2,054	1,122	932	478	269	209
Walking	35	30	41	48	44	53
With difficulty	32	28	36	43	39	47
Unable	3	2	4	5	4	6
Using stairs/inclines	34	31	39	44	39	52
With difficulty	28	26	30	33	29	39
Unable	6	5	8	11	10	13
Standing long periods	44	40	49	50	49	52
With difficulty	27	25	29	27	28	25
Unable	18	15	21	24	21	27

[Continued]

★ 542 ★

Prevalence and Severity of Selected Activity Limitations, by Race and Age
[Continued]

Activity[1]	All races			Blacks		
	Total age	69-74	75-84	Total age	69-74	75-84
Sitting long periods	19	19	20	26	24	29
With difficulty	15	15	14	18	20	16
Unable	5	4	6	8	5	13
Stooping/kneeling/crouching	46	44	50	51	45	59
With difficulty	31	32	31	30	24	37
Unable	15	12	18	21	20	22
Lifting/carrying up to 10 lbs.	22	18	26	35	32	40
With difficulty	10	9	11	15	13	17
Unable	12	9	15	20	18	22
Lifting/carrying heavy weights	57	53	61	63	61	66
With difficulty	19	20	18	16	16	16
Unable	38	34	42	47	45	50
Reaching	18	17	20	27	23	33
With difficulty	13	13	14	21	18	25
Unable	5	4	6	6	6	7
Using hands/fingers	16	14	19	23	19	30
With difficulty	14	13	16	20	17	24
Unable	2	1	3	4	2	6

Source: Herbert S. Parnes, Thomas N. Chirikos, Elizabeth G. Menaghan, Frank L. Mott, Gilbert Nestel, Lois B. Shaw, David G. Sommers, The NLS Older Male Sample Revisited: A Unique Data Base for Gerontological Research, Center for Human Resource Research, The Ohio State University, 1993, p. 24, reprinted with permission. Notes: 1. Number of sample cases on which weighted percentages are based. 2. Percentages "with difficulty" and "unable" may not add to total because of rounding.

498

★ 543 ★

Activities of Daily Living

Prevalence of Need for Help with Personal Care, by Type of Care, Race, and Age

[Data are in percentages]

Needs help with	All races			Blacks		
	Total age	69-74	75-84	Total age	69-74	75-84
n[1]	2,072	1,125	947	485	272	213
One or more personal care activities[2]	9	6	12	12	12	12
Bathing	7	4	10	9	9	10
Dressing	5	4	7	8	8	9
Eating	2	1	3	4	3	5
Getting in and out of bed	3	2	4	7	7	7
Walking	4	2	5	7	6	8
Using the toilet	3	2	4	6	6	7

Source: Herbert S. Parnes, Thomas N. Chirikos, Elizabeth G. Menaghan, Frank L. Mott, Gilbert Nestel, Lois B. Shaw, David G. Sommers, *The NLS Older Male Sample Revisited: A Unique Data Base for Gerontological Research*, Center for Human Resource Research, The Ohio State University, 1993, p. 26, reprinted with permission. *Notes:* 1. Number of sample cases on which weighted percentages are based. 2. Includes one or more of the activities listed.

Risk Behaviors

★ 544 ★

Cigarette Smoking

Percent of persons 18 years of age and over who currently smoked cigarettes, by sex, age, and selected characteristics: United States, 1990.

Characteristic	Both sexes 18 years and over	Male					Female				
		Total	18-29 years	30-44 years	45-64 years	65 years and over	Total	18-29 years	30-44 years	45-64 years	65 years and over
All persons[1]	25.5	28.4	28.6	33.6	29.3	14.6	22.8	25.3	25.8	24.8	11.5
Education level											
Less than 12 years	31.8	37.3	44.6	54.0	39.4	17.4	27.1	40.9	40.3	29.9	10.9
12 years	29.6	33.5	33.4	40.9	32.3	16.2	26.5	29.8	32.1	25.5	11.9
More than 12 years	18.3	20.0	16.1	23.9	21.5	8.7	16.6	14.5	17.2	20.5	11.8
13-15 years	23.0	26.2	20.4	34.3	27.6	8.9	20.2	17.3	23.5	22.8	13.0
16 years or more	13.5	14.5	8.8	16.0	17.6	8.6	12.3	9.3	11.1	18.2	10.2

[Continued]

★ 544 ★

Cigarette Smoking
[Continued]

Characteristic	Both sexes 18 years and over	Male					Female				
		Total	18-29 years	30-44 years	45-64 years	65 years and over	Total	18-29 years	30-44 years	45-64 years	65 years and over
Income											
Less than $10,000	31.6	37.3	30.6	59.7	47.0	21.1	28.6	31.9	46.6	33.2	13.2
$10,000-$19,999	29.8	34.1	35.8	44.7	40.7	16.4	26.3	31.9	36.5	26.1	12.2
$20,000-$34,999	26.9	30.3	30.6	37.0	30.5	13.0	23.5	22.3	27.1	26.5	12.1
$35,000-$49,999	23.4	25.5	22.8	28.4	27.4	10.9	21.0	19.7	22.4	22.5	10.2
$50,000 or more	19.3	21.3	20.6	24.1	20.7	10.1	17.2	17.7	16.2	19.0	12.3
Race											
White	25.6	28.0	29.1	33.0	28.7	13.7	23.4	27.1	26.1	25.4	11.5
Black	26.2	32.5	26.7	38.8	36.7	21.5	21.2	17.9	27.2	22.6	11.1
Hispanic origin											
Hispanic	23.0	30.9	28.5	35.9	30.2	19.4	16.3	15.7	18.6	18.1	5.1[2]
Non-Hispanic	25.7	28.2	28.6	33.4	29.3	14.4	23.4	26.7	26.6	25.3	11.7
Geographic region											
Northeast	23.9	26.8	28.0	31.1	26.7	15.0	21.3	25.9	24.6	22.2	10.3
Midwest	27.4	29.4	31.9	33.6	30.2	14.0	25.6	29.4	29.8	27.6	10.1
South	26.5	30.4	29.4	35.9	32.5	16.4	22.9	24.9	25.4	25.7	12.2
West	23.2	25.6	24.1	32.1	25.9	11.6	20.9	20.9	23.2	22.6	13.5
Marital status											
Currently married	24.6	27.1	32.2	31.5	27.0	12.6	22.1	27.6	23.1	21.9	10.5
Formerly married	30.3	41.1	43.9	49.3	44.4	23.8	25.9	44.3	37.9	33.5	12.4
Never married	24.3	26.7	25.4	32.6	28.8	12.7	21.3	20.2	28.0	23.2	8.8[2]
Employment status											
Currently employed	26.9	29.2	28.1	31.8	27.9	16.3	24.2	24.5	24.6	24.5	15.5
Unemployed	38.8	45.8	43.1	53.1	43.5	16.7[2]	31.2	29.8	38.1	25.1	6.4[2]
Not in labor force	21.3	23.3	25.5	51.7	33.3	14.2	20.3	26.5	28.1	25.2	11.0

Source: Health Promotion and Disease Prevention: United States, 1990, National Center for Health Statistics, Vital and Health Statistics, Series 10, No. 185, p. 46. *Notes:* Data are based on household interviews of the civilian noninstitutionalized population. The survey design, general qualifications, and information on the reliability of the estimates are given in appendix 1 in the original source. Denominator for each cell excludes unknowns. 1. Includes persons with unknown sociodemographic characteristics. 2. Figure does not meet standard of reliability or precision (more than 30-percent relative standard error in numerator of percent or rate).

★545★

Risk Behaviors

Cigarette Smoking: 25 or More Cigarettes per Day

Percent of current smokers 18 years of age and over who were smoking 25 cigarettes or more per day, by sex, age, and selected characteristics: United States, 1990.

Characteristic	Both sexes 18 years and over	Male					Female				
		Total	18-29 years	30-44 years	45-64 years	65 years and over	Total	18-29 years	30-44 years	45-64 years	65 years and over
All persons[1]	22.9	28.5	14.5	31.0	39.0	26.6	16.6	8.8	19.6	21.8	12.0
Education level											
Less than 12 years	22.2	25.1	15.2	31.6	30.8	19.3	18.7	10.6	25.1	24.8	11.5
12 years	23.4	29.6	15.4	33.6	39.2	35.1	17.2	8.7	21.4	21.1	13.7
More than 12 years	22.7	30.1	11.9	27.8	46.5	31.3	13.5	7.1	13.7	20.0	9.0[2]
13-15 years	23.1	30.6	12.3	29.2	53.2	36.3[2]	14.5	8.1	16.0	20.0	12.0[2]
16 years or more	22.0	29.3	10.5[2]	25.5	39.9	27.7[2]	11.6	3.5[2]	8.9	20.0	3.8[2]
Income											
Less than $10,000	17.3	20.9	10.2	30.2	27.4	13.5[2]	14.8	5.0[2]	24.4	17.4	14.8
$10,000-$19,999	22.3	27.2	18.7	26.4	38.2	30.9	17.2	12.0	23.2	21.3	7.8[2]
$20,000-$34,999	22.3	27.2	12.9	29.9	38.7	30.7	16.2	9.5	17.3	22.1	12.6[2]
$35,000-$49,999	25.3	31.2	18.2	31.1	42.0	27.2[2]	17.4	10.6	18.8	21.0	13.5[2]
$50,000 or more	28.1	35.4	9.1[2]	38.6	45.5	34.7[2]	18.3	5.1[2]	19.2	25.3	11.4[2]
Race											
White	25.4	32.1	16.2	35.1	43.6	30.3	18.0	9.4	21.6	23.6	12.8
Black	6.0	7.4	7.7[2]	7.4	6.9[2]	7.2[2]	4.2	3.8[2]	4.7[2]	4.9[2]	-[2]
Hispanic origin											
Hispanic	6.8	8.9	2.9[2]	11.3	13.2[2]	16.9[2]	3.5[2]	2.3[2]	4.1[2]	4.6[2]	-[2]
Non-Hispanic	24.1	30.3	15.9	32.8	40.8	27.1	17.4	9.3	20.6	22.7	12.2
Geographic region											
Northeast	21.3	26.3	14.2	27.7	36.3	26.0	15.9	10.2	16.4	22.3	11.4[2]
Midwest	24.2	30.9	18.4	35.0	39.2	27.0	17.2	8.2	20.9	22.6	12.1[2]
South	23.8	29.2	12.4	33.6	39.1	26.3	17.4	10.0	22.1	20.8	12.1
West	20.8	26.1	13.0	24.1	41.2	27.5	14.7	6.0[2]	16.4	21.7	12.1[2]
Marital status											
Currently married	25.2	31.8	15.8	32.0	40.7	31.4	17.2	10.4	19.3	21.6	8.9[2]
Formerly married	23.7	30.6	28.2	32.9	34.1	16.6	19.2	10.1[2]	22.2	22.7	13.8
Never married	13.5	16.3	12.3	23.1	31.3	19.7[2]	9.4	5.8	15.5	18.2[2]	14.1[2]
Employment status											
Currently employed	24.0	29.0	15.2	30.8	40.4	30.3	16.7	9.8	19.0	21.7	8.3[2]
Unemployed	23.9	28.2	12.6[2]	33.1	47.4	61.5[2]	17.0	8.5[2]	20.1	30.8[2]	-[2]
Not in labor force	19.8	26.3	11.1	31.9	32.4	25.4	16.2	6.7	21.1	21.5	12.6

Source: Health Promotion and Disease Prevention: United States, 1990, National Center for Health Statistics, Vital and Health Statistics, Series 10, No. 185, p. 47. *Notes:* Data are based on household interviews of the civilian noninstitutionalized population. The survey design, general qualifications, and information on the reliability of the estimates are given in appendix 1 in the original source. Denominator for each cell excludes unknowns. 1. Includes persons with unknown sociodemographic characteristics. 2. Figure does not meet standard of reliability or precision (more than 30-percent relative standard error in numerator of percent or rate).

★ 546 ★
Risk Behaviors

Percentage of Persons 65 and Over Who Smoked Cigarettes at Time of Survey, by Sex and Race: 1965 to 1987

Year	Male			Female		
	Total	White	Black	Total	White	Black
1965	28.5	27.7	36.4	9.6	9.8	7.1
1974	24.8	24.3	29.7	12.0	12.3	8.9
1979	20.9	20.5	26.2	13.2	13.8	8.5
1987	17.2	16.0	30.3	13.7	13.9	11.7

Source: Sixty-Five Plus in America, Cynthia M. Taeuber, U.S. Department of Commerce, Economics and Statistics Administration, Bureau of the Census, U.S. Government Printing Office, Washington, D.C., 1992, p. 3-9. Primary source: National Center for Health Statistics, *Health, United States, 1990*, Hyattsville, MD, Public Health Service, 1991, Table 55. *Notes:* Civilian noninstitutional population who smoked at least 100 cigarettes and who smoked at the time of the survey; includes occasional smokers. Excludes unknown smoking status.

★ 547 ★
Risk Behaviors

Smokers Who Are Aware of Its Dangers

Percent of current smokers 18 years of age and over who were aware that smoking increases one's chance of getting heart disease, by sex, age, and selected characteristics: United States, 1990.

Characteristic	Both sexes 18 years and over	Male					Female				
		Total	18-29 years	30-44 years	45-64 years	65 years and over	Total	18-29 years	30-44 years	45-64 years	65 years and over
All persons[1]	88.9	87.5	89.8	90.9	84.1	73.5	90.6	93.0	94.0	87.9	77.9
Education level											
Less than 12 years	81.3	79.4	82.6	84.5	76.7	67.4	83.6	88.5	88.1	78.9	74.7
12 years	90.5	88.5	91.5	90.5	84.3	77.3	92.4	94.5	94.8	90.3	79.0
More than 12 years	93.7	93.4	95.2	94.7	91.3	83.9	94.0	95.2	96.0	93.1	82.2
13-15 years	92.9	92.9	95.5	94.1	89.8	71.8	93.0	94.9	94.8	92.3	77.0
16 years or more	95.0	94.3	94.1	95.6	92.8	93.1	96.0	96.5	98.3	94.0	91.3
Income											
Less than $10,000	83.7	80.8	88.8	80.9	75.7	68.3	85.7	93.2	89.0	77.5	73.0
$10,000-$19,999	87.6	85.9	88.9	88.9	81.9	77.0	89.4	91.1	93.0	88.9	76.6
$20,000-$34,999	91.9	90.1	92.3	91.5	86.8	82.6	94.0	95.5	94.6	92.1	92.8
$35,000-$49,999	91.3	89.7	97.4	93.8	85.8	76.0	93.5	94.8	96.5	89.6	72.9
$50,000 or more	94.0	93.6	95.1	96.5	89.5	88.7	94.4	97.2	98.0	89.2	90.2
Race											
White	90.0	89.0	90.6	92.1	86.3	76.8	91.0	93.4	94.4	88.5	78.9

[Continued]

★ 547 ★

Smokers Who Are Aware of Its Dangers

[Continued]

Characteristic	Both sexes 18 years and over	Male					Female				
		Total	18-29 years	30-44 years	45-64 years	65 years and over	Total	18-29 years	30-44 years	45-64 years	65 years and over
Black	84.3	81.8	86.3	86.0	77.6	59.2	87.3	89.7	91.4	82.1	72.1
Hispanic origin											
Hispanic	83.8	82.3	77.6	84.9	86.3	79.2[2]	86.0	89.4	89.2	76.9	74.2[2]
Non-Hispanic	89.3	88.0	91.2	91.5	84.1	73.2	90.8	93.3	94.3	88.4	78.0
Geographic region											
Northeast	91.4	91.0	96.4	93.4	85.9	78.3	91.9	92.7	96.7	88.3	82.4
Midwest	91.1	90.4	93.3	93.4	86.8	75.5	91.8	95.8	93.4	89.0	78.8
South	85.9	84.3	84.0	89.1	81.6	70.9	87.8	90.0	91.9	86.3	72.0
West	89.1	86.3	88.6	88.8	83.6	70.1	92.5	95.0	95.8	88.9	82.7
Marital status											
Currently married	89.6	87.6	90.6	90.8	84.2	76.6	92.0	93.1	95.2	89.0	80.0
Formerly married	86.1	85.3	89.7	92.7	82.8	66.5	86.6	94.0	91.2	86.2	76.7
Never married	89.9	88.7	89.0	89.3	87.0	74.6[2]	91.8	92.6	92.8	85.6	76.6[2]
Employment status											
Currently employed	90.6	88.9	89.6	91.4	85.1	74.3	92.9	94.6	94.4	89.7	78.1
Unemployed	90.5	88.7	88.0	94.5	80.1	61.5[2]	93.4	96.6	93.8	82.5	100.0[2]
Not in labor force	84.5	80.9	91.8	84.0	81.1	73.5	86.4	88.6	92.7	85.7	77.8

Source: Health Promotion and Disease Prevention: United States, 1990, National Center for Health Statistics, Vital and Health Statistics, Series 10, No. 185, p. 49. Notes: Data are based on household interviews of the civilian noninstitutionalized population. The survey design, general qualifications, and information on the reliability of the estimates are given in appendix 1 in the original source. Denominator for each cell excludes unknowns. 1. Includes persons with unknown sociodemographic characteristics. 2. Figure does not meet standard of reliability or precision (more than 30-percent relative standard error in numerator of percent or rate).

★ 548 ★

Risk Behaviors

Smoke Detectors in Homes

Percent of persons 18 years of age and over who had at least 1 working smoke detector in their home, by sex, age, and selected characteristics: United States, 1990.

Characteristic	Both sexes 18 years and over	Male					Female				
		Total	18-29 years	30-44 years	45-64 years	65 years and over	Total	18-29 years	30-44 years	45-64 years	65 years and over
All persons[1]	78.6	78.6	76.4	81.7	77.4	77.5	78.6	77.9	82.4	78.3	73.5
Education level											
Less than 12 years	67.0	67.2	62.6	68.1	65.4	72.0	66.8	63.0	64.7	68.6	68.4
12 years	78.4	77.7	76.1	79.1	76.9	79.7	78.9	77.0	81.4	79.4	76.0
More than 12 years	85.1	85.0	83.3	86.7	84.3	83.9	85.1	85.0	87.4	83.9	79.2

[Continued]

★548★

Smoke Detectors in Homes
[Continued]

Characteristic	Both sexes 18 years and over	Male					Female				
		Total	18-29 years	30-44 years	45-64 years	65 years and over	Total	18-29 years	30-44 years	45-64 years	65 years and over
13-15 years	82.7	82.0	81.9	82.1	82.1	81.3	83.4	82.6	85.7	83.6	77.6
16 years or more	87.5	87.7	85.7	90.3	85.6	85.8	87.3	89.4	89.1	84.3	81.6
Income											
Less than $10,000	65.1	63.3	71.4	61.3	53.3	58.9	66.0	68.0	63.3	63.7	66.9
$10,000-$19,999	70.8	69.4	67.0	68.7	66.1	75.3	71.9	69.7	73.3	72.7	72.2
$20,000-$34,999	79.3	78.4	77.2	79.6	75.3	82.7	80.2	80.6	81.6	78.2	79.9
$35,000-$49,999	84.6	84.2	80.7	87.5	80.9	86.1	85.1	85.9	86.4	83.5	79.9
$50,000 or more	88.2	88.0	87.2	90.8	85.7	85.6	88.5	89.0	90.6	87.0	79.8
Race											
White	79.6	79.6	76.7	82.4	78.6	79.3	79.7	78.9	83.4	79.3	75.1
Black	71.2	71.5	75.4	75.7	66.0	59.1	71.1	72.5	76.4	70.1	56.0
Hispanic origin											
Hispanic	66.2	64.3	62.2	71.1	58.2	58.7	67.8	65.7	72.2	67.0	60.3
Non-Hispanic	79.7	79.8	78.3	82.6	78.6	78.2	79.6	79.6	83.4	79.0	73.9
Geographic region											
Northeast	84.0	84.1	80.9	87.0	82.8	84.6	84.0	83.3	87.2	83.1	81.0
Midwest	83.0	83.3	80.8	85.9	82.2	83.7	82.7	80.6	85.2	84.2	79.0
South	73.0	73.1	72.1	77.5	70.4	69.7	73.0	73.8	78.4	71.0	65.5
West	77.4	76.8	74.3	78.3	77.7	76.1	77.9	77.0	81.1	78.6	71.8
Marital status											
Currently married	81.0	81.2	78.9	84.0	79.4	80.1	80.8	79.1	84.4	79.4	75.6
Formerly married	73.2	70.3	75.6	73.1	66.6	69.4	74.4	75.1	76.6	76.5	71.9
Never married	75.1	74.2	74.8	75.2	69.4	62.9	76.1	77.0	76.3	69.9	71.7
Employment status											
Currently employed	80.6	80.2	77.4	82.7	79.4	80.4	81.0	80.1	83.3	79.7	70.3
Unemployed	73.2	71.4	69.3	76.0	68.1	73.3[2]	75.0	72.9	74.1	79.4	88.5
Not in labor force	75.1	74.1	73.1	67.9	70.2	77.0	75.6	73.5	80.8	76.2	73.8

Source: Health Promotion and Disease Prevention: United States, 1990, National Center for Health Statistics, Vital and Health Statistics, Series 10, No. 185, p. 63. *Notes:* Data are based on household interviews of the civilian noninstitutionalized population. The survey design, general qualifications, and information on the reliability of the estimates are given in appendix 1 in the original source. Denominator for each cell excludes unknowns. 1. Includes persons with unknown sociodemographic characteristics. 2. Figure does not meet standard of reliability or precision (more than 30-percent relative standard error in numerator of percent or rate).

★ 549 ★

Risk Behaviors

Alcohol Consumption

Percent of persons 18 years of age and over who had consumed an average of 1 ounce or more of ethanol a day (two or more drinks of beer, wine, or liquor) in the past 2 weeks, by sex, age, and selected characteristics: United States, 1990.

Characteristic	Both sexes 18 years and over	Male					Female				
		Total	18-29 years	30-44 years	45-64 years	65 years and over	Total	18-29 years	30-44 years	45-64 years	65 years and over
All persons[1]	5.5	9.7	10.3	9.7	9.8	8.5	1.7	1.7	1.6	2.0	1.7
Education level											
Less than 12 years	5.1	9.2	11.1	12.8	9.1	5.4	1.5	1.7[2]	2.9	1.1[2]	1.0
12 years	5.9	11.2	12.2	11.9	10.2	9.1	1.7	1.8	1.5	1.9	1.7
More than 12 years	5.4	8.7	8.2	7.5	9.9	12.0	1.9	1.5	1.5	2.6	3.3
13-15 years	5.5	9.3	8.6	9.6	10.0	8.6	2.1	1.5	1.7	2.8	3.9
16 years or more	5.3	8.2	7.4	5.9	9.8	14.5	1.7	1.5[2]	1.3	2.5	2.4[2]
Income											
Less than $10,000	4.8	10.0	11.3	12.6	9.0	5.8	2.0	2.6	3.5	1.8[2]	0.6[2]
$10,000-$19,999	4.9	8.8	11.4	9.2	8.3	5.7	1.7	1.4[2]	2.4	1.7[2]	1.6
$20,000-$34,999	5.8	10.3	10.8	10.5	10.5	8.3	1.5	1.6	1.2	1.6	1.8[2]
$35,000-$49,999	5.6	9.3	7.6	10.3	8.0	12.8	1.5	0.8[2]	1.3	1.8[2]	3.6[2]
$50,000 or more	6.7	10.7	10.3	8.2	12.5	16.7	2.3	1.1[2]	1.7	3.0	6.6[2]
Race											
White	5.8	10.1	11.0	9.7	10.4	9.0	1.8	1.9	1.6	2.1	1.9
Black	4.3	8.2	8.1	11.8	5.6	3.4[2]	1.2	0.6[2]	2.1	1.2[2]	0.4[2]
Hispanic origin											
Hispanic	4.6	8.8	6.6	9.6	11.9	7.4[2]	1.1	1.7[2]	0.6[2]	0.6[2]	1.3[2]
Non-Hispanic	5.6	9.8	10.8	9.7	9.7	8.5	1.8	1.6	1.8	2.1	1.7
Geographic region											
Northeast	5.4	9.9	10.9	9.9	9.4	8.9	1.6	2.4	1.2	1.3[2]	1.4[2]
Midwest	5.6	10.2	12.4	10.7	8.6	7.8	1.4	0.8[2]	1.9	1.8	1.0[2]
South	5.2	9.0	9.3	9.4	9.1	7.0	1.8	1.8	1.6	2.0	1.8
West	6.1	10.3	9.1	8.9	12.6	11.6	2.2	1.7	1.8	2.7	3.0
Marital status											
Currently married	5.3	8.9	9.6	8.8	9.0	8.7	1.6	1.3	1.4	1.9	2.4
Formerly married	5.3	13.8	15.7	14.8	16.5	8.0	1.8	2.8[2]	2.2	2.2	1.2
Never married	6.6	10.3	10.6	10.6	6.4[2]	6.5[2]	2.1	1.9	2.8	1.9[2]	1.9[2]
Employment status											
Currently employed	6.1	9.6	9.7	9.6	9.6	8.6	1.9	2.0	1.5	2.1	2.5[2]

[Continued]

★ 549 ★

Alcohol Consumption
[Continued]

Characteristic	Both sexes 18 years and over	Male					Female				
		Total	18-29 years	30-44 years	45-64 years	65 years and over	Total	18-29 years	30-44 years	45-64 years	65 years and over
Unemployed	9.0	15.8	20.6	12.4	11.1[2]	20.5[2]	1.6[2]	0.2[2]	2.4[2]	1.7[2]	9.0[2]
Not in labor force	4.0	9.2	10.2	9.6	10.3	8.4	1.6	1.0[2]	1.9	1.7	1.6

Source: *Health Promotion and Disease Prevention: United States, 1990*, National Center for Health Statistics, Vital and Health Statistics, Series 10, No. 185, p. 50. *Notes:* Data are based on household interviews of the civilian noninstitutionalized population. The survey design, general qualifications, and information on the reliability of the estimates are given in appendix 1 in the original source. Denominator for each cell excludes unknowns. 1. Includes persons with unknown sociodemographic characteristics. 2. Figure does not meet standard of reliability or precision (more than 30-percent relative standard error in numerator of percent or rate).

★ 550 ★

Risk Behaviors

Alcohol Consumption: Use Within the Past Year

Percent of persons 18 years of age and over who had at least one drink of beer, wine, or liquor in the past year, by sex, age, and selected characteristics: United States, 1990.

Characteristic	Both sexes 18 years and over	Male					Female				
		Total	18-29 years	30-44 years	45-64 years	65 years and over	Total	18-29 years	30-44 years	45-64 years	65 years and over
All persons[1]	60.7	71.8	75.6	78.3	68.4	55.6	50.7	58.5	58.2	47.6	31.3
Education level											
Less than 12 years	42.6	57.8	67.2	71.2	54.0	44.2	29.2	44.4	39.2	28.5	16.6
12 years	59.8	71.9	74.6	77.7	67.3	58.7	50.3	55.8	56.5	46.4	36.4
More than 12 years	71.0	78.5	80.6	80.5	77.1	68.5	63.3	67.0	64.1	63.1	51.2
13-15 years	68.0	76.2	79.1	78.2	74.0	61.5	60.8	64.4	61.7	59.7	49.2
16 years or more	74.2	80.6	83.3	82.3	79.1	73.5	66.4	71.8	66.4	66.5	53.9
Income											
Less than $10,000	44.9	60.8	72.9	70.8	51.5	36.6	36.3	54.4	46.0	29.5	17.5
$10,000-$19,999	51.6	63.3	71.9	72.4	55.7	49.4	42.1	53.2	49.7	36.7	29.1
$20,000-$34,999	61.7	72.2	75.0	76.7	67.0	63.7	51.7	58.6	56.2	44.1	40.5
$35,000-$49,999	68.2	75.0	77.5	78.4	70.1	64.2	60.6	66.3	62.4	53.7	55.7
$50,000 or more	76.0	83.6	83.2	87.1	81.2	77.3	67.9	71.2	69.9	65.0	58.4
Race											
White	63.1	73.6	78.5	80.1	70.2	56.9	53.6	63.3	61.7	50.4	33.0
Black	46.4	62.7	64.8	71.3	57.9	39.8	33.3	36.0	40.5	30.0	15.0
Hispanic origin											
Hispanic	52.3	69.2	66.1	76.8	66.1	54.3	37.9	41.7	42.2	29.5	23.5
Non-Hispanic	61.4	72.0	76.8	78.5	68.5	55.7	51.8	60.8	59.7	49.0	31.6
Geographic region											
Northeast	65.6	75.9	77.3	82.3	73.9	62.2	56.5	64.8	63.2	56.9	36.6

[Continued]

★ 550 ★

Alcohol Consumption: Use Within the Past Year
[Continued]

Characteristic	Both sexes 18 years and over	Male					Female				
		Total	18-29 years	30-44 years	45-64 years	65 years and over	Total	18-29 years	30-44 years	45-64 years	65 years and over
Midwest	66.4	77.1	84.1	81.9	73.4	60.2	56.5	67.0	65.4	52.7	32.6
South	52.2	65.0	69.9	74.1	59.8	45.0	40.9	49.8	49.1	35.3	22.6
West	63.2	72.6	73.3	77.2	71.0	62.0	54.5	58.0	59.5	53.0	39.9
Marital status											
Currently married	61.9	71.7	79.5	77.9	68.1	57.3	52.1	57.5	57.4	48.2	36.1
Formerly married	51.2	72.2	85.0	83.9	72.8	50.2	42.7	62.1	63.2	46.0	27.5
Never married	64.9	72.0	72.5	76.4	61.5	47.2	56.2	58.9	56.0	47.2	32.6
Employment status											
Currently employed	68.3	76.0	77.5	79.2	71.4	62.1	59.0	64.1	60.9	52.1	44.7
Unemployed	65.5	73.7	76.8	74.6	68.3	57.7[2]	56.5	56.6	58.3	51.9	62.8[2]
Not in labor force	44.6	56.8	63.0	66.4	55.3	54.2	38.7	45.2	49.6	40.9	29.5

Source: Health Promotion and Disease Prevention: United States, 1990, National Center for Health Statistics, Vital and Health Statistics, Series 10, No. 185, p. 51. *Notes:* Data are based on household interviews of the civilian noninstitutionalized population. The survey design, general qualifications, and information on the reliability of the estimates are given in appendix 1 in the original source. Denominator for each cell excludes unknowns. 1. Includes persons with unknown sociodemographic characteristics. 2. Figure does not meet standard of reliability or precision (more than 30-percent relative standard error in numerator of percent or rate).

★ 551 ★

Risk Behaviors

Seatbelt Use

Percent of persons 18 years of age and over who wore seatbelts all or most of the time when riding in a car, by sex, age, and selected characteristics: United States, 1990.

Characteristic	Both sexes 18 years and over	Male					Female				
		Total	18-29 years	30-44 years	45-64 years	65 years and over	Total	18-29 years	30-44 years	45-64 years	65 years and over
All persons[1]	67.0	62.3	55.7	64.2	63.5	67.3	71.3	66.8	73.8	72.0	72.2
Education level											
Less than 12 years	55.7	51.7	41.9	45.0	54.4	61.7	59.3	51.1	51.4	61.2	66.1
12 years	62.4	55.0	48.6	53.9	58.0	67.5	68.3	61.3	68.2	71.4	74.4
More than 12 years	77.2	73.3	69.5	75.5	72.6	75.3	81.3	78.7	83.7	80.3	80.5
13-15 years	72.7	67.0	63.7	69.1	67.8	68.6	77.8	75.8	79.6	77.0	79.2
16 years or more	81.8	78.8	79.4	80.4	75.7	80.1	85.5	84.0	87.7	83.8	82.3
Income											
Less than $10,000	57.8	53.0	55.4	46.8	48.4	58.0	60.4	58.6	51.3	61.4	66.6
$10,000-$19,999	59.6	55.2	50.0	53.8	52.2	65.1	63.1	59.3	58.8	63.5	70.2
$20,000-$34,999	64.2	58.1	53.7	58.0	58.0	67.4	70.1	66.5	72.1	68.3	75.2
$35,000-$49,999	71.5	66.2	58.5	68.7	66.0	76.7	77.3	75.3	78.6	76.2	79.7

[Continued]

★ 551 ★

Seatbelt Use
[Continued]

Characteristic	Both sexes 18 years and over	Male					Female				
		Total	18-29 years	30-44 years	45-64 years	65 years and over	Total	18-29 years	30-44 years	45-64 years	65 years and over
$50,000 or more	77.0	71.9	60.6	75.5	73.7	73.9	82.5	77.4	85.3	82.0	81.1
Race											
White	67.8	62.6	54.8	65.1	63.8	68.0	72.5	68.1	75.3	72.7	73.3
Black	58.3	56.4	56.7	54.4	56.2	52.3	59.7	56.2	60.7	62.9	59.6
Hispanic origin											
Hispanic	64.0	58.7	53.6	58.7	64.5	71.1	68.5	62.7	70.2	74.0	74.0
Non-Hispanic	67.3	62.5	55.9	64.7	63.5	67.2	71.5	67.4	74.1	71.8	72.2
Geographic region											
Northeast	59.6	54.8	44.6	58.1	59.8	55.5	63.9	58.2	67.9	64.2	63.7
Midwest	65.2	59.2	50.2	60.8	61.4	67.1	70.7	64.2	72.4	72.6	73.4
South	69.2	64.9	60.3	66.4	64.3	70.4	73.0	69.8	75.2	73.2	73.5
West	72.8	68.7	64.5	70.3	68.2	74.3	76.6	72.2	78.4	77.6	78.7
Marital status											
Currently married	68.7	64.0	55.7	64.5	64.7	69.3	73.5	67.7	75.8	74.1	73.7
Formerly married	65.7	59.6	53.9	62.5	56.8	60.4	68.1	60.0	66.3	66.9	71.1
Never married	62.1	57.8	55.8	63.9	59.4	57.9	67.4	66.7	69.6	65.7	71.7
Employment status											
Currently employed	67.3	62.4	56.7	64.8	64.5	64.8	73.1	69.5	75.1	73.7	75.1
Unemployed	57.8	52.4	42.6	60.2	55.0	88.0	63.8	61.8	65.7	61.3	85.9[2]
Not in labor force	67.3	63.2	55.6	55.1	60.6	67.7	69.3	60.9	70.8	70.0	71.8

Source: *Health Promotion and Disease Prevention: United States, 1990*, National Center for Health Statistics, Vital and Health Statistics, Series 10, No. 185, p. 64.
Notes: Data are based on household interviews of the civilian noninstitutionalized population. The survey design, general qualifications, and information on the reliability of the estimates are given in appendix 1 in the original source. Denominator for each cell excludes unknowns. 1. Includes persons with unknown sociodemographic characteristics. 2. Figure does not meet standard of reliability or precision (more than 30-percent relative standard error in numerator of percent or rate).

Drug Use

★ 552 ★

Marijuana for Medicinal Purposes: States with Programs

The listing shows states in which programs exist for permitting the medicinal use of marijuana. Marijuana is frequently used, where legal, to combat nausea caused by drug or irradiation treatment of cancer and other diseases.

State	State	State
Delaware	Kentucky	North Dakota
Hawaii	Maryland	Pennsylvania
Idaho	Mississippi	South Dakota
Indiana	Missouri	Utah
Kansas	Nebraska	Wyoming

Source: USA TODAY, November 27, 1992, p. 10A. Primary source: Drug policy foundation.

★ 553 ★

Drug Use

Treatments Associated with Office Visits for Persons 55 Years and Over

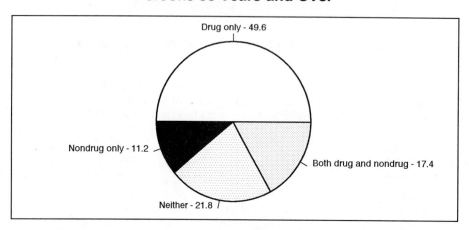

Of the estimated 205 million office visits by the 55-and-over population in 1985, the most common treatment modality was drug therapy alone, accounting for 50 percent of all treatments. Only 22 percent of office visits were associated with no form of treatment.

Therapy	Percent
Drug only	49.6
Neither	21.8
Nondrug only	11.2
Both drug and nondrug	17.4

Source: Health Data on Older Americans: United States, 1992, Centers for Disease Control and Prevention/National Center for Health Statistics, Vital and Health Statistics, Series 3: Analytic and Epidemiological Studies, No. 27, p. 188.

★ 554 ★

Drug Use

Drugs Most Frequently Prescribed by Office-Based Physicians, 1985

The top 50 drugs for each age cohort, by generic ingredient, are shown. The total of 297 million drug mentions resulted in 371 million drug ingredients (because a drug mention may contain multiple generic ingredients). Hydrochlorothiazide, alone or in combination with other drugs, was the most frequently reported generic ingredient for patients 55-64 and 65-74 years old. Digoxin replaced hydrochlorothiazide in the 75-and-over cohort, with hydrochlorothiazide ranking second. Digoxin was the only drug in the top 10 to show a consistent statistically significant increase in frequency of mention with age.

Age and generic ingredient	Number of mentions in thousands	Rank	Therapeutic use
55-64 years			
All drugs	125,143		
Acetaminophen	2,247	4	Analgesic, antipyretic
Allopurinol	776	34	Gout, hyperuricemia
Alprazolan	598	50	Anxiety disorders
Amitriptyline	739	38	Antidepressant
Ampicillin	629	49	Antibiotic
Aspirin	2,016	5	Analgesic, antipyretic, anti-inflammatory
Atenolol	1,787	10	Antihypertensive, angina pectoris
Bacitracin	621	49	Antibiotic
Cephalexin	985	25	Antibiotic
Chlorpheniramine	968	26	Antihistaminic
Chlorpropamide	816	31	Hypoglycemic
Cimetidine	1,035	24	Duodenal or gastric ulcer
Codeine	1,462	12	Analgesic, antitussive
Dexamethasone	770	35	Steroidal anti-inflammatory agent
Diazepam	694	42	Anxiety disorders
Digoxin	1,960	7	Cardiotonic
Dipyridamole	1,123	22	Angina pectoris
Erythromycin	1,415	15	Antibiotic
Estrogens	1,482	11	Estrogen replacement therapy, oral contraceptive
Furosemide	1,965	6	Diuretic, antihypertensive
Guaifenesin	662	43	Expectorant
Hydralazine	717	39	Antihypertensive
Hydrochlorothiazide	5,992	1	Diuretic, antihypertensive
Hydrocortisone	812	32	Steroidal anti-inflammatory agent
Ibuprofen	1,441	13	Nonsteroidal anti-inflammatory agent
Indomethacin	650	46	Nonsteroidal anti-inflammatory agent
Insulin	1,401	16	Hypoglycemic
Isosorbide	869	30	Vasodilator
Methyldopa	1,238	18	Antihypertensive
Metoprolol	1,164	20	Antihypertensive, angina pectoris
Naproxen	1,206	19	Nonsteroidal anti-inflammatory agent
Neomycin	942	27	Antibiotic
Nifedipine	657	44	Angina, antihypertensive
Nitroglycerin	1,836	8	Vasodilator

[Continued]

★ 554 ★

Drugs Most Frequently Prescribed by Office-Based Physicians, 1985
[Continued]

Age and generic ingredient	Number of mentions in thousands	Rank	Therapeutic use
Phenylephrine	1,156	21	Sympathomimetic
Phenylpropanolamine	1,056	23	Sympathomimetic
Polymixin B36	801	33	Antibiotic
Potassium replacement solutions	1,827	9	Replacement preparation
Prazosin	702	41	Antihypertensive
Prednisone	1,345	17	Steroidal anti-inflammatory agent
Propoxyphene	704	40	Analgesic
Propranolol	2,376	3	Arrhythmia, angina pectoris, antihypertensive, migraine
Sulfamethoxazole	912	28	Antibiotic
Theophylline	1,428	14	Bronchodilator
Timolol	762	36	Glaucoma
Triamcinolone	744	37	Steroidal anti-inflammatory agent
Triamterene	2,498	2	Diuretic, antihypertensive
Trimethoprim	894	29	Antibiotic
Vitamin B-12	653	45	Replacement preparation
Warfarin	641	47	Anticoagulant
65-74 years			
All drugs	136,256		
Acetaminophen	2,189	9	Analgesic, antipyretic
Albuterol	712	45	Bronchodilator
Aspirin	3,170	4	Analgesic, antipyretic, anti-inflammatory
Atenolol	1,148	20	Antihypertensive, angina pectoris
Calcium replacement agents	887	29	Replacement preparation
Captopril	734	43	Antihypertensive, congestive heart failure
Cephalexin	856	33	Antibiotic
Chlorpheniramine	884	31	Antihistaminic
Chlorpropamide	787	40	Hypoglycemic
Cimetidine	1,234	19	Duodenal or gastric ulcer
Codeine	905	28	Analgesic, antitussive
Dexamethasone	846	34	Steroidal anti-inflammatory agent
Digoxin	3,990	2	Cardiotonic
Diltiazem	723	44	Angina pectoris
Dipyridamole	1,674	11	Angina pectoris, anti-platelet
Ergocalciferol	698	47	Replacement preparation
Erythromycin	1,007	24	Antibiotic
Estrogens	884	30	Estrogen replacement therapy, oral contraceptive
Furosemide	3,098	5	Diuretic, antihypertensive
Hydralazine	694	48	Antihypertensive

[Continued]

★ 554 ★

Drugs Most Frequently Prescribed by Office-Based Physicians, 1985
[Continued]

Age and generic ingredient	Number of mentions in thousands	Rank	Therapeutic use
Hydrochlorothiazide	6,704	1	Diuretic, antihypertensive
Ibuprofen	1,557	15	Nonsteroidal anti-inflammatory agent
Insulin	1,638	12	Hypoglycemic
Isosorbide	1,514	16	Vasodilator
Levothyroxine	796	38	Thyroid replacement
Meclizine	687	49	Anti-emetic
Methyldopa	1,621	13	Antihypertensive
Metoprolol	979	25	Antihypertensive, angina pectoris
Naproxen	1,390	18	Nonsteroidal anti-inflammatory agent
Neomycin	1,029	23	Antibiotic
Nifedipine	811	37	Angina, antihypertensive
Nitroglycerin	2,451	7	Vasodilator
Phenylephrine	793	39	Sympathomimetic
Polymixin B36	966	26	Antibiotic
Potassium replacement solutions	3,182	3	Replacement preparation
Prazosin	704	46	Antihypertensive
Prednisolone	933	26	Steroidal anti-inflammatory agent
Prednisone	1,489	17	Steroidal anti-inflammatory agent
Propoxyphene	815	36	Analgesic
Propranolol	2,425	8	Arrhythmia, angina pectoris, antihypertensive, migraine
Reserpine	866	32	Antihypertensive
Spironolactone	741	42	Diuretic
Sulfamethoxazole	1,057	22	Antibiotic
Sulindac	673	50	Nonsteroidal anti-inflammatory agent
Tetracycline	785	41	Antibiotic
Theophylline	1,758	10	Bronchodilator
Timolol	1,578	14	Glaucoma
Triamterene	2,712	6	Diuretic, antihypertensive
Trimethoprim	1,131	21	Antibiotic
Warfarin	823	35	Anticoagulant

Source: *Health Data on Older Americans: United States, 1992*, Centers for Disease Control and Prevention/National Center for Health Statistics, Vital and Health Statistics, Series 3: Analytic and Epidemiological Studies, No. 27, pp. 196-197.

★ 555 ★
Drug Use

Drug Prescriptions, by Therapeutic Category

Data are based on reporting by a sample of office-based physicians.

Therapeutic category[1]	55-64 years		65-74 years		75 years and over	
	Number of mentions in thousands	Percent distribution	Number of mentions in thousands	Percent distribution	Number of mentions in thousands	Percent distribution
All drugs	99,132	100.0	109,785	100.0	88,797	100.0
Anti-infective agents (systemic)	7,860	7.9	7,651	7.0	4,722	5.3
Antibiotics	6,118	6.2	5,775	5.3	3,113	3.5
Cephalosporins	1,613	1.6	1,340	1.2	761	0.9
Erythromycins	1,407	1.4	905	0.8	574	0.6
Penicillins	1,765	1.8	1,828	1.7	933	1.1
Tetracyclines	903	0.9	1,230	1.1	594	0.7
Sulfonamides	1,021	1.0	1,173	1.1	906	1.0
All other anti-infective agents	721	0.7	703	0.6	703	0.8
Antineoplastic agents	1,464	1.5	1,527	1.4	908	1.0
Autonomic drugs	2,933	3.0	3,522	3.2	2,452	2.8
Anticholinergic agents	1,080	1.1	1,459	1.3	1,038	1.2
Sympathomimetic (adrenergic) agents	1,031	1.0	1,243	1.1	811	0.9
Skeletal muscle relaxants	759	0.8	387[2]	0.4[2]	206[2]	0.2[2]
Blood formation and coagulation agents	1,024	1.0	1,101	1.0	1,375	1.5
Anti-anemia drugs	369[2]	0.4[2]	258[2]	0.2[2]	628	0.7
Cardiovascular drugs	18,665	18.8	24,045	21.9	21,038	23.7
Cardiac drugs	6,959	7.0	10,157	9.3	8,990	10.1
Antihypertensive agents	7,518	7.6	7,756	7.1	6,053	6.8
Vasodilating agents	3,974	4.0	5,999	5.5	5,888	6.6
Analgesics and antipyretics	10,382	10.5	11,424	10.4	8,122	9.1
Nonsteroidal anti-inflammatory agents	7,612	7.7	8,711	7.9	5,863	6.6
Psychotropic drugs	7,060	7.1	6,527	5.9	4,738	5.3
Anxiolytics, sedatives, and hypnotics	4,231	4.3	4,147	3.8	2,785	3.1
Antidepressants	1,948	2.0	1,746	1.6	1,364	1.5
Major tranquilizers and antimanic drugs	881	0.9	634	0.5	589	0.7
Electrolyte, caloric, and water balance agents	11,558	11.7	15,013	13.7	14,164	16.0
Diuretics	8,293	8.4	10,280	9.4	9,808	11.0
Replacement solutions	2,289	2.3	3,913	3.6	3,614	4.1
Antihistamines, antitussives, expectorants, and mucolytic agents	4,233	4.3	3,141	2.9	1,888	2.1
Eye, ear, nose, and throat preparations	3,966	4.0	5,913	5.4	7,441	8.4
Anti-infectives	1,074	1.1	1,352	1.2	1,911	2.2
Antibiotics	687	0.7	958	0.9	1,466	1.7
Anti-inflammatory agents	596	0.6	1,120	1.0	1,188	1.3
Miotics	993	1.0	1,878	1.7	2,418	2.7

[Continued]

★ 555 ★

Drug Prescriptions, by Therapeutic Category
[Continued]

Therapeutic category[1]	55-64 years		65-74 years		75 years and over	
	Number of mentions in thousands	Percent distri-bution	Number of mentions in thousands	Percent distri-bution	Number of mentions in thousands	Percent distri-bution
Gastrointestinal drugs	4,158	4.2	5,256	4.8	3,844	4.3
Antacids and absorbents	594	0.6	698	0.6	509	0.6
Cathartics and laxatives	594	0.6	1,046	1.0	784	0.9
Emetics and anti-emetics	653	0.7	896	0.8	763	0.9
Miscellaneous gastrointestinal drugs (used chiefly in treating duodenal ulcer)	1,920	1.9	2,149	2.0	1,482	1.7
Hormones and synthetic substances	10,154	10.2	9,333	8.5	6,103	6.9
Adrenals	3,145	3.2	3,003	2.7	2,039	2.3
Estrogens	2,311	2.3	1,311	1.2	564	0.6
Antidiabetic agents	3,045	3.1	3,443	3.1	2,523	2.8
Insulins	1,401	1.4	1,631	1.5	881	1.0
Thyroid and antithyroid agents	1,061	1.1	1,320	1.2	891	1.0
Serums, toxins, and vaccines	780	0.8	833	0.8	843	1.0
Skin and mucous membrane agents	3,689	3.7	3,445	3.1	2,424	2.7
Anti-infectives	1,270	1.3	1,437	1.3	999	1.1
Fungicides	344[2]	0.3[2]	429[2]	0.4[2]	230[2]	0.3[2]
Anti-inflammatory agents	1,451	1.5	1,373	1.3	951	1.1
Keratolytic agents	118[2]	0.1[2]	28[2]	-	45[2]	-
Smooth muscle relaxants	1,895	1.9	2,092	1.9	1,465	1.7
Vitamins	1,359	1.4	1,516	1.4	2,015	2.3
Vitamin B complex	771	0.8	886	0.8	1,460	1.6
Multivitamin preparations	296[2]	0.3[2]	252	0.2	255[2]	0.3[2]
Other or undetermined	7,952	8.0	7,446	6.8	5,255	5.9

Source: Health Data on Older Americans: United States, 1992, Centers for Disease Control and Prevention/National Center for Health Statistics, Vital and Health Statistics, Series 3: Analytic and Epidemiological Studies, No. 27, pp. 202-203. Primary source: National Center for Health Statistics: Data from the National Ambulatory Medical Care Survey. *Notes:* Both mentions as the generic form of single-ingredient drugs and mentions as an ingredient of combination drugs are included. Vitamins, minerals, and vaccine are omitted. "-" indicates quantity is zero. 1. Based on American Hospital Formulary Service Classification System, Drug Product Information File, The American Druggist Blue Book Data Center, San Bruno, California, 1985. 2. Figure does not meet standard of reliability or precision.

★ 556 ★

Drug Use

Drug Prescriptions, by Physician's Specialty

Data are based on reporting by a sample of office-based physicians.

Patient age, physician identity, and specialty	Office visits		Drug mentions		Percent of office visits during which-	
	Number in thousands	Percent distri- bution	Number in thousands	Percent distri- bution	1 drug or more mentioned[1]	2 drugs or more mentioned[1]
55-64 years						
All physicians	75,044	100.0	99,132	100.0	64.9	34.8
Physician identity:						
Doctor of medicine	70,760	94.3	93,848	94.7	64.9	35.0
Doctor of osteopathy	4,284	5.7	5,284	5.3	65.4	32.8
Specialty:						
General or family practice	23,511	31.3	34,988	35.3	76.0	39.9
Internal medicine	12,644	16.8	23,664	23.9	81.1	51.0
Obstetrics and gynecology	2,398	3.2	2,054	2.1	60.0	17.5
Ophthalmology	5,937	7.9	3,806	3.8	39.5	16.7
Orthopedic surgery	4,285	5.7	2,420	2.4	38.0	12.0
General surgery	4,979	6.6	3,091	3.1	34.5	16.0
Dermatology	2,870	3.8	2,956	3.0	60.6	28.2
Psychiatry	1,859	2.5	2,308	2.3	62.8	36.0
Otolaryngology	1,983	2.6	1,363	1.4	47.2	17.8
Urologic surgery	2,090	2.8	1,230	1.2	47.4	8.7
Cardiology	2,820	3.7	7,810	7.9	85.8	72.4
Neurology	777	1.0	700	0.7	54.4	21.2
All other specialties	8,892	11.9	12,742	12.9	64.6	37.2
65-74 years						
All physicians	75,427	100.0	109,785	100.0	67.1	38.5
Physician identity:						
Doctor of medicine	71,833	95.2	104,073	94.8	66.7	38.4
Doctor of osteopathy	3,594	4.8	5,712	5.2	74.5	41.2
Specialty:						
General or family practice	21,735	28.8	37,061	33.8	80.2	46.0
Internal medicine	16,699	22.1	32,970	30.0	81.0	54.1
Obstetrics and gynecology	1,482	2.0	1,167	1.1	48.7	20.7
Ophthalmology	8,435	11.2	6,215	5.7	44.3	19.2
Orthopedic surgery	2,682	3.6	1,379	1.3	34.8	9.3
General surgery	4,790	6.4	3,989	3.6	43.5	21.0
Dermatology	2,617	3.5	2,177	2.0	52.5	19.5
Psychiatry	882	1.2	1,455	1.3	78.7	45.3
Otolaryngology	1,805	2.4	1,096	1.0	40.5	13.7
Urologic surgery	2,762	3.7	1,529	1.4	45.5	8.7

[Continued]

★ 556 ★

Drug Prescriptions, by Physician's Specialty
[Continued]

Patient age, physician identity, and specialty	Office visits		Drug mentions		Percent of office visits during which-	
	Number in thousands	Percent distri- bution	Number in thousands	Percent distri- bution	1 drug or more mentioned[1]	2 drugs or more mentioned[1]
Cardiology	2,950	3.9	8,235	7.5	85.8	72.3
Neurology	626	0.8	741	0.7	66.3	35.0
All other specialties	7,961	10.5	11,771	10.7	64.9	39.0
75 years and over						
All physicians	55,111	100.0	88,797	100.0	69.7	42.6
Physician identity:						
Doctor of medicine	52,620	95.5	84,677	95.4	69.4	42.4
Doctor of osteopathy	2,492	4.5	4,120	4.6	76.3	47.3
Specialty:						
General or family practice	16,206	29.4	31,054	35.0	82.5	51.0
Internal medicine	12,171	22.1	27,152	30.6	82.7	59.1
Obstetrics and gynecology	387[2]	0.7	403[2]	0.5[2]	63.1	23.1
Ophthalmology	9,127	16.6	8,188	9.2	53.5	25.6
Orthopedic surgery	1,699	3.1	719	0.8	31.4	9.2
General surgery	3,316	6.0	2,867	3.2	49.9	21.0
Dermatology	1,791	3.2	1,609	1.8	55.0	24.2
Psychiatry	293[2]	0.5[2]	674	0.8	82.9	67.7
Otolaryngology	933	1.7	612	0.7	40.6	15.5
Urologic surgery	1,872	3.4	1,134	1.3	47.3	10.8
Cardiology	2,065	3.7	6,378	7.2	87.0	78.3
Neurology	422[2]	0.8	419[2]	0.5	67.4	25.0
All other specialities	4,830	8.8	7,588	8.5	63.5	42.7

Source: Health Data on Older Americans: United States, 1992, Centers for Disease Control and Prevention/National Center for Health Statistics, Vital and Health Statistics, Series 3: Analytic and Epidemiological Studies, No. 27, pp. 204-205. Primary source: National Center for Health Statistics: Data from the National Ambulatory Medical Care Survey. *Notes:* Both mentions as the generic form of single-ingredient drugs and mentions as an ingredient of combination drugs are included. Vitamins, minerals, and vaccines are omitted. 1. Only mentions of drugs specifically intended for the principal (first-listed) diagnosis are included. Mentions of drugs associated with other-listed diagnosis or utilized for any other reason are not included. 2. Figure does not meet standard of reliability or precision.

★ 557 ★

Drug Use

Vitamin and Mineral Supplement Use

Data are based on household interviews of the civilian noninstitutionalized population.

Characteristic	Total number in thousands	Percent
Sex		
Male	21,652	35.0
Female	27,807	47.2
Age		
55-64 years	22,073	41.9
65-74 years	16,906	42.7
75-84 years	8,652	40.6
65 years and over	27,386	41.8
75 years and over	10,480	40.3
85 years and over	1,828	38.8
Race		
White	44,160	43.9
Black	4,360	21.6
All other	939	40.1
Education		
High school or less	37,543	39.0
More than high school	11,916	50.7
Income		
Less than $20,000	25,676	38.1
$20,000 or more	21,632	46.5
Respondent-assessed health status		
Excellent or very good	20,751	44.8
Good	15,944	21.8
Fair or poor	12,502	36.7

Source: Health Data on Older Americans: United States, 1992, Centers for Disease Control and Prevention/National Center for Health Statistics, Vital and Health Statistics, Series 3: Analytic and Epidemiological Studies, No. 27, p. 206. Primary source: National Center for Health Statistics: Data from the 1986 National Health Interview Survey Supplement on Vitamins and Minerals. *Notes:* Current usage includes those reporting nonprescription and prescription vitamin or mineral supplement use in the past 2 weeks.

★ 558 ★

Drug Use

Vitamin and Mineral Supplement Use, by Type Used

Data are based on household interviews of the civilian noninstitutionalized population.

Vitamin or mineral supplement used	Total	Sex		Age			
		Male	Female	55-64 years	65-74 years	75-84 years	85 years and over
				Percent			
Vitamin							
Vitamin A	24.2	21.6	26.3	24.9	24.1	23.8	20.3
Vitamin C	33.1	29.5	36.0	33.6	33.2	32.6	29.1
Vitamin D	25.9	21.4	29.4	25.9	26.3	25.9	22.0
Vitamin E	28.5	26.1	30.3	29.5	28.5	26.4	25.7
Vitamin B-6	27.5	24.3	29.9	28.3	26.6	27.4	25.1
Vitamin B-12	27.1	24.0	29.5	27.7	26.7	26.6	25.1
Folic acid	23.2	21.0	24.9	24.3	23.0	20.7	22.5
Niacin	27.1	24.4	29.3	28.1	26.6	26.5	23.5
Riboflavin	27.2	24.3	29.5	28.1	26.5	26.8	24.7
Thiamine	27.6	24.6	29.9	28.5	27.0	27.0	25.1
Mineral							
Calcium	22.5	15.5	28.1	22.7	24.3	19.3	19.7
Copper	14.9	13.3	16.1	14.8	15.8	13.3	15.8
Iodine	14.9	13.7	15.9	14.7	15.9	13.1	16.9
Iron	20.0	17.7	21.8	19.8	21.0	18.8	19.9
Magnesium	16.5	14.9	17.8	15.9	18.1	14.9	17.3
Phosphorus	9.8	8.8	10.7	9.7	10.3	9.0	11.6
Potassium	11.7	10.0	13.1	11.0	13.4	10.2	12.4
Selenium	9.5	8.0	10.7	9.1	10.7	8.1	10.8[1]
Zinc	17.3	15.8	18.5	17.3	18.5	15.1	18.2

Source: Health Data on Older Americans: United States, 1992, Centers for Disease Control and Prevention/National Center for Health Statistics, Vital and Health Statistics, Series 3: Analytic and Epidemiological Studies, No. 27, p. 207. Primary source: National Center for Health Statistics: Data from the 1986 National Health Interview Survey Supplement on Vitamins and Minerals. *Notes:* Current usage includes those reporting nonprescription and prescription vitamin or mineral supplement use in the past 2 weeks. 1. Figure does not meet standard of reliability or precision.

★ 559 ★

Drug Use

Commonly Prescribed Psychotropic Drugs and Their Side Effects: Antipsychotic (Neuroleptic) Drugs

Table shows the antipsychotic drugs most often prescribed and their degree of side effects ranging from minimal to marked.

Generic name	Brand name	Incidence of side effects			
		Sedation	Hypertension	Anti-cholinergic symptoms[1]	Extra-pyramidal symptoms[2]
Chloropromazine	Thorazine	Marked	Marked	Marked	Mild
Thioridizine	Mellaril	Marked	Marked	Marked	Mild
Acetophenazine	Tindal	Mild	Mild	Moderate	Mild
Perphenazine	Trilafon	Mild	Mild	Moderate	Moderate
Loxapine	Loxitane	Mild	Mild	Moderate	Moderate
Molindone	Moban	Mild	Mild	Moderate	Moderate
Trifluoperazine	Stelazine	Mild	Mild	Mild	Marked
Thiothixene	Navane	Mild	Mild	Mild	Marked
Fluphenazine	Prolixin	Mild	Mild	Mild	Marked
Haloperidol	Haldol	Minimal	Minimal	Mild	Marked

Source: U.S. Congress, "Resident Assessment: The Springboard to Quality of Care and Quality of Life for Nursing Home Residents," Workshop before the Special Committee on Aging, United States Senate, October 22, 1990, 101-30, U.S. Government Printing Office, Washington, D.C., p. 220. *Notes:* 1. Anticholinergic symptoms include: dry mouth, constipation, urinary retention, blurred vision, confusion, disorientation, short-term memory loss, hallucinations, insomnia, agitation and restlessness, picking behaviors, fever. 2. Extrapyramidal symptoms include: movement disorders, such as Parkinsonism, dyskinesias, and akathisia. Antidepressants (except Amoxapine) and antianxiety/hypnotics do not produce extrapyramidal side effects.

★ 560 ★

Drug Use

Commonly Prescribed Psychotropic Drugs and Their Side Effects: Antidepressant Drugs

Table shows the antidepressant drugs most often prescribed and their degree of side effects ranging from none to very strong.

Generic name	Brand name	Incidence of side effects		
		Sedation	Hypertension	Anti-cholinergic symptoms[3]
Cyclic antidepressants				
Imipramine	Tofranil	Mild	Moderate	Mod-strong
Desipramine	Norpramin	Mild	Mild-mod	Mild
Doxepin	Adapin Sinequan	Mod-strong	Moderate	Strong
Amitriptyline	Elavil Triavil	Strong	Moderate	Very strong

[Continued]

★ 560 ★

Commonly Prescribed Psychotropic Drugs and Their Side Effects: Antidepressant Drugs
[Continued]

Generic name	Brand name	Incidence of side effects		
		Sedation	Hypertension	Anti-cholinergic symptoms[3]
Nortriptyline	Aventyl Pamelor	Mild	Mild	Moderate
Maprotiline	Ludiomil	Mod-strong	Moderate	Moderate
Amoxapine[1]	Asendin	Mild	Moderate	Moderate
Fluoxetine	Prozac	Variable	Nil	Nil
Triazolopyridine Antidepressant				
Trazodone	Desyrel	Mod-strong	Moderate	Mild
MAO inhibitors[2]	Nardil	Mild	Moderate	Mild
Phenelzine	Parnate	Mild	Moderate	Mild
Tranylcypromine				
	Wellbutrin	None	Nil	Nil
Other				
Bupropion		May cause agitation High incidence of seizures		

Source: U.S. Congress, "Resident Assessment: The Springboard to Quality of Care and Quality of Life for Nursing Home Residents," Workshop before the Special Committee on Aging, United States Senate, October 22, 1990, 101-30, U.S. Government Printing Office, Washington, D.C., p. 220. *Notes:* 1. Also a neuroleptic drug with all the neuroleptic side effects. 2. Special diet required; many drug interactions. 3. Anticholinergic symptoms include: dry mouth, constipation, urinary retention, blurred vision, confusion, disorientation, short-term memory loss, hallucinations, insomnia, agitation and restlessness, picking behaviors, fever.

★ 561 ★

Drug Use

Commonly Prescribed Psychotropic Drugs and Their Side Effects: Antianxiety and Hypnotic Drugs

Generic name	Brand name	Duration of action
Benzodiazepines		
Triazolam	Halcion	Very short
Oxazepam	Serax	Short
Temazepam	Restoril	Short
Lorazepam	Activan	Short
Alprazolam	Xanax	Medium
Chlorodiazepoxide	Librium	Long
Diazepam	Valium	Long
Chlorazepate	Tranxene	Long

[Continued]

★ 561 ★

Commonly Prescribed Psychotropic Drugs and Their Side Effects: Antianxiety and Hypnotic Drugs
[Continued]

Generic name	Brand name	Duration of action
Flurazepam D	almane V	ery long
Barbiturates		
Antihistamines		
Dephenhydramine	Benadryl	Moderate
Hydroxyzine	Vistaril	Moderate
Chloral hydrate	Noctec	Long
Other		
Buspirone	Buspar	Not meaningful

Source: U.S. Congress, "Resident Assessment: The Springboard to Quality of Care and Quality of Life for Nursing Home Residents," Workshop before the Special Committee on Aging, United States Senate, October 22, 1990, 101-30, U.S. Government Printing Office, Washington, D.C., p. 221.

★ 562 ★

Drug Use

Number of Prescriptions for Medicare Beneficiaries 65 Years of Age or Older in 1987

Despite their much poorer health and greater need, older Blacks receive prescriptions, on the average, at about the same rate as elderly Whites. Moreover, the amount expended for prescriptions, on the average, is 10.9 percent less for elderly Blacks than elderly Whites: $238 vs. $267 in 1987.

	Prescriptions (in millions)	Average prescriptions per person
Total	487	15.3
White	421	15.4
Black	45	15.5

Source: U.S. Congress, "Profiles in Aging America: Meeting the Health Care Needs of the Nation's Black Elderly," Joint Hearing Before the Special Committee on Aging and the Congressional Black Caucus Health Braintrust, United States Senate, September 28, 1990, 101-29, U.S. Government Printing Office, Washington, D.C., p. 128. Primary source: "National Medical Expenditure Survey Prescribed Medicines: A Summary of Use and Expenditures by Medicare Beneficiaries," Research Findings 3, NCHSR, Dept. of Health and Human Services, Public Health Service, National Center for Health Services Research, and Health Care Technology Assessment, PHS-89-3448, Sept. 1989, p. 12.

★ 563 ★

Drug Use

Mixing Drugs

People over 65 run the greatest risk of a bad drug interaction since they make up 12 percent of the population and take 25 percent of all medications. Also, older Americans are heavy users of over-the-counter drugs. With advancing age, major changes occur in the body's ability to absorb and dispose of drugs and alcohol.

Source: U.S. Department of Health and Human Services, National Institute on Aging, *Bound for Good Health: A Collection of Age Pages.*

★ 564 ★

Drug Use

Arthritis Medicines

According to research conducted by the Food and Drug Administration, the medicines taken most by people over age 45 are those used to relieve the discomfort of arthritis.

Of the more than 100 forms of arthritis, osteoarthritis, rheumatoid arthritis, and gout are the most common. According to the Arthritis foundation, more than 9 million Americans over 65 have some symptoms of osteoarthritis.

Source: U.S. Department of Health and Human Services, National Institute on Aging, *Bound for Good Health: A Collection of Age Pages.*

★ 565 ★

Drug Use

Prescription Drug Use by the Elderly

People over 65 make up 13 percent of the American population, yet they take 30 percent of all prescription drugs sold in this country. As a group, older people tend to have more long-term illnesses—such as arthritis, diabetes, high-blood pressure, and heart disease—than younger people. And because they often have a number of diseases or disabilities at the same time, it is very common for them to be taking many different drugs.

Source: National Institute on Aging, *Bound for Good Health: A Collection of Age Pages.*

Self-Assessment of Health

★ 566 ★

Respondent-Assessed Health Status of Persons Aged 65+, by Sex and Family Income, 1989

Characteristic	All persons[1] (000)	Respondent-assessed health status (%)[2]					
		Total[3]	Excellent	Very good	Good	Fair	Poor
All persons 65+[4]	29,219	100.0	16.4	23.1	31.9	19.3	9.2
Sex							
Men	12,143	100.0	16.9	23.2	30.8	18.4	10.7
Women	17,076	100.0	16.1	23.0	32.8	20.0	8.1
Family income							
Under $10,000	5,612	100.0	10.3	19.4	29.7	25.0	15.6
$10,000 to $19,999	8,002	100.0	14.8	21.7	33.9	21.1	8.5
$20,000 to $34,999	5,242	100.0	20.2	25.7	32.5	15.7	5.9
$35,000 and over	3,484	100.0	26.0	26.8	30.3	11.7	5.1

Source: *Aging America, Trends and Projections*, prepared by the U.S. Senate Special Committee on Aging, the American Association of Retired Persons, the Federal Council on the Aging, and the U.S. Administration on Aging, 1991, Washington, D.C., p. 109. Primary source: National Center for Health Statistics, "Current Estimates from the National Health Interview Survey, 1989." *Vital and Health Statistics*, Series 10, No. 176, October 1990. Data are based on household interviews of the civilian, noninstitutional population. *Notes:* Percentages may not add to 100 percent due to rounding. 1. Includes unknown health status. 2. Excludes unknown health status. 3. The categories related to this concept result from asking the respondent, "Would you say—health is excellent, very good, good, fair, or poor?" As such, it is based on the respondent's opinion and not directly on any clinical evidence. 4. Includes unknown family income.

★ 567 ★

Self-Assessment of Health

Perception of Health Among Persons 65 Years of Age and Older in 1988

[Data are in percent]

	All races	White	Black
Excellent	16.3	17.0	9.0
Very Good	21.5	22.0	16.4
Good	32.8	33.3	26.4
Fair	19.9	19.1	29.3
Poor	9.5	8.6	18.9

Source: U.S. Congress, "Profiles in Aging America: Meeting the Health Care Needs of the Nation's Black Elderly," Joint Hearing Before the Special Committee on Aging and the Congressional Black Caucus Health Braintrust, United States Senate, September 28, 1990, 101-29, U.S. Government Printing Office, Washington, D.C., p. 115. Primary source: "Current Estimates from the National Health Interview Survey, 1988," U.S. Department of Health and Human Services, Public Health Service, Centers for Disease Control, National Center for Health Statistics, Series 10, No. 173, October 1989, p. 114.

Health Examinations

★ 568 ★

Pap Smears and Breast Examinations

Women 18 years of age and over who had had a Pap smear and who had had a breast examination, 1990.

Characteristic	Pap smear					Breast examination				
	Total	18-29 years	30-44 years	45-64 years	65 years and over	Total	18-29 years	30-44 years	45-64 years	65 years and over
All women[1]	50.1	63.9	55.2	43.6	30.4	53.1	62.2	55.6	49.1	42.0
Education level										
Less than 12 years	37.9	60.8	44.6	33.3	24.7	43.0	56.3	44.0	40.0	37.1
12 years	49.6	63.8	52.7	43.7	31.0	52.2	61.3	53.3	48.5	42.2
More than 12 years	57.2	65.1	60.0	50.2	40.0	59.7	65.5	60.3	55.8	51.0
13-15 years	54.6	64.0	56.2	47.3	35.3	56.9	63.7	56.3	52.2	48.1
16 years or more	60.3	67.1	63.6	53.2	46.8	63.2	68.7	64.1	59.6	55.0
Income										
Less than $10,000	41.0	60.8	43.5	31.4	25.1	45.5	59.5	43.1	38.6	36.7
$10,000-$19,999	44.0	62.3	46.6	36.2	29.2	47.0	60.0	45.8	40.8	40.2
$20,000-$34,999	50.1	64.1	53.6	40.0	32.2	53.0	62.7	53.8	45.5	44.8
$35,000-$49,999	55.2	67.2	56.0	46.6	40.9	58.3	66.5	57.2	54.1	52.5
$50,000 or more	58.9	64.3	62.5	54.7	37.5	61.4	64.5	63.2	59.0	50.3

[Continued]

★ 568 ★

Pap Smears and Breast Examinations
[Continued]

Characteristic	Pap smear					Breast examination				
	Total	18-29 years	30-44 years	45-64 years	65 years and over	Total	18-29 years	30-44 years	45-64 years	65 years and over
Race										
White	49.7	63.5	55.5	43.8	30.4	53.1	61.8	56.1	49.3	42.4
Black	54.3	71.8	55.8	42.6	29.2	55.3	68.4	55.1	48.0	38.0
Hispanic origin										
Hispanic	49.1	55.0	53.8	40.3	24.5	50.4	54.1	52.2	44.6	40.3
Non-Hispanic	50.1	65.1	55.3	43.7	30.6	53.4	63.4	55.9	49.3	42.1
Geographic region										
Northeast	47.9	62.8	56.3	41.5	26.0	53.4	62.9	58.5	48.3	41.7
Midwest	49.7	64.8	54.5	43.3	29.3	53.2	63.9	55.5	49.5	40.0
South	51.4	65.7	55.9	44.9	31.6	53.5	62.8	55.2	49.4	42.8
West	50.4	60.8	54.2	43.6	35.3	52.2	58.7	53.5	48.8	43.5
Marital status										
Currently married	53.5	70.7	56.6	46.2	33.2	55.8	67.7	56.6	51.4	44.7
Formerly married	39.1	68.4	52.5	37.4	28.4	45.5	63.9	53.0	43.1	40.3
Never married	51.5	55.4	49.2	34.1	28.6	53.1	55.7	51.0	44.0	36.6
Employment status										
Currently employed	54.7	64.2	55.0	46.0	35.3	55.9	62.4	55.3	51.2	42.8
Unemployed	51.1	63.1	50.2	30.3	18.9[2]	52.9	62.8	52.6	32.7	43.4[2]
Not in labor force	43.4	63.3	56.8	40.6	29.9	49.2	61.6	56.8	46.7	41.9

Source: Health Promotion and Disease Prevention: United States, 1990, National Center for Health Statistics, Vital and Health Statistics, Series 10, No. 185, p. 30. *Notes:* Data are based on household interviews of the civilian noninstitutionalized population. The survey design, general qualifications, and information on the reliability of the estimates are given in appendix 1 in the original source. Denominator for each cell excludes unknowns. 1. Includes women with unknown sociodemographic characteristics. 2. Figure does not meet standard of reliability or precision (more than 30-percent relative standard error in numerator of percent or rate).

★ 569 ★

Health Examinations

Breast Self-Examinations

Percent of women 18 years of age and over who knew how to do breast self-examination and percent of those who knew how to do breast self-examination who did the procedure at least 12 times a year, by age and selected characteristics: United States, 1990.

Characteristic	Knew breast self-examination					Did breast self-examination				
	Total	18-29 years	30-44 years	45-64 years	65 years and over	Total	18-29 years	30-44 years	45-64 years	65 years and over
All women[1]	88.1	84.9	92.7	90.6	80.5	43.1	36.6	43.6	47.1	45.4
Education level										
Less than 12 years	76.9	75.6	81.3	81.6	71.9	43.9	35.3	41.8	48.8	45.8
12 years	89.7	84.4	93.0	92.9	85.8	43.6	36.7	45.2	46.6	45.2
More than 12 years	92.8	89.5	95.4	94.1	88.6	42.2	36.8	42.7	46.5	45.2
13-15 years	91.7	88.3	95.0	92.4	89.9	43.1	38.5	45.1	44.4	46.6
16 years or more	94.0	91.7	95.7	95.8	86.8	41.3	33.7	40.4	48.6	43.1
Income										
Less than $10,000	80.0	81.0	84.8	79.6	76.4	42.2	36.2	40.5	49.0	45.9
$10,000-$19,999	85.3	82.2	90.9	87.2	82.1	43.0	39.4	41.5	47.0	44.6
$20,000-$34,999	90.6	86.8	93.2	93.8	86.2	42.3	33.9	44.0	47.2	45.3
$35,000-$49,999	93.3	89.2	95.7	94.1	89.2	43.1	39.9	43.0	47.4	38.7
$50,000 or more	92.5	87.1	94.9	94.0	83.2	41.5	31.3	42.6	44.4	48.2
Race										
White	88.8	85.6	93.5	91.2	81.9	42.3	35.6	42.7	46.1	44.3
Black	86.0	84.8	92.4	88.4	68.3	50.9	43.1	51.3	55.6	61.8
Hispanic origin										
Hispanic	74.7	70.4	77.9	78.0	71.7	44.1	37.7	46.2	47.1	53.6
Non-Hispanic	89.2	87.0	94.2	91.5	80.8	43.1	36.5	43.4	47.1	45.1
Geographic region										
Northeast	86.5	83.2	92.6	89.1	77.4	42.0	35.3	43.7	44.9	42.4
Midwest	90.5	88.0	94.9	92.5	83.3	41.3	33.0	43.1	44.1	44.9
South	89.2	88.3	94.3	90.9	79.3	46.0	39.8	47.0	49.0	49.3
West	84.8	77.2	88.0	89.3	83.1	41.6	36.2	38.6	50.2	42.6
Marital status										
Currently married	90.6	87.8	93.1	92.0	83.8	44.5	39.2	43.6	47.7	48.6
Formerly married	84.8	87.0	92.5	88.5	78.3	43.8	37.3	44.1	45.7	43.4
Never married	82.8	81.3	90.2	80.6	77.4	36.4	33.4	43.1	44.4	37.6
Employment status										
Currently employed	91.3	87.0	94.3	92.1	86.0	42.9	36.3	44.1	47.3	48.1

[Continued]

★ 569 ★

Breast Self-Examinations
[Continued]

Characteristic	Knew breast self-examination					Did breast self-examination				
	Total	18-29 years	30-44 years	45-64 years	65 years and over	Total	18-29 years	30-44 years	45-64 years	65 years and over
Unemployed	90.2	87.0	94.0	90.1	91.0	40.7	37.3	43.2	43.0	41.2[2]
Not in labor force	83.4	79.5	87.7	88.6	79.8	43.8	37.3	42.1	47.1	45.0

Source: Health Promotion and Disease Prevention: United States, 1990, National Center for Health Statistics, Vital and Health Statistics, Series 10, No. 185, p. 31. *Notes:* Data are based on household interviews of the civilian noninstitutionalized population. The survey design, general qualifications, and information on the reliability of the estimates are given in appendix 1 in the original source. Denominator for each cell excludes unknowns. 1. Includes women with unknown sociodemographic characteristics. 2. Figure does not meet standard of reliability or precision (more than 30-percent relative standard error in numerator of percent or rate).

★ 570 ★

Health Examinations

Mammograms: Women Who Ever Had Procedure

Percent of women 35 years of age and over who had ever had a mammogram, by age and selected characteristics: United States, 1990.

Characteristic	Total 35 years and over	35-39 years	40-49 years	50-59 years	60-69 years	70 years and over
All women[1]	57.7	39.5	64.3	67.9	61.7	50.1
Education level						
Less than 12 years	44.9	29.9	45.4	51.3	49.9	41.3
12 years	59.0	37.6	63.3	69.1	62.7	54.7
More than 12 years	65.5	43.0	71.3	78.8	74.3	63.4
13-15 years	63.2	40.2	69.0	76.3	72.3	60.6
16 years or more	67.9	45.7	73.4	81.5	76.6	67.4
Income						
Less than $10,000	40.9	28.1	43.2	44.5	43.2	41.3
$10,000-$19,999	50.3	26.7	49.1	55.1	57.0	51.6
$20,000-$34,999	58.9	37.8	63.1	68.1	64.6	56.8
$35,000-$49,999	62.9	43.0	66.9	76.2	72.0	58.7
$50,000 or more	71.4	47.4	76.8	82.2	77.2	64.9
Race						
White	58.9	40.9	65.6	69.2	63.5	50.2
Black	51.3	35.7	56.3	61.9	49.1	49.2
Hispanic origin						
Hispanic	49.4	35.5	50.2	58.3	55.8	48.6
Non-Hispanic	58.2	39.8	65.4	68.5	62.0	50.1

[Continued]

★ 570 ★

Mammograms: Women Who Ever Had Procedure
[Continued]

Characteristic	Total 35 years and over	35-39 years	40-49 years	50-59 years	60-69 years	70 years and over
Geographic region						
Northeast	58.4	41.4	60.4	70.7	63.5	51.0
Midwest	57.7	40.8	67.0	66.5	61.2	47.9
South	55.4	40.5	63.0	65.0	56.9	46.4
West	61.1	34.6	67.2	71.4	69.9	59.3
Marital status						
Currently married	61.5	40.8	66.6	71.0	64.0	59.9
Formerly married	51.7	35.3	60.3	60.5	57.7	44.8
Never married	47.4	36.4	48.4	55.1	59.5	47.7
Employment status						
Currently employed	60.5	40.5	65.8	70.3	65.2	57.4
Unemployed	52.9	34.6	54.8	63.0	72.0	60.0[2]
Not in labor force	55.1	36.6	60.6	64.2	60.2	49.6

Source: Health Promotion and Disease Prevention: United States, 1990, National Center for Health Statistics, Vital and Health Statistics, Series 10, No. 185, p. 58. *Notes:* Data are based on household interviews of the civilian noninstitutionalized population. The survey design, general qualifications, and information on the reliability of the estimates are given in appendix 1 in the original source. Denominator for each cell excludes unknowns. 1. Includes women with unknown sociodemographic characteristics. 2. Figure does not meet standard of reliability or precision (more than 30-percent relative standard error in numerator of percent or rate).

★ 571 ★

Health Examinations

Mammograms: Women Who Had Procedure in the Past 3 Years

Percent of women 35 years of age and over who had a mammogram in the past 3 years, by age and selected characteristics: United States, 1990.

Characteristic	Total 35 years and over	35-39 years	40-49 years	50-59 years	60-69 years	70 years and over
All women[1]	50.5	33.9	57.6	59.6	54.9	41.7
Education level						
Less than 12 years	37.4	26.1	39.5	42.5	42.5	33.0
12 years	51.8	31.9	56.0	61.3	55.8	46.6
More than 12 years	58.5	37.2	65.0	70.0	68.1	54.6
13-15 years	55.4	34.5	61.6	66.4	65.5	51.0
16 years or more	61.7	39.8	68.0	73.9	71.1	59.7

[Continued]

★571★

Mammograms: Women Who Had Procedure in the Past 3 Years
[Continued]

Characteristic	Total 35 years and over	35-39 years	40-49 years	50-59 years	60-69 years	70 years and over
Income						
Less than $10,000	32.7	21.9	33.0	34.1	36.4	33.1
$10,000-$19,999	42.5	22.5	41.0	44.9	49.0	44.4
$20,000-$34,999	52.0	31.2	56.0	61.0	58.6	49.1
$35,000-$49,999	56.6	38.9	60.7	67.2	66.7	50.8
$50,000 or more	64.5	41.3	70.6	74.3	70.0	55.3
Race						
White	51.5	35.1	58.8	60.7	56.5	41.8
Black	44.9	30.7	50.5	54.7	43.2	40.5
Hispanic origin						
Hispanic	42.3	30.7	44.4	49.1	46.0	41.7
Non-Hispanic	51.0	34.1	58.6	60.2	55.3	41.7
Geographic region						
Northeast	52.0	35.4	55.5	63.4	56.7	43.6
Midwest	50.4	34.9	60.6	57.8	52.9	40.8
South	48.0	35.1	55.8	55.8	51.1	37.4
West	53.4	29.5	59.0	64.1	63.3	48.9
Marital status						
Currently married	55.0	35.9	60.3	63.5	57.8	51.8
Formerly married	43.4	28.7	52.7	50.0	50.2	36.4
Never married	38.9	27.5	41.0	46.4	50.3	39.2
Employment status						
Currently employed	53.5	34.6	59.0	61.6	60.4	48.4
Unemployed	46.2	30.5	45.8	59.1	61.3[2]	48.5[2]
Not in labor force	47.5	31.9	54.6	56.2	52.6	41.2

Source: Health Promotion and Disease Prevention: United States, 1990, National Center for Health Statistics, Vital and Health Statistics, Series 10, No. 185, p. 59. *Notes:* Data are based on household interviews of the civilian noninstitutionalized population. The survey design, general qualifications, and information on the reliability of the estimates are given in appendix 1 in the original source. Denominator for each cell excludes unknowns. 1. Includes women with unknown sociodemographic characteristics. 2. Figure does not meet standard of reliability or precision (more than 30-percent relative standard error in numerator of percent or rate).

★ 572 ★
Health Examinations

Blood Pressure Checks

Percent of persons 18 years of age and over who had had their blood pressure checked in the past year, by sex, age, and selected characteristics: United States, 1990.

Characteristic	Both sexes 18 years and over	Male					Female				
		Total	18-29 years	30-44 years	45-64 years	65 years and over	Total	18-29 years	30-44 years	45-64 years	65 years and over
All persons[1]	87.0	82.7	77.6	80.6	85.8	90.9	90.8	92.1	89.9	90.0	91.7
Education level											
Less than 12 years	85.4	81.2	73.2	74.0	83.3	89.8	88.9	89.7	84.2	87.5	91.8
12 years	86.5	82.2	77.8	80.0	85.3	92.1	89.9	91.3	88.5	89.1	91.9
More than 12 years	88.2	83.9	79.3	82.5	87.4	91.4	92.7	93.7	92.4	92.7	91.1
13-15 years	87.6	82.6	79.5	81.4	85.7	92.0	92.0	93.6	90.8	91.9	91.5
16 years or more	88.8	85.0	79.1	83.3	88.5	91.0	93.4	93.9	93.9	93.4	90.6
Income											
Less than $10,000	86.2	79.8	78.0	73.9	82.4	86.2	89.5	91.1	83.4	89.6	91.5
$10,000-$19,999	85.5	80.8	73.9	76.5	82.6	91.2	89.2	90.9	85.6	87.0	92.7
$20,000-$34,999	86.1	81.6	77.0	79.1	84.5	91.9	90.4	92.4	89.7	90.1	88.8
$35,000-$49,999	87.3	83.9	78.2	82.6	88.3	94.5	91.0	92.5	91.0	89.9	90.0
$50,000 or more	88.7	85.1	81.2	84.0	87.0	91.8	92.6	94.0	92.6	91.6	93.2
Race											
White	86.9	82.9	78.0	80.3	85.8	91.2	90.6	92.0	89.8	89.6	91.4
Black	89.2	84.7	81.6	84.3	87.5	89.0	92.6	93.1	90.9	93.3	94.4
Hispanic origin											
Hispanic	81.8	73.3	68.9	72.1	78.7	85.7	88.3	88.2	88.6	86.3	92.7
Non-Hispanic	87.4	83.4	78.5	81.3	86.1	91.1	90.9	92.6	90.0	90.1	91.6
Geographic region											
Northeast	88.7	85.5	81.2	84.7	87.5	90.7	91.4	92.5	91.3	90.8	91.3
Midwest	87.2	83.2	78.8	80.8	85.3	92.3	90.8	92.2	90.1	89.7	91.7
South	87.1	82.3	76.7	80.5	86.1	89.5	91.2	92.7	90.0	90.5	92.2
West	84.9	80.2	74.5	76.6	84.3	92.0	89.2	90.4	88.2	88.3	90.9
Marital status											
Currently married	87.6	84.4	77.7	81.9	86.7	91.8	90.7	92.1	90.1	90.3	91.1
Formerly married	88.3	81.6	81.8	76.8	82.3	88.0	90.9	92.9	89.4	89.4	92.4
Never married	83.6	77.4	77.4	76.1	78.1	87.3	90.9	92.0	89.0	87.0	88.3
Employment status											
Currently employed	85.8	81.3	77.7	80.2	85.5	89.6	90.9	91.8	90.2	91.0	90.6

[Continued]

★ 572 ★

Blood Pressure Checks
[Continued]

Characteristic	Both sexes 18 years and over	Male					Female				
		Total	18-29 years	30-44 years	45-64 years	65 years and over	Total	18-29 years	30-44 years	45-64 years	65 years and over
Unemployed	84.9	79.3	76.5	83.4	79.8	68.9[2]	90.7	92.6	88.2	90.6	94.7
Not in labor force	89.7	88.1	77.9	85.1	87.7	91.4	90.5	92.5	89.0	88.4	91.8

Source: Health Promotion and Disease Prevention: United States, 1990, National Center for Health Statistics, Vital and Health Statistics, Series 10, No. 185, p. 32. Notes: Data are based on household interviews of the civilian noninstitutionalized population. The survey design, general qualifications, and information on the reliability of the estimates are given in appendix 1 in the original source. Denominator for each cell excludes unknowns. 1. Includes persons with unknown sociodemographic characteristics. 2. Figure does not meet standard of reliability or precision (more than 30-percent relative standard error in numerator of percent or rate).

★ 573 ★
Health Examinations

Cholesterol Checks

Percent of persons 18 years of age and over who had had their blood cholesterol checked, by sex, age, and selected characteristics: United States, 1990.

Characteristic	Both sexes 18 years and over	Male					Female				
		Total	18-29 years	30-44 years	45-64 years	65 years and over	Total	18-29 years	30-44 years	45-64 years	65 years and over
All persons[1]	52.7	49.9	24.5	48.2	65.9	71.4	55.3	32.2	53.2	69.4	70.5
Education level											
Less than 12 years	44.6	40.7	13.3	28.2	50.2	62.8	48.1	21.0	36.2	57.0	62.4
12 years	48.7	43.1	20.2	39.1	62.2	72.3	53.2	28.0	48.0	69.5	73.9
More than 12 years	60.8	60.0	34.2	59.1	77.1	82.8	61.5	40.8	61.7	77.8	80.6
13-15 years	54.0	51.5	29.7	52.1	72.6	77.9	56.2	35.9	57.1	74.1	79.0
16 years or more	67.7	67.6	42.0	64.5	80.1	86.4	67.9	49.6	66.1	81.5	82.7
Income											
Less than $10,000	40.8	32.3	21.0	26.4	44.9	49.0	45.4	24.0	35.9	58.5	64.5
$10,000-$19,999	46.0	40.8	18.3	32.0	51.4	68.9	50.3	27.4	39.9	61.9	72.3
$20,000-$34,999	50.6	46.8	26.3	43.0	59.0	77.2	54.4	34.6	51.5	70.0	72.4
$35,000-$49,999	55.7	52.7	22.9	53.3	70.2	84.9	58.9	38.3	58.5	73.3	79.1
$50,000 or more	65.3	65.0	34.1	64.7	77.7	87.4	65.5	41.4	65.1	77.7	78.9
Race											
White	54.7	52.4	25.8	50.6	67.9	73.2	56.8	33.2	54.6	70.1	71.5
Black	42.1	35.4	19.7	34.7	51.3	49.8	47.4	28.1	46.2	66.0	61.1
Hispanic origin											
Hispanic	37.5	30.0	14.7	31.6	47.9	57.2	43.9	27.7	45.0	63.9	62.2
Non-Hispanic	54.0	51.5	25.6	49.7	66.9	71.9	56.3	32.9	54.0	69.8	70.8

[Continued]

★ 573 ★

Cholesterol Checks
[Continued]

Characteristic	Both sexes 18 years and over	Male					Female				
		Total	18-29 years	30-44 years	45-64 years	65 years and over	Total	18-29 years	30-44 years	45-64 years	65 years and over
Geographic region											
Northeast	52.5	50.3	23.5	49.7	66.3	69.0	54.4	34.6	50.5	66.3	67.0
Midwest	54.7	52.2	26.8	50.5	67.1	75.0	57.0	32.7	54.4	72.0	72.8
South	51.8	48.1	24.7	46.2	63.5	67.3	55.1	32.1	54.3	68.5	69.6
West	52.2	49.9	22.4	47.3	67.6	76.8	54.4	29.6	52.7	71.0	73.3
Marital status											
Currently married	56.8	56.5	27.1	50.5	68.2	74.9	57.2	32.9	53.7	70.8	74.6
Formerly married	58.3	50.5	30.5	43.8	55.3	60.0	61.5	31.6	52.3	66.6	67.5
Never married	33.2	28.5	22.3	39.2	52.1	53.8	39.0	31.4	51.1	60.5	68.2
Employment status											
Currently employed	51.0	48.0	25.6	49.2	66.3	73.8	54.5	35.4	55.1	72.2	74.8
Unemployed	39.1	33.6	16.7	38.8	56.3	53.8[2]	45.1	30.8	48.5	65.5	83.3[2]
Not in labor force	57.7	59.0	20.8	37.0	65.3	71.0	57.1	24.6	47.9	65.4	69.9

Source: Health Promotion and Disease Prevention: United States, 1990, National Center for Health Statistics, Vital and Health Statistics, Series 10, No. 185, p. 36. *Notes:* Data are based on household interviews of the civilian noninstitutionalized population. The survey design, general qualifications, and information on the reliability of the estimates are given in appendix 1 in the original source. Denominator for each cell excludes unknowns. 1. Includes persons with unknown sociodemographic characteristics. 2. Figure does not meet standard of reliability or precision (more than 30-percent relative standard error in numerator of percent or rate).

★ 574 ★

Health Examinations

Place of Physician Contact, 1991
[Number per person per year and number of physician contacts]

Characteristic	Number per person per year[1]					Number in thousands[1]				
	All places[2]	Telephone	Office	Hospital	Other	All places[2]	Telephone	Office	Hospital	Other
All persons[3]	5.8	0.7	3.3	0.8	0.9	1,430,509	163,637	829,934	198,054	228,952
Age										
Under 5 years	7.1	1.2	4.3	1.0	0.6	137,908	22,583	83,920	18,526	12,169
5-17 years	3.4	0.4	2.1	0.5	0.4	157,649	17,459	94,878	24,341	20,005
18-24 years	3.9	0.5	2.0	0.6	0.8	96,236	11,184	49,804	15,836	18,887
25-44 years	5.1	0.6	3.0	0.7	0.7	410,158	50,975	242,241	55,063	59,013
45-64 years	6.6	0.7	3.8	1.0	1.0	312,248	35,184	180,743	48,348	46,131
65-74 years	9.2	0.8	5.6	1.2	1.5	168,621	15,291	102,129	21,619	28,007
75 years and over	12.3	0.9	6.4	1.2	3.7	147,688	10,960	76,220	14,320	44,740
Sex and age										
Male										
All ages	4.9	0.5	2.8	0.8	0.8	588,739	61,951	338,654	92,918	91,002
Under 18 years	4.7	0.6	2.8	0.7	0.5	156,371	21,035	94,595	23,878	15,759

[Continued]

★ 574 ★

Place of Physician Contact, 1991
[Continued]

Characteristic	Number per person per year[1]					Number in thousands[1]				
	All places[2]	Telephone	Office	Hospital	Other	All places[2]	Telephone	Office	Hospital	Other
18-44 years	3.4	0.4	1.9	0.5	0.7	178,733	18,754	96,647	27,421	34,351
45-64 years	5.8	0.6	3.4	1.1	0.7	131,513	12,791	77,013	24,473	16,523
65 years and over	9.7	0.7	5.6	1.4	1.9	122,122	9,370	70,399	17,146	24,369
Female										
All ages	6.6	0.8	3.8	0.8	1.1	841,771	101,686	491,280	105,136	137,949
Under 18 years	4.4	0.6	2.6	0.6	0.5	139,186	19,008	84,202	18,990	16,415
18-44 years	6.1	0.8	3.6	0.8	0.8	327,662	43,405	195,398	43,477	43,548
45-64 years	7.4	0.9	4.2	1.0	1.2	180,735	22,392	103,730	23,875	29,608
65 years and over	11.0	1.0	6.1	1.1	2.7	194,187	16,882	107,950	18,793	48,378
Race and age										
White										
All ages	6.0	0.7	3.5	0.8	0.9	1,243,100	149,106	733,957	1259,040	192,510
Under 18 years	4.8	0.7	3.0	0.6	0.5	252,755	35,842	157,547	31,988	25,892
18-44 years	5.0	0.6	2.9	0.6	0.7	436,147	56,517	254,422	57,003	65,238
45-64 years	6.6	0.8	3.9	0.9	0.9	268,848	31,746	159,286	38,408	37,954
65 years and over	10.5	0.9	6.0	1.2	2.3	285,350	25,002	162,702	31,642	63,427
Black										
All ages	4.9	0.3	2.5	1.0	1.0	152,111	10,574	77,814	30,954	31,584
Under 18 years	3.2	0.3	1.6	0.8	0.5	32,924	2,908	16,728	8,137	4,963
18-44 years	4.3	0.3	2.3	0.8	0.8	56,169	3,716	30,832	10,618	10,628
45-64 years	7.5	0.6	3.0	1.8	1.4	36,262	2,755	17,533	8,626	7,024
65 years and over	10.4	0.5[4]	5.0	1.4	3.5	26,755	1,195	12,722	3,572	8,969
Family income and age										
Under $10,000										
All ages	7.6	0.8	3.5	1.4	1.9	181,066	18,281	83,195	33,905	44,678
Under 18 years	5.1	0.4	2.4	1.3	0.9	34,542	2,540	16,704	8,865	6,213
18-44 years	6.1	0.7	2.6	1.1	1.7	56,442	6,126	24,446	9,825	15,810
45-64 years	12.0	1.7	5.2	2.8	2.3	36,443	5,191	15,699	8,486	7,031
65 years and over	11.4	0.9	5.6	1.4	3.3	53,639	4,425	26,346	6,729	15,624
$10,000-$19,999										
All ages	6.0	0.6	3.3	1.0	1.0	227,466	24,678	127,017	37,778	36,872
Under 18 years	4.0	0.5	2.2	0.7	0.6	40,398	4,737	22,138	7,331	6,067
18-44 years	4.7	0.6	2.5	0.9	0.7	69,198	9,121	36,320	13,339	10,135
45-64 years	8.0	0.7	4.6	1.4	1.3	46,142	4,245	26,193	8,125	7,186
65 years and over	9.5	0.9	5.6	1.2	1.8	71,728	6,574	42,366	8,983	13,484
$20,000-$34,999										
All ages	5.6	0.7	3.3	0.8	0.8	296,359	34,870	174,292	41,094	44,685
Under 18 years	4.2	0.6	2.6	0.6	0.5	61,787	9,030	37,771	8,087	6,644
18-44 years	4.8	0.6	2.7	0.7	0.7	115,225	14,102	65,704	17,622	17,415
45-64 years	6.5	0.8	3.9	1.0	0.9	58,175	6,699	34,308	8,767	8,171
65 years and over	10.6	0.9	6.3	1.1	2.2	61,172	5,038	36,509	6,618	12,455
$35,000 or more										
All ages	5.5	0.8	3.5	0.6	0.7	494,419	67,068	307,852	56,998	58,354
Under 18 years	5.2	0.8	3.4	0.5	0.4	125,521	20,319	82,375	13,092	8,796
18-44 years	5.0	0.7	3.1	0.5	0.6	205,179	28,774	125,927	21,850	26,554

[Continued]

★ 574 ★

Place of Physician Contact, 1991
[Continued]

Characteristic	Number per person per year[1]					Number in thousands[1]				
	All places[2]	Telephone	Office	Hospital	Other	All places[2]	Telephone	Office	Hospital	Other
45-64 years	6.1	0.7	3.7	0.9	0.8	119,552	13,425	73,321	16,810	15,152
65 years and over	10.0	1.0	6.0	1.2	1.8	44,166	4,549	26,229	5,245	7,852
Geographic region										
Northeast	5.5	0.6	3.3	0.8	0.8	277,763	28,379	167,707	40,610	39,835
Midwest	5.9	0.7	3.3	0.8	1.0	352,515	44,529	198,112	48,131	59,782
South	5.7	0.6	3.4	0.7	0.9	480,527	53,862	287,059	59,601	75,698
West	5.8	0.7	3.2	0.9	1.0	319,704	36,866	177,057	49,712	53,638
Place of residence										
MSA[5]	5.9	0.7	3.4	0.8	1.0	1,137,796	136,211	654,468	154,110	185,153
Central city	6.0	0.7	3.3	0.9	1.1	460,637	50,393	251,054	70,591	85,528
Not central city	5.8	0.7	3.4	0.7	0.8	677,160	85,819	403,414	83,519	99,626
Not MSA[5]	5.4	0.5	3.2	0.8	0.8	292,713	27,425	175,467	43,944	43,798

Source: Current Estimates From the National Health Interview Survey, 1991, National Center for Health Statistics, Vital and Health Statistics, Series 10, No. 184, pp. 114-115. *Notes:* Data are based on household interviews of the civilian noninstitutionalized population. The survey design, general qualifications, and information on the reliability of the estimates are given in appendix 1 in the original source. 1. Does not include physician contacts while an overnight patient in a hospital. 2. Includes unknown place of contact. 3. Includes other races and unknown family income. 4. Figure does not meet standard of reliability or precision. 5. MSA is metropolitan statistical area.

★ 575 ★

Health Examinations

Interval Since Last Physician Contact, 1991
[Percent distribution and number of persons]

Characteristic	Interval since last contact									
	Percent distribution[1]					Number in thousands[1]				
	All intervals[2]	Less than 1 year	1 year to less than 2 years	2 years to less than 5 years	5 years or more	All intervals[3]	Less than 1 year	1 year to less than 2 years	2 years to less than 5 years	5 years or more
All persons[4]	100.0	78.5	9.9	8.1	3.5	248,713	191,945	24,138	19,881	8,439
Age										
Under 5 years	100.0	94.4	4.5	1.0	0.1[5]	19,379	17,963	852	192	28
5-17 years	100.0	78.0	12.9	7.3	1.7	46,142	35,316	5,832	3,321	778
18-24 years	100.0	73.6	12.7	10.4	3.4	24,641	17,733	3,053	2,500	814
25-44 years	100.0	73.4	11.3	10.7	4.6	81,098	58,515	9,008	8,512	3,648
45-64 years	100.0	78.0	8.7	8.6	4.7	47,162	36,212	4,031	3,985	2,189
65-74 years	100.0	78.0	8.7	8.6	4.7	47,162	36,212	4,031	3,985	2,189
75 years and over	100.0	89.8	4.0	3.7	2.5	11,991	10,634	479	440	293
Sex and age										
Male										
All ages	100.0	73.0	11.4	10.7	4.9	120,724	86,437	13,448	12,658	5,795
Under 18 years	100.0	82.7	10.5	5.5	1.4	33,535	27,201	3,446	1,808	448
18-44 years	100.0	63.8	14.1	15.3	6.8	51,912	32,325	7,163	7,764	3,424
45-64 years	100.0	72.9	10.0	10.7	6.3	22,626	16,220	2,226	2,388	1,412
65 years and over	100.0	85.4	4.9	5.6	4.1	12,652	10,692	613	699	511

[Continued]

★ 575 ★

Interval Since Last Physician Contact, 1991
[Continued]

Characteristic	Percent distribution[1]					Number in thousands[1]				
	All intervals[2]	Less than 1 year	1 year to less than 2 years	2 years to less than 5 years	5 years or more	All intervals[3]	Less than 1 year	1 year to less than 2 years	2 years to less than 5 years	5 years or more
Female										
All ages	100.0	83.7	8.5	5.7	2.1	127,988	105,508	10,690	7,223	2,645
Under 18 years	100.0	83.1	10.3	5.4	1.1	31,986	26,079	3,239	1,706	359
18-44 years	100.0	82.7	9.2	6.1	2.0	53,827	43,923	4,897	3,249	1,038
45-64 years	100.0	82.7	7.5	6.6	3.2	24,536	19,992	1,805	1,597	777
65 years and over	100.0	89.1	4.3	3.9	2.7	17,640	15,514	748	672	471
Race and age										
White										
All ages	100.0	79.0	9.6	8.1	3.4	208,202	161,835	19,640	16,505	6,918
Under 18 years	100.0	83.8	9.8	5.3	1.1	52,593	43,348	5,062	2,716	577
18-44 years	100.0	73.9	11.4	10.6	4.2	87,785	63,769	9,797	9,127	3,617
45-64 years	100.0	77.9	8.8	8.6	4.7	40,628	31,167	3,524	3,454	1,868
65 years and over	100.0	87.6	4.7	4.5	3.2	27,197	23,551	1,257	1,209	856
Black										
All ages	100.0	77.6	11.4	7.8	3.2	30,896	23,433	3,441	2,343	966
Under 18 years	100.0	78.7	13.4	6.3	1.7	10,321	7,899	1,343	634	166
18-44 years	100.0	73.6	12.7	9.7	4.1	13,151	9,452	1,630	1,240	521
45-64 years	100.0	81.1	8.1	7.0	3.8	4,861	3,868	387	333	182
65 years and over	100.0	87.6	3.2	5.3	3.9	2,563	2,213	81	135	98
Family income and age										
Under $10,000										
All ages	100.0	80.0	8.2	7.6	4.1	23,892	18,847	1,942	1,802	968
Under 18 years	100.0	81.9	9.7	6.0	2.3	6,823	5,472	651	404	152
18-44 years	100.0	75.9	9.4	9.8	5.0	9,313	6,988	867	898	457
45-64 years	100.0	78.4	7.4	7.7	6.5	3,044	2,355	222	230	194
65 years and over	100.0	86.4	4.3	5.8	3.5	4,712	4,032	202	270	165
$10,000-$19,999										
All ages	100.0	77.0	9.5	9.0	4.5	37,984	28,806	3,544	3,383	1,689
Under 18 years	100.0	78.6	11.6	7.6	2.2	10,092	7,743	1,144	753	212
18-44 years	100.0	70.6	11.2	12.2	6.0	14,600	10,152	1,609	1,754	863
45-64 years	100.0	77.6	7.6	9.3	5.5	5,742	4,414	433	531	310
65 years and over	100.0	86.6	4.8	4.6	4.1	7,549	6,498	357	345	305
$20,000-$34,999										
All ages	100.0	77.2	10.5	8.8	3.5	53,182	40,596	5,499	4,648	1,830
Under 18 years	100.0	81.4	11.6	6.1	0.9	14,610	11,705	1,670	882	128
18-44 years	100.0	72.1	12.0	11.5	4.5	23,917	17,035	2,825	2,717	1,062
45-64 years	100.0	76.6	8.8	9.1	5.5	8,900	6,774	775	804	487
65 years and over	100.0	89.0	4.0	4.3	2.7	5,755	5,081	230	245	153
$35,000 or more										
All ages	100.0	80.9	9.4	7.2	2.5	89,200	71,217	8,312	6,326	2,198
Under 18 years	100.0	87.4	8.4	3.7	0.5	24,142	20,849	2,014	872	128
18-44 years	100.0	76.6	10.9	9.4	3.1	41,023	30,948	4,416	3,790	1,273
45-64 years	100.0	79.9	8.8	7.7	3.6	19,641	15,520	1,702	1,496	694
65 years and over	100.0	89.6	4.1	3.9	2.4	4,395	3,899	180	168	103
Geographic region										
Northeast	100.0	81.2	8.8	7.1	2.9	50,300	40,317	4,387	3,519	1,447
Midwest	100.0	79.5	9.6	7.9	3.0	59,735	46,871	5,657	4,666	1,766
South	100.0	76.8	11.0	8.7	3.5	84,008	63,138	9,009	7,162	2,918
West	100.0	77.7	9.5	8.5	4.3	54,670	41,620	5,086	4,534	2,308

[Continued]

★ 575 ★

Interval Since Last Physician Contact, 1991
[Continued]

Characteristic	Interval since last contact									
	Percent distribution[1]					Number in thousands[1]				
	All intervals[2]	Less than 1 year	1 year to less than 2 years	2 years to less than 5 years	5 years or more	All intervals[3]	Less than 1 year	1 year to less than 2 years	2 years to less than 5 years	5 years or more
Place of residence										
MSA[6]	100.0	79.0	9.7	7.9	3.4	194,020	150,879	18,558	14,996	6,448
Central city	100.0	79.1	9.7	7.7	3.4	76,512	59,574	7,324	5,828	2,554
Not central city	100.0	79.0	9.7	7.9	3.4	117,508	91,305	11,234	9,168	3,894
Not MSA[6]	100.0	76.7	10.4	9.1	3.7	54,693	41,066	5,580	4,885	1,991

Source: Current Estimates From the National Health Interview Survey, 1991, National Center for Health Statistics, Vital and Health Statistics, Series 10, No. 184, pp. 116-117. *Notes:* Data are based on household interviews of the civilian noninstitutionalized population. The survey design, general qualifications, and information on the reliability of the estimates are given in appendix 1 in the original source. 1. Includes physician contacts while an overnight patient in a hospital. 2. Excludes unknown interval. 3. Includes unknown interval. 4. Includes other races and unknown family income. 5. Figure does not meet standard of reliability or precision. 6. MSA is metropolitan statistical area.

★ 576 ★

Health Examinations

Diagnostic and Other Nonsurgical Procedures for Inpatients Discharged from Non-Federal Short-Stay Hospitals, 1980, 1988, 1989, and 1990

Data are based on a sample of hospital records.

Sex, age, and procedure category	Procedures in thousands				Procedures per 1,000 population			
	1980[1]	1988	1989[2]	1990	1980[1]	1988	1989[2]	1990
MALE								
All ages[2,3,4]	3,386	6,665	7,202	7,378	31.3	55.6	59.3	59.6
Angiocardiography using contrast material	174	749	767	833	1.6	6.4	6.5	6.9
Computerized axial tomography (CAT scan)	152	775	721	736	1.4	6.3	5.8	5.8
Diagnostic ultrasound	114	599	628	667	1.0	5.1	5.2	5.4
Cystoscopy	543	399	356	350	5.1	3.2	2.8	2.7
Radioisotope scan	236	315	287	268	2.1	2.6	2.3	2.1
Arteriography using contrast material	180	246	233	217	1.7	2.0	1.9	1.7
Endoscopy of large intestine without biopsy	228	170	158	148	2.1	1.4	1.2	1.2
Under 15 years[2,4]	217	424	566	546	8.3	15.6	20.5	19.4
Spinal tap	39	84	97	94	1.5	3.1	3.5	3.4
Diagnostic ultrasound	6[5]	51	49	47	0.2[5]	1.9	1.8	1.7
Computerized axial tomography (CAT scan)	17	42	46	41	0.7	1.5	1.7	1.5
Electroencephalogram	5[5]	15	17	17	0.2[5]	0.5	0.6	0.6
Radioisotope scan	8[5]	11	14	11	0.3[5]	0.4	0.5	0.4
Application of cast or splint	21	14	12	10	0.8	0.5	0.4	0.4
Cystoscopy	23	[5]	[5]	[5]	0.9	[5]	[5]	[5]
15-44 years[2,4]	884	1,382	1,477	1,584	17.3	24.4	25.9	27.6
Computerized axial tomography (CAT scan)	37	218	196	215	0.7	3.8	3.4	3.8
Diagnostic ultrasound	25	111	117	118	0.5	2.0	2.0	2.1
Angiocardiography using contrast material	30	89	98	102	0.6	1.6	1.7	1.8
Contrast myelogram	88	79	65	58	1.7	1.4	1.1	1.0
Radioisotope scan	48	62	58	47	0.9	1.1	1.0	0.8

[Continued]

★ 576 ★

Diagnostic and Other Nonsurgical Procedures for Inpatients Discharged from Non-Federal Short-Stay Hospitals, 1980, 1988, 1989, and 1990

[Continued]

Sex, age, and procedure category	Procedures in thousands				Procedures per 1,000 population			
	1980[1]	1988	1989[2]	1990	1980[1]	1988	1989[2]	1990
Arthroscopy of knee	94	55	55	43	1.8	1.0	1.0	0.7
Cystoscopy	80	36	37	35	1.6	0.6	0.6	0.6
Endoscopy of large intestine without biopsy	52	25	25	21	1.0	0.4	0.4	0.4
Application of cast or splint	54	27	25	22	1.1	0.5	0.4	0.4
45-64 years[2,4]	1,128	2,038	2,103	2,106	53.4	92.6	94.4	93.5
Angiocardiography using contrast material	106	388	386	428	5.0	17.6	17.3	19.0
Diagnostic ultrasound	41	173	188	184	1.9	7.9	8.5	8.1
Computerized axial tomography (CAT scan)	43	200	179	170	2.0	9.1	8.1	7.5
Radioisotope scan	75	102	88	81	3.5	4.7	3.9	3.6
Cystoscopy	153	93	84	80	7.3	4.2	3.8	3.6
Arteriography using contrast material	76	95	77	65	3.6	4.3	3.4	2.9
Endoscopy of large intestine without biopsy	86	48	36	42	4.0	2.2	1.6	1.9
65 years and over[2,4]	1,158	2,821	3,056	3,143	111.8	228.4	241.8	243.3
Computerized axial tomography (CAT scan)	54	316	299	309	5.2	25.6	23.7	23.9
Angiocardiography using contrast material	35	264	274	297	3.4	21.3	21.7	23.0
Diagnostic ultrasound	42	264	274	319	4.0	21.4	21.7	24.7
Cystoscopy	287	266	232	232	27.7	21.6	18.3	18.0
Endoscopy of small intestine without biopsy	35	113	131	123	3.3	9.1	10.4	9.5
Radioisotope scan	105	139	127	129	10.1	11.3	10.1	10.0
Arteriography using contrast material	72	110	117	109	7.0	8.9	9.3	8.4
Endoscopy of large intestine without biopsy	86	94	95	84	8.3	7.6	7.5	6.5
FEMALE								
All ages[2,3,4]	3,532	6,902	9,471	10,077	27.5	47.3	64.7	68.0
Diagnostic ultrasound	204	963	930	941	1.6	6.6	6.3	6.2
Computerized axial tomography (CAT scan)	154	838	798	770	1.2	5.6	5.3	4.9
Angiocardiography using contrast material	84	439	432	510	0.7	3.1	3.0	3.5
Radioisotope scan	289	390	347	335	2.1	2.6	2.3	2.1
Endoscopy of small intestine without biopsy	164	279	291	294	1.3	1.8	1.9	1.9
Endoscopy of large intestine without biopsy	307	238	255	250	2.3	1.5	1.6	1.5
Cystoscopy	324	143	131	135	2.6	1.0	0.9	0.9
Laparoscopy (excluding that for ligation and division of fallopian tubes)	235	133	125	147	1.8	0.9	0.9	1.0
Under 15 years[2,4]	191	356	418	403	7.6	13.8	15.9	15.0
Spinal tap	26	70	75	71	1.0	2.7	2.9	2.7
Computerized axial tomography (CAT scan)	10	39	37	27	0.4	1.5	1.4	1.0
Diagnostic ultrasound	5[5]	45	33	43	0.2[5]	1.7	1.3	1.6
Electroencephalogram	5	19	14	14	5	0.7	0.5	0.5
Angiocardiography using contrast material	5	5	11	6[5]	5	5	0.4	0.2[5]
Application of cast or splint	13	9[5]	7[5]	6[5]	0.5	0.3[5]	0.3[5]	0.2[5]
Radioisotope scan	6[5]	6[5]	6[5]	9[5]	0.2[5]	0.2[5]	0.2[5]	0.3[5]
Cystoscopy	38	5[5]	5	5	1.5	0.2[5]	5	5
15-44 years[2,4]	1,203	1,643	3,850	4,217	22.7	28.3	66.1	72.0
Diagnostic ultrasound	94	365	348	309	1.8	6.3	6.0	5.3
Computerized axial tomography (CAT scan)	36	156	157	144	0.7	2.7	2.7	2.5

[Continued]

★ 576 ★

Diagnostic and Other Nonsurgical Procedures for Inpatients Discharged from Non-Federal Short-Stay Hospitals, 1980, 1988, 1989, and 1990
[Continued]

Sex, age, and procedure category	Procedures in thousands				Procedures per 1,000 population			
	1980[1]	1988	1989[2]	1990	1980[1]	1988	1989[2]	1990
Laparoscopy (excluding that for ligation and division of fallopian tubes)	214	124	118	120	4.1	2.1	2.0	2.0
Biliary tract X-ray	60	109	94	102	1.1	1.9	1.6	1.7
Radioisotope scan	49	62	60	58	0.9	1.1	1.0	1.0
Contrast myelogram	66	57	46	36	1.2	1.0	0.8	0.6
Endoscopy of large intestine without biopsy	77	29	41	34	1.5	0.5	0.7	0.6
Cystoscopy	97	44	38	39	1.8	0.8	0.7	0.7
45-64 years[2,4]	1,030	1,711	1,771	1,861	44.2	71.4	73.3	76.3
Diagnostic ultrasound	44	176	190	174	1.9	7.3	7.9	7.1
Computerized axial tomography (CAT scan)	42	188	176	163	1.8	7.8	7.3	6.7
Angiocardiography using contrast material	49	189	173	214	2.1	7.9	7.2	8.8
Radioisotope scan	92	113	99	79	3.9	4.7	4.1	3.2
Biliary tract X-ray	48	63	73	64	2.1	2.6	3.0	2.6
Endoscopy of small intestine without biopsy	55	68	67	71	2.3	2.8	2.8	2.9
Endoscopy of large intestine without biopsy	94	54	58	59	4.0	2.3	2.4	2.4
Cystoscopy	93	33	37	37	4.0	1.4	1.5	1.5
65 years and over[2,4]	1,107	3,192	3,431	3,596	72.1	177.2	187.0	192.6
Computerized axial tomography (CAT scan)	66	455	428	436	4.3	25.3	23.3	23.3
Diagnostic ultrasound	62	377	359	415	4.0	20.9	19.6	22.2
Angiocardiography using contrast material	21	209	220	245	1.4	11.6	12.0	13.1
Radioisotope scan	143	209	182	189	9.3	11.6	9.9	10.1
Endoscopy of small intestine without biopsy	55	150	163	168	3.6	8.3	8.9	9.0
Endoscopy of large intestine without biopsy	131	154	155	156	8.5	8.6	8.4	8.4
Cystoscopy	96	61	51	56	6.2	3.4	2.8	3.0

Source: U.S. Department of Commerce, Economics and Statistics Administration, *National Economic, Social, and Environmental Data Bank, CD-ROM,* November 1992. Primary source: Division of Health Care Statistics, National Center for Health Statistics: Data from the National Hospital Discharge Survey. *Notes:* Excludes newborn infants. Data do not reflect total use of procedures because procedures for outpatients are not included in the National Hospital Discharge Survey. For example, CAT scans are frequently performed on outpatients. Rates are based on the civilian population. In each sex and age group, data are shown for the 5 most common procedures in 1980 and 1989. Procedure categories are based on the International Classification of Diseases, 9th Revision, Clinical Modification. For a listing of the code numbers, see Appendix II, table IX, in the primary source. 1. Comparisons of 1980 with later years should be made with caution as estimates of change may reflect improvements in the design (see Appendix I) rather than true changes in hospital use. 2. Beginning in 1989, the definition of some surgical and diagnostic and other nonsurgical procedures was revised, thus causing a discontinuity in the trends for the totals. See appendix II in the primary source. 3. Rates are age adjusted. 4. Includes nonsurgical procedures not shown. 5. Estimates based on fewer than 30 discharges are not shown; estimates based on 30-59 discharges should be used with caution.

★ 577 ★

Health Examinations

Average Annual Number of Physicians Visits

Data are based on household interviews of the civilian noninstitutionalized population. Number of visits per person per year.

Respondent-assessed health status and age	All races[1]		White		Black	
	Male	Female	Male	Female	Male	Female
All health statuses[2]						
55-59 years	4.2	4.7	4.1	4.5	4.8	6.2
60-64 years	4.8	5.2	4.7	5.1	5.9	6.5
65-69 years	4.9	5.4	4.8	5.3	6.0	7.0
70-74 years	5.4	5.8	5.3	5.5	5.7	8.4
75-79 years	5.5	5.9	5.5	5.8	5.5	6.6
80-84 years	5.9	6.3	5.9	6.3	6.5	7.4
65 years and over	5.4	5.8	5.4	5.7	5.9	7.4
75 years and over	6.0	6.2	6.0	6.1	6.1	6.9
85 years and over	7.5	6.6	7.5	6.6	7.7	6.9
Good or excellent health						
55-59 years	2.7	3.1	2.7	3.2	1.9	3.0
60-64 years	3.2	3.3	3.2	3.3	2.9	3.6
65-69 years	3.4	3.9	3.4	3.9	2.7	4.5
70-74 years	3.5	4.0	3.6	4.1	2.9	3.6
75-79 years	3.9	4.5	3.9	4.5	3.6	4.7
80-84 years	4.4	4.5	4.5	4.4	3.8	4.8
65 years and over	3.7	4.2	3.8	4.2	3.1	4.3
75 years and over	4.3	4.6	4.3	4.6	3.9	4.8
85 years and over	5.1	5.2	5.1	5.2	5.6	4.9
Fair or poor health						
55-59 years	10.5	10.6	10.2	10.6	10.6	11.1
60-64 years	9.8	11.0	9.7	11.2	10.0	10.4
65-69 years	8.9	9.6	8.8	9.5	9.7	10.0
70-74 years	9.5	10.1	9.5	9.4	9.8	14.2[3]
75-79 years	8.5	8.6	8.7	8.6	7.3	8.8
80-84 years	8.6	9.9	8.6	10.0	9.3	9.6
65 years and over	9.2	9.5	9.2	9.3	9.2	10.8
75 years and over	9.2	9.2	9.3	9.2	8.2	9.2
85 years and over	12.1	9.3	12.3	9.4	9.9	9.5

Source: Health Data on Older Americans: United States, 1992, Centers for Disease Control and Prevention/National Center for Health Statistics, Vital and Health Statistics, Series 3: Analytic and Epidemiological Studies, No. 27, p. 121. Primary source: National Center for Health Statistics: Data from the National Health Interview Survey. *Notes:* 1. Includes races other than White and Black. 2. Includes unknown respondent-assessed health status. 3. Figure does not meet standard of reliability or precision.

★ 578 ★

Health Examinations

Tests Commonly Performed by Office-Based Physicians

Data are based on reporting by a sample of office-based physicians.

Sex and age	Blood glucose	Urine glucose	Breast exam[1]	Pelvic exam[1]	Rectal exam	Visual acuity	Urin- alysis	Hema- tology	Pap test[1]	Blood pressure check	Electro- cardio- gram	Chest x ray
Total												
55-59 years	98	84	128	105	77	68	128	97	75	468	62	44
60-64 years	107	80	117	82	67	80	132	100	53	475	61	48
65-69 years	104	80	99	64	73	86	134	100	39	502	61	42
70-74 years	107	84	83	49	66	103	143	110	31	515	65	40
75-79 years	113	84	69	35	53	117	128	115	18^2	511	62	51
80-84 years	92	88	66	31	54^2	160	141	113	20^2	458	55	39
65 years and over	104	82	79	46	62	112	135	109	27	502	61	42
75 years and over	103	82	64	32	51	136	132	116	17	492	58	45
85 years and over	90	64	47^2	28^2	40	154	127	123	10^2	495	49	34^2
Male												
55-59 years	99	81	...	...	62	72	125	80	...	444	80	52
60-64 years	121	87	...	...	80	77	135	95	...	452	90	62
65-69 years	95	81	...	...	72	84	139	88	...	480	74	35
70-74 years	106	92	...	...	89	100	153	97	...	504	68	41
75-79 years	119	97	...	...	78	99	142	124	...	519	76	65
80-84 years	69	98	...	...	64	142	140	105	...	411	56	31
65 years and over	98	89	...	...	76	101	143	102	...	487	69	45
75 years and over	96	93	...	...	70	117	141	118	...	481	67	57
85 years and over	62^2	66^2	...	...	54^2	137	138	117	...	467	54^2	32
Female												
55-59 years	97	86	128	105	88	66	130	109	75	485	48	38
60-64 years	98	75	117	82	57	83	130	104	53	491	41	38
65-69 years	111	79	99	64	73	86	130	109	39	518	52	47
70-74 years	108	80	83	49	52	105	136	118	31	522	64	39
75-79 years	109	76	69	35	37	129	120	109	18^2	505	54	42
80-84 years	105	83	66	31	49	171	142	118	20^2	484	55	32
65 years and over	108	78	79	46	53	118	130	114	27	511	56	40
75 years and over	106	75	64	32	40	147	127	115	17	499	53	37
85 years and over	103	63	47^2	28^2	34^2	162	122	125	10^2	507	47^2	34^2

Source: Health Data on Older Americans: United States, 1992, Centers for Disease Control and Prevention/National Center for Health Statistics, Vital and Health Statistics, Series 3: Analytic and Epidemiological Studies, No. 27, p. 127. Primary source: National Center for Health Statistics: Data from the National Ambulatory Medical Care Survey. *Notes:* Three dots (...) means the category is not applicable. 1. Includes only visits by female patients. 2. Figure does not meet the standard for reliability or precision..

★ 579 ★

Health Examinations

Diagnostic Procedures Performed on Males

Number and rate of diagnostic and other nonsurgical procedures for males 55 years of age and over discharged from short-stay hospitals, by age and selected procedures: 1981 and 1987.

[Discharges from non-federal short-stay hospitals]

Age and procedure category	Number of procedures in thousands		Number of procedures per 10,000 population	
	1981	1987	1981	1987
55-59 years				
Angiocardiography using contrast material	50	102	92.3	192.9
Computerized axial tomography (CAT scan)	17	61	30.5	115.4
Diagnostic ultrasound	16	46	29.8	86.4
Arteriography using contrast material	29	32	52.9	58.2
Radioisotope scan	25	30	45.9	57.4
60-64 years				
Angiocardiography using contrast material	34	107	70.6	211.0
Computerized axial tomography (CAT scan)	12	72	25.8	142.6
Diagnostic ultrasound	13	62	26.1	122.2
Radioisotope scan	27	36	57.1	71.8
Arteriography using contrast material	28	32	57.8	63.2
65-69 years				
Angiocardiography using contrast material	31	99	79.4	220.3
Computerized axial tomography (CAT scan)	26	81	65.6	180.2
Diagnostic ultrasound	20	67	49.6	148.0
Radioisotope scan	42	42	106.9	94.4
Arteriography using contrast material	23	35	58.5	77.0
70-74 years				
Computerized axial tomography (CAT scan)	21	92	70.3	274.9
Diagnostic ultrasound	14	86	48.3	258.8
Angiocardiography using contrast material	12	58	42.4	174.5
Radioisotope scan	33	45	112.9	136.7
Arteriography using contrast material	25	42	84.2	127.2
75-79 years				
Computerized axial tomography (CAT scan)	17	69	89.4	304.0
Diagnostic ultrasound	10	62	52.1	275.1
Radioisotope scan	28	32	148.3	142.7
Angiocardiography using contrast material	3	30	18.1	131.8
Arteriography using contrast material	16	26	43.8	116.3

[Continued]

★579★

Diagnostic Procedures Performed on Males
[Continued]

Age and procedure category	Number of procedures in thousands		Number of procedures per 10,000 population	
	1981	1987	1981	1987
80-84 years				
Computerized axial tomography (CAT scan)	12	56	111.7	460.5
Diagnostic ultrasound	6	49	59.8	396.8
Radioisotope scan	13	30	124.8	241.1
Arteriography using contrast material	5	15	50.7	119.6
Angiocardiography using contrast material	Z[1]	9	9.7[1]	72.1
65 years and over				
Computerized axial tomography (CAT scan)	80	337	76.2	278.1
Diagnostic ultrasound	56	290	52.9	239.7
Angiocardiography using contrast material	49	196	46.3	162.0
Radioisotope scan	127	167	120.4	137.9
Arteriography using contrast material	74	121	70.0	99.7
75 years and over				
Computerized axial tomography (CAT scan)	34	165	92.2	383.1
Diagnostic ultrasound	22	138	60.2	320.8
Radioisotope scan	52	79	141.1	184.2
Arteriography using contrast material	26	44	71.0	102.1
Angiocardiography using contrast material	5	39	13.9	91.3
85 years and over				
Computerized axial tomography (CAT scan)	5	39	70.7	487.9
Diagnostic ultrasound	6	27	82.4	333.5
Radioisotope scan	10	17	146.0	214.5
Intravenous pyelogram	5	3	67.0	40.9
Arteriography using contrast material	5	3	67.1	35.9

Source: Health Data on Older Americans: United States, 1992, Centers for Disease Control and Prevention/National Center for Health Statistics, Vital and Health Statistics, Series 3: Analytic and Epidemiological Studies, No. 27, pp. 136-137. Primary source: National Center for Health Statistics: Data from the Hospital Discharge Survey. *Notes:* A Z stands for quantity more than zero but less than 500 where numbers are rounded to thousands. 1. Figure does not meet standard of reliability or precision.

★ 580 ★

Health Examinations

Diagnostic Procedures Performed on Females

Number and rate of diagnostic and other nonsurgical procedures for females 55 years of age and over discharged from short-stay hospitals, by age and selected procedures: 1981 and 1987.

[Discharges from non-federal short-stay hospitals]

Age and procedure category	Number of procedures in thousands		Number of procedures per 10,000 population	
	1981	1987	1981	1987
55-59 years				
Angiocardiography using contrast material	13	53	20.9	91.3
Computerized axial tomography (CAT scan)	19	53	30.9	90.8
Diagnostic ultrasound	13	46	21.1	79.7
Radioisotope scan	23	32	37.8	55.3
Arteriography using contrast material	18	16	29.4	26.8
60-64 years				
Computerized axial tomography (CAT scan)	20	64	35.2	110.4
Diagnostic ultrasound	21	59	38.4	101.9
Angiocardiography using contrast material	16	54	27.9	92.6
Radioisotope scan	43	37	77.3	63.3
Arteriography using contrast material	19	30	34.8	51.3
65-69 years				
Computerized axial tomography (CAT scan)	24	77	47.8	142.0
Diagnostic ultrasound	19	75	38.0	138.8
Angiocardiography using contrast material	17	64	35.1	119.4
Radioisotope scan	42	54	85.6	100.7
Arteriography using contrast material	25	29	50.5	53.4
70-74 years				
Computerized axial tomography (CAT scan)	21	95	52.2	213.5
Diagnostic ultrasound	19	90	46.9	202.6
Angiocardiography using contrast material	9	56	23.3	126.0
Radioisotope scan	33	46	80.3	103.6
Arteriography using contrast material	20	29	50.0	65.7
75-79 years				
Computerized axial tomography (CAT scan)	20	104	67.4	295.9
Diagnostic ultrasound	23	79	75.9	224.7
Radioisotope scan	29	51	96.8	144.1
Angiocardiography using contrast material	4	35	13.8	98.4
Arteriography using contrast material	13	26	43.9	73.5

[Continued]

★ 580 ★

Diagnostic Procedures Performed on Females
[Continued]

Age and procedure category	Number of procedures in thousands		Number of procedures per 10,000 population	
	1981	1987	1981	1987
80-84 years				
Computerized axial tomography (CAT scan)	15	92	73.5	400.4
Diagnostic ultrasound	12	76	60.0	328.9
Radioisotope scan	22	38	110.1	164.8
Arteriography using contrast material	8	19	40.9	83.5
Angiocardiography using contrast material	Z[1]	9	1.4	40.2
65 years and over				
Computerized axial tomography (CAT scan)	93	461	59.2	259.9
Diagnostic ultrasound	81	387	51.7	218.3
Radioisotope scan	143	219	91.2	123.7
Angiocardiography using contrast material	32	169	20.6	95.2
Arteriography using contrast material	72	107	46.1	60.5
75 years and over				
Computerized axial tomography (CAT scan)	48	289	71.9	367.0
Diagnostic ultrasound	43	222	64.6	281.6
Radioisotope scan	68	119	102.0	150.8
Arteriography using contrast material	27	49	40.4	62.5
Angiocardiography using contrast material	5	48	8.1	61.2
85 years and over				
Computerized axial tomography (CAT scan)	13	93	78.4	451.0
Diagnostic ultrasound	8	67	49.8	326.0
Radioisotope scan	17	30	101.7	146.5
Angiocardiography using contrast material	1	4	6.1	21.3
Arteriography using contrast material	6	4	33.5	20.1

Source: Health Data on Older Americans: United States, 1992, Centers for Disease Control and Prevention/National Center for Health Statistics, Vital and Health Statistics, Series 3: Analytic and Epidemiological Studies, No. 27, pp. 138-139. Primary source: National Center for Health Statistics: Data from the Hospital Discharge Survey. *Notes:* A Z stands for quantity more than zero but less than 500 where numbers are rounded to thousands. 1. Figure does not meet standard of reliability or precision.

Doctor Visits

★ 581 ★

Visits to Physicians per Person Per Year, 1970-1989
[Average number of visits]

Year	Sex		Race		Age					
	Male	Female	White	Black	Under 6	6 to 16	17 to 24	25 to 44	45 to 64	65 and over
1980	4.0	5.4	4.8	4.5	6.7	3.2	4.0	4.6	5.1	6.4
1985	4.4	6.1	5.4	4.7	6.3	3.1	4.2	4.9	6.1	8.3
1987	4.5	6.2	5.5	4.9	6.7	3.3	4.4	4.8	6.4	8.9
1988	4.5	6.2	5.6	4.6	7.0	3.4	3.8	5.1	6.1	8.7
1989	4.7	6.1	5.6	4.7	6.7	3.5	3.9	5.1	6.1	8.9

Source: U.S. Bureau of the Census. *Statistical Abstract of the United States 1992.* 112th edition. Washington, D.C.: U.S. Department of Commerce, 1992, p. 110. Primary source: U.S. National Center for Health Statistics, *Vital and Health Statistics*, series 10, and unpublished data.

Acute Conditions and Care

★ 582 ★

Acute Conditions Per 100 Persons, 1991
[Number of acute conditions per 100 persons per year]

Type of acute condition	All ages	Under 5 years	5-17 years	18-24 years	25-44 years	45 years and over		
						Total	45-64 years	65 years and over
All acute conditions	191.8	390.7	270.2	194.6	164.0	123.5	128.4	115.7
Infective and parasitic diseases	18.5	45.9	38.4	14.0	12.5	7.6	9.3	5.1
Common childhood diseases	1.8	10.6	4.7	0.3[1]	0.2[1]	0.1[1]	0.2[1]	-[1]
Intestinal virus, unspecified	4.0	8.5	8.4	3.1[1]	3.6	1.0[1]	1.3[1]	0.5[1]
Viral infections, unspecified	6.1	15.3	10.0	5.3	4.3	3.8	4.8	2.3[1]
Other	6.5	11.5	15.3	5.4	4.4	2.7	3.0	2.2[1]
Respiratory conditions	100.6	183.5	150.1	106.3	88.0	61.8	68.9	50.7
Common cold	28.6	67.2	38.7	34.1	22.9	17.2	17.4	17.0
Other acute upper respiratory infections	11.7	23.0	21.9	8.0	9.5	6.5	7.9	4.3
Influenza	52.1	68.1	78.6	58.1	51.1	31.5	38.2	20.9
Acute bronchitis	4.5	12.0	6.7	3.8	2.9	3.1	3.0	3.3
Pneumonia	1.7	6.5	1.4[1]	1.0[1]	0.8[1]	1.8	0.9[1]	3.3
Other respiratory conditions	2.0	6.8	2.8	1.3[1]	0.8[1]	1.7	1.5[1]	2.0[1]

[Continued]

★ 582 ★

Acute Conditions Per 100 Persons, 1991
[Continued]

Type of acute condition	All ages	Under 5 years	5-17 years	18-24 years	25-44 years	45 years and over		
						Total	45-64 years	65 years and over
Digestive system conditions	6.6	10.1	9.1	5.3	5.7	5.6	4.8	6.9
Dental conditions	1.4	3.3[1]	1.2[1]	0.8[1]	1.7	0.9[1]	1.2[1]	0.4[1]
Indigestion, nausea, and vomiting	2.9	2.0[1]	6.1	3.2[1]	2.5	1.4	1.0[1]	2.0[1]
Other digestive conditions	2.4	4.8	1.8	1.3[1]	1.5	3.3	2.5	4.5
Injuries	24.0	23.2	29.6	32.2	23.6	18.7	18.3	19.3
Fractures and dislocations	3.0	1.0[1]	5.0	3.7	2.8	2.3	2.0	2.7
Sprains and strains	5.4	1.1[1]	5.9	7.3	7.2	3.8	3.7	3.9
Open wounds and lacerations	4.7	6.1	6.9	7.6	4.5	2.4	2.9	1.5[1]
Contusions and superficial injuries	4.7	6.1	5.4	7.4	3.3	4.6	4.3	5.1
Other current injuries	6.1	8.9	6.3	6.1	5.8	5.7	5.4	6.0
Selected other acute conditions	30.1	105.0	34.3	25.0	23.9	17.1	15.6	19.2
Eye conditions	1.2	3.0[1]	1.0[1]	0.8[1]	0.7[1]	1.4	0.9[1]	2.2[1]
Acute ear infections	10.3	70.7	14.3	2.7[1]	3.9	1.9	2.5	1.0[1]
Other ear conditions	1.7	6.4	2.9	0.2[1]	1.3	0.8[1]	0.8[1]	0.8[1]
Acute urinary conditions	3.5	2.7[1]	1.7[1]	4.2	4.2	3.7	3.1	4.8
Disorders of menstruation	0.6	...	0.7[1]	1.5[1]	0.7[1]	0.2[1]	0.3[1]	-[1]
Other disorders of female genital tract	1.1	0.3[1]	-[1]	1.8[1]	1.8	1.1	1.0[1]	1.2[1]
Delivery and other conditions of pregnancy and puerperium	1.6	...	0.2[1]	6.5	2.5	-[1]	-[1]	...
Skin conditions	1.9	5.2	2.6	1.6[1]	1.0	1.8	0.9[1]	3.2
Acute musculoskeletal conditions	4.0	1.3[1]	2.7	3.2[1]	4.9	4.8	5.7	3.4
Headache, excluding migraine	1.3	-[1]	2.9	1.2[1]	1.4	0.7[1]	0.3[1]	1.1[1]
Fever, unspecified	2.9	15.4	5.3	1.3[1]	1.3	0.7[1]	0.1[1]	1.5[1]
All other acute conditions	11.9	23.1	8.6	11.7	10.3	12.7	11.5	14.6

Source: Current Estimates From the National Health Interview Survey, 1991, National Center for Health Statistics, Vital and Health Statistics, Series 10, No. 184, p. 13. *Notes:* Data are based on household interviews of the civilian noninstitutionalized population. The survey design, general qualifications, and information on the reliability of the estimates are given in appendix 1 in the original source. Excluded from these estimates are conditions involving neither medical attention nor activity restriction. A dash (-) represents zero. Three dots (...) indicate that the category is not applicable. 1. Figure does not meet standards of reliability or precision.

★ 583 ★
Acute Conditions and Care

Acute Conditions Reported by Persons 55 Years of Age and Over, 1985-87

Average annual number of selected reported acute conditions per 1,000 persons 55 years of age and over, by type of acute condition, race, sex, and age.

[Number per 1,000 persons]

Race, sex, and age	Type of acute condition			
	Respiratory	Digestive	Injury	Other[1]
Total[2]				
55-59 years	547.9	12.4[3]	158.0	253.6
60-64 years	554.5	39.3	198.0	256.7
65-69 years	487.4	49.1	177.8	241.5
70-74 years	416.5	48.5	194.6	325.5
75-79 years	374.6	94.3	222.3	270.4
80-84 years	454.6	63.7[3]	203.6	299.3
55-64 years	551.1	25.7	177.7	255.1
65-74 years	456.1	48.8	185.2	278.6
75-84 years	404.5	82.9	215.3	281.2
65 years and over	426.7	65.0	205.3	299.5
75 years and over	379.4	91.0	237.7	333.1
85 years and over	275.0	125.1[3]	331.1	549.2
White male				
55-64 years	501.0	20.5[3]	198.4	153.8
65-74 years	432.9	24.7[3]	139.2	236.3
75-84 years	364.6	34.9[3]	144.2	205.6
65 years and over	400.0	27.9	144.9	241.7
75 years and over	336.5	34.0[3]	155.9	252.2
85 years and over	204.8[3]	29.7[3]	210.8[3]	469.9
Black male				
55-64 years	426.4	-	135.3[3]	266.1[3]
65 years and over	153.5[3]	70.8[3]	173.0[3]	203.3[3]
White female				
55-64 years	625.7	29.7	174.7	328.9
65-74 years	490.8	49.5	234.0	314.5
75-84 years	437.2	118.9	254.3	339.5
65 years and over	460.0	83.0	253.6	348.9

[Continued]

★ 583 ★

Acute Conditions Reported by Persons 55 Years of Age and Over, 1985-87
[Continued]

Race, sex, and age	Type of acute condition			
	Respiratory	Digestive	Injury	Other[1]
75 years and over	416.8	129.8	281.0	397.0
85 years and over	338.3	171.6[3]	384.0	618.7
Black female				
55-64 years	403.6	62.1[3]	92.2[3]	319.2
65 years and over	479.0	119.9	154.8[3]	262.0

Source: Health Data on Older Americans: United States, 1992, Centers for Disease Control and Prevention/National Center for Health Statistics, Vital and Health Statistics, Series 3: Analytic and Epidemiological Studies, No. 27, p. 19. Primary source: National Center for Health Statistics: Data from the National Health Interview Survey. *Notes:* A dash (-) stands for zero. 1. Includes the following conditions: eye conditions; ear conditions; urinary tract infections; skin conditions; acute back, spine, or neck pain; other musculoskeletal conditions; headache, excluding migraine; and all other acute conditions. 2. Includes races other than white and black. 3. Figure does not meet standard of reliability or precision.

★ 584 ★

Acute Conditions and Care

Bed Days: Average Number Associated with Acute and Chronic Conditions for Persons 65 or Older

The perception of poorer health among older blacks is supported statistically by numerous indices. For example, the average number of bed days associated with acute and chronic conditions is 55.1 percent greater among elderly blacks than elderly whites: 21.4 days vs. 13.8 days.

	All races	White	Black
Total persons	28,683,000	25,817,000	2,401,000
Total bed days	412,094,000	355,233,000	51,345,000
Average bed days during year	14.4	13.8	21.4

Source: U.S. Congress, "Profiles in Aging America: Meeting the Health Care Needs of the Nation's Black Elderly," Joint Hearing Before the Special Committee on Aging and the Congressional Black Caucus Health Braintrust, United States Senate, September 28, 1990, 101-29, U.S. Government Printing Office, Washington, D.C., p. 115. Primary source: Unpublished data from the National Health Interview Survey, 1988, U.S. Dept. of Health and Human Services, Public Health Service, Centers for Disease Control, National Center for Health Statistics.

★ 585 ★

Acute Conditions and Care

Bed Days: Number Associated with Acute Conditions, 1991

[Number of bed days per 100 persons per year]

Type of acute condition	All ages	Under 5 years	5-17 years	18-24 years	25-44 years	45 years and over		
						Total	45-64 years	65 years and over
All acute conditions	313.6	420.7	334.2	324.1	280.6	305.7	269.6	361.8
Infective and parasitic diseases	27.6	75.9	54.3	28.0	15.4	12.4	11.0[1]	14.5[1]
Common childhood diseases	4.0	21.8[1]	10.6[1]	0.7[1]	0.3[1]	0.4[1]	0.6[1]	-[1]
Intestinal virus, unspecified	5.4	18.1[1]	11.8[1]	3.2[1]	3.7[1]	0.8[1]	0.6[1]	1.1[1]
Viral infections, unspecified	9.8	29.2[1]	14.2	7.8[1]	5.4[1]	7.5	7.5[1]	7.7[1]
Other	8.5	6.8[1]	17.8	16.2[1]	5.9[1]	3.7[1]	2.3[1]	5.8[1]
Respiratory conditions	166.4	227.0	219.1	156.3	140.9	149.7	141.8	161.9
Common cold	24.8	54.1	31.6	32.3	19.1	17.0	16.7	17.4[1]
Other acute upper respiratory infections	12.7	14.2[1]	25.0	10.2[1]	10.4	8.3	7.7[1]	9.2[1]
Influenza	100.3	114.7	137.7	95.1	93.2	83.7	94.8	66.4
Acute bronchitis	9.4	19.5[1]	10.7[1]	9.8[1]	7.9	7.4	10.1[1]	3.4[1]
Pneumonia	14.0	14.3[1]	7.9[1]	6.9[1]	8.1	26.0	9.5[1]	51.6
Other respiratory conditions	5.1	10.2[1]	6.2[1]	2.0[1]	2.2[1]	7.3[1]	3.1[1]	13.8[1]
Digestive system conditions	13.6	9.4[1]	10.0[1]	11.5[1]	12.5	18.8	14.8	24.9
Dental conditions	2.6	4.9[1]	2.7[1]	3.5[1]	2.7[1]	1.6[1]	1.9[1]	1.3[1]
Indigestion, nausea, and vomiting	2.9	3.0[1]	5.5[1]	3.6[1]	1.3[1]	2.7[1]	1.5[1]	4.6[1]
Other digestive conditions	8.1	1.41[1]	1.7[1]	4.4[1]	8.5	14.4	11.5[1]	19.0
Injuries	39.2	8.0[1]	14.8	58.0	41.8	52.8	43.5	67.4
Fractures and dislocations	10.7	1.2[1]	3.4[1]	14.0[1]	8.1	19.1	12.5	29.2
Sprains and strains	8.3	-[1]	2.8[1]	8.4[1]	15.9	5.8[1]	7.0[1]	3.8[1]
Open wounds and lacerations	3.8	1.4[1]	3.7[1]	7.6[1]	5.1[1]	1.7[1]	0.8[1]	3.1[1]
Contusions and superficial injuries	5.1	0.3[1]	1.4[1]	10.5[1]	3.6[1]	8.5	10.1[1]	5.9[1]
Other current injuries	11.3	5.1[1]	3.5[1]	17.5[1]	9.1	17.8	13.0	25.3
Selected other acute conditions	45.8	82.0	28.8	49.4	54.1	37.2	31.3	46.3
Eye conditions	0.2[1]	1.8[1]	-[1]	0.7[1]	-[1]	-[1]	-[1]	-[1]
Acute ear infections	9.5	56.6	12.0[1]	2.6[1]	5.2[1]	2.8[1]	2.4[1]	3.3[1]
Other ear conditions	1.0[1]	3.9[1]	2.1[1]	-[1]	0.6[1]	0.2[1]	0.3[1]	-[1]
Acute urinary conditions	4.7	1.1[1]	3.4[1]	2.7[1]	4.6[1]	7.2[1]	6.1[1]	9.0[1]
Disorders of menstruation	1.0[1]	...	0.3[1]	0.5[1]	2.6[1]	0.2[1]	0.3[1]	-[1]
Other disorders of female genital tract	1.3[1]	-[1]	-[1]	1.8[1]	2.5[1]	1.1[1]	0.7[1]	1.6[1]
Delivery and other conditions of pregnancy and puerperium	9.8	...	-[1]	32.8	20.0	-[1]	-[1]	...
Skin conditions	3.4	4.9[1]	2.8[1]	0.8[1]	1.9[1]	5.6[1]	4.1[1]	8.0[1]
Acute musculoskeletal conditions	8.1	-[1]	1.0[1]	2.7[1]	11.3	12.8	14.1	10.6[1]
Headache, excluding migraine	1.9[1]	-[1]	1.9[1]	2.6[1]	1.7[1]	2.4[1]	2.0[1]	3.0[1]

[Continued]

★ 585 ★

Bed Days: Number Associated with Acute Conditions, 1991
[Continued]

Type of acute condition	All ages	Under 5 years	5-17 years	18-24 years	25-44 years	45 years and over		
						Total	45-64 years	65 years and over
Fever, unspecified	5.0	13.6[1]	5.2[1]	2.2[1]	3.6[1]	4.9[1]	1.2[1]	10.7[1]
All other acute conditions	20.9	18.5[1]	7.2[1]	21.0[1]	16.0	34.9	27.2	46.8

Source: *Current Estimates From the National Health Interview Survey, 1991*, National Center for Health Statistics, Vital and Health Statistics, Series 10, No. 184, p. 43. *Notes:* Data are based on household interviews of the civilian noninstitutionalized population. The survey design, general qualifications, and information on the reliability of the estimates are given in appendix 1 in the original source. Excluded from these estimates are conditions involving neither medical attention nor activity restriction. A dash (-) represents zero. Three dots (...) indicate that the category is not applicable. 1. Figure does not meet standards of reliability or precision.

★ 586 ★

Acute Conditions and Care

Bed Days: Persons 65 Years of Age or Older with No Bed Days During the Preceding 12 Months

Elderly blacks are less likely than aged whites to have no bed days during the preceding year. In 1988, about three out of five (59.4 percent) of blacks 65 years of age or older had no bed days during the preceding twelve months, compared to two out of three (66.2 percent) aged whites.

	All races	White	Blacks
Total persons	28,683,000	25,817,000	2,401,000
Without bed days	18,837,000	17,102,000	1,426,000
Percent without bed days	65.7	66.2	59.4

Source: U.S. Congress, "Profiles in Aging America: Meeting the Health Care Needs of the Nation's Black Elderly," Joint Hearing Before the Special Committee on Aging, United States Senate, September 28, 1990, 101-29, U.S. Government Printing Office, Washington, D.C., p. 116. Primary source: Unpublished data from the National Health Interview Survey, 1988, U.S. Dept. of Health and Human Services, Public Health Service, Centers for Disease Controls, National Center for Health Statistics.

★ 587 ★

Acute Conditions and Care

Bone Fracture Diagnoses

Rate of patients discharged with a diagnosis of fractures, all sites, or hip fracture (fracture of neck of femur) for persons 55 years of age and over, by sex and age: 1981 and 1987.

Discharges from non-federal short-stay hospitals.

| Sex and age | Number of discharges per 1,000 population | | | |
| | Fractures, all sites | | Hip fracture | |
	1981	1987	1981	1987
Both sexes				
55-59 years	4.4	4.0	0.8	0.7
60-64 years	5.1	4.1	0.9	0.7
65-69 years	6.3	5.7	1.7	1.8
70-74 years	9.0	8.9	3.5	3.4
75-79 years	15.8	13.0	7.1	7.5
80-84 years	23.7	24.9	12.9	15.3
65 years and over	14.2	13.5	6.8	7.3
75 years and over	24.5	22.9	13.4	14.2
85 years and over	43.4	40.4	27.3	26.2
Male				
55-59 years	4.2	4.0	0.4	0.6
60-64 years	3.8	3.3	0.5	0.5
65-69 years	3.7	3.6	0.9	1.5
70-74 years	5.7	5.9	2.0	2.4
75-79 years	7.3	9.0	4.1	5.2
80-84 years	13.2	17.2	5.5	11.5
65 years and over	7.6	8.0	3.5	4.5
75 years and over	13.3	14.2	7.6	9.4
85 years and over	30.0	24.4	20.3	18.1
Female				
55-59 years	4.5	4.1	1.1	0.7
60-64 years	6.2	4.9	1.3	0.9
65-69 years	8.5	7.3	2.4	2.2
70-74 years	11.3	11.2	4.5	4.1
75-79 years	21.2	15.7	9.1	9.1
80-84 years	29.2	29.0	16.8	17.4
65 years and over	18.6	17.3	9.0	9.1
75 years and over	30.5	27.7	16.6	16.8
85 years and over	49.2	46.7	30.2	29.3

Source: Health Data on Older Americans: United States, 1992, Centers for Disease Control and Prevention/National Center for Health Statistics, Vital and Health Statistics, Series 3: Analytic and Epidemiological Studies, No. 27, p. 141. Primary source: National Center for Health Statistics: Data from the 1981 and 1987 National Hospital Discharge Surveys.

★ 588 ★

Acute Conditions and Care

Categorization of Acute-Illness Episodes in Nursing Home Residents by Disease Classification

The table is based on a study of 215 acute-illness episodes in residents of three West Coast nursing homes over a three-year period (1985-1988). The illnesses for which patients were hospitalized were typical of a nursing home population. The conditions most often responsible for transfer of residents to the hospital included respiratory conditions (25%), symptoms, signs, and ill-defined conditions (18%), and genitourinary problems (12%).

Disease diagnosis group	Classifi-fication[1]	Patients hospitalized (N = 83)		Patients treated in nursing homes (N = 132)	
		N	%	N	%
Infections and parasitic (exclusive of infections in other categories)	001-139	1	1.2	4	3.0
Neoplasms	140-239	3	3.6	3	2.3
Endocrine, nutritional, and metabolic disease and immune disorders	240-279	1	1.2	1	.7
Diseases of circulatory system	390-459	9	11	13	10.0
Diseases of respiratory system	460-519	21	25	32	24.2
Diseases of digestive system	520-579	9	11	11	8.3
Diseases of genitourinary system	580-629	10	12	24	18.2
Diseases of skin and subcutaneous tissue	680-709	5	6	2	1.5
Signs, symptoms, and ill-defined conditions	780-799	15	18	35	26.5
Injury and poisoning	800-999	9	11	3	2.3
Mental disorders	290-319	0	0	2	1.5
Disease of musculoskeletal system and connective tissue	710-739	0	0	2	1.5
Total		83	100	132	100.0

Source: U.S. Congress, "Resident Assessment: The Springboard to Quality of Care and Quality of Life for Nursing Home Residents," Workshop before the Special Committee on Aging, United States Senate, October 22, 1990, 101-30, U.S. Government Printing Office, Washington, D.C., p. 375. Primary source: *Quality Care Advocate*, July/August 1990. *Notes:* 1. Refers to the classification system of the International Classification of Disease Diagnosis Group.

★ 589 ★

Acute Conditions and Care

Categorization of Acute-Illness Episodes in Nursing Home Residents by Primary Symptoms

The table is based on a study of 215 acute-illness episodes in residents of three West Coast nursing homes over a three-year period (1985-1988).

International Classification of Disease Symptom	Patients hospitalized (N=83)		Patients treated in nursing home (N=132)	
	N	%	N	%
Fever	34	41.0	57	43.2
Dyspnea, cough, and chest pain	13	16.0	17	13.0
Lower body skeletal pain and swelling	8	9.8	6	4.5
Acute gastrointestinal symptoms	7	8.4	10	7.5
Changes in emotional and cognitive status	5	6.0	13	10.0
Changes in cardiovascular status	3	3.6	7	5.2
Nausea and vomiting	3	3.6	0	0
Wounds and skin injury	2	2.4	4	3.0
Genitourinary symptoms	2	2.4	8	6.0
Decubitus ulcers and cellulitis	2	2.4	5	3.8
Anorexia and weight loss	1	1.0	5	3.8
Fall	1	1.0	0	0
Other	2	2.4	0	0
Total	83	100	132	100

Source: U.S. Congress, "Resident Assessment: The Springboard to Quality of Care and Quality of Life for Nursing Home Residents," Workshop before the Special Committee on Aging, United States Senate, October 22, 1990, 101-30, U.S. Government Printing Office, Washington, D.C., p. 375. Primary source: *Quality Care Advocate*, July/August 1990.

★ 590 ★

Acute Conditions and Care

Health Status of Persons Discharged from Short-Stay Hospitals

Percent distribution of patients 55 years of age and over discharged from short-stay hospitals by disposition status, according to sex and age: 1981 and 1987.

[Discharges from non-federal short-stay hospitals]

Age and disposition status	Percent distribution			
	Male		Female	
	1981	1987	1981	1987
55-64 years				
Total	100.0	100.0	100.0	100.0
Routine discharge	82.5	87.3	83.3	88.6
Discharged to long-term care	1.3	2.3	1.4	2.4
Died	3.1	3.3	2.9	3.1

[Continued]

★ 590 ★

Health Status of Persons Discharged from Short-Stay Hospitals
[Continued]

Age and disposition status	Percent distribution			
	Male		Female	
	1981	1987	1981	1987
Other and unknown	13.1	7.1	12.4	5.9
65-74 years				
Total	100.0	100.0	100.0	100.0
Routine discharge	78.2	81.7	79.8	81.9
Discharged to long-term care	2.8	5.0	4.2	6.9
Died	6.2	5.7	3.7	4.0
Other and unknown	12.8	7.6	12.3	7.2
75-84 years				
Total	100.0	100.0	100.0	100.0
Routine discharge	71.9	73.4	72.1	70.9
Discharged to long-term care	7.6	11.5	10.6	15.7
Died	8.3	8.1	6.0	6.3
Other and unknown	12.2	7.0	11.3	7.1
65 years and over				
Total	100.0	100.0	100.0	100.0
Routine discharge	73.9	75.9	73.0	72.1
Discharged to long-term care	6.0	9.6	9.6	14.9
Died	7.6	7.2	5.7	5.9
Other and unknown	12.5	7.3	11.7	7.1
75 years and over				
Total	100.0	100.0	100.0	100.0
Routine discharge	68.5	69.6	67.2	64.5
Discharged to long-term care	10.1	14.6	14.3	21.2
Died	9.5	8.8	7.5	7.3
Other and unknown	11.9	7.0	11.0	7.0
85 years and over				
Total	100.0	100.0	100.0	100.0
Routine discharge	57.5	56.6	55.0	50.6
Discharged to long-term care	18.2	25.3	23.5	33.3
Died	13.3	11.4	11.2	9.6
Other and unknown	11.0	6.7	10.3	6.5

Source: Health Data on Older Americans: United States, 1992, Centers for Disease Control and Prevention/National Center for Health Statistics, Vital and Health Statistics, Series 3: Analytic and Epidemiological Studies, No. 27, p. 142. Primary source: National Center for Health Statistics: Data from the National Hospital Discharge Survey.

★ 591 ★

Acute Conditions and Care

Home Health Agency Visits for Pneumonia Patients per Episode

Type of home visit	Pre-prospective payment system visits	Post-prospective payment system visits
Skilled nursing	0.160	0.455
Home health aide	0.068	0.288

Source: U.S. Congress, "Medicare Fraud and Abuse: A Neglected Emergency?," Hearing before the Special Committee on Aging, United States Senate, October 2, 1991, 102-13, U.S. Government Printing Office, Washington, D.C., p. 227. Primary source: Abt Associates Inc.: "Episodes of Hospitalization and PPS - Working Paper," September 21, 1988.

★ 592 ★

Acute Conditions and Care

Hospitalization: Pneumonia and Influenza

Number of patients discharged, rate of discharges, and average length of stay for persons 55 years of age and over with a diagnosis of pneumonia or influenza, by sex and age: 1981 and 1987.

[Discharges from non-federal short-stay hospitals]

| Sex and age | Discharges | | | | Average length of stay | |
| | Number in thousands | | Number per 1,000 population | | Stay in days | |
	1981	1987	1981	1987	1981	1987
Both sexes						
55-59 years	46	37	4.0	3.3	8.1	7.7
60-64 years	47	52	4.6	4.7	9.7	8.3
65-69 years	63	68	7.1	6.9	9.8	9.3
70-74 years	72	87	10.2	11.2	10.9	10.1
75-79 years	69	92	14.1	15.9	11.0	9.4
80-84 years	61	94	19.8	26.7	11.7	10.2
65 years and over	351	454	13.4	15.2	11.0	9.9
75 years and over	216	299	20.9	24.5	11.4	10.0
85 years and over	86	113	36.3	39.3	11.6	10.2
Male						
55-59 years	20	18	3.6	3.3	8.0	9.0
60-64 years	21	26	4.4	5.1	10.3	8.3

[Continued]

★ 592 ★

Hospitalization: Pneumonia and Influenza
[Continued]

Sex and age	Discharges				Average length of stay Stay in days	
	Number in thousands		Number per 1,000 population			
	1981	1987	1981	1987	1981	1987
65-69 years	30	35	7.7	7.7	9.7	9.6
70-74 years	38	48	13.0	14.5	11.6	9.9
75-79 years	31	48	16.4	21.4	11.5	9.8
80-84 years	24	47	22.4	38.5	12.1	10.0
65 years and over	159	225	15.1	18.5	11.3	9.8
75 years and over	90	141	24.6	32.9	11.7	9.8
85 years and over	35	46	50.2	56.9	11.6	9.5
Female						
55-59 years	26	19	4.3	3.3	8.1	6.5
60-64 years	27	26	4.8	4.4	9.2	8.3
65-69 years	32	33	6.5	6.1	10.0	8.9
70-74 years	34	39	8.2	8.7	10.1	10.3
75-79 years	38	44	12.7	12.4	10.7	9.0
80-84 years	37	47	18.5	20.4	11.4	10.4
65 years and over	192	229	12.2	12.9	10.8	10.0
75 years and over	126	157	18.8	20.0	11.2	10.1
85 years and over	50	67	30.3	32.4	11.5	10.6

Source: Health Data on Older Americans: United States, 1992, Centers for Disease Control and Prevention/National Center for Health Statistics, Vital and Health Statistics, Series 3: Analytic and Epidemiological Studies, No. 27, p. 140. Primary source: National Center for Health Statistics: Data from the 1981 and 1987 National Hospital Discharge Surveys.

★ 593 ★

Acute Conditions and Care

Hospitalization: Selected Illnesses: Females
[Discharges from non-federal short-stay hospitals]

Age and first-listed diagnosis	Average length of stay in days	
	1981	1987
55-59 years		
Diseases of the heart	8.8	6.1
Malignant neoplasms	10.5	7.2
Cholelithiasis	9.2	6.0
Cerebrovascular disease	11.3	10.2
Fractures, all sites	9.3	6.5
Pneumonia, all forms	8.3	6.5

[Continued]

★ 593 ★

Hospitalization: Selected Illnesses: Females

[Continued]

Age and first-listed diagnosis	Average length of stay in days	
	1981	1987
60-64 years		
Diseases of the heart	9.6	7.3
Malignant neoplasms	10.6	7.6
Cerebrovascular disease	13.1	10.0
Fractures, all sites	11.5	8.4
Cholelithiasis	9.7	6.6
Pneumonia, all forms	10.1	8.6
65-69 years		
Diseases of heart	9.8	7.0
Malignant neoplasms	11.7	8.5
Cerebrovascular disease	12.6	10.9
Fractures, all sites	11.8	11.0
Pneumonia, all forms	10.4	9.0
Cholelithiasis	11.0	6.9
70-74 years		
Diseases of heart	10.0	7.3
Malignant neoplasms	13.3	9.6
Cerebrovascular disease	13.5	11.1
Fractures, all sites	14.9	9.2
Pneumonia, all forms	10.7	10.6
Cholelithiasis	12.1	8.4
75-79 years		
Diseases of heart	9.9	7.9
Malignant neoplasms	12.9	8.5
Cerebrovascular disease	13.4	10.2
Fractures, all sites	16.9	11.9
Pneumonia, all forms	11.0	9.0
Cholelithiasis	12.1	9.9
80-84 years		
Diseases of heart	11.1	8.0
Cerebrovascular disease	12.7	10.6
Fractures, all sites	16.7	12.1
Malignant neoplasms	14.1	10.5
Pneumonia, all forms	12.5	10.6
Urinary tract infection	11.2	11.0

[Continued]

★ 593 ★

Hospitalization: Selected Illnesses: Females
[Continued]

Age and first-listed diagnosis	Average length of stay in days	
	1981	1987
65 years and over		
Diseases of heart	10.4	7.6
Malignant neoplasms	12.9	9.5
Cerebrovascular disease	13.4	10.7
Fractures, all sites	16.6	11.7
Pneumonia, all forms	11.3	10.1
Cholelithiasis	12.0	9.2
75 years and over		
Diseases of the heart	10.7	8.0
Cerebrovascular disease	13.5	10.5
Fractures, all sites	17.9	12.4
Malignant neoplasms	13.5	10.0
Pneumonia, all forms	11.7	10.2
Urinary tract infection	10.5	9.8
85 years and over		
Diseases of the heart	11.5	8.0
Fractures, all sites	19.4	12.9
Cerebrovascular disease	14.5	10.8
Pneumonia, all forms	11.8	10.7
Malignant neoplasms	14.1	12.5
Volume depletion, dehydration	11.5	12.9

Source: Health Data on Older Americans: United States, 1992, Centers for Disease Control and Prevention/National Center for Health Statistics, Vital and Health Statistics, Series 3: Analytical and Epidemiological Studies, No. 27, pp. 130-131. Primary source: National Center for Health Statistics: Data from the National Hospital Discharge Survey.

★ 594 ★

Acute Conditions and Care

Hospitalization: Selected Illnesses: Males

[Discharges from non-federal short-stay hospitals]

Age and first-listed diagnosis	Average length of stay in days	
	1981	1987
55-59 years		
Diseases of the heart	8.1	5.9
Malignant neoplasms	10.5	9.3
Cerebrovascular disease	9.6	11.7
Inguinal hernia	4.8	2.1
Fractures, all sites	8.3	7.4
Hyperplasia of prostate	6.4	4.5
60-64 years		
Diseases of the heart	8.3	6.2
Malignant neoplasms	10.3	8.8
Cerebrovascular disease	11.7	8.9
Hyperplasia of prostate	7.2	4.8
Inguinal hernia	4.8	2.2
Pneumonia, all forms	10.8	8.4
65-69 years		
Diseases of heart	9.3	7.0
Malignant neoplasms	12.8	9.1
Cerebrovascular disease	11.2	8.9
Hyperplasia of prostate	8.5	5.0
Pneumonia, all forms	9.9	9.6
Inguinal hernia	5.4	2.6
70-74 years		
Diseases of heart	9.8	7.2
Malignant neoplasms	12.5	8.5
Cerebrovascular disease	10.9	9.1
Hyperplasia of prostate	8.9	5.3
Pneumonia, all forms	12.1	10.0
Inguinal hernia	6.1	3.5
75-79 years		
Diseases of heart	10.1	7.9
Malignant neoplasms	12.9	9.8
Cerebrovascular disease	14.7	9.4
Pneumonia, all forms	11.9	9.9
Hyperplasia of prostate	8.9	5.7
Fractures, all sites	16.5	11.7

[Continued]

★ 594 ★

Hospitalization: Selected Illnesses: Males
[Continued]

Age and first-listed diagnosis	Average length of stay in days	
	1981	1987
80-84 years		
Diseases of heart	10.3	7.4
Malignant neoplasms	12.7	10.5
Cerebrovascular disease	12.9	9.7
Pneumonia, all forms	12.7	10.0
Hyperplasia of prostate	10.3	6.2
Fractures, all sites	23.4	13.0
65 years and over		
Diseases of heart	9.9	7.3
Malignant neoplasms	12.8	9.3
Cerebrovascular disease	12.2	9.1
Pneumonia, all forms	11.7	9.8
Hyperplasia of prostate	9.3	5.7
Fractures, all sites	16.0	12.0
75 years and over		
Diseases of the heart	10.3	7.6
Malignant neoplasms	12.9	10.1
Cerebrovascular disease	13.4	9.3
Pneumonia, all forms	12.1	9.9
Hyperplasia of prostate	10.4	6.3
Fractures, all sites	18.2	12.5
85 years and over		
Diseases of the heart	10.7	7.1
Pneumonia, all forms	11.9	9.6
Malignant neoplasms	13.4	10.0
Cerebrovascular disease	11.6	8.6
Fractures, all sites	15.9	12.9
Hyperplasia of prostate	14.6	8.2

Source: Health Data on Older Americans: United States, 1992, Centers for Disease Control and Prevention/National Center for Health Statistics, Vital and Health Statistics, Series 3: Analytic and Epidemiological Studies, No. 27, pp. 128-129. Primary source: National Center for Health Statistics: Data from the National Hospital Discharge Survey.

★ 595 ★

Acute Conditions and Care

Medical Attention for Acute Conditions, 1991

[Percent of acute conditions medically attended]

Type of acute condition	All ages	Under 5 years	5-17 years	18-24 years	25-44 years	45 years and over		
						Total	45-64 years	65 years and over
All acute conditions	63.0	82.2	55.1	56.8	58.0	68.0	64.0	75.0
Infective and parasitic diseases	65.4	80.0	63.9	58.4	57.8	64.8	62.5	71.5
Common childhood diseases	70.5	81.4	58.2	100.0[1]	100.0[1]	58.0[1]	58.0[1]	_[1]
Intestinal virus, unspecified	36.3	69.7	27.2	24.2[1]	33.7	32.3[1]	31.9[1]	33.7[1]
Viral infections, unspecified	54.1	76.6	50.0	47.2[1]	44.8	52.1	51.7	53.3[1]
Other	92.4	90.8	94.9	86.7	89.0	95.1	92.9	100.0[1]
Respiratory conditions	46.6	74.4	41.2	35.6	39.0	50.8	47.2	58.6
Common cold	38.9	72.1	28.0	26.9	30.4	40.6	30.5	56.7
Other acute upper respiratory infections	76.6	92.6	67.5	60.4	79.6	82.1	79.0	91.1
Influenza	37.1	62.5	34.2	32.3	31.0	41.2	41.3	40.9
Acute bronchitis	90.3	93.0	86.2	93.9	88.5	93.3	92.5	94.5
Pneumonia	92.3	100.0	100.0[1]	32.9[1]	100.0[1]	88.4	100.0[1]	83.7
Other respiratory conditions	89.5	96.3	79.6	84.2[1]	83.8[1]	96.4	100.0[1]	92.1[1]
Digestive system conditions	66.3	74.5	45.6	87.4	62.2	80.7	78.7	82.9
Dental conditions	64.4	51.4[1]	67.3[1]	100.0[1]	71.0	50.8[1]	50.0[1]	54.6[1]
Indigestion, nausea, and vomiting	44.4	50.8[1]	29.0	78.9[1]	40.7	64.1[1]	71.0[1]	58.8[1]
Other digestive conditions	94.0	100.0	87.1[1]	100.0[1]	88.5	95.9	95.6	96.2
Injuries	88.3	93.5	89.7	90.9	86.3	86.5	89.3	82.3
Fractures and dislocations	99.2	100.0[1]	100.0	93.6	100.0	100.0	100.0	100.0
Sprains and strains	80.4	100.0[1]	79.9	81.2	78.0	83.7	91.1	72.9
Open wounds and lacerations	95.2	96.1	94.7	100.0	94.5	91.8	100.0	67.5[1]
Contusions and superficial injuries	87.5	88.4	88.2	97.1	85.8	83.0	83.4	82.4
Other current injuries	85.1	93.8	86.3	81.9	83.7	83.6	83.1	84.4
Selected other acute conditions	87.4	92.3	75.9	87.9	88.6	91.5	87.1	97.1
Eye conditions	98.3	91.7[1]	100.0[1]	100.0[1]	100.0[1]	100.0	100.0[1]	100.0[1]
Acute ear infections	98.4	99.1	97.8	100.0[1]	98.4	94.3	92.9	100.0[1]
Other ear conditions	87.6	88.5	82.0	100.0[1]	90.4	91.7[1]	86.5[1]	100.0[1]
Acute urinary conditions	98.7	100.0[1]	100.0[1]	100.0	97.0	99.6	99.2	100.0
Disorders of menstruation	63.7	...	37.4[1]	46.7[1]	89.6[1]	68.9[1]	68.9[1]	_[1]
Other disorders of female genital tract	100.0	100.0[1]	_[1]	100.0[1]	100.0	100.0	100.0[1]	100.0[1]
Delivery and other conditions of pregnancy and puerperium	98.7	...	100.0[1]	100.0	97.9	_[1]	_[1]	...
Skin conditions	97.8	100.0	91.2	100.0[1]	100.0	100.0	100.0[1]	100.0
Acute musculoskeletal conditions	81.8	100.0[1]	85.0	70.9[1]	79.8	83.9	79.7	94.8
Headache, excluding migraine	47.4	_[1]	25.9[1]	82.9[1]	64.9[1]	44.6[1]	_[1]	66.2[1]

[Continued]

★ 595 ★

Medical Attention for Acute Conditions, 1991
[Continued]

Type of acute condition	All ages	Under 5 years	5-17 years	18-24 years	25-44 years	45 years and over		
						Total	45-64 years	65 years and over
Fever, unspecified	43.2	57.9	21.5[1]	15.4[1]	38.6[1]	90.0[1]	-[1]	100.0[1]
All other acute conditions	83.5	94.3	66.6	74.1	82.4	89.2	88.3	90.3

Source: Current Estimates From the National Health Interview Survey, 1991, National Center for Health Statistics, Vital and Health Statistics, Series 10, No. 184, p. 25. Notes: Data are based on household interviews of the civilian noninstitutionalized population. The survey design, general qualifications, and information on the reliability of the estimates are given in appendix 1 in the original source. Excluded from these estimates are conditions involving neither medical attention nor activity restriction. A dash (-) represents zero. Three dots (...) indicate that the category is not applicable. 1. Figure does not meet standards of reliability or precision.

★ 596 ★

Acute Conditions and Care

Physician Contacts: Number of Contacts in 1989 and Reported Interval Since Last Contact, by Age

Data include office visits, telephone consultations, hospital contacts (including emergency room and outpatient visits but excluding inpatient visits) and other modes of contact. Data exclude people in institutions.

Age group who contacted physician	Contacts			Percent distribution of people, by interval since last contact			
	Number (thousands)	Percent distribution	Average number per person, per year	Less than 1 year	1 to less than 2 years	2 to less than 5 years	5 years or more
All ages	1,322,890	100.0	5.4	77.4	10.2	8.7	3.8
Under 5 years	126,309	9.5	6.7	93.3	5.0	1.2	0.4
5 to 17 years	157,698	11.9	3.5	76.3	13.4	8.1	2.3
18 to 24 years	98,233	7.4	3.9	72.2	13.0	11.2	3.6
25 to 44 years	398,368	30.1	5.1	72.8	11.3	11.2	4.7
45 to 64 years	283,351	21.4	6.1	76.5	9.2	9.0	5.3
65 +	258,931	19.6	8.9	85.9	4.7	4.9	3.5
65 to 74 years	145,949	11.0	8.2	85.1	5.3	5.6	4.0
75 +	112,982	8.5	9.9	89.1	4.0	4.0	2.9

Source: Aging America, Trends and Projections, prepared by the U.S. Senate Special Committee on Aging, the American Association of Retired Persons, the Federal Council on the Aging, and the U.S. Administration on Aging, 1991, Washington, D.C., p. 128. Primary source: National Center for Health Statistics, "Current Estimates from the National Health Interview Survey, 1989," Vital and Health Statistics, Series 10, No. 176, October 1990.

★ 597 ★

Acute Conditions and Care

Physician Contacts: Number per Year per Person 65 Years of Age and Older in 1988

Race	Total	Telephone	Office	Hospital	Other
White	8.7	0.9	5.4	1.0	1.3
Black	9.0	0.4	5.2	1.3	2.0

Source: U.S. Congress, "Profiles in Aging America: Meeting the Health Care Needs of the Nation's Black Elderly," Joint Hearing Before the Special Committee on Aging and the Congressional Black Caucus Health Braintrust, United States Senate, September 28, 1990, 101-29, U.S. Government Printing Office, Washington, D.C., p. 129. Primary source: "Current Estimates from the National Health Interview Survey, 1988," U.S. Dept. of Health and Human Services, Public Health Service, Centers for Disease Control, National Center for Health Statistics, Series 10, No. 173, Oct. 1989, p. 116.

★ 598 ★

Acute Conditions and Care

Physician Contacts: Projected Physician Visits for Years 2000 and 2030

[Number of people and visits in thousands]

Year	Age group		
	65 +	65 to 74	75 +
2000			
Noninstitutionalized population	34,882	18,243	16,639
Total physician contacts	295,613	147,480	148,133
% change in contacts, 1989-2000	14.2	1.0	31.1
2030			
Noninstitutionalized population	65,604	35,988	29,616
Total physician contacts	555,717	290,932	264,785
% change in contacts, 1989-2030	114.6	99.3	134.4

Source: Aging America, Trends and Projections, prepared by the U.S. Senate Special Committee on Aging, the American Association of Retired Persons, the Federal Council on the Aging, and the U.S. Administration on Aging, 1991, Washington, D.C., p. 129. Primary source: U.S. Administration on Aging. Unpublished projections based on physician visit rates from the 1989 National Health Interview Survey and population projections from the U.S. Bureau of the Census.

★ 599 ★

Acute Conditions and Care

Physician Contacts: Most Common Reasons Given for a Physician Visit

Data are based on reporting by a sample of office-based physicians.

Age and most common reason for a physician visit	Rank	Number of mentions per 1,000 visits	Rank	
			Male	Female
55-59 years				
Hypertension	1	56	1	2
General medical examination	2	50	4	1
Postoperative visit	3	49	2	3
Blood pressure test	4	41	3	4
Cough	5	37	6	5
Progress visit	6	27	5	12
Diabetes mellitus	7	26	7	9
Back pain	8	22	9	11
Shoulder pain	9	20	8	19
Headache	10	20	21	7
60-64 years				
General medical examination	1	60	3	1
Postoperative visit	2	55	1	2
Hypertension	3	53	2	3
Blood pressure test	4	39	5	4
Diabetes mellitus	5	38	4	7
Progress visit	6	37	6	6
Cough	7	30	12	5
Back pain	8	25	10	9
Anxiety	9	25	19	8
Chest pain (excluding heart pain)	10	24	8	15
65-69 years				
General medical examination	1	60	3	1
Postoperative visit	2	54	1	3
Hypertension	3	53	2	2
Blood pressure test	4	40	5	4
Progress visit	5	39	4	5
Diabetes mellitus	6	30	6	7
Cough	7	29	9	6
Vertigo	8	28	8	8
Chest pain (excluding heart pain)	9	25	7	10
Shortness of breath	10	21	13	11
70-74 years				
Postoperative visit	1	78	1	1
General medical examination	2	60	2	2

[Continued]

★ 599 ★

Physician Contacts: Most Common Reasons Given for a Physician Visit
[Continued]

Age and most common reason for a physician visit	Rank	Number of mentions per 1,000 visits	Rank	
			Male	Female
Hypertension	3	46	3	4
Progress visit	4	39	4	5
Blood pressure test	5	38	7	3
Diabetes mellitus	6	33	6	6
Cough	7	32	5	9
Diminished vision	8	26	10	7
Vertigo	9	24	16	8
Back pain	10	23	9	12
75-79 years				
Postoperative visit	1	74	1	1
General medical examination	2	62	2	3
Hypertension	3	51	4	2
Progress visit	4	44	3	4
Blood pressure test	5	37	9	5
Diabetes mellitus	6	31	6	8
Cataract	7	29	10	6
Cough	8	28	5	14
Vertigo	9	27	17	7
Diminished vision	10	27	11	9
80-84 years				
Postoperative visit	1	82	1	1
General medical examination	2	63	2	2
Progress visit	3	52	3	3
Diminished vision	4	40	6	4
Cataract	5	34	10	6
Hypertension	6	32	11	8
Vertigo	7	31	24	5
Shortness of breath	8	28	4	18
Diabetes mellitus	9	27	39	7
Cough	10	24	5	19
85 years and over				
General medical examination	1	64	1	3
Postoperative visit	2	64	2	1
Vertigo	3	44	16	2
Diminished vision	4	41	8	4
Cataract	5	40	5	7
Progress visit	6	38	3	10
Back pain	7	35	28	6

[Continued]

★ 599 ★

Physician Contacts: Most Common Reasons Given for a Physician Visit

[Continued]

Age and most common reason for a physician visit	Rank	Number of mentions per 1,000 visits	Rank	
			Male	Female
Hypertension	8	34[1]	43	5
Leg pain	9	32[1]	13	8
Skin lesion	10	30[1]	19	9

Source: Health Data on Older Americans: United States, 1992, Centers for Disease Control and Prevention/National Center for Health Statistics, Vital and Health Statistics, Series 3: Analytic and Epidemiological Studies, No. 27, pp. 122-123. Primary source: National Center for Health Statistics: Data from the National Ambulatory Medical Care Survey. *Note:* 1. Figure does not meet standard of reliability or precision.

★ 600 ★

Acute Conditions and Care

Physician Contacts: Most Frequent Diagnoses by Office-Based Physicians

Data are based on reporting by a sample of office-based physicians.

Age and frequent all-listed diagnoses[1]	Rank	Number of mentions per 1,000 visits	Rank	
			Male	Female
55-59 years				
Essential hypertension	1	143	1	1
Diabetes mellitus	2	61	2	2
Chronic ischemic heart disease	3	28	3	17
Neurotic disorders	4	26	9	4
Disorders of refraction and accommodation	5	26	6	5
Osteoarthritis and allied disorders	6	25	4	9
Arthropathies, other and unspecified	7	19	10	11
Obesity	8	16	27	10
Bronchitis	9	16	16	13
Acute upper respiratory infections	10	16	47	6
60-64 years				
Essential hypertension	1	159	1	1
Diabetes mellitus	2	83	2	2
Chronic ischemic heart disease	3	46	3	3
Osteoarthritis	4	28	5	5
Disorders of refraction and accommodation	5	26	8	4
Arthropathies	6	21	10	9
Chronic airway obstruction, not elsewhere classified	7	19	4	38
Neurotic disorders	8	19	19	7
Angina pectoris	9	19	6	22

[Continued]

★ 600 ★

Physician Contacts: Most Frequent Diagnoses by Office-Based Physicians
[Continued]

Age and frequent all-listed diagnoses[1]	Rank	Number of mentions per 1,000 visits	Rank	
			Male	Female
Cardiac dysrhythmias	10	17	16	11
65-69 years				
Essential hypertension	1	157	1	1
Diabetes mellitus	2	78	2	2
Chronic ischemic heart disease	3	47	3	5
Osteoarthritis and allied disorders	4	43	10	3
Cataract	5	30	8	4
Cardiac dysrhythmias	6	26	5	6
Angina pectoris	7	24	6	11
Chronic airway obstruction, not elsewhere classified	8	23	4	17
Arthropathies, other and unspecified	9	23	9	9
Disorders of refraction and accommodation	10	22	11	8
70-74 years				
Essential hypertension	1	145	1	1
Diabetes mellitus	2	81	2	2
Chronic ischemic heart disease	3	53	3	4
Cataract	4	48	5	3
Osteoarthritis and allied disorders	5	35	8	5
Cardiac dysrhythmias	6	27	6	10
Chronic airway obstruction, not elsewhere classified	7	24	4	12
Heart failure	8	25	9	8
Arthropathies	9	24	18	6
Glaucoma	10	24	14	7
75-79 years				
Essential hypertension	1	170	1	1
Diabetes mellitus	2	91	2	2
Chronic ischemic heart disease	3	67	3	4
Cataract	4	61	5	3
Osteoarthritis and allied disorders	5	48	7	5
Heart failure	6	37	6	7
Cardiac dysrhythmias	7	34	4	9
Glaucoma	8	32	8	6
Arthropathies, other and unspecified	9	27	12	8
Neurotic disorders	10	21	15	11

[Continued]

★ 600 ★

Physician Contacts: Most Frequent Diagnoses by Office-Based Physicians
[Continued]

Age and frequent all-listed diagnoses[1]	Rank	Number of mentions per 1,000 visits	Rank	
			Male	Female
80-84 years				
Essential hypertension	1	133	1	1
Cataract	2	74	5	2
Chronic ischemic heart disease	3	72	2	3
Diabetes mellitus	4	56	8	4
Heart failure	5	54	3	6
Osteoarthritis and allied disorders	6	54	6	5
Glaucoma	7	32	9	7
Cardiac dysrhythmias	8	30	7	11
Other eye disorders	9	27	14	8
Chronic airway obstruction, not elsewhere classified	10	27	4	26
85 years and over				
Essential hypertension	1	122	4	1
Chronic ischemic heart disease	2	77	1	3
Cataract	3	74	3	2
Heart failure	4	66	2	4
Diabetes mellitus	5	44	5	5
Osteoarthritis and allied disorders	6	37	9	6
Glaucoma	7	35	8	8
Cardiac dysrhythmias	8	33[2]	6	12
Other disorders of urethra and urinary tract	9	31[2]	16	9
Other skin cancer	10	31[2]	7	11

Source: *Health Data on Older Americans: United States, 1992*, Centers for Disease Control and Prevention/National Center for Health Statistics, Vital and Health Statistics, Series 3: Analytic and Epidemiological Studies, No. 27, pp. 125-126. Primary source: National Center for Health Statistics: Data from the National Ambulatory Medical Care Survey. *Notes:* 1. "All-listed" means listed as first, second, or third diagnosis. 2. Figure does not meet the standard for reliability or precision..

★ 601 ★

Acute Conditions and Care

Physician Contacts: Office Visits to Specialists

Data are based on reporting by a sample of office-based physicians.

Sex and age	Visits to all physicians Number in thousands	Specialty Percent						
		General practice	Internal medicine	General surgery	Ophthal-mology	Orthopedic surgery	Cardio-vascular specialty	Other specialty
Both sexes								
Total	205,582	29.9	20.2	6.4	11.4	4.2	3.8	10.3
55-59 years	37,218	29.6	16.8	6.7	7.4	6.4	3.2	12.6
60-64 years	37,826	33.1	16.9	6.6	8.4	5.0	4.3	10.5
65-69 years	39,781	28.8	22.3	6.0	10.4	4.2	4.0	10.4
70-74 years	35,646	28.8	22.0	6.8	12.1	2.9	3.9	10.6
75-79 years	29,354	28.6	22.3	7.1	14.7	3.5	4.1	9.2
80-84 years	16,227	29.2	21.4	4.9	19.1	2.6	3.5	8.6
65 years and over	130,539	29.1	22.1	6.2	13.5	3.4	3.8	9.7
75 years and over	55,111	29.4	22.1	6.0	16.6	3.1	3.8	8.5
85 years and over	9,530	32.3	22.5	4.5	18.1	2.6	3.1	6.3
Male								
Total	82,112	28.7	19.1	6.6	10.3	4.0	5.2	10.8
55-59 years	15,520	28.7	15.8	5.8	7.6	7.4	4.4	13.0
60-64 years	15,588	30.5	16.9	6.8	8.2	5.1	6.5	10.4
65-69 years	16,707	28.4	20.9	5.9	9.9	4.2	5.7	10.3
70-74 years	14,058	26.4	21.7	8.3	10.8	2.0	4.7	11.1
75-79 years	11,518	28.0	21.7	6.9	12.4	2.2	4.7	10.2
80-84 years	5,808	30.5	18.2	6.4	16.0	1.5	4.8	8.0
65 years and over	51,004	28.1	20.8	6.7	11.8	2.6	5.0	10.2
75 years and over	20,239	29.1	20.2	6.2	14.0	1.8	4.7	9.5
85 years and over	2,912	30.8	18.1	3.2	16.1	1.1	4.2	10.3
Female								
Total	123,469	30.7	20.9	6.2	12.2	4.4	2.9	10.0
55-59 years	21,698	30.2	17.5	7.2	7.3	5.7	2.3	12.2
60-64 years	22,237	34.9	16.8	6.5	8.6	4.9	2.9	10.5
65-69 years	23,074	29.1	23.3	6.1	10.7	4.2	2.7	10.4
70-74 years	21,588	30.4	22.2	5.7	12.9	3.5	3.3	10.3
75-79 years	17,835	29.0	22.7	7.3	16.2	4.4	3.7	8.6
80-84 years	10,419	28.5	23.2	4.1	20.8	3.2	2.7	8.9
65 years and over	79,535	29.7	23.0	5.9	14.5	3.8	3.1	9.3

[Continued]

★ 601 ★

Physician Contacts: Office Visits to Specialists

[Continued]

Sex and age	Visits to all physicians Number in thousands	Specialty Percent						
		General practice	Internal medicine	General surgery	Ophthal-mology	Orthopedic surgery	Cardio-vascular specialty	Other specialty
75 years and over	34,873	29.6	23.2	5.9	18.1	3.8	3.2	7.9
85 years and over	6,618	32.9	24.4	5.1	19.1	3.3	2.7	4.5

Source: Health Data on Older Americans: United States, 1992, Centers for Disease Control and Prevention/National Center for Health Statistics, Vital and Health Statistics, Series 3: Analytic and Epidemiological Studies, No. 27, p. 124. Primary source: National Center for Health Statistics: Data from the National Ambulatory Medical Care Survey.

★ 602 ★

Acute Conditions and Care

Restricted Activity Associated with Acute Conditions, 1991

[Number of restricted activity days per 100 persons per year]

Type of acute condition	All ages	Under 5 years	5-17 years	18-24 years	25-44 years	45 years and over		
						Total	45-64 years	65 years and over
All acute conditions	733.3	996.1	720.5	712.4	682.9	734.7	643.1	877.4
Infectious and parasitic diseases	62.2	155.9	124.2	56.3	35.2	32.0	29.8	35.5
Common childhood diseases	11.0	51.6	28.9	8.8[1]	1.7[1]	0.4[1]	0.7[1]	-[1]
Intestinal virus, unspecified	9.9	23.6[1]	19.5	9.6[1]	7.8	3.0[1]	2.4[1]	3.9[1]
Viral infections, unspecified	20.4	56.5	30.6	14.6[1]	11.9	16.1	16.9	14.9[1]
Other	21.0	24.1[1]	45.3	23.3	13.8	12.5	9.7[1]	16.7[1]
Respiratory conditions	341.6	526.3	407.2	297.7	285.8	328.7	309.4	358.7
Common cold	70.8	150.7	77.5	82.0	54.5	60.3	51.9	73.4
Other acute upper respiratory infections	31.5	50.8	49.4	18.2[1]	28.0	23.8	23.9	23.7
Influenza	184.5	236.9	235.2	169.1	166.2	165.1	181.6	139.3
Acute bronchitis	22.5	51.4	24.0	15.7[1]	17.0	22.3	25.1	18.1[1]
Pneumonia	23.0	24.1[1]	10.8[1]	10.6[1]	15.3	42.2	18.9	78.5
Other respiratory conditions	9.3	12.5[1]	10.3[1]	2.2[1]	4.8[1]	14.9	8.1[1]	25.6
Digestive system conditions	27.3	24.8[1]	18.5	19.7[1]	25.9	37.0	25.0	55.5
Dental conditions	5.6	13.3[1]	4.8[1]	5.5[1]	5.7[1]	4.0[1]	4.4[1]	3.4[1]
Indigestion, nausea, and vomiting	5.3	5.4[1]	9.6[1]	7.2[1]	3.4[1]	4.0[1]	1.9[1]	7.3[1]
Other digestive conditions	16.4	6.1[1]	4.1[1]	7.0[1]	16.8	28.9	18.7	44.8
Injuries	135.6	33.9	75.7	157.2	155.8	168.7	143.9	207.4
Fractures and dislocations	38.9	9.2[1]	27.4	44.8	30.9	59.6	40.8	88.7
Sprains and strains	37.3	-[1]	13.4	47.6	60.7	33.1	33.4	32.5
Open wounds and lacerations	11.1	7.3[1]	10.9[1]	19.9[1]	13.1	7.2[1]	7.6[1]	6.7[1]
Contusions and superficial injuries	18.5	2.6[1]	7.6[1]	13.5[1]	16.6	32.7	31.0	35.2
Other current injuries	29.8	14.7[1]	16.4	31.3	34.4	36.2	31.0	44.4

[Continued]

★ 602 ★

Restricted Activity Associated with Acute Conditions, 1991
[Continued]

Type of acute condition	All ages	Under 5 years	5-17 years	18-24 years	25-44 years	45 years and over		
						Total	45-64 years	65 years and over
Selected other acute conditions	116.3	210.6	74.2	125.2	133.2	97.2	82.4	120.1
Eye conditions	1.8[1]	4.6[1]	0.3[1]	4.5[1]	0.1[1]	3.0[1]	1.7[1]	4.9[1]
Acute ear infections	24.1	155.7	33.9	6.7[1]	9.4	6.1[1]	3.7[1]	9.9[1]
Other ear conditions	1.9[1]	7.9[1]	3.6[1]	-[1]	0.9[1]	0.9[1]	1.0[1]	0.6[1]
Acute urinary conditions	9.9	3.2[1]	4.3[1]	6.0[1]	10.3	15.7	13.4	19.3
Disorders of menstruation	1.7[1]	...	2.5[1]	1.4[1]	3.2[1]	0.2[1]	0.3[1]	-[1]
Other disorders of female genital tract	4.9	-[1]	-[1]	9.5[1]	8.0	4.4[1]	2.5[1]	7.5[1]
Delivery and other conditions of pregnancy and puerperium	25.1	...	1.7[1]	80.0	51.7	-[1]	-[1]	...
Skin conditions	5.6	6.5[1]	5.0[1]	1.5[1]	2.1[1]	10.8	7.5[1]	15.9[1]
Acute musculoskeletal conditions	28.1	2.5[1]	6.1[1]	5.4[1]	37.8	44.8	48.0	39.9
Headache, excluding migraine	5.2	-[1]	7.6[1]	4.9[1]	5.2[1]	5.1[1]	3.3[1]	8.0[1]
Fever, unspecified	8.0	30.1	9.3[1]	5.3[1]	4.6[1]	6.2[1]	1.2[1]	13.9[1]
All other acute conditions	50.4	44.6	20.6	56.2	47.0	71.2	52.5	100.3

Source: *Current Estimates From the National Health Interview Survey, 1991,* National Center for Health Statistics, Vital and Health Statistics, Series 10, No. 184, p. 31. *Notes:* Data are based on household interviews of the civilian noninstitutionalized population. The survey design, general qualifications, and information on the reliability of the estimates are given in appendix 1 in the original source. Excluded from these estimates are conditions involving neither medical attention nor activity restriction. A dash (-) represents zero. Three dots (...) indicate that the category is not applicable. 1. Figure does not meet standards of reliability or precision.

★ 603 ★

Acute Conditions and Care

Surgical Procedures Performed on Females

Number and rate of surgical procedures for females 55 years of age and over discharged from short-stay hospitals, by age and selected procedures: 1981 and 1987.

[Discharges from non-federal short-stay hospitals]

Age and first-listed diagnosis	Number of procedures in thousands		Number of procedures per 10,000 population	
	1981	1987	1981	1987
55-59 years				
Cardiac catheterization	17	43	27.2	73.3
Cholecystectomy	29	31	47.8	53.3
Hysterectomy	27	24	44.3	41.5
Oophorectomy and salpingo-oophorectomy	23	19	38.2	33.2
Reduction of fracture[1]	17	13	27.8	21.6

[Continued]

★ 603 ★

Surgical Procedures Performed on Females
[Continued]

Age and first-listed diagnosis	Number of procedures in thousands		Number of procedures per 10,000 population	
	1981	1987	1981	1987
60-64 years				
Cardiac catheterization	22	51	39.7	87.9
Cholecystectomy	31	31	55.7	52.8
Hysterectomy	26	25	47.3	43.1
Mastectomy	17	23	30.6	40.0
Reduction of fracture[1]	19	18	33.8	31.1
65-69 years				
Cardiac catheterization	20	56	40.4	103.8
Cholecystectomy	28	32	57.5	59.6
Hysterectomy	22	24	45.2	44.4
Reduction of fracture[1]	25	24	50.1	43.8
Resection of intestine	16	20	31.5	37.1
70-74 years				
Cardiac catheterization	12	47	28.6	106.4
Reduction of fracture[1]	19	29	47.2	64.9
Cholecystectomy	24	26	59.6	58.5
Resection of intestine	16	26	38.1	57.5
Arthroplasty and replacement of hip	16	19	39.7	43.7
75-79 years				
Cardiac catheterization	7	28	24.0	80.1
Reduction of fracture[1]	31	27	101.8	75.8
Arthroplasty and replacement of hip	17	24	56.9	67.0
Resection of intestine	13	19	41.7	53.6
Pacemaker insertion[2]	16	18	51.7	51.5
80-84 years				
Reduction of fracture[1]	29	33	141.9	142.9
Arthroplasty and replacement of hip	17	30	82.1	131.6
Pacemaker insertion[2]	16	19	80.2	82.3
Resection of intestine	11	13	55.1	58.3
Cholecystectomy	10	12	49.7	54.2
65 years and over				
Reduction of fracture[1]	134	169	85.2	95.2

[Continued]

★ 603 ★

Surgical Procedures Performed on Females

[Continued]

Age and first-listed diagnosis	Number of procedures in thousands		Number of procedures per 10,000 population	
	1981	1987	1981	1987
Cardiac catheterization	41	146	26.1	82.5
Arthroplasty and replacement of hip	82	115	52.5	65.1
Cholecystectomy	86	106	55.0	59.8
Resection of intestine	66	92	42.2	51.8
75 years and over				
Reduction of fracture[1]	90	116	134.2	147.2
Arthroplasty and replacement of hip	52	75	77.4	95.5
Pacemaker insertion[2]	45	53	67.5	67.4
Cholecystectomy	34	48	50.2	60.6
Resection of intestine	35	46	52.6	58.5
85 years and over				
Reduction of fracture[1]	30	56	184.1	273.7
Arthroplasty and replacement of hip	18	21	109.2	103.8
Pacemaker insertion[2]	13	16	80.7	77.9
Resection of intestine	11	14	69.4	67.2
Cholecystectomy	6	12	35.2	60.3

Source: *Health Data on Older Americans: United States, 1992,* Centers for Disease Control and Prevention/National Center for Health Statistics, Vital and Health Statistics, Series 3: Analytic and Epidemiological Studies, No. 27, pp. 134-135. Primary source: National Center for Health Statistics: Data from the National Hospital Discharge Survey. *Notes:* 1. Excluding skull, nose and jaw. 2. Including replacement, removal, and repair.

★ 604 ★

Acute Conditions and Care

Surgical Procedures Performed on Males

Number and rate of surgical procedures for males 55 years of age and over discharged from short-stay hospitals, by age and selected procedures: 1981 and 1987.

[Discharges from non-federal short-stay hospitals]

Age and first-listed diagnosis	Number of procedures in thousands		Number of procedures per 10,000 population	
	1981	1987	1981	1987
55-59 years				
Cardiac catheterization	48	84	88.3	157.7
Direct heart revascularization	26	40	46.6	75.1
Repair of inguinal hernia	40	26	73.9	49.1
Prostatectomy	24	24	43.8	46.2

[Continued]

★ 604 ★

Surgical Procedures Performed on Males
[Continued]

Age and first-listed diagnosis	Number of procedures in thousands		Number of procedures per 10,000 population	
	1981	1987	1981	1987
Reduction of fracture[1]	12	15	22.5	29.1
60-64 years				
Cardiac catheterization	40	89	83.3	176.0
Prostatectomy	45	56	94.0	109.9
Direct heart revascularization	25	44	52.9	87.6
Repair of inguinal hernia	42	32	87.5	62.6
Cholecystectomy	13	18	26.8	35.0
65-69 years				
Cardiac catheterization	34	87	85.0	194.2
Prostatectomy	64	79	161.5	175.4
Direct heart revascularization	23	48	58.8	106.7
Repair of inguinal hernia	42	28	107.2	62.1
Cholecystectomy	17	19	43.9	43.1
70-74 years				
Prostatectomy	80	85	271.0	256.5
Cardiac catheterization	17	53	58.3	159.6
Direct heart revascularization	10	39	32.8	116.1
Repair of inguinal hernia	34	26	115.8	77.1
Pacemaker insertion[2]	18	21	62.7	63.8
75-79 years				
Prostatectomy	57	77	298.5	338.9
Cardiac catheterization	7	30	35.5	134.6
Pacemaker insertion[2]	14	26	74.4	116.7
Repair of inguinal hernia	25	20	132.9	87.8
Cholecystectomy	10	16	50.3	70.7
80-84 years				
Prostatectomy	41	47	386.4	386.7
Pacemaker insertion[2]	13	18	118.7	146.4
Repair of inguinal hernia	13	13	123.8	109.4
Resection of intestine	9	12	84.5	102.0
Reduction of fracture[1]	4	10	41.5	81.5

[Continued]

★ 604 ★

Surgical Procedures Performed on Males
[Continued]

Age and first-listed diagnosis	Number of procedures in thousands		Number of procedures per 10,000 population	
	1981	1987	1981	1987
65 years and over				
Prostatectomy	263	318	248.7	262.7
Cardiac catheterization	60	182	56.9	149.8
Direct heart revascularization	36	105	34.2	86.8
Repair of inguinal hernia	122	96	115.2	79.2
Pacemaker insertion[2]	69	95	65.3	78.6
75 years and over				
Prostatectomy	119	154	324.5	358.8
Pacemaker insertion[2]	35	58	95.9	135.8
Repair of inguinal hernia	45	42	123.3	98.8
Cardiac catheterization	9	41	25.4	95.9
Resection of intestine	24	28	66.4	65.6
85 years and over				
Prostatectomy	21	30	301.1	372.5
Pacemaker insertion[2]	8	14	119.1	173.4
Reduction of fracture[1]	8	10	111.2	130.0
Repair of inguinal hernia	7	9	97.0	113.6
Arthroplasty and replacement of hip	5	7	77.0	87.8

Source: Health Data on Older Americans: United States, 1992, Centers for Disease Control and Prevention/National Center for Health Statistics, Vital and Health Statistics, Series 3: Analytic and Epidemiological Studies, No. 27, pp. 132-133. Primary source: National Center for Health Statistics: Data from the National Hospital Discharge Survey. *Notes:* 1. Excluding skull, nose and jaw. 2. Including replacement, removal, and repair.

Long-Term Conditions and Care

★ 605 ★

Chronic Conditions Reported by Persons 55 Years of Age and Over

Average annual number of selected reported chronic conditions per 1,000 persons 55 years of age and over, by type of chronic condition, sex, and age: 1979-81, 1982-84, and 1985-87.

[Number per 1,000 persons]

Sex and age	Ischemic heart disease			Hypertension			Diabetes		
	1979-81	1982-84	1985-87	1979-81	1982-84	1985-87	1979-81	1982-84	1985-87
Both sexes									
55-64 years	58.8	75.7	70.1	286.4	306.5	302.7	66.1	71.6	76.1
65-74 years	105.0	115.7	114.1	365.6	392.5	400.8	87.7	92.8	99.0
65 years and over	103.7	116.2	121.5	376.6	393.8	392.5	85.9	89.7	99.7
75 years and over	101.3	117.1	133.6	395.8	396.1	379.3	82.8	84.7	100.8
Male									
55-64 years	77.6	107.5	98.9	275.2	291.2	287.6	65.3	72.1	79.1
65-74 years	133.9	149.9	150.7	305.6	335.7	359.3	84.8	79.9	101.9
65 years and over	125.0	142.8	152.6	297.3	318.6	331.1	82.8	83.0	102.5
75 years and over	106.6	128.9	156.3	280.4	285.6	276.6	78.6	88.7	103.6
Female									
55-64 years	42.1	47.9	44.7	296.4	320.0	316.1	66.9	71.3	73.4
65-74 years	82.8	89.4	85.3	411.7	436.0	433.4	90.0	102.7	96.7
65 years and over	88.8	97.9	99.8	431.9	445.8	435.7	88.1	94.3	97.7
75 years and over	998.2	110.4	120.4	463.7	460.0	438.9	85.3	82.3	99.1

Source: Health Data on Older Americans: United States, 1992, Centers for Disease Control and Prevention/National Center for Health Statistics, Vital and Health Statistics, Series 3: Analytic and Epidemiological Studies, No. 27, p. 21. Primary source: National Center for Health Statistics: Data from the National Health Interview Survey. *Notes:* These rates are based on unduplicated counts; a person was counted only once for each condition regardless of the number of mentions of that condition.

★ 606 ★

Long-Term Conditions and Care

Number of People 65+ Living Alone Who Have Selected Chronic Health Problems, 1990-2020

From the source: "As the older population increases during the twenty-first century, the number of people with chronic health problems who live alone is expected to increase."

[Number in millions]

Condition	1990	2005	2020
Arthritis	5.2	6.1	8.2
Hearing/vision	4.8	5.8	7.6
Hypertension	4.4	5.1	6.8

Source: Aging America, Trends and Projections, prepared by the U.S. Senate Special Committee on Aging, the American Association of Retired Persons, the Federal Council on the Aging, and the U.S. Administration on Aging, 1991, Washington, D.C., p. 227. Primary source: Lewin/ICF estimates based on data from the 1984 *Supplement on Aging* and the Brookings/ICF Long-Term Care Financing Model, 1990.

★ 607 ★

Long-Term Conditions and Care

Proportion of People 65+ Living Alone Who Have Selected Chronic Health Problems, by Poverty Status, 1990

[Numbers in percent]

Condition	Poor	Non-poor
Arthritis	65.0	54.0
Hearing/vision	60.0	50.0
Hypertension	55.0	45.0

Source: Aging America, Trends and Projections, prepared by the U.S. Senate Special Committee on Aging, the American Association of Retired Persons, the Federal Council on the Aging, and the U.S. Administration on Aging, 1991, Washington, D.C., p. 226. Primary source: Lewin/ICF estimates based on data from the 1984 *Supplement on Aging* and the Brookings/ICF Long-Term Care Financing Model, 1990.

★ 608 ★

Long-Term Conditions and Care

Chronic Conditions Per 1,000 Persons, 1991

Type of chronic condition	All ages	Under 45 years			45-64 years	65 years and over		
		Total	Under 18 years	18-44 years		Total	65-74 years	75 years and over
Selected skin and musculoskeletal conditions								
Arthritis	125.2	29.8	1.6[1]	47.3	240.8	484.8	425.6	575.2
Gout, including gouty arthritis	8.6	2.5	-[1]	4.0	17.7	29.1	27.3	31.9
Intervertebral disc disorders	20.0	12.1	0.2[1]	19.4	43.8	27.6	31.1	22.3
Bone spur or tendinitis, unspecified	9.9	5.1	0.6[1]	8.0	21.4	18.7	19.3	17.8
Disorders of bone or cartilage	6.7	3.1	1.7[1]	3.9	10.4	21.3	19.4	24.2
Trouble with bunions	10.7	5.6	1.5[1]	8.1	17.3	29.6	24.0	38.4
Bursitis, unclassified	18.1	8.9	0.5[1]	14.1	41.1	34.0	39.9	24.9
Sebaceous skin cyst	4.7	4.4	1.6[1]	6.1	5.6	4.8[1]	6.6[1]	2.2[1]
Trouble with acne	20.4	28.0	26.5	28.8	4.9	1.6[1]	2.0[1]	1.0[1]
Psoriasis	9.4	7.1	2.6	10.0	15.4	12.8	11.5	14.7
Dermatitis	36.1	36.8	31.5	40.1	36.9	30.8	34.8	24.8
Trouble with dry (itching) skin, unclassified	19.8	16.0	11.5	18.8	23.2	36.2	24.4	54.4
Trouble with ingrown nails	23.8	17.9	7.8	24.2	26.6	52.2	50.2	55.4
Trouble with corns and calluses	19.4	10.7	0.7[1]	16.9	33.2	47.0	40.5	56.9
Impairments								
Visual impairment	32.1	19.6	5.4	28.4	47.5	79.2	56.8	113.3
Color blindness	9.9	8.4	2.7	11.9	13.1	12.9	12.0	14.3
Cataracts	26.5	2.3	1.4[1]	2.9	20.2	173.0	127.6	242.3
Glaucoma	10.4	1.7	0.4[1]	2.5	11.9	57.0	46.0	74.0
Hearing impairment	91.2	36.8	16.1	49.7	141.3	320.5	266.2	403.6
Tinnitus	26.1	9.5	1.7[1]	14.3	50.2	82.4	95.3	62.6
Speech impairment	11.2	11.7	16.7	8.6	10.0	10.3	6.1[1]	16.6
Absence of extremities (excludes tips of fingers or toes only)	5.9	2.9	0.9[1]	4.2	9.8	16.9	16.1	18.0
Paralysis of extremities, complete or partial	5.0	2.9	2.4[1]	3.2	7.1	14.0	8.3[1]	22.8
Deformity or orthopedic impairment	115.5	93.8	25.2	136.4	154.4	177.5	167.1	193.3
Back	71.2	59.0	9.1	89.9	99.3	96.2	95.8	96.7
Upper extremities	13.9	9.1	1.4[1]	13.9	22.1	28.2	30.0	25.4
Lower extremities	43.8	34.6	15.5	46.5	57.9	73.5	68.3	81.5
Selected digestive conditions								
Ulcer	15.0	9.7	1.1[1]	15.1	26.2	27.0	24.4	31.0
Hernia of abdominal cavity	19.7	7.0	2.9	9.5	40.6	58.9	55.0	64.8
Gastritis or duodenitis	11.8	7.9	1.6[1]	11.9	20.2	20.6	21.9	18.5
Frequent indigestion	23.0	16.4	2.2[1]	25.3	34.9	41.7	39.1	45.5
Enteritis or colitis	8.9	5.9	1.8[1]	8.5	11.7	21.5	17.5	27.8

[Continued]

★ 608 ★

Chronic Conditions Per 1,000 Persons, 1991

[Continued]

Type of chronic condition	All ages	Under 45 years			45-64 years	65 years and over		
		Total	Under 18 years	18-44 years		Total	65-74 years	75 years and over
Spastic colon	6.8	5.6	-[1]	9.0	11.1	7.5	9.8	3.9[1]
Diverticula of intestines	7.4	0.9[1]	-[1]	1.4[1]	12.2	36.7	39.8	31.9
Frequent constipation	18.5	11.1	6.2	14.1	19.1	59.7	41.4	87.7
Selected conditions of the genitourinary, nervous, endocrine, metabolic, and blood and blood-forming systems								
Goiter or other disorders of the thyroid	14.8	6.3	0.8[1]	9.6	28.3	41.7	45.8	35.4
Diabetes	29.0	8.8	1.1[1]	13.6	57.4	99.3	103.8	92.6
Anemias	14.3	12.5	6.8	16.0	13.2	26.1	22.5	31.5
Epilepsy	5.8	5.8	6.3	5.5	5.4	6.0	5.7[1]	6.3[1]
Migraine headache	38.4	39.1	12.6	55.5	47.2	20.6	19.6	22.3
Neuralgia or neuritis, unspecified	1.8	0.7[1]	-[1]	1.1[1]	3.2[1]	5.8	5.7[1]	6.0[1]
Kidney trouble	12.6	9.2	3.1	12.9	17.3	25.1	23.4	27.6
Bladder disorders	15.2	10.6	4.6	14.3	15.6	40.4	30.6	55.5
Diseases of prostate	7.2	0.9[1]	-[1]	1.5[1]	12.3	35.0	38.8	29.2
Diseases of female genital organs	19.5	19.9	3.1	30.4	24.4	9.7	13.4	4.0[1]
Selected circulatory conditions								
Rheumatic fever with or without heart disease	8.8	6.4	0.6[1]	9.9	15.1	13.0	13.9	11.6[1]
Heart disease	82.6	30.8	18.5	38.4	134.1	295.2	256.4	354.3
Ischemic heart disease	29.6	1.8	0.2[1]	2.8	61.1	138.3	127.2	155.3
Heart rhythm disorders	33.5	22.9	14.6	28.1	42.4	79.3	65.9	99.7
Tachycardia or rapid heart	8.4	3.3	1.6[1]	4.4	15.3	26.8	24.1	30.9
Heart murmurs	18.2	17.5	11.9	21.0	18.8	20.8	19.3	23.1
Other and unspecified heart rhythm disorders	6.9	2.1	1.1[1]	2.8	8.3	31.7	22.5	45.6
Other selected diseases of heart, excluding hypertension	19.4	6.1	3.8	7.5	30.5	77.7	63.4	99.5
High blood pressure (hypertension)	111.8	29.3	1.9[1]	46.3	244.0	372.2	376.6	365.5
Cerebrovascular disease	11.5	1.1	0.7[1]	1.4[1]	16.1	63.0	58.2	70.4
Hardening of the arteries	7.5	0.4[1]	-[1]	0.6[1]	11.1	42.7	36.4	52.1
Varicose veins of lower extremities	31.9	16.1	0.4[1]	25.9	58.7	79.5	90.4	62.8
Hemorrhoids	37.4	23.6	0.3[1]	38.0	68.1	67.5	75.7	55.0
Selected respiratory conditions								
Chronic bronchitis	50.5	49.2	53.1	46.7	53.9	52.5	56.2	46.7
Asthma	47.2	50.7	62.5	43.4	40.7	37.2	38.0	35.9

[Continued]

★ 608 ★

Chronic Conditions Per 1,000 Persons, 1991
[Continued]

Type of chronic condition	All ages	Under 45 years			45-64 years	65 years and over		
		Total	Under 18 years	18-44 years		Total	65-74 years	75 years and over
Hay fever or allergic rhinitis without asthma	97.5	99.2	64.6	120.6	107.1	72.9	79.4	62.9
Chronic sinusitis	129.3	116.0	59.6	151.0	171.1	139.5	156.4	113.7
Deviated nasal septum	6.1	6.0	1.6[1]	8.7	7.6	4.2[1]	4.5[1]	3.7[1]
Chronic disease of tonsils or adenoids	11.1	15.3	24.0	10.0	1.1[1]	2.8[1]	3.6[1]	1.8[1]
Emphysema	6.6	0.4[1]	-[1]	0.6[1]	12.8	32.4	32.7	31.9

Source: *Current Estimates From the National Health Interview Survey, 1991*, National Center for Health Statistics, Vital and Health Statistics, Series 10, No. 184, p. 82. Notes: Data are based on household interviews of the civilian noninstitutionalized population. The survey design, general qualifications, and information are given in appendix 1 of the original source. A dash (-) represents zero. 1. Figure does not meet standard of reliability or precision.

★ 609 ★

Long-Term Conditions and Care

Demographic Characteristics of Impaired Persons, Aged 65+, 1990

Sex	All persons age 65+		Impaired persons age 65+[1]	
	Number (000)	% of total	Number (000)	% of group[2]
Total	30,043	100.0	4,396	14.6
Men	12,469	41.5	1,408	11.3
Women	17,574	58.5	2,989	17.0

Source: *Aging America, Trends and Projections*, prepared by the U.S. Senate Special Committee on Aging, the American Association of Retired Persons, the Federal Council on the Aging, and the U.S. Administration on Aging, 1991, Washington, D.C., p. 145. Primary source: Lewin/ICF, unpublished data, 1990. Estimates based on data from 1984 *Survey on Aging* (SOA), *Current Population Survey* (CPS), and Brookings/ICF *Long-Term Care Financing Model*. Notes: Projections assume constant age, sex, and marital status rates of disability for persons living in the community. 1. Impaired older persons are persons age 65+ (living in the community) who have limitations in at least 1 of 5 activities of daily living. 2. Percentages are estimates which have been extracted from the numbers in column 1 by the editors of SROA.

★ 610 ★

Long-Term Conditions and Care

Expected Role of Private Long-Term Care Insurance

Year	Total LTC expenditures (in billions of 1989 dollars)	Percent of expenditures covered by private insurance
1990	46.0	2.0
2005	75.9	4.0
2020	132.6	6.6

Source: Aging America, Trends and Projections, prepared by the U.S. Senate Special Committee on Aging, the American Association of Retired Persons, the Federal Council on the Aging, and the U.S. Administration on Aging, 1991, Washington, D.C., p. 175. Primary source: Brookings/ICF *Long-Term Care Financing Model*, unpublished data, 1990.

★ 611 ★

Long-Term Conditions and Care

Living Arrangements of Impaired People Age 65+, 1990

Data refer to impaired older people, living in the community, who have limitations in at least 1 of 5 activities of daily living.

Living arrangement	All people age 65+		Impaired people age 65+	
	Number (000)	% of total	Number (000)	% of impaired
Total	30,043	100.0	4,396.0	100.0
Alone	9,172	30.5	1,458.0	33.2
With spouse	13,452	44.8	1,404.0	31.9
With spouse/others	2,621	8.7	326.0	7.4
With relatives	4,087	13.6	1,014.0	23.1
With nonrelatives	711	2.4	194.0	4.4

Source: Aging America, Trends and Projections, prepared by the U.S. Senate Special Committee on Aging, the American Association of Retired Persons, the Federal Council on the Aging, and the U.S. Administration on Aging, 1991, Washington, D.C., p. 146. Primary source: Lewin/ICF, unpublished data, 1990. Estimates based on data from 1984 *Survey on Aging* (SOA), *Current Population Survey* (CPS), and Brookings/ICF *Long-Term Care Financing Model*.

★ 612 ★

Long-Term Conditions and Care

Percentage of Ethnic Populations in Nursing Homes in 1980, by Age[1]

This table shows percentage of each ethnic group in older age cohorts utilizing long-term care services. While the data may *seem* to indicate that minority families are less likely to utilize long-term care, the original source points out that little data is available on this subject and that "if providers and planners (and the ethnic group itself) make such assumptions, potential barriers to utilization will not be identified."

Age	Black	Hispanic	Asian/ Pac. Isl.	Native Amer.	White
65+	3	3	2	4[2]	5
85+	12	10	10	13	23

Source: Yeo, Gwen, Ph.D., "Ethnogeriatric Education: Need and Recommendations," *Shortage of Health Care Professions Caring for the Elderly: Recommendations for Change,* Senate Select Committee on Aging, Comm. Pub. No. 102-915, p. 84. Primary source: American Association of Retired Persons (AARP) Minority Affairs Initiative, 1987. *Notes:* 1. Based on U.S. Census data. 2. Includes all institutionalized.

★ 613 ★

Long-Term Conditions and Care

Projections of Long-Term Care Issues

[Numbers in millions and dollars in billions (1987 dollars)]

Disabled elderly population	Baseline		Future	
	Year	Population	Year	Population
Disabled	1985[1]	6.80	2060	14.0-24.0
	1990[2]	11.10	2030	23.0-27.0
Using long-term care	1988[3]	6.30	2018	9.0-13.0
In a nursing home	1985[1]	1.30	2060	3.0-5.0
	1990[2]	1.80	2030	4.0-5.0
	1988[3]	2.30	2018	3.0-5.0
Disabled in community	1985[1]	5.50	2060	11.0-18.0
	1990[2]	9.20	2030	19.0-22.0
Using home care	1988[3]	4.00	2018	6.0-8.0
Home health aides	1985[4]	0.19	2040	0.3-1.3
Costs				
Costs of long-term care ($)	1988[3]	42.00	2018	93-150
	1988[3]	42.00	2048	355

[Continued]

★ 613 ★

Projections of Long-Term Care Issues
[Continued]

Disabled elderly population	Baseline		Future	
	Year	Population	Year	Population
Ratio[5] Ratio of working-age population to the elderly aged 65 and over				
Elderly in nursing homes	1985	111:1	2060	39:1
Disabled elderly	1985	21:1	2060	9:1

Source: U.S. General Accounting Office, *Long-Term Care: Projected Needs of the Aging Baby Boom Generation,* Report to the Honorable William S. Cohen, Special Committee on Aging, U.S. Senate, June 1991, p. 14. *Notes:* Projections cannot be compared across researchers because these sources used different surveys to define disability, used different projection methodologies, and beginning and end points for projections are not the same. 1. K. Manton, "Epidemiological, Demographic, and Social Correlates of Disability Among the Elderly" (*The Milbank Quarterly,* vol. 67, 1989). 2. S. Zedlewski and others, *The Needs of the Elderly in the 21st Century* (The Urban Institute, 1990). 3. A. Rivlin and others, *Caring for the Disabled Elderly: Who Will Pay?* (The Brookings Institution, 1988). 4. R. Suzman and K. Manton, "Forecasting Health and Functioning in Aging Societies," in *Aging, Health and Behavior,* eds., M. Ory and R. Ables (Sage Publications, 1991). 5. To calculate this ratio, original source divided the working-age population between the ages of 20 and 64 (from the Social Security Administration Annual Report) by the number of elderly in nursing homes (Manton, 1989). This produced the ratio of working-age population to nursing home elderly. A similar method was used to calculate the ratio of working-age population to disabled elderly.

★ 614 ★

Long-Term Conditions and Care

Reported Impairments per 1,000 Persons, 1985-87

Average annual selected reported impairments per 1,000 persons 55 years of age and over, by type of impairment, race, sex, and age.

[Number per 1,000 persons]

Race, sex, and age	Visual impairment[1]	Cataract	Hearing impairment[2]	Deformity or orthopedic impairment[3]
Total[4]				
55-59 years	43.0	21.0	214.1	173.6
60-64 years	59.8	46.5	278.1	184.3
65-69 years	56.4	74.0	335.5	183.7
70-74 years	81.0	130.4	368.8	200.6
75-79 years	113.8	218.2	405.6	225.3
80-84 years	107.6	259.7	425.5	203.9
55-64 years	51.3	33.6	245.7	178.8
65-74 years	69.7	71.1	365.0	220.2
75-84 years	133.9	197.0	697.6	380.8
65 years and over	89.5	155.7	383.0	203.2
75 years and over	125.2	246.9	435.7	222.4

[Continued]

★ 614 ★

Reported Impairments per 1,000 Persons, 1985-87

[Continued]

Race, sex, and age	Visual impairment[1]	Cataract	Hearing impairment[2]	Deformity or orthopedic impairment[3]
85 years and over	182.6	302.0	530.4	243.8
White male				
55-64 years	66.3	27.3	332.2	190.8
65-74 years	84.9	70.2	443.3	159.7
75-84 years	103.0	161.6	477.7	198.5
65 years and over	94.4	107.1	465.1	172.7
75 years and over	112.9	178.3	507.1	197.8
85 years and over	159.1	256.2	643.9	194.3
Black male				
55-64 years	66.8	32.7[5]	166.7	224.4
65 years and over	112.9	79.5	307.8	125.2
White female				
55-64 years	36.7	38.3	182.5	163.5
65-74 years	52.5	117.4	287.8	216.5
75-84 years	110.8	282.4	395.5	242.7
65 years and over	85.0	191.4	342.9	231.4
75 years and over	130.4	294.9	420.0	252.1
85 years and over	205.8	343.4	514.6	288.4
Black female				
55-64 years	52.3	20.4[5]	194.1[5]	188.5
65 years ad over	66.7	189.5	240.2	190.9

Source: Health Data on Older Americans: United States, 1992, Centers for Disease Control and Prevention/National Center for Health Statistics, Vital and Health Statistics, Series 3: Analytic and Epidemiological Studies, No. 27, p. 20. Primary source: National Center for Health Statistics: Data from the National Health Interview Survey. *Notes:* Data are based on household interviews of the civilian noninstitutionalized population. 1. Visual impairment includes blindness in both eyes and other visual impairments. 2. Hearing impairment included deafness in both ears, other hearing impairments, and tinnitus. 3. Deformity or orthopedic impairment includes back, upper extremities, and lower extremities. 4. Includes races other than white and black. 5. Figure does not meet standard of reliability or precision.

Hospitals

★ 615 ★

Cost of Hospital Care per Day for Medicare Enrollees by Geographic Region, 1980-1989

Region	Average charge per day		
	1980	1985	1989
New England	$295	$559	$838
Middle Atlantic	304	559	825
East North Central	298	623	971
West North Central	246	580	915
South Atlantic	277	613	963
East South Central	249	561	754
West South Central	259	599	1,003
Mountain	310	706	1,173
Pacific	424	907	1,480
U.S.	296	623	980

Source: National Center for Health Statistics. *Health United States 1991.* Washington, D.C.: U.S. Department of Health and Human Services, 1992, p. 296. Primary source: Bureau of Data Management and Strategy, Health Care Financing Administration: Unpublished data.

★ 616 ★
Hospitals

Days Hospitalized per Year by Race/Ethnicity, Age, and Income

[Days per person]

Characteristic	White	Black
Income, and hospitalization		
All family incomes[1]		
All ages	8.2	9.5
Under 18 years	6.4	8.8
18-44 years	5.9	7.1
45-64 years	9.7	12.3
65 years and over	11.7	14.0
Less than $20,000		
All ages	9.5	10.0
Under 18 years	6.5	9.4
18-44 years	6.6	7.4
45-64 years	11.7	13.5

[Continued]

★ 616 ★

Days Hospitalized per Year by Race/Ethnicity, Age, and Income

[Continued]

Characteristic	White	Black
65 years and over	12.1	13.5
$20,000 or more		
All ages	6.9	7.7
Under 18 years	6.2	7.4
18-44 years	5.4	6.2
45-64 years	8.4	10.6
65 years and over	10.5	13.7

Source: "Average Annual Number of Days Hospitalized per Person Hospitalized during the Year Preceding Interview by Race, Age, and Family Income: United States, 1985-87," *Health of Black and White Americans, 1985-87*, 1990, p. 21. Primary source: National Health Interview Survey, U.S. Department of Health and Human Services, Public Health Service, Centers for Disease Control, Division of Health Statistics, Hyattsville, MD, January 1990. *Note:* 1. Includes unknown family income.

★ 617 ★

Hospitals

Health Technology Facilities: Selected Countries

[Technology facilities per million persons]

	United States	Canada	Germany
MRI machines	3.69	0.46	0.94
Open-heart surgery units	3.26	1.23	0.74
Lithotripsy machines	0.94	0.16	0.34

Source: Sara Collins, "Cutting Edge Cures," *U.S. News & World Report*, June 7, 1993, p. 58. Primary source: *USN&WR*—Basic data: Dale Rublee, American Medical Association Center for Health Policy Research, OECD. *Notes:* Magnetic Resonance Imaging (MRI) machines are diagnostic tools. Lithotripsy machines dissolve kidney stones.

★ 618 ★

Hospitals

Hospital Beds Used per Day, by Age, 1989

Age group	Beds used per day[1]
1989, total	223
Age	
Under 1 year old	332
1 to 4 years old	53
5 to 14 years old	39
15 to 24 years old	112
25 to 34 years old	143
35 to 44 years old	138
45 to 64 years old	248
65 to 74 years old	580
75 years old and over	1,120

Source: U.S. Bureau of the Census. *Statistical Abstract of the United States 1992.* 112th edition. Washington, D.C.: U.S. Department of Commerce, 1992, p. 115. Primary source: U.S. National Center for Health Statistics, *Vital Health Statistics,* series 13 and unpublished data. *Notes:* 1. Average daily number of beds occupied per 100,000 civilian population.

★ 619 ★

Hospitals

Hospital Stay by Sex and Age, 1989

Age group	Average stay (days)		
	Total	Male	Female
1989, total	6.5	7.0	6.1
Age			
Under 1 year old	6.0	5.8	6.4
1 to 4 years old	3.5	3.5	3.5
5 to 14 years old	5.0	5.3	4.7
15 to 24 years old	4.1	5.7	3.5
25 to 34 years old	4.5	6.6	3.9
35 to 44 years old	5.6	6.2	5.1
45 to 64 years old	6.7	6.7	6.6
65 to 74 years old	8.2	7.9	8.5
75 years old and over	9.4	7.3	9.5

Source: U.S. Bureau of the Census. *Statistical Abstract of the United States 1992.* 112th edition. Washington, D.C.: U.S. Department of Commerce, 1992, p. 115. Primary source: U.S. National Center for Health Statistics, *Vital Health Statistics,* Series 13 and unpublished data.

★ 620 ★
Hospitals

Population of Community Hospitals, Nursing Homes, and Mental Care Facilities - Part I

Region, division, and state	Community hospitals[1]							Nursing homes, 1986[5]			
	Total (1,000)[3]		Personnel, FTE[2] Type, 1988			Average daily room charge[4] (Dol.)		Number	Beds		Residents (1,000)
			Physicians and dentists	Registered nurses	LPN's				Number (1,000)	Rate per 1,000 persons 65 yrs. and over	
	1988	1980				1989	1980				
United States	3,205	2,873	33.4	770.6	170.6	262	127	17,122	1,566	53.7	1,437.0
Northeast	787	693	16.3	183.7	33.1	NA	NA	3,088	335	50.1	317.6
New England	198	180	4.4	44.5	7.5	NA	NA	1,340	109	64.6	104.1
Maine	17	15	0.2	4.0	1.1	291	124	171	10	62.1	9.3
New Hampshire	13	10	Z	3.4	0.6	280	125	100	8	63.9	7.1
Vermont	6	6	Z	1.5	0.4	304	116	66	3	52.1	3.2
Massachusetts	105	99	3.0	23.0	3.2	301	151	649	52	65.2	48.7
Rhode Island	14	13	0.3	3.2	0.7	297	138	108	10	69.2	9.5
Connecticut	43	37	0.8	9.5	1.5	354	127	246	27	65.1	26.3
Middle Atlantic	590	513	12.0	139.1	25.6	NA	NA	1,748	226	45.2	213.5
New York	293	260	8.5	66.7	11.0	291	157	639	100	43.7	96.6
New Jersey	99	83	1.2	22.2	5.1	249	146	345	38	39.1	35.5
Pennsylvania	197	170	2.3	50.2	9.5	327	132	764	88	50.8	81.4
Midwest	852	822	6.9	206.0	38.4	NA	NA	5,647	526	71.1	479.5
East North Central	597	576	5.3	144.5	25.7	NA	NA	3,351	333	66.3	302.1
Ohio	167	151	1.0	41.8	8.4	269	139	954	84	63.2	76.0
Indiana	76	69	0.4	18.0	3.3	239	107	460	48	72.9	40.8
Illinois	168	169	1.9	40.6	5.4	283	144	769	97	70.0	88.2
Michigan	129	126	1.8	29.4	6.7	311	151	714	52	50.3	48.5
Wisconsin	57	62	0.1	14.7	2.0	194	104	454	53	84.7	48.6
West North Central	256	245	1.6	61.6	12.7	NA	NA	2,296	192	81.1	177.4
Minnesota	56	59	0.2	13.5	2.8	240	105	454	47	89.8	44.6
Iowa	41	39	0.1	10.9	1.4	213	107	445	35	84.5	32.5
Missouri	84	76	0.9	18.7	4.4	243	107	584	49	70.4	43.6
North Dakota	11	10	Z	2.6	0.6	217	93	83	7	81.7	6.8
South Dakota	9	8	Z	2.6	0.4	190	96	119	8	81.6	7.7
Nebraska	23	20	Z	5.6	1.4	189	100	234	19	88.6	18.1
Kansas	33	34	0.3	7.6	1.6	232	104	377	26	79.5	24.1
South	1,046	903	5.7	247.0	75.6	NA	NA	5,174	475	48.0	430.6
South Atlantic	535	441	3.8	131.5	31.6	NA	NA	2,233	195	37.2	183.7
Delaware	9	7	0.1	2.6	0.4	284	125	42	4	55.5	3.8
Maryland	55	49	0.6	13.8	1.6	248	119	214	25	53.5	24.0
District of Columbia	21	18	0.5	5.2	0.5	418	170	26	3	39.2	2.7
Virginia	67	58	0.6	16.7	4.8	194	101	248	26	43.0	24.7
West Virginia	26	27	0.2	6.2	2.0	202	110	103	8	31.9	7.8
North Carolina	79	65	0.9	20.5	4.6	174	87	374	27	37.4	26.0
South Carolina	36	31	0.1	8.3	2.9	201	80	189	14	39.1	13.4
Georgia	82	64	0.2	18.2	5.9	190	92	391	33	54.8	31.5

[Continued]

★ 620 ★

Population of Community Hospitals, Nursing Homes, and Mental Care Facilities - Part I
[Continued]

Region, division, and state	Community hospitals[1]							Nursing homes, 1986[5]			
	Personnel, FTE[2]				Average daily room charge[4] (Dol.)			Number	Beds		Residents (1,000)
	Total (1,000)[3]		Type, 1988						Number (1,000)	Rate per 1,000 persons 65 yrs. and over	
			Physicians and dentists	Registered nurses	LPN's						
	1988	1980				1989	1980				
Florida	160	123	0.6	40.1	8.9	240	109	646	54	26.3	49.7
East South Central	203	183	1.1	48.3	16.3	NA	NA	1,029	90	48.5	84.6
Kentucky	45	40	0.1	11.4	3.0	214	92	348	23	52.1	22.0
Tennessee	74	64	0.2	16.6	5.8	181	91	289	29	49.8	27.6
Alabama	53	50	0.7	13.5	4.5	195	96	237	23	46.1	21.3
Mississippi	32	29	0.1	6.8	3.1	167	67	155	14	44.7	13.6
West South Central	307	279	0.8	67.2	27.7	NA	NA	1,912	190	67.9	162.3
Arkansas	29	26	Z	6.2	3.6	161	86	235	22	63.6	19.8
Louisiana	57	52	0.1	11.8	4.5	208	89	283	34	72.6	29.7
Oklahoma	38	35	Z	8.1	3.0	204	101	371	30	74.2	26.1
Texas	183	166	0.6	41.2	16.6	212	91	1,023	104	65.8	86.7
West	520	455	4.5	133.9	23.5	NA	NA	3,213	230	44.2	209.3
Mountain	136	118	0.6	34.9	6.1	NA	NA	724	58	43.1	50.8
Montana	10	9	Z	2.1	0.5	275	113	92	6	61.7	5.6
Idaho	9	8	Z	2.3	0.7	254	110	78	5	46.1	4.5
Wyoming	5	4	Z	1.1	0.3	200	98	31	2	56.1	2.1
Colorado	36	33	0.2	9.2	0.9	262	124	212	18	62.0	16.3
New Mexico	13	11	Z	3.2	0.8	241	115	70	5	37.4	4.6
Arizona	36	30	0.1	9.9	1.3	230	106	109	11	27.8	9.8
Utah	17	14	0.2	4.3	0.9	279	112	97	6	45.6	5.2
Nevada	10	9	Z	2.8	0.5	256	125	35	3	28.0	2.6
Pacific	384	337	3.9	98.9	17.4	NA	NA	2,489	172	44.6	158.5
Washington	45	37	0.6	12.0	1.9	327	125	305	28	54.7	26.2
Oregon	30	25	0.2	8.7	1.1	333	133	206	16	44.9	14.6
California	295	264	2.9	74.9	13.7	382	161	1,881	123	43.2	114.0
Alaska	4	3	Z	1.0	0.1	363	189	17	1	66.8	1.0
Hawaii	11	8	0.1	2.3	0.6	303	127	80	3	27.6	2.7

Source: U.S. Department of Commerce, Bureau of the Census, *State and Metropolitan Area Data Book 1991*, August 1991, p. 219. *Notes:* Z = rounds to less than half the unit of measurement shown. 1. Data subject to copyright; see source citation in text of source. 2. Full-time equivalent. 3. Includes other salaried personnel, not shown separately. 4. As of January. Covers nongovernmental short-term general hospitals and represents average cost to patient for a semi-private room. 5. Covers nursing homes with 3 or more beds.

★ 621 ★

Hospitals

Population of Community Hospitals, Nursing Homes, and Mental Care Facilities - Part II

	Mental care hospitals, 1986				Facilities for the mentally retarded, 1988		
	State/county		Private		State		Non-state
	Residents (end of-year)	Total additions	Residents (end of-year)	Total additions	Resident patients June 30	Admissions (during year)[1]	resident patients June 30
United States	111,135	332,884	24,591	234,663	99,327	6,928[2]	171,414
Northeast	42,596	66,761	5,270	49,423	31,196	NA	38,066
New England	9,438	22,845	2,276	20,658	7,394	NA	10,289
Maine	372	1,853	91	638	325	154	1,748
New Hampshire	393	737	307	2,474	144	2	931
Vermont	188	478	96	850	186	2	381
Massachusetts	5,821	9,094	857	9,486	3,709	NA	3,801
Rhode Island	260	860	150	2,885	461	10	964
Connecticut	2,404	9,823	775	4,325	2,569	NA	2,464
Middle Atlantic	33,158	43,916	2,994	28,765	23,802	1,238	27,777
New York	22,033	28,530	988	9,565	13,836	1,075	14,270
New Jersey	4,346	9,004	524	3,847	5,360	70	3,092
Pennsylvania	6,779	6,382	1,482	15,353	4,606	93	10,415
Midwest	24,912	98,872	3,838	37,173	19,775	NA	59,553
East North Central	17,134	62,830	2,984	29,951	12,680	NA	37,886
Ohio	4,307	15,224	788	6,389	2,888	80	10,194
Indiana	2,389	4,119	518	8,095	2,015	37	3,709
Illinois	4,027	22,636	603	6,069	4,513	251	11,367
Michigan	4,891	9,859	915	8,361	1,436	NA	6,358
Wisconsin	1,520	10,992	160	1,037	1,828	90	6,258
West North Central	7,778	36,042	854	7,222	7,095	470	21,667
Minnesota	1,800	5,218	61	89	1,574	109	7,657
Iowa	816	5,249	-	-	1,056	70	3,361
Missouri	2,229	12,269	295	3,773	1,960	39	3,518
North Dakota	467	2,805	-	-	347	74	1,189
South Dakota	419	1,068	-	-	449	35	1,081
Nebraska	583	2,264	108	1,562	472	23	1,929
Kansas	1,464	7,169	390	1,798	1,237	120	2,932
South	32,777	133,201	11,204	99,241	34,958	NA	34,109
South Atlantic	19,852	73,818	6,490	53,941	15,134	NA	17,651
Delaware	516	2,005	43	713	374	11	314
Maryland	2,671	6,766	636	3,381	1,535	126	2,882
District of Columbia	1,500	4,059	134	1,716	356	NA	750

[Continued]

★ 621 ★

Population of Community Hospitals, Nursing Homes, and Mental Care Facilities - Part II
[Continued]

| | Mental care hospitals, 1986 | | | | Facilities for the mentally retarded, 1988 | | |
| | State/county | | Private | | State | | Non-state |
	Residents (end of-year)	Total additions	Residents (end of-year)	Total additions	Resident patients June 30	Admissions (during year)[1]	resident patients June 30
Virginia	3,122	8,571	2,308	12,863	2,846	200	1,434
West Virginia	593	1,313	63	1,220	461	42	634
North Carolina	2,994	9,640	591	6,535	2,845	122	2,338
South Carolina	2,016	8,471	193	2,242	2,446	85	1,388
Georgia	2,837	29,839	1,143	10,921	2,117	296	1,560
Florida	3,603	3,154	1,379	14,350	2,154	78	6,351
East South Central	6,018	19,416	1,224	14,133	5,943	449	4,473
Kentucky	1,017	4,942	424	4,853	846	109	1,094
Tennessee	1,790	7,265	525	4,713	2,075	219	1,722
Alabama	1,816	3,696	189	3,352	1,333	73	887
Mississippi	1,395	3,513	86	1,215	1,689	48	770
West South Central	6,907	39,967	3,490	31,167	13,881	336	11,985
Arkansas	259	4,395	84	866	1,314	44	806
Louisiana	1,669	7,619	860	7,935	2,819	106	3,611
Oklahoma	889	7,660	226	1,410	1,186	25	2,860
Texas	4,090	20,293	2,320	20,956	8,562	161	4,708
West	10,850	34,050	4,279	48,826	13,398	NA	39,686
Mountain	2,852	9,653	942	12,324	3,380	NA	8,666
Montana	354	921	42	747	243	4	978
Idaho	188	769	85	1,703	236	20	1,076
Wyoming	254	865	36	678	419	8	310
Colorado	892	3,346	314	3,714	803	65	2,223
New Mexico	219	1,085	86	1,188	507	49	832
Arizona	492	592	208	2,123	466	NA	1,751
Utah	317	370	74	719	533	45	1,204
Nevada	136	1,705	97	1,452	173	94	292
Pacific	7,998	24,397	3,337	36,502	10,018	NA	31,020
Washington	1,425	7,972	81	1,651	1,825	100	4,121
Oregon	969	4,448	71	1,316	1,098	27	2,207
California	5,210	10,101	3,088	32,033	6,826	638	24,171
Alaska	148	1,138	42	747	59	NA	282
Hawaii	246	738	55	755	210	4	239

Source: U.S. Department of Commerce, Bureau of the Census, *State and Metropolitan Area Data Book 1991*, August 1991, p. 219. *Notes:* 1. Additions comprise admissions and readmissions. Excludes facilities of fewer than 16 residents. 2. Estimated.

★ 622 ★

Hospitals

Trends in Hospital Usage by Persons Aged 65+, 1965-1988

Year	Number of discharges (in thousands)	Discharge rate (discharges per 1,000 people)	Average length of stay per discharge (in days)
1988	10,146	334.1	8.9
1987	10,459	350.5	8.6
1986	10,716	367.3	8.5
1985	10,508	368.2	8.7
1984	11,226	401.3	8.9
1983	11,302	412.1	9.7
1982	10,697	398.8	10.1
1981	10,408	396.7	10.5
1980	9,864	383.8	10.7
1979	9,086	361.5	10.8
1978	8,708	355.4	11.0
1977	8,344	349.2	11.1
1976	7,912	339.9	11.5
1975	7,654	337.3	11.6
1974	7,185	325.7	11.9
1973	6,937	322.3	12.1
1972	6,634	315.6	12.2
1971	5,986	291.1	12.6
1970	5,897	293.3	12.6
1969	5,694	289.3	14.0
1968	5,529	285.5	14.2
1967	5,210	273.2	14.1
1966	4,909	261.7	13.4
1965	4,602	248.2	13.1

Source: Aging America, Trends and Projections, prepared by the U.S. Senate Special Committee on Aging, the American Association of Retired Persons, the Federal Council on the Aging, and the U.S. Administration on Aging, 1991, Washington, D.C., p. 124. Primary source: National Center for Health Statistics, "Trends in Hospital Utilization: United States, 1965-1986," *Vital and Health Statistics* Series 13, No. 101, September 1989; "National Hospital Discharge Survey: Annual Summary, 1987," *Vital and Health Statistics*, Series 13, No. 99, April 1989, and "1988 Summary: National Hospital Discharge Survey," *Advance Data*, No.185, June 19, 1990.

Specific Illnesses

★ 623 ★

AIDS in the Elderly

The fact is that as many as 10 percent of all AIDS cases reported have involved people aged 50 and over. The older population also receives the highest rate of blood transfusions during routine medical care. As a result, the second most common cause of AIDS in people over age 50 (after homosexual and bisexual activity) has been exposure to contaminated blood transfusions received before 1985 when the public blood supply was not being screened for the virus.

Source: U.S. Department of Health and Human Services, National Institute on Aging, *Bound for Good Health: A Collection of Age Pages.*

★ 624 ★

Specific Illnesses

Probable Alzheimer's Disease for Persons Aged 65+

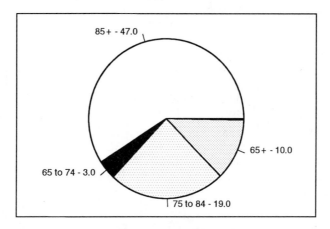

It is estimated that 10 percent of all persons over 65 years old have Alzheimer's Disease. It is much more prevalent in persons aged 85+, with almost half of that group estimated to have it in some degree. These data exclude persons in nursing homes or other institutions.

Age group	Percent
65+	10.0
65 to 74	3.0
75 to 84	19.0
85+	47.0

Source: Aging America, Trends and Projections, prepared by the U.S. Senate Special Committee on Aging, the American Association of Retired Persons, the Federal Council on the Aging, and the U.S. Administration on Aging, 1991, Washington, D.C., p. 116. Primary source: Dennis A. Evans, MD, et al. "Prevalence of Alzheimer's Disease in a Community Population of Older Persons," *Journal of the American Medical Association*, Vol. 262, No. 18, November 10, 1989.

★ 625 ★

Specific Illnesses

Arthritis

Data for 1960-84 are based on interviews of samples of the civilian noninstitutional population.

Sex, race, and age	Joint pain[1]		Physician-diagnosed arthritis[2]		
	1960-62	1976-80	1960-62	1976-80	1984
Total	41.5	48.9	37.2	44.3	47.7
55-59 years	37.9	49.9	34.7	38.9	38.4
60-64 years	45.1	50.0	37.0	44.2	44.6
65-69 years	37.7	47.5	35.9	48.4	48.8
70-74 years	49.1	47.6	42.1	48.0	55.5

[Continued]

★ 625 ★

Arthritis
[Continued]

Sex, race, and age	Joint pain[1]		Physician-diagnosed arthritis[2]		
	1960-62	1976-80	1960-62	1976-80	1984
75-79 years	38.8	...	39.7	...	54.2
80 years and over	...	...	...	...	55.6
Male	33.9	49.3	28.3	37.2	38.9
55-59 years	29.1	50.0	24.4	32.6	29.2
60-64 years	37.0	50.3	28.8	38.2	37.0
65-69 years	34.7	48.4	32.1	40.9	42.2
70-74 years	41.3	47.2	28.4	38.7	47.8
75-79 years	26.4	...	29.7	...	43.3
80 years and over	...	...	...	...	45.1
White male	33.1	49.7	28.1	37.3	38.2
55-59 years	27.2	50.5	22.8	33.5	28.2
60-64 years	36.0	50.0	28.8	38.0	36.1
65-69 years	34.9	49.1	32.0	40.3	41.3
70-74 years	40.8	48.4	29.2	38.9	47.4
75-79 years	26.8	...	30.5	...	42.4
80 years and over	...	...	...	...	44.8
Black male	41.4	44.7	30.2	36.4	47.5
55-64 years	45.5	49.1	33.6	31.9	43.3
65-74 years	38.9	38.4	26.8	42.8	51.7
75 years and over	21.4[3]	...	18.8[3]	...	51.1
Female	48.2	48.7	45.1	50.2	54.0
55-59 years	45.6	49.9	43.7	44.1	45.5
60-64 years	53.0	49.6	45.1	50.0	50.9
65-69 years	40.2	46.8	39.0	54.2	54.0
70-74 years	55.5	47.9	53.3	54.9	60.7
75-79 years	51.3	...	49.8	...	61.3
80 years and over	...	...	...	...	60.4
White female	47.3	48.5	45.1	49.2	53.2
55-59 years	47.5	49.4	43.1	42.2	45.5
60-64 years	49.1	50.2	44.5	49.6	50.4
65-69 years	38.5	46.2	39.4	52.8	52.9
70-74 years	54.8	47.9	53.1	55.2	59.3
75-79 years	50.7	...	53.0	...	60.2
80 years and over	...	...	...	...	59.3
Black female	58.4	50.0	45.0	59.7	61.2
55-64 years	55.8	49.9	49.9	58.5	50.1

[Continued]

★ 625 ★

Arthritis
[Continued]

Sex, race, and age	Joint pain[1]		Physician-diagnosed arthritis[2]		
	1960-62	1976-80	1960-62	1976-80	1984
65-74 years	62.8	50.2	44.5	61.3	69.9
75 years and over	57.0	...	19.7[3]	...	73.6

Source: *Health Data on Older Americans: United States, 1992*, Centers for Disease Control and Prevention/National Center for Health Statistics, Vital and Health Statistics, Series 3: Analytic and Epidemiological Studies, No. 27, pp. 283. Primary source: National Center for Health Statistics: 1960-62 data from the Health Examination Survey; 1976-80 data from the second National Health and Nutrition Examination Survey; 1984 data from the National Health Interview Survey Supplement on Aging. *Notes:* "..." indicates category not applicable. 1. Specific questions concerned "joint pains" and "pain in back, neck, or other joint." 2. Specific question: "Doctor confirm or ever told sample person that he/she had arthritis?" 3. Figure does not meet standard of reliability or precision.

★ 626 ★

Specific Illnesses

Arthritis Sufferers

Arthritis affects one American every 33 seconds, or about one million more every year. One in two people over the age of 65 has arthritis, and one in seven people in the American population as a whole. An average of one in three families is affected by this disease.

Source: Debra Lappin, (Chairperson, Government Affairs Committee, The Arthritis Foundation), U.S. House Committee on Appropriations, Depts. of Labor, Health and Human Services, Education... Appropriations. for 1991, Hearing, Washington, DC, 1990.

★ 627 ★

Specific Illnesses

High Blood Pressure

As many as 58 million Americans may have HBP [high blood pressure]. About 40 percent of whites and more than 50 percent of blacks age 65 and older suffer some form of HBP.

Source: National Institute on Aging, *Bound for Good Health: A Collection of Age Pages.*

★ 628 ★

Specific Illnesses

Persons Reporting High Blood Pressure

Percent of persons 18 years of age and over who had been told 2 or more different times that they had high blood pressure, by sex, age, and selected characteristics: United States, 1990.

Characteristic	Both sexes 18 years and over	Male					Female				
		Total	18-29 years	30-44 years	45-64 years	65 years and over	Total	18-29 years	30-44 years	45-64 years	65 years and over
All persons[1]	16.3	15.3	4.1	9.8	24.6	32.0	17.2	4.0	8.1	25.2	39.7
Education level											
Less than 12 years	24.5	20.8	5.0	11.0	29.8	31.6	27.8	4.6	14.5	33.8	42.4
12 years	15.7	14.2	3.3	9.9	24.7	31.7	16.9	4.3	7.7	25.5	39.6
More than 12 years	12.6	13.7	4.5	9.6	21.7	32.7	11.5	3.3	6.8	18.5	35.1
13-15 years	12.8	14.0	4.5	11.5	23.7	37.1	11.7	3.4	8.2	18.9	33.3
16 years or more	12.4	13.3	4.4	8.1	20.5	29.5	11.2	3.1	5.5	18.2	37.5
Income											
Less than $10,000	22.3	15.8	3.1	12.3	29.3	32.1	25.8	4.2	15.1	40.3	44.7
$10,000-$19,999	19.4	18.0	5.3	10.9	31.8	30.1	20.6	5.3	7.1	30.6	39.0
$20,000-$34,999	15.5	15.1	3.8	9.8	25.2	33.8	15.8	4.0	9.8	24.4	38.1
$35,000-$49,999	12.8	13.7	4.7	9.9	21.7	38.3	11.8	3.3	7.3	22.0	32.9
$50,000 or more	13.1	14.6	3.9	9.3	22.5	34.5	11.4	4.0	5.7	18.3	39.5
Race											
White	15.9	15.1	4.0	9.4	23.3	31.5	16.7	3.9	7.1	23.3	39.2
Black	21.3	20.0	5.5	14.2	38.6	38.6	22.3	4.5	15.0	41.2	47.2
Hispanic origin											
Hispanic	10.1	7.5	1.7[2]	5.6	17.8	21.2	12.3	2.9	8.7	23.9	41.1
Non-Hispanic	16.8	16.0	4.4	10.2	25.0	32.4	17.6	4.1	8.0	25.2	39.5
Geographic region											
Northeast	16.3	16.1	4.0	11.2	26.9	29.1	16.4	3.3	6.5	22.9	37.3
Midwest	16.9	15.8	4.3	11.4	22.9	33.5	17.9	4.1	7.7	25.6	43.0
South	17.6	15.9	4.2	9.1	26.7	33.1	19.1	4.9	10.5	28.2	40.6
West	13.5	13.3	3.7	7.9	21.1	30.8	13.7	2.9	6.1	21.6	36.1
Marital status											
Currently married	16.4	17.4	5.1	9.8	24.6	32.3	15.3	4.2	7.5	23.9	37.0
Formerly married	26.7	20.4	7.9[2]	11.0	25.0	31.8	29.3	6.2	10.4	28.9	42.5
Never married	6.6	6.2	3.2	9.1	21.9	27.0	7.1	3.3	8.5	23.8	29.7
Employment status											
Currently employed	11.2	11.8	4.0	9.5	21.1	30.0	10.6	3.6	7.6	20.0	33.7

[Continued]

★ 628 ★

Persons Reporting High Blood Pressure
[Continued]

Characteristic	Both sexes 18 years and over	Male					Female				
		Total	18-29 years	30-44 years	45-64 years	65 years and over	Total	18-29 years	30-44 years	45-64 years	65 years and over
Unemployed	10.3	11.2	6.7	9.9	21.9	13.3²	9.3	1.8²	8.2	25.3	29.5²
Not in labor force	27.3	28.2	3.3	16.0	40.1	32.6	26.9	5.1	9.5	32.6	40.4

Source: Health Promotion and Disease Prevention: United States, 1990, National Center for Health Statistics, Vital and Health Statistics, Series 10, No. 185, p. 33. *Notes:* Data are based on household interviews of the civilian noninstitutionalized population. The survey design, general qualifications, and information on the reliability of the estimates are given in appendix 1 in the original source. Denominator for each cell excludes unknowns. 1. Includes persons with unknown sociodemographic characteristics. 2. Figure does not meet standard of reliability or precision (more than 30-percent relative standard error in numerator of percent or rate).

★ 629 ★

Specific Illnesses

Persons Reporting High Blood Pressure Who Were Taking Medication for Hypertension

Percent of persons 18 years of age and over with 2 or more high blood pressure readings who were currently taking medicine for hypertension, by sex, age, and selected characteristics: United States, 1990.

Characteristic	Both sexes 18 years and over	Male					Female				
		Total	18-29 years	30-44 years	45-64 years	65 years and over	Total	18-29 years	30-44 years	45-64 years	65 years and over
All persons[1]	67.0	61.6	12.8	37.5	69.2	79.9	71.3	14.6	46.5	75.0	84.5
Education level											
Less than 12 years	72.8	67.6	10.8²	45.0	69.6	78.8	76.2	18.9²	51.2	75.3	84.3
12 years	67.1	62.4	10.5²	34.3	73.8	81.7	70.3	14.4²	40.2	76.3	84.5
More than 12 years	60.8	56.5	15.5²	37.7	64.6	80.1	66.0	12.4²	49.5	71.7	84.9
13-15 years	59.9	54.3	18.4²	36.3	67.4	75.0	65.9	10.6²	49.7	75.8	84.6
16 years or more	61.6	58.5	10.3²	39.2	62.5	84.7	66.2	15.1²	49.5	67.3	85.0
Income											
Less than $10,000	71.5	64.8	18.5²	46.9	64.7	79.7	73.8	16.5²	47.6	73.9	83.8
$10,000-$19,999	70.7	65.7	5.5²	35.1	77.2	80.9	74.2	14.8²	43.9	76.6	85.5
$20,000-$34,999	64.8	63.7	25.8²	41.1	71.5	78.8	65.7	20.0²	37.0	74.5	82.8
$35,000-$49,999	58.0	53.9	-²	39.3	65.7	74.9	63.1	3.6²	55.1	68.6	82.1
$50,000 or more	62.5	58.2	12.9²	31.4	66.5	86.4	68.5	9.3²	48.7	74.6	92.6
Race											
White	66.9	61.5	13.8	35.0	68.6	80.0	71.3	15.5	43.2	73.9	84.3
Black	70.1	64.9	9.6²	51.7	74.6	80.9	73.8	12.7²	57.8	82.1	86.6
Hispanic origin											
Hispanic	58.8	48.3	18.6²	28.1²	56.5	70.6²	64.2	7.1²	53.9	77.0	73.5
Non-Hispanic	67.4	62.1	126	37.9	69.7	80.1	71.7	15.4	45.7	74.8	84.9

[Continued]

★ 629 ★

Persons Reporting High Blood Pressure Who Were Taking Medication for Hypertension

[Continued]

Characteristic	Both sexes 18 years and over	Male					Female				
		Total	18-29 years	30-44 years	45-64 years	65 years and over	Total	18-29 years	30-44 years	45-64 years	65 years and over
Geographic region											
Northeast	69.5	62.9	2.9[2]	38.3	75.2	78.8	75.3	15.9[2]	55.4	79.8	82.6
Midwest	68.5	63.5	9.1[2]	41.5	71.7	83.0	72.6	23.5[2]	43.9	75.0	85.8
South	68.3	64.6	18.5[2]	43.3	70.9	79.5	70.9	11.6[2]	47.3	75.7	86.3
West	58.8	51.6	17.1[2]	18.8	55.4	77.1	65.4	7.0[2]	39.8	67.3	80.8
Marital status											
Currently married	66.9	64.7	16.3	39.6	70.4	80.8	69.4	14.9	46.4	74.6	86.3
Formerly married	73.4	59.9	16.0[2]	27.8	63.2	76.1	77.3	7.8[2]	44.9	75.3	83.6
Never married	44.0	36.7	8.5[2]	33.5	65.0	79.5	51.9	14.9[2]	51.2	78.6	80.0
Employment status											
Currently employed	55.5	52.1	11.1	35.1	66.4	82.8	60.1	15.5	45.7	72.6	83.2
Unemployed	48.4	43.1	3.7[2]	45.8[2]	64.5	54.5[2]	55.3	5.0[2]	45.0[2]	63.4	91.3[2]
Not in labor force	77.4	76.4	34.4[2]	58.2	75.8	79.4	77.9	13.6[2]	48.9	77.5	84.6

Source: Health Promotion and Disease Prevention: United States, 1990, National Center for Health Statistics, Vital and Health Statistics, Series 10, No. 185, p. 34. *Notes:* Data are based on household interviews of the civilian noninstitutionalized population. The survey design, general qualifications, and information on the reliability of the estimates are given in appendix 1 in the original source. Denominator for each cell excludes unknowns. A dash (-) stands for the quantity zero. 1. Includes persons with unknown sociodemographic characteristics. 2. Figure does not meet standard of reliability or precision (more than 30-percent relative standard error in numerator of percent or rate).

★ 630 ★

Specific Illnesses

Breast Cancer Cases by Age, 1992

Nearly half (47.6%) of all breast cancer cases in 1992 occurred among women aged 60 or older. Older women, however, are less likely to have had a mammogram than their younger counterparts.

Age range	Number of cases	Percent of total
40-44	13,100	7.3
45-49	15,800	8.8
50-54	14,900	8.3
55-59	15,800	8.8
60-64	20,700	11.5
65-69	23,800	13.2
70-74	22,000	12.2
75-79	19,300	10.7
Percent who have had mammogram:		
50-64	-	34.0

[Continued]

★ 630 ★

Breast Cancer Cases by Age, 1992

[Continued]

Age range	Number of cases	Percent of total
65-74	-	29.0
75-84	-	22.0
85+	-	13.0

Source: *Springfield News-Leader*, March 20, 1993, p. 4A. Primary source: American Cancer Society, National Cancer Institute. *Note:* A dash (-) stands for not reported by original source.

★ 631 ★

Specific Illnesses

Type II Diabetes by Age

Data show percent of all adults who get Type II diabetes. The largest percentage includes persons older than 75. Fourteen million people are afflicted with diabetes.

Age of occurrence	Percent of adults afflicted
20-44	2.0
45-64	6.0
65-75	9.0
75 and older	18.0

Source: *USA TODAY*, November 30, 1992, p. D1. Primary source: American Diabetes Association and *USA TODAY* research.

★ 632 ★

Specific Illnesses

Hearing Impairment in Older People

It has been estimated ... that about 30 percent of adults age 65 through 74 and about 50 percent of those age 75 through 79 suffer some degree of hearing loss. In the United States alone, more than 10 million older people are hearing impaired.

Source: National Institute on Aging, *Bound for Good Health: A Collection of Age Pages.*

★ 633 ★

Specific Illnesses

Black/White Ratio of Death Rates for Heart Disease, 1980

Death rates for coronary heart disease are lower for black males 65 or older than for white males in the same age bracket. The death rate is exactly the same for both black males and white males 55 to 64 years old. It is slightly higher, though, for black males 45 to 54 years old. Black females have a noticeably higher death rate from coronary heart disease than white females from age 45 to 64, a slightly higher death rate from age 65 to 74, and a lower death rate at age 75 or older.

Age	Black males/ White males	Black females/ White females
25-34	2.28	3.30
35-44	1.45	2.90
45-54	1.19	2.28
55-64	1.00	1.78
65-74	0.84	1.22
75-84	0.75	0.90
85 +	0.64	0.65

Source: U.S. Congress, "Profiles in Aging America: Meeting the Health Care Needs of the Nation's Black Elderly," Joint Hearing Before the Special Committee on Aging and the Congressional Black Caucus Health Braintrust, United States Senate, September 28, 1990, 101-29, U.S. Government Printing Office, Washington, D.C., p. 119. Primary source: "Report of the Secretary's Task Force on Black and Minority Health, Volume IV: Cardiovascular and Cerebrovascular Disease, Part I," U.S. Dept. of Health and Human Services, Jan. 1986, p. 97.

★ 634 ★

Specific Illnesses

Osteoporosis in the Elderly

All women should know about osteoporosis. This condition affects one in four women over age 60 and is a major cause of fractures in the spine, hip, wrist, and other parts of the skeleton.... White women are affected most often, particularly those who have a family history of osteoporosis or who have had their ovaries removed at an early age. Women with fair skin or small frames are also susceptible. Men are much less likely than women to get osteoporosis because of their denser bone structure and other factors. However, the risk of developing osteoporosis increases for men in their later years.

Source: National Institute on Aging, *Bound for Good Health: A Collection of Age Pages.*

★ 635 ★

Specific Illnesses

Prostate Enlargement in Elderly Males

Benign prostatic hypertrophy (BPH) is an enlargement of the prostate. This condition is common in older men; more than half of men in their 60s and as many as 90 percent of men in their 70s and 80s have some symptoms of BPH.

Source: National Institute on Aging, *Bound for Good Health: A Collection of Age Pages.*

★ 636 ★

Specific Illnesses

Prostate Cancer in Elderly Males

Prostate cancer is one of the most common forms of cancer among American men. About 80 percent of all cases are found in men over 65.

Source: National Institute on Aging, *Bound for Good Health: A Collection of Age Pages.*

★ 637 ★

Specific Illnesses

Urinary Incontinence in the Elderly

At least 1 in 10 persons age 65 or older suffers from incontinence.... Incontinence is not an inevitable result of aging. It is caused by specific changes in body function that often result from diseases or use of medications.... [It] may be brought on by an illness accompanied by fatigue, confusion, or hospital admission.

Source: National Institute on Aging, *Bound for Good Health: A Collection of Age Pages.*

★ 638 ★
Specific Illnesses

Home Medical Equipment, Supplies, and Services Used by Chronic Obstructive Pulmonary Disease (COPD) Patients[1]

It is assumed that all Chronic Obstructive Pulmonary Disease (COPD) patients will require home medical equipment services upon discharge from the hospital. It is further assumed that inpatient/home treatment patients will require an additional 1.4 days of home medical equipment costs.

Home medical equipment	Cost/month ($)	Source
Oxygen - stationary and portable	322.84	Sample of Medicare Fee schedules
Ventolin and aerosol inhaler	21.47	85% of Medi-Span, August 1990
Walker - wheeled	22.12	Sample of Medicare Fee schedules
Hospital bed - electric	195.73	Sample of Medicare Fee schedules
Bedside commode	30.15	Sample of Medicare Fee schedules
Overbed table	17.40	Homedco rental price
Monthly total	609.71	

Source: U.S. Congress, "Medicare Fraud and Abuse: A Neglected Emergency?," Hearing before the Special Committee on Aging, United States Senate, October 2, 1991, 102-13, U.S. Government Printing Office, Washington, D.C., p. 231. Primary source: Lewin/ICF *Note:* 1. COPD stands for Chronic Obstructive Pulmonary Disease.

Accidents

★ 639 ★

Motor Vehicle Traffic Fatalities by Age Group, 1991

Age (Years)	Percent of total traffic fatalities
Under 1	0.4
1-4	11.5
5-9	24.2
10-14	25.6
15-19	42.5
20-24	34.2
25-29	22.5
30-34	14.2
35-39	9.6
40-44	6.0
45-54	2.9

[Continued]

★ 639 ★

Motor Vehicle Traffic Fatalities by Age Group, 1991
[Continued]

Age (Years)	Percent of total traffic fatalities
55-64	1.2
Over 64	0.4

Source: National Center for Statistics and Analysis, National Highway Traffic Safety Administration, U.S. Department of Transportation, *1991 Traffic Fatality Facts*, p. 1.

★ 640 ★

Accidents

Involvement of the Older Population in Traffic Fatalities, 1975 and 1991

	1975			1991			Percent change, 1975-1991		
							Number		Percentage
	Total	Age 70+	Percent of total	Total	Age 70+	Percent of total	Total	Age 70+	Age 70+
Population (thousands)									
Total	215,465	14,564	6.8	252,177	21,717	8.6	+17.0	+49.0	+26.0
Male	104,876	5,669	5.4	122,979	8,300	6.7	+17.0	+46.0	+24.0
Female	110,589	8,895	8.0	129,198	13,417	10.4	+17.0	+51.0	+30.0
Licensed drivers (thousands)									
Total	129,791	6,736	5.2	169,183	14,065	8.3	+30.0	+109.0	+60.0
Male	70,505	4,267	6.1	86,791	7,242	8.3	+23.0	+69.0	+36.0
Female	59,286	2,469	4.2	82,392	6,823	8.3	+39.0	+176.0	+98.0
Drivers involved in fatal crashes									
Total	55,139	2,343	4.2	54,323	3,856	7.1	-1.0	+65.0	+69.0
Male	45,648	1,877	4.1	40,680	2,707	6.7	-11.0	+44.0	+63.0
Female	9,457	466	4.9	12,806	1,149	9.0	+35.0	+147.0	+84.0
Driver fatalities									
Total	23,649	1,483	6.3	23,904	2,486	10.4	+1.0	+68.0	+65.0
Male	19,864	1,202	6.1	18,105	1,741	9.6	-9.0	+45.0	+57.0
Female	3,784	281	7.4	5,799	745	12.8	+53.0	+165.0	+73.0
Total traffic fatalities									
Total	44,522	3,775	8.5	41,462	4,828	11.6	-7.0	+28.0	+36.0
Male	32,672	2,333	7.1	28,509	2,665	9.3	-13.0	+14.0	+30.0
Female	11,844	1,442	12.2	12,938	2,163	16.7	+9.0	+50.0	+37.0
Occupant fatalities									
Total	35,922	2,399	6.7	34,700	3,738	10.8	-13.0	+56.0	+61.0
Male	26,605	1,476	5.5	23,713	2,056	8.7	-11.0	+39.0	+58.0

[Continued]

★ 640 ★

Involvement of the Older Population in Traffic Fatalities, 1975 and 1991
[Continued]

| | 1975 | | | 1991 | | | Percent change, 1975-1991 | | |
| | Total | Age 70+ | Percent of total | Total | Age 70+ | Percent of total | Number | | Percentage |
							Total	Age 70+	Age 70+
Female	9,312	923	9.9	10,975	1,682	15.3	+18.0	+82.0	+55.0

Pedestrian fatalities

Total	7,516	1,348	17.9	5,797	1,041	18.0	-23.0	-23.0	+1.0
Male	5,196	832	16.0	3,983	567	14.2	-23.0	-32.0	-11.0
Female	2,319	516	22.3	1,812	474	26.6	-22.0	-8.0	+19.0

Source: National Center for Statistics and Analysis, National Highway Traffic Safety Administration, U.S. Department of Transportation, *1991 Older Driver Fatal Crash Facts*, p. 3. Primary source: Licensed drivers—Federal Highway Administration; population—Bureau of the Census.

★ 641 ★
Accidents

Driver Involvement Rates in Fatal Crashes by Age and Sex, 1991

| Age (years) | Drivers involved in fatal crashes | Population | | Licensed drivers | |
		Number (000)	Rate[1]	Number (000)	Rate[2]
		Male drivers			
16-20	5,940	9,231	64.35	6,657	89.23
21-24	5,293	7,688	68.85	7,196	73.55
25-34	11,000	21,427	51.34	20,986	52.42
35-44	7,213	19,432	37.12	18,506	38.98
45-54	4,176	12,563	33.24	12,158	34.35
55-64	2,771	9,932	27.90	9,706	28.55
65-69	1,134	4,491	25.25	4,316	26.27
70+	2,707	8,300	32.61	7,242	37.38
Total	40,234	93,064	43.23	86,767	46.37
		Female drivers			
16-20	2,049	8,760	23.39	5,939	34.50
21-24	1,444	7,427	19.44	6,650	21.71
25-34	3,130	21,450	14.59	20,010	15.64
35-44	2,262	19,840	11.40	17,920	12.62
45-54	1,277	13,177	9.69	11,651	10.96
55-64	915	11,073	8.26	9,211	8.26
65-69	469	5,546	8.46	4,168	11.25

[Continued]

★ 641 ★

Driver Involvement Rates in Fatal Crashes by Age and Sex, 1991
[Continued]

Age (years)	Drivers involved in fatal crashes	Population		Licensed drivers	
		Number (000)	Rate[1]	Number (000)	Rate[2]
70+	1,149	13,417	3.56	6,823	16.84
Total	12,695	100,690	12.61	82,372	15.41

Source: National Center for Statistics and Analysis, National Highway Traffic Safety Administration, U.S. Department of Transportation, *1991 Traffic Fatality Facts*, p. 3. Primary source: Licensed drivers—Federal Highway Administration; Population—Bureau of the Census. *Notes:* 1. Rate per 100,000 population. 2. Rate per 100,000 licensed drivers.

★ 642 ★

Accidents

Pedestrian Fatalities and Fatality Rates by Age and Sex, 1991

This table shows that persons younger than age 16 and persons older than age 70 constituted about one-third of all pedestrian fatalities in 1991.

Age (years)	Male			Female			Total		
	Fatalities	Population (000)	Fatality rate[1]	Fatalities	Population (000)	Fatality rate[1]	Fatalities	Population (000)	Fatality rate[1]
<5	144	9,836	1.46	100	9,386	1.07	244	19,222	1.27
5-9	216	9,337	2.31	101	8,900	1.13	317	18,237	1.74
10-15	191	10,741	1.78	104	10,223	1.02	295	20,964	1.41
16-20	251	9,231	2.72	115	8,760	1.31	366	17,992	2.03
21-24	277	7,688	3.60	85	7,427	1.14	363	15,114	2.40
25-34	752	21,427	3.51	234	21,450	1.09	986	42,877	2.30
35-44	613	19,432	3.15	199	19,840	1.00	812	39,272	2.07
45-54	397	12,563	3.16	150	13,177	1.14	547	25,739	2.13
55-64	368	9,932	3.71	136	11,073	1.23	504	21,005	2.40
65-69	148	4,491	3.30	99	5,546	1.79	247	10,037	2.46
70-79	301	6,013	5.01	255	8,509	3.00	556	14,521	3.83
80+	266	2,287	11.63	219	4,908	4.46	485	7,195	6.74
Unknown	59			15			75[2]		
Total	3,983	122,979	3.24	1,812	129,198	1.40	5,797[2]	252,177	2.30

Source: National Center for Statistics and Analysis, National Highway Traffic Safety Administration, U.S. Department of Transportation, *1991 Traffic Fatality Facts*, p. 4. Primary source: Population—Bureau of the Census. *Notes:* 1. Rate per 100,000 population. 2. Includes two fatalities of unknown sex.

★ 643 ★

Accidents

Pedalcyclist Fatalities and Fatality Rates by Age and Sex, 1991

[Rate is shown in per million population]

Age (years)	Male			Female			Total		
	Fatalities	Population (000)	Fatality rate	Fatalities	Population (000)	Fatality rate	Fatalities	Population (000)	Fatality rate
<5	14	9,836	1.42	3	9,386	0.32	17	19,222	0.88
5-9	80	9,337	8.57	21	8,900	2.36	101	18,237	5.54
10-15	153	10,741	14.24	36	10,223	3.52	189	20,964	9.02
16-20	55	9,231	5.96	7	8,760	0.80	62	17,992	3.45
21-24	47	7,688	6.11	11	7,427	1.48	58	15,114	3.84
25-34	117	21,427	5.46	15	21,450	0.70	132	42,877	3.08
35-44	82	19,432	4.22	15	19,840	0.76	97	39,272	2.47
45-54	69	12,563	5.49	4	13,177	0.30	73	25,739	2.84
55-64	45	9,932	4.53	4	11,073	0.36	49	21,005	2.33
65-69	15	4,491	3.34	1	5,546	0.18	16	10,037	1.59
70-79	24	6,013	3.99	3	8,509	0.35	24	14,521	1.86
80+	11	2,287	4.81	1	4,908	0.20	12	7,195	1.67
Unknown	8			0			8		
Total	720	122,979	5.85	121	129,198	0.94	841	252,177	3.33

Source: National Center for Statistics and Analysis, National Highway Traffic Safety Administration, U.S. Department of Transportation, *1991 Pedalcyclist Fatal Crash Facts*, p. 3. Primary source: Population—Bureau of the Census.

★ 644 ★

Accidents

Principal Impact Points in Two-Vehicle Fatal Crashes Involving an Older Driver and a Younger Driver

From the source: "In two-vehicle fatal crashes involving an older driver and a younger driver, the vehicle driven by the older person was 2.5 times more likely to be the one that was struck (53 percent vs. 20 percent). In half of these crashes, both vehicles were proceeding straight at the time of the collision. In 25 percent the older driver was turning left—8 times more often than the younger driver."

[Data are shown in percent]

Impact point on vehicle driven by older driver	Impact point on vehicle driven by younger driver			
	Front	Left side	Right side	Rear
Front	34.0	6.0	5.0	5.0
Left side	28.0	-	-	-
Right side	19.0	-	-	-
Rear	3.0	-	-	-

Source: National Center for Statistics and Analysis, National Highway Traffic Safety Administration, U.S. Department of Transportation, *1991 Older Driver Fatal Crash Facts*, p. 1.

★ 645 ★

Accidents

Alcohol Involvement for Drivers in Fatal Crashes, 1982 and 1991

Intoxication rates decreased between 1982 and 1991 for drivers of all ages involved in fatal crashes. The decrease was most significant for drivers 65 years of age and older, dropping from 9.9 percent in 1982 to 6.2 percent in 1991.

Drivers involved in fatal crashes	1982		1991		Change in percentage, 1982-1991
	Number of drivers	Percentage with BAC 0.10 g/dl or greater[1]	Number of drivers	Percentage with BAC 0.10 g/dl or greater[1]	
Total	56,029	30.0	54,323	23.9	-20.0
Drivers by age group (years)					
16-20	9,858	31.1	7,989	20.1	-35.0
21-24	9,018	40.0	6,738	33.7	-16.0
25-34	14,787	35.1	14,131	32.3	-8.0
35-44	7,984	27.9	9,475	25.2	-10.0
45-64	8,921	20.7	9,140	15.7	-24.0
Over 64	3,894	9.9	5,459	6.2	-37.0
Drivers by sex					
Male	44,370	32.4	40,680	26.9	-17.0
Female	10,675	18.9	12,806	13.6	-28.0
Drivers by vehicle type					
Passenger cars	34,121	30.6	31,045	23.4	-24.0
Light trucks	11,199	34.7	14,682	28.3	-18.0
Large trucks	4,582	4.3	4,285	2.0	-53.0
Motorcycles	4,490	40.5	2,819	38.6	-5.0

Source: National Center for Statistics and Analysis, National Highway Traffic Safety Administration, U.S. Department of Transportation, *1991 Alcohol Fatal Crash Facts*, p. 5. *Notes:* Numbers shown for groups of drivers do not add to the total number of drivers due to unknown or other data not included. 1. BAC stands for blood alcohol content and is measured in grams per deciliter.

★ 646 ★

Accidents

Alcohol Involvement for Nonoccupants Killed in Fatal Crashes, 1982 and 1991

Nonoccupant fatalities	1982		1991		Change in percentage, 1982-1991
	Number of nonoccupant fatalities	Percentage with BAC 0.10 g/dl or greater[2]	Number of nonoccupant fatalities	Percentage with BAC 0.10 g/dl or greater[2]	
Pedestrian fatalities by age group (years)					
16-20	721	47.0	366	34.0	-28.0
21-24	671	53.1	363	50.8	-4.0
25-34	1,109	53.2	986	56.4	+6.0
35-44	779	48.5	812	51.0	+5.0
45-64	1,264	40.7	1,051	36.0	-12.0
Over 64	1,449	13.8	1,288	9.8	-29.0
Total[1]	7,331	33.8	5,797	31.8	-6.0
Pedalcyclist fatalities					
Total	883	14.3	841	17.5	+22.0

Source: National Center for Statistics and Analysis, National Highway Traffic Safety Administration, U.S. Department of Transportation, *1991 Alcohol Fatal Crash Facts*, p. 6. *Notes:* 1. Includes pedestrians under 16 years old and pedestrians of unknown age. 2. BAC stands for blood alcohol content and is measured in grams per deciliter.

The following note is applicable to the next 13 tables:

"Data and estimates are based on injuries treated in hospital emergency rooms that patients say are *related* to products. Therefore it is *incorrect*, when using NEISS [National Electronic Injury Surveillance System] data, to say the injuries were *caused* by the product."

★ 647 ★
Accidents

Product-Related Injuries: Sports and Recreational Equipment

Data show product-related injuries in the United States and territories that were treated in hospital emergency departments.

Product	Number of cases	Estimated number of cases per 100,000 population Ages					
		All ages	00-04	05-14	15-24	25-64	65+
ATVs, mopeds, minibikes, etc.	1,359	50.0	14.5	103.2	129.0	27.9	7.2
Barbecue grills, stoves, equipment	185	6.2	23.4	7.5	3.5	4.9	2.5
Baseball	5,463	174.0	42.6	400.1	358.4	119.2	1.8
Basketball	8,641	257.5	9.9	469.1	885.2	114.9	2.4
Beach, picnic, camping equipment	243	8.1	21.6	17.7	5.1	5.4	3.3
Bicycles & accessories	7,739	233.3	266.5	949.9	256.5	75.3	20.2
Bowling	295	9.1	5.9	8.2	17.3	8.2	5.5
Cheerleading	156	5.0	-	13.5	20.7	-	-
Dancing	549	17.0	5.7	22.5	45.4	11.5	6.4
Exercise equipment	1,055	31.7	45.5	38.5	73.8	21.5	7.1
Fishing	798	27.9	16.5	50.6	30.9	25.4	16.0
Football	5,390	166.6	5.0	466.7	567.2	31.1	.5
Golf	504	16.6	9.8	31.3	13.5	13.9	19.3
Gymnastics & equipment	580	17.8	4.0	88.3	28.1	1.7	.2
Hockey, all kinds	646	19.7	2.7	38.7	68.4	7.5	.1
Horseback riding	876	29.9	7.2	41.8	48.5	30.8	3.9
Ice & roller skating	1,628	52.0	13.8	217.5	53.0	23.7	2.1
Lacrosse, rugby, misc. ball games	1,493	43.3	15.3	147.3	92.9	14.7	.4
Martial arts	354	10.2	.2	14.8	23.3	9.1	-
Nonpowder guns, BBs and pellets	321	9.7	8.1	40.3	15.8	2.0	.3
Playground equipment	3,316	101.7	402.8	465.8	19.3	4.9	2.2
Skateboards	1,085	33.1	14.6	155.8	59.0	2.5	.3
Snowskiing	1,228						
Soccer	1,795	56.2	2.0	167.3	160.7	16.6	.2
Swimming, pools, equipment	1,416	45.4	63.7	129.6	66.8	23.1	5.2
Tennis, badminton, squash	752	22.8	4.3	20.1	48.7	22.1	9.4
Toboggans, sleds, snow discs, etc.	315	11.5	9.8	44.8	15.2	4.1	.4
Track & field activities, equipment	853	23.9	-	41.9	61.8	16.7	2.6
Trampolines	350	13.1	16.1	66.1	11.6	1.6	-
Volleyball	1,510	50.5	-	63.7	142.6	39.5	1.0
Water skiing, tubing, surfing	336	12.1	1.1	6.2	31.1	12.6	.5
Wrestling	584	19.7	1.2	47.1	79.6	2.2	-
Other	575	19.7	16.1	32.9	40.7	14.6	2.6

Source: National Electronic Injury Surveillance System, *NEISS Data Highlights*, Jan.- Dec. 1990, Vol. 14.

★ 648 ★

Accidents

Product-Related Injuries: Home Communication, Entertainment, and Hobby

Product	Number of cases	Estimated Ages					
		All ages	00-04	05-14	15-24	25-64	65+
Misc. hobby equipment	188	5.8	15.8	9.8	10.3	3.0	1.0
Pet supplies, equipment	283	8.9	14.9	11.8	10.4	7.0	8.2
Sound recording & reproducing equip.	601	17.8	54.8	14.9	22.2	10.9	21.5
Television sets, stands	532	15.2	81.4	16.7	13.0	6.4	11.9
Other	18	.5	2.8	-	.2	.5	.4

Source: National Electronic Injury Surveillance System, *NEISS Data Highlights*, Jan.- Dec. 1990, Vol. 14.

★ 649 ★

Accidents

Product-Related Injuries: Personal Care Items

Product	Number of cases	Ages					
		All ages	00-04	05-14	15-24	25-64	65+
Cigarettes, lighters & fuel	264	7.8	38.7	6.4	8.1	5.1	1.5
Clothing, all	1,509	47.7	59.9	70.5	48.5	37.0	57.2
Grooming devices	406	11.6	63.7	10.6	17.2	5.1	1.3
Holders for personal items	232	6.8	12.7	10.2	3.7	5.6	8.0
Jewelry	762	19.7	88.4	35.4	20.6	8.8	3.9
Paper money & coins	482	11.9	105.3	25.0	1.5	.3	.5
Pencils, pens, other desk supplies	691	18.6	36.3	71.4	16.0	5.7	3.7
Razors, shavers, razor blades	683	18.8	20.1	14.4	35.6	17.3	9.0
Sewing equipment	427	11.9	20.2	18.4	16.6	8.8	7.0
Other	178	5.6	6.8	4.8	13.4	4.3	1.7

Source: National Electronic Injury Surveillance System, *NEISS Data Highlights*, Jan.- Dec. 1990, Vol. 14.

★ 650 ★
Accidents

Product-Related Injuries: Household Packaging and Containers

Product	Number of cases	Ages					
		All ages	00-04	05-14	15-24	25-64	65+
Cans, other containers	3,082	87.1	184.9	98.7	107.2	74.5	42.9
Glass bottles & jars	991	30.4	56.7	49.5	53.0	20.8	4.9
Paper/cardboard/plastic products	547	17.1	31.8	24.4	17.1	13.8	13.6

Source: National Electronic Injury Surveillance System, *NEISS Data Highlights*, Jan.- Dec. 1990, Vol. 14.

★ 651 ★
Accidents

Product-Related Injuries: Yard and Garden Equipment

Product	Number of cases	Ages					
		All ages	00-04	05-14	15-24	25-64	65+
Chain saws	424	15.8	1.0	2.9	16.1	22.8	10.4
Hand garden tools	415	14.2	17.2	24.2	11.0	12.3	12.7
Hatchets & axes	190	6.9	1.4	7.9	8.1	7.5	5.4
Lawn and garden care equipment	599	19.9	20.8	21.9	14.9	18.0	31.0
Lawn mowers, all types	897	31.1	13.6	19.1	24.1	37.9	36.0
Other power lawn equip.	255	9.2	4.2	5.2	8.9	11.5	8.2
Trimmers, small power garden tools	160	5.5	1.3	1.6	4.3	7.1	7.4
Other	118	4.0	6.0	9.7	2.6	2.6	4.2

Source: National Electronic Injury Surveillance System, *NEISS Data Highlights*, Jan.- Dec. 1990, Vol. 14.

★ 652 ★
Accidents

Product-Related Injuries: Home Workshop Equipment

Product	Number of cases	Ages					
		All ages	00-04	05-14	14-24	25-64	65+
Batteries, all types	162	5.0	13.4	5.4	7.1	3.9	1.2
Hoists, lifts, jacks, etc.	167	5.7	2.1	1.5	9.5	7.3	1.3
Miscellaneous workshop equipment	479	15.9	12.6	20.8	21.4	15.0	9.7
Power home tools, exc. saws	353	12.0	1.7	1.7	13.3	16.8	8.6
Power home workshop saws, all	1,127	37.7	5.4	8.8	36.3	45.7	58.9
Welding, soldering, cutting tools	229	7.8	1.0	-	15.8	10.4	.4

[Continued]

★ 652 ★

Product-Related Injuries: Home Workshop Equipment

[Continued]

Product	Number of cases	Ages					
		All ages	00-04	05-14	14-24	25-64	65+
Wires, cords, not specified	175	5.8	3.6	7.4	6.3	5.6	5.8
Workshop manual tools	1,455	47.5	23.6	27.5	64.2	57.9	21.7
Other	184	6.1	14.3	4.8	7.6	5.7	2.8

Source: National Electronic Injury Surveillance System, *NEISS Data Highlights*, Jan.- Dec. 1990, Vol. 14.

★ 653 ★

Accidents

Product-Related Injuries: Home Maintenance Equipment

Product	Number of cases	Ages					
		All ages	00-04	05-14	14-24	25-64	65+
Cleaning equip., non-caustic/detergent	333	9.8	17.2	10.8	8.5	8.5	11.0
Cleaning agents (exc. soaps)	582	16.3	92.8	6.6	15.1	10.8	4.8
Drain, oven cleaners, caustics	138	4.1	14.9	1.9	4.8	3.3	2.9
Miscellaneous household chemicals	250	7.5	23.8	9.1	8.9	5.4	2.6
Paints, solvents, lubricants	278	8.7	20.5	5.1	9.5	8.6	5.3
Other	163	4.3	24.4	1.5	2.8	2.6	4.3

Source: National Electronic Injury Surveillance System, *NEISS Data Highlights*, Jan.- Dec. 1990, Vol. 14.

★ 654 ★

Accidents

Product-Related Injuries: General Household Appliances

Product	Number of cases	Ages					
		All ages	00-04	05-14	15-24	25-64	65+
Cooking ranges, ovens, etc.	627	19.5	67.4	16.4	18.7	14.1	16.7
Irons, clothes steamers (not toys)	290	7.0	60.3	6.0	4.2	1.6	1.4
Misc. household appliances	400	12.4	27.0	9.2	12.7	10.7	14.1
Refrigerators, freezers	451	14.2	19.9	8.0	14.8	15.5	11.5
Washers & dryers	260	8.6	18.8	4.9	9.3	8.3	7.1

Source: National Electronic Injury Surveillance System, *NEISS Data Highlights*, Jan.- Dec. 1990, Vol. 14.

★ 655 ★
Accidents

Product-Related Injuries: Heating, Cooling, and Ventilating Equipment

Product	Number of cases	Ages					
		All ages	00-04	05-14	15-24	25-64	65+
Air conditioners	156	4.9	5.5	5.1	4.1	5.5	2.7
Chimneys, fireplaces	214	7.6	68.9	4.7	1.4	2.1	4.1
Fans (exc. stove exhaust fans)	239	7.7	17.0	6.7	8.2	6.7	7.1
Heating stoves & space heaters	410	13.4	87.4	14.9	6.1	6.2	5.0
Pipes, heating & plumbing	324	9.4	10.6	18.0	11.4	7.1	5.8
Radiators, all	321	7.6	50.1	9.1	3.5	3.0	4.2
Other	160	5.2	10.3	2.9	5.9	5.4	3.0

Source: National Electronic Injury Surveillance System, *NEISS Data Highlights*, Jan.- Dec. 1990, Vol. 14.

★ 656 ★
Accidents

Product-Related Injuries: Housewares

Product	Number of cases	Ages					
		All ages	00-04	05-14	15-24	25-64	65+
Cookware, pots and pans	443	13.3	27.8	13.6	15.9	11.4	8.4
Cutlery, knives, unpowered	5,872	179.5	76.6	170.0	293.6	190.5	70.8
Drinking glasses	1,796	53.5	53.8	47.8	101.3	50.6	14.3
Miscellaneous housewares	787	23.0	45.6	28.3	25.4	18.4	19.2
Scissors	360	10.8	21.6	25.3	11.4	6.6	4.4
Small kitchen appliances	566	17.5	26.3	10.4	21.9	18.3	11.8
Tableware and accessories	1,492	44.8	63.0	38.4	69.9	43.9	14.6
Other	118	3.9	4.8	8.3	2.6	3.4	1.7

Source: National Electronic Injury Surveillance System, *NEISS Data Highlights*, Jan.- Dec. 1990, Vol. 14.

★ 657 ★

Accidents

Product-Related Injuries: Home Furnishings and Accessories

Product	Number of cases	Ages					
		All ages	00-04	05-14	15-24	25-64	65+
Bathtub & shower structures	1,945	59.8	165.1	37.8	44.5	44.7	100.8
Beds, mattresses, pillows	4,960	141.6	663.8	188.1	72.6	49.6	230.7
Carpets and rugs	1,212	37.4	76.0	26.5	22.9	22.3	104.8
Chairs, sofas & sofa beds	4,910	148.5	653.9	157.5	83.7	71.0	226.4
Desks, cabinets, shelves, racks	2,811	83.1	291.3	119.4	68.2	49.3	72.1
Electric fixtures, lamps & equip.	660	20.0	44.9	26.1	22.6	15.2	15.1
Ladders, stools	2,174	68.8	63.1	29.0	38.1	80.9	104.8
Mirrors & mirror glass	306	8.7	16.9	9.7	18.1	5.8	3.0
Misc. household covers and fabrics	227	6.8	10.9	3.3	4.8	6.4	12.4
Other misc. furniture & accessories	645	19.0	38.4	10.5	15.9	21.0	12.7
Sinks & toilets	721	22.6	52.5	16.2	15.1	14.0	55.7
Tables, all types	4,331	127.3	798.9	139.0	71.5	48.9	94.6
Other	349	11.3	38.1	14.0	7.6	7.2	13.1

Source: National Electronic Injury Surveillance System, *NEISS Data Highlights*, Jan.- Dec. 1990, Vol. 14.

★ 658 ★

Accidents

Product-Related Injuries: Home Structures and Construction Materials

Product	Number of cases	Ages					
		All ages	00-04	05-14	15-24	25-64	65+
Cabinets or door hardware	298	8.8	32.3	12.7	7.8	4.7	8.5
Ceilings, walls, panels (inside)	3,199	88.3	182.4	156.8	150.3	48.0	44.3
Counters and counter tops	397	11.9	69.1	10.9	6.8	6.1	8.5
Fences	1,623	48.6	62.1	122.9	65.4	28.7	17.7
Glass doors, windows and panels	3,062	91.4	132.1	119.1	185.4	63.8	36.2
Handrails, railings and banisters	614	17.0	37.9	27.5	18.7	11.2	13.8
Misc. construction materials	1,074	36.9	29.2	49.8	43.0	35.9	24.2
Nails, carpet tacks, etc.	3,312	102.1	105.2	204.1	126.0	84.4	28.4
Non-glass doors and panels	5,079	138.9	396.2	231.5	162.6	81.2	86.3
Outside attached structures & materials	164	5.3	6.9	6.0	5.3	5.2	4.1
Porches, open side floors, etc.	1,439	47.9	105.3	63.9	39.9	38.2	44.7
Stairs, ramps, landings, floors	23,828	688.3	1,433.4	599.8	657.8	484.4	1,205.7
Windows, door sills, frames	674	20.9	68.9	22.3	22.1	11.4	27.7
Other	259	9.1	11.3	9.0	6.3	9.1	11.0

Source: National Electronic Injury Surveillance System, *NEISS Data Highlights*, Jan.- Dec. 1990, Vol. 14.

★ 659 ★

Accidents

Product-Related Injuries: Miscellaneous

Product	Number of cases	Ages					
		All ages	00-04	05-14	15-24	25-64	65+
Dollies, carts	548	16.5	109.6	14.6	6.6	7.0	12.9
Elevators, other lifts	231	5.8	10.2	4.2	4.9	4.2	13.0
Fireworks and flares	178	5.1	3.9	12.8	8.9	3.2	-
Gasoline and diesel fuels	237	8.2	21.8	7.4	13.0	6.3	3.0
Miscellaneous	1,520	45.6	79.8	124.5	71.3	18.1	17.3
Other	187	5.7	19.5	7.2	8.0	3.4	2.2

Source: National Electronic Injury Surveillance System, *NEISS Data Highlights*, Jan.- Dec. 1990, Vol. 14.

Health Costs

★ 660 ★

Personal Health Care Expenditures, by Age: 1977 and 1987

[Values in dollars] .

Age and type of expenditure	Aggregate amount (billions)			Per capita amount		
	1987	1977	1977[1]	1987	1977	1977[1]
Total expenditures						
All ages	447.0	150.3	281.9	1,776.0	658.0	1,234.1
Under 19 years	51.9	19.5	36.6	745.0	269.0	504.5
19 to 64 years	233.1	85.6	160.5	1,535.0	651.0	1,220.9
65 years and over	162.0	45.2	84.8	5,360.0	1,856.0	3,480.9
Private expenditures						
All ages	271.8	92.6	173.7	1,079.0	405.0	759.6
Under 19 years	38.1	14.4	27.0	547.0	198.0	371.3
19 to 64 years	173.0	62.3	116.8	1,139.0	474.0	889.0
65 years and over	60.6	15.9	29.8	2,004.0	653.0	1,224.7
Public expenditures						
All ages	175.3	57.8	108.4	696.0	253.0	474.5
Under 19	13.8	5.2	9.8	198.0	711.0	133.2

[Continued]

★ 660 ★

Personal Health Care Expenditures, by Age: 1977 and 1987
[Continued]

Age and type of expenditure	Aggregate amount (billions)			Per capita amount		
	1987	1977	1977[1]	1987	1977	1977[1]
19 to 64 years	60.0	23.2	43.5	395.0	177.0	332.0
65 years and over	101.5	29.3	55.0	3,356.0	1,204.0	2,258.1

Source: Health Care Financing Administration, Office of the Actuary, data from the Office of National Cost Estimates. Note: 1. 1977 in 1987 constant dollars.

★ 661 ★

Health Costs

Health Care Costs per Person, 65 Years Old or Older, 1991-2031

Data show average out-of-pocket medical expenses (not covered by Medicare or other insurance).

[Figures shown in dollars]

Year of retirement at age 65	Expenses
1991	1,680
2001	2,436
2011	3,261
2021	4,066
2031	4,826

Source: "Effect of Normal Medical Expenses on Single Person," *Management Review*, April 1992, p. 33. Primary source: Northwestern Life Insurance Co., November 1991.

★ 662 ★

Health Costs

Per Capita Personal Health Care Expenditures for Persons 65 Years and Over, by Age: 1987

Age and source of care	Total	Private	Public
65 years and over			
Total	5,360	2,004	3,356
Hospital care	2,248	333	1,915
Physicians' services	1,107	393	714

[Continued]

★ 662 ★

Per Capita Personal Health Care Expenditures for Persons 65 Years and Over, by Age: 1987

[Continued]

Age and source of care	Total	Private	Public
Nursing home care	1,085	634	451
Other personal care	920	644	276
65 to 69 years			
Total	3,728	1,430	2,298
Hospital care	1,682	312	1,370
Physicians' services	974	380	594
Nursing home care	165	94	71
Other personal care	907	644	263
70 to 74 years			
Total	4,424	1,564	2,860
Hospital care	2,062	327	1,735
Physicians' services	1,086	389	697
Nursing home care	360	205	155
Other personal care	916	644	262
75 to 79 years			
Total	5,455	1,843	3,612
Hospital care	2,536	341	2,195
Physicians' services	1,191	398	793
Nursing home care	802	461	341
Other personal care	925	644	281
80 to 84 years			
Total	6,717	2,333	4,384
Hospital care	2,935	355	2,580
Physicians' services	1,246	407	839
Nursing home care	1,603	927	676
Other personal care	934	644	290
85 years and over			
Total	9,178	3,631	5,547
Hospital care	3,231	376	2,855
Physicians' services	1,262	420	842
Nursing home care	3,738	2,191	1,547
Other personal care	947	645	302

Source: Health Care Financing Administration, Office of the Actuary, data from the Office of National Cost Estimates.

★ 663 ★

Health Costs

Health Care as a Proportion of Total Expenses

Average annual health care expenditures of elderly Americans are shown in dollars and as percent of total expenses. The 65 and over group spends nearly twice as much (in percent) as the younger group.

Category	65 and over		55 to 64	
	Actual ($)	Percent	Actual ($)	Percent
Total expenditures	19,692	100.0	31,945	100.0
Total health care expenditures	2,256	11.5	1,848	5.8
Health insurance	1,111	5.6	749	2.3
Medical services	579	2.9	672	2.1
Drugs	444	2.3	339	1.1
Medical supplies	122	0.6	88	0.3

Source: USA TODAY, December 30, 1992, p. 4B. Primary source: Bureau of Labor Statistics.

★ 664 ★

Health Costs

Annual Health Care Expenditures Distribution by Source of Funds

Type of service and age	Total	Source of funds			
		Private	Medicare	Medicaid	Other
All personal health care					
65-69 years	3,728	1,430	1,849	245	204
70-74 years	4,424	1,564	2,234	357	268
75-79 years	5,455	1,843	2,685	569	358
80-84 years	6,717	2,333	3,023	908	453
65 years and over	5,360	2,004	2,391	645	321
85 years and over	9,178	3,631	3,215	1,742	591
Hospital care					
65-69 years	1,682	312	1,144	67	158
70-74 years	2,062	327	1,431	93	212
75-79 years	2,536	341	1,786	127	283
80-84 years	2,935	355	2,070	161	348
65 years and over	2,248	333	1,566	110	239
85 years and over	3,231	376	2,246	198	411
Physician services					
65-69 years	974	380	558	14	22

[Continued]

★ 664 ★

Annual Health Care Expenditures Distribution by Source of Funds
[Continued]

Type of service and age	Total	Source of funds			
		Private	Medicare	Medicaid	Other
70-74 years	1,086	389	655	17	25
75-79 years	1,191	398	745	19	29
80-84 years	1,246	407	789	20	31
65 years and over	1,107	393	671	17	26
85 years and over	1,262	420	792	20	31
Nursing home care					
65-69 years	165	94	5	60	6
70-74 years	360	205	11	131	13
75-79 years	802	461	22	292	28
80-84 years	1,603	927	37	584	56
60 years and over	1,085	634	19	395	38
85 years and over	3,738	2,191	56	1,361	131
Other personal health care					
65-69 years	907	644	142	103	18
70-74 years	916	644	137	117	18
75-79 years	925	644	133	130	18
80-84 years	934	644	128	144	18
65 years and over	920	644	135	123	18
85 years and over	947	645	121	164	18

Percent distribution

All personal health care					
65-69 years	100.0	38.4	49.6	6.6	5.5
70-74 years	100.0	35.4	50.5	8.1	6.1
75-79 years	100.0	33.8	49.2	10.4	6.6
80-84 years	100.0	34.7	45.0	13.5	6.7
65 years and over	100.0	37.4	44.6	12.0	6.0
85 years and over	100.0	39.6	35.0	19.0	6.4
Hospital care					
65-69 years	100.0	18.6	68.0	4.0	9.4
70-74 years	100.0	15.9	69.4	4.5	10.3
75-79 years	100.0	13.5	70.4	5.0	11.2
80-84 years	100.0	12.1	70.5	5.5	11.9
65 years and over	100.0	14.8	69.7	4.9	10.6
85 years and over	100.0	11.6	69.5	6.1	12.7
Physician services					
65-69 years	100.0	39.0	57.3	1.4	2.3
70-74 years	100.0	35.8	60.3	1.6	2.3

[Continued]

★ 664 ★

Annual Health Care Expenditures Distribution by Source of Funds

[Continued]

Type of service and age	Total	Source of funds			
		Private	Medicare	Medicaid	Other
75-79 years	100.0	33.4	62.6	1.6	2.4
80-84 years	100.0	32.7	63.3	1.6	2.5
65 years and over	100.0	35.5	60.6	1.5	2.4
85 years and over	100.0	33.3	62.8	1.6	2.5
Nursing home care					
65-69 years	100.0	57.0	3.0	36.4	3.6
70-74 years	100.0	56.9	3.1	36.4	3.6
75-79 years	100.0	57.5	2.7	36.4	3.5
80-84 years	100.0	57.8	2.3	36.4	3.5
65 years and over	100.0	58.4	1.8	36.4	3.5
85 years and over	100.0	58.6	1.5	36.4	3.5
Other personal health care					
65-69 years	100.0	71.0	15.7	11.4	2.0
70-74 years	100.0	70.3	15.0	12.8	2.0
75-79 years	100.0	69.6	14.4	14.0	2.0
80-84 years	100.0	69.0	13.7	15.4	1.9
65 years and over	100.0	70.0	14.7	13.4	2.0
85 years and over	100.0	68.1	12.8	17.3	1.9

Source: Health Data on Older Americans: United States, 1992, Centers for Disease Control and Prevention/National Center for Health Statistics, Vital and Health Statistics, Series 3: Analytic and Epidemiological Studies, No. 27, pp. 225-226. Primary source: Waldo D., Sonnefeld S., McKusick D., Arnett R. "Health expenditures by age group, 1977 and 1987." Health Care Financing Review 10(4):111-20. 1989. Notes: Hospital care and physician services include both inpatient and outpatient care. Percents may not add to 100 because of rounding.

★ 665 ★

Health Costs

Federal Pension and Health Programs as a Percentage of GNP and the Budget, 1965-2040

From the source: "Rising health care costs, rather than spending for retirement income, account for most of the current increase in public spending on the elderly... Social Security retirement and disability benefits, which grew from 2.5 percent of GNP in 1965 to 5.2 percent in 1983, are projected to decline to 4.2 percent by 2005, and then increase slightly to 5.7 percent by 2030. Other pension benefits paid from the federal budget are expected to decline from 2 percent of GNP currently to about 1.2 percent of GNP by 2030."

Year	Pension programs as a percent of GNP[1]	Health programs as a percent of GNP[1]	Total as a percent of of GNP[1]	Total as a percent of of budget[2]
1965	4.1	0.3	4.4	24.9
1970	4.7	1.4	6.1	30.0
1975	6.4	2.0	8.4	37.1
1980	6.5	2.3	8.8	38.2
1982	7.1	2.7	9.7	39.6
1984	7.0	2.8	9.8	39.7
1986	6.6	3.0	9.6	39.4
1988	6.4	3.2	9.6	39.4
1990	6.6[3]	3.1[3]	9.7	40.4
1995	6.2	3.7	9.9	41.3
2000	5.8	4.0	9.8	40.8
2005	5.6	4.4	10.0	41.7
2010	6.0	4.7	10.7	44.6
2015	6.0	5.0	11.0	45.8
2020	6.5	5.4	11.9	49.6
2025	7.0	5.9	12.9	53.9
2030	7.1	6.4	13.5	56.3
2035	7.1	7.0	14.1	58.8
2040	7.0	7.5	14.5	60.4

Source: Aging America, Trends and Projections, prepared by the U.S. Senate Special Committee on Aging, the American Association of Retired Persons, the Federal Council on the Aging, and the U.S. Administration on Aging, 1991, Washington, D.C., p. 242. Primary source: John L. Palmer and Barbara B. Torrey, "Health Care Financing and Pension Programs," Paper prepared for the Urban Institute Conference on "Federal Budget Policy in the 1980s, September 29-30, 1983. *Notes:* 1. Estimates for 1984-1988 are based on Congressional Budget Office baseline assumptions, August 1983; forecasts for 1990 and beyond are based on intermediate assumptions of the Social Security and Medicare actuaries. 2. Forecasts for 1990 and beyond are based on the assumption that the budget accounts for 24 percent of GNP. 3. The discontinuity in the estimates of pension and health benefits as a percent of GNP between 1986 and 1990 is due to the Social Security trustees assuming that Old-Age, Survivors, and Disability Insurance (OASDI) will grow at a faster rate in the late 1980s than Congressional Budget Office assumes, and the Health Insurance trustees assuming that Medicare will grow at a slower rate than CBO assumes.

★ 666 ★

Health Costs

Percentage of Government Medical Care Expenditure on the Elderly Population, Compared to Other Countries, 1980-2025

From the source: "With the shift in the age structure of the population, an associated change will take place in the underlying structure of demand for services, creating imbalances between available physical capacity and professional manpower resources and the structure of demand. This change will undoubtedly create short-term transitional adjustment difficulties. For example, the share of government expenditure on medical care consumed by the age group 65 and over will substantially increase. In the Federal Republic of Germany, Italy, and the United Kingdom, it will increase by 7-9 percentage points between 1980 and 2025; in Canada, Japan, and the United States, the increase will be even more dramatic. This increased share will be reflected in a change in the demand for particular services, with obviously increased needs for nursing home facilities and for professionals and paraprofessionals trained in geriatric care. An associated problem will be the need to 'retool' plants and retrain professionals in specialties less in demand."

Country	1980	2000	2010	2025
Canada	33.3	38.0	40.9	53.1
Germany, Fed. Rep. of[1]	33.1	33.6	39.0	42.6
Italy	31.8	36.2	37.4	40.6
Japan	27.4	37.7	43.8	48.3
United Kingdom	42.1	44.1	44.3	49.4
United States	50.0	54.4	55.6	64.6

Source: Aging and Social Expenditure in the Major Industrial Countries, 1980-2025, Peter S. Heller, Richard Hemming, Peter W. Kohnert et. al., International Monetary Fund, September, 1986, p. 45. *Notes:* Gross Domestic Product excludes expenditure on medical research and education, administration, and capital investment in the medical sector. 1. People included are those over age sixty.

★ 667 ★

Health Costs

Health Care Expenditures as Percent of GDP: Worldwide, 1991

Medical technology costs have contributed to the world's rising health care expenditures.

[Total health care expenditures as a percentage of GDP, 1991]

Country	Percent
United States	13.4
Canada	10.0
Germany	8.5
Japan	6.6
United Kingdom	6.6

Source: Sara Collins, "Cutting Edge Cures," *U.S. News & World Report*, June 7, 1993, p. 58.
Note: GDP stands for gross domestic product.

★ 668 ★

Health Costs

Projected Increases in Real Government Expenditures on Medical Care for Selected Countries, 2000 and 2025

Data show increases in expenditures using 1980 as the reference year.

[Index: 1980 = 100]

Country	Year		
	1980	2000	2025
Japan, medical care costs			
United States	100.0	130.0	180.0
France	100.0	117.0	130.0
West Germany	100.0	104.0	103.0
Italy	100.0	113.0	121.0
United Kingdom	100.0	105.0	115.0
Canada	100.0	128.0	174.0
Japan	100.0	130.0	147.0

Source: Aging America, Trends and Projections, prepared by the U.S. Senate Special Committee on Aging, the American Association of Retired Persons, the Federal Council on the Aging, and the U.S. Administration on Aging, 1991, Washington, D.C., p. 270. Primary source: International Monetary Fund (IMF), *Aging and Social Expenditure in the Major Industrial Countries, 1980-2025*, by Peter S. Heller, Richard Hemming, Peter W. Kohnert, and IMF staff. Occasional Paper 47, September 1986.

★ 669 ★

Health Costs

Projected Home Care Expenditures for People Age 65+, by Source of Payment: 1990, 2005, and 2020

[Numbers in billions of 1989 dollars]

Source of payment	1990	2005	2020
Medicare	2.2	3.9	5.7
Medicaid	1.7	2.6	3.5
Other public payers	1.4	2.5	3.9
Out-of-pocket	2.6	4.5	6.7
Total	7.9	13.5	19.8

Source: Aging America, Trends and Projections, prepared by the U.S. Senate Special Committee on Aging, the American Association of Retired Persons, the Federal Council on the Aging, and the U.S. Administration on Aging, 1991, Washington, D.C., p. 174. Primary source: Brookings/ICF *Long Term Care Financing Model*, unpublished data, 1990.

★ 670 ★

Health Costs

Projected Percent Increase in Spending on Medicare and Social Security Each Fiscal Year, 1992-1997

	1992	1993	1994	1995	1996	1997
Medicare	12.3	10.9	11.3	11.4	11.4	11.2
Social Security	6.7	5.6	5.6	5.7	5.4	5.6

Source: "Entitlements for the Retired Take Ever More Money," *New York Times*, August 30, 1992, p. 4E. Primary source: Social Security Administration.

★ 671 ★

Health Costs

Percent of Federal Budget Spent on the Medicaid and Social Security Programs, 1980-1997

	1980	1985	1990	1991	1992	1993	1994	1995	1996	1997
Total Social Security and Medicare	25.5	27.1	28.3	28.8	28.4	29.4	31.2	33.2	34.5	34.4
Social Security	19.8	19.7	19.7	20.2	19.6	19.9	20.8	21.7	22.1	21.7
Medicare	5.8	7.4	8.5	8.6	8.8	9.5	10.4	11.5	12.4	12.7

Source: "Entitlements for the Retired Take Ever More Money," *New York Times,* August 30, 1992, p. 4E. Primary source: Congressional Budget Office. *Note:* Numbers may not add due to rounding.

★ 672 ★

Health Costs

Expenditures on Hospital Care, Nursing Home Care, Physician Services, and All Other Personal Health Care Expenditures: U.S., 1960-90

Data are compiled by the Health Care Financing Administration.

Service and year	Total ($ bil.)	Percent distribution					
		Non-government				Government	
		Out-of pocket payments	Private health insurance	Other private funds	Total[1]	Medicaid	Medicare
Hospital care							
1960	9.3	20.7	35.6	1.2	42.5	-	-
1965	14.0	19.6	40.9	1.9	37.6	-	-
1970	27.9	9.0	34.4	3.2	53.4	8.1	18.8
1975	52.4	8.4	34.4	2.8	54.5	8.8	21.9
1980	102.4	5.2	36.6	4.9	53.3	9.4	25.8
1983	147.2	5.2	36.6	4.9	53.3	9.0	28.0
1984	157.5	5.1	36.1	4.6	54.1	9.1	28.8
1985	168.3	5.2	35.3	4.9	54.5	9.2	28.9
1986	179.8	4.8	35.2	5.0	55.0	9.2	28.5
1987	194.2	4.5	35.6	5.0	54.9	9.5	27.8
1988	212.0	5.3	35.6	5.3	53.9	9.4	27.1
1989	232.6	5.2	35.8	5.4	53.6	9.9	26.7
1990	256.0	5.0	34.9	5.4	54.7	11.1	26.7
Nursing home care							
1960	1.0	80.0	0.0	6.4	13.6	-	-
1965	1.7	64.5	0.1	5.8	29.5	-	-
1970	4.9	48.2	0.3	4.9	46.6	28.0	5.0
1975	9.9	42.1	0.7	4.8	52.3	47.5	2.9

[Continued]

★ 672 ★

Expenditures on Hospital Care, Nursing Home Care, Physician Services, and All Other Personal Health Care Expenditures: U.S., 1960-90

[Continued]

Service and year	Total ($ bil.)	Percent distribution					
		Non-government				Government	
		Out-of pocket payments	Private health insurance	Other private funds	Total[1]	Medicaid	Medicare
1980	20.0	43.3	0.9	3.1	52.7	48.6	2.1
1983	28.9	47.1	1.0	2.3	49.5	45.7	1.8
1984	31.2	47.8	1.1	2.1	48.9	44.9	1.8
1985	34.1	48.6	1.0	1.9	48.5	44.6	1.7
1986	36.7	49.1	1.0	1.9	48.0	44.1	1.6
1987	39.7	47.9	1.0	1.9	49.2	45.2	1.6
1988	42.8	48.1	1.1	1.9	48.9	44.4	2.2
1989	47.7	43.7	1.1	1.9	53.3	43.2	8.0
1990	53.1	44.9	1.1	1.9	52.1	45.4	4.7
Physician services							
1960	5.3	62.7	30.2	0.1	7.1	-	-
1965	8.2	60.6	32.5	0.1	6.8	-	-
1970	13.6	42.8	35.2	0.1	21.9	4.6	11.8
1975	23.3	32.8	39.3	0.1	27.9	7.1	14.6
1980	41.9	26.9	42.9	0.1	30.2	5.1	19.0
1983	60.6	24.1	43.9	0.0	32.0	4.0	22.0
1984	67.1	23.4	45.2	0.0	31.4	3.8	21.6
1985	74.0	21.8	45.6	0.0	32.6	3.9	22.5
1986	82.1	20.8	45.6	0.0	33.5	3.9	23.2
1987	93.0	20.4	45.7	0.0	33.8	3.8	23.4
1988	105.1	19.9	46.7	0.0	33.4	3.6	23.0
1989	113.6	18.8	46.5	0.0	34.7	3.7	24.1
1990	125.7	18.7	46.3	0.0	35.0	4.2	23.9
All other personal health care[2]							
1960	8.4	87.8	1.4	2.7	8.0	-	-
1965	11.7	87.4	2.2	2.6	7.8	-	-
1970	18.5	80.6	4.3	2.7	12.4	4.4	0.7
1975	31.0	72.2	8.5	3.0	16.4	6.2	1.7
1980	55.1	62.1	17.5	3.5	16.9	6.0	3.1
1983	78.3	58.2	21.1	3.8	16.8	6.0	4.4
1984	85.5	57.4	21.9	4.0	16.7	6.1	4.7
1985	93.4	56.6	21.9	4.3	17.2	6.5	4.8
1986	102.2	56.1	22.2	4.1	17.7	6.9	4.8
1987	112.4	55.3	22.9	3.9	17.9	7.3	4.7
1988	122.9	54.3	23.7	3.9	18.1	7.6	4.7

[Continued]

★ 672 ★

Expenditures on Hospital Care, Nursing Home Care, Physician Services, and All Other Personal Health Care Expenditures: U.S., 1960-90

[Continued]

Service and year	Total ($ bil.)	Percent distribution					
		Non-government				Government	
		Out-of pocket payments	Private health insurance	Other private funds	Total[1]	Medicaid	Medicare
1989	136.1	52.8	24.3	4.0	18.9	8.4	5.1
1990	150.5	50.4	25.2	4.2	20.1	9.0	5.4

Source: U.S. Department of Commerce, Economics and Statistics Administration, *National Economic, Social, and Environmental Data Bank, CD-ROM,* November 1992. Primary source: Office of National Health Statistics, Office of the Actuary: *National Health Expenditures, 1990. Health Care Financing Review. Vol. 13, No. 1. HCFA Pub. No. 03321.* Health Care Financing Administration. Washington. U.S. Government Printing Office, October 1991. *Notes:* These data include revisions back to 1978 and differ from previous editions of *Health, United States.* A dash (-) indicates that data were not available in the original source. 1. Includes other government expenditures for these health care services, for example, care funded by the Department of Veterans Affairs and State and locally financed subsidies to hospitals. 2. Includes expenditures for dental services, other professional services, home health care, drugs and other medical nondurables, vision products and other medical durables, and other personal health care.

★ 673 ★

Health Costs

Drugs: Cost of Drugs

Due to inflation, a drug today costing the average American $53.76, cost only $20 in 1980, a 268 percent increase. At the current rate of inflation, that same drug will cost $77.06 in 1995 (a 365% increase), and $120.88 in the year 2000 (a 604% increase).

Source: "Communism Collapses...but Nothing Changes the Pharmaceutical Industry's Skyrocketing Pricing Practices," David Pryor, *Congressional Record,* September 10, 1991, pS.12618.

★ 674 ★

Health Costs

Drugs: Frequency of Price Increases and Percentage Increases - Drug Specific: Ansaid

[Increase in price per pill in dollars]

Date	Ansaid 100 mg price increase	Ansaid 50 mg price increase
01-01-89	0.8000	0.5125
09-17-89	0.8480	0.5433
03-05-90	0.9659	0.6188
01-11-91	1.0576	0.6775
01-03-92	1.0999	0.7046
Percent increase	37.49	37.48

Source: U.S. Congress, "The Effects of Escalating Drug Costs on the Elderly," Hearing before the Special Committee on Aging, United States Senate, April 22, 1992, 102-21, U.S. Government Printing Office, Washington, D.C., p. 54.

★ 675 ★

Health Costs

Drugs: Frequency of Price Increases and Percentage Increases - Drug Specific: Axid

[Increase in price per pill in dollars]

Date	Axid 300 mg price increase
05-01-88	1.8257
04-27-89	1.9353
04-10-90	2.0707
03-14-91	2.3813
01-03-92	2.5720
Percent increase	40.88

Source: U.S. Congress, "The Effects of Escalating Drug Costs on the Elderly," Hearing before the Special Committee on Aging, United States Senate, April 22, 1992, 102-21, U.S. Government Printing Office, Washington, D.C., p. 55.

★ 676 ★

Health Costs

Drugs: Frequency of Price Increases and Percentage Increases - Drug Specific: Ceclor

[Increase in price per pill in dollars]

Date	Ceclor 250 mg caps price increase
09-01-88	1.2783
04-01-89	1.3933
12-01-89	1.4908
10-15-90	1.6101
05-25-91	1.7550
03-15-92	1.8322
Percent increase	31.50

Source: U.S. Congress, "The Effects of Escalating Drug Costs on the Elderly," Hearing before the Special Committee on Aging, United States Senate, April 22, 1992, 102-21, U.S. Government Printing Office, Washington, D.C., p. 56.

★ 677 ★

Health Costs

Drugs: Frequency of Price Increases and Percentage Increases - Drug Specific: Ceftin

[Increase in price per pill in dollars]

Date	Ceftin 250 mg price increase	Ceftin 500 mg price increase
07-10-88	2.0150	3.7090
08-01-89	2.1960	4.1067
01-05-90	2.3495	4.3940
10-09-90	2.5375	4.7455
08-29-91	2.7666	5.1728
03-06-92	2.8885	5.4020
Percent increase	43.35	45.65

Source: U.S. Congress, "The Effects of Escalating Drug Costs on the Elderly," Hearing before the Special Committee on Aging, United States Senate, April 22, 1992, 102-21, U.S. Government Printing Office, Washington, D.C., p. 55.

★ 678 ★

Health Costs

Drugs: Frequency of Price Increases and Percentage Increases - Drug Specific: Premarin

[Increase in price per pill in dollars]

Date	Premarin 1.2 mg price increase	Premarin .626 mg price increase
04-01-89	0.2935	0.2143
07-28-89	0.3521	0.2574
03-16-90	0.3853	0.2816
09-01-90	0.42155	0.3081
03-15-91	0.4528	0.3309
02-24-92	0.4726	0.3454
Percent increase	61.02	61.18

Source: U.S. Congress, "The Effects of Escalating Drug Costs on the Elderly," Hearing before the Special Committee on Aging, United States Senate, April 22, 1992, 102-21, U.S. Government Printing Office, Washington, D.C., p. 55.

★ 679 ★

Health Costs

Drugs: Frequency of Price Increases and Percentage Increases - Drug Specific: Prozac

[Increase in price per pill in dollars]

Date	Prozac 20 mg price increase
01-04-88	1.3201
01-13-89	1.4389
09-28-89	1.5684
08-30-90	1.6782
05-09-91	1.8292
01-10-92	1.9298
Percent increase	46.19

Source: U.S. Congress, "The Effects of Escalating Drug Costs on the Elderly," Hearing before the Special Committee on Aging, United States Senate, April 22, 1992, 102-21, U.S. Government Printing Office, Washington, D.C., p. 54.

★ 680 ★

Health Costs

Drugs: Frequency of Price Increases and Percentage Increases - Drug Specific: Ventolin

[Increase in price per pill in dollars]

Date	Ventolin refill price increase per pill, tablet, etc.
12-18-88	0.7865
07-03-89	0.8953
07-02-90	0.9712
01-24-91	1.0106
06-29-91	1.0559
03-06-92	1.1036
Percent increase	40.32

Source: U.S. Congress, "The Effects of Escalating Drug Costs on the Elderly," Hearing before the Special Committee on Aging, United States Senate, April 22, 1992, 102-21, U.S. Government Printing Office, Washington, D.C., p. 54.

★ 681 ★

Health Costs

Drugs: Frequency of Price Increases and Percentage Increases - Drug Specific: Xanax

[Increase in price per pill in dollars]

Date	Xanax 0.5 mg price increase
04-01-88	0.3914
04-01-89	0.4461
07-17-89	0.4774
03-05-90	0.5438
01-11-91	0.5976
01-03-92	0.8490
Percent increase	65.82

Source: U.S. Congress, "The Effects of Escalating Drug Costs on the Elderly," Hearing before the Special Committee on Aging, United States Senate, April 22, 1992, 102-21, U.S. Government Printing Office, Washington, D.C., p. 56.

★ 682 ★

Health Costs

Drugs: Frequency of Price Increases - Drug Specific

[Increase in price per pill in dollars]

Drug	Dates of increases					
Axid	5-88	4-89	4-90	3-91	1-92	-
Cardizem	5-90	10-90	2-91	7-91	-	2-92
Ceclor	9-88	4-89	12-89	10-90	6-91	3-92
Cipro	7-88	5-89	1-90	10-90	6-91	3-92
Dolobid	12-87	11-88	7-89	3-90	2-91	1-92
Humulin	10-87	9-88	8-89	9-90	9-91	-
Nicorette	10-89	3-90	9-90	2-91	7-91	2-92
Premarin	4-89	7-89	3-90	9-90	3-91	2-92
Seldane	10-89	3-90	9-90	2-91	7-91	2-92
Ventolin	12-88	7-89	7-90	1-91	6-91	3-92
Verelan	6-90	12-90	4-91	3-92	-	-
Xanax	4-88	4-89	9-89	3-90	11-91	1-92

Source: U.S. Congress, "The Effects of Escalating Drug Costs on the Elderly," Hearing before the Special Committee on Aging, United States Senate, April 22, 1992, 102-21, U.S. Government Printing Office, Washington, D.C., p. 56.

★ 683 ★

Health Costs

Drugs: Prescription Expenditures for Medicare Beneficiaries 65 Years of Age or Older in 1987

[Increase in price per pill in dollars]

	Amount (in millions)	Average per person (in dollars)
Total	$8,318	$262
White	7,291	267
Black	694	238

Source: U.S. Congress, "Profiles in Aging America: Meeting the Health Care Needs of the Nation's Black Elderly," Joint Hearing Before the Special Committee on Aging and the Congressional Black Caucus Health Braintrust, United States Senate, September 28, 1990, 101-29, U.S. Government Printing Office, Washington, D.C., p. 128. Primary source: "National Medical Expenditure Survey Prescribed Medicines: A Summary of Use and Expenditures by Medicare Beneficiaries," Research Findings 3, NCHSR, Dept. of Health and Human Services, Public Health Service, National Center for Health Services Research, and Health Care Technology Assessment, PHS 89-3448, Sept. 1989, p. 12.

★ 684 ★

Health Costs

Drugs: The Price of Drugs, California and Mexico

[Average price in dollars]

Drug	Strength (mg)	Number of tablets	Average price	
			California	Mexico
Cardizem	60	30	$24.04	$6.12
Cector	250	15	35.87	6.87
Mevacor	20	30	67.62	42.08
Prozac	20	14	33.22	23.49
Tagamet	300	100	77.08	19.60
Xanax	.25	90	64.08	NA
Zantac	160	60	92.31	21.91

Source: "Medicines Across the Border," *Detroit Free Press*, November 26, 1992, p. 23A. Primary source: Families USA Foundation. *Note:* NA stands for not available.

★ 685 ★

Health Costs

Health Care Costs per Family Headed by a 65-Year-Old, 1961-1991

[Figures shown in dollars]

Type of care	Average out-of-pocket costs per family		
	1961	1972	1991
Hospital	228	175	90
Doctor	316	184	408
Nursing home	287	582	1,194
Private insurance	304	309	653
Medicare	---	214	320
Other	454	390	640

Source: "Health Costs," *The Wall Street Journal*, February 26, 1992, p. B6. Primary source: Families USA.

★ 686 ★

Health Costs

Hip Fractures: Cost Comparison of Inpatient and Inpatient/Home Treatment of Hip Fractures

Inpatient/home treatment saves $2,016.19 per episode. Inpatient/home treatment saves $2,337.88 per quality-adjusted episode.

Cost component	Inpatient treatment strategy 1 ($)	Inpatient/home treatment strategy 2 ($)
Hospital inpatient costs	6,500.21	4,383.83
Physician inpatient costs	+ 207.93	none
Outpatient hospital and physician costs	none	+ 93.49
Personnel	none	+ 165.57
Home medical equipment, supplies and services	none	+ 49.16
Total	6,708.14	4,692.05
Quality of life adjustment	+ 321.79	none
Adjusted total	7,029.93	4,692.05

Source: U.S. Congress, "Medicare Fraud and Abuse: A Neglected Emergency?," Hearing before the Special Committee on Aging, United States Senate, October 2, 1991, 102-13, U.S. Government Printing Office, Washington, D.C., p. 225. *Notes:* A plus in one column reflects an incremental cost. Total costs are used for comparison only and do not reflect total cost of an episode.

★ 687 ★

Health Costs

Hip Fractures: Expenditures

[Data are in 1977 dollars]

	($)
Outpatient and emergency room institutional service	22.00
Outpatient diagnostic and therapeutic services	214.35
Physician office, outpatient, and emergency room	88.87
Drugs (prescription in a physician setting)	29.91
Total	355.13

Source: U.S. Congress, "Medicare Fraud and Abuse: A Neglected Emergency?," Hearing before the Special Committee on Aging, United States Senate, October 2, 1991, 102-13, U.S. Government Printing Office, Washington, D.C., p. 224. Primary source: Grazier L.K., Holbrook T.L., and Kelsey J.L.: *The Frequency of Occurrence, Impact, and Costs of Musculoskeletal Conditions in the United States*, American Academy of Orthopedic Surgeons, 1984.

★ 688 ★

Health Costs

Home Health Agency Visits per Patient Episode

From the source: "A recent paper reports home health utilization by Medicare patients for specific diagnoses. Estimates of per visit charges are based on 1987 allowed charges inflated to 1990 dollars at a rate of 5.5% per year. Length of therapy for the inpatient strategy is assumed to be 9 weeks; while patients receiving inpatient and home therapy incur an additional 5.8 days of services at a charge of $194.79. When 85% of charges are used as a proxy for costs, the total cost attributable to combination therapy is $165.57."

	Visits	Charge/visit ($)	Total charge
Skilled nursing	8.56	74	633.44
Home health aide	7.63	55	419.65
Physical therapy	12.83	75	962.25
Occup/speech/social work	1.21	83	100.43
Total			2,115.77

Source: U.S. Congress, "Medicare Fraud and Abuse: A Neglected Emergency?," Hearing before the Special Committee on Aging, United States Senate, October 2, 1991, 102-13, U.S. Government Printing Office, Washington, D.C., p. 224. Primary source: Branch L., Goldberg H., Chen V. et al: "Medicare Home Health Clients: Who Are They and What Services Do They Receive During an Episode of Care?" Submitted to the *Health Care Financing Review*, April 1990.

★ 689 ★

Health Costs

Home Medical Equipment, Supplies, and Services per Episode, 1990

In 1981 27.3% of the patients discharged from the hospital needed home medical equipment (HME). By 1986 the percentage had increased to 35.0%.

Home medical equipment	Rental/ purchase	Fee/price (9 weeks) ($)	Source
Hospital bed, manual	Rental	192.53	Sample of Medicare fee schedules
Walker - wheeled	Rental	49.77	Sample of Medicare fee schedules
Drop-arm commode	Rental	67.84	Sample of Medicare fee schedules
Toilet safety rails	Purchase	41.40	85% of price
Transfer bath bench	Purchase	98.58	85% of price
Total cost (9 weeks)		450.12	

Source: U.S. Congress, "Medicare Fraud and Abuse: A Neglected Emergency?," Hearing before the Special Committee on Aging, United States Senate, October 2, 1991, 102-13, U.S. Government Printing Office, Washington, D.C., p.224.

★ 690 ★

Health Costs

Home Medical Equipment, Supplies, and Services Used by Amyotrophic Lateral Sclerosis (ALS) Patients

Amounts are in 1990 dollars. Table displays the monthly cost associated with home medical equipment, supplies and service ($940.88). The cost associated with 1.3 days of equipment is $40.21.

Home medical equipment	Cost/month	Source
Oxygen - portable	322.84	Sample of Medicare Fee Schedules
Oxygen - stationary	275.51	Sample of Medicare Fee Schedules
Hospital bed - electric	195.73	Sample of Medicare Fee Schedules
Bed trapeze	40.57	Sample of Medicare Fee Schedules
Walker	22.12	Sample of Medicare Fee Schedules
Bedside commode	30.15	Sample of Medicare Fee Schedules
Flotation mattress	46.18	Sample of Medicare Fee Schedules
Toilet safety rails	2.30	85% of purchase price/18 months
Bathtub/shower chair	5.48	85% of purchase price/18 months
Total costs per month	940.88	

Source: U.S. Congress, "Medicare Fraud and Abuse: A Neglected Emergency?," Hearing before the Special Committee on Aging, United States Senate, October 2, 1991, 102-13, U.S. Government Printing Office, Washington, D.C., p. 228. Primary source: Lewin/ICF.

★ 691 ★

Health Costs

Pneumonia: Cost Comparison of Treatment of Pneumonia in Amyotrophic Lateral Sclerosis (ALS) Patients

From the source: "Approximately 4,600 Americans develop Amyotrophic Lateral Sclerosis (ALS) each year. ALS, also known as Lou Gehrig's disease, is a degenerative disease that is diagnosed around age 65. The disease paralyzes voluntary muscles but leaves people alert and able to think clearly. Eventually, muscles associated with breathing begin to weaken and patients are susceptible to life threatening infections such as pneumonia. Once diagnosed as having ALS, the mean survival rate is three years. At some point during those three years, ALS patients will require home medical equipment services... Inpatient/home treatment saves $259.28 per episode and inpatient/home treatment saves $304.78 per quality-adjusted episode.

Cost component	Inpatient treatment strategy 1[1] ($)	Inpatient/home treatment strategy 2[2] ($)
Hospital inpatient costs	3,704.85	3,422.93
Physician inpatient costs	+ 46.41	none
Personnel	none	+ 28.84
Home medical equipment, supplies, and service	none	+ 40.21

[Continued]

★ 691 ★

Pneumonia: Cost Comparison of Treatment of Pneumonia in Amyotrophic Lateral Sclerosis (ALS) Patients

[Continued]

Cost component	Inpatient treatment strategy 1[1] ($)	Inpatient/home treatment strategy 2[2] ($)
Total	3,751.26	3,491.98
Quality of life adjustment	+ 45.50	none
Adjusted total	3,796.76	3,491.98

Source: U.S. Congress, "Medicare Fraud and Abuse: A Neglected Emergency?," Hearing before the Special Committee on Aging, United States Senate, October 2, 1991, 102-13, U.S. Government Printing Office, Washington, D.C., p. 229. *Notes:* A plus value in one column reflects an incremental cost. Total costs are used for comparison only and do not reflect total cost of an episode. 1. Strategy 1: Inpatient treatment for ALS-related pneumonia—the patient requires inpatient treatment for 8.5 days and then is released to the home setting for follow-up treatment. All ALS patients require home medical equipment upon discharge. 2. Strategy 2: Shorter inpatient stay combined with more intensive home therapy—the patient receives only 7.2 days of inpatient therapy and substitutes the additional 1.3 days of inpatient therapy seen in Strategy 1 for 1.3 days of care in the home using medical equipment for support.

★ 692 ★

Health Costs

Pulmonary Disease: Cost Comparison of Treatment of Chronic Obstructive Pulmonary Disease (COPD) Patients

From the source: "The results of the cost-identification analysis, detailed in the table, indicate that the reduction of inpatient stay of COPD patients in inpatient/home treatment saves approximately $450 per patient in health care resources. When quality of life is factored into the analysis, the cost savings attributed to inpatient/home therapy increases to $520 per patient. Thus, less intensive inpatient treatment of COPD is both cheaper and more cost-effective than the longer inpatient strategies."

Cost component	Inpatient treatment strategy 1[1] ($)	Inpatient/home treatment strategy 2[2] ($)
Hospital inpatient costs	3,497.68	3,019.91
Physician inpatient costs	+ 50.19	none
Outpatient hospital and physician costs	none	+ 4.92
Personnel	none	+ 16.05
Home medical equipment, supplies and services	none	+ 28.06

[Continued]

★ 692 ★

Pulmonary Disease: Cost Comparison of Treatment of Chronic Obstructive Pulmonary Disease (COPD) Patients

[Continued]

Cost component	Inpatient treatment strategy 1[1] ($)	Inpatient/home treatment strategy 2[2] ($)
Total	3,547.87	3,097.75
Quality of life adjustment	+ 73.13	none
Adjusted total	3,621.00	3,097.75

Source: U.S. Congress, "Medicare Fraud and Abuse: A Neglected Emergency?," Hearing before the Special Committee on Aging, United States Senate, October 2, 1991, 102-13, U.S. Government Printing Office, Washington, D.C., p. 232. Notes: A plus value in a column reflects an incremental cost. Total costs are used for comparison only and do not reflect total cost of an episode. 1. Strategy 1: inpatient treatment for COPD— the patient requires inpatient treatment for 7.5 days and is then released to the home setting for follow-up treatment. All patients will require home medical equipment. 2. Strategy 2: Shorter inpatient stay with more intensive home treatment—the patient receives only 6.1 days of inpatient therapy before being released to treatment in the home setting.

★ 693 ★

Health Costs

Pulmonary Disease: Home Health Agency Visits per Chronic Obstructive Pulmonary Disease (COPD) Patient

From the source: "The number of home health visits to patients and the cost of a home health visit are provided in the table below. Estimates for charge per visit are 1987 charges inflated to 1990 dollars at a rate of 5.5% per year. Assuming the length of an episode is three months, the charge per day can be calculated by dividing the total charges by the total days. The charge for an additional 1.4 days of home health visits totals $18.88. When 85% of charges is used as a proxy for costs, the total cost attributable to combination therapy is $16.05."

	Visits	Charge/visit	Total charge
Skilled nursing	10.61	74	785.14
Home health aide	5.24	55	288.20
Physical therapy	1.19	75	89.25
Occup/speech/social work	0.72	83	51.12
Total			1,213.71

Source: U.S. Congress, "Medicare Fraud and Abuse: A Neglected Emergency?," Hearing before the Special Committee on Aging, United States Senate, October 2, 1991, 102-13, U.S. Government Printing Office, Washington, D.C., p. 231. Primary source: Branch L, Goldberg H, Chet V et al.: "Medicare Home Health Clients: Who Are They and What Service Do They Receive During an Episode of Care?" Submitted to *Health Care Financing Review*, April 1990.

★ 694 ★

Health Costs

Cost Effectiveness of Home Care Savings to Society per Quality Adjusted Episode

From the source: "The pressure on providers to reduce length of inpatient stay as well as the development of locally managed home medical equipment services that allow for more care in the home are largely responsible for these savings. Physicians are increasingly aware of the availability of home medical equipment and home health care services and factor these choices into their practice decisions. Full realization of the potential of home health care services and home medical equipment services can achieve significant cost savings as well as improve patient satisfaction."

Type of patient	Savings per episode ($)	Prevalence (per year)	Annual savings ($)
Hip fracture	2,300	250,000	575,000,000
Amyotrophic Lateral Sclerosis with pneumonia (ALS)	300	1,533	459,900
Chronic Obstructive Pulmonary Disease (COPD)	520	93,184	48,455,680

Source: U.S. Congress, "Medicare Fraud and Abuse: A Neglected Emergency?," Hearing before the Special Committee on Aging, United States Senate, October 2, 1991, 102-13, U.S. Government Printing Office, Washington, D.C., p. 217. Primary source: Lewin/ICF.

★ 695 ★

Health Costs

Medicare: Short-Stay Hospital Charges for Hospital Insurance, by State, Geographic Division, and Outside Area, 1975-91

Average covered charge per covered day of care is shown[1].

Census division and state[2]	Short-stay hospitals							
	1975	1980	1985	1987[3]	1988[3]	1989[3]	1990[3]	1991[3]
Total[4]	$143	$292	$584	$707	$868	$999	$1,105	$1,279
United States[5]	144	293	586	709	871	1,003	1,110	1,285
New England	159	298	546	638	749	860	988	1,142
Connecticut	167	287	559	683	846	983	1,177	1,367
Maine	133	284	572	587	697	802	924	1,069
Massachusetts	168	316	553	655	741	829	940	1,079
New Hampshire	123	264	533	610	758	904	1,021	1,186
Rhode Island	154	284	486	540	634	750	852	972
Vermont	124	230	487	572	694	814	922	1,069
Middle Atlantic	163	304	536	619	738	896	943	1,075
New Jersey	157	300	464	514	593	637	725	893
New York	176	301	516	564	656	736	836	927

[Continued]

★ 695 ★

Medicare: Short-Stay Hospital Charges for Hospital Insurance, by State, Geographic Division, and Outside Area, 1975-91

[Continued]

Census division and state[2]	Short-stay hospitals							
	1975	1980	1985	1987[3]	1988[3]	1989[3]	1990[3]	1991[3]
Pennsylvania	145	312	705	777	936	1,446	1,236	1,371
East North Central	140	294	604	710	864	978	1,097	1,250
Illinois	148	322	649	757	942	1,071	1,203	1,388
Indiana	116	236	524	633	772	892	997	1,153
Michigan	156	332	650	807	958	1,070	1,193	1,360
Ohio	134	277	545	665	809	911	1,031	1,145
Wisconsin	128	251	543	591	714	822	933	1,080
West North Central	117	248	594	670	817	919	1,052	1,224
Iowa	110	239	490	606	718	800	901	1,049
Kansas	113	244	605	679	827	934	1,093	1,263
Minnesota	124	248	605	684	858	979	1,132	1,297
Missouri	119	257	603	702	864	976	1,108	1,286
Nebraska	116	251	585	654	806	883	1,045	1,251
North Dakota	118	237	571	651	782	854	937	1,081
South Dakota	107	228	566	597	703	811	915	1,106
South Atlantic	135	273	544	693	866	979	1,106	1,290
Delaware	153	274	562	679	827	972	1,191	1,348
District of Columbia	174	373	710	832	1,063	1,215	1,374	1,524
Florida	161	321	689	850	1,058	1,209	1,361	1,585
Georgia	125	258	573	676	838	940	1,081	1,238
Maryland	164	274	495	571	675	735	813	913
North Carolina	101	214	466	555	696	806	932	1,093
South Carolina	106	229	530	606	780	913	1,020	1,191
Virginia	118	247	507	604	781	890	1,023	1,207
West Virginia	108	247	557	660	800	902	1,009	1,155
East South Central	115	243	533	644	806	908	1,021	1,183
Alabama	126	282	604	753	935	1,063	1,179	1,367
Kentucky	107	216	520	600	764	869	967	1,111
Mississippi	98	213	451	549	679	768	866	993
Tennessee	122	250	559	644	807	891	1,013	1,181
West South Central	117	253	603	714	874	999	1,139	1,317
Arkansas	104	231	554	594	710	799	927	1,036
Louisiana	116	265	616	740	905	1,025	1,180	1,343
Oklahoma	128	271	592	681	790	878	997	1,126
Texas	118	250	612	743	925	1,075	1,212	1,429
Mountain	142	305	673	823	1,026	1,192	1,350	1,558
Arizona	155	325	682	879	1,078	1,273	1,443	1,677
Colorado	144	288	623	789	981	1,140	1,308	1,558

[Continued]

★ 695 ★

Medicare: Short-Stay Hospital Charges for Hospital Insurance, by State, Geographic Division, and Outside Area, 1975-91
[Continued]

Census division and state[2]	Short-stay hospitals							
	1975	1980	1985	1987[3]	1988[3]	1989[3]	1990[3]	1991[3]
Idaho	129	273	611	723	882	1,017	1,140	1,318
Montana	116	262	620	680	832	929	1,037	1,184
Nevada	177	424	994	1,216	1,543	1,753	2,030	2,197
New Mexico	133	293	684	782	913	1,055	1,140	1,328
Utah	142	316	620	748	1,001	1,141	1,283	1,437
Wyoming	109	245	614	662	813	942	1,094	1,251
Pacific	196	416	852	1,022	1,280	1,463	1,650	1,974
Alaska	228	379	706	897	1,252	1,330	1,477	1,555
California	206	448	893	1,087	1,377	1,576	1,796	2,151
Hawaii	148	333	713	854	1,031	1,142	1,224	1,539
Oregon	158	329	741	838	981	1,136	1,275	1,491
Washington	163	293	646	744	912	1,021	1,162	1,339
Outlying areas	77	152	283	421	502	745	910	1,211
Puerto Rico	77	151	311	362	436	475	505	555
Virgin Islands	92	161	264	401	385	498	747	901
Other	88	263	273	501	685	1,263	1,478	2,178

Source: *Annual Statistical Supplement, 1992 to the Social Security Bulletin*, U.S. Department of Health and Human Services, Social Security Administration, January 1993, p. 301. *Notes:* 1. Based on bills approved in each year and recorded in the Health Care Financing Administration before December 27, 1991. Includes data for services rendered to both aged and disabled persons. 2. Geographic distribution reflects the beneficiaries' area of residence. 3. Preliminary data. 4. Excludes claims for persons residing in foreign countries. 5. Includes claims for persons whose place of residence is unknown.

★ 696 ★

Health Costs

Medicare: Skilled-Nursing Facility Charges for Hospital Insurance, by State, 1975-91

Average covered charge per covered day of care is shown[1].

Census division and state[2]	Skilled-nursing facilities							
	1975	1980	1985	1987[3]	1988[3]	1989[3]	1990[3]	1991[3]
Total[4]	$43	$70	$119	$163	$171	$156	$184	$228
New England	50	77	115	141	147	140	164	189
Connecticut	35	51	95	108	125	133	156	183
Maine	52	100	146	216	244	230	282	239
Massachusetts	63	98	139	177	182	145	173	194
New Hampshire	41	86	129	165	181	178	212	246
Rhode Island	43	59	93	102	110	113	128	146
Vermont	38	62	105	119	139	123	145	197

[Continued]

★ 696 ★

Medicare: Skilled-Nursing Facility Charges for Hospital Insurance, by State, 1975-91
[Continued]

Census division and state[2]	Skilled-nursing facilities							
	1975	1980	1985	1987[3]	1988[3]	1989[3]	1990[3]	1991[3]
Middle Atlantic	50	73	115	149	145	143	164	189
New Jersey	45	81	124	285	144	135	157	184
New York	61	80	120	136	144	148	165	182
Pennsylvania	40	65	105	135	148	139	165	196
East North Central	40	68	108	145	149	136	159	196
Illinois	37	77	118	209	210	183	206	248
Indiana	35	60	101	124	139	141	172	215
Michigan	45	60	93	108	109	107	126	146
Ohio	41	69	114	146	144	129	148	188
Wisconsin	35	64	111	133	140	130	144	169
West North Central	45	82	148	205	185	159	187	225
Iowa	46	84	175	217	236	233	263	296
Kansas	39	66	151	171	209	221	249	284
Minnesota	46	94	137	213	109	102	119	148
Missouri	47	95	163	263	281	231	255	297
Nebraska	41	71	127	160	180	182	202	222
North Dakota	43	49	88	108	118	105	114	136
South Dakota	33	61	106	161	156	141	159	165
South Atlantic	34	59	97	129	148	136	158	204
Delaware	31	50	76	91	98	104	124	176
District of Columbia	34	64	110	129	152	159	177	246
Florida	34	59	101	136	166	151	182	238
Georgia	34	71	108	129	135	120	138	179
Maryland	37	56	99	116	129	121	134	173
North Carolina	31	52	91	110	120	113	128	151
South Carolina	26	46	74	138	158	129	150	182
Virginia	42	68	103	135	143	142	163	195
West Virginia	36	64	91	120	135	131	157	218
East South Central	37	56	98	122	138	122	147	188
Alabama	33	38	73	106	123	108	134	172
Kentucky	36	58	114	117	131	123	147	182
Mississippi	45	105	124	157	174	136	150	192
Tennessee	41	70	99	125	142	132	155	205
West South Central	45	94	159	228	257	210	260	323
Arkansas	44	84	163	222	238	181	228	258
Louisiana	43	83	231	353	408	330	363	477
Oklahoma	60	145	176	296	328	286	315	353
Texas	43	78	117	167	197	181	229	288

[Continued]

★ 696 ★

Medicare: Skilled-Nursing Facility Charges for Hospital Insurance, by State, 1975-91

[Continued]

Census division and state[2]	Skilled-nursing facilities							
	1975	1980	1985	1987[3]	1988[3]	1989[3]	1990[3]	1991[3]
Mountain	38	64	126	158	190	176	214	265
Arizona	41	71	130	172	183	178	225	279
Colorado	42	73	143	182	234	206	246	306
Idaho	27	46	83	120	136	129	146	186
Montana	30	44	87	104	117	104	120	143
Nevada	37	66	132	159	166	164	221	276
New Mexico	57	122	122	202	240	233	260	293
Utah	36	75	128	162	209	216	257	288
Wyoming	36	49	121	136	164	165	199	270
Pacific	45	81	142	194	215	204	253	329
Alaska	68	115	130	270	271	266	272	335
California	46	87	150	202	225	215	269	355
Hawaii	49	83	152	161	184	168	196	260
Oregon	40	63	119	151	166	164	197	240
Washington	34	62	111	144	158	153	186	228
Outlying areas	51	96	92	160	176	161	200	237
Puerto Rico	51	97	101	115	126	164	189	220
Virgin Islands	43	104	82	214	236	161	214	299
Other	52	79	94	151	165	157	195	192

Source: *Annual Statistical Supplement, 1992 to the Social Security Bulletin*, U.S. Department of Health and Human Services, Social Security Administration, January 1993, p. 302. *Notes:* 1. Based on bills approved in each year and recorded in the Health Care Financing Administration before December 27, 1991. Includes data for services rendered to both aged and disabled persons. 2. Geographic distribution reflects the beneficiaries' area of residence. 3. Preliminary data. 4. Excludes claims for persons residing in foreign countries.

★ 697 ★

Health Costs

Overview of the EFMI Program[1]

Overview of the Emergency Fund for the Medically Indigent, Inc. (EFMI) Program, 1985-1991.

Year	Total income ($)	Total patients	Patient cost ($)[2]	Pharmacy patients	Pharmacy cost ($)
1985	2,154.00	114	1,731.00	46	515.68
1986	3,477.28	193	3,008.64	76	1,245.39
1987	4,840.31	253	4,007.17	129	1,944.54
1988	5,571.24	253	4,709.01	151	3,096.36
1989	7,460.04	276	5,812.87	169	3,920.62

[Continued]

★ 697 ★

Overview of the EFMI Program
[Continued]

Year	Total income ($)	Total patients	Patient cost ($)[2]	Pharmacy patients	Pharmacy cost ($)
1990	7,471.27	379	8,819.61[3]	270	6,877.11
1991	9,309.73	414	10,462.38[3]	290	8,589.38

Source: U.S. Congress, "The Effects of Escalating Drug Costs on the Elderly," Hearing before the Special Committee on Aging, United States Senate, April 22, 1992, 102-21, U.S. Government Printing Office, Washington, D.C., p. 28. Primary source: Emergency Fund for the Medically Indigent, Inc., 141 Lakeshore Circle N.E., Milledgeville, GA 31061. *Notes:* 1. EFMI stands for Emergency Fund for the Medically Indigent, Inc. and is a United Way Agency. 2. Does not include administrative costs, which are about $150 per year. 3. Deficit covered by money ($2,000) from Governor's Contingency fund awarded in August 1989.

★ 698 ★

Health Costs

Savings to Society per Quality Adjusted Episode

Type of patient	Savings per episode ($)	Prevalence per/year	Annual savings ($)
Hip fracture	2,300	250,000	575,000,000
Amyotrophic Lateral Sclerosis (ALS) with pneumonia	300	1,533	459,900
Chronic Obstructive Pulmonary Disease (COPD)	520	93,184	48,455,680

Source: U.S. Congress, "Medicare Fraud and Abuse: A Neglected Emergency?," Hearing before the Special Committee on Aging, United States Senate, October 2, 1991, 102-13, U.S. Government Printing Office, Washington, D.C., p. 233. Primary source: Lewin/ICF.

★ 699 ★

Health Costs

Whether Widow Provided Nursing Care for Husband and Whether Such Care Limited Her Employment, by Race and Age[1]

[Percentages]

Item	All races				Blacks
	Total age	Less than 65	65-74	75 and over	
Whether provided care					
n[2]	1,210	129	630	451	319
Percent	35	38	39	29	39
Did care limit employment[3]					
n[2]	430	50	239	141	119
Percent yes	32	49	33	25	42

Source: Herbert S. Parnes, Thomas N. Chirikos, Elizabeth G. Menaghan, Frank L. Mott, Gilbert Nestel, Lois B. Shaw, David G. Sommers, *The NLS Older Male Sample Revisited: A Unique Data Base for Gerontological Research*, Center for Human Resource Research, The Ohio State University, 1993, p. 102, reprinted with permission. *Notes:* 1. Sample limited to women married to sample person at time of his death. 2. Number of sample cases on which weighted percentages are based. 3. Sample limited to women providing care.

Geriatrics Professionals

★ 700 ★

Training Capacity for Geriatrics Faculty Per Year, 1991

This table shows the capacity to train physicians as geriatrics faculty and the effect of a decrease in available training faculty due to retirement or entrance into clinical practice. From the source: "Projected net loss in the numbers of geriatrics physician faculty will continue each year in each specialty to the year 2000, ranging from two in neurology to 30 in family practice." Data refer to physicians only.

	Specialty				
	Internal medicine	Family practice	Neur- ology	Psychi- atry	Physical medicine
Number of graduating geriatrics fellows (estimated)	66	16	19	40	2
Number of junior faculty entering as faculty[1]	35	8	10	18	1
Number of mid-career entering as faculty	14	7	2	2	1
Total new geriatrics faculty/year	49	15	12	20	2
Number of junior faculty leaving academics[2]	65	38	14	24	6
Number of faculty retiring[3]	10	8	5	8	1

[Continued]

★ 700 ★

Training Capacity for Geriatrics Faculty Per Year, 1991
[Continued]

	Specialty				
	Internal medicine	Family practice	Neur-ology	Psychi-atry	Physical medicine
Total geriatrics faculty leaving/year	75	46	29	32	7
Net gain/loss of geriatrics faculty per year	-26	-31	-7	-12	-5

Source: Reuben, David B., M.D., "The Adequacy of Geriatrician Supply", *Shortage of Health Care Professions Caring for the Elderly: Recommendations for Change*, Senate Select Committee on Aging, Comm. Pub. No. 102-915, p. 11. *Notes:* 1. Based on approximately 50% of physicians completing fellowships in geriatrics entering academics. 2. Based on the percent of geriatrics faculty that leave academics before reaching senior faculty status (amortized over 8 years) i.e., 10%/ yr. 3. Based on a 25-year career in academics, i.e., 4% retire each year.

★ 701 ★

Geriatrics Professionals

Nursing Services Demand: 1990 to 2020

This table shows the increasing number of FTE (full-time equivalent) nursing personnel needed to meet U.S. demand for nursing services through the year 2020. The increasing need for nursing personnel for older Americans contributes to a greater need for service to the overall population.

Year	Demand for full-time equivalent nurses for older Americans					All settings for all ages	Percent of total demand attributed to older Americans
	All hospitals	Nursing homes	Home health	Other	All settings		
RNs							
1990	420,600	94,900	29,600	38,900	584,000	1,476,000	39.6
1995	469,300	119,800	32,600	42,900	665,000	1,610,000	41.3
2000	510,100	147,900	35,300	45,800	739,000	1,736,000	42.6
2005	556,400	174,700	37,300	48,900	817,000	1,854,000	44.1
2010	609,200	201,900	39,200	54,100	904,000	1,964,000	46.0
2015	681,300	209,600	41,300	62,000	994,000	2,052,000	48.4
2020	783,900	223,900	45,800	72,200	1,126,000	2,155,000	52.3
LP/VNs							
1990	98,100	112,100	2,300	19,500	232,000	476,000	48.7
1995	97,400	126,700	2,500	20,900	248,000	490,000	50.6
2000	93,400	141,200	2,700	21,600	259,000	500,000	51.8
2005	89,900	154,100	2,900	22,500	269,000	513,000	52.4
2010	88,500	166,900	3,000	24,300	283,000	527,000	53.7
2015	90,200	164,800	3,200	27,100	285,000	529,000	53.9
2020	101,100	167,300	3,500	30,800	303,000	538,000	56.3
Aides							
1990	159,100	421,900	16,400	-	597,000	860,000	69.4
1995	173,000	483,200	19,100	-	675,000	942,000	71.7
2000	183,400	545,500	21,700	-	751,000	1,023,000	73.4

[Continued]

★ 701 ★

Nursing Services Demand: 1990 to 2020
[Continued]

Year	Demand for full-time equivalent nurses for older Americans					All settings for all ages	Percent of total demand attributed to older Americans
	All hospitals	Nursing homes	Home health	Other	All settings		
2005	193,100	602,200	23,900	-	819,000	1,097,000	74.7
2010	207,100	658,500	26,000	-	892,000	1,168,000	76.4
2015	227,700	655,500	28,100	-	911,000	1,178,000	77.3
2020	257,000	671,100	32,000	-	960,000	1,211,000	79.3

Source: "Health Sources and Services Administration: Bureau of Health Professions Response," *Shortage of Health Care Professions Caring for the Elderly: Recommendations for Change*, Senate Select Committee on Aging, Comm. Pub. No. 102-915, pp. 40-41. Primary source: Projections prepared by Division of Nursing, Bureau of Health Professions, Health Resources and Services Administration, U.S. Department of Health and Human Services, 1992. *Notes:* RN stands for registered nurse; LPN stands for licensed pratical nurse; VN stands for vocational nurse.

★ 702 ★

Geriatrics Professionals

Supply and Demand for Full-Time Equivalent Registered Nurses: 1990-2020

From the source: "These data show that the supply for RNs [registered nurses] will increase into the middle of the first decade in the next century but will decline thereafter."

Year	DFTERN[1] to provide nursing service to older Americans	Supply of FTE[2] registered nurses	Percent of supply needed to satisfy demand
1990	584,000	1,435,000	40.7
1995	665,000	1,585,000	41.9
2000	739,000	1,647,000	44.9
2005	817,000	1,676,000	48.7
2010	904,000	1,637,000	55.2
2015	994,000	1,623,000	61.2
2020	1,126,000	1,555,000	72.4

Source: "Health Sources and Services Administration: Bureau of Health Professions Response," *Shortage of Health Care Professions Caring for the Elderly: Recommendations for Change*, Senate Select Committee on Aging, Comm. Pub. No. 102-915, p. 42. Primary source: Projections prepared by Division of Nursing, Bureau of Health Professions, Health Resources and Services Administration, U.S. Department of Health and Human Services, 1992. *Notes:* 1. DFTERN stands for demand for full-time equivalent registered nurses. 2. FTE stands for full-time equivalent.

Health: Worldwide

★ 703 ★

Availability and Use of Health Services, by Selected Countries, 1988

	Inpatient beds per 1000 population	Inpatient days per capita	Admissions as percent of total population	Average length-of-stay (days)	Inpatient occupancy rate	Physicians per 1,000 population	Physicians' contacts per capita
Canada[2]	6.9	2.0	14.5	13.2	82.7	2.2	6.6
France	10.2	3.0	22.3	13.1	81.2	2.6	7.1
Germany	10.9	3.5	21.5	16.6	86.5	2.9	11.5
Japan	15.6	4.1	7.8	52.1	84.1	1.6[2]	12.9[2]
United Kingdom	6.5	2.0	15.9	15.0[2]	80.6[1]	1.4	4.5[1]
United States	5.1	1.3	13.8	9.3	69.2	2.3	5.3
Average	9.2	2.7	16.0	19.9	80.7	2.2	8.0

Source: U.S. Congress, "Cutting Health Care Costs: Experiences in France, Germany, and Japan," Joint Hearing before the Committee on Governmental Affairs and the Special Committee on Aging, United States Senate, November 19, 1991, 102-15, U.S. Government Printing Office, Washington, D.C., p. 175. Primary source: George J. Schieber, Jean-Pierre Poullier, and Leslie Greenwald, "Health Care Systems in Twenty-Four Countries," *Health Affairs*, Fall 1991: 22-38. *Notes:* 1. 1986. 2. 1987.

★ 704 ★

Health: Worldwide

Population and Health Outcome Measures, by Selected Countries, 1988

	Infant mortality, live births per 1,000	Life expectancy (years)				Percent of population over 64
		At birth		At age 80		
		Males	Females	Males	Females	
Canada	7.2	73.0[1]	79.7[1]	6.9[1]	8.9[1]	11.1
France	7.7	72.3	80.6	6.8	8.6	13.6
Germany	7.6	71.8	78.4	6.1[2]	7.6[2]	15.4
Japan	4.8	75.5	81.3	6.9	8.4	11.2
United Kingdom	9.0	72.4	78.1	6.4	8.1	15.6
United States	10.0	71.5	78.3	6.9	8.7	12.3
Average	7.7	72.8	79.4	6.7	8.4	13.2

Source: U.S. Congress, "Cutting Health Care Costs: Experiences in France, Germany, and Japan," Joint Hearing before the Committee on Governmental Affairs and the Special Committee on Aging, United States Senate, November 19, 1991, 102-15, U.S. Government Printing Office, Washington, D.C., p. 176. Primary source: George J. Schieber, Jean-Pierre Poullier, and Leslie Greenwald, "Health Care Systems in Twenty-Four Countries," *Health Affairs*, Fall 1991: 22-38. *Notes:* 1. 1986. 2. 1987.

Dental Health

★ 705 ★

Dental Visits: In the Past Year

Percent of persons 18 years of age and over who had gone to the dentist at least once in the past 12 months, by sex, age, and selected characteristics: United States, 1990.

Characteristic	Both sexes 18 years and over	Male					Female				
		Total	18-29 years	30-44 years	45-64 years	65 years and over	Total	18-29 years	30-44 years	45-64 years	65 years and over
All persons[1]	62.5	59.0	57.9	62.9	60.5	48.7	65.7	67.4	74.0	64.9	50.2
Education level											
Less than 12 years	40.4	38.3	45.2	39.5	39.3	30.6	42.2	51.8	52.7	40.7	33.0
12 years	61.3	55.9	55.1	59.0	53.9	53.6	65.5	65.4	70.7	65.5	55.7
More than 12 years	75.3	71.4	66.7	70.9	77.3	69.4	79.3	75.8	81.8	81.2	74.7
13-15 years	71.5	66.3	66.4	65.8	70.0	58.9	76.1	75.5	78.4	75.9	71.1
16 years or more	79.2	75.9	67.2	74.8	81.9	77.1	83.1	76.3	85.2	86.5	79.8
Income											
Less than $10,000	44.5	40.3	58.5	35.2	30.2	19.3	46.8	60.7	50.7	41.7	34.2
$10,000-$19,999	49.1	43.5	48.5	47.7	37.5	37.8	53.6	60.6	57.8	50.7	45.6
$20,000-$34,999	63.2	58.1	58.1	58.7	58.5	55.9	68.0	69.3	71.9	63.6	64.1
$35,000-$49,999	72.5	67.3	62.3	71.3	63.0	74.0	78.1	74.4	82.1	75.0	76.8
$50,000 or more	78.2	74.6	67.5	74.2	77.9	79.2	82.1	78.8	84.5	81.9	76.5
Race											
White	64.1	60.8	59.6	64.8	62.6	50.5	67.2	68.9	75.4	66.6	52.2
Black	51.8	46.0	51.4	48.9	42.5	29.2	56.4	59.1	66.4	53.2	31.1
Hispanic origin											
Hispanic	54.0	47.7	44.3	50.5	53.6	32.1	59.3	55.5	65.8	62.0	42.1
Non-Hispanic	63.3	59.9	59.6	64.0	61.0	49.2	66.3	69.2	74.8	65.1	50.5
Geographic region											
Northeast	66.6	63.9	63.2	70.3	62.5	52.3	69.0	73.1	77.7	68.0	52.6
Midwest	65.0	61.0	59.6	66.0	62.9	48.8	68.7	73.4	75.6	68.4	50.8
South	57.3	53.0	54.4	56.4	52.7	43.4	61.2	62.9	69.7	60.1	45.9
West	64.2	61.5	56.9	62.6	68.2	54.6	66.7	63.3	75.4	65.8	54.9
Marital status											
Currently married	64.4	59.8	53.4	64.4	62.0	51.2	69.0	65.1	75.6	67.8	57.1
Formerly married	53.8	52.5	55.1	59.7	53.2	39.9	54.4	61.0	68.6	57.3	44.4
Never married	63.8	59.1	61.0	56.9	54.9	38.6	69.5	71.2	69.8	60.6	58.5
Employment status											
Currently employed	66.8	62.3	58.0	64.6	63.7	57.3	72.3	70.7	76.7	68.6	60.4

[Continued]

★ 705 ★

Dental Visits: In the Past Year

[Continued]

Characteristic	Both sexes 18 years and over	Male					Female				
		Total	18-29 years	30-44 years	45-64 years	65 years and over	Total	18-29 years	30-44 years	45-64 years	65 years and over
Unemployed	56.9	48.2	49.8	48.0	46.5	38.5[2]	66.4	67.1	64.5	69.9	57.7[2]
Not in labor force	54.2	49.3	60.7	43.5	49.0	46.9	56.6	59.5	66.9	59.2	49.0

Source: Health Promotion and Disease Prevention: United States, 1990, National Center for Health Statistics, Vital and Health Statistics, Series 10, No. 185, p. 55.
Notes: Data are based on household interviews of the civilian noninstitutionalized population. The survey design, general qualifications, and information on the reliability of the estimates are given in appendix 1 in the original source. Denominator for each cell excludes unknowns. 1. Includes persons with unknown sociodemographic characteristics. 2. Figure does not meet standard of reliability or precision (more than 30-percent relative standard error in numerator of percent or rate).

★ 706 ★

Dental Health

Tooth Loss: Complete Loss of Permanent Teeth, 1990

Percent of persons 18 years of age and over who had lost all their permanent teeth, by sex, age, and selected characteristics: United States, 1990.

Characteristic	Both sexes 18 years and over	Male					Female				
		Total	18-29 years	30-44 years	45-64 years	65 years and over	Total	18-29 years	30-44 years	45-64 years	65 years and over
All persons[1]	10.6	9.6	1.4	3.0	14.4	30.9	11.5	1.7	3.4	15.0	33.7
Education level											
Less than 12 years	23.6	21.0	1.4[2]	5.3	26.9	42.4	25.9	1.3[2]	7.9	27.5	46.9
12 years	9.8	8.9	1.3	3.2	16.1	28.8	10.5	2.0	3.4	14.6	30.0
More than 12 years	4.5	4.6	1.5	2.4	6.3	17.0	4.4	1.6	2.3	6.8	14.9
13-15 years	5.4	5.6	1.3	2.7	9.0	25.6	5.3	1.4	2.5	8.9	18.4
16 years or more	3.6	3.7	1.8[2]	2.1	4.6	10.8	3.4	2.0[2]	2.0	4.7	9.9
Income											
Less than $10,000	20.3	16.6	1.0[2]	4.1[2]	30.1	46.5	22.3	1.7[2]	4.8	28.6	48.0
$10,000-$19,999	15.9	15.4	0.6[2]	3.4	20.6	41.6	16.3	2.1	4.9	20.6	36.8
$20,000-$34,999	9.1	9.0	2.3	3.3	15.1	26.5	9.2	2.3	3.5	16.8	23.4
$35,000-$49,999	6.3	7.0	1.1[2]	3.5	15.9	16.8	5.6	1.5[2]	3.9	9.9	15.2
$50,000 or more	4.6	4.6	1.6[2]	2.0	7.4	13.6	4.6	1.5[2]	2.3	7.3	16.7
Race											
White	10.8	9.9	1.4	2.8	14.7	31.4	11.7	1.6	3.5	15.2	32.7
Black	9.3	7.6	1.3[2]	3.6	11.9	29.3	10.6	2.9	2.8	13.5	41.5
Hispanic origin											
Hispanic	4.9	4.4	1.1[2]	1.7[2]	10.2	21.8	5.3	1.6[2]	2.0[2]	6.7	33.1
Non-Hispanic	11.0	10.0	1.4	3.1	14.7	31.2	12.0	1.8	3.5	15.5	33.8

[Continued]

★ 706 ★

Tooth Loss: Complete Loss of Permanent Teeth, 1990
[Continued]

Characteristic	Both sexes 18 years and over	Male					Female				
		Total	18-29 years	30-44 years	45-64 years	65 years and over	Total	18-29 years	30-44 years	45-64 years	65 years and over
Geographic region											
Northeast	10.8	9.7	2.2	2.0	15.8	29.4	11.7	2.1	2.5	14.0	33.3
Midwest	11.5	10.7	1.4	3.6	16.1	34.5	12.3	1.7	3.7	16.8	35.3
South	11.0	10.0	0.7[2]	3.2	15.8	31.8	11.9	1.5	3.8	15.0	35.4
West	8.4	7.3	1.9	3.2	9.0	26.1	9.4	1.7	3.2	13.7	28.9
Marital status											
Currently married	9.9	10.7	1.5	3.2	14.4	29.4	9.1	2.0	3.4	13.2	28.6
Formerly married	21.1	15.1	2.6[2]	2.5	15.7	36.7	23.5	1.5[2]	3.5	20.2	38.7
Never married	3.3	3.1	1.3	2.7	10.6	35.5	3.4	1.5	2.7	13.9	19.1
Employment status											
Currently employed	5.8	5.7	1.5	2.9	12.2	21.7	6.0	1.7	3.4	12.3	25.5
Unemployed	5.0	5.8	1.1[2]	2.6[2]	18.0	24.4[2]	4.0	1.5[2]	2.6[2]	9.4[2]	24.4[2]
Not in labor force	20.9	23.5	0.9[2]	5.7	23.2	33.0	19.6	1.9	3.4	19.2	34.8

Source: Health Promotion and Disease Prevention: United States, 1990, National Center for Health Statistics, Vital and Health Statistics, Series 10, No. 185, p. 56. *Notes:* Data are based on household interviews of the civilian noninstitutionalized population. The survey design, general qualifications, and information on the reliability of the estimates are given in appendix 1 in the original source. Denominator for each cell excludes unknowns. 1. Includes persons with unknown sociodemographic characteristics. 2. Figure does not meet standard of reliability or precision (more than 30-percent relative standard error in numerator of percent or rate).

★ 707 ★

Dental Health

Tooth Loss: Complete Loss of Permanent Teeth, 1986 and 1989

Percent of persons 45 years of age and over who were edentulous, by age, sex, and race: United States, 1986 and 1989.

Characteristic	Total 45 years and over		45-54 years		55-64 years		65-74 years		75 years and over	
	1986	1989	1986	1989	1986	1989	1986	1989	1986	1989
Population[1]	24.0	21.9	11.7	10.0	21.7	19.0	29.7	28.4	46.3	43.0
Sex										
Male	22.4	20.7	11.3	9.7	20.4	18.4	28.3	28.3	47.6	43.2
Female	25.4	22.9	12.0	10.4	22.7	19.5	30.8	28.5	45.6	42.8
Race										
White	24.1	22.1	12.0	10.4	21.8	19.0	29.4	28.4	45.5	41.9
Black	24.6	22.1	10.5	8.6	22.1	20.4	33.0	29.1	56.8	53.0

Source: Dental Services and Oral Health: United States, 1989, National Center for Health Statistics, Vital and Health Statistics, Series 10, No. 185, p. 5. *Note:* 1. Includes persons of other races not shown separately.

★ 708 ★

Dental Health

Dental Visits: Reasons Given for Not Visiting a Dentist

Percent of persons by reasons reported for no dental visit in past year, according to selected demographic characteristics: United States, 1989.

Age	All with no visits in past year	Percent distribution						
		Fear	Cost	Access problems	No dental problem	No teeth	Not important	Other reason
All ages	100.0	4.3	13.7	1.7	46.8	14.3	2.3	8.7
2-17 years	100.0	1.3	15.0	1.5	56.8	0.2	1.9	11.9
18-34 years	100.0	5.9	19.1	2.4	52.4	0.7	3.2	9.5
35-64 years	100.0	5.8	12.8	1.5	43.3	17.8	2.2	8.4
65 years and over	100.0	2.2	4.1	1.1	31.2	49.7	1.1	3.9

Source: Dental Services and Oral Health: United States, 1989, National Center for Health Statistics, Vital and Health Statistics, Series 10, No. 185, p. 56.

★ 709 ★

Dental Health

Dental Visits: Intervals Between Visits, by Sex

Percent distribution of persons 2 years of age and over by interval since last dental visit: United States, 1989.

Characteristic	All intervals[1]	Less than 1 year			1 year to less than 2 years	2 years to less than 5 years	5 years or more	Never
		Total	Less than 6 months	6-11 months				
Age								
All ages	100.0	57.2	36.2	19.1	9.5	12.3	11.1	4.7
2-4 years	100.0	32.1	20.6	10.2	2.8	1.0	...	55.0
5-17 years	100.0	69.0	44.5	21.8	9.5	7.7	2.1	7.2
18-34 years	100.0	56.9	33.6	21.4	11.8	15.8	8.7	1.5
35-54 years	100.0	61.4	39.2	20.3	9.7	12.9	10.6	0.6
55-64 years	100.0	54.0	36.8	15.9	8.2	13.5	18.7	0.3
65 years and over	100.0	43.2	29.1	13.1	7.0	13.1	30.6	0.5
65-74 years	100.0	47.6	32.2	14.4	7.4	13.3	26.5	0.4
75 years and over	100.0	36.3	24.3	11.0	6.3	13.0	37.0	0.6
Sex								
Male								
All ages	100.0	54.9	34.3	18.9	9.6	13.3	11.7	5.1
2-4 years	100.0	31.4	19.8	10.2	2.7	0.7	...	56.1
5-11 years	100.0	68.7	43.5	22.5	8.8	6.3	1.0	10.5
12-17 years	100.0	66.8	42.7	21.1	11.2	10.5	3.5	3.5
18-34 years	100.0	51.5	29.6	20.4	11.9	18.2	10.9	1.8

[Continued]

★ 709 ★

Dental Visits: Intervals Between Visits, by Sex

[Continued]

Characteristic	All intervals[1]	Less than 1 year			1 year to less than 2 years	2 years to less than 5 years	5 years or more	Never
		Total	Less than 6 months	6-11 months				
35-44 years	100.0	59.6	37.8	20.0	10.1	13.9	10.6	1.0
45-54 years	100.0	57.2	36.2	19.5	9.2	13.8	14.2	0.5
55-64 years	100.0	53.2	35.5	16.5	8.1	14.1	18.9	0.4
65 years and over	100.0	43.0	28.8	13.1	6.9	13.7	30.8	0.6
65-74 years	100.0	47.4	31.8	14.5	7.4	13.4	27.0	0.5[2]
75 years and over	100.0	34.6	23.2	10.3	6.1	14.3	37.8	0.8[2]
Female								
All ages	100.0	59.4	38.1	19.4	9.4	11.3	10.6	4.2
2-4 years	100.0	32.9	21.4	10.2	2.9	1.4	...	53.8
5-11 years	100.0	69.7	45.3	21.6	8.6	6.0	1.0	10.1
12-17 years	100.0	70.9	46.6	21.7	9.7	9.0	3.3	3.1
18-34 years	100.0	62.0	37.4	22.5	11.7	13.5	6.7	1.2
35-44 years	100.0	66.1	41.9	22.0	9.9	11.8	7.3	0.4
45-54 years	100.0	61.1	39.9	19.0	9.1	12.3	12.2	0.4
55-64 years	100.0	54.8	37.9	15.4	8.4	12.9	18.5	0.3[2]
65 years and over	100.0	43.4	29.3	13.1	7.0	12.7	30.5	0.4[2]
65-74 years	100.0	47.8	32.4	14.2	7.5	13.1	26.1	0.3[2]
75 years and over	100.0	37.3	25.0	11.4	6.4	12.2	36.5	0.4[2]

Source: *Dental Services and Oral Health: United States, 1989*, National Center for Health Statistics, Vital and Health Statistics, Series 10, No. 185, p. 23. *Notes:* Three dots (...) means that the category is not applicable. 1. Includes unknown interval not shown separately. 2. Figure does not meet standard reliability or precision (more than 30- percent relative standard error in numerator of percent or rate).

★ 710 ★

Dental Health

Dental Visits: Intervals Between Visits, by Socio-Economic Characteristics

Percent distribution of persons 45 and over by interval since last dental visit, according to selected socioeconomic characteristics: United States, 1989.

Characteristic	All intervals[1]	Less than 1 year			1 year to less than 2 years	2 years to less than 5 years	5 years or more	Never
		Total	Less than 6 months	6-11 months				
Education level[1]								
Less than 9 years								
All ages, 22 years and over	100.0	27.8	16.4	10.1	8.3	17.3	38.0	3.1
45-54 years	100.0	30.8	17.4	11.6	10.3	21.0	30.7	2.3
55-64 years	100.0	28.3	16.9	10.6	11.3	19.1	34.8	1.3
65 years and over	100.0	24.2	14.9	8.4	6.3	15.0	47.6	1.0

[Continued]

★ 710 ★

Dental Visits: Intervals Between Visits, by Socio-Economic Characteristics
[Continued]

Characteristic	All intervals[1]	Less than 1 year			1 year to less than 2 years	2 years to less than 5 years	5 years or more	Never
		Total	Less than 6 months	6-11 months				
9-11 years								
All ages, 22 years and over	100.0	38.2	22.7	14.2	10.3	19.8	25.5	1.1
45-54 years	100.0	36.6	20.2	15.1	12.1	20.7	25.7	0.3
55-64 years	100.0	37.1	23.5	11.7	9.1	19.3	28.8	0.4
65 years and over	100.0	33.7	21.7	11.2	7.2	15.9	37.9	0.3
12 years								
All ages, 22 years and over	100.0	54.8	34.1	19.0	10.6	15.0	14.1	0.6
45-54 years	100.0	57.4	36.4	19.2	9.8	13.6	13.7	0.4
55-64 years	100.0	56.9	37.7	17.7	8.5	12.8	17.0	0.1
65 years and over	100.0	49.3	33.5	14.4	8.2	12.8	24.5	0.3
13 years or more								
All ages, 22 years and over	100.0	70.1	45.8	22.6	8.9	10.5	6.3	0.2
45-54 years	100.0	74.9	50.2	22.6	7.4	8.5	5.2	0.1
55-64 years	100.0	73.7	53.7	18.9	6.0	8.6	7.6	0.2
65 years and over	100.0	67.1	47.5	18.7	6.1	9.7	13.2	0.1
Family income[2]								
Less than $10,000								
All ages	100.0	40.9	23.2	16.3	10.2	15.6	22.1	7.5
45-54 years	100.0	30.7	17.5	11.8	11.6	21.5	30.9	1.0
55-64 years	100.0	29.1	16.6	11.3	9.3	18.1	38.6	0.8
65 years and over	100.0	25.8	16.5	8.8	5.7	15.0	49.2	0.9
65-74 years	100.0	27.4	17.5	9.4	6.4	16.4	45.5	0.7
75 years and over	100.0	24.1	15.5	8.2	4.9	13.5	53.0	1.1
$10,000-$19,999								
All ages	100.0	43.4	25.7	16.2	11.4	17.1	17.3	6.6
45-54 years	100.0	40.8	23.8	15.2	10.5	19.9	23.2	1.0
55-64 years	100.0	41.7	25.9	14.5	9.7	16.6	27.8	0.4
65 years and over	100.0	39.0	25.4	12.6	7.6	16.1	32.8	0.4
65-74 years	100.0	40.6	26.2	13.4	8.0	15.7	31.4	0.5
75 years and over	100.0	36.5	24.2	11.4	6.9	16.7	35.0	0.4
$20,000-$34,999								
All ages	100.0	58.3	36.2	20.4	10.5	13.2	9.9	5.0
45-54 years	100.0	54.5	33.0	19.9	11.1	15.1	16.4	0.4
55-64 years	100.0	54.1	36.3	16.3	9.3	15.6	17.3	0.2
65 years and over	100.0	54.6	38.6	14.9	8.4	12.1	22.3	0.3
65-74 years	100.0	57.4	40.3	16.1	8.6	12.4	19.5	0.2
75 years and over	100.0	48.2	34.7	12.3	8.0	11.5	28.6	0.4

[Continued]

★ 710 ★

Dental Visits: Intervals Between Visits, by Socio-Economic Characteristics
[Continued]

Characteristic	All intervals[1]	Less than 1 year			1 year to less than 2 years	2 years to less than 5 years	5 years or more	Never
		Total	Less than 6 months	6-11 months				
$35,000 or more								
All ages	100.0	73.0	49.1	21.6	8.0	8.5	4.9	2.8
45-54 years	100.0	72.2	49.0	21.2	7.8	9.8	7.3	0.2
55-64 years	100.0	72.3	51.8	19.3	6.9	9.0	9.3	0.2
65 years and over	100.0	67.7	49.0	16.8	5.7	8.8	14.2	0.2
65-74 years	100.0	72.4	52.9	17.3	5.5	8.6	10.5	0.1
75 years and over	100.0	55.8	39.1	15.6	6.4	9.3	23.8	0.4
Dental insurance coverage[3]								
Having private dental insurance								
All ages	100.0	71.4	47.5	21.8	8.9	9.1	5.7	3.4
45-54 years	100.0	71.2	47.1	22.0	8.4	10.2	8.6	0.2
55-64 years	100.0	66.9	48.6	16.7	7.9	11.1	12.7	0.2
65 years and over	100.0	61.0	43.2	16.6	7.6	10.7	17.7	0.2
65-74 years	100.0	63.9	44.8	17.9	8.3	10.8	15.1	0.2
75 years and over	100.0	53.6	39.0	13.6	6.0	10.5	24.4	0.3
Without private dental insurance								
All ages	100.0	50.0	30.2	18.1	10.3	15.2	15.5	5.9
45-54 years	100.0	50.8	31.7	17.4	10.6	16.8	18.5	0.7
55-64 years	100.0	48.8	31.5	16.0	8.8	15.7	23.4	0.5
65 years and over	100.0	42.1	28.1	13.0	7.1	14.1	33.0	0.5
65-74 years	100.0	46.2	30.8	14.3	7.5	14.2	29.0	0.4
75 years and over	100.0	36.0	24.0	11.0	6.6	13.9	38.9	0.7

Source: Dental Services and Oral Health: United States, 1989, National Center for Health Statistics, Vital and Health Statistics, Series 10, No. 185, p. 28. *Notes:* 1. Persons with unknown education level not shown separately. 2. Persons with unknown income not shown separately. 3. Persons with unknown insurance coverage not shown separately.

★ 711 ★

Dental Health

Dental Visits per Person by Selected Characteristics, 1987

Characteristic	Dental visits Number per person		
	1964	1983	1989
Total	1.6	1.9	2.1
Age			
2-14 years	1.3	2.0	2.1

[Continued]

★ 711 ★

Dental Visits per Person by Selected Characteristics, 1987

[Continued]

Characteristic	Dental visits Number per person		
	1964	1983	1989
2-4 years	0.3	0.7	0.9
5-14 years	1.9	2.5	2.5
15-44 years	1.9	1.9	2.0
45-64 years	1.7	2.0	2.4
65 years and over	0.8	1.5	2.0
65-74 years	0.9	1.8	2.2
75 years and over	0.6	1.1	1.8
Sex			
Male	1.4	1.7	2.0
Female	1.7	2.1	2.3
Race			
White	1.7	2.0	2.3
Black	0.8	1.2	1.2
Family income			
Less than $14,000	0.9	1.2	1.3
$14,000-$24,999	0.9	1.5	1.6
$25,000-$34,999	1.4	2.2	2.2
$35,000-$49,999	1.9	2.5	2.7
$50,000 or more	2.7	2.9	3.1
Geographic region			
Northeast	2.1	2.4	2.2
Midwest	1.6	1.9	2.1
South	1.2	1.6	1.8
West	1.7	2.0	2.4

Source: National Center for Health Statistics. *Health United States 1991*. Washington, D.C.: U.S. Department of Health and Human Services, 1992, p. 223. Primary source: Division of Health Interview Statistics, National Center for Health Statistics: Data from the National Health Interview Survey.

Chapter 11
HEALTH INSURANCE

Tables on health and health care will be found in the previous chapter. This chapter presents information on health insurance in its various aspects, including sections on Coverage, Sources, Benefits, Abuses, Politics of Health Insurance, Dental Plans, and an extensive section on Medicare and Medicaid.

Information of a related nature will be found in the chapters on *Social Security, Health and Health Care,* and *Income, Assets, and Spending.*

Coverage

★ 712 ★

Health Care Coverage for Persons Aged 65+, by Type of Coverage and Selected Characteristics: 1980, 1984, and 1989

From the source: "Denominators for 1980 include people with unknown health insurance (less than 1 percent). In 1989, 5.2 percent of all people 65+ had no Medicare but only 0.9 percent were without health insurance."

[Numbers in percent]

Characteristic	Medicare and private insurance			Medicare and Medicaid[1]			Medicare only[2]		
	1980	1984	1989	1980	1984	1989	1980	1984	1989
Total[4]	64.4	70.9	73.5	8.1	5.4	5.7	22.7	20.0	16.8
Age									
65 to 74 years	67.0	73.3	74.2	6.8	4.5	5.0	20.6	17.7	15.5
75+	59.9	66.8	72.3	10.3	7.0	6.8	26.4	24.1	19.0
75 to 84 years	61.9	69.2	74.1	9.7	6.5	6.4	24.8	22.0	17.4
85+	51.2	56.2	64.8	12.7	9.3	8.5	33.0	33.4	26.1

[Continued]

★ 712 ★

Health Care Coverage for Persons Aged 65+, by Type of Coverage and Selected Characteristics: 1980, 1984, and 1989
[Continued]

Characteristic	Medicare and private insurance			Medicare and Medicaid[1]			Medicare only[2]		
	1980	1984	1989	1980	1984	1989	1980	1984	1989
Sex[3]									
Men	65.6	71.6	73.9	5.7	3.3	4.0	23.1	20.8	17.2
Women	63.6	70.5	73.4	9.6	6.9	6.8	22.4	19.4	16.4
Race[3]									
White	68.3	74.4	77.3	6.6	4.0	4.5	21.0	18.5	14.7
Black	26.5	38.1	39.3	23.3	19.9	16.5	40.6	35.4	37.9

Source: Aging America, Trends and Projections, prepared by the U.S. Senate Special Committee on Aging, the American Association of Retired Persons, the Federal Council on the Aging, and the U.S. Administration on Aging, 1991, Washington, D.C., p. 132. Primary source: Table excerpted from National Center for Health Statistics, Health United States, 1990, U.S. Department of Health and Human Services, Pub. No. (PHS)91-1232, March 1991. Notes: 1. Includes people receiving Aid to Families with Dependent Children or Supplementary Security Income, or those with current Medicaid cards. 2. Includes people not covered by private insurance or Medicaid and a small portion of people with other types of coverage, such as CHAMPUS or public assistance. CHAMPUS stands for Civilian Health and Medical Program of the Uniformed Services. 3. Age adjusted. 4. Age adjusted and includes all other races not shown separately.

★ 713 ★
Coverage

Health Care Coverage for Persons 65 Years and Over, by Type of Coverage: 1980 and 1989
[Data are in percent and are from the civilian noninstitutional population]

	1980	1989
Medicare and private insurance		
65 to 74 years	67.0	74.2
75 to 84 years	61.9	74.1
85 years and over	51.2	64.8
Medicare only[1]		
65 to 74 years	20.6	15.5
75 to 84 years	24.8	17.4
85 years and over	33.0	26.1

Source: Sixty-Five Plus in America, Cynthia M. Taeuber, U.S. Department of Commerce, Economics and Statistics Administration, Bureau of the Census, U.S. Government Printing Office, Washington, D.C., 1992, p. 3-17. Primary source: National Center for Health Statistics, Health, United States, 1990, Hyattsville, MD, Public Health Service, 1991, Table 125. Notes: 1. Includes persons covered by Civilian Health and Medical Program of the Uniformed Serives (CHAMPUS) and public assistance. Does not include persons covered by Medicaid.

★ 714 ★

Coverage

Health Care Coverage for Persons 65 Years of Age and Over, by Type of Coverage: U.S., 1980, 1984, and 1989

[Percent of population]

Age group	Medicare/private insurance			Medicare/Medicaid[1]			Medicare only[2]		
	1980	1984	1989	1980	1984	1989	1980	1984	1989
Total[3,4]	64.4	70.9	73.5	8.1	5.4	5.7	22.7	20.0	16.8
65-74 years	67.0	73.3	74.2	6.8	4.5	5.0	20.6	17.7	15.5
75 years and over	59.9	66.8	72.3	10.3	7.0	6.8	26.4	24.1	19.0
75-84 years	61.9	69.2	74.1	9.7	6.5	6.4	24.8	22.0	17.4
85 years and over	51.2	56.2	64.8	12.7	9.3	8.5	33.0	33.4	26.1

Source: U.S. Department of Commerce, Economics and Statistics Administration, *National Economic, Social, and Environmental Data Bank,* *CD-ROM,* November 1992. Primary source: Division of Health Interview Statistics and Division of Analysis, National Center for Health Statistics: Data from the National Health Interview Survey. *Notes:* Persons with Medicare, private insurance, and Medicaid appear in both columns. 1980 denominators include persons with unknown health insurance (less than 1 percent). In 1989, 5.2 percent of all persons 65 years of age and over had no Medicare but only 0.9 percent were without health insurance. 1. Includes persons receiving Aid to Families with Dependent Children or Supplemental Security Income or those with current Medicaid cards. 2. Includes persons not covered by private insurance or Medicaid and a small proportion of persons with other types of coverage, such as CHAMPUS (Civilian Health and Medical Program of the Uniformed Services) or public assistance. 3. Age adjusted. 4. Includes all other races not shown separately and unknown family income.

★ 715 ★

Coverage

Health Insurance Coverage for Low-Income Persons Aged 65+, 1989

[Numbers in percent]

Type of coverage	Poor elderly	Near-poor elderly
Medicare/private insurance	34.0	59.0
Medicare only	34.0	31.0
Medicare/medicaid	29.0	10.0
Uninsured	3.0	-

Source: Aging America, Trends and Projections, prepared by the U.S. Senate Special Committee on Aging, the American Association of Retired Persons, the Federal Council on the Aging, and the U.S. Administration on Aging, 1991, Washington, D.C., p. 142. Primary source: Diane Rowland, "Fewer Resources, Greater Burdens: Medical Care Coverage for Low-Income Elderly People," *Bipartisan Commission on Comprehensive Health Care,* May 10, 1990. *Notes:* Low-income elderly refers to persons aged 65+ with incomes below 200% of poverty.

★ 716 ★

Coverage

Health Insurance Coverage, by Poverty Status, 1991

Due to government health programs, such as Medicare and Medicaid, the proportion of older Americans who have health insurance is much greater than other age groups.

[Numbers in thousands]

| Age | Total pop-ulation | Covered by some form of health insurance all or part of year | | | | | Not covered |
		Total	Private insurance[1]	Medicaid[1]	Medicare[1]	CHAMPUS, VA or military health plan	
NUMBER							
All income levels							
Total	251,179	215,821	181,331	26,739	32,907	9,807	35,358
45 to 64 years	48,173	42,213	38,450	2,420	2,260	2,535	5,961
65 years and over	30,590	30,301	20,715	2,891	29,377	1,178	289
Income below poverty level							
Total	35,708	25,488	7,941	16,888	4,586	644	10,220
45 to 64 years	4,306	2,688	1,128	1,301	557	127	1,618
65 years and over	3,781	3,677	1,229	1,187	3,619	71	104
PERCENT DISTRIBUTION							
All income levels							
Total	100.0	85.9	72.2	10.6	13.1	3.9	14.1
45 to 64 years	100.0	87.6	79.8	5.0	4.7	5.3	12.4
65 years and over	100.0	99.1	67.7	9.5	96.0	3.9	0.9
Income below poverty level							
Total	100.0	71.4	22.2	47.3	12.8	1.8	28.6
45 to 64 years	100.0	62.4	26.2	30.2	12.9	2.9	37.6
65 years and over	100.0	97.2	32.5	31.4	95.7	1.9	2.7

Source: Poverty in the United States: 1991, Current Population Reports, Series P-60, No. 181, U.S. Department of Commerce, Bureau of the Census, August 1992, p. xviii. *Note:* 1. Includes those also covered by other insurance.

★ 717 ★

Coverage

Uninsured Elderly

Approximately 37 million people, 17 percent of the population, carried no health insurance in 1991. Of these, 1 percent (or about 370,000) fell into the "elderly" category—which was not defined more precisely.

	Percentage
Working family head	34.4
Working dependent	21.6
Children	26.0
Elderly	1.0
Unemployed	17.0

Source: USA TODAY, February 23, 1993, p. 4A. Primary source: Employee Benefits Research Institute.

★ 718 ★

Coverage

Percentage of Persons 65 Years or Older With or Without a Usual Source of Care in 1987

	White	Black
With a usual source of care	91.5	88.0
Without a usual source of care	8.5	12.0

Source: U.S. Congress, "Profiles in Aging America: Meeting the Health Care Needs of the Nation's Black Elderly," Joint Hearing Before the Special Committee on Aging and the Congressional Black Caucus Health Braintrust, United States Senate, September 28, 1990, 101-29, U.S. Government Printing Office, Washington, D.C., p. 130. Primary source: Unpublished data from the 1987 National Medical Expenditure Survey: Household Component, U.S. Dept. of Health and Human Services, Public Health Service, National Center for Health Service Research and Health Care Technology Assessment.

★ 719 ★
Coverage

Satisfaction with Health Insurance Coverage

Data show responses of 10,000 respondents to a survey in percent.

	Percent
Somewhat satisfied	32.0
Neutral; no answer	30.0
Somewhat dissatisfied	12.0
Completely satisfied	11.0
Complete dissatisfied	10.0
No coverage	5.0

Source: Modern Maturity, Vol. 36, Number 3, June-July 1993, p. 12.

★ 720 ★
Coverage

Percent of Elderly Insured by Blue Cross of Western Pennsylvania

The table presents a sampling of elderly (65 and over) covered by Blue Cross. This example shows coverage of elderly by Blue Cross of Western Pennsylvania.

Age group	Total population 65 and older	Population insured by Blue Cross	Percent of total age group
65 to 69	217,300	131,000	60.3
70 and older	457,600	323,500	70.7
Total	674,000	454,500	67.3

Source: Modern Healthcare, December 23/30, 1991, p. 42. Primary source: Blue Cross of Western Pennsylvania.

★ 721 ★

Coverage

Hospital Insurance

Individuals who are eligible for Social Security or Railroad Retirement are eligible for premium-free Hospital Insurance benefits when they attain age 65, whether they have claimed monthly benefits or not. Also, individuals and their spouses with a sufficient period of Medicare-only coverage in Federal, State or local government employment are eligible at age 65.... In addition, HI protection is provided to disabled beneficiaries (but not their dependents) who have been entitled to Social Security or Railroad Retirement disability benefits for at least 24 months (or government employees with Medicare-only coverage disabled for more than 29 months), and to insured workers (and their spouses and children) with end-stage renal disease who require renal dialysis or a kidney transplant.... Also eligible for HI enrollment under transitional provisions are persons aged 65 or older with specified amounts of earnings credits less than those required for monthly benefit eligibility. (Not eligible under the transitional provisions are retired Federal employees covered by the Federal Employees' Health Benefits Act of 1959 or aliens admitted for permanent residence unless they have 5 consecutive years of residence and the required covered quarters under these provisions.

Source: Annual Statistical Supplement, 1992 to the Social Security Bulletin, U.S. Department of Health and Human Services, Social Security Administration, January 1993, p. 65.

★ 722 ★

Coverage

Supplemental Medical Insurance (SMI)

Except for aliens, all persons aged 65 or older and all disabled persons entitled to coverage under HI (Health Insurance) are eligible to enroll in the SMI (Supplemental Medical Insurance) program on a voluntary basis by paying a monthly premium.... In 1993, enrolled individuals pay a monthly premium of $36.60 deducted from their Social Security benefit, Railroad Retirement annuity, or Federal Civil Service Retirement annuity.... Individuals may either pay the premium or be eligible to have the State social service or medical assistance agency pay the premium on their behalf.

Source: Annual Statistical Supplement, 1992 to the Social Security Bulletin, U.S. Department of Health and Human Services, Social Security Administration, January 1993, pp. 67-68.

Sources

★ 723 ★

Sources of Health Insurance

Numbers are in percent. Many respondents have multiple sources of health insurance.

Source	Working in career job	Working in bridge job	Not working
None	5.5	10.9	14.5
Current employer	75.6	52.4	-
Previous employer	3.8	18.6	35.7
Self-purchased	29.0	29.4	31.5
Medicare	3.0	3.2	11.8
Other	14.6	17.6	20.7
Current employer only	48.7	31.3	-

Source: Ruhm, Christopher J., "Bridge Employment and Job Stopping in the 1980s," *The Commonwealth Fund, Americans Over 55 at Work Program*, May 1991, p. 16. *Notes:* Data are based on a survey of 3,509 Americans aged 50 to 64 conducted by Louis Harris Associates for The Commonwealth Fund between March and September 1989. The survey is a national cross section but excludes Alaska and Hawaii and people in prisons, hospitals, nursing homes, or religious and educational institutions.

★ 724 ★
Sources

Source of Payment by Hospital Discharge

[Discharges from non-federal short-stay hospitals]

Sex and age	Total discharges (numbers in thousands)	Discharges (number per 1,000 persons)	Expected principal source of payment (%)						
			Medicare	Medicaid	Blue Cross/ Blue Shield	Other commercial insurance	Worker's compen-sation	Self-pay	Other or no charge
Both sexes									
55-64 years	4,049	183.9	16.1	6.5	25.4	40.5	1.5	5.2	4.8
65-74 years	4,963	280.9	91.5	1.1	1.7	3.7	0.9	0.7	0.4
75-84 years	3,968	426.6	94.8	0.7	0.7	2.5	0.6	0.5	0.2
65 years and over	10,459	350.5	93.4	0.9	1.1	3.0	0.7	0.5	0.4
75 years and over	5,496	451.7	95.1	0.7	0.6	2.3	0.6	0.4	0.3
85 years and over	1,528	533.0	96.1	0.8	0.3	1.7	0.6	0.3	0.2
Male									
55-64 years	2,077	200.4	18.1	4.4	24.2	42.0	2.2	4.6	4.5

[Continued]

★ 724 ★

Source of Payment by Hospital Discharge

[Continued]

Sex and age	Total discharges (numbers in thousands)	Discharges (number per 1,000 persons)	Expected principal source of payment (%)						
			Medicare	Medicaid	Blue Cross/ Blue Shield	Other commercial insurance	Worker's compen- sation	Self- pay	Other or no charge
65-74 years	2,416	308.8	90.4	1.0	2.0	4.4	1.0	0.6	0.6
75-84 years	1,714	491.3	93.7	0.6	0.7	3.4	0.7	0.5	0.4
65 years and over	4,629	382.0	92.2	0.8	1.4	3.8	0.9	0.5	0.4
75 years and over	2,213	515.3	94.1	0.6	0.7	3.1	0.7	0.4	0.4
85 years and over	499	619.1	95.6	0.6	0.5	2.0	0.7	0.4	0.2
Female									
55-64 years	1,972	169.2	14.1	8.8	26.6	39.0	0.8	5.9	4.8
65-74 years	2,547	258.7	92.6	1.1	1.3	3.1	0.8	0.7	0.4
75-84 years	2,254	387.9	95.6	0.7	0.7	1.9	0.5	0.5	0.1
65 years and over	5,830	329.1	94.4	0.9	0.9	2.4	0.6	0.6	0.2
75 years and over	3,283	417.0	95.8	0.8	0.6	1.8	0.5	0.4	0.1
85 years and over	1,029	499.3	96.3	1.0	0.3	1.6	0.5	0.3	-

Source: *Health Data on Older Americans: United States, 1992*, Centers for Disease Control and Prevention/National Center for Health Statistics, Vital and Health Statistics, Series 3: Analytic and Epidemiological Studies, No. 27, p. 219. Primary source: National Center for Health Statistics: Data from the National Hospital Discharge Survey. *Note:* "-" indicates quantity is zero.

★ 725 ★

Sources

Source of Payment for Nursing Home Residents

[Data are based on reporting by a sample of nursing homes]

Primary source of payment	Both sexes				Male				Female			
	55-64 years	65-74 years	75-84 years	85 years and over	55-64 years	65-74 years	75-84 years	85 years and over	55-64 years	65-74 years	75-84 years	85 years and over
All sources												
Number of residents (in thousands)	88	209	502	604	43	79	140	114	45	130	362	490
Average monthly charge	1,358	1,367	1,471	1,492	1,415	1,330	1,457	1,510	1,304	1,389	1,476	1,487
Own income or family support												
Number of residents (in thousands)	27	71	229	272	14	27	63	62	12	44	167	210
Average monthly charge	1,118	1,425	1,450	1,513	1,258	1,349	1,455	1,535	953	1,472	1,448	1,506
Medicare												
Number of residents (in thousands)	1[2]	5[2]	10	5[2]	1[2]	2[2]	3[2]	1[2]	-	3[2]	7	4[2]
Average monthly charge	3,507	1,748	2,360	1,966	3,507	1,903	2,676	2,289	-	1,614	2,220	1,901
Medicaid												
Skilled nursing facility benefit:												
Number of residents (in thousands)	17	31	82	110	7	0	22	17	11	22	60	93
Average monthly charge	1,981	1,846	1,904	1,839	1,963	1,810	1,889	1,912	1,992	1,860	1,909	1,826
Intermediate care facility benefit:												
Number of residents (in thousands)	30	78	159	192	12	28	42	28	18	49	117	165
Average monthly charge	1,291	1,229	1,295	1,303	1,400	1,248	1,244	1,283	1,222	1,218	1,314	1,306
Other government assistance or welfare												
Number of residents (in thousands)	6[2]	14	12	11	4[2]	5[2]	5[2]	2[2]	3[2]	9	6[2]	9

[Continued]

★ 725 ★

Source of Payment for Nursing Home Residents
[Continued]

Primary source of payment	Both sexes				Male				Female			
	55-64 years	65-74 years	75-84 years	85 years and over	55-64 years	65-74 years	75-84 years	85 years and over	55-64 years	65-74 years	75-84 years	85 years and over
Average monthly charge	710	770	908	1,185	641	797	1,058	1,042	801	758	789	1,217
All other sources[1]												
Number of residents (in thousands)	7	10	10	13	6[2]	8	5[2]	4[2]	1[2]	3[2]	6[2]	9
Average monthly charge	1,414	1,136	997	957	1,460	1,126	1,044	1,078	1,209	1,166	957	897

Source: Health Data on Older Americans: United States, 1992, Centers for Disease Control and Prevention/National Center for Health Statistics, Vital and Health Statistics, Series 3: Analytic and Epidemiological Studies, No. 27, p. 221. Primary source: National Center for Health Statistics: Data from the National Hospital Discharge Survey. Notes: "-" indicates quantity is zero. 1. Includes religious organizations, Veterans' Administration contracts, initial payment-life care funds, and unknown. 2. Figure does not meet standard of reliability or precision.

Benefits

★ 726 ★

Cutting Retiree Health Insurance Benefits

Data are based on a survey of 2,000 companies conducted by the consulting firm of A. Foster Higgins. Survey samples were not necessarily representative of all companies.

	Number of companies surveyed	Percentage who:	
		Have ended[1] or plan to end[2] benefits	Have reduced[1] or plan to reduce[2] benefits
1989	1,380	3.0	43.0
1990	1,180	5.0	58.0
1991	1,114	7.0	65.0

Source: New York Times, June 28, 1992, p. 15. Primary source: A. Foster Higgins, a consulting firm. Notes: 1. In 1990 or 1991. 2. In 1992 or 1993.

Abuses

★ 727 ★

Complaints That Were Not Properly Referred for Investigation by Insurance Carriers

[Figures represent number of complaints]

Carrier	Instructed or allowed to settle with provider	Instructed to submit in writing	Not recognized as potential fraud/abuse	Other[1]	Total
Aetna Life and Casualty Co. (AZ)	2	4	0	0	6
Blue Cross and Blue Shield of Florida	1	5	0	1	7
Blue Shield of Massachusetts	1	0	0	0	1
Blue Cross and Blue Shield of Texas	1	0	1	0	2
Transamerica Occidental Life Insurance Co. (CA)	7	5	3	0	15
Total	12	14	4	1	31

Source: U.S. Congress, "Medicare Fraud and Abuse: A Neglected Emergency?," Hearing before the Special Committee on Aging, United States Senate, October 2, 1991, 102-13, U.S. Government Printing Office, Washington, D.C., p. 162. Notes: 1. The carrier representative instructed the beneficiary to contact another carrier regarding the complaint but failed to give the beneficiary the carrier's address or telephone number.

★ 728 ★

Abuses

Referred Cases Indicating Potential Insurance Fraud and Abuse

[Figures represent number of complaints]

Carrier	Cases where providers had recent prior substantiated complaints[1]		Cases that strongly suggested fraudulent or abusive behavior	
	Fully investigated	Not fully investigated	Fully investigated	Not fully investigated
Aetna Life and Casualty Co. (AZ)	0	2	0	1
Blue Cross and Blue Shield of Florida	2	1	0	1
Blue Shield of Massachusetts	1	2	0	0
Blue Cross and Blue Shield of Texas	1	1	0	1

[Continued]

★ 728 ★

Referred Cases Indicating Potential Insurance Fraud and Abuse

[Continued]

Carrier	Cases where providers had recent prior substantiated complaints[1]		Cases that strongly suggested fraudulent or abusive behavior	
	Fully investigated	Not fully investigated	Fully investigated	Not fully investigated
Transamerica Occidental Life Insurance Co. (CA)	0	2	0	0
Total	4	8	0	3

Source: U.S. Congress, "Medicare Fraud and Abuse: A Neglected Emergency?," Hearing before the Special Committee on Aging, United States Senate, October 2, 1991, 102-13, U.S. Government Printing Office, Washington, D.C., p. 163. *Note:* 1. Two or more similar, substantiated complaints in the past 2 years.

Politics of Health Insurance

★ 729 ★

Leading Health and Insurance PACs

[Ranked by 1993 contributions through May]

Group	Contributions (dollars)		
	1991	1993	Change
Nat'l Assn. of Life Underwriters	138,250	155,500	17,250
American Medical Association	104,650	148,736	44,086
American Hospital Association[1]	61,350	123,250	61,900
Ind. Insurance Agents of America	126,868	105,906	-20,962
Podiatry PAC	82,250	95,500	13,250
American Council of Life Insurance	85,327	87,000	1,673
American Dental PAC	71,325	82,397	11,072
American Health Care Association	52,000	80,700	28,700
American Family PAC	81,500	79,900	-1,600
Mass. Mutual Life Insurance Co.	66,800	72,500	5,750
American Chiropractic Association	21,500	63,930	42,430
Metropolitan Employees	66,750	58,500	-8,250
American Optometric Association	49,550	55,200	5,650
American Physical Therapy	37,950	54,300	16,350
Blue Cross and Blue Shield Assn.	34,650	53,541	18,891
American Int'l. Group Employee	24,528	45,700	21,172
Aetna Life and Casualty Co.	32,450	45,300	12,850
Am. Society of Anesthesiologists	0	45,300	45,300

[Continued]

★ 729 ★

Leading Health and Insurance PACs
[Continued]

Group	Contributions (dollars)		
	1991	1993	Change
Cigna Corp.	56,350	38,750	-17,600
Schering-Plough	15,500	37,000	21,500

Source: Dana Priest, "Health Plan Worries Spur PACs: Industry Group Donations Up 20%", *Washington Post*, July 17, 1993, p. A19. Primary source: Federal Election Commission records compiled by Citizen Action. *Notes:* PAC stands for political action committee. 1. Most recent month for which data is available is April 1993; 1991 figure is also April.

Costs

★ 730 ★

Cost of Insurance in Missouri

The cost of health insurance in the state of Missouri is shown, by age, in dollars.

Companies	Age			
	65	70	75	80
Blue Cross/Blue Shield, St. Louis	$390	$456	$627	$681
Blue Cross/Blue Shield, Kansas City	360	372	564	744
Bankers Life and Casualty	374	425	496	588
Equitable Life and Casualty	486	552	564	564
United American Insurance	639	719	775	812

Source: St. Louis Post Dispatch, July 22, 1993, p.1. Missouri Department of Insurance. *Notes:* The rates are for women who smoke. Policy costs for men will be higher. For women who do not smoke costs will be lower. The cost may vary by 10 percent depending on whether the policyholder lives in a rural or urban area.

Dental Plans

★ 731 ★

Dental Insurance: Type of Private Insurance Plan

Percent distribution of persons 2 years of age and over by private dental insurance status, according to selected demographic characteristics: United States, 1989.

Characteristic	Total population	Without private dental insurance	With private dental insurance				
			Total	Comprehensive plan only	Single service plan only	Both plans	With unknown coverage
Age							
All ages	100.0	51.9	40.5	32.7	6.8	1.0	7.7
2-4 years	100.0	54.3	39.9	32.8	6.6	0.6	5.8
5-17 years	100.0	48.4	45.4	35.9	8.3	1.1	6.2
18-34 years	100.0	50.6	40.7	33.6	6.2	0.9	8.7
35-54 years	100.0	42.8	50.0	39.7	9.0	1.4	7.2
55-64 years	100.0	55.2	37.1	29.9	6.3	0.8	7.7
65 years and over	100.0	75.8	15.0	13.0	1.9	0.2	9.2
65-74 years	100.0	74.1	17.7	15.2	2.3	0.2[1]	8.2
75 years and over	100.0	78.3	10.8	9.5	1.2	0.2[1]	10.8

Source: *Dental Services and Oral Health: United States, 1989*, National Center for Health Statistics, Vital and Health Statistics, Series 10, No. 185, p. 48.

★ 732 ★

Dental Plans

Dental Insurance: Type of Private Insurance Plan, by Socio-Economic Characteristics

Percent distribution of persons 45 years old and over by private dental insurance status, according to selected socioeconomic characteristics: United States, 1989.

Characteristic	Total population	Without private dental insurance	With private dental insurance				With unknown coverage
			Total	Comprehensive plan only	Single service plan only	Both plans	
Education level[1]							
Less than 9 years							
All 22 years old and over	100.0	77.8	14.1	12.4	1.4	0.3	8.2
45-54 years	100.0	69.2	23.2	19.9	2.5	0.8[4]	7.6
55-64 years	100.0	72.7	20.0	17.6	2.3	0.2[4]	7.3
65 years and over	100.0	81.9	8.5	7.8	0.6	0.1[4]	9.6

[Continued]

★ 732 ★

Dental Insurance: Type of Private Insurance Plan, by Socio-Economic Characteristics
[Continued]

Characteristic	Total population	Without private dental insurance	With private dental insurance				With unknown coverage
			Total	Comprehensive plan only	Single service plan only	Both plans	
9-11 years							
All 22 years old and over	100.0	67.8	24.3	21.0	3.0	0.3	7.9
45-54 years	100.0	56.2	36.4	31.3	4.6	0.5[4]	7.4
55-64 years	100.0	65.2	28.0	23.4	4.2	0.5[4]	6.8
65 years and over	100.0	78.7	11.0	9.5	1.5	0.0[4]	10.3
12 years							
All 22 years old and over	100.0	52.6	39.6	32.5	6.1	0.9	7.8
45-54 years	100.0	43.3	49.0	40.0	7.9	1.1	7.7
55-64 years	100.0	52.3	39.7	32.0	6.8	0.9	8.0
65 years and over	100.0	74.9	16.9	14.9	1.8	0.2[4]	8.2
13 years or more							
All 22 years old and over	100.0	41.6	51.4	40.3	9.6	1.4	7.0
45-54 years	100.0	35.4	58.5	45.3	11.2	2.0	6.0
55-64 years	100.0	45.3	48.0	37.7	9.0	1.3	6.7
65 years and over	100.0	68.7	24.1	19.7	3.9	0.4[4]	7.3
Family income[2]							
Less than $10,000							
All ages	100.0	83.9	10.2	9.3	0.8	0.1[4]	5.9
45-54 years	100.0	89.7	7.5	6.3	0.8[4]	0.3[4]	2.9
55-64 years	100.0	88.3	6.8	6.0	0.8[4]	-	4.9
65 years and over	100.0	84.5	5.7	5.5	0.2[4]	0.0[4]	9.8
65-74 years	100.0	84.1	6.7	6.6	0.1[4]	-	9.2
75 years and over	100.0	84.8	4.7	4.4	0.3[4]	0.1[4]	10.4
$10,000-$19,999							
All ages	100.0	70.4	23.0	19.8	3.0	0.2	6.6
45-54 years	100.0	68.2	25.4	21.2	3.8	0.3[4]	6.5
55-64 years	100.0	70.3	23.1	20.0	3.0	0.[4]	6.6
65 years and over	100.0	79.9	12.7	11.6	1.0	0.1[4]	7.3
65-74 years	100.0	79.1	14.0	12.9	1.0	0.1[4]	7.0
75 years and over	100.0	81.3	10.7	9.6	0.9[4]	0.2[4]	8.0
$20,000-$34,999							
All ages	100.0	49.1	45.5	37.3	7.5	0.8	5.4
45-54 years	100.0	44.0	50.3	41.9	7.8	0.6[4]	5.7
55-64 years	100.0	53.7	40.0	32.7	6.7	0.6[4]	6.4
65 years and over	100.0	72.3	21.5	17.9	3.4	0.2[4]	6.2
65-74 years	100.0	70.3	24.4	20.0	4.1	0.3[4]	5.3
75 years and over	100.0	76.8	15.1	13.1	1.8[4]	0.1[4]	8.1

[Continued]

★ 732 ★

Dental Insurance: Type of Private Insurance Plan, by Socio-Economic Characteristics
[Continued]

Characteristic	Total population	Without private dental insurance	With private dental insurance				With unknown coverage
			Total	Comprehensive plan only	Single service plan only	Both plans	
$35,000 or more							
All ages	100.0	33.8	60.8	46.8	12.0	2.0	5.4
45-54 years	100.0	30.7	64.4	49.5	12.5	2.3	4.9
55-64 years	100.0	39.0	55.7	42.4	11.3	1.9	5.3
65 years and over	100.0	67.9	26.3	21.0	4.8	0.6[4]	5.8
65-74 years	100.0	65.3	29.3	23.4	5.2	0.7[4]	5.5
75 years and over	100.0	74.3	18.9	14.8	3.6[4]	0.4[4]	6.8
Poverty index[3]							
Below poverty threshold							
All ages	100.0	83.8	11.0	9.8	1.1	0.1[4]	5.2
45-54 years	100.0	89.3	7.6	7.0	0.4[4]	0.2[4]	3.2
55-64 years	100.0	89.5	6.1	5.4	0.7[4]	-	4.4
65 years and over	100.0	87.8	4.4	4.3	0.1[4]	-	7.8
65-74 years	100.0	86.6	5.5	5.5	-	-	8.0
75 years and over	100.0	89.0	3.3	3.1	0.2[4]	-	7.7
At or above poverty threshold							
All ages	100.0	46.6	46.8	37.6	8.1	1.2	6.5
45-54 years	100.0	40.1	53.7	42.8	9.3	1.5	6.2
55-64 years	100.0	51.6	41.7	33.4	7.3	1.0	6.7
65 years and over	100.0	75.0	17.3	14.8	2.3	0.2	7.8
65-74 years	100.0	73.2	19.9	17.0	2.7	0.2[4]	6.9
75 years and over	100.0	78.0	12.6	11.0	1.5	0.2[4]	9.3

Source: Dental Services and Oral Health: United States, 1989, National Center for Health Statistics, Vital and Health Statistics, Series 10, No. 185, p. 52. *Notes:* A dash (-) stands for zero. 1. Persons with unknown education level not shown separately. 2. Persons with unknown income not shown separately. 3. Persons with unknown poverty status not shown separately. 4. Figure does not meet standard of reliability or precision (more than 30-percent relative standard error in numerator of percent or rate).

★ 733 ★

Dental Plans

Dental Insurance: Private Dental Health Insurance

Selected dental variables, by private dental health insurance status and selected demographic characteristics: United States, 1989.

Age	Total population[1] Number in thousands	Rate of dental visit per person per year	Dental visit in previous year Percent		
			1 or more visits	3 or more visits	Edentulous person
All ages					
Having insurance	95,436	2.7	71.4	19.3	3.7
Without insurance	122,368	1.7	50.0	12.2	10.5
2-4 years					
Having insurance	4,430	1.1	40.1	2.9	-
Without insurance	6,022	0.8	27.8	2.4	-
5-17 years					
Having insurance	20,531	3.2	81.6	19.4	-
Without insurance	21,894	1.8	61.4	12.8	-
18-34 years					
Having insurance	27,791	2.4	70.2	17.8	0.3
Without insurance	34,517	1.4	49.9	11.1	0.5
35-54 years					
Having insurance	30,346	2.7	72.8	21.7	4.3
Without insurance	25,971	1.9	53.2	14.2	7.3
55-64 years					
Having insurance	7,949	3.4	66.9	23.9	14.7
Without insurance	11,824	1.9	48.8	14.9	22.6
65 years or more					
Having insurance	4,389	3.0	61.0	20.2	23.3
Without insurance	22,141	1.9	42.1	12.3	36.4

Source: *Dental Services and Oral Health: United States, 1989,* National Center for Health Statistics, Vital and Health Statistics, Series 10, No. 185, p. 67. *Notes:* A dash (-) represents a quantity of zero. 1. Total includes persons of other races or unknown income (not shown separately). Persons with unknown insurance coverage are excluded.

Medicare and Medicaid

★ 734 ★

Medicare

Medicare is a federal program for aged and disabled persons who are insured under the Social Security program.... It consists of two separate but coordinated programs: Part A is Hospital Insurance (HI) and Part B is Supplementary Medical Insurance (SMI).

Source: Annual Statistical Supplement, 1992 to the Social Security Bulletin, U.S. Department of Health and Human Services, Social Security Administration, January 1993, p. 64.

★ 735 ★

Medicare and Medicaid

Medicaid

The program, known as Medicaid, became law in 1965 as a jointly funded cooperative venture between the federal and state governments to assist states in the provision of more adequate medical care to eligible needy persons. Medicaid is the largest program providing medical and health-related services to America's poor people.

Within broad national guidelines, which the federal government provides, each of the States: (1) establishes its own eligibility standards; (2) determines the type, amount, duration, and scope of services; (3) sets the rate of payment for services; and (4) administers its own program. Thus, the Medicaid program varies considerably from state to state, as well as within each state.... The total outlay for the Medicaid program in fiscal year 1991 was $90.5 billion ($51.5 billion federal and $39 billion state monies), plus administrative costs.

Source: Annual Statistical Supplement, 1992 to the Social Security Bulletin, U.S. Department of Health and Human Services, Social Security Administration, January 1993, p. 77.

★ 736 ★

Medicare and Medicaid

Medicare and Medicaid Relationship

Some aged and/or disabled persons are covered under both Medicaid and Medicare (title XVIII of the Social Security Act). These recipients are known as "dual beneficiaries" or "dual eligibles." The Medicare program provides Hospital Insurance (HI, also known as Part A) and Supplementary Medical Insurance (SMI, known as Part B). For those persons aged 65 or older (and for certain disabled persons) who have insured status under Social Security, coverage for HI is automatic.... Additional help is provided for certain Medicare recipients known as "qualified Medicare beneficiaries" or "QMBs": those beneficiaries with resources at or below twice the standard allowed under the SSI program, and with incomes below 100 percent of Federal poverty guidelines. For these, the Medicaid program in most States pays the Medicare premiums, deductibles and certain coinsurance costs, if the recipient applies for this help. In addition, States are required to cover the Part B Supplementary Medical Insurance premiums (but no other cost sharing) for Medicare beneficiaries with resources below twice the SSI level and with income below 110 percent of Federal poverty guidelines in 1993, and below 120 percent in 1995. These new QMBs are not quite poor enough to qualify for Medicaid services; they benefit because their Medicare cost-sharing expenses are paid by the State Medicaid programs.

Source: Annual Statistical Supplement, 1992 to the Social Security Bulletin, U.S. Department of Health and Human Services, Social Security Administration, January 1993, p. 79.

★ 737 ★

Medicare and Medicaid

Medicare and Medicaid - Part I

Region, division, and state	Persons enrolled (1,000)[1,2]			Persons served, 1987[2] (1,000)		Benefit payments (mil. dol.)[2,3]				
				Persons 65 yr. old and over	Disabled	1988 (Prel.)	1987		1985, total	1980, total
	1988 (Prel.)	1985	1980				Total[4]	Aged		
United States	32,297	30,437	27,890	21,980	2,076	86,038	79,957	70,883	70,261	35,561
Northeast	7,293	7,043	6,636	5,244	454	20,577	19,690	17,658	17,789	9,071
New England	1,844	1,772	1,647	1,308	106	5,112	4,436	4,013	4,266	2,238
Maine	178	169	158	132	13	361	360	321	353	177
New Hampshire	132	124	112	91	7	301	272	248	247	120
Vermont	72	69	65	52	5	157	134	119	138	68
Massachusetts	850	824	779	592	47	2,663	2,245	2,034	2,226	1,179
Rhode Island	155	149	138	113	10	426	350	316	315	189
Connecticut	456	436	394	328	24	1,204	1,074	975	988	505
Middle Atlantic	5,449	5,271	4,989	3,936	348	15,465	15,253	13,645	13,523	6,833
New York	2,480	2,425	2,365	1,799	167	6,444	7,036	6,286	6,236	3,409

[Continued]

★ 737 ★

Medicare and Medicaid - Part I
[Continued]

Region, division, and state	Persons enrolled (1,000)[1,2]			Persons served, 1987[2] (1,000)		Benefit payments (mil. dol.)[2,3]				
				Persons 65 yr. old and over	Disabled	1988 (Prel.)	1987		1985, total	1980, total
	1988 (Prel.)	1985	1980				Total[4]	Aged		
New Jersey	1,066	1,024	943	752	64	2,882	2,787	2,484	2,625	1,198
Pennsylvania	1,902	1,822	1,681	1,384	116	6,138	5,431	4,875	4,662	2,226
Midwest	8,188	7,825	7,315	5,570	507	21,961	19,728	17,559	17,724	9,507
East North Central	5,612	5,338	4,948	3,863	372	16,032	14,382	12,752	12,648	6,720
Ohio	1,491	1,408	1,303	1,043	101	4,071	3,940	3,489	3,137	1,606
Indiana	737	696	642	481	47	1,802	1,612	1,415	1,367	719
Illinois	1,500	1,441	1,351	990	86	4,554	4,040	3,592	3,744	2,046
Michigan	1,190	1,130	1,034	853	94	3,957	3,282	2,898	3,029	1,620
Wisconsin	695	664	617	496	43	1,646	1,508	1,360	1,371	729
West North Central	2,575	2,487	2,366	1,707	135	5,929	5,346	4,806	5,077	2,787
Minnesota	573	549	514	290	26	1,017	863	764	1,024	594
Iowa	449	435	416	332	23	890	928	836	821	453
Missouri	761	737	706	523	49	2,216	1,905	1,699	1,639	888
North Dakota	97	93	87	71	5	231	226	211	212	109
South Dakota	108	104	98	77	5	224	215	199	188	96
Nebraska	233	227	219	160	10	443	422	381	441	234
Kansas	355	342	326	255	17	909	787	717	752	413
South	10,992	10,227	9,234	7,407	770	27,241	25,973	22,759	21,752	10,412
South Atlantic	5,825	5,366	4,724	3,961	399	14,139	13,704	12,050	11,525	5,555
Delaware	84	77	66	59	6	229	199	176	160	87
Maryland	517	480	422	367	32	1,505	1,481	1,310	1,252	622
District of Columbia	78	79	79	58	5	315	301	259	285	149
Virginia	686	634	558	465	53	1,561	1,517	1,305	1,260	614
West Virginia	300	290	276	194	27	683	626	542	550	260
North Carolina	843	774	680	558	68	1,567	1,585	1,349	1,303	642
South Carolina	418	380	329	253	36	803	780	653	624	302
Georgia	699	653	587	463	67	1,754	1,642	1,376	1,263	601
Florida	2,201	2,000	1,726	1,548	106	5,723	5,572	5,080	4,828	2,278
East South Central	2,103	1,999	1,859	1,385	183	5,218	4,820	4,134	3,813	1,878
Kentucky	518	493	463	333	44	1,163	1,134	973	875	437
Tennessee	665	629	579	433	55	1,867	1,571	1,359	1,231	594
Alabama	563	533	491	387	49	1,401	1,349	1,157	1,056	523
Mississippi	357	344	326	232	35	787	767	644	651	324
West South Central	3,064	2,862	2,651	2,061	188	7,884	7,448	6,576	6,414	2,979
Arkansas	381	367	349	259	29	877	815	712	697	333
Louisiana	513	474	443	326	40	1,525	1,385	1,188	977	467
Oklahoma	437	420	402	301	24	1,078	983	888	853	443
Texas	1,732	1,600	1,458	1,174	94	4,405	4,266	3,788	3,887	1,736

[Continued]

★ 737 ★

Medicare and Medicaid - Part I

[Continued]

Region, division, and state	Persons enrolled (1,000)[1,2]			Persons served, 1987[2] (1,000)		Benefit payments (mil. dol.)[2,3]				
				Persons 65 yr. old and over	Disabled	1988 (Prel.)	1987		1985, total	1980, total
	1988 (Prel.)	1985	1980				Total[4]	Aged		
West	5,800	5,319	4,679	3,751	346	16,243	14,502	12,844	12,981	6,529
Mountain	1,521	1,364	1,155	979	81	3,731	3,255	2,908	2,752	1,304
Montana	113	106	94	73	6	268	229	206	199	99
Idaho	126	117	104	90	6	244	244	224	199	97
Wyoming	49	45	41	33	2	125	110	101	88	44
Colorado	334	303	268	209	18	862	682	610	657	315
New Mexico	167	150	130	99	10	365	323	278	292	137
Arizona	462	407	328	307	25	1,224	1,096	982	860	383
Utah	149	136	118	101	7	333	291	259	214	110
Nevada	121	100	73	67	7	309	280	248	243	119
Pacific	4,279	3,956	3,524	2,772	265	12,513	11,248	9,935	10,229	5,225
Washington	584	535	469	394	33	1,271	1,226	1,096	1,005	507
Oregon	403	374	331	254	21	743	749	672	762	385
California	3,152	2,927	2,630	2,049	204	10,196	9,013	7,943	8,227	4,219
Alaska	22	18	13	13	1	55	52	46	40	18
Hawaii	118	102	81	63	6	248	208	179	195	96

Source: U.S. Department of Commerce, Bureau of the Census, *State and Metropolitan Area Data Book 1991*, August 1991, p. 220. *Notes:* 1. As of July 1. Cover persons enrolled for hospital and/or medical insurance. 2. U.S. totals include data for enrollees with residence unknown. 3. For calendar year. 4. Include disabled.

★ 738 ★

Medicare and Medicaid

Medicare and Medicaid - Part II

Region, division, and State	Medicaid[1]					
	Recipients (1,000)			Payments (million dols.)		
	1988 (prel.)	1985	1980	1988 (Prel.)	1985	1980
United States	21,628	20,225	20,205	48,575	37,364	23,213
Northeast	4,900	4,948	5,578	16,992	13,247	8,139
New England	1,069	1,054	1,363	3,815	2,717	1,782
Maine	119	124	145	324	232	131
New Hampshire	33	38	45	166	118	72
Vermont	51	50	54	113	89	59
Massachusetts	555	523	775	2,043	1,433	1,009
Rhode Island	98	101	128	332	250	160
Connecticut	213	217	217	837	595	350

[Continued]

★ 738 ★

Medicare and Medicaid - Part II
[Continued]

| Region, division, and State | Medicaid[1] | | | | | |
| | Recipients (1,000) | | | Payments (million dols.) | | |
	1988 (prel.)	1985	1980	1988 (Prel.)	1985	1980
Middle Atlantic	3,831	3,895	4,214	13,177	10,530	6,357
New York	2,212	2,242	2,288	9,209	7,588	4,543
New Jersey	533	581	676	1,718	1,145	756
Pennsylvania	1,086	1,071	1,251	2,250	1,797	1,058
Midwest	5,273	5,230	4,572	11,149	9,146	5,637
East North Central	3,970	3,999	3,460	8,043	6,626	4,114
Ohio	1,118	1,045	809	2,359	1,767	809
Indiana	301	284	205	1,036	747	354
Illinois	1,043	1,063	1,049	1,857	1,653	1,192
Michigan	1,105	1,133	973	1,806	1,517	1,072
Wisconsin	403	473	425	985	942	687
West North Central	1,303	1,231	1,112	3,106	2,520	1,523
Minnesota	336	357	325	1,098	1,001	590
Iowa	228	212	178	472	360	230
Missouri	379	356	321	686	525	295
North Dakota	44	37	31	161	117	47
South Dakota	41	34	35	124	94	55
Nebraska	105	94	71	227	167	109
Kansas	170	142	149	338	256	197
South	6,510	5,630	5,586	12,522	9,056	5,559
South Atlantic	2,980	2,594	2,613	6,353	4,331	2,513
Delaware	37	41	49	101	71	45
Maryland	320	3229	313	843	584	322
District of Columbia	97	98	127	360	298	168
Virginia	326	303	320	756	547	360
West Virginia	221	211	199	283	173	104
North Carolina	411	343	377	957	647	401
South Carolina	263	238	298	455	309	258
Georgia	537	469	430	1,105	760	462
Florida	768	562	501	1,493	943	392
East South Central	1,563	1,386	1,396	2,437	1,767	1,150
Kentucky	413	408	410	689	540	296
Tennessee	479	362	354	890	578	380
Alabama	305	316	324	444	375	263
Mississippi	366	300	307	414	274	211

[Continued]

★ 738 ★

Medicare and Medicaid - Part II
[Continued]

Region, division, and State	Medicaid[1]					
	Recipients (1,000)			Payments (million dols.)		
	1988 (prel.)	1985	1980	1988 (Prel.)	1985	1980
West South Central	1,967	1,650	1,577	3,732	2,958	1,896
Arkansas	227	197	222	432	358	235
Louisiana	433	416	385	775	725	415
Oklahoma	245	270	254	581	460	265
Texas	1,062	767	716	1,944	1,414	981
West	4,944	4,417	4,469	7,912	5,914	3,878
Mountain	554	441	426	1,253	840	505
Montana	81	47	46	136	96	62
Idaho	46	39	44	123	76	52
Wyoming	20	20	11	33	28	14
Colorado	180	147	155	464	316	182
New Mexico	105	87	88	217	148	70
Arizona	X	X	X	X	X	X
Utah	86	72	57	185	110	80
Nevada	36	28	25	95	66	45
Pacific	4,391	3,976	4,043	6,659	5,075	3,373
Washington	403	326	315	852	584	329
Oregon	189	153	186	331	239	179
California	3,675	3,381	3,418	5,226	4,045	2,728
Alaska	33	24	18	95	66	28
Hawaii	91	92	107	155	140	109

Source: U.S. Department of Commerce, Bureau of the Census, *State and Metropolitan Area Data Book 1991*, August 1991, p. 220. *Notes:* X = Figure not applicable because column heading and stub line make an entry impossible, absurd, or meaningless. 1. For fiscal years ending September 30.

★ 739 ★

Medicare and Medicaid

Where the Medicaid Dollar for the Elderly Goes, 1989

Nursing homes - 69.0

Home health - 8.0

Hospitals - 8.0

Prescription drugs - 7.0

Other - 7.0

Physicians - 1.0

Type of expense	Percent
Nursing homes	69.0
Home health	8.0
Hospitals	8.0
Prescription drugs	7.0
Physicians	1.0
Other	7.0

Source: Aging America, Trends and Projections, prepared by the U.S. Senate Special Committee on Aging, the American Association of Retired Persons, the Federal Council on the Aging, and the U.S. Administration on Aging, 1991, Washington, D.C., p. 139. Primary source: Thomas W. Reilly, Steven B. Clauser, and David K. Baugh, "Trends in Medicaid Payments and Utilization, 1975-1989," *Health Care Financing Review,* 1990 Annual Supplement.

★ 740 ★

Medicare and Medicaid

Medicare and Medicaid Beneficiaries, 1983-1991

Between 1968 and 1975 (when the programs were new), beneficiaries increased substantially. Since 1975, the rate has been just over 20 million people.

[Number of beneficiaries in thousands]

Fiscal year	Medicare aged benef.	Medicare disabled benef.	Medicaid benef.
1983	26,670	2,918	21,554
1984	27,112	2,884	21,607
1985	27,123	2,944	21,814
1986	27,728	2,986	22,515
1987	28,239	3,042	23,109
1988	28,779	3,115	22,907
1989	29,358	3,200	23,511

[Continued]

★ 740 ★

Medicare and Medicaid Beneficiaries, 1983-1991
[Continued]

Fiscal year	Medicare aged benef.	Medicare disabled benef.	Medicaid benef.
1990[1]	29,951	3,251	24,600
1991[1]	30,480	3,297	25,600

Source: Medicare and Medicaid's 25th Anniversary—Much Promised, Accomplished, and Left Unfinished: A Report Presented by the Chairman of the Select Committee on Aging, U.S. Government Printing Office, 1990. Primary source: Health Care Financing Administration and Congressional Budget Office, 1990. *Note:* 1. Estimate.

★ 741 ★

Medicare and Medicaid

Medicare Users by Age

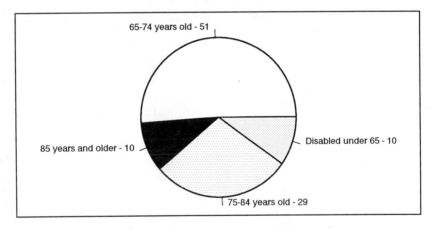

Data show use of Medicare funds by the disabled and the elderly (65 and over) by age bracket.

	Percent
Disabled under 65	10
65-74 years old	51
75-84 years old	29
85 years and older	10

Source: USA TODAY, March 10, 1993, p. 1A. Primary source: Health Care Financing Administration.

★ 742 ★

Medicare and Medicaid

Medicare Enrollees, Expenditures, and Expenditure Percent Distribution, by Type of Service: United States, Selected Years, 1967-90

[Data are compiled by the Health Care Financing Administration]

Type of service	1967	1970	1975	1980	1985	1988	1989	1990[1]
	Enrollees (number in millions)[2]							
Total[3]	19.5	20.5	25.0	28.5	31.1	33.0	33.6	34.2
Hospital insurance	19.5	20.4	24.6	28.1	30.6	32.4	33.0	33.7
Supplementary medical insurance	17.9	19.6	23.9	27.4	30.0	31.6	32.1	32.6
	Expenditures (amount in millions)							
Total	4,737	7,493	16,316	36,822	72,294	88,561	100,586	110,984
Total hospital insurance[4]	3,430	5,281	11,581	25,577	48,414	53,331	60,803	66,997
Inpatient hospital	3,034	4,827	10,877	24,082	44,680	49,062	53,822	59,301
Skilled nursing facility	282	246	278	401	577	816	2,978	2,876
Home health agency	29	51	160	568	2,144	2,313	2,765	3,517
Hospice	-	-	-	-	43	156	238	356
Administrative expenses[5]	77	157	266	512	834	815	792	758
Total supplementary medical insurance	1,307	2,212	4,735	11,245	23,880	35,230	39,783	43,987
Physician	1,128	1,790	3,415	8,188	17,311	24,372	27,057	29,628
Outpatient hospital	33	114	652	1,935	4,304	6,534	7,662	8,475
Home health agency	10	34	87	195	54	62	73	81
Group practice ~ prepayment	19	26	80	203	720	2,019	2,308	2,827
Independent laboratory	7	11	39	114	558	983	1,194	1,457
Administrative expenses	110	237	462	610	933	1,260	1,489	1,519
	Expenditures (percent distribution)							
Total hospital insurance[4]	100.0	100.0	100.0	100.0	100.0	100.0	100.0	100.0
Inpatient hospital	88.5	91.4	93.9	94.2	92.3	92.0	89.3	88.5
Skilled nursing facility	8.2	4.7	0.5	1.6	1.2	1.6	4.6	4.3
Home health agency	0.8	1.0	1.4	2.2	4.4	4.4	4.3	5.2
Hospice	-	-	-	-	0.0	0.2	0.2	0.5
Administrative expenses[5]	2.2	3.0	2.3	2.0	1.7	1.5	1.3	1.1
Total supplementary medical insurance	100.0	100.0	100.0	100.0	100.0	100.0	100.0	100.0

[Continued]

★ 742 ★

Medicare Enrollees, Expenditures, and Expenditure Percent Distribution, by Type of Service: United States, Selected Years, 1967-90
[Continued]

Type of service	1967	1970	1975	1980	1985	1988	1989	1990[1]
Physician	86.3	80.9	72.1	72.8	72.5	69.2	68.0	67.4
Outpatient hospital	2.5	5.2	13.8	17.2	18.0	18.5	19.3	19.3
Home health agency	0.8	1.5	1.8	1.7	0.2	0.2	0.2	0.2
Group practice prepayment	1.5	1.2	1.7	1.8	3.0	5.7	5.8	6.4
Independent laboratory	0.5	0.5	0.8	1.0	2.3	2.8	3.0	3.3
Administrative expenses	8.4	10.7	9.8	5.4	3.9	3.6	3.7	3.5

Source: U.S. Department of Commerce, Economics and Statistics Administration, *National Economic, Social, and Environmental Data Bank, CD-ROM,* November 1992. Primary source: Office of Medicare Cost Estimates, Office of the Actuary and Bureau of Data Management and Strategy. Health Care Financing Administration. Washington. April 1991. *Notes:* A dash (-) indicates that data were not applicable. 1. Preliminary figures. 2. Includes the U.S. population residing in the United States, Puerto Rico, Virgin Islands, Guam, other outlying areas, and foreign countries, and residence unknown. 3. Number enrolled in the hospital insurance and/or supplementary medical insurance programs on July 1. 4. Includes coverage for outpatient hospital diagnostic service under hospital insurance terminated after Mar. 31, 1968, and Medicaid and Maternal and Child Health Professional Standard Review Organization activity through 1981, Peer Review Organization activity after 1983; is counted as an inpatient hospital benefit in other actuarial tables presenting benefit payments by type of benefit. 5. Includes costs of experiments and demonstration projects.

★ 743 ★
Medicare and Medicaid

Medicare Enrollment, Persons Served, and Payments for Medicare Enrollees 65 Years of Age and Over: U.S. and Other Areas, Selected Years, 1967-89
[Data are compiled by the Health Care Financing Administration]

Age	Enrollment in millions[1]				Persons served per 1,000 enrollees[2]				Payments per person served ($)[3]			
	1967	1977	1987	1989	1967	1977	1987	1989	1967	1977	1987	1989
Total	19.5	23.8	29.4	30.4	367	570	754	785	592	1,332	3,025	3,445
65-66 years	2.8	3.3	4	3.9	300	533	700	730	496	1,075	2,214	2,381
67-68 years	2.6	3.2	3.7	3.9	326	511	667	703	521	1,173	2,536	2,864
69-70 years	2.4	2.9	3.4	3.5	339	531	705	732	530	1,211	2,700	3,029
71-72 years	2.3	2.6	3.1	3.2	351	555	740	764	560	1,228	2,904	3,204
73-74 years	2.1	2.3	2.9	2.9	369	576	762	795	574	1,319	3,048	3,486
75-79 years	3.9	4.5	5.7	5.9	398	597	787	820	624	1,430	3,312	3,755
80-84 years	2.2	3	3.7	3.9	430	623	828	857	693	1,549	3,496	4,074
85 years and over	1.3	2.1	3	3.2	465	652	841	869	740	1,636	3,708	4,384

Source: U.S. Department of Commerce, Economics and Statistics Administration, *National Economic, Social, and Environmental Data Bank, CD-ROM,* November 1992. Primary source: Bureau of Data Management and Strategy, Health Care Financing Administration: Unpublished data. *Notes:* Data include the United States, residence unknown, Puerto Rico, Virgin Islands, Guam, other outlying areas and foreign countries. 1. Includes fee-for-service and Health Maintenance Organization (HMO) enrollees and is as of July 1 each year. 2. Excludes HMO enrollees. 3. Excludes amounts for HMO services.

★ 744 ★

Medicare and Medicaid

Use of Selected Community Health and Social Services

Data are based on personal interviews of the functionally impaired Medicare eligibles living in the community.

Race, sex, age, and help with ADLs	Number of persons (in thousands)	Health and social services					
		Hospital-ization last year	Physician office care	Auxiliary health services[1]	Mental health services	Rehabil-itation therapist[2]	Senior centers
Race							
White	4,872	34.7	38.8	19.1	0.9	3.5	6.5
All other	782	27.4	41.7	12.9	0.8[4]	3.2	6.5
Sex							
Male	1,951	35.9	37.7	15.0	0.9	3.3	5.0
Female	3,703	32.5	40.0	19.9	0.9	3.5	7.3
Age							
65-74 years	2,083	34.6	41.5	19.0	1.8	4.3	5.9
75-84 years	2,459	34.8	39.5	18.2	0.5[4]	3.3	7.7
65 years and over	5,654	33.7	39.2	18.2	0.9	3.5	6.5
75 years and over	3,571	33.2	37.9	17.7	0.4[4]	3.0	6.9
85 years and over	1,133	29.7	34.3	16.8	0.0[4]	2.2	5.1
Help with ADLs[3]							
No help received	4,023	29.3	38.8	19.0	0.8	2.3	7.8
Help with 1	765	38.4	42.0	17.9	1.3[4]	3.7	4.3
Help with 2	318	41.8	44.7	17.9	1.3[4]	4.4	3.5
Help with 3-5	548	55.1	35.4	12.6	1.6[4]	11.1	1.8[4]

Source: Health Data on Older Americans: United States, 1992, Centers for Disease Control and Prevention/National Center for Health Statistics, Vital and Health Statistics, Series 3: Analytic and Epidemiological Studies, No. 27, p. 181. Primary source: National Long Term Care Survey, 1984. *Notes:* 1. Includes dentists, podiatrists, optometrists, and chiropractors. 2. Includes physical therapists, occupational therapists, speech therapists, and hearing therapists. 3. Receives help of another person with the following activities of daily living (ADL): bathing, dressing, transferring, toileting, eating. 4. Figure does not meet standard of reliability or precision.

★ 745 ★

Medicare and Medicaid

Medicare: Enrollment and Reimbursements of Aged Persons, 1967-90

Type of coverage and service	1967	1975	1980	1985	1988	1989	1990	Average annual rate change (percent) 1967-90
				Persons enrolled (in thousands)				
Hospital Insurance and/or Supplementary Medical Insurance	19,521	22,790	25,515	28,176	29,879	30,409	30,948	2.0
Hospital Insurance	19,494	22,472	25,104	27,683	29,312	29,869	30,464	2.0
Supplementary Medical Insurance	17,893	21,945	24,680	27,311	28,780	29,216	29,685	2.2
				Persons served (in thousands)				
Hospital Insurance and/or Supplementary Medical Insurance	7,154	12,032	16,271	20,347	22,942	23,868	24,809	5.6
Hospital Insurance	3,960	4,963	6,024	6,058	6,082	6,155	6,367	2.1
Inpatient hospital	3,601	4,913	5,951	5,714	5,779	5,725	5,906	2.2
Skilled-nursing services	354	260	248	304	371	613	615	2.4
Home health services[1]	126	329	675	1,448	1,485	1,580	1,818	12.3
Supplementary Medical Insurance	6,523	11,762	16,099	20,186	22,808	23,746	24,687	6.0
Physicians' and other medical services	6,415	11,396	15,627	19,590	22,270	23,283	24,193	5.9
Outpatient services	1,511	3,768	6,629	9,889	12,795	13,291	14,055	10.2
Home health services[1]	118	161	302	27	32	36	38	-4.8
				Persons served per 1,000 enrollees				
Hospital Insurance and/or Supplementary Medical Insurance	367	528	638	722	768	785	802	3.5
Hospital Insurance	203	221	240	219	208	206	209	.1
Inpatient hospital	185	219	237	206	197	192	194	.2
Skilled-nursing services	18	12	10	11	13	21	20	.5
Home health services[1]	7	15	27	52	51	53	60	9.8
Supplementary Medical Insurance	365	536	652	739	793	813	832	3.6
Physicians' and other medical services	359	519	633	717	774	797	815	3.6
Outpatient services	77	172	269	362	445	455	474	8.2
Home health services[1]	7	7	12	1	1	1	1	-8.1
				Amount reimbursed (in millions)				
Hospital Insurance and/or Supplementary Medical Insurance	$4,239	$12,689	$29,134	$56,199	$72,900	$82,222	$88,778	14.1
Hospital Insurance	2,967	9,209	20,353	37,360	45,703	50,448	54,244	13.5
Inpatient hospital	2,659	8,840	19,583	35,313	43,112	45,439	48,952	13.5
Skilled-nursing services	274	233	331	464	811	2,806	1,886	8.7
Home health services[1]	26	136	440	1,583	1,781	2,202	3,406	23.6
Supplementary Medical Insurance	1,272	3,481	8,781	18,839	27,196	31,774	34,533	15.4
Physicians' and other medical services	1,224	3,050	7,361	15,309	20,143	25,310	27,379	14.5
Outpatient services	38	374	1,261	3,499	5,843	6,407	7,077	25.5
Home health services[1]	17	56	159	31	43	57	78	6.8
				Amount reimbursed per person served				
Hospital Insurance and/or Supplementary Medical Insurance	$592	$1,055	$1,791	$2,762	$3,178	$3,445	$3,578	8.1
Hospital Insurance	749	1,855	3,379	6,167	7,515	8,196	8,520	11.2
Inpatient hospital	738	1,799	3,291	6,181	7,461	7,937	8,289	11.1
Skilled-nursing services	774	896	1,336	1,525	2,184	4,580	3,068	6.2
Home health services[1]	204	413	652	1,093	1,199	1,394	1,874	10.1
Supplementary Medical Insurance	195	296	545	933	1,192	1,338	1,399	8.9
Physicians' and other medical services	191	268	471	781	957	1,087	1,132	8.0
Outpatient services	25	99	190	354	457	482	503	13.9
Home health services[1]	145	347	526	1,122	1,359	1,614	2,033	12.2

[Continued]

★ 745 ★

Medicare: Enrollment and Reimbursements of Aged Persons, 1967-90
[Continued]

Type of coverage and service	1967	1975	1980	1985	1988	1989	1990	Average annual rate change (percent) 1967-90
	Amount reimbursed per enrollee							
Hospital Insurance and/or Supplementary Medical Insurance	$217	$557	$1,142	$1,995	$2,440	$2,704	$2,869	11.9
Hospital Insurance	152	410	811	1,350	1,559	1,689	1,781	11.3
Inpatient hospital	137	394	780	1,276	1,471	1,521	1,607	11.3
Skilled-nursing services	14	11	13	17	28	94	62	6.7
Home health services[1]	1	6	18	57	61	74	112	22.8
Supplementary Medical Insurance	71	159	356	690	945	1,088	1,163	12.9
Physicians' and other medical services	69	139	298	561	740	866	922	11.9
Outpatient services	2	17	51	128	180	219	238	23.1
Home health services[1]	1	2	6	1	1	2	3	4.9

Source: *Annual Statistical Supplement, 1992 to the Social Security Bulletin*, U.S. Department of Health and Human Services, Social Security Administration, January 1993, p. 293. *Notes:* 1. The Omnibus Reconciliation Act of 1980 (Public Law 96-499) eliminated the 100-visit limit on home health services and the 3-day prior hospitalization requirement. This made the coverage of home health services under Hospital Insurance the same as under Supplementary Medical Insurance. Because section 1833(d) of the Social Security Act requires that services that can be paid under Hospital Insurance cannot be paid under Supplementary Medical Insurance, virtually all home health services are now paid under the Hospital Insurance program.

★ 746 ★

Medicare and Medicaid

Medicare: Hospital Insurance Enrollees, by State, Geographic Division and Outlying Area, 1966-91

The health insurance program for the aged (Medicare) went into effect July 1, 1966.

[Number in thousands]

Census division and state	Aged persons									
	1966	1967	1970	1975	1980	1985	1988	1989	1990	1991
Total	19,082	19,494	20,361	22,472	25,104	27,683	29,312	29,869	30,464	31,043
United States[1]	18,798	19,189	20,015	22,062	24,617	27,144	28,737	29,282	29,866	30,435
New England	1,233	1,248	1,275	1,367	1,487	1,612	1,672	1,692	1,722	1,745
Connecticut	273	278	288	318	358	400	419	426	432	438
Maine	116	117	120	129	141	152	158	161	163	165
Massachusetts	619	625	632	662	705	751	770	776	792	800
New Hampshire	77	79	82	91	102	114	121	123	125	128
Rhode Island	100	101	105	113	123	134	139	141	143	146
Vermont	48	48	50	54	58	62	65	66	67	68
Middle Atlantic	3,788	3,833	3,928	4,144	4,428	4,724	4,880	4,925	4,980	5,048
New Jersey	655	666	693	757	840	923	963	975	988	1,002
New York	1,903	1,924	1,962	2,020	2,089	2,156	2,193	2,202	2,214	2,227
Pennsylvania	1,230	1,244	1,273	1,367	1,499	1,644	1,724	1,748	1,778	1,818

[Continued]

★ 746 ★

Medicare: Hospital Insurance Enrollees, by State, Geographic Division and Outlying Area, 1966-91
[Continued]

Census division and state	Aged persons									
	1966	1967	1970	1975	1980	1985	1988	1989	1990	1991
East North Central	3,685	3,732	3,825	4,064	4,410	4,790	5,012	5,088	5,168	5,253
Illinois	1,064	1,076	1,094	1,144	1,221	1,306	1,352	1,367	1,382	1,397
Indiana	477	483	494	529	576	627	659	672	683	695
Michigan	726	737	764	822	906	999	1,051	1,069	1,090	1,111
Ohio	966	977	995	1,056	1,144	1,251	1,320	1,342	1,366	1,394
Wisconsin	453	460	476	513	563	607	630	637	646	656
West North Central	1,862	1,889	1,926	2,033	2,166	2,286	2,358	2,382	2,409	2,435
Iowa	347	350	354	365	384	403	414	417	421	424
Kansas	259	262	268	284	301	318	329	332	335	339
Minnesota	396	402	413	439	475	509	528	534	542	549
Missouri	540	549	559	592	631	662	683	691	699	708
Nebraska	178	180	184	193	204	212	217	218	220	222
North Dakota	65	65	68	74	81	86	89	90	90	91
South Dakota	78	80	81	85	91	96	99	100	101	103
South Atlantic	2,544	2,644	2,870	3,433	4,089	4,721	5,136	5,283	5,461	5,605
Delaware	42	43	45	51	59	68	75	77	79	81
District of Columbia	67	67	66	66	66	67	66	67	67	67
Florida	757	807	931	1,230	1,549	1,820	2,001	2,070	2,165	2,221
Georgia	336	347	365	418	484	551	593	606	622	647
Maryland	265	274	291	328	373	428	462	472	484	495
North Carolina	375	387	416	486	577	670	732	752	773	796
South Carolina	176	181	193	227	271	321	354	365	375	385
Virginia	334	344	364	415	481	553	599	615	632	647
West Virginia	191	193	199	212	229	244	253	259	263	267
East South Central	1,190	1,221	1,276	1,415	1,570	1,704	1,790	1,817	1,854	1,888
Alabama	299	309	326	369	416	456	481	489	497	505
Kentucky	324	331	340	363	392	418	437	443	449	454
Mississippi	210	215	224	248	271	287	297	300	303	312
Tennessee	357	366	386	434	491	542	575	585	605	616
West South Central	1,667	1,719	1,821	2,057	2,315	2,541	2,704	2,783	2,837	2,895
Arkansas	220	226	237	265	296	318	330	335	338	346
Louisiana	280	289	304	339	375	408	432	443	450	457
Oklahoma	277	284	296	324	353	378	393	403	410	415
Texas	890	920	985	1,129	1,290	1,437	1,550	1,602	1,639	1,677
Mountain	623	644	698	837	1,030	1,233	1,372	1,421	1,473	1,522
Arizona	127	135	158	215	291	367	418	435	451	467
Colorado	177	181	189	209	240	274	300	309	318	327
Idaho	64	66	69	79	94	108	116	118	121	124
Montana	67	68	70	75	85	96	101	104	105	107

[Continued]

★ 746 ★

Medicare: Hospital Insurance Enrollees, by State, Geographic Division and Outlying Area, 1966-91

[Continued]

Census division and state	Aged persons									
	1966	1967	1970	1975	1980	1985	1988	1989	1990	1991
Nevada	25	27	31	44	64	89	109	118	127	136
New Mexico	63	66	73	90	111	132	146	151	157	161
Utah	69	71	77	90	107	126	137	141	146	150
Wyoming	29	30	31	34	38	42	45	46	47	49
Pacific	2,190	2,250	2,389	2,693	3,102	3,515	3,792	3,868	3,954	4,033
Alaska	6	6	7	8	11	5	19	20	22	23
California	1,634	1,681	1,788	2,010	2,298	2,579	2,770	2,817	2,875	2,928
Hawaii	38	40	45	56	72	92	105	111	115	119
Oregon	208	214	226	257	299	341	368	378	387	396
Washington	304	309	323	362	422	487	529	543	556	567
Residence unknown	15	9	9	19	20	17	21	21	9	11
Outlying areas	145	154	178	222	270	309	329	336	344	351
Puerto Rico	141	150	174	216	263	300	322	329	337	343
Virgin Islands	2	3	3	4	5	5	6	6	6	7
Other	1	2	2	2	2	3	1	1	1	1
Foreign countries	140	151	168	189	217	230	250	254	258	

Source: *Annual Statistical Supplement, 1992 to the Social Security Bulletin*, U.S. Department of Health and Human Services, Social Security Administration, January 1993, p. 295. *Notes:* 1. Represents those in 50 States, District of Columbia, and with residence unknown.

★ 747 ★

Medicare and Medicaid

Medicare: Enrollment, by Type of Coverage and Selected Characteristics, 1966-91

From the source: "Medicare is a Federal program for aged and disabled persons who are insured under the Social Security program.... It consists of two separate but coordinated programs: Part A is Hospital Insurance (HI) and Part B is Supplementary Medical Insurance (SMI)." Medicare is free to all eligible Social Security recipients, while SMI requires a payment of monthly premiums. Data here are shown for persons aged 65 or older.

[Number in thousands]

Age, sex, race and census region	1966	1970	1975	1980	1982	1984	1985	1986	1988	1989	1990	1991
	Hospital Insurance											
Total	19,082	20,361	22,472	25,104	26,115	27,112	27,683	28,257	29,312	30,464	30,464	31,043
Age												
65-74	11,990	12,316	13,426	14,894	15,386	15,805	16,111	16,424	16,916	17,151	17,394	17,621

[Continued]

★ 747 ★

Medicare: Enrollment, by Type of Coverage and Selected Characteristics, 1966-91

[Continued]

Age, sex, race and census region	1966	1970	1975	1980	1982	1984	1985	1986	1988	1989	1990	1991
75 or older	7,092	8,045	9,046	10,210	10,728	11,306	11,572	11,833	12,395	12,718	13,071	13,423
Sex												
Men	8,133	8,507	9,168	10,156	10,538	10,920	11,146	11,378	11,811	12,038	12,280	12,523
Women	10,950	11,855	13,304	14,948	15,577	16,192	16,536	16,879	17,500	17,831	18,184	18,520
Race												
White	17,042	18,187	19,996	22,244	23,104	23,945	24,424	24,902	25,728	26,156	26,591	26,948
All other races	1,445	1,608	1,870	2,160	2,265	2,374	2,444	2,515	2,688	2,799	2,931	3,067
Unknown	596	566	607	699	745	792	815	840	896	914	942	1,028
Census region												
United States[1]	18,798	20,015	22,062	24,617	25,612	26,587	27,144	27,705	28,737	29,282	29,866	30,435
Northeast	5,021	5,202	5,511	5,915	6,087	6,241	6,337	6,418	6,553	6,618	6,702	6,793
Midwest	5,548	5,750	6,097	6,576	6,790	6,979	7,076	7,179	7,370	7,470	7,577	7,688
South	5,402	5,966	6,905	7,974	8,348	8,736	8,966	9,195	9,630	9,883	10,152	10,288
West	2,813	3,087	3,530	4,132	4,367	4,614	4,747	4,896	5,164	5,290	5,427	5,555

Supplementary Medical Insurance

	1966	1970	1975	1980	1982	1984	1985	1986	1988	1989	1990	1991
Total	17,736	19,584	21,945	24,680	25,707	26,764	27,310	27,863	28,780	29,216	29,685	30,185
Age												
65-74	11,186	11,873	13,215	14,726	15,192	15,633	15,884	16,148	16,482	16,603	16,747	16,918
75 or older	6,550	7,711	8,730	9,954	10,515	11,131	11,426	11,715	12,298	12,613	12,938	13,267
Sex												
Men	7,534	8,132	8,873	9,868	10,250	10,652	10,852	11,058	11,403	11,569	11,758	11,971
Women	10,202	11,452	13,073	14,813	15,457	16,112	16,459	16,805	17,377	17,647	17,927	18,214
Race												
White	15,938	17,576	19,575	21,876	22,738	23,619	24,060	24,498	25,187	25,513	25,849	26,172
All other races	1,264	1,472	1,781	2,114	2,231	2,358	2,441	2,528	2,704	2,799	2,910	3,030
Unknown	534	537	589	691	738	787	810	837	889	904	927	983
Census region												
United States[1]	17,626	19,459	21,795	24,468	25,478	26,519	27,059	27,603	28,512	28,944	29,408	29,900
Northeast	4,782	5,062	5,437	5,884	6,056	6,223	6,307	6,376	6,468	6,506	6,561	6,625
Midwest	5,172	5,594	6,007	6,520	6,742	6,944	7,031	7,122	7,281	7,359	7,450	7,545
South	5,012	5,786	6,845	7,949	8,327	8,735	8,966	9,199	9,560	9,804	10,005	10,210
West	2,653	3,012	3,488	4,095	4,335	4,601	4,739	4,891	5,145	5,258	5,385	5,512

Source: *Annual Statistical Supplement, 1992 to the Social Security Bulletin*, U.S. Department of Health and Human Services, Social Security Administration, January 1993, p. 297. *Notes:* 1. Represents those in the 50 States, District of Columbia, and with residence unknown.

★ 748 ★

Medicare and Medicaid

Medicare: Hospital Insurance Bills Approved and Reimbursements, 1966-91

The number of bills approved for payment and the amount reimbursed are shown, by type of benefit and type of beneficiary, 1966-91.

[Number in thousands]

Year approved	Total[1]		Inpatient hospital[2]		Home health		Skilled-nursing facilities[3]	
	Number	Amount reimbursed	Number	Amount reimbursed	Number	Amount reimbursed	Number	Amount reimbursed
All persons								
1966	1,979	824,367	1,866	821,362	34	2,113	...	...
1970	7,512	4,855,161	6,313	4,578,080	571	46,896	627	230,183
1975	10,318	10,414,195	8,687	10,006,206	1,078	145,631	553	262,358
1979	12,831	19,321,096	10,314	18,615,371	1,997	377,732	520	327,992
1980	13,866	23,200,897	11,088	22,367,454	2,266	473,805	512	359,638
1981	14,896	27,701,752	11,508	26,639,308	2,875	666,260	513	396,185
1982	16,737	33,080,071	11,996	31,579,763	4,223	1,068,162	518	432,147
1983	17,312	36,133,754	12,107	34,337,127	4,661	1,337,527	543	459,100
1984	16,483	36,046,031	10,985	34,007,966	4,958	1,577,714	540	460,351
1985	15,615	37,533,351	10,352	35,414,544	4,747	1,656,411	515	462,396
1986	16,000	39,045,165	10,474	36,679,676	4,974	1,829,759	551	535,730
1987	15,406	39,584,874	10,262	37,225,007	4,663	1,807,762	481	552,105
1988	15,391	40,859,263	10,180	38,216,668	4,614	1,891,160	597	751,435
1989	16,325	44,955,779	9,940	40,144,211	4,979	2,224,408	1,406	2,587,160
1990	18,232	49,331,647	10,395	43,779,106	6,431	3,330,256	1,406	2,222,285
1991	20,428	55,258,108	10,658	47,969,767	8,388	5,047,391	1,381	2,240,950
Persons aged 65 or older [4]								
1973	8,080	6,550,708	6,980	6,297,814	624	60,549	476	192,345
1975	9,389	9,429,866	7,844	9,041,321	1,009	135,687	536	252,859
1979	11,385	16,999,417	9,040	16,337,003	1,847	347,921	502	314,493
1980	12,287	20,357,667	9,705	19,580,817	2,097	436,589	485	340,250
1981	13,254	24,378,817	10,098	23,384,330	2,661	613,719	495	380,769
1982	14,962	29,170,229	10,555	27,772,783	3,906	981,067	501	416,380
1983	15,540	31,959,130	10,700	30,284,469	4,315	1,231,532	525	443,129
1984	14,871	32,040,872	9,754	30,139,771	4,595	1,456,125	523	444,976
1985	14,063	33,325,618	9,160	31,348,094	4,404	1,530,937	499	446,587
1986	14,363	34,579,907	9,218	32,373,793	4,612	1,690,046	532	516,068
1987	13,882	35,322,516	9,090	33,119,345	4,327	1,671,678	465	531,493
1988	13,917	36,602,037	9,047	34,124,594	4,294	1,754,560	577	722,883
1989	14,751	40,044,850	8,774	35,522,207	4,630	2,060,815	1,347	2,461,828
1990	16,525	44,015,084	9,191	38,806,251	5,984	3,086,110	1,350	2,122,723
1991	18,548	49,332,113	9,406	42,498,728	7,812	4,682,130	1,331	2,151,255

[Continued]

★ 748 ★

Medicare: Hospital Insurance Bills Approved and Reimbursements, 1966-91
[Continued]

Year approved	Total[1]		Inpatient hospital[2]		Home health		Skilled-nursing facilities[3]	
	Number	Amount reimbursed	Number	Amount reimbursed	Number	Amount reimbursed	Number	Amount reimbursed

Disabled persons[5]

1973	215	173,178	206	170,850	6	692	4	1,637
1975	929	984,329	843	964,885	69	9,944	17	9,499
1979	1,443	2,321,679	1,274	2,278,368	150	29,811	18	13,499
1980	1,545	2,773,750	1,357	2,722,587	168	37,199	18	13,965
1981	1,642	3,322,935	1,410	3,254,978	214	52,541	18	15,416
1982	1,775	3,909,842	1,441	3,806,980	317	87,095	17	15,767
1983	1,772	4,174,624	1,407	4,052,658	346	105,995	18	15,971
1984	1,612	4,005,159	1,232	3,868,195	363	121,589	17	15,375
1985	1,552	4,207,733	1,192	4,066,450	343	125,474	16	15,809
1986	1,637	4,465,258	1,256	4,305,883	362	139,713	19	19,662
1987	1,524	4,262,358	1,172	4,105,662	335	136,084	16	20,612
1988	1,474	4,257,226	1,135	4,092,074	321	136,600	20	28,552
1989	1,574	4,910,929	1,166	4,622,004	349	163,593	59	125,332
1990	1,706	5,316,563	1,203	4,972,855	447	244,146	56	99,562
1991	1,879	5,925,995	1,253	5,471,039	577	365,261	50	89,695

Source: Annual Statistical Supplement, 1992 to the Social Security Bulletin, U.S. Department of Health and Human Services, Social Security Administration, January 1993, p. 299. *Notes:* Three dots (...) means not applicable. 1. Included in total but not shown separately are data on approved bills for outpatient diagnostic services rendered before Apr. 1, 1968. Beginning in April 1968, outpatient diagnostic services, formerly covered under Hospital Insurance are covered under Supplementary Medical Insurance. 2. The Social Security Amendments of 1983 (Public Law 98-21) replace (for most hospitals) the retrospective cost reimbursement system and the cost-per-case limits and rate of increase ceiling created by the Tax Equity and Fiscal Responsibility Act of 1982. Effective with hospital cost-ting periods beginning on or after Oct. 1, 1983, Medicare payments for inpatient operating costs are to be based on a fixed amount, determined in advance, for each case, according to one of 475 diagnosis related groups (DRG's) into which a case is classified. The prospective payment is considered payment in full; hospitals are prohibited from charging beneficiaries more than the statutory deductible and coinsurance. Additional payments, determined by nondiagnostic criteria, are made to hospitals by the program for various "pass-through" costs and additional adjustments. These additional payments are not included in the inpatient hospital billing amounts reimbursed shown in this table. 3. Coverage began Jan. 1, 1967. Benefit payments shown for 1985 are incomplete due to billing lags. 4. Beginning Oct. 1, 1978, includes a relatively small number of persons entitled to benefits solely because of end-stage renal disease. 5. Includes a relatively small number of persons under age 65 entitled to benefits solely because of end-stage renal disease.

★ 749 ★

Medicare and Medicaid

Medicare: Number of Participating Health Agencies, by Type of Facility, 1967-91

Year	Hospitals			Skilled-nursing facilities	Home health agencies	Independent laboratories
	All hospitals	General[1]	Psychiatric			
Facilities						
1967	6,829	6,501	328	4,405	1,890	2,355
1968	6,831	6,492	339	4,787	2,173	2,645
1969	6,791	6,447	344	4,786	2,311	2,676
1970	6,779	6,444	335	4,494	2,333	2,750
1971	6,741	6,401	340	4,084	2,256	2,808
1972	6,744	6,392	352	3,981	2,212	2,906
1973	6,746	6,388	358	3,961	2,222	2,961
1974	6,707	6,349	358	3,892	2,254	2,991
1975	6,770	6,383	387	3,932	2,290	3,174
1976	6,774	6,368	406	3,992	2,353	3,156
1977	6,755	6,353	402	4,461	2,496	3,249
1978	6,848	6,432	416	4,982	2,715	3,384
1979	6,780	6,372	408	5,055	2,858	3,448
1980	6,736	6,325	411	5,155	3,012	3,374
1981	6,749	6,335	414	5,295	3,169	3,511
1982	6,737	6,321	416	5,510	3,627	3,643
1983	6,687	6,257	430	5,760	4,235	3,708
1984	6,676	6,228	448	6,183	5,237	3,890
1985	6,710	6,209	501	6,725	5,932	4,029
1986	6,731	6,189	542	7,148	5,953	4,298
1987	6,715	6,130	585	7,379	5,769	4,487
1988	6,658	6,044	614	7,683	5,673	4,676
1989	6,547	5,891	656	8,688	5,661	4,828
1990	6,522	5,848	674	9,008	5,730	4,881
1991	6,471	5,759	712	10,061	5,963	4,898
Beds						
1967	1,141,155	837,211	303,944	308,843	...	...
1968	1,166,173	852,643	313,530	337,937	...	...
1969	1,182,843	863,876	318,967	360,049	...	...
1970	1,190,309	878,509	311,800	325,415	...	...
1971	1,172,353	888,205	284,148	296,090	...	...
1972	1,155,270	906,280	248,990	287,533	...	...
1973	1,147,501	919,832	227,669	290,060	...	...
1974	1,132,435	925,772	206,663	289,416	...	...

[Continued]

★ 749 ★

Medicare: Number of Participating Health Agencies, by Type of Facility, 1967-91
[Continued]

Year	Hospitals			Skilled-nursing facilities	Home health agencies	Independent laboratories
	All hospitals	General[1]	Psychiatric			
1975	1,136,908	939,717	197,191	287,468	...	...
1976	1,169,433	980,805	188,628	332,515	...	...
1977	1,130,519	976,465	154,054	381,715	...	...
1978	1,154,250	1,015,645	138,605	414,188	...	...
1979	1,152,088	1,016,525	135,563	433,715	...	...
1980	1,145,245	1,017,794	127,451	448,007	...	...
1981	1,152,877	1,032,042	120,835	463,715	...	...
1982	1,146,480	1,044,427	102,053	497,056	...	...
1983	1,143,544	1,046,674	96,870	519,551	...	...
1984	1,146,093	1,050,832	95,261	548,201	...	...
1985	1,144,589	1,046,889	97,700	[2]	...	...
1986	1,137,853	1,043,430	94,423	444,326	...	....
1987	1,124,928	1,030,556	94,372	449,867	...	...
1988	1,115,809	1,022,116	93,693	476,447	...	...
1989	1,106,295	1,008,845	97,450	507,475	...	...
1990	1,104,703	1,005,480	99,223	512,107	...	...
1991	1,102,286	1,003,147	99,139	583,116	...	...

Source: *Annual Statistical Supplement, 1992 to the Social Security Bulletin*, U.S. Department of Health and Human Services, Social Security Administration, January 1993, p. 305. *Notes:* Three dots (...) stands for not applicable. 1. Includes short-stay and other long-stay hospitals. 2. Data not available.

★ 750 ★

Medicare and Medicaid

Medicare: Participating Hospitals and Beds for the Hospital Insurance Program, by State, 1991

Census division and state	All hospitals		Short-stay			Long stay	
	Hospitals	Beds	Hospitals	Beds	Beds per 1,000 enrollees[1]	Hospitals	Beds
Total	6,471	1,102,286	5,450	965,357	31.1	1,021	136,929
United States	6,411	1,091,206	5,393	954,962	31.4	1,018	136,244
New England	299	57,272	226	45,215	25.9	73	12,057
Connecticut	52	14,429	35	11,131	25.4	17	3,298
Maine	42	4,593	39	4,390	26.6	3	203
Massachusetts	141	28,099	99	21,186	26.5	42	6,913
New Hampshire	31	3,758	26	3,168	24.7	5	590

[Continued]

★ 750 ★

Medicare: Participating Hospitals and Beds for the Hospital Insurance Program, by State, 1991
[Continued]

Census division and state	All hospitals		Short-stay			Long stay	
	Hospitals	Beds	Hospitals	Beds	Beds per 1,000 enrollees[1]	Hospitals	Beds
Rhode Island	16	4,220	12	3,341	23.0	4	879
Vermont	17	2,173	15	1,999	29.3	2	174
Middle Atlantic	678	177,901	554	142,081	28.1	124	35,820
New Jersey	115	35,242	91	30,332	30.3	24	4,910
New York	289	91,997	244	69,904	31.4	45	22,093
Pennsylvania	274	50,662	219	41,845	23.0	55	8,817
East North Central	947	194,821	814	178,812	34.0	133	16,009
Illinois	232	52,827	206	49,871	35.7	26	2,956
Indiana	153	28,638	116	25,904	37.3	37	2,734
Michigan	194	35,944	175	33,203	29.9	19	2,741
Ohio	219	55,485	188	50,187	36.0	31	5,298
Wisconsin	149	21,927	129	19,647	29.9	20	2,280
West North Central	805	92,710	739	84,383	34.7	66	8,327
Iowa	127	14,220	123	13,530	31.9	4	690
Kansas	146	13,854	131	12,096	35.7	15	1,758
Minnesota	161	19,649	151	17,509	31.9	10	2,140
Missouri	156	28,734	132	26,419	37.3	24	2,315
Nebraska	100	8,289	92	7,432	33.5	8	857
North Dakota	54	4,355	51	3,925	43.0	3	430
South Dakota	61	3,609	59	3,472	33.9	2	137
South Atlantic	996	189,640	807	166,168	29.6	189	23,472
Delaware	11	2,479	7	2,174	26.7	4	305
District of Columbia	14	5,043	10	3,946	59.3	4	1,097
Florida	286	59,350	219	53,925	24.3	67	5,425
Georgia	192	28,808	162	25,265	39.1	30	3,543
Maryland	69	18,201	51	13,621	27.5	18	4,580
North Carolina	149	27,902	129	24,282	30.5	20	3,620
South Carolina	83	13,690	70	11,944	31.0	13	1,746
Virginia	122	23,914	99	21,418	33.1	23	2,496
West Virginia	70	10,253	60	9,593	36.0	10	660
East South Central	519	80,843	461	75,340	39.9	58	5,503
Alabama	128	21,074	115	20,015	39.6	13	1,059
Kentucky	121	18,310	104	16,352	36.0	17	1,958
Mississippi	111	13,146	105	12,683	40.6	6	463
Tennessee	159	28,313	137	26,290	42.7	22	2,023
West South Central	939	122,728	760	107,608	37.2	179	15,120
Arkansas	101	12,995	84	11,222	32.4	17	1,773

[Continued]

★ 750 ★

Medicare: Participating Hospitals and Beds for the Hospital Insurance Program, by State, 1991
[Continued]

Census division and state	All hospitals		Short-stay			Long stay	
	Hospitals	Beds	Hospitals	Beds	Beds per 1,000 enrollees[1]	Hospitals	Beds
Louisiana	178	25,615	141	21,945	48.1	37	3,670
Oklahoma	147	16,845	126	15,120	36.4	21	1,725
Texas	513	67,273	409	59,321	35.4	104	7,952
Mountain	460	50,742	373	41,980	27.6	87	8,762
Arizona	90	12,722	69	10,864	23.3	21	1,858
Colorado	88	14,529	66	10,615	32.4	22	3,914
Idaho	51	3,177	44	2,814	22.7	7	363
Montana	61	3,378	57	3,208	29.9	4	170
Nevada	30	3,754	25	3,307	24.3	5	447
New Mexico	57	5,597	45	4,918	30.5	12	679
Utah	51	5,682	40	4,492	29.9	11	1,190
Wyoming	32	1,903	27	1,762	36.2	5	141
Pacific	768	124,549	659	113,375	28.1	109	11,174
Alaska	25	1,646	22	1,392	60.5	3	254
California	544	96,718	453	88,454	30.2	91	8,264
Hawaii	26	2,745	22	2,344	19.7	4	401
Oregon	71	8,622	66	8,184	20.7	5	438
Washington	102	14,818	96	13,001	22.9	6	1,817
Outlying areas	60	11,080	57	10,395	29.7	3	685
Puerto Rico	56	10,581	53	9,896	28.8	3	685
Virgin Islands	1	160	1	160	24.4	...	...
Other	3	339	3	339	1.5	...	...

Source: Annual Statistical Supplement, 1992 to the Social Security Bulletin, U.S. Department of Health and Human Services, Social Security Administration, January 1993, p. 306. *Notes:* Three dots (...) means not applicable. 1. Based on number of persons aged 65 or older enrolled in the Hospital Insurance program as of July 1, 1991.

★ 751 ★

Medicare and Medicaid

Medicare: Participating Skilled-Nursing Facilities and Other Health Care Fields, by State, 1991

Data show the number of participating skilled-nursing facilities, home health agencies, independent laboratories, and end-stage renal disease facilities.

Census division and state	Skilled-nursing facilities			Home health agencies	Inde-pendent labor-atories	End-stage renal disease facilities
	Number	Beds	Beds per 1,000 enrollees[1]			
Total	10,061	583,116	18.8	5,963	4,898	2,211
United States	10,054	582,790	19.1	5,919	4,622	2,187
New England	728	47,411	27.2	338	341	80
Connecticut	211	21,013	48.0	101	91	20
Maine	34	1,076	6.5	22	19	6
Massachusetts	354	19,991	25.0	152	162	40
New Hampshire	18	394	3.1	36	20	6
Rhode Island	86	3,775	25.9	14	46	6
Vermont	25	1,162	17.0	13	3	2
Middle Atlantic	1,434	163,220	32.3	510	633	274
New Jersey	219	19,303	19.3	56	100	37
New York	588	99,870	44.8	202	256	116
Pennsylvania	627	44,047	24.2	252	277	121
East North Central	1,827	95,840	18.2	955	557	271
Illinois	420	10,843	7.8	255	161	92
Indiana	289	9,154	13.2	142	69	38
Michigan	329	21,111	19.0	158	126	53
Ohio	579	42,692	30.6	247	148	53
Wisconsin	210	12,040	18.3	153	53	35
West North Central	1,052	57,718	23.7	757	262	152
Iowa	63	1,679	4.0	153	29	16
Kansas	90	1,740	5.1	126	58	18
Minnesota	424	38,151	69.5	194	33	34
Missouri	300	6,688	9.5	187	86	54
Nebraska	58	1,816	8.2	49	24	13
North Dakota	82	6,883	75.4	29	19	10
South Dakota	35	761	7.4	19	13	7
South Atlantic	1,655	79,269	14.1	846	713	515
Delaware	33	2,243	27.6	18	22	7
District of Columbia	11	508	7.6	14	12	21
Florida	523	20,864	9.4	254	278	152
Georgia	215	6,771	10.5	78	104	81
Maryland	168	15,062	30.4	75	110	53
North Carolina	326	14,366	18.1	132	70	65
South Carolina	150	11,469	29.8	55	26	46

[Continued]

★ 751 ★

Medicare: Participating Skilled-Nursing Facilities and Other Health Care Fields, by State, 1991
[Continued]

Census division and state	Skilled-nursing facilities			Home health agencies	Inde- pendent labor- atories	End-stage renal disease facilities
	Number	Beds	Beds per 1,000 enrollees[1]			
Virginia	164	4,521	7.0	161	58	75
West Virginia	65	3,465	13.0	59	33	15
East South Central	630	28,546	15.1	556	340	168
Alabama	211	9,838	19.5	126	98	42
Kentucky	216	9,799	21.6	103	89	28
Mississippi	49	1,388	4.4	79	51	33
Tennessee	154	7,521	12.2	248	102	65
West South Central	631	18,485	6.4	1,002	520	298
Arkansas	66	2,136	6.2	176	40	37
Louisiana	75	3,688	8.1	229	89	73
Oklahoma	39	699	1.7	92	53	34
Texas	451	11,962	7.1	505	338	154
Mountain	599	23,382	15.4	412	240	121
Arizona	131	3,078	6.6	63	65	45
Colorado	151	3,700	11.3	118	62	19
Idaho	71	2,143	17.3	32	19	7
Montana	92	3,968	37.0	44	11	7
Nevada	35	3,554	26.1	24	26	6
New Mexico	29	569	3.5	56	25	19
Utah	63	5,497	36.6	41	19	16
Wyoming	27	873	17.9	34	13	2
Pacific	1,498	68,919	17.1	543	1,016	308
Alaska	7	235	10.2	9	7	2
California	1,147	59,788	20.4	395	835	254
Hawaii	31	1,937	16.3	23	30	12
Oregon	110	2,044	5.2	61	51	16
Washington	203	4,915	8.7	55	93	24
Outlying areas	7	326	.9	44	276	24
Puerto Rico	6	290	.8	42	270	21
Virgin Islands	...	...	...	1	...	...
Other	1	36	51.1	1	6	3

Source: *Annual Statistical Supplement, 1992 to the Social Security Bulletin*, U.S. Department of Health and Human Services, Social Security Administration, January 1993, p. 307. *Notes:* Three dots (...) means not applicable. 1. Based on number of persons aged 65 or older enrolled in the Hospital Insurance program as of July 1, 1991.

★ 752 ★

Medicare and Medicaid

Medicaid Recipients and Amounts Spent, by Category of Recipient, 1972-1991

Data show the unduplicated number of recipients, total vendor payments, and average amounts spent on each group, by type of eligibility category for fiscal years 1972-91[1].

Fiscal year	Total	Aged 65 or older	Blindness	Permanent and total disability	Dependent children under age 21	Adults in families with dependent children	Other
Number (in thousands)							
1972	17,606	3,318	108	1,625	7,841	3,137	1,576
1975	22,007	3,615	109	2,355	9,598	4,529	1,800
1976	22,815	3,612	97	2,572	9,924	4,774	1,836
1977	22,832	3,636	92	2,710	9,651	4,785	1,959
1978	21,965	3,376	82	2,636	9,376	4,643	1,852
1979	21,520	3,364	79	2,674	9,106	4,570	1,727
1980	21,605	3,440	92	2,819	9,333	4,877	1,499
1981	21,980	3,367	86	2,993	9,581	5,187	1,364
1982	21,603	3,240	84	2,806	9,563	5,356	1,434
1983	21,554	3,371	77	2,844	9,535	5,592	1,129
1984	21,607	3,238	79	2,834	9,684	5,600	1,187
1985	21,814	3,061	80	2,937	9,757	5,518	1,214
1986	22,515	3,140	82	3,100	10,029	5,647	1,362
1987	23,109	3,224	85	3,296	10,168	5,599	1,418
1988	22,907	3,159	86	3,401	10,037	5,503	1,343
1989	23,511	3,132	95	3,496	10,318	5,717	1,175
Amount (in millions)							
1972	$6,300	$1,925	$45	$1,354	$1,139	$962	$875
1975	12,242	4,358	93	3,052	2,186	2,062	492
1976	14,091	4,910	96	3,824	2,431	2,288	542
1977	16,239	5,499	116	4,767	2,610	2,606	641
1978	17,992	6,308	116	5,505	2,748	2,673	643
1979	20,472	7,046	108	6,774	2,884	3,021	638
1980	23,311	8,739	124	7,497	3,123	3,231	596
1981	27,204	9,926	154	9,301	3,508	3,763	552
1982	29,399	10,739	172	10,233	3,473	4,093	689
1983	32,391	11,954	183	11,184	3,836	4,487	747
1984	33,891	12,815	219	11,758	3,979	4,420	700
1985	37,508	14,096	249	13,203	4,414	4,746	798
1986	41,005	15,097	277	14,635	5,135	4,880	980
1987	45,050	16,037	309	16,507	5,508	5,592	1,078
1988	48,710	17,135	344	18,250	5,848	5,883	1,198

[Continued]

★ 752 ★

Medicaid Recipients and Amounts Spent, by Category of Recipient, 1972-1991
[Continued]

Fiscal year	Total	Aged 65 or older	Blindness	Permanent and total disability	Dependent children under age 21	Adults in families with dependent children	Other
1989	54,500	18,558	409	20,476	6,892	6,897	1,268
1990	64,859	21,508	434	23,969	9,100	8,590	1,257
1991	77,048	25,453	475	27,798	11,690	10,439	1,193
Average amount							
1972	$358	$580	$417	$833	$145	$307	$555
1975	556	1,205	850	1,296	228	455	273
1976	618	1,359	990	1,487	245	479	295
1977	711	1,512	1,258	1,759	270	545	327
1978	819	1,869	1,412	2,088	293	576	347
1979	951	2,094	1,369	2,534	317	661	369
1980	1,079	2,540	1,358	2,659	335	663	398
1981	1,238	2,948	1,784	3,108	366	725	405
1982	1,361	3,315	2,047	3,646	363	764	480
1983	1,503	3,545	2,379	3,932	402	802	662
1984	1,569	3,957	2,766	4,149	411	789	590
1985	1,719	4,605	3,104	4,496	452	860	658
1986	1,821	4,808	3,401	4,721	512	864	719
1987	1,949	4,975	3,644	5,008	542	999	761
1988	2,126	5,425	4,005	5,366	583	1,069	891
1989	2,318	5,926	4,317	5,858	668	1,206	1,079
1990	2,568	6,717	5,212	6,595	811	1,429	1,138
1991	2,725	7,577	5,572	6,979	871	1,540	1,813

Source: Annual Statistical Supplement, 1992 to the Social Security Bulletin, U.S. Department of Health and Human Services, Social Security Administration, January 1993, p. 309. *Notes:* 1. Fiscal year 1977 began in October 1976 and was the first year of the new Federal fiscal cycle. Before 1977, the fiscal year began in July. Beginning in fiscal year 1980, recipients' categories do not add to unduplicated total because of the small number of recipients that are in more than one category during the year.

Chapter 12
NURSING HOMES AND RESIDENT CARE

The topics covered in this chapter include Population Summary, Population Characteristics, Nursing Home Costs, Causes for Admission, Cognitive Disabilities, Mental Illness, Mobility Impairment, Effects of Restraints, and Safety Issues. The word "population," as used here, refers to nursing home populations.

Information of a related nature may be found in the chapters on *Health and Health Care*, *Health Insurance*, and *Demography*.

Population Summary

★ 753 ★

Nursing Home Population, by Region, Division, and State: 1980 and 1990

Region, division, and State	Number			Percent change, 1980 to 1990	Percentage of population in 1990
	1980	1990	Change, 1980 to 1990		
United States	1,426,371	1,772,032	345,661	24.2	0.7
Northeast	327,319	399,329	72,010	22.0	0.8
New England	106,344	119,646	13,302	12.5	0.9
Middle Atlantic	220,975	279,683	58,708	26.6	0.7
Midwest	472,568	544,650	72,082	15.3	0.9
East North Central	296,088	346,243	50,155	16.9	0.8
West North Central	176,480	198,407	21,927	12.4	1.1
South	396,554	558,382	161,828	40.8	0.7
South Atlantic	163,080	270,930	107,850	66.1	0.6
East South Central	77,060	102,900	25,840	33.5	0.7

[Continued]

★ 753 ★

Nursing Home Population, by Region, Division, and State: 1980 and 1990

[Continued]

Region, division, and State	Number			Percent change, 1980 to 1990	Percentage of population in 1990
	1980	1990	Change, 1980 to 1990		
West South Central	156,414	184,552	28,138	18.0	0.7
West	229,930	269,671	39,741	17.3	0.5
Mountain	47,139	65,842	18,703	39.7	0.5
Pacific	182,791	203,829	21,038	11.5	0.5
New England	106,344	119,646	13,302	12.5	0.9
Maine	9,570	9,855	285	3.0	0.8
Vermont	4,354	4,809	455	10.5	0.9
New Hampshire	6,673	8,202	1,529	22.9	0.7
Massachusetts	49,728	55,662	5,934	11.9	0.9
Rhode Island	8,146	10,156	2,010	24.7	1.0
Connecticut	27,873	30,962	3,089	11.1	0.9
Middle Atlantic	220,975	279,683	58,708	26.6	0.7
New York	114,276	126,175	11,899	10.4	0.7
New Jersey	34,414	47,054	12,640	36.7	0.6
Pennsylvania	72,285	106,454	34,169	47.3	0.9
East North Central	296,088	346,243	50,155	16.9	0.8
Ohio	71,479	93,769	22,290	31.2	0.9
Indiana	40,112	50,845	10,733	26.8	0.9
Illinois	80,410	93,662	13,252	16.5	0.8
Michigan	55,805	57,622	1,817	3.3	0.6
Wisconsin	48,282	50,345	2,063	4.3	1.0
West North Central	176,480	198,407	21,927	12.4	1.1
Minnesota	44,553	47,051	2,498	5.6	1.1
Iowa	36,217	36,455	238	0.7	1.3
Missouri	37,942	52,060	14,118	37.2	1.0
North Dakota	7,486	8,159	673	9.0	1.3
South Dakota	8,087	9,356	1,269	15.7	1.3
Nebraska	17,650	19,171	1,521	8.6	1.2
Kansas	24,545	26,155	1,610	6.6	1.1
South Atlantic	163,080	270,930	107,850	66.1	0.6
Delaware	2,771	4,596	1,825	65.9	0.7
Maryland	19,821	26,884	7,063	35.6	0.6
District of Columbia	2,866	7,008	4,142	144.5	1.2
Virginia	24,323	37,762	13,439	55.3	0.6
West Virginia	6,355	12,591	6,236	98.1	0.7
North Carolina	29,596	47,014	17,418	58.9	0.7
South Carolina	11,666	18,228	6,562	56.2	0.5

[Continued]

★ 753 ★

Nursing Home Population, by Region, Division, and State: 1980 and 1990
[Continued]

Region, division, and State	Number			Percent change, 1980 to 1990	Percentage of population in 1990
	1980	1990	Change, 1980 to 1990		
Georgia	29,376	36,549	7,173	24.4	0.6
Florida	36,306	80,298	43,992	121.2	0.6
East South Central	77,060	102,900	25,840	33.5	0.7
Kentucky	23,591	27,874	4,283	18.2	0.8
Tennessee	22,014	35,192	13,178	59.9	0.7
Alabama	18,702	24,031	5,329	28.5	0.6
Mississippi	12,753	15,803	3,050	23.9	0.6
West South Central	156,414	184,552	28,138	18.0	0.7
Arkansas	18,631	21,809	3,178	17.1	0.9
Louisiana	22,776	32,072	9,296	40.8	0.8
Oklahoma	25,732	29,666	3,934	15.3	0.9
Texas	89,275	101,005	11,730	13.1	0.6
Mountain	47,139	65,842	18,703	39.7	0.5
Montana	5,479	7,764	2,285	41.7	1.0
Idaho	5,084	6,318	1,234	24.3	0.6
Wyoming	2,198	2,679	481	21.9	0.6
Colorado	16,109	18,506	2,397	14.9	0.6
New Mexico	2,585	6,276	3,691	142.8	0.4
Arizona	8,424	14,472	6,048	71.8	0.4
Utah	4,921	6,222	1,301	26.4	0.4
Nevada	2,339	3,605	1,266	54.1	0.3
Pacific	182,791	203,829	21,038	11.5	0.5
Washington	27,970	32,840	4,870	17.4	0.7
Oregon	16,052	18,200	2,148	13.4	0.6
California	134,756	148,362	13,606	10.1	0.5
Alaska	854	1,202	348	40.7	0.2
Hawaii	3,159	3,225	66	2.1	0.3

Source: Sixty-Five Plus in America, Cynthia M. Taeuber, U.S. Department of Commerce, Economics and Statistics Administration, Bureau of the Census, U.S. Government Printing Office, Washington, D.C., 1992, pp. 6-11 - 6-12. Primary source: U.S. Bureau of the Census, 1980 from 1980 Census of Population, *Persons in Institutions and Other Group Quarters*, PC80-2-4D; 1990 from 1990 Census of Population and Housing, Summary Tape File 1A.

★ 754 ★
Population Summary

Nursing Homes with 25 or More Beds and Number of Beds, According to Geographic Division and State: United States, 1976, 1982, and 1986

[Data are based on reporting by facilities]

Geographic division and state	Nursing homes				Number of beds			
	1976	1982	1986		1976	1982	1986	
			Number	% of U.S. total			Number	% of U.S. total
United States	14,133	14,565	16,033	100.0	1,291,632	1,469,357	1,615,771	100.0
New England	1,211	1,246	1,235	7.7	91,885	105,293	108,474	6.7
Maine	121	155	144	0.9	7,027	9,717	9,685	0.6
New Hampshire	68	70	75	0.5	5,633	6,729	6,987	0.4
Vermont	53	51	47	0.3	3,477	3,196	3,083	0.2
Massachusetts	645	620	612	3.8	47,169	50,366	51,126	3.2
Rhode Island	85	95	101	0.6	6,766	8,885	9,927	0.6
Connecticut	239	255	256	1.6	21,813	26,400	27,666	1.7
Middle Atlantic	1,567	1,587	1,921	12.0	187,435	210,010	243,962	15.1
New York	708	732	777	4.8	97,489	108,898	114,192	7.1
New Jersey	313	332	356	2.2	31,147	36,638	39,071	2.4
Pennsylvania	546	523	788	4.9	58,799	64,474	90,699	5.6
East North Central	2,904	2,966	2,999	18.7	281,144	326,171	330,342	20.4
Ohio	750	830	886	5.5	60,680	74,276	82,522	5.1
Indiana	420	449	449	2.8	35,799	47,196	47,257	2.9
Illinois	805	809	775	4.8	84,085	99,777	96,684	6.0
Michigan	508	471	480	3.0	53,966	55,349	53,651	3.3
Wisconsin	421	407	409	2.6	46,614	49,573	50,228	3.1
West North Central	1,965	2,171	2,142	13.4	157,057	185,774	187,781	11.6
Minnesota	385	390	399	2.5	38,177	42,500	44,357	2.7
Iowa	440	475	440	2.7	31,785	38,150	34,942	2.2
Missouri	408	530	552	3.4	32,539	46,403	50,204	3.1
North Dakota	82	80	81	0.5	6,413	6,402	6,789	0.4
South Dakota	117	116	114	0.7	8,047	7,938	7,918	0.5
Nebraska	210	225	214	1.3	18,408	18,516	18,132	1.1
Kansas	323	355	342	2.1	21,688	25,865	25,439	1.6
South Atlantic	1,475	1,745	2,152	13.4	142,245	177,495	212,382	13.1
Delaware	22	27	36	0.2	2,123	2,194	3,345	0.2
Maryland	165	179	200	1.2	18,559	21,164	24,402	1.5
District of Columbia	17	16	19	0.1	2,604	2,556	3,029	0.2
Virginia	208	267	288	1.8	23,816	29,251	29,653	1.8
West Virginia	73	95	103	0.6	4,858	7,505	8,692	0.5
North Carolina	276	346	402	2.5	20,903	28,156	34,049	2.1
South Carolina	102	130	157	1.0	8,311	11,560	14,071	0.9
Georgia	304	306	298	1.9	28,732	32,194	31,738	2.0
Florida	308	379	649	4.0	32,339	42,915	63,403	3.9

[Continued]

★ 754 ★

Nursing Homes with 25 or More Beds and Number of Beds, According to Geographic Division and State: United States, 1976, 1982, and 1986

[Continued]

Geographic division and state	Nursing homes				Number of beds			
	1976	1982	1986		1976	1982	1986	
			Number	% of U.S. total			Number	% of U.S. total
East South Central	856	865	887	5.5	66,994	85,565	90,180	5.6
Kentucky	267	276	277	1.7	19,929	25,837	26,426	1.6
Tennessee	258	251	267	1.7	19,448	26,111	28,599	1.8
Alabama	209	190	203	1.3	19,207	20,490	21,736	1.3
Mississippi	122	148	140	0.9	8,410	13,127	13,419	0.8
West South Central	1,740	1,789	1,922	12.0	157,173	177,237	189,920	11.8
Arkansas	208	200	237	1.5	19,322	19,327	21,910	1.4
Louisiana	200	224	276	1.7	18,969	24,836	32,747	2.0
Oklahoma	341	359	382	2.4	25,990	28,902	30,359	1.9
Texas	991	1,006	1,027	6.4	92,892	104,172	104,904	6.5
Mountain	495	529	631	3.9	41,881	47,857	57,414	3.6
Montana	69	59	57	0.4	4,725	5,120	4,804	0.3
Idaho	54	47	60	0.4	4,263	4,102	5,240	0.3
Wyoming	22	25	27	0.2	1,753	2,060	2,301	0.1
Colorado	174	157	183	1.1	17,792	16,848	18,402	1.1
New Mexico	30	31	56	0.3	2,489	2,351	4,915	0.3
Arizona	67	109	134	0.8	5,832	9,888	12,740	0.8
Utah	63	76	84	0.5	3,707	5,025	5,995	0.4
Nevada	16	25	30	0.2	1,320	2,463	3,017	0.2
Pacific	1,920	1,667	2,144	13.4	165,818	153,955	195,316	12.1
Washington	318	309	328	2.0	29,415	30,017	32,021	2.0
Oregon	202	177	214	1.3	15,758	15,711	17,404	1.1
California	1,369	1,148	1,569	9.8	118,144	105,325	143,179	8.9
Alaska	8	10	10	0.1	738	1,031	1,082	0.1
Hawaii	23	23	23	0.1	1,763	1,871	1,630	0.1

Source: U.S. Department of Commerce, Economics and Statistics Administration, *National Economic, Social, and Environmental Data Bank, CD-ROM,* November 1992. Primary source: Division of Health Care Statistics, National Center for Health Statistics: *Trends in Nursing and Related Care Homes and Hospitals, United States, Selected Years 1969-80,* by G. W. Strahan. Vital and Health Statistics. Series 14, No. 30. DHHS Pub. No. (PHS) 84-1825. Public Health Service. Washington. U.S. Government Printing Office, Mar. 1984; *Nursing and Related Care Homes as reported from the 1982 National Master Facility Inventory Survey,* by D. A. Roper. Vital and Health Statistics. Series 14, No. 32. DHHS Pub. No. (PHS) 86-1827. Public Health Service. Washington. U.S. Government Printing Office, Sept. 1986; data from the National Master Facility Inventory; Final data from the 1986 Inventory of Long-Term Care Places; Resident population computed by the Division of Analysis, National Center for Health Statistics from the Compressed Mortality File, a county-level national mortality and population data base. *Notes:* The 1982 inventory excluded certain types of nursing homes that the 1976 and 1986 inventories included (nursing home units of hospitals, nursing homes for the blind, etc.). To make the data comparable, these types of homes and their beds were subtracted from the 1976 and 1986 figures. 1. Number of beds per 1,000 resident population 85 years of age and over.

★ 755 ★

Population Summary

Nursing Home Residents

Nursing home residents 65 years of age and over per 1,000 population, according to age, sex, and race: 1963, 1973-74, 1977, and 1985.

Age, sex, and race	Residents per 1,000 population[1]			
	1963	1973-74[2]	1977[3]	1985
Age				
All ages	25.4	44.7	47.1	46.2
65-74 years	7.9	12.3	14.4	12.5
75-84 years	39.6	57.7	64.0	57.7
85 years and over	148.4	257.3	225.9	220.3
Sex				
Male	18.1	30.0	30.3	29.0
65-74 years	6.8	11.3	12.6	10.8
75-84 years	29.1	39.9	44.9	43.0
85 years and over	105.6	182.7	146.3	145.7
Female	31.1	54.9	58.6	57.9
65-74 years	8.8	13.1	15.8	13.8
75-84 years	47.5	68.9	75.4	66.4
85 years and over	175.1	294.9	262.4	250.1
Race[4]				
White	26.6	46.9	48.9	47.7
65-74 years	8.1	12.5	14.2	12.3
75-84 years	41.7	60.3	67.0	59.1
85 years and over	157.7	270.8	234.2	228.7
Black	10.3	22.0	30.7	5.0
65-74 years	5.9	11.1	17.6	15.4
75-84 years	13.8	26.7	33.4	45.3
85 years and over	41.8	105.7	133.6	141.5

Source: Health Data on Older Americans: United States, 1992, Centers for Disease Control and Prevention/National Center for Health Statistics, Vital and Health Statistics, Series 3: Analytic and Epidemiological Studies, No. 27, p. 144. *Notes:* 1. Residents per 1,000 population for 1973-74 and 1977 differ from those presented in the original source reports because the rates have been recomputed using revised census estimates for these years. 2. Excludes residents in personal care or domiciliary care homes. 3. Includes residents in domiciliary care homes. 4. For data years 1973-74 and 1977, all people of Hispanic origin were included in the white category. For 1963, "black" includes all other races.

★ 756 ★

Population Summary

Nursing Home Residents 65 Years of Age and Older by Age, Sex, and Race in the United States in 1985

Age, sex, and race	Residents	Percent	Number of residents 65 years and older per 1,000 population 65 years and older
Total	1,318,000	100.0	46.2
Age			
65-74 years	212,100	16.1	12.5
75-84 years	509,000	38.6	57.7
85 years or older	597,300	45.3	220.3
Sex			
Male	334,400	25.4	29.0
Female	983,900	74.6	57.9
Race			
White	1,227,400	93.1	42.7
Black	82,000	6.2	35.0
Other	8,900	0.7	20.1

Source: U.S. Congress, "Profiles in Aging America: Meeting the Health Care Needs of the Nation's Black Elderly," Joint Hearing Before the Special Committee on Aging and the Congressional Black Caucus Health Braintrust, United States Senate, September 28, 1990, 101-29, U.S. Government Printing Office, Washington, D.C., p. 132. Primary source: *The National Nursing Home Survey: 1985 Summary for the United States*, Hing, E., Sekscenski, E., Strahan, G., "Vital Health Statistics," Series 13, No. 97, U.S. Dept. of Health and Human Services, Public Health Service, National Center for Health Statistics, Jan. 1989, pp. 23-4. *Note:* Figures may not add to 100 because of rounding.

★ 757 ★

Population Summary

Nursing Home Concerns of Families

Category	What troubled them[1] (N=51)	How many see this as their top concern (N=21)
Admission process	8 (15.7%)	5 (23.8%)
Elder leaving own home	3	2
Elder resisting admission	3	2
Selecting a nursing home	2	1

[Continued]

★ 757 ★

Nursing Home Concerns of Families
[Continued]

Category	What troubled them[1] (N=51)	How many see this as their top concern (N=21)
Care provided by staff	16 (31.4%)	5 (23.8%)
Inadequate environment	3	0
Inadequate care	12	5
Use of restraints	1	0
Feelings of family members	7 (13.7%)	3 (14.3%)
Guilt	4	2
Fear that placement will be permanent	3	1
Feelings of residents	15 (29.4%)	6 (28.6%)
Depression	4	0
Loneliness	6	4
Loss of independence	3	1
Unhappiness	2	1
Financing nursing home care	5 (9.8%)	2 (9.5%)

Source: Valarie L. Sorrels, "Nursing Home Fears", *Geriatric Nursing*, September- October 1991, p. 237.
Note: 1. Family members listed more than one concern.

Population Characteristics

★ 758 ★

Nursing Home Residents, According to Selected Functional Status and Age: United States, 1977 and 1985

[Data are based on a sample of nursing homes]

Functional status	1977					1985				
	All ages	Under 65 years	65-74 years	75-84 years	85 years and over	All ages	Under 65 years	65-74 years	75-84 years	85 years and over
					Number of residents					
	1,303,100	177,100	211,400	464,700	449,900	1,491,400	173,100	212,100	509,000	597,300
					Percent distribution					
Total	100.0	100.0	100.0	100.0	100.0	100.0	100.0	100.0	100.0	100.0
Dressing										
Independent	30.6	44.8	38.8	27.5	24.2	24.6	41.1	29.8	24.1	18.3
Requires assistance[1]	69.4	55.2	61.2	72.5	75.8	75.4	58.9	70.2	75.9	81.7
Using toilet room										
Independent	47.5	61.8	53.1	45.7	41.0	39.1	57.1	43.4	39.7	32.0
Requires assistance	42.5	28.1	37.8	44.7	48.0	48.9	31.5	45.8	47.8	55.9
Does not use	10.1	10.1	9.1	9.6	11.0	12.0	11.4	10.8	12.6	12.1
Mobility										
Walks independently	33.9	53.6	43.2	33.2	22.5	29.3	51.0	39.6	30.4	18.4
Walks with assistance	28.8	15.7	21.4	30.5	35.6	24.8	13.5	20.4	24.7	29.6
Chairfast	32.0	25.5	30.5	31.5	35.9	39.5	29.3	33.7	38.7	45.1
Bedfast	5.3	5.2	5.0	4.9	6.1	6.5	6.2	6.3	6.1	6.9
Continence										
No difficulty controlling bowel or bladder	54.7	68.0	62.4	52.9	47.8	48.1	67.7	57.1	45.0	41.9
Difficulty controlling--										
Bowel	3.7	3.0	3.7	4.0	3.8	1.9	1.5[3]	2.0[3]	1.7	2.2
Bladder	9.0	5.8	6.5	9.4	11.1	10.3	6.4	6.8	11.0	12.0
Bowel and bladder	25.9	16.8	20.6	26.9	30.8	31.7	16.8	27.5	33.6	35.8
Ostomy in either bowel or bladder	6.7	6.4	6.8	6.9	6.5	8.1	7.5	6.6	8.7	8.1
Eating										
Independent	67.4	73.8	72.9	66.2	63.5	60.7	68.5	66.6	60.9	56.1
Requires assistance[2]	32.6	26.2	27.1	33.8	36.5	39.3	31.5	33.4	39.1	43.9
Vision										
Not impaired	67.2	81.0	75.4	67.9	57.2	75.9	88.5	83.3	77.8	68.1
Partially impaired	19.0	10.9	13.4	19.6	24.1	14.6	5.9	10.0	14.2	19.1
Severely impaired	6.6	2.2	3.3	6.1	10.4	5.6	1.9[3]	4.3	4.1	8.4

[Continued]

★ 758 ★

Nursing Home Residents, According to Selected Functional Status and Age: United States, 1977 and 1985

[Continued]

Functional status	1977					1985				
	All ages	Under 65 years	65-74 years	75-84 years	85 years and over	All ages	Under 65 years	65-74 years	75-84 years	85 years and over
Completely lost	2.9	2.2	2.6	2.6	3.8	2.5	2.5[3]	1.3[3]	2.1	3.2
Unknown	4.3	3.8	5.3	3.9	4.5	1.4	1.2[3]	1.0[3]	1.8	1.2
Hearing										
Not impaired	69.5	87.6	81.0	71.6	54.9	78.5	96.1	90.4	82.6	65.7
Partially impaired	21.7	6.6	11.4	21.2	33.1	16.7	3.1[3]	7.4	14.8	25.5
Severely impaired	4.3	0.4[3]	1.9	3.0	8.4	3.4	0.1[3]	1.1[3]	1.5	6.8
Completely lost	0.7	1.1[3]	0.7[3]	0.6[3]	0.7[3]	0.6	0.1[3]	0.4[3]	0.6[3]	0.8[3]
Unknown	3.7	4.4	5.0	3.6	3.0	0.8	0.5[3]	0.7[3]	0.5[3]	1.1

Source: U.S. Department of Commerce, Economics and Statistics Administration, *National Economic, Social, and Environmental Data Bank, CD-ROM,* November 1992. Primary source: Division of Health Care Statistics, National Center for Health Statistics: *Characteristics of Nursing Home Residents, Health Status, and Care Received: National Nursing Home Survey, United States, May-December 1977,* by E. Hing. Vital and Health Statistics. Series 13, No. 51. DHHS Pub. No. (PHS) 81-1712. Public Health Service. Washington. U.S. Government Printing Office, April 1981; *The National Nursing Home Survey: 1985 Summary for the United States,* by E. Hing, E. Sekscenski, and G. Strahan. Vital and Health Statistics. Series 13, No. 97. DHHS Pub. No. (PHS) 89-1758. Public Health Service. Washington. U.S. Government Printing Office, Jan. 1989. *Notes:* 1. Includes those who do not dress. 2. Includes those who are tube or intravenously fed. 3. Relative standard error greater than 30 percent.

★ 759 ★
Population Characteristics

Nursing Home Residents with Selected Cognitive Disabilities Who Have Depression/Anxiety Disorders - Part I

Percent of nursing home residents, by presence of selected cognitive disabilities, sex, age, race, and presence of depression or anxiety: 1985. Data are based on personal interviews of the nursing home staff most knowledgeable about the residents sampled.

Sex, age, and race	Total	No cognitive disabilities	Cognitive dis- abilities[1]	Organic brain syndromes	Alzheimer's disease	Schizophrenia and other psychoses
			Number			
All residents	1,489,500	485,100	1,004,400	68,000	79,200	194,200
			Percent			
All statuses	100.0	100.0	100.0	100.0	100.0	100.0
Depression	23.6	12.3	29.1	25.3	24.9	34.9
Anxiety	25.4	10.4	32.7	31.0	31.6	37.3
Neither	57.1	74.4	48.8	50.7	50.5	44.2
Sex						
Male						
Depression	6.3	3.2	7.7	6.2	7.7	11.1
Anxiety	6.5	2.6	8.4	7.4	10.0	9.6

[Continued]

★ 759 ★

Nursing Home Residents with Selected Cognitive Disabilities Who Have Depression/Anxiety Disorders - Part I

[Continued]

Sex, age, and race	Total	No cognitive disabilities	Cognitive dis-abilities[1]	Organic brain syndromes	Alzheimer's disease	Schizophrenia and other psychoses
Neither	17.4	22.2	15.1	13.0	14.4	15.6
Female						
Depression	17.3	9.0	21.3	19.0	16.9	23.8
Anxiety	18.9	7.9	24.3	23.6	21.7	27.6
Neither	39.7	52.0	33.7	37.7	35.8	28.6
Age						
Under 65 years						
Depression	3.1	1.3	3.9	1.5	1.4[3]	11.1
Anxiety	2.9	0.7[3]	3.9	1.6	2.3[3]	10.2
Neither	6.4	5.0	7.1	2.2	3.3[3]	10.4
65-74 years						
Depression	4.1	2.4	5.0	3.9	5.8[3]	8.2
Anxiety	4.1	1.5	5.3	4.0	7.1[3]	8.3
Neither	7.3	8.9	6.6	5.1	9.4	10.4
75-84 years						
Depression	8.4	4.6	10.2	9.1	11.0	8.7
Anxiety	8.4	3.7	10.7	10.3	12.8	9.9
Neither	19.6	27.3	16.0	18.3	22.9	12.2
65 years and over						
Depression	20.4	11.0	25.0	23.6	23.4	23.5
Anxiety	22.5	9.7	28.7	29.2	29.2	26.7
Neither	50.3	68.6	41.5	48.4	47.3	33.6
75 years and over						
Depression	16.3	8.6	20.0	19.7	17.8	15.1
Anxiety	18.4	8.2	23.3	25.1	22.2	18.5
Neither	43.0	59.7	35.0	43.2	38.0	23.1
85 years and over						
Depression	7.9	3.9	9.9	10.6	6.7[3]	6.5
Anxiety	10.0	4.6	12.6	14.9	9.4	8.6
Neither	23.4	32.4	19.0	25.0	14.9	10.9
Race[2]						
White						
Depression	21.9	11.6	26.9	23.3	22.7	33.1
Anxiety	24.0	10.1	30.7	29.0	29.3	34.9
Neither	52.3	67.8	44.9	46.5	48.2	38.9
Black						
Depression	1.5	0.6[3]	1.9	1.7	2.0[3]	1.7[3]

[Continued]

★ 759 ★

Nursing Home Residents with Selected Cognitive Disabilities Who Have Depression/Anxiety Disorders - Part I

[Continued]

Sex, age, and race	Total	No cognitive disabilities	Cognitive disabilities[1]	Organic brain syndromes	Alzheimer's disease	Schizophrenia and other psychoses
Anxiety	1.3	0.2[3]	1.8	1.8	2.2[3]	2.2[3]
Neither	4.3	5.8	3.5	4.0	1.4[3]	4.6

Source: Health Data on Older Americans: United States, 1992, Centers for Disease Control and Prevention/National Center for Health Statistics, Vital and Health Statistics, Series 3: Analytic and Epidemiological Studies, No. 27, pp. 167-168. Primary source: National Center for Health Statistics: Data from the National Nursing Home Survey. Notes: Presence of depression or anxiety means that depression or anxiety is displayed to such a degree that functioning is restricted. Column percents may exceed 100 because a resident may have had both depression and anxiety. 1. Includes residents with all types of cognitive disabilities. Residents with multiple disabilities are counted only once in the total. 2. Excludes races other than White and Black. 3. Figure does not meet standard of reliability or precision.

★ 760 ★

Population Characteristics

Nursing Home Residents with Selected Cognitive Disabilities Who Have Depression/Anxiety Disorders - Part II

Percent of nursing home residents, by presence of selected cognitive disabilities, sex, age, race, and presence of depression or anxiety: 1985. Data are based on personal interviews of the nursing home staff most knowledgeable about the residents sampled.

Sex, age, and race	Total	Depressive disorders	Anxiety disorders	Alcohol and drug abuse	Mental retardation
			Number		
All residents	1,489,500	214,800	215,000	58,700	82,800
			Percent		
All statuses	100.0	100.0	100.0	100.0	100.0
Depression	23.6	71.4	50.9	28.8	14.9
Anxiety	25.4	49.1	71.7	34.9	28.4
Neither	57.1	20.2	18.6	50.7	63.7
Sex					
Male					
Depression	6.3	17.8	13.3	17.2	6.4
Anxiety	6.5	11.6	18.8	19.8	13.4
Neither	17.4	6.2	5.6	34.5	28.2
Female					
Depression	17.3	53.6	37.6	11.4	8.4
Anxiety	18.9	37.4	52.9	14.9	15.0
Neither	39.7	14.0	12.9	16.1	35.7

[Continued]

★ 760 ★

Nursing Home Residents with Selected Cognitive Disabilities Who Have Depression/Anxiety Disorders - Part II
[Continued]

Sex, age, and race	Total	Depressive disorders	Anxiety disorders	Alcohol and drug abuse	Mental retardation
Age					
Under 65 years					
Depression	3.1	10.6	8.0	8.3[3]	5.3[3]
Anxiety	2.9	7.4	8.6	8.5[3]	9.8
Neither	6.4	2.9	4.4	15.5	38.8
65-74 years					
Depression	4.1	12.4	9.2	6.3[3]	3.9[3]
Anxiety	4.1	9.3	12.4	10.6[3]	9.5
Neither	7.3	4.1	2.1[3]	16.3	12.4
75-84 years					
Depression	8.4	26.5	19.3	8.3[3]	3.9[3]
Anxiety	8.4	18.3	26.7	10.5	5.6[3]
Neither	19.6	7.8	5.9	13.5	9.5
65 years and over					
Depression	20.4	60.4	42.6	19.7	9.6
Anxiety	22.5	41.5	62.8	26.3	18.6
Neither	50.3	17.1	13.6	34.5	24.4
75 years and over					
Depression	16.3	47.9	33.3	13.2	5.6[3]
Anxiety	18.4	32.2	50.4	15.9	8.9
Neither	43.0	13.1	11.6	18.6	11.6
85 years and over					
Depression	7.9	21.5	14.0	5.0[3]	1.7[3]
Anxiety	10.0	13.8	23.8	5.3[3]	3.4[3]
Neither	23.4	5.3	5.7	5.3[3]	2.1[3]
Race[2]					
White					
Depression	21.9	66.2	47.2	27.2	13.0
Anxiety	24.0	46.0	66.4	31.0	26.3
Neither	52.3	19.6	17.0	43.8	59.3
Black					
Depression	1.5	4.0	3.4	1.5[3]	1.3[3]

[Continued]

★ 760 ★

Nursing Home Residents with Selected Cognitive Disabilities Who Have Depression/Anxiety Disorders - Part II
[Continued]

Sex, age, and race	Total	Depressive disorders	Anxiety disorders	Alcohol and drug abuse	Mental retardation
Anxiety	1.3	2.4[3]	4.7	3.6[3]	1.6[3]
Neither	4.3	0.8[3]	1.1[3]	6.0[3]	3.5[3]

Source: *Health Data on Older Americans: United States, 1992*, Centers for Disease Control and Prevention/National Center for Health Statistics, Vital and Health Statistics, Series 3: Analytic and Epidemiological Studies, No. 27, pp. 167-168. Primary source: National Center for Health Statistics: Data from the National Nursing Home Survey. *Notes:* Presence of depression or anxiety means that depression or anxiety is displayed to such a degree that functioning is restricted. Column percents may exceed 100 because a resident may have had both depression and anxiety. 1. Includes residents with all types of cognitive disabilities. Residents with multiple disabilities are counted only once in the total. 2. Excludes races other than White and Black. 3. Figure does not meet standard of reliability or precision.

★ 761 ★
Population Characteristics

Nursing Home Residents with Selected Cognitive Disabilities, by Prior Living Arrangement, 1985 - Part I

Data are based on the personal interviews of the nursing home staff most knowledgeable about the residents sampled.

Age and living arrangement prior to admission	Total	No cognitive disabilities	Cognitive disabilities[1]	Organic brain syndromes	Alzheimer's disease	Schizophrenia and other psychoses
			Number			
All ages	1,441,600	470,300	971,300	664,600	78,253	185,500
			Percent			
All arrangements	100.0	100.0	100.0	100.0	100.0	100.0
Private or semiprivate residence[2]	39.3	42.8	37.5	40.5	46.3	26.8
Alone	13.9	18.1	11.9	12.5	10.0	9.9
With others	22.4	21.1	23.0	25.0	34.2	14.8
Another health facility[2]	60.7	57.2	62.5	59.5	53.7	73.2
Nursing home	5.3	5.4	5.3	5.4	4.9[3]	4.2
Mental hospital, unit, or center	5.1	0.2[3]	7.4	3.5	2.7[3]	22.5
65 years and over						
Private or semiprivate residence[2]	36.3	40.6	34.2	39.5	44.8	22.3

[Continued]

★ 761 ★

Nursing Home Residents with Selected Cognitive Disabilities, by Prior Living Arrangement, 1985 - Part I

[Continued]

Age and living arrangement prior to admission	Total	No cognitive disabilities	Cognitive disabi-lities[1]	Organic brain syndromes	Alzheimer's disease	Schizophrenia and other psychoses
Alone	13.4	18.0	11.2	12.2	9.9	8.3
With others	20.2	19.3	20.7	24.4	33.9	12.1
Another health facility[2]	52.2	51.8	52.4	55.7	48.1	50.7
Nursing home	4.8	4.8	4.8	5.2	4.9[3]	3.6
Mental hospital, unit, or center	2.7	0.2[3]	3.9	2.6	2.3[3]	11.4
75 years and over						
Private or semiprivate residence[2]	32.1	35.7	30.4	36.0	36.7	17.5
Alone	12.2	16.1	10.3	11.5	9.2	7.1
With others	17.5	16.5	18.0	21.8	26.7	9.1
Another health facility[2]	42.3	43.9	41.5	47.4	35.1	32.9
Nursing home	4.0	4.0	4.0	4.6	-	2.8[3]
Mental hospital, unit, or center	1.6	0.1[3]	2.3	2.0	1.8[3]	5.3
85 years and over						
			Percent			
Private or semiprivate residence[2]	18.1	20.4	17.0	20.8	16.0	9.7
Alone	7.2	9.2	6.3	7.3	4.9[3]	3.8
With others	9.4	9.2	9.5	11.7	10.9	4.7
Another health facility[2]	22.5	23.1	22.2	27.8	14.5	13.8
Nursing home	1.8	1.9	1.8	2.3	0.6[3]	1.0[3]
Mental hospital, unit, or center	0.5	0.1[3]	0.7	0.8[3]	1.0[3]	1.7[3]

Source: *Health Data on Older Americans: United States, 1992,* Centers for Disease Control and Prevention/National Center for Health Statistics, Vital and Health Statistics, Series 3: Analytic and Epidemiological Studies, No. 27, pp. 177-178. Primary source: National Center for Health Statistics: Data from the National Nursing Home Survey. *Notes:* Column percents may not add to 100 because of rounding. "-" indicates quantity is zero. 1. Includes residents with all types of cognitive disabilities. Residents with multiple disabilities are counted only once in the total. 2. Does not add to total shown because of missing information and other categories. 3. Figure does not meet standard of reliability or precision.

★ 762 ★

Population Characteristics

Nursing Home Residents with Selected Cognitive Disabilities, by Prior Living Arrangement, 1985 - Part II

Data are based on the personal interviews of the nursing home staff most knowledgeable about the residents sampled.

Age and living arrangement prior to admission	Total	Depressive disorders	Anxiety disorders	Alcohol and drug abuse	Mental retardation
			Number		
All ages	1,441,600	206,600	209,900	55,800	79,600
			Percent		
All arrangements	100.0	100.0	100.0	100.0	100.0
Private or semiprivate residence[2]	39.3	36.4	35.3	29.4	28.5
Alone	13.9	13.5	13.0	12.2	4.0[3]
With others	22.4	20.8	20.0	15.6	22.7
Another health facility[2]	60.7	63.6	64.7	70.6	71.5
Nursing home	5.3	5.8	5.9	7.5[3]	4.4[3]
Mental hospital, unit, or center	5.1	6.7	7.3	6.4[3]	25.4
65 years and over					
Private or semiprivate residence[2]	36.3	32.7	31.2	23.4	12.5
Alone	13.4	12.4	11.6	10.4[3]	2.7[3]
With others	20.2	18.5	17.5	11.5	9.2
Another health facility[2]	52.2	52.8	53.4	47.2	35.0
Nursing home	4.8	5.3	5.5	6.6[3]	2.8[3]
Mental hospital, unit, or center	2.7	3.9	3.2	2.9[3]	9.4
75 years and over					
Private or semiprivate residence[2]	32.1	28.9	27.6	16.6	5.2[3]
Alone	12.2	11.5	10.1	8.2[3]	1.1[3]
With others	17.5	15.7	15.6	7.7[3]	4.1[3]
Another health facility[2]	42.3	38.6	41.0	25.1	16.9
Nursing home	4.0	4.4	4.5	4.1[3]	0.7[3]
Mental hospital, unit, or center	1.6	1.3[3]	1.3[3]	1.1[3]	5.5[3]

[Continued]

★ 762 ★

Nursing Home Residents with Selected Cognitive Disabilities, by Prior Living Arrangement, 1985 - Part II

[Continued]

Age and living arrangement prior to admission	Total	Depressive disorders	Anxiety disorders	Alcohol and drug abuse	Mental retardation
85 years and over					
			Percent		
Private or semiprivate residence[2]	18.1	13.5	13.9	7.5[3]	1.0[3]
Alone	7.2	6.3	4.6	4.1[3]	-
With others	9.4	6.2	7.6	3.1[3]	0.8[3]
Another health facility[2]	22.5	16.9	18.7	5.8[3]	4.5[3]
Nursing home	1.8	1.6[3]	1.9[3]	0.4[3]	-
Mental hospital, unit, or center	0.5	0.4[3]	0.2[3]	0.7[3]	0.4[3]

Source: *Health Data on Older Americans: United States, 1992,* Centers for Disease Control and Prevention/National Center for Health Statistics, Vital and Health Statistics, Series 3: Analytic and Epidemiological Studies, No. 27, pp. 177-178. Primary source: National Center for Health Statistics: Data from the National Nursing Home Survey. *Notes:* Column percents may not add to 100 because of rounding. "-" indicates quantity is zero. 1. Includes residents with all types of cognitive disabilities. Residents with multiple disabilities are counted only once in the total. 2. Does not add to total shown because of missing information and other categories. 3. Figure does not meet standard of reliability or precision.

★ 763 ★

Population Characteristics

Primary Nursing: Questionnaire Results

Based on results of a questionnaire distributed to nurses one year after the primary nurse concept was introduced at the Primary Nurse Convention of 1977. Nurses were asked to evaluate the effects of primary nursing with respect to care delivered, professional nursing practice, relationship with other disciplines, and job satisfaction. Those who had worked under both team nursing and primary nursing were asked to rate each category against both types. The results are shown in the table below.

Care delivered	Primary nursing	Team nursing	Percentage difference
Individualized	4.18	3.0	+23.0
Knowledge of resident	4.1	3.0	+22.0
Meeting of resident needs	3.9	2.6	-26.0
Maximizing resident potential	3.8	2.8	+20.0
Perceptions of resident's response to nursing care	4.3	3.2	+22.0
Perceptions of family's response to nursing care	4.5	3.0	+30.0

[Continued]

★ 763 ★

Primary Nursing: Questionnaire Results

[Continued]

Care delivered	Primary nursing	Team nursing	Percentage difference
Relationship with others			
Interaction with peers/same shift	4.0	3.2	+16.0
Collaboration with other disciplines	4.0	3.0	+20.0
Interaction with peers/other shifts	3.3	2.3	+20.0
Staff meetings	3.8	2.8	+20.0
Relationship with nursing administration	3.8	2.7	+22.0
Professional nursing practice			
Professional satisfaction	3.9	2.6	+26.0
Level of accountability	4.6	3.2	+26.0
Ability to implement nursing decisions	4.4	2.4	+40.0
Ability to implement nursing care using nursing process	4.2	3.1	+22.0

Source: U.S. Congress, "Resident Assessment: The Springboard to Quality of Care and Quality of Life for Nursing Home Residents," Workshop before the Special Committee on Aging, United States Senate, October 22, 1990, 101-30, U.S. Government Printing Office, Washington, D.C., p. 299. Primary source: National League for Nursing, 10 Columbus Circle, New York, NY 10019, "Partnerships Between Nursing and Nursing Home Residents," Associate Degree Nursing.

Nursing Home Costs

★ 764 ★

Projected Nursing Home Expenditures for Persons Aged 65+, by Source of Payment: 1990, 2005, and 2020

[Numbers in billions of 1989 dollars]

Source of payment	1990	2005	2020
Medicare	1.1	1.8	3.2
Medicaid	15.7	27.0	45.0
Out-of-pocket	20.8	35.2	64.4
Total	37.6	64.0	112.6

Source: Aging America, Trends and Projections, prepared by the U.S. Senate Special Committee on Aging, the American Association of Retired Persons, the Federal Council on the Aging, and the U.S. Administration on Aging, 1991, Washington, D.C., p. 172. Primary source: Brookings/ICF *Long Term-Care Financing Model,* unpublished data, 1990.

★ 765 ★

Nursing Home Costs

Nursing Home Residents with Selected Cognitive Disabilities, by Primary Source of Payment, 1985 - Part I

Data are based on personal interviews of the nursing home staff most knowledgeable about the residents sampled.

Age and primary source of payment in last month	Total	No cognitive disabilities	Cognitive disabi-lities[1]	Organic brain syndromes	Alzheimer's disease	Schizophrenia and other psychoses
			Number			
All sources	1,470,100	476,300	993,800	682,100	79,400	191,100
All ages						
			Percent			
Total	100.0	100.0	100.0	100.0	100.0	100.0
Own income or family support	42.2	48.2	39.4	41.2	52.4	32.8
Medicare	1.4	2.5	0.9	1.1	0.4[3]	1.1[3]
Medicaid:						
Total	51.0	44.3	54.3	54.4	43.5	56.1
Skilled care	17.8	14.8	19.2	20.0	16.8	17.1
Intermediate care	33.2	29.4	35.0	34.4	26.4	39.3
Veteran's Administration contract	1.1	1.0[3]	1.2	1.0	1.9[3]	2.5[3]
All other[2]	4.2	4.0	4.3	2.1	1.6[3]	7.2
65 years and over						
All sources	88.4	92.0	86.7	94.9	93.4	72.8
Own income or family support	39.0	45.8	35.7	39.7	51.2	24.3
Medicare	1.4	2.4	0.9	1.1	0.4[3]	1.1[3]
Medicaid:						
Total	44.3	39.7	46.6	51.5	39.4	42.3
Skilled care	15.2	12.8	16.3	18.7	15.5	11.7
Intermediate care	29.1	27.0	30.2	32.7	24.3	30.7
Veteran's Administration contract	0.7	0.7[3]	0.7	0.7[3]	1.6[3]	1.2[3]
All other[2]	3.1	3.5	2.9	1.9	0.7[3]	4.0
75 years and over						
All sources	74.5	79.8	72.0	83.2	71.7	50.4
Own income or family support	34.1	40.2	31.3	35.5	42.4	19.2
Medicare	1.0	1.6	0.8	1.0	0.4[3]	0.7[3]

[Continued]

★ 765 ★

Nursing Home Residents with Selected Cognitive Disabilities, by Primary Source of Payment, 1985 - Part I

[Continued]

Age and primary source of payment in last month	Total	No cognitive disabilities	Cognitive disabi- lities[1]	Organic brain syndromes	Alzheimer's disease	Schizophrenia and other psychoses
Medicaid:						
Total	36.9	35.0	37.9	44.9	28.7	27.8
Skilled care	13.1	11.4	13.8	16.8	13.3	8.9
Intermediate care	23.9	23.6	24.0	28.0	15.0	18.9
Veteran's Administration						
contract	0.4[3]	0.4[3]	0.3[3]	0.4[3]	0.3[3]	0.3[3]
All other[2]	2.1	2.8	1.7	1.5	0.5[3]	2.3[3]
85 years and over						
			Percent			
All sources	40.6	43.7	39.1	48.4	30.1	23.1
Own income or family						
support	18.5	22.0	16.9	20.2	15.1	9.3
Medicare	0.4[3]	0.7[3]	0.2[3]	0.3[3]	-	0.3[3]
Medicaid:						
Total	20.6	19.1	21.3	26.9	14.9	13.0
Skilled care	7.5	6.0	8.2	10.3	6.7[3]	5.0
Intermediate care	13.1	13.1	13.1	16.6	8.2	7.9
Veteran's Administration						
contract	0.1[3]	0.2[3]	0.1[3]	0.2[3]	-	0.1[3]
All other[2]	1.0	1.7	0.7	0.9[3]	0.3[3]	0.6[3]

Source: *Health Data on Older Americans: United States, 1992*, Centers for Disease Control and Prevention/National Center for Health Statistics, Vital and Health Statistics, Series 3: Analytic and Epidemiological Studies, No. 27, pp. 175-176. Primary source: National Center for Health Statistics: Data from the National Nursing Home Survey. *Notes:* Column percents may not add to 100 because of rounding. "-" indicates quantity is zero. 1. Includes residents with all types of cognitive disabilities. Residents with multiple disabilities are counted only once in the total. 2. Includes other Government assistance or welfare, religious or volunteer agencies, life care, and other sources. 3. Figure does not meet standard of reliability or precision.

★ 766 ★

Nursing Home Costs

Nursing Home Residents with Selected Cognitive Disabilities, by Primary Source of Payment, 1985 - Part II

Data are based on personal interviews of the nursing home staff most knowledgeable about the residents sampled.

Age and primary source of payment in last month	Total	Depressive disorders	Anxiety disorders	Alcohol and drug abuse	Mental retardation
			Number		
All sources	1,470,100	211,700	213,200	57,300	82,300
All ages					
			Percent		
Total	100.0	100.0	100.0	100.0	100.0
Own income or family support	42.2	41.3	40.5	32.5	18.1
Medicare	1.4	0.7[3]	1.0[3]	1.1[3]	0.5[3]
Medicaid:					
Total	51.0	52.8	52.1	51.0	64.7
Skilled care	17.8	16.9	20.3	20.5	16.9
Intermediate care	33.2	35.8	31.8	30.7	48.6
Veteran's Administration contract	1.1	1.4[3]	1.0[3]	6.1[3]	0.4[3]
All other[2]	4.2	4.1	5.4	8.2[3]	16.3
65 years and over					
All sources	88.4	86.6	84.2	72.6	45.8
Own income or family support	39.0	36.8	36.0	26.0	8.4
Medicare	1.4	0.7[3]	1.0[3]	0.7[3]	0.5[3]
Medicaid:					
Total	44.3	45.9	42.8	37.5	30.1
Skilled care	15.2	14.1	16.4	12.1	7.6
Intermediate care	29.1	31.8	26.3	25.4	22.4
Veteran's Administration contract	0.7	0.2[3]	0.5[3]	3.5[3]	-
All other[2]	3.1	2.7[3]	3.9	4.7[3]	7.4
75 years and over					
All sources	74.5	68.3	67.8	42.0	21.3
Own income or family support	34.1	29.9	29.9	14.9	4.3[3]

[Continued]

★ 766 ★

Nursing Home Residents with Selected Cognitive Disabilities, by Primary Source of Payment, 1985 - Part II

[Continued]

Age and primary source of payment in last month	Total	Depressive disorders	Anxiety disorders	Alcohol and drug abuse	Mental retardation
Medicare	1.0	0.6[3]	0.8[3]	0.5[3]	0.5[3]
Medicaid:					
Total	36.9	35.6	34.6	24.6	14.5
Skilled care	13.1	11.2	13.6	7.7[3]	3.7[3]
Intermediate care	23.9	24.5	21.1	16.5	10.7
Veteran's Administration contract	0.4[3]	0.2[3]	-	1.7[3]	-
All other[2]	2.1	1.7[3]	2.5[3]	1.1[3]	2.6[3]
85 years and over					
			Percent		
All sources	40.6	30.4	32.5	13.5	5.8[3]
Own income or family support	18.5	13.0	13.9	6.6[3]	1.0[3]
Medicare	0.4[3]	0.2[3]	0.3[3]	-	0.5[3]
Medicaid:					
Total	20.6	16.3	17.2	6.9[3]	3.7[3]
Skilled care	7.5	6.0	7.2	1.7[3]	2.0[3]
Intermediate care	13.1	10.3	10.0	5.0[3]	1.6[3]
Veteran's Administration contract	0.1[3]	-	-	-	-
All other[2]	1.0	1.1[3]	1.2[3]	-	0.1[3]

Source: Health Data on Older Americans: United States, 1992, Centers for Disease Control and Prevention/National Center for Health Statistics, Vital and Health Statistics, Series 3: Analytic and Epidemiological Studies, No. 27, pp. 175-176. Primary source: National Center for Health Statistics: Data from the National Nursing Home Survey. *Notes:* Column percents may not add to 100 because of rounding. "-" indicates quantity is zero. 1. Includes residents with all types of cognitive disabilities. Residents with multiple disabilities are counted only once in the total. 2. Includes other Government assistance or welfare, religious or volunteer agencies, life care, and other sources. 3. Figure does not meet standard of reliability or precision.

★ 767 ★

Nursing Home Costs

Average Total Monthly Charge of Nursing Home Residents, by Mental Condition and Selected Resident Characteristics: United States, 1985

[Data are shown in dollars]

Resident characteristic	All residents	Mental condition	
		With mental disorders	Without mental disorders
Age			
Under 65 years	1,379	1,275	1,704
65 years and over	1,466	1,488	1,426
65-74 years	1,372	1,360	1,398
75-84 years	1,468	1,487	1,435
85 years and over	1,497	1,539	1,427
Sex			
Male	1,438	1,395	1,519
Female	1,463	1,485	1,420
Race			
White	1,454	1,459	1,443
Black and other	1,481	1,466	1,506
Black	1,451	1,400	1,540
Hispanic origin			
Hispanic	1,400	1,457	1,225
Non-Hispanic[1]	1,457	1,460	1,453
Current marital status			
Married	1,540	1,470	1,676
Widowed[1]	1,472	1,513	1,403
Divorced or separated	1,362	1,288	1,505
Never married	1,382	1,364	1,430
Has living children			
Yes	1,485	1,505	1,451
No or unknown	1,413	1,398	1,444

Source: U.S. Department of Health and Human Services, National Center for Health Statistics, Vital and Health Statistics, *Mental Illness in Nursing Homes: United States, 1985*, Series 13: Data from the National Health Survey, No. 105, p. 12. *Notes:* Figures may not add to totals because of rounding. 1. Includes a small number of unknowns.

Causes for Admission

★ 768 ★

Prior Living Arrangements of Nursing Home Residents with Next of Kin: United States, 1985

Usual living arrangement prior to admission[1]	Mental condition					
	With mental disorders			Without mental disorders		
	All residents with next of kin	Under 65 years	65 years and over	All residents with next of kin	Under 65 years	65 years and over
Total	100.0	100.0	100.0	100.0	100.0	100.0
Usual living quarters						
Private or semi-private residence	67.5	47.4	70.4	75.0	57.2	76.3
Own home or apartment	37.7	19.4	40.3	46.6	31.5	47.8
Relative's home or apartment	20.2	18.9	20.3	19.6	19.6	19.6
Other private home or apartment	3.6	6.2	3.2	3.5	1.9	3.6
Retirement home	4.4	0.8	4.9	3.6	5	3.9
Boarding house, rooming house, or rented room	1.7	2.2	1.6	1.7	4.1	1.5
Another health facility	27.5	42.0	25.4	20.0	36.7	18.7
Another nursing home	18.3	14.3	18.9	13.4	23.8	12.6
General or short-term hospital	4.5	8.8	3.9	5.7	11.3	5.3
Mental hospital	3.5	14.7	1.9	0.1	5	0.1
Chronic disease or other long-term care hospital	1.0	4.2	0.6	0.8	1.7	0.8
Other place or unknown	5.0	10.6	4.2	5.1	6.1	5.0
Type of usual living arrangement						
Lived alone	22.7	8.1	24.8	34.0	7.7	36.0
Lived with spouse only	10.9	2.3	12.1	9.5	10.2	9.5
Lived with spouse and other relatives	1.7	2.5	1.6	1.9	5.8	1.6
Lived with son or daughter	13.6	3.7	15.0	13.8	7.2	14.4
Lived with other relatives	8.7	20.5	7.0	8.0	20.7	7.0
Lived with unrelated persons	3.6	5.1	3.3	2.2	1.4	2.3
Group quarters[2]	6.1	2.8	6.5	5.3	4.1	5.4
Another health facility, other place, or unknown[3]	32.9	54.9	29.7	25.3	43.1	23.9
Who lived with resident[4]						
Spouse	13.0	4.8	14.1	11.5	16.0	11.2
Children	14.8	5.6	16.2	15.2	12.2	15.4
Parents	2.3	14.3	0.6	1.4	14.9	0.4
Siblings	4.2	6.3	3.9	4.2	8.6	3.9

[Continued]

★ 768 ★

Prior Living Arrangements of Nursing Home Residents with Next of Kin: United States, 1985

[Continued]

Usual living arrangement prior to admission[1]	Mental condition					
	With mental disorders			Without mental disorders		
	All residents with next of kin	Under 65 years	65 years and over	All residents with next of kin	Under 65 years	65 years and over
Grandchildren	5.9	2.8	6.3	6.7	3.9	6.9
Other relatives	12.2	9.3	12.6	12.5	13.0	12.4
Nonrelatives	6.5	7.3	6.4	5.2	2.2	5.4

Source: U.S. Department of Health and Human Services, National Center for Health Statistics, Vital and Health Statistics, Mental Illness in Nursing Homes: United States, 1985, Series 13: Data from the National Health Survey, No. 105, p. 33. Notes: 1. Living arrangements are as reported by next of kin. 2. Includes retirement home, boarding house, rooming house, and rented room. 3. Includes a small number of residents with usual living quarters in a private or semi-private residence but whose usual living arrangements are unknown. 4. Includes persons who usually lived with the resident in a private or semi-private residence prior to admission. 5. Data not available.

★ 769 ★

Causes for Admission

Distribution of Nursing Home Residents with Next of Kin, by Reason for Admission, Prior State of Health, Age, Sex, and Race: United States, 1985

[Distribution is in percent]

Reason for admission and prior state of health[1]	All residents with mental disorders and next of kin	Age					Sex		Race	
		Under 65 years	Total	65 years and over			Male	Female	White	Black and other
				65-74 years	75-84 years	85 years and over				
Total	100.0	100.0	100.0	100.0	100.0	100.0	100.0	100.0	100.0	100.0
Main medical reason for admission										
Hip fracture	5.3	1.1	5.9	2.5	3.4	9.3	2.3	6.4	5.7	0.8
Other fracture	1.2	0.3	1.3	0.5	1.0	1.8	0.3	1.5	1.2	0.3
Arthritis	1.4	3	1.6	1.3	1.6	1.8	0.8	1.7	1.5	1.1
Other condition of bones, muscles, or joints	2.2	1.1	2.4	0.9	2.3	3.1	1.7	2.4	2.4	0.4
Stroke	9.7	4.8	10.4	13.5	11.2	8.6	10.3	9.5	9.4	13.6
Atherosclerosis	4.2	3	4.8	1.3	5.9	5.1	3.0	4.6	4.4	1.4
Other heart or circulatory condition	4.4	2.3	4.7	3.8	5.2	4.5	3.9	4.6	4.3	4.6
Cancer, all types	1.3	3.1	1.1	1.0	1.3	0.9	2.7	0.8	1.4	0.4
Alzheimer's disease	9.6	3.3	10.5	14.9	13.9	6.0	9.3	9.6	9.9	4.9
Confused or forgetful	4.9	0.5	5.5	1.1	4.7	7.7	3.2	5.5	4.7	7.4
Senility	5.7	0.7	6.4	3.0	6.5	7.6	2.8	6.8	5.7	6.3
Other emotional, mental, or nervous condition	14.0	47.9	9.1	21.5	8.8	5.1	21.1	11.4	13.5	20.6
Parkinson's disease	1.7	1.4	1.7	1.1	2.9	0.9	2.7	1.3	1.8	0.4
Central nervous system diseases or injuries	2.5	9.3	1.5	3.9	1.4	0.8	4.4	1.8	2.6	1.7
Dizziness, fainting, or falls	1.1	0.8	1.2	0.1	0.7	1.9	0.5	1.4	1.2	0.4
Loss of vision or hearing	2.0	0.8	2.1	2.5	2.0	2.1	1.9	2.0	1.8	3.2
Respiratory condition	1.6	0.5	1.7	2.7	1.9	1.3	1.4	1.7	1.7	0.4
Diseases of the digestive or endocrine systems	2.6	2.3	2.7	4.3	2.1	2.6	2.9	2.5	2.4	5.5
Genitourinary diseases	0.8	0.3	0.8	0.2	1.0	0.9	0.8	0.8	0.8	0.8

[Continued]

★ 769 ★

Distribution of Nursing Home Residents with Next of Kin, by Reason for Admission, Prior State of Health, Age, Sex, and Race: United States, 1985

[Continued]

Reason for admission and prior state of health[1]	All residents with mental disorders and next of kin	Age					Sex		Race	
		Under 65 years	Total	65 years and over			Male	Female	White	Black and other
				65-74 years	75-84 years	85 years and over				
No main medical reason	2.7	0.8	3.0	2.0	2.9	3.5	1.9	3.1	2.7	3.6
Old age or general debilitation	2.7	0.7	3.0	0.9	2.6	4.2	2.4	2.8	2.8	1.7
Other medical reason or unknown	18.4	18.3	18.4	17.0	16.8	20.3	19.7	17.9	18.3	20.1
General reason for admission[2]										
Recuperation from surgery or illness	29.6	19.5	31.0	34.2	30.3	30.5	28.1	30.1	29.5	30.9
No one at home to provide care	62.4	54.9	63.4	58.8	64.0	64.6	59.6	63.4	62.1	65.2
Not enough money to purchase nursing care at home	41.0	45.0	40.4	46.3	42.2	36.9	40.6	41.2	40.0	53.9
Required more care than household members could give	79.1	74.1	79.8	79.1	79.9	79.9	79.4	78.9	79.1	79.0
Problems in doing everyday activities	72.6	62.6	74.0	71.4	73.4	75.4	67.7	74.4	72.3	75.2
Because spouse entered	2.6	0.3	2.9	1.9	2.3	3.9	3.4	2.4	2.7	2.0
State of health before admission										
Suddenly ill or injured	14.3	8.9	15.1	12.1	12.5	18.4	13.2	14.8	14.4	13.9
Gradually worsening	51.6	28.3	54.9	46.5	59.3	54.3	46.0	53.7	51.6	52.2
In poor condition most of year	15.7	23.6	14.6	20.4	14.8	12.5	19.7	14.3	15.6	17.3
Other health status	15.1	30.9	12.8	17.5	10.2	13.5	16.7	14.5	15.2	13.6
Unknown	3.2	8.3	2.5	3.6	3.3	1.3	4.4	2.7	3.2	3.2

Source: U.S. Department of Health and Human Services, National Center for Health Statistics, Vital and Health Statistics, *Mental Illness in Nursing Homes: United States, 1985*, Series 13: Data from the National Health Survey, No. 105, p. 34. *Notes:* 1. Reasons for admission and prior states of health are as reported by next of kin. 2. Figures may not add to totals because resident may have had more than one reason for admission to nursing home. 3. Data not available.

★ 770 ★

Causes for Admission

Nursing Home Residents with Next of Kin, by Reason for Admission, Prior State of Health, Age, and Mental Condition: United States, 1985

[Distribution is in percent]

Reason for admission and prior state of health	Mental condition					
	With mental disorders			Without mental disorders		
	All residents with next of kin	Under 65 years	65 years and over	All residents with next of kin	Under 65 years	65 years and over
Total	100.0	100.0	100.0	100.0	100.0	100.0
Main medical reason for admission						
Hip fracture	5.3	1.1	5.9	6.8	0.8	7.3
Other fracture	1.2	0.3	1.3	2.1	[1]	2.2
Arthritis	1.4	[1]	1.6	4.3	0.8	4.6
Other condition of bones, muscles, or joints	2.2	1.1	2.4	3.9	1.9	4.1
Stroke	9.7	4.8	10.4	19.4	22.7	19.2
Atherosclerosis	4.2	[1]	4.8	1.6	1.9	1.6
Other heart or circulatory condition	4.4	2.3	4.7	6.5	4.1	6.7
Cancer, all types	1.3	3.1	1.1	3.0	1.9	3.1

[Continued]

★ 770 ★

Nursing Home Residents with Next of Kin, by Reason for Admission, Prior State of Health, Age, and Mental Condition: United States, 1985

[Continued]

Reason for admission and prior state of health	Mental condition					
	With mental disorders			Without mental disorders		
	All residents with next of kin	Under 65 years	65 years and over	All residents with next of kin	Under 65 years	65 years and over
Alzheimer's disease	9.6	3.3	10.5	0.4	[1]	0.5
Confused or forgetful	4.9	0.5	5.5	2.2	[1]	2.3
Senility	5.7	0.7	6.4	1.4	[1]	1.5
Other emotional, mental, or nervous condition	14.0	47.9	9.1	2.4	5.0	2.2
Parkinson's disease	1.7	1.4	1.7	2.1	3.3	2.0
Central nervous system diseases or injuries	2.5	9.3	1.5	4.5	30.7	2.5
Dizziness, fainting, or falls	1.1	0.8	1.2	1.3	[1]	1.4
Loss of vision or hearing	2.0	0.8	2.1	2.8	1.7	2.9
Respiratory condition	1.6	0.5	1.7	2.4	0.8	2.6
Diseases of the digestive or endocrine systems	2.6	2.3	2.7	3.9	2.8	4.0
Genitourinary diseases	0.8	0.3	0.8	1.2	[1]	1.3
No main medical reason	2.7	0.8	3.0	4.8	0.8	5.1
Old age or general debilitation	2.7	0.7	3.0	2.7	[1]	2.9
Other medical reason or unknown	18.4	18.3	18.4	19.9	21.0	19.9
General reason for admission						
Recuperation from surgery or illness	29.6	19.5	31.0	42.9	38.1	43.3
No one at home to provide care	62.4	54.9	63.4	66.8	59.1	67.4
Not enough money to purchase nursing care at home	41.0	45.0	40.4	39.7	47.8	39.1
Required more care than household members could give	79.1	74.1	79.8	74.6	82.0	74.0
Problems in doing everyday activities	72.6	62.6	74.0	76.4	74.9	76.6
Because spouse entered	2.6	0.3	2.9	3.4	0.8	3.6
State of health before admission						
Suddenly ill or injured	14.3	8.9	15.1	22.4	24.9	22.3
Gradually worsening	51.6	28.3	54.9	45.4	28.5	46.7
In poor condition most of year	15.7	23.6	14.6	16.8	22.7	16.3
Other health status	15.1	30.9	12.8	13.8	21.3	13.2
Unknown	3.2	8.3	2.5	1.6	3.0	1.5

Source: U.S. Department of Health and Human Services, National Center for Health Statistics, Vital and Health Statistics, *Mental Illness in Nursing Homes: United States, 1985*, Series 13: Data from the National Health Survey, No. 105, p. 35. *Notes:* Figures may not add to totals because resident may have had more than one reason for admission to nursing home. 1. Data not available.

Cognitive Disabilities

★ 771 ★

Nursing Home Residents with Selected Cognitive Disabilities per 1000 Persons
United States, 1985]

Cognitive disabilities	Average rate	Age				Race		Sex	
		Under 65 years	65-74 years	75-84 years	85 years and over	White	Black	Male	Female
None	326	207	294	346	351	324	343	324	326
One or more	674	793	706	654	649	676	657	676	674
Organic brain syndromes	461	186	385	477	551	460	479	397	486
Alzheimer's disease and other degeneration of the brain	53	31[1]	82	66	40	55	34[1]	55	52
Schizophrenia and other psychoses	130	316	212	103	74	128	153	152	122
Depressive disorders	144	178	186	159	108	147	101	129	150
Anxiety disorders	144	195	165	152	116	145	135	137	147
Alcohol and drug abuse	39	101	81	33	13	38	60	89	20
Mental retardation	56	263	98	27	1[1]	56	45[1]	89	42

Source: *Health Data on Older Americans: United States, 1992,* Centers for Disease Control and Prevention/National Center for Health Statistics, Vital and Health Statistics, Series 3: Analytic and Epidemiological Studies, No. 27, p. 146. *Note:* 1. Figure does not meet the standard of reliability or precision.

★ 772 ★

Cognitive Disabilities

Cognitive Disabilities of Nursing Home Discharges

Rate of cognitive disabilities per 1,000 nursing home discharges: 1984-85.

Cognitive disabilities	Rate
None	727
One or more	273
Organic brain syndromes	141
Alzheimer's disease and other degeneration of the brain	39
Schizophrenia and other psychoses	62
Depressive disorders	24
Anxiety disorders	11
Alcohol and drug abuse	22
Mental retardation	10

Source: *Health Data on Older Americans: United States, 1992,* Centers for Disease Control and Prevention/National Center for Health Statistics, Vital and Health Statistics, Series 3: Analytic and Epidemiological Studies, No. 27, p. 152.

★ 773 ★

Cognitive Disabilities

Nursing Home Residents with Selected Cognitive Disabilities, by Race - Part I

Number and percent of nursing home residents, by presence of selected cognitive disabilities, sex, age, and race: 1985. Data are based on personal interviews of the nursing home staff most knowledgeable about the residents sampled.

Sex, age, and race	Total	No cognitive disabilities	Cognitive disabilities[1]	Organic brain syndromes	Alzheimer's disease	Schizophrenia and other psychoses
			Number			
All residents	1,489,500	485,100	1,004,400	686,000	79,200	194,200
Sex						
Male	422,600	137,100	285,500	167,700	23,300	64,300
Female	1,066,900	348,000	718,900	518,300	55,900	129,900
Age						
Under 65 years	166,500	34,400	132,100	31,000	5,100[3]	52,600
65-74 years	209,100	61,400	147,700	80,400	17,100	44,300
75-84 years	501,800	173,500	328,300	239,300	32,900	51,700
65 years and over	1,314,700	446,800	867,900	652,300	74,000	140,400
75 years and over	1,105,700	385,500	720,200	571,900	57,000	96,100
85 years and over	603,900	212,000	391,900	332,600	24,000	44,400[3]
Race[2]						
White	1,373,100	445,100	928,000	631,900	75,300	176,400
Black	104,000	35,700	68,300	49,800	3,500[3]	15,900[3]
			Percent			
All residents	100.0	100.0	100.0	100.0	100.0	100.0
Sex						
Male	28.4	28.3	28.4	24.4	29.4	33.1
Female	71.6	71.7	71.6	75.6	70.6	66.9
Age						
Under 65 years	11.2	7.1	13.2	4.5	6.4[3]	27.1
65-74 years	14.0	12.7	14.7	11.7	21.6	22.8
75-84 years	33.7	35.8	32.7	34.9	41.5	26.6
65 years and over	88.3	92.1	86.4	95.1	93.4	72.3
75 years and over	74.2	79.5	71.7	83.4	72.0	49.5
85 years and over	40.5	43.7	39.0	48.5	30.3	22.9

[Continued]

★ 773 ★

Nursing Home Residents with Selected Cognitive Disabilities, by Race - Part I

[Continued]

Sex, age, and race	Total	No cognitive disabilities	Cognitive dis-abilities[1]	Organic brain syndromes	Alzheimer's disease	Schizophrenia and other psychoses
Race[2]						
White	92.2	91.8	92.4	92.1	95.1	90.8
Black	7.0	7.4	6.8	7.3	4.4[3]	8.2

Source: Health Data on Older Americans: United States, 1992, Centers for Disease Control and Prevention/National Center for Health Statistics, Vital and Health Statistics, Series 3: Analytic and Epidemiological Studies, No. 27, p. 160. Primary source: National Center for Health Statistics: Data from the National Nursing Home Survey. Notes: Column percents may not add to 100 because of rounding. 1. Includes residents with all types of cognitive disabilities; residents with multiple disabilities are counted only once in the total. 2. Excludes races other than white and black. 3. Figure does not meet standard of reliability or precision.

★ 774 ★

Cognitive Disabilities

Nursing Home Residents with Selected Cognitive Disabilities, by Race - Part II

Number and percent of nursing home residents, by presence of selected cognitive disabilities, sex, age, and race: 1985. Data are based on personal interviews of the nursing home staff most knowledgeable about the residents sampled.

Sex, age, and race	Total	Depressive disorders	Anxiety disorders	Alcohol and drug abuse	Mental retardation
		Number			
All residents	1,489,500	214,800	215,000	58,700	82,800
Sex					
Male	422,600	54,700	57,800	37,700	37,700
Female	1,066,900	160,200	157,200	21,000	45,200
Age					
Under 65 years	166,500	29,700	32,400	16,800	43,800
65-74 years	209,100	38,900	34,500	16,900	20,400
75-84 years	501,800	79,700	76,500	16,600	13,400
65 years and over	1,314,700	183,800	180,900	41,300	38,300
75 years and over	1,105,700	144,900	146,400	24,400	17,900
85 years and over	603,900	65,200	69,900	7,800	4,500[3]
Race[2]					
White	1,373,100	201,600	198,500	51,800	76,700
Black	104,000	10,500	14,000	6,200	4,700[3]

[Continued]

★774★

Nursing Home Residents with Selected Cognitive Disabilities, by Race - Part II

[Continued]

Sex, age, and race	Total	Depressive disorders	Anxiety disorders	Alcohol and drug abuse	Mental retardation
			Percent		
All residents	100.0	100.0	100.0	100.0	100.0
Sex					
Male	28.4	25.5	26.9	64.2	45.5
Female	71.6	74.6	73.1	35.8	54.6
Age					
Under 65 years	11.2	13.8	15.1	28.6	52.9
65-74 years	14.0	18.1	16.0	28.8	24.6
75-84 years	33.7	37.1	35.6	28.3	16.2
65 years and over	88.3	85.6	84.1	70.4	46.3
75 years and over	74.2	67.5	68.1	41.6	21.6
85 years and over	40.5	30.4	32.5	13.3	5.4[3]
Race[2]					
White	92.2	93.9	92.3	88.2	92.6
Black	7.0	4.9	6.5	10.6	5.7[3]

Source: Health Data on Older Americans: United States, 1992, Centers for Disease Control and Prevention/National Center for Health Statistics, Vital and Health Statistics, Series 3: Analytic and Epidemiological Studies, No. 27, p. 160. Primary source: National Center for Health Statistics: Data from the National Nursing Home Survey. *Notes:* Column percents may not add to 100 because of rounding. 1. Includes residents with all types of cognitive disabilities; residents with multiple disabilities are counted only once in the total. 2. Excludes races other than white and black. 3. Figure does not meet standard of reliability or precision.

★ 775 ★
Cognitive Disabilities

Nursing Home Residents with Selected Cognitive Disabilities Who Need Help with Activities of Daily Living (ADL), 1985 - Part I

Data are based on personal interviews of the nursing home staff most knowledgeable about the residents sampled.

Age and ADLs for which help of another person is required	Total	No cognitive disabilities	Cognitive disabi- lities[1]	Organic brain syndromes	Alzheimer's disease	Schizophrenia and other psychoses
			Number			
All ages	1,489,500	484,600	1,004,900	685,500	78,800	194,300
			Percent			
Number:						
None	8.2	10.5	7.1	2.8	2.6[3]	17.2
1-2	20.1	24.1	18.2	14.5	8.7	28.4
3-4	27.9	26.5	28.5	30.1	33.2	25.2
5-7	43.8	38.9	46.2	52.6	55.5	29.2
Type:						
Eating	37.0	25.6	42.5	51.0	60.1	27.0
Toileting	48.2	42.2	51.0	58.1	65.5	33.6
Dressing	73.7	65.7	77.6	85.7	87.8	59.9
Bathing	88.0	84.6	89.6	95.4	96.4	77.6
Transferring[2]	59.2	55.7	60.9	69.1	69.4	37.2
Walking	34.1	33.8	34.3	37.4	38.7	25.4
Getting outside	36.7	40.7	34.8	31.7	36.1	36.0
65 years and over						
Number:						
None	5.5	9.2	3.7	1.9	2.4[3]	6.8
1-2	17.3	22.8	14.6	13.4	7.8	19.1
3-4	25.0	24.9	25.1	28.8	30.3	19.0
5-7	40.5	35.2	43.0	51.1	52.8	27.3
Type:						
Eating	33.7	22.5	39.1	49.3	57.3	24.0
Toileting	44.7	38.4	47.8	56.6	62.5	31.2
Dressing	67.2	60.6	70.5	82.7	82.6	50.5
Bathing	79.9	78.6	80.5	91.6	90.5	63.1
Transferring[2]	54.7	50.6	56.7	67.1	65.1	34.0
Walking	31.9	31.6	32.0	36.2	36.7	22.7
Getting outside	31.9	37.3	29.2	29.9	32.5	26.6

[Continued]

★ 775 ★

Nursing Home Residents with Selected Cognitive Disabilities Who Need Help with Activities of Daily Living (ADL), 1985 - Part I
[Continued]

Age and ADLs for which help of another person is required	Total	No cognitive disabilities	Cognitive disabi-lities[1]	Organic brain syndromes	Alzheimer's disease	Schizophrenia and other psychoses
75 years and over						
Number:						
None	3.8	7.6	2.0	1.2	2.0[3]	2.4[3]
1-2	14.1	19.8	11.3	11.3	7.2[3]	11.1
3-4	21.4	22.2	21.0	25.0	22.7	14.6
5-7	34.9	29.9	37.3	45.8	40.2	21.4
Type:						
Eating	29.2	19.3	34.0	44.1	44.2	18.8
Toileting	38.3	32.8	40.9	50.1	46.3	24.1
Dressing	57.5	52.0	60.2	73.3	63.1	38.8
Bathing	68.1	68.2	68.0	80.0	69.4	45.4
Transferring[2]	47.4	43.5	49.2	60.0	48.3	27.2
Walking	27.7	27.8	27.7	32.4	27.3	18.5
Getting outside	26.9	32.6	24.1	26.2	23.9	18.3
85 years and over						
Number:						
None	1.5	3.5	0.6[3]	0.4[3]	0.9[3]	0.6[3]
1-2	6.7	11.1	4.6	5.2	1.8[3]	3.9
3-4	12.0	12.4	11.8	14.6	9.1	7.1
5-7	20.3	16.6	22.0	28.3	18.8	11.4
Type:						
Eating	16.8	10.2	20.0	26.8	20.3	10.7
Toileting	22.5	18.9	24.3	31.1	20.0	13.5
Dressing	32.7	29.0	34.4	43.7	27.8	19.5
Bathing	37.8	37.8	37.8	47.4	29.3	21.8
Transferring[2]	27.6	23.7	29.5	37.5	24.0	15.0
Walking	15.9	15.6	16.0	19.5	12.0	9.3
Getting outside	14.3	18.2	12.5	14.6	9.2	7.5

Source: Health Data on Older Americans: United States, 1992, Centers for Disease Control and Prevention/National Center for Health Statistics, Vital and Health Statistics, Series 3: Analytic and Epidemiological Studies, No. 27, pp. 169-170. Primary source: National Center for Health Statistics: Data from the National Nursing Home Survey. *Notes:* Column percents may not add to 100 because of rounding. "-" indicates quantity is zero. 1. Includes residents with all types of cognitive disabilities. Residents with multiple disabilities are counted only once in the total. 2. Transferring means getting in and out of a bed or chair. 3. Figure does not meet standard of reliability or precision.

★ 776 ★

Cognitive Disabilities

Nursing Home Residents with Selected Cognitive Disabilities Who Need Help with Activities of Daily Living (ADL), 1985 - Part II

Data are based on personal interviews of the nursing home staff most knowledgeable about the residents sampled.

Age and ADLs for which help of another person is required	Total	Depressive disorders	Anxiety disorders	Alcohol and drug abuse	Mental retardation
			Number		
All ages	1,489,500	214,700	215,200	58,800	83,200
			Percent		
Number:					
None	8.2	10.2	8.2	21.9	8.4
1-2	20.1	18.4	20.6	32.1	25.6
3-4	27.9	25.5	24.5	20.5	29.9
5-7	43.8	45.9	46.7	25.5	36.1
Type:					
Eating	37.0	37.0	39.2	18.8	33.8
Toileting	48.2	49.5	48.0	29.3	39.7
Dressing	73.7	73.7	74.5	50.5	70.0
Bathing	88.0	87.3	87.7	73.6	83.5
Transferring[2]	59.2	60.0	58.2	33.0	41.4
Walking	34.1	36.4	37.3	24.2	23.8
Getting outside	36.7	36.9	36.8	35.3	47.3
65 years and over					
Number:					
None	5.5	5.3	4.3	9.7[3]	0.7[3]
1-2	17.3	15.2	15.9	22.8	12.4
3-4	25.0	22.9	20.8	15.9	13.0
5-7	40.5	42.1	42.9	21.6	20.3
Type:					
Eating	33.7	33.7	35.2	15.4	15.7
Toileting	44.7	45.9	44.3	26.1	24.0
Dressing	67.2	66.7	66.1	40.9	36.1
Bathing	79.9	78.1	77.4	58.7	42.9
Transferring[2]	54.7	55.1	53.4	27.7	22.5
Walking	31.9	33.9	35.5	19.4	16.6
Getting outside	31.9	31.8	31.1	25.8	18.8

[Continued]

★ 776 ★

Nursing Home Residents with Selected Cognitive Disabilities Who Need Help with Activities of Daily Living (ADL), 1985 - Part II
[Continued]

Age and ADLs for which help of another person is required	Total	Depressive disorders	Anxiety disorders	Alcohol and drug abuse	Mental retardation
75 years and over					
Number:					
None	3.8	2.9	2.3[3]	2.4[3]	0.8[3]
1-2	14.1	11.7	12.4	14.6	5.3[3]
3-4	21.4	18.0	16.9	9.8[3]	6.5[3]
5-7	34.9	34.9	36.5	15.0	9.4
Type:					
Eating	29.2	28.2	30.5	11.1	7.3
Toileting	38.3	37.7	37.6	16.5	11.0
Dressing	57.5	53.9	55.0	27.7	17.5
Bathing	68.1	62.8	64.1	38.0	19.5
Transferring[2]	47.4	45.7	45.2	18.0	11.9
Walking	27.7	27.7	29.4	13.4	8.9
Getting outside	26.9	26.5	25.7	18.4	6.7[3]
85 years and over					
Number:					
None	1.5	-	0.6[3]	-	-
1-2	6.7	4.3	4.8	3.9[3]	0.6[3]
3-4	12.0	8.8	8.1	2.4[3]	2.1[3]
5-7	20.3	16.7	19.1	6.7[3]	2.9[3]
Type:					
Eating	16.8	13.1	15.9	5.9[3]	2.1[3]
Toileting	22.5	18.1	19.5	6.3[3]	4.0[3]
Dressing	32.7	25.9	28.1	11.6	4.7[3]
Bathing	37.8	29.1	31.2	13.4	5.4[3]
Transferring[2]	27.6	22.4	23.7	8.4[3]	4.5[3]
Walking	15.9	14.0	15.1	4.4[3]	2.3[3]
Getting outside	14.3	11.5	11.3	6.2[3]	1.3[3]

Source: Health Data on Older Americans: United States, 1992, Centers for Disease Control and Prevention/National Center for Health Statistics, Vital and Health Statistics, Series 3: Analytic and Epidemiological Studies, No. 27, pp. 169-170. Primary source: National Center for Health Statistics: Data from the National Nursing Home Survey. *Notes:* Column percents may not add to 100 because of rounding. "-" indicates quantity is zero. 1. Includes residents with all types of cognitive disabilities. Residents with multiple disabilities are counted only once in the total. 2. Transferring means getting in and out of a bed or chair. 3. Figure does not meet standard of reliability or precision.

★ 777 ★
Cognitive Disabilities

Nursing Home Residents with Selected Cognitive Disabilities Who Need Help with Instrumental Activities of Daily Living (IADL) - Part I

Data are based on personal interviews of the nursing home staff most knowledgeable about the residents sampled.

Age and IADLs for which help of another person is required	Total	No cognitive disabilities	Cognitive disabi-lities[1]	Organic brain syndromes	Alzheimer's disease	Schizophrenia and other psychoses
			Number			
All ages	1,489,600	485,300	1.004,300	685,400	78,700	194,300
			Percent			
Number:						
None	15.3	25.7	10.2	5.5	3.2[3]	18.6
1-2	14.9	19.9	12.5	9.3	5.6[3]	13.9
3-4	69.9	54.5	77.3	85.2	91.2	67.5
Type:						
Care of personal possessions	73.4	59.3	80.3	87.8	93.1	68.7
Handling money	75.3	61.3	82.1	87.7	94.0	75.6
Securing personal items[2]	76.2	63.9	82.2	89.0	93.7	71.9
Using the telephone	62.7	49.6	69.0	77.1	84.2	58.2
65 years and over						
Number:						
None	12.3	23.0	7.1	4.6	3.0[3]	9.4
1-2	12.6	18.7	9.7	8.5	5.5[5]	8.1
3-4	63.4	50.4	69.6	82.1	85.1	54.9
Type:						
Care of personal possessions	66.4	54.6	72.1	84.3	86.7	55.5
Handling money	67.6	57.1	72.7	84.1	88.3	58.1
Securing personal items[2]	69.0	59.5	73.6	85.4	87.4	57.6
Using the telephone	57.1	45.8	62.6	74.1	78.9	48.6
75 years and over						
Number:						
None	9.7	19.4	5.0	3.7	2.2[3]	4.0
1-2	10.4	16.2	7.6	7.4	3.7[3]	5.1
3-4	54.1	43.8	59.0	72.4	66.5	40.2

[Continued]

★ 777 ★

Nursing Home Residents with Selected Cognitive Disabilities Who Need Help with Instrumental Activities of Daily Living (IADL) - Part I

[Continued]

Age and IADLs for which help of another person is required	Total	No cognitive disabilities	Cognitive disabi- lities[1]	Organic brain syndromes	Alzheimer's disease	Schizophrenia and other psychoses
Type:						
Care of personal possessions	56.5	47.7	60.7	74.2	67.3	40.3
Handling money	57.6	49.8	61.3	74.1	67.5	42.4
Securing personal items[2]	58.8	51.6	62.3	75.5	69.0	41.9
Using the telephone	48.8	39.7	53.2	65.0	60.0	36.3
85 years and over						
Number:						
None	4.4	9.4	2.0	1.6	1.4[3]	1.2[3]
1-2	5.5	9.4	3.5	3.7	0.7[3]	2.0[3]
3-4	30.7	24.8	33.5	43.2	28.4	19.8
Type:						
Care of personal possessions	31.7	27.2	33.9	43.6	27.6	19.7
Handling money	32.4	28.3	34.4	43.9	28.2	20.4
Securing personal items[2]	33.3	29.5	35.2	44.9	29.0	20.7
Using the telephone	27.4	22.5	29.7	38.3	25.4	17.4

Source: Health Data on Older Americans: United States, 1992, Centers for Disease Control and Prevention/National Center for Health Statistics, Vital and Health Statistics, Series 3: Analytic and Epidemiological Studies, No. 27, pp. 171-172. Primary source: National Center for Health Statistics: Data from the National Nursing Home Survey. *Notes:* Column percents may not add to 100 because of rounding. "-" indicates quantity is zero. 1. Includes residents with all types of cognitive disabilities. Residents with multiple disabilities are counted only once in the total. 2. Securing personal items means shopping for items such as newspapers, toilet articles, and snack foods. 3. Figure does not meet standard of reliability or precision.

★ 778 ★

Cognitive Disabilities

Nursing Home Residents with Selected Cognitive Disabilities Who Need Help with Instrumental Activities of Daily Living (IADL) - Part II

Data are based on personal interviews of the nursing home staff most knowledgeable about the residents sampled.

Age and IADLs for which help of another person is required	Total	Depressive disorders	Anxiety disorders	Alcohol and drug abuse	Mental retardation
			Number		
All ages	1,489,600	214,600	214,700	58,900	82,700
			Percent		
Number:					
None	15.3	13.3	12.5	25.8	8.0
1-2	14.9	15.4	15.3	22.9	19.0
3-4	69.9	71.3	72.2	51.2	73.0
Type:					
Care of personal possessions	73.4	74.9	76.4	55.7	79.4
Handling money	75.3	76.3	77.9	62.8	86.8
Securing personal items[2]	76.2	77.2	78.3	61.7	78.3
Using the telephone	62.7	65.3	65.7	44.4	59.9
65 years and over					
Number:					
None	12.3	8.7	8.6	13.9	2.9[3]
1-2	12.6	12.5	10.8	17.6	8.6
3-4	63.4	64.7	65.1	38.4	35.4
Type:					
Care of personal possessions	66.4	67.3	67.7	43.7	38.3
Handling money	67.6	68.5	68.0	46.2	39.0
Securing personal items[2]	69.0	68.9	69.4	48.8	37.3
Using the telephone	57.1	59.1	58.6	36.1	27.8
75 years and over					
Number:					
None	9.7	6.3	6.5	5.7[3]	1.2[3]
1-2	10.4	9.8	8.5	11.6	3.9[3]
3-4	54.1	51.4	53.3	24.6	16.6

[Continued]

★ 778 ★

Nursing Home Residents with Selected Cognitive Disabilities Who Need Help with Instrumental Activities of Daily Living (IADL) - Part II

[Continued]

Age and IADLs for which help of another person is required	Total	Depressive disorders	Anxiety disorders	Alcohol and drug abuse	Mental retardation
Type:					
Care of personal possessions	56.5	53.7	55.7	27.1	18.3
Handling money	57.6	54.8	55.5	30.6	17.6
Securing personal items[2]	58.8	54.3	56.3	28.2	18.0
Using the telephone	48.8	47.7	48.4	23.4	13.2
85 years and over					
Number:					
None	4.4	2.3[3]	2.0[3]	0.7[3]	-
1-2	5.5	3.8	4.0	3.7[3]	1.0[3]
3-4	30.7	24.3	26.6	8.5[3]	4.4[3]
Type:					
Care of personal possessions	31.7	24.7	27.7	9.6[3]	5.7[3]
Handling money	32.4	25.9	28.4	11.5	4.7[3]
Securing personal items[2]	33.3	25.4	27.5	10.1[3]	4.8[3]
Using the telephone	27.4	21.7	23.6	9.0[3]	3.9[3]

Source: *Health Data on Older Americans: United States, 1992*, Centers for Disease Control and Prevention/National Center for Health Statistics, Vital and Health Statistics, Series 3: Analytic and Epidemiological Studies, No. 27, pp. 171-172. Primary source: National Center for Health Statistics: Data from the National Nursing Home Survey. *Notes:* Column percents may not add to 100 because of rounding. "-" indicates quantity is zero. 1. Includes residents with all types of cognitive disabilities. Residents with multiple disabilities are counted only once in the total. 2. Securing personal items means shopping for items such as newspapers, toilet articles, and snack foods. 3. Figure does not meet standard of reliability or precision.

★ 779 ★

Cognitive Disabilities

Nursing Home Residents with Selected Cognitive Disabilities, by Type of Therapy Received

Data are based on personal interviews of the nursing home staff most knowledgeable about the residents sampled.

Age and therapy received in past month[1]	Total	No cognitive disabilities	Cognitive disabi- lities[2]	Organic brain syndromes	Alzheimer's disease	Schizophrenia and other psychoses	Depressive disorders	Anxiety disorders	Alcohol and drug abuse	Mental retardation
Number										
Total[3]	1,464,500	476,500	988,000	677,800	77,500	189,100	213,100	212,000	58,200	81,400
All ages										
Percent										
Total	100.0	100.0	100.0	100.0	100.0	100.0	100.0	100.0	100.0	100.0
No therapy	70.0	70.7	69.8	72.7	72.0	64.5	63.6	65.5	47.3	63.1
Mental health evaluation or treatment	6.2	3.2	7.6	4.7	5.2^5	18.5	11.6	9.8	9.5	12.4
Social services by social worker	11.3	9.9	11.9	11.2	10.7	11.6	14.7	12.6	8.8	19.7
Other[4]	23.4	26.1	22.1	20.9	22.6	21.2	26.3	24.6	16.2	28.5
65 years and over										
No therapy	63.2	65.7	62.1	69.9	68.0	49.7	55.5	58.0	49.3	29.9
Mental health evaluation or treatment	4.2	2.6	4.9	4.1	5.2^5	9.0	8.5	6.2	7.4^5	4.2^5
Social services by social worker	9.6	9.0	9.9	10.5	10.3	8.1	12.9	9.4	6.4^3	8.0
Other[4]	19.9	22.8	18.6	19.6	21.2	15.3	22.6	19.9	16.0	11.6
75 years and over										
No therapy	53.6	57.1	52.0	61.3	52.3	34.8	44.1	48.0	31.4	14.5
Mental health evaluation or treatment	3.1	2.2	3.5	3.3	4.1^5	4.7	5.4	3.8	2.1^5	2.7^5
Social services by social worker	8.0	8.1	8.1	9.2	8.0	5.1	9.2	7.3	2.4^5	3.9^5
Other[4]	16.4	19.2	15.0	17.0	14.8	10.0	17.6	15.9	9.1^5	4.1^5
85 years and over										
No therapy	29.7	31.6	28.8	35.8	19.5	16.2	21.1	22.3	10.8	4.9^5
Mental health evaluation or treatment	1.5	1.3	1.7	1.9	2.3^5	2.2^5	2.4^5	1.5^5	0.4^5	-
Social services by social worker	4.6	5.2	4.3	5.3	6.2^5	2.8^5	3.7	4.6	0.5^5	0.2^5
Other[4]	8.6	10.2	7.9	9.7	8.4	5.2	7.8	8.5	1.7^5	0.6^5

Source: Health Data on Older Americans: United States, 1992, Centers for Disease Control and Prevention/National Center for Health Statistics, Vital and Health Statistics, Series 3: Analytic and Epidemiological Studies, No. 27, p. 174. Primary source: National Center for Health Statistics: Data from the National Nursing Home Survey. *Notes:* Column percents may not add to more than 100 because a person may have received several types of therapy. "-" indicates quantity is zero. 1. Therapy received either inside or outside the nursing home. 2. Includes residents with all types of cognitive disabilities. Residents with multiple disabilities are counted only once in the total. 3. Residents with more than one type of therapy are counted only once. 4. Includes physical, occupational, recreational, and speech or hearing therapy. 5. Figure does not meet standard of reliability or precision.

★ 780 ★

Cognitive Disabilities

Nursing Home Residents with Selected Cognitive Disabilities, by Duration of Stay, 1984-85

Data are based on personal interviews of the nursing home staff most knowledgeable about the discharged patients sampled.

Age, duration of stay, and discharge status	Total	No cognitive disabilities	Cognitive disabi- lities[1]	Organic brain syndromes	Alzheimer's disease	Schizophrenia and other psychoses	Depressive disorders	Anxiety disorders	Alcohol and drug abuse	Mental retardation
					Number					
All ages	1,221,300	887,900	333,400	172,200	47,600	75,700	29,300	13,400	26,900	12,200
All ages										
					Percent					
Duration of stay:										
Total	100.0	100.0	100.0	100.0	100.0	100.0	100.0	100.0	100.0	100.0
Less than 6 months	56.3	59.3	48.3	43.5	46.2	48.1	58.6	61.4	66.5	45.0
6 months to less than 1 year	17.7	17.5	18.2	19.1	18.6	18.8	16.2	12.9[2]	18.5	14.1[2]
1 year to less than 3 years	15.1	13.4	19.7	21.0	28.3	20.3	17.0	11.0[2]	6.2[2]	19.7[2]
3 years or more	10.9	9.8	13.7	16.7	6.1[2]	12.5	7.7[2]	16.8[2]	6.9[2]	27.2[2]
Discharge status:										
Alive	71.7	69.8	76.7	70.7	66.2	82.1	89.6	91.3	94.5	86.6
Dead	28.1	29.9	23.3	29.7	33.1	17.7	9.4[2]	10.2[2]	3.8[2]	13.4[2]
65 years and over										
Duration of stay:										
Total	88.3	89.9	84.1	96.5	92.9	72.7	84.6	80.3	48.2	44.2
Less than 6 months	49.3	53.1	39.0	41.6	43.0	33.4	49.3	44.8	29.1	14.8[2]
6 months to less than 1 year	15.5	15.5	15.5	18.3	18.3	14.0	12.9[2]	9.9[2]	8.5[2]	3.1[2]
1 year to less than 3 years	13.5	12.0	17.3	20.0	25.9	14.8	14.6[2]	7.4[2]	5.5[2]	9.4[2]
3 years or more	10.0	9.2	12.2	16.4	5.1[2]	10.2	7.9[2]	14.6[2]	2.7[2]	16.0[2]
Discharge status:										
Alive	61.5	61.5	61.5	67.2	61.5	54.6	76.9	67.1	42.0	36.9
Dead	26.7	28.3	22.4	28.9	30.8	17.2	8.9[2]	9.7[2]	3.6[2]	10.7[2]
75 years and over										
Duration of stay:										
Total	74.3	76.1	69.4	86.4	74.3	53.9	68.1	-	20.3	22.3[2]
Less than 6 months	40.2	43.4	31.8	36.8	37.1	25.3	41.9	40.2	12.8[2]	4.0[2]
6 months to less than 1 year	13.3	13.5	12.6	16.3	14.7	9.4	9.4[2]	4.8[2]	2.4[2]	-
1 year to less than 3 years	11.5	10.5	14.3	17.7	19.2	12.1	10.1[2]	6.3[2]	4.2[2]	4.6[2]
3 years or more	9.2	8.7	10.6	15.6	3.8[2]	7.3	6.5[2]	10.9[2]	1.7[2]	12.0[2]
Discharge status:										
Alive	50.5	50.9	49.6	59.1	47.9	40.7	61.1	50.5	18.4	10.1[2]
Dead	23.6	25.1	19.7	27.2	26.7	13.0	6.9[2]	10.7[2]	1.1[2]	7.1[2]
85 years and over										
Duration of stay:										
Total	38.1	38.7	36.6	51.4	25.4	19.7	23.8	38.1	5.2[2]	7.6[2]
Less than 6 months	18.0	19.1	15.2	20.2	9.3[2]	7.3	15.0[2]	29.5[2]	2.5[2]	-
6 months to less than 1 year	6.6	6.9	6.0	8.6	3.9[2]	3.7[2]	1.1[2]	0.6[2]	1.2[2]	-
1 year to less than 3 years	6.8	6.3	8.1	10.4	10.5	6.3	5.1[2]	1.2[2]	1.9[2]	1.4[2]
3 years or more	6.6	6.4	7.4	12.1	1.5[2]	2.7[2]	3.3[2]	7.3[2]	0.6[2]	6.0[2]

[Continued]

★ 780 ★

Nursing Home Residents with Selected Cognitive Disabilities, by Duration of Stay, 1984-85
[Continued]

Age, duration of stay, and discharge status	Total	No cognitive disabilities	Cognitive disabi- lities[1]	Organic brain syndromes	Alzheimer's disease	Schizophrenia and other psychoses	Depressive disorders	Anxiety disorders	Alcohol and drug abuse	Mental retardation
Discharge status:										
Alive	23.5	23.4	23.8	32.4	12.1	13.3	22.6	34.2	6.4[2]	4.7[2]
Dead	14.5	15.2	12.8	19.0	13.8	6.6	1.8[2]	6.6[2]	-	2.9[2]

Source: Health Data on Older Americans: United States, 1992, Centers for Disease Control and Prevention/National Center for Health Statistics, Vital and Health Statistics, Series 3: Analytic and Epidemiological Studies, No. 27, pp. 179-180. Primary source: National Center for Health Statistics: Data from the National Nursing Home Survey. *Notes:* Column percents may not add to 100 because of rounding. "-" indicates quantity is zero. 1. Includes residents with all types of cognitive disabilities. Residents with multiple disabilities are counted only once in the total. 2. Figure does not meet standard of reliability or precision.

Mental Illness

★ 781 ★

Mental Illness in Nursing Homes, by Type: United States, 1985

About 88 percent of the nation's 1.45 million nursing home residents are 65 years and older. Of the total 1.45 million residents, about 65% suffer some form of mental illness. Data show number and percent of residents with mental disorders and percent of total residents, by selected mental disorders.

Mental disorder	Total[1]	Percent of residents with mental disorders[1]	Percent of total residents
Total	974,300	100.0	65.3
Mental retardation	83,200	8.5	5.6
Alcohol and drug abuse	58,700	6.0	3.9
Organic brain syndromes (including Alzheimer's disease)	696,800	71.5	46.7
Depressive disorders	167,000	17.1	11.2
Schizophrenia and other psychoses	195,400	20.0	13.1
Anxiety disorders	163,700	16.8	11.0
Other mental illness	17,700	1.8	1.2

Source: U.S. Department of Health and Human Services, National Center for Health Statistics, Vital and Health Statistics, *Mental Illness in Nursing Homes: United States, 1985*, Series 13: Data from the National Health Survey, No. 105. *Notes:* 1. Subgroups add to more than the total because residents with multiple disorders are counted only once in the total.

★ 782 ★

Mental Illness

Mental Illness and Age in Nursing Homes

About 20 percent of all residents under 65 years of age had a diagnosis of OBS[1]. The percent of residents with OBS increases with age to 55.6 percent of the total for those 85 years of age and over. The number of residents with each of the other mental disorders all declined with age. The greatest decline was among those residents with mental retardation and schizophrenia and other psychoses.

Source: U.S. Department of Health and Human Services, National Center for Health Statistics, Vital and Health Statistics, *Mental Illness in Nursing Homes: United States, 1985,* Series 13: Data from the National Health Survey, No. 105, p. 4. *Notes:* 1. OBS stands for Organic brain syndromes. This category includes Alzheimer's disease.

★ 783 ★

Mental Illness

Characteristics of Nursing Home Residents with Mental Disorders

[Data are shown in percent]

Characteristic	Percent
Female	65.4
Male	65.1
Age	
Under 65 years	75.8
65-74 years	67.8
75-84 years	63.4
85 years and over	63.0
Race	
White	65.4
Black and other	64.0

Source: U.S. Department of Health and Human Services, National Center for Health Statistics, Vital and Health Statistics, *Mental Illness in Nursing Homes: United States, 1985,* Series 13: Data from the National Health Survey, No. 105, p. 5.

★ 784 ★

Mental Illness

Number and Distribution of Nursing Home Residents by Selected Resident Characteristics, According to Mental Conditions: United States, 1985

Resident characteristic	All residents (number)	Percent distribution	Residents with mental disorders (number)	Percent distribution	Percent of total	Residents without mental disorders (number)	Percent distribution	Percent of total
Total	1,491,400	100.00	974,300	100.0	65.3	517,200	100.0	34.7
Age								
Under 65 years	173,100	11.6	131,200	13.5	75.8	41,900	8.1	24.2
65 years and over	1,318,300	88.4	843,000	86.5	64.0	475,300	91.9	36.1
65-74 years	212,100	14.2	143,800	14.8	67.8	68,300	13.2	32.2
75-84 years	509,000	34.1	322,700	33.1	63.4	186,300	36.0	36.6
85 years and over	597,300	40.0	376,500	38.6	63.0	220,800	42.7	37.0
Sex								
Male	423,800	28.4	276,200	28.3	65.2	147,500	28.5	34.8
Female	1,067,700	71.6	698,100	71.7	65.4	369,600	71.5	34.6
Race								
White	1,374,600	92.2	899,600	92.3	65.4	475,100	91.9	34.6
Black and other	116,800	7.8	74,700	7.7	64.0	42,100	8.1	36.0
Hispanic origin								
Hispanic	41,000	2.7	30,900	3.2	75.4	10,100	2.0	24.6
Non-Hispanic	1,450,400	97.3	943,300	96.8	65.0	507,100	98.0	35.0

Source: U.S. Department of Health and Human Services, National Center for Health Statistics, Vital and Health Statistics, *Mental Illness in Nursing Homes: United States, 1985*, Series 13: Data from the National Health Survey, No. 105, p. 6. *Note:* Figures may not add to totals because of rounding.

★ 785 ★

Mental Illness

Average Number of Dependencies of Nursing Home Residents, by Mental Condition, Age, Sex, and Race: United States: 1985

Data represent the average number of persons needing assistance with daily living activities.

Age, sex, and race	All residents	Mental condition	
		With mental disorders	Without mental disorders
Total	3.8	4.0	3.3
Age			
Under 65 years	2.8	2.4	3.8
65-74 years	3.4	3.5	3.2
75-84 years	3.8	4.1	3.3
85 years and over	4.1	4.7	3.2
Sex			
Male	3.3	3.5	3.1
Female	3.9	4.2	3.4
Race			
White	3.7	4.0	3.2
Black and other	3.9	4.0	3.9

Source: U.S. Department of Health and Human Services, National Center for Health Statistics, Vital and Health Statistics, *Mental Illness in Nursing Homes: United States, 1985,* Series 13: Data from the National Health Survey, No. 105, p. 7.

★ 786 ★

Mental Illness

Nursing Home Residents, by Mental Condition, Age, and Functional Status: United States, 1985

[Data are shown in percent]

Functional status	Mental condition					
	With mental disorders			Without mental disorders		
	All residents	Under 65 years	65 years and over	All residents	Under 65 years	65 years and over
Requires assistance bathing	90.3	67.2	93.9	85.8	83.1	86.0
Requires assistance dressing[1]	79.4	53.4	83.5	67.8	76.1	67.1
Requires assistance eating[2]	45.4	26.6	48.4	27.7	46.8	26.1
Requires assistance with mobility[3]	68.8	38.1	73.6	74.2	83.1	73.5
Requires assistance transferring[4]	61.6	30.3	66.5	56.7	68.7	55.7
Requires assistance using toilet room[5]	65.3	34.5	70.0	52.6	69.2	51.1
Continence--difficulty with bowel and/ or bladder control	59.7	30.5	64.2	37.3	37.9	37.3
Receives help in instrumental activities of daily living	90.0	76.2	92.1	74.9	71.6	75.2

Source: U.S. Department of Health and Human Services, National Center for Health Statistics, Vital and Health Statistics, *Mental Illness in Nursing Homes: United States, 1985*, Series 13: Data from the National Health Survey, No. 105, p. 8. *Notes:* 1. Includes those who do not dress. 2. Includes those who are tube or intravenously fed. 3. Includes those who are chairfast or bedfast. 4. Transferring refers to getting in or out of bed or chair. 5. Includes those who do not use toilet room.

★ 787 ★

Mental Illness

Dependency in the Activities of Daily Living, by Age and Mental Condition: United States, 1985

85 years and over - 98.5	
75-84 years - 93.9	
65-74 years - 87.6	
Under 65 years - 69.7	

Chart shows data from column 1.

Percent of nursing home residents with at least one dependency in the activities of daily living.

Age	Mental condition	
	With disorders	Without disorders
Under 65 years	69.7	85.4
65-74 years	87.6	85.1
75-84 years	93.9	87.0
85 years and over	98.5	89.6

Source: U.S. Department of Health and Human Services, National Center for Health Statistics, Vital and Health Statistics, *Mental Illness in Nursing Homes: United States, 1985*, Series 13: Data from the National Health Survey, No. 105, p. 8.

★ 788 ★

Mental Illness

Average Length of Stay Since Admission of Nursing Home Resident, by Mental Condition and Selected Resident Characteristics: United States, 1985

[Length of stay is shown in days]

Resident characteristic	All residents	Mental condition	
		With mental disorders	Without mental disorders
		Length of stay	
Total	1,059	1,139	907
Age			
Under 65 years	1,311	1,464	829
65 years and over	1,026	1,089	914
65-74 years	1,055	1,161	833
75-84 years	948	997	864
85 years and over	1,081	1,140	981

[Continued]

★ 788 ★

Average Length of Stay Since Admission of Nursing Home Resident, by Mental Condition and Selected Resident Characteristics: United States, 1985

[Continued]

Resident characteristic	All residents	Mental condition	
		With mental disorders	Without mental disorders
Race			
White	1,061	1,140	515
Black and other	1,037	1,136	451
Current marital status			
Married	675	724	293
Widowed	990	1,032	545
Divorced or separated	997	1,114	350
Never married	1,582	1,721	629
Has living children			
Yes	933	989	479
No or unknown	1,244	1,343	541

Source: U.S. Department of Health and Human Services, National Center for Health Statistics, Vital and Health Statistics, *Mental Illness in Nursing Homes: United States, 1985*, Series 13: Data from the National Health Survey, No. 105, p. 10.

★ 789 ★

Mental Illness

Nursing Home Length of Stay Since Admission, by Mental Condition and Facility Type: United States, 1985

Facility characteristics	Mental condition			
	With mental disorders		Without mental disorders	
	Number	Length of stay in days	Number	Length of stay in days
Total	974,300	1,139	517,200	907
Ownership				
Proprietary	692,600	1,103	331,300	773
Voluntary nonprofit	195,300	1,166	146,300	1,085
Government	86,400	1,374	39,600	1,371
Certification				
Skilled nursing facility only	178,300	948	97,000	690

[Continued]

★ 789 ★

Nursing Home Length of Stay Since Admission, by Mental Condition and Facility Type: United States, 1985
[Continued]

Facility characteristics	Mental condition			
	With mental disorders		Without mental disorders	
	Number	Length of stay in days	Number	Length of stay in days
Skilled nursing facility and intermediate care facility	438,800	1,043	235,900	916
Intermediate care facility only	254,000	1,354	117,400	1,012
Not certified	103,100	1,351	66,900	1,007
Bed size				
Less than 50 beds	93,900	1,506	39,400	785
50-99 beds	263,100	1,108	149,100	912
100-199 beds	418,400	1,015	226,300	841
200 beds or more	198,900	1,268	102,400	1,092

Source: U.S. Department of Health and Human Services, National Center for Health Statistics, Vital and Health Statistics, *Mental Illness in Nursing Homes: United States, 1985*, Series 13: Data from the National Health Survey, No. 105, p. 10. *Note:* Figures may not add to totals because of rounding.

★ 790 ★

Mental Illness

Number of Nursing Home Residents with Mental Disorders, by Selected Patient Characteristics: United States, 1985

[Number of residents]

Patient characteristic	All residents	All residents with mental disorders[1]	Mental retardation	Alcohol and drug abuse	Organic brain syndromes[2]	Depressive disorders	Schizophrenia and other psychoses	Anxiety disorders	Other mental illness
Total	1,491,400	974,300	83,200	58,700	696,800	167,000	195,400	163,700	17,700
Sex									
Male	423,800	276,200	37,700	37,700	170,800	40,700	64,700	44,500	8,400
Female	1,067,700	698,100	45,500	21,000	526,000	126,200	130,700	119,200	9,300
Age									
Under 65 years	173,100	131,200	44,500	18,200	33,800	24,900	54,100	22,400	5,600[3]
65 years and over	1,318,300	843,000	38,700	40,500	663,000	142,000	141,300	141,300	12,100
65-74 years	212,100	143,800	20,200	16,100	81,000	28,900	44,000	28,000	3,900[3]
75-84 years	509,000	322,700	14,000	16,900	249,800	64,500	53,500	61,800	3,400[3]
85 years and over	597,300	376,500	4,600[3]	7,500	332,200	48,600	43,800	51,500	4,800[3]
Race									
White	1,374,600	899,600	77,000	51,800	642,200	155,600	177,600	151,600	16,800
Black and other	116,800	74,700	6,200	6,900	54,500	11,300	17,800	12,100	900[3]
Black	104,400	66,600	4,700[3]	6,200	50,300	8,500	15,900	10,500	900[3]

[Continued]

★ 790 ★

Number of Nursing Home Residents with Mental Disorders, by Selected Patient Characteristics: United States, 1985

[Continued]

Patient characteristic	All residents	All residents with mental disorders[1]	Mental retardation	Alcohol and drug abuse	Organic brain syndromes[2]	Depressive disorders	Schizophrenia and other psychoses	Anxiety disorders	Other mental illness
Hispanic origin									
Hispanic	41,000	30,900	2,200[3]	2,100[3]	23,900	4,900[3]	7,700	4,900[3]	800[3]
Non-Hispanic	1,450,400	943,300	81,000	56,500	672,900	162,100	187,700	158,800	16,800

Source: U.S. Department of Health and Human Services, National Center for Health Statistics, Vital and Health Statistics, *Mental Illness in Nursing Homes: United States, 1985*, Series 13: Data from the National Health Survey, No. 105, p. 18. *Notes:* 1. Subgroups add to more than the total because residents with multiple disorders are counted only once in the total. 2. Includes Alzheimer's disease. 3. Figure does not meet standard of reliability or precision (more than 30-percent relative standard error).

★ 791 ★

Mental Illness

Age and Number of Nursing Home Residents with Mental Disorders: United States, 1985

	All residents with mental disorders	Age					Sex		Race		
		Under 65 years	65 years and over							Black and other	
			Total	65-74 years	75-84 years	85 years and over	Male	Female	White	Total	Black
Age in years											
Average resident age	79	51	83	70	80	90	73	81	79	75	76
Median resident age	82	55	83	70	80	90	76	83	82	77	77
Number											
Total residents	974,300	131,200	843,000	143,800	322,700	376,500	276,200	698,100	899,600	74,700	66,600

Source: U.S. Department of Health and Human Services, National Center for Health Statistics, Vital and Health Statistics, *Mental Illness in Nursing Homes: United States, 1985*, Series 13: Data from the National Health Survey, No. 105, p. 19. *Note:* Figures may not add to totals because of rounding.

★ 792 ★

Mental Illness

Nursing Home Residents with Mental Disorders, by Age, Sex, Race, and Facility Type: United States, 1985

Facility Characteristic	All residents with mental disorders	Age					Sex		Race		
		Under 65 years	65 years and over				Male	Female	White	Black and other	
			Total	65-74 years	75-84 years	85 years and over				Total	Black
Number											
Ownership											
Proprietary	692,600	101,300	591,300	110,400	221,500	259,400	199,400	493,200	637,000	55,600	50,500
Voluntary nonprofit	195,300	10,600	184,700	21,400	71,000	92,300	43,800	151,500	182,200	13,000	12,100
Government	86,400	19,400	67,000	12,000	30,200	24,800	33,000	53,400	80,300	6,100	4,100
Certification											
Skilled nursing facility only	178,300	19,000	159,300	23,200	56,500	79,600	44,900	133,400	160,900	17,400	13,300
Skilled nursing and intermediate care facility	438,800	47,800	391,100	60,400	153,300	177,300	115,300	323,500	406,600	32,300	30,800
Intermediate care facility only	254,000	29,500	224,500	40,700	85,300	98,500	75,100	178,900	234,300	19,800	18,200
Not certified	103,100	34,900	68,100	19,500	27,500	21,100	40,800	62,200	97,800	5,300[1]	4,300[1]
Bed size											
Less than 50 beds	93,900	24,800	69,100	18,000	27,200	23,900	30,100	63,800	86,100	7,800	6,900
50-99 beds	263,100	23,800	239,300	40,900	80,800	117,600	68,700	194,400	249,700	13,400	12,200
100-199 beds	418,400	49,600	368,800	56,500	152,700	159,600	113,900	304,500	383,700	34,700	30,300
200 beds or more	198,900	33,000	165,900	28,400	62,100	75,400	63,500	135,400	180,000	18,800	17,200

Source: U.S. Department of Health and Human Services, National Center for Health Statistics, Vital and Health Statistics, *Mental Illness in Nursing Homes: United States, 1985*, Series 13: Data from the National Health Survey, No. 105, p. 19. *Notes:* Figures may not add to totals because of rounding. 1. Figure does not meet standard of reliability or precision (more than 30-percent relative standard error).

★ 793 ★

Mental Illness

Nursing Home Residents with Mental Disorders, by Age, Sex, Race, and Facility Affiliation: United States, 1985

Facility affiliation	All residents with mental disorders	Age					Sex		Race		
		Under 65 years	65 years and over				Male	Female	White	Black and other	
			Total	65-74 years	75-84 years	85 years and over				Total	Black
Number											
Chain	471,100	53,000	418,100	72,000	157,100	189,000	129,000	342,000	438,200	32,900	30,600
Independent	409,600	57,900	351,700	59,200	131,900	160,700	111,100	298,500	374,300	35,300	31,700
Government	86,400	19,400	67,000	12,000	30,200	24,800	33,000	53,400	80,300	6,100	4,100[1]
Unknown	7,100	1,000[1]	6,200	600[1]	3,600[1]	2,000[1]	3,000[1]	4,100[1]	6,700	400[1]	300[1]

Source: U.S. Department of Health and Human Services, National Center for Health Statistics, Vital and Health Statistics, *Mental Illness in Nursing Homes: United States, 1985*, Series 13: Data from the National Health Survey, No. 105, p. 19. *Notes:* Figures may not add to totals because of rounding. 1. Figure does not meet standard of reliability or precision (more than 30-percent relative standard error).

★ 794 ★

Mental Illness

Nursing Home Residents with Mental Disorders, by Age, Sex, Race, and Sensory Impairment: United States, 1985

Functional status	All residents with mental disorders	Age					Sex		Race		
		Under 65 years	65 years and over				Male	Female	White	Black and other	
			Total	65-74 years	75-84 years	85 years and over				Total	Black
Total	974,300	131,200	843,000	143,800	322,700	376,500	276,200	698,100	899,600	74,700	66,600
Aids used[1]											
Eyeglass or contacts	560,600	46,300	514,300	70,400	192,600	251,300	129,200	431,500	537,400	23,200	20,500
Hearing aid	52,900	1,500[4]	51,400	2,600[4]	14,000	34,800	13,800	39,100	52,000	900[4]	900[4]
Vision[2]											
Not impaired	725,800	116,800	609,000	116,600	242,000	250,300	215,200	510,600	669,500	56,200	49,700
Partially impaired[3]	145,500	8,000	137,500	16,600	49,500	71,400	36,500	109,000	134,500	11,000	10,000
Severely impaired	58,700	1,800[4]	56,900	7,400	14,600	34,900	13,200	45,500	56,500	2,200[4]	2,000[4]
Completely lost	28,600	3,100[4]	25,500	2,000[4]	8,600	14,800	6,900	21,700	23,800	4,800[4]	4,500[4]
Unknown	15,700	1,600[4]	14,100	1,100[4]	8,000	5,000[4]	4,400[4]	11,300	15,300	400[4]	400[4]
Hearing[2]											
Not impaired	761,900	126,300	635,600	127,800	264,900	242,800	222,100	539,800	700,200	61,700	55,100
Partially impaired[3]	160,500	3,900[4]	156,600	11,600	47,900	97,000	41,600	118,900	149,600	10,800	9,400
Severely impaired	37,000	200[4]	36,800	2,300[4]	6,100	28,400	9,100	28,000	35,500	1,500[4]	1,500[4]
Completely lost	6,000	0[4]	5,900	700[4]	2,100[4]	3,100[4]	1,400[4]	4,600[4]	5,500[4]	400[4]	400[4]
Unknown	8,900	800[4]	8,100	1,300[4]	1,700[4]	5,100[4]	2,100[4]	6,900	8,700	300[4]	300[4]

Source: U.S. Department of Health and Human Services, National Center for Health Statistics, Vital and Health Statistics, *Mental Illness in Nursing Homes: United States, 1985*, Series 13: Data from the National Health Survey, No. 105, pp. 22-23. *Notes:* Figures may not add to totals because of rounding. 1. Figures do not add to totals because resident may not have used glasses, contacts, or hearing aid. 2. Status at best correction, that is, with corrective lenses or hearing aid, if applicable. 3. Includes a small number of residents who were impaired but whose level of impairment is unknown. 4. Figure does not meet standard of reliability or precision (more than 30-percent relative standard error).

★ 795 ★

Mental Illness

Nursing Home Residents with Mental Disorders, by Age, Sex, Race, and Dependency Status: United States, 1985

Dependency status	All residents with mental disorders	Age					Sex		Race		
		Under 65 years	65 years and over				Male	Female	White	Black and other	
			Total	65-74 years	75-84 years	85 years and over				Total	Black
Total	974,300	131,200	843,000	143,800	322,700	376,500	276,200	698,100	899,600	74,700	66,600
Bathing											
Independent[1]	94,700	43,000	51,700	20,000	22,900	8,900	48,800	45,900	87,500	7,300	6,100
Requires assistance	879,500	88,200	791,300	123,800	299,900	367,600	227,400	652,200	812,100	67,500	60,600
Dressing											
Independent[1]	200,300	61,200	139,100	42,200	60,700	36,200	82,800	117,500	186,800	13,600	11,600
Requires assistance; includes those who do not dress	773,900	70,000	703,900	101,600	262,000	340,300	193,400	580,600	712,800	61,100	55,000

[Continued]

★ 795 ★

Nursing Home Residents with Mental Disorders, by Age, Sex, Race, and Dependency Status: United States, 1985

[Continued]

Dependency status	All residents with mental disorders	Age					Sex		Race		
		Under 65 years	65 years and over				Male	Female	White	Black and other	
			Total	65-74 years	75-84 years	85 years and over				Total	Black
Eating											
Independent[1]	531,500	96,400	435,100	91,500	172,600	171,000	173,600	357,900	489,900	41,600	35,900
Requires assistance; includes those who are tube or intravenously fed	442,800	34,900	407,900	52,300	150,100	205,500	102,600	340,100	409,600	33,100	30,800
Mobility											
Walks independently[1]	303,600	81,200	222,400	62,300	102,900	57,300	114,300	189,300	280,900	22,700	19,300
Walks with assistance	206,300	15,400	191,000	27,500	68,400	95,100	55,700	150,700	189,600	16,700	15,700
Chairfast	393,500	28,400	365,100	44,400	128,000	192,700	93,700	299,800	362,100	31,400	28,200
Bedfast	70,800	6,300	64,500	9,700	23,500	31,400	12,500	58,300	66,900	3,900[2]	3,500[2]

Source: U.S. Department of Health and Human Services, National Center for Health Statistics, Vital and Health Statistics, *Mental Illness in Nursing Homes: United States, 1985*, Series 13: Data from the National Health Survey, No. 105, pp. 22-23. Notes: Figures may not add to totals because of rounding. 1. Includes a small number of unknowns. 2. Figure does not meet standard of reliability or precision (more than 30-percent relative standard error).

★ 796 ★

Mental Illness

Nursing Home Residents with Mental Disorders, by Age, Sex, Race, and Functional Status: United States, 1985

Functional status	All residents with mental disorders	Age					Sex		Race		
		Under 65 years	65 years and over				Male	Female	White	Black and other	
			Total	65-74 years	75-84 years	85 years and over				Total	Black
Total	974,300	131,200	843,000	143,800	322,700	376,500	276,200	698,100	899,600	74,700	66,600
Transferring[2]											
Independent[1]	374,400	91,500	282,900	71,400	124,600	86,900	134,800	239,600	344,900	29,500	25,100
Requires assistance	599,900	39,700	560,200	72,400	198,200	289,600	141,400	458,500	554,700	45,200	41,600
Using toilet room											
Independent[1]	338,500	86,000	252,500	62,600	109,700	80,300	124,800	213,700	311,300	27,100	23,600
Requires assistance	504,500	33,200	471,300	66,400	167,800	237,100	123,400	381,100	469,000	35,500	32,700
Does not use toilet room	131,300	12,100	119,200	14,800	45,300	59,100	28,000	103,300	119,300	12,100	10,300
Continence											
No difficulty in controlling bowels or bladder[1]	392,900	91,200	301,700	75,900	115,700	110,100	127,400	265,500	359,700	33,200	28,300
Difficulty controlling bowels	16,800	2,700[3]	14,200	2,600[3]	4,000[3]	7,600	6,000	10,800	15,700	1,100[3]	1,100[3]
Difficulty controlling bladder	103,800	8,400	95,400	10,500	39,000	45,900	27,600	76,100	98,000	5,800	4,900[3]
Difficulty controlling both bowels and bladder	387,900	21,700	366,300	47,500	139,400	179,400	95,300	292,700	359,100	28,900	26,700
Ostomy in either bowels or bladder	72,800	7,300	65,500	7,400	24,700	33,500	19,900	52,900	67,100	5,800	5,600[3]

Source: U.S. Department of Health and Human Services, National Center for Health Statistics, Vital and Health Statistics, *Mental Illness in Nursing Homes: United States, 1985*, Series 13: Data from the National Health Survey, No. 105, pp. 22-23. Notes: Figures may not add to totals because of rounding. 1. Includes a small number of unknowns. 2. Transferring refers to getting in and out of a bed or chair. 3. Figure does not meet standard of reliability or precision (more than 30-percent relative standard error).

★ 797 ★

Mental Illness

Nursing Home Residents with Mental Disorders, by Age, Sex, Race, and Dependency Status: United States, 1985

Functional status	All residents with mental disorders	Age					Sex		Race		
		Under 65 years	65 years and over				Male	Female	White	Black and other	
			Total	65-74 years	75-84 years	85 years and over				Total	Black
Total	974,300	131,200	843,000	143,800	322,700	376,500	276,200	698,100	899,600	74,700	66,600
Number of dependencies in activities of daily living[2]											
None	82,700	39,700	43,100	17,800	19,700	5,600[3]	43,600	39,100	76,400	6,300	5,100[3]
1	89,800	17,300	72,400	20,100	31,200	21,100	31,900	57,800	84,500	5,300[3]	4,800[3]
2	94,300	20,100	74,200	16,300	30,700	27,200	27,100	67,100	86,700	7,600	6,600
3	68,100	10,500	57,600	11,600	23,900	22,100	20,100	48,000	59,600	8,600	7,700
4	109,700	10,100	99,600	17,700	36,000	45,900	26,800	82,900	99,800	9,900	7,600
5	186,300	12,700	173,700	20,900	65,300	87,500	48,700	137,700	174,300	12,100	11,400
6	343,400	20,900	322,400	39,400	115,900	167,100	78,000	265,400	318,400	25,000	23,500
Instrumental activities of daily living											
Does not receive help[1]	97,700	31,300	66,400	20,100	29,700	16,600	42,300	55,400	89,200	8,500	7,300
Receives help	876,600	100,000	776,600	123,700	293,100	359,800	233,900	642,600	810,400	66,200	59,300
Care of personal possessions	786,500	78,600	707,900	110,200	267,400	330,300	201,200	585,300	723,400	63,000	56,700
Handling money	807,000	91,900	715,000	111,700	268,400	335,000	213,400	593,600	7747,400	59,600	52,700
Securing personal items such as newspapers, toilet articles, snack food	803,800	81,500	722,200	110,100	269,600	342,500	209,800	594,000	743,200	60,600	54,900
Using the telephone	677,200	62,300	614,900	92,700	232,900	289,300	172,800	504,400	623,600	53,600	49,300

Source: U.S. Department of Health and Human Services, National Center for Health Statistics, Vital and Health Statistics, *Mental Illness in Nursing Homes: United States, 1985*, Series 13: Data from the National Health Survey, No. 105, pp. 22-23. *Notes:* Figures may not add to totals because of rounding. 1. Includes a small number of unknowns. 2. Activities of daily living include bathing, dressing, eating, transferring, using toilet room, and continence. Unknowns were considered not dependent. 3. Figure does not meet standard of reliability or precision (more than 30-percent relative standard error).

★ 798 ★

Mental Illness

Nursing Home Residents with Mental Disorders and Percent Distribution of Length of Stay

Sex and age of resident	All residents with mental disorders Number	Percent distribution							Stay in days	
		Total	Length of stay since admission						Average length of stay since admission	Median length of stay since admission
			Less than 3 months	3 months to less than 6 months	6 months to less than 12 months	1 year to less than 3 years	3 years to less than 5 years	5 years or more		
Sex and age										
Both sexes, all ages	974,300	100.0	10.8	9.3	13.4	32.1	14.6	19.8	1,139	674
Under 65 years	131,200	100.0	12.2	12.3	10.7	24.8	12.2	27.7	1,464	740
65 years and over	843,000	100.0	10.6	8.8	13.8	33.2	14.9	18.6	1,089	663
65-74 years	143,800	100.0	12.9	10.2	13.9	28.9	14.6	19.4	1,161	591
75-84 years	322,700	100.0	10.3	8.4	15.6	35.8	14.3	15.7	997	624
85 years and over	376,500	100.0	9.9	8.7	12.3	32.6	15.6	20.8	1,140	742

[Continued]

★ 798 ★

Nursing Home Residents with Mental Disorders and Percent Distribution of Length of Stay

[Continued]

Sex and age of resident	All residents with mental disorders Number	Percent distribution							Stay in days	
			Length of stay since admission						Average length of stay since admission	Median length of stay since admission
		Total	Less than 3 months	3 months to less than 6 months	6 months to less than 12 months	1 year to less than 3 years	3 years to less than 5 years	5 years or more		
Male, all ages	276,200	100.0	13.4	10.2	12.6	31.7	12.6	19.5	1,141	624
Under 65 years	68,200	100.0	14.3	13.6	11.8	27.2	8.7	24.4	1,322	588
65 years and over	208,000	100.0	13.0	9.1	12.9	33.1	13.9	17.9	1,082	629
65-74 years	56,100	100.0	13.0	8.8	13.2	28.3	15.8	21.0	1,281	684
75-84 years	85,500	100.0	12.1	8.8	14.0	35.9	12.5	16.7	1,006	617
85 years and over	66,400	100.0	14.2	9.7	11.3	33.8	14.3	16.7	1,011	625
Female, all ages	698,100	100.0	9.8	9.0	13.7	32.2	15.4	20.0	1,139	700
Under 65 years	63,000	100.0	9.0	11.0	9.5	22.1	16.1	31.4	1,619	994
65 years and over	635,000	100.0	9.7	8.8	14.1	33.2	15.3	18.9	1,091	683
65-74 years	87,700	100.0	12.9	11.1	14.4	29.3	13.9	18.4	1,084	517
75-84 years	237,300	100.0	9.6	8.2	16.1	35.8	15.0	15.3	993	630
85 years and over	310,100	100.0	9.0	8.5	12.6	32.4	15.9	21.7	1,168	774

Source: U.S. Department of Health and Human Services, National Center for Health Statistics, Vital and Health Statistics, *Mental Illness in Nursing Homes: United States, 1985*, Series 13: Data from the National Health Survey, No. 105, p. 26. *Note:* Figures may not add to totals because of rounding.

★ 799 ★

Mental Illness

Nursing Home Residents with Mental Disorders, Percent Distribution by Length of Stay and Facility Type

Facility characteristic	All residents with mental disorders Number	Percent distribution							Stay in days	
			Length of stay since admission						Average length of stay since admission	Median length of stay since admission
		Total	Less than 3 months	3 months to less than 6 months	6 months to less than 12 months	1 year to less than 3 years	3 years to less than 5 years	5 years or more		
Ownership										
Proprietary	692,600	100.0	11.1	10.3	13.4	31.6	14.4	19.2	1,103	657
Voluntary nonprofit	195,300	100.0	9.0	7.6	13.1	33.6	15.9	20.8	1,166	742
Government	86,400	100.0	12.2	4.8	14.5	32.3	13.2	23.0	1,374	689
Certification										
Skilled nursing facility only	178,300	100.0	14.0	11.7	12.9	33.3	14.0	14.2	948	590
Skilled nursing facility and intermediate care facility	438,800	100.0	10.9	9.0	15.3	34.0	14.0	16.8	1,043	629
Intermediate care facility only	254,000	100.0	7.6	8.1	12.0	29.7	15.9	26.6	1,354	855
Not certified	103,100	100.0	12.6	9.6	9.8	27.6	14.7	25.7	1,351	814
Bed size										
Less than 50 beds	93,900	100.0	9.4	9.7	10.7	28.8	14.2	27.3	1,506	834
50-99 beds	263,100	100.0	11.2	9.4	14.4	30.9	13.8	20.3	1,108	664
100-199 beds	418,400	100.0	11.0	9.6	13.4	34.0	15.3	16.7	1,015	653
200 beds or more	198,900	100.0	10.5	8.5	13.4	31.1	14.3	22.3	1,268	685

Source: U.S. Department of Health and Human Services, National Center for Health Statistics, Vital and Health Statistics, *Mental Illness in Nursing Homes: United States, 1985*, Series 13: Data from the National Health Survey, No. 105, p. 27. *Note:* Figures may not add to totals because of rounding.

★ 800 ★

Mental Illness

Nursing Home Residents with Mental Disorders, Percent Distribution by Length of Stay and Facility Affiliation

Facility affiliation	All residents with mental disorders Number	Percent distribution							Stay in days	
			Length of stay since admission						Average length of stay since admission	Median length of stay since admission
		Total	Less than 3 months	3 months to less than 6 months	6 months to less than 12 months	1 year to less than 3 years	3 years to less than 5 years	5 years or more		
Chain	471,100	100.0	12.2	10.0	14.4	30.1	15.6	17.8	1,047	629
Independent	409,600	100.0	8.9	9.6	11.9	34.5	13.6	21.6	1,200	715
Government	86,400	100.0	12.2	4.8	14.5	32.3	13.2	23.0	1,374	689
Unknown	7,100	100.0	9.4	6.6	23.1	25.9	18.9	16.0	910	521

Source: U.S. Department of Health and Human Services, National Center for Health Statistics, Vital and Health Statistics, *Mental Illness in Nursing Homes: United States, 1985*, Series 13: Data from the National Health Survey, No. 105, p. 27. *Note:* Figures may not add to totals because of rounding.

★ 801 ★

Mental Illness

Prior Living Arrangements of Nursing Home Residents with Mental Disorders, by Age, Sex, and Race: United States, 1985

Usual living arrangement prior to admission[1]	All residents with mental disorders and next of kin	Age					Sex		Race		
		Under 65 years	65 years and over				Male	Female	White	Black and other	
			Total	65-74 years	75-84 years	85 years and over				Total	Black
Total	100.0	100.0	100.0	100.0	100.0	100.0	100.0	100.0	100.0	100.0	100.0
Usual living quarters											
Private or semi-private residence	67.5	47.4	70.4	56.6	70.5	75.3	59.8	70.4	67.6	67.2	67.1
Own home or apartment	37.7	19.4	40.3	33.0	41.3	42.1	37.2	37.9	38.5	28.3	29.1
Relative's home or apartment	20.2	18.9	20.3	15.1	18.4	23.8	13.4	22.6	19.6	27.5	26.1
Other private home or apartment	3.6	6.2	3.2	5.1	3.3	2.5	4.7	3.2	3.2	8.0	8.9
Retirement home	4.4	1.0	4.9	1.6	6.2	5.0	3.2	4.8	4.5	2.8	2.7
Boarding house, rooming house, or rented room	1.7	2.2	1.6	1.5	1.2	1.9	1.3	1.8	1.7	0.7	0.5
Another health facility	27.5	42.0	25.4	37.8	25.3	21.0	33.3	25.3	27.3	29.2	29.3
Another nursing home	18.3	14.4	18.9	23.7	18.5	17.5	17.2	18.8	18.3	18.7	19.9
General or short-term hospital	4.5	9.0	3.9	7.3	4.0	2.7	7.1	3.6	4.5	5.2	4.9
Mental hospital	3.5	14.7	1.9	6.0	1.7	0.7	6.8	2.4	3.4	5.1	4.1
Chronic disease or other long-term care hospital	1.0	4.2	0.6	1.0	1.2	5	2.5	0.5	1.1	0.4	0.5
Other place or unknown	5.0	10.6	4.2	5.5	4.3	3.6	6.9	4.3	5.1	3.5	3.6
Type of usual living arrangement											
Lived alone	22.7	8.1	24.8	17.8	24.3	27.6	14.0	25.8	23.1	17.4	18.3
Lived with spouse only	10.9	2.3	12.1	13.5	14.3	9.7	17.7	8.4	11.3	5.5	5.0
Lived with spouse and other relatives	1.7	2.5	1.6	2.2	1.2	1.8	3.6	1.1	1.8	1.1	1.3
Lived with son or daughter	13.6	3.7	15.0	6.0	14.0	19.0	6.7	16.1	13.3	16.6	15.5

[Continued]

★ 801 ★

Prior Living Arrangements of Nursing Home Residents with Mental Disorders, by Age, Sex, and Race: United States, 1985
[Continued]

Usual living arrangement prior to admission[1]	All residents with mental disorders and next of kin	Age					Sex		Race		
		Under 65 years	65 years and over				Male	Female	White	Black and other	
			Total	65-74 years	75-84 years	85 years and over				Total	Black
Lived with other relatives	8.7	21.0	7.0	10.9	6.4	6.1	10.0	8.2	8.0	17.5	17.7
Lived with unrelated persons	3.6	5.1	3.3	3.0	2.6	4.2	2.7	3.9	3.5	3.8	4.2
Group quarters[2]	6.1	2.8	6.5	3.2	7.4	6.9	4.5	6.6	6.3	3.5	3.1
Another health facility, other place or unknown[3]	32.9	54.8	29.7	43.7	29.7	24.8	40.9	29.9	32.7	34.5	34.6
Who lived with resident[4]											
Spouse	13.0	4.8	14.1	15.9	15.8	12.1	22.2	9.6	13.5	6.6	6.4
Children	14.8	5.6	16.2	7.9	14.9	20.3	8.9	17.0	14.6	17.4	16.0
Parents	2.3	14.3	0.6	3.3	0.3	5	3.7	1.8	2.5	0.7	0.5
Siblings	4.2	6.3	3.9	7.0	4.0	2.7	4.6	4.1	4.1	6.6	7.4
Grandchildren	5.9	2.7	6.3	5.5	5.9	6.9	4.5	6.4	5.6	9.0	7.4
Other relatives	6.5	7.3	6.4	6.1	5.2	7.5	4.7	7.1	6.6	5.8	6.4
Nonrelatives	6.5	7.3	6.4	6.1	5.2	7.5	4.7	7.1	6.6	5.8	6.4

Source: U.S. Department of Health and Human Services, National Center for Health Statistics, Vital and Health Statistics, *Mental Illness in Nursing Homes: United States, 1985*, Series 13: Data from the National Health Survey, No. 105, p. 31. *Notes:* 1. Living arrangements are as reported by next of kin. 2. Includes retirement home, boarding house, rooming house, and rented room. 3. Includes a small number of residents with usual living quarters in a private or semi-private residence but whose usual living arrangements are unknown. 4. Includes persons who usually lived with the resident in a private or semi-private residence prior to admission. 5. Data not available.

Mobility Impairment

★ 802 ★

Mobility Impairments in Nursing Home Residents Over Age 75

From the source: "As with home-dwelling frail older persons... physical disabilities are the sole or primary cause of many persons' nursing home needs."

	Number Impaired	Percent of Residents
Chairfast	464,000	42.0
Walk with assistance	301,000	27.0
Walk independently	260,000	24.0
Bedfast	79,000	7.0

Source: National Institute on Aging, *Physical Frailty*: A Reducible Barrier to Independence for Older Americans, Report to Congress, pp. 5-6.

Effects of Restraints

★ 803 ★

Detrimental Effects of Physical and Chemical Restraints on Nursing Home Residents: Cardiovascular

These effects may be due to restraints and/or other conditions.

Effect	Cause	Prevention
Swelling of ankle or lower leg/rings too tight/ shoes too tight	Older people may have a less efficient circulatory system. Without enough exercise, and changing of position, fluid collects in hands and feet.	Release, exercise every 2 hrs/change position often. Lie flat in bed every two hours. Use alternative methods.
Death	Cardiovascular stress response as fearful resident struggles to be free from restraint	Use alternative methods.

Source: U.S. Congress, "Resident Assessment: The Springboard to Quality of Care and Quality of Life for Nursing Home Residents," Workshop before the Special Committee on Aging, United States Senate, October 22, 1990, 101-30, U.S. Government Printing Office, Washington, D.C., p. 381. Primary source: *Quality Care Advocate*, July/August 1990. Developed by the National Citizens' Coalition for Nursing Home Reform for the National Center for State Long Term Care Ombudsman Resources funded by the Administration on Aging.

★ 804 ★

Effects of Restraints

Detrimental Effects of Physical and Chemical Restraints on Nursing Home Residents: Gastro-Intestinal Genito-Urinary

These effects may be due to restraints and/or other conditions.

Effect	Cause	Prevention
Decrease in appetite/weight loss/sunken cheek bones/sores around mouth	Broken spirit/not interested in life. Discomfort of restraint/preoccupation with discomfort. No activity to work up appetite. Too drowsy from drug use to eat.	Use alternative methods. Release, exercise at least every two hours. Decrease drug dose.
Dehydration. Dry skin/dry mouth/sunken eyes/ fever/acute confusion	Cannot reach water. Too drowsy to drink. Too depressed to drink. Does not recognize decreased sense of thirst.	Use alternative methods. Leave water within reach at all times. Offer fluids/encourage to drink between meals and at meals.
Urinary retention Distended lower belly/complains of needing to go to the bathroom/dribbling when toileted instead of good stream/presence of catheter with no other apparent cause	Many psychoactive drugs effect ability to release urine.	Discontinue drug. Use alternative methods. Use alternative drug. Discontinue catheter use.
Incontinence Wet/complains of not being taken to the bathroom/ agitation especially for resident with dementia/ presence of catheter for no other apparent reason	Not taken to the bathroom/toileting done according to facility rather than individual pattern/drug action may cause incontinence	Release, toilet, exercise every two hours or more often if necessary. Use alternative methods. Discontinue drug use. Use alternative drug.

[Continued]

★ 804 ★

Detrimental Effects of Physical and Chemical Restraints on Nursing Home Residents: Gastro-Intestinal Genito-Urinary
[Continued]

Effect	Cause	Prevention
Urinary tract infections/pain and frequency of urination, fever	Catheter use, not voiding regularly, low fluid intake	Toilet to avoid incontinence, increase fluid intake, use alternative methods.
Constipation/impaction Resident complains of stomach ache/constipation restlessness, decreased appetite/confusion Preoccupied with bowels	Lack of activity. Inability to get enough fluids. Not taken to the bathroom according to lifelong bowel pattern. meals.	Release, exercise, toilet every two hours or more if necessary. Toilet according to life-pattern. Offer fluids between meals and at Leave water within reach. Use alternative methods.

Source: U.S. Congress, "Resident Assessment: The Springboard to Quality of Care and Quality of Life for Nursing Home Residents," Workshop before the Special Committee on Aging, United States Senate, October 22, 1990, 101-30, U.S. Government Printing Office, Washington, D.C., pp. 382-383. Primary source: *Quality Care Advocate*, July/August 1990. Developed by the National Citizens' Coalition for Nursing Home Reform for the National Center for State Long Term Care Ombudsman Resources funded by the Administration on Aging.

★ 805 ★
Effects of Restraints

Detrimental Effects of Physical and Chemical Restraints on Nursing Home Residents: Musculo-Skeleton

These effects may be due to restraints and/or other conditions.

Effect	Cause	Prevention
Decrease in mobility such as unable to walk, move own wheelchair. Wasting of muscles over time. Contractures in extremities recognized by hands in fist, bent elbows, knees bent toward chest and moved, if at all, only with difficulty and pain. Increased fractures.	Prolonged inactivity causes loss of muscle in all ages, so that the person gradually loses ability to use them; bone loss results in increased fracture risk.	Use alternative methods: physical therapy, release, weight bearing exercise every 2 hours or more often if necessary. Range of motion exercises, fit chair to individual, use cushions, wedges and pillows for comfort.

Source: U.S. Congress, "Resident Assessment: The Springboard to Quality of Care and Quality of Life for Nursing Home Residents," Workshop before the Special Committee on Aging, United States Senate, October 22, 1990, 101-30, U.S. Government Printing Office, Washington, D.C., p. 383. Primary source: *Quality Care Advocate*, July/August 1990. Developed by the National Citizens' Coalition for Nursing Home Reform for the National Center for State Long Term Care Ombudsman Resources funded by the Administration on Aging.

★ 806 ★
Effects of Restraints

Detrimental Effects of Physical and Chemical Restraints on Nursing Home Residents: Nervous System

These effects may be due to restraints and/or other conditions.

Effect	Cause	Prevention
Complains of tension or exhibits signs of tension.	Restraints are not relaxing; stressful from having movement restricted.	Use alternative methods, use restraints for very short periods of time. Discontinue drug or lower dose. Use alternative drug without that particular side effect.
Tardive dyskinesia/repetitive movements of head, tongue, hands, and feet.	Caused by some chemical restraints. Haldol is a commonly used drug with this effect and is irreversible.	Use lowest drug dose for shortest period of time. Keep in mind general rule: 1/2 adult dose for elderly--1/4 dose for elderly with dementia. (Of course there are exceptions to this) Note that continuous long-term drug use is seldom necessary.
Coma/death	Too large dose of psychoactive drug	Use small doses for short periods of time.

Source: U.S. Congress, "Resident Assessment: The Springboard to Quality of Care and Quality of Life for Nursing Home Residents," Workshop before the Special Committee on Aging, United States Senate, October 22, 1990, 101-30, U.S. Government Printing Office, Washington, D.C., p. 384. Primary source: *Quality Care Advocate*, July/August 1990. Developed by the National Citizens' Coalition for Nursing Home Reform for the National Center for State Long Term Care Ombudsman Resources funded by the Administration on Aging.

★ 807 ★
Effects of Restraints

Detrimental Effects of Physical and Chemical Restraints on Nursing Home Residents: Psychological

These effects may be due to restraints and/or other conditions.

Effect	Cause	Prevention
Panic/anxious expression/combative/ increased confusion	Frightened by physical restraints. Does not like restraints. Does not understand why they are being used. Paradoxical reaction to a psychoactive drug.	Use alternative methods. Use CR and PR for are being used for short periods only. Use different drug, lower dose or no drug.
Lethargy/depression/decreased social interaction	Person gives up when restrained, withdraws, broken spirit. Staff ignore restrained resident. Drug in too large dose.	Use alternative methods. Increase opportunity to socialize. Frequent staff interaction. Decrease time restraints are used. Decrease drug dose or change drugs.
Screaming/yelling/calling out	Use alternative options, identify and meet needs, comfort	Use alternative options, identify and meet needs, comfort

Source: U.S. Congress, "Resident Assessment: The Springboard to Quality of Care and Quality of Life for Nursing Home Residents," Workshop before the Special Committee on Aging, United States Senate, October 22, 1990, 101-30, U.S. Government Printing Office, Washington, D.C., p. 385. Primary source: *Quality Care Advocate*, July/August 1990. Developed by the National Citizens' Coalition for Nursing Home Reform for the National Center for State Long Term Care Ombudsman Resources funded by the Administration on Aging. *Note:* CR stands for chemical restraint; PR stands for physical restraint.

★ 808 ★

Effects of Restraints

Detrimental Effects of Physical and Chemical Restraints on Nursing Home Residents: Respiratory

These effects may be due to restraints and/or other conditions.

Effect	Cause	Prevention
Resident complains that chest feels tight/ says "can't breathe"/appears anxious	Chest/vest restraint is too tight. Resident fears restraint and has anxiety attack. Lack of movement	Use alternative methods. Loosen restraint. Decrease use of drugs. Exercise every two hours or more often if necessary.
Pneumonia Acute confusion/shortness of breath/ chest pain	Lack of movement allows secretions to pool, decreases efficiency of lungs with decreased oxygen exchange and increased confusion.	Same as above Shortness of breath when active.
Death	Incorrectly applied restraint leads to death by strangulation	Apply restraint correctly/use alternative methods.

Source: U.S. Congress, "Resident Assessment: The Springboard to Quality of Care and Quality of Life for Nursing Home Residents," Workshop before the Special Committee on Aging, United States Senate, October 22, 1990, 101-30, U.S. Government Printing Office, Washington, D.C., p. 386. Primary source: *Quality Care Advocate*, July/August 1990. Developed by the National Citizens' Coalition for Nursing Home Reform for the National Center for State Long Term Care Ombudsman Resources funded by the Administration on Aging.

★ 809 ★

Effects of Restraints

Detrimental Effects of Physical and Chemical Restraints on Nursing Home Residents: Skin

These effects may be due to restraints and/or other conditions.

Effect	Cause	Prevention
Bruising/cuts/redness	Incorrectly applied restraint or improper size or type of restraint. Resident struggles against restraint.	Apply restraint correctly according to manufacturer's direction. Use alternative methods. Apply restraint for short periods of time.
Pressure sores	Resident in one position too long. Studies show two times number of pressure sores in restrained residents.	Release, exercise, at least every 2 hrs.-- more often if necessary. Use alternative methods.

Source: U.S. Congress, "Resident Assessment: The Springboard to Quality of Care and Quality of Life for Nursing Home Residents," Workshop before the Special Committee on Aging, United States Senate, October 22, 1990, 101-30, U.S. Government Printing Office, Washington, D.C., p. 386. Primary source: *Quality Care Advocate*, July/August 1990. Developed by the National Citizens' Coalition for Nursing Home Reform for the National Center for State Long Term Care Ombudsman Resources funded by the Administration on Aging.

Safety Issues

★ 810 ★

State Requirements for Compliance by Nursing Facilities with the Life Safety Code (LSC) Editions

The Life Safety Code (LSC), a specific type of fire code, establishes minimum requirements which provide a reasonable degree of safety from fire in buildings and structures. It is the most widely used fire code in the U.S. and is developed by the National Fire Protection Association. Nursing facilities must comply with the 1967, 1973, 1981, and 1985 editions of the LSC to receive Medicare and Medicaid funding. Many states require nursing facilities to abide by more recent editions.

States	Numbers	Percent
States requiring facilities to comply with the 1985, 1988, or 1991 LSC edition	26	51.0
States requiring facilities to comply with the 1981, 1985, 1988, or 1991 LSC editions	6	12.0
States requiring facilities to comply with the 1967, 1973, 1981, or 1985 LSC editions	14	27.0
No comment or N/A	5	10

Source: U.S. Congress, "A State-by-State Analysis of Fire Safety in Nursing Facilities," A Staff Report of the Special Committee on Aging, United States Senate, May, 1992, 102-M, U.S. Government Printing Office, Washington, D.C., p. 13.

★ 811 ★
Safety Issues

State Requirements for Automatic Fire Sprinklers in Nursing Facilities

States	Numbers	Percent
States with a sprinkler requirement for all facilities	12	24.0
States with a sprinkler requirement for only new facilities	15	29.0
States with no sprinkler requirements	24	47.0

Source: U.S. Congress, "A State-by-State Analysis of Fire Safety in Nursing Facilities," A Staff Report of the Special Committee on Aging, United States Senate, May, 1992, 102-M, U.S. Government Printing Office, Washington, D.C., p. 14.

★ 812 ★

Safety Issues

State Requirements for Automatic Fire Sprinklers in New Nursing Facilities

Dates	Numbers	Percent
States requiring fire sprinklers in 1991	3	20
States requiring fire sprinklers in 1981-90	7	47
States requiring fire sprinklers in 1971-80	3	20
No response	2	13

Source: U.S. Congress, "A State-by-State Analysis of Fire Safety in Nursing Facilities," A Staff Report of the Special Committee on Aging, United States Senate, May, 1992, 102-M, U.S. Government Printing Office, Washington, D.C., p. 14.

★ 813 ★

Safety Issues

State Requirements for Emergency Preparedness Plans in Nursing Facilities

States	Numbers	Percent
States with a requirement for emergency preparedness plans in nursing facilities	45	88
States with no emergency preparedness plan requirement for nursing facilities	5	10
Unknown	1	2

Source: U.S. Congress, "A State-by-State Analysis of Fire Safety in Nursing Facilities," A Staff Report of the Special Committee on Aging, United States Senate, May, 1992, 102-M, U.S. Government Printing Office, Washington, D.C., p. 15.

★ 814 ★

Safety Issues

State Requirements for Agency Responsible for the Review of Nursing Facilities' Emergency Preparedness Plans

States	Numbers	Percent
States where the fire authority reviews the plans	33	65
States where another agency solely reviews the plans	9	18
States where both the fire authority and another agency review the plans	7	14
States where no agency reviews the plans	2	3

Source: U.S. Congress, "A State-by-State Analysis of Fire Safety in Nursing Facilities," A Staff Report of the Special Committee on Aging, United States Senate, May, 1992, 102-M, U.S. Government Printing Office, Washington, D.C., p. 16.

★ 815 ★

Safety Issues

State Requirements for Frequency of Nursing Facilities' Emergency Preparedness Plan Reviews

States	Numbers	Percent
States with a quarterly review of plans	1	2
States with an annual review of plans	38	75
States with a varying review of plans	2	4
States with one time only review of plans	1	2
Unknown	9	18

Source: U.S. Congress, "A State-by-State Analysis of Fire Safety in Nursing Facilities," A Staff Report of the Special Committee on Aging, United States Senate, May, 1992, 102-M, U.S. Government Printing Office, Washington, D.C., p. 16.

★ 816 ★

Safety Issues

State Requirements for Smoke Detectors in Nursing Facilities

States	Numbers	Percent
States requiring smoke detectors in both bedrooms and corridors	10	20
States requiring smoke detectors in corridors only	28	55
States requiring no smoke detectors in all facilities	13	25

Source: U.S. Congress, "A State-by-State Analysis of Fire Safety in Nursing Facilities," A Staff Report of the Special Committee on Aging, United States Senate, May, 1992, 102-M, U.S. Government Printing Office, Washington, D.C., p. 16.

★ 817 ★

Safety Issues

State Requirements for Fire Safety Training of Nursing Facility Employees

States	Numbers	Percent
States requiring training annually	22	43
States requiring training only once	4	8
States requiring training at other frequencies	19	37
States requiring no training	5	10
No response	1	2

Source: U.S. Congress, "A State-by-State Analysis of Fire Safety in Nursing Facilities," A Staff Report of the Special Committee on Aging, United States Senate, May, 1992, 102-M, U.S. Government Printing Office, Washington, D.C., p. 17.

★ 818 ★

Safety Issues

State Requirements for Life Safety Code (LSC) in Nursing Homes

State	Editions of LSC	LSC adopted	LSC enforced for facilities' funding only
Alabama	1967; 1973; 1981; 1985	x	
Alaska	1967; 1973; 1981; 1985		X-by reference to uniform Fire Code
Arizona	1985	x-Adopted by Department of Health	
Arkansas	1967; 1973; 1981; 1985	x	
California	1967; 1973 1981; 1985		x
Colorado			x
Connecticut	1988	x	
Delaware	1985	x	
District of Columbia	1981; 1985		x
Florida	1988	x	
Georgia	1985	x	
Hawaii	N/A		x
Idaho	1988		X-By reference to Uniform Fire Code
Illinois	1985	x	
Indiana	1981; 1985		x
Iowa	1967; 1973 1981; 1985		x
Kansas	1981; 1985 1988	x	
Kentucky	1967; 1973 1981; 1985; 1988	x	
Louisiana	1988	x	
Maine	1991	x	
Maryland	1988	x	
Massachusetts			x
Michigan	1967; 1981 1985	x-Adopted 1985 L.S.C. with amendments	
Minnesota	1988	x	
Mississippi	1985	x	
Missouri	1967; 1973; 1981; 1985	x	
Montana	1967; 1973;		

[Continued]

★ 818 ★

State Requirements for Life Safety Code (LSC) in Nursing Homes
[Continued]

State	Editions of LSC	LSC adopted	LSC enforced for facilities' funding only
Nebraska	1981; 1985 1985	x	x
Nevada	1988	x-L.S.C. & ICBO Codes	
New Hampshire	1988	x	
New Jersey	N/A		x-by reference to uniform Fire Code
New Mexico	1988	x	
New York	1985	x-1985 L.S.C. with an amendment	
North Carolina	1985		x
North Dakota	1967; 1973; 1981; 1985; 1988		x
Ohio	1981	x	
Oklahoma	1988	x	
Oregon	1981; 1985		x
Pennsylvania	1967; 1973; 1981; 1985		x
Rhode Island	1988	x-Health Care Section only adopted by state	
South Carolina	N/A		x-By reference to Standard Fire Prevention Code
South Dakota	1967; 1973; 1981; 1985	x	
Tennessee	1981	x-L.S.C. & Standard Building Code	
Texas	1985	x	
Utah	1991	x	
Vermont	1988	x	
Virginia	1967; 1973; 1981; 1985		x
Washington	1985	x-By reference to Uniform Fire Code	
West Virginia	1988	x	

[Continued]

★ 818 ★

State Requirements for Life Safety Code (LSC) in Nursing Homes
[Continued]

State	Editions of LSC	LSC adopted	LSC enforced for facilities' funding only
Wisconsin	1985	x	
Wyoming	1967; 1973; 1981; 1985; 1988; 1991	x	

Source: U.S. Congress, "A State-by-State Analysis of Fire Safety in Nursing Facilities," A Staff Report of the Special Committee on Aging, United States Senate, May, 1992, 102-M, U.S. Government Printing Office, Washington, D.C., pp. 34-36. *Note:* ICBO stands for International Conference of Building Officials.

★ 819 ★

Safety Issues

State Requirements for Fire Sprinklers in Nursing Facilities

States	Installed in new facilities	Installed in all facilities	Proposed legislation	Sprinklers throughout structure
Alabama	x - 1988			
Alaska	x - 1980	x - 1980		x
Arizona	x - 1979			
Arkansas			No response	
California	x - 1971	x - 1971		x
Colorado			x	
Connecticut				
Delaware	x - 1989			
District of Columbia			Unknown	
Florida				
Georgia			x	
Hawaii	x			
Idaho	x			
Illinois			Unknown	
Indiana	x - 1985			
Iowa				
Kansas				
Kentucky				
Louisiana				
Maine	x - 1965	x - 1965		x
Maryland	x - 1975			
Massachusetts	x	x		x
Michigan	x - 1991			

[Continued]

★ 819 ★

State Requirements for Fire Sprinklers in Nursing Facilities
[Continued]

States	Installed in new facilities	Installed in all facilities	Proposed legislation	Sprinklers throughout structure
Minnesota	x - 1973			
Mississippi				
Missouri	x - 1981		Unknown	
Montana	x - 1988			
Nebraska				
Nevada	x - 1973	x - 1973		x
New Hampshire	x - 1986	x - 1986		x
New Jersey	x - 1991		x	
New Mexico				
New York				
North Carolina			Unknown	
North Dakota				
Ohio	x - 1976	x - 1976		x
Oklahoma				
Oregon	x - 1975	x - 1975		x
Pennsylvania				
Rhode Island	x - 1990			
South Carolina	x - 1984		Unknown	
South Dakota				
Tennessee				
Texas				
Utah	x	x		x
Vermont				
Virginia	x - 1975	x - 1990		x
Washington	x - 1977	x - 1986		x
West Virginia	x - 1968	x - 1968		x
Wisconsin				
Wyoming	x - 1991			

Source: U.S. Congress, "A State-by-State Analysis of Fire Safety in Nursing Facilities," A Staff Report of the Special Committee on Aging, United States Senate, May, 1992, 102-M, U.S. Government Printing Office, Washington, D.C., pp. 37-40.

★ 820 ★

Safety Issues

State Requirements for Emergency Preparedness Plans in Nursing Facilities

States	All facilities required to have plans	Plans reviewed by fire authority	Plans reviewed by other authority	Frequency of plans' review
Alabama	x		Department of Public Health	Annually
Alaska	x	x		Annually
Arizona	x	x		Annually
Arkansas	x	x		Annually
California	x	x		Annually
Colorado		x	Department of Health	Unknown
Connecticut	x	x		Annually
Delaware	x		Board of Health	Once
District of Columbia	x	x		Annually
Florida	x	x		Annually
Georgia			Health & Human Services	Unknown
Hawaii	x	x		Annually
Idaho	x	x	Health & Welfare	Unknown
Illinois	x		Department of Public Health	Unknown
Indiana		x		Annually
Iowa				Unknown
Kansas	x	x		Annually
Kentucky	x	x		Annually
Louisiana	x	x	Health & Human Services	Annually
Maine	x	x		Annually
Maryland	x	x		Annually
Massachusetts	x	x		Quarterly
Michigan	x	x		Annually
Minnesota	x	x		Annually
Mississippi	x	x	Department of Health	Annually
Missouri	x		Department of Aging	Annually
Montana	x	x		Annually
Nebraska	x	x		Annually
Nevada	x	x		Unknown
New Hampshire	x	x		Annually
New Jersey	x	x		As prepared or revised
New Mexico	x	x	State Health Certification	

[Continued]

★ 820 ★

State Requirements for Emergency Preparedness Plans in Nursing Facilities

[Continued]

States	All facilities required to have plans	Plans reviewed by fire authority	Plans reviewed by other authority	Frequency of plans' review
New York	x		Agency Department of Health	Annually Varies
North Carolina	x	x		Annually
North Dakota	x	x		Annually
Ohio	x	x	Department of Health	Annually
Oklahoma	Unknown		Department of Health	Unknown
Oregon	x	x		Annually
Pennsylvania	x			Unknown
Rhode Island	x	x		Annually
South Carolina	x		Law Enforcement Division	Unknown
South Dakota		x		Annually
Tennessee	x	x	Department of Health	Annually
Texas	x	x		Annually
Utah	x	x		Annually
Vermont	x	x		Annually
Virginia	x	x		Annually
Washington	x	x		Annually
West Virginia	x	x		Annually
Wisconsin	x		Health & Social Services	Annually
Wyoming	x	x		Annually

Source: U.S. Congress, "A State-by-State Analysis of Fire Safety in Nursing Facilities," A Staff Report of the Special Committee on Aging, United States Senate, May, 1992, 102-M, U.S. Government Printing Office, Washington, D.C., pp. 41-44.

★ 821 ★
Safety Issues
State Requirements for Smoke Detectors in Nursing Facilities

States	All facilities install smoke detectors	All facilities install smoke detectors in bedrooms & halls
Alabama	X	
Alaska	X	X
Arizona	X	
Arkansas	X	
California	X	
Colorado		
Connecticut		
Delaware	X	
District of Columbia	X	
Florida	X	
Georgia		
Hawaii		
Idaho	X	X
Illinois	X	
Indiana		
Iowa		
Kansas	X	
Kentucky	X	
Louisiana	X	
Maine		
Maryland	X	
Massachusetts	X	X
Michigan		
Minnesota		
Mississippi	X	X
Missouri		
Montana	X	X
Nebraska	X	
Nevada	X	X
New Hampshire	X	X
New Jersey	X	
New Mexico		
New York	X	X
North Carolina	X	
North Dakota	X	
Ohio	X	X
Oklahoma	X	
Oregon	X	
Pennsylvania	X	
Rhode Island	X	

[Continued]

★ 821 ★

State Requirements for Smoke Detectors in Nursing Facilities
[Continued]

States	All facilities install smoke detectors	All facilities install smoke detectors in bedrooms & halls
South Carolina	x	
South Dakota		
Tennessee	x	
Texas	x	
Utah	x	
Vermont	x	
Virginia	x	
Washington	x	x
West Virginia	x	
Wisconsin	x	
Wyoming		

Source: U.S. Congress, "A State-by-State Analysis of Fire Safety in Nursing Facilities," A Staff Report of the Special Committee on Aging, United States Senate, May, 1992, 102-M, U.S. Government Printing Office, Washington, D.C., pp. 45-48.

★ 822 ★

Safety Issues

State Requirements for Frequency of Fire Safety Training for Nursing Facility Employees

States	Annually	Once only	Never	Other
Alabama	x			
Alaska				
Arizona				Quarterly Requirement for inservice
Arkansas	x			
California				
Colorado				Quarterly Once only/ never
Connecticut	x			
Delaware				Once only/ Annually
District of Columbia		x		
Florida				Annually/ quarterly
Georgia				Periodically
Hawaii	x			

[Continued]

★ 822 ★

State Requirements for Frequency of Fire Safety Training for Nursing Facility Employees
[Continued]

States	Annually	Once only	Never	Other
Idaho			x	
Illinois				Quarterly
Indiana				Quarterly fire drills
Iowa			x	
Kansas	x			
Kentucky	x			
Louisiana			x	
Maine	x			
Maryland		x		
Massachusetts	No response	No response	No response	No response
Michigan			x	
Minnesota	x			
Mississippi				Fire drills
Missouri	x			
Montana	x			
Nebraska	x			
Nevada	x			
New Hampshire				Quarterly fire drills
New Jersey				Quarterly fire drills
New Mexico	x			
New York				Quarterly fire drills
North Carolina				No state requirement/ Determined at local level
North Dakota				Fire drills
Ohio	x			
Oklahoma	x			
Oregon				Monthly
Pennsylvania	x			
Rhode Island				Quarterly fire drills
South Carolina		x		
South Dakota				Quarterly fire drills
Tennessee			x	
Texas				Quarterly fire drills
Utah	x			
Vermont	x			
Virginia	x			

[Continued]

★ 822 ★

State Requirements for Frequency of Fire Safety Training for Nursing Facility Employees

[Continued]

States	Annually	Once only	Never	Other
Washington	X			
West Virginia	X			
Wisconsin	X			
Wyoming		X		

Source: U.S. Congress, "A State-by-State Analysis of Fire Safety in Nursing Facilities," A Staff Report of the Special Committee on Aging, United States Senate, May, 1992, 102-M, U.S. Government Printing Office, Washington, D.C., pp. 49-52.

★ 823 ★

Safety Issues

State Requirements for Specific Components of Fire Safety Training Programs in Nursing Facilities

States	Closing doors for fire control	Function of sprinklers	Operation of extinguishers	Knowledge of emergency plan	Fire prevention	Action to take in a fire	Notify fire department
Alabama	X		X	X	X	X	X
Alaska	X			X		X	
Arizona				X		X	X
Arkansas	X	X	X	X	X	X	X
California	X	X	X	X	X	X	X
Colorado	X	X	X	X	X	X	X
Connecticut	X	X	X	X	X	X	X
Delaware	X	X	X	X	X	X	X
District of Columbia	X	X	X	X	X	X	X
Florida	X	X	X	X	X	X	X
Georgia	X	X	X	X	X	X	X
Hawaii			X	X	X	X	X
Idaho							
Illinois	X		X	X	X	X	X
Indiana	X	X	X	X	X	X	X
Iowa							
Kansas	X		X	X	X	X	X
Kentucky	X	X	X	X	X	X	X
Louisiana							
Maine	X	X	X	X	X	X	X
Maryland	X	X	X	X	X	X	X
Massachusetts	NR	NR	NR	NR	NR	NR	NR
Michigan							
Minnesota	X		X	X	X	X	X
Mississippi							
Missouri	X	X	X	X	X	X	X

[Continued]

★ 823 ★

State Requirements for Specific Components of Fire Safety Training Programs in Nursing Facilities

[Continued]

States	Closing doors for fire control	Function of sprinklers	Operation of extinguishers	Knowledge of emergency plan	Fire prevention	Action to take in a fire	Notify fire department
Montana	x		x	x	x	x	x
Nebraska	NR	NR	NR	NR	NR	NR	NR
Nevada	x	x	x	x		x	x
New Hampshire	x	x	x	x	x	x	x
New Jersey							
New Mexico	x		x	x	x	x	x
New York							
North Carolina							
North Dakota	x		x	x		x	x
Ohio	x	x	x	x	x	x	x
Oklahoma			x		x	x	x
Oregon	x	x	x	x	x	x	x
Pennsylvania	x	x	x	x	x	x	x
Rhode Island	x		x	x	x	x	x
South Carolina	x		x		x	x	x
South Dakota					x	x	x
Tennessee	N/A	N/A	N/A	N/A	N/A	N/A	N/A
Texas	x	x	x	x	x	x	x
Utah	x		x	x	x	x	x
Vermont			x	x		x	x
Virginia	NR	NR	NR	NR	NR	NR	NR
Washington	x	x	x	x	x	x	x
West Virginia	x	x	x		x	x	x
Wisconsin	x	x	x	x	x	x	x
Wyoming	NR	NR	NR	NR	NR	NR	NR

Source: U.S. Congress, "A State-by-State Analysis of Fire Safety in Nursing Facilities," A Staff Report of the Special Committee on Aging, United States Senate, May, 1992, 102-M, U.S. Government Printing Office, Washington, D.C., pp. 53-57. *Note:* NR stands for No response.

★ 824 ★

Safety Issues

State Requirements for Fire Safety Enforcement in Nursing Facilities

States	Fire sprinklers	Smoke detectors	Fire doors	Door latches	Extinguishers
Alabama	x	x	x	x	x
Alaska	x	x	x	x	x
Arizona	x	x	x	x	x
Arkansas	x	x	x	x	x
California	x	x	x	x	x

[Continued]

★ 824 ★

State Requirements for Fire Safety Enforcement in Nursing Facilities

[Continued]

States	Fire sprinklers	Smoke detectors	Fire doors	Door latches	Extinguishers
Colorado					
Connecticut	x	x	x	x	x
Delaware	x	x	x	x	x
District of Columbia	x	x	x	x	x
Florida	x	x	x	x	x
Georgia	x	x	x	x	x
Hawaii	x	x	x	x	x
Idaho	x	x	x	x	x
Illinois			x	x	x
Indiana	x	x	x	x	x
Iowa	x	x	x	x	x
Kansas	x	x	x	x	x
Kentucky	x	x	x	x	x
Louisiana	x	x	x	x	x
Maine	x	x	x	x	x
Maryland	x	x	x	x	x
Massachusetts	x	x	x	x	x
Michigan	x	x	x	x	x
Minnesota	x	x	x	x	x
Mississippi	No response	No response	No response	No response	No response
Missouri	x	x	x	x	x
Montana	x	x	x	x	x
Nebraska	x	x	x	x	x
Nevada	x	x	x	x	x
New Hampshire	x	x	x	x	x
New Jersey	x	x	x	x	x
New Mexico	x	x	x	x	x
New York	No response	No response	No response	No response	No response
North Carolina	x	x	x	x	x
North Dakota	x	x	x	x	x
Ohio	x	x	x	x	x
Oklahoma	x	x	x	x	x
Oregon	x	x	x	x	x
Pennsylvania		x	x	x	x
Rhode Island	x	x	x	x	x
South Carolina	x	x	x	x	x
South Dakota	x	x	x	x	x
Tennessee	x	x	x	x	x
Texas	x	x	x	x	x
Utah	x	x	x	x	x
Vermont	x	x	x	x	x
Virginia	x	x	x	x	x
Washington	x	x	x	x	x
West Virginia	x	x	x	x	x

[Continued]

★ 824 ★

State Requirements for Fire Safety Enforcement in Nursing Facilities
[Continued]

States	Fire sprinklers	Smoke detectors	Fire doors	Door latches	Extinguishers
Wisconsin	X	X	X	X	X
Wyoming			X	X	X

Source: U.S. Congress, "A State-by-State Analysis of Fire Safety in Nursing Facilities," A Staff Report of the Special Committee on Aging, United States Senate, May, 1992, 102-M, U.S. Government Printing Office, Washington, D.C., pp. 58-61.

Chapter 13
CULTURE AND LIFESTYLE

This chapter brings together diverse statistical information on the elderly, including Religious Preferences, Cultural Characteristics, Entertainment, Television, Eating Out, Senior Discounts, and Transportation. Similar information is presented in the chapters on *Public Life*, and *Opinions*.

Religion

★ 825 ★

Religious Preferences of Persons Age 50 Years and Older

Data show results of a national survey conducted by the Gallup Organization for the Princeton Religion Research Organization. The following question was asked: "What is your religious preference?—Protestant, Catholic, Jewish, or an Orthodox Church, such as the Greek or Russian Orthodox Church?"

	Ages of respondents	
	18 years and older	50 years and older
Protestant	56.0	64.0
Roman Catholic	25.0	23.0
Jewish	2.0	2.0
Orthodox Church	1.0	[1]

Source: Personal communication from Ms. Alison Gallup of the Princeton Religion Research Organization. Primary source: *Religion in America 1992-1993* (25th anniversary edition), p. 37. *Notes:* 1. Less than one percent .

Cultural Characteristics

★ 826 ★

Cultural Characteristics of Centenarians by Age Group: 1980

Characteristic	Number of persons		
	100 and over	100 to 104 years	105 years and over
Year of immigration			
Total	14,170	12,838	1,332
Born a citizen	11,553	10,556	997
1950-1980	338	338	0
Before 1950	2,279	1,944	335
Language spoken at home			
Total	14,170	12,838	1,332
Only English	12,035	10,929	1,106
Other than English	2,135	1,909	226
Ability to speak English			
Total	14,170	12,838	1,332
Only speaks English	12,035	10,929	1,106
Speaks another language at home	2,135	1,909	226
Speaks English well	1,278	1,116	162
Does not speak English well	857	793	64

Source: Gregory Spencer, Arnold A. Goldstein, and Cynthia M. Taeuber, *America's Centenarians: Data from the 1980 Census*, National Institute on Aging, Washington, DC, June 1987, Table A-1. *Notes:* 1. A problem with 1980 Census allocation procedures resulted in an inflation of the count of the centenarian population by about one-fourth. This data reflects unallocated age data only and therefore may be subject to sampling error due to incorrect reporting, overreporting by respondents, or incomplete documentation.

★ 827 ★
Cultural Characteristics

Ancestry of Centenarians by Age Group: 1980

Area of origin	Number of persons		
	100 and over	100 to 104 years	105 Years and over
Total persons[1]	13,879	12,625	1,254
Western European	6,214	5,740	474
Eastern European and Russia	437	373	64
Hispanic Americas, Caribbean	313	313	0
Africa	123	123	
Asia and the Pacific	0	0	0
Canada, Non-Hispanic Caribbean	3,486	2,885	601
Other, not reported	3,306	3,191	115
Male			
Western European	1,293	1,206	87
Eastern European and Russia	148	148	0
Hispanic Americas, Caribbean	85	85	0
Africa	0	0	0
Canada and Non-Hispanic Caribbean	1,181	1,114	67
Other, not reported	825	757	68
Female			
Western Europe	4,921	4,534	387
Eastern Europe and Russia	289	225	64
Hispanic Americas, Caribbean	228	228	0
Africa	123	123	0
Asia and the Pacific	0	0	0
Canada and Non-Hispanic Caribbean	2,305	1,771	534
Other, not reported	2,481	2,434	47

Source: Gregory Spencer, Arnold A. Goldstein, and Cynthia M. Taeuber, *America's Centenarians: Data from the 1980 Census*, National Institute on Aging, Washington, DC, June 1987, Table A-1. *Notes:* 1. A problem with 1980 Census allocation procedures resulted in an inflation of the count of the centenarian population by about one-fourth. This data reflects unallocated age data only and therefore may be subject to sampling error due to incorrect reporting, overreporting by respondents, or incomplete documentation.

Entertainment

★ 828 ★

Television's Representation of the U.S. Population, by Age

Data show percent distribution of the U.S. population in real life and as represented by prime time television programs.

Age	Real life	On TV
Children (0-12)	19.0	4.0
Teens (13-17)	7.0	6.0
Young adults (18-35)	30.0	42.0
Middle age (36-59)	27.0	40.0
Seniors (60-over)	17.0	8.0

Source: USA TODAY, July 6, 1993, p. 3D.

★ 829 ★

Entertainment

Movie Viewing

Data show older Americans as percent of all persons who saw at least three movies within the past month.

Age	Percent of viewers
55-64	4.6
65 or older	9.7

Source: Brandweek, April 5, 1993, p. 32.

★ 830 ★

Entertainment

Average Annual Expenditures of All Consumers for Entertainment and Reading, by Age: 1990

[In dollars, except as indicated]

Age	Entertainment and reading		Entertainment				Reading
	Total	Percent of total expenditures	Total	Fees and admissions	Television, radios, and sound equipment	Other equipment and services[1]	
All consumers	1,575	5.6	1,422	371	454	597	153
Under 25 years old	908	5.5	833	218	344	272	75
25 to 34 years old	1,606	5.7	1,472	342	503	628	134
35 to 44 years old	2,025	5.7	1,837	527	583	726	188
45 to 54 years old	2,150	5.8	1,966	438	592	937	184
55 to 64 years old	1,670	5.7	1,507	365	390	752	163
65 to 74 years old	1,070	5.1	914	329	307	277	156
75 years old and over	535	3.5	423	153	161	109	112

Source: U.S. Bureau of the Census, *Statistical Abstract of the United States*: 1992 (112th edition.) Washington, DC, 1992, p. 235. Primary source: U.S. Bureau of Labor Statistics, *Consumer Expenditure Survey*, annual. *Notes:* 1. Other equipment and services includes pets, toys, and playground equipment, and sports, exercise, and photographic equipment.

Television

★ 831 ★

Where the Elderly View Television

Older Americans are less likely than younger ones to watch television in bed or in the car—and more likely to watch in the dining area. Data show percent of population with a working television set placed in the following places. Data are for 1992.

	18 to 24	25 to 44	45 to 59	60 and older
Living room, family room or den	86	95	95	93
Own bedroom	60	58	57	45
Child's bedroom	22	31	28	8
Kitchen	9	12	20	20
Dining area	9	10	10	19
Bathroom	2	3	2	4
Garage	-	2	2	2

[Continued]

★ 831 ★

Where the Elderly View Television
[Continued]

	18 to 24	25 to 44	45 to 59	60 and older
Patio or porch	2	1	5	4
Car	2	2	-	-

Source: American Demographics, March 1993, p. 18. Primary source: Peter D. Hart Research Associates for *TV Guide*.

★ 832 ★

Television

Top-Ranked Television Programs

Table shows the 10 television programs most popular with people aged 50 and over. Ratings shown indicate percent of the total age-group that watches the program.

Program	Ratings among viewers 50-plus	Network
Murder, She Wrote	25.4	CBS
60 Minutes	24.0	CBS
In the Heat of the Night	19.0	CBS
Sunday Night Movie	17.9	CBS
Evening Shade	16.6	CBS
Murphy Brown	16.3	CBS
Hearts Afire	15.1	CBS
Unsolved Mysteries	15.0	NBC
Golden Palace	13.7	CBS
48 Hours	13.6	CBS
20/20	13.6	ABC

Source: Advertising Age, November 16, 1992, p. 56. Primary source: Nielsen Media Research.

Eating Out

★ 833 ★

Full Service vs. Quick Service Restaurant Preferences

Distribution of restaurant meals and snacks by age group. Table shows where people take their meals, indicating that with advancing age people show greater preference for full service restaurants.

[Values in percent]

	Full service	Quick service
All customers	31	69
50-64 years	45	55
65 and over	51	49

Source: *Nation's Restaurant News*, June 22, p. 14. Primary source: NDP Crest.

Senior Discounts

★ 834 ★

Senior Citizen Discount Use

Data show responses from a survey of 374 women age 65 and older in the Greater Kansas City metro area.

[Percentage of discount users]

	Frequency of use		Life satisfaction		Living arrangements	
	Heavy	Light/none	Satisfied	Dissatisfied	Independent	Dependent
Travel	34	12	23	3	20	5
Restaurants	64	22	39	14	55	12
Groceries	36	13	22	9	32	7
Entertainment	39	14	24	11	36	6
Prescription drugs	64	30	43	20	55	22

Source: Lisa D. Spiller and Richard A. Hamilton, "Senior Citizen Discount Programs: Which Seniors to Target and Why," *Journal of Consumer Marketing*, pp. 44-45.

Transportation

★ 835 ★

Licensed Older Male Drivers, by Age, 1990

Data are compiled for the calendar year from reports of state authorities and other sources.

[Number]

State	55-59	60-64	65-69	70-74[3]	75-79[3,4]	80-84[3,4]	85 and over[3,4]
Alabama	77,209	68,861	54,103	37,465	21,779	10,337	-
Alaska	7,200	5,500	3,600	2,200	1,300	400	150
Arizona[1]	67,099	64,347	62,235	102,956	-	-	-
Arkansas[2]	51,679	50,325	48,864	41,099	30,083	17,936	9,032
California	542,442	496,217	445,688	669,623	-	-	-
Colorado	53,362	48,231	42,074	31,196	19,908	10,570	4,314
Connecticut	64,952	66,196	59,889	47,033	31,871	16,234	7,433
Delaware	14,329	14,214	12,608	9,246	5,318	2,561	964
District of Columbia	12,602	11,677	9,947	7,179	7,464	-	-
Florida[1]	262,225	281,822	293,746	250,463	178,743	101,585	51,115
Georgia	119,419	104,207	87,775	134,137	-	-	-
Hawaii	19,600	20,391	18,882	25,503	-	-	-
Idaho	19,786	18,763	17,658	14,544	10,039	5,213	2,059
Illinois	214,660	212,318	188,315	141,329	92,657	65,477	-
Indiana	97,208	99,020	93,382	73,286	114,646	-	-
Iowa	55,181	56,384	53,146	94,590	-	-	-
Kansas	47,842	47,595	45,074	35,513	26,423	15,125	8,542
Kentucky	72,710	68,959	61,061	95,452	-	-	-
Louisiana	75,287	72,604	63,368	44,148	26,978	13,021	4,577
Maine	26,309	25,397	23,274	17,492	12,224	6,566	3,136
Maryland	93,443	88,213	75,135	116,705	34,792	18,026	8,135
Massachusetts	116,992	116,976	105,804	82,620	54,838	29,052	13,222
Michigan[2]	179,292	182,318	160,430	118,008	77,591	39,557	18,719
Minnesota	75,298	73,984	69,204	139,728	-	-	-
Mississippi	53,122	52,621	48,440	41,594	78,293	-	-
Missouri	108,279	106,302	97,468	73,804	98,226	-	-
Montana[1]	23,541	19,435	14,789	29,155	-	-	-
Nebraska	31,294	31,262	29,295	22,807	32,288	-	-
Nevada	27,613	25,879	23,579	30,767	-	-	-
New Hampshire	21,448	20,289	16,077	14,208	9,116	4,519	1,491
New Jersey	191,608	194,556	165,077	268,251	-	-	-
New Mexico[2]	33,223	27,417	25,965	31,436	-	-	-
New York	329,095	326,322	281,329	209,104	139,220	108,919	-
North Carolina	132,618	125,613	113,061	163,994	-	-	-
North Dakota	12,234	12,625	11,632	9,830	14,037	-	-
Ohio	222,859	228,074	205,329	338,116	-	-	-
Oklahoma	65,907	62,099	57,935	102,219	-	-	-
Oregon[1]	58,685	61,782	59,328	116,707	-	-	-
Pennsylvania	268,738	287,951	252,566	389,441	-	-	-

[Continued]

★ 835 ★

Licensed Older Male Drivers, by Age, 1990
[Continued]

State	55-59	60-64	65-69	70-74[3]	75-79[3,4]	80-84[3,4]	85 and over[3,4]
Rhode Island	19,695	20,540	17,245	11,280	6,434	2,413	13,335
South Carolina	66,646	62,016	57,515	85,749	-	-	-
South Dakota	13,731	14,423	14,061	11,352	8,398	4,965	2,855
Tennessee	100,327	94,395	85,517	63,690	44,525	35,780	-
Texas	310,885	285,920	247,455	179,159	120,321	65,691	30,286
Utah	25,929	24,232	22,041	17,461	11,640	6,252	2,878
Vermont	11,571	10,918	9,607	7,423	5,117	2,874	1,362
Virginia	123,719	113,780	98,932	147,224	-	-	-
Washington	92,594	87,482	81,961	139,988	-	-	-
West Virginia	39,737	42,246	39,617	66,630	-	-	-
Wisconsin[2]	95,053	96,591	87,325	68,718	50,219	28,680	14,477
Wyoming	9,170	9,176	7,898	5,852	4,001	2,121	944
Total	4,855,447	4,738,465	4,266,307	4,977,473	1,368,489	613,874	199,026

Source: U.S. Department of Transportation, Federal Highway Administration, *Highway Statistics 1990*, p. 34. *Notes:* FHWA stands for Federal Highway Administration. 1. Number of licensed drivers estimated by FHWA. 2. Age/sex distribution estimated by FHWA. 3. Data for older age groups may be included for those states for which there is no further age breakout. 4. Where dash appears, age group data is not available and is included with last reported column value to the left.

★ 836 ★

Transportation

Licensed Older Female Drivers, by Age, 1990

Data are compiled for the calendar year from reports of state authorities and other sources.

[Number]

State	55-59	60-64	65-69	70-74[3]	75-79[3,4]	80-84[3,4]	85 and over[3,4]
Alabama	77,167	68,622	52,677	36,594	19,931	7,627	-
Alaska	5,800	4,600	3,600	1,900	1,700	700	250
Arizona[1]	63,549	65,415	63,293	100,657	-	-	-
Arkansas[2]	50,890	50,304	47,870	39,406	28,508	15,825	6,366
California	486,183	464,588	443,169	657,631	-	-	-
Colorado	52,060	48,298	43,621	31,929	21,251	11,185	3,762
Connecticut	66,812	66,882	62,169	49,470	32,043	15,829	5,783
Delaware	14,037	13,695	12,479	8,920	5,310	2,571	800
District of Columbia	10,729	10,366	9,592	6,764	6,336	-	-
Florida[1]	251,242	279,171	291,594	242,004	170,130	94,930	39,357
Georgia	116,852	104,585	91,550	142,160	-	-	-
Hawaii	17,282	17,275	13,458	13,640	-	-	-
Idaho	19,055	18,650	18,012	14,662	10,043	5,071	1,662
Illinois	202,016	197,342	178,728	134,197	85,254	55,072	-
Indiana	93,387	95,138	91,394	73,623	109,172	-	-
Iowa	56,133	57,069	55,119	104,938	-	-	-

[Continued]

★ 836 ★

Licensed Older Female Drivers, by Age, 1990

[Continued]

State	55-59	60-64	65-69	70-74[3]	75-79[3,4]	80-84[3,4]	85 and over[3,4]
Kansas	49,106	49,079	48,148	40,804	31,644	18,876	9,116
Kentucky	67,637	63,381	55,587	85,556	-	-	-
Louisiana	74,014	70,910	60,782	42,580	26,019	12,053	3,395
Maine	24,691	24,962	22,709	17,690	12,183	6,524	2,765
Maryland	86,073	80,837	72,790	106,633	32,377	16,274	5,830
Massachusetts	109,584	110,986	103,678	81,434	54,215	28,357	10,575
Michigan[2]	180,044	180,045	164,719	126,268	83,462	42,471	16,113
Minnesota	71,482	69,789	64,695	128,573	-	-	-
Mississippi	51,049	49,786	44,502	36,079	59,979	-	-
Missouri	105,803	103,630	96,261	76,221	97,643	-	-
Montana[1]	17,867	13,823	9,777	12,435	-	-	-
Nebraska	31,163	30,867	28,424	24,066	33,767	-	-
Nevada	23,638	22,408	20,528	26,296	-	-	-
New Hampshire	19,798	19,494	16,734	13,650	8,758	4,342	1,433
New Jersey	171,974	179,912	142,871	193,140	-	-	-
New Mexico[2]	30,667	24,278	22,681	26,186	-	-	-
New York	284,773	280,800	243,844	181,558	114,835	77,986	-
North Carolina	134,127	126,626	112,045	158,657	-	-	-
North Dakota	12,272	12,326	11,083	9,720	13,656	-	-
Ohio	216,173	217,181	198,841	325,500	-	-	-
Oklahoma	68,104	64,580	60,991	120,495	-	-	-
Oregon[1]	56,144	59,220	56,553	104,471	-	-	-
Pennsylvania	243,092	254,113	219,423	294,462	-	-	-
Rhode Island	19,398	20,389	17,137	11,408	6,332	2,103	11,970
South Carolina	67,034	62,004	57,671	86,099	-	-	-
South Dakota	13,809	14,411	13,520	11,807	9,216	5,555	2,611
Tennessee	101,020	93,751	85,198	62,823	42,484	31,157	-
Texas	293,592	272,547	245,683	184,605	133,942	76,050	32,120
Utah	26,163	24,628	22,569	17,968	12,254	6,465	2,273
Vermont	10,503	10,315	9,317	7,335	5,214	3,047	1,297
Virginia	115,375	106,882	95,445	136,364	-	-	-
Washington	86,310	84,027	82,154	135,992	-	-	-
West Virginia	37,370	37,876	33,877	52,112	-	-	-
Wisconsin[2]	90,835	90,741	82,832	67,094	48,051	25,528	9,208
Wyoming	8,734	8,431	7,447	5,855	4,171	2,368	974
Total	4,582,612	4,497,035	4,108,841	4,670,431	1,319,880	567,966	167,660

Source: U.S. Department of Transportation, Federal Highway Administration, *Highway Statistics 1990*, p. 33. Notes: FHWA stands for Federal Highway Administration. 1. Number of licensed drivers estimated by FHWA. 2. Age/sex distribution estimated by FHWA. 3. Data for older age groups may be included for those states for which there is no further age breakout. 4. Where dash appears, age group data is not available and is included with last reported column value to the left.

★ 837 ★

Transportation

Distribution of Licensed Drivers, by Sex and Percentage in Each Age Group, 1990

Age	Male drivers			Female drivers		
	Number	Percent of male drivers	Percent of age cohort[1]	Number	Percent of female drivers	Percent of age cohort[1]
55-59	4,855,447	5.7	94.8	4,582,612	5.6	81.8
60-64	4,738,465	5.5	93.3	4,497,035	5.5	77.7
65-69	4,266,307	5.0	92.2	4,108,841	5.1	74.2
70 and over	7,158,862	8.3	89.5	6,725,937	8.3	52.5

Source: U.S. Department of Transportation, Federal Highway Administration, *Highway Statistics 1990*, p. 32. *Notes:* 1. The distribution of 1990 population by age and sex was not available at the time of printing, therefore this distribution was computed using the 1989 age and sex estimates of the Bureau of the Census, Series P-25 adjusted to the 1990 total population.

★ 838 ★

Transportation

Average Annual Miles by Driver Age, 1990

Age group	Miles per year
55-59	12,595
60-64	10,198
65-69	8,290
70 and over	6,264
All ages	13,181
Male	16,632
Female	9,543

Source: U.S. Department of Transportation, Federal Highway Administration, *Highway Statistics 1990*, p. 220. Primary source: Driver's annual estimate.

★ 839 ★

Transportation

Work Transportation

[Numbers are shown in thousands]

Characteristics	Total occupied units	Tenure		Housing unit characteristics				Household characteristics			
		Owner	Renter	New construction 4 yrs.	Mobile homes	Physical problems		Black	Hispanic	Moved in past year	Below poverty level
						Severe	Moderate				
Principal means of transportation to work last week											
Drives self	3,997	3,536	461	84	151	123	164	287	149	139	156
Carpool	585	485	100	5	25	16	32	104	55	17	48
2 person	444	376	68	5	22	6	18	76	26	14	29
3 person	80	62	18	-	2	3	13	16	21	2	9
4+ person	61	48	13	-	-	7	-	11	8	-	9
Mass transportation	290	180	111	4	-	5	12	89	19	7	10
Taxicab	17	15	2	3	-	4	-	2	-	3	-
Bicycle or motorcycle	26	23	2	-	3	-	2	4	-	-	2
Walks only	239	170	69	3	17	18	11	21	15	5	11
Other means	48	42	6	9	6	2	-	14	7	-	4
Works at home	268	240	28	4	2	2	9	5	4	11	36

Source: U.S. Department of Commerce and U.S. Department of Housing and Urban Development, Current Housing Reports H151/89, *Supplement to the American Housing Survey for the United States in 1989*, October 1992, p. 82. *Note:* A dash (-) means zero or rounds to zero.

★ 840 ★

Transportation

Transportation Distance From Work

[Numbers are shown in thousands]

Characteristics	Total occupied units	Tenure		Housing unit characteristics				Household characteristics			
		Owner	Renter	New construction 4 yrs.	Mobile homes	Physical problems		Black	Hispanic	Moved in past year	Below poverty level
						Severe	Moderate				
Distance from home to work											
Less than 1 mile	505	431	74	3	26	18	25	44	36	10	26
1 to 4 miles	1,435	1,221	214	32	43	20	63	139	64	49	68
5 to 9 miles	1,085	909	176	15	50	47	41	115	49	48	41
10 to 19 miles	1,131	954	177	27	44	49	63	138	52	34	41
20 to 29 miles	385	333	52	10	13	12	16	34	21	12	24
30 to 49 miles	172	154	18	3	3	4	5	12	13	5	4
50 miles or more	55	50	5	-	-	4	-	5	-	-	-
Works at home	268	240	28	4	2	2	9	5	4	11	36
No fixed place of work	434	399	35	17	23	13	8	35	9	13	27
Median	7	7	7	8	7	9	7	8	7	7	6

Source: U.S. Department of Commerce and U.S. Department of Housing and Urban Development, Current Housing Reports H151/89, *Supplement to the American Housing Survey for the United States in 1989*, October 1992, p. 82. *Note:* A dash (-) means zero or rounds to zero.

Chapter 14
PUBLIC LIFE

This chapter presents information on Politics, Voter Participation, and Volunteerism. Related information is also contained in the chapters on *Culture and Lifestyle* and *Opinions*.

Politics

★ 841 ★

Members of Congress, by Age and Seniority: 1977 to 1991
[As of beginning of first session of each Congress (January 3)]

Members of congress and years served	Age (in years)						Seniority[1]				
	Under 40	40 to 49	50 to 59	60 to 69	70 to 79	80 and over	Less than 2 years	2 to 9 years	10 to 19 years	20 to 29 years	30 years or more
Representatives[2]											
95th Cong., 1977	81	121	147	71	15	-	71	207	116	33	8
96th Cong., 1979	86	125	145	63	14	-	80	206	105	32	10
97th Cong., 1981	94	142	132	54	12	1	77	231	96	23	8
98th Cong., 1983	86	145	132	57	13	1	83	224	88	28	11
99th Cong., 1985	71	154	131	59	17	2	49	237	104	34	10
100th Cong., 1987	63	153	137	56	24	2	51	221	114	37	12
101st Cong., 1989	41	163	133	74	20	2	39	207	139	35	13
102d Cong., 1991	39	152	134	86	20	4	55	178	147	44	11
Senators											
95th Cong., 1977	6	26	35	21	10	2	18	41	24	12	5
96th Cong., 1979	10	31	33	17	8	1	20	41	23	12	4
97th Cong., 1981	9	35	36	14	6	-	19	51	17	11	2
98th Cong., 1983	7	28	39	20	3	3	5	61	21	10	3
99th Cong., 1985	4	27	38	25	4	2	8	56	27	7	2
100th Cong., 1987	5	30	36	22	5	2	14	41	36	7	2

[Continued]

★ 841 ★

Members of Congress, by Age and Seniority: 1977 to 1991
[Continued]

Members of congress and years served	Age (in years)						Seniority[1]				
	Under 40	40 to 49	50 to 59	60 to 69	70 to 79	80 and over	Less than 2 years	2 to 9 years	10 to 19 years	20 to 29 years	30 years or more
101st Cong., 1989	-	30	40	22	6	2	23	22	43	10	2
102d Cong., 1991	-	23	46	24	5	2	5	34	47	10	4

Source: U.S. Bureau of the Census, *Statistical Abstract of the United States: 1992* (112th edition.) Washington, DC, 1992, p. 264. Primary source: U.S. Bureau of the Census from data published in *Congressional Directory*, biennial. *Notes:* (-) A dash represents zero. 1. Represents consecutive years of service. 2. Figures for Representatives exclude vacancies.

★ 842 ★
Politics

Reported Voting and Registration, by Age, Sex, and Years of School Completed

Data are for November 1988.

[Numbers in thousands]

Age, sex and years of school completed	All persons	Reported registered		Reported voted		Reported that they did not vote[1]				
						Total	Registered	Not registered		
		No.	%	No.	%			Total[2]	Not a U.S. citizen	Do not know and not reported on registration[3]
55 to 64 years										
Both sexes										
Total	21,585	16,658	77.2	14,964	69.3	6,621	1,694	4,928	762	914
Elementary:										
0 to 4 years	705	270	38.3	201	28.4	505	70	435	156	44
5 to 7 years	1,257	680	54.1	510	40.6	747	170	577	132	59
8 years	1,415	830	58.6	695	49.2	719	134	585	69	95
High school:										
1 to 3 years	3,122	2,164	69.3	1,816	58.2	1,306	348	958	64	120
4 years	8,748	7,056	80.7	6,377	72.9	2,370	678	1,692	202	395
College:										
1 to 3 years	2,866	2,527	88.2	2,372	82.7	495	156	339	47	88
4 years	1,874	1,662	88.7	1,581	84.4	293	81	212	72	63
5 or more years	1,598	1,468	91.9	1,412	88.4	186	56	130	20	50
Male										
Total	10,164	7,869	77.4	7,090	69.8	3,075	779	2,295	320	440
Elementary:										
0 to 4 years	411	166	40.4	724	30.2	287	42	245	80	33
5 to 7 years	622	353	56.7	293	47.1	329	60	270	45	26
8 years	767	448	58.4	379	49.4	388	69	320	36	54

[Continued]

★ 842 ★

Reported Voting and Registration, by Age, Sex, and Years of School Completed
[Continued]

Age, sex and years of school completed	All persons	Reported registered		Reported voted		Reported that they did not vote[1]				
								Not registered		
		No.	%	No.	%	Total	Registered	Total[2]	Not a U.S. citizen	Do not know and not reported on registration[3]
High school:										
1 to 3 years	1,462	1,044	71.5	878	60.0	584	167	417	21	47
4 years	3,512	2,800	79.7	2,521	71.8	990	278	712	79	172
College:										
1 to 3 years	1,269	1,126	88.7	1,046	82.4	223	80	144	18	40
4 years	1,083	981	90.6	934	86.2	149	47	102	25	37
5 or more years	1,038	952	91.7	915	88.1	123	37	86	16	32
Female										
Total	11,421	8,789	77.0	7,874	68.9	3,547	914	2,632	443	474
Elementary:										
0 to 4 years	294	104	35.4	76	26.0	218	28	190	75	11
5 to 7 years	635	327	51.6	217	34.2	418	110	307	87	34
8 years	647	382	59.0	316	48.8	331	66	266	33	41
High school:										
1 to 3 years	1,660	1,119	67.4	938	56.5	722	181	541	43	73
4 years	5,236	4,256	81.3	3,856	73.6	1,380	400	980	124	223
College:										
1 to 3 years	1,597	1,402	87.8	1,326	83.0	271	76	196	29	48
4 years	791	681	86.1	648	81.9	144	34	110	47	26
5 or more years	560	517	92.3	497	88.8	63	19	43	4	18
65 Years and Over										
Both sexes										
Total	28,803	22,580	78.4	19,818	68.8	8,986	2,763	6,223	578	1,377
Elementary:										
0 to 4 years	1,541	819	53.1	567	36.8	974	252	722	135	117
5 to 7 years	2,833	1,783	62.9	1,406	49.6	1,426	377	1,050	122	184
8 years	4,099	2,842	69.3	2,333	56.9	1,765	508	1,257	67	233
High school:										
1 to 3 years	4,619	3,605	78.0	3,109	67.3	1,510	495	1,014	37	198
4 years	9,397	7,853	83.6	7,115	75.7	2,282	738	1,543	132	421
College:										
1 to 3 years	3,071	2,726	88.8	2,542	82.8	529	185	344	30	106
4 years	1,893	1,693	89.4	1,567	82.7	327	126	201	33	93
5 or more years	1,351	1,260	93.2	1,179	87.2	172	81	91	22	25
Male										
Total	11,949	9,748	81.6	8,762	73.3	3,187	986	2,201	206	547

[Continued]

★ 842 ★

Reported Voting and Registration, by Age, Sex, and Years of School Completed
[Continued]

Age, sex and years of school completed	All persons	Reported registered		Reported voted		Reported that they did not vote[1]				
						Total	Registered	Not registered		
		No.	%	No.	%			Total[2]	Not a U.S. citizen	Do not know and not reported on registration[3]
Elementary:										
0 to 4 years	748	427	57.2	293	39.3	454	134	320	45	65
5 to 7 years	1,193	815	68.3	688	57.7	505	127	378	40	73
8 years	1,690	1,254	74.2	1,073	63.5	617	181	436	24	97
High school:										
1 to 3 years	1,840	1,517	82.5	1,315	71.5	524	202	323	8	64
4 years	3,511	3,035	86.5	2,839	80.9	672	196	476	39	154
College:										
1 to 3 years	1,238	1,102	89.0	1,033	83.5	205	68	136	9	50
4 years	918	839	91.4	802	87.4	116	37	79	24	34
5 or more years	812	759	93.5	718	88.4	94	41	53	17	10
Female										
Total	16,854	12,832	76.1	11,055	65.6	5,799	1,777	4,022	371	830
Elementary:										
0 to 4 years	793	391	49.3	273	34.4	520	118	402	90	53
5 to 7 years	1,640	968	59.0	718	43.8	922	250	672	82	111
8 years	2,409	1,588	65.9	1,261	52.3	1,148	327	821	43	136
High school:										
1 to 3 years	2,779	2,087	75.1	1,794	64.5	985	294	692	29	134
4 years	5,886	4,818	81.9	4,276	72.6	1,610	542	1,068	93	267
College:										
1 to 3 years	1,833	1,625	88.7	1,508	82.3	324	116	208	21	56
4 years	975	853	87.5	764	78.3	211	89	122	9	59
5 or more years	539	501	92.8	461	85.5	78	40	39	4	15

Source: U.S. Department of Commerce, Bureau of the Census, Current Population Reports, Series P-20, No. 440, *Voting and Registration in the Election of November 1988*, U.S. Government Printing Office, Washington, DC, 1989, p. 47. *Notes:* 1. Includes persons reported as "did not vote," "do not know," and "not reported" on voting. 2. In addition to those reported as "not registered," total includes those "not a U.S. citizen," and "do not know" and "not reported" on registration. 3. Includes "do not know" and "not reported" on citizenship.

★ 843 ★

Politics

Reported Voting and Registration, by Age, Sex, Employment Status, and Class of Worker

Data are for November 1988.

[Numbers in thousands]

Age, sex, employment status and class of worker	65 Years and Over									
	All persons	Reported registered		Reported voted		Reported that they did not vote[1]				
						Total	Registered	Not registered		
								Total[2]	Not a U.S. citizen	Do not know and not reported on registration[3]
		No.	%	No.	%					
Both sexes										
Total	28,803	22,580	78.4	19,818	68.8	8,986	2,763	6,223	578	1,377
In civilian labor force	3,511	2,999	85.4	2,774	79.0	737	225	512	71	128
Employed	3,407	2,918	85.6	2,705	79.4	702	213	490	64	121
Agricultural industries	266	233	87.4	200	75.0	67	33	33	4	4
Self-employed workers[4]	209	186	88.7	166	79.4	43	19	24	2	4
Wage and salary workers	57	47	(B)	34	(B)	23	14	10	2	-
Nonagricultural industries	3,141	2,685	85.5	2,505	79.8	636	180	456	60	117
Private wage and salary workers	2,043	1,708	83.6	1,579	77.3	464	128	335	53	70
Government workers	474	439	92.5	413	87.1	61	26	35	3	10
Self-employed workers[4]	624	538	86.3	513	82.3	111	25	85	5	38
Unemployed	104	81	78.3	69	66.3	35	13	22	7	6
Not in labor force	25,293	19,581	77.4	17,044	67.4	8,249	2,538	5,711	507	1,249
Male										
Total	11,949	9,748	81.6	8,762	73.3	3,187	986	2,201	206	547
In civilian labor force	2,007	1,745	87.0	1,625	81.0	382	120	261	43	74
Employed	1,943	1,695	87.2	1,583	81.5	360	112	248	38	71
Agricultural industries	218	190	87.3	163	74.7	55	27	28	2	4
Self-employed workers[4]	175	155	88.8	136	77.9	39	19	20	-	4
Wage and salary workers	43	35	(B)	27	(B)	16	8	8	2	-
Nonagricultural industries	1,725	1,505	87.2	1,420	82.3	305	85	220	36	66
Private wage and salary workers	1,109	963	86.9	899	81.0	210	65	146	29	32
Government workers	200	186	92.9	176	87.9	24	10	14	3	2
Self-employed workers[4]	416	355	85.4	345	83.0	71	10	61	5	32
Unemployed	64	50	(B)	42	(B)	22	8	13	6	3
Not in labor force	9,942	8,003	80.5	7,138	71.8	2,805	865	1,939	163	473
Female										
Total	16,854	12,832	76.1	11,055	65.6	5,799	1,777	4,022	371	830
In civilian labor force	1,504	1,254	83.3	1,149	76.4	355	105	251	28	54
Employed	1,464	1,223	83.5	1,122	76.6	342	100	241	26	51
Agricultural industries	49	43	(B)	37	(B)	11	6	6	2	-
Self-employed workers[4]	34	30	(B)	30	(B)	4	-	4	2	-
Wage and salary workers	14	12	(B)	7	(B)	7	5	2	-	-
Nonagricultural industries	1,416	1,180	83.3	1,085	76.7	331	95	236	24	51
Private wage and salary workers	934	745	79.7	681	72.9	253	64	190	24	38
Government workers	274	252	92.2	237	86.4	37	16	21	-	7
Self-employed workers[4]	208	183	88.2	168	80.8	40	15	25	-	6
Unemployed	40	31	(B)	27	(B)	13	4	9	1	3
Not in labor force	15,350	11,578	75.4	9,906	64.5	5,444	1,672	3,772	344	777

Source: U.S. Department of Commerce, Bureau of the Census, Current Population Reports, Series P-20, No. 440, *Voting and Registration in the Election of November 1988,* U.S. Government Printing Office, Washington, DC, 1989, p. 55. *Notes:* 1. Includes persons reported as "did not vote," "do not know," and "not reported" on voting. 2. In addition to those reported as "not registered," total includes those "not a U.S. citizen," and "do not know" and "not reported" on registration. 3. Includes "do not know" and "not reported" on citizenship. 4. Includes unpaid family workers. B= Population of less than 75,000 persons.

★ 844 ★

Politics

Reported Voting and Registration of Family Members, by Age and Family Income

Data are for November 1988.

[Numbers in thousands]

Age and family income	All persons	Reported registered		Reported voted		Reported that they did not vote[1]				
						Total	Registered	Not registered		
		No.	%	No.	%			Total[2]	Not a U.S. citizen	Do not know and not reported on registration[3]
65 to 74 years										
Total	13,113	10,802	82.4	9,845	75.1	3,269	957	2,311	250	526
Under $5,000	413	276	66.8	203	49.1	210	73	137	20	22
$5,000 to $9,999	1,616	1,172	72.5	1,011	62.5	606	162	444	45	46
$10,000 to $14,999	2,686	2,163	80.5	1,958	72.9	728	204	523	61	59
$15,000 to $19,999	3,083	2,606	84.5	2,395	77.7	687	211	477	19	130
$20,000 to $24,999	951	856	90.0	782	82.2	170	75	95	16	30
$25,000 to $34,999	1,423	1,274	89.5	1,207	84.8	216	67	150	19	29
$35,000 to $49,999	1,057	959	90.8	908	85.9	149	51	98	25	22
$50,000 and over	640	587	91.8	570	89.2	69	17	53	18	15
Income not reported	1,244	909	73.1	810	65.1	434	99	335	28	173
75 years and over										
Total	6,499	4,840	74.5	4,136	63.6	2,364	704	1,659	174	336
Under $5,000	330	214	64.8	169	51.4	160	44	116	20	20
$5,000 to $9,999	1,248	893	71.6	725	58.1	523	168	355	30	60
$10,000 to $14,999	1,399	1,072	76.6	906	64.8	493	166	327	18	43
$15,000 to $19,999	1,293	982	76.0	879	68.0	414	103	311	41	70
$20,000 to $24,999	409	311	76.0	269	65.8	140	42	98	13	9
$25,000 to $34,999	550	436	79.3	370	67.2	180	66	114	16	14
$35,000 to $49,999	387	295	76.2	249	64.5	137	46	92	16	11
$50,000 and over	261	209	80.1	193	73.8	69	17	52	10	13
Income not reported	622	427		376	60.4	247	52	195	10	96

Source: U.S. Department of Commerce, Bureau of the Census, Current Population Reports, Series P-20, No. 440, *Voting and Registration in the Election of November 1988*, U.S. Government Printing Office, Washington, DC, 1989, p. 64. *Notes:* 1. Includes persons reported as "did not vote," "do not know," and "not reported" on voting. 2. In addition to those reported as "not registered," total includes those "not a U.S. citizen," and "do not know" and "not reported" on registration. 3. Includes "do not know" and "not reported" on citizenship.

★ 845 ★

Politics

Persons Registered Specifically for the 1988 Election: November 1988

[Numbers in thousands]

Age	All persons	Total registered	Registered specifically for 1988			Previously registered	Not reported whether previously registered
			Total[1]	First time	Not first time		
Number							
United States							
Total	178,098	118,589	11,656	3,885	6,364	106,543	390
18 and 19 years	7,295	3,118	1,613	1,416	50	1,487	19
20 and 21 years	7,025	3,385	870	664	110	2,501	15
22 to 24 years	11,250	5,818	1,070	473	455	4,720	27
25 to 29 years	21,210	11,502	2,010	482	1,278	9,421	71
30 to 34 years	21,467	13,172	1,866	370	1,308	11,253	52
35 to 44 years	35,186	24,392	2,054	278	1,527	22,247	91
45 to 54 years	24,277	17,964	877	107	657	17,049	38
55 to 64 years	21,585	16,658	611	51	464	16,022	25
65 to 74 years	17,578	14,233	482	38	348	13,719	32
75 years and over	11,226	8,347	202	5	168	8,124	21
Percent distribution							
Total	178,098	100.0	9.8	3.3	5.4	89.8	0.3
18 and 19 years	7,295	100.0	51.7	45.4	1.6	47.7	0.6
20 and 21 years	7,025	100.0	25.7	19.6	3.2	73.9	0.4
22 to 24 years	11,250	100.0	18.4	8.1	7.8	81.1	0.5
25 to 29 years	21,210	100.0	17.5	4.2	11.1	81.9	0.6
30 to 34 years	21,467	100.0	14.2	2.8	9.9	85.4	0.4
35 to 44 years	35,186	100.0	8.4	1.1	6.3	91.2	0.4
45 to 54 years	24,277	100.0	4.9	0.6	3.7	94.9	0.2
55 to 64 years	21,585	100.0	3.7	0.3	2.8	96.2	0.2
65 to 74 years	17,578	100.0	3.4	0.3	2.4	96.4	0.2
75 years and over	11,226	100.0	2.4	0.1	2.0	97.3	0.3

Source: U.S. Department of Commerce, Bureau of the Census, Current Population Reports, Series P-20, No. 440, *Voting and Registration in the Election of November 1988*, U.S. Government Printing Office, Washington, DC, 1989, pp. 66-67. *Notes:* 1. Includes 1,406,000 persons who said they had registered specifically for the 1988 election, but who did not report whether they were first time registrants in 1988.

★ 846 ★
Politics

Persons Who Registered Specifically for and Voted in the 1988 Election: November 1988

[Numbers in thousands]

Age	Total registered specifically for this election	First-time registrants			Not first-time registrants			Not reported whether first-time registrants
		Total[1]	Voted	Did not vote	Total[1]	Voted	Did not vote	
Number								
United States								
Total	11,656	3,885	3,261	534	6,364	5,828	506	1,406
18 and 19 years	1,613	1,416	1,173	183	50	35	10	146
20 and 21 years	870	664	555	91	110	94	15	96
22 to 24 years	1,071	473	382	85	455	408	41	142
25 to 29 years	2,010	482	426	55	1,278	1,195	82	251
30 to 34 years	1,866	370	301	66	1,308	1,183	118	189
35 to 44 years	2,054	278	245	30	1,527	1,429	91	249
45 to 54 years	877	107	93	14	657	599	57	113
55 to 64 years	611	51	42	9	464	418	46	95
65 to 74 years	482	38	38	-	348	320	28	96
75 years and over	202	5	5	-	168	148	20	29
Percent Distribution								
Total	100.0	33.3	28.0	4.6	54.6	50.0	4.3	12.1
18 and 19 years	100.0	87.8	72.7	11.3	3.1	2.2	0.6	9.1
20 and 21 years	100.0	76.3	63.8	10.5	12.6	10.8	1.7	11.0
22 to 24 years	100.0	44.2	35.7	7.9	42.5	38.1	3.8	13.3
25 to 29 years	100.0	24.0	21.2	2.7	63.6	59.5	4.1	12.5
30 to 34 years	100.0	19.8	16.1	3.5	70.1	63.4	6.3	10.1
35 to 44 years	100.0	13.5	11.9	1.5	74.3	69.6	4.4	12.1
45 to 54 years	100.0	12.2	10.6	1.6	74.9	68.3	6.5	12.9
55 to 64 years	100.0	8.3	6.9	1.5	75.9	68.4	7.5	15.5
65 to 74 years	100.0	7.9	7.9	-	72.2	66.4	5.8	19.9
75 years and over	100.0	2.5	2.5	-	83.2	73.3	9.9	14.4

Source: U.S. Department of Commerce, Bureau of the Census, Current Population Reports, Series P-20, No. 440, *Voting and Registration in the Election of November 1988*, U.S. Government Printing Office, Washington, DC, 1989, pp. 68-69. *Note:* 1. Includes persons who did not report whether they had voted.

★ 847 ★

Politics

Political Party Identification of the Adult Population, by Degree of Attachment, by Age: 1990

Data covers citizens of voting-age living in private housing units in the contiguous United States.

[In percent]

Age	Total	Strong Democratic	Weak Democratic	Independent Democrat	Independent	Independent Republican	Weak Republican	Strong Republican	Apolitical
1990, total[1]	100	20	19	12	11	12	15	10	2
Year of birth									
1959 or later (Under 32)	100	11	17	15	15	14	16	9	2
1943 to 1958 (32 to 47)	100	20	22	14	10	10	15	8	2
1927 to 1942 (48 to 63)	100	24	17	11	9	14	13	10	1
1911 to 1926 (64 to 79)	100	30	22	7	6	10	13	13	1
1895 to 1910 (80 to 95)	100	43	14	9	5	2	19	9	(Z)

Source: U.S. Bureau of the Census, *Statistical Abstract of the United States: 1992*, (112th edition.) Washington, DC, 1992, p. 270. Primary source: Center for Political Studies, University of Michigan, Ann Arbor, MI, unpublished data. *Notes:* A (Z) stands for less than 0.5 percent. 1. Includes other characteristics, not shown separately.

Voter Participation

★ 848 ★

Reported Voting in National Elections, by Age Group, 1980-1988

Data exclude persons in institutions.

[Number in thousands]

Age group	1980		1982		1984		1986		1988	
	Number	Percent	Number	Percent	Number	Percent	Number	Percent	Number	Percent
18+	93,066	59.2	80,310	48.5	101,878	59.9	79,954	46.0	102,224	57.4
18 to 20	4,387	35.7	2,390	19.8	4,131	36.7	1,993	18.6	3,570	33.2
21 to 24	6,838	43.1	4,749	28.4	7,276	43.5	3,789	24.2	5,684	38.3
25 to 34	19,498	54.6	15,667	40.4	21,978	54.5	14,720	35.1	20,468	48.0
35 to 44	16,460	64.4	14,676	52.2	19,514	63.5	16,283	49.3	21,550	61.2
45 to 54	15,174	67.5	13,350	60.1	15,035	67.5	12,544	54.8	16,170	66.6
55 to 64	15,031	71.3	14,141	64.4	15,889	72.1	13,761	62.7	14,964	69.3
65+	15,677	65.1	15,336	59.9	18,055	67.7	16,865	60.9	19,818	68.8

[Continued]

★ 848 ★

Reported Voting in National Elections, by Age Group, 1980-1988

[Continued]

Age group	1980		1982		1984		1986		1988	
	Number	Percent	Number	Percent	Number	Percent	Number	Percent	Number	Percent
65 to 74	10,622	69.3	10,312	64.8	11,761	71.8	11,117	65.1	12,840	73.0
75 +	5,055	57.6	5,024	51.9	6,294	67.7	5,748	54.0	6,978	62.2

Source: Aging America, Trends and Projections, prepared by the U.S. Senate Special Committee on Aging, the American Association of Retired Persons, the Federal Council on the Aging, and the U.S. Administration on Aging, 1991, Washington, D.C., p. 201. Primary source: Bureau of the Census, "Voting and Registration in the Election of November 1980," Current Population Reports, Series P-20, No. 370, April 1982; "Voting and Registration in the Election of November 1982," Current Population Reports, Series P-20, No. 383, November 1983; "Voting and Registration in the Election of November 1984," Current Population Reports, Series P-20, No. 405, March 1986; "Voting and Registration in the Election of November 1986," Current Population Reports, Series P-20, No. 414, September 1987; and "Voting and Registration in the Election of November 1988," Current Population Reports, Series P-20, No. 440, October 1989.

★ 849 ★

Voter Participation

Reported Voting in Elections, by Sex, Race, and Hispanic Origin: 1984, 1986, and 1988

Data exclude people in institutions.

[Numbers in percent]

Race and Hispanic origin	65 to 74 years		75 and over	
	Men	Women	Men	Women
1984 election				
Total	73.9	70.2	68.3	57.2
White	75.0	71.2	69.6	57.8
Black	65.9	57.9	64.0	55.0
Hispanic[1]	49.7	44.6	30.3	29.2
1986 election				
Total	68.7	62.2	63.1	48.8
White	70.1	63.3	64.2	49.5
Black	58.9	55.8	52.1	43.9
Hispanic[1]	43.7	35.8	32.6	30.9
1988 election				
Total	75.0	71.5	70.2	57.5
White	75.9	72.1	71.9	58.7
Black	68.5	70.2	59.4	49.9
Hispanic[1]	52.0	48.2	53.1	29.1

Source: Aging America, Trends and Projections, prepared by the U.S. Senate Special Committee on Aging, the American Association of Retired Persons, the Federal Council on the Aging, and the U.S. Administration on Aging, 1991, Washington, D.C., p. 203. Primary source: U.S. Bureau of the Census, "Voting and Registration in the Election of November 1984," Current Population Reports, Series P-20, No. 405, March 1980; "Voting and Registration in the Election of November 1986," Current Population Reports, Series P-20, No. 414, September 1987; and "Voting and Registration in the Election of November 1988," Current Population Reports, Series P-20, No. 440, October 1989.

★ 850 ★
Voter Participation

Change in Voter Turnout Between the 1988 and 1992 Presidential Elections, by Age

Data show a sharp decrease in the voter turnout of people aged 60 and older. Figures are estimated and factor out the population increase between 1988 and 1992 to normalize results.

Age group	Change in voter turnout, 1988 to 1992 in percent
18-29	20.0
30-44	18.0
45-59	19.0
60+	-21.0

Source: New York Times, November 8, 1992, p. 2. Primary source: Voter Research and surveys.

Volunteerism

★ 851 ★

Unpaid Volunteer Workers, by Sex, May 1989

Data exclude people in institutions.

[Numbers in thousands]

Sex	Age		
	16+	55-64	65+
Both sexes, total	186,181	21,373	29,153
Unpaid volunteers	38,042	4,455	4,934
As % of total	20.4	20.8	16.9
Men, total	88,656	10,053	12,135
Unpaid volunteers	16,681	1,987	1,917
As % of total	18.8	19.8	15.8
Women, total	97,525	11,320	17,017

[Continued]

★ 851 ★

Unpaid Volunteer Workers, by Sex, May 1989
[Continued]

Sex	Age		
	16+	55-64	65+
Unpaid volunteers	21,361	2,468	3,016
As % of total	21.9	21.8	17.7

Source: Aging America, Trends and Projections, prepared by the U.S. Senate Special Committee on Aging, the American Association of Retired Persons, the Federal Council on the Aging, and the U.S. Administration on Aging, 1991, Washington, D.C., p. 204. Primary source: U.S. Department of Labor, Bureau of Labor Statistics, "Thirty-Eight Million Persons Do Volunteer Work," Press Release USDL 90-154, March 29, 1990. Data are from *Current Population Survey,* May 1989.

★ 852 ★

Volunteerism

Unpaid Volunteer Workers, by Selected Characteristics, May 1989

Data exclude people in institutions.

[Numbers in percent]

Characteristic	Age		
	16+	55-64	65+
Type of organization for which work was performed			
Hospital or other health organization	10.4	12.4	17.8
School or other educational institution	15.1	6.7	4.3
Social or welfare organization	9.9	16.1	14.5
Civic or political organization	13.2	16.1	11.1
Sport or recreation organization	7.8	2.5	1.8
Church or other religious organization	37.4	45.7	43.3
Other organizations	6.3	5.7	7.2
Hours worked per week			
Median hours worked	4.3	4.4	4.7
Less than 5 hours	60.0	58.9	53.6
5 to 9 hours	19.9	19.9	23.8
10 to 19 hours	10.8	11.7	11.0
20 to 34 hours	5.8	6.1	7.4
35 hours and over	3.6	3.4	4.2
Weeks worked per year			
Median weeks worked	25.2	30.5	34.9
Less than 5 weeks	20.2	17.5	14.4
5 to 14 weeks	21.2	18.8	16.6

[Continued]

★ 852 ★

Unpaid Volunteer Workers, by Selected Characteristics, May 1989

[Continued]

Characteristic	Age		
	16+	55-64	65+
15 to 26 weeks	14.4	12.8	14.8
27 to 49 weeks	15.9	15.9	16.9
50 to 52 weeks	28.3	35.1	37.2

Source: *Aging America, Trends and Projections*, prepared by the U.S. Senate Special Committee on Aging, the American Association of Retired Persons, the Federal Council on the Aging, and the U.S. Administration on Aging, 1991, Washington, D.C., p. 204. Primary source: U.S. Department of Labor, Bureau of Labor Statistics, "Thirty-Eight Million Persons Do Volunteer Work," Press Release USDL 90-154, March 29, 1990. Data are from, *Current Population Survey*, May 1989.

★ 853 ★

Volunteerism

Percent of Adult Population Doing Volunteer Work, by Age: 1989

Data include civilian non-institutional population, 16 years old and over. A volunteer is a person who performed unpaid work for an organization such as a church, the Boy or Girl Scouts, a school, Little League, etc. during the year. Persons who did work on their own such as helping out neighbors or relatives are excluded.

[For year ending May]

Age	Volunteer workers		Percent distribution of volunteers, by type of organization[1]							
	Number (1,000)	Percent of population	Total	Churches, other religious	Schools, other educational	Civic or political	Hospitals, other health	Social or welfare	Sport or or recreational	Other
Total	38,042	20.4	100.0	37.4	15.1	13.2	10.4	9.9	7.8	6.3
16 to 19 years old	1,902	13.4	100.0	34.4	26.8	8.9	9.2	7.0	8.2	5.5
20 to 24 years old	2,064	11.4	100.0	30.5	18.5	12.7	11.9	11.6	8,9	6.8
25 to 34 years old	8,680	20.2	100.0	34.9	18.3	13.3	9.1	9.3	8.9	6.1
35 to 44 years old	10,337	28.9	100.0	33.1	20.3	12.6	7.4	8.5	12.1	6.1
45 to 54 years old	5,670	23.0	100.0	40.8	11.8	15.1	10.1	8.8	7.1	6.3
55 to 64 years old	4,455	20.8	100.0	45.7	6.7	16.1	12.4	10.9	2.5	5.7
65 years old and over	4,934	16.9	100.0	43.3	4.3	11.1	17.8	14.5	1.8	7.2

Source: U.S. Bureau of the Census, *Statistical Abstract of the United States: 1992* (112th edition.) Washington, DC, 1992, p. 374. Primary source: U.S. Bureau of Labor Statistics, *News*, USDL 90-154, March 29, 1990. *Note:* 1. Organization for which most work was done.

Chapter 15
OPINIONS

This chapter holds results of opinion surveys or polls on the subjects of Advertising, Baseball, Entertainment, Health Care, Life Satisfaction, Longevity, Retirement, Sexual Orientation, and Shopping. Related information is also contained in the chapters on *Culture and Lifestyle* and *Public Life*.

Advertising

★ 854 ★

Advertising's Presentation of the Elderly

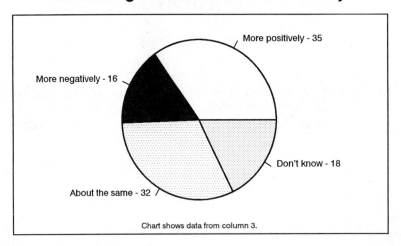

Chart shows data from column 3.

Data show survey responses to the question, "How are older Americans portrayed in advertising today compared with a few years ago?" The sample included 1,002 persons aged 18 and older.

[Data are shown in percent]

	All respondents	Under 50	50 or over
More positively	38	40	35
More negatively	12	11	16
About the same	35	37	32
Don't know	15	13	18

Source: Advertising Age, November 16, 1992, p. S-1. Primary source: The Roper Organization.

★ 855 ★

Advertising

Advertising's Presentation of the U.S. Population

Data show survey responses to the question, "How fairly do you think the following are represented in advertising?" The survey included 1,002 persons aged 18 and older.

[Data are shown in percent]

	Under-represented	Over-represented	About right
Handicapped people	57	5	27
Hispanics	41	8	38
People 50 or over	37	6	47
Blacks	29	16	45
Housewives	29	12	46
Employed women	23	10	52
People in their 30s or 40s	20	10	59
Teenagers & young adults	9	35	47

Source: Advertising Age, November 16, 1992, p. S-1. Primary source: The Roper Organization.

★ 856 ★

Advertising

Advertising's Use of Elderly Fears

Responses to the survey question, "Do agree with the following statement?: Advertisers try to take advantage of older people's fears of death to sell insurance and health care products that won't really help them."

[Response is shown in percent]

	All respondents	Under 50	50 or older
Agree	65.0	65.0	64.0
Disagree	20.0	20.0	18.0
Don't know	16.0	15.0	18.0

Source: Advertising Age, November 16, 1992, p. S-8. Primary source: The Roper Organization.

Baseball

★ 857 ★

Views of Elderly on Changes in Baseball

Elderly Americans (50 and over) are consistently less enthusiastic than younger people about changing the way baseball in organized and played.

	Percent who favor		
	All ages	Under 50	50 and over
Interleague play between American and National league teams during the regular season	62	68	54
Expansion of two or four teams	65	72	53
Expanding the baseball playoffs to include wild-card teams, like the National Football League	51	58	37

Source: USA TODAY, March 4, 1993, p. 10C. Primary source: USA TODAY, CNN, Gallup joint nationwide poll conducted February 12- 14, 1993.

Entertainment

★ 858 ★

Leading Television Shows Among Older Americans

Program	Network	Ratings among viewers 50-plus
Murder, She Wrote	CBS	25.4
60 Minutes	CBS	24.0
In the Heat of the Night	CBS	19.0
Sunday Night Movie	CBS	17.9
Evening Shade	CBS	16.6
Murphy Brown	CBS	16.3
Hearts Afire	CBS	15.1
Unsolved Mysteries	NBC	15.0
Golden Palace	CBS	13.7

[Continued]

★ 858 ★

Leading Television Shows Among Older Americans
[Continued]

Program	Network	Ratings among viewers 50-plus
48 Hours[1]	CBS	13.6
20/20[1]	ABC	13.6

Source: Advertising Age, November 16, 1992, p. S1. Primary source: Nielsen Media Research, Season-to-date through Nov. 1. *Note:* 1. Tied in ratings.

★ 859 ★

Entertainment

Television's Presentation of the Elderly
[Response is shown in percent]

Portrayed	All respondents	Under 50	50 or over
Do the portrayals of older Americans in advertising fit the qualities you think of as typical for this age group?			
Physically active			
Right balance	50.0	52.0	45.0
Not enough that way	29.0	28.0	31.0
Don't know	12.0	11.0	16.0
Too much that way	9.0	9.0	8.0
Adventurous			
Right balance	43.0	45.0	39.0
Not enough that way	33.0	32.0	33.0
Don't know	16.0	14.0	21.0
Too much that way	9.0	9.0	7.0
Economically disadvantaged			
Not enough that way	33.0	33.0	31.0
Right balance	33.0	35.0	29.0
Don't know	19.0	17.0	24.0
Too much that way	15.0	15.0	16.0
Serious			
Right balance	50.0	53.0	43.0
Don't know	18.0	15.0	24.0
Not enough that way	20.0	18.0	23.0
Too much that way	12.0	13.0	10.0

[Continued]

★ 859 ★

Television's Presentation of the Elderly
[Continued]

Portrayed	All respondents	Under 50	50 or over
Family oriented			
Right balance	58.0	63.0	49.0
Not enough that way	22.0	20.0	25.0
Don't know	14.0	12.0	19.0
Too much that way	6.0	6.0	7.0
Carefree			
Right balance	47.0	48.0	44.0
Don't know	17.0	14.0	22.0
Not enough that way	24.0	26.0	20.0
Too much that way	13.0	12.0	14.0
Frail, unhealthy			
Right balance	38.0	40.0	33.0
Too much that way	27.0	27.0	27.0
Don't know	17.0	15.0	21.0
Not enough that way	19.0	19.0	19.0
Dependent			
Right balance	42.0	44.0	37.0
Don't know	18.0	16.0	23.0
Not enough that way	21.0	21.0	21.0
Too much that way	19.0	19.0	19.0
Generous			
Right balance	50.0	53.0	45.0
Don't know	20.0	17.0	26.0
Not enough that way	25.0	25.0	25.0
Too much that way	5.0	5.0	4.0
Forgetful and mentally slow			
Right balance	38.0	42.0	31.0
Too much that way	24.0	23.0	26.0
Don't know	22.0	19.0	26.0
Not enough that way	17.0	16.0	17.0

Source: *Advertising Age*, November 16, 1992, p. S-8. Primary source: The Roper Organization.

★ 860 ★

Entertainment

Television's Elderly as Role Models

Responses to the survey question, "How do you feel about the following statement?: There's not enough advertising that shows older Americans as role models to be looked up to and admired."

[Response is shown in percent]

	All respondents	Under 50	50 and older
Agree	62.0	63.0	59.0
Disagree	22.0	21.0	22.0
Don't know	16.0	15.0	19.0

Source: Advertising Age, November 16, 1992, p. S-8. Primary source: The Roper Organization.

Health Care

★ 861 ★

Stress Reduction for Healthier Living

Data show percent of survey respondents who said they intentionally reduced stress in the last five years in order to live a healthier life.

[Data are shown in percent.]

Age	Percent[1]
18-39	44.0
40+	56.0

Source: Health and Longevity, Belden & Russonello, The Alliance for Aging Research, December 1992, p. 17. *Notes:* Data represent the results of a national telephone survey conducted in December 1992. A total of 906 adults responded. Elderly Americans (50 years or older) represented 34 percent of the sample. 1. Percentages are weighted.

★ 862 ★

Health Care

Opinions on Research Spending and Health Care Costs

Data show survey responses to the question, "Spending money now on medical research to find cures for major diseases will reduce future health care costs. Do you agree or disagree?"

[Data are shown in percent]

	Agree strongly	Agree somewhat	Disagree somewhat	Disagree strongly	Don't know
Totals	48.0	28.0	11.0	8.0	5.0
Totals collapsed					
Agree	76.0				
Disagree			19.0		
Age					
18-29	48.0	32.0	9.0	5.0	6.0
30-39	53.0	25.0	10.0	10.0	2.0
40-49	53.0	24.0	10.0	12.0	2.0
50-64	50.0	29.0	12.0	6.0	3.0
65+	34.0	28.0	17.0	8.0	13.0
Presidential vote					
Clinton	55.0	21.0	12.0	27.0	5.0
Bush	41.0	34.0	9.0	9.0	5.0
Perot	41.0	32.0	13.0	11.0	4.0

Source: Health and Longevity, Belden & Russonello, The Alliance for Aging Research, December 1992, p. 28. *Notes:* Data represent the results of a national telephone survey conducted in December 1992. A total of 906 adults responded. Elderly Americans (50 years or older) represented 34 percent of the sample. Percentages are weighted.

★ 863 ★

Health Care

Opinions on Medical Research and Health Care Reform

Data show survey responses to the question, "Any type of health care reform should include more government emphasis on medical research to cure and prevent diseases. Do you agree or disagree?"

[Data are shown in percent]

	Agree strongly	Agree somewhat	Disagree somewhat	Disagree strongly	Don't know
Totals	51.0	31.0	10.0	4.0	3.0
Totals collapsed					
Agree	82.0				
Disagree			14.0		
Age					
18-29	51.0	37.0	10.0	2.0	1.0
30-39	49.0	33.0	11.0	5.0	3.0
40-49	50.0	32.0	10.0	4.0	4.0
50-64	60.0	24.0	10.0	4.0	2.0
65 +	49.0	28.0	11.0	6.0	4.0
Presidential vote					
Clinton	59.0	32.0	6.0	2.0	2.0
Bush	37.0	37.0	17.0	7.0	1.0
Perot	38.0	38.0	14.0	5.0	4.0

Source: Health and Longevity, Belden & Russonello, The Alliance for Aging Research, December 1992, p. 29. *Notes:* Data represent the results of a national telephone survey conducted in December 1992. A total of 906 adults responded. Elderly Americans (50 years or older) represented 34 percent of the sample. Percentages are weighted.

★ 864 ★

Health Care

Fetal Tissue Use in Medical Research

Data show survey responses to the question, "Scientists should be able to use fetal tissue from abortions to find cures for deadly diseases such as Alzheimer's and Parkinson's. Do you agree or disagree?"

[Data are shown in percent]

	Agree strongly	Agree somewhat	Disagree somewhat	Disagree strongly	Don't know
Totals	38.0	25.0	8.0	24.0	5.0
Totals collapsed					
Agree	63.0				
Disagree			32.0		
Education					
High school or less	33.0	23.0	10.0	28.0	7.0
Some college/vocational	37.0	30.0	6.0	23.0	4.0
College degree or more	48.0	24.0	5.0	19.0	4.0
Household occupation					
Professional white-collar	43.0	21.0	9.0	22.0	4.0
Managerial white-collar	44.0	24.0	5.0	23.0	4.0
Blue-collar	33.0	28.0	8.0	25.0	6.0
Household income					
Less than $15,000	26.0	26.0	7.0	33.0	7.0
$15,000-$34,999	35.0	25.0	10.0	24.0	5.0
$35,000-$49,999	45.0	25.0	5.0	20.0	4.0
$50,000 or more	47.0	23.0	6.0	21.0	2.0
Age					
18-29	32.0	33.0	10.0	23.0	2.0
30-39	32.0	23.0	7.0	31.0	7.0
40-49	41.0	29.0	5.0	22.0	4.0
50-64	43.0	20.0	9.0	22.0	6.0
65+	46.0	16.0	7.0	23.0	7.0
Sex					
Male	43.0	26.0	7.0	19.0	4.0
Female	33.0	23.0	8.0	29.0	6.0

Source: Health and Longevity, Belden & Russonello, The Alliance for Aging Research, December 1992, p. 31. *Notes:* Data represent the results of a national telephone survey conducted in December 1992. A total of 906 adults responded. Elderly Americans (50 years or older) represented 34 percent of the sample. Percentages are weighted.

★ 865 ★

Health Care

Dissatisfaction with Physicians

Data show responses to the question, "My doctor does not spend enough time listening to me about my health. Do you agree or disagree?" From the source: "When Americans are asked to consider how well their doctors listen to them, a slim majority (51%) voice satisfaction, while four in 10 (42%) are less than satisfied. The satisfaction, with doctors as listeners increases with age; women over age 64 are the most likely to be pleased."

[Data are shown in percent]

	Agree strongly	Agree somewhat	Disagree somewhat	Disagree strongly	Don't know
Totals	23.0	19.0	22.0	29.0	6.0
Age					
18-29	23.0	21.0	32.0	18.0	6.0
30-39	24.0	17.0	21.0	30.0	7.0
40-49	24.0	21.0	17.0	29.0	6.0
50-64	22.0	21.0	20.0	30.0	5.0
65+	23.0	13.0	17.0	40.0	7.0
Women					
Under 40	24.0	17.0	26.0	27.0	6.0
Over 40	23.0	19.0	15.0	40.0	3.0

Source: Health and Longevity, Belden & Russonello, The Alliance for Aging Research, December 1992, p. 32. *Notes:* Data represent the results of a national telephone survey conducted in December 1992. A total of 906 adults responded. Elderly Americans (50 years or older) represented 34 percent of the sample. Percentages are weighted.

★ 866 ★

Health Care

Opinions on Doctor-Assisted Suicide

Data show survey responses to the question, "Doctors should be allowed by law to help their terminally ill patients commit suicide. Do you agree or disagree?"

[Data are shown in percent]

	Agree strongly	Agree somewhat	Disagree somewhat	Disagree strongly	Don't know
Totals	24.0	19.0	12.0	38.0	6.0
Totals collapsed					
Agree	43.0				
Disagree			50.0		
Sex					
Male	26.0	22.0	12.0	35.0	4.0

[Continued]

★ 866 ★

Opinions on Doctor-Assisted Suicide
[Continued]

	Agree strongly	Agree somewhat	Disagree somewhat	Disagree strongly	Don't know
Female	21.0	17.0	12.0	41.0	8.0
Age					
18-29	20.0	22.0	13.0	44.0	2.0
30-39	23.0	24.0	13.0	34.0	6.0
40-49	28.0	19.0	8.0	38.0	7.0
50-64	25.0	16.0	15.0	37.0	8.0
65+	24.0	14.0	14.0	38.0	9.0
Race					
White	25.0	21.0	13.0	35.0	6.0
African-American	14.0	15.0	8.0	58.0	5.0
Household income					
Less than $15,000	16.0	13.0	11.0	53.0	7.0
$15,000-$34,999	26.0	18.0	12.0	38.0	5.0
$35,000-$49,999	23.0	24.0	13.0	34.0	6.0
$50,000 or more	27.0	25.0	13.0	31.0	4.0
Household occupation					
Professional white-collar	29.0	22.0	11.0	32.0	4.0
Managerial white-collar	24.0	26.0	10.0	32.0	7.0
Blue-collar	20.0	15.0	16.0	43.0	6.0
Household children					
None	26.0	21.0	13.0	32.0	7.0
18 and under	21.0	17.0	12.0	45.0	4.0

Source: Health and Longevity, Belden & Russonello, The Alliance for Aging Research, December 1992, p. 34.
Notes: Data represent the results of a national telephone survey conducted in December 1992. A total of 906 adults responded. Elderly Americans (50 years or older) represented 34 percent of the sample. Percentages are weighted.

Life Satisfaction

★ 867 ★

Life Satisfaction

Data are based on a survey of 3,509 Americans aged 50 to 64 conducted by Louis Harris Associates for The Commonwealth Fund between March and September 1989. The survey is a national cross section but excludes Alaska and Hawaii and people in prison, hospitals, nursing homes, or religious and educational institutions.

Extent of life satisfaction:
—Sixty percent of older people are very satisfied with life.
—Four percent are not at all satisfied with life, and 36 percent are somewhat satisfied.

Relationship to work:
—People who are not working are five times more likely than people who are working full time to be not at all satisfied with life.
—Sixty-three percent of people working full time are very satisfied with life, compared with 55 percent of people not working.

Relationship to demographic characteristics:
—Unmarried people are 3.5 times as likely to be not at all satisfied with life as married people.
—Life satisfaction does not vary by gender.
—Men between the ages of 60 and 64 are more likely than men between the ages of 55 and 59 to be satisfied (65 percent versus 58 percent).
—Extreme dissatisfaction does not vary by race or ethnicity; however,

Hispanics are somewhat more likely than other older people to be very satisfied with life. White men are less likely to be satisfied than black and Hispanic men at the same income level.

Relationship to economic characteristics:
—Low-income (less than $7,500) people are much more likely than very high-income people (more than $50,000) to be not at all satisfied with life (17 percent versus 0.4 percent).
—High-income people are two-thirds more likely than low-income people to say that they are very satisfied with life.
—People with less than a high school education are four times more likely than people with a college education to be dissatisfied with life.

Relationship to health status:
—Sixty-six percent of persons in excellent or good health are very satisfied with life, compared with 38 percent of those in fair or poor health.
—Those in fair or poor health are almost eight times as likely to be very

[Continued]

★ 867 ★

Life Satisfaction
[Continued]

dissatisfied with life.

These are some of the most significant determinants of life satisfaction among older adults:
—Being employed full time
—Being married
—Having family income in excess of $15,000
—Being in good or excellent health

These results suggest that life planning early in life can help shape satisfaction in older life. The plan should include:
—Getting a good education that leads to stable employment and higher income
—Developing and maintaining a good marital relationship
—Maintaining good health habits that prevent or delay the onset of chronic disease and disability

Source: Davis, Karen, "Life Satisfaction and Older Adults," *The Commonwealth Fund, Americans Over 55 at Work Program*, September 1991, pp. v-vi.

★ 868 ★

Life Satisfaction

Life Satisfaction Among the Population Ages 50-64, by Selected Characteristics, 1989

Characteristic	Percent of population		
	Very satisfied	Somewhat satisfied	Not at all satisfied
Total	60.1	36.4	3.5
Employment status			
Full time	63.2	35.5	1.3
Part time	65.0	32.6	2.5
Not working	54.6	38.5	6.9
Age			
50-54	59.9	37.3	2.8
55-59	57.3	38.7	4.0
Men	58.5	38.0	3.5
Women	56.2	39.2	4.6
60-64	65.4	31.3	3.3
Gender			
Male	63.0	33.8	3.2
Female	57.5	38.6	3.9

[Continued]

★ 868 ★

Life Satisfaction Among the Population Ages 50-64, by Selected Characteristics, 1989
[Continued]

Characteristic	Percent of population		
	Very satisfied	Somewhat satisfied	Not at all satisfied
Marital status			
Not married	46.2	45.9	7.9
Married	64.2	33.5	2.3
Race			
White	59.7	36.9	3.4
Black	59.1	36.5	4.4
Hispanic	69.0	26.8	4.2
Other	52.0	42.3	5.7
Income			
Less than $7,500	42.8	40.3	16.9
$7,500-$14,999	49.0	41.3	9.7
$15,000-$24,999	56.0	40.7	3.3
$25,000-$34,999	58.1	39.6	2.3
$35,000-$49,999	64.5	34.3	1.2
$50,000+	71.3	28.3	0.4
Total sample	60.1	36.4	3.5
Education (years)			
<12	57.2	36.1	6.7
12-15	58.4	38.2	3.4
16+	66.0	32.4	1.6+
Health status			
Excellent/good	65.7	32.7	1.5
Fair/poor	37.8	50.7	11.5

Source: Davis, Karen, "Life Satisfaction and Older Adults," *The Commonwealth Fund, Americans Over 55 at Work Program*, September 1991, pp. 13-14. *Notes:* Data are based on a survey of 3,509 Americans aged 50 to 64 conducted by Louis Harris Associates for The Commonwealth Fund between March and September 1989. The survey is a national cross section but excludes Alaska and Hawaii and people in prison, hospitals, nursing homes, or religious and educational institutions.

★ 869 ★

Life Satisfaction

Life Satisfaction Among Population Aged 50-64, 1989

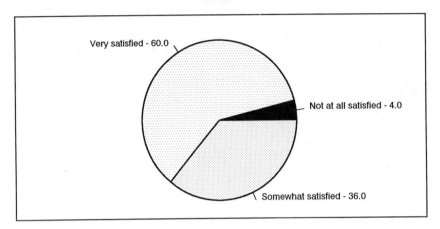

Very satisfied - 60.0

Not at all satisfied - 4.0

Somewhat satisfied - 36.0

Response	Percent
Very satisfied	60.0
Somewhat satisfied	36.0
Not at all satisfied	4.0

Source: Davis, Karen, "Life Satisfaction and Older Adults," *The Commonwealth Fund, Americans Over 55 at Work Program*, September 1991, p. 21. *Notes:* Data are based on a survey of 3,509 Americans aged 50 to 64 conducted by Louis Harris Associates for The Commonwealth Fund between March and September 1989. The survey is a national cross section but excludes Alaska and Hawaii and people in prison, hospitals, nursing homes, or religious and educational institutions.

★ 870 ★

Life Satisfaction

Percent of the Population Aged 50-64 Not At All Satisfied with Life, by Employment Status, 1989

Employment status	Percent
Not working	6.90
Part-time	2.41
Full-time	1.31

Source: Davis, Karen, "Life Satisfaction and Older Adults," *The Commonwealth Fund, Americans Over 55 at Work Program*, September 1991, p. 22. *Notes:* Data are based on a survey of 3,509 Americans aged 50 to 64 conducted by Louis Harris Associates for The Commonwealth Fund between March and September 1989. The survey is a national cross section but excludes Alaska and Hawaii and people in prison, hospitals, nursing homes, or religious and educational institutions.

★ 871 ★

Life Satisfaction

Percent of the Population Aged 50-64 Very Satisfied with Life, by Employment Status, 1989

Employment status	Percent
Part-time	65.0
Full-time	63.0
Not working	55.0

Source: Davis, Karen, "Life Satisfaction and Older Adults," *The Commonwealth Fund, Americans Over 55 at Work Program*, September 1991, p. 23. *Notes:* Data are based on a survey of 3,509 Americans aged 50 to 64 conducted by Louis Harris Associates for The Commonwealth Fund between March and September 1989. The survey is a national cross section but excludes Alaska and Hawaii and people in prison, hospitals, nursing homes, or religious and educational institutions.

★ 872 ★

Life Satisfaction

Percent of Population Aged 50-64 Very Satisfied with Life, by Age, 1989

Age	Percent
50-54	60.0
55-59	57.0
60-64	65.0

Source: Davis, Karen, "Life Satisfaction and Older Adults," *The Commonwealth Fund, Americans Over 55 at Work Program*, September 1991, p. 24. *Notes:* Data are based on a survey of 3,509 Americans aged 50 to 64 conducted by Louis Harris Associates for The Commonwealth Fund between March and September 1989. The survey is a national cross section but excludes Alaska and Hawaii and people in prison, hospitals, nursing homes, or religious and educational institutions.

★ 873 ★

Life Satisfaction

Life Satisfaction Among Population Aged 50-64, by Sex, 1989

Response	Male	Female
Very satisfied	63.0	58.0
Somewhat satisfied	34.0	39.0
Not at all satisfied	3.0	4.0

Source: Davis, Karen, "Life Satisfaction and Older Adults," *The Commonwealth Fund, Americans Over 55 at Work Program*, September 1991, p. 25. *Notes:* Data are based on a survey of 3,509 Americans aged 50 to 64 conducted by Louis Harris Associates for The Commonwealth Fund between March and September 1989. The survey is a national cross section but excludes Alaska and Hawaii and people in prison, hospitals, nursing homes, or religious and educational institutions.

★ 874 ★

Life Satisfaction

Percent of Population Aged 50-64 Very Satisfied with Life, by Race, 1989

Race	Percent
Hispanic	69.0
White	60.0
Black	59.0
Other	52.0

Source: Davis, Karen, "Life Satisfaction and Older Adults," *The Commonwealth Fund, Americans Over 55 at Work Program*, September 1991, p. 26. *Notes:* Data are based on a survey of 3,509 Americans aged 50 to 64 conducted by Louis Harris Associates for The Commonwealth Fund between March and September 1989. The survey is a national cross section but excludes Alaska and Hawaii and people in prison, hospitals, nursing homes, or religious and educational institutions.

★ 875 ★

Life Satisfaction

Life Satisfaction Among Population Aged 50-64, by Marital Status, 1989

[Numbers are in percent]

Response	Married	Not married
Very satisfied	64.0	46.0
Somewhat satisfied	34.0	46.0
Not at all satisfied	2.0	8.0

Source: Davis, Karen, "Life Satisfaction and Older Adults," *The Commonwealth Fund, Americans Over 55 at Work Program*, September 1991, p. 27. *Notes:* Data are based on a survey of 3,509 Americans aged 50 to 64 conducted by Louis Harris Associates for The Commonwealth Fund between March and September 1989. The survey is a national cross section but excludes Alaska and Hawaii and people in prison, hospitals, nursing homes, or religious and educational institutions.

★ 876 ★

Life Satisfaction

Percent of Population Aged 50-64 Very Satisfied with Life, by Annual Family Income, 1989

Annual family income	Percent
$7,500 or less	43.0
$7,501-$15,000	49.0
$15,001-$25,000	56.0
$25,001-$35,000	58.0
$35,001-$50,000	65.0
$50,000 or more	71.0

Source: Davis, Karen, "Life Satisfaction and Older Adults," *The Commonwealth Fund, Americans Over 55 at Work Program*, September 1991, p. 28. *Notes:* Data are based on a survey of 3,509 Americans aged 50 to 64 conducted by Louis Harris Associates for The Commonwealth Fund between March and September 1989. The survey is a national cross section but excludes Alaska and Hawaii and people in prison, hospitals, nursing homes, or religious and educational institutions.

★ 877 ★

Life Satisfaction

Percent of Population Aged 50-64 Very Satisfied with Life, by Education, 1989

Education attained (yrs.)	Percent
Less than 12 years	57.0
12-15 years	58.0
More than 16 years	66.0

Source: Davis, Karen, "Life Satisfaction and Older Adults," *The Commonwealth Fund, Americans Over 55 at Work Program*, September 1991, p. 29. *Notes:* Data are based on a survey of 3,509 Americans aged 50 to 64 conducted by Louis Harris Associates for The Commonwealth Fund between March and September 1989. The survey is a national cross section but excludes Alaska and Hawaii and people in prison, hospitals, nursing homes, or religious and educational institutions.

★ 878 ★

Life Satisfaction

Life Satisfaction Among Population Aged 50-64, by Health Status, 1989

Response	Excellent/ good health	Fair/ poor health
Somewhat satisfied	33.0	51.0
Very satisfied	66.0	38.0
Not at all satisfied	2.0	12.0

Source: Davis, Karen, "Life Satisfaction and Older Adults," *The Commonwealth Fund, Americans Over 55 at Work Program*, September 1991, p. 30. *Notes:* Data are based on a survey of 3,509 Americans aged 50 to 64 conducted by Louis Harris Associates for The Commonwealth Fund between March and September 1989. The survey is a national cross section but excludes Alaska and Hawaii and people in prison, hospitals, nursing homes, or religious and educational institutions.

★ 879 ★

Life Satisfaction

Expectations of Quality of Life

Data show survey responses to the question, "Do you think you will enjoy life more, or less, when you get older?"

[Data are shown in percent]

	More	Less	About as much	Don't know/ Not available
Total	50.0	30.0	11.0	9.0
Age				
18-29	55.0	30.0	6.0	9.0
30-39	64.0	21.0	7.0	8.0
40-49	47.0	36.0	9.0	8.0
50-64	50.0	28.0	12.0	11.0
65+	30.0	39.0	24.0	8.0
Age collapsed				
18-39	59.0	26.0	6.0	9.0
40+	42.0	34.0	15.0	9.0
Household income				
Less than $15,000	48.0	30.0	8.0	14.0
$15,000-$34,999	49.0	37.0	9.0	5.0
$35,000-$49,999	51.0	27.0	14.0	8.0
$50,000 or more	57.0	23.0	12.0	8.0

Source: Health and Longevity, Belden & Russonello, The Alliance for Aging Research, December 1992, p. 15. *Notes:* Data represent the results of a national telephone survey conducted in December 1992. A total of 906 adults responded. Elderly Americans (50 years or older) represented 34 percent of the sample. Percentages are weighted.

Longevity

★ 880 ★

Desire to be 100 Years Old

Data show survey responses to the question, "If it were possible, would you like to live to be 100 years old?"

[Data are shown in percent]

	Yes	No	Don't know
Total	61.0	34.0	5.0
Sex			
Male	65.0	30.0	4.0
Female	57.0	39.0	5.0
Race			
White	58.0	37.0	5.0
African-American	76.0	17.0	7.0
Age			
18-29	65.0	32.0	3.0
30-39	69.0	26.0	4.0
40-49	61.0	64.0	5.0
50-64	54.0	40.0	6.0
65 +	52.0	43.0	5.0

Source: *Health and Longevity*, Belden & Russonello, The Alliance for Aging Research, December 1992, p. 10. *Notes:* Data represent the results of a national telephone survey conducted in December 1992. A total of 906 adults responded. Elderly Americans (50 years or older) represented 34 percent of the sample. Percentages are weighted.

★ 881 ★

Longevity

Expectations of Longevity, by Respondent Age

Data show survey responses to the question, "How old do you expect to live to be? Until what age?"

[Data are shown in percent]

Age	1991[1]	1992
Less than age 70	8.0	9.0
70 to 74	12.0	14.0
75 to 79	13.0	13.0
80 to 84	25.0	24.0
85 to 94	14.0	12.0

[Continued]

★ 881 ★

Expectations of Longevity, by Respondent Age
[Continued]

Age	1991[1]	1992
90 to 99	11.0	8.0
100 or older	6.0	4.0
Don't know	11.0	14.0
Subtotal: 80 or older	56.0	48.0

Source: Health and Longevity, Belden & Russonello, The Alliance for Aging Research, December 1992, p. 12. *Notes:* Data represent the results of a national telephone survey conducted in December 1992. A total of 906 adults responded. Elderly Americans (50 years or older) represented 34 percent of the sample. Percentages are weighted. 1. Alliance for Aging Research, National Public Opinion Survey (Belden & Russell), November 1991.

★ 882 ★

Longevity

Expectations of Longevity, by Educational and Professional Status

Data show survey responses to the question, "How old do you expect to live to be? Until what age?"

[Data are shown in percent]

	Less than 80	More than 80	Don't know
Total	36.0	49.0	14.0
Education			
High school or less	36.0	45.0	18.0
Some college/vocational	46.0	41.0	12.0
College degree or more	27.0	63.0	10.0
Household occupation			
Professional white collar	28.0	59.0	13.0
Managerial/technical/sales white collar	40.0	51.0	7.0
Blue collar	38.0	42.0	18.0

Source: Health and Longevity, Belden & Russonello, The Alliance for Aging Research, December 1992, p. 13. *Notes:* Data represent the results of a national telephone survey conducted in December 1992. A total of 906 adults responded. Elderly Americans (50 years or older) represented 34 percent of the sample. Percentages are weighted.

★ 883 ★

Longevity

Fear of Dependence in Old Age

Data show survey responses to the question, "Please tell me if you agree strongly, agree somewhat, disagree somewhat, or disagree strongly with the following statements: losing my independence and having to spend the last years of my life in a nursing home are what I fear most about old age."

[Data are shown in percent.]

	Agree strongly	Agree somewhat	Disagree somewhat	Disagree strongly	Don't know
Total	50.0	20.0	13.0	14.0	3.0
Total collapsed					
Agree	70.0				
Disagree			27.0		
Sex					
Male	45.0	23.0	13.0	16.0	3.0
Female	55.0	18.0	13.0	11.0	3.0
Household income					
Less than $15,000	56.0	19.0	10.0	9.0	6.0
$15,000-$34,999	55.0	17.0	11.0	15.0	2.0
$35,000-$49,999	48.0	20.0	15.0	14.0	3.0
$50,000 or more	41.0	27.0	14.0	14.0	3.0
Education					
High school or less	53.0	16.0	10.0	17.0	4.0
Some college/vocational	54.0	20.0	14.0	10.0	2.0
College degree/more	41.0	27.0	18.0	12.0	2.0

Source: Health and Longevity, Belden & Russonello, The Alliance for Aging Research, December 1992, p. 20. *Notes:* Data represent the results of a national telephone survey conducted in December 1992. A total of 906 adults responded. Elderly Americans (50 years or older) represented 34 percent of the sample. Percentages are weighted.

Retirement

★ 884 ★

Retirement Expectations

Data show survey responses to the question, "At what age do you expect to retire completely?"

	Percent[1]
45 and under	3.0
46-59	15.0
60	14.0
61-64	9.0
65	29.0
66-69	2.0
70-79	10.0
80 or older	2.0
Would not like to retire	12.0
Categories collapsed	
Under 65	42.0
65	29.0
Over 65	26.0

Source: Health and Longevity, Belden & Russonello, The Alliance for Aging Research, December 1992, p. 22. *Notes:* Data represent the results of a national telephone survey conducted in December 1992. A total of 906 adults responded. Elderly Americans (50 years or older) represented 34 percent of the sample. 1. Percentages are weighted.

★ 885 ★

Retirement

Retirement Expectations for Next Generation

Data show survey responses to the question, "Do you think your children's generation will retire, on average, at an earlier age, a later age, or the same age as your generation?"

	Percent
Later age	37.0
Earlier age	26.0
Same age	29.0
Don't know	7.0

Source: Health and Longevity, Belden & Russonello, The Alliance for Aging Research, December 1992, p. 23. *Notes:* Data represent the results of a national telephone survey conducted in December 1992. A total of 906 adults responded. Elderly Americans (50 years or older) represented 34 percent of the sample. 1. Percentages are weighted.

★ 886 ★

Retirement

Retirement Activity Preferences

Data show survey responses to the question, "If you could choose, how would you like to spend most of your time in retirement?"

Activity	Percent[1]
Watching television	1.0
Spending time with family and friends	16.0
Traveling	43.0
Volunteering	7.0
Working at a part-time job	8.0
Doing sports and other recreational activities	13.0
Caring for someone else in your family	5.0
Something else	6.0
Don't know	1.0

Source: Health and Longevity, Belden & Russonello, The Alliance for Aging Research, December 1992, p. 25. *Notes:* Data represent the results of a national telephone survey conducted in December 1992. A total of 906 adults responded. Elderly Americans (50 years or older) represented 34 percent of the sample. 1. Percentages are weighted.

Sexual Orientation

★ 887 ★

Views on Homosexuals in the Clergy

Data show results of a telephone survey of 1,002 persons who responded to the question: "Do you think homosexuals should or should not be hired for the clergy?" Approval is given less by older persons.

[Data are shown in percent]

	Should	Should not
National	43.0	50.0
Protestant	37.0	57.0
Catholic	48.0	45.0
Age 18-29	49.0	46.0
Age 30-49	48.0	47.0
Age 50-64	37.0	53.0
Age 65 and older	28.0	61.0
College graduates	56.0	40.0

[Continued]

★ 887 ★

Views on Homosexuals in the Clergy

[Continued]

	Should	Should not
Attended college	46.0	49.0
No college	36.0	55.0

Source: Princeton Religion Research Center, "Public Divided on the Issue of Hiring of Homosexuals for the Clergy," *Emerging Trends*, November 1992, p. 5. Primary source: The Gallup Organization. *Note:* "No opinion" (7 percent nationally) is not shown.

Shopping

★ 888 ★

Supermarket Performance Ratings: Variety Attributes

Table is based on 600 telephone interviews conducted in February 1991, or on a subsample of those 600 interviews. The focus groups were located in Princeton, New Jersey; Minneapolis, Minnesota; Dallas, Texas; and Los Angeles, California.

	Base	Easy to find sales	Variety	Items in stock	New items	National brands	Store brands	Easy to find items
All shoppers	(600)	8.32	8.50	8.24	7.76	8.39	8.45	8.25
Age								
Under 30	(119)	8.33	8.65	8.39	7.66	8.50	8.50	8.44
30-44	(233)	8.24	8.18	8.03	7.52	8.17	8.38	8.16
45-54	(88)	8.36	8.60	8.31	7.80	8.45	8.32	8.14
55+	(142)	8.55	8.89	8.50	8.30	8.67	8.80	8.46

Source: Food Marketing Institute, *The Service Advantage: How Consumers Evaluate Service in Their Supermarket, 1991*, p. 48. Published with permission.

★ 889 ★

Shopping

Supermarket Performance Ratings: Merchandise Attributes

Table is based on 600 telephone interviews conducted in February 1991, or on a subsample of those 600 interviews. The focus groups were located in Princeton, New Jersey; Minneapolis, Minnesota; Dallas, Texas; and Los Angeles, California.

	Base	Displays	Prepared foods	Samples	Recipes
All shoppers	(600)	7.23	6.90	6.69	5.25
Age					
Under 30	(119)	7.14	7.42	6.59	5.25
30-44	(233)	6.91	6.65	6.63	5.10
45-54	(88)	7.28	7.17	6.25	5.58
55+	(142)	7.85	6.95	7.26	5.45

Source: Food Marketing Institute, *The Service Advantage: How Consumers Evaluate Service in Their Supermarket, 1991*, p. 49. Published with permission.

★ 890 ★

Shopping

Supermarket Performance Ratings: Courtesy Desk

Table is based on 600 telephone interviews conducted in February 1991, or on a subsample of those 600 interviews. The focus groups were located in Princeton, New Jersey; Minneapolis, Minnesota; Dallas, Texas; and Los Angeles, California.

	Courtesy desk				Price	
	Base	Returns	Respond	Pay by check	Keep low	Lowest price
All shoppers	(600)	8.65	8.25	9.09	7.89	7.56
Age						
Under 30	(119)	8.18	7.84	8.87	8.03	7.78
30-44	(233)	8.53	8.14	9.16	7.61	7.49
45-54	(88)	8.88	8.25	9.00	7.70	7.06
55+	(142)	9.22	8.85	9.23	8.39	7.90

Source: Food Marketing Institute, *The Service Advantage: How Consumers Evaluate Service in Their Supermarket, 1991*, p. 50. Published with permission.

★ 891 ★

Shopping

Supermarket Performance Ratings: Personnel

Table is based on 600 telephone interviews conducted in February 1991, or on a subsample of those 600 interviews. The focus groups were located in Princeton, New Jersey; Minneapolis, Minnesota; Dallas, Texas; and Los Angeles, California.

	Base	Helpful personnel							
		Attentive cashiers	Help avail.	Helpful empl.	Careful baggers	Short lines	Help to car	Consistent service	Line limits
All shoppers	(600)	8.39	7.59	7.91	7.70	7.49	7.00	8.54	8.00
Age									
Under 30	(119)	8.35	7.48	7.90	7.43	7.26	6.61	8.47	7.73
30-44	(233)	8.09	7.40	7.70	7.31	7.29	6.77	8.35	7.92
45-54	(88)	8.61	7.76	8.00	8.26	7.78	7.31	8.53	8.15
55+	(142)	8.84	8.05	8.32	8.25	7.92	7.61	8.96	8.32

Source: Food Marketing Institute, *The Service Advantage: How Consumers Evaluate Service in Their Supermarket, 1991*, p. 51. Published with permission.

★ 892 ★

Shopping

Supermarket Performance Ratings: Facility and Maintenance

Table is based on 600 telephone interviews conducted in February 1991, or on a subsample of those interviews. The focus groups were located in Princeton, New Jersey; Minneapolis, Minnesota; Dallas, Texas; and Los Angeles, California.

	Base	Remove damaged	Remove expired	Clean	Enough carts	Location	Rest rooms
All shoppers	(600)	8.78	8.54	8.79	8.97	9.12	6.42
Age							
Under 30	(119)	8.61	8.68	8.80	8.96	8.98	6.50
30-44	(233)	8.66	8.38	8.63	8.92	9.07	6.28
45-54	(88)	9.03	8.61	8.90	9.17	9.08	6.84
55+	(142)	9.03	8.70	9.08	9.03	9.39	6.40

Source: Food Marketing Institute, *The Service Advantage: How Consumers Evaluate Service in Their Supermarket, 1991*, p. 52. Published with permission.

Chapter 16
CRIMINALS AND VICTIMS

This chapter deals with elderly Americans as criminals under the heading of Offenders and with the elderly as victims of crime under the heading of Victimization. Related information on Neighborhoods may be found in the chapter on *Housing*.

Offenders

★ 893 ★

Arrests of Elderly People, 1990

The table summarizes data from 10,206 agencies.

Offense charged	Total all ages	55-59	60-64	65 and over
Total	11,250,083	120,657	78,527	84,251
Percent distribution[1]	100.0	1.1	.7	.7
Murder and nonnegligent manslaughter	18,298	192	146	188
Forcible rape	30,966	310	204	227
Robbery	136,300	256	116	110
Aggravated assault	376,917	4,027	2,625	2,741
Burglary	341,192	828	376	434
Larceny-theft	1,241,236	12,965	9,845	15,003
Motor vehicle theft	168,338	284	152	174
Arson	14,974	138	84	84
Violent crime[2]	562,481	4,785	3,091	3,266
Percent distribution[1]	100.0	.9	.5	.6
Property crime[3]	1,765,740	14,215	10,457	15,695
Percent distribution[1]	100.0	.8	.6	.9
Other assaults	801,425	7,302	4,370	4,797

[Continued]

★ 893 ★

Arrests of Elderly People, 1990

[Continued]

Offense charged	Total all ages	55-59	60-64	65 and over
Forgery and counterfeiting	74,393	416	209	206
Fraud	279,776	2,987	1,804	1,796
Embezzlement	12,055	104	65	50
Stolen property: buying, receiving, possessing	131,656	567	352	319
Vandalism	256,558	930	565	710
Weapons: carrying, possessing, etc.	176,137	1,750	1,221	1,202
Prostitution and commercialized vice	91,093	623	398	495
Sex offenses (except forcible rape and prostitution)	84,852	1,909	1,397	1,749
Drug abuse violations	869,155	3,705	1,910	1,362
Gambling	15,443	941	712	764
Offenses against family and children	65,992	635	358	367
Driving under the influence	1,390,906	27,815	18,329	17,073
Liquor laws	552,039	3,676	2,356	2,169
Drunkenness	716,504	17,579	11,730	11,297
Disorderly conduct	579,674	4,763	3,257	3,625
Vagrancy	31,237	671	406	306
All other offenses (except traffic)	2,572,491	25,184	15,496	16,957
Suspicion	17,753	100	44	46

Source: *Crime in the United States*, Uniform Crime Reports, 1990, Federal Bureau of Investigation, U.S. Department of Justice, Washington, DC 20535, pp. 184-185. *Notes:* 1. Because of rounding, the percentages may not add to total. 2. Violent crimes are offenses of murder, forcible rape, robbery, and aggravated assault. 3. Property crimes are offenses of burglary, larceny-theft, motor vehicle theft, and arson.

★ 894 ★

Offenders

Elderly Female Arrests, 1990

Offense charged	Total all ages	Age		
		55-59	60-64	65 and over
Total	2,068,153	17,551	11,455	14,963
Percent distribution[1]	100.0	.8	.6	.7
Murder and nonnegligent manslaughter	1,911	23	23	26
Forcible rape	336	3	1	-
Robbery	11,285	25	12	11
Aggravated assault	50,137	447	245	258
Burglary	29,972	114	59	72
Larceny-theft	397,385	5,484	4,418	6,663

[Continued]

★ 894 ★

Elderly Female Arrests, 1990
[Continued]

Offense charged	Total all ages	Age		
		55-59	60-64	65 and over
Motor vehicle theft	16,889	31	10	9
Arson	1,950	27	14	12
Violent crime[2]	63,669	498	281	295
Percent distribution[1]	100.0	.8	.4	.5
Property crime[3]	446,196	5,656	4,501	6,756
Percent distribution[1]	100.0	1.3	1.0	1.5
Other assaults	128,970	984	543	694
Forgery and counterfeiting	25,726	84	41	66
Fraud	123,656	1,110	572	615
Embezzlement	4,972	42	16	24
Stolen property: buying, receiving, possessing	15,792	79	37	49
Vandalism	27,686	116	64	103
Weapons: carrying, possessing, etc.	13,082	152	89	103
Prostitution and commercialized vice	58,323	41	24	19
Sex offenses (except forcible rape and prostitution)	6,561	28	13	24
Drug abuse violations	145,826	476	213	206
Gambling	2,129	133	75	81
Offenses against family and children	11,776	85	50	53
Driving under the influence	177,690	2,680	1,618	1,380
Liquor laws	103,141	336	193	228
Drunkenness	71,910	923	656	599
Disorderly conduct	110,619	721	403	591
Vagrancy	3,930	42	14	34
All other offenses (except traffic)	427,774	3,358	2,049	3,038
Suspicion	2,662	7	3	5

Source: Crime in the United States, Uniform Crime Reports, 1990, Federal Bureau of Investigation, U.S. Department of Justice, Washington, DC 20535, pp. 188-189. *Notes:* 1. Because of rounding, percentages may not add to total. 2. Violent crimes are offenses of murder, forcible rape, robbery, and aggravated assault. 3. Property crimes are offenses of burglary, larceny-theft, motor vehicle theft, and arson.

★ 895 ★

Offenders

Elderly Male Arrests, 1990

Offense charged	Total all ages	Age		
		55-59	60-64	65 and over
Total	9,181,930	103,106	67,072	69,288
Percent distribution[1]	100.0	1.1	.7	.8
Murder and nonnegligent manslaughter	16,387	169	123	162
Forcible rape	30,630	307	203	227
Robbery	125,015	231	104	99
Aggravated assault	326,780	3,580	2,380	2,483
Burglary	311,220	714	317	362
Larceny-theft	843,851	7,481	5,427	8,340
Motor vehicle theft	151,449	253	142	165
Arson	13,024	111	70	72
Violent crime[2]	498,812	4,287	2,810	2,971
Percent distribution[1]	100.0	.9	.6	.6
Property crime[3]	1,319,544	8,559	5,956	8,939
Percent distribution[1]	100.0	.6	.5	.7
Other assaults	672,455	6,318	3,827	4,103
Forgery and counterfeiting	48,667	332	168	140
Fraud	156,120	1,877	1,232	1,181
Embezzlement	7,083	62	49	26
Stolen property: buying, receiving, possessing	115,864	488	315	270
Vandalism	228,872	814	501	607
Weapons: carrying, possessing, etc.	163,055	1,598	1,132	1,099
Prostitution and commercialized vice	32,770	582	374	476
Sex offenses (except forcible rape and prostitution)	78,291	1,881	1,384	1,725
Drug abuse violations	723,329	3,229	1,697	1,156
Gambling	13,314	808	637	683
Offenses against family and children	54,216	550	308	314
Driving under the influence	1,213,216	25,135	16,711	15,693
Liquor laws	448,898	3,340	2,163	1,941
Drunkenness	644,594	16,656	11,074	10,698
Disorderly conduct	469,055	4,042	2,854	3,034
Vagrancy	27,307	629	392	272
All other offenses (except traffic)	2,144,717	21,826	13,447	13,919
Suspicion	15,091	93	41	41

Source: Crime in the United States, Uniform Crime Reports, 1990, Federal Bureau of Investigation, U.S. Department of Justice, Washington, DC 20535, pp. 186-187. *Notes:* 1. Because of rounding, percentages may not add to total. 2. Violent crimes are offenses of murder, forcible rape, robbery, and aggravated assault. 3. Property crimes are offenses of burglary, larceny-theft, motor vehicle theft, and arson.

★ 896 ★

Offenders

City Arrests, Distribution by Age, 1991

Offenses charged	Age						
	35-39	40-44	45-49	50-54	55-59	60-64	65 and over
Total	789,840	474,171	247,641	141,268	83,763	53,170	59,807
Percent distribution[1]	9.4	5.7	3.0	1.7	1.0	0.6	0.7
Murder and nonnegligent manslaughter	1,015	610	291	225	108	91	113
Forcible rape	2,229	1,273	608	381	193	133	146
Robbery	7,156	3,148	1,170	496	214	98	132
Aggravated assault	28,743	17,073	9,110	5,031	2,815	1,777	1,965
Burglary	16,332	7,667	2,935	1,300	654	286	312
Larceny-theft	84,481	51,024	25,945	15,517	10,357	7,691	11,904
Motor vehicle theft	5,227	2,497	1,063	439	209	92	109
Arson	634	415	210	157	89	41	65
Violent crime[2]	39,143	22,104	11,179	6,133	3,330	2,099	2,356
Percent distribution[1]	8.6	4.8	2.5	1.3	.7	.5	.5
Property crime[3]	106,674	61,603	30,153	17,413	11,309	8,110	12,390
Percent distribution[1]	7.5	4.3	2.1	1.2	.8	.6	.9
Crime index total[4]	145,817	83,707	41,332	23,546	14,639	10,209	14,746
Percent distribution[1]	7.7	4.4	2.2	1.2	.8	.5	.8
Other assaults	61,093	34,781	17,443	9,203	5,051	3,039	3,536
Forgery and counterfeiting	6,048	3,220	1,386	685	296	141	160
Fraud	21,877	13,592	6,725	3,250	1,772	852	1,317
Embezzlement	718	444	220	207	91	28	33
Stolen property: buying, receiving, possessing	6,825	3,544	1,635	884	415	241	230
Vandalism	10,023	5,304	2,563	1,310	695	399	531
Weapons: carrying, possessing, etc.	9,757	6,126	3,448	1,948	1,173	738	920
Prostitution and commercialized vice	8,765	3,928	1,738	849	483	283	372
Sex offenses (except forcible rape and prostitution)	6,604	4,470	2,708	1,771	1,176	886	1,121
Drug abuse violations	67,517	34,815	14,022	6,051	2,628	1,235	1,106
Gambling	1,212	1,052	847	698	528	382	477
Offenses against family and children	5,465	3,059	1,374	669	374	230	266
Driving under the influence	104,084	69,901	41,855	25,357	15,579	10,479	10,055
Liquor laws	13,173	8,996	5,475	3,442	2,457	1,530	1,316
Drunkenness	75,711	51,157	31,393	20,569	13,594	8,415	8,262
Disorderly conduct	40,988	23,937	12,298	7,125	3,943	2,575	2,985

[Continued]

★ 896 ★

City Arrests, Distribution by Age, 1991

[Continued]

Offenses charged	Age						
	35-39	40-44	45-49	50-54	55-59	60-64	65 and over
Vagrancy	4,884	2,886	1,761	1,108	583	328	264
All other offenses (except traffic)	197,839	118,451	59,116	32,442	18,225	11,143	12,069
Suspicion	1,440	801	302	154	61	37	41

Source: Federal Bureau of Investigation, *Uniform Crime Reports for the United States 1991*, p. 237. *Notes:* 1. Because of rounding, the percentages may not add to total. 2. Violent crimes are offenses of murder, forcible rape, robbery, and aggravated assault. 3. Property crimes are offenses of burglary, larceny-theft, motor vehicle theft, and arson. 4. Includes arson.

★ 897 ★

Offenders

Suburban Area Arrests, Distribution by Age, 1991

Data show number of arrests for each offense. Suburban areas include suburban city and county law enforcement agencies within metropolitan areas. Central cities are not included.

Offense charged	Age						
	35-39	40-44	45-49	50-54	55-59	60-64	65 and over
Total	328,972	200,952	108,964	61,639	35,952	23,157	24,790
Percent distribution[1]	9.2	5.6	3.1	1.7	1.0	.6	.7
Murder and nonnegligent manslaughter	284	224	121	106	38	30	56
Forcible rape	846	563	268	169	92	56	66
Robbery	1,504	705	269	118	59	29	37
Aggravated assault	10,386	6,393	3,488	1,841	1,052	706	735
Burglary	5,138	2,378	959	408	231	114	115
Larceny-theft	30,929	19,073	10,242	6,079	4,123	3,151	4,687
Motor vehicle theft	1,660	862	433	180	105	46	66
Arson	291	193	108	55	39	22	26
Violent crime[2]	13,020	7,885	4,146	2,234	1,241	821	894
Percent distribution[3]	9.0	5.5	2.9	1.5	.9	.6	.6
Property crime[3]	38,018	22,506	11,742	6,722	4,498	3,333	4,894
Percent distribution[1]	6.7	4.0	2.1	1.2	.8	.6	.9
Crime index total[4]	51,038	30,391	15,888	8,956	5,739	4,154	5,788
Percent distribution[1]	7.2	4.3	2.2	1.3	.8	.6	.8
Other assaults	25,004	14,781	7,727	4,373	2,446	1,417	1,617
Forgery and counterfeiting	2,886	1,524	633	295	149	87	63
Fraud	14,050	8,691	4,449	2,219	1,181	597	703

[Continued]

★ 897 ★

Suburban Area Arrests, Distribution by Age, 1991
[Continued]

Offense charged	Age						
	35-39	40-44	45-49	50-54	55-59	60-64	65 and over
Embezzlement	353	249	133	53	38	11	24
Stolen property: buying, receiving, possessing	2,743	1,507	712	411	190	114	117
Vandalism	3,598	1,921	955	556	276	187	242
Weapons: carrying possessing, etc.	3,520	2,301	1,374	798	472	306	348
Prostitution and commercialized vice	820	437	224	137	75	35	59
Sex offenses (except forcible rape and prostitution)	2,787	1,955	1,197	813	496	398	521
Drug abuse violations	21,594	10,742	4,404	1,830	819	419	352
Gambling	188	194	179	168	132	80	90
Offenses against family and children	5,388	3,282	1,508	713	346	192	191
Driving under the influence	74,254	50,478	29,760	18,048	10,880	6,962	6,238
Liquor laws	3,925	2,466	1,363	854	514	370	307
Drunkenness	26,415	17,312	10,554	6,489	4,090	2,715	2,481
Disorderly conduct	13,244	8,048	4,245	2,411	1,354	901	1,105
Vagrancy	465	280	155	97	41	27	39
All other offenses (except traffic)	76,562	44,303	23,449	12,393	6,705	4,177	4,494
Suspicion	138	90	55	25	9	7	11

Source: Federal Bureau of Investigation, *Uniform Crime Reports for the United States 1991*, p. 264. *Notes:* 1. Because of rounding, the percentages may not add to total. 2. Violent crimes are offenses of murder, forcible rape, robbery, and aggravated assault. 3. Property crimes are offenses of burglary, larceny-theft, motor vehicle theft, and arson. 4. Includes arson.

★ 898 ★
Offenders

Suburban County Arrests, Distribution by Age, 1991

Offense charged	Age						
	35-39	40-44	45-49	50-54	55-59	60-64	65 and over
Total	155,480	95,074	51,520	28,569	16,559	9,968	9,839
Percent distribution[1]	10.3	6.3	3.4	1.9	1.1	.7	.7
Murder and nonnegligent manslaughter	183	148	79	75	24	19	31
Forcible rape	481	314	144	90	58	28	32

[Continued]

★ 898 ★

Suburban County Arrests, Distribution by Age, 1991
[Continued]

Offense charged	Age						
	35-39	40-44	45-49	50-54	55-59	60-64	65 and over
Robbery	649	316	111	59	23	14	9
Aggravated assault	5,199	3,229	1,791	944	564	357	362
Burglary	2,393	1,145	472	186	109	54	54
Larceny-theft	10,296	6,525	3,373	1,892	1,271	910	1,169
Motor vehicle theft	927	488	244	103	63	22	48
Arson	184	101	73	32	19	17	9
Violent crime[2]	6,512	4,007	2,125	1,168	669	418	434
Percent distribution[1]	9.7	5.9	3.2	1.7	1.0	.6	.6
Property crime[3]	13,800	8,259	4,162	2,213	1,462	1,003	1,280
Percent distribution[1]	7.0	4.2	2.1	1.1	.7	.5	.6
Crime index total[4]	20,312	12,266	6,287	3,381	2,131	1,421	1,714
Percent distribution[1]	7.6	4.6	2.4	1.3	.8	.5	.6
Other assaults	10,979	6,507	3,536	1,980	1,164	653	727
Forgery and counterfeiting	1,328	739	310	164	69	60	32
Fraud	7,759	4,986	2,523	1,246	660	338	358
Embezzlement	204	155	90	31	21	9	4
Stolen property: buying, receiving, possessing	1,216	667	325	189	91	58	56
Vandalism	1,345	738	386	261	108	67	114
Weapons: carrying possessing, etc.	1,671	1,121	671	389	249	169	161
Prostitution and commercialized vice	382	208	103	61	30	19	27
Sex offenses (except forcible rape and prostitution)	1,484	1,057	660	463	298	216	294
Drug abuse violations	11,571	5,934	2,515	1,057	523	270	198
Gambling	116	107	125	100	93	60	50
Offenses against family and children	3,775	2,328	1,109	509	221	106	95
Driving under the influence	38,811	26,361	15,501	9,428	5,771	3,500	2,873
Liquor laws	1,423	883	515	354	179	114	121
Drunkenness	8,678	5,659	3,247	1,993	1,243	752	739
Disorderly conduct	3,284	1,898	1,058	604	341	208	259
Vagrancy	185	119	65	56	12	16	32

[Continued]

★ 898 ★

Suburban County Arrests, Distribution by Age, 1991
[Continued]

Offense charged	Age						
	35-39	40-44	45-49	50-54	55-59	60-64	65 and over
All other offenses (except traffic)	40,926	23,315	12,481	6,294	3,354	1,929	1,984
Suspicion	31	26	13	9	1	3	1

Source: Federal Bureau of Investigation, *Uniform Crime Reports for the United States 1991*, p. 246. *Notes:* 1. Because of rounding, the percentages may not add to total. 2. Violent crimes are offenses of murder, forcible rape, robbery, and aggravated assault. 3. Property crimes are offenses of burglary, larceny-theft, motor vehicle theft, and arson. 4. Includes arson.

★ 899 ★
Offenders

Rural County Arrests, Distribution by Age, 1991

Offense charged	Age						
	35-39	40-44	45-49	50-54	55-59	60-64	65 and over
Total	92,796	60,425	34,738	20,865	12,856	8,154	9,185
Percent distribution[1]	10.7	6.9	4.0	2.4	1.5	.9	1.1
Murder and nonnegligent manslaughter	191	113	78	47	26	13	29
Forcible rape	281	169	104	65	44	32	26
Robbery	163	77	32	28	11	5	6
Aggravated assault	3,033	1,953	1,236	733	400	246	355
Burglary	1,362	695	323	147	80	52	79
Larceny-theft	3,420	2,237	1,313	844	551	330	508
Motor vehicle theft	374	222	97	63	33	12	15
Arson	136	80	49	26	12	11	16
Violent crime[2]	3,668	2,312	1,450	873	481	296	416
Percent distribution[1]	11.0	7.0	4.4	2.6	1.4	.9	1.3
Property crime[3]	5,292	3,234	1,782	1,080	676	405	618
Percent distribution[1]	5.8	3.6	2.0	1.2	.7	.4	.7
Crime index total[4]	8,960	5,546	3,232	1,953	1,157	701	1,034
Percent distribution[1]	7.2	4.5	2.6	1.6	.9	.6	.8
Other assaults	6,957	4,550	2,511	1,454	837	557	613
Forgery and counterfeiting	782	411	206	110	41	27	30
Fraud	7,303	4,711	2,629	1,363	838	537	591
Embezzlement	139	100	73	43	31	12	5

[Continued]

★ 899 ★

Rural County Arrests, Distribution by Age, 1991

[Continued]

Offense charged	Age						
	35-39	40-44	45-49	50-54	55-59	60-64	65 and over
Stolen property: buying, receiving, possessing	498	323	168	110	63	29	38
Vandalism	1,067	581	304	138	110	46	103
Weapons: carrying possessing, etc.	954	716	435	267	166	122	137
Prostitution and commercialized vice	29	19	11	8	12	3	4
Sex offenses (except forcible rape and prostitution)	941	635	368	417	215	171	237
Drug abuse violations	5,668	2,983	1,308	618	271	154	151
Gambling	78	65	74	74	55	31	62
Offenses against family and children	1,539	898	476	212	98	68	77
Driving under the influence	24,956	17,583	10,619	6,644	4,313	2,817	2,798
Liquor laws	1,353	843	574	357	236	142	204
Drunkenness	7,152	4,945	3,116	2,110	1,333	855	858
Disorderly conduct	2,981	1,905	1,054	618	446	286	338
Vagrancy	35	27	14	10	5	-	2
All other offenses (except traffic)	21,323	13,549	7,546	4,344	2,624	1,591	1,895
Suspicion	81	35	20	15	5	5	8

Source: Federal Bureau of Investigation, *Uniform Crime Reports for the United States 1991*, p. 255. *Notes:* 1. Because of rounding, the percentages may not add to total. 2. Violent crimes are offenses of murder, forcible rape, robbery, and aggravated assault. 3. Property crimes are offenses of burglary, larceny-theft, motor vehicle theft, and arson. 4. Includes arson.

★ 900 ★

Offenders

Licensed Drivers and Estimated Arrests for Driving Under the Influence, by Age: 1975 and 1986

[Total drivers and arrests in thousands]

Age	1975			1986			Percent change in rate, 1975-86
	Drivers	Arrests	Arrests per 100,000 drivers	Drivers	Arrests	Arrests per 100,000 drivers	
Total[1]	129,671	946	729	158,494	1,792	1,130	55
Percent Distribution	100.0	100.0	(X)	100.0	100.0	(X)	(X)
16 to 17 years old	3.7	1.8	352	2.6	1.5	647	84

[Continued]

★ 900 ★

Licensed Drivers and Estimated Arrests for Driving Under the Influence, by Age: 1975 and 1986

[Continued]

Age	1975			1986			Percent change in rate, 1975-86
	Drivers	Arrests	Arrests per 100,000 drivers	Drivers	Arrests	Arrests per 100,000 drivers	
18 to 24 years old	18.9	25.3	979	15.7	28.8	2,075	112
25 to 29 years old	12.9	15.0	847	13.0	22.0	1,909	125
30 to 34 years old	10.3	12.2	867	12.2	15.8	1,471	70
35 to 39 years old	8.5	10.6	909	10.9	11.1	1,158	27
40 to 44 years old	7.9	9.8	904	8.5	7.2	968	7
45 to 49 years old	8.0	8.9	812	6.9	4.9	805	-1
50 to 54 years old	7.9	7.3	675	6.3	3.4	609	-10
55 to 59 years old	6.8	4.6	490	6.3	2.4	434	-11
60 to 64 years old	5.7	2.7	347	5.9	1.6	299	-14
65 years old and over	9.5	1.8	141	11.9	1.2	118	-16

Source: U.S. Bureau of the Census, *Statistical Abstract of the United States: 1992* (112th edition.) Washington, DC, 1992, p. 612. Primary source: U.S. Bureau of Justice Statistics, *Drunk Driving, Special Report. Notes:* (X) indicates not applicable. 1. Represents licensed drivers and arrests for those 16 years old and over.

★ 901 ★

Offenders

State Prison Inmates, by Age: 1979 and 1986

Based on a sample survey of about 13,711 inmates in 1986 and 11,397 inmates in 1979; subject to sampling variability.

Age	Number		Percent of prison inmates	
	1979	1986	1979	1986
Total[1]	274,564	450,416	100.0	100.0
Under 18 years old	2,220	2,057	0.8	0.5
18 to 24 years old	97,860	120,384	35.6	26.7
25 to 34 years old	116,284	205,817	42.4	45.7
35 to 44 years old	37,926	87,502	13.8	19.4
45 to 54 years old	13,987	23,524	5.1	5.2
55 to 64 years old	4,786	8,267	1.7	1.8
65 years old and over	1,499	2,808	0.5	0.6

Source: U.S. Bureau of the Census, *Statistical Abstract of the United States: 1992* (112th edition.) Washington, DC, 1992, p. 197. Primary source: U.S. Bureau of Justice Statistics, *Profile of State Prison Inmates, 1986*, January 1988. *Note:* 1. For 1986, includes data not reported.

★ 902 ★

Offenders

Inmates of Institutions 100 Years and Over, by Age, Sex, and Age Allocation: 1980

These data show that more than 30 percent of the centenarian population are prison inmates. One might suggest a correlation between old age and criminal tendencies—however, it is much more likely that an elderly person residing in an institution is receiving proper nutritional and medical care, thus ensuring longevity.

Age	Total	Male	Female
Total persons[1]	22,012	6,367	15,645
Total inmates	8,473	1,065	6,868
100-104	7,657	1,424	6,233
105-109	769	169	600
110+	47	12	35

Source: Gregory Spencer, Arnold A. Goldstein, and Cynthia M. Taeuber, *America's Centenarians: Data from the 1980 Census,* National Institute on Aging, Washington, DC, June 1987, p. B2. *Notes:* 1. A problem with 1980 Census allocation procedures resulted in an inflation of the count of the centenarian population by about one-fourth. This data reflects unallocated age data only and therefore may be subject to sampling error due to incorrect reporting, overreporting by respondents, or incomplete documentation.

★ 903 ★

Offenders

Age, Sex, and Race of Murder Offenders, 1991

From the source: "Supplemental data were reported for 24,578 murder offenders in 1991. Of those for whom sex and age were reported, 90 percent were males, and 87 percent were persons 18 years of age or older. Seventy-seven percent were aged 15 through 34 years. Of offenders for whom race was known, 55 percent were black, 43 percent were white, and the remainder were persons of other races."

Age	Total	Sex			Race			
		Male	Female	Unknown	White	Black	Other	Unknown
Total	24,578	15,577	1,737	7,264	7,368	9,453	331	7,426
Percent distribution[1]	100.0	63.4	7.1	29.6	30.0	38.5	1.3	30.2
Under 18[2]	2,136	2,009	125	2	763	1,304	54	15
18 and over[2]	14,162	12,579	1,567	16	6,294	7,534	261	73
Infant (under 1)	-	-	-	-	-	-	-	-
1 to 4	-	-	-	-	-	-	-	-
5 to 9	5	5	-	-	3	1	1	-
10 to 14	236	212	24	-	81	143	9	3
15 to 19	4,099	3,873	223	3	1,428	2,568	77	26
20 to 24	3,950	3,631	315	4	1,482	2,381	71	16

[Continued]

★ 903 ★

Age, Sex, and Race of Murder Offenders, 1991
[Continued]

Age	Total	Sex			Race			
		Male	Female	Unknown	White	Black	Other	Unknown
25 to 29	2,550	2,260	288	2	1,187	1,310	38	15
30 to 34	2,013	1,710	300	3	984	974	45	10
35 to 39	1,238	1,034	203	1	640	567	28	3
40 to 44	819	688	131	-	432	360	22	5
45 to 49	500	421	77	2	280	204	10	6
50 to 54	313	267	45	1	193	115	4	1
55 to 59	195	167	28	-	120	72	3	-
60 to 64	135	112	23	-	77	52	6	-
65 to 69	100	81	18	1	53	45	-	2
70 to 74	65	61	4	-	44	21	-	-
75 and over	79	65	13	1	53	24	1	1
Unknown	8,281	990	45	7,246	311	615	16	7,338

Source: Federal Bureau of Investigation, *Uniform Crime Reports for the United States 1991*, p. 16. *Notes:* 1. Because of rounding, percentages may not add to totals. 2. Does not include unknown ages.

★ 904 ★

Offenders

Prisoners Sentenced to Death, by Age

Elderly prisoners sentenced to death (55 and older) represent 2.5 percent of prisoners under sentence of death.

Region and state	Prisoners under sentence of death							
	All ages	Under 20 years	20 to 24 years	25 to 29 years	30 to 34 years	35 to 39 years	40 to 54 years	55 years and older
All prisoners U.S. total	2,250	6	191	487	593	394	523	56
Northeast	132	0	9	27	37	23	34	2
Connecticut	2	0	0	0	1	0	1	0
New Jersey	18	0	1	5	5	3	4	0
Pennsylvania	112	0	8	22	31	20	29	2
Midwest	345	0	34	86	86	68	64	7
Illinois	115	0	9	21	33	26	24	2
Indiana	48	0	6	15	11	7	8	1
Missouri	72	0	5	23	16	14	13	1
Nebraska	12	0	0	1	2	5	3	1
Ohio	98	0	14	26	24	16	16	2
South	1,310	6	119	281	348	223	299	34
Alabama	106	0	8	26	24	20	25	3
Arkansas	33	0	2	2	7	8	13	1

[Continued]

★ 904 ★

Prisoners Sentenced to Death, by Age

[Continued]

Region and state	Prisoners under sentence of death							
	All ages	Under 20 years	20 to 24 years	25 to 29 years	30 to 34 years	35 to 39 years	40 to 54 years	55 years and older
Delaware	7	0	1	2	2	0	2	0
Florida	289	0	20	52	67	49	93	8
Georgia	90	0	6	15	26	15	25	3
Kentucky	29	0	0	6	7	11	5	0
Louisiana	35	1	2	7	12	7	6	0
Maryland	16	0	0	6	3	4	3	0
Mississippi	44	0	5	12	12	6	6	3
North Carolina	88	2	10	13	22	11	27	3
Oklahoma	109	2	13	23	30	20	16	5
South Carolina	42	0	8	7	16	3	7	1
Tennessee	75	0	6	13	24	17	12	3
Texas	304	1	37	82	82	46	52	4
Virginia	43	0	1	15	14	6	7	0
West	463	0	29	93	122	80	126	13
Arizona	84	0	8	16	16	10	32	2
California	254	0	9	54	67	51	66	7
Colorado	3	0	0	0	1	0	2	0
Idaho	18	0	0	3	10	3	2	0
Montana	8	0	1	1	3	1	2	0
Nevada	52	0	8	11	12	8	12	1
New Mexico	1	0	0	0	1	0	0	0
Oregon	23	0	3	3	7	4	3	3
Utah	11	0	0	3	4	1	3	0
Washington	7	0	0	2	1	2	2	0
Wyoming	2	0	0	0	0	0	2	0

Source: U.S. Department of Justice, Office of Justice Programs, Bureau of Justice Statistics, *Correctional Populations in the United States, 1989*, NCJ-130445, October 1991, pp. 130-131.

★ 905 ★

Offenders

Prisoners Under Sentence of Death, by Age: 1980 to 1990

[As of December 31]

Age	1980	1985	1988	1989	1990
Total[1]	688	1,575	2,117	2,243	2,356
Under 20 years	11	13	11	6	8
20 to 24 years	173	212	195	191	168
25 to 34 years	334	804	1,048	1,080	1,110

[Continued]

★ 905 ★

Prisoners Under Sentence of Death, by Age: 1980 to 1990

[Continued]

Age	1980	1985	1988	1989	1990
35 to 54 years	186	531	823	917	1,006
55 years and over	10	31	47	56	64

Source: U.S. Bureau of the Census, *Statistical Abstract of the United States: 1992* (112th edition.) Washington, DC, 1992, p. 199. Primary source: U.S. Bureau of Justice Statistics, *Capital Punishment,* annual. *Notes:* Excludes prisoners under sentence of death who remained within local correctional systems pending exhaustion of appellate process or who had not been committed to prison. 1. For 1980 to 1989, revisions to the total number of prisoners were not carried to the characteristics except for race.

Victimization

★ 906 ★

Victimization Rates, 1990

Older Americans (50 and older) had lower rates of victimization—measured in incidents per 1,000 persons—than any other age group in 1990.

[Rate per 1,000 persons in each age group]

Type of crime	12-15	16-19	20-24	25-34	35-49	50-64	65 and over
All personal crimes	160.3	187.8	174.8	114.0	76.6	44.0	24.6
Crimes of violence	68.8	74.4	63.1	36.4	19.2	7.5	3.5
Completed	27.3	28.6	28.5	14.8	7.3	2.6	1.6
Attempted	41.5	45.8	34.7	21.7	11.9	4.9	1.9
Rape	1.8	1.4	1.9	0.6	0.4	0.1	0.1
Robbery	13.6	9.5	12.3	7.6	3.2	2.2	1.5
Completed	9.0	6.6	9.0	5.0	2.5	1.5	1.1
Attempted	4.6	2.9	3.3	2.6	0.8	0.7	0.4
Assault	53.3	63.5	48.9	28.2	15.6	5.3	1.9
Aggravated	13.9	26.2	16.8	9.9	4.7	1.4	1.1
Simple	39.4	37.2	32.1	18.3	10.9	3.9	0.8
Crimes of theft	91.5	113.4	111.6	77.5	57.5	36.5	21.2
Completed	89.2	107.2	104.4	72.4	53.1	33.9	19.8
Attempted	2.3	6.2	7.2	5.1	4.4	2.6	1.4
Personal larceny with contact	1.8	4.0	5.5	3.5	2.4	2.6	3.3
Purse snatching	0.3	0.1	1.4	1.0	0.6	0.8	1.0
Pocket picking	1.5	3.8	4.1	2.4	1.8	1.7	2.4
Personal larceny without contact	89.7	109.4	106.1	74.1	55.0	33.9	17.9
Completed	87.5	103.3	99.3	69.2	50.9	31.6	16.6

[Continued]

★ 906 ★

Victimization Rates, 1990
[Continued]

Type of crime	12-15	16-19	20-24	25-34	35-49	50-64	65 and over
Less than $50	61.0	46.0	33.5	24.0	17.4	11.8	6.7
$50 or more	22.9	53.2	61.2	42.8	31.0	18.0	8.5
Amount not available	3.6	4.1	4.5	2.3	2.5	1.8	1.3
Attempted	2.2	6.2	6.8	4.9	4.1	2.4	1.3
Total population (mil.)	13.5	13.7	18.0	43.2	52.1	32.9	30.0

Source: Criminal Victimization in the United States, 1990, U.S. Department of Justice, February 1992, NCJ-134126, p. 23.
Note: Detail may not add to total shown because of rounding.

★ 907 ★

Victimization

Victimization Rate by Age

Data show occurrence of violent crime, theft, and household crime per 1,000 people for the years 1987-1989.

Age	Violence	Theft	Household
12-19	86.2	128.2	410.5
20-24	72.7	142.2	336.8
25-34	47.6	101.8	283.5
34-49	29.2	80.5	261.9
50-64	14.4	50.4	193.5
65 and older	7.8	24.3	115.2

Source: USA TODAY, December 4, 1992, p. 9A. Primary source: Bureau of Justice statistics.

★ 908 ★

Victimization

Victimization Rates for Violent Crimes, 1990

Sex and age	Total population	Crimes of violence	Completed violent crimes	Attempted violent crimes	Rape	Robbery Total	With injury	Without injury	Assault Total	Aggravated assault
Male										
12-15	6,899,480	92.2	37.5	54.7	0.3[1]	20.6	4.5	16.1	71.3	20.6
16-19	6,930,150	94.7	34.3	60.3	0.4[1]	12.5	2.0[1]	10.5	81.8	39.6
20-24	8,815,790	78.4	30.4	47.9	0.2[1]	17.1	4.7	12.5	61.0	23.5
25-34	21,437,380	44.3	16.7	27.7	0.4[1]	9.7	3.7	6.0	34.2	13.8
35-49	25,580,960	21.6	7.8	13.8	0.3[1]	3.7	1.6	2.2	17.6	6.2

[Continued]

★ 908 ★

Victimization Rates for Violent Crimes, 1990
[Continued]

| Sex and age | Total population | Crimes of violence | Completed violent crimes | Attempted violent crimes | Rape | Robbery | | | Assault | |
						Total	With injury	Without injury	Total	Aggravated assault
50-64	15,689,980	8.9	2.4	6.5	0.0[1]	2.0	0.8[1]	1.3[1]	6.9	2.0
65 and over	12,483,090	3.7	1.6[1]	2.1	0.0[1]	1.7	1.1[1]	0.6[1]	2.0	1.4[1]
Female										
12-15	6,569,620	44.1	16.5	27.6	3.4	6.3	2.3[1]	4.0	34.4	6.9
16-19	6,808,710	53.8	22.7	31.1	2.5[1]	6.5	2.1[1]	4.4	44.8	12.6
20-24	9,201,300	48.5	26.6	22.0	3.5	7.8	2.5	5.2	37.3	10.5
25-34	21,740,780	28.6	12.9	15.8	0.9[1]	5.6	2.3	3.2	22.2	6.0
35-49	26,481,020	16.8	6.7	10.1	0.5[1]	2.8	1.4	1.4	13.6	3.2
50-64	17,198,280	6.3	2.8	3.5	0.1[1]	2.3	0.9[1]	1.4	3.9	0.8[1]
65 and over	17,437,250	3.3	1.6	1.7	0.1[1]	1.3	0.5[1]	0.8[1]	1.9	0.9[1]

Source: Criminal Victimization in the United States, 1990, U.S. Department of Justice, February 1992, NCJ-134126, p. 24. *Notes:* Detail may not add to total shown because of rounding. 1. Estimate is based on about 10 or fewer sample cases.

★ 909 ★

Victimization

Victimization Rates for Crimes of Violence, by Race and Type of Crime, 1990
[Rate per 1,000 persons in each age group.]

| Race and age | Total population | Rate per 1,000 persons in each age group | | | | | | |
| | | Crimes of violence | Completed violent crimes | Attempted violent crimes | Rape | Robbery | | |
						Total	With injury	Without injury
White								
12-15	10,812,490	66.3	26.3	40.0	1.7[1]	11.4	3.4	8.0
16-19	10,990,530	72.5	28.1	44.3	1.6[1]	6.3	1.6[1]	4.7
20-24	14,930,980	64.7	28.6	36.0	2.1	11.9	3.9	7.9
25-34	36,233,820	35.6	13.5	22.1	0.7	6.3	2.5	3.8
35-49	44,486,380	18.8	6.6	12.2	0.4[1]	2.5	1.0	1.5
50-64	28,693,580	7.1	2.1	5.0	0.1[1]	1.6	0.7[1]	1.0
65 and over	26,961,350	2.9	1.2	1.7	0.0[1]	1.1	0.5[1]	0.6[1]
Black								
12-15	2,138,670	86.5	37.5	49.1	3.1[1]	26.6	3.4[1]	23.2
16-19	2,164,810	81.3	30.3	51.0	0.9[1]	24.5	4.1[1]	20.4
20-24	2,448,480	64.7	33.3	31.4	0.8[1]	17.0	0.7[1]	16.3
25-34	5,449,920	42.9	23.2	19.7	0.0[1]	15.6	6.4	9.2
35-49	5,608,560	23.9	12.6	11.2	0.7[1]	7.5	3.7	3.8

[Continued]

★ 909 ★

Victimization Rates for Crimes of Violence, by Race and Type of Crime, 1990

[Continued]

Race and age	Total population	Rate per 1,000 persons in each age group						
		Crimes of violence	Completed violent crimes	Attempted violent crimes	Rape	Robbery		
						Total	With injury	Without injury
50-64	3,411,110	10.7	6.8	3.9[1]	0.0[1]	6.2	2.5[1]	3.6[1]
65 and over	2,507,160	7.2[1]	5.5[1]	1.7[1]	0.0[1]	3.7[1]	2.9[1]	0.8[1]

Source: Criminal Victimization in the United States, 1990, U.S. Department of Justice, February 1992, NCJ-134126, p. 28. *Notes:* Detail may not add to total shown because of rounding. 1. Estimate is based on about 10 or fewer sample cases.

★ 910 ★

Victimization

Victimization Rates for Assaults, Thefts, and Larceny, by Race and Type of Crime, 1990

[Rate per 1,000 persons in each age group]

Race and age	Total	Assault		Thefts			Personal larceny	
		Aggravated	Simple	Total	Completed	Attempted	With contact	Without contact
White								
12-15	53.2	11.8	41.5	96.4	93.7	2.7	1.9	94.5
16-19	64.6	25.5	39.0	120.5	113.0	7.5	2.4	118.1
20-24	50.7	16.8	33.8	111.2	103.5	7.7	5.4	105.8
25-34	28.7	9.6	19.1	77.3	72.0	5.3	3.1	74.2
35-49	15.9	4.6	11.2	58.4	54.1	4.2	2.3	56.1
50-64	5.4	1.3	4.0	36.2	33.4	2.8	2.3	33.9
65 and over	1.8	1.0	0.8	20.5	19.0	1.4	2.9	17.5
Black								
12-15	56.8	24.6	32.2	77.2	76.2	1.1[1]	2.0[1]	75.3
16-19	55.9	30.0	25.8	75.1	74.0	1.1[1]	10.1	65.0
20-24	46.9	21.2	25.6	116.8	112.1	4.8[1]	7.2[1]	109.7
25-34	27.3	12.5	14.8	79.4	75.7	3.7[1]	5.4	73.9
35-49	15.6	6.4	9.2	47.5	41.4	6.1	3.1[1]	44.4
50-64	4.5[1]	2.4[1]	2.1[1]	39.9	38.8	1.1[1]	4.4[1]	35.5
65 and over	3.4[1]	2.7[1]	0.7[1]	28.1	28.1	0.0[1]	8.0[1]	20.1

Source: Criminal Victimization in the United States, 1990, U.S. Department of Justice, February 1992, NCJ-134126, p. 28. *Notes:* Detail may not add to total shown because of rounding. 1. Estimate is based on about 10 or fewer sample cases.

★ 911 ★

Victimization

Victimization Rates by Race, Sex, Age, and Type of Crime, 1990

Race, sex, and age	Total population	Rate per 1,000 persons in each age group	
		Crimes of violence	Crimes of theft
White			
Male			
12-15	5,517,930	89.2	94.4
16-19	5,536,190	93.4	129.1
20-24	7,384,690	79.9	114.2
25-34	18,241,240	43.1	82.3
35-49	22,146,820	20.2	57.7
50-64	13,798,320	8.3	35.3
65 and over	11,270,280	3.1	21.1
Female			
12-15	5,294,550	42.5	98.5
16-19	5,454,340	51.3	111.7
20-24	7,546,290	49.8	108.3
25-34	17,992,570	28.0	72.2
35-49	22,339,560	17.4	59.0
50-64	14,895,250	5.9	37.0
65 and over	15,691,070	2.8	20.1
Black			
Male			
12-15	1,088,170	113.4	85.3
16-19	1,074,310	111.3	84.2
20-24	1,106,570	82.0	139.3
25-34	2,510,530	54.5	95.7
35-49	2,523,030	31.5	46.8
50-64	1,527,930	12.4[1]	56.1
65 and over	1,016,850	9.4[1]	17.7[1]
Female			
12-15	1,050,490	58.6	68.9
16-19	1,090,490	51.6	66.0
20-24	1,341,910	50.3	98.3
25-34	2,939,380	33.0	65.4
35-49	3,085,520	17.7	48.1
50-64	1,883,180	9.3[1]	26.7
65 and over	1,490,300	5.7[1]	35.1

Source: Criminal Victimization in the United States, 1990, U.S. Department of Justice, February 1992, NCJ-134126, p. 29. *Note:* 1. Estimate is based on about 10 or fewer sample cases.

★ 912 ★

Victimization

Percent Distribution of Multiple Offender Victimizations, 1990

Type of crime and race of victim	Number of multiple - offender victimizations	Percent of multiple-offender victimizations					
			Perceived race of offenders				
		Total	All white	All black	All other	Mixed races	Not known and not available
Crimes of violence[1]							
White	1,343,400	100.0	47.3	26.1	9.4	13.2	4.0
Black	357,250	100.0	5.6	83.0	7.6	1.0[2]	2.7[2]
Robbery							
White	344,950	100.0	26.5	41.4	17.1	13.3	1.7[2]
Black	141,340	100.0	6.1[2]	86.0	2.0[2]	2.6[2]	3.3[2]
Assault							
White	978,790	100.0	55.3	20.4	6.7	12.8	4.9
Black	215,900	100.0	5.3[2]	81.1	11.3	0.0[2]	2.3[2]

Source: Criminal Victimization in the United States, 1990, U.S. Department of Justice, February 1992, NCJ-134126, p. 65. *Notes:* Detail may not add to total shown because of rounding. 1. Includes data on rape, not shown separately. 2. Estimate is based on about 10 or fewer sample cases.

★ 913 ★

Victimization

Percent Distribution of Crime Victims Needing Hospital Care, 1990

Characteristic	Percent of victimizations		
	Crimes of violence[1]	Robbery	Assault
Sex			
Both sexes	8.2	8.7	7.7
Male	7.8	8.7	7.6
Female	8.8	8.6	8.0
Age			
12-19	6.5	4.1[2]	6.7
20-34	9.6	9.6	9.1
35-49	6.5	10.6[2]	5.8
50-64	10.5	14.4[2]	8.9[2]
65 and over	11.3[2]	12.4[2]	10.9[2]

[Continued]

★ 913 ★

Percent Distribution of Crime Victims Needing
Hospital Care, 1990
[Continued]

Characteristic	Percent of victimizations		
	Crimes of violence[1]	Robbery	Assault
Race			
White	8.1	8.5	7.7
Black	8.8	8.9	8.3
Victim-offender relationship			
Strangers	7.9	7.9	7.8
Non-strangers	8.5	11.9	7.7

Source: Criminal Victimization in the United States, 1990, U.S. Department of Justice, February 1992, NCJ-134126, p. 91. *Notes:* 1. Includes data on rape, not shown separately. 2. Estimate is based on about 10 or fewer sample cases.

★ 914 ★

Victimization

Percent Distribution of Injured Crime Victims
Needing Hospital Care, 1990

Characteristic	Percent of injured victims receiving care		
	Crimes of violence[1]	Robbery	Assault
Sex			
Both sexes	24.2	25.1	23.5
Male	25.4	27.6	25.1
Female	22.7	21.6	21.4
Age			
12-19	20.4	17.4[2]	20.3
20-34	26.9	27.2	26.0
35-49	19.7	23.2[2]	19.0
50-64	39.3	37.3[2]	40.7[2]
65 and over	30.6[2]	23.5[2]	41.3[2]
Race			
White	23.8	23.6	23.5
Black	26.4	30.8	23.5

[Continued]

★ 914 ★

Percent Distribution of Injured Crime Victims
Needing Hospital Care, 1990
[Continued]

Characteristic	Percent of injured victims receiving care		
	Crimes of violence[1]	Robbery	Assault
Victim-offender relationship			
Strangers	26.6	25.2	26.8
Nonstrangers	21.4	24.9	20.2

Source: *Criminal Victimization in the United States, 1990,* U.S. Department of Justice, February 1992, NCJ-134126, p. 91. *Notes:* 1. Includes data on rape, not shown separately. 2. Estimate is based on about 10 or fewer sample cases.

★ 915 ★

Victimization

Age, Sex, and Race of Elderly Murder Victims, 1990

Age	Total	Sex		Race			
		Male	Female	White	Black	Other	Unknown
Total, all ages	20,045	15,628	4,399	9,724	9,744	345	232
55 to 59	451	332	119	271	159	18	3
60 to 64	422	322	100	261	152	5	4
65 to 69	284	195	89	180	98	5	1
70 to 74	234	129	105	167	61	5	1
75 and over	450	205	245	293	153	1	3

Source: *Crime in the United States,* Uniform Crime Reports, 1990, Federal Bureau of Investigation, U.S. Department of Justice, Washington, DC 20535, p. 11.

★ 916 ★

Victimization

Age, Sex, and Race of Murder Victims, 1991

Age	Total	Sex			Race			
		Male	Female	Unknown	White	Black	Other	Unknown
Total	21,505	16,781	4,693	31	10,135	10,660	531	179
Percent distribution[1]	100.0	78.0	21.8	0.1	47.1	49.6	2.5	0.8
Under 18[2]	2,233	1,595	637	1	1,038	1,131	52	12

[Continued]

★ 916 ★

Age, Sex, and Race of Murder Victims, 1991
[Continued]

Age	Total	Sex			Race			
		Male	Female	Unknown	White	Black	Other	Unknown
18 and over[2]	18,898	14,925	3,971	2	8,943	9,376	473	106
Infant (under 1)	304	160	143	1	178	116	5	5
1 to 4	371	193	178	-	178	177	15	1
5 to 9	110	54	56	-	66	39	5	-
10 to 14	290	201	89	-	152	129	7	2
15 to 19	2,702	2,335	367	-	1,035	1,600	49	18
20 to 24	3,948	3,312	636	-	1,571	2,278	76	23
25 to 29	3,362	2,703	659	-	1,450	1,806	90	16
30 to 34	2,898	2,237	660	1	1,355	1,455	76	12
35 to 39	2,145	1,689	456	-	1,074	994	66	11
40 to 44	1,496	1,148	347	1	775	666	48	7
45 to 49	981	744	237	-	574	374	26	7
50 to 54	658	515	143	-	399	226	27	6
55 to 59	459	346	113	-	289	155	11	4
60 to 64	421	302	119	-	255	154	12	-
65 to 69	321	226	95	-	206	110	4	1
70 to 74	241	156	85	-	148	87	5	1
75 and over	424	199	225	-	276	141	3	4
Unknown	374	261	85	28	154	153	6	61

Source: Federal Bureau of Investigation, *Uniform Crime Reports for the United States 1991*, p. 16. *Notes:* 1. Because of rounding, percentages may not add to totals. 2. Does not include unknown ages.

★ 917 ★

Victimization

Elderly Murder Victims - Weapons Used, 1990 - Part I

Age	Total	Weapons					
		Firearm	Cutting or stabbing instrument	Blunt object (club, hammer, etc.)	Personal[1] weapons (hands, fists, feet, etc.)	Poison	Explosives
Total, all ages	20,045	12,847	3,503	1,075	1,112	11	14
50 to 54	586	336	106	56	34	1	3
55 to 59	451	227	111	47	24	-	1
60 to 64	422	179	110	38	42	-	1
65 to 69	284	125	74	29	22	1	-

[Continued]

★ 917 ★

Elderly Murder Victims - Weapons Used, 1990 - Part I
[Continued]

Age	Total	Weapons					
		Firearm	Cutting or stabbing instrument	Blunt object (club, hammer, etc.)	Personal[1] weapons (hands, fists, feet, etc.)	Poison	Explosives
70 to 74	234	75	60	39	25	-	-
75 and over	450	132	99	87	60	3	1

Source: *Crime in the United States*, Uniform Crime Reports, 1990, Federal Bureau of Investigation, U.S. Department of Justice, Washington, DC 20535, p. 12. *Note:* 1. "Pushed" is included in personal weapons.

★ 918 ★

Victimization

Elderly Murder Victims - Weapons Used, 1990 - Part II

Age	Total	Weapons				
		Arson	Narcotics	Strangulation	Asphyxiation	Other weapon or weapon not stated
Total, all ages	20,045	287	29	312	96	759
50 to 54	586	9	-	10	6	25
55 to 59	451	9	2	9	2	19
60 to 64	422	8	-	18	3	23
65 to 69	284	7	-	9	5	12
70 to 74	234	11	-	7	3	14
75 and over	450	13	2	18	7	28

Source: *Crime in the United States*, Uniform Crime Reports, 1990, Federal Bureau of Investigation, U.S. Department of Justice, Washington, DC 20535, p. 12.

★ 919 ★

Victimization

States Which Have Statutes for Reporting Elder Abuse and Neglect

This information is current through June 1, 1990. M stands for mandatory. V stands for voluntary.

State	Reporting requirement	State	Reporting requirement
Alabama	M	Montana	M
Alaska	M	Nebraska	M
Arizona	M	Nevada	M
Arkansas	M	New Hampshire	M
California	M	New Jersey	M
Colorado	V	New Mexico	M
Connecticut	M	New York	M
Delaware	M	North Carolina	M
District of Columbia	M	North Dakota	V
Florida	M	Ohio	M
Georgia	M	Oklahoma	M
Hawaii	M	Oregon	M
Idaho	M	Pennsylvania	V
Illinois	M	Rhode Island	M
Indiana	M	South Carolina	M
Iowa	M	South Dakota	
Kansas	M	Tennessee	M
Kentucky	M	Texas	M
Louisiana	M	Utah	M
Maine	M	Vermont	M
Maryland	M	Virginia	M
Massachusetts	M	Washington	M
Michigan	M	West Virginia	M
Minnesota	M	Wisconsin	V
Mississippi	M	Wyoming	M
Missouri	M		

Source: U.S. Congress, "Elder Abuse and Neglect: Prevention and Intervention," Hearing before the Special Committee on Aging, United States Senate, June 29, 1991, 102-5, U.S. Government Printing Office, Washington, D.C., p. 48. *Note:* - no information provided in the source.

SOURCES

This appendix lists the 143 sources from which *Statistical Record of Older Americans* was drawn. Each item is followed by a listing of the table number or numbers which cite the source.

- "A Comparison of Income, Income Sources, and Expenditures of Older Adults by Educational Attainment," *Family Economics Review*, 1992, Vol. 5, No. 4, Tables 135, 136, 137, 138, 139, 140, 141, 255, 308

- *Advertising Age*, November 16, 1992, Tables 38, 832, 854, 855, 856, 858, 859, 860

- "Age at Retirement," *Family Economics Review*, 1992, Vol. 5., No.4, Table 391

- *Aging America, Trends and Projections*, prepared by the U.S. Senate Special Committee on Aging, the American Association of Retired Persons, the Federal Council on the Aging, and the U.S. Administration on Aging, 1991, Washington, D.C., Tables 12, 23, 26, 45, 54, 58, 62, 63, 64, 67, 70, 75, 78, 79, 80, 82, 83, 87, 90, 91, 127, 129, 157, 158, 159, 160, 161, 162, 164, 165, 166, 167, 168, 169, 170, 171, 172, 174, 200, 201, 202, 206, 207, 208, 213, 214, 218, 219, 221, 222, 230, 231, 248, 249, 250, 251, 257, 267, 268, 270, 273, 276, 277, 278, 283, 284, 285, 286, 287, 300, 301, 373, 403, 404, 405, 410, 411, 415, 416, 417, 418, 419, 423, 424, 426, 437, 438, 492, 510, 511, 523, 524, 525, 566, 596, 598, 606, 607, 609, 610, 611, 622, 624, 665, 668, 669, 712, 715, 739, 764, 848, 849, 851, 852

- Allen, Steven G., Robert L. Clark, Ann A. McDermed, "Post-Retirement Benefits Increases in the 1980s," in *Trends in Pensions 1992*, U.S. Department of Labor, Pension and Welfare Benefits Administration, U.S. Government Printing Office, Washington, DC, Tables 344, 345

- *American Demographics*
  - December 1992, Tables 173, 217
  - March 1993, Table 831

- *Annual Statistical Supplement, 1992 to the Social Security Bulletin*, U.S. Department of Health and Human Services, Social Security Administration, January 1993, Tables 238, 239, 259, 356, 357, 358, 359, 360, 361, 374, 375, 377, 378, 379, 380, 381, 382, 383, 384, 385, 386, 387, 388, 389, 390, 392, 395, 396, 397, 398, 399, 400, 401, 402, 406, 430, 695, 696, 721, 722, 734, 735, 736, 745, 746, 747, 748, 749, 750, 751, 752

- "Average Annual Number of Days Hospitalized per Person Hospitalized during the Year Preceding Interview by Race, Age, and Family Income: United States, 1985-87," *Health of Black and White Americans, 1985-87*, 1990, Table 616

- Beller, David J. and Helen H. Lawrence, "Trends in Private Pension Coverage," in *Trends in Pen-*

sions 1992, U.S. Department of Labor, Pension and Welfare Benefits Administration, U.S. Government Printing Office, Washington, DC, 1992, Tables 329, 333

● Beller, David J. and David D. McCarthy, "Private Pension Benefits," in *Trends in Pensions 1992*, U.S. Department of Labor, Pension and Welfare Benefits Administration, U.S. Government Printing Office, Washington, DC, 1992, Tables 321, 322, 323, 328, 433

● Bernan, Phillip, "Make Positive Images of Aging Pay Off for You," *Bank Marketing*, February 1993, Table 215

● Billingsley, Andrew, "Understanding African-American Family Diversity," *State of Black America*, Janet Dewart, ed., National Urban League, Inc., 1990, Table 30

● Bortnick, Steven M. and Ports, Michelle Harrison, "Job search methods and results: tracking the unemployed, 1991," *Monthly Labor Review*, December 1992, Table 439

● *Brandweek*, April 5, 1993, Table 829

● *Business Week*, April 12, 1993, Table 264

● Callis, Robert R., U.S. Bureau of the Census, *Homeownership Trends in the 1980's*, Series H-121, No. 2, U.S. Government Printing Office, Washington, DC, December 1990, Tables 472, 473

● Coates, Joseph F., Jennifer Jarratt, and John B. Mahaffie, "Future Work," *The Futurist* 25, No. 3, May-June, 1993, Table 409

● "Cost of Food at Home," *Family Economics Review*, 1992, Vol. 5, No. 4, Table 309

● Collins, Sara, "Cutting Edge Cures," *U.S. News & World Report*, June 7, 1993, Tables 617, 667

● *Crime in the United States*, Uniform Crime Reports, 1990, Federal Bureau of Investigation, U.S. Department of Justice, Washington, DC 20535, Tables 893, 894, 895, 918

● *Criminal Victimization in the United States, 1990*, U.S. Department of Justice, February 1992, NCJ-134126, Tables 906, 908, 909, 910, 911, 912, 913, 914

● *Current Estimates From the National Health Interview Survey, 1991*, National Center for Health Statistics, Vital and Health Statistics, Series 10, No. 184, Tables 529, 530, 574, 575, 582, 585, 595, 602, 608

● Daily, Lorna M. and John A. Turner, "U.S. Private Pensions in World Perspective: 1970-89," in *Trends in Pensions 1992*, U.S. Department of Labor, Pension and Welfare Benefits Administration, U.S. Government Printing Office, Washington, DC, 1992, Tables 336, 337, 338, 339, 340

● Davis, Karen, "Life Satisfaction and Older Adults," *The Commonwealth Fund, Americans Over 55 at Work Program*, September 1991, Tables 867, 868, 869, 870, 871, 872, 873, 874, 875, 876, 877, 878

● *Dental Services and Oral Health: United States, 1989*, National Center for Health Statistics, Vital and Health Statistics, Series 10, No. 185, Tables 707, 708, 709, 710, 731, 732, 733

● *Detroit Free Press*, April 4, 1993, Tables 368, 370, 376, 394

● *Detroit News*
  – March 14, 1993, Table 223
  – November 30, 1992, Table 258

● Dietrich, Robert, "Looking Toward the 1990s," *Supermarket Business* 44, No. 3, March, 1989, Tables 304, 305, 306

- "Effect of Normal Medical Expenses on Single Person," *Management Review*, April 1992, Table 661

- *Elderly Households, a Profile*, Senate Select Committee on Aging, Comm. Pub. No. 102-912, 1992, Tables 256, 294, 295, 296, 487, 488, 489

- "Entitlements for the Retired Take Ever More Money," *New York Times*, August 30, 1992, Tables 670, 671

- *Family Economics Review*, 1992, Vol. 5, No. 4, Tables 128, 307

- Federal Bureau of Investigation, *Uniform Crime Reports for the United States 1991*, Tables 896, 897, 898, 899, 903, 916

- Fullerton, Howard Jr., Bureau of Labor Statistics, "Labor Force Projections: The Baby Boom Moves On," *Monthly Labor Review*, Vol. 114, No. 11, November 1991, Table 413

- Gallup, Alison, personal communication, August 31, 1993, Princeton Religion Research Organization, Table 825

- German, Brad, "Starter Homes," *Builder* 15, No. 1, January, 1992, Table 153

- *Health and Longevity*, Belden & Russonello, The Alliance for Aging Research, December 1992, Tables 861, 862, 863, 864, 865, 866, 879, 880, 881, 882, 883, 884, 885, 886

- Health Care Financing Administration, Office of the Actuary, data from the Office of National Cost Estimates, Tables 660, 662

- "Health Costs," *The Wall Street Journal*, February 26, 1992, Table 685

- *Health Data on Older Americans: United States, 1992*, Centers for Disease Control and Preven-tion/National Center for Health Statistics, Vital and Health Statistics, Series 3: Analytic and Epidemiological Studies, No. 27, Tables 81, 99, 106, 111, 112, 113, 114, 122, 531, 532, 533, 534, 535, 536, 537, 553, 554, 555, 556, 557, 558, 577, 578, 579, 580, 583, 587, 590, 592, 593, 594, 599, 600, 601, 603, 604, 605, 614, 625, 664, 724, 725, 744, 755, 759, 760, 761, 762, 765, 766, 771, 772, 773, 774, 775, 776, 777, 778, 779, 780

- *Health Promotion and Disease Prevention: United States, 1990*, National Center for Health Statistics, Vital and Health Statistics, Series 10, No. 185, Tables 515, 516, 517, 518, 519, 520, 521, 522, 544, 545, 547, 548, 549, 550, 551, 568, 569, 570, 571, 572, 573, 628, 629, 705, 706

- Heller, Peter S, Richard Hemming, Peter W. Koh-nert et. al., *Aging and Social Expenditure in the Major Industrial Countries, 1980-2025*, International Monetary Fund, September, 1986, Table 666

- *Highlights from Health Data on Older Americans: United States, 1992*, Centers for Disease Control and Prevention/National Center for Health Statistics, Vital and Health Statistics, Series 3: Analytic and Epidemiological Studies, No. 27, Table 538

- "Historical Perspectives," *Statistical Bulletin* 71, No. 3, July-September, 1990, Tables 13, 14

- Intindola, Brenda, "75 Million Dangerously Weak Savers", *National Underwriter*, April 5, 1993, Table 347

- Isaacs III, McAllister, "Focus on Everybody's Customer – The Consumer," *Textile World* 139, No. 11, November, 1989, Table 302

- Jaynes, Gerald David and Robin M. Williams, eds., "Black Americans' Health," *A Common Destiny: Blacks and American Society*, National Academy Press, Washington, DC, 1989, Table 20

• Jaynes, Gerald David and Robin M. Williams, Jr., eds., "Children and Families," *A Common Destiny: Blacks and American Society*, National Academy Press, Washington, DC, 1989, Table 31

• Katsura, Harold M., Raymond J. Struyk, and Sandra J. Newman, *Housing for the Elderly in 2010: Projections and Policy Options*, Urban Institute Report 89-4. Washington, DC, The Urban Institute Press, 1989, Table 154

• Katsura, Harold M., Raymond J. Struyk, and Sandra J. Newman, *Projected Changes in the Characteristics and Housing Situation of the Elderly Population if Current Policies Continue*, Housing for the Elderly in 2010, Washington, DC, The Urban Institute Press, Table 152

• Kolata, Gina, "New Views on Life Spans Alter Forecasts on Elderly," *New York Times*, November 16, 1992, Table 28

• Korczyk, Sophie M., "Gender and Pension Coverage," in *Trends in Pensions 1992*, U.S. Department of Labor, Pension and Welfare Benefits Administration, U.S. Government Printing Office, Washington, DC, 1992, Tables 320, 325, 326, 330, 331, 332, 427, 428, 434

• Lappin, Debra, Government Affairs Committee, The Arthritis Foundation, U.S. House Committee on Appropriations, Depts. of Labor, Health and Human Services and Education, "Appropriations for 1991," Hearing, Washington, DC, 1990, Table 626

• Lichtenstein, Jules H., Ph.D., "Pension Availability and Coverage in Small and Large Firms," in *Trends in Pensions 1992*, U.S. Department of Labor, Pension and Welfare Benefits Administration, U.S. Government Printing Office, Washington, DC, 1992, Tables 319, 324

• Littman, Mark, U.S. Bureau of the Census, *Poverty in the United States: 1990*, Current Population Reports, Series P-60, No. 175, U.S. Government Printing Office, Washington, DC, 1991, Tables 5, 275

• *Marital Status and Living Arrangements: March 1990*, Current Population Reports, Series P-20, No. 450, May 1991, U.S. Bureau of the Census, Tables 142, 143, 144, 145, 146, 147, 148, 149, 150, 175, 176, 177, 178, 179, 180, 181, 182, 183, 184, 185, 186, 187, 188, 189, 190, 191

• Masnick, George S., Working Paper W89-1 for the Joint Center for Housing Studies of Harvard University, *U.S. Household Trends: The 1980s and Beyond*, 1989, Table 155

• *Medicare and Medicaid's 25th Anniversary— Much Promised, Accomplished, and Left Unfinished: A Report Presented by the Chairman of the Select Committee on Aging*, U.S. Government Printing Office, 1990, Table 740

• "Medicines Across the Border," *Detroit Free Press*, November 26, 1992, Table 684

• Meisenheimer III, Joseph R., "How do immigrants fare in the U.S. labor market?" *Monthly Labor Review*, December 1992, Tables 227, 228, 229, 414, 446, 447, 448

• Mitchell, Olivia S., "Trends in Pension Benefit Formulas and Retirement Provisions," in *Trends in Pensions 1992*, U.S. Department of Labor, Pension and Welfare Benefits Administration, U.S. Government Printing Office, Washington, DC, 1992, Tables 334, 335, 343

• *Modern Healthcare*, December 23-30, 1991, Table 720

• *Modern Maturity*, Vol. 36, Number 3, June-July 1993, Table 719

• National Center for Health Statistics. *Health United States 1991*, Washington, DC, U.S. Department of Health and Human Services, 1992, Tables 615, 711

• National Center for Statistics and Analysis, National Highway Traffic Safety Administration, U.S. Department of Transportation, *1991 Alcohol Fatal Crash Facts*, Tables 645, 646

• National Center for Statistics and Analysis, National Highway Traffic Safety Administration, U.S. Department of Transportation, *1991 Older Driver Fatal Crash Facts*, Tables 640, 644

• National Center for Statistics and Analysis, National Highway Traffic Safety Administration, U.S. Department of Transportation, *1991 Pedalcyclist Fatal Crash Facts*, Table 643

• National Center for Statistics and Analysis, National Highway Traffic Safety Administration, U.S. Department of Transportation, *1991 Traffic Fatality Facts*, Tables 639, 641, 642

• National Electronic Injury Surveillance System, *NEISS Data Highlights*, Jan.-Dec. 1990, Vol. 14., Tables 647, 648, 649, 650, 651, 652, 653, 654, 655, 656, 657, 658, 659

• National Institute on Aging, *Bound for Good Health: A Collection of Age Pages*, Tables 118, 563, 564, 565, 623, 627, 632, 634, 635, 636, 637

• National Institute on Aging, *Physical Frailty: A Reducible Barrier to Independence for Older Americans*, September 1991, Department of Health and Human Services, Public Health Service, National Institutes of Health, Report to Congress, Tables 540, 802

• *Nation's Restaurant News*, June 22, Table 833

• *New York Times*,
  – June 28, 1992, Table 726
  – August 20, 1992, Tables 352, 369
  – August 30, 1992, Table 371

  – November 8, 1992, Table 850
  – November 10, 1992, Table 37
  – February 11, 1993, Table 350
  – March 14, 1993, Table 351
  – March 21, 1993, Table 105
  – July 13, 1993, Table 60

• Parnes, Herbert S., Thomas N. Chirikos, Elizabeth G. Menaghan, Frank L. Mott, Gilbert Nestel, Lois B. Shaw, David G. Sommers, *The NLS Older Male Sample Revisited: A Unique Data Base for Gerontological Research*, Center for Human Resource Research, The Ohio State University, 1993, Tables 193, 194, 195, 196, 197, 198, 199, 241, 242, 243, 244, 245, 429, 541, 542, 543, 699

• Philips, Kristen, "State and Local Government Pension Benefits," in *Trends in Pensions 1992*, U.S. Department of Labor, Pension and Welfare Benefits Administration, U.S. Government Printing Office, Washington, DC, 1992, Tables 316, 317, 318

• "Population 65 Years Old and Over, by Age Group and Sex, 1960 to 1989, and Projections, 2000," *Statistical Abstract of the United States*, 1991, Table 53

• *Population Census, 1990*, U.S. Bureau of the Census, Table 35

• *Poverty in the United States: 1991*, Current Population Reports, Series P-60, No. 181, U.S. Department of Commerce, Bureau of the Census, August 1992, Tables 130, 151, 288, 289, 290, 291, 292, 293, 716

• Priest, Dana, "Health Plan Worries Spur PACs: Industry Group Donations Up 20%," *Washington Post*, July 17, 1993, Table 729

• Princeton Religion Research Center, "Public Divided on the Issue of Hiring of Homosexuals for the Clergy," *Emerging Trends*, November 1992, Table 887

- "Projections of the Hispanic Population, by Age and Sex: 1995 to 2010," *Statistical Abstract of the United States*, 1991, Table 48

- "Projections of the Total Population by Age, Sex, and Race: 1995 to 2010," *Statistical Abstract of the United States*, 1991, Table 46

- Pryor, David, "Communism Collapses...but Nothing Changes the Pharmaceutical Industry's Skyrocketing Pricing Practices,", *Congressional Record*, September 10, 1991, Table 673

- Quinn, Joseph F. and Richard V. Berkhauser, "Retirement Preferences and Plans of Older American Workers," *The Commonwealth Fund, Americans Over 55 at Work Program*, October 1990, Tables 342, 348, 349, 441, 442, 443, 444, 445

- Reuben, David B., M.D., "The Adequacy of Geriatrician Supply," *Shortage of Health Care Professions Caring for the Elderly: Recommendations for Change*, Senate Select Committee on Aging, Comm. Pub. No. 102-915, Table 700

- Ruhm, Christopher J., "Bridge Employment and Job Stopping in the 1980s," *The Commonwealth Fund, Americans Over 55 at Work Program*, May 1991, Tables 254, 425, 431, 435, 436, 440, 723

- *St. Louis Post Dispatch*, July 22, 1993, Table 730

- *Social Security Bulletin*, Vol. 55, No. 3, Fall 1992, Tables 220, 269, 353, 354, 355

- *The Service Advantage: How Consumers Evaluate Service in Their Supermarket, 1991*, Food Marketing Institute, Tables 888, 889, 890, 891, 892

- *Shortage of Health Care Professions Caring for the Elderly: Recommendations for Change*, Health Sources and Services Administration: Bureau of Health Professions Response, Senate

- Select Committee on Aging, Comm. Pub. No. 102-915, Tables 701, 702

- Sorrels, Valarie L., "Nursing Home Fears," *Geriatric Nursing*, September-October 1991, Table 757

- Spencer, Gregory, Arnold A. Goldstein, and Cynthia M. Taeuber, *America's Centenarians: Data from the 1980 Census*, National Institute on Aging, Washington, DC, June 1987, Tables 134, 192, 247, 826, 827, 902

- Spiller, Lisa D. and Richard A. Hamilton, "Senior Citizen Discount Programs: Which Seniors to Target and Why," *Journal of Consumer Marketing*, Table 834

- *Springfield News-Leader*, March 20, 1993, Table 630

- *Statistical Abstract of the United States: 1991*, U.S. National Center for Health Statistics, *Vital Statistics of the United States*, annual; and unpublished data, Table 74

- Stevens, James, "Projected Consumer Spending in the 90s," *Appliances*, Vol. 47, No. 12, December, 1990, Table 303

- Taeuber, Cynthia M., *Sixty-Five Plus in America*, U.S. Department of Commerce, Economics and Statistics Administration, Bureau of the Census, U.S. Government Printing Office, Washington, DC, 1992, Tables 17, 18, 19, 21, 22, 27, 44, 50, 51, 57, 61, 68, 71, 73, 77, 97, 101, 102, 108, 109, 156, 224, 225, 252, 253, 271, 279, 372, 412, 526, 527, 528, 546, 713, 753

- Thompson, Roger, "A Decline in Covered Workers," *Nation's Business*, March 1993, Table 346

- U.S. Bureau of the Census, 1980 and 1990 Censuses of Population: for 1980, *General Population*

Characteristics, PC80-1-B1, Table 67; for 1990, Summary Tape File 1A, Tables 49, 56

● U.S. Bureau of the Census, 1990 Census of Population and Housing, Summary Tape File 1A, Table 163

● U.S. Bureau of the Census, 1990 Census of Population and Housing, Summary Tape File 1A; 2000 and 2010 from *Projections of the Population of the United States, by Age, Sex, and Race: 1989 to 2010*, U.S. Government Printing Office, Washington, DC, 1990, Table 52

● U.S. Bureau of the Census, Housing and Household Economic Statistics Division, Income Branch, unpublished tabulations from March 1990 Current Population Survey, Tables 232, 233, 234, 235, 236, 237

● U.S. Bureau of the Census, "1950 Nonwhite Population by Race," Special Report P-E, No. 3B, Washington, DC, U.S. Government Printing Office, 1951, Table 16

● U.S. Bureau of the Census, *Statistical Abstract of the United States: 1992* (112th edition), Washington, DC, 1992, Tables 34, 43, 88, 89, 131, 133, 216, 246, 263, 407, 420, 421, 422, 449, 450, 471, 830, 841, 847, 581, 618, 619, 853, 900, 901, 905

● U.S. Congress, "A State-by-State Analysis of Fire Safety in Nursing Facilities," A Staff Report of the Special Committee on Aging, United States Senate, May, 1992, 102-M, U.S. Government Printing Office, Washington, DC, Tables 810, 811, 812, 813, 814, 815, 816, 817, 818, 819, 820, 821, 822, 823, 824

● U.S. Congress, "Consumer Fraud and the Elderly: Easy Prey?," Hearing before the Special Committee on Aging, United States Senate, September 24, 1992, 102-25, U.S. Government Printing Of-

fice, Washington, DC, Tables 311, 312, 313, 314, 315

● U.S. Congress, "Crimes Committed Against the Elderly," Hearing before the Special Committee on Aging, United States Senate, August 6, 1991, 102-11, U.S. Government Printing Office, Washington, DC, Table 39

● U.S. Congress, "Cutting Health Care Costs: Experiences in France, Germany, and Japan," Joint Hearing before the Committee on Governmental Affairs and the Special Committee on Aging, United States Senate, November 19, 1991, Tables 703, 704

● U.S. Congress, "Elder Abuse and Neglect: Prevention and Intervention," Hearing before the Special Committee on Aging, United States Senate, June 29, 1991, 102-5, U.S. Government Printing Office, Washington, DC, Table 919

● U.S. Congress, "Medicare Fraud and Abuse: A Neglected Emergency?," Hearing before the Special Committee on Aging, United States Senate, October 2, 1991, 102-13, U.S. Government Printing Office, Washington, DC, Tables 591, 638, 686, 687, 688, 689, 690, 691, 692, 693, 694, 698, 727, 728

● U.S. Congress, "Profiles in Aging America: Meeting the Health Care Needs of the Nation's Black Elderly," United States Senate, Joint Hearing Before the Special Committee on Aging and the Congressional Black Caucus Health Braintrust, September 28, 1990, U.S. Government Printing Office, Washington, DC, Tables 76, 95, 96, 120, 121, 280, 512, 559, 560, 561, 562, 567, 584, 586, 588, 589, 597, 633, 683, 718, 756 763, 803, 804, 805, 806, 807, 808, 809

● U.S. Congress, "Resident Assessment: The Springboard to Quality of Care and Quality of Life for Nursing Home Residents," Workshop before the Special Committee on Aging, United States

Senate, October 22, 1990, 101-30, Tables 559, 560, 561,

• U.S. Congress, "The Effects of Escalating Drug Costs on the Elderly," Hearing before the Special Committee on Aging, United States Senate, April 22, 1992, 102-21, U.S. Government Printing Office, Washington, DC, Tables 674, 675, 676, 677, 678, 679, 680, 681, 682, 697

• U.S. Department of Commerce and U.S. Department of Housing and Urban Development, Current Housing Reports, H150/89, *American Housing Survey for the United States in 1989*, July 1991, Tables 226, 262, 465, 466, 467, 468 475, 476, 481, 482, 484, 485, 486, 493, 494, 495, 496, 497, 498, 499, 501, 502, 505, 508, 509

• U.S. Department of Commerce and U.S. Department of Housing and Urban Development, Current Housing Reports H151/89, *Supplement to the American Housing Survey for the United States in 1989*, October 1992, Tables 469, 470, 477, 478, 483, 490, 491, 500, 503, 504, 506, 507, 839, 840

• U.S. Department of Commerce, Bureau of the Census, Current Population Reports, Series P-20, No. 440, *Voting and Registration in the Election of November 1988*, U.S. Government Printing Office, Washington, DC, 1989, Tables 842, 843, 844, 845, 846

• U.S. Department of Commerce, Bureau of the Census, Current Population Reports, Special Studies, Series P-23, No. 160, *Labor Force Status and Other Characteristics of Persons With a Work Disability: 1981 to 1988*, U.S. Government Printing Office, Tables 432, 456, 457, 458, 459, 460, 461, 462, 463, 464

• U.S. Department of Commerce, Bureau of the Census, *1990 Census of Population and Housing, Summary Tape File 1C, United States Summary*, CD900- 1C, February 1992, Tables 32, 33, 36, 40, 41

• U.S. Department of Commerce, Bureau of the Census, *Geographical Mobility: March 1987 to March 1990*, Current Population Reports, Population Characteristics, Series P-20, No. 456, Tables 123, 124, 125, 126

• U.S. Department of Commerce, Bureau of the Census, *State and Metropolitan Area Data Book 1991*, August 1991, Tables 365, 366, 620, 737, 738

• U.S. Department of Commerce, Economics and Statistics Administration, Bureau of the Census, International Population Reports P95/92-3: *An Aging World II*, by Kevin Kinsella and Cynthia M. Taeuber, February 1993, Tables 59, 65, 66, 132

• U.S. Department of Commerce, Economics and Statistics Administration, *National Economic, Social, and Environmental Data Bank, CD-ROM*, November 1992, Tables 69, 72, 86, 92, 93, 98, 100, 103, 104, 107, 110, 539, 576, 672, 714, 742, 743, 754, 758

• U.S. Department of Health and Human Services, National Center for Health Statistics, Vital and Health Statistics, *Mental Illness in Nursing Homes: United States, 1985*, Series 13: Data from the National Health Survey, No. 105, Tables 767, 768, 769, 770, 781, 782, 783, 784, 785, 786, 787, 788, 789, 790, 791, 792, 793, 794, 795, 796, 797, 798, 799, 800, 801

• U.S. Department of Health and Human Services, National Center for Health Statistics, *National Hospital Discharge Survey: Annual Summary, 1988*, Series 13, No. 106, Table 119

• U.S. Department of Health and Human Services, National Institute on Aging, *Profiles of America's Elderly: Growth of America's Elderly in the 1980's*, December 1991, Tables 24, 25, 29, 55

• U.S. Department of Health and Human Services, Social Security Administration, *Income of the Aged Chartbook, 1990*, U.S. Government Printing

Office, Washington, DC, September 1992, Tables 203, 204, 205, 209, 210, 211, 212, 240, 260, 261, 281, 282, 362, 363, 364, 393

- U.S. Department of Justice, Office of Justice Programs, Bureau of Justice Statistics, *Correctional Populations in the United States, 1989*, NCJ-130445, October 1991, Table 904

- U.S. Department of Labor, Pension and Welfare Benefits Administration, *Trends in Pensions 1992*, U.S. Government Printing Office, Washington, DC, 1992, Table 327

- U.S. Department of Transportation, Federal Highway Administration, *Highway Statistics 1990*, Tables 835, 836, 837, 838

- U.S. Department of Veterans Affairs, Demographics Division, *1990 Census Data on Veterans, United States*, Table 42

- U.S. Department of Veterans Affairs, Veterans Benefits Administration, *Servicemen's and Veterans' Group Life Insurance Programs: Twenty-Seventh Annual Report, Year Ending June 30, 1992*, Tables 115, 116, 117

- U.S. Equal Employment Opportunity Commission, *Fiscal Year 1989 Annual Report*, Tables 451, 452, 453, 454, 455

- U.S. General Accounting Office, *Long-Term Care: Projected Needs of the Aging Baby Boom Generation*, Report to the Honorable William S. Cohen, Special Committee on Aging, U.S. Senate, June 1991, Table 613

- U.S. General Accounting Office, *Poverty Trends 1980-88: Changes in Family Composition and Income Sources Among the Poor*, GAO/PEMD-92-34, September 1992, Tables 265, 266, 272, 274, 298, 299

- USA Today
  - November 27, 1992, Table 552
  - November 30, 1992, Table 631
  - December 4, 1992, Table 907
  - December 30, 1992, Table 663
  - February 23, 1993, Table 717
  - February 24, 1993, Table 85
  - March 4, 1993, Table 857
  - March 10, 1993, Table 741
  - June 1, 1993, Table 474
  - July 6, 1993, Table 828

- Waldrop, Judith, "You'll Know It's the 21st Century When ...," *American Demographics* 12, No. 12, December, 1990

- *Wall Street Journal*, February 15, 1993, Table 367

- "Who Gives to the Arts and Humanities," *The Chronicle of Philanthropy*, Table 310

- "Workers With Low Earnings: 1964 to 1990," *Family Economics Review*, 1992, Vol. 5, No. 4, Table 297

- *Workforce 2000: Work and Workers for the Twenty-First Century*, Hudson Institute, Indianapolis, Indiana, 1987, Table 408

- Yeo, Gwen, Ph.D., "Ethnogeriatric Education: Need and Recommendations," *Shortage of Health Care Professions Caring for the Elderly: Recommendations for Change*, Senate Select Committee on Aging, Comm. Pub. No. 102-915, Tables 513, 514, 612

- Wade, Alice H., "Social Security Area Population Projections," Office of the Actuary, Social Security Administration, *Social Security Bulletin* 51, No. 2, February, 1988, Tables 15, 84

- Wilcox, Melynda Dovel, "The High Cost of Working in Retirement," *Kiplinger's Personal Finance Magazine*, August 1993, Table 341

KEYWORD INDEX

The *Keyword Index* holds references to more than 1,500 subjects and names, including, concepts, public and private organizations, programs, diseases, place names, and the like. The index was generated, in part, from the descriptive tags in the tables; additional index terms were added by the editors. Each entry is followed by one or more page numbers marked p. or pp. After the page references, table references are provided within brackets. The phrase *p. 340 [339]* means that the item appears on page 340 in Table 339. Acronymic phrases are usually also referenced by full name elsewhere. Thus *AIDS* and *Acquired immune deficiency syndrome* will both be found in the index. Such phrases are *not* cross-referenced unless they refer to different tables. In other cases, *See* references are provided. Thus *HIV* is referred to *Human immunodeficiency virus.*

Alabama continued:
— Medicare and Medicaid, pp. 678, 680 [737-738]
— nursing home safety, pp. 767, 769, 771, 773-774, 776-777
　　[818-824]
— nursing homes, p. 706 [754]
— population, pp. 39, 45 [36, 41]
— population 65 and older, pp. 40, 53, 57, 59 [37, 49, 52, 54]
— population 65 and older living alone, p. 173 [163]
— population 85 and older, p. 62 [56]
— skilled nursing charges, p. 644 [696]
— skilled nursing facilities, p. 699 [751]
— Social Security, pp. 335, 337 [365-366]
— Social Security beneficiaries, p. 371 [396]
— Social Security benefits, pp. 369, 374 [395, 398]
— Social Security benefits, by state, p. 373 [397]
— SSI benefits received, pp. 376-377 [399-400]
— veteran population, p. 45 [42]

Alaska
— age discrimination in, p. 418 [453]
— drivers licenses, pp. 787-788 [835-836]
— elderly in nursing homes, p. 704 [753]
— elderly population, pp. 38, 42 [35, 38]
— hospital insurance charges, p. 643 [695]
— medical facilities, pp. 590, 592 [620-621]
— Medicare, pp. 690, 697 [746, 750]
— Medicare and Medicaid, pp. 679, 681 [737-738]
— nursing home safety, pp. 767, 769, 771, 773-774, 776-777
　　[818-824]
— nursing homes, p. 706 [754]
— population, p. 39 [36]
— population 65 and older, pp. 40, 54, 57, 59 [37, 49, 52, 54]
— population 65 and older living alone, p. 173 [163]
— population 85 and older, p. 63 [56]
— skilled nursing charges, p. 645 [696]
— skilled nursing facilities, p. 699 [751]
— Social Security, pp. 336, 338 [365-366]
— Social Security beneficiaries, p. 371 [396]
— Social Security benefits, pp. 369, 374 [395, 398]
— Social Security benefits, by state, p. 373 [397]
— SSI benefits received, pp. 376-377 [399-400]
— veteran population, p. 45 [42]

Alaska Natives
— and health risks, p. 467 [513]

Albany, NY
— population, pp. 23, 29 [21-22]

Albuquerque, NM
— population, pp. 19, 25 [21-22]

Albuterol
— and patients aged 55-74 years, p. 512 [554]

Alcohol
— and nursing home discharges, p. 729 [772]
— and nursing home residents, p. 729 [771]
— and traffic fatalities, pp. 609-610 [645-646]
— in nursing homes, pp. 743, 750 [781, 790]

Alcona County, MI
— percent over 55 years old, p. 36 [33]

Aleutians East Borough, AK
— percent over 55 years old, p. 35 [32]

Aleutians West Census Area, AK
— percent over 55 years old, p. 35 [32]

Alexandria, VA
— affluent elderly in, p. 219 [217]
— population, pp. 23, 28 [21-22]

All-terrain vehicles
— product-related injuries, p. 611 [647]

Allentown, PA
— population, pp. 23, 29 [21-22]

Allopurinol
— and patients aged 55-74 years, p. 511 [554]

Alprazolan
— and patients aged 55-74 years, p. 511 [554]

ALS, pp. 638, 641, 646 [690-691, 694, 698]

Alzheimer's disease, pp. 726, 728 [769-770]
— and nursing home discharges, p. 729 [772]
— in nursing homes, pp. 729, 743-744, 750 [771, 781-782, 790]
— opinions on research, p. 814 [864]
— prevalence, by age, p. 595 [624]

Amarillo, TX
— population, pp. 21, 27 [21-22]

American Chiropractic Association PAC, p. 670 [729]
American Council of Life Insurance PAC, p. 670 [729]
American Dental PAC, p. 670 [729]
American Family PAC, p. 670 [729]
American Health Care Association PAC, p. 670 [729]
American Hospital Association PAC, p. 670 [729]
American Indians, pp. 17, 98 [19, 94]
American International Group Employee PAC, p. 670 [729]
American Medical Association PAC, p. 670 [729]
American Optometric Association PAC, p. 670 [729]
American Physical Therapy PAC, p. 670 [729]
American Samoa
— Social Security benefits, p. 370 [395]
American Society of Anesthesiologists PAC, p. 670 [729]

Amitriptyline
— and patients aged 55-74 years, p. 511 [554]

Ampicillin
— and patients aged 55-74 years, p. 511 [554]

Amyotrophic Lateral Sclerosis, pp. 638, 641, 646 [690-691,
　　694, 698]
— and cost effectiveness, p. 641 [694]

Anaheim, CA
— population, pp. 20, 25 [21-22]

Analgesics and antipyretics
— and patients aged 55 to 75+ years, p. 514 [555]

Ancestry
— of centenarians, p. 781 [826]

Anchorage Borough, AK
— percent over 55 years old, p. 36 [32]

Anchorage, AK
— affluent elderly in, p. 219 [217]
— population, pp. 20, 25 [21-22]

Anemias
— incidence, p. 580 [608]

Angina pectoris
— and frequent diagnoses, pp. 567-568 [600]

Angiocardiography
— and females, pp. 544-545 [580]

Numbers following p. or pp. are page references. Numbers in [ ] are table references.

Angiocardiography continued:
— and males, pp. 542-543 [579]
Ann Arbor, MI
— population, pp. 23, 28 [21-22]
Annuities, p. 245 [255]
— and gender, pp. 295, 297 [322-323]
— from former employer, p. 297 [323]
Antacids and absorbents
— and patients aged 55 to 75+ years, p. 515 [555]
Anti-anemia drugs
— and patients aged 55 to 75+ years, p. 514 [555]
Anti-infectives
— and patients aged 55 to 75+ years, p. 514 [555]
Anti-inflammatory agents
— and patients aged 55 to 75+ years, pp. 514-515 [555]
Antibiotics
— and patients aged 55 to 75+ years, p. 514 [555]
Anticholinergic agents
— and patients aged 55 to 75+ years, p. 514 [555]
Antidepressants
— and patients aged 55 to 75+ years, p. 514 [555]
Antidiabetic agents
— and patients aged 55 to 75+ years, p. 515 [555]
Antihistamines
— antitussives, p. 514 [555]
Antihypertensive agents
— and patients aged 55 to 75+ years, p. 514 [555]
Antineoplastic agents
— and patients aged 55 to 75+ years, p. 514 [555]
Anxiety, pp. 711, 713 [759-760]
— and blacks, pp. 711, 713 [759-760]
— and doctors visits, p. 565 [599]
— and nursing home discharges, p. 729 [772]
— and nursing home residents, pp. 729, 743, 750 [771, 781, 790]
— and whites, pp. 711, 713 [759-760]
Anxiolytics
— sedatives, and hypnotics, and patients aged 55 to 75+ years, p. 514 [555]
Apartments, pp. 725, 757 [768, 801]
Apparel and services
— expenditures, pp. 282 [307-308]
Appliances
— product-related injuries, pp. 614-615 [654, 656]
Apprentices
— employment discrimination charges, p. 417 [452]
Argentina
— elderly population, p. 66 [61]
Arizona
— age discrimination in, p. 418 [453]
— death sentences, p. 847 [904]
— drivers licenses, pp. 787-788 [835-836]
— elderly in nursing homes, p. 704 [753]
— elderly population, pp. 38, 42 [35, 38]
— hospital insurance charges, p. 642 [695]
— medical facilities, pp. 590, 592 [620-621]
— Medicare, pp. 689, 697 [746, 750]
— Medicare and Medicaid, pp. 679, 681 [737-738]
— nursing home safety, pp. 767, 769, 771, 773-774, 776-777

Arizona continued:
[818-824]
— nursing homes, p. 706 [754]
— population, p. 39 [36]
— population 65 and older, pp. 40, 53, 57, 59 [37, 49, 52, 54]
— population 65 and older living alone, p. 173 [163]
— population 85 and older, p. 63 [56]
— skilled nursing charges, p. 645 [696]
— skilled nursing facilities, p. 699 [751]
— Social Security, pp. 336, 338 [365-366]
— Social Security beneficiaries, p. 371 [396]
— Social Security benefits, pp. 369, 374 [395, 398]
— Social Security benefits, by state, p. 373 [397]
— SSI benefits received, pp. 376-377 [399-400]
— veteran population, p. 45 [42]
Arkansas
— age discrimination in, p. 418 [453]
— death sentences, p. 846 [904]
— drivers licenses, pp. 787-788 [835-836]
— elderly in nursing homes, p. 704 [753]
— elderly population, pp. 38, 42 [35, 38]
— hospital insurance charges, p. 642 [695]
— medical facilities, pp. 590, 592 [620-621]
— Medicare, pp. 689, 696 [746, 750]
— Medicare and Medicaid, pp. 678, 681 [737-738]
— nursing home safety, pp. 767, 769, 771, 773-774, 776-777 [818-824]
— nursing homes, p. 706 [754]
— population, pp. 39, 45 [36, 41]
— population 65 and older, pp. 40, 53, 57, 59 [37, 49, 52, 54]
— population 65 and older living alone, p. 173 [163]
— population 85 and older, p. 62 [56]
— skilled nursing charges, p. 644 [696]
— skilled nursing facilities, p. 699 [751]
— Social Security, pp. 335, 338 [365-366]
— Social Security beneficiaries, p. 371 [396]
— Social Security benefits, pp. 369, 374 [395, 398]
— Social Security benefits, by state, p. 373 [397]
— SSI benefits received, p. 376 [399]
— veteran population, p. 45 [42]
Arlington, TX
— population, pp. 20, 25 [21-22]
Arlington, VA
— affluent elderly in, p. 219 [217]
— population, pp. 21, 26 [21-22]
Arson
— arrests for, pp. 838, 841-842 [896, 898-899]
— elderly charged with, p. 834 [893]
— elderly females arrested, p. 836 [894]
— elderly males charged, p. 837 [895]
Arteriography
— and females, pp. 544-545 [580]
— and males, pp. 542-543 [579]
Arthritis, pp. 523, 595, 597, 726-727 [564, 625-626, 769-770]
— and females, p. 595 [625]
— and males, p. 595 [625]
— incidence, p. 579 [608]
— older Americans with, p. 465 [510]
— physician diagnosed, p. 595 [625]

Numbers following p. or pp. are page references. Numbers in [ ] are table references.

Arthropathies
— and frequent diagnoses, pp. 567-568 [600]
Arthroplasty, p. 573 [603]
Arts
— philanthropy, p. 284 [310]
Asia
— elderly population, p. 70 [65]
— percent 65 and older in, p. 68 [63]
Asian or Pacific Islanders
— 65 and older, p. 17 [19]
Asians
— and health risks, p. 467 [513]
— death rates, p. 98 [94]
— health care utilization, p. 583 [612]
Aspirin
— and patients aged 55-74 years, pp. 511-512 [554]
Assault
— multiple-offender, p. 853 [912]
— victimization rate, pp. 848-849, 851, 853-854 [906, 908, 910, 913-914]
Assets, pp. 217, 224 [215, 225]
— at financial institutions, p. 222 [222]
— business, p. 224 [225]
— checking accounts, p. 222 [222]
— financial investments, p. 224 [225]
— impaired elderly, p. 219 [218]
— income from, pp. 213-214, 247-248, 334 [210-211, 260-261, 364]
— IRAs, pp. 222, 224 [222, 225]
— KEOGH accounts, pp. 222, 224 [222, 225]
— motor vehicles, p. 222 [222]
— mutual fund shares, pp. 222, 224 [222, 225]
— of families, p. 218 [216]
— own home, p. 222 [222]
— real estate, p. 222 [222]
— savings account, p. 222 [222]
— stocks, pp. 222, 224 [222, 225]
— United States savings bonds, p. 222 [222]
— unsecured, p. 222 [222]
Assisted activities
— in nursing homes, pp. 747-748 [786-787]
Assisted living, p. 755 [797]
— finances, p. 250 [264]
— in nursing homes, pp. 746, 753 [785, 795]
Associate's degrees, p. 139 [133]
Asthma
— incidence, p. 580 [608]
Atenolol
— and patients aged 55-74 years, pp. 511-512 [554]
Atherosclerosis, pp. 726-727 [769-770]
— deaths from, pp. 85-86 [81-82]
Atlanta, GA
— age discrimination in, p. 421 [455]
— population, pp. 19, 25 [21-22]
ATVs
— product-related injuries, p. 611 [647]
Audio equipment
— entertainment expenditures, p. 784 [830]
— product-related injuries, p. 612 [648]

Auditory impairments
— in nursing homes, p. 753 [794]
Aurora, CO
— population, pp. 20, 26 [21-22]
Austin, TX
— population, pp. 19, 24 [21-22]
Australia
— and diseases, p. 124 [122]
— and mortality, p. 124 [122]
— life expectancy, pp. 74-75 [72]
— life expectancy at 65, p. 77 [73]
— life expectancy at birth, p. 77 [73]
— pensions in, pp. 312-315 [336-340]
— suicide rate, p. 93 [88]
Austria
— elderly population, p. 65 [59]
— life expectancy, pp. 74-75 [72]
— life expectancy at 65, p. 77 [73]
— life expectancy at birth, p. 77 [73]
— shared social security agreements with United States, p. 383 [406]
— Social Security programs, p. 384 [407]
— suicide rate, p. 93 [88]
Autonomic drugs
— and patients aged 55 to 75+ years, p. 514 [555]
Autos
— accidents, pp. 605-606 [640-641]
— drivers licenses, pp. 787-788, 790 [835-837]
— miles driven, p. 790 [838]
— traffic fatalities, p. 604 [639]
Axes
— product-related injuries, p. 613 [651]
Bachelor's degrees, p. 139 [133]
Bacitracin
— and patients aged 55-74 years, p. 511 [554]
Back pain
— and doctors visits, pp. 565-566 [599]
Badminton
— product-related injuries, p. 611 [647]
Bakersfield, CA
— population, pp. 21, 26 [21-22]
Baltimore, MD
— age discrimination in, p. 421 [455]
— population, pp. 19, 24 [21-22]
Bangladesh
— elderly population, p. 66 [61]
Banisters
— product-related injuries, p. 616 [658]
Barbecue grills
— product-related injuries, p. 611 [647]
Baseball, p. 808 [857]
— product-related injuries, p. 611 [647]
Basketball
— product-related injuries, p. 611 [647]
Bathing
— nursing home assistance, pp. 747, 753 [786, 795]
Bathtubs
— product-related injuries, p. 616 [657]

Numbers following p. or pp. are page references. Numbers in [ ] are table references.

Baton Rouge, LA
— population, pp. 20, 26 [21-22]
Batteries
— product-related injuries, p. 613 [652]
Baxter County, AR
— percent over 55 years old, p. 36 [33]
Beach products
— product-related injuries, p. 611 [647]
Beaumont, TX
— population, pp. 22, 28 [21-22]
Bed days, pp. 549, 551 [584, 586]
Beds and bedding
— product-related injuries, p. 616 [657]
Beer
— expenditures on, p. 280 [304]
Belgium
— aging population, p. 65 [60]
— and diseases, p. 124 [122]
— and mortality, p. 124 [122]
— elderly population, p. 65 [59]
— life expectancy, pp. 75-76 [72]
— life expectancy at 65, p. 77 [73]
— life expectancy at birth, p. 77 [73]
— shared social security agreements with United States 383 [406]
— Social Security programs, p. 384 [407]
Benefits
— employment discrimination charges, p. 417 [452]
— in-kind, p. 211 [207]
— non-cash Social Security, p. 328 [357]
— percent of income from Social Security, p. 363 [389]
— retirement, p. 366 [391]
— shared social security agreements with other countries 383 [406]
— Social Security, pp. 325-327, 344-345 [353-356, 374-375]
— Social Security beneficiaries, by state, p. 371 [396]
— Social Security benefits, by state, p. 373 [397]
— Social Security for women, p. 352 [381]
— Social Security paid, by state, p. 369 [395]
— Social Security withheld due to earnings, p. 367 [392]
— Social Security, by state, p. 374 [398]
Benign prostatic hypertrophy
See: BPH
Bergen, NJ
— affluent elderly in, p. 219 [217]
Berkeley, CA
— population, pp. 23, 29 [21-22]
Bethel, AK
— percent over 55 years old, p. 35 [32]
Bicycles & accessories
— product-related injuries, p. 611 [647]
Birmingham, AL
— age discrimination in, p. 421 [455]
— population, pp. 20, 25 [21-22]
Blacks
— age of householder, p. 435 [470]
— and health risks, p. 467 [513]
— and housing characteristics, p. 432 [466]
— and housing costs, p. 453 [495]

Blacks continued:
— and income, pp. 207, 333 [203, 363]
— and nursing home assistance, p. 746 [785]
— and poverty, p. 263 [282]
— and property insurance, p. 456 [499]
— and public transportation, p. 461 [506]
— and shopping, p. 462 [507]
— cost of living, p. 454 [496]
— death rates, p. 98 [94]
— desire for longevity, p. 826 [880]
— educational attainment, p. 142 [137]
— geographic mobility, p. 463 [509]
— health care utilization, pp. 468, 583 [514, 612]
— home maintenance costs, p. 455 [497]
— household characteristics, p. 458 [502]
— housing characteristics, pp. 431-433, 438, 440-444, 446-447, 453, 455, 457, 460 [465, 467-468, 475-482, 484-486, 494, 498, 501, 505]
— housing tenure, p. 434 [469]
— in advertising, p. 807 [855]
— living arrangements, pp. 173, 177 [162, 167]
— mental disorders in nursing homes, pp. 745, 750 [784, 790]
— neighborhood conditions, pp. 459, 462 [504, 508]
— rent collected by, p. 452 [493]
— savings and investments of, p. 225 [226]
Bladder control, p. 754 [796]
Bladder disorders
— incidence, p. 580 [608]
Blood cholesterol
— checks, p. 532 [573]
Blood formation and coagulation agents
— and patients aged 55 to 75+ years, p. 514 [555]
Blood glucose, p. 541 [578]
Blood pressure, pp. 531-532, 541, 598-599 [572-573, 578, 628-629]
Blood pressure tests, p. 531 [572]
— and doctors visits, pp. 565-566 [599]
Blue Cross and Blue Shield Association PAC, p. 670 [729]
Blue Cross of Western Pennsylvania, p. 664 [720]
Boarding houses, pp. 725, 757 [768, 801]
Body weight
— health and age, pp. 477-478 [521-522]
— obesity, pp. 477-478 [521-522]
— trying to lose, p. 478 [522]
Boise City, ID
— population, pp. 22, 28 [21-22]
Bonds
— as assets, p. 218 [216]
Bone conditions, pp. 602, 726-727 [634, 769-770]
Bone fractures, p. 552 [587]
Bone spur or tendinitis
— incidence, p. 579 [608]
Books
— entertainment expenditures, p. 784 [830]
Boston, MA
— population, pp. 19, 24 [21-22]
Bottles
— product-related injuries, p. 613 [650]
Bowel control, p. 754 [796]

Numbers following p. or pp. are page references. Numbers in [ ] are table references.

Numbers following p. or pp. are page references. Numbers in [ ] are table references.

Cardiac catheterization, pp. 572-576 [603-604]
Cardiac drugs
— and patients aged 55 to 75 + years, p. 514 [555]
Cardiac dysrhythmias
— and frequent diagnoses, pp. 568-569 [600]
Cardiovascular drugs
— and patients aged 55 to 75 + years, p. 514 [555]
Cardizem
— cost of, p. 635 [684]
Care at home, p. 727 [769]
Career jobs
— employment, p. 406 [435]
— hours preferred, p. 409 [440]
Caribbean
— elderly population, p. 70 [65]
— percent 65 and older in, p. 69 [63]
Carpets and rugs
— product-related injuries, p. 616 [657]
Carrying weapons
— elderly charged with, p. 834 [893]
— elderly males charged with, p. 837 [895]
Carts
— product-related injuries, p. 617 [659]
Cash assistance
— participation in government programs, p. 270 [293]
Cash contributions
— expenditures, pp. 277, 282-283 [300, 307-308]
Cataracts
— and doctors visits, p. 566 [599]
— and frequent diagnoses, pp. 568-569 [600]
— incidence, p. 579 [608]
— older Americans with, p. 465 [510]
Cathartics and laxatives
— and patients aged 55 to 75 + years, p. 515 [555]
Caustics
— product-related injuries, p. 614 [653]
Cector
— cost of, p. 635 [684]
Cedar Rapids, IA
— population, pp. 23, 28 [21-22]
Ceilings
— product-related injuries, p. 616 [658]
Centenarians
— educational attainment, p. 139 [134]
— income of, p. 239 [247]
— language and ancestry, p. 781 [826]
— marital status of, p. 199 [192]
Central America
— percent 65 and older in, p. 68 [63]
Central nervous system diseases, pp. 726-728 [769-770]
Cephalexin
— and patients aged 55-74 years, pp. 511-512 [554]
Cephalosporins
— and patients aged 55 to 75 + years, p. 514 [555]
Cerebrovascular death rates, p. 101 [98]
Cerebrovascular diseases, pp. 116, 124 [112, 122]
— and hospital stays, pp. 557-561 [593-594]
— blacks, p. 100 [97]
— death rates, pp. 101, 116 [98, 112]

Cerebrovascular diseases continued:
— deaths from, pp. 83-87 [81-83]
— incidence, p. 580 [608]
— persons 65 and older, p. 100 [97]
Certificates of deposit
— as assets, p. 218 [216]
Chain saws
— product-related injuries, p. 613 [651]
Chairs
— product-related injuries, p. 616 [657]
Charitable donations, p. 284 [310]
Charlotte County, FL
— percent over 55 years old, p. 36 [33]
Charlotte, NC
— age discrimination in, p. 421 [455]
— population, pp. 19, 25 [21-22]
Chattahoochee County, GA
— percent over 55 years old, p. 35 [32]
Chattanooga, TN
— population, pp. 21, 27 [21-22]
CHD, p. 123 [120]
Checking accounts
— as assets, p. 218 [216]
Cheerleading
— product-related injuries, p. 611 [647]
Chemicals
— product-related injuries, p. 614 [653]
Chesapeake, VA
— population, pp. 21, 27 [21-22]
Chest pain
— and doctors visits, p. 565 [599]
Chest X-rays, p. 541 [578]
Chicago, IL
— age discrimination in, p. 421 [455]
— population, pp. 18, 24 [21-22]
Chile
— life expectancy, pp. 75-76 [72]
— life expectancy at 65, p. 77 [73]
— life expectancy at birth, p. 77 [73]
Chimneys
— product-related injuries, p. 615 [655]
China
— elderly population, pp. 66, 70 [61, 65]
— population 65 and older, p. 67 [62]
Chlorpheniramine
— and patients aged 55-74 years, pp. 511-512 [554]
Chlorpropamide
— and patients aged 55-74 years, pp. 511-512 [554]
Cholecystectomy, pp. 572-575 [603-604]
Cholelithiasis
— and hospital stays, pp. 557-559 [593]
Chronic airway obstruction, pp. 567-569 [600]
Chronic bronchitis
— incidence, p. 580 [608]
Chronic health conditions, p. 579 [608]
Chronic ischemic heart disease
— and frequent diagnoses, pp. 567-569 [600]
Chronic liver disease and cirrhosis
— deaths from, pp. 83-85 [81]

Numbers following p. or pp. are page references. Numbers in [ ] are table references.

Chronic obstructive pulmonary disease, pp. 604, 639-641, 646 [638, 692-694, 698]
— and cost effectiveness, p. 641 [694]
— deaths from, pp. 83-86 [81-82]
Chronic sinusitis, pp. 465, 581 [510, 608]
Chula Vista, CA
— population, pp. 22, 27 [21-22]
Cigarette smoking, p. 502 [546]
Cigarettes and lighters
— product-related injuries, p. 612 [649]
Cigna Corp. PAC, p. 671 [729]
Cimetidine
— and patients aged 55-74 years, pp. 511-512 [554]
Cincinnati, OH
— population, pp. 19, 25 [21-22]
Circulatory conditions, pp. 726-727 [769-770]
Cities
— housing in, p. 433 [468]
Citrus County, FL
— percent over 55 years old, p. 36 [33]
Citrus Heights, CA
— population, pp. 23, 29 [21-22]
Civil Rights Act of 1964, p. 420 [454]
Cleaning equipment
— product-related injuries, p. 614 [653]
Cleaning solutions
— product-related injuries, p. 614 [653]
Clergy
— opinions on homosexuals in, p. 830 [887]
Clerical employment, p. 406 [435]
Cleveland, OH
— age discrimination in, p. 421 [455]
— population, pp. 19, 24 [21-22]
Clothes dryers, p. 279 [303]
Clothes steamers
— product-related injuries, p. 614 [654]
Clothing
— expenditures, p. 277 [300]
— product-related injuries, p. 612 [649]
Codeine
— and patients aged 55-74 years, pp. 511-512 [554]
Cognitive disabilities, pp. 715, 717, 720, 722, 729-731, 742 [761-762, 765-766, 771, 773-774, 780]
College, p. 133 [127]
— completion of, pp. 138-139 [131, 133]
— persons with, p. 136 [130]
Color blindness
— incidence, p. 579 [608]
Colorado
— age discrimination in, p. 418 [453]
— death sentences, p. 847 [904]
— drivers licenses, pp. 787-788 [835-836]
— elderly in nursing homes, p. 704 [753]
— elderly population, pp. 38, 42 [35, 38]
— hospital insurance charges, p. 642 [695]
— medical facilities, pp. 590, 592 [620-621]
— Medicare, pp. 689, 697 [746, 750]
— Medicare and Medicaid, pp. 679, 681 [737-738]
— nursing home safety, pp. 767, 769, 771, 773-774, 776, 778

Colorado continued:
[818-824]
— nursing homes, p. 706 [754]
— population, p. 39 [36]
— population 65 and older, pp. 40, 53, 57, 59 [37, 49, 52, 54]
— population 65 and older living alone, p. 173 [163]
— population 85 and older, p. 63 [56]
— skilled nursing charges, p. 645 [696]
— skilled nursing facilities, p. 699 [751]
— Social Security, pp. 336, 338 [365-366]
— Social Security beneficiaries, p. 371 [396]
— Social Security benefits, pp. 369, 374 [395, 398]
— Social Security benefits, by state, p. 373 [397]
— SSI benefits received, pp. 376-377 [399-400]
— veteran population, p. 45 [42]
Colorado Springs, CO
— population, pp. 20, 25 [21-22]
Columbus, GA
— population, pp. 21, 26 [21-22]
Columbus, OH
— population, pp. 19, 24 [21-22]
Commercialized vice
— elderly charged with, p. 834 [893]
— elderly females arrested, p. 835 [894]
— elderly males charged with, p. 837 [895]
Common childhood diseases
— incidence, pp. 546, 550, 562, 571 [582, 585, 595, 602]
Common cold
— incidence, pp. 546, 550, 562, 571 [582, 585, 595, 602]
Communications industry
— retirement plans, p. 320 [346]
Community health services, p. 686 [744]
Community hospitals, pp. 589, 591 [620-621]
Community services
— use by persons living alone, p. 267 [287]
Community social services, p. 686 [744]
Computerized axial tomography (CAT scan), pp. 542-545 [579-580]
Concord, CA
— population, pp. 23, 28 [21-22]
Condominiums
— housing characteristics, p. 432 [466]
Connecticut
— age discrimination in, p. 418 [453]
— death sentences, p. 846 [904]
— drivers licenses, pp. 787-788 [835-836]
— elderly in nursing homes, p. 703 [753]
— elderly population, pp. 38, 42 [35, 38]
— hospital insurance charges, p. 641 [695]
— medical facilities, pp. 589, 591 [620-621]
— Medicare, pp. 688, 695 [746, 750]
— Medicare and Medicaid, pp. 677, 679 [737-738]
— nursing home safety, pp. 767, 769, 771, 773-774, 776, 778 [818-824]
— nursing homes, p. 705 [754]
— population, p. 39 [36]
— population 65 and older, pp. 40, 52, 56, 59 [37, 49, 52, 54]
— population 65 and older living alone, p. 173 [163]
— population 85 and older, p. 62 [56]

Numbers following p. or pp. are page references. Numbers in [ ] are table references.

Numbers following p. or pp. are page references. Numbers in [ ] are table references.

Numbers following p. or pp. are page references. Numbers in [ ] are table references.

Numbers following p. or pp. are page references. Numbers in [ ] are table references.

Numbers following p. or pp. are page references. Numbers in [ ] are table references.

Numbers following p. or pp. are page references. Numbers in [ ] are table references.

Numbers following p. or pp. are page references. Numbers in [ ] are table references.

Numbers following p. or pp. are page references. Numbers in [ ] are table references.

Folic acid
— and health, p. 519 [558]
Food
— expenditures, pp. 277, 282-283 [300, 307-309]
Food and Drug Administration, p. 523 [564]
Food stamp use
— and housing characteristics, p. 249 [262]
Food stamps
— federal govenment expenditures on, p. 343 [373]
— in-kind benefit, p. 211 [207]
— participation in government programs, p. 270 [293]
Football
— product-related injuries, p. 611 [647]
Foreign countries
— Medicare, p. 690 [746]
— Social Security benefits, p. 371 [395]
Forgery, pp. 840, 842 [898-899]
— arrests for, pp. 838, 841-842 [896, 898-899]
— elderly charged with, pp. 834-835 [893]
— elderly females arrested, pp. 835-836 [894]
— elderly males charged, p. 837 [895]
— elderly males charged with, p. 837 [895]
Fort Lauderdale, FL
— population, pp. 21, 27 [21-22]
Fort Wayne, IN
— population, pp. 21, 26 [21-22]
Fort Worth, TX
— population, pp. 19, 24 [21-22]
Fractures, pp. 572-576 [603-604]
— hospital stays, pp. 557-561 [593-594]
— incidence, pp. 547, 550, 562, 571 [582, 585, 595, 602]
France
— aging population, p. 65 [60]
— and diseases, p. 124 [122]
— and mortality, p. 124 [122]
— elderly population, pp. 64-66, 69-70 [58-59, 61, 64-66]
— expenditures on social programs, p. 382 [404]
— health services, p. 650 [703]
— labor force participation, pp. 390, 392 [417, 420]
— life expectancy, pp. 74-75, 79, 650 [72, 75, 704]
— life expectancy at 65, p. 77 [73]
— life expectancy at birth, p. 77 [73]
— medical care costs, p. 625 [668]
— pension expenditures, p. 382 [405]
— pensions in, pp. 312-315 [336-340]
— population, p. 31 [26]
— population 65 and older, pp. 67-68 [62]
— ratios of men to women, p. 71 [67]
— shared social security agreements with United States 383 [406]
— Social Security in, p. 384 [407]
— Social Security programs, p. 384 [407]
— suicide rate, p. 93 [88]
— support ratios, p. 381 [403]
Fraud
— arrests for, pp. 838, 841-842 [896, 898-899]
— elderly charged with, p. 835 [893]
— elderly females arrested, p. 836 [894]
— elderly males charged, p. 837 [895]

Fraud continued:
— insurance, pp. 669 [727-728]
Freezers
— product-related injuries, p. 614 [654]
Fremont, CA
— population, pp. 21, 26 [21-22]
Frequent constipation
— incidence, p. 580 [608]
Frequent indigestion
— incidence, p. 579 [608]
Fresno, CA
— population, pp. 19, 25 [21-22]
Friendships
— blacks, p. 203 [198]
Fuels, p. 277 [300]
— cost to elderly households, pp. 453-454 [495-496]
— product-related injuries, p. 617 [659]
Fullerton, CA
— population, pp. 22, 28 [21-22]
Funding
— health care programs, p. 645 [697]
Fungicides
— and patients aged 55 to 75 + years, p. 515 [555]
Furnishings, p. 277 [300]
Furniture
— product-related injuries, p. 616 [657]
Furosemide
— and patients aged 55-74 years, pp. 511-512 [554]
Gambling
— arrests for, pp. 838, 841, 843 [896, 898-899]
— elderly charged with, p. 835 [893]
— elderly females arrested, p. 836 [894]
— elderly males charged, p. 837 [895]
Garden equipment
— product-related injuries, p. 613 [651]
Garden Grove, CA
— population, pp. 21, 27 [21-22]
Garland, TX
— population, pp. 21, 26 [21-22]
Gary, IN
— population, pp. 22, 28 [21-22]
Gas (natural gas)
— cost in elderly households, p. 453 [495]
Gasoline
— product-related injuries, p. 617 [659]
Gastritis or duodenitis
— incidence, p. 579 [608]
Gastrointestinal drugs
— and patients aged 55 to 75 + years, p. 515 [555]
Genitourinary diseases, pp. 580, 726, 728 [608, 769-770]
Geographic mobility
— reason for move, p. 463 [509]
Georgia
— age discrimination in, p. 419 [453]
— death sentences, p. 847 [904]
— drivers licenses, pp. 787-788 [835-836]
— elderly in nursing homes, p. 704 [753]
— elderly population, pp. 38, 42 [35, 38]
— hospital insurance charges, p. 642 [695]

Numbers following p. or pp. are page references. Numbers in [ ] are table references.

Numbers following p. or pp. are page references. Numbers in [ ] are table references.

Numbers following p. or pp. are page references. Numbers in [ ] are table references.

Numbers following p. or pp. are page references. Numbers in [ ] are table references.

Health insurance continued:
— coverage, p. 664 [719]
— coverage by poverty status, p. 662 [716]
— expenditures, p. 278 [301]
— for people with low-income, p. 661 [715]
— hospital bills, approved by Medicare, p. 692 [748]
— hospital bills, reimbursements by Medicare, p. 692 [748]
— Medicaid, pp. 661, 676, 682, 700 [715, 735, 739, 752]
— Medicare, pp. 661, 676-677, 684-685 [715, 734, 736, 742-743]
— Medicare enrollment and reimbursements, 1967 to 1990, p. 687 [745]
— Medicare enrollment by type, p. 690 [747]
— Medicare enrollment, by state, p. 688 [746]
— military, p. 662 [716]
— participating hospitals and beds for Medicare, p. 695 [750]
— participating skilled nursing facilities in Medicare, p. 698 [751]
— percent who receive, p. 328 [357]
— private, p. 662 [716]
— sources of, p. 666 [723]
— type of coverage, p. 659 [712]
Hearing aids, p. 753 [794]
Hearing impairment, p. 601 [632]
— in nursing homes, p. 753 [794]
— incidence, p. 579 [608]
— older Americans with, p. 465 [510]
Heart conditions, pp. 726-727 [769-770]
Heart disease, pp. 116, 124 [113, 122]
— blacks, p. 105 [102]
— death rates, pp. 103, 105, 116 [100, 102, 113]
— death rates, females, p. 105 [102]
— death rates, males, p. 105 [102]
— deaths, pp. 87, 104 [83, 101]
— health, p. 104 [101]
— incidence, p. 580 [608]
— older Americans with, p. 465 [510]
— whites, p. 105 [102]
Heart failure
— and frequent diagnoses, pp. 568-569 [600]
Heart murmurs
— incidence, p. 580 [608]
Heart revascularization, pp. 575-576 [604]
— and males, p. 574 [604]
Heart rhythm disorders
— incidence, p. 580 [608]
Heating
— in elderly households, pp. 438, 446 [475, 484]
Heating and cooling
— in elderly households, p. 446 [485]
Heating equipment
— product-related injuries, p. 615 [655]
Hematology, p. 541 [578]
Hemorrhoids
— incidence, p. 580 [608]
Hernando County, FL
— percent over 55 years old, p. 36 [33]
Hernia of abdominal cavity
— incidence, p. 579 [608]

Hialeah, FL
— population, pp. 20, 26 [21-22]
Hickory County, MO
— percent over 55 years old, p. 36 [33]
High blood pressure, pp. 580, 597 [608, 627]
High school, p. 133 [127]
— completion of, pp. 136, 138-139 [130-131, 133]
Highlands County, FL
— percent over 55 years old, p. 36 [33]
Hip fractures, pp. 636, 641, 726-727 [686, 694, 769-770]
Hiring
— employment discrimination charges, p. 417 [452]
Hispanics
— age of householder, p. 435 [470]
— and health risks, p. 467 [513]
— and housing characteristics, p. 432 [466]
— and housing costs, p. 453 [495]
— and income, pp. 207, 333 [203, 363]
— and poverty, p. 263 [282]
— and property insurance, p. 456 [499]
— and public transportation, p. 461 [506]
— and shopping, p. 462 [507]
— cost of living, p. 454 [496]
— death rates, p. 98 [94]
— educational attainment, p. 142 [137]
— geographic mobility, p. 463 [509]
— health care utilization, pp. 468, 583 [514, 612]
— home maintenance costs, p. 455 [497]
— household characteristics, p. 458 [502]
— housing characteristics, pp. 431-433, 438, 440-442, 444, 446-447, 453, 455, 457, 460 [465, 467-468, 475-480, 482, 484-486, 494, 498, 501, 505]
— housing tenure, p. 434 [469]
— in advertising, p. 807 [855]
— living arrangements, pp. 173, 177 [162, 167]
— mental disorders in nursing homes, pp. 745, 750 [784, 790]
— neighborhood conditions, pp. 459, 462 [504, 508]
— rent collected by, p. 452 [493]
— savings and investments of, p. 225 [226]
HIV
See: Human immunodeficiency virus
Hobby equipment
— product-related injuries, p. 612 [648]
Hockey
— all kinds, product-related injuries, p. 611 [647]
Hoists
— product-related injuries, p. 613 [652]
Holders for personal items
— product-related injuries, p. 612 [649]
Hollywood, FL
— population, pp. 22, 28 [21-22]
Home care
— source of payment, p. 626 [669]
Home equity, p. 250 [263]
— households, p. 242 [251]
Home furnishings
— product-related injuries, p. 616 [657]
Home health
— Medicaid expenditures on, p. 682 [739]

Numbers following p. or pp. are page references. Numbers in [ ] are table references.

Numbers following p. or pp. are page references. Numbers in [ ] are table references.

Numbers following p. or pp. are page references. Numbers in [ ] are table references.

Numbers following p. or pp. are page references. Numbers in [ ] are table references.

India
— elderly population, pp. 66, 70 [61, 65]
— population 65 and older, pp. 67-68 [62]
Indian River County, FL
— percent over 55 years old, p. 36 [33]
Indiana
— age discrimination in, p. 419 [453]
— death sentences, p. 846 [904]
— drivers licenses, pp. 787-788 [835-836]
— elderly in nursing homes, p. 703 [753]
— elderly population, pp. 38, 42 [35, 38]
— hospital insurance charges, p. 642 [695]
— medical facilities, pp. 589, 591 [620-621]
— Medicare, pp. 689, 696 [746, 750]
— Medicare and Medicaid, pp. 678, 680 [737-738]
— nursing home safety, pp. 767, 769, 771, 773, 775-776, 778
   [818-824]
— nursing homes, p. 705 [754]
— population, p. 39 [36]
— population 65 and older, pp. 40, 52, 56, 59 [37, 49, 52, 54]
— population 65 and older living alone, p. 174 [163]
— population 85 and older, p. 62 [56]
— skilled nursing charges, p. 644 [696]
— skilled nursing facilities, p. 698 [751]
— Social Security, pp. 335, 337 [365-366]
— Social Security beneficiaries, p. 371 [396]
— Social Security benefits, pp. 370, 374 [395, 398]
— Social Security benefits, by state, p. 373 [397]
— SSI benefits received, pp. 376-377 [399-400]
— veteran population, p. 46 [42]
Indianapolis, IN
— age discrimination in, p. 421 [455]
— population, pp. 19, 24 [21-22]
Indigestion
— incidence, pp. 547, 550, 562, 571 [582, 585, 595, 602]
Individual retirement accounts
   See: IRAs
Indomethacin
— and patients aged 55-74 years, p. 511 [554]
Indonesia
— elderly population, p. 66 [61]
— population 65 and older, p. 67 [62]
Infectious and parasitic diseases
— incidence, pp. 546, 550, 562, 571 [582, 585, 595, 602]
Infective diseases
— incidence, pp. 550, 562, 571 [585, 595, 602]
Inflation
— and drug costs, p. 629 [673]
Influenza
— deaths from, p. 86 [82]
— in females, p. 556 [592]
— in males, p. 556 [592]
— incidence, pp. 546, 550, 562, 571 [582, 585, 595, 602]
Inglewood, CA
— population, pp. 23, 28 [21-22]
Inguinal hernia, pp. 574-576 [604]
— and hospital stays, p. 560 [594]
Injuries, p. 726 [769]
— from sports and recreational equipment, p. 611 [647]

Injuries continued:
— incidence, pp. 547, 550, 562, 571 [582, 585, 595, 602]
— product-related, pp. 611-617 [647-659]
Inpatient health care, p. 636 [686]
Instrumental activities of daily living
— and nursing home residents, pp. 737, 739 [777-778]
Insulin
— and patients aged 55-74 years, pp. 511, 513 [554]
— and patients aged 55 to 75+ years, p. 515 [555]
Insurance, p. 669 [728]
— abuse, p. 669 [727]
— assistance from, p. 321 [347]
— complaints, pp. 669 [727-728]
— cost per family, p. 635 [685]
— costs, p. 671 [730]
— costs for long-term care, p. 582 [610]
— coverage, p. 661 [714]
— dental, pp. 672, 675 [731-733]
— fraud, p. 669 [727]
— fraud potential, p. 669 [728]
— health, pp. 620, 659, 664, 684 [663, 712, 720, 742]
— hospital bills, approved by Medicare, p. 692 [748]
— hospital bills, reimbursements by Medicare, p. 692 [748]
— Medicaid, pp. 676, 682 [735, 739]
— Medicaid participation, p. 700 [752]
— Medicare and Medicaid relationship, p. 677 [736]
— Medicare enrollees, p. 685 [743]
— Medicare enrollment and reimbursements, 1967 to 1990
   687 [745]
— Medicare enrollment by type of coverage, p. 690 [747]
— Medicare enrollment, by state, p. 688 [746]
— property, p. 456 [499]
— short-stay hospital charges, p. 641 [695]
— skilled nursing facility charges, p. 643 [696]
— Social Security, p. 365 [390]
— Social Security benefits, pp. 354, 356-357 [383-385]
— worldwide, p. 384 [407]
Insurance carriers, p. 669 [727]
Insurance industry
— older workers, p. 396 [424]
Insurance PAC, p. 670 [729]
Interest
— as income, p. 245 [255]
Intermediate care facilities, pp. 749, 752, 756 [789, 792, 799]
Internal medicine
— geriatrics, p. 647 [700]
Intervertebral disc disorders
— incidence, p. 579 [608]
Intestinal virus
— unspecified, incidence, pp. 546, 550, 562, 571 [582, 585, 595,
   602]
Intimidation
— employment discrimination charges, p. 417 [452]
Intravenous pyelogram
— and males, p. 543 [579]
Investment
— income, p. 246 [258]
Investment portfolios, p. 217 [215]

Numbers following p. or pp. are page references. Numbers in [ ] are table references.

Investments
— and housing characteristics, p. 225 [226]
Iodine
— and health, p. 519 [558]
Iowa
— age discrimination in, p. 419 [453]
— drivers licenses, pp. 787-788 [835-836]
— elderly in nursing homes, p. 703 [753]
— elderly population, pp. 38, 42 [35, 38]
— hospital insurance charges, p. 642 [695]
— medical facilities, pp. 589, 591 [620-621]
— Medicare, pp. 689, 696 [746, 750]
— Medicare and Medicaid, pp. 678, 680 [737-738]
— nursing home safety, pp. 767, 769, 771, 773, 775-776, 778
   [818-824]
— nursing homes, p. 705 [754]
— population, pp. 39, 45 [36, 41]
— population 65 and older, pp. 40, 52, 56, 59 [37, 49, 52, 54]
— population 65 and older living alone, p. 174 [163]
— population 85 and older, pp. 44, 62 [40, 56]
— skilled nursing charges, p. 644 [696]
— skilled nursing facilities, p. 698 [751]
— Social Security, pp. 335, 337 [365-366]
— Social Security beneficiaries, p. 371 [396]
— Social Security benefits, pp. 370, 374 [395, 398]
— Social Security benefits, by state, p. 373 [397]
— SSI benefits received, p. 376 [399]
— veteran population, p. 46 [42]
Iran
— elderly population, p. 67 [61]
IRAs, pp. 222, 224 [222, 225]
Ireland
— aging population, p. 66 [60]
— life expectancy, pp. 75-76 [72]
— life expectancy at 65, p. 77 [73]
— life expectancy at birth, p. 77 [73]
— Social Security in, p. 384 [407]
— Social Security programs, p. 384 [407]
Iron
— and health, p. 519 [558]
Ironing
— product-related injuries, p. 614 [654]
Irvine, CA
— population, pp. 23, 28 [21-22]
Irving, TX
— population, pp. 21, 27 [21-22]
Ischemic heart disease
— incidence, p. 580 [608]
Isosorbide
— and patients aged 55-74 years, pp. 511, 513 [554]
Israel
— and diseases, p. 124 [122]
— and mortality, p. 124 [122]
— life expectancy, pp. 74, 76 [72]
— life expectancy at 65, p. 77 [73]
— life expectancy at birth, p. 77 [73]
Italy
— aging population, p. 65 [60]
— and diseases, p. 124 [122]

Italy continued:
— and mortality, p. 124 [122]
— elderly population, pp. 64-66, 69-70 [58-59, 61, 64-65]
— expenditures on social programs, p. 382 [404]
— labor force participation, pp. 392-393 [420]
— labor force participation rates, p. 390 [417]
— life expectancy, pp. 74-75, 79 [72, 75]
— life expectancy at 65, p. 77 [73]
— life expectancy at birth, p. 77 [73]
— medical care costs, p. 625 [668]
— medical care expenditures, p. 624 [666]
— pension expenditures, p. 382 [405]
— population, p. 31 [26]
— population 65 and older, pp. 67-68 [62]
— ratios of men to women, p. 71 [67]
— shared social security agreements with United States, p. 383
   [406]
— Social Security in, p. 384 [407]
— Social Security programs, p. 384 [407]
— suicide rate, p. 93 [88]
— support ratios, p. 381 [403]
Jacks
— product-related injuries, p. 613 [652]
Jackson, MS
— population, pp. 20, 26 [21-22]
Jacksonville, FL
— population, pp. 19, 24 [21-22]
Japan
— and diseases, p. 124 [122]
— and mortality, p. 124 [122]
— elderly population, pp. 64-66, 69-70 [58-59, 61, 64-66]
— expenditures on social programs, p. 382 [404]
— health care, p. 625 [667]
— health services, p. 650 [703]
— labor force participation, pp. 392-393 [420]
— labor force participation rates, p. 391 [417]
— life expectancy, pp. 74-75, 79, 650 [72, 75, 704]
— life expectancy at 65, p. 77 [73]
— life expectancy at birth, p. 77 [73]
— medical care expenditures, p. 624 [666]
— pension expenditures, p. 383 [405]
— pensions in, pp. 312-315 [336-340]
— population, p. 31 [26]
— population 65 and older, p. 67 [62]
— ratios of men to women, p. 71 [67]
— Social Security in, p. 384 [407]
— Social Security programs, p. 384 [407]
— suicide rate, p. 94 [89]
— support ratios, p. 381 [403]
Jars
— product-related injuries, p. 613 [650]
Jersey City, NJ
— population, pp. 20, 25 [21-22]
Jewelry
— product-related injuries, p. 612 [649]
Job classification
— employment discrimination charges, p. 417 [452]
Joint conditions, pp. 726-727 [769-770]
Joint pain, p. 595 [625]

Numbers following p. or pp. are page references. Numbers in [ ] are table references.

Numbers following p. or pp. are page references. Numbers in [ ] are table references.

Numbers following p. or pp. are page references. Numbers in [ ] are table references.

Numbers following p. or pp. are page references. Numbers in [ ] are table references.

Numbers following p. or pp. are page references. Numbers in [ ] are table references.

897

Numbers following p. or pp. are page references. Numbers in [ ] are table references.

Numbers following p. or pp. are page references. Numbers in [ ] are table references.

Minnesota continued:
— Social Security, pp. 335, 337 [365-366]
— Social Security beneficiaries, p. 371 [396]
— Social Security benefits, pp. 370, 375 [395, 398]
— Social Security benefits, by state, p. 373 [397]
— SSI benefits received, pp. 376, 378 [399-400]
— veteran population, p. 46 [42]
Minorities
— aging population, p. 30 [23]
Miotics
— and patients aged 55 to 75+ years, p. 514 [555]
Mirrors
— product-related injuries, p. 616 [657]
Mississippi
— age discrimination in, p. 419 [453]
— death sentences, p. 847 [904]
— drivers licenses, pp. 787, 789 [835-836]
— elderly in nursing homes, p. 704 [753]
— elderly population, pp. 38, 42 [35, 38]
— hospital insurance charges, p. 642 [695]
— medical facilities, pp. 590, 592 [620-621]
— Medicare, pp. 689, 696 [746, 750]
— Medicare and Medicaid, pp. 678, 680 [737-738]
— nursing home safety, pp. 767, 770-771, 773, 775-776, 778 [818-824]
— nursing homes, p. 706 [754]
— population, p. 39 [36]
— population 65 and older, pp. 41, 53, 57, 59 [37, 49, 52, 54]
— population 65 and older living alone, p. 174 [163]
— population 85 and older, p. 62 [56]
— skilled nursing charges, p. 644 [696]
— skilled nursing facilities, p. 699 [751]
— Social Security, pp. 335, 337 [365-366]
— Social Security beneficiaries, p. 371 [396]
— Social Security benefits, pp. 370, 375 [395, 398]
— Social Security benefits, by state, p. 373 [397]
— SSI benefits received, p. 376 [399]
— veteran population, p. 46 [42]
Missouri
— age discrimination in, p. 419 [453]
— and health insurance, p. 671 [730]
— death sentences, p. 846 [904]
— drivers licenses, pp. 787, 789 [835-836]
— elderly in nursing homes, p. 703 [753]
— elderly population, pp. 38, 42 [35, 38]
— hospital insurance charges, p. 642 [695]
— medical facilities, pp. 589, 591 [620-621]
— Medicare, pp. 689, 696 [746, 750]
— Medicare and Medicaid, pp. 678, 680 [737-738]
— nursing home safety, pp. 767, 770-771, 773, 775-776, 778 [818-824]
— nursing homes, p. 705 [754]
— population, pp. 39, 45 [36, 41]
— population 65 and older, pp. 41, 52, 56, 59 [37, 49, 52, 54]
— population 65 and older living alone, p. 174 [163]
— population 85 and older, pp. 44, 62 [40, 56]
— skilled nursing charges, p. 644 [696]
— skilled nursing facilities, p. 698 [751]
— Social Security, pp. 335, 337 [365-366]

Missouri continued:
— Social Security beneficiaries, p. 371 [396]
— Social Security benefits, pp. 370, 375 [395, 398]
— Social Security benefits, by state, p. 373 [397]
— SSI benefits received, pp. 376, 378 [399-400]
— veteran population, p. 46 [42]
Mobile homes, p. 431 [465]
— and geographic area, p. 433 [468]
— and government subsidies, p. 455 [498]
— and public transportation, p. 461 [506]
— and shopping, p. 462 [507]
— building conditions, p. 442 [479]
— building security, p. 460 [505]
— cost of utilities, p. 454 [496]
— energy costs in, p. 453 [495]
— heating and cooling, p. 446 [484]
— heating in, p. 446 [485]
— lot and unit size, p. 443 [481]
— maintenance cost to elderly, pp. 438, 455 [476, 497]
— neighborhood conditions, p. 459 [504]
— plumbing in, p. 447 [486]
— property insurance, p. 456 [499]
— purchase price, p. 458 [502]
— quality, p. 438 [475]
— space per person, p. 444 [482]
— street conditions near, p. 462 [508]
— units in structure, p. 432 [466]
— value of, p. 457 [501]
— year built, p. 432 [467]
Mobile, AL
— population, pp. 20, 26 [21-22]
Mobility, pp. 125, 130-131 [123, 125-126]
— and blacks, p. 125 [123]
— and Hispanics, p. 125 [123]
— and housing, pp. 432-433 [466-468]
— nursing home assistance, pp. 747, 753-754 [786, 795-796]
Mobility impairments
— of nursing home residents, p. 758 [802]
Moderate physical problems
— in elderly households, p. 438 [475]
Modesto, CA
— population, pp. 21, 26 [21-22]
Money market accounts
— as assets, p. 218 [216]
Montana
— age discrimination in, p. 419 [453]
— death sentences, p. 847 [904]
— drivers licenses, pp. 787, 789 [835-836]
— elderly in nursing homes, p. 704 [753]
— elderly population, pp. 38, 42 [35, 38]
— hospital insurance charges, p. 643 [695]
— medical facilities, pp. 590, 592 [620-621]
— Medicare, pp. 689, 697 [746, 750]
— Medicare and Medicaid, pp. 679, 681 [737-738]
— nursing home safety, pp. 767, 770-771, 773, 775, 777-778 [818-824]
— nursing homes, p. 706 [754]
— population, p. 39 [36]
— population 65 and older, pp. 41, 53, 57, 59 [37, 49, 52, 54]

Numbers following p. or pp. are page references. Numbers in [ ] are table references.

Numbers following p. or pp. are page references. Numbers in [ ] are table references.

Numbers following p. or pp. are page references. Numbers in [ ] are table references.

Numbers following p. or pp. are page references. Numbers in [ ] are table references.

Numbers following p. or pp. are page references. Numbers in [ ] are table references.

Numbers following p. or pp. are page references. Numbers in [ ] are table references.

Numbers following p. or pp. are page references. Numbers in [ ] are table references.

Numbers following p. or pp. are page references. Numbers in [ ] are table references.

Physician visits
— and black females, p. 540 [577]
— and black males, p. 540 [577]
— and blacks, p. 540 [577]
— and white females, p. 540 [577]
— and white males, p. 540 [577]
— and whites, p. 540 [577]
Physicians
— contact projections, p. 564 [598]
— contacts, p. 563 [596]
— geriatrics, p. 647 [700]
— Medicaid expenditures on, p. 682 [739]
— opinions on, p. 815 [865]
— patient visits annually, p. 546 [581]
Picnic equipment
— product-related injuries, p. 611 [647]
Pillows
— product-related injuries, p. 616 [657]
Pipes, heating and plumbing
— product-related injuries, p. 615 [655]
Pitkin, CO
— affluent elderly in, p. 218 [217]
Pittsburgh, PA
— population, pp. 19, 25 [21-22]
Plano, TX
— population, pp. 22, 28 [21-22]
Plastic
— product-related injuries, p. 613 [650]
Playground equipment
— product-related injuries, p. 611 [647]
Plumbing
— in elderly households, p. 438 [475]
Pneumonia, p. 646 [698]
— deaths from, p. 86 [82]
— hospital stays, pp. 557-561 [593-594]
— in females, p. 556 [592]
— in males, p. 556 [592]
— incidence, pp. 546, 550, 562, 571 [582, 585, 595, 602]
Pneumonia and influenza
— deaths from, pp. 84-86 [81-82]
Podiatry PAC, p. 670 [729]
Poland
— elderly population, pp. 66, 70 [61, 65]
— life expectancy, pp. 75-76 [72]
— life expectancy at 65, p. 78 [73]
— life expectancy at birth, p. 78 [73]
— suicide rate, p. 94 [89]
Political action committees
  See: PAC
Politics, pp. 793, 796-799 [842-846]
— party preference, p. 800 [847]
— voting participation, pp. 800-801 [848-849]
Polymixin B36
— and patients aged 55-74 years, pp. 512-513 [554]
Pomona, CA
— population, pp. 22, 27 [21-22]
Pools
— product-related injuries, p. 611 [647]
Population, pp. 11-12, 18, 34, 49, 58, 82, 650 [13-14, 20, 30,

Population continued:
46, 53, 80, 704]
— 1950-1989, p. 14 [16]
— 1990, p. 38 [35]
— 2010, p. 38 [35]
— 65 and older, pp. 30, 40, 54, 68, 216 [23, 37, 50, 63, 214]
— 85 and older, pp. 33, 63 [28, 57]
— age 62, p. 51 [47]
— aged 50-64 life satisfaction, p. 820 [869]
— aging, p. 48 [45]
— black, p. 35 [31]
— black female, p. 14 [16]
— black male, p. 14 [16]
— by age group and state, p. 39 [36]
— by country, p. 65 [59]
— by marital status, p. 12 [15]
— by state, pp. 42, 44-45 [38, 40-41]
— by state and age group, p. 39 [36]
— centenarians, p. 781 [826]
— counties with the least older Americans, p. 35 [32]
— counties with the most older Americans, p. 36 [33]
— elderly, pp. 18, 61, 257, 702 [21, 56, 273, 753]
— elderly living alone, pp. 173, 177 [162, 167]
— elderly support, p. 216 [214]
— elderly to youth ratio, p. 16 [17]
— growth, pp. 30, 54, 60 [24, 50, 55]
— growth projection, p. 48 [45]
— growth rates in selected countries, p. 64 [58]
— Hispanic, p. 51 [48]
— Hispanic female, p. 14 [16]
— Hispanic male, p. 14 [16]
— in selected countries, pp. 31, 69 [26, 64]
— life satisfaction, p. 820 [870]
— mortality rate, p. 650 [704]
— of elderly by state ranking, pp. 18, 24 [21-22]
— persons 65 and older, p. 45 [41]
— persons 85 +, p. 44 [40]
— ratios of men to women in selected countries, p. 71 [67]
— sandwich generation, p. 63 [57]
— support of parents, p. 63 [57]
— support ratios, p. 63 [57]
— under 18, p. 216 [214]
— veterans, pp. 45, 47 [42-43]
— white female, p. 14 [16]
— white male, p. 14 [16]
— women to men ratio, p. 31 [25]
— world regions, p. 68 [63]
— worldwide, pp. 70 [65-66]
Porches
— product-related injuries, p. 616 [658]
Portland, OR
— population, pp. 19, 24 [21-22]
Portsmouth, VA
— population, pp. 23, 29 [21-22]
Portugal
— aging population, p. 66 [60]
— elderly population, p. 65 [59]
— life expectancy, pp. 75-76 [72]
— life expectancy at 65, p. 77 [73]

Numbers following p. or pp. are page references. Numbers in [ ] are table references.

908

Numbers following p. or pp. are page references. Numbers in [ ] are table references.

Property crimes
— arrests for, pp. 838, 841-842 [896, 898-899]
— elderly charged with, p. 834 [893]
— elderly females arrested, p. 836 [894]
— elderly males charged, p. 837 [895]
Property insurance, p. 456 [499]
Propoxyphene
— and patients aged 55-74 years, pp. 512-513 [554]
Propranolol
— and patients aged 55-74 years, pp. 512-513 [554]
Prospective payment system (PPS), p. 556 [591]
Prostate cancer, p. 603 [636]
Prostate enlargement, p. 603 [635]
Prostatectomy, pp. 574-576 [604]
Prostitution
— arrests for, pp. 838, 841, 843 [896, 898-899]
— elderly charged with, pp. 834-835 [893]
— elderly females arrested, pp. 835-836 [894]
— elderly males charged, p. 837 [895]
— elderly males charged with, p. 837 [895]
Protestantism, p. 780 [825]
Providence, RI
— population, pp. 21, 27 [21-22]
Prozac
— cost of, p. 635 [684]
Psoriasis
— incidence, p. 579 [608]
Psychiatrics
— geriatrics, p. 647 [700]
Psychoses
— in nursing homes, pp. 743, 750 [781, 790]
Psychotropic drugs
— and patients aged 55 to 75+ years, p. 514 [555]
Public administration
— older workers, p. 396 [424]
Public assistance
— as income, pp. 214, 247-248 [211, 260-261]
— cash, p. 270 [293]
— food stamps, p. 270 [293]
— Medicaid, p. 270 [293]
— participation in, p. 270 [293]
— subsidized housing, p. 270 [293]
Public housing
— in-kind benefit, p. 211 [207]
— participation in government programs, p. 270 [293]
— rent subsidy, p. 453 [494]
Public services, p. 277 [300]
Public transportation, p. 461 [506]
Public utilities
— retirement plans, p. 320 [346]
Puerto Rico
— age discrimination in, p. 420 [453]
— hospital insurance charges, p. 643 [695]
— life expectancy, p. 75 [72]
— life expectancy at 65, p. 77 [73]
— life expectancy at birth, p. 77 [73]
— Medicare, pp. 690, 697 [746, 750]
— skilled nursing charges, p. 645 [696]
— skilled nursing facilities, p. 699 [751]

Puerto Rico continued:
— Social Security beneficiaries, p. 372 [396]
— Social Security benefits, p. 370 [395]
— Social Security benefits, by state, p. 373 [397]
Pulmonary disease
— deaths from, p. 86 [82]
Race
— and educational attainment, p. 142 [137]
— pension plans, p. 299 [324]
— private pension plans, p. 291 [319]
— Supplemental Security Income, p. 379 [402]
— and income, p. 234 [240]
Radiators
— product-related injuries, p. 615 [655]
Radioisotope scan
— and females, pp. 544-545 [580]
— and males, pp. 542-543 [579]
Radios
— entertainment expenditures, p. 784 [830]
Railings
— product-related injuries, p. 616 [658]
Railroad Retirement, p. 245 [255]
— as income, pp. 214, 248, 334 [211, 261, 364]
Raleigh, NC
— population, pp. 20, 26 [21-22]
Ramps
— product-related injuries, p. 616 [658]
Rancho Cucamonga, CA
— population, pp. 23, 29 [21-22]
Ranges
— product-related injuries, p. 614 [654]
Rape
— arrests for, pp. 838, 841, 843 [896, 898-899]
— victimization rate, pp. 848-850, 854 [906, 908-909, 914]
Razors and blades
— product-related injuries, p. 612 [649]
Reading
— entertainment expenditures, p. 784 [830]
Real estate
— as debt, p. 250 [263]
— older workers, p. 396 [424]
Receiving stolen property
— elderly females arrested, p. 835 [894]
— elderly males charged with, p. 837 [895]
Recreation
— and retirement, p. 830 [886]
Recreation equipment
— product-related injuries, p. 611 [647]
Rectal examinations, p. 541 [578]
Recuperation, pp. 727-728 [769-770]
Referrals
— employment discrimination charges, p. 418 [452]
Refrigerators
— product-related injuries, p. 614 [654]
Registered nurses
— geriatrics, pp. 648-649 [701-702]
Reinstatements
— employment discrimination charges, p. 418 [452]

Numbers following p. or pp. are page references. Numbers in [ ] are table references.

Numbers following p. or pp. are page references. Numbers in [ ] are table references.

911

Numbers following p. or pp. are page references. Numbers in [ ] are table references.

Numbers following p. or pp. are page references. Numbers in [ ] are table references.

913

Numbers following p. or pp. are page references. Numbers in [ ] are table references.

Numbers following p. or pp. are page references. Numbers in [ ] are table references.

Numbers following p. or pp. are page references. Numbers in [ ] are table references.

Numbers following p. or pp. are page references. Numbers in [ ] are table references.

Transportation industry
— older workers, p. 396 [424]
— retirement plans, p. 320 [346]
Travel
— and retirement, p. 830 [886]
— senior citizen discounts, p. 786 [834]
Triamcinolone
— and patients aged 55-74 years, p. 512 [554]
Triamterene
— and patients aged 55-74 years, pp. 512-513 [554]
Trimethoprim
— and patients aged 55-74 years, pp. 512-513 [554]
Tucson, AZ
— population, pp. 19, 24 [21-22]
Tulsa, OK
— population, pp. 19, 25 [21-22]
Tumors
— death rates, p. 110 [107]
— deaths from, p. 87 [83]
Turkey
— 1985, education attainment in, p. 138 [132]
— elderly population, p. 66 [61]
TV programs
— ratings, p. 808 [858]
Ulcer
— incidence, p. 579 [608]
Unemployment, p. 407 [437]
— displaced workers, p. 408 [438]
Unions
— employment discrimination charges, p. 418 [452]
— member earnings, p. 415 [449]
— membership, p. 416 [450]
United Kingdom
— elderly population, pp. 64-66, 69-70 [58-59, 61, 64-65]
— expenditures on social programs, p. 382 [404]
— gross income of elderly in, p. 228 [231]
— health care, p. 625 [667]
— health services, p. 650 [703]
— labor force participation, p. 392 [420]
— labor force participation rates, pp. 391, 393 [417, 420]
— life expectancy, pp. 79, 650 [75, 704]
— medical care costs, p. 625 [668]
— medical care expenditures, p. 624 [666]
— pension expenditures, p. 382 [405]
— pensions in, pp. 312-315 [336-340]
— population, p. 31 [26]
— population 65 and older, pp. 67-68 [62]
— ratios of men to women, p. 71 [67]
— shared social security agreements with United States 383 [406]
— Social Security in, p. 384 [407]
— Social Security programs, p. 384 [407]
— suicide rate, p. 94 [89]
— support ratios, p. 381 [403]
United States
— 1991, education attainment in, p. 138 [132]
— and diseases, p. 125 [122]
— and mortality, p. 125 [122]
— elderly in nursing homes, p. 702 [753]

United States continued:
— elderly population, pp. 64-66, 69-70 [58-59, 61, 64-66]
— expenditures on social programs, p. 382 [404]
— gross income of elderly in, p. 228 [231]
— health care, p. 625 [667]
— health services, p. 650 [703]
— hospital insurance charges, p. 641 [695]
— labor force participation, p. 392 [420]
— labor force participation rates, p. 390 [417]
— life expectancy, pp. 75-76, 79, 650 [72, 75, 704]
— life expectancy at 65, p. 77 [73]
— life expectancy at birth, p. 77 [73]
— medical care costs, p. 625 [668]
— medical care expenditures, p. 624 [666]
— medical facilities, pp. 589, 591 [620-621]
— Medicare, pp. 688, 690, 695 [746-747, 750]
— Medicare and Medicaid, pp. 677, 679 [737-738]
— nursing homes, p. 705 [754]
— pension expenditures, p. 382 [405]
— population, p. 31 [26]
— population 65 and older, pp. 52, 55, 67 [49, 52, 62]
— population 65 and older living alone, p. 173 [163]
— population 85 and older, p. 61 [56]
— ratios of men to women, p. 71 [67]
— skilled nursing facilities, p. 698 [751]
— Social Security, pp. 334, 336 [365-366]
— Social Security budget, p. 339 [367]
— Social Security programs, p. 384 [407]
— support ratios, p. 381 [403]
Upper respiratory infections
— and frequent diagnoses, p. 567 [600]
Urban areas
— housing in, p. 433 [468]
Urinary conditions, p. 603 [635]
— and hospital stays of females, pp. 558-559 [593]
— incidence, pp. 547, 550, 562, 571-572 [582, 585, 595, 602]
— incontinence, p. 603 [637]
Urine glucose, p. 541 [578]
Utah
— age discrimination in, p. 419 [453]
— death sentences, p. 847 [904]
— drivers licenses, pp. 788-789 [835-836]
— elderly in nursing homes, p. 704 [753]
— elderly population, pp. 39, 42 [35, 38]
— hospital insurance charges, p. 643 [695]
— medical facilities, pp. 590, 592 [620-621]
— Medicare, pp. 690, 697 [746, 750]
— Medicare and Medicaid, pp. 679, 681 [737-738]
— nursing home safety, pp. 768, 770, 772, 774-775, 777-778 [818-824]
— nursing homes, p. 706 [754]
— population, p. 40 [36]
— population 65 and older, pp. 41, 53, 57, 60 [37, 49, 52, 54]
— population 65 and older living alone, p. 174 [163]
— population 85 and older, p. 63 [56]
— skilled nursing charges, p. 645 [696]
— skilled nursing facilities, p. 699 [751]
— Social Security, pp. 336, 338 [365-366]
— Social Security beneficiaries, p. 372 [396]

Numbers following p. or pp. are page references. Numbers in [ ] are table references.

Numbers following p. or pp. are page references. Numbers in [ ] are table references.

Virginia Beach, VA
— population, pp. 19, 25 [21-22]
Visual acuity, p. 541 [578]
Visual impairments
— in nursing homes, p. 753 [794]
— incidence, p. 579 [608]
— older Americans with, p. 465 [510]
Vitamin A
— and health, p. 519 [558]
Vitamin B-12
— and health, p. 519 [558]
— and patients aged 55-74 years, p. 512 [554]
Vitamin B-6
— and health, p. 519 [558]
Vitamin B complex
— and patients aged 55 to 75+ years, p. 515 [555]
Vitamin C
— and health, p. 519 [558]
Vitamin D
— and health, p. 519 [558]
Vitamin E
— and health, p. 519 [558]
Vitamin use, p. 518 [557]
Vitamins
— and blacks, p. 518 [557]
— and health, p. 519 [558]
— and patients aged 55 to 75+ years, p. 515 [555]
— and whites, p. 518 [557]
Vocational nurses
— geriatrics, p. 648 [701]
Vocational school
— completion of, p. 139 [133]
Volleyball
— product-related injuries, p. 611 [647]
Volunteerism, pp. 802, 804, 830 [851, 853, 886]
Vomiting
— incidence, pp. 550, 562, 571 [585, 595, 602]
Voter registration
— by age, pp. 797-799 [844-846]
— females, p. 796 [843]
— males, p. 796 [843]
Voter turnout, p. 802 [850]
Voting, p. 796 [843]
— behavior, p. 793 [842]
— by age, pp. 797, 799 [844, 846]
— by race, p. 801 [849]
— participation in elections, pp. 800-801 [848-849]
Waco, TX
— population, pp. 23, 29 [21-22]
Wade Hampton Census Area, AK
— percent over 55 years old, p. 35 [32]
Wage and salary workers
— English-language proficiency, p. 227 [229]
— foreign born, pp. 226-227 [228-229]
— full time, pp. 226-227 [228-229]
— men, pp. 226-227 [228-229]
— women, pp. 226-227 [228-229]
Wages
— employment discrimination charges, p. 418 [452]

Wages continued:
— of year-round, full-time workers, p. 275 [297]
Walls
— product-related injuries, p. 616 [658]
Warfarin
— and patients aged 55-74 years, pp. 512-513 [554]
Warrant officers
— mortality rate, p. 119 [116]
Warren, MI
— population, pp. 21, 27 [21-22]
Washing machines, p. 279 [303]
— product-related injuries, p. 614 [654]
Washington
— age discrimination in, p. 419 [453]
— death sentences, p. 847 [904]
— drivers licenses, pp. 788-789 [835-836]
— elderly in nursing homes, p. 704 [753]
— elderly population, pp. 39, 43 [35, 38]
— hospital insurance charges, p. 643 [695]
— medical facilities, pp. 590, 592 [620-621]
— Medicare, pp. 690, 697 [746, 750]
— Medicare and Medicaid, pp. 679, 681 [737-738]
— nursing home safety, pp. 768, 770, 772, 774, 776-778 [818-824]
— nursing homes, p. 706 [754]
— population, p. 40 [36]
— population 65 and older, pp. 41, 53, 57, 60 [37, 49, 52, 54]
— population 65 and older living alone, p. 174 [163]
— population 85 and older, p. 63 [56]
— skilled nursing charges, p. 645 [696]
— skilled nursing facilities, p. 699 [751]
— Social Security, pp. 336, 338 [365-366]
— Social Security beneficiaries, p. 372 [396]
— Social Security benefits, pp. 370, 375 [395, 398]
— Social Security benefits, by state, p. 373 [397]
— SSI benefits received, p. 377 [399]
— veteran population, p. 46 [42]
Washington, DC
— population, pp. 19, 24 [21-22]
Water
— cost to elderly households, p. 454 [496]
Water facilities
— in elderly households, p. 447 [486]
Water skiing
— product-related injuries, p. 611 [647]
— tubing, surfing, product-related injuries, p. 611 [647]
Waterbury, CT
— population, pp. 23, 28 [21-22]
Weapons
— arrests for, p. 841 [898]
— arrests for carrying, p. 843 [899]
— carrying and possessing, elderly charged with, pp. 835-838 [893-896]
— used on elderly murder victims, pp. 856-857 [917-918]
Welding
— product-related injuries, p. 613 [652]
West Germany
See also: German Democratic Republic; Germany; Germany, Federal Republic
— expenditures on social programs, p. 382 [404]

Numbers following p. or pp. are page references. Numbers in [ ] are table references.

Numbers following p. or pp. are page references. Numbers in [ ] are table references.

Wisconsin
— age discrimination in, p. 419 [453]
— drivers licenses, pp. 788-789 [835-836]
— elderly in nursing homes, p. 703 [753]
— elderly population, pp. 39, 43 [35, 38]
— hospital insurance charges, p. 642 [695]
— medical facilities, pp. 589, 591 [620-621]
— Medicare, pp. 689, 696 [746, 750]
— Medicare and Medicaid, pp. 678, 680 [737-738]
— nursing home safety, pp. 769-770, 772, 774, 776-777, 779 [818-824]
— nursing homes, p. 705 [754]
— population, p. 40 [36]
— population 65 and older, pp. 41, 52, 56, 60 [37, 49, 52, 54]
— population 65 and older living alone, p. 175 [163]
— population 85 and older, p. 62 [56]
— skilled nursing charges, p. 644 [696]
— skilled nursing facilities, p. 698 [751]
— Social Security, pp. 335, 337 [365-366]
— Social Security beneficiaries, p. 372 [396]
— Social Security benefits, pp. 370, 375 [395, 398]
— Social Security benefits, by state, p. 373 [397]
— SSI benefits received, p. 377 [399]
— veteran population, p. 46 [42]

Worcester, MA
— population, pp. 21, 26 [21-22]

Work disabilities
— and blacks, p. 422 [456]
— and Hispanics, p. 422 [456]
— and whites, p. 422 [456]
— by age, pp. 402, 422, 427-430 [432, 456, 460-464]
— by race, p. 422 [456]
— by sex, p. 422 [456]
— females, pp. 402, 425-430 [432, 458-464]
— males, pp. 402, 425-430 [432, 458-464]

Workers
— by industry, p. 396 [424]
— by occupation, p. 395 [423]
— full- or part-time status, p. 397 [426]
— growth projections, p. 386 [410]
— labor force participation rates, pp. 389-390 [415-416]
— labor force participation rates in selected countries, p. 390 [417]
— self-employed workers, p. 400 [430]
— unemployment, p. 407 [437]
— volunteer, pp. 802-803 [851-852]

Workshop equipment
— product-related injuries, p. 613 [652]

Wounds
— incidence, pp. 550, 562, 571 [585, 595, 602]

Wrestling
— product-related injuries, p. 611 [647]

Wyoming
— age discrimination in, p. 419 [453]
— death sentences, p. 847 [904]
— drivers licenses, pp. 788-789 [835-836]
— elderly in nursing homes, p. 704 [753]
— elderly population, pp. 39, 43 [35, 38]
— hospital insurance charges, p. 643 [695]

Wyoming continued:
— medical facilities, pp. 590, 592 [620-621]
— Medicare, pp. 690, 697 [746, 750]
— Medicare and Medicaid, pp. 679, 681 [737-738]
— nursing home safety, pp. 769-770, 772, 774, 776-777, 779 [818-824]
— nursing homes, p. 706 [754]
— population, p. 40 [36]
— population 65 and older, pp. 41, 53, 57, 60 [37, 49, 52, 54]
— population 65 and older living alone, p. 175 [163]
— population 85 and older, p. 63 [56]
— skilled nursing charges, p. 645 [696]
— skilled nursing facilities, p. 699 [751]
— Social Security, pp. 336, 338 [365-366]
— Social Security beneficiaries, p. 372 [396]
— Social Security benefits, pp. 370, 375 [395, 398]
— Social Security benefits, by state, p. 373 [397]
— SSI benefits received, pp. 377-378 [399-400]
— veteran population, p. 46 [42]

Xanax
— cost of, p. 635 [684]

Yard equipment
— product-related injuries, p. 613 [651]

Yonkers, NY
— population, pp. 20, 26 [21-22]

Yugoslavia
— elderly population, p. 67 [61]
— life expectancy, pp. 75-76 [72]
— life expectancy at 65, p. 77 [73]
— life expectancy at birth, p. 77 [73]

Zantac
— cost of, p. 635 [684]

Zinc
— and health, p. 558 [519]

Numbers following p. or pp. are page references. Numbers in [ ] are table references.

ABBREVIATIONS AND ACRONYMS

Abbreviations are usually explained within the context of data presented. The following listing shows the abbreviations used together with an explanation. The same abbreviations are used by different authors in different ways. Where more than one use is possible, both are shown.

AARP	American Association of Retired Persons	B	Base population is less than 75,000 — too small to show derived measures (Statistics)
AB	Aid to the Blind (Social Security Administration)		
		BAC	Blood Alcohol Content
ADEA	Age Discrimination in Employment Act	BPH	Benign Prostatic Hypertrophy
ADL	Activities of Daily Living	C	Confidence level (Statistics)
AFDC	Aid to Families with Dependent Children		
		CAT	Computerized Axial Tomography (CAT scan)
AIDS	Acquired Immune Deficiency Syndrome	CBO	Congressional Budget Office
ALS	Amyotrophic Lateral Sclerosis (Lou Gehrig's Disease)	CDC	Centers for Disease Control
APTD	Aid to the Permanently and Totally Disabled	CDP	Census Designated Place
		CD-ROM	Compact Disc - Read-Only Memory
ATV	All-Terrain Vehicle		

CE	Consumer Expenditures Survey		EPA	Equal Pay Act
CHAMPUS	Civilian Health and Medical Program of the Uniformed Services		Exc	Except
			Exc	Excluding
			FEPAs	Fair Employment Practices Agencies
CHD	Coronary Heart Disease			
COPD	Chronic Obstructive Pulmonary Disease		FHWA	Federal Highway Administration
CPH	Census of Population and Housing		FRG	Federal Republic of Germany (West Germany)
CPI	Consumer Price Index		FTE	Full-Time Equivalent
CPS	Current Population Survey		FY	Fiscal Year
CR	Chemical Restraint (Nursing facilities)		GAO	General Accounting Office
			g/dl	Grams per deciliter
DFTERN	Demand for Full-Time Equivalent Registered Nurses		GDP	Gross Domestic Product
			GNP	Gross National Product
DHHS	Department of Health and Human Services		GPO	Government Printing Office
DI	Disability Insurance (Social Security Administration)		HBP	High Blood Pressure
			HCFA	Health Care Financing Administration
Dol	Dollar		HH	Households
EBS	Employee Benefits Survey		HI	Hospital Insurance
EEOC	Equal Employment Opportunity Commission		HIV	Human Immunodeficiency Virus
EFMI	Emergency Fund for the Medically Indigent, Inc. (United Way)		HME	Home Medical Equipment

HMO	Health Maintenance Organization		Mil	Million
HU	Heavy Users		NA	Not Applicable
HUD	United States Department of Housing and Urban Development		NA	Not Available
			NCHSR	National Center for Health Services Research
IADL	Instrumental Activities of Daily Living		NEISS	National Electronic Injury Surveillance System
ICBO	International Conference of Building Officials		NIA/USC	National Institute on Aging/University of Southern California
ICF	Intermediate Care Facility		NIH	National Institutes of Health
IMF	International Monetary Fund			
IRA	Individual Retirement Account		OAA	Old Age Assistance
			OASDI	Old-Age, Survivors, and Disability Insurance
IRS	Internal Revenue Service		OASI	Old-Age and Survivors Insurance
LPN	Licensed Practical Nurse			
LSC	Life Safety Code (National Fire Protection Association)		OBRA	Omnibus Budget Reconciliation Act
			OBS	Organic Brain Syndrome
LTC	Long-Term Care		OECD	Organization for Economic Cooperation and Development
M	Mandatory			
MAO	Monoamine Oxidase		OGC	Office of the General Counsel
mg	Milligram			
MRI	Magnetic Resonance Imaging		OTC	Over the Counter
			PAC	Political Action Committee
MSA	Metropolitan Statistical Area		PHS	Public Health Service

925

PMSA	Primary Metropolitan Statistical Area		SSI	Supplemental Security Income (Social Security Administration)
PPS	Prospective Payment System (Medicare)		SSI	Supplemental Security Insurance
PR	Physical Restraint (Nursing facilities)		USDA	United States Department of Agriculture
PRA	Post Retirement Adjustment		USDL	United States Department of Labor
QC	Quarter of Coverage (Social Security Administration)		V	Voluntary
			VA	Department of Veterans' Affairs
QMBs	Qualified Medicare Beneficiaries		VN	Vocational Nurse
RN	Registered Nurse		WIC	Women, Infants, and Children (Supplemental food program)
SGLI	Servicemen's Group Life Insurance			
SIPP	Survey of Income and Program Participation (Social Security Administration)		WIN	Work Incentive Program
			WHAT	Wechsler's Hearing Aid Test
SMI	Supplementary Medical Insurance (Social Security Administration)		X	Not Applicable
			Z	Less than .05 percent
SNF	Skilled Nursing Facility			
SOA	Survey on Aging			
SROA	Statistical Record of Older Americans			
SS	Social Security			
SSA	Social Security Administration			